Oxford Essential Italian Dictionary

Oxford Essential Italian Dictionary

ITALIAN–ENGLISH
ENGLISH–ITALIAN

ITALIANO–INGLESE
INGLESE–ITALIANO

OXFORD
UNIVERSITY PRESS

Great Clarendon Street, Oxford OX2 6DP

Oxford University Press is a department of the University of Oxford. It furthers the University's objective of excellence in research, scholarship, and education by publishing worldwide in

Oxford New York

Auckland Cape Town Dar es Salaam Hong Kong Karachi Kuala Lumpur Madrid Melbourne Mexico City Nairobi New Delhi Shanghai Taipei Toronto

With offices in

Argentina Austria Brazil Chile Czech Republic France Greece Guatemala Hungary Italy Japan Poland Portugal Singapore South Korea Switzerland Thailand Turkey Ukraine Vietnam

Oxford is a registered trade mark of Oxford University Press in the UK and in certain other countries

Previously published as the *Oxford Italian Mini Dictionary*, 2005

First edition 2009

British Library Cataloguing in Publication Data

Data available

Library of Congress Cataloging in Publication Data

Data available

ISBN 978-0-19-957641-8

9

Typeset by Interactive Sciences Ltd, Gloucester
Printed in Great Britain by Clays Ltd, St Ives plc

Contents/Indice

List of contributors

Joyce Andrews

Debora Mazza, Donatella Boi,
Sonia Tinagli-Baxter, Peter Terrell,
Jane Goldie, Francesca Logi, Carla Zipoli

Nicholas Rollin

Introduzione

Destinato a utenti italiani e inglesi, l'*Oxford Essential Italian Dictionary* contiene le parole, i termini e le espressioni più utili d'uso corrente.

Il dizionario costituisce un'opera di consultazione pratica e completa, e fornisce risposte rapide e puntuali alle esigenze di traduzione di viaggiatori, studenti e professionisti.

Allo scopo di fornire il maggior numero possibile di informazioni riguardo all'inglese e all'italiano, questo dizionario ricorre ad alcune convenzioni per sfruttare al meglio lo spazio disponibile.

All'interno della voce un trattino ondulato ~ è utilizzato al posto del lemma.

Qualora il lemma contenga una barra verticale |, il trattino ondulato sostituisce solo la parte del lemma che precede la barra. Ad es.:
dark|en *vt oscurare*. **~ness** *n* buio *m* (la seconda parola in neretto va letta **darkness**).

Vengono forniti indicatori per indirizzare l'utente verso la traduzione del senso voluto di una parola. I tipi di indicatori sono:

- etichette semantiche, indicanti lo specifico settore d'uso di una parola o di un senso (commercio, informatica, fotografia ecc.);
- indicatori di significato, ad es.: **redazione** *f* (ufficio) editorial office; (di testi) editing;
- soggetti tipici di verbi, ad es.: **trovarsi** *vr* (luogo:) be;
- complementi oggetti tipici di verbi, collocati dopo la traduzione del verbo stesso, ad es.: **superare** *vt* overtake (veicolo); pass (esame);
- sostantivi che ricorrono tipicamete con certi aggettivi, ad es.: **solare** *adj* (energia, raggi) solar; (crema) sun.

Il pallino nero indica che la stessa parola viene tradotta come una diversa parte del discorso, ad es.: **calcolatore** *adj* ... • *m* ...

La pronuncia inglese è trascritta usando l'Alfabetico Fonetico Internazionale (vedi pag. viii).

L'accento tonico nelle parole italiane è indicato dal segno ' collocato davanti alla sillaba accentata.

Le parentesi quadre racchiudono parti di espressioni che possono essere omesse senza alterazioni di significato.

Introduction

The *Oxford Essential Italian Dictionary* has been written for speakers of both Italian and English and contains the most useful words and expressions in use today.

The dictionary provides a handy and comprehensive reference work for tourists, students, and business people who require quick and reliable answers to their translation needs.

In order to give the maximum information about English and Italian in the space available, this new dictionary uses certain space-saving conventions.

A swung dash ~ is used to replace the headword within the entry.

Where the headword contains a vertical bar | the swung dash replaces only the part of the headword that comes before the |. For example:
efficien|te *adj* efficient. **~za** *f* efficiency (the second bold word reads efficienza).

Indicators are provided to guide the user to the best translation for a specific sense of a word. Types of indicator are:

- field labels, which indicate a general area of usage (commercial, computing, photography etc);
- sense indicators, eg: **bore** *n* (of gun) calibro *m*; (person) seccatore, -trice *mf*;
- typical subjects of verbs, eg: **bond** *vt* (glue:) attaccare;
- typical objects of verbs, placed after the translation of the verb, eg: **boost** *vt* stimolare (sales); sollevare (morale);
- nouns that typically go together with certain adjectives, eg: **rich** *adj* ricco; (food) pesante;

A bullet point means that a headword has changed its part of speech within an entry, eg: **partition** *n* ... • vt ...

English pronunciation is given for the Italian user in the International Phonetic Alphabet (see p vii).

Italian stress is shown by a ' placed in front of the stressed syllable in a word.

Square brackets are used around parts of an expression which can be omitted without altering its sense.

Pronunciation of Italian/ Pronuncia inglese

Vowels

a is broad like *a* in *father*: **casa**

e has two sounds: closed like *ey* in *they*: **sera**; open like e in egg: **sette**

i is like *ee* in *feet*: **venire**.

o 1. closed like *o* in *show*: **croma**.
2. open like *o* in *dog*: **bocca**.

u is like *oo* in *moon*: **luna**

When two or more vowels come together each vowel is pronounced separately: **buono; baia.**

Consonants

b, d, f, l, m, n, p, t, v are pronounced as in English. When these are double, they are pronounced as separate sounds: **bello.**

c before **a, o** or **u** and before consonants is like *k* in *king*: **cane.** Before **e** or **i** it is like *ch* in *church*: **cena.**

ch is also like *k* in *king*: **chiesa**

g before **a, o** or **u** is hard like *g* in *got*: **gufo**. Before **e** or **i** it is like *j* in *jelly*: **gentile.**

gh is like *g* in *gun*: **ghiaccio.**

gl when followed by **a, e, o** and **u** is like *gl* in *glass*: **gloria.**

gli is like *lli* in *million*: **figlio.**

gn is like *ni* in *onion*: **bagno.**

h is silent.

ng is like *ng* in *finger*: **ringraziare.**

r is pronounced distinctly.

s between two vowels is like *s* in *rose*: **riso.** At the beginning of a word it is like *s* in *soap*: **sapone.**

sc before *e* or *i* is like *sh* in *shell*: **scienza.**

z sounds like *ts* within a word: **fazione;** like dz at the beginning: **zoo.**

Stress is shown by the sign ' printed before the stressed syllable.

Simboli fonetici

Vocali e dittonghi

iː	*see*	ɔː	*saw*	eɪ	*page*	ɔɪ	*join*
ɪ	*sit*	ʊ	*put*	əʊ	*home*	ɪə	*near*
e	*ten*	uː	*too*	aɪ	*five*	eə	*hair*
æ	*hat*	ʌ	*cup*	aɪə	*fire*	ʊə	*poor*
ɑː	*arm*	ɜː	*fur*	aʊ	*now*		
ɒ	*got*	ə	*ago*	aʊə	*flour*		

Consonanti

p	*pen*	tʃ	*chin*	s	*so*	n	*no*
b	*bad*	dʒ	*June*	z	*zoo*	ŋ	*sing*
t	*tea*	f	*fall*	ʃ	*she*	l	*leg*
d	*dip*	v	*voice*	ʒ	*measure*	r	*red*
k	*cat*	θ	*thin*	h	*how*	j	*yes*
g	*got*	ð	*then*	m	*man*	w	*wet*

Note: ' precede la sillaba accentata.

Abbreviations/Abbreviazioni

adjective	*adj*	aggettivo
abbreviation	*abbr*	abbreviazione
administration	*Admin*	amministrazione
adverb	*adv*	avverbio
aeronautics	*Aeron*	aeronautica
American	*Am*	americano
anatomy	*Anat*	anatomia
archaeology	*Archeol*	archeologia
architecture	*Archit*	architettura
astrology	*Astr*	astrologia
attributive	*attrib*	attributo
automobiles	*Auto*	automobile
auxiliary	*aux*	ausiliario
biology	*Biol*	biologia
botany	*Bot*	botanica
British English	*Br*	inglese britannico
chemistry	*Chem*	chimica
commerce	*Comm*	commercio
computers	*Comput*	informatica
conjunction	*conj*	congiunzione
cooking	*Culin*	cucina
definite article	*def art*	articolo determinativo
et cetera	*ecc*	eccetera
electricity	*Electr*	elettricità
et cetera	*etc*	eccetera
feminine	*f*	femminile
figurative	*fig*	figurato
formal	*fml*	formale
geography	*Geog*	geografia
geology	*Geol*	geologia
grammar	*Gram*	grammatica
humorous	*hum*	umoristico
indefinite article	*indef art*	articolo indeterminativo
interjection	*int*	interiezione
interrogative	*inter*	interrogativo
invariable	*inv*	invariabile
law	*Jur*	legge/giuridico
literary	*liter*	letterario
masculine	*m*	maschile
mathematics	*Math*	matematica
mechanics	*Mech*	meccanica
medicine	*Med*	medicina
masculine or feminine	*mf*	maschile o femminile
military	*Mil*	militare

music	*Mus*	musica
noun	*n*	sostantivo
nautical	*Naut*	nautica
pejorative	*pej*	peggiorativo
personal	*pers*	personale
photography	*Phot*	fotografia
physics	*Phys*	fisica
plural	*pl*	plurale
politics	*Pol*	politica
possessive	*poss*	possessivo
past participle	*pp*	participio passato
prefix	*pref*	prefisso
preposition	*prep*	preposizione
present tense	*pres*	presente
pronoun	*pron*	pronome
psychology	*Psych*	psicologia
past tense	*pt*	tempo passato
someone	*qcno*	qualcuno
something	*qcsa*	qualcosa
rail	*Rail*	ferrovia
reflexive	*refl*	riflessivo
religion	*Relig*	religione
relative pronoun	*rel pron*	pronome relativo
somebody	*sb*	qualcuno
school	*Sch*	scuola
singular	*sg*	singolare
something	*sth*	qualcosa
technical	*Techn*	tecnico
telephone	*Teleph*	telefono
theatrical	*Theat*	teatrale
television	*TV*	televisione
typography	*Typ*	tipografia
university	*Univ*	università
auxiliary verb	*v aux*	verbo ausiliare
intransitive verb	*vi*	verbo intransitivo
reflexive verb	*vr*	verbo riflessivo
transitive verb	*vt*	verbo transitivo
transitive and intransitive verb	*vt/i*	verbo transitivo e intransitivo
vulgar	*vulg*	volgare
familiar	[!]	familiare
slang	[✱]	gergo
cultural equivalent	≈	equivalenza culturale

Aa

a (**ad** *before vowel*) *prep* to; (*stato in luogo, tempo, età*) at; (*con mese, città*) in; (*mezzo, modo*) by; **dire qcsa a qcno** tell sb sth; **alle tre** at three o'clock; **a vent'anni** at the age of twenty; **a Natale** at Christmas; **a dicembre** in December; **ero al cinema** I was at the cinema; **vivo a Londra** I live in London; **a due a due** two by two; **a piedi** on *o* by foot; **maglia a maniche lunghe** long-sleeved sweater; **casa a tre piani** house with three floors; **giocare a tennis** play tennis; **50 km all'ora** 50 km an hour; **4 euro al chilo** 4 euros a kilo; **al mattino/alla sera** in the morning/evening; **a venti chilometri/due ore da qui** twenty kilometres/two hours away

a'bate *m* abbot

abbacchi'ato *adj* downhearted

ab'bacchio *m* [young] lamb

abbagli'ante *adj* dazzling ● *m* headlight, high beam

abbagli'are *vt* dazzle. **ab'baglio** *m* blunder; **prendere un ~** make a blunder

abbai'are *vi* bark

abba'ino *m* dormer window

abbando'na|re *vt* abandon; leave (luogo); give up (piani ecc). **~rsi** *vr* let oneself go; **~rsi a** give oneself up to (ricordi ecc). **~to** *adj* abandoned. **ab-ban'dono** *m* abandoning; *fig* abandon; (*stato*) neglect

abbassa'mento *m* (*di temperatura, prezzi ecc*) drop

abbas'sar|e *vt* lower; turn down (radio, tv); **~e i fari** dip the headlights. **~si** *vr* stoop; (sole ecc:) sink; *fig* demean oneself

ab'basso *adv* below ● *int* down with

abba'stanza *adv* enough; (*alquanto*) quite

ab'batter|e *vt* demolish; shoot down (aereo); put down (animale); topple (regime); (*fig: demoralizzare*) dishearten. **~si** *vr* (*cadere*) fall; *fig* be discouraged

abbatti'mento *m* (*morale*) despondency

abbat'tuto *adj* despondent

abba'zia *f* abbey

abbel'lir|e *vt* embellish. **~si** *vr* adorn oneself

abbeve'ra|re *vt* water. **~'toio** *m* drinking trough

abbi'ente *adj* well-to-do

abbiglia'mento *m* clothes *pl*; (*industria*) clothing industry

abbigli'ar|e *vt* dress. **~si** *vr* dress up

abbina'mento *m* combining

abbi'nare *vt* combine; match (colori)

abbindo'lare *vt* cheat

abbocca'mento *m* interview; (*conversazione*) talk

abboc'care *vi* bite; (tubi:) join; *fig* swallow the bait

abboc'cato *adj* (vino) fairly sweet

abbof'farsi *vr* stuff oneself

abbona'mento *m* subscription; (*ferroviario ecc*) season-ticket; **fare l'~** take out a subscription

abbo'na|re *vt* make a subscriber. **~rsi** *vr* subscribe (**a** to); take out a season-ticket (**a** for) (teatro, stadio). **~to, -a** *mf* subscriber

abbon'dan|te *adj* abundant; (quantità) copious; (nevicata) heavy; (vestiario) roomy. **~te di** abounding in. **~te'mente** *adv* (mangiare) copiously. **~za** *f* abundance

abbon'dare *vi* abound

abbor'da|bile *adj* (persona) approachable; (prezzo) reasonable. **~ggio** *m* (*Mil*) boarding. **~re** *vt* board (nave); approach (persona); ([!]: *attaccar bottone a*) chat up; tackle (compito ecc)

abbotto'na|re *vt* button up. **~'tura** *f* [row of] buttons. **~to** *adj fig* tight-lipped

abboz'zare *vt* sketch [out]; **~ un sorriso** give a hint of a smile. **ab'bozzo** *m* sketch

abbracci'are *vt* embrace; take up

(professione); *fig* include. **ab'braccio** *m* hug

abbrevi'a|re *vt* shorten; (*ridurre*) curtail; abbreviate (parola). **~zi'one** *f* abbreviation

abbron'zante *m* sun-tan lotion

abbron'za|re *vt* bronze; tan (pelle). **~rsi** *vr* get a tan. **~to** *adj* tanned. **~'tura** *f* [sun-]tan

abbrusto'lire *vt* toast; roast (caffè ecc)

abbruti'mento *m* brutalization. **abbru'tire** *vt* brutalize. **abbru'tirsi** *vr* become brutalized

abbuf'fa|rsi *vr* [!] stuff oneself. **~ta** *f* blowout

abbuo'nare *vt* reduce

abbu'ono *m* allowance; *Sport* handicap

abdi'ca|re *vi* abdicate. **~zi'one** *f* abdication

aber'rante *adj* aberrant

a'bete *m* fir

abi'etto *adj* despicable

'abil|e *adj* able; (*idoneo*) fit; (*astuto*) clever. **~ità** *f inv* ability; (*idoneità*) fitness; (*astuzia*) cleverness. **~'mente** *adv* ably; (*con astuzia*) cleverly

abili'ta|re *vt* qualify. **~to** *adj* qualified. **~zi'one** *f* qualification; (*titolo*) diploma

abis'sale *adj* abysmal. **a'bisso** *m* abyss

abi'tabile *adj* inhabitable

abi'tacolo *m* (*Auto*) passenger compartment

abi'tante *mf* inhabitant

abi'ta|re *vi* live. **~to** *adj* inhabited ● *m* built-up area. **~zi'one** *f* house

'abito *m* (*da donna*) dress; (*da uomo*) suit. **~ da cerimonia/da sera** formal/evening dress

abitu'al|e *adj* usual. **~'mente** *adv* usually

abitu'ar|e *vt* accustom. **~si a** *vr* get used to

abitudi'nario, -a *adj* of fixed habits ● *mf* person of fixed habits

abi'tudine *f* habit; **d'~** usually; **per ~** out of habit; **avere l'~ di fare qcsa** be in the habit of doing sth

abnegazi'one *f* self-sacrifice

ab'norme *adj* abnormal

abo'li|re *vt* abolish; repeal (legge). **~zi'one** *f* abolition; repeal

abomi'nevole *adj* abominable

abor'rire *vt* abhor

abor'ti|re *vi* miscarry; (*volontariamente*) have an abortion; *fig* fail. **~vo** *adj* abortive. **a'borto** *m* miscarriage; (*volontario*) abortion. **~sta** *adj* pro-choice

abras|i'one *f* abrasion. **abra'sivo** *adj & m* abrasive

abro'ga|re *vt* repeal. **~zi'one** *f* repeal

'abside *f* apse

abu'lia *f* apathy. **a'bulico** *adj* apathetic

abu's|are *vi* **~ di** abuse; over-indulge in (alcol); (*approfittare di*) take advantage of; (*violentare*) rape. **~ivo** *adj* illegal

a'buso *m* abuse. **~ di confidenza** breach of confidence

a.C. *abbr* (avanti Cristo) BC

'acca *f* [!] **non ho capito un'~** I understood damn all

acca'demi|a *f* academy. **A~a di Belle Arti** Academy of Fine Arts. **~co, -a** *adj* academic ● *mf* academician

acca'd|ere *vi* happen; **accada quel che accada** come what may. **~uto** *m* event

accalappi'are *vt* catch; *fig* allure

accal'carsi *vr* crowd

accal'da|rsi *vr* get overheated; *fig* get excited. **~to** *adj* overheated

accalo'rarsi *vr* get excited

accampa'mento *m* camp. **accam'pare** *vt fig* put forth. **accam'parsi** *vr* camp

accani'mento *m* tenacity; (*odio*) rage

acca'ni|rsi *vr* persist; (*infierire*) rage. **~to** *adj* persistent; (odio) fierce; *fig* inveterate

ac'canto *adv* near; **~ a** *prep* next to

accanto'nare *vt* set aside; (*Mil*) billet

accaparra'mento *m* hoarding; (*Comm*) cornering

accapar'ra|re *vt* hoard. **~rsi** *vr* grab; corner (mercato). **~'tore, ~'trice** *mf* hoarder

accapigli'arsi *vr* scuffle; (*litigare*) squabble

accappa'toio *m* bathrobe; (*per spiaggia*) beachrobe

accappo'nare *vt* **fare ~ la pelle a qcno** make sb's flesh creep

accarez'zare *vt* caress; *fig* cherish

accartocci'ar|e *vt* scrunch up. **~si** *vr* curl up

acca'sarsi *vr* get married

accasci'arsi *vr* flop down; *fig* lose heart

accata'stare *vt* pile up

accatti'vante *adj* beguiling

accatti'varsi *vr* **~ le simpatie/la stima/l'affetto di qcno** gain sb's sympathy/respect/affection

accatto'naggio *m* begging. **accat'tone, -a** *mf* beggar

accaval'lar|e *vt* cross (gambe). **~si** *vr* pile up; *fig* overlap

acce'cante *adj* (luce) blinding

acce'care *vt* blind ● *vi* go blind

ac'cedere *vi* **~ a** enter; (*acconsentire*) comply with

accele'ra|re *vi* accelerate ● *vt* accelerate. **~to** *adj* rapid. **~'tore** *m* accelerator. **~zi'one** *f* acceleration

ac'cender|e *vt* light; turn on (luce, TV ecc); *fig* inflame; **ha da ~e?** have you got a light?. **~si** *vr* catch fire; (*illuminarsi*) light up; (TV ecc:) turn on; *fig* become inflamed

accendi'gas *m inv* gas lighter; (*su cucina*) automatic ignition

accen'dino *m* lighter

accendi'sigari *m* cigar-lighter

accen'nare *vt* indicate; hum (melodia) ● *vi* **~ a** beckon to; *fig* hint at; (*far l'atto di*) make as if to; **accenna a piovere** it looks like rain. **ac'cenno** *m* gesture; (*con il capo*) nod; *fig* hint

accensi'one *f* lighting; (*di motore*) ignition

accen'ta|re *vt* accent; (*con accento tonico*) stress. **~zi'one** *f* accentuation. **ac'cento** *m* accent; (*tonico*) stress

accentra'mento *m* centralizing

accen'trare *vt* centralize

accentu'a|re *vt* accentuate. **~rsi** *vr* become more noticeable. **~to** *adj* marked

accerchia'mento *m* surrounding

accerchi'are *vt* surround

accerta'mento *m* check

accer'tare *vt* ascertain; (*controllare*) check; assess (reddito)

ac'ceso *adj* lighted; (radio, TV ecc) on; (colore) bright

acces'sibile *adj* accessible; (persona) approachable; (spesa) reasonable

ac'cesso *m* access; (*Med: di rabbia*) fit; **vietato l'~** no entry

acces'sorio *adj* accessory; (*secondario*) of secondary importance ● *m* accessory; **accessori** *pl* (*rifiniture*) fittings

ac'cetta *f* hatchet

accet'tabile *adj* acceptable

accet'tare *vt* accept; (*aderire a*) agree to

accettazi'one *f* acceptance; (*luogo*) reception. **~ [bagagli]** check-in. **[banco] ~** check-in [desk]

ac'cetto *adj* agreeable; **essere bene ~** be very welcome

accezi'one *f* meaning

acchiap'pare *vt* catch

acchito *m* **di primo ~** at first

acciac'ca|re *vt* crush; *fig* prostrate. **~to, -a** *adj* **essere ~to** ache all over. **acci'acco** *m* infirmity; **acciacchi** *pl* aches and pains

acciaie'ria *f* steelworks

acci'aio *m* steel; **~ inossidabile** stainless steel

acciden'ta|le *adj* accidental. **~l'mente** *adv* accidentally. **~to** *adj* (terreno) uneven

acci'dente *m* accident; (*Med*) stroke; **non capisce un ~** [!] he doesn't understand a damn thing. **acci'denti!** *int* damn!

accigli'a|rsi *vr* frown. **~to** *adj* frowning

ac'cingersi *vr* **~ a** be about to

acci'picchia *int* good Lord!

acciuf'fare *vt* catch

acci'uga *f* anchovy

accla'ma|re *vt* applaud; (*eleggere*) acclaim. **~zi'one** *f* applause

acclima'tar|e *vt* acclimatize. **~si** *vr* get acclimatized

ac'clu|dere *vt* enclose. **~so** *adj* enclosed

accocco'larsi *vr* squat

accogli'en|te *adj* welcoming; (*confortevole*) cosy. **~za** *f* welcome

ac'cogliere *vt* receive; (*con piacere*) welcome; (*contenere*) hold

accol'larsi *vr* take on (responsabilità, debiti, doveri). **accol'lato** *adj* high-necked

accoltel'lare *vt* knife

accomia'tar|e *vt* dismiss. **~si** *vr* take one's leave (**da** of)

accomo'dante *adj* accommodating

accomo'dar|e *vt* (*riparare*) mend; (*disporre*) arrange. **~si** *vr* make oneself at home; **si accomodi!** come in!; (*si sieda*) take a seat!

accompagna'mento *m* accompaniment; (*seguito*) retinue

accompa'gna|re *vt* accompany; **~re qcno a casa** see sb home; **~re qcno alla porta** show sb out. **~'tore, ~'trice** *mf* companion; (*di comitiva*) escort; (*Mus*) accompanist

accomu'nare *vt* pool

acconci'a|re *vt* arrange. **~'tura** *f* hair-style; (*ornamento*) head-dress

accondiscen'den|te *adj* too obliging. **~za** *f* excessive desire to please

accondi'scendere *vi* **~ a** condescend; comply with (desiderio); (*acconsentire*) consent to

acconsen'tire *vi* consent

acconten'tar|e *vt* satisfy. **~si** *vr* be content (**di** with)

ac'conto *m* deposit; **in ~** on account; **lasciare un ~** leave a deposit

accop'pare *vt* [!] bump off

accoppia'mento *m* coupling; (*di animali*) mating

accoppi'a|re *vt* couple; mate (animali). **~rsi** *vr* pair off; mate. **~ta** *f* (*scommessa*) *bet on two horses for first and second place*

acco'rato *adj* sorrowful

accorci'ar|e *vt* shorten. **~si** *vr* get shorter

accor'dar|e *vt* concede; match (colori ecc); (*Mus*) tune. **~si** *vr* agree

ac'cordo *m* agreement; (*Mus*) chord; (*armonia*) harmony; **andare d'~** get on well; **d'~!** agreed!; **essere d'~** agree; **prendere accordi con qcno** make arrangements with sb

ac'corgersi *vr* **~ di** notice; (*capire*) realize

accorgi'mento *m* shrewdness; (*espediente*) device

ac'correre *vi* hasten

accor'tezza *f* (*previdenza*) forethought

ac'corto *adj* shrewd; **mal ~** incautious

accosta'mento *m* combination

acco'star|e *vt* draw close to; approach (persona); set ajar (porta ecc). **~si** *vr* **~si a** come near to

accovacci'a|rsi *vr* crouch

accoz'zaglia *f* jumble; (*di persone*) mob

accoz'zare *vt* **~ colori** mix colours that clash

accredita'mento *m* credit; **~ tramite bancogiro** Bank Giro Credit

accredi'tare *vt* confirm (notizia); (*Comm*) credit

ac'cresc|ere *vt* increase. **~ersi** *vr* grow larger. **~i'tivo** *adj* augmentative

accucci'arsi *vr* (cane:) lie down; (persona:) crouch

accu'dire *vi* **~ a** attend to

accumu'la|re *vt* accumulate. **~rsi** *vr* accumulate. **~'tore** *m* accumulator; (*Auto*) battery. **~zi'one** *f* accumulation.

accura'tezza *f* care

accu'rato *adj* careful

ac'cusa *f* accusation; (*Jur*) charge; **essere in stato di ~** have been charged; **la Pubblica A~** the public prosecutor

accu'sa|re *vt* accuse; (*Jur*) charge; complain of (dolore); **~re ricevuta di** acknowledge receipt of. **~to, -a** *mf* accused. **~'tore** *m* prosecutor

a'cerbo *adj* sharp; (*non maturo*) unripe

'acero *m* maple

a'cerrimo *adj* implacable

a'ceto *m* vinegar

ace'tone *m* nail-polish remover

A.C.I. *abbr* (Automobile Club d'Italia) Italian Automobile Association

acidità *f* acidity. **~ di stomaco** acid stomach

'acido *adj* acid; (persona) sour ● *m* acid

a'cidulo *adj* slightly sour

'acino *m* berry; (*chicco*) grape

'acne *f* acne

'acqua *f* water; **fare ~** leak; **~ in bocca!** *fig* mum's the word!. **~ corrente** running water. **~ dolce** fresh water. **~ minerale** mineral water. **~ minerale gassata** fizzy mineral water.

~ **naturale** still mineral water. ~ **potabile** drinking water. ~ **salata** salt water. ~ **tonica** tonic water
acqua'forte *f* etching
ac'quaio *m* sink
acquama'rina *adj* aquamarine
acqua'rello *m* = **ACQUERELLO**
ac'quario *m* aquarium; (*Astr*) Aquarius
acqua'santa *f* holy water
acqua'scooter *m inv* water-scooter
ac'quatico *adj* aquatic
acquat'tarsi *vr* crouch
acqua'vite *f* brandy
acquaz'zone *m* downpour
acque'dotto *m* aqueduct
'acqueo *adj* **vapore** ~ water vapour
acque'rello *m* water-colour
acqui'rente *mf* purchaser
acqui'si|re *vt* acquire. **~to** *adj* acquired. **~zi'one** *f* attainment
acqui'st|are *vt* purchase; (*ottenere*) acquire. **ac'quisto** *m* purchase; **uscire per ~i** go shopping; **fare ~i** shop
acqui'trino *m* marsh
acquo'lina *f* **far venire l'~ in bocca a qcno** make sb's mouth water
ac'quoso *adj* watery
'acre *adj* acrid; (*al gusto*) sour; *fig* harsh
a'crilico *m* acrylic
a'croba|ta *mf* acrobat. **~'zia** *f* acrobatics *pl*
a'cronimo *m* acronym
acu'ir|e *vt* sharpen. **~si** *vr* become more intense
a'culeo *m* sting; (*Bot*) prickle
acumi'nato *adj* pointed
a'custic|a *f* acoustics *pl*. **~o** *adj* acoustic
acu'tezza *f* acuteness
acutiz'zarsi *vr* become worse
a'cuto *adj* sharp; (suono) shrill; (freddo, odore) intense; (*Gram, Math, Med*) acute ● *m* (*Mus*) high note
ad *prep* = **A** (*davanti a vocale*)
adagi'ar|e *vt* lay down. **~si** *vr* lie down
a'dagio *adv* slowly ● *m* (*Mus*) adagio; (*proverbio*) adage
adattabilità *f* adaptability
adatta'mento *m* adaptation; **avere spirito di** ~ be adaptable
adat'ta|re *vt* adapt; (*aggiustare*) fit. **~rsi** *vr* adapt. **~'tore** *m* adaptor. **a'datto** *adj* suitable (**a** for); (*giusto*) right
addebita'mento *m* debit. ~ **diretto** direct debit
addebi'tare *vt* debit; ascribe (colpa)
ad'debito *m* charge
addensa'mento *m* thickening; (*di persone*) gathering
adden'sar|e *vt* thicken. **~si** *vr* thicken; (*affollarsi*) gather
adden'tare *vt* bite
adden'trarsi *vr* penetrate
ad'dentro *adv* deeply; **essere ~ in** be in on
addestra'mento *m* training
adde'strar|e *vt* train. **~si** *vr* train
ad'detto, -a *adj* assigned ● *mf* employee; (*diplomatico*) attaché. ~ **stampa** press officer
addiaccio *m* **dormire all'~** sleep in the open
addi'etro *adv* (*indietro*) back; (*nel passato*) before
ad'dio *m & int* goodbye. ~ **al celibato** stag party
addirit'tura *adv* (*perfino*) even; (*assolutamente*) absolutely; **~!** really!
ad'dirsi *vr* ~ **a** suit
addi'tare *vt* point at; (*in mezzo a un gruppo*) point out; *fig* point to
addi'tivo *adj & m* additive
addizio'nal|e *adj* additional. **~'mente** *adv* additionally
addizio'nare *vt* add [up]. **addizi'one** *f* addition
addob'bare *vt* decorate. **ad'dobbo** *m* decoration
addol'cir|e *vt* sweeten; tone down (colore); *fig* soften. **~si** *vr fig* mellow
addolo'ra|re *vt* grieve. **~rsi** *vr* be upset (**per** by). **~to** *adj* distressed
ad'dom|e *m* abdomen. **~i'nale** *adj* abdominal; **[muscoli] addominali** *pl* abdominals
addomesti'ca|re *vt* tame. **~'tore** *m* tamer
addormen'ta|re *vt* put to sleep. **~rsi** *vr* go to sleep. **~to** *adj* asleep; *fig* slow
addos'sar|e *vt* **~e a** (*appoggiare*) lean

against; (*attribuire*) lay on. **~si** *vr* (*ammassarsi*) crowd; shoulder (responsabilità ecc)

ad'dosso *adv* on; **~ a** *prep* on; (*molto vicino*) right next to; **mettere gli occhi ~ a qcno/qcsa** hanker after sb/sth; **non mettermi le mani ~!** keep your hands off me!; **stare ~ a qcno** *fig* be on sb's back

ad'durre *vt* produce (prova, documento); give (pretesto, esempio)

adegua'mento *m* adjustment

adegu'a|re *vt* adjust. **~rsi** *vr* conform. **~to** *adj* adequate; (*conforme*) consistent

a'dempi|ere *vt* fulfil. **~'mento** *m* fulfilment

ade'noidi *fpl* adenoids

ade'ren|te *adj* adhesive; (vestito) tight ● *mf* follower. **~za** *f* adhesion. **~ze** *pl* connections

ade'rire *vi* **~ a** adhere to; support (petizione); agree to (richiesta)

adesca'mento *m* (*Jur*) soliciting

ade'scare *vt* bait; *fig* entice

adesi'one *f* adhesion; *fig* agreement

ade'sivo *adj* adhesive ● *m* sticker; (*Auto*) bumper sticker

a'desso *adv* now; (*poco fa*) just now; (*tra poco*) any moment now; **da ~ in poi** from now on; **per ~** for the moment

adia'cente *adj* adjacent; **~ a** next to

adi'bire *vt* **~ a** put to use as

'adipe *m* adipose tissue

adi'ra|rsi *vr* get irate. **~to** *adj* irate

a'dire *vt* resort to; **~ le vie legali** take legal proceedings

'adito *m* **dare ~ a** give rise to

adocchi'are *vt* eye; (*con desiderio*) covet

adole'scen|te *adj & mf* adolescent. **~za** *f* adolescence. **~zi'ale** *adj* adolescent

adom'brar|e *vt* darken; *fig* veil. **~si** *vr* (*offendersi*) take offence

adope'rar|e *vt* use. **~si** *vr* take trouble

ado'rabile *adj* adorable

ado'ra|re *vt* adore. **~zi'one** *f* adoration

ador'nare *vt* adorn

adot't|are *vt* adopt. **~ivo** *adj* adoptive. **adozi'one** *f* adoption

adrena'lina *f* adrenalin

adri'atico *adj* Adriatic ● *m* **l'A~** the Adriatic

adu'la|re *vt* flatter. **~'tore, ~'trice** *mf* flatterer. **~zi'one** *f* flattery

adulte'ra|re *vt* adulterate. **~to** *adj* adulterated

adul'terio *m* adultery. **a'dultero, -a** *adj* adulterous ● *m* adulterer ● *f* adulteress

a'dulto, -a *adj & mf* adult; (*maturo*) mature

adu'nanza *f* assembly

adu'na|re *vt* gather. **~ta** *f* (*Mil*) parade

a'dunco *adj* hooked

ae'rare *vt* air (stanza)

a'ereo *adj* aerial; (*dell'aviazione*) air *attrib* ● *m* aeroplane, plane

ae'robic|a *f* aerobics. **~o** *adj* aerobic

aerodi'namic|a *f* aerodynamics *sg*. **~o** *adj* aerodynamic

aero'nautic|a *f* aeronautics *sg*; (*Mil*) Air Force. **~o** *adj* aeronautical

aero'plano *m* aeroplane

aero'porto *m* airport

aero'scalo *m* cargo and servicing area

aero'sol *m inv* aerosol

'afa *f* sultriness

af'fabil|e *adj* affable. **~ità** *f* affability

affaccen'da|rsi *vr* busy oneself (**a** with). **~to** *adj* busy

affacci'arsi *vr* show oneself; **~ alla finestra** appear at the window

affa'ma|re *vt* starve [out]. **~to** *adj* starving

affan'na|re *vt* leave breathless. **~rsi** *vr* busy oneself; (*agitarsi*) get worked up. **~to** *adj* breathless; **dal respiro ~to** wheezy. **af'fanno** *m* breathlessness; *fig* worry

af'fare *m* matter; (*Comm*) deal; (*occasione*) bargain; **affari** *pl* business; **non sono affari tuoi** it's none of your business. **affa'rista** *mf* wheeler-dealer

affasci'nante *adj* fascinating; (persona, sorriso) bewitching

affasci'nare *vt* bewitch; *fig* charm

affatica'mento *m* fatigue

affati'car|e *vt* tire; (*sfinire*) exhaust. **~si** *vr* tire oneself out; (*affannarsi*) strive

af'fatto *adv* completely; **non... ~** not... at all; **niente ~!** not at all!

affer'ma|re *vt* affirm; (*sostenere*) assert. **~rsi** *vr* establish oneself

affermativa'mente *adv* in the affirmative

afferma'tivo *adj* affirmative

affermazi'one *f* assertion; (*successo*) achievement

affer'rar|e *vt* seize; catch (oggetto); (*capire*) grasp; **~e al volo** *fig* be quick on the uptake. **~si** *vr* **~si a** grasp at

affet'ta|re *vt* slice; (*ostentare*) affect. **~to** *adj* sliced; (maniere) affected ● *m* cold meat.

affet'tivo *adj* affective; **rapporto ~** emotional tie

af'fetto[1] *m* affection

af'fetto[2] *adj* **~ da** suffering from

affettuosità *f inv* (*gesto*) affectionate gesture

affettu'oso *adj* affectionate

affezio'na|rsi *vr* **~rsi a** grow fond of. **~to** *adj* devoted (**a** to)

affian'car|e *vt* put side by side; (*Mil*) flank; *fig* support. **~si** *vr* come side by side; *fig* stand together; **~si a qcno** *fig* help sb out

affiata'mento *m* harmony

affia'ta|rsi *vr* get on well together. **~to** *adj* close-knit; **una coppia ~ta** a very close couple

affibbi'are *vt* **~ qcsa a qcno** saddle sb with sth; **~ un pugno a qcno** let fly at sb

affi'dabil|e *adj* dependable. **~ità** *f* dependability

affida'mento *m* (*Jur: dei minori*) custody; **fare ~ su qcno** rely on sb; **non dare ~** not inspire confidence

affi'dar|e *vt* entrust. **~si** *vr* **~si a** rely on

affievo'lirsi *vr* grow weak

af'figgere *vt* affix

affi'lare *vt* sharpen

affili'ar|e *vt* affiliate. **~si** *vr* become affiliated

affi'nare *vt* sharpen; (*perfezionare*) refine

affinché *conj* so that, in order that

af'fin|e *adj* similar. **~ità** *f* affinity

affiora'mento *m* emergence; (*Naut*) surfacing

affio'rare *vi* emerge; *fig* come to light

af'fisso *m* bill; (*Gram*) affix

affitta'camere *m inv* landlord ● *f inv* landlady

affit'tare *vt* rent; **'af'fittasi'** 'for rent'

af'fitt|o *m* rent; **contratto d'~o** lease; **dare in ~o** let; **prendere in ~o** rent. **~u'ario, -a** *mf* (*Jur*) lessee

af'fligger|e *vt* torment. **~si** *vr* distress oneself

af'fli|tto *adj* distressed. **~zi'one** *f* distress; *fig* affliction

afflosci'arsi *vr* become floppy; (*accasciarsi*) flop down; (morale:) decline

afflu'en|te *adj & m* tributary. **~za** *f* flow; (*di gente*) crowd

afflu'ire *vi* flow; *fig* pour in

af'flusso *m* influx

affo'ga|re *vt/i* drown; (*Culin*) poach; **~re in** *fig* be swamped with. **~to** *adj* (persona) drowned; (uova) poached. **~to al caffè** *m ice cream with hot espresso poured over it*

affol'la|re *vt*, **~rsi** *vr* crowd. **~to** *adj* crowded

affonda'mento *m* sinking

affon'dare *vt/i* sink

affossa'mento *m* pothole

affran'ca|re *vt* redeem (bene); stamp (lettera); free (schiavo). **~rsi** *vr* free oneself. **~'trice** *f* franking machine. **~'tura** *f* stamping; (*di spedizione*) postage

af'franto *adj* prostrated; (*esausto*) worn out

af'fresco *m* fresco

affret'ta|re *vt* speed up. **~rsi** *vr* hurry. **~ta'mente** *adv* hastily. **~to** *adj* hasty

affron'tar|e *vt* face; confront (nemico); meet (spese). **~si** *vr* clash

af'fronto *m* affront, insult; **fare un ~ a qcno** insult sb

affumi'ca|re *vt* fill with smoke; (*Culin*) smoke. **~to** *adj* (prosciutto, formaggio) smoked

affuso'la|re *vt* taper [off]. **~to** *adj* tapering

afo'risma *m* aphorism

a'foso *adj* sultry
'Africa *f* Africa. **afri'cano, -a** *agg & mf* African
afrodi'siaco *adj & m* aphrodisiac
a'genda *f* diary
agen'dina *f* pocket-diary
a'gente *m* agent; **agenti** *pl* **atmosferici** atmospheric agents. **~ di cambio** stockbroker. **~ di polizia** police officer
agen'zia *f* agency; (*filiale*) branch office; (*di banca*) branch. **~ di viaggi** travel agency. **~ immobiliare** estate agency
agevo'la|re *vt* facilitate. **~zi'one** *f* facilitation
a'gevol|e *adj* easy; (strada) smooth. **~'mente** *adv* easily
agganci'ar|e *vt* hook up; (*Rail*) couple. **~si** *vr* (vestito:) hook up
ag'geggio *m* gadget
agget'tivo *m* adjective
agghiacci'ante *adj* terrifying
agghiacci'ar|e *vt fig* **~ qcno** make sb's blood run cold. **~si** *vr* freeze
agghin'da|re *vt* [!] dress up. **~rsi** *vr* [!] doll oneself up. **~to** *adj* dressed up
aggiorna'mento *m* up-date
aggior'na|re *vt* (*rinviare*) postpone; (*mettere a giorno*) bring up to date. **~rsi** *vr* get up to date. **~to** *adj* up-to-date; (versione) updated
aggi'rar|e *vt* surround; (*fig: ingannare*) trick. **~si** *vr* hang about; **~si su** (discorso ecc:) be about; (somma:) be around
aggiudi'car|e *vt* award; (*all'asta*) knock down. **~si** *vr* win
aggi'un|gere *vt* add. **~ta** *f* addition. **~'tivo** *adj* supplementary. **~to** *adj* added ● *adj & m* (*assistente*) assistant
aggiu'star|e *vt* mend; (*sistemare*) settle; ([!]: *mettere a posto*) fix. **~si** *vr* adapt; (*mettersi in ordine*) tidy oneself up; (*decidere*) sort things out; (tempo:) clear up
agglomera'mento *m* conglomeration
agglome'rato *m* built-up area
aggrap'par|e *vt* grasp. **~si** *vr* **~si a** cling to
aggra'vante (*Jur*) *f* aggravation ● *adj* aggravating
aggra'var|e *vt* (*peggiorare*) make worse; increase (pena); (*appesantire*) weigh down. **~si** *vr* worsen
aggrazi'ato *adj* graceful
aggre'dire *vt* attack
aggre'ga|re *vt* add; (*associare a un gruppo ecc*) admit. **~rsi** *vr* **~rsi a** join. **~to** a associated ● *m* aggregate; (*di case*) block
aggressi'one *f* aggression; (*atto*) attack
aggres's|ivo *adj* aggressive. **~ività** *f* aggressiveness. **~ore** *m* aggressor
aggrin'zare, aggrin'zire *vt* wrinkle
aggrot'tare *vt* **~ le ciglia/la fronte** frown
aggrovigli'a|re *vt* tangle. **~rsi** *vr* get entangled; *fig* get complicated. **~to** *adj* entangled; *fig* confused
agguan'tare *vt* catch
aggu'ato *m* ambush; (*tranello*) trap; **stare in ~** lie in wait
agguer'rito *adj* fierce
agia'tezza *f* comfort
agi'ato *adj* (persona) well off; (vita) comfortable
a'gibil|e *adj* (palazzo) fit for human habitation. **~ità** *f* fitness for human habitation
'agil|e *adj* agile. **~ità** *f* agility
'agio *m* ease; **mettersi a proprio ~** make oneself at home
a'gire *vi* act; (*comportarsi*) behave; (*funzionare*) work; **~ su** affect
agi'ta|re *vt* shake; wave (mano); (*fig: turbare*) trouble. **~rsi** *vr* toss about; (*essere inquieto*) be restless; (mare:) get rough. **~to** *adj* restless; (mare) rough. **~'tore, ~'trice** *mf* (*persona*) agitator. **~zi'one** *f* agitation; **mettere in ~zione qcno** make sb worried
'agli = A + GLI
'aglio *m* garlic
a'gnello *m* lamb
agno'lotti *mpl* ravioli *sg*
a'gnostico, -a *adj & mf* agnostic
'ago *m* needle
ago'ni|a *f* agony. **~z'zare** *vi* be on one's deathbed
ago'nistic|a *f* competition. **~o** *adj* competitive
agopun'tura *f* acupuncture

a'gosto *m* August

a'grari|a *f* agriculture. **~o** *adj* agricultural ● *m* landowner

a'gricol|o *adj* agricultural. **~'tore** *m* farmer. **~'tura** *f* agriculture

agri'foglio *m* holly

agritu'rismo *m* farm holidays, agrotourism

Agriturismo In the 1980s many farmers began to supplement their falling incomes by offering tourists an authentic experience of the Italian countryside. *Agriturismo* is now a very popular form of tourism in Italy. Guests can learn traditional skills and crafts, such as cooking and wine-making, all of which helps to preserve a threatened way of life.

'agro *adj* sour

agroalimen'tare *adj* food *attrib*

agro'dolce *adj* bitter-sweet; (*Culin*) sweet-and-sour; **in ~** sweet and sour

agrono'mia *f* agronomy

a'grume *m* citrus fruit; (*pianta*) citrus tree

aguz'zare *vt* sharpen; **~ le orecchie** prick up one's ears; **~ la vista** look hard

aguz'zino *m* slave-driver; (*carceriere*) jailer

ahimè *int* alas

'ai = A + I

'aia *f* threshing-floor

'Aia *f* **L'~** The Hague

Aids *mf* Aids

ai'rone *m* heron

ai'tante *adj* sturdy

aiu'ola *f* flower-bed

aiu'tante *mf* assistant ● *m* (*Mil*) adjutant. **~ di campo** aide-de-camp

aiu'tare *vt* help

ai'uto *m* help, aid; (*assistente*) assistant

aiz'zare *vt* incite; **~ contro** set on

al = A+IL

'ala *f* wing; **fare ~** make way

ala'bastro *m* alabaster

'alacre *adj* brisk

a'lano *m* Great Dane

'alba *f* dawn

Alba'n|ia *f* Albania. **a~ese** *adj & mf* Albanian

albeggi'are *vi* dawn

albe'ra|to *adj* wooded; (viale) tree-lined. **~'tura** *f* (*Naut*) masts *pl*. **albe'rello** *m* sapling

al'berg|o *m* hotel. **~o diurno** *hotel where rooms are rented during the daytime*. **~a'tore, ~a'trice** *mf* hotel-keeper. **~hi'ero** *adj* hotel *attrib*

'albero *m* tree; (*Naut*) mast; (*Mech*) shaft. **~ genealogico** family tree. **~ maestro** (*Naut*) mainmast. **~ di Natale** Christmas tree

albi'cocc|a *f* apricot. **~o** *m* apricot-tree

al'bino, -a *mf* albino

'albo *m* register; (*libro ecc*) album; (*per avvisi*) notice board

'album *m* album. **~ da disegno** sketch-book

al'bume *m* albumen

'alce *m* elk

'alcol *m* alcohol; (*Med*) spirit; (*liquori forti*) spirits *pl*; **darsi all'~** take to drink. **al'colici** *mpl* alcoholic drinks. **al'colico** *adj* alcoholic. **alco'lismo** *m* alcoholism. **~iz'zato, -a** *adj & mf* alcoholic

alco'test® *m inv* Breathalyser®

al'cova *f* alcove

al'cun, al'cuno *adj & pron* any; **non ha ~ amico** he hasn't any/has no friends. **alcuni** *pl* some, a few; **~i suoi amici** some of his friends

alea'torio *adj* unpredictable

a'letta *f* (*Mech*) fin

alfa'betico *adj* alphabetical

alfabetizzazi'one *f* **~ della popolazione** teaching people to read and write

alfa'beto *m* alphabet

alfi'ere *m* (*negli scacchi*) bishop

al'fine *adv* eventually, in the end

'alga *f* seaweed

'algebra *f* algebra

Alge'ri|a *f* Algeria. **a~no, -a** *agg & mf* Algerian

ali'ante *m* glider

'alibi *m inv* alibi

alie'na|re *vt* alienate. **~rsi** *vr* become estranged; **~rsi le simpatie di qcno**

a

lose sb's good will. **~to, -a** *adj* alienated ● *mf* lunatic

a'lieno, -a *mf* alien ● *adj* **è ~ da invidia** envy is foreign to him

alimen'ta|re *vt* feed; *fig* foment ● *adj* food *attrib*; (abitudine) dietary ● *m* **~ri** *pl* food-stuffs. **~'tore** *m* power unit. **~zi'one** *f* feeding

> **Alimentari** *Alimentari* are food shops offering a range of products, from groceries, fruit, and vegetables to prepared foods like cheeses, cured hams, and salamis. Some even bake their own bread. An *alimentari* will also usually prepare *panini* (filled rolls) using their own ingredients. Small villages which have no other shops usually have an *alimentari*.

ali'mento *m* food; **alimenti** *pl* food; (*Jur*) alimony

a'liquota *f* share; (*di imposta*) rate

ali'scafo *m* hydrofoil

'alito *m* breath

'alla = **A + LA**

allaccia'mento *m* connection

allacci'ar|e *vt* fasten (cintura); lace up (scarpe); do up (vestito); (*collegare*) connect; form (amicizia). **~si** *vr* do up, fasten

allaga'mento *m* flooding

alla'gar|e *vt* flood. **~si** *vr* become flooded

allampa'nato *adj* lanky

allarga'mento *m* (*di strada, ricerche*) widening

allar'gar|e *vt* widen; open (braccia, gambe); let out (vestito ecc); *fig* extend. **~si** *vr* widen

allar'mante *adj* alarming

allar'ma|re *vt* alarm. **~to** *adj* panicky

al'larme *m* alarm; **dare l'~** raise the alarm; **falso ~** *fig* false alarm. **~ aereo** air raid warning

allar'mis|mo *m* alarmism. **~ta** *mf* alarmist

allatta'mento *m* (*di animale*) suckling; (*di neonato*) feeding

allat'tare *vt* suckle (animale); feed (neonato)

'alle = **A + LE**

alle'a|nza *f* alliance. **~to, -a** *adj* allied ● *mf* ally

alle'ar|e *vt* unite. **~si** *vr* form an alliance

alle'ga|re[1] *vt* (*Jur*) allege

alle'ga|re[2] *vt* (*accludere*) enclose; set on edge (denti). **~to** *adj* enclosed ● *m* enclosure; **in ~to** attached. **~zi'one** *f* (*Jur*) allegation

allegge'rir|e *vt* lighten; *fig* alleviate. **~si** *vr* become lighter; (*vestirsi leggero*) put on lighter clothes

allego'ria *f* allegory. **alle'gorico** *adj* allegorical

allegra'mente *adv* breezily

alle'gria *f* gaiety

al'legro *adj* cheerful; (colore) bright; (*brillo*) tipsy ● *m* (*Mus*) allegro

alle'luia *int* hallelujah!

allena'mento *m* training

alle'na|re *vt*, **~rsi** *vr* train. **~'tore, ~'trice** *mf* trainer, coach

allen'tar|e *vt* loosen; *fig* relax. **~si** *vr* become loose; (*Mech*) work loose

aller'gia *f* allergy. **al'lergico** *adj* allergic

all'erta *f* stare **~** be alert

allesti'mento *m* preparation. **~ scenico** (*Theat*) set

alle'stire *vt* prepare; stage (spettacolo); (*Naut*) fit out

allet'tante *adj* alluring

allet'tare *vt* entice

alleva'mento *m* breeding; (*processo*) bringing up; (*luogo*) farm; (*per piante*) nursery; **pollo di ~** battery chicken

alle'vare *vt* bring up (bambini); breed (animali); grow (piante)

allevi'are *vt* alleviate; *fig* lighten

alli'bito *adj* astounded

allibra'tore *m* bookmaker

allie'tar|e *vt* gladden. **~si** *vr* rejoice

alli'evo, -a *mf* pupil ● *m* (*Mil*) cadet

alliga'tore *m* alligator

allinea'mento *m* alignment

alline'ar|e *vt* line up; (*Typ*) align; *Fin* adjust. **~si** *vr* fall into line

'allo = **A + LO**

al'locco *m* *Zool* tawny owl

al'lodola *f* [sky]lark

alloggi'are *vt* put up; (casa:) provide accommodation for; (*Mil*) billet ● *vi* stay; (*Mil*) be billeted. **al'loggio** *m* apartment; (*Mil*) billet

allontana'mento *m* removal

allonta'nar|e *vt* move away; (*licenziare*) dismiss; avert (pericolo). **~si** *vr* go away

al'lora *adv* then; (*a quel tempo*) at that time; (*in tal caso*) in that case; **d'~ in poi** from then on; **e ~?** what now?; (*e con ciò?*) so what?; **fino ~** until then

al'loro *m* laurel; (*Culin*) bay

'alluce *m* big toe

alluci'na|nte *adj* [!] incredible; **sostanza ~nte** hallucinogen. **~to, -a** *mf* [!] space cadet. **~zi'one** *f* hallucination

allucino'geno *adj* (sostanza) hallucinatory

al'ludere *vi* **~ a** allude to

allu'minio *m* aluminium

allun'gar|e *vt* lengthen; stretch [out] (gamba); extend (tavolo); (*diluire*) dilute; **~e il collo** crane one's neck. **~e le mani su qcno** touch sb up. **~e il passo** quicken one's step. **~si** *vr* grow longer; (*crescere*) grow taller; (*sdraiarsi*) lie down

allusi'one *f* allusion

allu'sivo *adj* allusive

alluvio'nale *adj* alluvial

alluvi'one *f* flood

al'meno *adv* at least; **[se] ~ venisse il sole!** if only the sun would come out!

a'logeno *m* halogen ● *adj* **lampada alogena** halogen lamp

a'lone *m* halo

'Alpi *fpl* **le ~** the Alps

alpi'nis|mo *m* mountaineering. **~ta** *mf* mountaineer

al'pino *adj* Alpine ● *m* (*Mil*) **gli alpini** the Alpine troops

al'quanto *adj* a certain amount of ● *adv* rather

alt *int* stop

alta'lena *f* swing; (*tavola in bilico*) seesaw

altale'nare *vi fig* vacillate

alta'mente *adv* highly

al'tare *m* altar

alta'rino *m* **scoprire gli altarini di qcno** reveal sb's guilty secrets

alte'ra|re *vt* alter; adulterate (vino); (*falsificare*) falsify. **~rsi** *vr* be altered; (cibo:) go bad; (merci:) deteriorate; (*arrabbiarsi*) get angry. **~to** *adj* (vino) adulterated. **~zi'one** *f* alteration; (*di vino*) adulteration

al'terco *m* altercation

alter'nanza *f* alternation

alter'na|re *vt*, **~rsi** *vr* alternate. **~'tiva** *f* alternative. **~'tivo** *adj* alternate. **~to** *adj* alternating. **~'tore** *m* (*Electr*) alternator

al'tern|o *adj* alternate; **a giorni ~i** every other day

al'tero *adj* haughty

al'tezza *f* height; (*profondità*) depth; (*suono*) pitch; (*di tessuto*) width; (*titolo*) Highness; **essere all'~ di** be on a level with; *fig* be up to

altezzos|a'mente *adv* haughtily. **~ità** *f* haughtiness

altez'zoso *adj* haughty

al'ticcio *adj* tipsy, merry

altipi'ano *m* plateau

alti'tudine *f* altitude

'alto *adj* high; (*di statura*) tall; (*profondo*) deep; (suono) high-pitched; (tessuto) wide; (*Geog*) northern; **a notte alta** in the middle of the night; **avere degli alti e bassi** have some ups and downs; **ad alta fedeltà** high-fidelity; **a voce alta, ad alta voce** in a loud voice; (leggere) aloud; **essere in ~ mare** be on the high seas. **alta finanza** *f* high finance. **alta moda** *f* high fashion. **alta tensione** *f* high voltage ● *adv* high; **in ~** at the top; (guardare:) up; **mani in ~!** hands up!

alto'forno *m* blast-furnace

altolà *int* halt there!

altolo'cato *adj* highly placed

altopar'lante *m* loudspeaker

altopi'ano *m* plateau

altret'tanto *adj & pron* as much; (*pl*) as many ● *adv* likewise; **buona fortuna! – grazie, ~** good luck! – thank you, the same to you

altri'menti *adv* otherwise

'altro *adj* other; **un ~, un'altra** another; **l'altr'anno** last year; **domani l'~** the day after tomorrow; **l'ho visto l'~ giorno** I saw him the other day ● *pron* other [one]; **un ~, un'altra** another [one]; **ne vuoi dell'~?** would you like some more?; **l'un l'~** one another; **nessun ~** nobody else; **gli altri** (*la gente*) other people ● *m* something else; **non fa ~ che lavorare** he does nothing but work; **desidera ~?** (*in negozio*) anything else?; **più che ~, sono stanco** I'm tired more than anything; **se non ~** at least; **senz'~** certainly; **tra l'~** what's more; **~ che!** and how!

altroi'eri *m* **l'~** the day before yesterday

al'tronde *adv* **d'~** on the other hand

al'trove *adv* elsewhere

al'trui *adj* other people's ● *m* other people's belongings *pl*

al'tura *f* high ground; (*Naut*) deep sea

a'lunno, -a *mf* pupil

alve'are *m* hive

al'za|re *vt* lift; (*costruire*) build; (*Naut*) hoist; **~re le spalle** shrug one's shoulders. **~rsi** *vr* rise; (*in piedi*) stand up; (*da letto*) get up; **~rsi in piedi** get to one's feet. **~ta** *f* lifting; (*aumento*) rise; (*da letto*) getting up; (*Archit*) elevation. **~to** *adj* up

a'mabile *adj* lovable; (vino) sweet

a'maca *f* hammock

amalga'mar|e *vt*, **~si** *vr* amalgamate

a'mante *adj* **~ di** fond of ● *m* lover ● *f* mistress, lover

a'ma|re *vt* love; like (musica, ecc). **~to, -a** *adj* loved ● *mf* beloved

ama'rena *f* sour black cherry

ama'retto *m* macaroon

ama'rezza *f* bitterness; (*dolore*) sorrow

a'maro *adj* bitter ● *m* bitterness; (*liquore*) bitters *pl*

ama'rognolo *adj* rather bitter

ama'tore, -'trice *mf* lover

ambasci'a|ta *f* embassy; (*messaggio*) message. **~'tore, ~'trice** *m* ambassador ● *f* ambassadress

ambe'due *adj & pron* both

ambien'ta|le *adj* environmental. **~'lista** *adj & mf* environmentalist

ambien'tar|e *vt* acclimatize; set (personaggio, film ecc). **~si** *vr* get acclimatized

ambi'ente *m* environment; (*stanza*) room; *fig* milieu

ambiguità *f inv* ambiguity; (*di persona*) shadiness

am'biguo *adj* ambiguous; (persona) shady

am'bire *vi* **~ a** aspire to

'ambito *m* sphere

ambiva'len|te *adj* ambivalent. **~za** *f* ambivalence

ambizi'o|ne *f* ambition. **~so** *adj* ambitious

ambu'lante *adj* wandering; **venditore ~** hawker

ambu'lanza *f* ambulance

ambula'torio *m* (*di medico*) surgery; (*di ospedale*) out-patients'

a'meba *f* amoeba

a'meno *adj* pleasant

A'merica *f* America. **~ del Sud** South America. **ameri'cano, -a** *agg & mf* American

ami'anto *m* asbestos

ami'chevole *adj* friendly

ami'cizia *f* friendship; **fare ~ con qcno** make friends with sb; **amicizie** *pl* (*amici*) friends

a'mico, -a *mf* friend; **~ del cuore** bosom friend

'amido *m* starch

ammac'ca|re *vt* dent; bruise (frutto). **~rsi** *vr* (metallo:) get dented; (frutto:) bruise. **~to** *adj* dented; (frutto) bruised. **~'tura** *f* dent; (*livido*) bruise

ammae'stra|re *vt* (*istruire*) teach; train (animale). **~to** *adj* trained

ammai'nare *vt* lower (bandiera); furl (vele)

amma'la|rsi *vr* fall ill. **~to, -a** *adj* ill ● *mf* sick person; (*paziente*) patient

ammali'are *vt* bewitch

am'manco *m* deficit

ammanet'tare *vt* handcuff

ammani'cato *adj* **essere ~** have connections

amma'raggio *m* splashdown

amma'rare *vi* put down on the sea; (nave spaziale:) splash down

ammas'sar|e *vt* amass. **~si** *vr* crowd together. **am'masso** *m* mass; (*mucchio*) pile

ammat'tire *vi* go mad

ammaz'zar|e *vt* kill. **~si** *vr* (*suicidarsi*) kill oneself; (*rimanere ucciso*) be killed

am'menda *f* amends *pl*; (*multa*) fine; **fare ~ di qcsa** make amends for sth
am'messo *pp di* **ammettere** ● *conj* **~ che** supposing that
am'mettere *vt* admit; (*riconoscere*) acknowledge; (*supporre*) suppose
ammic'care *vi* wink
ammini'stra|re *vt* administer; (*gestire*) run. **~'tivo** *adj* administrative. **~'tore, ~'trice** *mf* administrator; (*di azienda*) manager; (*di società*) director. **~tore delegato** managing director. **~zi'one** *f* administration; **fatti di ordinaria ~zione** *fig* routine matters
ammi'ragli|o *m* admiral. **~'ato** *m* admiralty
ammi'ra|re *vt* admire. **~to** *adj* **restare/essere ~to** be full of admiration. **~'tore, ~'trice** *mf* admirer. **~zi'one** *f* admiration. **ammi'revole** *adj* admirable
ammis'sibile *adj* admissible
ammissi'one *f* admission; (*approvazione*) acknowledgement
ammobili'a|re *vt* furnish. **~to** *adj* furnished
am'modo *adj* proper ● *adv* properly
am'mollo *m* **in ~** soaking
ammo'niaca *f* ammonia
ammoni'mento *m* warning; (*di rimprovero*) admonishment
ammo'ni|re *vt* warn; (*rimproverare*) admonish. **~'tore** *adj* admonishing. **~zi'one** *f Sport* warning
ammon'tare *vi* **~ a** amount to ● *m* amount
ammonticchi'are *vt* heap up
ammorbi'dente *m* (*per panni*) softener
ammorbi'dir|e *vt*, **~si** *vr* soften
ammorta'mento *m* (*Comm*) amortization
ammor'tare *vt* pay off (spesa); (*Comm*) amortize (debito)
ammortiz'za|re *vt* (*Comm*) = **AMMORTARE**; (*Mech*) damp. **~'tore** *m* shock-absorber
ammosci'ar|e *vt* make flabby. **~si** *vi* get flabby
ammucchi'a|re *vt*, **~rsi** *vr* pile up. **~ta** *f* (☒: *orgia*) orgy
ammuf'fi|re *vi* go mouldy. **~to** *adj* mouldy
ammutina'mento *m* mutiny
ammuti'narsi *vr* mutiny
ammuto'lire *vi* be struck dumb
amni'stia *f* amnesty
'amo *m* hook; *fig* bait
a'more *m* love; **fare l'~** make love; **per l'amor di Dio/del cielo!** for heaven's sake!; **andare d'~ e d'accordo** get on like a house on fire; **amor proprio** self-respect; **è un ~** (persona) he/she is a darling; **per ~ di** for the sake of; **amori** *pl* love affairs. **~ggi'are** *vi* flirt. **amo'revole** *adj* loving
a'morfo *adj* shapeless; (fig) grey
amo'roso *adj* loving; (sguardo ecc) amorous; (lettera, relazione) love
ampi'ezza *f* (*di esperienza*) breadth; (*di stanza*) spaciousness; (*di gonna*) fullness; (*importanza*) scale
'ampio *adj* ample; (esperienza) wide; (stanza) spacious; (vestito) loose; (gonna) full; (pantaloni) baggy
am'plesso *m* embrace
amplia'mento *m* (*di casa, porto*) enlargement; (*di strada*) widening
ampli'are *vt* broaden (conoscenze)
amplifi'ca|re *vt* amplify; *fig* magnify. **~'tore** *m* amplifier. **~zi'one** *f* amplification
am'polla *f* cruet
ampu'ta|re *vt* amputate. **~zi'one** *f* amputation
amu'leto *m* amulet
anabbagli'ante *adj* (*Auto*) dipped ● *mpl* **anabbaglianti** dipped headlights
anacro'nis|mo *m* anachronism. **~tico** *adj* anachronistic
a'nagrafe *f* (*ufficio*) register office; (*registro*) register of births, marriages and deaths
ana'grafico *adj* **dati** *mpl* **anagrafici** personal data
ana'gramma *m* anagram
anal'colico *adj* non-alcoholic ● *m* soft drink, non-alcoholic drink
analfa'be|ta *adj & mf* illiterate. **~'tismo** *m* illiteracy
anal'gesico *m* painkiller
a'nalisi *f inv* analysis; (*Med*) test. **~ grammaticale/del periodo/logica** parsing. **~ del sangue** blood test
ana'li|sta *mf* analyst. **~tico** *adj* analyt-

ical. **~z'zare** *vt* analyse; (*Med*) test

anal'lergico *adj* hypoallergenic

analo'gia *f* analogy. **a'nalogo** *adj* analogous

'ananas *m inv* pineapple

anar'chi|a *f* anarchy. **a'narchico, -a** *adj* anarchic ● *mf* anarchist. **~smo** *m* anarchism

A.N.A.S. *f abbr* (Azienda Nazionale Autonoma delle Strade) *national road maintenance authority*

anato'mia *f* anatomy. **ana'tomico** *adj* anatomical; (sedia) contoured

'anatra *f* duck

ana'troccolo *m* duckling

'anca *f* hip; (*di animale*) flank

ance'strale *adj* ancestral

'anche *conj* also, too; (*persino*) even; **~ se** even if

anchilo'sato *adj fig* stiff

an'cora¹ *adv* still, yet; (*di nuovo*) again; (*di più*) some more; **~ una volta** once more

'anco|ra² *f* anchor; **gettare l'~ra** drop anchor. **~'raggio** *m* anchorage. **~'rare** *vt* anchor

anda'mento *m* (*del mercato, degli affari*) trend

an'dante *adj* (*corrente*) current; (*di poco valore*) cheap ● *m* (*Mus*) andante

an'da|re *vi* go; (*funzionare*) work; **~ via** (*partire*) leave; (macchia:) come out; **~ [bene]** (*confarsi*) suit; (taglia:) fit; **ti va bene alle tre?** does three o'clock suit you?; **non mi va di mangiare** I don't feel like eating; **~ di fretta** be in a hurry; **~ fiero di** be proud of; **~ di moda** be in fashion; **va per i 20 anni** he's nearly 20; **ma va' [là]!** come on!; **come va?** how are things?; **~ a male** go off; **~ a fuoco** go up in flames; **va spedito [entro] stamattina** it must be sent this morning; **ne va del mio lavoro** my job is at stake; **come è andata a finire?** how did it turn out?; **cosa vai dicendo?** what are you talking about?. **~rsene** go away; (*morire*) pass away ● *m* going; **a lungo ~re** eventually

'andito *m* passage

an'drone *m* entrance

a'neddoto *m* anecdote

ane'lare *vt* **~ a** long for. **a'nelito** *m* longing

a'nello *m* ring; (*di catena*) link

ane'mia *f* anaemia. **a'nemico** *adj* anaemic

a'nemone *m* anemone

aneste'si|a *f* anaesthesia; (*sostanza*) anaesthetic. **~'sta** *mf* anaesthetist. **ane'stetico** *adj & m* anaesthetic

an'fibi *mpl* (*stivali*) army boots

an'fibio *m* (*animale*) amphibian ● *adj* amphibious

anfite'atro *m* amphitheatre

'anfora *f* amphora

an'fratto *m* ravine

an'gelico *adj* angelic

'angelo *m* angel. **~ custode** guardian angel

angli'c|ano *adj* Anglican.

angli'smo *m* Anglicism

an'glofilo, -a *adj & mf* Anglophile

an'glofono, -a *mf* English-speaker

anglo'sassone *adj & mf* Anglo-Saxon

ango'la|re *adj* angular. **~zi'one** *f* angle shot

'angolo *m* corner; (*Math*) angle. **~ [di] cottura** kitchenette

ango'loso *adj* angular

an'gosci|a *f* anguish. **~'are** *vt* torment. **~'ato** *adj* agonized. **~'oso** *adj* (*disperato*) anguished; (*che dà angoscia*) distressing

angu'illa *f* eel

an'guria *f* water-melon

an'gusti|a *f* (*ansia*) anxiety; (*penuria*) poverty. **~'are** *vt* distress. **~'arsi** *vr* be very worried (**per** about)

an'gusto *adj* narrow

'anice *m* anise; (*Culin*) aniseed; (*liquore*) anisette

ani'dride *f* **~ carbonica** carbon dioxide

'anima *f* soul; **non c'era ~ viva** there was not a soul about; **all'~!** good grief!; **un'~ in pena** a soul in torment. **~ gemella** soul mate

ani'ma|le *adj & m* animal; **~li domestici** *pl* pets. **~'lesco** *adj* animal

ani'ma|re *vt* give life to; (*ravvivare*) enliven; (*incoraggiare*) encourage. **~rsi** *vr* come to life; (*accalorarsi*) become animated. **~to** *adj* animate; (discussione) animated; (paese) lively. **~'tore, ~'trice** *mf* leading spirit; *Cinema* animator. **~zi'one** *f* animation

'animo *m* (*mente*) mind; (*indole*) disposition; (*cuore*) heart; **perdersi d'~** lose heart; **farsi ~** take heart. **~sità** *f* animosity

ani'moso *adj* brave; (*ostile*) hostile

'anitra *f* = **ANATRA**

annac'qua|re *vt* water down. **~to** *adj* watered down

annaffi'a|re *vt* water. **~'toio** *m* watering-can

an'nali *mpl* annals

anna'spare *vi* flounder

an'nata *f* year; (*importo annuale*) annual amount; (*di vino*) vintage

annebbia'mento *m* fog build-up; *fig* clouding

annebbi'ar|e *vt* cloud (vista, mente). **~si** *vr* become foggy; (vista, mente:) grow dim

annega'mento *m* drowning

anne'ga|re *vt/i* drown

anne'rir|e *vt/i* blacken. **~si** *vr* become black

annessi'one *f* (*di nazione*) annexation

an'nesso *pp di* **annettere** ● *adj* attached; (stato) annexed

an'nettere *vt* add; (*accludere*) enclose; annex (stato)

annichi'lire *vt* annihilate

anni'darsi *vr* nest

annienta'mento *m* annihilation

annien'tar|e *vt* annihilate. **~si** *vr* abase oneself

anniver'sario *adj & m* anniversary. **~ di matrimonio** wedding anniversary

'anno *m* year; **Buon A~!** Happy New Year!; **quanti anni ha?** how old are you?; **Tommaso ha dieci anni** Thomas is ten [years old]. **~ bisestile** leap year

anno'dar|e *vt* knot; do up (cintura); *fig* form. **~si** *vr* become knotted

annoi'a|re *vt* bore; (*recare fastidio*) annoy. **~rsi** *vr* get bored; (*condizione*) be bored. **~to** *adj* bored

anno'ta|re *vt* note down; annotate (testo). **~zi'one** *f* note

annove'rare *vt* number

annu'a|le *adj* annual, yearly. **~rio** *m* year-book

annu'ire *vi* nod; (*acconsentire*) agree

annulla'mento *m* annulment; (*di appuntamento*) cancellation

annul'lar|e *vt* annul; cancel (appuntamento); (*togliere efficacia a*) undo; disallow (gol); (*distruggere*) destroy. **~si** *vr* cancel each other out

annunci'a|re *vt* announce; (*preannunciare*) foretell. **~'tore, ~'trice** *mf* announcer. **A~zi'one** *f* Annunciation

an'nuncio *m* announcement; (*pubblicitario*) advertisement; (*notizia*) news. **annunci** *pl* **economici** classified advertisements

'annuo *adj* annual, yearly

annu'sare *vt* sniff

annuvo'lar|e *vt* cloud. **~si** *vr* cloud over

'ano *m* anus

a'nomalo *adj* anomalous

anoni'mato *m* **mantenere l'~** remain anonymous

a'nonimo, -a *adj* anonymous ● *mf* (*pittore, scrittore*) anonymous painter/writer

ano'ressico, -a *mf* anorexic

anor'mal|e *adj* abnormal ● *mf* deviant. **~ità** *f inv* abnormality

'ansa *f* handle; (*di fiume*) bend

an'sare *vi* pant

'ansia, ansietà *f* anxiety; **stare/essere in ~ per** be anxious about

ansi'oso *adj* anxious

antago'nis|mo *m* antagonism. **~ta** *mf* antagonist

an'tartico *adj & m* Antarctic

antece'dente *adj* preceding ● *m* precedent

ante'fatto *m* prior event

ante'guerra *adj* pre-war ● *m* pre-war period

ante'nato, -a *mf* ancestor

an'tenna *f* (*Radio, TV*) aerial; (*di animale*) antenna; (*Naut*) yard. **~ parabolica** satellite dish

ante'porre *vt* put before

ante'prima *f* preview; **vedere qcsa in ~** have a sneak preview of sth

anteri'ore *adj* front *attrib*; (*nel tempo*) previous

antia'ereo *adj* anti-aircraft *attrib*
antial'lergico *adj* hypoallergenic
antia'tomico *adj* **rifugio ~** fallout shelter
antibi'otico *adj & m* antibiotic
anti'caglia *f* (*oggetto*) piece of old junk
antica'mente *adv* long ago
anti'camera *f* ante-room; **far ~** be kept waiting
antichità *f inv* antiquity; (*oggetto*) antique
antici'clone *m* anticyclone
antici'pa|re *vt* advance; (*Comm*) pay in advance; (*prevedere*) anticipate; (*prevenire*) forestall ● *vi* be early. **~ta'mente** *adv* in advance. **~zi'one** *f* anticipation; (*notizia*) advance news
an'ticipo *m* advance; (*caparra*) deposit; **in ~** early; (*nel lavoro*) ahead of schedule
an'tico *adj* ancient; (mobile ecc) antique; (*vecchio*) old; **all'antica** old-fashioned ● *mpl* **gli antichi** the ancients
anticoncezio'nale *adj & m* contraceptive
anticonfor'mis|mo *m* unconventionality. **~ta** *mf* nonconformist. **~tico** *adj* unconventional
anticonge'lante *adj & m* anti-freeze
anticostituzio'nale *adj* unconstitutional
anti'crimine *adj inv* (squadra) crime *attrib*
antidemo'cratico *adj* undemocratic
antidolo'rifico *m* painkiller
an'tidoto *m* antidote
anti'droga *adj inv* (campagna) anti-drugs; (squadra) drug *attrib*
antie'stetico *adj* ugly
antifa'scismo *m* anti-fascism
antifa'scista *adj & mf* anti-fascist
anti'furto *m* anti-theft device; (*allarme*) alarm ● *adj inv* (sistema) anti-theft
anti'gelo *m* antifreeze; (*parabrezza*) defroster
antigi'enico *adj* unhygienic
An'tille *fpl* **le ~** the West Indies
an'tilope *f* antelope
antin'cendio *adj inv* **allarme ~** fire alarm; **porta ~** fire door
anti'nebbia *m inv* (*Auto*) **[faro] ~** foglamp
antinfiamma'torio *adj & m* anti-inflammatory
antinucle'are *adj* anti-nuclear
antio'rario *adj* anti-clockwise
anti'pasto *m* hors d'oeuvre
an'tipodi *mpl* antipodes; **essere agli ~** *fig* be poles apart
antiquari'ato *m* antique trade
anti'quario, -a *mf* antique dealer
anti'quato *adj* antiquated
anti'ruggine *m inv* rust-inhibitor
anti'rughe *adj inv* anti-wrinkle *attrib*
anti'scippo *adj inv* theft-proof
anti'settico *adj & m* antiseptic
antisoci'ale *adj* anti-social
antista'minico *m* antihistamine
anti'stante a *prep* in front of
anti'tarlo *m inv* woodworm treatment
antiterro'ristico *adj* antiterrorist *attrib*
an'titesi *f inv* antithesis
'antivirus *m inv* virus checker
antolo'gia *f* anthology
'antro *m* cavern
antropolo'gia *f* anthropology. **an'tro'pologo, -a** *mf* anthropologist
anu'lare *m* ring-finger
'anzi *conj* in fact; (*o meglio*) or better still; (*al contrario*) on the contrary
anzianità *f* old age; (*di servizio*) seniority
anzi'ano, -a *adj* elderly; (*di grado*) senior ● *mf* elderly person
anziché *conj* rather than
anzi'tempo *adv* prematurely
anzi'tutto *adv* first of all
a'orta *f* aorta
apar'titico *adj* unaligned
apa'tia *f* apathy. **a'patico** *adj* apathetic
'ape *f* bee; **nido di api** honeycomb
aperi'tivo *m* aperitif
aperta'mente *adv* openly
a'perto *adj* open; **all'aria aperta** in the open air; **all'~** open-air
aper'tura *f* opening; (*inizio*) beginning; (*ampiezza*) spread; (*di arco*) span; (*Pol*) overtures *pl*; (*Phot*) aperture; **~ mentale** openness

'apice *m* apex
apicol'tura *f* beekeeping
ap'nea *f* **immersione in ~** free diving
a'polide *adj* stateless ● *mf* stateless person
a'postolo *m* apostle
apostro'fare *vt* (*mettere un apostrofo a*) write with an apostrophe; reprimand (persona)
a'postrofo *m* apostrophe
appaga'mento *m* fulfilment
appa'ga|re *vt* satisfy. **~rsi** *vr* **~rsi di** be satisfied with
appai'are *vt* pair; mate (animali)
appallotto'lare *vt* roll into a ball
appalta'tore *m* contractor
ap'palto *m* contract; **dare in ~** to contract
appan'naggio *m* (*in denaro*) annuity; *fig* prerogative
appan'nar|e *vt* mist (vetro); dim (vista). **~si** *vr* mist over; (vista:) grow dim
appa'rato *m* apparatus; (*pompa*) display
apparecchi'a|re *vt* prepare ● *vi* lay the table. **~'tura** *f* (*impianti*) equipment
appa'recchio *m* apparatus; (*congegno*) device; (*radio, tv ecc*) set; (*aeroplano*) aircraft. **~ acustico** hearing aid
appa'ren|te *adj* apparent. **~te'mente** *adv* apparently. **~za** *f* appearance; **in ~za** apparently.
appa'ri|re *vi* appear; (*sembrare*) look. **~'scente** *adj* striking; *pej* gaudy. **~zi'one** *f* apparition
apparta'mento *m* apartment
appar'ta|rsi *vr* withdraw. **~to** *adj* secluded
apparte'nenza *f* membership
apparte'nere *vi* belong
appassio'nante *adj* (storia, argomento) exciting
appassio'na|re *vt* excite; (*commuovere*) move. **~rsi** *vr* **~rsi a** become excited by. **~to** *adj* passionate; **~to di** (*entusiastico*) fond of
appas'sir|e *vi* wither. **~si** *vr* fade
appel'larsi *vr* **~ a** appeal to
ap'pello *m* appeal; (*chiamata per nome*) rollcall; (*esami*) exam session; **fare l'~** call the roll
ap'pena *adv* just; (*a fatica*) hardly ● *conj* **[non] ~** as soon as
ap'pendere *vt* hang [up]
appen'dice *f* appendix. **appendi'cite** *f* appendicitis
Appen'nini *mpl* **gli ~** the Apennines
appesan'tir|e *vt* weigh down. **~si** *vr* become heavy
ap'peso *pp di* **appendere** *adj* hanging; (*impiccato*) hanged
appe'ti|to *m* appetite; **aver ~to** be hungry; **buon ~to!** enjoy your meal!. **~'toso** *adj* appetizing; *fig* tempting
appezza'mento *m* plot of land
appia'nar|e *vt* level; *fig* smooth over. **~si** *vr* improve
appiat'tir|e *vt* flatten. **~si** *vr* flatten oneself
appic'care *vt* **~ il fuoco a** set fire to
appicci'car|e *vt* stick; **~e a** (*fig: appioppare*) palm off on ● *vi* be sticky. **~si** *vr* stick; (cose:) stick together; **~si a qcno** *fig* stick to sb like glue
appiccica'ticcio *adj* sticky; *fig* clingy
appicci'coso *adj* sticky; *fig* clingy
appie'dato *adj* **sono ~** I don't have the car; **sono rimasto ~** I was stranded
appi'eno *adv* fully
appigli'arsi *vr* **~ a** get hold of; *fig* stick to. **ap'piglio** *m* fingerhold; (*per piedi*) foothold; *fig* pretext
appiop'pare *vt* **~ a** palm off on; ([!]: *dare*) give
appiso'larsi *vr* doze off
applau'dire *vt/i* applaud. **ap'plauso** *m* applause
appli'cabile *adj* applicable
appli'ca|re *vt* apply; enforce (legge ecc). **~rsi** *vr* apply oneself. **~'tore** *m* applicator. **~zi'one** *f* application; (*di legge*) enforcement
appoggi'ar|e *vt* lean (**a** against); (*mettere*) put; (*sostenere*) back. **~si** *vr* **~si a** lean against; *fig* rely on. **ap'poggio** *m* support
appollai'arsi *vr fig* perch
ap'porre *vt* affix
appor'tare *vt* bring; (*causare*) cause. **ap'porto** *m* contribution
apposita'mente *adv* especially
ap'posito *adj* proper

a

ap'posta *adv* on purpose; (*espressamente*) specially

apposta'mento *m* ambush; (*caccia*) lying in wait

appo'star|e *vt* post (soldati). **~si** *vr* lie in wait

ap'prend|ere *vt* understand; (*imparare*) learn. **~i'mento** *m* learning

appren'di|sta *mf* apprentice. **~'stato** *m* apprenticeship

apprensi'one *f* apprehension; **essere in ~ per** be anxious about. **appren'sivo** *adj* apprehensive

ap'presso *adv & prep* (*vicino*) near; (*dietro*) behind; **come ~** as follows

appre'star|e *vt* prepare. **~si** *vr* get ready

apprez'za|bile *adj* appreciable. **~'mento** *m* appreciation; (*giudizio*) opinion

apprez'za|re *vt* appreciate. **~to** *adj* appreciated

ap'proccio *m* approach

appro'dare *vi* land; **~ a** *fig* come to; **non ~ a nulla** come to nothing. **ap'prodo** *m* landing; (*luogo*) landing-stage

approfit'ta|re *vi* take advantage (**di** of), profit (**di** by). **~'tore, ~'trice** *mf* chancer

approfondi'mento *m* deepening; **di ~** *fig*: (esame) further

approfon'di|re *vt* deepen. **~rsi** *vr* (divario:) widen. **~to** *adj* (studio, ricerca) in-depth

appropri'a|rsi *vr* (*essere adatto a*) suit; **~rsi di** take possession of. **~to** *adj* appropriate. **~zi'one** *f* (*Jur*) appropriation. **~zione indebita** (*Jur*) embezzlement

approssi'ma|re *vt* **~re per eccesso/difetto** round up/down. **~rsi** *vr* draw near. **~tiva'mente** *adv* approximately. **~'tivo** *adj* approximate. **~zi'one** *f* approximation

appro'va|re *vt* approve of; approve (legge). **~zi'one** *f* approval

approvvigiona'mento *m* supplying; **approvvigionamenti** *pl* provisions

approvvigio'nar|e *vt* supply. **~si** *vr* stock up

appunta'mento *m* appointment; **fissare un ~** make an appointment; **darsi ~** decide to meet

appun'tar|e *vt* (*annotare*) take notes; (*fissare*) fix; (*con spillo*) pin; (*appuntire*) sharpen. **~si** *vr* **~si su** (teoria:) be based on

appun'ti|re *vt* sharpen. **~to** *adj* (mento) pointed

ap'punto[1] *m* note; (*piccola critica*) niggle

ap'punto[2] *adv* exactly; **per l'~!** exactly!; **stavo ~ dicendo...** I was just saying...

appu'rare *vt* verify

a'pribile *adj* that can be opened

apribot'tiglie *m inv* bottle-opener

a'prile *m* April; **il primo d'~** April Fools' Day

a'prir|e *vt* open; turn on (acqua ecc); (*con chiave*) unlock; open up (ferita ecc). **~si** *vr* open; (*spaccarsi*) split; (*confidarsi*) confide (**con** in)

apri'scatole *f inv* tin-opener

aqua'planing *m* **andare in ~** aquaplane

'aquil|a *f* eagle; **non è un'~a!** he is no genius!. **~'lino** *adj* aquiline

aqui'lone *m* (*giocattolo*) kite

ara'besco *m* arabesque; *hum* scribble

A'rabia Sau'dita *f* **l'~** Saudi Arabia

'arabo, -a *adj* Arab; (lingua) Arabic ● *mf* Arab ● *m* (*lingua*) Arabic

a'rachide *f* peanut

ara'gosta *f* lobster

a'ranci|a *f* orange. **~'ata** *f* orangeade. **~o** *m* orange-tree; (*colore*) orange. **~'one** *adj & m* orange

a'ra|re *vt* plough. **~tro** *m* plough

ara'tura *f* ploughing

a'razzo *m* tapestry

arbi'trar|e *vt* arbitrate in; *Sport* referee. **~ietà** *f* arbitrariness. **~io** *adj* arbitrary

ar'bitrio *m* will; **è un ~** it's very high-handed

'arbitro *m* arbiter; *Sport* referee; (*nel baseball*) umpire

ar'busto *m* shrub

'arca *f* ark; (*cassa*) chest

ar'ca|ico *adj* archaic. **~'ismo** *m* archaism

ar'cangelo *m* archangel

ar'cata *f* arch; (*serie di archi*) arcade

arche|olo'gia *f* archaeology. **~o'lo-**

gico *adj* archaeological. **~'ologo, -a** *mf* archaeologist

ar'chetto *m* (*Mus*) bow

architet'tare *vt fig* devise; **cosa state architettando?** *fig* what are you plotting?

archi'tet|to *m* architect. **~'tonico** *adj* architectural. **~'tura** *f* architecture

archivi'are *vt* file; (*Jur*) close

ar'chivio *m* archives *pl*; (*Comput*) file

archi'vista *mf* filing clerk

ar'cigno *adj* grim

arci'pelago *m* archipelago

arci'vescovo *m* archbishop

'arco *m* arch; (*Math*) arc; (*Mus, arma*) bow; **nell'~ di una giornata/due mesi** in the space of a day/two months

arcoba'leno *m* rainbow

arcu'a|re *vt* bend. **~rsi** *vr* bend. **~to** *adj* bent, curved

ar'dente *adj* burning; *fig* ardent. **~'mente** *adv* ardently

'ardere *vt/i* burn

ar'desia *f* slate

ar'di|re *vi* dare. **~to** *adj* daring; (*coraggioso*) bold; (*sfacciato*) impudent

ar'dore *m* (*calore*) heat; *fig* ardour

'arduo *adj* arduous; (*ripido*) steep

'area *f* area. **~ di rigore** (*nel calcio*) penalty area. **~ di servizio** service area

a'rena *f* arena

are'narsi *vr* run aground; *fig*: (trattative) reach deadlock; **mi sono arenato** I'm stuck

'argano *m* winch

argen'tato *adj* silver-plated

argente'ria *f* silver[ware]

ar'gento *m* silver

ar'gil|la *f* clay. **~'loso** *adj* (terreno) clayey

argi'nare *vt* embank; *fig* hold in check, contain

'argine *m* embankment; (*diga*) dike

argomen'tare *vi* argue

argo'mento *m* argument; (*motivo*) reason; (*soggetto*) subject

argu'ire *vt* deduce

ar'gu|to *adj* witty. **~zia** *f* wit; (*battuta*) witticism

'aria *f* air; (*aspetto*) appearance; (*Mus*) tune; **andare all'~** *fig* come to nothing; **avere l'~...** look...; **corrente d'~** draught; **mandare all'~ qcsa** *fig* ruin sth

aridità *f* aridity, dryness

'arido *adj* arid

arieggi'a|re *vt* air. **~to** *adj* airy

ari'ete *m* ram. **A~** (*Astr*) Aries

ari'etta *f* (*brezza*) breeze

a'ringa *f* herring

ari'oso *adj* (locale) light and airy

aristo'cra|tico, -a *adj* aristocratic • *mf* aristocrat. **~'zia** *f* aristocracy

arit'metica *f* arithmetic

arlec'chino *m* Harlequin; *fig* buffoon

'arma *f* weapon; **armi** *pl* arms; (*forze armate*) [armed] forces; **chiamare alle armi** call up; **sotto le armi** in the army; **alle prime armi** *fig* inexperienced. **~ da fuoco** firearm. **armi** *mpl* **di distruzione di massa** weapons of mass destruction.

armadi'etto *m* locker, cupboard

ar'madio *m* cupboard; (*guardaroba*) wardrobe

armamen'tario *m* tools *pl*; *fig* paraphernalia

arma'mento *m* armament; (*Naut*) fitting out

ar'ma|re *vt* arm; (*equipaggiare*) fit out; (*Archit*) reinforce. **~rsi** *vr* arm oneself (**di** with). **~ta** *f* army; (*flotta*) fleet. **~'tore** *m* shipowner. **~'tura** *f* framework; (*impalcatura*) scaffolding; (*di guerriero*) armour

armeggi'are *vi fig* manoeuvre

armi'stizio *m* armistice

armo'ni|a *f* harmony. **ar'monica** *f* **~ [a bocca]** mouth organ. **ar'monico** *adj* harmonic. **~'oso** *adj* harmonious

armoniz'zar|e *vt* harmonize • *vi* match. **~si** *vr* (colori:) match

ar'nese *m* tool; (*oggetto*) thing; (*congegno*) gadget; **male in ~** in bad condition

'arnia *f* beehive

a'roma *m* aroma; **aromi** *pl* herbs. **~tera'pia** *f* aromatherapy

aro'matico *adj* aromatic

aromatiz'zare *vt* flavour

'arpa *f* harp

ar'peggio *m* arpeggio

a

ar'pia *f* harpy
arpi'one *m* hook; (*pesca*) harpoon
arrabat'tarsi *vr* do all one can
arrabbi'a|rsi *vr* get angry. **~to** *adj* angry. **~'tura** *f* rage; **prendersi una ~tura** fly into a rage
arraf'fare *vt* grab
arrampi'ca|rsi *vr* climb [up]. **~ta** *f* climb. **~'tore, ~'trice** *mf* climber. **~'tore sociale** social climber
arran'care *vi* limp, hobble
arrangia'mento *m* arrangement
arrangi'ar|e *vt* arrange. **~si** *vr* manage; **~si alla meglio** get by; **ar'rangiati!** get on with it!
arra'parsi *vr* [!] get randy
arre'care *vt* bring; (*causare*) cause
arreda'mento *m* interior decoration; (*l'arredare*) furnishing; (*mobili ecc*) furnishings *pl*
arre'da|re *vt* furnish. **~'tore, ~'trice** *mf* interior designer. **ar'redo** *m* furnishings *pl*
ar'rendersi *vr* surrender
arren'devo|le *adj* (persona) yielding. **~'lezza** *f* softness
arre'star|e *vt* arrest; (*fermare*) stop. **~si** *vr* halt. **ar'resto** *m* stop; (*Med, Jur*) arrest; **la dichiaro in [stato d'] arresto** you are under arrest; **mandato di arresto** warrant. **arresti** *pl* **domiciliari** (*Jur*) house arrest
arre'tra|re *vt/i* withdraw; pull back (giocatore). **~to** *adj* (paese ecc) backward; (*Mil: posizione*) rear; **numero ~to** (*di rivista*) back number; **del lavoro ~to** a backlog of work ● *m* (*di stipendio*) back pay
arre'trati *mpl* arrears
arricchi'mento *m* enrichment
arric'chi|re *vt* enrich. **~rsi** *vr* get rich. **~to, -a** *mf* nouveau riche
arricci'are *vt* curl; **~ il naso** turn up one's nose
ar'ringa *f* harangue; (*Jur*) closing address
arrischi'a|rsi *vr* dare. **~to** *adj* risky; (*imprudente*) rash
arri'va|re *vi* arrive; **~re a** (*raggiungere*) reach; (*ridursi*) be reduced to. **~to, -a** *adj* successful; **ben ~to!** welcome! ● *mf* successful person
arrive'derci *int* goodbye; **~ a domani** see you tomorrow
arri'vis|mo *m* social climbing; (*nel lavoro*) careerism. **~ta** *mf* social climber; (*nel lavoro*) careerist
ar'rivo *m* arrival; *Sport* finish
arro'gan|te *adj* arrogant. **~za** *f* arrogance
arro'garsi *vr* **~ il diritto di fare qcsa** take it upon oneself to do sth
arrossa'mento *m* reddening
arros'sar|e *vt* make red (occhi). **~si** *vr* go red
arros'sire *vi* blush, go red
arro'stire *vt* roast; toast (pane); (*ai ferri*) grill. **ar'rosto** *adj & m* roast
arroto'lare *vt* roll up
arroton'dar|e *vt* round; (*Math ecc*) round off. **~si** *vr* become round; (persona:) get plump
arrovel'larsi *vr* **~ il cervello** rack one's brains
arroven'ta|re *vt* make red-hot. **~rsi** *vr* become red-hot. **~to** *adj* red-hot
arruf'fa|re *vt* ruffle; *fig* confuse. **~to** *adj* (capelli) ruffled
arruffianarsi *vr* **~ qcno** *fig* butter sb up
arruggi'ni|re *vt* rust. **~rsi** *vr* go rusty; *fig* (*fisicamente*) stiffen up; (conoscenze:) go rusty. **~to** *adj* rusty
arruola'mento *m* enlistment
arruo'lar|e *vt/i*, **~si** *vr* enlist
arse'nale *m* arsenal; (*cantiere*) [naval] dockyard
ar'senico *m* arsenic
'arso *pp di* **ardere** ● *adj* burnt; (*arido*) dry. **ar'sura** *f* burning heat; (*sete*) parching thirst
'arte *f* art; (*abilità*) craftsmanship; **le belle arti** the fine arts. **arti figurative** figurative arts
arte'fa|re *vt* adulterate (vino); disguise (voce). **~tto** *adj* fake; (vino) adulterated
ar'tefice *mf* craftsman; craftswoman; *fig* author
ar'teria *f* artery. **~ [stradale]** arterial road
arterioscle'rosi *f* arteriosclerosis
'artico *adj & m* Arctic
artico'la|re *adj* articular ● *vt* articulate; (*suddividere*) divide. **~rsi** *vr fig*

~rsi in consist of. **~to** *adj* (*Auto*) articulated; *fig* well-constructed. **~zi'one** *f* (*Anat*) articulation

ar'ticolo *m* article. **~ di fondo** leader

artifici'ale *adj* artificial

arti'fici|o *m* artifice; (*affettazione*) affectation. **~'oso** *adj* artful; (*affettato*) affected

artigia'nal|e *adj* made by hand; *hum* amateurish. **~'mente** *adv* with craftsmanship; *hum* amateurishly

artigi|a'nato *m* craftsmanship; (*ceto*) craftsmen *pl*. **~'ano, -a** *m* craftsman • *f* craftswoman

artigli|'ere *m* artilleryman. **~e'ria** *f* artillery

ar'tiglio *m* claw; *fig* clutch

ar'tist|a *mf* artist. **~ica'mente** *adv* artistically. **~ico** *adj* artistic

'arto *m* limb

ar'trite *f* arthritis

ar'trosi *f* rheumatism

arzigogo'lato *adj* bizarre

ar'zillo *adj* sprightly

a'scella *f* armpit

ascen'den|te *adj* ascending • *m* (*antenato*) ancestor; (*influenza*) ascendancy; (*Astr*) ascendant

ascensi'one *f* ascent; **l'A~** the Ascension

ascen'sore *m* lift, elevator *Am*

a'scesa *f* ascent; (*al trono*) accession; (*al potere*) rise

a'scesso *m* abscess

a'sceta *mf* ascetic

'ascia *f* axe

asciugabianche'ria *m inv* (*stenditoio*) clothes horse

asciugaca'pelli *m inv* hair dryer

asciuga'mano *m* towel

asciu'gar|e *vt* dry. **~si** *vr* dry oneself; (*diventare asciutto*) dry up

asci'utto *adj* dry; (*magro*) wiry; (risposta) curt; **essere all'~** *fig* be hard up

ascol'ta|re *vt* listen to • *vi* listen. **~'tore, ~'trice** *mf* listener

a'scolto *m* listening; **dare ~ a** listen to; **mettersi in ~** *Radio* tune in

asfal'tare *vt* asphalt

a'sfalto *m* asphalt

asfis'si|a *f* asphyxia. **~'ante** *adj* oppressive; *fig*: (persona) annoying. **~'are** *vt* asphyxiate; *fig* annoy

'Asia *f* Asia. **asi'atico, -a** *agg & mf* Asian

a'silo *m* shelter; (*d'infanzia*) nursery school. **~ nido** day nursery. **~ politico** political asylum

asim'metrico *adj* asymmetrical

'asino *m* donkey; (*fig: persona stupida*) ass

'asma *f* asthma. **a'smatico** *adj* asthmatic

asoci'ale *adj* asocial

'asola *f* buttonhole

a'sparagi *mpl* asparagus *sg*

a'sparago *m* asparagus spear

asperità *f inv* harshness; (*di terreno*) roughness

aspet'ta|re *vt* wait for; (*prevedere*) expect; **~re un bambino** be expecting [a baby]; **fare ~re qcno** keep sb waiting • *vi* wait. **~rsi** *vr* expect. **~'tiva** *f* expectation

a'spetto[1] *m* appearance; (*di problema*) aspect; **di bell'~** good-looking

a'spetto[2] *m* **sala** *f* **d'~** waiting room

aspi'rante *adj* aspiring; (pompa) suction *attrib* • *mf* (*a un posto*) applicant; (*al trono*) aspirant; **gli aspiranti al titolo** the contenders for the title

aspira'polvere *m inv* vacuum cleaner

aspi'ra|re *vt* inhale; (*Mech*) suck in • *vi* **~re a** aspire to. **~'tore** *m* extractor fan. **~zi'one** *f* inhalation; (*Mech*) suction; (*ambizione*) ambition

aspi'rina *f* aspirin

aspor'tare *vt* take away

aspra'mente *adv* (*duramente*) severely

a'sprezza *f* (*al gusto*) sourness; (*di clima*) severity; (*di suono*) harshness; (*di odore*) pungency

'aspro *adj* (*al gusto*) sour; (clima) severe; (suono, parole) harsh; (odore) pungent; (litigio) bitter

assag|gi'are *vt* taste. **~'gini** *mpl* (*Culin*) samples. **as'saggio** *m* tasting; (*piccola quantità*) taste

as'sai *adv* very; (*moltissimo*) very much; (*abbastanza*) enough

assa'li|re *vt* attack. **~'tore, ~'trice** *mf* assailant

as'salto *m* attack; **prendere d'~** storm (città); *fig* mob (persona); hold up (banca)

assapo'rare *vt* savour

assassi'nare *vt* murder, assassinate

assas'sin|io *m* murder, assassination. **~o, -a** *adj* murderous ● *m* murderer ● *f* murderess

'asse *f* board ● *m* (*Techn*) axle; (*Math*) axis. **~ da stiro** ironing board

assecon'dare *vt* satisfy; (*favorire*) support

assedi'are *vt* besiege. **as'sedio** *m* siege

assegna'mento *m* allotment; **fare ~ su** rely on

asse'gna|re *vt* allot; award (premio). **~'tario** *mf* recipient. **~zi'one** *f* (*di alloggio, borsa di studio*) allocation; (*di premio*) award

as'segno *m* allowance; (*bancario*) cheque; **contro ~** cash on delivery. **~ circolare** bank draft. **assegni** *pl* **familiari** family allowance. **~ non trasferibile** non-transferable cheque.

assem'blea *f* assembly; (*adunanza*) gathering

assembra'mento *m* gathering

assen'nato *adj* sensible

as'senso *m* assent

assen'tarsi *vr* go away; (*da stanza*) leave the room

as'sen|te *adj* absent; (*distratto*) absent-minded ● *mf* absentee. **~te'ismo** *m* absenteeism. **~te'ista** *mf* frequent absentee. **~za** *f* absence; (*mancanza*) lack

asse'r|ire *vt* assert. **~'tivo** *adj* assertive. **~zi'one** *f* assertion

assesso'rato *m* department

asses'sore *m* councillor

assesta'mento *m* settlement

asse'star|e *vt* arrange; **~e un colpo** deal a blow. **~si** *vr* settle oneself

asse'tato *adj* parched

as'setto *m* order; (*Aeron, Naut*) trim

assicu'ra|re *vt* assure; (*Comm*) insure; register (posta); (*fissare*) secure; (*accertare*) ensure. **~rsi** *vr* (*con contratto*) insure oneself; (*legarsi*) fasten oneself; **~rsi che** make sure that. **~'tivo** *adj* insurance *attrib*. **~'tore, ~'trice** *mf* insurance agent ● *adj* insurance *attrib*. **~zi'one** *f* assurance; (*contratto*) insurance

assidera'mento *m* exposure. **assi'derato** *adj* (*Med*) suffering from exposure; [!] frozen

assidu|a'mente *adv* assiduously. **~ità** *f* assiduity

as'siduo *adj* assiduous; (cliente) regular

assil'lante *adj* (persona, pensiero) nagging

assil'lare *vt* pester

as'sillo *m* worry

assimi'la|re *vt* assimilate. **~zi'one** *f* assimilation

as'sise *fpl* assizes; **Corte d'A~** Court of Assize[s]

assi'sten|te *mf* assistant. **~te sociale** social worker. **~te di volo** flight attendant. **~za** *f* assistance; (*presenza*) presence. **~za sociale** social work

assistenzi'a|le *adj* welfare *attrib*. **~'lismo** *m* welfare

as'sistere *vt* assist; (*curare*) nurse ● *vi* **~ a** (*essere presente*) be present at; watch (spettacolo ecc)

'asso *m* ace; **piantare in ~** leave in the lurch

associ'a|re *vt* join; (*collegare*) associate. **~rsi** *vr* join forces; (*Comm*) enter into partnership. **~rsi a** join. **~zi'one** *f* association

assogget'tar|e *vt* subject. **~si** *vr* submit

asso'lato *adj* sunny

assol'dare *vt* recruit

as'solo *m* (*Mus*) solo

as'solto *pp di* **assolvere**

assoluta'mente *adv* absolutely

assolu'tismo *m* absolutism

asso'lu|to *adj* absolute. **~zi'one** *f* acquittal; (*Relig*) absolution

as'solvere *vt* perform (compito); (*Jur*) acquit; (*Relig*) absolve

assomigli'ar|e *vi* **~e a** resemble. **~si** *vr* resemble each other

assom'marsi *vr* combine; **~ a qcsa** add to sth

asso'nanza *f* assonance

asson'nato *adj* drowsy

asso'pirsi *vr* doze off

assor'bente *adj & m* absorbent. **~ igienico** sanitary towel

assor'bire *vt* absorb

assor'da|re *vt* deafen. **~nte** *adj* deafening

assorti'mento *m* assortment

assor'ti|re *vt* match (colori). **~to** *adj* assorted; (colori, persone) matched

as'sorto *adj* engrossed

assottigli'ar|e *vt* make thin; (*aguzzare*) sharpen; (*ridurre*) reduce. **~si** *vr* grow thin; (finanze:) be whittled away

assue'fa|re *vt* accustom. **~rsi** *vr* **~rsi a** get used to. **~tto** *adj* (*a caffè, aspirina*) immune to the effects; (*a droga*) addicted. **~zi'one** *f* (*a caffè, aspirina*) immunity to the effects; (*a droga*) addiction

as'sumere *vt* assume; take on (impiegato); **~ informazioni** make inquiries

as'sunto *pp di* **assumere** ● *m* task. **assunzi'one** *f* (*di impiegato*) employment

assurdità *f inv* absurdity; **~** *pl* nonsense

as'surdo *adj* absurd

'asta *f* pole; (*Mech*) bar; (*Comm*) auction; **a mezz'~** at half-mast

a'stemio *adj* abstemious

aste'n|ersi *vr* abstain (**da** from). **~si'one** *f* abstention

aste'nuto, -a *mf* abstainer

aste'risco *m* asterisk

astig'ma|tico *adj* astigmatic. **~'tismo** *m* astigmatism

'asti|o *m* rancour; **avere ~o contro qcno** bear sb a grudge. **~'oso** *adj* resentful

a'stratto *adj* abstract

astrin'gente *adj & m* astringent

'astro *m* star

astrolo'gia *f* astrology. **a'strologo, -a** *mf* astrologer

astro'nauta *mf* astronaut

astro'nave *f* spaceship

astr|ono'mia *f* astronomy. **~o'nomico** *adj* astronomical. **a'stronomo** *m* astronomer

astrusità *f* abstruseness

a'stuccio *m* case

a'stu|to *adj* shrewd; (*furbo*) cunning. **~zia** *f* shrewdness; (*azione*) trick

ate'ismo *m* atheism

A'tene *f* Athens

'ateo, -a *adj & mf* atheist

a'tipico *adj* atypical

at'lant|e *m* atlas. **~ico** *adj* Atlantic; **l' [Oceano] A~ico** the Atlantic [Ocean]

at'let|a *mf* athlete. **~ica** *f* athletics *sg*. **~ica leggera** track and field events. **~ica pesante** *weight-lifting, boxing, wrestling, etc*. **~ico** *adj* athletic

atmo'sfer|a *f* atmosphere. **~ico** *adj* atmospheric

a'tomic|a *f* atom bomb. **~o** *adj* atomic

'atomo *m* atom

'atrio *m* entrance hall

a'troc|e *adj* atrocious; (*terrible*) dreadful. **~ità** *f inv* atrocity

atrofiz'zarsi *vr* atrophy

attaccabot'toni *mf inv* [crashing] bore

attacca'brighe *mf inv* troublemaker

attacca'mento *m* attachment

attacca'panni *m inv* [coat-]hanger; (*a muro*) clothes hook

attac'car|e *vt* attach; (*legare*) tie; (*appendere*) hang; (*cucire*) sew on; (*contagiare*) pass on; (*assalire*) attack; (*iniziare*) start ● *vi* stick; (*diffondersi*) catch on. **~si** *vr* cling; (*affezionarsi*) become attached; (*litigare*) quarrel

attacca'ticcio *adj* sticky

at'tacco *m* attack; (*punto d'unione*) junction

attar'darsi *vr* stay late; (*indugiare*) linger

attec'chire *vi* take; (moda ecc:) catch on

atteggia'mento *m* attitude

atteggi'ar|e *vt* assume. **~si** *vr* **~si a** pose as

attem'pato *adj* elderly

at'tender|e *vt* wait for ● *vi* **~e a** attend to. **~si** *vr* expect

atten'dibil|e *adj* reliable. **~ità** *f* reliability

atte'nersi *vr* **~ a** stick to

attenta'mente *adv* attentively

atten'ta|re *vi* **~re a** make an attempt on. **~to** *m* act of violence; (*contro politico ecc*) assassination attempt. **~'tore, ~'trice** *mf* (*a scopo politico*) terrorist

at'tento *adj* attentive; (*accurato*) careful; **~!** look out!; **stare ~** pay attention

attenu'ante *f* extenuating circumstance

attenu'a|re *vt* attenuate; (*minimizzare*) minimize; subdue (colori ecc); calm (dolore); soften (colpo). **~rsi** *vr* diminish. **~zi'one** *f* lessening

attenzi'one *f* attention; **~!** watch out!

atter'ra|ggio *m* landing. **~re** *vt* knock down • *vi* land

atter'rir|e *vt* terrorize. **~si** *vr* be terrified

at'tes|a *f* waiting; (*aspettativa*) expectation; **in ~a di** waiting for. **~o** *pp di* **attendere**

atte'sta|re *vt* state; (*certificare*) certify. **~to** *m* certificate. **~zi'one** *f* certificate; (*dichiarazione*) declaration

'attico *m* attic

at'tiguo *adj* adjacent

attil'lato *adj* (vestito) close-fitting

'attimo *m* moment

atti'nente *adj* **~ a** pertaining to

at'tingere *vt* draw; *fig* obtain

atti'rare *vt* attract

atti'tudine *f* (*disposizione*) aptitude; (*atteggiamento*) attitude

atti'v|are *vt* activate. **~ismo** *m* activism. **~ista** *mf* activist. **attività** *f inv* activity; (*Comm*) assets *pl*. **~o** *adj* active; (*Comm*) productive • *m* assets *pl*

attiz'za|re *vt* poke; *fig* stir up. **~'toio** *m* poker

'atto *m* act; (*azione*) action; (*Comm, Jur*) deed; (*certificato*) certificate; **atti** *pl* (*di società ecc*) proceedings; **mettere in ~** put into effect

at'tonito *adj* astonished

attorcigli'ar|e *vt* twist. **~si** *vr* get twisted

at'tore *m* actor

attorni'ar|e *vt* surround. **~si** *vr* **~si di** surround oneself with

at'torno *adv* around, about • *prep* **~ a** around, about

attrac'care *vt/i* dock

attra'ente *adj* attractive

at'tra|rre *vt* attract. **~rsi** *vr* be attracted to each other. **~t'tiva** *f* charm

attraversa'mento *m* crossing. **~ pedonale** crossing, crosswalk *Am*

attraver'sare *vt* cross; (*passare*) go through

attra'verso *prep* through; (*obliquamente*) across

attrazi'on|e *f* attraction. **~i** *pl* **turistiche** tourist attractions

attrez'za|re *vt* equip; (*Naut*) rig. **~rsi** *vr* kit oneself out; **~'tura** *f* equipment; (*Naut*) rigging

at'trezzo *m* tool; **attrezzi** *pl* equipment; *Sport* appliances *pl*; (*Theat*) props *pl*

attribu'ir|e *vt* attribute. **~si** *vr* ascribe to oneself; **~si il merito di** claim credit for

attri'bu|to *m* attribute. **~zi'one** *f* attribution

at'trice *f* actress

at'trito *m* friction

attu'abile *adj* feasible

attu'al|e *adj* present; (*di attualità*) topical; (*effettivo*) actual. **~ità** *f* topicality; (*avvenimento*) news; **programma di ~ità** current affairs programme. **~iz'zare** *vt* update. **~'mente** *adv* at present

attu'a|re *vt* carry out. **~rsi** *vr* be realized. **~zi'one** *f* carrying out

attu'tire *vt* deaden; **~ il colpo** soften the blow

au'dac|e *adj* audacious;. **~ia** *f* boldness; (*insolenza*) audacity

'audience *f inv* (*telespettatori*) audience

'audio *m* audio

audiovi'sivo *adj* audiovisual

audi'torio *m* auditorium

audizi'one *f* audition; (*Jur*) hearing

'auge *m* height; **essere in ~** be popular

augu'rar|e *vt* wish. **~si** *vr* hope. **au'gurio** *m* wish; (*presagio*) omen; **auguri!** all the best!; (*a Natale*) Happy Christmas!; **tanti auguri** best wishes

'aula *f* classroom; (*università*) lecture-hall; (*sala*) hall. **~ magna** (*in università*) great hall. **~ del tribunale** courtroom

aumen'tare *vt/i* increase. **au'mento** *m* increase; (*di stipendio*) [pay] rise

au'reola *f* halo

au'rora *f* dawn

auscul'tare *vt* (*Med*) auscultate

ausili'are *adj & mf* auxiliary

auspicabile *adj* **è ~ che...** it is to be hoped that...
auspi'care *vt* hope for
au'spicio *m* omen; **auspici** (*pl: protezione*) auspices
austerità *f* austerity
au'stero *adj* austere.
Au'strali|a *f* Australia. **a~'ano, -a** *adj & mf* Australian
'Austria *f* Austria. **au'striaco, -a** *agg & mf* Austrian
autar'chia *f* autarchy. **au'tarchico** *adj* autarchic
autenti'c|are *vt* authenticate. **~ità** *f* authenticity
au'tentico *adj* authentic; (*vero*) true
au'tista *m* driver
'auto+ *pref* self +; auto-
autoabbron'zante *m* self-tan • *adj* self-tanning
autoambu'lanza *f* ambulance
autoartico'lato *m* articulated lorry
autobio|gra'fia *f* autobiography. **~'grafico** *adj* autobiographical
auto'botte *f* tanker
'autobus *m inv* bus
auto'carro *m* lorry
autocommiserazi'one *f* self-pity
autoconcessio'nario *m* car dealer
auto'critica *f* self-criticism
autodi'fesa *f* self-defence
auto'gol *m inv* own goal
au'tografo *adj & m* autograph
autolesio'nis|mo *m fig* self-destruction. **~tico** *adj* self-destructive
auto'linea *f* bus line
au'toma *m* robot
automatica'mente *adv* automatically
auto'matico *adj* automatic • *m* (*bottone*) press-stud; (*fucile*) automatic
automatiz'za|re *vt* automate. **~zi'one** *f* automation
auto'mezzo *m* motor vehicle
auto'mobi|le *f* [motor] car. **~'lismo** *m* motoring. **~'lista** *mf* motorist. **~'listico** *adj* (industria) automobile *attrib*
autonoma'mente *adv* autonomously
autono'mia *f* autonomy; (*Auto*) range; (*di laptop, cellulare*) battery life.
au'tonomo *adj* autonomous
auto'psia *f* autopsy
auto'radio *f inv* car radio; (*veicolo*) radio car
au'tore, -'trice *mf* author; (*di pinti*) painter; (*di furto ecc*) perpetrator; **quadro d'~** genuine master
auto'revo|le *adj* authoritative; (*che ha influenza*) influential. **~'lezza** *f* authority
autori'messa *f* garage
autori|tà *f inv* authority. **~'tario** *adj* autocratic. **~ta'rismo** *m* authoritarianism
autori'tratto *m* self-portrait
autoriz'za|re *vt* authorize. **~zi'one** *f* authorization
auto'scontro *m inv* bumper car
autoscu'ola *f* driving school
auto'stop *m* hitch-hiking; **fare l'~** hitch-hike. **~'pista** *mf* hitch-hiker
auto'strada *f* motorway
autostra'dale *adj* motorway *attrib*
autosuffici'en|te *adj* self-sufficient. **~za** *f* self-sufficiency
autotrasporta'|tore, ~'trice *mf* haulier, carrier
auto'treno *m* articulated lorry
autove'icolo *m* motor vehicle
Auto'velox® *m inv* speed camera
autovet'tura *f* motor vehicle
autun'nale *adj* autumn[al]
au'tunno *m* autumn
aval'lare *vt* endorse
a'vallo *m* endorsement
avam'braccio *m* forearm
avangu'ardia *f* vanguard; *fig* avant-garde; **essere all'~** be in the forefront; (*Techn*) be at the leading edge
a'vanti *adv* (*in avanti*) forward; (*davanti*) in front; (*prima*) before; **~!** (*entrate*) come in!; (*suvvia*) come on!; (*su semaforo*) cross now; **va' ~!** go ahead!; **andare ~** (*precedere*) go ahead; (orologio:) be fast; **~ e indietro** backwards and forwards • *adj* before • *prep* **~ a** before; (*in presenza di*) in the presence of
avanti'eri *adv* the day before yesterday
avanza'mento *m* progress; (*promozione*) promotion
avan'za|re *vi* advance; (*progredire*) pro-

gress; (*essere d'avanzo*) be left [over] ● *vt* advance; (*superare*) surpass; (*promuovere*) promote. **~rsi** *vr* advance; (*avvicinarsi*) approach. **~ta** *f* advance. **~to** *adj* advanced; (*nella notte*) late; **in età ~ta** elderly. **a'vanzo** *m* remainder; (*Comm*) surplus; **avanzi** *pl* (*rovine*) remains; (*di cibo*) left-overs

ava'ri|a *f* (*di motore*) engine failure. **~'ato** *adj* (frutta, verdura) rotten; (carne) tainted

ava'rizia *f* avarice. **a'varo, -a** *adj* stingy ● *mf* miser

a'vena *f* oats *pl*

a'vere

! Si può usare **have** o **have got** per parlare di ciò che si possiede. *have got* non si usa nell'inglese americano

● *vt* have; (*ottenere*) get; (*indossare*) wear; (*provare*) feel; **ho trent'anni** I'm thirty; **ha avuto il posto** he got the job; **~ fame/freddo** be hungry/cold; **ho mal di denti** I've got toothache; **cos'ha a che fare con lui?** what has it got to do with him?; **~ da fare** be busy; **che hai?** what's the matter with you?; **nei hai per molto?** will you be long?; **quanti ne abbiamo oggi?** what date is it today?; **avercela con qcno** have it in for sb

● *v aux* have; **non l'ho visto** I haven't seen him; **lo hai visto?** have you seen him?; **l'ho visto ieri** I saw him yesterday

● *m* **averi** *pl* wealth *sg*

avia|'tore *m* flyer, aviator. **~zi'one** *f* aviation; (*Mil*) Air Force

avidità *f* avidness. **'avido** *adj* avid

avio'getto *m* jet

'avo, -a *mf* ancestor

avo'cado *m inv* avocado

a'vorio *m* ivory

Avv. *abbr* avvocato

avva'lersi *vr* avail oneself (**di** of)

avvalla'mento *m* depression

avvalo'rare *vt* bear out (tesi); endorse (documento); (*accrescere*) enhance

avvam'pare *vi* flare up; (*arrossire*) blush

avvantaggi'ar|e *vt* favour. **~si** *vr* **~si di** benefit from; (*approfittare*) take advantage of

avve'd|ersi *vr* (*accorgersi*) notice; (*capire*) realize. **~uto** *adj* shrewd

avvelena'mento *m* poisoning

avvele'na|re *vt* poison. **~rsi** *vr* poison oneself. **~to** *adj* poisoned

avve'nente *adj* attractive

avveni'mento *m* event

avve'nire[1] *vi* happen; (*aver luogo*) take place

avve'ni|re[2] *m* future. **~'ristico** *adj* futuristic

avven'ta|rsi *vr* fling oneself. **~to** *adj* (decisione) rash

av'vento *m* advent; (*Relig*) Advent

avven'tore *m* regular customer

avven'tu|ra *f* adventure; (*amorosa*) affair; **d'~** (film) adventure *attrib.* **~'rarsi** *vr* venture. **~ri'ero, -a** *m* adventurer ● *f* adventuress. **~'roso** *adj* adventurous

avve'ra|bile *adj* (previsione) that may come true. **~rsi** *vr* come true

av'verbio *m* adverb

avver'sar|e *vt* oppose. **~io, -a** *adj* opposing ● *mf* opponent

avversi|'one *f* aversion. **~tà** *f inv* adversity

av'verso *adj* (*sfavorevole*) adverse; (*contrario*) averse

avver'tenza *f* (*cura*) care; (*avvertimento*) warning; (*avviso*) notice; (*premessa*) foreword; **avvertenze** *pl* (*istruzioni*) instructions

avverti'mento *m* warning

avver'tire *vt* warn; (*informare*) inform; (*sentire*) feel

avvez'zar|e *vt* accustom. **~si** *vr* accustom oneself. **av'vezzo** *adj* **avvezzo a** used to

avvia'mento *m* starting; (*Comm*) goodwill

avvi'a|re *vt* start. **~rsi** *vr* set out. **~to** *adj* under way; **bene ~to** thriving

avvicenda'mento *m* (*in agricoltura*) rotation; (*nel lavoro*) replacement

avvicen'darsi *vr* alternate

avvicina'mento *m* approach

avvici'nar|e *vt* bring near; approach (persona). **~si** *vr* approach; **~si a** approach

avvi'lente *adj* demoralizing; (*umiliante*) humiliating

avvili'mento *m* despondency; (*degradazione*) degradation

avvi'li|re *vt* dishearten; (*degradare*) degrade. **~rsi** *vr* lose heart; (*degradarsi*) degrade oneself. **~to** *adj* disheartened; (*degradato*) degraded

avvilup'par|e *vt* envelop. **~si** *vr* wrap oneself up; (*aggrovigliarsi*) get entangled

avvinaz'zato *adj* drunk

avvin'cente *adj* (libro ecc) enthralling. **av'vincere** *vt* enthral

avvinghi'ar|e *vt* clutch. **~si** *vr* cling

av'vio *m* start-up; **dare l'~ a qcsa** get sth under way; **prendere l'~** get under way

avvi'sare *vt* inform; (*mettere in guardia*) warn

av'viso *m* notice; (*annuncio*) announcement; (*avvertimento*) warning; (*pubblicitario*) advertisement; **a mio ~** in my opinion. **~ di garanzia** (*Jur*) *notification that one is to be the subject of a legal enquiry*

avvi'stare *vt* catch sight of

avvi'tare *vt* screw in; screw down (coperchio)

avviz'zire *vi* wither

avvo'ca|to *m* lawyer; *fig* advocate. **~'tura** *f* legal profession

av'volger|e *vt* wrap [up]. **~si** *vr* wrap oneself up

avvol'gibile *m* roller blind

avvol'toio *m* vulture

aza'lea *f* azalea

azi'en|da *f* business. **~ agricola** farm. **~ di soggiorno** tourist bureau. **~'dale** *adj* (politica) corporate; (giornale) in-house

aziona'mento *m* operation

azio'nare *vt* operate

azio'nario *adj* share *attrib*

azi'one *f* action; *Fin* share; **d'~** (romanzo, film) action[-packed]. **azio'nista** *mf* shareholder

a'zoto *m* nitrogen

azzan'nare *vt* seize with its teeth; sink its teeth into (gamba)

azzar'd|are *vt* risk. **~arsi** *vr* dare. **~ato** *adj* risky; (*precipitoso*) rash. **az'zardo** *m* hazard; **gioco d'azzardo** game of chance

azzec'care *vt* hit; (*indovinare*) guess

azzuf'farsi *vr* come to blows

az'zur|ro *adj & m* blue; **il principe ~** Prince Charming. **~'rognolo** *adj* bluish

Bb

bab'beo *adj* foolish • *m* idiot

'babbo *m* [!] dad, daddy. **B~ Natale** Father Christmas

bab'buccia *f* slipper

babbu'ino *m* baboon

ba'bordo *m* (*Naut*) port side

baby'sitter *mf inv* baby-sitter; **fare la ~** babysit

ba'cato *adj* wormeaten

'bacca *f* berry

baccalà *m inv* dried salted cod

bac'cano *m* din

bac'cello *m* pod

bac'chetta *f* rod; (*magica*) wand; (*di direttore d'orchestra*) baton; (*di tamburo*) drumstick

ba'checa *f* showcase; (*in ufficio*) notice board. **~ elettronica** (*Comput*) bulletin board

bacia'mano *m* kiss on the hand; **fare il ~ a qcno** kiss sb's hand

baci'ar|e *vt* kiss. **~si** *vr* kiss [each other]

ba'cillo *m* bacillus

baci'nella *f* basin

ba'cino *m* basin; (*Anat*) pelvis; (*di porto*) dock; (*di minerali*) field

'bacio *m* kiss

'baco *m* worm. **~ da seta** silkworm

ba'cucco *adj* **un vecchio ~** a senile old man

'bada *f* **tenere qcno a ~** keep sb at bay

ba'dante *mf* carer

ba'dare *vi* take care (**a** of); (*fare attenzione*) look out; **bada ai fatti tuoi!** mind your own business!

b

ba'dia *f* abbey
ba'dile *m* shovel
'badminton *m* badminton
'baffi *mpl* moustache *sg*; (*di animale*) whiskers; **mi fa un baffo** I don't give a damn; **ridere sotto i ~** laugh up one's sleeve
baf'futo *adj* moustached
ba'gagli *mpl* baggage. **~'aio** *m* (*Rail*) baggage car; (*Auto*) boot
ba'gaglio *m* baggage; **un ~** a piece of baggage. **~ a mano** hand baggage
baggia'nata *f* **non dire baggianate** don't talk nonsense
bagli'ore *m* glare; (*improvviso*) flash; (*fig: di speranza*) glimmer
ba'gnante *mf* bather
ba'gna|re *vt* wet; (*inzuppare*) soak; (*immergere*) dip; (*innaffiare*) water; (mare:) wash; (fiume:) flow through. **~rsi** *vr* get wet; (*al mare ecc*) bathe.
ba'gnato *adj* wet
ba'gnino, -a *mf* life guard
'bagno *m* bath; (*stanza*) bathroom; (*gabinetto*) toilet; (*in casa*) toilet; (*al mare*) bathe; **bagni** *pl* (*stabilimento*) lido; **fare il ~** have a bath; (*nel mare ecc*) [have a] swim; **andare in ~** go to the toilet; **mettere a ~** soak. **~ turco** Turkish bath
bagnoma'ria *m* bain marie
bagnoschi'uma *m inv* bubble bath
'baia *f* bay
baio'netta *f* bayonet
'baita *f* mountain chalet
bala'ustra, balaus'trata *f* balustrade
balbet't|are *vt/i* stammer; (bambino:) babble. **~io** *m* stammering; babble
bal'buzi|e *f* stutter. **~'ente** *adj* stuttering ● *mf* stutterer
Bal'can|i *mpl* Balkans. **b~ico** *adj* Balkan
balco'nata *f* (*Theat*) balcony
balcon'cino *m* **reggiseno a ~** underwired bra
bal'cone *m* balcony
baldac'chino *m* canopy; **letto a ~** four-poster bed
bal'dan|za *f* boldness. **~'zoso** *adj* bold
bal'doria *f* revelry; **far ~** have a riotous time
ba'lena *f* whale
bale'nare *vi* lighten; *fig* flash; **mi è balenata un'idea** I've just had an idea
bale'niera *f* whaler
ba'leno *m* **in un ~** in a flash
ba'lera *f* dance hall
ba'lia *f* **in ~ di** at the mercy of
'balla *f* bale; (**!**: *frottola*) tall story
bal'labile *adj* good for dancing to
bal'la|re *vi* dance. **~ta** *f* ballad
balla'toio *m* (*nelle scale*) landing
balle'rino, -a *mf* dancer; (*classico*) ballet dancer; **ballerina** (*classica*) ballet dancer, ballerina
bal'letto *m* ballet
'ballo *m* dance; (*il ballare*) dancing; **sala da ~** ballroom; **essere in ~** (lavoro, vita:) be at stake; (persona:) be committed; **tirare qcno in ~** involve sb
ballonzo'lare *vi* skip about
ballot'taggio *m* second count (*of votes*)
balne'a|re *adj* bathing *attrib*. **stagione ~** swimming season. **stazione ~** seaside resort. **~zi'one** *f* **è vietata la ~zione** no swimming
ba'lordo *adj* foolish; (*stordito*) stunned; **tempo ~** nasty weather
'balsamo *m* balsam; (*per capelli*) conditioner; (*lenimento*) remedy
'baltico *adj* Baltic. **il [mar] B~** the Baltic [Sea]
balu'ardo *m* bulwark
'balza *f* crag; (*di abito*) flounce
bal'zano *adj* (*idea*) weird
bal'zare *vi* bounce; (*saltare*) jump; **~ in piedi** leap to one's feet. **'balzo** *m* bounce; (*salto*) jump; **prendere la palla al balzo** seize an opportunity
bam'bagia *f* cotton wool
bambi'nata *f* childish thing to do/say
bam'bi|no, -a *mf* child; (*appena nato*) baby; **avere un ~no** have a baby. **~'none, -a** *mf pej* big *or* overgrown child
bam'boccio *m* chubby child; (*sciocco*) simpleton; (*fantoccio*) rag doll
'bambo|la *f* doll. **~'lotto** *m* male doll
bambù *m* bamboo
ba'nal|e *adj* banal; **~ità** *f inv* banality;

~**iz'zare** *vt* trivialize
ba'nan|a *f* banana. ~**o** *m* banana-tree
'banca *f* bank. ~ **[di] dati** databank
banca'rella *f* stall
ban'cario, -a *adj* banking *attrib*; **trasferimento** ~ bank transfer ● *mf* bank employee
banca'rotta *f* bankruptcy; **fare** ~ go bankrupt
banchet'tare *vi* banquet. **ban'chetto** *m* banquet
banchi'ere *m* banker
ban'china *f* (*Naut*) quay; (*in stazione*) platform; (*di strada*) path; ~ **non transitabile** soft verge
ban'chisa *f* floe
'banco *m* (*di scuola*) desk; (*di negozio*) counter; (*di officina*) bench; (*di gioco, banca*) bank; (*di mercato*) stall; (*degli imputati*) dock; **sotto** ~ under the counter; **medicinale da** ~ over the counter medicines. ~ **informazioni** information desk. ~ **di nebbia** fog bank
'bancomat® *m inv* cashpoint, ATM; (*carta*) bank card
ban'cone *m* counter; (*in bar*) bar
banco'nota *f* banknote, bill *Am*; **banco'note** *pl* paper currency
'banda *f* band; (*di delinquenti*) gang. ~ **d'atterraggio** landing strip. ~ **larga** broad band. ~ **rumorosa** rumble strip
banderu'ola *f* weathercock; (*Naut*) pennant
bandi'e|ra *f* flag. ~**'rina** *f* (*nel calcio*) corner flag. ~**'rine** *pl* bunting *sg*
ban'di|re *vt* banish; (*pubblicare*) publish; *fig* dispense with (formalità, complimenti). ~**to** *m* bandit. ~**'tore** *m* (*di aste*) auctioneer
'bando *m* proclamation; ~ **di concorso** job advertisement (*published in an official gazette for a job for which a competitive examination has to be taken*)
bar *m inv* bar

> **Bar** In Italy a bar is first and foremost a place where coffee is drunk, although alcoholic and soft drinks are also served. Italians tend to drink their coffee standing up at the bar, and there is usually an additional charge for sitting at a table.

'bara *f* coffin
ba'rac|ca *f* hut; (*catapecchia*) hovel; **mandare avanti la** ~**ca** keep the ship afloat. ~**'cato** *m person living in a makeshift shelter.* ~**'chino** *m* (*di gelati, giornali*) kiosk; *Radio* CB radio. ~**'cone** *m* (*roulotte*) circus caravan; (*in luna park*) booth. ~**'copoli** *f inv* shanty town
bara'onda *f* chaos
ba'rare *vi* cheat
'baratro *m* chasm
barat'tare *vt* barter. **ba'ratto** *m* barter
ba'rattolo *m* jar; (*di latta*) tin
'barba *f* beard; (🅸: *noia*) bore; **farsi la** ~ shave; **è una** ~ (*noia*) it's boring
barbabi'etola *f* beetroot. ~ **da zucchero** sugar-beet
bar'barico *adj* barbaric. **bar'barie** *f* barbarity. **'barbaro** *adj* barbarous ● *m* barbarian
'barbecue *m inv* barbecue
barbi'ere *m* barber; (*negozio*) barber's
barbi'turico *m* barbiturate
bar'bone *m* (*vagabondo*) vagrant; (*cane*) poodle
bar'boso *adj* 🅸 boring
barbu'gliare *vi* mumble
bar'buto *adj* bearded
'barca *f* boat. ~ **a motore** motorboat. ~ **da pesca** fishing boat. ~ **a remi** rowing boat. ~ **di salvataggio** lifeboat. ~ **a vela** sailing boat. ~**i'olo** *m* boatman
barcame'narsi *vr* manage
barcol'lare *vi* stagger
bar'cone *m* barge; (*di ponte*) pontoon
bar'dar|e *vt* harness. ~**si** *vr hum* dress up
ba'rel|la *f* stretcher. ~**li'ere** *m* stretcher-bearer
'Barents: **il mare di** ~ the Barents Sea
bari'centro *m* centre of gravity
ba'ri|le *m* barrel. ~**'lotto** *m fig* tub of lard
ba'rista *m* barman ● *f* barmaid
ba'ritono *m* baritone
bar'lume *m* glimmer; **un** ~ **di speranza** a glimmer of hope
'barman *m inv* barman
'baro *m* cardsharper
ba'rocco *adj & m* baroque

b

ba'rometro *m* barometer
ba'rone *m* baron; **i baroni** *fig* the top brass. **baro'nessa** *f* baroness
'barra *f* bar; (*lineetta*) oblique; (*Naut*) tiller. **~ spazio** (*Comput*) space bar. **~ strumenti** (*Comput*) tool bar
bar'rare *vt* block off (strada)
barri'ca|re *vt* barricade. **~ta** *f* barricade
barri'era *f* barrier; (*stradale*) roadblock; (*Geol*) reef. **~ razziale** colour bar
bar'ri|re *vi* trumpet. **~to** *m* trumpeting
barzel'letta *f* joke; **~ sporca** *o* **spinta** dirty joke
basa'mento *m* base
ba'sar|e *vt* base. **~si** *vr* **~si su** be based on; **mi baso su ciò che ho visto** I'm going on [the basis of] what I saw
'basco, -a *mf & adj* Basque ● *m* (*copricapo*) beret
'base *f* basis; (*fondamento*) foundation; (*Mil*) base; (*Pol*) rank and file; **a ~ di** containing; **in ~ a** on the basis of. **~ dati** database
'baseball *m* baseball
ba'setta *f* sideburn
basi'lare *adj* basic
ba'silica *f* basilica
ba'silico *m* basil
ba'sista *m* grass roots politician; (*di un crimine*) mastermind
'basket *m* basketball
bas'sezza *f* lowness; (*di statura*) shortness; (*viltà*) vileness
bas'sista *mf* bassist
'basso *adj* low; (*di statura*) short; (acqua) shallow; (televisione) quiet; (*vile*) despicable; **parlare a bassa voce** speak in a low voice; **la bassa Italia** southern Italy ● *m* lower part; (*Mus*) bass. **guardare in ~** look down
basso'fondo *m* (*pl* **bassifondi**) shallows *pl*; **bassifondi** *pl* (*quartieri poveri*) slums
bassorili'evo *m* bas-relief
bas'sotto *m* dachshund
ba'stardo, -a *adj* bastard; (*di animale*) mongrel ● *mf* bastard; (*animale*) mongrel
ba'stare *vi* be enough; (*durare*) last; **basta!** that's enough!; **basta che** (*purché*) provided that; **basta così** that's enough; **basta così?** is that enough?; (*in negozio*) anything else?; **basta andare alla posta** you only have to go to the post office
Basti'an con'trario *m* contrary old so-and-so
basti'one *m* bastion
basto'nare *vt* beat
baston'cino *m* ski pole. **~ di pesce** fish finger, fish stick *Am*
ba'stone *m* stick; (*da golf*) club; (*da passeggio*) walking stick
ba'tosta *f* blow
bat'tagli|a *f* battle; (*lotta*) fight. **~'are** *vi* battle; *fig* fight
bat'taglio *m* (*di campana*) clapper; (*di porta*) knocker
battagli'one *m* battalion
bat'tello *m* boat; (*motonave*) steamer
bat'tente *m* (*di porta*) wing; (*di finestra*) shutter; (*battaglio*) knocker
'batter|e *vt* beat; (*percorrere*) scour; thresh (grano); break (record) ● *vi* (*bussare, urtare*) knock; (cuore:) beat; (ali ecc:) flap; *Tennis* serve; **~e a macchina** type; **~e le palpebre** blink; **~e le mani** clap [one's hands]; **~e le ore** strike the hours. **~si** *vr* fight
bat'teri *mpl* bacteria
batte'ria *f* battery; (*Mus*) drums *pl*
bat'terio *m* bacterium. **~'logico** *adj* bacteriological
batte'rista *mf* drummer
bat'tesimo *m* baptism
battez'zare *vt* baptize
battiba'leno *m* **in un ~** in a flash
batti'becco *m* squabble
batticu'ore *m* palpitation; **mi venne il ~** I was scared
bat'tigia *f* water's edge
batti'mano *m* applause
batti'panni *m inv* carpetbeater
batti'stero *m* baptistery
batti'strada *m inv* outrider; (*di pneumatico*) tread; *Sport* pacesetter
battitap'peto *m inv* carpet sweeper
'battito *m* [heart]beat; (*alle tempie*) throbbing; (*di orologio*) ticking; (*della pioggia*) beating
bat'tuta *f* beat; (*colpo*) knock; (*spirito-*

saggine) wisecrack; (*osservazione*) remark; (*Mus*) bar; *Tennis* service; (*Theat*) cue; (*dattilografia*) stroke

ba'tuffolo *m* flock

ba'ule *m* trunk

'bava *f* dribble; (*di cane ecc*) slobber; **aver la ~ alla bocca** foam at the mouth

bava'glino *m* bib

ba'vaglio *m* gag

'bavero *m* collar

ba'zar *m inv* bazaar

baz'zecola *f* trifle

bazzi'care *vt/i* haunt

be'arsi *vr* delight (**di** in)

beati'tudine *f* bliss. **be'ato** *adj* blissful; (*Relig*) blessed; **beato te!** lucky you!

beauty-'case *m inv* toilet bag

bebè *m inv* baby

bec'caccia *f* woodcock

bec'ca|re *vt* peck; *fig* catch. **~rsi** *vr* (*litigare*) quarrel. **~ta** *f* peck

beccheggi'are *vi* pitch

bec'chino *m* grave-digger

'bec|co *m* beak; (*di caffettiera ecc*) spout. **~'cuccio** *m* spout

be'fana *f* Epiphany; (*donna brutta*) old witch

> **Befana** *La Befana*, whose name is derived from *Epifania* (Epiphany), is an old woman who is said to visit children on 6 January, bringing presents and sweets. *Befana* is also the name for the Epiphany holiday and usually signals the end of the Christmas celebrations and the return to school.

'beffa *f* hoax; **farsi beffe di qcno** mock sb. **bef'fardo** *adj* derisory; (persona) mocking

bef'far|e *vt* mock. **~si** *vr* **~si di** make fun of

'bega *f* quarrel; **è una bella ~** it's really annoying

'beige *adj & m* beige

be'la|re *vi* bleat. **~to** *m* bleating

'belga *adj & mf* Belgian

'Belgio *m* Belgium

'bella *f* (*in carte, Sport*) decider

bel'lezza *f* beauty; **che ~!** how lovely!; **chiudere/finire in ~** end on a high note

'belli|co *adj* war *attrib*. **~'coso** *adj* warlike. **~ge'rante** *adj & mf* belligerent

'bello *adj* nice; (*di aspetto*) beautiful; (uomo) handsome; (*moralmente*) good; **cosa fai di ~ stasera?** what are you up to tonight?; **oggi fa ~** it's a nice day; **una bella cifra** a lot; **un bel piatto di pasta** a big plate of pasta; **nel bel mezzo** right in the middle; **un bel niente** absolutely nothing; **bell'e fatto** over and done with; **bell'amico!** [a] fine friend he is/you are!; **questa è bella!** that's a good one!; **scamparla bella** have a narrow escape ● *m* (*bellezza*) beauty; (*innamorato*) sweetheart; **sul più ~** at the crucial moment; **il ~ è che...** the funny thing is that...

'belva *f* wild beast

be'molle *m* (*Mus*) flat

ben ▷**BENE**

benché *conj* though, although

'benda *f* bandage; (*per occhi*) blindfold. **ben'dare** *vt* bandage; blindfold (occhi)

'bene *adv* well; **ben ~** thoroughly; **~!** good!; **star ~** (*di salute*) be well; (vestito, stile:) suit; (*finanziariamente*) be well off; **non sta ~** (*non è educato*) it's not nice; **sta/va ~!** all right!; **ti sta ~!** [it] serves you right!; **ti auguro ogni ~** I wish you well; **di ~ in meglio** better and better; **fare ~** (*aver ragione*) do the right thing; **fare ~ a** (cibo:) be good for; **una persona per ~** a good person; **per ~** (fare) properly; **è ben difficile** it's very difficult; **come tu ben sai** as you well know; **lo credo ~!** I can well believe it! ● *m* good; **per il tuo ~** for your own good. **beni** *mpl* (*averi*) property *sg*; **un ~ di famiglia** a family heirloom

bene'detto *adj* blessed

bene'di|re *vt* bless. **~zi'one** *f* blessing

benedu'cato *adj* well-mannered

benefat|'tore, -'trice *m* benefactor ● *f* benefactress

benefi'care *vt* help

benefi'cenza *f* charity

benefici'ar|e *vi* **~e di** profit by. **~io, -a** *adj & mf* beneficiary. **bene'ficio** *m* benefit. **be'nefico** *adj* beneficial; (*di beneficenza*) charitable

bene'placito *m* approval

b

be'nessere *m* well-being
bene'stante *adj* well-off ● *mf* well-off person
bene'stare *m* consent
be'nevolo *adj* benevolent
ben'fatto *adj* well-made
'beni *mpl* property *sg*; *Fin* assets; **~ di consumo** consumer goods
benia'mino *m* favourite
be'nigno *adj* kindly; (*Med*) benign
beninfor'mato *adj* well-informed
benintenzio'nato, -a *adj* well-meaning ● *mf* well-meaning person
benin'teso *adv* of course
benpen'sante *adj* selfrighteous
benser'vito *m* **dare il ~ a qcno** fire sb
bensì *conj* but rather
benve'nuto *adj & m* welcome
ben'visto *adj* **essere ~** go down well (**da** with)
benvo'lere *vt* **farsi ~ da qcno** win sb's affection; **prendere qcno in ~** take a liking to sb; **essere benvoluto da tutti** to be well-liked by everyone
ben'zina *f* petrol, gas *Am*; **far ~** get petrol. **~ verde** unleaded petrol. **ben-zi'naio, -a** *mf* petrol station attendant
'bere *vt* drink; (*assorbire*) absorb; *fig* swallow ● *m* drinking; (*bevande*) drinks *pl*
berga'motto *m* bergamot
ber'lina *f* (*Auto*) saloon
Ber'lino *m* Berlin
ber'muda *mpl* (*pantaloni*) Bermuda shorts
ber'noccolo *m* bump; (*disposizione*) flair
ber'retto *m* beret, cap
bersagli'are *vt fig* bombard. **ber'saglio** *m* target
be'stemmi|a *f* swear-word; (*maledizione*) oath; (*sproposito*) blasphemy. **~'are** *vi* swear
'besti|a *f* animal; (*persona brutale*) beast; (*persona sciocca*) fool; **andare in ~a** [!] blow one's top. **~'ale** *adj* bestial; (espressione, violenza) brutal; [!]: (freddo, fame) terrible. **~alità** *f inv* bestiality; *fig* nonsense. **~'ame** *m* livestock
'bettola *f fig* dive
be'tulla *f* birch
be'vanda *f* drink
bevi|'tore, -'trice *mf* drinker
be'vut|a *f* drink. **~o** *pp di* **bere**
bi'ada *f* fodder
bianche'ria *f* linen. **~ intima** underwear
bi'anco *adj* white; (foglio, pagina ecc) blank ● *m* white; **mangiare in ~** not eat rich food; **in ~ e nero** (film, fotografia) black and white; **passare una notte in ~** have a sleepless night
bian'core *m* whiteness
bianco'spino *m* hawthorn
biasci'care *vt* (*mangiare*) eat noisily; (*parlare*) mumble
biasi'mare *vt* blame. **bi'asimo** *m* blame
'Bibbia *f* Bible
bibe'ron *m inv* [baby's] bottle
'bibita *f* [soft] drink
'biblico *adj* biblical
bibliogra'fia *f* bibliography
biblio'te|ca *f* library; (*mobile*) bookcase. **~'cario, -a** *mf* librarian
bicarbo'nato *m* bicarbonate
bicchi'ere *m* glass
bicchie'rino *m* [!] tipple
bici'cletta *f* bicycle; **andare in ~** ride a bicycle
bico'lore *adj* two-coloured
bidè *m inv* bidet
bi'dello, -a *mf* janitor
bido'nata *f* [!] swindle
bi'done *m* bin; ([!]: *truffa*) swindle; **fare un ~ a qcno** [!] stand sb up
bien'nale *adj* biennial
bi'ennio *m* two-year period
bi'etola *f* beet
bifo'cale *adj* bifocal
bi'folco, -a *mf fig* boor
bifor'c|arsi *vr* fork. **~azi'one** *f* fork. **~uto** *adj* forked
biga'mia *f* bigamy. **'bigamo, -a** *adj* bigamous ● *mf* bigamist
bighello'nare *vi* loaf around. **bighel'lone** *m* loafer
bigiotte'ria *f* costume jewellery; (*negozio*) jeweller's
bigliet't|aio *m* booking clerk; (*sui treni*) ticket-collector. **~e'ria** *f* ticket-

office; (*Theat*) box-office
bigli'et|to *m* ticket; (*lettera breve*) note; (*cartoncino*) card; (*di banca*) banknote. **~to da visita** business card. **~'tone** *m* (🅸: *soldi*) big one
bignè *m inv* cream puff
bigo'dino *m* roller
bi'gotto *m* bigot
bi'kini *m inv* bikini
bi'lanci|a *f* scales *pl*; (*Comm*) balance; **B~a** (*Astr*) Libra. **~'are** *vt* balance; *fig* weigh. **~o** *m* budget; (*Comm*) balance sheet; **fare il ~o** balance the books; *fig* take stock
'bil|e *f* bile; *fig* rage
bili'ardo *m* billiards *sg*
'bilico *m* equilibrium; **in ~** in the balance
bi'lingue *adj* bilingual
bili'one *m* billion
bilo'cale *adj* two-room
'bimbo, -a *mf* child
bimen'sile *adj* fortnightly
bime'strale *adj* bimonthly
bi'nario *m* track; (*piattaforma*) platform
bi'nocolo *m* binoculars *pl*
bio'chimica *f* biochemistry
biodegra'dabile *adj* biodegradable
bio'etica *f* bioethics
bio'fisica *f* biophysics
biogra'fia *f* biography. **bio'grafico** *adj* biographical. **bi'ografo, -a** *mf* biographer
biolo'gia *f* biology. **bio'logico** *adj* biological; (*alimento, agricoltura*) organic. **bi'ologo, -a** *mf* biologist
bi'ond|a *f* blonde. **~o** *adj* blond • *m* fair colour; (*uomo*) fair-haired man
bio'sfera *f* biosphere
bi'ossido *m* **~ di carbonio** carbon dioxide
bioterro'rismo *m* bioterrorism
biparti'tismo *m* two-party system
'birba *f*, **bir'bante** *m* rascal, rogue. **bir'bone** *adj* wicked
biri'chino, -a *adj* naughty • *mf* little devil
bi'rillo *m* skittle
'birr|a *f* beer; **a tutta ~a** *fig* flat out. **~a chiara** lager. **~a scura** brown ale. **~e'ria** *f* beer-house; (*fabbrica*) brewery
bis *m inv* encore
bi'saccia *f* haversack
bi'sbetic|a *f* shrew. **~o** *adj* bad-tempered
bisbigli'are *vt/i* whisper. **bi'sbiglio** *m* whisper
'bisca *f* gambling-house
'biscia *f* snake
bi'scotto *m* biscuit
bisessu'ale *adj & mf* bisexual
bise'stile *adj* **anno ~** leap year
bisettima'nale *adj* fortnightly
bi'slacco *adj* peculiar
bis'nonno, -a *mf* great-grandfather; great-grandmother
biso'gn|are *vi* **~a agire subito** we must act at once; **~a farlo** it is necessary to do it; **non ~a venire** you don't have to come. **~o** *m* need; (*povertà*) poverty; **aver ~o di** need. **~oso** *adj* needy; (*povero*) poor; **~oso di** in need of
bi'sonte *m* bison
bi'stecca *f* steak
bisticci'are *vi* quarrel. **bi'sticcio** *m* quarrel; (*gioco di parole*) pun
bistrat'tare *vt* mistreat
bi'torzolo *m* lump
'bitter *m inv* (bitter) aperitif
bi'vacco *m* bivouac
'bivio *m* crossroads; (*di strada*) fork
bizan'tino *adj* Byzantine
'bizza *f* tantrum; **fare le bizze** (bambini:) play up
biz'zarro *adj* bizarre
biz'zeffe *adv* **a ~** galore
blan'dire *vt* soothe; (*allettare*) flatter. **'blando** *adj* mild
bla'sone *m* coat of arms
'blatta *f* cockroach
blin'da|re *vt* armour-plate. **~to** *adj* armoured
blitz *m inv* blitz
bloc'car|e *vt* block; (*isolare*) cut off; (*Mil*) blockade; (*Comm*) freeze. **~si** *vr* (*Mech*) jam
blocca'sterzo *m* steering lock
'blocco *m* block; (*Mil*) blockade; (*dei fitti*) restriction; (*di carta*) pad; (*unione*) coalition; **in ~** (*Comm*) in bulk. **~ stradale** road-block
bloc-'notes *m inv* writing pad
blog'gista *mf* blogger

blu *adj & m* blue
blue-'jeans *mpl* jeans
bluff *m inv* (*carte, fig*) bluff
'blusa *f* blouse
'boa *m* boa [constrictor]; (*sciarpa*) [feather] boa ● *f* (*Naut*) buoy
bo'ato *m* rumbling
bo'bina *f* spool; (*di film*) reel; (*Electr*) coil
'bocca *f* mouth; **a ~ aperta** *fig* dumbfounded; **in ~ al lupo!** [!] break a leg!; **fare la respirazione ~ a ~ a qcno** give sb mouth to mouth resuscitation *or* the kiss of life
boc'caccia *f* grimace; **far boccacce** make faces
boc'caglio *m* nozzle
boc'cale *m* jug; (*da birra*) tankard
bocca'porto *m* (*Naut*) hatch
boc'cata *f* (*di fumo*) puff; **prendere una ~ d'aria** get a breath of fresh air
boc'cetta *f* small bottle
boccheggi'are *vi* gasp
boc'chino *m* cigarette holder; (*Mus, di pipa*) mouthpiece
'bocc|ia *f* (*palla*) bowl; **~e** *pl* (*gioco*) bowls *sg*
bocci'a|re *vt* (*agli esami*) fail; (*respingere*) reject; (*alle bocce*) hit; **essere ~to** fail; (*ripetere*) repeat a year. **~'tura** *f* failure
bocci'olo *m* bud
boccon'cino *m* morsel
boc'cone *m* mouthful; (*piccolo pasto*) snack
boc'coni *adv* face downwards
'boia *m* executioner
boi'ata *f* [!] rubbish
boicot'tare *vt* boycott
bo'lero *m* bolero
'bolgia *f* (*caos*) bedlam
'bolide *m* meteor; **passare come un ~** shoot past [like a rocket]
Bo'livi|a *f* Bolivia. **b~'ano, -a** *agg & mf* Bolivian
'bolla *f* bubble; (*pustola*) blister
bol'la|re *vt* stamp; *fig* brand. **~to** *adj fig* branded; **carta ~ta** *paper with stamp showing payment of duty*
bol'lente *adj* boiling [hot]
bol'let|ta *f* bill; **essere in ~ta** be hard up. **~'tino** *m* bulletin; (*Comm*) list
bol'lino *m* coupon
bol'li|re *vt/i* boil. **~to** *m* boiled meat. **~'tore** *m* boiler; (*per l'acqua*) kettle. **~'tura** *f* boiling
'bollo *m* stamp
bol'lore *m* boil; (*caldo*) intense heat; *fig* ardour
'bomba *f* bomb; **a prova di ~** bombproof
bombarda'mento *m* shelling; (*con aerei*) bombing; *fig* bombardment. **~ aereo** air raid
bombar'd|are *vt* shell; (*con aerei*) bomb; *fig* bombard. **~i'ere** *m* bomber
bom'betta *f* bowler [hat]
'bombola *f* cylinder. **~ di gas** gas cylinder
bombo'lone *m* doughnut
bomboni'era *f* wedding keep-sake
bo'naccia *f* (*Naut*) calm
bonacci'one, -a *mf* good-natured person ● *adj* good-natured
bo'nario *adj* kindly
bo'nifica *f* land reclamation. **bonifi'care** *vt* reclaim
bo'nifico *m* (*Comm*) discount; (*bancario*) [credit] transfer
bontà *f* goodness; (*gentilezza*) kindness
'bora *f* bora (*cold north-east wind in the upper Adriatic*)
'borchi|a *f* stud. **~'ato** *adj* studded
bor'da|re *vt* border. **~'tura** *f* border
bor'deaux *adj inv* maroon
bor'dello *m* brothel; *fig* bedlam; (*disordine*) mess
'bordo *m* border; (*estremità*) edge; **a ~** (*Aeron, Naut*) on board
bor'gata *f* hamlet
bor'ghese *adj* bourgeois; (abito) civilian; **in ~** in civilian dress; (poliziotto) in plain clothes
borghe'sia *f* middle classes *pl*
'borgo *m* village
'bori|a *f* conceit. **~'oso** *adj* conceited
bor'lotto *m* **[fagiolo] ~** borlotto bean
boro'talco *m* talcum powder
bor'raccia *f* flask
'bors|a *f* bag; (*borsetta*) handbag; (*valori*) Stock Exchange. **~a dell'acqua calda** hot-water bottle. **~a frigo** cool-box. **~a della spesa** shopping bag. **~a di studio** scholarship. **~ai'olo** *m* pick-

pocket. **~el'lino** *m* purse. **bor'sista** *mf Fin* speculator; (*Sch*) scholarship holder

bor'se|llo *m* purse; (*borsetto*) man's handbag. **~tta** *f* handbag. **~tto** *m* man's handbag

bo'scaglia *f* woodlands *pl*

boscai'olo *m* woodman; (*guardaboschi*) forester

'bosco *m* wood. **bo'scoso** *adj* wooded

'Bosnia *f* Bosnia

'bossolo *m* cartridge case

bo'tanic|a *f* botany. **~o** *adj* botanical • *m* botanist

'botta *f* blow; (*rumore*) bang; **fare a botte** come to blows. **~ e risposta** *fig* thrust and counter-thrust

'botte *f* barrel

bot'te|ga *f* shop; (*di artigiano*) workshop. **~'gaio, -a** *mf* shopkeeper. **~'ghino** *m Theatr* boxoffice; (*del lotto*) lottery-shop

bot'tigli|a *f* bottle; **in ~a** bottled. **~e'ria** *f* wine shop

bot'tino *m* loot; (*Mil*) booty

'botto *m* bang; **di ~** all of a sudden

bot'tone *m* button; (*Bot*) bud

bo'vino *adj* bovine; **bovini** *pl* cattle

box *m inv* (*per cavalli*) loosebox; (*recinto per bambini*) play-pen

'boxe *f* boxing

'bozza *f* draft; (*Typ*) proof; (*bernoccolo*) bump. **boz'zetto** *m* sketch

'bozzolo *m* cocoon

brac'care *vt* hunt

brac'cetto *m* **a ~** arm in arm

bracci'a|le *m* bracelet; (*fascia*) armband. **~'letto** *m* bracelet; (*di orologio*) watch-strap

bracci'ante *m* day labourer

bracci'ata *f* (*nel nuoto*) stroke

'bracci|o *m* (*pl f* **braccia**) arm; (*di fiume, pl* **bracci**) arm. **~'olo** *m* (*di sedia*) arm[rest]; (*da nuoto*) armband

'bracco *m* hound

bracconi'ere *m* poacher

'brac|e *f* embers *pl*; **alla ~e** chargrilled. **~i'ere** *m* brazier. **~i'ola** *f* chop

'brado *adj* **allo stato ~** in the wild

'brama *f* longing. **bra'mare** *vt* long for. **bramo'sia** *f* yearning

'branca *f* branch

'branchia *f* gill

'branco *m* (*di cani*) pack; (*pej: di persone*) gang

branco'lare *vi* grope

'branda *f* camp-bed

bran'dello *m* scrap; **a brandelli** in tatters

bran'dire *vt* brandish

'brano *m* piece; (*di libro*) passage

Bra'sil|e *m* Brazil. **b~i'ano, -a** *agg & mf* Brazilian

bra'vata *f* bragging

'bravo *adj* good; (*abile*) clever; (*coraggioso*) brave; **~!** well done!. **bra'vura** *f* skill

'breccia *f* breach; **sulla ~** *fig* very successful, at the top

bre'saola *f dried, salted beef sliced thinly and eaten cold*

bre'tella *f* shoulder-strap; **bretelle** *pl* (*di calzoni*) braces

'breve *adj* brief; **in ~** briefly; **tra ~** shortly

brevet'tare *vt* patent. **bre'vetto** *m* patent; (*attestato*) licence

brevità *f* shortness

'brezza *f* breeze

'bricco *m* jug

bric'cone *m* blackguard; *hum* rascal

'briciol|a *f* crumb; *fig* grain. **~o** *m* fragment

'briga *f* (*fastidio*) trouble; (*lite*) quarrel; **attaccar ~** pick a quarrel; **prendersi la ~ di fare qcsa** go to the trouble of doing sth

brigadi'ere *m* (*dei carabinieri*) sergeant

bri'gante *m* bandit; *hum* rogue

bri'gare *vi* intrigue

bri'gata *f* brigade; (*gruppo*) group

briga'tista *mf* (*Pol*) member of the Red Brigades

'briglia *f* rein; **a ~ sciolta** at breakneck speed

bril'lante *adj* brilliant; (*scintillante*) sparkling • *m* diamond

bril'lare *vi* shine; (metallo:) glitter; (*scintillare*) sparkle

'brillo *adj* tipsy

'brina *f* hoar-frost

brin'dare *vi* toast; **~ a qcno** drink a toast to sb

'brindisi *m inv* toast

bri'tannico *adj* British

'brivido *m* shiver; (*di paura ecc*) shudder; (*di emozione*) thrill
brizzo'lato *adj* greying
'brocca *f* jug
broc'cato *m* brocade
'broccoli *mpl* broccoli *sg*
'brodo *m* broth; (*per cucinare*) stock. ~ **ristretto** consommé
'broglio *m* ~ **elettorale** gerrymandering
bron'chite *f* bronchitis
'broncio *m* sulk; **fare il** ~ sulk
bronto'l|are *vi* grumble; (tuono ecc:) rumble. ~**io** *m* grumbling; (*di tuono*) rumbling. ~**one, -a** *mf* grumbler
'bronzo *m* bronze
bros'sura *f* **edizione in** ~ paperback
bru'care *vt* (pecora:) graze
bruciacchi'are *vt* scorch
brucia'pelo *adv* **a** ~ point-blank
bruci'a|re *vt* burn; (*scottare*) scald; (*incendiare*) set fire to ● *vi* burn; (*scottare*) scald. ~**rsi** *vr* burn oneself. ~**to** *adj* burnt; *fig* burnt-out. ~**'tore** *m* burner. ~**'tura** *f* burn. **bruci'ore** *m* burning sensation
'bruco *m* grub
'brufolo *m* spot
brughi'era *f* heath
bruli'c|are *vi* swarm
'brullo *adj* bare
'bruma *f* mist
'bruno *adj* brown; (occhi, capelli) dark
brusca'mente *adv* (*di colpo*) suddenly
bru'schetta *f toasted bread rubbed with garlic and sprinkled with olive oil*
'brusco *adj* sharp; (persona) brusque; (*improvviso*) sudden
bru'sio *m* buzzing
bru'tal|e *adj* brutal. ~**ità** *f inv* brutality. ~**iz'zare** *vt* brutalize. **'bruto** *adj & m* brute
brut'tezza *f* ugliness
'brut|to *adj* ugly; (tempo, tipo, situazione, affare) nasty; (*cattivo*) bad; ~**ta copia** rough copy; ~**to tiro** dirty trick. ~**'tura** *f* ugly thing
'buca *f* hole; (*avvallamento*) hollow. ~ **delle lettere** (*a casa*) letter-box
buca'neve *m inv* snowdrop
bu'car|e *vt* make a hole in; (*pungere*) prick; punch (biglietti) ● *vi* have a puncture. ~**si** *vr* prick oneself; (*con droga*) shoot up
bu'cato *m* washing
'buccia *f* peel, skin
bucherel'lare *vt* riddle
'buco *m* hole
bu'dello *m* (*pl f* **budella**) bowel
bu'dino *m* pudding
'bue *m* (*pl* **buoi**) ox; **carne di** ~ beef
'bufalo *m* buffalo
bu'fera *f* storm; (*di neve*) blizzard
buf'fetto *m* cuff
'buffo *adj* funny; (*Theat*) comic ● *m* funny thing. ~**'nata** *f* (*scherzo*) joke. **buf'fone** *m* buffoon; **fare il buffone** play the fool
bu'gi|a *f* lie; ~**a pietosa** white lie. ~**'ardo, -a** *adj* lying ● *mf* liar
bugi'gattolo *m* cubby-hole
'buio *adj* dark ● *m* darkness; **al** ~ in the dark; ~ **pesto** pitch dark
'bulbo *m* bulb; (*dell'occhio*) eyeball
Bulga'ria *f* Bulgaria. **'bulgaro, -a** *adj & mf* Bulgarian
'bullo *m* bully
bul'lone *m* bolt
'bunker *m inv* bunker
buona'fede *f* good faith
buona'notte *int* good night
buona'sera *int* good evening
buon'giorno *int* good morning; (*di pomeriggio*) good afternoon
buon'grado: **di** ~ *adv* willingly
buongu'staio, -a *mf* gourmet. **buon'gusto** *m* good taste
bu'ono *adj* good; (momento) right; **dar** ~ (*convalidare*) accept; **alla buona** easy-going; (cena) informal; **buona notte/sera** good night/evening; **buon compleanno/Natale!** happy birthday/merry Christmas!; **buon senso** common sense; **di buon'ora** early; **una buona volta** once and for all; **buona parte di** the best part of; **tre ore buone** three good hours ● *m* good; (*in film*) goody; (*tagliando*) voucher; (*titolo*) bond; **con le buone** gently; ~ **sconto** money-off coupon ● *mf* **buono, -a a nulla** dead loss
buontem'pone, -a *mf* happy-go-lucky person
buonu'more *m* good temper

buonu'scita *f* retirement bonus; (*di dirigente*) golden handshake

burat'tino *m* puppet

'burbero *adj* surly; (*nei modi*) rough

bu'rocra|te *m* bureaucrat. **buro'cratico** *adj* bureaucratic. **~'zia** *f* bureaucracy

bur'ra|sca *f* storm. **~'scoso** *adj* stormy

'burro *m* butter

bur'rone *m* ravine

bu'scar|e *vt*, **~si** *vr* catch

bus'sare *vt* knock

'bussola *f* compass; **perdere la ~** lose one's bearings

'busta *f* envelope; (*astuccio*) case. **~ paga** pay packet. **~'rella** *f* bribe. **bu'stina** *f* (*di tè*) tea bag; (*per medicine*) sachet

'busto *m* bust; (*indumento*) girdle

but'tar|e *vt* throw; **~e giù** (*demolire*) knock down; (*inghiottire*) gulp down; scribble down (scritto); ! put on (pasta); (*scoraggiare*) dishearten; **~e via** throw away. **~si** *vr* throw oneself; (*saltare*) jump

butte'rato *adj* pock-marked

Cc

caba'ret *m inv* cabaret

ca'bina *f* (*Aeron, Naut*) cabin; (*balneare*) beach hut. **~ elettorale** polling booth. **~ di pilotaggio** cockpit. **~ telefonica** telephone box. **cabi'nato** *m* cabin cruiser

ca'cao *m* cocoa

'cacca *f* ! pooh

'caccia *f* hunt; (*con fucile*) shooting; (*inseguimento*) chase; (*selvaggina*) game • *m inv* (*Aeron*) fighter; (*Naut*) destroyer

cacciabombardi'ere *m* fighter-bomber

cacciagi'one *f* game

cacci'a|re *vt* hunt; (*mandar via*) chase away; (*scacciare*) drive out; (*ficcare*) shove • *vi* go hunting. **~rsi** *vr* (*nascondersi*) hide; (*andare a finire*) get to; **~rsi nei guai** get into trouble; **alla ~'tora** *adj* (*Culin*) chasseur. **~'tore, ~'trice** *mf* hunter. **~tore di frodo** poacher

caccia'vite *m inv* screwdriver

ca'chet *m inv* (*Med*) capsule; (*colorante*) colour rinse; (*stile*) cachet

'cachi *m inv* (*albero, frutta*) persimmon

'cacio *m* (*formaggio*) cheese

'cactus *m inv* cactus

ca'da|vere *m* corpse. **~'verico** *adj fig* deathly pale

ca'dente *adj* falling; (casa) crumbling

ca'denza *f* cadence; (*ritmo*) rhythm; (*Mus*) cadenza

ca'dere *vi* fall; (capelli ecc:) fall out; (*capitombolare*) tumble; (vestito ecc:) hang; **far ~** (*di mano*) drop; **~ dal sonno** feel very sleepy; **lasciar ~** drop; **~ dalle nuvole** *fig* be taken aback

ca'detto *m* cadet

ca'duta *f* fall; (*di capelli*) loss; *fig* downfall

caffè *m inv* coffee; (*locale*) café. **~ corretto** espresso coffee with a dash of liqueur. **~ lungo** weak black coffee. **~ macchiato** coffee with a dash of milk. **~ ristretto** strong espresso coffee. **~ solubile** instant coffee. **caffe'ina** *f* caffeine. **caffe l'latte** *m inv* white coffee.

> *i*
> **Caffè** If you ask for a *caffè* in an Italian bar you will be served an *espresso*, a small amount of very strong coffee in a small cup. A *macchiato* is the same, but with the addition of a little frothy milk. *Cappuccino* is drunk in the morning or afternoon, never at the end of a meal. A *corretto* has a dash of spirits in it.

caffetti'era *f* coffee-pot

cafo'naggine *f* boorishness

cafo'nata *f* boorishness

ca'fone, -a *mf* boor

ca'gare *vi* ! crap

cagio'nare *vt* cause

cagio'nevole *adj* delicate

cagli'ar|e *vi*, **~si** *vr* curdle

'cagna *f* bitch

ca'gnara *f* ! din

C

ca'gnesco *adj* **guardare qcno in ~** scowl at sb

'cala *f* creek

cala'brone *m* hornet

cala'maio *m* inkpot

cala'mari *mpl* squid *sg*

cala'mita *f* magnet

calamità *f inv* calamity

ca'lar|e *vi* come down; (vento:) drop; (*diminuire*) fall; (*tramontare*) set • *vt* (*abbassare*) lower; (*nei lavori a maglia*) decrease • *m* (*di luna*) waning. **~si** *vr* lower oneself

'calca *f* throng

cal'cagno *m* heel

cal'care[1] *m* limestone

cal'care[2] *vt* tread; (*premere*) press [down]; **~ la mano** *fig* exaggerate; **~ le orme di qcno** *fig* follow in sb's footsteps

'calce[1] *f* lime

'calce[2] *m* **in ~** at the foot of the page

calce'struzzo *m* concrete

cal'cetto *m Sport* five-a-side [football]

calci'a|re *vt* kick. **~'tore** *m* footballer

cal'cina *f* mortar

calci'naccio *m* (*pezzo di intonaco*) flake of plaster

'calcio[1] *m* kick; (*Sport*) football; (*di arma da fuoco*) butt; **dare un ~ a** kick. **~ d'angolo** corner [kick]

'calcio[2] *m* (*chimica*) calcium

'calco *m* tracing; (*arte*) cast

calco'la|re *vt* calculate; (*considerare*) consider. **~'tore** *adj* calculating • *m* calculator; (*macchina elettronica*) computer

'calcolo *m* calculation; (*Med*) stone

cal'daia *f* boiler

caldar'rosta *f* roast chestnut

caldeggi'are *vt* support

'caldo *adj* warm; (*molto caldo*) hot • *m* heat; **avere ~** be warm/hot; **fa ~** it is warm/hot

calen'dario *m* calendar

'calibro *m* calibre; (*strumento*) callipers *pl*; **di grosso ~** (persona) top *attrib*

'calice *m* goblet; (*Relig*) chalice

ca'ligine *m* fog; (*industriale*) smog

'call centre *m inv* call centre

calligra'fia *f* handwriting; (cinese) calligraphy

cal'lista *mf* chiropodist. **'callo** *m* corn; **fare il callo a** become hardened to. **cal'loso** *adj* callous

'calma *f* calm. **cal'mante** *adj* calming • *m* sedative. **cal'mare** *vt* calm [down]; (*lenire*) soothe. **cal'marsi** *vr* calm down; (vento:) drop; (dolore:) die down. **'calmo** *adj* calm

'calo *m* (*Comm*) fall; (*di volume*) shrinkage; (*di peso*) loss

ca'lore *m* heat; (*moderato*) warmth; **in ~** (animale) on heat. **calo'roso** *adj* warm

calo'ria *f* calorie

ca'lorico *adj* calorific

calo'rifero *m* radiator

calorosa'mente *adv* (*cordialmente*) warmly

calpe'stare *vt* trample [down]; *fig* trample on (diritti, sentimenti); **vietato ~ l'erba** keep off the grass

calpe'stio *m* (*passi*) footsteps

ca'lunni|a *f* slander. **~'are** *vt* slander. **~'oso** *adj* slanderous

ca'lura *f* heat

cal'vario *m* Calvary; *fig* trial

cal'vizie *f* baldness. **'calvo** *adj* bald

'calz|a *f* (*da donna*) stocking; (*da uomo*) sock. **~a'maglia** *f* tights *pl*; (*per danza*) leotard

cal'zante *adj fig* fitting

cal'za|re *vt* (*indossare*) wear; (*mettersi*) put on • *vi* fit

calza'scarpe *m inv* shoehorn

calza'tura *f* footwear

calzaturi'ficio *m* shoe factory

cal'zetta *f* **è una mezza ~** *fig* he's no use

calzet'tone *m* knee-length woollen sock. **cal'zino** *m* sock

calzo'l|aio *m* shoemaker. **~e'ria** *f* (*negozio*) shoe shop

calzon'cini *mpl* shorts. **~ da bagno** swimming trunks

cal'zone *m folded pizza with tomato and mozzarella or ricotta*

cal'zoni *mpl* trousers, pants *Am*

camale'onte *m* chameleon

cambi'ale *f* bill of exchange

cambia'mento *m* change

cambi'ar|e *vt/i* change; move (casa); (*fare cambio di*) exchange; **~e rotta**

(*Naut*) alter course. **~si** *vr* change. '**cambio** *m* change; (*Comm, scambio*) exchange; (*Mech*) gear; **dare il ~ a qcno** relieve sb; **in ~ di** in exchange for

'**camera** *f* room; (*mobili*) [bedroom] suite; (*Phot*) camera; **C~** (*Comm, Pol*) Chamber. **~ ardente** funeral parlour. **~ d'aria** inner tube. **C~ di Commercio** Chamber of Commerce. **C~ dei Deputati** (*Pol*) ≈House of Commons. **~ doppia** double room. **~ da letto** bedroom. **~ matrimoniale** double room. **~ oscura** darkroom. **~ singola** single room

came'rata[1] *f* (*dormitorio*) dormitory; (*Mil*) barrack room

came'ra|ta[2] *mf* (*amico*) mate; (*Pol*) comrade. **~'tismo** *m* comradeship

cameri'era *f* maid; (*di ristorante*) waitress; (*in albergo*) chamber-maid; (*di bordo*) stewardess

cameri'ere *m* manservant; (*di ristorante*) waiter; (*di bordo*) steward

came'rino *m* dressing-room

'**camice** *m* overall. **cami'cetta** *f* blouse. **ca'micia** *f* shirt; **uovo in ~** poached egg. **camicia da notte** nightdress

cami'netto *m* fireplace

ca'mino *m* chimney; (*focolare*) fireplace

'**camion** *m inv* truck, lorry *Br*

camion'cino *m* van

camio'netta *f* jeep

camio'nista *mf* truck driver

cam'mello *m* camel; (*tessuto*) camelhair • *adj inv* (*colore*) camel

cam'meo *m* cameo

cammi'na|re *vi* walk; (auto, orologio:) go. **~ta** *f* walk; **fare una ~ta** go for a walk. **cam'mino** *m* way; **essere in ~** be on the way; **mettersi in ~** set out

camo'milla *f* camomile; (*bevanda*) camomile tea

ca'morra *f* local mafia

ca'moscio *m* chamois; (*pelle*) suede

cam'pagna *f* country; (*paesaggio*) countryside; (*Comm, Mil*) campaign; **in ~** in the country. **~ elettorale** election campaign. **~ pubblicitaria** marketing campaign. **campa'gnolo, -a** *adj* rustic • *m* countryman • *f* countrywoman

cam'pale *adj* field *attrib*; **giornata ~** *fig* strenuous day

cam'pa|na *f* bell; (*di vetro*) belljar. **~'nella** *f* (*di tenda*) curtain ring. **~'nello** *m* door-bell; (*cicalino*) buzzer

campa'nile *m* belfry

campani'lismo *m* parochialism

campani'lista *mf* person with a parochial outlook

cam'panula *f* (*Bot*) campanula

cam'pare *vi* live; (*a stento*) get by

cam'pato *adj* **~ in aria** unfounded

campeggi'a|re *vi* camp; (*spiccare*) stand out. **~'tore, ~'trice** *mf* camper. **cam'peggio** *m* camping; (*terreno*) campsite

cam'pestre *adj* rural

'**camping** *m inv* campsite

campio'nari|o *m* [set of] samples • *adj* samples; **fiera ~a** trade fair

campio'nato *m* championship

campiona'tura *f* (*di merce*) range of samples

campi'on|e *m* champion; (*Comm*) sample; (*esemplare*) specimen. **~'essa** *f* ladies' champion

'**campo** *m* field; (*accampamento*) camp. **~ da calcio** football pitch. **~ di concentramento** concentration camp. **~ da golf** golf course. **~ da tennis** tennis court. **~ profughi** refugee camp

campo'santo *m* cemetery

camuf'far|e *vt* disguise. **~si** *vr* disguise oneself

'**Cana|da** *m* Canada. **~'dese** *agg & mf* Canadian

ca'naglia *f* scoundrel; (*plebaglia*) rabble

ca'nal|e *m* channel; (*artificiale*) canal. **~iz'zare** *vt* channel (acque). **~izzazi'one** *f* channelling; (*rete*) pipes *pl*

'**canapa** *f* hemp

cana'rino *m* canary

cancel'la|re *vt* cross out; (*con la gomma*) rub out; (*annullare*) cancel; (*Comput*) delete. **~'tura** *f* erasure. **~zi'one** *f* cancellation; (*Comput*) deletion

cancelle'ria *f* chancellery; (*articoli per scrivere*) stationery

cancelli'ere *m* chancellor; (*di tribunale*) clerk

can'cello *m* gate

cance'ro|geno *m* carcinogen • *adj*

C

carcinogenic. **~'so** *adj* cancerous
can'crena *f* gangrene
'cancro *m* cancer. **C~** (*Astr*) Cancer
candeg'gi|na *f* bleach. **~'are** *vt* bleach. **can'deggio** *m* bleaching
can'de|la *f* candle; (*Auto*) spark plug. **~li'ere** *m* candlestick
candi'da|rsi *vr* stand as a candidate. **~to, -a** *mf* candidate. **~'tura** *f* (*Pol*) candidacy; (*per lavoro*) application
'candido *adj* snow-white; (*sincero*) candid; (*puro*) pure
can'dito *adj* candied
can'dore *m* whiteness; *fig* innocence
'cane *m* dog; (*di arma da fuoco*) cock; **un tempo da cani** foul weather. **~ da caccia** hunting dog
ca'nestro *m* basket
cangi'ante *adj* iridescent; **seta ~** shot silk
can'guro *m* kangaroo
ca'nile *m* kennel; (*di allevamento*) kennels *pl*. **~ municipale** dog pound
ca'nino *adj & m* canine
'canna *f* reed; (*da zucchero*) cane; (*di fucile*) barrel; (*bastone*) stick; (*di bicicletta*) crossbar; (*asta*) rod; ([!]: *hascish*) joint; **povero in ~** destitute. **~ da pesca** fishing rod
can'nella *f* cinnamon
can'neto *m* bed of reeds
can'niba|le *m* cannibal. **~'lismo** *m* cannibalism
cannocchi'ale *m* telescope
canno'nata *f* cannon shot; **è una ~** *fig* it's brilliant
cannon'cino *m* (*dolce*) cream horn
can'none *m* cannon; *fig* ace
can'nuccia *f* [drinking] straw; (*di pipa*) stem
ca'noa *f* canoe
'canone *m* canon; (*affitto*) rent; **equo ~** fair rents act
ca'noni|co *m* canon. **~z'zare** *vt* canonize. **~zzazi'one** *f* canonization
ca'noro *adj* melodious
ca'notta *f* (*estiva*) vest top
canot'taggio *m* canoeing; (*voga*) rowing
canotti'era *f* singlet
canotti'ere *m* oarsman
ca'notto *m* [rubber] dinghy
cano'vaccio *m* (*trama*) plot; (*straccio*) duster
can'tante *mf* singer
can't|are *vt/i* sing. **~au'tore, ~au'trice** *mf* singer-songwriter. **~icchi'are** *vt* sing softly; (*a bocca chiusa*) hum
canti'ere *m* yard; (*Naut*) shipyard; (*di edificio*) construction site. **~ navale** naval dockyard
canti'lena *f* singsong; (*ninna-nanna*) lullaby
can'tina *f* cellar; (*osteria*) wine shop
'canto¹ *m* singing; (*canzone*) song; (*Relig*) chant; (*poesia*) poem
'canto² *m* (*angolo*) corner; (*lato*) side; **dal ~ mio** for my part; **d'altro ~** on the other hand
canto'nata *f* **prendere una ~** *fig* be sadly mistaken
can'tone *m* canton; (*angolo*) corner
can'tuccio *m* nook
canzo'na|re *vt* tease. **~'torio** *adj* teasing. **~'tura** *f* teasing
can'zo|ne *f* song. **~'netta** *f* [!] pop song. **~ni'ere** *m* songbook

> *i*
> **Canzone** Italians are very proud of their tradition of popular song and it is celebrated at the Festival of Sanremo (*Festival della Canzone Italiana*). The festival has been held since 1951 and is watched by millions on Italian TV every year. The festival includes a competition for the best new song and the winner is guaranteed chart success.

'caos *m* chaos. **ca'otico** *adj* chaotic
C.A.P. *m abbr* (Codice di Avviamento Postale) post code, zip code *Am*
ca'pac|e *adj* able; (*esperto*) skilled; (stadio, contenitore) big; **~e di** (*disposto a*) capable of. **~ità** *f inv* ability; (*attitudine*) skill; (*capienza*) capacity
capaci'tarsi *vr* **~ di** (*rendersi conto*) understand; (*accorgersi*) realize
ca'panna *f* hut
capan'nello *m* **fare ~ intorno a qcno/qcsa** gather round sb/sth
capan'none *m* shed; (*Aeron*) hangar
ca'parbio *adj* obstinate
ca'parra *f* deposit
capa'tina *f* short visit; **fare una ~ in**

città/da qcno pop into town/in on sb

ca'pel|lo *m* hair; **~li** *pl* (*capigliatura*) hair *sg*. **~'lone** *m* hippie. **~'luto** *adj* hairy

capez'zale *m* bolster; *fig* bedside

ca'pezzolo *m* nipple

capi'en|te *adj* capacious. **~za** *f* capacity

capiglia'tura *f* hair

ca'pire *vt* understand; **~ male** misunderstand; **si capisce!** naturally!; **sì, ho capito** yes, I see

capi'ta|le *adj* (*Jur*) capital; (*principale*) main ● *f* (*città*) capital ● *m* (*Comm*) capital. **~'lismo** *m* capitalism. **~'lista** *mf* capitalist. **~'listico** *adj* capitalist

capitane'ria *f* **~ di porto** port authorities *pl*

capi'tano *m* captain

capi'tare *vi* (*giungere per caso*) come; (*accadere*) happen

capi'tello *m* (*Archit*) capital

capito'la|re *vi* capitulate. **~zi'one** *f* capitulation

ca'pitolo *m* chapter

capi'tombolo *m* headlong fall; **fare un ~** tumble down

'capo *m* head; (*chi comanda*) boss [!]; (*di vestiario*) item; (*Geog*) cape; (*in tribù*) chief; (*parte estrema*) top; **a ~** new paragraph; **da ~** over again; **in ~ a un mese** within a month; **giramento di ~** dizziness; **mal di ~** headache; **~ d'abbigliamento** item of clothing. **~ d'accusa** (*Jur*) charge. **~ di bestiame** head of cattle

capo'banda *m* (*Mus*) bandmaster; (*di delinquenti*) ringleader

ca'poccia *m* ([!]: *testa*) nut

capocci'one, -a *mf* [!] brainbox

capo'danno *m* New Year's Day

capofa'miglia *m* head of the family

capo'fitto *m* **a ~** headlong

capo'giro *m* giddiness

capola'voro *m* masterpiece

capo'linea *m* terminus

capo'lino *m* **fare ~** peep in

capolu'ogo *m* main town

capo'rale *m* lance-corporal

capo'squadra *mf Sport* team captain

capo'stipite *mf* (*di famiglia*) progenitor

capo'tavola *mf* head of the table

capo'treno *m* guard

capouf'ficio *mf* head clerk

capo'verso *m* first line

capo'vol|gere *vt* overturn; *fig* reverse. **~gersi** *vr* overturn; (barca:) capsize; *fig* be reversed. **~to** *pp di* **capovolgere** ● *adj* upside-down

'cappa *f* cloak; (*di camino*) cowl; (*di cucina*) hood

cap'pel|la *f* chapel. **~'lano** *m* chaplain

cap'pello *m* hat. **~ a cilindro** top hat

'cappero *m* caper

'cappio *m* noose

cap'pone *m* capon

cap'potto *m* [over]coat

cappuc'cino *m* (*frate*) Capuchin; (*bevanda*) white coffee

cap'puccio *m* hood; (*di penna stilografica*) cap

'capra *f* goat. **ca'pretto** *m* kid

ca'pricci|o *m* whim; (*bizzarria*) freak; **fare i capricci** have tantrums. **~'oso** *adj* capricious; (bambino) naughty

Capri'corno *m* (*Astr*) Capricorn

capri'ola *f* somersault

capri'olo *m* roe-deer

'capro *m* [billy-]goat. **~ espiatorio** scapegoat.

ca'prone *m* [billy] goat

'capsula *f* capsule; (*di proiettile*) cap; (*di dente*) crown

cap'tare *vt* (*Radio, TV*) pick up; catch (attenzione)

cara'bina *f* carbine

carabini'ere *m* carabiniere; **carabini'eri** *pl Italian police*

> i
>
> **Carabinieri** The *Carabinieri* are a national Italian police force which is part of the army. They deal with issues of public order and serious crimes, but there is a certain amount of overlap with the duties of the *Polizia di Stato*, which is not part of the army and is controlled by the Interior Ministry. *Carabinieri* wear a distinctive dark uniform with a red stripe.

ca'raffa *f* carafe

Ca'raibi *mpl* (*zona*) Caribbean *sg*; (*isole*) Caribbean Islands; **il mar dei ~** the Caribbean [Sea]

C

C

cara'mella *f* sweet
cara'mello *m* caramel
ca'rato *m* carat
ca'ratte|re *m* character; (*caratteristica*) characteristic; (*Typ*) type; **di buon ~re** good-natured. **~'ristico, -a** *adj* characteristic; (*pittoresco*) quaint ● *f* characteristic. **~riz'zare** *vt* characterize
carbon'cino *m* charcoal
car'bone *m* coal
carbu'rante *m* fuel
carbura'tore *m* carburettor
car'cassa *f* carcass; *fig* old wreck
carce'ra|rio *adj* prison *attrib.* **~to, -a** *mf* prisoner. **~zi'one** *f* imprisonment. **~zione preventiva** preventive detention
'carcer|e *m* prison; (*punizione*) imprisonment. **~i'ere, -a** *mf* gaoler
carci'ofo *m* artichoke
cardi'nale *adj & m* cardinal
'cardine *m* hinge
cardio|chi'rurgo *m* heart surgeon. **~lo'gia** *f* cardiology. **cardi'ologo** *m* heart specialist. **~'tonico** *m* heart stimulant
'cardo *m* thistle
ca'rena *f* (*Naut*) bottom
ca'ren|te *adj* **~te di** lacking in. **~za** *f* lack; (*scarsità*) scarcity
care'stia *f* famine; (*mancanza*) dearth
ca'rezza *f* caress
cari'a|rsi *vi* decay. **~to** *adj* decayed
'carica *f* office; (*Electr, Mil*) charge; *fig* drive. **cari'care** *vt* load; (*Electr, Mil*) charge; wind up (orologio). **~'tore** *m* (*per proiettile*) magazine
carica'tu|ra *f* caricature. **~'rale** *adj* grotesque. **~'rista** *mf* caricaturist
'carico *adj* loaded (**di** with); (colore) strong; (orologio) wound [up]; (batteria) charged ● *m* load; (*di nave*) cargo; (*il caricare*) loading; **a ~ di** (*Comm*) to be charged to; (persona) dependent on
'carie *f* [tooth] decay
ca'rino *adj* pretty; (*piacevole*) agreeable
ca'risma *m* charisma
carit|à *f* charity; **per ~à!** (*come rifiuto*) God forbid!. **~a'tevole** *adj* charitable
carnagi'one *f* complexion
car'naio *m fig* shambles
car'nale *adj* carnal; **cugino ~** first cousin
'carne *f* flesh; (*alimento*) meat; **~ di manzo/maiale/vitello** beef/pork/veal
car'nefi|ce *m* executioner. **~'cina** *f* slaughter
carne'va|le *m* carnival. **~'lesco** *adj* carnival
car'noso *adj* fleshy
'caro, -a *adj* dear; **cari saluti** kind regards ● *mf* 🗈 darling, dear; **i miei cari** my nearest and dearest
ca'rogna *f* carcass; *fig* bastard
caro'sello *m* merry-go-round
ca'rota *f* carrot
caro'vana *f* caravan; (*di veicoli*) convoy
caro'vita *m* high cost of living
'carpa *f* carp
carpenti'ere *m* carpenter
car'pire *vt* seize; (*con difficoltà*) extort
car'poni *adv* on all fours
car'rabile *adj* suitable for vehicles; **passo ~** ▹**CARRAIO**
car'raio *adj* **passo ~** *entrance to driveway, garage etc where parking is forbidden*
carreggi'ata *f* roadway; **doppia ~** dual carriageway, divided highway *Am*
carrel'lata *f* (*TV*) pan
car'rello *m* trolley; (*di macchina da scrivere*) carriage; (*Aeron*) undercarriage; (*Cinema, TV*) dolly. **~ d'atterraggio** (*Aeron*) landing gear
car'retto *m* cart
carri'e|ra *f* career; **di gran ~ra** at full speed; **fare ~ra** get on. **~'rismo** *m* careerism
carri'ola *f* wheelbarrow
'carro *m* cart. **~ armato** tank. **~ attrezzi** breakdown vehicle. **~ funebre** hearse. **~ merci** truck
car'rozza *f* carriage; (*Rail*) car. **~ cuccette** sleeping car. **~ ristorante** restaurant car
carroz'zella *f* (*per bambini*) pram; (*per disabili*) wheelchair
carrozze'ria *f* bodywork; (*officina*) bodyshop
carroz'zina *f* pram; (*pieghevole*) pushchair, stroller *Am*
carroz'zone *m* (*di circo*) caravan
'carta *f* paper; (*da gioco*) card; (*statuto*) charter; (*Geog*) map. **~ d'argento** ≈

senior citizens' railcard. ~ **assorbente** blotting-paper. ~ **di credito** credit card. ~ **geografica** map. ~ **d'identità** identity card. ~ **igienica** toilet-paper. ~ **di imbarco** boarding card *or* pass. ~ **da lettere** writing-paper. ~ **da parati** wallpaper. ~ **stagnola** silver paper; (*Culin*) aluminium foil. ~ **straccia** waste paper. ~ **stradale** road map. ~ **velina** tissue-paper. ~ **verde** (*Auto*) green card. ~ **vetrata** sand-paper

cartacar'bone *f* carbon paper

car'taccia *f* waste paper

carta'modello *m* pattern

cartamo'neta *f* paper money

carta'pesta *f* papier mâché

carta'straccia *f* waste paper

cartave'trare *vt* sand [down]

car'tel|la *f* briefcase; (*di cartone*) folder; (*di scolaro*) satchel. **~la clinica** medical record. **~'lina** *f* folder

cartel'lino *m* (*etichetta*) label; (*dei prezzi*) price-tag; (*di presenza*) time-card; **timbrare il** ~ clock in; (*all'uscita*) clock out

car'tel|lo *m* sign; (*pubblicitario*) poster; (*stradale*) road sign; (*di protesta*) placard: (*Comm*) cartel. **~'lone** *m* poster; (*Theat*) bill

carti'era *f* paper-mill

car'tina *f* map

car'toccio *m* paper bag; **al** ~ (*Culin*) baked in foil

carto'|laio, -a *mf* stationer. **~le'ria** *f* stationer's. **~libre'ria** *f* stationer's and book shop

carto'lina *f* postcard. ~ **postale** postcard

carto'mante *mf* fortune-teller

carton'cino *m* (*materiale*) card

car'tone *m* cardboard; (*arte*) cartoon. ~ **animato** [animated] cartoon

car'tuccia *f* cartridge

'casa *f* house; (*abitazione propria*) home; (*ditta*) firm; **amico di** ~ family friend; **andare a** ~ go home; **essere di** ~ be like one of the family; **fatto in** ~ home-made; **padrone di** ~ (*di pensione ecc*) landlord; (*proprietario*) house owner. ~ **di cura** nursing home. ~ **popolare** council house. ~ **dello studente** hall of residence

ca'sacca *f* military coat; (*giacca*) jacket

ca'saccio *adv* **a** ~ at random

casa'ling|a *f* housewife. **~o** *adj* domestic; (*fatto in casa*) home-made; (*amante della casa*) home-loving; (*semplice*) homely

ca'scante *adj* falling; (*floscio*) flabby

ca'sca|re *vi* fall [down]. **~ta** *f* (*di acqua*) waterfall

ca'schetto *m* **[capelli a]** ~ bob

ca'scina *f* farm building

'casco *m* crash-helmet; (*asciuga-capelli*) [hair-]drier; ~ **di banane** bunch of bananas

caseggi'ato *m* apartment block

casei'ficio *m* dairy

ca'sella *f* pigeon-hole. ~ **postale** post office box; (*Comput*) mailbox

casel'lante *mf* (*per treni*) signalman

casel'lario *m* ~ **giudiziario** record of convictions; **avere il** ~ **giudiziario vergine** have no criminal record

ca'sello [autostra'dale] *m* [motorway] toll booth

case'reccio *adj* home-made

ca'serma *f* barracks *pl*; (*dei carabinieri*) [police] station

casi'nista *mf* [!] muddler. **ca'sino** *m* [!] (*bordello*) brothel; (*fig: confusione*) racket; (*disordine*) mess; **un casino di** loads of

casinò *m inv* casino

ca'sistica *f* (*classificazione*) case records *pl*

'caso *m* chance; (*Gram, Med*), (fatto, circostanza) case; **a** ~ at random; ~ **mai** if need be; **far** ~ **a** pay attention to; **non far** ~ **a** take no account of; **per** ~ by chance. ~ **[giudiziario]** [legal] case

caso'lare *m* farmhouse

'caspita *int* good gracious!

'cassa *f* till; cash; (*luogo di pagamento*) cash desk; (*mobile*) chest; (*istituto bancario*) bank. ~ **automatica prelievi** cash dispenser, ATM. ~ **da morto** coffin. ~ **toracica** ribcage

cassa'forte *f* safe

cassa'panca *f* linen chest

casseru'ola *f* saucepan

cas'setta *f* case; (*per registratore*) cassette. ~ **delle lettere** letterbox. ~ **di sicurezza** strong-box

C

cas'set|to *m* drawer. **~'tone** *m* chest of drawers

cassi'ere, -a *mf* cashier; (*di supermercato*) checkout assistant; (*di banca*) teller

'casta *f* caste

ca'stagn|a *f* chestnut. **casta'gneto** *m* chestnut grove. **~o** *m* chestnut[-tree]

ca'stano *adj* chestnut

ca'stello *m* castle; (*impalcatura*) scaffold

casti'gare *vt* punish

casti'gato *adj* (*casto*) chaste

ca'stigo *m* punishment

castità *f* chastity. **'casto** *adj* chaste

ca'storo *m* beaver

ca'strare *vt* castrate

casu'al|e *adj* chance *attrib.* **~'mente** *adv* by chance

ca'supola *f* little house

cata'clisma *m fig* upheaval

cata'comba *f* catacomb

cata'fascio *m* **andare a ~** go to rack and ruin

cata'litico *adj* **marmitta catalitica** (*Auto*) catalytic converter

cataliz'za|re *vt* heighten. **~'tore** *m* (*Auto*) catalytic converter

catalo'gare *vt* catalogue. **ca'talogo** *m* catalogue

catama'rano *m* (*da diporto*) catamaran

cata'pecchia *f* hovel; ⊡ dump

catapul'tar|e *vt* eject. **~si** *vr* (*precipitarsi*) dive

catarifran'gente *m* reflector

ca'tarro *m* catarrh

ca'tasta *f* pile

ca'tasto *m* land register

ca'tastrofe *f* catastrophe. **cata'strofico** *adj* catastrophic

cate'chismo *m* catechism

cate|go'ria *f* category. **~'gorico** *adj* categorical

ca'tena *f* chain. **~ montuosa** mountain range. **catene** *pl* **da neve** tyre-chains. **cate'naccio** *m* bolt

cate'|nella *f* (*collana*) chain. **~'nina** *f* chain

cate'ratta *f* cataract

ca'terva *f* **una ~ di** heaps of

cati'nell|a *f* basin; **piovere a ~e** bucket down

ca'tino *m* basin

ca'trame *m* tar

'cattedra *f* (*tavolo di insegnante*) desk; (*di università*) chair

catte'drale *f* cathedral

catti'veria *f* wickedness; (*azione*) wicked action

cattività *f* captivity

cat'tivo *adj* bad; (bambino) naughty

cattoli'cesimo *m* Catholicism

cat'tolico, -a *adj & mf* [Roman] Catholic

cat'tu|ra *f* capture. **~'rare** *vt* capture

caucciù *m* rubber

'causa *f* cause; (*Jur*) lawsuit; **far ~ a qcno** sue sb. **cau'sare** *vt* cause

'caustico *adj* caustic

cauta'mente *adv* cautiously

cau'tela *f* caution

caute'lar|e *vt* protect. **~si** *vr* take precautions

cauteriz'z|are *vt* cauterize. **cauterizzazi'one** *f* cauterization

'cauto *adj* cautious

cauzi'one *f* security; (*per libertà provvisoria*) bail

'cava *f* quarry; *fig* mine

caval'ca|re *vt* ride; (*stare a cavalcioni*) sit astride. **~ta** *f* ride; (*corteo*) cavalcade. **~'via** *m* flyover

cavalci'oni: **a ~** *adv* astride

cavali'ere *m* rider; (*titolo*) knight; (*accompagnatore*) escort; (*al ballo*) partner

cavalle|'resco *adj* chivalrous. **~'ria** *f* chivalry; (*Mil*) cavalry. **~'rizzo, -a** *m* horseman ● *f* horsewoman

caval'letta *f* grasshopper

caval'letto *m* trestle; (*di macchina fotografica*) tripod; (*di pittore*) easel

caval'lina *f* (*ginnastica*) horse

ca'vallo *m* horse; (*misura di potenza*) horsepower; (*scacchi*) knight; (*dei pantaloni*) crotch; **a ~** on horseback; **andare a ~** go horse-riding. **~ a dondolo** rocking-horse

caval'lone *m* (*ondata*) roller

caval'luccio ma'rino *m* sea horse

ca'var|e *vt* take out; (*di dosso*) take off; **~sela** get away with it; **se la cava bene** he's doing all right

cava'tappi *m inv* corkscrew

ca'ver|na *f* cave. **~'noso** *adj* (voce) deep
'cavia *f* guinea-pig
cavi'ale *m* caviar
ca'viglia *f* ankle
cavil'lare *vi* quibble. **ca'villo** *m* quibble
cavità *f inv* cavity
'cavo *adj* hollow • *m* cavity; (*di metallo*) cable; (*Naut*) rope
cavo'lata *f* ! rubbish
cavo'letto *m* **~ di Bruxelles** Brussels sprout
cavolfi'ore *m* cauliflower
'cavolo *m* cabbage; **~!** ! sugar!
caz'zo *int vulg* fuck!
caz'zott|o *m* punch; **prendere qcno a ~i** beat sb up
cazzu'ola *f* trowel
c/c *abbr* (conto corrente) c/a
CD-Rom *m inv* CD-Rom
ce *pers pron* (*a noi*) (to) us • *adv* there; **~ ne sono molti** there are many
'cece *m* chick-pea
cecità *f* blindness
ceco, -a *adj & mf* Czech; **la Repubblica Ceca** the Czech Republic
'cedere *vi* (*arrendersi*) surrender; (*concedere*) yield; (*sprofondare*) subside • *vt* give up; make over (proprietà ecc). **ce'devole** *adj* (terreno ecc) soft; *fig* yielding. **cedi'mento** *m* (*di terreno*) subsidence
'cedola *f* coupon
'cedro *m* (*albero*) cedar; (*frutto*) citron
'ceffo *m* (*muso*) snout; (*pej: persona*) mug
cef'fone *m* slap
ce'lar|e *vt* conceal. **~si** *vr* hide
cele'bra|re *vt* celebrate. **~zi'one** *f* celebration
'celebr|e *adj* famous. **~ità** *f inv* celebrity
'celere *adj* swift
ce'leste *adj* (*divino*) heavenly • *agg & m* (*colore*) sky-blue
celi'bato *m* celibacy
'celibe *adj* single • *m* bachelor
'cella *f* cell
'cellofan *m inv* cellophane; (*Culin*) cling film
'cellula *f* cell. **~ fotoelettrica** electronic eye
cellu'lare *m* (*telefono*) cellular phone • *adj* **[furgone] ~** *m* police van. **[telefono] ~** *m* cellular phone
cellu'lite *f* cellulite
cellu'loide *adj* celluloid
cellu'losa *f* cellulose
'Celt|i *mpl* Celts. **~ico** *adj* Celtic
cemen'tare *vt* cement. **ce'mento** *m* cement. **cemento armato** reinforced concrete
'cena *f* dinner; (*leggera*) supper

> *i*
> **Cena** *Cena* is the evening meal, traditionally a lighter meal than *pranzo*, although it too may start with a primo (often small pasta shapes in broth). A *cena* can also be a dinner party or a dinner at a restaurant, two of the principal ways in which Italians socialize.

ce'nacolo *m* circle
ce'nare *vi* have dinner
'cenci|o *m* rag; (*per spolverare*) duster. **~'oso** *adj* in rags
'cenere *f* ash; (*di carbone ecc*) cinders
ce'netta *f* (*cena semplice*) informal dinner
'cenno *m* sign; (*col capo*) nod; (*con la mano*) wave; (*allusione*) hint; (*breve resoconto*) mention
ce'none *m* **il ~ di Capodanno/Natale** *special New Year's Eve/Christmas Eve dinner*
censi'mento *m* census
cen's|ore *m* censor. **~ura** *f* censorship. **~u'rare** *vt* censor
'cent *m inv* cent
centelli'nare *vt* sip
cente'n|ario, -a *adj & mf* centenarian • *m* centenary. **~'nale** *adj* centennial
cen'tesimo *adj* hundredth • *m* (*di moneta*) cent; **non avere un ~** be penniless
cen'ti|grado *adj* centigrade. **~metro** *m* centimetre
centi'naio *m* hundred
'cento *adj & m* one *or* a hundred; **per ~** per cent
centome'trista *mf Sport* one hundred metres runner

C

cento'mila *m* one *or* a hundred thousand

cen'trale *adj* central ● *f* (*di società ecc*) head office. **~ atomica** atomic power station. **~ elettrica** power station. **~ nucleare** nuclear power station. **~ telefonica** [telephone] exchange

centra'li|na *f* (*Teleph*) switchboard. **~'nista** *mf* operator

centra'lino *m* (*Teleph*) exchange; (*di albergo ecc*) switchboard

centra'li|smo *m* centralism. **~z'zare** *vt* centralize

cen'trare *vt* **~ qcsa** hit sth in the centre; (*fissare nel centro*) centre; *fig* hit on the head (idea)

cen'trifu|ga *f* spin-drier. **centrifuga [asciugaverdure]** shaker. **~'gare** *vt* centrifuge; (lavatrice:) spin

'centro *m* centre. **~ [città]** city centre. **~ commerciale** mall. **~ di accoglienza** reception centre. **~ sociale** community centre

> **Centro storico** The layout and much of the fabric of most Italian town and city centres derive from medieval or even Roman times, with the result that the *centro storico* is a place of narrow streets. Some (like Lucca) are surrounded by city walls. This makes life difficult for the motorist, and cars have been banned from many city centres.

'ceppo *m* (*di albero*) stump; (*da ardere*) log; (*fig: gruppo*) stock

'cera *f* wax; (*aspetto*) look. **~ per il pavimento** floor-polish

ce'ramica *f* (*arte*) ceramics; (*materia*) pottery; (*oggetto*) pot

ce'rato *adj* (tela) waxed

cerbi'atto *m* fawn

'cerca *f* **andare in ~ di** look for

cercaper'sone *m inv* beeper

cer'care *vt* look for ● *vi* **~ di** try to

'cerchi|a *f* circle. **~'are** *vt* circle (parola). **~'ato** *adj* (occhi) black-ringed. **~'etto** *m* (*per capelli*) hairband

'cerchi|o *m* circle; (*giocattolo*) hoop. **~'one** *m* alloy wheel

cere'ale *m* cereal

cere'brale *adj* cerebral

'cereo *adj* waxen

ce'retta *f* depilatory wax

ceri'moni|a *f* ceremony. **~'ale** *m* ceremonial. **~'oso** *adj* ceremonious

ce'rino *m* [wax] match

cerni'era *f* hinge; (*di borsa*) clasp. **~ lampo** zip[-fastener], zipper *Am*

'cernita *f* selection

'cero *m* candle

ce'rone *m* grease-paint

ce'rotto *m* [sticking] plaster

certa'mente *adv* certainly

cer'tezza *f* certainty

certifi'ca|re *vt* certify. **~to** *m* certificate

'certo *adj* certain; (notizia) definite; (*indeterminativo*) some; **sono ~ di riuscire** I am certain to succeed; **certi giorni** some days; **un ~ signor Giardini** a Mr Giardini; **una certa Anna** somebody called Anna; **certa gente** *pej* some people; **ho certi dolori!** I'm in such pain!. **certi** *pron pl* some; (*alcune persone*) some people ● *adv* of course; **sapere per ~** know for certain; **di ~** surely; **~ che sì!** of course!

cer'vello *m* brain.

'cervo *m* deer

ce'sareo *adj* (*Med*) Caesarean

cesel'la|re *vt* chisel. **~to** *adj* chiselled. **ce'sello** *m* chisel

ce'soie *fpl* shears

ce'spugli|o *m* bush. **~'oso** *adj* (terreno) bushy

ces'sa|re *vi* stop, cease ● *vt* stop. **~te il fuoco** ceasefire

cessi'one *f* handover

'cesso *m* ☒ (*gabinetto*) bog, john *Am*; (*fig: locale, luogo*) dump

'cesta *f* [large] basket. **ce'stello** *m* (*di lavatrice*) drum

cesti'nare *vt* throw away. **ce'stino** *m* [small] basket; (*per la carta straccia*) waste-paper basket. **'cesto** *m* basket

'ceto *m* [social] class

'cetra *f* lyre

cetrio'lino *m* gherkin. **cetri'olo** *m* cucumber

cfr *abbr* (confronta) cf.

chat'tare *vi* (*Comput*) chat

che

- *pron rel* (*persona*: *soggetto*) who; (*persona*: *oggetto*) that, who, whom *fml*; (*cosa, animale*) that, which; **questa è la casa ~ ho comprato** this is the house [that] I've bought; **il ~ mi sorprende** which surprises me; **dal ~ deduco che...** from which I gather that...; **avere di ~ vivere** have enough to live on; **grazie! – non c'è di ~!** thank you! – don't mention it!; **il giorno ~ ti ho visto** [!] the day I saw you
- *adj inter* which, what; (*esclamativo*: *con aggettivo*) how; (*con nome*) what a; **~ macchina prendiamo, la tua o la mia?** which car are we taking, yours or mine?; **~ bello!** how nice!; **~ idea!** what an idea!; **~ bella giornata!** what a lovely day!
- *pron inter* what; **a ~ pensi?** what are you thinking about?
- *conj* that; (*con comparazioni*) than; **credo ~ abbia ragione** I think [that] he is right; **era così commosso ~ non riusciva a parlare** he was so moved [that] he couldn't speak; **aspetto ~ telefoni** I'm waiting for him to phone; **è da un po' ~ non lo vedo** it's been a while since I saw him; **mi piace più Roma ~ Milano** I like Rome better than Milan; **~ ti piaccia o no** whether you like it or not; **~ io sappia** as far as I know

checché *indef pron* whatever
chemiotera'pia *f* chemotherapy
chero'sene *m* paraffin
cheti'chella: **alla ~** *adv* silently
'cheto *adj* quiet

chi

- *rel pron* whoever; (*coloro che*) people who; **ho trovato ~ ti può aiutare** I found somebody who can help you; **c'è ~ dice che...** some people say that...; **senti ~ parla!** listen to who's talking!
- *inter pron* (*soggetto*) who; (*oggetto, con preposizione*) who, whom *fml*; (*possessivo*) **di ~** whose; **~ sei?** who are you?; **~ hai incontrato?** who did you meet?; **di ~ sono questi libri?** whose books are these?; **con ~ parli?** who are you talking to?; **a ~ lo dici!** tell me about it!

chi'acchie|ra *f* chat; (*pettegolezzo*) gossip. **~'rare** *vi* chat; (*far pettegolezzi*) gossip. **~'rato** *adj* **essere ~rato** (*persona*:) be the subject of gossip; **~re** *pl* chitchat; **far quattro ~re** have a chat. **~'rone, -a** *adj* talkative ● *mf* chatterer
chia'ma|re *vt* call; (*far venire*) send for; **come ti chiami?** what's your name?; **mi chiamo Roberto** my name is Robert; **~re alle armi** call up. **~rsi** *vr* be called. **~ta** *f* call; (*Mil*) call-up
chi'appa *f* [!] cheek
chiara'mente *adv* clearly
chia'rezza *f* clarity; (*limpidezza*) clearness
chiarifi'ca|re *vt* clarify. **~'tore** *adj* clarificatory. **~zi'one** *f* clarification
chiari'mento *m* clarification
chia'rir|e *vt* make clear; (*spiegare*) clear up. **~si** *vr* become clear
chi'aro *adj* clear; (*luminoso*) bright; (colore) light. **chia'rore** *m* glimmer
chiaroveg'gente *adj* clear-sighted ● *mf* clairvoyant
chi'as|so *m* din. **~'soso** *adj* rowdy
chi'av|e *f* key; **chiudere a ~e** lock. **~e inglese** spanner. **~i'stello** *m* latch
chiaz|za *f* stain. **~'zare** *vt* stain
chic *adj inv* chic
chicches'sia *pron* anybody
'chicco *m* grain; (*di caffé*) bean; (*d'uva*) grape
chi'eder|e *vt* ask; (*per avere*) ask for; (*esigere*) demand. **~si** *vr* wonder
chi'esa *f* church
chi'esto *pp di* **chiedere**
'chiglia *f* keel
'chilo *m* kilo
chilo'grammo *m* kilogram[me]
chilome'traggio *m* (*Auto*) mileage
chilo'metrico *adj* in kilometres
chi'lometro *m* kilometre
chi'mera *f fig* illusion
'chimic|a *f* chemistry. **~o, -a** *adj* chemical ● *mf* chemist
'china *f* (*declivio*) slope; **inchiostro di ~** Indian ink

C

chi'nar|e *vt* lower. **~si** *vr* stoop

chincaglie'rie *fpl* knick-knacks

chinesitera'pia *f* physiotherapy

chi'nino *m* quinine

'chino *adj* bent

chi'notto *m sparkling soft drink*

chi'occia *f* sitting hen

chi'occiola *f* snail; (*Comput*) at sign; **scala a ~** spiral staircase

chi'odo *m* nail; (*idea fissa*) obsession. **~ di garofano** clove

chi'oma *f* head of hair; (*fogliame*) foliage

chi'osco *m* kiosk

chi'ostro *m* cloister

chiro'man|te *mf* palmist. **~'zia** *f* palmistry

chirur'gia *f* surgery. **chi'rurgico** *adj* surgical. **chi'rurgo** *m* surgeon

chissà *adv* who knows; **~ quando arriverà** I wonder when he will arrive

chi'tar|ra *f* guitar. **~'rista** *mf* guitarist

chi'uder|e *vt* close; (*con la chiave*) lock; turn off (luce, acqua); (*per sempre*) close down (negozio ecc); (*recingere*) enclose ● *vi* shut, close. **~si** *vr* shut; (tempo:) cloud over; (ferita:) heal up.

chi'unque *pron* anyone, anybody ● *rel pron* whoever

chi'usa *f* enclosure; (*di canale*) lock; (*conclusione*) close

chi'u|so *pp di* **chiudere** ● *adj* shut; (tempo) overcast; (persona) reserved. **~'sura** *f* closing; (*sistema*) lock; (*allacciatura*) fastener. **~sura lampo** zip, zipper *Am*

ci

● *pron* (*personale*) us; (*riflessivo*) ourselves; (*reciproco*) each other; (*a ciò, di ciò ecc*) about it; **non ci disturbare** don't disturb us; **aspettateci** wait for us; **ci ha detto tutto** he told us everything; **ce lo manderanno** they'll send it to us; **ci consideriamo...** we consider ourselves...; **ci laviamo le mani** we wash our hands; **ci odiamo** we hate each other; **non ci penso mai** I never think about it; **pensaci!** think about it!

● *adv* (*qui*) here; (*lì*) there; (*moto per luogo*) through it; **ci siamo** we are here; **ci siete?** are you there?; **ci siamo passati tutti** we all went through it; **c'è** there is; **ce ne sono molti** there are many; **ci vuole pazienza** it takes patience; **non ci vedo/sento** I can't see/hear

cia'bat|ta *f* slipper. **~'tare** *vi* shuffle

ciabat'tino *m* cobbler

ci'alda *f* wafer

cial'trone *m* scoundrel

ciam'bella *f* (*Culin*) ring-shaped cake; (*salvagente*) lifebelt; (*gonfiabile*) rubber ring

cianci'are *vi* gossip

cia'notico *adj* (colorito) puce

ci'ao *int* [!] (*all' arrivo*) hello!, hi!; (*alla partenza*) bye-bye!

ciar'la|re *vi* chat. **~'tano** *m* charlatan

cias'cuno *adj* each ● *pron* everyone, everybody; (*distributivo*) each [one]; **per ~** each

ci'bar|e *vt* feed. **~ie** *fpl* provisions **~si** *vr* eat; **~si di** live on

ciber'netico *adj* cybernetic

'cibo *m* food

ci'cala *f* cicada

cica'lino *m* buzzer

cica'tri|ce *f* scar. **~z'zante** *m* ointment

cicatriz'zarsi *vr* heal [up]. **cicatrizzazi'one** *f* healing

'cicca *f* cigarette end; ([!]: *sigaretta*) fag; ([!]: *gomma*) [chewing] gum

cic'chetto *m* [!] (*bicchierino*) nip; (*rimprovero*) telling-off

'ciccia *f* fat, flab

cice'rone *m* guide

cicla'mino *m* cyclamen

ci'clis|mo *m* cycling. **~ta** *mf* cyclist

'ciclo *m* cycle; (*di malattia*) course

ciclomo'tore *m* moped

ci'clone *m* cyclone

ci'cogna *f* stork

ci'coria *f* chicory

ci'eco, -a *adj* blind ● *m* blind man ● *f* blind woman

ci'elo *m* sky; (*Relig*) heaven; **santo ~!** good heavens!
'cifra *f* figure; (*somma*) sum; (*monogramma*) monogram; (*codice*) code
ci'fra|re *vt* embroider with a monogram; (*codificare*) code. **~to** *adj* monogrammed; coded
'ciglio *m* (*bordo*) edge; (*pl f* **ciglia**: *delle palpebre*) eyelash
'cigno *m* swan
cigo'l|are *vi* squeak. **~io** *m* squeak
'Cile *m* Chile
ci'lecca *f* **far ~** miss
ci'leno, -a *adj & mf* Chilean
cili'egi|a *f* cherry. **~o** *m* cherry [tree]
cilin'drata *f* cubic capacity; **macchina di alta ~** highpowered car
ci'lindro *m* cylinder; (*cappello*) top hat
'cima *f* top; (*fig: persona*) genius; **da ~ a fondo** from top to bottom
ci'melio *m* relic
cimen'tar|e *vt* put to the test. **~si** *vr* (*provare*) try one's hand
'cimice *f* bug; (*puntina*) drawing pin, thumbtack *Am*
cimini'era *f* chimney; (*Naut*) funnel
cimi'tero *m* cemetery
ci'murro *m* distemper
'Cina *f* China
cin cin! *int* cheers!
cincischi'are *vi* fiddle
'cine *m* [!] cinema
cine'asta *mf* film maker
'cinema *m inv* cinema. **cine'presa** *f* cine-camera
ci'nese *adj & mf* Chinese
cine'teca *f* film collection
'cingere *vt* (*circondare*) surround
'cinghia *f* strap; (*cintura*) belt
cinghi'ale *m* wild boar; **pelle di ~** pigskin
cinguet't|are *vi* twitter. **~io** *m* twittering
'cinico *adj* cynical
ci'niglia *f* (*tessuto*) chenille
ci'nismo *m* cynicism
ci'nofilo *adj* dog-loving
cin'quanta *adj & m* fifty. **cinquan'tenne** *adj & mf* fifty-year-old. **cinquan'tesimo** *adj* fiftieth. **cinquan'tina** *f* **una cinquantina di** about fifty
'cinque *adj & m* five
cinquecen'tesco *adj* sixteenth-century
cinque'cento *adj* five hundred • *m* **il C~** the sixteenth century
cinque'mila *adj & m* five thousand
'cinta *f* (*di pantaloni*) belt; **muro di ~** [boundary] wall. **cin'tare** *vt* enclose
'cintola *f* (*di pantaloni*) belt
cin'tura *f* belt. **~ di salvataggio** lifebelt. **~ di sicurezza** (*Aeron*), (*Auto*) seat-belt
cintu'rino *m* **~ dell'orologio** watch-strap
ciò *pron* this; that; **~ che** what; **~ nondimeno** nevertheless
ci'occa *f* lock
ciocco'la|ta *f* chocolate; (*bevanda*) [hot] chocolate. **~'tino** *m* chocolate. **~to** *m* chocolate. **~to al latte/fondente** milk/plain chocolate
cioè *adv* that is
ciondo'lare *vi* dangle. **ci'ondolo** *m* pendant
cionono'stante *adv* nonetheless
ci'otola *f* bowl
ci'ottolo *m* pebble
ci'polla *f* onion; (*bulbo*) bulb
ci'presso *m* cypress
'cipria *f* [face] powder
'Cipro *m* Cyprus. **cipri'ota** *adj & mf* Cypriot
'circa *adv & prep* about
'circo *m* circus
circo'la|re *adj* circular • *f* circular; (*di metropolitana*) circle line • *vi* circulate. **~'torio** *adj* (*Med*) circulatory. **~zi'one** *f* circulation; (*traffico*) traffic
'circolo *m* circle; (*società*) club
circon'ci|dere *vt* circumcise. **~si'one** *f* circumcision
circon'dar|e *vt* surround. **~io** *m* (*amministrativo*) administrative district. **~si di** *vr* surround oneself with
circonfe'renza *f* circumference. **~ dei fianchi** hip measurement
circonvallazi'one *f* ring road
circo'scritto *adj* limited
circoscrizi'one *f* area. **~ elettorale** constituency
circo'spetto *adj* wary
circospezi'one *f* **con ~** warily

C

circo'stante *adj* surrounding
circo'stanza *f* circumstance; (*occasione*) occasion
circu'ire *vt* (*ingannare*) trick
cir'cuito *m* circuit
circumnavi'ga|re *vt* circumnavigate. **~zi'one** *f* circumnavigation
ci'sterna *f* cistern; (*serbatoio*) tank
'cisti *f inv* cyst
ci'ta|re *vt* quote; (*come esempio*) cite; (*Jur*) summons. **~zi'one** *f* quotation; (*Jur*) summons *sg*
citofo'nare *vt* buzz. **ci'tofono** *m* entry phone; (*in ufficio, su aereo ecc*) intercom
ci'trullo, -a *mf* [!] dimwit
città *f inv* town; (*grande*) city
citta'della *f* citadel
citta|di'nanza *f* citizenship; (*popolazione*) citizens *pl*. **~'dino, -a** *mf* citizen; (*abitante di città*) city dweller
ciucci'are *vt* [!] suck. **ci'uccio** *m* [!] dummy
ci'uffo *m* tuft
ci'urma *f* (*Naut*) crew
ci'vet|ta *f* owl; (*fig: donna*) flirt; **[auto] ~ta** unmarked police car. **~'tare** *vi* flirt. **~te'ria** *f* coquettishness
'civico *adj* civic
ci'vil|e *adj* civil. **~iz'zare** *vt* civilize. **~iz'zato** *adj* (paese) civilized. **~izzazi'one** *f* civilization. **~'mente** *adv* civilly
civiltà *f inv* civilization; (*cortesia*) civility
'clacson *m inv* (car) horn
clacsonare *vi* hoot; honk
cla'mo|re *m* clamour; **fare ~re** cause a sensation. **~rosa'mente** *adv* (sbagliare) sensationally. **~'roso** *adj* noisy; (sbaglio) sensational
clan *m inv* clan; *fig* clique
clandestinità *f* secrecy
clande'stino *adj* secret; **movimento ~** underground movement; **passeggero ~** stowaway
clari'netto *m* clarinet
'classe *f* class. **~ turistica** tourist class
classi'cis|mo *m* classicism. **~ta** *mf* classicist
'classico *adj* classical; (*tipico*) classic ● *m* classic
clas'sifi|ca *f* classification; *Sport* results *pl*. **~'care** *vt* classify. **~'carsi** *vr* be placed. **~ca'tore** *m* (*cartella*) folder. **~cazi'one** *f* classification
clas'sista *mf* class-conscious person
'clausola *f* clause
claustro|fo'bia *f* claustrophobia. **~'fobico** *adj* claustrophobic
clau'sura *f* (*Relig*) enclosed order
clavi'cembalo *m* harpsichord
cla'vicola *f* collar-bone
cle'men|te *adj* merciful; (tempo) mild. **~za** *f* mercy
cleri'cale *adj* clerical. **'clero** *m* clergy
clic *m* (*Comput*) click; **fare ~ su** click on; **fare doppio ~ su** double-click on
clic'care *vi* click (**su** on)
cli'en|te *mf* client; (*di negozio*) customer. **~'tela** *f* customers *pl*
'clima *m* climate. **cli'matico** *adj* climatic; **stazione climatica** health resort
'clinica *f* clinic. **clinico** *adj* clinical ● *m* clinician
clo'na|re *vt* clone. **~'zione** *f* cloning
'cloro *m* chlorine
clou *adj inv* **i momenti ~** the highlights
coabi'ta|re *vi* live together. **~zi'one** *f* cohabitation
coagu'la|re *vt*, **~rsi** *vr* coagulate. **~zi'one** *f* coagulation
coaliz|i'one *f* coalition. **~'zarsi** *vr* unite
co'atto *adj* (*Jur*) compulsory
'cobra *m inv* cobra
coca'ina *f* cocaine. **cocai'nomane** *mf* cocaine addict
cocci'nella *f* ladybird
'coccio *m* earthenware; (*frammento*) fragment
cocci|u'taggine *f* stubbornness. **~'uto** *adj* stubborn
'cocco *m* coconut palm; [!] love; **noce di ~** coconut
cocco'drillo *m* crocodile
cocco'lare *vt* cuddle
co'cente *adj* (sole) burning
'cocktail *m inv* (*ricevimento*) cocktail party
co'comero *m* watermelon
co'cuzzolo *m* top; (*di testa, cappello*) crown
'coda *f* tail; (*di abito*) train; (*fila*) queue;

fare la ~ queue [up], stand in line *Am.* **~ di cavallo** (*acconciatura*) ponytail.

co'dardo, -a *adj* cowardly • *mf* coward

'codice *m* code. **~ di avviamento postale** postal code, zip code *Am.* **~ a barre** bar-code. **~ fiscale** tax code. **~ della strada** highway code.

codifi'care *vt* codify

coe'ren|te *adj* consistent. **~za** *f* consistency

coesi'one *f* cohesion

coe'taneo, -a *adj & mf* contemporary

cofa'netto *m* casket. **'cofano** *m* chest; (*Auto*) bonnet, hood *Am*

'cogliere *vt* pick; (*sorprendere*) catch; (*afferrare*) seize; (*colpire*) hit

co'gnato, -a *mf* brother-in-law; sister-in-law

cognizi'one *f* knowledge

co'gnome *m* surname

'coi = **CON + I**

coinci'denza *f* coincidence; (*di treno ecc*) connection

coin'cidere *vi* coincide

coinqui'lino *m* flatmate

coin'vol|gere *vt* involve. **~gi'mento** *m* involvement. **~to** *adj* involved

'coito *m* coitus

col = **CON + IL**

colà *adv* there

cola|'brodo *m inv* strainer; **ridotto a un ~brodo** [!] full of holes. **~'pasta** *m inv* colander

co'la|re *vt* strain; (*versare lentamente*) drip • *vi* (*gocciolare*) drip; (*perdere*) leak; **~re a picco** (*Naut*) sink. **~ta** *f* (*di metallo*) casting; (*di lava*) flow

colazi'one *f* (*del mattino*) breakfast; (*di mezzogiorno*) lunch; **prima ~** breakfast; **far ~** have breakfast/lunch. **~ al sacco** packed lunch

co'lei *pron f* the one

co'lera *m* cholera

coleste'rolo *m* cholesterol

colf *f abbr* (collaboratrice familiare) home help

'colica *f* colic

co'lino *m* [tea] strainer

'colla *f* glue; (*di farina*) paste. **~ di pesce** gelatine

collabo'ra|re *vi* collaborate. **~'tore, ~'trice** *mf* collaborator. **~zi'one** *f* collaboration

col'lana *f* necklace; (*serie*) series

col'lant *m inv* tights *pl*

col'lare *m* collar

col'lasso *m* collapse

collau'dare *vt* test. **col'laudo** *m* test

'colle *m* hill

col'lega *mf* colleague

collega'mento *m* connection; (*Mil*) liaison; *Radio* link; **~ ipertestuale** hypertext link. **colle'gar|e** *vt* connect. **~si** *vr* link up

collegi'ale *mf* boarder • *adj* (responsabilità, decisione) collective

col'legio *m* (*convitto*) boarding-school. **~ elettorale** constituency

'collera *f* anger; **andare in ~** get angry. **col'lerico** *adj* irascible

col'letta *f* collection

collet|tività *f inv* community. **~'tivo** *adj* collective; (interesse) general; **biglietto ~tivo** group ticket

col'letto *m* collar

collezi|o'nare *vt* collect. **~'one** *f* collection. **~o'nista** *mf* collector

colli'mare *vi* coincide

col'li|na *f* hill. **~'noso** *adj* (terreno) hilly

col'lirio *m* eyewash

collisi'one *f* collision

'collo *m* neck; (*pacco*) package; **a ~ alto** high-necked. **~ del piede** instep

colloca'mento *m* placing; (*impiego*) employment

collo'ca|re *vt* place. **~rsi** *vr* take one's place. **~zi'one** *f* placing

colloqui'ale *adj* (termine) colloquial. **col'loquio** *m* conversation; (*udienza ecc*) interview; (*esame*) oral [exam]

collusi'one *f* collusion

colluttazi'one *f* scuffle

col'mare *vt* fill [to the brim]; bridge (divario); **~ qcno di gentilezze** overwhelm sb with kindness. **'colmo** *adj* full • *m* top; *fig* height; **al colmo della disperazione** in the depths of despair; **questo è il colmo!** (*con indignazione*) this is the last straw!; (*con stupore*) I don't believe it!

co'lomb|a *f* dove. **~o** *m* pigeon

co'loni|a[1] *f* colony; **~a [estiva]** (*per*

C

bambini) holiday camp. **~'ale** *adj* colonial

co'lonia² *f* **[acqua di] ~** [eau de] Cologne

co'lonico *adj* (terreno, casa) farm

coloniz'za|re *vt* colonize. **~'tore, ~'trice** *mf* colonizer

co'lon|na *f* column. **~ sonora** soundtrack. **~ vertebrale** spine. **~'nato** *m* colonnade

colon'nello *m* colonel

co'lono *m* tenant farmer

colo'rante *m* colouring

colo'rare *vt* colour; colour in (disegno)

co'lore *m* colour; **a colori** in colour; **di ~** coloured. **colo'rito** *adj* coloured; (viso) rosy; (racconto) colourful ● *m* complexion

co'loro *pron pl* the ones

colos'sale *adj* colossal. **co'losso** *m* colossus

'colpa *f* fault; (*biasimo*) blame; (*colpevolezza*) guilt; (*peccato*) sin; **dare la ~ a** blame; **essere in ~** be at fault; **per ~ di** because of. **col'pevole** *adj* guilty ● *mf* culprit

col'pire *vt* hit, strike

'colpo *m* blow; (*di arma da fuoco*) shot; (*urto*) knock; (*emozione*) shock; (*Med, Sport*) stroke; (*furto*) raid; **di ~** suddenly; **far ~** make a strong impression; **far venire un ~ a qcno** *fig* give sb a fright; **perdere colpi** (motore:) keep missing; **a ~ d'occhio** at a glance; **a ~ sicuro** for certain. **~ d'aria** chill. **~ di sole** sunstroke; **colpi di sole** (*su capelli*) highlights. **~ di stato** coup [d'état]. **~ di telefono** ring; **dare un ~ di telefono a qn** give sb a ring. **~ di testa** [sudden] impulse. **~ di vento** gust of wind

col'poso *adj* **omicidio ~** manslaughter

coltel'lata *f* stab. **col'tello** *m* knife

colti'va|re *vt* cultivate. **~'tore, ~'trice** *mf* farmer. **~zi'one** *f* farming; (*di piante*) growing

'colto *pp di* **cogliere** ● *adj* cultured

'coltre *f* blanket

col'tura *f* cultivation

co'lui *pron inv m* the one

'coma *m* coma; **in ~** in a coma

comanda'mento *m* commandment

coman'dante *m* commander; (*Aeron, Naut*) captain

coman'dare *vt* command; (*Mech*) control ● *vi* be in charge. **co'mando** *m* command; (*di macchina*) control

co'mare *f* (*madrina*) godmother

combaci'are *vi* fit together; (testimonianze:) concur

combat'tente *adj* fighting ● *m* combatant. **ex ~** ex-serviceman

com'bat|tere *vt/i* fight. **~ti'mento** *m* fight; (*Mil*) battle; **fuori ~timento** (pugilato) knocked out. **~'tuto** *adj* (gara) hard fought

combi'na|re *vt/i* arrange; (*mettere insieme*) combine; (!: *fare*) do; **cosa stai ~ndo?** what are you doing?. **~rsi** *vr* combine; (*mettersi d'accordo*) come to an agreement. **~zi'one** *f* combination; (*caso*) coincidence; **per ~zione** by chance

com'briccola *f* gang

combu'sti|bile *adj* combustible ● *m* fuel. **~'one** *f* combustion

com'butta *f* gang; **in ~** in league

'come

● *adv* like; (*in qualità di*) as; (*interrogativo, esclamativo*) how; **questo vestito è ~ il tuo** this dress is like yours; **~ stai?** how are you?; **~ va?** how are things?; **~ mai?** how come?; **~?** what?; **non sa ~ fare** he doesn't know what to do; **~ sta bene!** how well he looks!; **~ no!** that will be right!; **~ tu sai** as you know; **fa ~ vuoi** do as you like; **~ se** as if

● *conj* (*non appena*) as soon as

co'meta *f* comet

'comico, -a *adj* comic ● *m* funny side ● *mf* (*attore*) comedian ● *f* (*a torte in faccia*) slapstick sketch

co'mignolo *m* chimney-pot

cominci'are *vt/i* begin, start; **a ~ da oggi** from today.

comi'tato *m* committee

comi'tiva *f* party, group

co'mizio *m* meeting

com'mando *m inv* commando

com'medi|a *f* comedy; (*opera teatrale*)

play; *fig* sham. **~a musicale** musical. **~'ante** *mf* comedian; *fig pej* phoney. **~'ografo, -a** *mf* playwright

commemo'ra|re *vt* commemorate. **~zi'one** *f* commemoration

commen'sale *mf* fellow diner

commen't|are *vt* comment on; (*annotare*) annotate. **~ario** *m* commentary. **~a'tore, ~a'trice** *mf* commentator. **com'mento** *m* comment

commerci'a|le *adj* commercial; (relazioni, trattative) trade; (attività) business. **centro ~le** shopping centre. **~'lista** *mf* business consultant; (*contabile*) accountant. **~liz'zare** *vt* market. **~lizzazi'one** *f* marketing

commerci'ante *mf* trader; (*negoziante*) shopkeeper. **~ all'ingrosso** wholesaler

commerci'are *vi* **~ in** deal in

com'mercio *m* commerce; (*internazionale*) trade; (*affari*) business; **in ~** (prodotto) on sale. **~ all'ingrosso** wholesale trade. **~ al minuto** retail trade

com'messo, -a *pp di* **commettere** • *mf* shop assistant. **~ viaggiatore** commercial traveller • *f* (*ordine*) order

comme'stibile *adj* edible. **commestibili** *mpl* groceries

com'mettere *vt* commit; make (sbaglio)

commi'ato *m* leave; **prendere ~ da** take leave of

commise'rar|e *vt* commiserate with. **~si** *vr* feel sorry for oneself

commissari'ato *m* (*di polizia*) police station

commis's|ario *m* [police] superintendent; (*membro di commissione*) commissioner; *Sport* steward; (*Comm*) commission agent. **~ario d'esame** examiner. **~i'one** *f* (*incarico*) errand; (*comitato ecc*) commission; (*Comm: di merce*) order; **~ioni** *pl* (*acquisti*) **fare ~ioni** go shopping. **~ione d'esame** board of examiners. **C~ione Europea** European Commission

commit'tente *mf* purchaser

com'mo|sso *pp di* **commuovere** • *adj* moved. **~'vente** *adj* moving

commozi'one *f* emotion. **~ cerebrale** concussion

commu'over|e *vt* touch, move. **~si** *vr* be touched

commu'tare *vt* change; (*Jur*) commute

comò *m inv* chest of drawers

comoda'mente *adv* comfortably

como'dino *m* bedside table

comodità *f inv* comfort; (*convenienza*) convenience

'comodo *adj* comfortable; (*conveniente*) convenient; (*spazioso*) roomy; (*facile*) easy; **stia ~!** don't get up!; **far ~** be useful • *m* comfort; **fare il proprio ~** do as one pleases

compae'sano, -a *mf* fellow countryman

com'pagine *f* (*squadra*) team

compa'gnia *f* company; (*gruppo*) party; **fare ~ a qcno** keep sb company; **essere di ~** be sociable. **~ aerea** airline

com'pagno, -a *mf* companion; (*Comm, Sport, in coppia*) partner; (*Pol*) comrade. **~ di scuola** schoolmate

compa'rabile *adj* comparable

compa'ra|re *vt* compare. **~'tivo** *adj & m* comparative. **~zi'one** *f* comparison

com'pare *m* (*padrino*) godfather; (*testimone di matrimonio*) witness

compa'rire *vi* appear; (*spiccare*) stand out; **~ in giudizio** appear in court

com'parso, -a *pp di* **comparire** • *f* appearance; *Cinema* extra

compartecipazi'one *f* sharing; (*quota*) share

comparti'mento *m* compartment; (*amministrativo*) department

compas'sato *adj* calm and collected

compassi'o|ne *f* compassion; **aver ~ne per** feel pity for; **far ~ne** arouse pity. **~'nevole** *adj* compassionate

com'passo *m* [pair of] compasses *pl*

compa'tibil|e *adj* (*conciliabile*) compatible; (*scusabile*) excusable. **~ità** *f* compatibility. **~'mente** *adv* **~mente con i miei impegni** if my commitments allow

compa'tire *vt* pity; (*scusare*) make allowances for

compat'tezza *f* (*di materia*) compactness. **com'patto** *adj* compact; (*denso*) dense; (*solido*) solid; *fig* united

compene'trare *vt* pervade

compen'sar|e *vt* compensate; (*sup-

plire) make up for. **~si** *vr* balance each other out

compen'sato *m* (*legno*) plywood

compensazi'one *f* compensation

C **com'penso** *m* compensation; (*retribuzione*) remuneration; **in ~** (*in cambio*) in return; (*d'altra parte*) on the other hand; (*invece*) instead

'comper|a *f* purchase; **far ~e** do some shopping

compe'rare *vt* buy

compe'ten|te *adj* competent. **~za** *f* competence; (*responsabilità*) responsibility

com'petere *vi* compete; **~ a** (compito:) be the responsibility of

competi|tività *f* competitiveness. **~'tivo** *adj* (prezzo, carattere) competitive. **~'tore, ~'trice** *mf* competitor. **~zi'one** *f* competition

compia'cen|te *adj* obliging. **~za** *f* obligingness

compia'c|ere *vt/i* please. **~ersi** *vr* (*congratularsi*) congratulate. **~ersi di** (*degnarsi*) condescend. **~i'mento** *m* satisfaction; *pej* smugness. **~i'uto** *adj* satisfied; (aria, sorriso) smug

compi'an|gere *vt* pity; (*per lutto ecc*) sympathize with. **~to** *adj* lamented • *m* grief

'compier|e *vt* (*concludere*) complete; commit (delitto); **~e gli anni** have one's birthday. **~si** *vr* end; (*avverarsi*) come true

compi'la|re *vt* compile; fill in (modulo). **~zi'one** *f* compilation

compi'mento *m* **portare a ~ qcsa** conclude sth

com'pire *vt* = COMPIERE

compi'tare *vt* spell

com'pito[1] *adj* poilte

'compito[2] *m* task; (*Sch*) homework

compi'ut|o *adj* **avere 30 anni ~i** be over 30

comple'anno *m* birthday

complemen'tare *adj* complementary; (*secondario*) subsidiary

comple'mento *m* complement; (*Mil*) draft. **~ oggetto** direct object

comples|sità *f* complexity. **~siva'mente** *adv* on the whole. **~'sivo** *adj* comprehensive; (*totale*) total. **com'plesso** *adj* complex; (*difficile*) complicated • *m* complex; (*di cantanti ecc*) group; (*di circostanze, fattori*) combination; **in ~so** on the whole

completa'mente *adv* completely

comple'tare *vt* complete

com'pleto *adj* complete; (*pieno*) full [up]; **essere al ~** (teatro:) be sold out; **la famiglia al ~** the whole family • *m* (*vestito*) suit; (*insieme di cose*) set

compli'ca|re *vt* complicate. **~rsi** *vr* become complicated. **~to** complicated. **~zi'one** *f* complication; **salvo ~zioni** all being well

'complic|e *mf* accomplice • *adj* (sguardo) knowing. **~ità** *f* complicity

complimen'tar|e *vt* compliment. **~si** *vr* **~si con** congratulate

compli'menti *mpl* (*ossequi*) regards; (*congratulazioni*) congratulations; **far ~** stand on ceremony

compli'mento *m* compliment

complot'tare *vi* plot

compo'nente *adj & m* component • *mf* member

compo'nibile *adj* (cucina) fitted; (mobili) modular

componi'mento *m* composition; (*letterario*) work

com'por|re *vt* compose; (*ordinare*) put in order; (*Typ*) set. **~si** *vr* **~si di** be made up of

comporta'mento *m* behaviour

compor'tar|e *vt* involve; (*consentire*) allow. **~si** *vr* behave

composi|'tore, -'trice *mf* composer; (*Typ*) compositor. **~zi'one** *f* composition

com'posta *f* stewed fruit; (*concime*) compost

compo'stezza *f* composure

com'posto *pp di* **comporre** • *adj* composed; (*costituito*) comprising; **stai ~!** sit properly! • *m* (*Chem*) compound

com'pra|re *vt* buy. **~'tore, ~'trice** *mf* buyer

compra'vendita *f* buying and selling

com'pren|dere *vt* understand; (*includere*) comprise. **~'sibile** *adj* understandable. **~sibil'mente** *adv* understandably. **~si'one** *f* understanding. **~'sivo** *adj* understanding; (*che include*) inclusive. **com'preso** *pp di* **compren-**

dere ● *adj* included; **tutto compreso** (prezzo) all-in

com'pressa *f* compress; (*pastiglia*) tablet

compressi'one *f* compression. **com'presso** *pp di* **comprimere** ● *adj* compressed

com'primere *vt* press; (*reprimere*) repress

compro'me|sso *pp di* **compromettere** ● *m* compromise. **~t'tente** *adj* compromising. **~ttere** *vt* compromise

comproprietà *f* multiple ownership

compro'vare *vt* prove

compu'tare *vt* calculate

com'puter *m inv* computer. **~iz'zare** *vt* computerize. **~iz'zato** *adj* computerized

computiste'ria *f* book-keeping. **'computo** *m* calculation

comu'nale *adj* municipal

co'mune *adj* common; (*condiviso*) mutual; (*ordinario*) ordinary ● *m* borough; (*amministrativo*) commune; **fuori del ~** extraordinary. **~'mente** *adv* commonly

comuni'ca|re *vt* communicate; pass on (malattia); (*Relig*) administer Communion to. **~rsi** *vr* receive Communion. **~'tiva** *f* communicativeness. **~'tivo** *adj* communicative. **~to** *m* communiqué. **~to stampa** press release. **~zi'one** *f* communication; (*Teleph*) [phone] call; **avere la ~zione** get through; **dare la ~zione a qcno** put sb through

comuni'one *f* communion; (*Relig*) [Holy] Communion

comu'nis|mo *m* communism. **~ta** *adj & mf* communist

comunità *f inv* community. **C~ [Economica] Europea** European [Economic] Community

co'munque *conj* however ● *adv* anyhow

con *prep* with; (*mezzo*) by; **~ facilità** easily; **~ mia grande gioia** to my great delight; **è gentile ~ tutti** he is kind to everyone; **col treno** by train; **~ questo tempo** in this weather

co'nato *m* **~ di vomito** retching

'conca *f* basin; (*valle*) dell

concate'na|re *vt* link together. **~zi'one** *f* connection

'concavo *adj* concave

con'ceder|e *vt* grant; award (premio); (*ammettere*) admit. **~si** *vr* allow oneself (pausa)

concentra'mento *m* concentration

concen'tra|re *vt*, **~rsi** *vr* concentrate. **~to** *adj* concentrated ● *m* **~to di pomodoro** tomato pureé. **~zi'one** *f* concentration

concepi'mento *m* conception

conce'pire *vt* conceive (bambino); (*capire*) understand; (*figurarsi*) conceive of; devise (piano ecc)

con'cernere *vt* concern

concer'tar|e *vt* (*Mus*) harmonize; (*organizzare*) arrange. **~si** *vr* agree

concer'tista *mf* concert performer. **con'certo** *m* concert; (*composizione*) concerto

concessio'nario *m* agent

concessi'one *f* concession

con'cesso *pp di* **concedere**

con'cetto *m* concept; (*opinione*) opinion

concezi'one *f* conception; (*idea*) concept

con'chiglia *f* [sea] shell

'concia *f* tanning; (*di tabacco*) curing

conci'a|re *vt* tan; cure (tabacco); **~re qcno per le feste** give sb a good hiding. **~rsi** *vr* (*sporcarsi*) get dirty; (*vestirsi male*) dress badly. **~to** *adj* (pelle, cuoio) tanned

concili'abile *adj* compatible

concili'a|re *vt* reconcile; settle (contravvenzione); (*favorire*) induce. **~rsi** *vr* go together; (*mettersi d'accordo*) become reconciled. **~zi'one** *f* reconciliation; (*Jur*) settlement

con'cilio *m* (*Relig*) council; (*riunione*) assembly

conci'mare *vt* feed (pianta). **con'cime** *m* fertilizer; (*chimico*) fertilizer

concisi'one *f* conciseness. **con'ciso** *adj* concise

conci'tato *adj* excited

concitta'dino, -a *mf* fellow citizen

con'clu|dere *vt* conclude; (*finire con successo*) achieve. **~dersi** *vr* come to an end. **~si'one** *f* conclusion; **in ~sione** (*insomma*) in short. **~'sivo** *adj* conclusive. **~so** *pp di* **concludere**

C

concomi'tanza *f* (*di circostanze, fatti*) combination

concor'da|nza *f* agreement. **~re** *vt* agree; (*Gram*) make agree. **~to** *m* agreement; (*Comm, Jur*) arrangement

con'cord|e *adj* in agreement; (*unanime*) unanimous

concor'ren|te *adj* concurrent; (*rivale*) competing ● *mf* (*Comm*), *Sport* competitor; (*candidato*) candidate. **~za** *f* competition. **~zi'ale** *adj* competitive

con'cor|rere *vi* (*contribuire*) concur; (*andare insieme*) go together; (*competere*) compete. **~so** *pp di* **concorrere** ● *m* competition; **fuori ~so** not in the official competition. **~so di bellezza** beauty contest

concreta'mente *adv* specifically

concre|'tare *vt* (*concludere*) achieve. **~tiz'zare** *vt* put into concrete form (idea, progetto)

con'creto *adj* concrete; **in ~** in concrete terms

concussi'one *f* extortion

con'danna *f* sentence; **pronunziare una ~** pass a sentence. **condan'nare** *vt* condemn; (*Jur*) sentence. **condan'nato, -a** *mf* convict

conden'sa|re *vt*, **~rsi** *vr* condense. **~zi'one** *f* condensation

condi'mento *m* seasoning; (*salsa*) dressing. **con'dire** *vt* flavour; dress (insalata)

condiscen'den|te *adj* indulgent; *pej* condescending. **~za** *f* indulgence; *pej* condescension

condi'videre *vt* share

condizio'na|le *adj & m* conditional ● *f* (*Jur*) suspended sentence

condizio'na|re *vt* condition. **~to** *adj* conditional. **~'tore** *m* air conditioner

condizi'one *f* condition; **a ~ che** on condition that

condogli'anze *fpl* condolences; **fare le ~ a** offer condolences to

condomini'ale *adj* (spese) common. **condo'minio** *m* joint ownership; (*edificio*) condominium

condo'nare *vt* remit. **con'dono** *m* remission

con'dotta *f* conduct, (*circoscrizione di medico*) district; (*di gara ecc*) management; (*tubazione*) piping

con'dotto *pp di* **condurre** ● *adj* **medico ~** district doctor ● *m* pipe; (*Anat*) duct

condu'cente *m* driver

con'du|rre *vt* lead; drive (veicoli); (*accompagnare*) take; conduct (gas, elettricità ecc); (*gestire*) run. **~rsi** *vr* behave. **~t'tore, ~t'trice** *mf* (*TV*) presenter; (*di veicolo*) driver ● *m* (*Electr*) conductor. **~t'tura** *f* duct

confabu'lare *vi* have a confab

confa'cente *adj* suitable. **con'farsi** *vr* **confarsi a** suit

confederazi'one *f* confederation

confe'renz|a *f* (*discorso*) lecture; (*congresso*) conference. **~a stampa** news conference. **~i'ere, -a** *mf* lecturer

confe'rire *vt* (*donare*) give ● *vi* confer

con'ferma *f* confirmation. **confer'mare** *vt* confirm

confes's|are *vt*, **~arsi** *vr* confess. **~io'nale** *adj & m* confessional. **~i'one** *f* confession. **~ore** *m* confessor

con'fetto *m* sugared almond

confet'tura *f* jam

confezio'na|re *vt* manufacture; make (abiti); package (merci). **~to** *adj* (vestiti) off-the-peg; (gelato) wrapped

confezi'one *f* manufacture; (*di abiti*) tailoring; (*di pacchi*) packaging; **confezioni** *pl* clothes. **~ regalo** gift pack

confic'car|e *vt* thrust. **~si** *vr* run into

confi'd|are *vi* **~are in** trust ● *vt* confide. **~arsi** *vr* **~arsi con** confide in. **~ente** *adj* confident ● *mf* confidant

confi'denz|a *f* confidence; (*familiarità*) familiarity; **prendersi delle ~e** take liberties. **~i'ale** *adj* confidential; (rapporto, tono) familiar

configu'ra|re *vt* (*Comput*) configure. **~zi'one** *f* configuration

confi'nante *adj* neighbouring

confi'na|re *vi* (*relegare*) confine ● *vi* **~re con** border on. **~rsi** *vr* withdraw. **~to** *adj* confined

con'fin|e *m* border; (*tra terreni*) boundary. **~o** *m* political exile

con'fi|sca *f* (*di proprietà*) forfeiture. **~'scare** *vt* confiscate

con'flitt|o *m* conflict. **~u'ale** *adj* adversarial

conflu'enza *f* confluence; (*di strade*) junction

conflu'ire *vi* (fiumi:) flow together; (strade:) meet

con'fonder|e *vt* confuse; (*turbare*) confound; (*imbarazzare*) embarrass. **~si** *vr* (*mescolarsi*) mingle; (*turbarsi*) become confused; (*sbagliarsi*) be mistaken

confor'ma|re *vt* adapt. **~rsi** *vr* conform. **~zi'one** *f* conformity (**a** with); (*del terreno*) composition

con'forme *adj* according. **~'mente** *adv* accordingly

confor'mi|smo *m* conformity. **~sta** *mf* conformist. **~tà** *f* (*a norma*) conformity

confor'tante *adj* comforting

confor't|are *vt* comfort. **~evole** *adj* (*comodo*) comfortable. **con'forto** *m* comfort

confron'tare *vt* compare

con'fronto *m* comparison; **in ~ a** by comparison with; **nei tuoi confronti** towards you; **senza ~** far and away

confusi|o'nario *adj* (persona) muddle-headed. **~'one** *f* confusion; (*baccano*) racket; (*disordine*) mess; (*imbarazzo*) embarrassment. **con'fuso** *pp di* **confondere** ● *adj* confused; (*indistinto*) indistinct; (*imbarazzato*) embarrassed

conge'dar|e *vt* dismiss; (*Mil*) discharge. **~si** *vr* take one's leave

con'gedo *m* leave; **essere in ~** be on leave. **~ malattia** sick leave. **~ maternità** maternity leave

conge'gnare *vt* devise; (*mettere insieme*) assemble. **con'gegno** *m* device

congela'mento *m* freezing; (*Med*) frost-bite

conge'la|re *vt* freeze. **~to** *adj* (cibo) deep-frozen. **~'tore** *m* freezer

congeni'ale *adj* congenial

con'genito *adj* congenital

congestio'na|re *vt* congest. **~to** *adj* (traffico) congested. **congesti'one** *f* congestion

conget'tura *f* conjecture

congi'unger|e *vt* join; combine (sforzi). **~si** *vr* join

congiunti'vite *f* conjunctivitis

congiun'tivo *m* subjunctive

congi'unto *pp di* **congiungere** ● *adj* joined ● *m* relative

congiun'tu|ra *f* joint; (*circostanza*) juncture; (*situazione*) situation. **~'rale** *adj* economic

congiunzi'one *f* conjunction

congi'u|ra *f* conspiracy. **~'rare** *vi* conspire

conglome'rato *m* conglomerate; *fig* conglomeration; (*da costruzione*) concrete

congratu'la|rsi *vr* **~rsi con qcno per** congratulate sb on. **~zi'oni** *fpl* congratulations

con'grega *f* band

congre'ga|re *vt*, **~rsi** *vr* congregate. **~zi'one** *f* congregation

con'gresso *m* congress

'congruo *adj* proper; (*giusto*) fair

conguagli'are *vt* balance. **congu'aglio** *m* balance

coni'are *vt* coin

'conico *adj* conical

co'nifera *f* conifer

co'niglio *m* rabbit

coniu'gale *adj* marital; (vita) married

coniu'ga|re *vt* conjugate. **~rsi** *vr* get married. **~zi'one** *f* conjugation

'coniuge *mf* spouse

connessi'one *f* connection. **con'nesso** *pp di* **connettere**

con'netter|e *vt* connect ● *vi* think rationally. **~rsi** *vr* go online

conni'vente *adj* conniving

conno'ta|re *vt* connote. **~to** *m* distinguishing feature; **~ti** *pl* description

con'nubio *m fig* union

'cono *m* cone

cono'scen|te *mf* acquaintance. **~za** *f* knowledge; (*persona*) acquaintance; (*sensi*) consciousness; **perdere ~za** lose consciousness; **riprendere ~za** regain consciousness

co'nosc|ere *vt* know; (*essere a conoscenza di*) be acquainted with; (*fare la conoscenza di*) meet. **~i'tore, ~i'trice** *mf* connoisseur. **~i'uto** *pp di* **conoscere** ● *adj* well-known

con'quist|a *f* conquest. **conqui'stare** *vt* conquer; *fig* win

consa'cra|re *vt* consecrate; ordain (sacerdote); (*dedicare*) dedicate. **~rsi** *vr* devote oneself

consangu'ineo, -a *mf* bloodrelation

consa'pevo|le *adj* conscious. **~'lezza**

C

f consciousness. **~l'mente** *adv* consciously

'conscio *adj* conscious

consecu'tivo *adj* consecutive; (*seguente*) next

con'segna *f* delivery; (*merce*) consignment; (*custodia*) care; (*di prigioniero*) handover; (*Mil: ordine*) orders *pl*; (*Mil: punizione*) confinement; **pagamento alla ~** cash on delivery

conse'gnare *vt* deliver; (*affidare*) give in charge; (*Mil*) confine to barracks

consegu'en|te *adj* consequent. **~za** *f* consequence; **di ~za** (*perciò*) consequently

consegui'mento *m* achievement

consegu'ire *vt* achieve ● *vi* follow

con'senso *m* consent

consensu'ale *adj* consensus-based

consen'tire *vi* consent ● *vt* allow

con'serva *f* preserve; (*di frutta*) jam; (*di agrumi*) marmalade. **~ di pomodoro** tomato sauce

conser'var|e *vt* preserve; (*mantenere*) keep. **~si** *vr* keep; **~si in salute** keep well

conserva|'tore, -'trice *mf* (*Pol*) conservative

conserva'torio *m* conservatory

conservazi'one *f* preservation; **a lunga ~** long-life

conside'ra|re *vt* consider; (*stimare*) regard. **~to** *adj* (*stimato*) esteemed. **~zi'one** *f* consideration; (*osservazione, riflessione*) remark

conside'revole *adj* considerable

consigli'abile *adj* advisable

consigli|'are *vt* advise; (*raccomandare*) recommend. **~'arsi** *vr* **~arsi con qcno** ask sb's advice. **~'ere, -a** *mf* adviser; (*membro di consiglio*) councillor

con'siglio *m* advice; (*ente*) council. **~ d'amministrazione** board of directors. **C~ dei Ministri** Cabinet

consi'sten|te *adj* substantial; (*spesso*) thick; (*fig: argomento*) valid

con'sistere *vi* **~ in** consist of

consoci'ata *f* associate company

conso'lar|e[1] *vt* console; (*rallegrare*) cheer. **~si** *vr* console oneself

conso'la|re[2] *adj* consular. **~to** *m* consulate

consolazi'one *f* consolation; (*gioia*) joy

'console *m* consul

consoli'dar|e *vt*, **~si** *vr* consolidate

conso'nante *f* consonant

'consono *adj* consistent

con'sorte *mf* consort

con'sorzio *m* consortium

con'stare *vi* **~ di** consist of; (*risultare*) appear; **a quanto mi consta** as far as I know; **mi consta che** it appears that

consta'ta|re *vt* ascertain. **~zi'one** *f* observation

consu'e|to *adj* & *m* usual. **~tudi'nario** *adj* (diritto) common; (persona) set in one's ways. **~'tudine** *f* habit; (*usanza*) custom

consu'len|te *mf* consultant. **~za** *f* consultancy

consul'ta|re *vt* consult. **~rsi con** consult with. **~zi'one** *f* consultation

consul't|ivo *adj* consultative. **~orio** *m* clinic

consu'ma|re *vt* (*usare*) consume; wear out (abito, scarpe); consummate (matrimonio); commit (delitto). **~rsi** *vr* consume; (abito, scarpe:) wear out; (*struggersi*) pine

consu'mato *adj* (politico) seasoned; (scarpe, tappeto) worn

consuma|'tore, -'trice *mf* consumer. **~zi'one** *f* (*bibita*) drink; (*spuntino*) snack

consu'mis|mo *m* consumerism. **~ta** *mf* consumerist

con'sumo *m* consumption; (*di abito, scarpe*) wear; (*uso*) use; **generi di ~** consumer goods *or* items. **~ [di carburante]** [fuel] consumption

consun'tivo *m* **[bilancio] ~** final statement

conta'balle *mf* [!] storyteller

con'tabil|e *adj* book-keeping ● *mf* accountant. **~ità** *f* accounting; **tenere la ~ità** keep the accounts

contachi'lometri *m inv* mileometer, odometer *Am*

conta'dino, -a *mf* farm-worker; (*medievale*) peasant

contagi|'are *vt* infect. **con'tagio** *m* infection. **~'oso** *adj* infectious

conta'gocce *m inv* dropper

contami'na|re *vt* contaminate.

~zi'one *f* contamination

con'tante *m* cash; **pagare in contanti** pay cash

con'tare *vt/i* count; (*tenere conto di*) take into account; (*proporsi*) intend

conta'scatti *m inv* (*Teleph*) time-unit counter

conta'tore *m* meter

contat'tare *vt* contact. **con'tatto** *m* contact

'conte *m* count

conteggi'are *vt* put on the bill ● *vi* calculate. **con'teggio** *m* calculation. **conteggio alla rovescia** countdown

con'te|gno *m* behaviour; (*atteggiamento*) attitude. **~'gnoso** *adj* dignified

contem'pla|re *vt* contemplate; (*fissare*) gaze at. **~zi'one** *f* contemplation

con'tempo *m* **nel ~** in the meantime

contempo|ranea'mente *adv* at once. **~'raneo, -a** *adj & mf* contemporary

conten'dente *mf* competitor. **con'tendere** *vi* compete; (*litigare*) quarrel ● *vt* contend

conte'n|ere *vt* contain; (*reprimere*) repress. **~ersi** *vr* contain oneself. **~i'tore** *m* container

conten'tarsi *vr* **~ di** be content with

conten'tezza *f* joy

conten'tino *m* placebo

con'tento *adj* glad; (*soddisfatto*) contented

conte'nuto *m* contents *pl*; (*soggetto*) content

contenzi'oso *m* legal department

con'tes|a *f* disagreement; *Sport* contest. **~o** *pp di* **contendere** ● *adj* contested

con'tessa *f* countess

conte'sta|re *vt* contest; (*Jur*) notify. **~'tario** *adj* anti-establishment. **~'tore, ~'trice** *mf* protester. **~zi'one** *f* (*disputa*) dispute

con'testo *m* context

con'tiguo *adj* adjacent

continen'tale *adj* continental. **conti'nente** *m* continent

conti'nenza *f* continence

contin'gen|te *m* contingent; (*quota*) quota. **~za** *f* contingency

continua'mente *adv* (*senza interruzione*) continuously; (*frequentemente*) continually

continu|'are *vt/i* continue; (*riprendere*) resume. **~a'tivo** *adj* permanent. **~azi'one** *f* continuation. **~ità** *f* continuity

con'tinu|o *adj* continuous; (*molto frequente*) continual. **corrente ~a** direct current; **di ~o** continually

'conto *m* calculation; (*Comm*) account; (*di ristorante ecc*) bill; (*stima*) consideration; **a conti fatti** all things considered; **far ~ di** (*supporre*) suppose; (*proporsi*) intend; **far ~ su** rely on; **in fin dei conti** when all is said and done; **per ~ di** on behalf of; **per ~ mio** (*a mio parere*) in my opinion; (*da solo*) on my own; **starsene per ~ proprio** be on one's own; **rendersi ~ di qcsa** realize sth; **sul ~ di qcno** (voci, informazioni) about sb; **tener ~ di qcsa** take sth into account; **tenere da ~ qcsa** look after sth. **~ corrente** current account, checking account *Am.* **~ alla rovescia** countdown

con'torcer|e *vt* twist. **~si** *vr* twist about

contor'nare *vt* surround

con'torno *m* contour; (*Culin*) vegetables *pl*

contorsi'one *f* contortion. **con'torto** *pp di* **contorcere** ● *adj* twisted

contrabban|'dare *vt* smuggle. **~di'ere, -a** *mf* smuggler. **contrab'bando** *m* contraband

contrab'basso *m* double bass

contraccambi'are *vt* return. **contrac'cambio** *m* return

contracce|t'tivo *m* contraceptive. **~zi'one** *f* contraception

contrac'col|po *m* rebound; (*di arma da fuoco*) recoil; *fig* repercussion

con'trada *f* (*rione*) district

contrad'detto *pp di* **contraddire**

contrad'di|re *vt* contradict. **~t'torio** *adj* contradictory. **~zi'one** *f* contradiction

contraddi'stin|guere *vt* differentiate. **~to** *adj* distinct

contra'ente *mf* contracting party

contra'ereo *adj* anti-aircraft

C

C

contraf'fa|re *vt* disguise; (*imitare*) imitate; (*falsificare*) forge. **~tto** *adj* forged. **~zi'one** *f* disguising; (*imitazione*) imitation; (*falsificazione*) forgery

con'tralto *m* countertenor ● *f* contralto

contrap'peso *m* counterbalance

contrap'por|re *vt* counter; (*confrontare*) compare. **~si** *vr* contrast; **~si a** be opposed to

contraria'mente *adv* contrary (**a** to)

contrari|'are *vt* oppose; (*infastidire*) annoy. **~'arsi** *vr* get annoyed. **~età** *f inv* adversity; (*ostacolo*) set-back

con'trario *adj* contrary; (direzione) opposite; (*sfavorevole*) unfavourable ● *m* contrary; **al ~** on the contrary

con'trarre *vt* contract

contras|se'gnare *vt* mark. **~'segno** *m* mark; **[in] ~segno** (*spedizione*) cash on delivery

contra'stare *vt* oppose; (*contestare*) contest ● *vi* clash. **con'trasto** *m* contrast; (*litigio*) dispute

contrattac'care *vt* counterattack. **contrat'tacco** *m* counter-attack

contrat'ta|re *vt/i* negotiate; (*mercanteggiare*) bargain. **~zi'one** *f* (*salariale*) bargaining

contrat'tempo *m* hitch

con'tratt|o *pp di* **contrarre** ● *m* contract. **~o a termine** fixed-term contract. **~u'ale** *adj* contractual

contravve'n|ire *vi* contravene. **~zi'one** *f* contravention; (*multa*) fine

contrazi'one *f* contraction; (*di prezzi*) reduction

contribu'ente *mf* contributor; (*del fisco*) taxpayer

contribu|'ire *vi* contribute. **contri'buto** *m* contribution

'contro *prep* against; **~ di me** against me ● *m* **i pro e i ~** the pros and cons

contro'battere *vt* counter

controbilanci'are *vt* counterbalance

controcor'rente *adj* non-conformist ● *adv* upriver; *fig* upstream

controffen'siva *f* counter-offensive

controfi'gura *f* stand-in

controindicazi'one *f* (*Med*) contraindication

control'la|re *vt* control; (*verificare*) check; (*collaudare*) test. **~rsi** *vr* have self-control. **~to** *adj* controlled

con'trol|lo *m* control; (*verifica*) check; (*Med*) check-up. **~lo delle nascite** birth control. **~'lore** *m* controller; (*sui treni ecc*) [ticket] inspector. **~lore di volo** air-traffic controller

contro'mano *adv* in the wrong direction

contromi'sura *f* countermeasure

contropi'ede *m* **prendere in ~** catch off guard

controprodu'cente *adj* self-defeating

con'trordin|e *m* counter order; **salvo ~i** unless I/you hear to the contrary

contro'senso *m* contradiction in terms

controspio'naggio *m* counter-espionage

contro'vento *adv* against the wind

contro'vers|ia *f* controversy; (*Jur*) dispute. **~o** *adj* controversial

contro'voglia *adv* unwillingly

contu'macia *f* default; **in ~** in one's absence

contun'dente *adj* (corpo, arma) blunt

contur'ba|nte *adj* perturbing

contusi'one *f* bruise

convale'scen|te *adj* convalescent

con'vali|da *f* validation. **~'dare** *vt* confirm; validate (atto, biglietto)

con'vegno *m* meeting; (*congresso*) congress

conve'nevol|e *adj* suitable; **~i** *pl* pleasantries

conveni'en|te *adj* convenient; (prezzo) attractive; (*vantaggioso*) advantageous. **~za** *f* convenience; (*interesse*) advantage; (*di prezzo*) attractiveness

conve'nire *vi* (*riunirsi*) gather; (*concordare*) agree; (*ammettere*) admit; (*essere opportuno*) be convenient ● *vt* agree on; **ci conviene andare** it is better to go; **non mi conviene stancarmi** I'd better not tire myself out

con'vento *m* (*di suore*) convent; (*di frati*) monastery

conve'nuto *adj* fixed

convenzi|o'nale *adj* conventional. **~'one** *f* convention

conver'gen|te *adj* converging. **~za** *f* *fig* confluence
con'vergere *vi* converge
conver'sa|re *vi* converse. **~zi'one** *f* conversation
conversi'one *f* conversion
con'verso *pp di* **convergere**
conver'tibile *f* (*Auto*) convertible
conver'ti|re *vt* convert. **~rsi** *vr* be converted. **~to, -a** *mf* convert
con'vesso *adj* convex
convin'cente *adj* convincing
con'vin|cere *vt* convince. **~to** *adj* convinced. **~zi'one** *f* conviction
con'vitto *m* boarding school
convi'ven|te *m* common-law husband • *f* common-law wife. **~za** *f* cohabitation. **con'vivere** *vi* live together
convivi'ale *adj* convivial
convo'ca|re *vt* convene. **~zi'one** *f* convening
convogli'are *vt* convey; convoy (navi) **con'voglio** *m* convoy; (*ferroviario*) train
convulsi'one *f* convulsion. **con'vulso** *adj* convulsive; (*febbrile*) feverish
coope'ra|re *vi* co-operate. **~'tiva** *f* co-operative. **~zi'one** *f* co-operation
coordina'mento *m* co-ordination
coordi'na|re *vt* co-ordinate. **~ta** *f* (*Math*) coordinate. **~te bancarie** bank (account) details. **~zi'one** *f* co-ordination
co'perchio *m* lid; (*copertura*) cover
co'perta *f* blanket; (*copertura*) cover; (*Naut*) deck
coper'tina *f* cover; (*di libro*) dust-jacket
co'perto *pp di* **coprire** • *adj* covered; (cielo) overcast • *m* (*a tavola*) place; (*prezzo del coperto*) cover charge; **al ~** under cover
coper'tone *m* tarpaulin; (*gomma*) tyre
coper'tura *f* covering; (*Comm, Fin*) cover
'copia *f* copy; **bella/brutta ~** fair/rough copy; **~ carbone** carbon copy. **~ su carta** hardcopy. **copi'are** *vt* copy
copi'one *m* script
copi'oso *adj* plentiful
'coppa *f* (*calice*) goblet; (*per gelato ecc*) dish; *Sport* cup. **~ [di] gelato** ice-cream (*served in a dish*)
cop'petta *f* bowl; (*di gelato*) small tub
'coppia *f* couple; (*in carte*) pair
co'prente *adj* (*cipria, vernice*) covering
copri'capo *m* headgear
coprifu'oco *m* curfew
copri'letto *m* bedspread
copripiu'mino *m* duvet cover
co'prir|e *vt* cover; drown (suono); hold (carica). **~si** *vr* (*vestirsi*) cover up; *fig* cover oneself; (cielo:) become overcast
coque *f* **alla ~** (uovo) soft-boiled
co'raggi|o *m* courage; (*sfacciataggine*) nerve; **~o!** come on. **~'oso** *adj* courageous
co'rale *adj* choral
co'rallo *m* coral
Co'rano *m* Koran
co'raz|za *f* armour; (*di animali*) shell. **~'zata** *f* battleship. **~'zato** *adj* (nave) armour-clad
corbelle'ria *f* nonsense; (*sproposito*) blunder
'corda *f* cord; (*Mus, spago*) string; (*fune*) rope; (*cavo*) cable; **essere giù di ~** be depressed; **dare ~ a qcno** encourage sb. **corde vocali** vocal cords
cordi'al|e *adj* cordial • *m* (*bevanda*) cordial; **~i saluti** best wishes. **~ità** *f* cordiality
'cordless *m inv* cordless phone
cor'doglio *m* grief; (*lutto*) mourning
cor'done *m* cord; (*schieramento*) cordon
core|ogra'fia *f* choreography. **~'ografo, -a** *mf* choreographer
cori'andoli *mpl* confetti *sg*
cori'andolo *m* (*spezia*) coriander
cori'car|e *vt* put to bed. **~si** *vr* go to bed
co'rista *mf* choir member
corna ▷CORNO
cor'nacchia *f* crow
corna'musa *f* bagpipes *pl*
cor'nett|a *f* (*Mus*) cornet; (*del telefono*) receiver. **~o** *m* (*brioche*) croissant
cor'ni|ce *f* frame. **~ci'one** *m* cornice
'corno *m* (*pl f* **corna**) horn; **fare le corna a qcno** be unfaithful to sb; **fare le corna** (*per scongiuro*) touch wood. **cor'nuto** *adj* horned • *m* ([!]: *marito tradito*) cuckold; (*insulto*) bastard
'coro *m* chorus; (*Relig*) choir

C

co'rolla *f* corolla

co'rona *f* crown; (*di fiori*) wreath; (*rosario*) rosary. **~'mento** *m* (*di impresa*) crowning. **coro'nare** *vt* crown; (sogno) fulfil

cor'petto *m* bodice

'corpo *m* body; (*Mil, diplomatico*) corps *inv*; **~ a ~** man to man; **andare di ~** move one's bowels. **~ di ballo** corps de ballet. **~ insegnante** teaching staff. **~ del reato** incriminating item

corpo'rale *adj* corporal

corporati'vismo *m* corporatism

corpora'tura *f* build

corporazi'one *f* corporation

cor'poreo *adj* bodily

cor'poso *adj* full-bodied

corpu'lento *adj* stout

cor'puscolo *m* corpuscle

corre'dare *vt* equip

corre'dino *m* (*per neonato*) layette

cor'redo *m* (*nuziale*) trousseau

cor'reggere *vt* correct; lace (bevanda)

corre'lare *vt* correlate

cor'rente *adj* running; (*in vigore*) current; (*frequente*) everyday; (inglese ecc) fluent ● *f* current; (*d'aria*) draught; **essere al ~** be up to date. **~'mente** *adv* (parlare) fluently

'correre *vi* run; (*affrettarsi*) hurry; *Sport* race; (notizie:) circulate; **~ dietro a** run after ● *vt* run; **~ un pericolo** run a risk; **lascia ~!** don't bother!

corre|tta'mente *adv* correctly. **cor'retto** *pp di* **correggere** ● *adj* correct; (caffè) with a drop of alcohol. **~zi'one** *f* correction

cor'rida *f* bullfight

corri'doio *m* corridor; (*Aeron*) aisle

corri'|dore, -'trice *mf* racer; (*a piedi*) runner

corri'era *f* coach, bus

corri'ere *m* courier; (*posta*) mail; (*spedizioniere*) carrier

corri'mano *m* bannister

corrispet'tivo *m* amount due

corrispon'den|te *adj* corresponding ● *mf* correspondent. **~za** *f* correspondence; **scuola/corsi per ~za** correspondence course; **vendite per ~za** mail-order [shopping]. **corri'spondere** *vi* correspond; (stanza:) communicate; **corrispondere a** (*contraccambiare*) return

corri'sposto *adj* (amore) reciprocated

corrobo'rare *vt* strengthen; *fig* corroborate

cor'roder|e *vt*, **~si** *vr* corrode

cor'rompere *vt* corrupt; (*con denaro*) bribe

corrosi'one *f* corrosion. **corro'sivo** *adj* corrosive

cor'roso *pp di* **corrodere**

cor'rotto *pp di* **corrompere** ● *adj* corrupt

corrucci'a|rsi *vr* be vexed. **~to** *adj* upset

corru'gare *vt* wrinkle; **~ la fronte** knit one's brows

corruzi'one *f* corruption; (*con denaro*) bribery

'corsa *f* running; (*rapida*) dash; *Sport* race; (*di treno ecc*) journey; **di ~** at a run; **fare una ~** run

cor'sia *f* gangway; (*di ospedale*) ward; (*Auto*) lane; (*di supermercato*) aisle

cor'sivo *m* italics *pl*

'corso *pp di* **correre** ● *m* course; (*strada*) main street; (*Comm*) circulation; **lavori in ~** work in progress; **nel ~ di** during. **~ d'acqua** watercourse

'corte *f* [court]yard; (*Jur, regale*) court; **fare la ~ a qcno** court sb. **~ d'appello** court of appeal

cor'teccia *f* bark

corteggia'mento *m* courtship

corteggi'a|re *vt* court. **~'tore** *m* admirer

cor'teo *m* procession

cor'te|se *adj* courteous. **~'sia** *f* courtesy; **per ~sia** please

cortigi'ano, -a *mf* courtier ● *f* courtesan

cor'tile *m* courtyard

cor'tina *f* curtain; (*schermo*) screen

'corto *adj* short; **essere a ~ di** be short of. **~ circuito** *m* short [circuit]

cortome'traggio *m Cinema* short

cor'vino *adj* jet-black

'corvo *m* raven

'cosa *f* thing; (*faccenda*) matter; *inter, rel* what; **[che] ~** what; **nessuna ~**

nothing; **ogni ~** everything; **per prima ~** first of all; **tante cose** so many things; (*augurio*) all the best

'cosca *f* clan

'coscia *f* thigh; (*Culin*) leg

cosci'en|te *adj* conscious. **~za** *f* conscience; (*consapevolezza*) consciousness

co'scri|tto *m* conscript. **~zi'one** *f* conscription

così *adv* so; (*in questo modo*) like this, like that; (*perciò*) therefore; **le cose stanno ~** that's how things stand; **fermo ~!** hold it; **proprio ~!** exactly!; **basta ~!** that will do!; **ah, è ~?** it's like that, is it?; **~ ~** so-so; **e ~ via** and so on; **per ~ dire** so to speak; **più di ~** any more; **una ~ cara ragazza!** such a nice girl!; **è stato ~ generoso da aiutarti** he was kind enough to help you ● *conj* (*allora*) so ● *adj inv* (*tale*) like that; **una ragazza ~** a girl like that

cosicché *conj* and so

cosid'detto *adj* so-called

co'smesi *f* cosmetics

co'smetico *adj & m* cosmetic

'cosmico *adj* cosmic

'cosmo *m* cosmos

cosmopo'lita *adj* cosmopolitan

co'spargere *vt* sprinkle; (*disseminare*) scatter

co'spetto *m* **al ~ di** in the presence of

co'spicuo *adj* conspicuous; (somma ecc) considerable

cospi'ra|re *vi* conspire. **~'tore, ~'trice** *mf* conspirator. **~zi'one** *f* conspiracy

'costa *f* coast; (*Anat*) rib

costà *adv* there

co'stan|te *adj & f* constant. **~za** *f* constancy

co'stare *vi* cost; **quanto costa?** how much is it?

co'stata *f* chop

costeggi'are *vt* (*per mare*) coast; (*per terra*) skirt

co'stei *pers pron* ▷**COSTUI**

costellazi'one *f* constellation

coster'na|to *adj* dismayed. **~zi'one** *f* consternation

costi'er|a *f* stretch of coast. **~o** *adj* coastal

costi'pa|to *adj* constipated. **~zi'one** *f* constipation; (*raffreddore*) bad cold

costitu'ir|e *vt* constitute; (*formare*) form; (*nominare*) appoint. **~si** *vr* (*Jur*) give oneself up

costituzio'nale *adj* constitutional. **costituzi'one** *f* constitution; (*fondazione*) setting up

'costo *m* cost; **ad ogni ~** at all costs; **a nessun ~** on no account

'costola *f* rib; (*di libro*) spine

costo'letta *f* cutlet

co'storo *pron* ▷**COSTUI**

co'stoso *adj* costly

co'stretto *pp di* **costringere**

co'stri|ngere *vt* compel; (*stringere*) constrict. **~t'tivo** *adj* coercive

costru|'ire *vt* build. **~t'tivo** *adj* constructive. **~zi'one** *f* construction

co'stui, co'stei, *pl* **co'storo** *pron* (*soggetto*) he, she, *pl* they; (*complemento*) him, her, *pl* them

co'stume *m* (*usanza*) custom; (*condotta*) morals *pl*; (*indumento*) costume. **~ da bagno** swim-suit; (*da uomo*) swimming trunks

co'tenna *f* pigskin; (*della pancetta*) rind

coto'letta *f* cutlet

co'tone *m* cotton. **~ idrofilo** cotton wool, absorbent cotton *Am*

'cottimo *m* **lavorare a ~** do piecework

'cotto *pp di* **cuocere** ● *adj* done; ([!]: *infatuato*) in love; ([!]: *sbronzo*) drunk; **ben ~** (carne) well done

'cotton fi'oc® *m inv* cotton bud

cot'tura *f* cooking

co'vare *vt* hatch; sicken for (malattia); harbour (odio) ● *vi* smoulder

'covo *m* den

co'vone *m* sheaf

'cozza *f* mussel

coz'zare *vi* **~ contro** bump into. **'cozzo** *m fig* clash

C.P. *abbr* (Casella Postale) PO Box

'crampo *m* cramp

'cranio *m* skull

cra'tere *m* crater

cra'vatta *f* tie; (*a farfalla*) bow-tie

cre'anza *f* politeness; **mala ~** bad manners

cre'a|re *vt* create; (*causare*) cause. **~ti-**

vità *f* creativity. **~'tivo** *adj* creative. **~to** *m* creation. **~'tore, ~'trice** *mf* creator. **~zi'one** *f* creation

crea'tura *f* creature; (*bambino*) baby; **povera ~!** poor thing!

C

cre'den|te *mf* believer. **~za** *f* belief; (*Comm*) credit; (*mobile*) sideboard. **~zi'ali** *fpl* credentials

'creder|e *vt* believe; (*pensare*) think ● *vi* **~e in** believe in; **credo di sì** I think so; **non ti credo** I don't believe you. **~si** *vr* think oneself to be. **cre'dibile** *adj* credible. **credibilità** *f* credibility

'credi|to *m* credit; (*stima*) esteem; **comprare a ~to** buy on credit. **~'tore, ~'trice** *mf* creditor

credulità *f* credulity

'credu|lo *adj* credulous. **~'lone, -a** *mf* simpleton

'crema *f* cream; (*di uova e latte*) custard. **~ idratante** moisturizer. **~ pasticciera** egg custard. **~ solare** suntan lotion

cre'ma|re *vt* cremate. **~'torio** *m* crematorium. **~zi'one** *f* cremation

'crème cara'mel *f* crème caramel

creme'ria *f* dairy (*also selling ice cream and cakes*)

'crepa *f* crack

cre'paccio *m* cleft; (*di ghiacciaio*) crevasse

crepacu'ore *m* heart-break

crepa'pelle: **a ~** *adv* fit to burst; **ridere a ~** split one's sides with laughter

cre'pare *vi* crack; ([!]: *morire*) kick the bucket; **~ dal ridere** laugh fit to burst

crepa'tura *f* crevice

crêpe *f inv* pancake

crepi'tare *vi* crackle

cre'puscolo *m* twilight

cre'scendo *m* crescendo

'cresc|ere *vi* grow; (*aumentare*) increase ● *vt* (*allevare*) bring up; (*aumentare*) increase. **~ita** *f* growth; (*aumento*) increase. **~i'uto** *pp di* **crescere**

'cresi|ma *f* confirmation. **~'mare** *vt* confirm

'crespo *adj* frizzy ● *m* crêpe

'cresta *f* crest; (*cima*) peak

'creta *f* clay

'Creta *f* Crete

cre'tino, -a *adj* stupid ● *mf* idiot

cric *m inv* jack

cri'ceto *m* hamster

crimi'nal|e *adj & mf* criminal. **~ità** *f* crime. **'crimine** *m* crime

crimi'noso *adj* criminal

'crin|e *m* horsehair. **~i'era** *f* mane

'cripta *f* crypt

crisan'temo *m* chrysanthemum

'crisi *f inv* crisis; (*Med*) fit

cristal'lino *m* crystalline

cristalliz'zar|e *vt*, **~si** *vr* crystallize; *fig*: (parola, espressione:) become part of the language

cri'stallo *m* crystal

Cristia'nesimo *m* Christianity

cristi'ano, -a *adj & mf* Christian

'Cristo *m* Christ; **un povero c~** a poor beggar

cri'terio *m* criterion; (*buon senso*) [common] sense

'criti|ca *f* criticism; (*recensione*) review. **criti'care** *vt* criticize. **~co** *adj* critical ● *m* critic. **~cone, -a** *mf* faultfinder

crivel'lare *vt* riddle (**di** with)

cri'vello *m* sieve

Cro'azia *f* Croatia

croc'cante *adj* crisp ● *m type of crunchy nut biscuit*

croc'chetta *f* croquette

'croce *f* cross; **a occhio e ~** roughly. **C~ Rossa** Red Cross

croce'via *m inv* crossroads *sg*

croci'ata *f* crusade

cro'cicchio *m* crossroads *sg*

croci'era *f* cruise; (*Archit*) crossing

croci'fi|ggere *vt* crucify. **~ssi'one** *f* crucifixion. **~sso** *pp di* **crocifiggere** ● *adj* crucified ● *m* crucifix

crogio'larsi *vr* bask

crogi[u]'olo *m* crucible; *fig* melting pot

crol'lare *vi* collapse; (prezzi:) slump. **'crollo** *m* collapse; (*dei prezzi*) slump

cro'mato *adj* chromium-plated. **'cromo** *m* chrome. **cromo'soma** *m* chromosome

'cronaca *f* chronicle; (*di giornale*) news; (*Radio, TV*) commentary; **fatto di ~** news item. **~ nera** crime news

'cronico *adj* chronic

cro'nista *mf* reporter

crono'logico *adj* chronological
cronome'trare *vt* time
cro'nometro *m* chronometer
'crosta *f* crust; (*di formaggio*) rind; (*di ferita*) scab; (*quadro*) daub
cro'staceo *m* shellfish
cro'stata *f* tart
cro'stino *m* croûton
crucci'arsi *vr* worry. **'cruccio** *m* worry
cruci'ale *adj* crucial
cruci'verba *m inv* crossword [puzzle]
cru'del|e *adj* cruel. **~tà** *f inv* cruelty
'crudo *adj* raw; (*rigido*) harsh
cru'ento *adj* bloody
cru'miro *m* blackleg, scab
'crusca *f* bran
cru'scotto *m* dashboard
'Cuba *f* Cuba
cu'betto *m* **~ di ghiaccio** ice cube
'cubico *adj* cubic
cubi'tal|e *adj* **a caratteri ~i** in enormous letters
'cubo *m* cube
cuc'cagna *f* abundance; (*baldoria*) merry-making; **paese della ~** land of plenty
cuc'cetta *f* (*su un treno*) couchette; (*Naut*) berth
cucchia'ino *m* teaspoon
cucchi'a|io *m* spoon; **al ~io** (dolce) creamy. **~i'ata** *f* spoonful
'cuccia *f* dog's bed; **fa la ~!** lie down!
cuccio'lata *f* litter
'cucciolo *m* puppy
cu'cina *f* kitchen; (*il cucinare*) cooking; (*cibo*) food; (*apparecchio*) cooker; **far da ~** cook; **libro di ~** cook[ery] book. **~ a gas** gas cooker
cuci'n|are *vt* cook. **~ino** *m* kitchenette
cu'ci|re *vt* sew; **macchina per ~re** sewing-machine. **~to** *m* sewing. **~'tura** *f* seam
cucù *m inv* cuckoo
'cuculo *m* cuckoo
'cuffia *f* bonnet; (*da bagno*) bathing-cap; (*ricevitore*) headphones *pl*
cu'gino, -a *mf* cousin
'cui *pron rel* (*persona: con prep*) who, whom *fml*; (*cose, animali: con prep*) which; (*tra articolo e nome*) whose; **la persona con ~ ho parlato** the person [who] I spoke to; **la ditta per ~ lavoro** the company I work for, the company for which I work; **l'amico il ~ libro è stato pubblicato** the friend whose book was published; **in ~** (*dove*) where; (*quando*) that; **per ~** (*perciò*) so; **la città in ~ vivo** the city I live in, the city where I live; **il giorno in ~ l'ho visto** the day [that] I saw him
culi'nari|a *f* cookery. **~o** *adj* culinary
'culla *f* cradle. **cul'lare** *vt* rock
culmi'na|nte *adj* culminating. **~re** *vi* culminate. **'culmine** *m* peak
'culto *m* cult; (*Relig*) religion; (*adorazione*) worship
cul'tu|ra *f* culture. **~ra generale** general knowledge. **~'rale** *adj* cultural
cultu'ris|mo *m* body-building
cumula'tivo *adj* cumulative; **biglietto ~** group ticket
'cumulo *m* pile; (*mucchio*) heap; (*nuvola*) cumulus
'cuneo *m* wedge
cu'netta *f* gutter
cu'ocere *vt/i* cook; fire (ceramica)
cu'oco, -a *mf* cook
cu'oio *m* leather. **~ capelluto** scalp
cu'ore *m* heart; **cuori** *pl* (*carte*) hearts; **nel profondo del ~** in one's heart of hearts; **di [buon] ~** (persona) kind-hearted; **nel ~ della notte** in the middle of the night; **stare a ~ a qcno** be very important to sb
cupi'digia *f* greed
'cupo *adj* gloomy; (suono) deep
'cupola *f* dome
'cura *f* care; (*amministrazione*) management; (*Med*) treatment; **a ~ di** edited by; **in ~** under treatment. **~ dimagrante** diet. **cu'rante** *adj* **medico curante** GP, doctor
cu'rar|e *vt* take care of; (*Med*) treat; (*guarire*) cure; edit (testo). **~si** *vr* take care of oneself; (*Med*) follow a treatment; **~si di** (*badare a*) mind
cu'rato *m* parish priest
cura'tore, -'trice *mf* trustee; (*di testo*) editor
'curia *f* curia
curio's|are *vi* be curious; (*mettere il naso*) pry (**in** into); (*nei negozi*) look around. **~ità** *f inv* curiosity. **curi'oso**

C

adj curious; (*strano*) odd

cur'sore *m* (*Comput*) cursor

'curva *f* curve; (*stradale*) bend. **~ a gomito** U-bend. **cur'vare** *vti* curve; (strada:) bend. **cur'varsi** *vr* bend. **'curvo** *adj* curved; (*piegato*) bent

cusci'netto *m* pad; (*Mech*) bearing

cu'scino *m* cushion; (*guanciale*) pillow. **~ d'aria** air cushion

'cuspide *f* spire

cu'stod|e *m* caretaker. **~e giudiziario** official receiver. **~ia** *f* care; (*Jur*) custody; (*astuccio*) case. **custo'dire** *vt* keep; (*badare*) look after

cu'taneo *adj* skin *attrib*

'cute *f* skin

Dd

da *prep* from; (*con verbo passivo*) by; (*moto a luogo*) to; (*moto per luogo*) through; (*stato in luogo*) at; (*continuativo*) for; (*causale*) with; (*in qualità di*) as; (*con caratteristica*) with; (*come*) like; (*temporale*) since, for

> **!** *da* si traduce con **for** quando si tratta di un periodo di tempo e con **since** quando si riferisce al momento in cui qualcosa è cominciato. Nota che in inglese si usa il passato prossimo invece del presente: **aspetto da mesi** I've been waiting for months; **aspetto da lunedì** I've been waiting since Monday

····➤ **da Roma a Milano** from Rome to Milan; **staccare un quadro dalla parete** take a picture off the wall; **i bambini dai 5 ai 10 anni** children between 5 and 10; **vedere qcsa da vicino/lontano** see sth from up close/from a distance; **scritto da** written by; **andare dal panettiere** go to the baker's; **passo da te più tardi** I'll come over to your place later; **passiamo da qui** let's go this way; **un appuntamento dal dentista** an appointment at the dentist's; **il treno passa da Venezia** the train goes through Venice; **dall'anno scorso** since last year; **vivo qui da due anni** I've been living here for two years; **da domani** from tomorrow; **piangere dal dolore** cry with pain; **ho molto da fare** I have a lot to do; **occhiali da sole** sunglasses; **qualcosa da mangiare** something to eat; **un uomo dai capelli scuri** a man with dark hair; **è un oggetto da poco** it's not worth much; **l'ho fatto da solo** I did it by myself; **si è fatto da sé** he is a self-made man; **non è da lui** it's not like him

dac'capo *adv* again; (*dall'inizio*) from the beginning

dacché *conj* since

'dado *m* dice; (*Culin*) stock cube; (*Techn*) nut

daf'fare *m* work

'dagli = DA + GLI. **'dai** = DA + I

'dai *int* come on!

'daino *m* deer; (*pelle*) buckskin

dal = DA + IL. **'dalla** = DA + LA. **'dalle** = DA + LE. **'dallo** = DA + LO

'dalia *f* dahlia

dal'tonico *adj* colour-blind

'dama *f* lady; (*nei balli*) partner; (*gioco*) draughts *sg*

dami'gella *f* (*di sposa*) bridesmaid

damigi'ana *f* demijohn

dam'meno *adv* **non essere ~ (di qcno)** be no less good (than sb)

da'naro *m* = DENARO

dana'roso *adj* ([!]: *ricco*) loaded

da'nese *adj* Danish ● *mf* Dane ● *m* (*lingua*) Danish

Dani'marca *f* Denmark

dan'na|re *vt* damn; **far ~re qcno** drive sb mad. **~to** *adj* damned. **~zi'one** *f* damnation

danneggi|a'mento *m* damage. **~'are** *vt* damage; (*nuocere*) harm

'danno *m* damage; (*a persona*) harm. **dan'noso** *adj* harmful

'danza *f* dance; (*il danzare*) dancing. **dan'zare** *vi* dance

dapper'tutto *adv* everywhere

dap'poco *adj* worthless
dap'prima *adv* at first
'dardo *m* dart
'dar|e *vt* give; take (esame); have (festa); **~ qcsa a qcno** give sb sth; **~ da mangiare a qcno** give sb something to eat; **~ il benvenuto a qcno** welcome sb; **~ la buonanotte a qcno** say good night to sb; **~ del tu/del lei a qcno** address sb as "tu"/ "lei"; **~ del cretino a qcno** call sb an idiot; **~ qcsa per scontato** take sth for granted; **cosa danno alla TV stasera?** what's on TV tonight? ● *vi* **~ nell'occhio** be conspicuous; **~ alla testa** go to one's head; **~ su** (finestra, casa:) look on to; **~ sui** *o* **ai nervi a qcno** get on sb's nerves ● *m* (*Comm*) debit. **~si** *vr* (*scambiarsi*) give each other; **~si da fare** get down to it; **si è dato tanto da fare!** he went to so much trouble!; **~si a** (*cominciare*) take up; **~si al bere** take to drink; **~si per** (malato) pretend to be; **~si per vinto** give up; **può ~si** maybe
'darsena *f* dock
'data *f* date. **~ di emissione** date of issue. **~ di nascita** date of birth. **~ di scadenza** cut-off date
da'ta|re *vt* date; **a ~re da** as from. **~to** *adj* dated
'dato *adj* given; (*dedito*) addicted; **~ che** given that ● *m* datum. **~ di fatto** well-established fact; **dati** *pl* data. **da'tore** *m* giver. **datore, datrice** *mf* **di lavoro** employer
'dattero *m* date
dattilogra'f|are *vt* type. **~ia** *f* typing. **datti'lografo, -a** *mf* typist
dat'torno *adv* **togliersi ~** clear off
da'vanti *adv* before; (*dirimpetto*) opposite; (*di fronte*) in front ● *adj inv* front ● *m* front; **~ a** *prep* in front of
da'vanzo *adv* more than enough
dav'vero *adv* really; **per ~** in earnest; **dici ~?** honestly?
'dazio *m* duty; (*ufficio*) customs *pl*
d.C. *abbr* (dopo Cristo) AD
'dea *f* goddess
debel'lare *vt* defeat
debili'ta|nte *adj* weakening. **~re** *vt* weaken. **~rsi** *vr* become weaker
debita'mente *adv* duly
'debi|to *adj* due; **a tempo ~to** in due course ● *m* debt. **~'tore, ~'trice** *mf* debtor
'debo|le *adj* weak; (luce) dim; (suono) faint ● *m* weak point; (*preferenza*) weakness. **~'lezza** *f* weakness
debor'dare *vi* overflow
debosci'ato *adj* debauched
debut'ta|nte *m* (*attore*) actor making his début ● *f* actress making her début. **~re** *vi* make one's début. **de'butto** *m* début
deca'den|te *adj* decadent. **~'tismo** *m* decadence. **~za** *f* decline; (*Jur*) loss. **deca'dere** *vi* lapse. **decadi'mento** *m* (*delle arti*) decline
decaffei'nato *adj* decaffeinated ● *m* decaffeinated coffee
decan'tare *vt* (*lodare*) praise
decapi'ta|re *vt* decapitate; behead (condannato). **~zi'one** *f* decapitation; beheading
decappot'tabile *adj* convertible
de'ce|dere *vi* (*morire*) die. **~'duto** *adj* deceased
decele'rare *vt* decelerate
decen'nale *adj* ten-yearly. **de'cennio** *m* decade
de'cen|te *adj* decent. **~te'mente** *adv* decently. **~za** *f* decency
decentra'mento *m* decentralization
de'cesso *m* death; **atto di ~** death certificate
de'cider|e *vt* decide; settle (questione). **~si** *vr* make up one's mind
deci'frare *vt* decipher; (*documenti cifrati*) decode
deci'male *adj* decimal
deci'mare *vt* decimate
'decimo *adj* tenth
de'cina *f* (*Math*) ten; **una ~ di** (*circa dieci*) about ten
decisa'mente *adv* definitely
decisio'nale *adj* decision-making
deci|si'one *f* decision. **~'sivo** *adj* decisive. **de'ciso** *pp di* **decidere** ● *adj* decided
decla'ma|re *vt/i* declaim. **~'torio** *adj* (stile) declamatory
declas'sare *vt* downgrade
decli'na|re *vt* decline; **~re ogni responsabilità** disclaim all responsibility

d

• *vi* go down; (*tramontare*) set. **~zi'one** *f* declension. **de'clino** *m* decline; **in declino** on the decline
decodificazi'one *f* decoding
decol'lare *vi* take off
décolle'té *m inv* décolleté
d
de'collo *m* take-off
decolo'ra|nte *m* bleach. **~re** *vt* bleach
decolorazi'one *f* bleaching
decom'po|rre *vt*, **~rsi** *vr* decompose. **~sizi'one** *f* decomposition
deconcen'trarsi *vr* become distracted
deconge'lare *vt* defrost
decongestio'nare *vt* relieve congestion in
deco'ra|re *vt* decorate. **~'tivo** *adj* decorative. **~to** *adj* (*ornato*) decorated. **~'tore, ~'trice** *mf* decorator. **~zi'one** *f* decoration
de'coro *m* decorum
decorosa'mente *adv* decorously. **decoroso** *adj* dignified
decor'renza *f* **~ dal...** starting from...
de'correre *vi* pass; **a ~ da** with effect from. **de'corso** *pp di* **decorrere** • *m* passing; (*Med*) course
de'crepito *adj* decrepit
decre'scente *adj* decreasing. **de'crescere** *vi* decrease; (prezzi:) go down; (acque:) subside
decre'tare *vt* decree. **de'creto** *m* decree. **decreto legge** *decree which has the force of law*
'dedalo *m* maze
'dedica *f* dedication
dedi'car|e *vt* dedicate. **~si** *vr* dedicate oneself
'dedi|to *adj* **~ a** given to; (*assorto*) engrossed in; addicted to (vizi). **~zi'one** *f* dedication
de'dotto *pp di* **dedurre**
dedu'cibile *adj* (tassa) allowable
de'du|rre *vt* deduce; (*sottrarre*) deduct. **~t'tivo** *adj* deductive. **~zi'one** *f* deduction
defal'care *vt* deduct
defe'rire *vt* (*Jur*) remit
defezi|o'nare *vi* (*abbandonare*) defect. **~'one** *f* defection
defici'en|te *adj* (*mancante*) deficient; (*Med*) mentally deficient • *mf* mental defective **~za** *f* deficiency; (*lacuna*) gap; (*Med*) mental deficiency
'defici|t *m inv* deficit. **~'tario** *adj* (bilancio) deficit *attrib*
defi'larsi *vr* (*scomparire*) slip away
défilé *m inv* fashion show
defi'ni|re *vt* define; (*risolvere*) settle. **~tiva'mente** *adv* for good. **~'tivo** *adj* definitive. **~to** *adj* definite. **~zi'one** *f* definition; (*soluzione*) settlement
deflazi'one *f* deflation
deflet'tore *m* (*Auto*) quarterlight
deflu'ire *vi* (liquidi:) flow away; (persone:) stream out
de'flusso *m* (*di marea*) ebb
defor'mar|e *vt* deform (arto); *fig* distort. **~si** *vr* lose its shape. **de'form|e** *adj* deformed. **~ità** *f* deformity
defor'ma|to *adj* warped. **~zi'one** *f* (*di fatti*) distortion
defrau'dare *vt* defraud
de'funto, -a *adj & mf* deceased
degene'ra|re *vi* degenerate. **~to** *adj* degenerate. **~zi'one** *f* degeneration. **de'genere** *adj* degenerate
de'gen|te *mf* patient. **~za** *f* confinement
'degli = DI + GLI
deglu'tire *vt* swallow
de'gnare *vt* **~ qcno di uno sguardo** deign to look at sb
'degno *adj* worthy; (*meritevole*) deserving
degrada'mento *m* degradation
degra'da|re *vt* degrade. **~rsi** *vr* lower oneself; (città:) fall into disrepair. **~zi'one** *f* degradation
de'grado *m* damage; **~ ambientale** *m* environmental damage
degu'sta|re *vt* taste. **~zi'one** *f* tasting
'dei = DI + I. **'del** = DI + IL
dela|'tore, **-'trice** *mf* [police] informer. **~zi'one** *f* informing
'delega *f* proxy
dele'ga|re *vt* delegate. **~to** *m* delegate. **~zi'one** *f* delegation
dele'terio *adj* harmful
del'fino *m* dolphin; (*stile di nuoto*) butterfly [stroke]

de'libera *f* bylaw
delibe'ra|re *vt/i* deliberate; **~ su/in** rule on/in. **~to** *adj* deliberate
delicata'mente *adv* delicately
delica'tezza *f* delicacy; (*fragilità*) frailty; (*tatto*) tact
deli'cato *adj* delicate
delimi'tare *vt* delimit
deline'a|re *vt* outline. **~rsi** *vr* be outlined; *fig* take shape. **~to** *adj* defined
delin'quen|te *mf* delinquent. **~za** *f* delinquency
deli'rante *adj* (*Med*) delirious; (*assurdo*) insane
deli'rare *vi* be delirious. **de'lirio** *m* delirium; *fig* frenzy
de'litt|o *m* crime. **~u'oso** *adj* criminal
de'lizi|a *f* delight. **~'are** *vt* delight. **~'oso** *adj* delightful; (*cibo*) delicious
'della = DI + LA. **'delle** = DI + LE. **'dello** = DI + LO
delocaliz'zare *vt* relocate
'delta *m inv* delta
delta'plano *m* hang-glider; **fare ~** go hang-gliding
delucidazi'one *f* clarification
delu'dente *adj* disappointing
de'lu|dere *vt* disappoint. **~si'one** *f* disappointment. **de'luso** *adj* disappointed
demar'ca|re *vt* demarcate. **~zi'one** *f* demarcation
de'men|te *adj* demented. **~za** *f* dementia. **~zi'ale** *adj* (*assurdo*) zany
demilitariz'za|re *vt* demilitarize. **~zi'one** *f* demilitarization
demistificazi'one *f* debunking
demo'cra|tico *adj* democratic. **~'zia** *f* democracy
democristi'ano, -a *adj & mf* Christian Democrat
demogra'fia *f* demography. **demo'grafico** *adj* demographic
demo'li|re *vt* demolish. **~zi'one** *f* demolition
'demone *m* demon. **de'monio** *m* demon
demoraliz'zar|e *vt* demoralize. **~si** *vr* become demoralized
de'mordere *vi* give up
demoti'vato *adj* demotivated
de'nari *mpl* (*nelle carte*) diamonds
de'naro *m* money
deni'gra|re *vt* denigrate. **~'torio** *adj* denigratory
denomi'na|re *vt* name. **~'tore** *m* denominator. **~zi'one** *f* denomination; **~zione di origine controllata** *guarantee of a wine's quality*
deno'tare *vt* denote
densità *f inv* density. **'denso** *adj* dense
den'ta|le *adj* dental. **~rio** *adj* dental. **~ta** *f* bite. **~'tura** *f* teeth *pl*
'dente *m* tooth; (*di forchetta*) prong; **al ~** (*Culin*) slightly firm. **~ del giudizio** wisdom tooth. **~ di latte** milk tooth. **denti'era** *f* false teeth *pl*
denti'fricio *m* toothpaste
den'tista *mf* dentist
'dentro *adv* in, inside; (*in casa*) indoors; **da ~** from within; **qui ~** in here ● *prep* in, inside; (*di tempo*) within, by ● *m* inside
denu'dar|e *vt* bare. **~si** *vr* strip
de'nunci|a, de'nunzia *f* denunciation; (*alla polizia*) report; (*dei redditi*) [income] tax return. **~'are** *vt* denounce; (*accusare*) report
denutrizi'one *f* malnutrition
deodo'rante *adj & m* deodorant
dépendance *f inv* outbuilding
depe'ri|bile *adj* perishable. **~'mento** *m* wasting away; (*di merci*) deterioration. **~re** *vi* waste away
depi'la|re *vt* depilate. **~rsi** *vr* shave (gambe); pluck (sopracciglia). **~'torio** *m* depilatory
deplo'rabile *adj* deplorable
deplo'r|are *vt* deplore; (*dolersi di*) grieve over. **~evole** *adj* deplorable
de'porre *vt* put down; lay (uova); (*togliere da una carica*) depose; (*testimoniare*) testify
depor'ta|re *vt* deport. **~to, -a** *mf* deportee. **~zi'one** *f* deportation
deposi'tar|e *vt* deposit; (*lasciare in custodia*) leave; (*in magazzino*) store. **~io, -a** *mf* (*di segreto*) repository. **~si** *vr* settle
de'posi|to *m* deposit; (*luogo*) warehouse; (*Mil*) depot. **~to bagagli** left-luggage office. **~zi'one** *f* deposition; (*da una carica*) removal
depra'va|re *vt* deprave. **~to** *adj* depraved

d

depre'ca|bile *adj* appalling. **~re** *vt* deprecate

depre'dare *vt* plunder

depressi'one *f* depression. **de'presso** *pp di* **deprimere** • *adj* depressed

deprez'zar|e *vt* depreciate. **~si** *vr* depreciate

depri'mente *adj* depressing

de'primer|e *vt* depress. **~si** *vr* become depressed

depu'ra|re *vt* purify. **~'tore** *m* purifier

depu'ta|re *vt* delegate. **~to, -a** *mf* Member of Parliament, MP

deraglia'mento *m* derailment

deragli'are *vi* go off the lines; **far ~** derail

'derby *m inv Sport* local Derby

deregolamentazi'one *f* deregulation

dere'litto *adj* derelict

dere'tano *m* backside, bottom

de'ri|dere *vt* deride. **~si'one** *f* derision. **~'sorio** *adj* derisory

deri'va|re *vi* **~re da** (*provenire*) derive from • *vt* derive; (*sviare*) divert. **~zi'one** *f* derivation; (*di fiume*) diversion

dermato|lo'gia *f* dermatology. **der'ma'tologo, -a** *mf* dermatologist

'deroga *f* dispensation. **dero'gare** *vi* **derogare a** depart from

der'rat|a *f* merchandise. **~e alimentari** foodstuffs

deru'bare *vt* rob

descrit'tivo *adj* descriptive. **des'critto** *pp di* **descrivere**

des'cri|vere *vt* describe. **~'vibile** *adj* describable. **~zi'one** *f* description

de'serto *adj* uninhabited • *m* desert

deside'rabile *adj* desirable

deside'rare *vt* wish; (*volere*) want; (*intensamente*) long for; **desidera?** can I help you?; **lasciare a ~** leave a lot to be desired

desi'de|rio *m* wish; (*brama*) desire; (*intenso*) longing. **~'roso** *adj* desirous; (*bramoso*) longing

desi'gnare *vt* designate; (*fissare*) fix

de'sistere *vi* **~ da** desist from

'desktop 'publishing *m* desktop publishing

deso'la|re *vt* distress. **~to** desolate; (*spiacente*) sorry. **~zi'one** *f* desolation

'despota *m* despot

de'star|e *vt* waken; *fig* awaken. **~si** *vr* waken; *fig* awaken

desti'na|re *vt* destine; (*nominare*) appoint; (*assegnare*) assign; (*indirizzare*) address. **~'tario** *m* addressee. **~zi'one** *f* destination; *fig* purpose

de'stino *m* destiny; (*fato*) fate

destitu|'ire *vt* dismiss. **~zi'one** *f* dismissal

'desto *adj liter* awake

'destra *f* (*parte*) right; (*mano*) right hand; **prendere a ~** turn right

destreggi'ar|e *vi*, **~si** *vr* manoeuvre

de'strezza *f* dexterity, skill

'destro *adj* right; (*abile*) skilful

detei'nato *adj* tannin-free

dete'n|ere *vt* hold; (polizia:) detain. **~uto, -a** *mf* prisoner. **~zi'one** *f* detention

deter'gente *adj* cleaning; (latte, crema) cleansing • *m* detergent; (*per la pelle*) cleanser

deteriora'mento *m* deterioration

deterio'rar|e *vt* deteriorate. **~si** *vr* deteriorate

determi'nante *adj* decisive

determi'na|re *vt* determine. **~rsi** *vr* **~rsi a** resolve to. **~'tezza** *f* determination. **~'tivo** *adj* (*Gram*) definite. **~to** *adj* (*risoluto*) determined; (*particolare*) specific. **~zi'one** *f* determination; (*decisione*) decision

deter'rente *adj & m* deterrent

deter'sivo *m* detergent. **~ per i piatti** washing-up liquid

dete'stare *vt* detest, hate

deto'nare *vi* detonate

de'tra|rre *vt* deduct (**da** from). **~zi'one** *f* deduction

detri'mento *m* detriment; **a ~ di** to the detriment of

de'trito *m* debris

'detta *f* **a ~ di** according to

dettagli'ante *mf* retailer

dettagli'a|re *vt* detail. **~ta'mente** *adv* in detail

det'taglio *m* detail; **al ~** (*Comm*) retail

det'ta|re *vt* dictate. **~to** *m*, **~'tura** *f* dictation

'detto *adj* said; (*chiamato*) called; (*soprannominato*) nicknamed; **~ fatto** no sooner said than done ● *m* saying

detur'pare *vt* disfigure

deva'sta|re *vt* devastate. **~to** *adj* devastated

devi'a|re *vi* deviate ● *vt* divert. **~zi'one** *f* deviation; (*stradale*) diversion

devitaliz'zare *vt* deaden (dente)

devo'lu|to *pp di* **devolvere** ● *adj* devolved. **~zi'one** *f* devolution

de'volvere *vt* devolve

de'vo|to *adj* devout; (*affezionato*) devoted. **~zi'one** *f* devotion

di *prep* of; (*partitivo*) some; (*scritto da*) by; (parlare, pensare ecc) about; (*con causa, mezzo*) with; (*con provenienza*) from; (*in comparazioni*) than; (*con infinito*) to; **la casa di mio padre/dei miei genitori** my father's house/my parents' house; **compra del pane** buy some bread; **hai del pane?** do you have any bread?; **un film di guerra** a war film; **piangere di dolore** cry with pain; **coperto di neve** covered with snow; **sono di Genova** I'm from Genoa; **uscire di casa** leave one's house; **più alto di te** taller than you; **è ora di partire** it's time to go; **crede di aver ragione** he thinks he's right; **dire di sì** say yes; **di domenica** on Sundays; **di sera** in the evening; **una pausa di un'ora** an hour's break; **un corso di due mesi** a two-month course

dia'bet|e *m* diabetes. **~ico, -a** *adj & mf* diabetic

dia'bolico *adj* diabolical

dia'dema *m* diadem; (*di donna*) tiara

di'afano *adj* diaphanous

dia'framma *m* diaphragm; (*divisione*) screen

di'agnos|i *f inv* diagnosis. **~ti'care** *vt* diagnose

diago'nale *adj & f* diagonal

dia'gramma *m* diagram

dia'letto *m* dialect

Dialetto As Italy was not unified until 1861, standard Italian was slow to become widely used except by the cultural elite. As a result dialects are used by many Italians, with 60% using their dialect regularly. Ranging from Neapolitan and Sicilian to Milanese and Venetian, they vary considerably from each other. Tuscan dialects are the closest to standard Italian.

di'alogo *m* dialogue

dia'mante *m* diamond

di'ametro *m* diameter

di'amine *int* **che ~...** what on earth...

diaposi'tiva *f* slide

di'ario *m* diary

diar'rea *f* diarrhoea

di'avolo *m* devil

di'batt|ere *vt* debate. **~ersi** *vr* struggle. **~ito** *m* debate; (*meno formale*) discussion

dica'stero *m* office

di'cembre *m* December

dice'ria *f* rumour

dichia'ra|re *vt* state; (*ufficialmente*) declare. **~rsi** *vr* **si dichiara innocente** he says he's innocent. **~zi'one** *f* statement; (*documento, di guerra*) declaration

dician'nove *adj & m* nineteen

dicias'sette *adj & m* seventeen

dici'otto *adj & m* eighteen

dici'tura *f* wording

didasca'lia *f* (*di film*) subtitle; (*di illustrazione*) caption

di'dattico *adj* didactic; (televisione) educational

di'dentro *adv* inside

didi'etro *adv* behind ● *m hum* hindquarters *pl*

di'eci *adj & m* ten

die'cina = DECINA

'diesel *adj & f inv* diesel

di'esis *m inv* sharp

di'eta *f* diet; **essere a ~** be on a diet. **die'tetico** *adj* diet. **die'tista** *mf* dietician. **die'tologo, -a** *mf* dietician

di'etro *adv* behind ● *prep* behind; (*dopo*) after ● *adj* back; (*di zampe*) hind ● *m* back; **le stanze di ~** the back rooms

dietro'front *m inv* about-turn; *fig* U-turn

di'fatti *adv* in fact

di'fen|dere *vt* defend. **~dersi** *vr* defend oneself. **~'siva** *f* **stare sulla ~siva** be on the defensive. **~'sivo** *adj* defensive. **~'sore** *m* defender; **avvocato ~sore** defence counsel

di'fes|a *f* defence; **prendere le ~e di qcno** come to sb's defence. **~o** *pp di* **difendere**

difet't|are *vi* be defective; **~are di** lack. **~ivo** *adj* defective

di'fet|to *m* defect; (*morale*) fault, flaw; (*mancanza*) lack; (*in tessuto, abito*) flaw; **essere in ~to** be at fault; **far ~to** be lacking. **~'toso** *adj* defective; (abito) flawed

diffa'ma|re *vt* (*con parole*) slander; (*per iscritto*) libel. **~'torio** *adj* slanderous; (*per iscritto*) libellous. **~zi'one** *f* slander; (*scritta*) libel

diffe'ren|te *adj* different. **~za** *f* difference; **a ~za di** unlike; **non fare ~za** make no distinction (**fra** between). **~zi'ale** *adj & m* differential

differenzi'ar|e *vt* differentiate. **~si** *vr* **~si da** differ from

diffe'ri|re *vt* postpone ● *vi* be different. **~ta** *f* **in ~ta** (*TV*) prerecorded

dif'ficil|e *adj* difficult; (*duro*) hard; (*improbabile*) unlikely ● *m* difficulty. **~'mente** *adv* with difficulty

difficoltà *f inv* difficulty

dif'fida *f* warning

diffi'd|are *vi* **~are di** distrust ● *vt* warn. **~ente** *adj* mistrustful. **~enza** *f* mistrust

dif'fonder|e *vt* spread; diffuse (calore, luce ecc). **~si** *vr* spread. **diffusi'one** *f* diffusion; (*di giornale*) circulation

dif'fu|so *pp di* **diffondere** ● *adj* common; (malattia) widespread; (luce) diffuse

difi'lato *adv* straight; (*subito*) straightaway

'diga *f* dam; (*argine*) dike

dige'ribile *adj* digestible

dige|'rire *vt* digest; [!] stomach. **~sti'one** *f* digestion. **~'stivo** *adj* digestive ● *m* digestive; (*dopo cena*) liqueur

digi'tale *adj* digital; (*delle dita*) finger *attrib* ● *f* (*fiore*) foxglove

digitaliz'zare *vt* digitize

digi'tare *vt* key in

digiu'nare *vi* fast

digi'uno *adj* **essere ~** have an empty stomach ● *m* fast; **a ~** (bere ecc) on an empty stomach

digni|tà *f* dignity. **~'tario** *m* dignitary. **~'toso** *adj* dignified

digressi'one *f* digression

digri'gnare *vi* **~ i denti** grind one's teeth

dila'gare *vi* flood; *fig* spread

dilani'are *vt* tear to pieces

dilapi'dare *vt* squander

dila'ta|re *vt*, **~rsi** *vr* dilate; (metallo, gas:) expand

dilazio'nabile *adj* postponable

dilazi|o'nare *vt* delay. **~'one** *f* delay

dilegu'ar|e *vt* disperse. **~si** *vr* disappear

di'lemma *m* dilemma

dilet'tante *mf* amateur

dilet'tare *vt* delight

di'letto, -a *adj* beloved ● *m* delight ● *mf* (*persona*) beloved

dili'gen|te *adj* diligent; (lavoro) accurate. **~za** *f* diligence

dilu'ire *vt* dilute

dilun'gar|e *vt* prolong. **~si** *vr* **~si su** dwell on (argomento)

diluvi'are *vi* pour [down]. **di'luvio** *m* downpour; *fig* flood

dima'gr|ante *adj* slimming. **~i'mento** *m* weight loss. **~ire** *vi* slim

dime'nar|e *vt* wave; wag (coda). **~si** *vr* be agitated

dimensi'one *f* dimension; (*misura*) size

dimenti'canza *f* forgetfulness; (*svista*) oversight

dimenti'car|e *vt*, **~si** *vr* **~ [di]** forget. **dimentico** *adj* **dimentico di** (*che non ricorda*) forgetful of

di'messo *pp di* **dimettere** ● *adj* humble; (*trasandato*) shabby; (voce) low

dimesti'chezza *f* familiarity

di'metter|e *vt* dismiss; (*da ospedale ecc*) discharge. **~si** *vr* resign

dimez'zare *vt* halve

diminu|'ire *vt/i* diminish; (*in maglia*)

decrease. **~'tivo** *adj & m* diminutive. **~zi'one** *f* decrease; (*riduzione*) reduction

dimissi'oni *fpl* resignation *sg*; **dare le ~** resign

di'mo|ra *f* residence. **~'rare** *vi* reside

dimo'strante *mf* demonstrator

dimo'stra|re *vt* demonstrate; (*provare*) prove; (*mostrare*) show. **~rsi** *vr* prove [to be]. **~'tivo** *adj* demonstrative. **~zi'one** *f* demonstration; (*Math*) proof

di'namico, -a *adj* dynamic. **dina'mismo** *m* dynamism

dinami'tardo *adj* **attentato ~** bomb attack

dina'mite *f* dynamite

'dinamo *f inv* dynamo

di'nanzi *adv* in front ● *prep* **~ a** in front of

dina'stia *f* dynasty

dini'ego *m* denial

dinocco'lato *adj* lanky

dino'sauro *m* dinosaur

din'torn|i *mpl* outskirts; **nei ~i di** in the vicinity of. **~o** *adv* around

'dio *m* (*pl* **'dei**) god; **D~** God

di'ocesi *f inv* diocese

dipa'nare *vt* wind into a ball; *fig* unravel

diparti'mento *m* department

dipen'den|te *adj* depending ● *mf* employee. **~za** *f* dependence; (*edificio*) annexe

di'pendere *vi* **~ da** depend on; (*provenire*) derive from; **dipende** it depends

di'pinger|e *vt* paint; (*descrivere*) describe. **~si** *vr* (*truccarsi*) make up. **di'pinto** *pp di* **dipingere** ● *adj* painted ● *m* painting

di'plo|ma *m* diploma. **~'marsi** *vr* graduate

diplo'matico *adj* diplomatic ● *m* diplomat; (*pasticcino*) millefeuille (*with alcohol*)

diplo'mato *mf person with school-leaving qualification* ● *adj* qualified

diploma'zia *f* diplomacy

di'porto *m* **imbarcazione da ~** pleasure craft

dira'dar|e *vt* thin out; make less frequent (visite). **~si** *vr* thin out; (nebbia:) clear

dira'ma|re *vt* issue ● *vi*, **~rsi** *vr* branch out; (*diffondersi*) spread. **~zi'one** *f* (*di strada*) fork

'dire *vt* say; (*raccontare, riferire*) tell; **~ quello che si pensa** speak one's mind; **voler ~** mean; **volevo ben ~!** I wondered!; **~ di sì/no** say yes/no; **si dice che...** rumour has it that...; **come si dice "casa" in inglese?** what's the English for "casa"?; **che ne dici di...?** how about...?; **non c'è che ~** there's no disputing that; **e ~ che...** to think that...; **a dir poco/tanto** at least/most ● *vi* **~ bene/male di** speak highly/ill of; **dica pure** how can I help you?; **dici sul serio?** are you serious?

diretta'mente *adv* directly

diret'tissima *f* **per ~** (*Jur*) omitting normal procedure

diret'tissimo *m* fast train

diret'tiva *f* directive

di'retto *pp di* **dirigere** ● *adj* direct. **~ a** (*inteso*) meant for. **essere ~ a** be heading for. **in diretta** (trasmissione) live ● *m* (*treno*) through train

diret|'tore, -'trice *mf* manager; manageress; (*di scuola*) headmaster; headmistress. **~tore d'orchestra** conductor

direzi'one *f* direction; (*di società*) management; (*Sch*) headmaster's/headmistress's office (*primary school*)

diri'gen|te *adj* ruling ● *mf* executive; (*Pol*) leader. **~za** *f* management. **~zi'ale** *adj* managerial

di'riger|e *vt* direct; conduct (orchestra); run (impresa). **~si** *vr* **~si verso** head for

dirim'petto *adv* opposite ● *prep* **~ a** facing

di'ritto¹, dritto *adj* straight; (*destro*) right ● *adv* straight; **andare ~** go straight on ● *m* right side; (*Tennis*) forehand

di'ritt|o² *m* right; (*Jur*) law. **~i** *pl* **d'autore** royalties

dirit'tura *f* straight line; *fig* honesty. **~ d'arrivo** *Sport* home straight

diroc'cato *adj* tumbledown

dirom'pente *adj fig* explosive

dirot'ta|re *vt* reroute (treno, aereo); (*illegalmente*) hijack; divert (traffico) ● *vi*

d

alter course. **~'tore, ~'trice** *mf* hijacker

di'rotto *adj* (pioggia) pouring; (pianto) uncontrollable; **piovere a ~** rain heavily

di'rupo *m* precipice

dis'abile *mf* disabled person

disabi'tato *adj* uninhabited

disabitu'arsi *vr* **~ a** get out of the habit of

disac'cordo *m* disagreement

disadat'tato, -a *adj* maladjusted ● *mf* misfit

disa'dorno *adj* unadorned

disa'gevole *adj* (*scomodo*) uncomfortable

disagi'ato *adj* poor; (vita) hard

di'sagio *m* discomfort; (*difficoltà*) inconvenience; (*imbarazzo*) embarrassment; **sentirsi a ~** feel uncomfortable; **disagi** *pl* (*privazioni*) hardships

disappro'va|re *vt* disapprove of. **~zi'one** *f* disapproval

disap'punto *m* disappointment

disar'mante *adj fig* disarming

disar'mare *vt/i* disarm. **di'sarmo** *m* disarmament

disa'strato, -a *adj* devastated

di'sastro *m* disaster; ([!]: *grande confusione*) mess; ([!]: *persona*) disaster area. **disa'stroso** *adj* disastrous

disat'ten|to *adj* inattentive. **~zi'one** *f* inattention; (*svista*) oversight

disatti'vare *vt* de-activate

disa'vanzo *m* deficit

disavven'tura *f* misadventure

dis'brigo *m* dispatch

dis'capito *m* **a ~ di** to the detriment of

dis'carica *f* scrap-yard

discen'den|te *adj* descending ● *mf* descendant. **~za** *f* descent; (*discendenti*) descendants *pl*

di'scendere *vt/i* descend; (*dal treno*) get off; (*da cavallo*) dismount; (*sbarcare*) land. **~ da** (*trarre origine da*) be a descendant of

di'scepolo, -a *mf* disciple

di'scernere *vt* discern

di'sces|a *f* descent; (*pendio*) slope; **~a in picchiata** (*di aereo*) nosedive; **essere in ~a** (strada:) go downhill. **~a libera** (*in sci*) downhill race. **disce'sista** *mf* (*sciatore*) downhill skier. **~o** *pp di* **discendere**

dis'chetto *m* (*Comput*) diskette

dischi'uder|e *vt* open; (*svelare*) disclose. **~si** *vr* open up

disci'oglier|e *vt*, **~si** *vr* dissolve; (*fondersi*) melt. **disci'olto** *pp di* **disciogliere**

disci'pli|na *f* discipline. **~'nare** *adj* disciplinary **~'nato** *adj* disciplined

'disco *m* disc; (*Comput*) disk; *Sport* discus; (*Mus*) record; **ernia del ~** slipped disc. **~ fisso** (*Comput*) hard disk. **~ volante** flying saucer

discogra'fia *f* (*insieme di incisioni*) discography. **disco'grafico** *adj* (industria) recording; **casa discografica** recording company

'discolo *mf* rascal ● *adj* unruly

discol'par|e *vt* clear. **~si** *vr* clear oneself

disconnet'tersi *vr* go offline

disco'noscere *vt* disown (figlio)

discontinuità *f* (*nel lavoro*) irregularity. **discon'tinuo** *adj* intermittent; (rendimento) uneven

discor'dan|te *adj* discordant. **~za** *f* mismatch

discor'dare *vi* (opinioni:) conflict. **di-s'corde** *adj* clashing. **dis'cordia** *f* discord; (*dissenso*) dissension

dis'cor|rere *vi* talk (**di** about). **~'sivo** *adj* colloquial. **dis'corso** *pp di* **discorrere** ● *m* speech; (*conversazione*) talk

dis'costo *adj* distant ● *adv* far away; **stare ~** stand apart

disco'te|ca *f* disco; (*raccolta*) record library

discre'pan|te *adj* contradictory. **~za** *f* discrepancy

dis'cre|to *adj* discreet; (*moderato*) moderate; (*abbastanza buono*) fairly good. **~zi'one** *f* discretion; (*giudizio*) judgement; **a ~zione di** at the discretion of

discrimi'nante *adj* extenuating

discrimi'na|re *vt* discriminate. **~'torio** *adj* (atteggiamento) discriminatory. **~zi'one** *f* discrimination

discussi'one *f* discussion; (*alterco*) argument. **dis'cusso** *pp di* **discutere** ● *adj* controversial

dis'cutere *vt* discuss; (*formale*) debate; (*litigare*) argue; ~ **sul prezzo** bargain. **discu'tibile** *adj* debatable; (gusto) questionable

disde'gnare *vt* disdain. **dis'degno** *m* disdain

dis'dett|a *f* retraction; (*sfortuna*) bad luck; (*Comm*) cancellation. **~o** *pp di* **disdire**

disdi'cevole *adj* unbecoming

dis'dire *vt* retract; (*annullare*) cancel

diseduca'tivo *adj* boorish

dise'gna|re *vt* draw; (*progettare*) design. **~'tore, ~'trice** *mf* designer. **di'segno** *m* drawing; (*progetto, linea*) design

diser'bante *m* herbicide • *adj* herbicidal

disere'da|re *vt* disinherit • *mf* **i ~ti** the dispossessed

diser|'tare *vt/i* desert; **~tare la scuola** stay away from school. **~'tore** *m* deserter. **~zi'one** *f* desertion

disfaci'mento *m* decay

dis'fa|re *vt* undo; strip (letto); (*smantellare*) take down; (*annientare*) defeat; **~re le valigie** unpack [one's bags]. **~rsi** *vr* fall to pieces; (*sciogliersi*) melt; **~rsi di** (*liberarsi di*) get rid of; **~rsi in lacrime** dissolve into tears. **~tta** *f* defeat. **~tto** *adj fig* worn out

disfat'tis|mo *m* defeatism. **~ta** *adj & mf* defeatist

disfunzi'one *f* disorder

dis'gelo *m* thaw

dis'grazi|a *f* misfortune; (*incidente*) accident; (*sfavore*) disgrace. **~ata'mente** *adv* unfortunately. **~'ato, -a** *adj* unfortunate • *mf* wretch

disgre'gar|e *vt* break up. **~si** *vr* disintegrate

disgu'ido *m* **~ postale** mistake in delivery

disgu'st|are *vt* disgust. **~arsi** *vr* **~arsi di** be disgusted by. **dis'gusto** *m* disgust. **~oso** *adj* disgusting

disidra'ta|re *vt* dehydrate. **~to** *adj* dehydrated

disil'lu|dere *vt* disenchant. **~si'one** *f* disenchantment. **~so** *adj* disillusioned

disimbal'lare *vt* unpack

disimpa'rare *vt* forget

disimpe'gnar|e *vt* release; (*compiere*) fulfil; redeem (oggetto dato in pegno). **~si** *vr* disengage oneself; (*cavarsela*) manage. **disim'pegno** *m* (*locale*) vestibule

disincan'tato *adj* (*disilluso*) disillusioned

disinfe'sta|re *vt* disinfest. **~zi'one** *f* disinfestation

disinfet'tante *adj & m* disinfectant

disinfe|t'tare *vt* disinfect. **~zi'one** *f* disinfection

disinfor'mato *adj* uninformed

disini'bito *adj* uninhibited

disinne'scare *vt* defuse (mina). **disin'nesco** *m* (*di bomba*) bomb disposal

disinse'rire *vt* disconnect

disinte'gra|re *vt*, **~rsi** *vr* disintegrate. **~zi'one** *f* disintegration

disinteres'sarsi *vr* **~ di** take no interest in. **disinte'resse** *m* indifference; (*oggettività*) disinterestedness

disintossi'ca|re *vt* detoxify. **~rsi** *vr* come off drugs. **~zi'one** *f* giving up alcohol/drugs

disin'volto *adj* natural. **disinvol'tura** *f* confidence

disles'sia *f* dyslexia

disli'vello *m* difference in height; *fig* inequality

dislo'care *vt* (*Mil*) post

dismi'sura *f* excess; **a ~** excessively

disobbedi'ente *adj* disobedient

disobbe'dire *vt* disobey

disoccu'pa|to, -a *adj* unemployed • *mf* unemployed person. **~zi'o-ne** *f* unemployment

disonestà *f* dishonesty. **diso'nesto** *adj* dishonest

disono'rare *vt* dishonour. **diso'nore** *m* dishonour

di'sopra *adv* above • *adj* upper • *m* top

disordi'na|re *vt* disarrange. **~ta'mente** *adv* untidily. **~to** *adj* untidy; (*sregolato*) immoderate. **di'sordine** *m* disorder

disorganiz'za|re *vt* disorganize. **~to** *adj* disorganized. **~zi'one** *f* disorganization

disorienta'mento *m* disorientation

disorien'ta|re *vt* disorientate. **~rsi** *vr* lose one's bearings. **~to** *adj fig* bewildered

di'sotto *adv* below • *adj* lower • *m* bottom

dis'paccio *m* dispatch

dispa'rato *adj* disparate

'dispari *adj* odd. **~tà** *f inv* disparity

dis'parte *adv* **in ~** apart; **stare in ~** stand aside

d

dis'pendi|o *m* (*spreco*) waste. **~'oso** *adj* expensive

dis'pen|sa *f* pantry; (*distribuzione*) distribution; (*mobile*) cupboard; (*Jur*) exemption; (*Relig*) dispensation; (*pubblicazione periodica*) number. **~'sare** *vt* distribute; (*esentare*) exonerate

dispe'ra|re *vi* despair (**di** of). **~rsi** *vr* despair. **~ta'mente** (piangere) desperately. **~to** *adj* desperate. **~zi'one** *f* despair

dis'per|dere *vt*, **~dersi** *vr* disperse. **~si'one** *f* dispersion; (*di truppe*) dispersal. **~'sivo** *adj* disorganized. **~so** *pp di* **disperdere** • *adj* scattered; (*smarrito*) lost • *m* missing soldier

dis'pet|to *m* spite; **a ~to di** in spite of. **~'toso** *adj* spiteful

dispia'c|ere *m* upset; (*rammarico*) regret; (*dolore*) sorrow; (*preoccupazione*) worry • *vi* **mi dispiace** I'm sorry; **non mi dispiace** I don't dislike it; **se non ti dispiace** if you don't mind. **~i'uto** *adj* upset; (*dolente*) sorry

dispo'nibil|e *adj* available; (*gentile*) helpful. **~ità** *f* availability; (*gentilezza*) helpfulness

dis'por|re *vt* arrange • *vi* dispose; (*stabilire*) order; **~re di** have at one's disposal. **~si** *vr* line up

disposi'tivo *m* device

disposizi'one *f* disposition; (*ordine*) order; (*libera disponibilità*) disposal. **dis'posto** *pp di* **disporre** • *adj* ready; (*incline*) disposed; **essere ben disposto verso** be favourably disposed towards

di'spotico *adj* despotic

dispregia'tivo *adj* disparaging

disprez'zare *vt* despise. **dis'prezzo** *m* contempt

'disputa *f* dispute

dispu'tar|e *vi* dispute; (*gareggiare*) compete. **~si** *vr* **~si qcsa** contend for sth

dissacra'torio *adj* debunking

dissangua'mento *m* loss of blood

dissangu'a|re *vt*, **~rsi** *vr* bleed. **~rsi** *vr fig* become impoverished. **~to** *adj* bloodless; *fig* impoverished

dissa'pore *m* disagreement

dissec'car|e *vt*, **~si** *vr* dry up

dissemi'nare *vt* disseminate; (*notizie*) spread

dis'senso *m* dissent; (*disaccordo*) disagreement

dissente'ria *f* dysentery

dissen'tire *vi* disagree (**da** with)

dissertazi'one *f* dissertation

disser'vizio *m* poor service

disse'sta|re *vt* upset; (*Comm*) damage. **~to** *adj* (strada) uneven. **dis'sesto** *m* ruin

disse'tante *adj* thirst-quenching

disse'ta|re *vt* **~re qcno** quench sb's thirst

dissi'dente *adj & mf* dissident

dis'sidio *m* disagreement

dis'simile *adj* unlike, dissimilar

dissimu'lare *vt* conceal; (*fingere*) dissimulate

dissi'pa|re *vt* dissipate; (*sperperare*) squander. **~rsi** *vr* (nebbia:) clear; (dubbio:) disappear. **~to** *adj* dissipated. **~zi'one** *f* squandering

dissoci'ar|e *vt*, **~si** *vr* dissociate

disso'dare *vt* till

dis'solto *pp di* **dissolvere**

disso'luto *adj* dissolute

dis'solver|e *vt*, **~si** *vr* dissolve; (*disperdere*) dispel

disso'nanza *f* dissonance

dissua|'dere *vt* dissuade. **~si'one** *f* dissuasion. **~'sivo** *adj* dissuasive

distac'car|e *vt* detach; *Sport* leave behind. **~si** *vr* be detached. **di'stacco** *m* detachment; (*separazione*) separation; *Sport* lead

di'stan|te *adj* far away; *fig*: (person) detached • *adv* far away **~za** *f* distance. **~zi'are** *vt* space out; *Sport* outdistance

di'stare *vi* be distant; **quanto dista?** how far is it?

di'sten|dere *vt* stretch out (parte del corpo); (*spiegare*) spread; (*deporre*) lay. **~dersi** *vr* stretch; (*sdraiarsi*) lie down; (*rilassarsi*) relax. **~si'one** *f* stretching;

(*rilassamento*) relaxation; (*Pol*) détente. **~'sivo** *adj* relaxing

di'steso, -a *pp di* **distendere** • *f* expanse

distil'l|are *vt/i* distil. **~azi'one** *f* distillation. **~e'ria** *f* distillery

di'stinguer|e *vt* distinguish. **~si** *vr* distinguish oneself. **distin'guibile** *adj* distinguishable

di'stinta *f* (*Comm*) list. **~ di pagamento** receipt. **~ di versamento** paying-in slip

distinta'mente *adv* individually; (*chiaramente*) clearly

distin'tivo *adj* distinctive • *m* badge

di'stin|to, -a *pp di* **distinguere** • *adj* distinct; (*signorile*) distinguished; **~ti saluti** Yours faithfully. **~zi'one** *f* distinction

di'stogliere *vt* **~ da** remove from; (*dissuadere*) dissuade from. **di'stolto** *pp di* **distogliere**

di'storcere *vt* twist

distorsi'one *f* (*Med*) sprain; (*alterazione*) distortion

di'stra|rre *vt* distract; (*divertire*) amuse. **~rsi** *vr* get distracted; (*svagarsi*) amuse oneself; **non ti distrarre!** pay attention!. **~tta'mente** *adv* absently. **~tto** *pp di* **distrarre** • *adj* absent-minded; (*disattento*) inattentive. **~zi'one** *f* absent-mindedness; (*errore*) inattention; (*svago*) amusement

di'stretto *m* district

distribu|'ire *vt* distribute; (*disporre*) arrange; deal (carte). **~'tore** *m* distributor; (*di benzina*) petrol pump; (*automatico*) slot-machine. **~zi'one** *f* distribution

distri'car|e *vt* disentangle; **~si da qcsa** *vr fig* get out of sth

di'stru|ggere *vt* destroy. **~t'tivo** *adj* destructive; (critica) negative. **~tto** *pp di* **distruggere**. **~zi'one** *f* destruction

distur'bar|e *vt* disturb; (*sconvolgere*) upset. **~si** *vr* trouble oneself. **di'sturbo** *m* bother; (*indisposizione*) trouble; (*Med*) problem; (*Radio, TV*) interference; **disturbi** *pl* (*Radio, TV*) static. **disturbi di stomaco** stomach trouble

disubbidi'en|te *adj* disobedient. **~za** *f* disobedience

disubbi'dire *vi* **~ a** disobey

disugu|agli'anza *f* disparity. **~'ale** *adj* unequal; (*irregolare*) irregular

di'suso *m* **cadere in ~** fall into disuse

di'tale *m* thimble

di'tata *f* poke; (*impronta*) finger-mark

'dito *m* (*pl f* **dita**) finger; (*di vino*) finger. **~ del piede** toe

'ditta *f* firm

dit'tafono *m* dictaphone

ditta'tor|e *m* dictator. **~i'ale** *adj* dictatorial. **ditta'tura** *f* dictatorship

dit'tongo *m* diphthong

di'urno *adj* daytime; **spettacolo ~** matinée

'diva *f* diva

diva'ga|re *vi* digress. **~zi'one** *f* digression

divam'pare *vi* burst into flames; *fig* spread like wildfire

di'vano *m* sofa. **~ letto** sofa bed

divari'care *vt* open

di'vario *m* discrepancy; **un ~ di opinioni** a difference of opinion

dive'n|ire *vi* = DIVENTARE. **~uto** *pp di* **divenire**

diven'tare *vi* become; (*lentamente*) grow; (*rapidamente*) turn

di'verbio *m* squabble

diver'gen|te *adj* divergent. **~za** *f* divergence; **~za di opinioni** difference of opinion. **di'vergere** *vi* diverge

diversa'mente *adv* otherwise; (*in modo diverso*) differently

diversifi'ca|re *vt* diversify. **~rsi** *vr* differ. **~zi'one** *f* diversification

diver|si'one *f* diversion. **~sità** *f inv* difference. **~'sivo** *m* diversion. **di'verso** *adj* different; **diversi** *pl* (*parecchi*) several • *pron* several [people]

diver'tente *adj* amusing. **diverti'mento** *m* amusement

diver'tir|e *vt* amuse. **~si** *vr* enjoy oneself

divi'dendo *m* dividend

di'vider|e *vt* divide; (*condividere*) share. **~si** *vr* (*separarsi*) separate

divi'eto *m* prohibition; **~ di sosta** no parking

divinco'larsi *vr* wriggle

divinità *f inv* divinity. **di'vino** *adj* divine

di'visa *f* uniform; (*Comm*) currency

divisi'one *f* division

d

di'vismo *m* worship; (*atteggiamento*) superstar mentality
di'vi|so *pp di* **dividere. ~'sore** *m* divisor. **~'sorio** *adj* dividing
'divo, -a *mf* star
divo'rar|e *vt* devour. **~si** *vr* **~si da** be consumed with
divorzi'a|re *vi* divorce. **~to, -a** *mf* divorcee. **di'vorzio** *m* divorce
divul'ga|re *vt* divulge; (*rendere popolare*) popularize. **~rsi** *vr* spread. **~'tivo** *adj* popular. **~zi'one** *f* popularization
dizio'nario *m* dictionary
dizi'one *f* diction
do *m* (*Mus*) C

> *i*
> **DOC** Italian wines which are grown in certain specified areas and which conform to certain regulations may be styled *DOC* (*Denominazione di Origine Controllata*). The classification *DOCG* (*Denominazione di Origine Controllata e Garantita*) is awarded to DOC wines of particular quality. Wines must conform to the DOC criteria for at least five years before they can be classified as DOCG.

'doccia *f* shower; (*grondaia*) gutter; **fare la ~** have a shower
do'cen|te *adj* teaching ● *mf* teacher; (*Univ*) lecturer. **~za** *f* (*Univ*) lecturer's qualification
'docile *adj* docile
documen'tar|e *vt* document. **~si** *vr* gather information (**su** about)
documen'tario *adj & m* documentary
documen'ta|to *adj* well-documented; (persona) well-informed. **~zi'one** *f* documentation
docu'mento *m* document
dodi'cesimo *adj & m* twelfth. **'dodici** *adj & m* twelve
do'gan|a *f* customs *pl*; (*dazio*) duty. **doga'nale** *adj* customs. **~i'ere** *m* customs officer
'doglie *fpl* labour pains
'dogma *m* dogma. **dog'matico** *adj* dogmatic. **~'tismo** *m* dogmatism
'dolce *adj* sweet; (clima) mild; (voce, consonante) soft; (acqua) fresh ● *m* (*portata*) dessert; (*torta*) cake; **non mangio dolci** I don't eat sweet things. **~'mente** *adv* sweetly. **dol'cezza** *f* sweetness; (*di clima*) mildness
dolce'vita *adj inv* (*maglione*) rollneck
dolci'ario *adj* confectionery
dolci'astro *adj* sweetish
dolcifi'cante *m* sweetener ● *adj* sweetening
dolci'umi *mpl* sweets
do'lente *adj* painful; (*spiacente*) sorry
do'le|re *vi* ache, hurt; (*dispiacere*) regret. **~rsi** *vr* regret; (*protestare*) complain; **~rsi di** be sorry for
'dollaro *m* dollar
'dolo *m* (*Jur*) malice; (*truffa*) fraud
Dolo'miti *fpl* **le ~** the Dolomites
do'lore *m* pain; (*morale*) sorrow. **dolo'roso** *adj* painful
do'loso *adj* malicious
do'manda *f* question; (*richiesta*) request; (*scritta*) application; (*Comm*) demand; **fare una ~ (a qcno)** ask (sb) a question. **~ di impiego** job application
doman'dar|e *vt* ask; (*esigere*) demand; **~e qcsa a qcno** ask sb for sth. **~si** *vr* wonder
do'mani *adv* tomorrow; **~ sera** tomorrow evening ● *m* **il ~** the future; **a ~** see you tomorrow
do'ma|re *vt* tame; *fig* control (emozioni). **~'tore** *m* tamer
domat'tina *adv* tomorrow morning
do'meni|ca *f* Sunday. **~'cale** *adj* Sunday *attrib*
do'mestico, -a *adj* domestic ● *m* servant ● *f* maid
domicili'are *adj* **arresti domiciliari** (*Jur*) house arrest
domicili'arsi *vr* settle
domi'cilio *m* domicile; (*abitazione*) home; **recapitiamo a ~** we do home deliveries
domi'na|re *vt* dominate; (*controllare*) control ● *vi* rule over; (*prevalere*) be dominant. **~rsi** *vr* control oneself. **~'tore, ~'trice** *mf* ruler; **~zi'one** *f* domination
do'minio *m* control; (*Pol*) dominion; (*ambito*) field; **di ~ pubblico** common knowledge
don *m inv* (*ecclesiastico*) Father
do'na|re *vt* give; donate (sangue, or-

gano) • *vi* **~re a** (*giovare esteticamente*) suit. **~'tore, ~'trice** *mf* donor. **~zi'one** *f* donation

dondo'l|are *vt* swing; (*cullare*) rock • *vi* sway. **~arsi** *vr* swing. **~io** *m* rocking. **'dondolo** *m* swing; **cavallo/sedia a dondolo** rocking-horse/chair

dongio'vanni *m inv* Romeo

'donna *f* woman. **~ di servizio** domestic help

don'naccia *f pej* whore

'dono *m* gift

'dopo *prep* after; (*a partire da*) since • *adv* afterwards; (*più tardi*) later; (*in seguito*) later on; **~ di me** after me

dopo'barba *m inv* aftershave

dopo'cena *m inv* evening

dopodiché *adv* after which

dopodo'mani *adv* the day after tomorrow

dopogu'erra *m inv* post-war period

dopo'pranzo *m inv* afternoon

dopo'sci *adj & nm inv* après-ski

doposcu'ola *m inv* after-school activities *pl*

dopo-'shampoo *m inv* conditioner • *adj inv* conditioning

dopo'sole *m inv* aftersun cream • *adj inv* aftersun

dopo'tutto *adv* after all

doppi'aggio *m* dubbing

doppia'mente *adv* doubly

doppi'a|re *vt* double; *Sport* lap; *Cinema* dub. **~'tore, ~'trice** *mf* dubber

'doppio *adj & adv* double. **~ clic** *m* (*Comput*) double click. **~ fallo** *m Tennis* double fault. **~ gioco** *m* double-dealing. **~ mento** *m* double chin. **~ senso** *m* double entendre. **doppi vetri** *mpl* double glazing • *m* double; *Tennis* doubles *pl*. **~ misto** *Tennis* mixed doubles

doppi'one *m* duplicate

doppio'petto *adj* double-breasted

dop'pista *mf* doubles player

do'ra|re *vt* gild; (*Culin*) brown. **~to** *adj* gilt; (*color oro*) golden. **~'tura** *f* gilding

dormicchi'are *vi* doze

dormigli'one, -a *mf* sleepyhead; *fig* lazy-bones

dor'mi|re *vi* sleep; (*essere addormentato*) be asleep; *fig* be asleep. **~ta** *f* good sleep. **~'tina** *f* nap. **~'torio** *m* dormitory

dormi'veglia *m* **essere in ~** be half asleep

dor'sale *adj* dorsal • *f* (*di monte*) ridge

'dorso *m* back; (*di libro*) spine; (*di monte*) crest; (*nel nuoto*) backstroke

do'saggio *m* dosage

do'sare *vt* dose; *fig* measure; **~ le parole** weigh one's words

dosa'tore *m* measuring jug

'dose *f* dose; **in buona ~** *fig* in good measure. **~ eccessiva** overdose

dossi'er *m inv* file

'dosso *m* (*dorso*) back; **levarsi di ~ gli abiti** take off one's clothes

do'ta|re *vt* endow; (*di accessori*) equip. **~to** *adj* (persona) gifted; (*fornito*) equipped. **~zi'one** *f* (*attrezzatura*) equipment; **in ~zione** at one's disposal

'dote *f* dowry; (*qualità*) gift

'dotto *adj* learned • *m* scholar; (*Anat*) duct

dotto|'rato *m* doctorate. **dot'tore, ~'ressa** *mf* doctor

dot'trina *f* doctrine

'dove *adv* where; **di ~ sei?** where do you come from; **fin ~?** how far?; **per ~?** which way?

do'vere *vi* (*obbligo*) have to, must; **devo andare** I have to go, I must go; **devo venire anch'io?** do I have to come too?; **avresti dovuto dirmelo** you should have told me, you ought to have told me; **devo sedermi un attimo** I must sit down for a minute, I need to sit down for a minute; **dev'essere successo qualcosa** something must have happened; **come si deve** properly • *vt* (*essere debitore di, derivare*) owe; **essere dovuto a** be due to • *m* duty; **per ~** out of duty. **dove'roso** *adj* only right and proper

do'vunque *adv* (*dappertutto*) everywhere; (*in qualsiasi luogo*) anywhere • *conj* wherever

do'vuto *adj* due; (*debito*) proper

doz'zi|na *f* dozen. **~'nale** *adj* cheap

dra'gare *vt* dredge

'drago *m* dragon

'dramm|a *m* drama. **dram'matico** *adj* dramatic. **~atiz'zare** *vt* dramatize.

~a'turgo *m* playwright. **dram'mone** *m* (*film*) tear-jerker

drappeggi'are *vt* drape. **drap'peggio** *m* drapery

drap'pello *m* (*Mil*) squad; (*gruppo*) band

d e

'drastico *adj* drastic

dre'nare *vt* drain

drib'blare *vt* (*in calcio*) dribble

'dritta *f* (*mano destra*) right hand; (*Naut*) starboard; (*informazione*) pointer, tip; **a ~ e a manca** left, right and centre

'dritto *adj* = DIRITTO[1] ● *mf* [!] crafty so-and-so

driz'zar|e *vt* straighten; (*rizzare*) prick up. **~si** *vr* straighten [up]; (*alzarsi*) raise

'dro|ga *f* drug. **~'gare** *vt* drug. **~'garsi** *vr* take drugs. **~'gato, -a** *mf* drug addict

drogh|e'ria *f* grocery. **~i'ere, -a** *mf* grocer

'dubbi|o *adj* doubtful; (*ambiguo*) dubious ● *m* doubt; (*sospetto*) suspicion; **mettere in ~o** doubt; **essere fuori ~o** be beyond doubt; **essere in ~o** be doubtful. **~'oso** *adj* doubtful

dubi'ta|re *vi* doubt; **~re di** doubt; (*diffidare*) mistrust; **dubito che venga** I doubt whether he'll come. **~'tivo** *adj* ambiguous

'duca, du'chessa *mf* duke; duchess

'due *adj & m* two

due'cento *adj & m* two hundred

du'ello *m* duel

due'mila *adj & m* two thousand

due'pezzi *m inv* (*bikini*) bikini

du'etto *m* duo; (*Mus*) duet

'duna *f* dune

'dunque *conj* therefore; (*allora*) well [then]

'duo *m inv* duo; (*Mus*) duet

du'omo *m* cathedral

dupli'ca|re *vt* duplicate. **~to** *m* duplicate. **'duplice** *adj* double; **in duplice** in duplicate

dura'mente *adv* (lavorare) hard; (rimproverare) harshly

du'rante *prep* during

du'r|are *vi* last; (cibo:) keep; (*resistere*) hold out. **~ata** *f* duration. **~a'turo, ~evole** *adj* lasting, enduring

du'rezza *f* hardness; (*di carne*) toughness; (*di voce, padre*) harshness

'duro, -a *adj* hard; (persona, carne) tough; (voce) harsh; (pane) stale ● *mf* tough person

du'rone *m* hardened skin

'duttile *adj* (materiale) ductile; (carattere) malleable

DVD *m inv* DVD

Ee

e, ed *conj* and

'ebano *m* ebony

eb'bene *conj* well [then]

eb'brezza *f* inebriation; (*euforia*) elation; **guida in stato di ~** drink-driving. **'ebbro** *adj* inebriated; (*di gioia*) ecstatic

'ebete *adj* stupid

ebollizi'one *f* boiling

e'braico *adj* Hebrew ● *m* (*lingua*) Hebrew. **e'breo, -a** *adj* Jewish ● *mf* Jew

eca'tombe *f* **fare un'~** wreak havoc

ecc *abbr* (eccetera) etc

ecce'den|te *adj* (peso, bagaglio) excess. **~za** *f* excess; (*d'avanzo*) surplus; **avere qcsa in ~za** have an excess of sth; **bagagli in ~za** excess baggage. **~za di cassa** surplus. **ec'cedere** *vt* exceed ● *vi* go too far; **eccedere nel bere** drink too much

eccel'len|te *adj* excellent. **~za** *f* excellence; (*titolo*) Excellency; **per ~za** par excellence. **ec'cellere** *vi* excel (**in** at)

ec'centrico, -a *adj & mf* eccentric

eccessiva'mente *adv* excessively. **ecces'sivo** *adj* excessive

ec'cesso *m* excess; **andare agli eccessi** go to extremes; **all'~** to excess. **~ di velocità** speeding

ec'cetera *adv* et cetera

ec'cetto *prep* except; **~ che** (*a meno che*) unless. **eccettu'are** *vt* except

eccezio'nal|e *adj* exceptional. **~'mente** *adv* exceptionally; (*contrariamente alla regola*) as an exception

eccezi'one *f* exception; (*Jur*) objection; **a ~ di** with the exception of

eccita'mento *m* excitement. **ecci'tante** *adj* exciting; (sostanza) stimulant ● *m* stimulant

ecci'ta|re *vt* excite. **~rsi** *vr* get excited. **~to** *adj* excited

eccitazi'one *f* excitement

ecclesi'astico *adj* ecclesiastical ● *m* priest

'ecco *adv* (*qui*) here; (*là*) there; **~!** exactly!; **~ fatto** there we are; **~ la tua borsa** here is your bag; **~ [lì] mio figlio** there is my son; **~mi** here I am; **~ tutto** that is all

ec'come *adv & int* and how!

echeggi'are *vi* echo

e'clissi *f inv* eclipse

'eco *f* (*pl m* **echi**) echo

ecogra'fia *f* scan

ecolo'gia *f* ecology. **eco'logico** *adj* ecological; (prodotto) environmentally friendly

e commerci'ale *f* ampersand

econo'm|ia *f* economy; (*scienza*) economics; **fare ~ia** economize (**di** on). **eco'nomico** *adj* economic; (*a buon prezzo*) cheap. **~ista** *mf* economist. **~iz'zare** *vt/i* economize; save (tempo, denaro). **e'conomo, -a** *adj* thrifty ● *mf* (*di collegio*) bursar

é'cru *adj inv* raw

ec'zema *m* eczema

ed *conj vedi* **e**

'edera *f* ivy

e'dicola *f* [newspaper] kiosk

edifi'cabile *adj* (area, terreno) *classified as suitable for development*

edifi'cante *adj* edifying

edifi'care *vt* build

edi'ficio *m* building; *fig* structure

e'dile *adj* building *attrib*

edi'lizi|a *f* building trade. **~o** *adj* building *attrib*

edi|'tore, -'trice *adj* publishing ● *mf* publisher; (*curatore*) editor. **~to'ria** *f* publishing. **~tori'ale** *adj* publishing ● *m* editorial

edizi'one *f* edition; (*di manifestazione*) performance. **~ ridotta** abridg[e]ment. **~ della sera** (*di telegiornale*) evening news

edu'ca|re *vt* educate; (*allevare*) bring up. **~'tivo** *adj* educational. **~to** *adj* polite. **~'tore, ~'trice** *mf* educator. **~zi'one** *f* education; (*di bambini*) upbringing; (*buone maniere*) [good] manners *pl*. **~zione fisica** physical education

e'felide *f* freckle

effemi'nato *adj* effeminate

efferve'scente *adj* effervescent; (*frizzante*) fizzy; (aspirina) soluble

effettiva'mente *adv* **è troppo tardi - ~** it's too late - so it is

effet'tivo *adj* actual; (*efficace*) effective; (personale) permanent; (*Mil*) regular ● *m* sum total

ef'fett|o *m* effect; (*impressione*) impression; **in ~i** in fact; **~i personali** personal belongings. **~u'are** *vt* carry out (controllo, sondaggio). **~u'arsi** *vr* take place

effi'cac|e *adj* effective. **~ia** *f* effectiveness

effici'en|te *adj* efficient. **~za** *f* efficiency

ef'fimero *adj* ephemeral

effusi'one *f* effusion

E'geo *m* **l'~** the Aegean [Sea]

E'gitto *m* Egypt. **egizi'ano, -a** *agg & mf* Egyptian

'egli *pers pron* he; **~ stesso** he himself

ego'centrico, -a *adj* egocentric

ego'is|mo *m* selfishness. **~ta** *adj* selfish ● *mf* selfish person. **~tico** *adj* selfish

e'gregio *adj* distinguished; **E~ Signore** Dear Sir

eiaculazi'one *f* ejaculation

elabo'ra|re *vt* elaborate; process (dati). **~to** *adj* elaborate. **~zi'one** *f* elaboration; (*di dati*) processing. **~zione [di] testi** word processing

elar'gire *vt* lavish

elastici|tà *f* elasticity. **~z'zato** *adj* (stoffa) elasticated. **e'lastico** *adj* elastic; (tessuto) stretch; (orario, mente) flexible; (persona) easygoing ● *m* elastic; (*fascia*) rubber band

ele'fante *m* elephant

ele'gan|te *adj* elegant. **~za** *f* elegance

e'leggere *vt* elect. **eleg'gibile** *adj* eligible

e

e

elemen'tare *adj* elementary; **scuola ~** primary school
ele'mento *m* element; **elementi** *pl* (*fatti*) data; (*rudimenti*) elements
ele'mosina *f* charity; **chiedere l'~** beg. **elemosi'nare** *vt/i* beg
elen'care *vt* list
e'lenco *m* list. **~ abbonati** telephone directory. **~ telefonico** telephone directory
elet'tivo *adj* (carica) elective. **e'letto, -a** *pp di* **eleggere** • *adj* chosen • *mf* elected member
eletto'ra|le *adj* electoral. **~to** *m* electorate
elet|'tore, -'trice *mf* voter
elet'trauto *m inv garage for electrical repairs*
elettri'cista *m* electrician
elettri|cità *f* electricity. **e'lettrico** *adj* electric. **~z'zante** *adj* (notizia, gara) electrifying. **~z'zare** *vt fig* electrify. **~z'zato** *adj fig* electrified
elettrocardio'gramma *m* electrocardiogram
e'lettrodo *m* electrode
elettrodo'mestico *m* [electrical] household appliance
elet'trone *m* electron
elet'tronico, -a *adj* electronic • *f* electronics
ele'va|re *vt* raise; (*promuovere*) promote; (*erigere*) erect; (*fig: migliorare*) better; **~ al quadrato/cubo** square/cube. **~rsi** *vr* rise; (edificio:) stand. **~to** *adj* high. **~zi'one** *f* elevation
elezi'one *f* election
'elica *f* (*Aeron, Naut*) propeller; (*del ventilatore*) blade
eli'cottero *m* helicopter
elimi'na|re *vt* eliminate. **~'toria** *f Sport* preliminary heat. **~zi'one** *f* elimination
é'li|te *f inv* élite. **~'tista** *adj* élitist
'ella *pers pron* she
el'metto *m* helmet
elogi'are *vt* praise
elo'quen|te *adj* eloquent; *fig* tell-tale. **~za** *f* eloquence
e'lu|dere *vt* elude; evade (sorveglianza). **~'sivo** *adj* elusive
el'vetico *adj* Swiss
emaci'ato *adj* emaciated
'e-mail *f* e-mail; **indirizzo ~** e-mail address. **~ spazzatura** junk e-mail
ema'na|re *vt* give off; pass (legge) • *vi* emanate
emanci'pa|re *vt* emancipate. **~rsi** *vr* become emancipated. **~to** *adj* emancipated. **~zi'one** *f* emancipation
emargi'na|to *m* marginalized person. **~zi'one** *f* marginalization
em'bargo *m* embargo
em'ble|ma *m* emblem. **~'matico** *adj* emblematic
embrio'nale *adj* embryonic. **embri'one** *m* embryo
emen|da'mento *m* amendment. **~'dare** *vt* amend
emer'gen|te *adj* emergent. **~za** *f* emergency; **in caso di ~za** in an emergency
e'mergere *vi* emerge; (sottomarino:) surface; (*distinguersi*) stand out
e'merso *pp di* **emergere**
e'messo *pp di* **emettere**
e'mettere *vt* emit; give out (luce, suono); let out (grido); (*mettere in circolazione*) issue
emi'crania *f* migraine
emi'gra|re *vi* emigrate. **~to, -a** *mf* immigrant. **~zi'one** *f* emigration
emi'nen|te *adj* eminent. **~za** *f* eminence
e'miro *m* emir
emis'fero *m* hemisphere
emis'sario *m* emissary
emissi'one *f* emission; (*di denaro*) issue; (*trasmissione*) broadcast
emit'tente *adj* issuing; (*trasmittente*) broadcasting • *f* transmitter
emorra'gia *f* haemorrhage
emor'roidi *fpl* piles
emotività *f* emotional make-up. **emo'tivo** *adj* emotional
emozio'na|nte *adj* exciting; (*commovente*) moving. **~re** *vt* excite; (*commuovere*) move. **~rsi** *vr* become excited; (*commuoversi*) be moved. **~to** *adj* excited; (*commosso*) moved. **emozi'one** *f* emotion; (*agitazione*) excitement
'empio *adj* impious; (*spietato*) pitiless; (*malvagio*) wicked
em'pirico *adj* empirical

em'porio *m* emporium; (*negozio*) general store
emu'la|re *vt* emulate. **~zi'one** *f* emulation
emulsi'one *f* emulsion
en'ciclica *f* encyclical
enciclope'dia *f* encyclopaedia
encomi'are *vt* commend. **en'co-mio** *m* commendation
en'demico *adj* endemic
endo've|na *f* intravenous injection. **~'noso** *adj* intravenous; **per via ~nosa** intravenously
ener'getico *adj* (risorse, crisi) energy *attrib*; (alimento) energy-giving
ener'gia *f* energy. **e'nergico** *adj* energetic; (*efficace*) strong
'enfasi *f* emphasis
en'fati|co *adj* emphatic. **~z'zare** *vt* emphasize
e'nigma *m* enigma. **enig'matico** *adj* enigmatic. **enig'mistica** *f* puzzles *pl*
E.N.I.T. *m abbr* (Ente Nazionale Italiano per il Turismo) Italian State Tourist Office
en'nesimo *adj* (*Math*) nth; [!] umpteenth
e'norm|e *adj* enormous. **~e'mente** *adv* massively. **~ità** *f inv* enormity; (*assurdità*) absurdity
eno'teca *f* wine-tasting shop
'ente *m* board; (*società*) company; (*filosofia*) being
entità *f inv* entity; (*gravità*) seriousness; (*dimensione*) extent
entou'rage *m inv* entourage
en'trambi *adj & pron* both
en'tra|re *vi* go in, enter; **~re in** go into; (*stare in, trovar posto in*) fit into; (*arruolarsi*) join; **~rci** (*avere a che fare*) have to do with; **tu che c'entri?** what has it got to do with you? **~ta** *f* entrance; **~te** *pl* (*Comm*) takings; (*reddito*) income *sg*
'entro *prep* (*tempo*) within
entro'terra *m inv* hinterland
entusias'mante *adj* fascinating
entusias'mar|e *vt* arouse enthusiasm in. **~si** *vr* be enthusiastic (**per** about)
entusi'as|mo *m* enthusiasm. **~ta** *adj* enthusiastic ● *mf* enthusiast. **~tico** *adj* enthusiastic
enume'ra|re *vt* enumerate. **~zi'one** *f* enumeration
enunci'a|re *vt* enunciate. **~zi'one** *f* enunciation
epa'tite *f* hepatitis
'epico *adj* epic
epide'mia *f* epidemic
epi'dermide *f* epidermis
Epifa'nia *f* Epiphany
epi'gramma *m* epigram
epil|es'sia *f* epilepsy. **epi'lettico, -a** *adj & mf* epileptic
e'pilogo *m* epilogue
epi'sodi|co *adj* episodic; **caso ~co** one-off case. **~o** *m* episode
'epoca *f* age; (*periodo*) period; **a quell'~** in those days; **auto d'~** vintage car
ep'pure *conj* [and] yet
epu'rare *vt* purge
equa'tore *m* equator. **equatori'ale** *adj* equatorial
equazi'one *f* equation
e'questre *adj* equestrian; **circo ~** circus
equili'bra|re *vt* balance. **~to** *adj* well-balanced. **equi'librio** *m* balance; (*buon senso*) common sense; (*di bilancia*) equilibrium
equili'brismo *m* **fare ~** do a balancing act
e'quino *adj* horse *attrib*
equi'nozio *m* equinox
equipaggia'mento *m* equipment
equipaggi'are *vt* equip; (*di persone*) man
equi'paggio *m* crew; (*Aeron*) cabin crew
equipa'rare *vt* make equal
é'quipe *f inv* team
equità *f* equity
equitazi'one *f* riding
equiva'len|te *adj & m* equivalent. **~za** *f* equivalence
equiva'lere *vi* **~ a** be equivalent to
equivo'care *vi* misunderstand
e'quivoco *adj* equivocal; (*sospetto*) suspicious ● *m* misunderstanding
'equo *adj* fair, just
'era *f* era
'erba *f* grass; (*aromatica, medicinale*) herb.

~ **cipollina** chives *pl*. **er'baccia** *f* weed. **er'baceo** *adj* herbaceous
erbi'cida *m* weed-killer
erbo'rist|a *mf* herbalist. **~e'ria** *f* herbalist's shop
er'boso *adj* grassy
er'culeo *adj* (forza) herculean
e'red|e *mf* heir; heiress. **~ità** *f inv* inheritance; (*Biol*) heredity. **~i'tare** *vt* inherit. **~itarietà** *f* heredity. **~i'tario** *adj* hereditary
ere'sia *f* heresy. **e'retico, -a** *adj* heretical ● *mf* heretic
e're|tto *pp di* **erigere** ● *adj* erect. **~zi'one** *f* erection; (*costruzione*) building
er'gastolo *m* life sentence; (*luogo*) prison
'erica *f* heather
e'rigere *vt* erect; (*fig: fondare*) found
eri'tema *m* (*cutaneo*) inflammation; (*solare*) sunburn
er'metico *adj* hermetic; (*a tenuta d'aria*) airtight
'ernia *f* hernia
e'rodere *vi* erode
e'ro|e *m* hero. **~ico** *adj* heroic. **~'ismo** *m* heroism
ero'ga|re *vt* distribute; (*fornire*) supply. **~zi'one** *f* supply
ero'ina *f* heroine; (*droga*) heroin
erosi'one *f* erosion
e'rotico *adj* erotic.
er'rante *adj* wandering. **er'rare** *vi* wander; (*sbagliare*) be mistaken
er'rato *adj* (*sbagliato*) mistaken
erronea'mente *adv* mistakenly
er'rore *m* error; (*di stampa*) misprint; **essere in ~** be wrong
'erta *f* **stare all'~** be on the alert
eru'di|rsi *vr* get educated. **~to** *adj* learned
erut'tare *vt* (vulcano:) erupt ● *vi* (*ruttare*) belch. **eruzi'one** *f* eruption; (*Med*) rash
esage'ra|re *vt* exaggerate ● *vi* exaggerate; (*nel comportamento*) go over the top; **~re nel mangiare** eat too much. **~ta'mente** *adv* excessively. **~to** *adj* exaggerated; (prezzo) exorbitant ● *m* **è un ~to** he exaggerates. **~zi'one** *f* exaggeration; **è costato un'~zione** it cost the earth
esa'lare *vt/i* exhale
esal'ta|re *vt* exalt; (*entusiasmare*) elate. **~to** *adj* (*fanatico*) fanatical ● *m* fanatic. **~zi'one** *f* exaltation; (*in discorso*) fervour
e'same *m* examination, exam; **dare un ~** take an exam; **prendere in ~** examine. **~ del sangue** blood test. **esami** *pl* **di maturità** ≈ A-levels
esami'na|re *vt* examine. **~'tore, ~'trice** *mf* examiner
e'sangue *adj* bloodless
e'sanime *adj* lifeless
esaspe'rante *adj* exasperating
esaspe'ra|re *vt* exasperate. **~rsi** *vr* get exasperated. **~zi'one** *f* exasperation
esat|ta'mente *adv* exactly. **~'tez-za** *f* exactness; (*precisione*) precision; (*di risultato*) accuracy
e'satto *pp di* **esigere** ● *adj* exact; (risposta, risultato) correct; (orologio) right; **hai l'ora esatta?** do you have the right time?; **sono le due esatte** it's two o'clock exactly
esat'tore *m* collector
esau'dire *vt* grant; fulfil (speranze)
esauri'ente *adj* exhaustive
esau'ri|re *vt* exhaust. **~rsi** *vr* exhaust oneself; (merci ecc:) run out. **~to** *adj* exhausted; (merci) sold out; (libro) out of print; **fare il tutto ~to** (spettacolo:) play to a full house
'esca *f* bait
escande'scenz|a *f* outburst; **dare in ~e** lose one's temper
escla'ma|re *vi* exclaim. **~'tivo** *adj* exclamatory. **~zi'one** *f* exclamation
es'clu|dere *vt* exclude (possibilità, ipotesi). **~si'one** *f* exclusion. **~'siva** *f* exclusive right; **in ~siva** exclusive. **~siva'mente** *adv* exclusively. **~'sivo** *adj* exclusive. **~so** *pp di* **escludere** ● *adj* **non è ~so che ci sia** it's not out of the question that he'll be there
escogi'tare *vt* contrive
escursi'one *f* excursion; (*scorreria*) raid; (*di temperatura*) range
ese'cra|bile *adj* abominable. **~re** *vt* abhor
esecu|'tivo *adj & m* executive. **~'tore,**

~'trice *mf* executor; (*Mus*) performer. **~zi'one** *f* execution; (*Mus*) performance

esegu'ire *vt* carry out; (*Jur*) execute; (*Mus*) perform

e'sempio *m* example; **ad** *o* **per ~** for example; **dare l'~ a qcno** set sb an example; **fare un ~** give an example

esem'plare *m* specimen; (*di libro*) copy

esen'tar|e *vt* exempt. **~si** *vr* free oneself. **e'sente** *adj* exempt. **esente da imposta** duty-free. **esente da IVA** VAT-exempt

esen'tasse *adj* duty-free

e'sequie *fpl* funeral rites

eser'cente *mf* shopkeeper

eserci'ta|re *vt* exercise; (*addestrare*) train; (*fare uso di*) exert; (*professione*) practise. **~rsi** *vr* practise. **~zi'one** *f* exercise; (*Mil*) drill

e'sercito *m* army

eser'cizio *m* exercise; (*pratica*) practice; (*Comm*) financial year; (*azienda*) business; **essere fuori ~** be out of practice

esi'bi|re *vt* show off; produce (documenti). **~rsi** *vr* (*Theat*) perform; *fig* show off. **~zi'one** *f* (*Theat*) performance; (*di documenti*) production

esibizio'nis|mo *m* showing off

esi'gen|te *adj* exacting; (*pignolo*) fastidious. **~za** *f* demand; (*bisogno*) need. **e'sigere** *vt* demand; (*riscuotere*) collect

e'siguo *adj* meagre

esila'rante *adj* exhilarating

'esile *adj* slender; (voce) thin

esili'a|re *vt* exile. **~'rsi** *vr* go into exile. **~to, -a** *adj* exiled • *mf* exile. **e'silio** *m* exile

e'simer|e *vt* release. **~si** *vr* **~si da** get out of

esi'sten|te *adj* existing. **~za** *f* existence.

e'sistere *vi* exist

esi'tante *adj* hesitating; (voce) faltering

esi'ta|re *vi* hesitate. **~zi'one** *f* hesitation

'esito *m* result; **avere buon ~** be a success

'esodo *m* exodus

e'sofago *m* oesophagus

esone'rare *vt* exempt. **e'sonero** *m* exemption

esorbi'tante *adj* exorbitant

esorciz'zare *vt* exorcize

esordi'ente *mf* *person making his/her début*. **e'sordio** *m* opening; (*di attore*) début. **esor'dire** *vi* début

esor'tare *vt* (*pregare*) beg; (*incitare*) urge

e'sotico *adj* exotic

espa'drillas *fpl* espadrilles

es'pan|dere *vt* expand. **~dersi** *vr* expand; (*diffondersi*) extend. **~si'one** *f* expansion. **~'sivo** *adj* expansive; (persona) friendly

espatri'are *vi* leave one's country. **es'patrio** *m* expatriation

espedi'ente *m* expedient; **vivere di ~i** live by one's wits

es'pellere *vt* expel

esperi|'enza *f* experience; **parlare per ~enza** speak from experience. **~'mento** *m* experiment

es'perto, -a *adj & mf* expert

espi'a|re *vt* atone for. **~'torio** *adj* expiatory

espi'rare *vt/i* breathe out

espli'care *vt* carry on

esplicita'mente *adv* explicitly. **es'plicito** *adj* explicit

es'plodere *vi* explode • *vt* fire

esplo'ra|re *vt* explore. **~'tore, ~'trice** *mf* explorer; **giovane ~tore** boy scout. **~zi'one** *f* exploration

esplo|si'one *f* explosion. **~'sivo** *adj & m* explosive

es'por|re *vt* expose; display (merci); (*spiegare*) expound; exhibit (quadri ecc). **~si** *vr* (*compromettersi*) compromise oneself; (*al sole*) expose oneself

espor'ta|re *vt* export. **~'tore, ~'trice** *mf* exporter. **~zi'one** *f* export

esposizi'one *f* (*mostra*) exhibition; (*in vetrina*) display; (*spiegazione ecc*) exposition; (*posizione, fotografia*) exposure. **es'posto** *pp di* **esporre** • *adj* exposed; **esposto a** (*rivolto*) facing • *m* (*Jur*) statement

espressa'mente *adv* expressly; **non l'ha detto ~** he didn't put it in so many words

e

espres|si'one *f* expression. **~'sivo** *adj* expressive

es'presso *pp di* **esprimere** ● *adj* express ● *m* (*lettera*) express letter; (*treno*) express train; (*caffè*) espresso; **per ~** (spedire) [by] express [post]

es'primer|e *vt* express. **~si** *vr* express oneself

e

espropri'a|re *vt* dispossess. **~zi'one** *f* (*Jur*) expropriation. **es'proprio** *m* expropriation

espulsi'one *f* expulsion. **es'pulso** *pp di* **espellere**

es'senz|a *f* essence. **~i'ale** *adj* essential ● *m* important thing. **~ial'mente** *adj* essentially

'essere

● *vi* be; **c'è** there is; **ci sono** there are; **che ora è? – sono le dieci** what time is it? – it's ten o'clock; **chi è? – sono io** who is it? – it's me; **ci sono!** (*ho capito*) I've got it!; **ci siamo!** (*siamo arrivati*) here we are at last!; **siamo in due** there are two of us; **questa camicia è da lavare** this shirt is to be washed; **non è da te** it's not like you; **~ di** (*provenire da*) be from; **~ per** (*favorevole*) be in favour of; **se fossi in te,...** if I were you,...; **sarà!** if you say so!; **come sarebbe a dire?** what are you getting at?

● *v aux* have; (*in passivi*) be; **siamo arrivati** we have arrived; **ci sono stato ieri** I was there yesterday; **sono nato a Torino** I was born in Turin; **è riconosciuto come...** he is recognized as...; **è stato detto che** it has been said that

● *m* being. **~ umano** human being. **~ vivente** living creature

essic'cato *adj* dried

'esso, -a *pers pron* he, she; (*cosa, animale*) it

est *m* east

'estasi *f* ecstasy; **andare in ~ per** go into raptures over

e'state *f* summer

e'sten|dere *vt* extend. **~dersi** *vr* spread; (*allungarsi*) stretch. **~si'one** *f* extension; (*ampiezza*) expanse; (*Mus*) range. **~'sivo** *adj* extensive

estenu'ante *adj* exhausting

estenu'a|re *vt* wear out; deplete (risorse, casse). **~rsi** *vr* wear oneself out

esteri'or|e *adj & m* exterior. **~'mente** *adv* externally; (*di persone*) outwardly

esterna'mente *adv* on the outside

ester'nare *vt* express, show

e'sterno *adj* external; **per uso ~** for external use only ● *m* (*allievo*) day-boy; (*Archit*) exterior; (*in film*) location shot

'estero *adj* foreign ● *m* foreign countries *pl*; **all'~** abroad

esterre'fatto *adj* horrified

e'steso *pp di* **estendere** ● *adj* extensive; (*diffuso*) widespread; **per ~** (scrivere) in full

e'stetic|a *f* aesthetics *sg*. **~a'mente** *adv* aesthetically. **~o, -a** *adj* aesthetic; (chirurgia, chirurgo) plastic. **este'tista** *f* beautician

'estimo *m* estimate

e'stin|guere *vt* extinguish. **~guersi** *vr* die out. **~to, -a** *pp di* **estinguere** ● *mf* deceased. **~'tore** *m* [fire] extinguisher. **~zi'one** *f* extinction; (*di incendio*) putting out

estir'pa|re *vt* uproot; extract (dente); *fig* eradicate (crimine, malattia). **~zi'one** *f* eradication; (*di dente*) extraction

e'stivo *adj* summer

e'stor|cere *vt* extort. **~si'one** *f* extortion. **~to** *pp di* **estorcere**

estradizi'one *f* extradition

e'straneo, -a *adj* extraneous; (*straniero*) foreign ● *mf* stranger

estrani'ar|e *vt* estrange. **~si** *vr* become estranged

e'stra|rre *vt* extract; (*sorteggiare*) draw. **~tto** *pp di* **estrarre** ● *m* extract; (*brano*) excerpt; (*documento*) abstract. **~tto conto** statement [of account], bank statement. **~zi'one** *f* extraction; (*sorte*) draw

estrema'mente *adv* extremely

estre'mis|mo *m* extremism. **~ta** *mf* extremist

estremità *f inv* extremity; (*di una corda*) end ● *fpl* (*Anat*) extremities

e'stremo *adj* extreme; (*ultimo*) last; **misure estreme** drastic measures; **l'E~ Oriente** the Far East • *m* (*limite*) extreme. **estremi** *pl* (*di documento*) main points; (*di reato*) essential elements; **essere agli estremi** be at the end of one's tether

'estro *m* (*disposizione artistica*) talent; (*ispirazione*) inspiration; (*capriccio*) whim. **e'stroso** *adj* talented; (*capriccioso*) unpredictable

estro'mettere *vt* expel

estro'verso *adj* extroverted • *m* extrovert

estu'ario *m* estuary

esube'ran|te *adj* exuberant. **~za** *f* exuberance

'esule *mf* exile

esul'tante *adj* exultant

esul'tare *vi* rejoice

esu'mare *vt* exhume

età *f inv* age; **raggiungere la maggiore ~** come of age; **un uomo di mezz'~** a middle-aged man

'etere *m* ether. **e'tereo** *adj* ethereal

eterna'mente *adv* eternally

eternità *f* eternity; **è un'~ che non la vedo** I haven't seen her for ages

e'terno *adj* eternal; (questione, problema) age-old; **in ~** [!] for ever

eterosessu'ale *mf* heterosexual

'etica *f* ethics

eti'chetta[1] *f* label; price-tag

eti'chetta[2] *f* etiquette

etichet'tare *vt* label

'etico *adj* ethical

eti'lometro *m* Breathalyzer®

Eti'opia *f* Ethiopia

'etnico *adj* ethnic

e'trusco *adj & mf* Etruscan

'ettaro *m* hectare

'etto, etto'grammo *m* hundred grams, ≈ quarter pound

eucari'stia *f* Eucharist

eufe'mismo *m* euphemism

eufo'ria *f* elation; (*Med*) euphoria. **eu'forico** *adj* elated; (*Med*) euphoric

'euro *m inv Fin* euro

Euro'city *m* international Intercity

eurodepu'tato *m* Euro MP, MEP

Eu'ropa *f* Europe. **euro'peo, -a** *agg & mf* European

eutana'sia *f* euthanasia

evacu'a|re *vt* evacuate. **~zi'one** *f* evacuation

e'vadere *vt* evade; (*sbrigare*) deal with • *vi* **~ da** escape from

evane'scente *adj* vanishing

evan'gel|ico *adj* evangelical. **evange'lista** *m* evangelist

evapo'ra|re *vi* evaporate. **~zi'one** *f* evaporation

evasi'one *f* escape; (*fiscale*) evasion; *fig* escapism. **eva'sivo** *adj* evasive

e'vaso *pp di* **evadere** • *m* fugitive

eva'sore *m* **~ fiscale** tax evader

eveni'enza *f* eventuality

e'vento *m* event

eventu'al|e *adj* possible. **~ità** *f inv* eventuality

evi'den|te *adj* evident; **è ~te che** it is obvious that. **~te'mente** *adv* evidently. **~za** *f* evidence; **mettere in ~za** emphasize; **mettersi in ~za** make oneself conspicuous

evidenzi'a|re *vt* highlight. **~'tore** *m* (*penna*) highlighter

evi'tare *vt* avoid; (*risparmiare*) spare

evo'care *vt* evoke

evo'lu|to *pp di* **evolvere** • *adj* evolved; (*progredito*) progressive; (civiltà, nazione) advanced; **una donna evoluta** a modern woman. **~zi'one** *f* evolution; (*di ginnasta, aereo*) circle

e'volver|e *vt* develop. **~si** *vr* evolve

ev'viva *int* hurray; **~ il Papa!** long live the Pope!; **gridare ~** cheer

ex+ *pref* ex+, former

'extra *adj inv* extra; (qualità) first-class • *m inv* extra

extracomuni'tario *adj* non-EU

extrater'restre *mf* extra-terrestrial

> *i*
>
> **Extravergine** Olive oil which is obtained from the first pressing of the olives is called *extravergine* (extra virgin). It has a distinctive peppery flavour and is often a cloudy greenish colour. A less refined grade, suitable for cooking, is obtained by using chemical methods. This is called simply *olio d'oliva*.

e

Ff

fa[1] *m inv* (*Mus*) F
fa[2] *adv* ago; **due mesi ~** two months ago
fabbi'sogno *m* requirements *pl*
'fabbrica *f* factory
fabbri'cabile *adj* (area, terreno) that can be built on
fabbri'cante *m* manufacturer
fabbri'ca|re *vt* build; (*produrre*) manufacture; (*fig: inventare*) fabricate. **~to** *m* building. **~zi'one** *f* manufacturing; (*costruzione*) building
'fabbro *m* blacksmith
fac'cend|a *f* matter; **~e** *pl* (*lavori domestici*) housework *sg*. **~i'ere** *m* wheeler-dealer
fac'chino *m* porter
'facci|a *f* face; (*di foglio*) side; **~a a ~a** face to face; **~a tosta** cheek; **voltar ~a** change sides; **di ~a** (palazzo) opposite; **alla ~a di** (!: *a dispetto di*) in spite of. **~'ata** *f* façade; (*di foglio*) side; (*fig: esteriorità*) outward appearance
fa'ceto *adj* facetious; **tra il serio e il ~** half joking
fa'chiro *m* fakir
'facil|e *adj* easy; (*affabile*) easygoing; **essere ~e alle critiche** be quick to criticize; **essere ~e al riso** laugh a lot; **~e a farsi** easy to do; **è ~e che piova** it's likely to rain. **~ità** *f* ease; (*disposizione*) aptitude; **avere ~ità di parola** express oneself well
facili'ta|re *vt* facilitate. **~zi'one** *f* facility; **~zioni** *pl* special terms
facil'mente *adv* (*con facilità*) easily; (*probabilmente*) probably
faci'lone *adj* slapdash. **~'ria** *f* slapdash attitude
facino'roso *adj* violent
facoltà *f inv* faculty; (*potere*) power. **facolta'tivo** *adj* optional; **fermata facoltativa** request stop
facol'toso *adj* wealthy
'faggio *m* beech
fagi'ano *m* pheasant
fagio'lino *m* French bean
fagi'olo *m* bean; **a ~** (arrivare, capitare) at the right time
fagoci'tare *vt* gobble up (società)
fa'gotto *m* bundle; (*Mus*) bassoon
'faida *f* feud
fai da te *m* do-it-yourself, DIY
fal'cata *f* stride
'falc|e *f* scythe. **fal'cetto** *m* sickle. **~i'are** *vt* cut; *fig* mow down. **~ia'trice** *f* [lawn-]mower
'falco *m* hawk
fal'cone *m* falcon
'falda *f* stratum; (*di neve*) flake; (*di cappello*) brim; (*pendio*) slope
fale'gname *m* carpenter. **~'ria** *f* carpentry
'falla *f* leak
fal'lace *adj* deceptive
fallimen'tare *adj* disastrous; (*Jur*) bankruptcy. **falli'mento** *m Fin* bankruptcy; *fig* failure
fal'li|re *vi Fin* go bankrupt; *fig* fail • *vt* miss (colpo). **~to, -a** *adj* unsuccessful; *Fin* bankrupt • *mf* failure; *Fin* bankrupt
'fallo *m* fault; (*errore*) mistake; *Sport* foul; (*imperfezione*) flaw; **senza ~** without fail
falò *m inv* bonfire
fal'sar|e *vt* alter; (*falsificare*) falsify. **~io, -a** *mf* forger; (*di documenti*) counterfeiter
falsifi'ca|re *vt* fake; (*contraffare*) forge. **~zi'one** *f* (*di documento*) falsification
falsità *f* falseness
'falso *adj* false; (*sbagliato*) wrong; (opera d'arte ecc) fake; (gioielli, oro) imitation • *m* forgery; **giurare il ~** commit perjury
'fama *f* fame; (*reputazione*) reputation
'fame *f* hunger; **aver ~** be hungry; **fare la ~** barely scrape a living. **fa'melico** *adj* ravenous
famige'rato *adj* infamous
fa'miglia *f* family
famili'ar|e *adj* family *attrib*; (*ben noto*) familiar; (*senza cerimonie*) informal • *mf* relative, relation **~ità** *f* familiarity; (*informalità*) informality. **~iz'zarsi** *vr* familiarize oneself
fa'moso *adj* famous
fa'nale *m* lamp; (*Auto*) light. **fanali** *pl* **posteriori** (*Auto*) rear lights

fa'natico, -a *adj* fanatical; **essere ~ di calcio** be a football fanatic ● *mf* fanatic. **fana'tismo** *m* fanaticism

fanci'ul|la *f* young girl. **~'lezza** *f* childhood. **~lo** *m* young boy

fan'donia *f* lie; **fandonie!** nonsense!

fan'fara *f* fanfare; (*complesso*) brass band

fanfaro'nata *f* brag. **fanfa'rone, -a** *mf* braggart

fan'ghiglia *f* mud. **'fango** *m* mud. **fan'goso** *adj* muddy

fannul'lone, -a *mf* idler

fantasci'enza *f* science fiction

fanta'si|a *f* fantasy; (*immaginazione*) imagination; (*capriccio*) fancy; (*di tessuto*) pattern. **~'oso** *adj* (stilista, ragazzo) imaginative; (resoconto) improbable

fan'tasma *m* ghost

fantasti'c|are *vi* day-dream. **~he'ria** *f* day-dream. **fan'tastico** *adj* fantastic; (racconto) fantasy

'fante *m* infantryman; (*nelle carte*) jack. **~'ria** *m* infantry

fan'tino *m* jockey

fan'toccio *m* puppet

fanto'matico *adj* phantom *attrib*

fara'butto *m* trickster

fara'ona *f* (*uccello*) guinea-fowl

far'ci|re *vt* stuff; fill (torta). **~to** *adj* stuffed; (dolce) filled

far'dello *m* bundle; *fig* burden

'fare

● *vt* do; make (dolce, letto ecc); (*recitare la parte di*) play; (*trascorrere*) spend; **~ una pausa/un sogno** have a break/a dream; **~ colpo su** impress; **~ paura a** frighten; **~ piacere a** please; **farla finita** put an end to it; **~ l'insegnante** be a teacher; **~ lo scemo** play the idiot; **~ una settimana al mare** spend a week at the seaside; **3 più 3 fa 6** 3 and 3 makes 6; **quanto fa? – fanno 10 000 euro** how much is it? – it's 10,000 euros; **far ~ qcsa a qcno** get sb to do sth; (*costringere*) make sb do sth; **~ vedere** show; **fammi parlare** let me speak; **niente a che ~ con** nothing to do with; **non c'è niente da ~** (*per problema*) there is nothing we/you/etc. can do; **fa caldo/buio** it's warm/dark; **non fa niente** it doesn't matter; **strada facendo** on the way; **farcela** (*riuscire*) manage

● *vi* **fai in modo di venire** try and come; **~ da** act as; **~ per** make as if to; **~ presto** be quick; **non fa per me** it's not for me

● *m* way; **sul far del giorno** at daybreak.

● **farsi** *vr* (*diventare*) get; **farsi avanti** come forward; **farsi i fatti propri** mind one's own business; **farsi la barba** shave; **farsi il ragazzo** [!] find a boyfriend; **farsi male** hurt oneself; **farsi strada** (*aver successo*) make one's way in the world

fa'retto *m* spot[light]

far'falla *f* butterfly

farfal'lino *m* (*cravatta*) bow tie

farfugli'are *vt* mutter

fa'rina *f* flour. **fari'nacei** *mpl* starchy food *sg*

fa'ringe *f* pharynx

fari'noso *adj* (neve) powdery; (mela) soft; (patata) floury

farma|'ceutico *adj* pharmaceutical. **~'cia** *f* pharmacy; (*negozio*) chemist's [shop]. **~cia di turno** duty chemist. **~'cista** *mf* chemist. **'farmaco** *m* drug

i **Farmacia** A *farmacia* in Italy sells medicines and health-related products, whereas a *profumeria* sells not only perfume, but also beauty and personal hygiene products. For film and developing services it is necessary to go to a shop specializing in photographic equipment.

'faro *m* (*Auto*) headlight; (*Aeron*) beacon; (*costruzione*) lighthouse

'farsa *f* farce

'fasci|a *f* band; (*zona*) area; (*ufficiale*) sash; (*benda*) bandage. **~'are** *vt* bandage; cling to (fianchi). **~a'tura** *f* dressing; (*azione*) bandaging

fa'scicolo *m* file; (*di rivista*) issue; (*libretto*) booklet

'fascino *m* fascination

f

'fascio *m* bundle; (*di fiori*) bunch
fa'scis|mo *m* fascism. **~ta** *mf* fascist
'fase *f* phase
fa'stidi|o *m* nuisance; (*scomodo*) inconvenience; **dar ~o a qcno** bother sb; **~i** *pl* (*preoccupazioni*) worries; (*disturbi*) troubles. **~'oso** *adj* tiresome
'fasto *m* pomp. **fa'stoso** *adj* sumptuous
fa'sullo *adj* bogus
'fata *f* fairy
fa'tale *adj* fatal; (*inevitabile*) fated
fata'l|ismo *m* fatalism. **~ista** *mf* fatalist. **~ità** *f inv* fate; (*caso sfortunato*) misfortune. **~'mente** *adv* inevitably
fa'tica *f* effort; (*lavoro faticoso*) hard work; (*stanchezza*) fatigue; **a ~** with great difficulty; **è ~ sprecata** it's a waste of time; **fare ~ a fare qcsa** find it difficult to do sth; **fare ~ a finire qcsa** struggle to finish sth. **fati'caccia** *f* pain
fati'ca|re *vi* toil; **~re a** (*stentare*) find it difficult to. **~ta** *f* effort; (*sfacchinata*) grind. **fati'coso** *adj* tiring; (*difficile*) difficult
'fato *m* fate
fat'taccio *m hum* foul deed
fat'tezze *fpl* features
fat'tibile *adj* feasible
'fatto *pp di* **fare** • *adj* done, made; **~ a mano** hand-made • *m* fact; (*azione*) action; (*avvenimento*) event; **bada ai fatti tuoi!** mind your own business; **di ~** in fact; **in ~ di** as regards
fat'to|re *m* (*Math, causa*) factor; (*di fattoria*) farm manager. **~'ria** *f* farm; (*casa*) farmhouse
fatto'rino *m* messenger [boy]
fattucchi'era *f* witch
fat'tura *f* (*stile*) cut; (*lavorazione*) workmanship; (*Comm*) invoice
fattu'ra|re *vt* invoice; (*adulterare*) adulterate. **~to** *m* turnover, sales *pl*. **~zi'one** *f* invoicing, billing
'fatuo *adj* fatuous
fau'tore *m* supporter
'fava *f* broad bean
fa'vella *f* speech
fa'villa *f* spark
'favo|la *f* fable; (*fiaba*) story; (*oggetto di pettegolezzi*) laughing-stock; (*meraviglia*) dream. **~'loso** *adj* fabulous
fa'vore *m* favour; **essere a ~ di** be in favour of; **per ~** please; **di ~** (condizioni, trattamento) preferential. **~ggia'mento** *m* (*Jur*) aiding and abetting. **favo'revole** *adj* favourable. **~vol'mente** *adv* favourably
favo'ri|re *vt* favour; (*promuovere*) promote; **vuol ~re?** (*a cena, pranzo*) will you have some?; (*entrare*) will you come in?. **~to, -a** *adj & mf* favourite
fax *m inv* fax. **fa'xare** *vt* fax
fazi'one *f* faction
faziosità *f* bias. **fazi'oso** *m* sectarian
fazzolet'tino *m* **~ [di carta]** [paper] tissue
fazzo'letto *m* handkerchief; (*da testa*) headscarf
feb'braio *m* February
'febbre *f* fever; **avere la ~** have *o* run a temperature. **~ da fieno** hay fever. **feb'brile** *adj* feverish
'feccia *f* dregs *pl*
'fecola *f* potato flour
fecon'da|re *vt* fertilize. **~'tore** *m* fertilizer. **~zi'one** *f* fertilization. **~zione artificiale** artificial insemination. **fe'condo** *adj* fertile
'fede *f* faith; (*fiducia*) trust; (*anello*) wedding-ring; **in buona/mala ~** in good/bad faith; **prestar ~ a** believe; **tener ~ alla parola** keep one's word. **fe'dele** *adj* faithful • *mf* believer; (*seguace*) follower. **~l'mente** *adv* faithfully. **~ltà** *f* faithfulness
'federa *f* pillowcase
fede'ra|le *adj* federal. **~'lismo** *m* federalism. **~zi'one** *f* federation
fe'dina *f* **avere la ~ penale sporca/pulita** have a/no criminal record
'fegato *m* liver; *fig* guts *pl*
'felce *f* fern
fe'lic|e *adj* happy; (*fortunato*) lucky. **~ità** *f* happiness
felici'ta|rsi *vr* **~rsi con** congratulate. **~zi'oni** *fpl* congratulations
'felpa *f* (*indumento*) sweatshirt
fel'pato *adj* brushed; (passo) stealthy
'feltro *m* felt; (*cappello*) felt hat
'femmin|a *f* female. **femmi'nile** *adj* feminine; (abbigliamento) women's; (sesso) female • *m* feminine. **~ilità** *f* femininity. **femmi'nismo** *m* feminism
'femore *m* femur

'fend|ere *vt* split. **~i'tura** *f* split; (*in roccia*) crack

feni'cottero *m* flamingo

fenome'nale *adj* phenomenal. **fe'nomeno** *m* phenomenon

'feretro *m* coffin

feri'ale *adj* weekday; **giorno ~** weekday

'ferie *fpl* holidays; (*di università, tribunale ecc*) vacation *sg*; **andare in ~** go on holiday

feri'mento *m* wounding

fe'ri|re *vt* wound; (*in incidente*) injure; *fig* hurt. **~rsi** *vr* injure oneself. **~ta** *f* wound. **~to** *adj* wounded • *m* wounded person; (*Mil*) casualty

'ferma *f* (*Mil*) period of service

fermaca'pelli *m inv* hairslide

ferma'carte *m inv* paperweight

fermacra'vatta *m inv* tiepin

fer'maglio *m* clasp; (*spilla*) brooch; (*per capelli*) hair slide

ferma'mente *adv* firmly

fer'ma|re *vt* stop; (*fissare*) fix; (*Jur*) detain • *vi* stop. **~rsi** *vr* stop. **~ta** *f* stop. **~ta dell'autobus** bus-stop. **~ta a richiesta** request stop

fermen'ta|re *vi* ferment. **~zi'one** *f* fermentation. **fer'mento** *m* ferment; (*lievito*) yeast

fer'mezza *f* firmness

'fermo *adj* still; (veicolo) stationary; (*stabile*) steady; (orologio) not working • *m* (*Jur*) detention; (*Mech*) catch; **in stato di ~** in custody

fe'roc|e *adj* ferocious; (bestia) wild; (dolore) unbearable. **~e'mente** *adv* fiercely. **~ia** *f* ferocity

fer'raglia *f* scrap iron

ferra'gosto *m* 15 August (*bank holiday in Italy*); (*periodo*) August holidays *pl*

ferra'menta *fpl* ironmongery *sg*; **negozio di ~** ironmonger's

fer'ra|re *vt* shoe (cavallo). **~to** *adj* **~to in** (*preparato in*) well up on

'ferreo *adj* iron

'ferro *m* iron; (*attrezzo*) tool; (*di chirurgo*) instrument; **bistecca ai ferri** grilled steak; **di ~** (memoria) excellent; (alibi) cast-iron; **salute di ~** iron constitution. **~ battuto** wrought iron. **~ da calza** knitting needle. **~ di cavallo** horseshoe. **~ da stiro** iron

ferro'vecchio *m* scrap merchant

ferro'vi|a *f* railway. **~'ario** *adj* railway. **~'ere** *m* railwayman

'fertil|e *adj* fertile. **~ità** *f* fertility. **~iz'zante** *m* fertilizer

fer'vente *adj* blazing; *fig* fervent

'fervere *vi* (preparativi:) be well under way

'fervid|o *adj* fervent; **~i auguri** best wishes

fer'vore *m* fervour

fesse'ria *f* nonsense

'fesso *pp di* **fendere** • *adj* cracked; ([!]: *sciocco*) foolish • *m* [!] (*idiota*) fool; **far ~ qcno** con sb

fes'sura *f* crack; (*per gettone ecc*) slot

'festa *f* feast; (*giorno festivo*) holiday; (*compleanno*) birthday; (*ricevimento*) party; *fig* joy; **fare ~ a qcno** welcome sb; **essere in ~** be on holiday; **far ~** celebrate. **~i'olo** *adj* festive

festeggia'mento *m* celebration; (*manifestazione*) festivity

festeggi'are *vt* celebrate; (*accogliere festosamente*) give a hearty welcome to

fe'stino *m* party

festività *fpl* festivities. **fe'stivo** *adj* holiday; (*lieto*) festive. **festivi** *mpl* public holidays

fe'stoso *adj* merry

fe'tente *adj* evil smelling; *fig* revolting • *mf* [!] bastard

fe'ticcio *m* fetish

'feto *m* foetus

fe'tore *m* stench

'fetta *f* slice; **a fette** sliced. **~ biscottata** *slices of crispy toast-like bread*

fet'tuccia *f* tape; (*con nome*) name tape

feu'dale *adj* feudal. **'feudo** *m* feud

FFSS *abbr* (Ferrovie dello Stato) Italian state railways

fi'aba *f* fairy-tale. **fia'besco** *adj* fairytale

fi'acc|a *f* weariness; (*indolenza*) laziness; **battere la ~a** be sluggish. **fiac'care** *vt* weaken. **~o** *adj* weak; (*indolente*) slack; (*stanco*) weary; (partita) dull

fi'acco|la *f* torch. **~'lata** *f* torchlight procession

fi'ala *f* phial

fi'amma *f* flame; (*Naut*) pennant; **in**

fiamme aflame. **andare in fiamme** go up in flames. **~ ossidrica** blowtorch

fiam'ma|nte *adj* flaming; **nuovo ~nte** brand new. **~ta** *f* blaze

fiammeggi'are *vi* blaze

fiam'mifero *m* match

fiam'mingo, -a *adj* Flemish ● *mf* Fleming ● *m* (*lingua*) Flemish

fiancheggi'are *vt* border; *fig* support

fi'anco *m* side; (*di persona*) hip; (*di animale*) flank; (*Mil*) wing; **al mio ~** by my side; **~ a ~** (lavorare) side by side

fi'asco *m* flask; *fig* fiasco; **fare ~** be a fiasco

fia'tare *vi* breathe; (*parlare*) breathe a word

fi'ato *m* breath; (*vigore*) stamina; **strumenti a ~** wind instruments; **senza ~** breathlessly; **tutto d'un ~** (bere, leggere) all in one go

'fibbia *f* buckle

'fibra *f* fibre; **fibre** *pl* (*alimentari*) roughage. **~ ottica** optical fibre

ficca'naso *mf* nosey parker

fic'car|e *vt* thrust; drive (chiodo ecc); (!: *mettere*) shove. **~si** *vr* thrust oneself; (*nascondersi*) hide; **~si nei guai** get oneself into trouble

fiche *f inv* (*gettone*) chip

'fico *m* (*albero*) fig-tree; (*frutto*) fig. **~ d'India** prickly pear

'fico, -a ! *mf* cool sort ● *adj* cool

fidanza'mento *m* engagement

fidan'za|rsi *vr* get engaged. **~to, -a** *mf* (*ufficiale*) fiancé; fiancée

fi'da|rsi *vr* **~rsi di** trust. **~to** *adj* trustworthy

'fido *m* devoted follower; (*Comm*) credit

fi'duci|a *f* confidence; **degno di ~a** trustworthy; **persona di ~a** reliable person; **di ~a** (fornitore) usual. **~'oso** *adj* trusting

fi'ele *m* bile; *fig* bitterness

fie'nile *m* barn. **fi'eno** *m* hay

fi'era *f* fair

fie'rezza *f* (*dignità*) pride. **fi'ero** *adj* proud

fi'evole *adj* faint; (luce) dim

'fifa *f* ! jitters; **aver ~** have the jitters

'figli|a *f* daughter; **~a unica** only child. **~'astra** *f* stepdaughter. **~'astro** *m* stepson. **~o** *m* son; (*generico*) child. **~o unico** only child

> **i** **Figlio di papà** With the rapid rise in living standards which took place in Italy after 1945, many more children grow up in affluent families than was previously the case, and *figli unici* (only children) are often the norm. Children, both young and grown-up, are often given considerable financial help by their parents, and are sometimes termed *figli di papà*, implying that they are also spoilt.

figli'occi|a *f* goddaughter. **~o** *m* godson

figli'o|la *f* girl. **~'lanza** *f* offspring. **~lo** *m* boy

'figo, -a ▷FICO, -A

fi'gura *f* figure; (*aspetto esteriore*) shape; (*illustrazione*) illustration; **far bella/brutta ~** make a good/bad impression; **mi hai fatto fare una brutta ~** you made me look a fool; **che ~!** how embarrassing!. **figu'raccia** *f* bad impression

figu'ra|re *vt* represent; (*simboleggiare*) symbolize; (*immaginare*) imagine ● *vi* (*far figura*) cut a dash; (*in lista*) appear. **~rsi** *vr* (*immaginarsi*) imagine; **~ti!** imagine that!; **posso? – [ma] ~ti!** may I? – of course!. **~'tivo** *adj* figurative

figu'rina *f* ≈ cigarette card

figu|ri'nista *mf* dress designer. **~'rino** *m* fashion sketch. **~'rone** *m* **fare un ~rone** make an excellent impression

'fila *f* line; (*di soldati ecc*) file; (*di oggetti*) row; (*coda*) queue; **di ~** in succession; **fare la ~** queue [up], stand in line *Am*

fi'lare *vt* spin; (*Naut*) pay out ● *vi* (*andarsene*) run away; (liquido:) trickle; **fila!** ! scram!; **~ con** (!: *amoreggiare*) go out with

filar'monica *f* (*orchestra*) orchestra

fila'strocca *f* rigmarole; (*per bambini*) nursery rhyme

fi'la|to *adj* spun; (*ininterrotto*) running; (*continuato*) uninterrupted; **di ~to** (*subito*) immediately ● *m* yarn

fil di 'ferro *m* wire

fi'letto *m* (*bordo*) border; (*di vite*) thread; (*Culin*) fillet

fili'ale *adj* filial ● *f* (*Comm*) branch

fili'grana *f* filigree; (*su carta*) watermark

film *m inv* film. ~ **giallo** thriller. ~ **a lungo metraggio** feature film

fil'ma|re *vt* film. ~**to** *m* short film. **fil'mino** *m* cine film

'filo *m* thread; (*tessile*) yarn; (*metallico*) wire; (*di lama*) edge; (*venatura*) grain; (*di perle*) string; (*d'erba*) blade; (*di luce*) ray; **con un ~ di voce** in a whisper; **fare il ~ a qcno** fancy sb; **perdere il ~** lose the thread. ~ **spinato** barbed wire

'filobus *m inv* trolleybus

filodiffusi'one *f* rediffusion

fi'lone *m* vein; (*di pane*) long loaf

filoso'fia *f* philosophy. **fi'losofo, -a** *mf* philosopher

fil'trare *vt* filter. **'filtro** *m* filter

'filza *f* string

fin ▷**FINE, FINO**[1]

fi'nal|e *adj* final ● *m* end ● *f Sport* final. **fina'lista** *mf* finalist. ~**ità** *f inv* finality; (*scopo*) aim. ~**'mente** *adv* at last; (*in ultimo*) finally

fi'nanz|a *f* finance; ~**i'ario** *adj* financial. ~**i'ere** *m* financier; (*guardia di finanza*) customs officer. ~**ia'mento** *m* funding

finanzi'a|re *vt* fund, finance. ~**'tore,** ~**'trice** *mf* backer

finché *conj* until; (*per tutto il tempo che*) as long as

'fine *adj* fine; (*sottile*) thin; (udito, vista) keen; (*raffinato*) refined ● *f* end; **alla ~** in the end; **alla fin ~** after all; **in fin dei conti** when all's said and done; **senza ~** endless ● *m* aim. ~ **settimana** weekend

fi'nestra *f* window. **fine'strella** *f* **di aiuto** (*Comput*) help box. **fine'strino** *m* (*Auto, Rail*) window

fi'nezza *f* fineness; (*sottigliezza*) thinness; (*raffinatezza*) refinement

'finger|e *vt* pretend; feign (affetto ecc). ~**si** *vr* pretend to be

fini'menti *mpl* finishing touches; (*per cavallo*) harness *sg*

fini'mondo *m* end of the world; *fig* pandemonium

fi'ni|re *vt/i* finish, end; (*smettere*) stop; (*diventare, andare a finire*) end up; ~**scila!** stop it!. ~**to** *adj* finished; (*abile*) accomplished. ~**'tura** *f* finish

finlan'dese *adj* Finnish ● *mf* Finn ● *m* (*lingua*) Finnish

Fin'landia *f* Finland

'fino[1] *prep* ~ **a** till, until; (*spazio*) as far as; ~ **all'ultimo** to the last; **fin da** (*tempo*) since; (*spazio*) from; **fin qui** as far as here; **fin troppo** too much; ~ **a che punto** how far

'fino[2] *adj* fine; (*acuto*) subtle; (*puro*) pure

fi'nocchio *m* fennel; ([!]: *omosessuale*) poof

fi'nora *adv* so far, up till now

'finta *f* sham; *Sport* feint; **far ~ di** pretend to; **far ~ di niente** act as if nothing had happened; **per ~** (*per scherzo*) for a laugh

'fint|o, -a *pp di* **fingere** ● *adj* false; (*artificiale*) artificial; **fare il ~o tonto** act dumb

finzi'one *f* pretence

fi'occo *m* bow; (*di neve*) flake; (*nappa*) tassel; **coi fiocchi** *fig* excellent. ~ **di neve** snowflake

fi'ocina *f* harpoon

fi'oco *adj* weak; (luce) dim

fi'onda *f* catapult

fio'raio, -a *mf* florist

fiorda'liso *m* cornflower

fi'ordo *m* fiord

fi'ore *m* flower; (*parte scelta*) cream; **fiori** *pl* (*nelle carte*) clubs; **a fior d'acqua** on the surface of the water; **fior di** (*abbondanza*) a lot of; **ha i nervi a fior di pelle** his nerves are on edge; **a fiori** flowery

fioren'tino *adj* Florentine

fio'retto *m* (*scherma*) foil; (*Relig*) act of mortification

fio'rire *vi* flower; (albero:) blossom; *fig* flourish

fio'rista *mf* florist

fiori'tura *f* (*di albero*) blossoming

fi'otto *m* **scorrere a fiotti** pour out; **piove a fiotti** the rain is pouring down

Fi'renze *f* Florence

'firma *f* signature; (*nome*) name

fir'ma|re *vt* sign. ~**'tario, -a** *mf* signatory. ~**to** *adj* (abito, borsa) designer *attrib*

fisar'monica *f* accordion

f

fi'scale *adj* fiscal
fischi'are *vi* whistle • *vt* whistle; (*in segno di disapprovazione*) boo
fischiet't|are *vt* whistle. **~io** *m* whistling
fischi'etto *m* whistle. **'fischio** *m* whistle
'fisco *m* treasury; (*tasse*) taxation; **il ~** the taxman
'fisica *f* physics
'fisico, -a *adj* physical • *mf* physicist • *m* physique
'fisima *f* whim
fisio|lo'gia *f* physiology. **~'logico** *adj* physiological
fisiono'mia *f* features, face; (*di paesaggio*) appearance
fisiotera'pi|a *f* physiotherapy. **~sta** *mf* physiotherapist
fis'sa|re *vt* fix, fasten; (*guardare fissamente*) stare at; arrange (appuntamento, ora). **~rsi** *vr* (*stabilirsi*) settle; (*fissare lo sguardo*) stare; **~rsi su** (*ostinarsi*) set one's mind on; **~rsi di fare qcsa** become obsessed with doing sth. **~to** *m* obsessive. **~zi'one** *f* fixation; (*ossessione*) obsession
'fisso *adj* fixed; **un lavoro ~** a regular job; **senza fissa dimora** of no fixed abode
fit'tizio *adj* fictitious
fitto[1] *adj* thick; **~ di** full of • *m* depth
fitto[2] *m* (*affitto*) rent; **dare a ~** let; **prendere a ~** rent; (*noleggiare*) hire
fiu'mana *f* swollen river; *fig* stream
fi'ume *m* river; *fig* stream
fiu'tare *vt* smell. **fi'uto** *m* [sense of] smell; *fig* nose
'flaccido *adj* flabby
fla'cone *m* bottle
fla'gello *m* scourge
fla'grante *adj* flagrant; **in ~** in the act
fla'nella *f* flannel
'flash *m inv Journ* newsflash
'flauto *m* flute
'flebile *adj* feeble
'flemma *f* calm; (*Med*) phlegm
fles'sibil|e *adj* flexible. **~ità** *f* flexibility
flessi'one *f* (*del busto in avanti*) forward bend
'flesso *pp di* **flettere**
flessu'oso *adj* supple
'flettere *vt* bend
flir'tare *vi* flirt
F.lli *abbr* (fratelli) Bros
'floppy disk *m inv* floppy disk
'florido *adj* flourishing
'floscio *adj* limp; (*flaccido*) flabby
'flotta *f* fleet. **flot'tiglia** *f* flotilla
flu'ente *adj* fluent
flu'ido *m* fluid
flu'ire *vi* flow
fluore'scente *adj* fluorescent
flu'oro *m* fluorine
'flusso *m* flow; (*Med*) flux; (*del mare*) flood[-tide]; **~ e riflusso** ebb and flow
fluttu'ante *adj* fluctuating
fluttu'a|re *vi* (prezzi, moneta:) fluctuate. **~zi'one** *f* fluctuation
fluvi'ale *adj* river
fo'bia *f* phobia
'foca *f* seal
fo'caccia *f* (*pane*) flat bread; (*dolce*) ≈ raisin bread
fo'cale *adj* (distanza, punto) focal. **focaliz'zare** *vt* get into focus (fotografia); focus (attenzione); define (problema)
'foce *f* mouth
foco'laio *m* (*Med*) focus; *fig* centre
foco'lare *m* hearth; (*caminetto*) fireplace; (*Techn*) furnace
fo'coso *adj* fiery
'foder|a *f* lining; (*di libro*) dust-jacket; (*di poltrona ecc*) loose cover. **fode'rare** *vt* line; cover (libro). **~o** *m* sheath
'foga *f* impetuosity
'foggi|a *f* fashion; (*maniera*) manner; (*forma*) shape. **~'are** *vt* mould
'foglia *f* leaf; (*di metallo*) foil
fogli'etto *m* (*pezzetto di carta*) piece of paper
'foglio *m* sheet; (*pagina*) leaf. **~ elettronico** (*Comput*) spreadsheet. **~ rosa** (*Auto*) provisional licence
'fogna *f* sewer. **~'tura** *f* sewerage
fo'lata *f* gust
fol'clo|re *m* folklore. **~'ristico** *adj* folk; (*bizzarro*) weird
folgo'ra|re *vi* (*splendere*) shine • *vt* (*con un fulmine*) strike. **~zi'one** *f* (*da fulmine, elettrica*) electrocution; (*idea*) brainwave

'folgore *f* thunderbolt
'folla *f* crowd
'folle *adj* mad; **in ~** (*Auto*) in neutral
folle'mente *adv* madly
fol'lia *f* madness; **alla ~** (amare) to distraction
'folto *adj* thick
fomen'tare *vt* stir up
fond'ale *m* (*Theat*) backcloth
fonda'men|ta *fpl* foundations. **~'tale** *adj* fundamental. **~to** *m* (*di principio, teoria*) foundation
fon'da|re *vt* establish; base (ragionamento, accusa). **~to** *adj* (ragionamento) well-founded. **~zi'one** *f* establishment; **~zioni** *pl* (*di edificio*) foundations
fon'delli *mpl* **prendere qcno per i ~** [!] pull sb's leg
fon'dente *adj* (cioccolato) dark
'fonder|e *vt/i* melt; (colori:) blend. **~si** *vr* melt; (*Comm*) merge
'fondi *mpl* (*denaro*) funds; (*di caffè*) grounds
'fondo *adj* deep; **è notte fonda** it's the middle of the night • *m* bottom; (*fine*) end; (*sfondo*) background; (*indole*) nature; (*somma di denaro*) fund; (*feccia*) dregs *pl*; **andare a ~** (nave:) sink; **da cima a ~** from beginning to end; **in ~** after all; **in ~ in ~** deep down; **fino in ~** right to the end; (capire) thoroughly. **~ d'investimento** investment trust
fondo'tinta *m* foundation cream
fon'duta *f* ≈ fondue
fo'netic|a *f* phonetics. **~o** *adj* phonetic
fon'tana *f* fountain
'fonte *f* spring; *fig* source • *m* font
fo'raggio *m* forage
fo'rar|e *vt* pierce; punch (biglietto) • *vi* puncture. **~si** *vr* (gomma, pallone:) go soft
'forbici *fpl* scissors
forbi'cine *fpl* (*per le unghie*) nail scissors
'forca *f* fork; (*patibolo*) gallows *pl*
for'cella *f* fork; (*per capelli*) hairpin
for'chet|ta *f* fork. **~'tata** *f* (*quantità*) forkful
for'cina *f* hairpin
'forcipe *m* forceps *pl*
for'cone *m* pitchfork
fo'resta *f* forest. **fore'stale** *adj* forest *attrib*
foresti'ero, -a *adj* foreign • *mf* foreigner
for'fait *m inv* fixed price; **dare ~** (*abbandonare*) give up
'forfora *f* dandruff
'forgi|a *f* forge. **~'are** *vt* forge
'forma *f* form; (*sagoma*) shape; (*Culin*) mould; (*da calzolaio*) last; **essere in ~** be in good form; **a ~ di** in the shape of; **forme** *pl* (*del corpo*) figure *sg*; (*convenzioni*) appearances
formag'gino *m* processed cheese. **for'maggio** *m* cheese
for'mal|e *adj* formal. **~ità** *f inv* formality. **~iz'zarsi** *vr* stand on ceremony. **~'mente** *adv* formally
for'ma|re *vt* form. **~rsi** *vr* form; (*svilupparsi*) develop. **~to** *m* size; (*di libro*) format; **~to tessera** (fotografia) passportsize
format'tare *vt* format
formazi'one *f* formation; *Sport* line-up. **~ professionale** vocational training
formico'l|are *vi* (braccio ecc:) tingle; **~are di** be swarming with; **mi ~a la mano** I have pins and needles in my hand. **~io** *m* swarming; (*di braccio ecc*) pins and needles *pl*
formi'dabile *adj* (*tremendo*) formidable; (*eccezionale*) tremendous
for'mina *f* mould
for'moso *adj* shapely
'formula *f* formula. **formu'lare** *vt* formulate; (*esprimere*) express
for'nace *f* furnace; (*per laterizi*) kiln
for'naio *m* baker; (*negozio*) bakery
for'nello *m* stove; (*di pipa*) bowl
for'ni|re *vt* supply (**di** with). **~'tore** *m* supplier. **~'tura** *f* supply
'forno *m* oven; (*panetteria*) bakery; **al ~** roast. **~ a microonde** microwave [oven]
'foro *m* hole; (*romano*) forum; (*tribunale*) [law] court
'forse *adv* perhaps, maybe; **essere in ~** be in doubt
forsen'nato, -a *adj* mad • *mf* madman; madwoman

'forte *adj* strong; (colore) bright; (suono) loud; (*resistente*) tough; (spesa) considerable; (dolore) severe; (pioggia) heavy; (*a tennis, calcio*) good; ([!]: *simpatico*) great; (taglia) large ● *adv* strongly; (parlare) loudly; (*velocemente*) fast; (piovere) heavily ● *m* (*fortezza*) fort; (*specialità*) strong point

for'tezza *f* fortress; (*forza morale*) fortitude

fortifi'care *vt* fortify

for'tino *m* (*Mil*) blockhouse

for'tuito *adj* fortuitous; **incontro ~** chance encounter

for'tuna *f* fortune; (*successo*) success; (*buona sorte*) luck. **atterraggio di ~** forced landing; **aver ~** be lucky; **buona ~!** good luck!; **di ~** makeshift; **per ~** luckily. **fortu'nato** *adj* lucky, fortunate; (impresa) successful. **~ta'mente** *adv* fortunately

fo'runcolo *m* pimple; (*grosso*) boil

'forza *f* strength; (*potenza*) power; (*fisica*) force; **di ~** by force; **a ~ di** by dint of; **con ~** hard; **~!** come on!; **~ di volontà** will-power; **~ maggiore** circumstances beyond one's control; **la ~ pubblica** the police; **per ~** against one's will; (*naturalmente*) of course; **farsi ~** bear up; **mare ~ 8** force 8 gale; **bella ~!** [!] big deal!. **le forze armate** the armed forces

for'za|re *vt* force; (*scassare*) break open; (*sforzare*) strain. **~to** *adj* forced; (sorriso) strained ● *m* convict

forzi'ere *m* coffer

for'zuto *adj* strong

fo'schia *f* haze

'fosco *adj* dark

fo'sfato *m* phosphate

'fosforo *m* phosphorus

'fossa *f* pit; (*tomba*) grave. **~ biologica** cesspool. **fos'sato** *m* (*di fortificazione*) moat

fos'setta *f* dimple

'fossile *m* fossil

'fosso *m* ditch; (*Mil*) trench

'foto *f inv* [!] photo; **fare delle ~** take some photos

foto'camera *f* camera

foto'cellula *f* photocell

fotocomposizi'one *f* filmsetting, photocomposition

foto'copi|a *f* photocopy. **~'are** *vt* photocopy. **~a'trice** *f* photocopier

foto'finish *m inv* photo finish

fotogra|'fare *vt* photograph. **~'fia** *f* (*arte*) photography; (*immagine*) photograph; **fare ~fie** take photographs. **foto'grafico** *adj* photographic; **macchina fotografica** camera. **fo'tografo, -a** *mf* photographer

foto'gramma *m* frame

fotomo'dello, -a *mf* [photographer's] model

fotoro'manzo *m* photo story

fou'lard *m inv* scarf

fra *prep* (*in mezzo a due*) between; (*in un insieme*) among; (*tempo, distanza*) in; **detto ~ noi** between you and me; **~ sé e sé** to oneself; **~ l'altro** what's more; **~ breve** soon; **~ quindici giorni** in two weeks' time; **~ tutti, siamo in venti** there are twenty of us altogether

fracas'sar|e *vt* smash. **~si** *vr* shatter

fra'casso *m* din; (*di cose che cadono*) crash

'fradicio *adj* (*bagnato*) soaked; (*guasto*) rotten; **ubriaco ~** blind drunk

'fragil|e *adj* fragile; *fig* frail. **~ità** *f* fragility; *fig* frailty

'fragola *f* strawberry

fra'go|re *m* uproar; (*di cose rotte*) clatter; (*di tuono*) rumble. **~'roso** *adj* uproarious; (tuono) rumbling; (suono) clanging

fra'gran|te *adj* fragrant. **~za** *f* fragrance

frain'te|ndere *vt* misunderstand. **~ndersi** *vr* be at cross-purposes. **~so** *pp di* **fraintendere**

frammen'tario *adj* fragmentary

'frana *f* landslide. **fra'nare** *vi* slide down

franca'mente *adv* frankly

fran'cese *adj* French ● *mf* Frenchman; Frenchwoman ● *m* (*lingua*) French

fran'chezza *f* frankness

'Francia *f* France

'franco[1] *adj* frank; (*Comm*) free; **farla franca** get away with sth

'franco[2] *m* (*moneta*) franc

franco'bollo *m* stamp

fran'gente *m* (*onda*) breaker; (*scoglio*) reef; (*fig: momento difficile*) crisis; **in quel**

~ given the situation

'frangia *f* fringe

fra'noso *adj* subject to landslides

fran'toio *m* olive-press

frantu'mar|e *vt*, **~si** *vr* shatter. **fran'tumi** *mpl* splinters; **andare in frantumi** be smashed to pieces

frappé *m inv* milkshake

frap'por|re *vt* interpose. **~si** *vr* intervene

fra'sario *m* vocabulary; (*libro*) phrase book

'frase *f* sentence; (*espressione*) phrase. **~ fatta** cliché

'frassino *m* ash[-tree]

frastagli'a|re *vt* make jagged. **~to** *adj* jagged

frastor'na|re *vt* daze. **~to** *adj* dazed

frastu'ono *m* racket

'frate *m* friar; (*monaco*) monk

fratel'la|nza *f* brotherhood. **~stro** *m* half-brother

fra'tell|i *mpl* (*fratello e sorella*) brother and sister. **~o** *m* brother

fraterniz'zare *vi* fraternize. **fra'terno** *adj* brotherly

frat'taglie *fpl* (*di pollo ecc*) giblets

frat'tanto *adv* in the meantime

frat'tempo *m* **nel ~** meanwhile, in the meantime

frat'tu|ra *f* fracture. **~'rare** *vt*, **~'rarsi** *vr* break

fraudo'lento *adj* fraudulent

frazi'one *f* fraction; (*borgata*) hamlet

'frecci|a *f* arrow; (*Auto*) indicator. **~'ata** *f* (*osservazione pungente*) cutting remark

fredda'mente *adv* coldly

fred'dare *vt* cool; (*fig: con sguardo, battuta*) cut down; (*uccidere*) kill

fred'dezza *f* coldness

'freddo *adj & m* cold; **aver ~** be cold; **fa ~** it's cold

freddo'loso *adj* sensitive to cold

fred'dura *f* pun

fre'ga|re *vt* rub; ([!]: *truffare*) cheat; ([!]: *rubare*) swipe. **~rsene** [!] not give a damn; **chi se ne frega!** what the heck!. **~si** *vr* rub (occhi). **~ta** *f* rub. **~'tura** *f* [!] (*truffa*) swindle; (*delusione*) letdown

'fregio *m* (*Archit*) frieze; (*ornamento*) decoration

'frem|ere *vi* quiver. **~ito** *m* quiver

fre'na|re *vt* brake; *fig* restrain; hold back (lacrime) ● *vi* brake. **~rsi** *vr* check oneself. **~ta** *f* **fare una ~ta brusca** brake sharply

frene'sia *f* frenzy; (*desiderio smodato*) craze. **fre'netico** *adj* frenzied

'freno *m* brake; *fig* check; **togliere il ~** release the brake; **usare il ~** apply the brake; **tenere a ~** restrain. **~ a mano** handbrake

frequen'tare *vt* frequent; attend (scuola ecc); mix with (persone)

fre'quen|te *adj* frequent; **di ~te** frequently. **~za** *f* frequency; (*assiduità*) attendance

fre'schezza *f* freshness; (*di temperatura*) coolness

'fresco *adj* fresh; (temperatura) cool; **stai ~!** you're for it! ● *m* coolness; **far ~** be cool; **mettere/tenere in ~** put/keep in a cool place

'fretta *f* hurry, haste; **aver ~** be in a hurry; **far ~ a qcno** hurry sb; **in ~ e furia** in a great hurry. **frettolosa'mente** *adv* hurriedly. **fretto'loso** *adj* (persona) in a hurry; (lavoro) rushed, hurried

fri'abile *adj* crumbly

'friggere *vt* fry; **vai a farti ~!** get lost! ● *vi* sizzle

friggi'trice *f* chip pan

frigidità *f* frigidity. **'frigido** *adj* frigid

fri'gnare *vi* whine

'frigo *m inv* fridge

frigo'bar *m inv* minibar

frigo'rifero *adj* refrigerating ● *m* refrigerator

frit'tata *f* omelette

frit'tella *f* fritter; ([!]: *macchia d'unto*) grease stain

'fritto *pp di* **friggere** ● *adj* fried; **essere ~** be done for ● *m* fried food. **~ misto** mixed fried fish/vegetables. **frit'tura** *f* fried dish

frivo'lezza *f* frivolity. **'frivolo** *adj* frivolous

frizio'nare *vt* rub. **frizi'one** *f* friction; (*Mech*) clutch; (*di pelle*) rub

friz'zante *adj* fizzy; (vino) sparkling; (aria) bracing

f

'frizzo *m* gibe
fro'dare *vt* defraud
'frode *f* fraud. **~ fiscale** tax evasion
'frollo *adj* tender; (selvaggina) high; (persona) spineless; **pasta frolla** short-[crust] pastry
'fronda *f* [leafy] branch; *fig* rebellion. **fron'doso** *adj* leafy
fron'tale *adj* frontal; (scontro) head-on
'fronte *f* forehead; (*di edificio*) front; **di ~** opposite; **di ~ a** opposite, facing; (*a paragone*) compared with; **far ~ a** face ● *m* (*Mil, Pol*) front. **~ggi'are** *vt* face
fronti'era *f* frontier, border
fron'tone *m* pediment
'fronzolo *m* frill
'frotta *f* swarm; (*di animali*) flock
'frottola *f* fib; **frottole** *pl* nonsense *sg*
fru'gale *adj* frugal
fru'gare *vi* rummage ● *vt* search
frul'la|re *vt* (*Culin*) whisk ● *vi* (ali:) whirr. **~to** *m* **~to di frutta** *fruit drink with milk and crushed ice.* **~'tore** *m* [electric] mixer. **frul'lino** *m* whisk
fru'mento *m* wheat
frusci'are *vi* rustle
fru'scio *m* rustle; (*radio, giradischi*) background noise; (*di acque*) murmur
'frusta *f* whip; (*frullino*) whisk
fru'sta|re *vt* whip. **~ta** *f* lash. **fru'stino** *m* riding crop
fru'stra|re *vt* frustrate. **~to** *adj* frustrated. **~zi'one** *f* frustration
'frutt|a *f* fruit; (*portata*) dessert. **frut'tare** *vi* bear fruit ● *vt* yield. **frut'teto** *m* orchard. **~i'vendolo, -a** *mf* greengrocer. **~o** *m* fruit; *Fin* yield; **~i di bosco** fruits of the forest. **~i di mare** seafood *sg*. **~u'oso** *adj* profitable
f.to *abbr* (firmato) signed
fu *adj* (*defunto*) late; **il ~ signor Rossi** the late Mr Rossi
fuci'la|re *vt* shoot. **~ta** *f* shot
fu'cile *m* rifle
fu'cina *f* forge
'fuga *f* escape; (*perdita*) leak; (*Mus*) fugue; **darsi alla ~** escape
fu'gace *adj* fleeting
fug'gevole *adj* short-lived
fuggi'asco, -a *mf* fugitive
fuggi'fuggi *m* stampede
fug'gi|re *vi* flee; (innamorati:) elope; *fig* fly. **~'tivo, -a** *mf* fugitive
'fulcro *m* fulcrum
ful'gore *m* splendour
fu'liggine *f* soot
fulmi'nar|e *vt* strike by lightning; (*con sguardo*) look daggers at; (*con scarica elettrica*) electrocute. **~si** *vr* burn out. **'fulmine** *m* lightning. **ful'mineo** *adj* rapid
'fulvo *adj* tawny
fumai'olo *m* funnel; (*di casa*) chimney
fu'ma|re *vt/i* smoke; (*in ebollizione*) steam. **~'tore, ~'trice** *mf* smoker; **non fumatori** non-smoker, non-smoking
fu'metto *m* comic strip; **fumetti** *pl* comics
'fumo *m* smoke; (*vapore*) steam; *fig* hot air; **andare in ~** vanish. **fu'moso** *adj* smoky; (discorso) vague
fu'nambolo, -a *mf* tightrope walker
'fune *f* rope; (*cavo*) cable
'funebre *adj* funeral; (*cupo*) gloomy
fune'rale *m* funeral
fu'nesto *adj* sad
'fungere *vi* **~ da** act as

> *i*
> **Funghi** Wild mushrooms are an Italian passion, and the most prized is the *porcino* (cep), which can be bought fresh or dried. However, many Italians are also avid mushroom-pickers and are expert at differentiating edible mushrooms (*funghi commestibili*) from poisonous ones. Local authorities often have a department controlling the picking and selling of mushrooms.

'fungo *m* mushroom; (*Bot*) fungus
funico'lare *f* funicular [railway]
funi'via *f* cableway
funzio'nal|e *adj* functional. **~ità** *f* functionality
funziona'mento *m* functioning
funzio'nare *vi* work, function; **~ da** (*fungere da*) act as
funzio'nario *m* official
funzi'one *f* function; (*carica*) office; (*Relig*) service; **entrare in ~** take up office

fu'oco *m* fire; (*fisica, fotografia*) focus; **far ~** fire; **dar ~ a** set fire to; **prendere ~** catch fire. **fuochi** *pl* **d'artificio** fireworks
fuorché *prep* except
fu'ori *adv* out; (*all'esterno*) outside; (*all'aperto*) outdoors; **andare di ~** (*traboccare*) spill over; **essere ~ di sé** be beside oneself; **essere in ~** (*sporgere*) stick out; **far ~** ! do in; **~ luogo** (*inopportuno*) out of place; **~ mano** out of the way; **~ moda** old-fashioned; **~ pasto** between meals; **~ pericolo** out of danger; **~ questione** out of the question; **~ uso** out of use • *m* outside
fuori'bordo *m* speedboat (*with outboard motor*)
fuori'classe *mf inv* champion
fuorigi'oco *m & adv* offside
fuori'legge *mf* outlaw
fuori'serie *adj* custom-made • *f* (*Auto*) custom-built model
fuori'strada *m* off-road vehicle
fuorvi'are *vt* lead astray • *vi* go astray
furbe'ria *f* cunning. **fur'bizia** *f* cunning
'furbo *adj* cunning; (*intelligente*) clever; (*astuto*) shrewd; **bravo ~!** nice one!; **fare il ~** try to be clever
fu'rente *adj* furious
fur'fante *m* scoundrel
furgon'cino *m* delivery van. **fur'gone** *m* van
'furi|a *f* fury; (*fretta*) haste; **a ~a di** by dint of. **~'bondo, ~'oso** *adj* furious
fu'rore *m* fury; (*veemenza*) frenzy; **far ~** be all the rage. **~ggi'are** *vi* be a great success
furtiva'mente *adv* covertly. **fur'tivo** *adj* furtive
'furto *m* theft; (*con scasso*) burglary; **commettere un ~** steal. **~ d'identità** identity theft
'fusa *fpl* **fare le ~** purr
fu'scello *m* (*di legno*) twig; (*di paglia*) straw; **sei un ~** you're as light as a feather
fu'seaux *mpl* leggings
fu'sibile *m* fuse
fusi'one *f* fusion; (*Comm*) merger
'fuso *pp di* **fondere** • *adj* melted • *m* spindle. **~ orario** time zone
fusoli'era *f* fuselage
fu'stagno *m* corduroy
fu'stino *m* (*di detersivo*) box
'fusto *m* stem; (*tronco*) trunk; (*recipiente di metallo*) drum; (*di legno*) barrel
'futile *adj* futile
fu'turo *adj & m* future

Gg

gab'bar|e *vt* cheat. **~si** *vr* **~si di** make fun of
'gabbia *f* cage; (*da imballaggio*) crate. **~ degli imputati** dock. **~ toracica** rib cage
gabbi'ano *m* [sea]gull
gabi'netto *m* consulting room; (*Pol*) cabinet; (*bagno*) lavatory; (*laboratorio*) laboratory
'gaffe *f inv* blunder
gagli'ardo *adj* vigorous
gai'ezza *f* gaiety. **'gaio** *adj* cheerful
'gala *f* gala
ga'lante *adj* gallant. **~'ria** *f* gallantry. **galantu'omo** *m* (*pl* **galantuomini**) gentleman
ga'lassia *f* galaxy
gala'teo *m* [good] manners *pl*; (*trattato*) book of etiquette
gale'otto *m* (*rematore*) galley-slave; (*condannato*) convict
ga'lera *f* (*nave*) galley; ! prison
'galla *f* (*Bot*) gall; **a ~** *adv* afloat; **venire a ~** surface
galleggi'are *vi* float
galle'ria *f* tunnel; (*d'arte*) gallery; (*Theat*) circle; (*arcata*) arcade. **~ d'arte** art gallery
'Galles *m* Wales. **gal'lese** *adj* welsh • *m* Welshman; (*lingua*) Welsh • *f* Welshwoman
gal'letto *m* cockerel; **fare il ~** show off
gal'lina *f* hen
gal'lismo *m* machismo
'gallo *m* cock
gal'lone *m* stripe; (*misura*) gallon

f g

galop'pare *vi* gallop. **ga'loppo** *m* gallop; **al galoppo** at a gallop
'gamba *f* leg; (*di lettera*) stem; **a quattro gambe** on all fours; **essere in ~** (*essere forte*) be strong; (*capace*) be smart
gamba'letto *m* pop sock
gambe'retto *m* shrimp. **'gambero** *m* prawn; (*di fiume*) crayfish
'gambo *m* stem; (*di pianta*) stalk
'gamma *f* (*Mus*) scale; *fig* range
ga'nascia *f* jaw; **ganasce** *pl* **del freno** brake shoes

g

'gancio *m* hook
'ganghero *m* **uscire dai gangheri** *fig* get into a temper
'gara *f* competition; (*di velocità*) race; **fare a ~** compete
ga'rage *m inv* garage
ga'ran|te *mf* guarantor. **~'tire** *vt* guarantee; (*rendersi garante*) vouch for; (*assicurare*) assure. **~'zia** *f* guarantee; **in ~zia** under guarantee
gar'ba|re *vi* like; **non mi garba** I don't like it. **~to** *adj* courteous
'garbo *m* courtesy; (*grazia*) grace; **con ~** graciously
gareggi'are *vi* compete
garga'nella *f* **a ~** from the bottle
garga'rismo *m* gargle; **fare i gargarismi** gargle
ga'rofano *m* carnation
'garza *f* gauze
gar'zone *m* boy. **~ di stalla** stableboy
gas *m inv* gas; **dare ~** (*Auto*) accelerate; **a tutto ~** flat out. **~ lacrimogeno** tear gas. **~** *pl* **di scarico** exhaust fumes
gas'dotto *m* natural gas pipeline
ga'solio *m* diesel oil
ga'sometro *m* gasometer
gas's|are *vt* aerate; (*uccidere col gas*) gas. **~ato** *adj* gassy. **~oso, -a** *adj* gassy; (bevanda) fizzy ● *f* lemonade
'gastrico *adj* gastric. **ga'strite** *f* gastritis
gastro|no'mia *f* gastronomy. **~'nomico** *adj* gastronomic. **ga'stronomo, -a** *mf* gourmet
'gatta *f* **una ~ da pelare** a headache
gatta'buia *f hum* clink
gat'tino, -a *mf* kitten
'gatto, -a *mf* cat. **~ delle nevi** snowmobile
gat'toni *adv* on all fours
gay *adj inv* gay
'gazza *f* magpie
gaz'zarra *f* racket
gaz'zella *f* gazelle; (*Auto*) police car
gaz'zetta *f* gazette
gaz'zosa *f* clear lemonade
'geco *m* gecko
ge'la|re *vt/i* freeze. **~ta** *f* frost
gela't|aio, -a *mf* ice-cream seller; (*negozio*) ice-cream shop. **~e'ria** *f* ice-cream parlour. **~i'era** *f* ice-cream maker
gela'ti|na *f* gelatine; (*dolce*) jelly. **~na di frutta** fruit jelly.
ge'lato *adj* frozen ● *m* ice-cream
'gelido *adj* freezing
'gelo *m* (*freddo intenso*) freezing cold; (*brina*) frost; *fig* chill
ge'lone *m* chilblain
gelosa'mente *adv* jealously
gelo'sia *f* jealousy. **ge'loso** *adj* jealous
'gelso *m* mulberry[-tree]
gelso'mino *m* jasmine
gemel'laggio *m* twinning
ge'mello, -a *adj & mf* twin; (*di polsino*) cuff-link; **Gemelli** *pl* (*Astr*) Gemini *sg*
'gem|ere *vi* groan; (*tubare*) coo. **~ito** *m* groan
'gemma *f* gem; (*Bot*) bud
'gene *m* gene
genealo'gia *f* genealogy
gene'ral|e[1] *adj* general; **spese ~i** overheads
gene'rale[2] *m* (*Mil*) general
generalità *f* (*qualità*) generality, general nature; **~** *pl* (*dati personali*) particulars
generaliz'za|re *vt* generalize. **~zi'one** *f* generalization. **general'mente** *adv* generally
gene'ra|re *vt* give birth to; (*causare*) breed; (*Techn*) generate. **~'tore** *m* (*Techn*) generator. **~zi'one** *f* generation
'genere *m* kind; (*Biol*) genus; (*Gram*) gender; (*letterario, artistico*) genre; (*prodotto*) product; **il ~ umano** mankind;

in ~ generally. **generi** *pl* **alimentari** provisions
ge'nerico *adj* generic; **medico** ~ general practitioner
'genero *m* son-in-law
generosità *f* generosity. **gene'roso** *adj* generous
'genesi *f inv* genesis
ge'netico, -a *adj* genetic • *f* genetics
gen'giva *f* gum
geni'ale *adj* ingenious; (*congeniale*) congenial
'genio *m* genius; **andare a** ~ be to one's taste. ~ **civile** civil engineering. ~ **[militare]** Engineers
geni'tale *adj* genital. **genitali** *mpl* genitals
geni'tore *m* parent
gen'naio *m* January
'Genova *f* Genoa
gen'taglia *f* rabble
'gente *f* people *pl*
gen'til|e *adj* kind; **G~e Signore** (*in lettere*) Dear Sir. **genti'lezza** *f* kindness; **per gentilezza** (*per favore*) please. **~'mente** *adv* kindly. **~u'omo** (*pl* **~u'omini**) *m* gentleman
genu'ino *adj* genuine; (cibo, prodotto) natural
geogra'fia *f* geography. **geo'grafico** *adj* geographical. **ge'ografo, -a** *mf* geographer
geolo'gia *f* geology. **geo'logico** *adj* geological. **ge'ologo, -a** *mf* geologist
ge'ometra *mf* surveyor
geome'tria *f* geometry
ge'ranio *m* geranium
gerar'chia *f* hierarchy
ge'rente *m* manager • *f* manageress
'gergo *m* slang; (*di professione ecc*) jargon
geria'tria *f* geriatrics *sg*
Ger'mania *f* Germany
'germe *m* germ; (*fig: principio*) seed
germogli'are *vi* sprout. **ger'moglio** *m* sprout
gero'glifico *m* hieroglyph
'gesso *m* chalk; (*Med, scultura*) plaster
gestazi'one *f* gestation
gestico'lare *vi* gesticulate
gesti'one *f* management
ge'stir|e *vi* manage. **~si** *vr* budget one's time and money
'gesto *m* gesture; (*azione pl f* **gesta**) deed
ge'store *m* manager
Gesù *m* Jesus. ~ **bambino** baby Jesus
gesu'ita *m* Jesuit
get'ta|re *vt* throw; (*scagliare*) fling; (*emettere*) spout; (*Techn*), *fig* cast; **~re via** throw away. **~rsi** *vr* throw oneself; **~rsi in** (fiume:) flow into. **~ta** *f* throw
'getto *m* throw; (*di liquidi, gas*) jet; **a** ~ **continuo** in a continuous stream; **di** ~ straight off
getto'nato *adj* popular. **get'tone** *m* token; (*per giochi*) counter
'ghetto *m* ghetto
ghiacci'aio *m* glacier
ghiacci'a|re *vt/i* freeze. **~to** *adj* frozen; (*freddissimo*) ice-cold
ghi'acci|o *m* ice; (*Auto*) black ice. **~'olo** *m* icicle; (*gelato*) ice lolly
ghi'aia *f* gravel
ghi'anda *f* acorn
ghi'andola *f* gland
ghigliot'tina *f* guillotine
ghi'gnare *vi* sneer
ghi'ot|to *adj* greedy; (*appetitoso*) appetizing. **~'tone, -a** *mf* glutton. **~tone'ria** *f* (*qualità*) gluttony; (*cibo*) tasty morsel
ghir'landa *f* (*corona*) wreath; (*di fiori*) garland
'ghiro *m* dormouse; **dormire come un** ~ sleep like a log
'ghisa *f* cast iron
già *adv* already; (*un tempo*) formerly; **~!** indeed!; ~ **da ieri** since yesterday
gi'acca *f* jacket. ~ **a vento** windcheater
giacché *conj* since
giac'cone *m* jacket
gia'cere *vi* lie
giaci'mento *m* deposit. ~ **di petrolio** oil deposit
gia'cinto *m* hyacinth
gi'ada *f* jade
giaggi'olo *m* iris
giagu'aro *m* jaguar
gial'lastro *adj* yellowish
gi'allo *adj & m* yellow; **[libro]** ~ thriller

Giap'pone *m* Japan. **giappo'nese** *adj & mf* Japanese
giardi'n|aggio *m* gardening. **~i'ere, -a** *mf* gardener ● *f* (*Auto*) estate car; (*sottaceti*) pickles *pl*
giar'dino *m* garden. **~ d'infanzia** kindergarten. **~ pensile** roofgarden. **~ zoologico** zoo
giarretti'era *f* garter
giavel'lotto *m* javelin
gi'gan|te *adj* gigantic ● *m* giant. **~'tesco** *adj* gigantic
g
gigantogra'fia *f* blow-up
'giglio *m* lily
gilè *m inv* waistcoat
gin *m inv* gin
gineco|lo'gia *f* gynaecology. **~'logico** *adj* gynaecological. **gine'cologo, -a** *mf* gynaecologist
gi'nepro *m* juniper
gingil'larsi *vr* fiddle; (*perder tempo*) potter. **gin'gillo** *m* plaything; (*ninnolo*) knick-knack
gin'nasio *m* ≈ grammar school
gin'nast|a *mf* gymnast. **~ica** *f* gymnastics; (*esercizi*) exercises *pl*
ginocchi'ata *f* **prendere una ~** bang one's knee
gi'nocchi|o *m* (*pl m* **ginocchi** *o f* **ginocchia**) knee; **in ~o** on one's knees; **mettersi in ~o** kneel down; (*per supplicare*) go down on one's knees. **~'oni** *adv* kneeling
gio'ca|re *vt/i* play; (*giocherellare*) toy; (*d'azzardo*) gamble; (*puntare*) stake; (*ingannare*) trick. **~rsi la carriera** throw one's career away. **~'tore, ~'trice** *mf* player; (*d'azzardo*) gambler
gio'cattolo *m* toy
giocherel'l|are *vi* toy; (*nervosamente*) fiddle. **~one** *adj* skittish
gi'oco *m* game; (*Techn*) play; (*d'azzardo*) gambling; (*scherzo*) joke; (*insieme di pezzi ecc*) set; **fare il doppio ~ con qcno** double-cross sb
giocoli'ere *m* juggler
gio'coso *adj* playful
gi'oia *f* joy; (*gioiello*) jewel; (*appellativo*) sweetie
gioiell|e'ria *f* jeweller's [shop]. **~i'ere, -a** *mf* jeweller; (*negozio*) jeweller's. **gioi'ello** *m* jewel; **gioielli** *pl* jewellery
gioi'oso *adj* joyous
gio'ire *vi* **~ per** rejoice at
Gior'dania *f* Jordan
giorna'laio, -a *mf* newsagent
gior'nale *m* [news]paper; (*diario*) journal. **~ di bordo** logbook. **~ radio** news bulletin
giornali'ero *adj* daily ● *m* (*per sciare*) day pass
giorna'lino *m* comic
giorna'lis|mo *m* journalism. **~ta** *mf* journalist
giornal'mente *adv* daily
gior'nata *f* day; **in ~** today
gi'orno *m* day; **al ~** per day; **al ~ d'oggi** nowadays; **di ~** by day; **un ~ sì, un ~ no** every other day
gi'ostra *f* merry-go-round
giova'mento *m* **trarre ~ da** derive benefit from
gi'ova|ne *adj* young; (*giovanile*) youthful ● *m* young man ● *f* young woman. **~'nile** *adj* youthful. **~'notto** *m* young man
gio'var|e *vi* **~e a** be useful to; (*far bene a*) be good for. **~si** *vr* **~si di** avail oneself of
giovedì *m inv* Thursday. **~ grasso** *last Thursday before Lent*
gioventù *f* youth; (*i giovani*) young people *pl*
giovi'ale *adj* jovial
giovi'nezza *f* youth
gira'dischi *m inv* record-player
gi'raffa *f* giraffe; *Cinema* boom
gi'randola *f* (*fuoco d'artificio*) Catherine wheel; (*giocattolo*) windmill; (*banderuola*) weathercock
gi'ra|re *vt* turn; (*andare intorno, visitare*) go round; (*Comm*) endorse; *Cinema* shoot ● *vi* turn; (aerei, uccelli:) circle; (*andare in giro*) wander; **~re al largo** steer clear. **~rsi** *vr* turn [round]; **mi gira la testa** I'm dizzy
girar'rosto *m* spit
gira'sole *m* sunflower
gi'rata *f* turn; (*Comm*) endorsement; (*in macchina ecc*) ride; **fare una ~** (*a piedi*) go for a walk; (*in macchina*) go for a ride
gira'volta *f* spin; *fig* U-turn

gi'rello *m* (*per bambini*) babywalker; (*Culin*) topside
gi'revole *adj* revolving
gi'rino *m* tadpole
'giro *m* turn; (*circolo*) circle; (*percorso*) round; (*viaggio*) tour; (*passeggiata*) short walk; (*in macchina*) drive; (*in bicicletta*) ride; (*circolazione di denaro*) circulation; **nel ~ di un mese** within a month; **senza giri di parole** without beating about the bush; **a ~ di posta** by return mail. **~ d'affari** (*Comm*) turnover. **giri** *pl* **al minuto** rpm. **~ turistico** sightseeing tour. **~ vita** waist measurement
giro'collo *m* choker; **a ~** crewneck
gi'rone *m* round
gironzo'lare *vi* wander about
girova'gare *vi* wander about. **gi'rovago** *m* wanderer
'gita *f* trip; **andare in ~** go on a trip. **~ scolastica** school trip. **gi'tante** *mf* tripper
giù *adv* down; (*sotto*) below; (*dabbasso*) downstairs; **a testa in ~** (*a capofitto*) headlong; **essere ~** be down; (*di salute*) be run down; **~ di corda** down; **~ di lì, su per ~** more or less; **non andare ~ a qcno** stick in sb's craw
gi'ub|ba *f* jacket; (*Mil*) tunic. **~'botto** *m* bomber jacket
giudi'care *vt* judge; (*ritenere*) consider
gi'udice *m* judge. **~ conciliatore** justice of the peace. **~ di gara** umpire. **~ di linea** linesman
giu'dizi|o *m* judg[e]ment; (*opinione*) opinion; (*senno*) wisdom; (*processo*) trial; (*sentenza*) sentence; **mettere ~o** become wise. **~'oso** *adj* sensible
gi'ugno *m* June
giu'menta *f* mare
gi'ungere *vi* arrive; **~ a** (*riuscire*) succeed in ● *vt* (*unire*) join
gi'ungla *f* jungle
gi'unta *f* addition; (*Mil*) junta; **per ~** in addition. **~ comunale** district council
gi'unto *pp di* **giungere** ● *m* (*Mech*) joint
giun'tura *f* joint
giuo'care, giu'oco = **GIOCARE, GIOCO**
giura'mento *m* oath; **prestare ~** take the oath
giu'ra|re *vt/i* swear. **~to, -a** *adj* sworn ● *mf* juror
giu'ria *f* jury
giu'ridico *adj* legal
giurisdizi'one *f* jurisdiction
giurispru'denza *f* jurisprudence
giu'rista *mf* jurist
giustifi'ca|re *vt* justify. **~zi'one** *f* justification
giu'stizi|a *f* justice. **~'are** *vt* execute. **~'ere** *m* executioner
gi'usto *adj* just, fair; (*adatto*) right; (*esatto*) exact ● *m* (*uomo retto*) just man; (*cosa giusta*) right ● *adv* exactly; **~ ora** just now
glaci'ale *adj* glacial
gla'diolo *m* gladiolus
'glassa *f* (*Culin*) icing
gli *def art mpl* (*before vowel and s + consonant, gn, ps, z*) the; ▷**IL** ● *pron* (*a lui*) [to] him; (*a esso*) [to] it; (*a loro*) [to] them
glice'rina *f* glycerine
'glicine *m* wisteria
gli'e|lo, -a *pron* [to] him/her/them; (*forma di cortesia*) [to] you; **~ chiedo** I'll ask him/her/them/you; **gliel'ho prestato** I've lent it to him/her/them/you. **~ne** (*di ciò*) [of] it; **~ne ho dato un po'** I gave him/her/them/you some
glo'bal|e *adj* global; *fig* overall. **~izza'zione** *f* globalization. **~'mente** *adv* globally
'globo *m* globe. **~ oculare** eyeball. **~ terrestre** globe
'globulo *m* globule; (*Med*) corpuscle. **~ bianco** white corpuscle. **~ rosso** red corpuscle
'glori|a *f* glory. **~'arsi** *vr* **~arsi di** be proud of. **~'oso** *adj* glorious
glos'sario *m* glossary
glu'cosio *m* glucose
'gluteo *m* buttock
'gnorri *m* **fare lo ~** play dumb
'gobb|a *f* hump. **~o, -a** *adj* hunchbacked ● *mf* hunchback
'gocci|a *f* drop; (*di sudore*) bead; **è stata l'ultima ~a** it was the last straw. **~o'lare** *vi* drip. **~o'lio** *m* dripping
go'der|e *vi* (*sessualmente*) come; **~e di** enjoy. **~sela** have a good time. **~si** *vr* **~si qcsa** enjoy sth

g

g

godi'mento *m* enjoyment
goffa'mente *adv* awkwardly. **'goffo** *adj* awkward
'gola *f* throat; (*ingordigia*) gluttony; (*Geog*) gorge; (*di camino*) flue; **avere mal di ~** have a sore throat; **far ~ a qcno** tempt sb
golf *m inv* jersey; *Sport* golf
'golfo *m* gulf
golosità *f inv* greediness; (*cibo*) tasty morsel. **go'loso** *adj* greedy
'golpe *m inv* coup
gomi'tata *f* nudge
'gomito *m* elbow; **alzare il ~** raise one's elbow
go'mitolo *m* ball
'gomma *f* rubber; (*colla, da masticare*) gum; (*pneumatico*) tyre. **~ da masticare** chewing gum
gommapi'uma *f* foam rubber
gom'mista *m* tyre specialist
gom'mone *m* [rubber] dinghy
'gondol|a *f* gondola. **~i'ere** *m* gondolier
gonfa'lone *m* banner
gonfi'abile *adj* inflatable
gonfi'ar|e *vi* swell ● *vt* blow up; pump up (pneumatico); (*esagerare*) exaggerate. **~si** *vr* swell; (acque:) rise. **'gonfio** *adj* swollen; (pneumatico) inflated. **gonfi'ore** *m* swelling
gongo'la|nte *adj* overjoyed. **~re** *vi* be overjoyed
'gonna *f* skirt. **~ pantalone** culottes *pl*
goo'glare *vt/i* google
gorgogli'are *vi* gurgle
go'rilla *m inv* gorilla; (*guardia del corpo*) bodyguard
'gotico *adj & m* Gothic
gover'nante *f* housekeeper
gover'na|re *vt* govern; (*dominare*) rule; (*dirigere*) manage; (*curare*) look after. **~'tore** *m* governor
go'verno *m* government; (*dominio*) rule; **al ~** in power
gps *m* gps
gracchi'are *vi* caw; *fig*: (persona:) screech
graci'dare *vi* croak
'gracile *adj* delicate
gra'dasso *m* braggart
gradata'mente *adv* gradually
gradazi'one *f* gradation. **~ alcoolica** alcohol[ic] content
gra'devol|e *adj* agreeable.
gradi'mento *m* liking; **indice di ~** (*Radio, TV*) popularity rating; **non è di mio ~** it's not to my liking
gradi'nata *f* flight of steps; (*di stadio*) stand; (*di teatro*) tiers *pl*
gra'dino *m* step
gra'di|re *vt* like; (*desiderare*) wish. **~to** *adj* pleasant; (*bene accetto*) welcome
'grado *m* degree; (*rango*) rank; **di buon ~** willingly; **essere in ~ di fare qcsa** be in a position to do sth: (*essere capace a*) be able to do sth
gradu'ale *adj* gradual
gradu'a|re *vt* graduate. **~to** *adj* graded; (*provvisto di scala graduata*) graduated ● *m* (*Mil*) noncommissioned officer. **~'toria** *f* list. **~zi'one** *f* graduation
'graffa *f* clip
graf'fetta *f* staple
graffi'a|re *vt* scratch. **~'tura** *f* scratch
'graffio *m* scratch
gra'fia *f* [hand]writing; (*ortografia*) spelling
'grafic|a *f* graphics; **~a pubblicitaria** commercial art. **~a'mente** *adv* graphically. **~o** *adj* graphic ● *m* graph; (*persona*) graphic designer
gra'migna *f* weed
gram'matica *f* grammar
'grammo *m* gram[me]
gran *adj* ▷**GRANDE**
'grana *f* grain; (*formaggio*) parmesan; ([!]: *seccatura*) trouble; ([!]: *soldi*) readies *pl*
gra'naio *m* barn
gra'nat|a *f* (*Mil*) grenade; (*frutto*) pomegranate. **~i'ere** *m* (*Mil*) grenadier
Gran Bre'tagna *f* Great Britain
'granchio *m* crab; (*errore*) blunder; **prendere un ~** make a blunder
grandango'lare *m* wide-angle lens
'grande (*a volte* **gran**) *adj* (*ampio*) large; (*grosso*) big; (*alto*) tall; (*largo*) wide; (*fig*: *senso morale*) great; (*grandioso*) grand; (*adulto*) grown-up; **ho una**

gran fame I'm very hungry; **fa un gran caldo** it is very hot; **in ~** on a large scale; **in gran parte** to a great extent; **un gran ballo** a grand ball ● *mf* (*persona adulta*) grown-up; (*persona eminente*) great man/woman. **~ggi'are** *vi* **~ggiare su** tower over; (*darsi arie*) show off

gran'dezza *f* greatness; (*ampiezza*) largeness; (*larghezza*) width, breadth; (*dimensione*) size; (*fasto*) grandeur; (*prodigalità*) lavishness; **a ~ naturale** life-size

grandi'nare *vi* hail; **grandina** it's hailing. **'grandine** *f* hail

grandiosità *f* grandeur. **grandi'oso** *adj* grand

gran'duca *m* grand duke

gra'nello *m* grain; (*di frutta*) pip

gra'nita *f crushed ice drink*

gra'nito *m* granite

'grano *m* grain; (*frumento*) wheat

gran'turco *m* maize

'granulo *m* granule

'grappa *f* grappa; (*morsa*) cramp

'grappolo *m* bunch. **~ d'uva** bunch of grapes

gras'setto *m* bold [type]

gras'sezza *f* fatness

'gras|so *adj* fat; (cibo) fatty; (*unto*) greasy; (terreno) rich; (*grossolano*) coarse ● *m* fat; (*sostanza*) grease. **~'soccio** *adj* plump

'grata *f* grating. **gra'tella, gra'ticola** *f* (*Culin*) grill

gra'tifica *f* bonus. **~zi'one** *f* satisfaction

grati'na|re *vt* cook au gratin. **~to** *adj* au gratin

grati'tudine *f* gratitude. **'grato** *adj* grateful; (*gradito*) pleasant

gratta'capo *m* trouble

grattaci'elo *m* skyscraper

'gratta e 'vinci *m inv* scratch card

grat'tar|e *vt* scratch; (*raschiare*) scrape; (*grattugiare*) grate; ([!]: *rubare*) pinch ● *vi* grate. **~si** *vr* scratch oneself

grat'tugi|a *f* grater. **~'are** *vt* grate

gratuita'mente *adv* free [of charge]. **gra'tuito** *adj* free [of charge]; (*ingiustificato*) gratuitous

gra'vare *vt* burden ● *vi* **~ su** weigh on

'grave *adj* (*pesante*) heavy; (*serio*) serious; (*difficile*) hard; (voce, suono) low; (*fonetica*) grave; **essere ~** (*ammalato*) be seriously ill. **~'mente** *adv* seriously

gravi'danza *f* pregnancy. **'gravido** *adj* pregnant

gravità *f* seriousness; (*Phys*) gravity

gra'voso *adj* onerous

'grazi|a *f* grace; (*favore*) favour; (*Jur*) pardon; **entrare nelle ~e di qcno** get into sb's good books. **~'are** *vt* pardon

'grazie *int* thank you!, thanks!; **~ mille!** many thanks!

grazi'oso *adj* charming; (*carino*) pretty

'Grec|ia *f* Greece. **g~o, -a** *agg & mf* Greek

'gregge *m* flock

'greggio *adj* raw ● *m* crude oil

grembi'ale, grembi'ule *m* apron

'grembo *m* lap; (*utero*) womb; *fig* bosom

gre'mi|re *vt* pack. **~rsi** *vr* become crowded (**di** with). **~to** *adj* packed

'gretto *adj* stingy; (*di vedute ristrette*) narrow-minded

'grezzo *adj* = GREGGIO

gri'dare *vi* shout; (*di dolore*) scream; (animale:) cry ● *vt* shout

'grido *m* (*pl m* **gridi** *o f* **grida**) shout; (*di animale*) cry; **l'ultimo ~** the latest fashion

'grigio *adj & m* grey

'griglia *f* grill; **alla ~** grilled

gril'letto *m* trigger

'grillo *m* cricket; (*fig: capriccio*) whim

'grinfia *f fig* clutch

'grin|ta *f* grit. **~'toso** *adj* determined

'grinza *f* wrinkle; (*di stoffa*) crease

grip'pare *vi* (*Mech*) seize

gris'sino *m* bread-stick

'gronda *f* eaves *pl*

gron'daia *f* gutter

gron'dare *vi* pour; (*essere bagnato fradicio*) be dripping

'groppa *f* back

'groppo *m* knot

gros'sezza *f* size; (*spessore*) thickness

gros'sista *mf* wholesaler

g

'grosso *adj* big, large; (*spesso*) thick; (*grossolano*) coarse; (*grave*) serious • *m* big part; (*massa*) bulk; **farla grossa** do a stupid thing

grosso|lanità *f inv* (*qualità*) coarseness; (*di errore*) grossness; (*azione, parola*) coarse thing. **~'lano** *adj* coarse; (errore) gross

grosso'modo *adv* roughly

'grotta *f* cave, grotto

grovi'era *m* Gruyère

gro'viglio *m* tangle; *fig* muddle

g

gru *f inv* (*uccello, edilizia*) crane

'gruccia *f* (*stampella*) crutch; (*per vestito*) hanger

gru'gni|re *vi* grunt. **~to** *m* grunt

'grugno *m* snout

'grullo *adj* silly

'grumo *m* clot; (*di farina ecc*) lump. **gru'moso** *adj* lumpy

'gruppo *m* group; (*comitiva*) party. **~ sanguigno** blood group

gruvi'era *m* Gruyère

'gruzzolo *m* nest-egg

guada'gnare *vt* earn; gain (tempo, forza ecc). **gua'dagno** *m* gain; (*profitto*) profit; (*entrate*) earnings *pl*

gu'ado *m* ford; **passare a ~** ford

gua'ina *f* sheath; (*busto*) girdle

gu'aio *m* trouble; **che ~!** that's just brilliant!; **essere nei guai** be in a fix; **guai a te se lo tocchi!** don't you dare touch it!

gu'anci|a *f* cheek. **~'ale** *m* pillow

gu'anto *m* glove. **guantoni** *pl* **[da boxe]** boxing gloves

guarda'coste *m inv* coastguard

guarda'linee *m inv Sport* linesman

guar'dar|e *vt* look at; (*osservare*) watch; (*badare a*) look after; (*dare su*) look out on • *vi* look; (*essere orientato verso*) face. **~si** *vr* look at oneself; **~si da** beware of; (*astenersi*) refrain from

guarda'rob|a *m inv* wardrobe; (*di locale pubblico*) cloakroom. **~i'ere, -a** *mf* cloakroom attendant

gu'ardia *f* guard; (*poliziotto*) policeman; (*vigilanza*) watch; **essere di ~** be on guard; (medico:) be on duty; **fare la ~ a** keep guard over; **mettere in ~ qcno** warn sb. **~ carceraria** prison warder. **~ del corpo** bodyguard. **~ di finanza** ≈ Fraud Squad. **~ forestale** forest ranger. **~ medica** duty doctor

guardi'ano, -a *mf* caretaker. **~ notturno** night watchman

guar'dingo *adj* cautious

guardi'ola *f* gatekeeper's lodge

guarigi'one *f* recovery

gua'rire *vt* cure • *vi* recover; (ferita:) heal [up]

guarnigi'one *f* garrison

guar'ni|re *vt* trim; (*Culin*) garnish. **~zi'one** *f* trimming; (*Culin*) garnish; (*Mech*) gasket

gua'star|e *vt* spoil; (*rovinare*) ruin; break (meccanismo). **~si** *vr* spoil; (*andare a male*) go bad; (tempo:) change for the worse; (meccanismo:) break down. **gu'asto** *adj* broken; (ascensore, telefono) out of order; (auto) broken down; (cibo, dente) bad • *m* breakdown; (*danno*) damage

guazza'buglio *m* muddle

guaz'zare *vi* wallow

gu'ercio *adj* cross-eyed

gu'err|a *f* war; (*tecnica bellica*) warfare. **~ mondiale** world war. **~eggi'are** *vi* wage war. **guer'resco** *adj* (*di guerra*) war; (*bellicoso*) warlike. **~i'ero** *m* warrior

guer'rigli|a *f* guerrilla warfare. **~'ero, -a** *mf* guerrilla

'gufo *m* owl

'guglia *f* spire

gu'id|a *f* guide; (*direzione*) guidance; (*comando*) leadership; (*Auto*) driving; (*tappeto*) runner; **~a a destra/sinistra** right-/left-hand drive. **~a telefonica** telephone directory. **~a turistica** tourist guide. **gui'dare** *vt* guide; (*Auto*) drive; steer (nave). **~a'tore, ~a'trice** *mf* driver

guin'zaglio *m* leash

guiz'zare *vi* dart; (luce:) flash. **gu'izzo** *m* dart; (*di luce*) flash

'guscio *m* shell

gu'stare *vt* taste • *vi* like. **'gusto** *m* taste; (*piacere*) liking; **mangiare di gusto** eat well; **prenderci gusto** develop a taste for. **gu'stoso** *adj* tasty; *fig* delightful

guttu'rale *adj* guttural

habitué *mf inv* regular
ham'burger *m inv* hamburger
'handicap *m inv* handicap
handicap'pa|re *vt* handicap. **~to, -a** *mf* disabled person • *adj* disabled
'hascisc *m* hashish
henné *m* henna
hi-fi *m inv* hi-fi
'hippy *adj* hippy
hockey *m* hockey. **~ su ghiaccio** ice hockey. **~ su prato** hockey
hollywoodi'ano *adj* Hollywood
ho'tel *m inv* hotel

i *def art mpl* the; ▷**IL**
iber'na|re *vi* hibernate. **~zi'one** *f* hibernation
i'bisco *m* hibiscus
'ibrido *adj & m* hybrid
'iceberg *m inv* iceberg
i'cona *f* icon
Id'dio *m* God
i'dea *f* idea; (*opinione*) opinion; (*ideale*) ideal; (*indizio*) inkling; (*piccola quantità*) hint; (*intenzione*) intention; **cambiare ~** change one's mind; **neanche per ~!** not on your life!; **chiarirsi le idee** get one's ideas straight. **~ fissa** obsession
ide'a|le *adj & m* ideal. **~'lista** *mf* idealist. **~liz'zare** *vt* idealize
ide'a|re *vt* conceive. **~'tore, ~'trice** *mf* originator
'idem *adv* the same
i'dentico *adj* identical
identifi'cabile *adj* identifiable
identifi'ca|re *vt* identify. **~zi'one** *f* identification
identità *f inv* identity
ideolo'gia *f* ideology. **ideo'logico** *adj* ideological
idi'oma *m* idiom. **idio'matico** *adj* idiomatic
idi'ota *adj* idiotic • *mf* idiot. **idio'zia** *f* (*cosa stupida*) idiocy
idola'trare *vt* worship
idoleggi'are *vt* idolize. **'idolo** *m* idol
idoneità *f* suitability; (*Mil*) fitness; **esame di ~** qualifying examination. **i'doneo** *adj* **idoneo a** suitable for; (*Mil*) fit for
i'drante *m* hydrant
idra'ta|nte *adj* (crema, gel) moisturizing. **~zi'one** *f* moisturizing
i'draulico *adj* hydraulic • *m* plumber
'idrico *adj* water *attrib*
idrocar'buro *m* hydrocarbon
idroe'lettrico *adj* hydroelectric
i'drofilo *adj* ▷**COTONE**
i'drogeno *m* hydrogen
i'ella *f* [!] bad luck; **portare ~** be bad luck. **iel'lato** *adj* [!] jinxed, plagued by bad luck
i'ena *f* hyena
i'eri *adv* yesterday; **~ l'altro, l'altro ~** the day before yesterday; **~ pomeriggio** yesterday afternoon; **il giornale di ~** yesterday's paper
ietta|'tore, -'trice *mf* jinx. **~ tura** *f* (*sfortuna*) bad luck
igi'en|e *f* hygiene. **~ico** *adj* hygienic. **igie'nista** *mf* hygienist
i'gnaro *adj* unaware
i'gnobile *adj* base; (*non onorevole*) dishonourable
igno'ran|te *adj* ignorant • *mf* ignoramus. **~za** *f* ignorance
igno'rare *vt* (*non sapere*) be unaware of; (*trascurare*) ignore
i'gnoto *adj* unknown

il *def art m* the

> **!** L'articolo determinativo in inglese non si usa quando si parla in generale: **Il latte fa bene** milk is good for you

····➤ **il signor Magnetti** Mr Magnetti; **il dottor Piazza** Dr Piazza; **ha il naso storto** he has a bent nose; **mettiti il cappello** put your hat on; **il lunedì** on Mondays; **il 1986** 1986; **5 euro il chilo** 5 euros a kilo

'ilar|e *adj* merry. **~ità** *f* hilarity
illazi'one *f* inference
illecita'mente *adv* illicitly. **il'lecito** *adj* illicit
ille'gal|e *adj* illegal. **~ità** *f* illegality. **~'mente** *adv* illegally
illeg'gibile *adj* illegible; (libro) unreadable
illegittimità *f* illegitimacy. **ille'gittimo** *adj* illegitimate
il'leso *adj* unhurt
illette'rato, -a *adj & mf* illiterate
illimi'tato *adj* unlimited
illivi'dire *vt* bruise • *vi* (*per rabbia*) become livid
il'logico *adj* illogical
il'luder|e *vt* deceive. **~si** *vr* deceive oneself
illumi'na|re *vt* light [up]; *fig* enlighten; **~re a giorno** floodlight. **~rsi** *vr* light up. **~zi'one** *f* lighting; *fig* enlightenment
Illumi'nismo *m* Enlightenment
illusi'one *f* illusion; **farsi illusioni** delude oneself
il'luso, -a *pp di* **illudere** • *adj* deluded • *mf* day-dreamer.
illu'stra|re *vt* illustrate. **~'tivo** *adj* illustrative. **~'tore, ~'trice** *mf* illustrator. **~zi'one** *f* illustration
il'lustre *adj* distinguished
imbacuc'ca|re *vt*, **~rsi** *vr* wrap up. **~to** *adj* wrapped up
imbal'la|ggio *m* packing. **~re** *vt* pack; (*Auto*) race
imbalsa'ma|re *vt* embalm; stuff (animale). **~to** *adj* embalmed; (animale) stuffed
imbambo'lato *adj* vacant
imbaraz'zante *adj* embarrassing
imbaraz'za|re *vt* embarrass; (*ostacolare*) encumber. **~to** *adj* embarrassed
imba'razzo *m* embarrassment; (*ostacolo*) hindrance; **trarre qcno d'~** help sb out of a difficulty. **~ di stomaco** indigestion
imbarca'dero *m* landing-stage
imbar'ca|re *vt* embark; (❗: *rimorchiare*) score. **~rsi** *vr* embark. **~zi'one** *f* boat. **~zione di salvataggio** lifeboat. **im'barco** *m* embarkation; (*banchina*) landing-stage
imba'sti|re *vt* tack; *fig* sketch. **~'tura** *f* tacking, basting
im'battersi *vr* **~ in** run into
imbat't|ibile *adj* unbeatable. **~uto** *adj* unbeaten
imbavagli'are *vt* gag
imbe'cille *adj* stupid • *mf* imbecile
imbel'lire *vt* embellish
imbestia'li|re *vi*, **~rsi** *vr* fly into a rage. **~to** *adj* enraged
im'bever|e *vt* imbue (**di** with). **~si** *vr* absorb
imbe'v|ibile *adj* undrinkable. **~uto** *adj* **~uto di** (acqua) soaked in; (nozioni) imbued with
imbian'c|are *vt* whiten • *vi* turn white. **~hino** *m* house painter
imbizzar'rir|e *vi*, **~si** *vr* become restless; (*arrabbiarsi*) get angry
imboc'ca|re *vt* feed; (*entrare*) enter; *fig* prompt. **~'tura** *f* opening; (*ingresso*) entrance; (*Mus: di strumento*) mouthpiece. **im'bocco** *m* entrance
imbo'scar|e *vt* hide. **~si** *vr* (*Mil*) shirk military service
imbo'scata *f* ambush
imbottigli'a|re *vt* bottle. **~rsi** *vr* get snarled up in a traffic jam. **~to** *adj* (vino, acqua) bottled
imbot'ti|re *vt* stuff; pad (giacca); (*Culin*) fill. **~rsi** *vr* **~rsi di** (*fig: di pasticche*) stuff oneself with. **~ta** *f* quilt. **~to** *adj* (spalle) padded; (cuscino) stuffed; (panino) filled. **~'tura** *f* stuffing; (*di giacca*) padding; (*Culin*) filling
imbra'nato *adj* clumsy
imbrat'tar|e *vt* mark. **~si** *vr* dirty oneself
imbroc'car|e *vt* hit; **~la giusta** hit the nail on the head
imbrogli|'are *vt* muddle; (*raggirare*) cheat. **im'broglio** *m* tangle; (*pasticcio*) mess; (*inganno*) trick. **~'one, -a** *mf* cheat
imbronci'a|re *vi*, **~rsi** *vr* sulk. **~to** *adj* sulky
imbru'nire *vi* get dark; **all'~** at dusk
imbrut'tire *vt* make ugly • *vi* become ugly

imbu'care *vt* post, mail; (*nel biliardo*) pot
imbur'rare *vt* butter
im'buto *m* funnel
imi'ta|re *vt* imitate. **~'tore, ~'trice** *mf* imitator. **~zi'one** *f* imitation
immaco'lato *adj* immaculate
immagazzi'nare *vt* store
immagi'na|re *vt* imagine; (*supporre*) suppose; **s'immagini!** imagine that!. **~rio** *adj* imaginary. **~zi'one** *f* imagination. **im'magine** *f* image; (*rappresentazione, idea*) picture
imman'cabil|e *adj* unfailing. **~'mente** *adv* without fail
im'mane *adj* huge; (*orribile*) terrible
imma'nente *adj* immanent
immangi'abile *adj* inedible
immatrico'la|re *vt* register. **~rsi** *vr* (studente:) matriculate. **~zi'one** *f* registration; (*di studente*) matriculation
immaturità *f* immaturity. **imma'turo** *adj* unripe; (persona) immature; (*precoce*) premature
immedesi'ma|rsi *vr* **~rsi in** identify oneself with. **~zi'one** *f* identification
immedia|ta'mente *adv* immediately. **~'tezza** *f* immediacy. **immedi'ato** *adj* immediate
immemo'rabile *adj* immemorial
immens|a'mente *adv* enormously. **~ità** *f* immensity. **im'menso** *adj* immense
immensu'rabile *adj* immeasurable
im'merger|e *vt* immerse. **~si** *vr* plunge; (sommergibile:) dive; **~si in** immerse oneself in
immersi'one *f* immersion; (*di sommergibile*) dive. **im'merso** *pp di* **immergere**
immi'gra|nte *adj & mf* immigrant. **~re** *vi* immigrate. **~to, -a** *mf* immigrant. **~zi'one** *f* immigration
immi'nen|te *adj* imminent. **~za** *f* imminence
immischi'ar|e *vt* involve. **~si** *vr* **~si in** meddle in
immis'sario *m* tributary
immissi'one *f* insertion
im'mobile *adj* motionless
im'mobili *mpl* real estate. **~'are** *adj* società **~are** building society, savings and loan *Am*
immobili|tà *f* immobility. **~z'zare** *vt* immobilize; (*Comm*) tie up
immo'lare *vt* sacrifice
immondez'zaio *m* rubbish tip. **immon'dizia** *f* filth; (*spazzatura*) rubbish. **im'mondo** *adj* filthy
immo'ral|e *adj* immoral. **~ità** *f* immorality
immorta'lare *vt* immortalize. **immor'tale** *adj* immortal
immoti'vato *adj* (gesto) unjustified
im'mun|e *adj* exempt; (*Med*) immune. **~ità** *f* immunity. **~iz'zare** *vt* immunize. **~izzazi'one** *f* immunization
immunodefici'enza *f* immunodeficiency
immuso'ni|rsi *vr* sulk. **~to** *adj* sulky
immu'ta|bile *adj* unchangeable. **~to** *adj* unchanging
impacchet'tare *vt* wrap up
impacci'a|re *vt* hamper; (*disturbare*) inconvenience; (*imbarazzare*) embarrass. **~to** *adj* embarrassed; (*goffo*) awkward. **im'paccio** *m* embarrassment; (*ostacolo*) hindrance; (*situazione difficile*) awkward situation
im'pacco *m* compress
impadro'nirsi *vr* **~ di** take possession of; (*fig: imparare*) master
impa'gabile *adj* priceless
impagi'na|re *vt* paginate. **~zi'one** *f* pagination
impagli'are *vt* stuff (animale)
impa'lato *adj fig* stiff
impalca'tura *f* scaffolding; *fig* structure
impalli'dire *vi* turn pale; (*fig: perdere d'importanza*) pale into insignificance
impa'nare *vt* roll in breadcrumbs
impanta'narsi *vr* get bogged down
impape'rarsi, impappi'narsi *vr* falter, stammer
impa'rare *vt* learn
impareggi'abile *adj* incomparable
imparen'ta|rsi *vr* **~ con** become related to. **~to** *adj* related
'impari *adj* unequal; (*dispari*) odd
impar'tire *vt* impart
imparzi'al|e *adj* impartial. **~ità** *f* impartiality

impas'sibile *adj* impassive
impa'sta|re *vt* (*Culin*) knead; blend (colori). **im'pasto** *m* (*Culin*) dough; (*miscuglio*) mixture
im'patto *m* impact
impau'rir|e *vt* frighten. **~si** *vr* become frightened
im'pavido *adj* fearless
impazi'en|te *adj* impatient; **~te di fare qcsa** eager to do sth. **~'tirsi** *vr* lose patience. **~za** *f* impatience
impaz'zata *f* **all'~** full speed
impaz'zire *vi* go mad; (maionese:) separate; **far ~ qcno** drive sb mad; **~ per** be crazy about; **da ~** (mal di testa) blinding
i
impec'cabile *adj* impeccable
impedi'mento *m* hindrance; (*ostacolo*) obstacle
impe'dire *vt* **~ di** prevent from; (*impacciare*) hinder; (*ostruire*) obstruct; **~ a qcno di fare qcsa** prevent sb [from] doing sth
impe'gna|re *vt* (*dare in pegno*) pawn; (*vincolare*) bind; (*prenotare*) reserve; (*assorbire*) take up. **~rsi** *vr* apply oneself; **~rsi a fare qcsa** commit oneself to doing sth. **~'tiva** *f* referral. **~'tivo** *adj* binding; (lavoro) demanding. **~ato** *adj* engaged; (*Pol*) committed. **im'pegno** *m* engagement; (*Comm*) commitment; (*zelo*) care
impel'lente *adj* pressing
impen'na|rsi *vr* (cavallo:) rear; *fig* bristle. **~ta** *f* sharp rise; (*di cavallo*) rearing; (*di moto*) wheelie
impen'sa|bile *adj* unthinkable. **~to** *adj* unexpected
impensie'rir|e *vt*, **~si** *vr* worry
impe'ra|nte *adj* prevailing. **~re** *vi* reign; (tendenza:) prevail
impera'tivo *adj & m* imperative
impera'tore, -'trice *m* emperor ● *f* empress
impercet'tibile *adj* imperceptible
imperdo'nabile *adj* unforgivable
imper'fe|tto *adj & m* imperfect. **~zi'one** *f* imperfection
imperi'a|le *adj* imperial. **~'lismo** *m* imperialism
imperi'oso *adj* imperious; (*impellente*) urgent
impe'rizia *f* lack of skill
imperme'abile *adj* waterproof ● *m* raincoat
imperni'ar|e *vt* pivot; (*fondare*) base. **~si** *vr* **~si su** be based on
im'pero *m* empire; (*potere*) rule
imperscru'tabile *adj* inscrutable
imperso'nale *adj* impersonal
imperso'nare *vt* personify; (*interpretare*) act [the part of]
imper'territo *adj* undaunted
imperti'nen|te *adj* impertinent. **~za** *f* impertinence
imperver'sare *vi* rage
im'pervio *adj* inaccessible
'impet|o *m* impetus; (*impulso*) impulse; (*slancio*) transport. **~u'oso** *adj* impetuous; (vento) blustering
impet'tito *adj* stiff
impian'tare *vt* install; set up (azienda)
impi'anto *m* plant; (*sistema*) system; (*operazione*) installation. **~ radio** (*Auto*) car stereo system
impia'strare *vt* plaster; (*sporcare*) dirty. **impi'astro** *m* poultice; (*persona noiosa*) bore; (*pasticcione*) cack-handed person
impic'car|e *vt* hang. **~si** *vr* hang oneself
impicci|'arsi *vr* meddle. **im'piccio** *m* hindrance; (*seccatura*) bother. **~'one, -a** *mf* nosey parker
impie'ga|re *vt* employ; (*usare*) use; spend (tempo, denaro); *Fin* invest; **l'autobus ha ~to un'ora** it took the bus an hour. **~rsi** *vr* get [oneself] a job
impiega'tizio *adj* clerical
impie'gato, -a *mf* employee. **~ di banca** bank clerk. **impi'ego** *m* employment; (*posto*) job; *Fin* investment
impieto'sir|e *vt* move to pity. **~si** *vr* be moved to pity
impie'trito *adj* petrified
impigli'ar|e *vt* entangle. **~si** *vr* get entangled
impi'grir|e *vt* make lazy. **~si** *vr* get lazy
impli'ca|re *vt* implicate; (*sottintendere*) imply. **~rsi** *vr* become involved. **~zi'one** *f* implication
implicita'mente *adv* implicitly. **im'plicito** *adj* implicit

implo'ra|re *vt* implore. **~zi'one** *f* entreaty

impolve'ra|re *vt* cover with dust. **~rsi** *vr* get covered with dust. **~to** *adj* dusty

imponde'rabile *adj* imponderable; (causa, evento) unpredictable

impo'nen|te *adj* imposing. **~za** *f* impressiveness

impo'nibile *adj* taxable ● *m* taxable income

impopo'lar|e *adj* unpopular. **~ità** *f* unpopularity

im'por|re *vt* impose; (*ordinare*) order. **~si** *vr* assert oneself; (*aver successo*) be successful; **~si di** (*prefiggersi di*) set oneself the task of

impor'tan|te *adj* important ● *m* important thing. **~za** *f* importance

impor'ta|re *vt* import; (*comportare*) cause ● *vi* matter; (*essere necessario*) be necessary. **non ~!** it doesn't matter!; **non me ne ~ niente!** I couldn't care less!. **~'tore, ~'trice** *mf* importer. **~zi'one** *f* importation; (*merce importata*) import

im'porto *m* amount

importu'nare *vt* pester. **impor'tuno** *adj* troublesome; (*inopportuno*) untimely

imposizi'one *f* imposition; (*imposta*) tax

imposses'sarsi *vr* **~ di** seize

impos'sibil|e *adj* impossible ● *m* **fare l'~e** do absolutely all one can. **~ità** *f* impossibility

im'posta[1] *f* tax; **~ sul reddito** income tax; **~ sul valore aggiunto** value added tax

im'posta[2] *f* (*di finestra*) shutter

impo'sta|re *vt* (*progettare*) plan; (*basare*) base; (*Mus*) pitch; (*imbucare*) post, mail; set out (domanda, problema). **~zi'one** *f* planning; (*di voce*) pitching

im'posto *pp di* **imporre**

impo'store, -a *mf* impostor

impo'ten|te *adj* powerless; (*Med*) impotent. **~za** *f* powerlessness; (*Med*) impotence

impove'rir|e *vt* impoverish. **~si** *vr* become poor

imprati'cabile *adj* impracticable; (strada) impassable

imprati'chir|e *vt* train. **~si** *vr* **~si in** *o* **a** get practice in

impre'care *vi* curse

impreci's|abile *adj* indeterminable. **~ato** *adj* indeterminate. **~i'one** *f* inaccuracy. **impre'ciso** *adj* inaccurate

impre'gnar|e *vt* impregnate; (*imbevere*) soak; *fig* imbue. **~si** *vr* become impregnated with

imprendi'tor|e, -'trice *mf* entrepreneur. **~i'ale** *adj* entrepreneurial

imprepa'rato *adj* unprepared

im'presa *f* undertaking; (*gesta*) exploit; (*azienda*) firm

impre'sario *m* impresario; (*appaltatore*) contractor

imprescin'dibile *adj* inescapable

impressio'na|bile *adj* impressionable. **~nte** *adj* impressive; (*spaventoso*) frightening

impressi|o'nare *vt* impress; (*spaventare*) frighten; expose (foto). **~o'narsi** *vr* be affected; (*spaventarsi*) be frightened. **~'one** *f* impression; (*sensazione*) sensation; (*impronta*) mark; **far ~one a qcno** upset sb

impressio'nis|mo *m* impressionism. **~ta** *mf* impressionist

im'presso *pp di* **imprimere** ● *adj* printed

impre'stare *vt* lend

impreve'dibile *adj* unforeseeable; (persona) unpredictable

imprevi'dente *adj* improvident

impre'visto *adj* unforeseen ● *m* unforeseen event

imprigio|na'mento *m* imprisonment. **~'nare** *vt* imprison

im'primere *vt* impress; (*stampare*) print; (*comunicare*) impart

impro'babil|e *adj* unlikely, improbable. **~ità** *f* improbability

improdut'tivo *adj* unproductive

im'pronta *f* impression; *fig* mark. **~ digitale** fingerprint. **~ del piede** footprint

impro'perio *m* insult; **improperi** *pl* abuse *sg*

im'proprio *adj* improper

improvvi'sa|re *vt/i* improvise. **~rsi** *vr* turn oneself into a. **~ta** *f* surprise. **~zi'one** *f* improvisation

i

improv'viso *adj* sudden; **all'~** unexpectedly
impru'den|te *adj* imprudent. **~za** *f* imprudence
impu'gna|re *vt* grasp; (*Jur*) contest. **~'tura** *f* grip; (*manico*) handle
impulsività *f* impulsiveness. **impul'sivo** *adj* impulsive
im'pulso *m* impulse; **agire d'~** act on impulse
impune'mente *adv* with impunity. **impu'nito** *adj* unpunished
impun'tura *f* stitching
impurità *f inv* impurity. **im'puro** *adj* impure
impu'tabile *adj* attributable (**a** to)
i
impu'ta|re *vt* attribute; (*accusare*) charge. **~to, -a** *mf* accused. **~zi'one** *f* charge
imputri'dire *vi* rot
in *prep* in; (*moto a luogo*) to; (*su*) on; (*entro*) within; (*mezzo*) by; (*con materiale*) made of; **essere in casa/ufficio** be at home/at the office; **in mano/tasca** in one's hand/pocket; **andare in Francia/campagna** go to France/the country; **salire in treno** get on the train; **versa la birra nel bicchiere** pour the beer into the glass; **in alto** up there; **in giornata** within the day; **nel 1997** in 1997; **una borsa in pelle** a bag made of leather, a leather bag; **in macchina** (viaggiare, venire) by car; **in contanti** [in] cash; **in vacanza** on holiday; **se fossi in te** if I were you; **siamo in sette** there are seven of us
inabbor'dabile *adj* unapproachable
i'nabil|e *adj* incapable; (*fisicamente*) unfit. **~ità** *f* incapacity
inabi'tabile *adj* uninhabitable
inacces'sibile *adj* inaccessible; (persona) unapproachable
inaccet'tabil|e *adj* unacceptable. **~ità** *f* unacceptability
inacer'bi|re *vt* embitter; exacerbate (rapporto). **~si** *vr* grow bitter
inaci'dir|e *vt* turn sour. **~si** *vr* go sour; (persona:) become bitter
ina'datto *adj* unsuitable
inadegu'ato *adj* inadequate
inadempi|'ente *mf* defaulter. **~'mento** *m* nonfulfilment
inaffer'rabile *adj* elusive
ina'la|re *vt* inhale. **~'tore** *m* inhaler. **~zi'one** *f* inhalation
inalbe'rar|e *vt* hoist. **~si** *vr* (cavallo:) rear [up]; (*adirarsi*) lose one's temper
inalte'ra|bile *adj* unchangeable; (colore) fast. **~to** *adj* unchanged
inami'da|re *vt* starch. **~to** *adj* starched
inammis'sibile *adj* inadmissible
inamovi'bile *adj* irremovable
inani'mato *adj* inanimate; (*senza vita*) lifeless
inappa'ga|bile *adj* unsatisfiable. **~to** *adj* unfulfilled
inappe'tenza *f* lack of appetite
inappli'cabile *adj* inapplicable
inappun'tabile *adj* faultless
inar'car|e *vt* arch; raise (sopracciglia). **~si** *vr* (legno:) warp; (ripiano:) sag; (linea:) curve
inari'dir|e *vt* parch; empty of feelings (persona). **~si** *vr* dry up; (persona:) become empty of feelings
inartico'lato *adj* inarticulate
inaspettata'mente *adv* unexpectedly. **inaspet'tato** *adj* unexpected
inaspri'mento *m* embitterment; (*di conflitto*) worsening
ina'sprir|e *vt* embitter. **~si** *vr* become embittered
inattac'cabile *adj* unassailable; (*irreprensibile*) irreproachable
inatten'dibile *adj* unreliable. **inat'teso** *adj* unexpected
inattività *f* inactivity. **inat'tivo** *adj* inactive
inattu'abile *adj* impracticable
inau'dito *adj* unheard of
inaugu'rale *adj* inaugural; **viaggio ~** maiden voyage
inaugu'ra|re *vt* inaugurate; open (mostra); unveil (statua); christen (lavastoviglie ecc). **~zi'one** *f* inauguration; (*di mostra*) opening; (*di statua*) unveiling
inavver't|enza *f* inadvertence. **~ita'mente** *adv* inadvertently
incagli'ar|e *vi* ground • *vt* hinder. **~si** *vr* run aground
incalco'labile *adj* incalculable
incal'li|rsi *vr* grow callous; (*abituarsi*)

become hardened. **~to** *adj* callous; (*abituato*) hardened

incal'za|nte *adj* (ritmo) driving; (richiesta) urgent. **~re** *vt* pursue; *fig* press

incame'rare *vt* appropriate

incammi'nar|e *vt* get going; (*fig: guidare*) set off. **~si** *vr* set out

incana'lar|e *vt* canalize; *fig* channel. **~si** *vr* converge on

incande'scen|te *adj* incandescent; (discussione) burning

incan'ta|re *vt* enchant. **~rsi** *vr* stand spellbound; (*incepparsi*) jam. **~'tore, ~'trice** *m* enchanter ● *f* enchantress

incan'tesimo *m* spell

incan'tevole *adj* enchanting

in'canto *m* spell; *fig* delight; (*asta*) auction; **come per ~** as if by magic

incanu'ti|re *vt* turn white. **~to** *adj* white

inca'pac|e *adj* incapable. **~ità** *f* incapability

incapo'nirsi *vr* be set (**a fare** on doing)

incap'pare *vi* **~ in** run into

incappucci'arsi *vr* wrap up

incapricci'arsi *vr* **~ di** take a fancy to

incapsu'lare *vt* seal; crown (dente)

incarce'ra|re *vt* imprison. **~zi'one** *f* imprisonment

incari'ca|re *vt* charge. **~rsi** *vr* take upon oneself; **me ne incarico io** I will see to it. **~to, -a** *adj* in charge ● *mf* representative. **in'carico** *m* charge; **per incarico di** on behalf of

incar'na|re *vt* embody. **~rsi** *vr* become incarnate

incarta'mento *m* documents *pl*. **in-car'tare** *vt* wrap [in paper]

incas'sa|re *vt* pack; (*Mech*) embed; box in (mobile, frigo); (*riscuotere*) cash; take (colpo). **~to** *adj* set; (fiume) deeply embanked. **in'casso** *m* collection; (*introito*) takings *pl*

incasto'na|re *vt* set. **~'tura** *f* setting. **~to** *adj* embedded; (anello) inset (**di** with)

inca'strar|e *vt* fit in; ([!]: *in situazione*) corner. **~si** *vr* fit. **in'castro** *m* joint; **a incastro** (pezzi) interlocking

incate'nare *vt* chain

incatra'mare *vt* tar

incatti'vire *vt* turn nasty

in'cauto *adj* imprudent

inca'va|re *vt* hollow out. **~to** *adj* hollow. **~'tura** *f* hollow. **in'cavo** *m* hollow; (*scanalatura*) groove

incendi'ar|e *vt* set fire to; *fig* inflame. **~si** *vr* catch fire. **~io, -a** *adj* incendiary; *fig*: (discorso) inflammatory; *fig*: (bellezza) sultry ● *mf* arsonist. **in'cendio** *m* fire. **incendio doloso** arson

incene'ri|re *vt* burn to ashes; (*cremare*) cremate. **~rsi** *vr* be burnt to ashes. **~'tore** *m* incinerator

in'censo *m* incense

incensu'rato *adj* blameless; **essere ~** (*Jur*) have a clean record

incenti'vare *vt* motivate. **incen'tivo** *m* incentive

incen'trarsi *vr* **~ su** centre on

incep'par|e *vt* block; *fig* hamper. **~si** *vr* jam

ince'rata *f* oilcloth

incerot'tato *adj* with a plaster on

incer'tezza *f* uncertainty. **in'certo** *adj* uncertain ● *m* uncertainty

inces'sante *adj* unceasing. **~'mente** *adv* incessantly

in'cest|o *m* incest. **~u'oso** *adj* incestuous

in'cetta *f* buying up; **fare ~ di** stockpile

inchi'esta *f* investigation

inchi'nar|e *vt*, **~si** *vr* bow. **in'chino** *m* bow; (*di donna*) curtsy

inchio'dare *vt* nail; nail down (coperchio); **~ a letto** (malattia:) confine to bed

inchi'ostro *m* ink

inciam'pare *vi* stumble; **~ in** (*imbattersi*) run into. **inci'ampo** *m* hindrance

inciden'tale *adj* incidental

inci'den|te *m* (*episodio*) incident; (*infortunio*) accident. **~za** *f* incidence

in'cidere *vt* cut; (*arte*) engrave; (*registrare*) record ● *vi* **~ su** (*gravare*) weigh upon

in'cinta *adj* pregnant

incipi'ente *adj* incipient

incipri'ar|e *vt* powder. **~si** *vr* powder one's face

in'circa *adv* **all'~** more or less

i

incisi'one *f* incision; (*arte*) engraving; (*acquaforte*) etching; (*registrazione*) recording

inci'sivo *adj* incisive ● *m* (*dente*) incisor

in'ciso *m* **per ~** incidentally

incita'mento *m* incitement. **inci'tare** *vt* incite

inci'vil|e *adj* uncivilized; (*maleducato*) impolite. **~tà** *f* barbarism; (*maleducazione*) rudeness

incle'men|te *adj* harsh

incli'nabile *adj* reclining

incli'na|re *vt* tilt ● *vi* **~re a** be inclined to. **~rsi** *vr* list. **~to** *adj* tilted; (terreno) sloping. **~zi'one** *f* slope, inclination. **in'cline** *adj* inclined

i

in'clu|dere *vt* include; (*allegare*) enclose. **~si'one** *f* inclusion. **~'sivo** *adj* inclusive. **~so** *pp di* **includere** ● *adj* included; (*compreso*) inclusive; (*allegato*) enclosed

incoe'ren|te *adj* (*contraddittorio*) inconsistent. **~za** *f* inconsistency

in'cognit|a *f* unknown quantity. **~o** *adj* unknown ● *m* **in ~o** incognito

incol'lar|e *vt* stick; (*con colla liquida*) glue. **~si** *vr* stick to; **~si a qcno** stick close to sb

incolle'ri|rsi *vr* lose one's temper. **~to** *adj* enraged

incol'mabile *adj* (differenza) unbridgeable; (vuoto) unfillable

incolon'nare *vt* line up

inco'lore *adj* colourless

incol'pare *vt* blame

in'colto *adj* uncultivated; (persona) uneducated

in'colume *adj* unhurt

incom'ben|te *adj* impending. **~za** *f* task

in'combere *vi* **~ su** hang over; **~ a** (*spettare*) be incumbent on

incominci'are *vt/i* begin, start

incomo'dar|e *vt* inconvenience. **~si** *vr* trouble. **in'comodo** *adj* uncomfortable; (*inopportuno*) inconvenient ● *m* inconvenience

incompa'rabile *adj* incomparable

incompe'ten|te *adj* incompetent. **~za** *f* incompetence

incompi'uto *adj* unfinished

incom'pleto *adj* incomplete

incompren'si|bile *adj* incomprehensible. **~'one** *f* lack of understanding; (*malinteso*) misunderstanding. **incom'preso** *adj* misunderstood

inconce'pibile *adj* inconceivable

inconclu'dente *adj* inconclusive; (persona) ineffectual

incondizio|nata'mente *adv* unconditionally. **~'nato** *adj* unconditional

inconfes'sabile *adj* unmentionable

inconfon'dibile *adj* unmistakable

incongru'ente *adj* inconsistent

in'congruo *adj* inadequate

inconsa'pevol|e *adj* unaware; (*inconscio*) unconscious. **~'mente** *adv* unwittingly

inconscia'mente *adv* unconsciously. **in'conscio** *adj & m* (*Psych*) unconscious

inconsi'sten|te *adj* insubstantial; (notizia ecc) unfounded. **~za** *f* (*di ragionamento, prove*) flimsiness

inconsu'eto *adj* unusual

incon'sulto *adj* rash

incontami'nato *adj* uncontaminated

inconte'nibile *adj* irrepressible

inconten'tabile *adj* insatiable; (*esigente*) hard to please

inconti'nen|te *adj* incontinent. **~za** *f* incontinence

incon'trar|e *vt* meet; encounter, meet with (difficoltà). **~si** *vr* meet (**con qcno** sb)

incon'trario: **all'~** *adv* the other way around; (*in modo sbagliato*) the wrong way around

incontra'sta|bile *adj* incontrovertible. **~to** *adj* undisputed

in'contro *m* meeting; *Sport* match. **~ al vertice** summit meeting ● *prep* **~ a** towards; **andare ~ a qcno** go to meet sb; *fig* meet sb half way

inconveni'ente *m* drawback

incoraggi|a'mento *m* encouragement. **~'ante** *adj* encouraging. **~'are** *vt* encourage

incornici'a|re *vt* frame. **~'tura** *f* framing

incoro'na|re *vt* crown. **~zi'one** *f* coronation

incorpo'rar|e *vt* incorporate; (*mescolare*) blend. **~si** *vr* blend; (territori:) merge

incorreg'gibile *adj* incorrigible

in'correre *vt* ~ **in** incur; ~ **nel pericolo di...** run the risk of...
incorrut'tibile *adj* incorruptible
incosci'en|te *adj* unconscious; (*irresponsabile*) reckless ● *mf* irresponsible person. **~za** *f* unconsciousness; recklessness
inco'stan|te *adj* changeable; (persona) fickle. **~za** *f* changeableness; (*di persona*) fickleness
incre'dibile *adj* unbelievable, incredible
incredulità *f* incredulity. **in'credulo** *adj* incredulous
incremen'tare *vt* increase; (*intensificare*) step up. **incre'mento** *m* increase. **incremento demografico** population growth
incresci'oso *adj* regrettable
incre'spar|e *vt* ruffle; wrinkle (tessuto); make frizzy (capelli); **~e la fronte** frown. **~si** *vr* (acqua:) ripple; (tessuto:) wrinkle; (capelli:) go frizzy
incrimi'na|re *vt* indict; *fig* incriminate. **~zi'one** *f* indictment
incri'na|re *vt* crack; *fig* affect (amicizia). **~rsi** *vr* crack; (amicizia:) be affected. **~'tura** *f* crack
incroci'a|re *vt* cross ● *vi* (*Aeron, Naut*) cruise. **~rsi** *vr* cross. **~'tore** *m* cruiser
in'crocio *m* crossing; (*di strade*) crossroads *sg*
incrol'labile *adj* indestructible
incro'sta|re *vt* encrust. **~zi'one** *f* encrustation
incuba|'trice *f* incubator. **~zi'one** *f* incubation
'incubo *m* nightmare
in'cudine *f* anvil
incu'rabile *adj* incurable
incu'rante *adj* careless
incurio'sir|e *vt* make curious. **~si** *vr* become curious
incursi'one *f* raid. ~ **aerea** air raid
incurva'mento *m* bending
incur'va|re *vt*, **~rsi** *vr* bend. **~'tura** *f* bending
in'cusso *pp di* **incutere**
incusto'dito *adj* unguarded
in'cutere *vt* arouse
'indaco *m* indigo
indaffa'rato *adj* busy
inda'gare *vt/i* investigate
in'dagine *f* research; (*giudiziaria*) investigation. ~ **di mercato** market survey
indebi'tar|e *vt*, **~si** *vr* get into debt
in'debito *adj* undue
indeboli'mento *m* weakening
indebo'lir|e *vt*, **~si** *vr* weaken
inde'cen|te *adj* indecent. **~za** *f* indecency; (*vergogna*) disgrace
indeci'frabile *adj* indecipherable
indecisi'one *f* indecision. **inde'ciso** *adj* undecided
inde'fesso *adj* tireless
indefi'ni|bile *adj* indefinable. **~to** *adj* indefinite
indefor'mabile *adj* crushproof
in'degno *adj* unworthy
indelica'tezza *f* indelicacy; (*azione*) tactless act. **indeli'cato** *adj* indiscreet; (*grossolano*) indelicate
in'denn|e *adj* uninjured; (*da malattia*) unaffected. **~ità** *f inv* allowance; (*per danni*) compensation. **~ità di trasferta** travel allowance. **~iz'zare** *vt* compensate. **inden'nizzo** *m* compensation
indero'gabile *adj* binding
indeside'ra|bile *adj* undesirable. **~to** *adj* (figlio, ospite) unwanted
indetermi'na|bile *adj* indeterminable. **~'tezza** *f* vagueness. **~to** *adj* indeterminate
'Indi|a *f* India. **i~'ano, -a** *adj & mf* Indian; **in fila i~ana** in single file
indiavo'lato *adj* possessed; (*vivace*) wild
indi'ca|re *vt* show, indicate; (*col dito*) point at; (*far notare*) point out; (*consigliare*) advise. **~'tivo** *adj* indicative ● *m* (*Gram*) indicative. **~'tore** *m* indicator; (*Techn*) gauge; (*prontuario*) directory. **~zi'one** *f* indication; (*istruzione*) direction
'indice *m* (*dito*) forefinger; (*lancetta*) pointer; (*di libro, statistica*) index; (*fig: segno*) sign
indietreggi'are *vi* draw back; (*Mil*) retreat
indi'etro *adv* back, behind; **all'~** backwards; **avanti e ~** back and forth; **essere ~** be behind; (*mentalmente*) be backward; (*con pagamenti*) be in arrears; (*di orologio*) be slow; **fare marcia ~** reverse; **rimandare ~** send

back; **rimanere ~** be left behind; **torna ~!** come back!
indi'feso *adj* undefended; (*inerme*) helpless
indiffe'ren|te *adj* indifferent; **mi è ~te** it is all the same to me. **~za** *f* indifference
in'digeno, -a *adj* indigenous ● *mf* native
indi'gen|te *adj* needy. **~za** *f* poverty
indigesti'one *f* indigestion. **indi'gesto** *adj* indigestible
indi'gna|re *vt* make indignant. **~rsi** *vr* be indignant. **~to** *adj* indignant. **~zi'one** *f* indignation
indimenti'cabile *adj* unforgettable
indipen'den|te *adj* independent. **~te'mente** *adv* independently; **~temente dal tempo** regardless of the weather, whatever the weather. **~za** *f* independence
in'dire *vt* announce
indiretta'mente *adv* indirectly. **indi'retto** *adj* indirect
indiriz'zar|e *vt* address; (*mandare*) send; (*dirigere*) direct. **~si** *vr* direct one's steps. **indi'rizzo** *m* address; (*direzione*) direction
indisci'pli|na *f* lack of discipline. **~'nato** *adj* undisciplined
indi'scre|to *adj* indiscreet. **~zi'one** *f* indiscretion
indi'scusso *adj* unquestioned
indiscu'tibil|e *adj* unquestionable. **~'mente** *adv* unquestionably
indispen'sabile *adj* essential, indispensable
indispet'tir|e *vt* irritate. **~si** *vr* get irritated
indi'spo|rre *vt* antagonize. **~sto** *pp di* **indisporre** ● *adj* indisposed. **~sizi'one** *f* indisposition
indisso'lubile *adj* indissoluble
indistin'guibile *adj* indiscernible
indistinta'mente *adv* without exception. **indi'stinto** *adj* indistinct
indistrut'tibile *adj* indestructible
indistur'bato *adj* undisturbed
in'divia *f* endive
individu'a|le *adj* individual. **~'lista** *mf* individualist. **~lità** *f* individuality. **~re** *vt* individualize; (*localizzare*) locate; (*riconoscere*) single out
indi'viduo *m* individual
indivi'sibile *adj* indivisible. **indi'viso** *adj* undivided
indizi'a|re *vt* throw suspicion on. **~to, -a** *adj* suspected ● *mf* suspect. **in'dizio** *m* sign; (*Jur*) circumstantial evidence
'indole *f* nature
indolenzi'mento *m* stiffness
indolen'zi|rsi *vr* go stiff. **~to** *adj* stiff
indo'lore *adj* painless
indo'mani *m* **l'~** the following day
Indo'nesia *f* Indonesia
indo'rare *vt* gild
indos'sa|re *vt* wear; (*mettere addosso*) put on. **~'tore, ~'trice** *mf* model
in'dotto *pp di* **indurre**
indottri'nare *vt* indoctrinate
indovi'n|are *vt* guess; (*predire*) foretell. **~ato** *adj* successful; (*scelta*) well-chosen. **~ello** *m* riddle. **indo'vino, -a** *mf* fortune-teller
indubbia'mente *adv* undoubtedly. **in'dubbio** *adj* undoubted
indugi'ar|e *vi*, **~si** *vr* linger. **in'dugio** *m* delay
indul'gen|te *adj* indulgent. **~za** *f* indulgence
in'dul|gere *vi* **~gere a** indulge in. **~to** *pp di* **indulgere** ● *m* (*Jur*) pardon
indu'mento *m* garment; **indumenti** *pl* clothes
induri'mento *m* hardening
indu'rir|e *vt*, **~si** *vr* harden
in'durre *vt* induce
in'dustri|a *f* industry. **~'ale** *adj* industrial ● *mf* industrialist
industrializ'za|re *vt* industrialize. **~to** *adj* industrialized. **~zi'one** *f* industrialization
industri|'arsi *vr* try one's hardest. **~'oso** *adj* industrious
induzi'one *f* induction
inebe'tito *adj* stunned
inebri'ante *adj* intoxicating, exciting
i'nedia *f* starvation
i'nedito *adj* unpublished
ineffi'cace *adj* ineffective
inefficì'en|te *adj* inefficient. **~za** *f* inefficiency
ineguagli'abile *adj* incomparable

inegu'ale *adj* unequal; (superficie) uneven
inelut'tabile *adj* inescapable
ine'rente *adj* **~ a** concerning
i'nerme *adj* unarmed; *fig* defenceless
inerpi'carsi *vr* **~ su** clamber up; (pianta:) climb up
i'ner|te *adj* inactive; (*Phys*) inert. **~zia** *f* inactivity; (*Phys*) inertia
inesat'tezza *f* inaccuracy. **ine'satto** *adj* inaccurate; (*erroneo*) incorrect; (*non riscosso*) uncollected
inesau'ribile *adj* inexhaustible
inesi'sten|te *adj* non-existent. **~za** *f* non-existence
inesperi'enza *f* inexperience. **ine'sperto** *adj* inexperienced
inespli'cabile *adj* inexplicable
ine'sploso *adj* unexploded
inesti'mabile *adj* inestimable
inetti'tudine *f* ineptitude. **i'netto** *adj* inept; **inetto a** unsuited to
ine'vaso *adj* (pratiche) pending; (corrispondenza) unanswered
inevi'tabil|e *adj* inevitable. **~'mente** *adv* inevitably
i'nezia *f* trifle
infagot'tar|e *vt* wrap up. **~si** *vr* wrap [oneself] up
infal'libile *adj* infallible
infa'ma|re *vt* defame. **~'torio** *adj* defamatory
in'fam|e *adj* infamous; ([!]: *orrendo*) awful, shocking. **~ia** *f* infamy
infan'garsi *vr* get muddy
infan'tile *adj* children's; (ingenuità) childlike; *pej* childish
in'fanzia *f* childhood; (*bambini*) children *pl*; **prima ~** infancy
infar'cire *vi* pepper (discorso) (**di** with)
infari'na|re *vt* flour; **~re di** sprinkle with. **~'tura** *f fig* smattering
in'farto *m* coronary
infasti'dir|e *vt* irritate. **~si** *vr* get irritated
infati'cabile *adj* untiring
in'fatti *conj* as a matter of fact; (*veramente*) indeed
infatu'a|rsi *vr* become infatuated (**di** with). **~to** *adj* infatuated. **~zi'one** *f* infatuation
infe'condo *adj* infertile
infe'del|e *adj* unfaithful. **~tà** *f* unfaithfulness; **~** *pl* affairs
infe'lic|e *adj* unhappy; (*inappropriato*) unfortunate; (*cattivo*) bad. **~ità** *f* unhappiness
infel'tri|rsi *vr* get matted. **~to** *adj* matted
inferi'or|e *adj* (*più basso*) lower; (qualità) inferior • *mf* inferior. **~ità** *f* inferiority
inferme'ria *f* infirmary; (*di nave*) sick-bay
infermi'er|a *f* nurse. **~e** *m* [male] nurse
infermità *f* sickness. **~ mentale** mental illness. **in'fermo, -a** *adj* sick • *mf* invalid
infer'nale *adj* infernal; (*spaventoso*) hellish
in'ferno *m* hell; **va all'~!** go to hell!
infero'cirsi *vr* become fierce
inferri'ata *f* grating
infervo'rar|e *vt* arouse enthusiasm in. **~si** *vr* get excited
infe'stare *vt* infest
infet't|are *vt* infect. **~arsi** *vr* become infected. **~ivo** *adj* infectious. **in'fetto** *adj* infected. **infezi'one** *f* infection
infiac'chir|e *vt/i*, **~si** *vr* weaken
infiam'mabile *adj* [in]flammable
infiam'ma|re *vt* set on fire; (*Med, fig*) inflame. **~rsi** *vr* catch fire; (*Med*) become inflamed. **~zi'one** *f* (*Med*) inflammation
in'fido *adj* treacherous
infie'rire *vi* (*imperversare*) rage; **~ su** attack furiously
in'figger|e *vt* drive. **~si** *vr* **~si in** penetrate
infi'lar|e *vt* thread; (*mettere*) insert; (*indossare*) put on. **~si** *vr* slip on (vestito); **~si in** (*introdursi in*) slip into
infil'tra|rsi *vr* infiltrate. **~zi'one** *f* infiltration; (*d'acqua*) seepage; (*Med: iniezione*) injection
infil'zare *vt* pierce; (*infilare*) string; (*conficcare*) stick
'infimo *adj* lowest
in'fine *adv* finally; (*insomma*) in short
infinità *f* infinity; **un'~ di** masses of. **infi'nito** *adj* infinite; (*Gram*) infinitive • *m* infinite; (*Gram*) infinitive; (*Math*) in-

i

finity; **all'infinito** endlessly

infinocchi'are *vt* [!] hoodwink

infischi'arsi *vr* ~ **di** not care about; **me ne infischio** [!] I couldn't care less

in'fisso *pp di* **infiggere** ● *m* fixture; (*di porta, finestra*) frame

infit'tir|e *vt/i*, **~si** *vr* thicken

inflazi'one *f* inflation

infles'sibil|e *adj* inflexible. **~ità** *f* inflexibility

inflessi'one *f* inflexion

in'fli|ggere *vt* inflict. **~tto** *pp di* **infliggere**

influ'en|te *adj* influential. **~za** *f* influence; (*Med*) influenza

influen'za|bile *adj* (mente, opinione) impressionable. **~re** *vt* influence. **~to** *adj* (*malato*) with the flu

influ'ire *vi* ~ **su** influence

in'flusso *m* influence

info'carsi *vr* catch fire; (viso:) go red; (discussione:) become heated

infol'tire *vt/i* thicken

infon'dato *adj* unfounded

in'fondere *vt* instil

infor'care *vt* fork up; get on (bici); put on (occhiali)

infor'male *adj* informal

infor'ma|re *vt* inform. **~rsi** *vr* inquire (**di** about).

infor'matic|a *f* computing, IT. **~o** *adj* computer *attrib*

infor'ma|tivo *adj* informative. **infor'mato** *adj* informed; **male informato** ill-informed. **~'tore, ~'trice** *mf* (*di polizia*) informer. **~zi'one** *f* information (*solo sg*); **un'~zione** a piece of information

in'forme *adj* shapeless

infor'nare *vt* put into the oven

infortu'narsi *vr* have an accident.

infor'tu|nio *m* accident. **~nio sul lavoro** industrial accident

infos'sa|rsi *vr* sink; (guance, occhi:) become hollow. **~to** *adj* sunken, hollow

infradici'ar|e *vt* drench. **~si** *vr* get drenched; (*diventare marcio*) rot

infra'dito *m pl* (*scarpe*) flip-flops

in'frang|ere *vt* break; (*in mille pezzi*) shatter. **~ersi** *vr* break. **~'gibile** *adj* unbreakable

in'franto *pp di* **infrangere** ● *adj* shattered; (cuore) broken

infra'rosso *adj* infra-red

infrastrut'tura *f* infrastructure

infrazi'one *f* offence

infredda'tura *f* cold

infreddo'li|rsi *vr* feel cold. **~to** *adj* cold

infruttu'oso *adj* fruitless

infuo'ca|re *vt* make red-hot. **~to** *adj* burning

infu'ori *adv* **all'~** outwards; **all'~ di** except

infuri'a|re *vi* rage. **~rsi** *vr* fly into a rage. **~to** *adj* blustering

infusi'one *f* infusion. **in'fuso** *pp di* **infondere** ● *m* infusion

Ing. *abbr* ingegnere

ingabbi'are *vt* cage; (*fig: mettere in prigione*) jail

ingaggi'are *vt* engage; sign up (calciatori ecc); begin (lotta, battaglia). **in'gaggio** *m* engagement; (*di calciatore*) signing [up]

ingan'nar|e *vt* deceive; (*essere infedele a*) be unfaithful to. **~si** *vr* deceive oneself; **se non m'inganno** if I am not mistaken

ingan'nevole *adj* deceptive. **in'ganno** *m* deceit; (*frode*) fraud

ingarbugli'a|re *vt* entangle; (*confondere*) confuse. **~rsi** *vr* get entangled; (*confondersi*) become confused. **~to** *adj* confused

inge'gnarsi *vr* do one's best

inge'gnere *m* engineer. **ingegne'ria** *f* engineering

in'gegno *m* brains *pl*; (*genio*) genius; (*abilità*) ingenuity. **~sa'mente** *adv* ingeniously

ingelo'sir|e *vt* make jealous. **~si** *vr* become jealous

in'gente *adj* huge

ingenu|a'mente *adv* naïvely. **~ità** *f* naïvety. **in'genuo** *adj* ingenuous; (*credulone*) naïve

inge'renza *f* interference

inge'rire *vt* swallow

inges'sa|re *vt* put in plaster. **~'tura** *f* plaster

Inghil'terra *f* England

inghiot'tire *vt* swallow

in'ghippo *m* trick
ingial'li|re *vi*, **~rsi** *vr* turn yellow. **~to** *adj* yellowed
ingigan'tir|e *vt* magnify ● *vi*, **~si** *vr* grow to enormous proportions
inginocchi'a|rsi *vr* kneel [down]. **~to** *adj* kneeling. **~'toio** *m* prie-dieu
ingiù *adv* down; **all'~** downwards; **a testa ~** head downwards
ingi'un|gere *vt* order. **~zi'one** *f* injunction. **~zione di pagamento** final demand
ingi'uri|a *f* insult; (*torto*) wrong; (*danno*) damage. **~'are** *vt* insult; (*fare un torto a*) wrong. **~'oso** *adj* insulting
ingiu'stizia *f* injustice. **ingi'usto** *adj* unjust, unfair
in'glese *adj* English ● *m* Englishman; (*lingua*) English ● *f* Englishwoman
ingoi'are *vt* swallow
ingol'far|e *vt* flood (motore). **~si** *vr fig* get involved; (motore:) flood
ingom'bra|nte *adj* cumbersome. **~re** *vt* clutter up; *fig* cram (mente)
in'gombro *m* encumbrance; **essere d'~** be in the way
ingor'digia *f* greed. **in'gordo** *adj* greedy
ingor'gar|e *vt* block. **~si** *vr* be blocked [up]. **in'gorgo** *m* blockage; (*del traffico*) jam
ingoz'zar|e *vt* gobble up; (*nutrire eccessivamente*) stuff; fatten (animali)
ingra'na|ggio *m* gear; *fig* mechanism. **~re** *vt* engage ● *vi* be in gear
ingrandi'mento *m* enlargement
ingran'di|re *vt* enlarge; (*esagerare*) magnify. **~rsi** *vr* become larger; (*aumentare*) increase
ingras'sar|e *vt* fatten up; (*Mech*) grease ● *vi*, **~si** *vr* put on weight
ingrati'tudine *f* ingratitude. **in'grato** *adj* ungrateful; (*sgradevole*) thankless
ingredi'ente *m* ingredient
in'gresso *m* entrance; (*accesso*) admittance; (*sala*) hall; **~ gratuito/libero** admission free; **vietato l'~** no entry; no admittance
ingros'sar|e *vt* make big; (*gonfiare*) swell ● *vi*, **~si** *vr* grow big; (*gonfiare*) swell
in'grosso: **all'~** *adv* wholesale; (*pressappoco*) roughly
ingua'ribile *adj* incurable
'inguine *m* groin
ingurgi'tare *vt* gulp down
ini'bi|re *vt* inhibit; (*vietare*) forbid. **~to** *adj* inhibited. **~zi'one** *f* inhibition; (*divieto*) prohibition
iniet'tar|e *vt* inject. **~si** *vr* **~si di sangue** (occhi:) become bloodshot. **iniezi'one** *f* injection
inimic'arsi *vr* make an enemy of. **inimi'cizia** *f* enmity
inimi'tabile *adj* inimitable
ininter|rotta'mente *adv* continuously. **~'rotto** *adj* continuous
iniquità *f* iniquity. **i'niquo** *adj* iniquitous
inizi'are *vt* begin; (*avviare*) open; **~ qcno a qcsa** initiate sb in sth ● *vi* begin
inizia'tiva *f* initiative; **prendere l'~** take the initiative
inizi'a|to, -a *adj* initiated ● *mf* initiate; **gli ~ti** the initiated. **~'tore, ~'trice** *mf* initiator. **~zi'one** *f* initiation
i'nizio *m* beginning, start; **dare ~ a** start; **avere ~** get under way
innaffi'a|re *vt* water. **~'toio** *m* watering-can
innal'zar|e *vt* raise; (*erigere*) erect. **~si** *vr* rise
innamo'ra|rsi *vr* fall in love (**di** with). **~ta** *f* girl-friend. **~to** *adj* in love ● *m* boy-friend
in'nanzi *adv* (*stato in luogo*) in front; (*di tempo*) ahead; (*avanti*) forward; (*prima*) before; **d'ora ~** from now on ● *prep* (*prima*) before; **~ a** in front of. **~'tutto** *adv* first of all; (*soprattutto*) above all
in'nato *adj* innate
innatu'rale *adj* unnatural
inne'gabile *adj* undeniable
innervo'sir|e *vt* make nervous. **~si** *vr* get irritated
inne'scare *vt* prime. **in'nesco** *m* primer
inne'stare *vt* graft; (*Mech*) engage; (*inserire*) insert. **in'nesto** *m* graft; (*Mech*) clutch; (*Electr*) connection
inne'vato *adj* covered in snow

i

'inno *m* hymn. ~ **nazionale** national anthem

inno'cen|te *adj* innocent ~**te'mente** *adv* innocently

in'nocuo *adj* innocuous

inno'va|re *vt* make changes in. ~**'tivo** *adj* innovative. ~**'tore** *adj* trail-blazing. ~**zi'one** *f* innovation

innume'revole *adj* innumerable

ino'doro *adj* odourless

inoffen'sivo *adj* harmless

inol'trar|e *vt* forward. ~**si** *vr* advance

inol'trato *adj* late

i'noltre *adv* besides

inon'da|re *vt* flood. ~**zi'one** *f* flood

i

inope'roso *adj* idle

inoppor'tuno *adj* untimely

inorgo'glir|e *vt* make proud. ~**si** *vr* become proud

inorri'dire *vt* horrify ● *vi* be horrified

inosser'vato *adj* unobserved; (*non rispettato*) disregarded; **passare** ~ go unnoticed

inossi'dabile *adj* stainless

'inox *adj inv* (acciaio) stainless

inqua'dra|re *vt* frame; *fig* put in context (scrittore, problema). ~**rsi** *vr* fit into. ~**'tura** *f* framing

inqualifi'cabile *adj* unspeakable

inquie'tar|e *vt* worry. ~**si** get worried; (*impazientirsi*) get cross. **inqui'eto** *adj* restless; (*preoccupato*) worried. **inquie'tudine** *f* anxiety

inqui'lino, -a *mf* tenant

inquina'mento *m* pollution

inqui'na|re *vt* pollute. ~**to** *adj* polluted

inqui'rente *adj* (*Jur*) (magistrato) examining; **commissione** ~ commission of enquiry

inqui'si|re *vt/i* investigate. ~**to** *adj* under investigation. ~**'tore,** ~**'trice** *adj* inquiring ● *mf* inquisitor. ~**zi'one** *f* inquisition

insabbi'are *vt* shelve

insa'lat|a *f* salad. ~**a belga** endive. ~**i'era** *f* salad bowl

insa'lubre *adj* unhealthy

insa'nabile *adj* incurable

insangui'na|re *vt* cover with blood. ~**to** *adj* bloody

insa'po|re *adj* tasteless. ~**'rire** *vt* flavour

insa'puta *f* **all'**~ **di** unknown to

insazi'abile *adj* insatiable

insce'nare *vt* stage

inscin'dibile *adj* inseparable

insedia'mento *m* installation

insedi'ar|e *vt* install. ~**si** *vr* install oneself

in'segna *f* sign; (*bandiera*) flag; (*decorazione*) decoration; (*emblema*) insignia *pl*; (*stemma*) symbol. ~ **luminosa** neon sign

insegna'mento *m* teaching. **inse'gnante** *adj* teaching ● *mf* teacher

inse'gnare *vt/i* teach; ~ **qcsa a qcno** teach sb sth

insegui'mento *m* pursuit

insegu'i|re *vt* pursue. ~**'tore,** ~**'trice** *mf* pursuer

insemi'na|re *vt* inseminate. ~**zi'one** *f* insemination. ~**zione artificiale** artificial insemination

insena'tura *f* inlet

insen'sato *adj* senseless; (*folle*) crazy

insen'sibil|e *adj* insensitive; (braccio ecc) numb. ~**ità** *f* insensitivity

inseri'mento *m* insertion

inse'rir|e *vt* insert; place (annuncio); (*Electr*) connect. ~**si** *vr* ~**si in** get into. **in'serto** *m* file; (*in un film ecc*) insert

inservi'ente *mf* attendant

inserzi'o|ne *f* insertion; (*avviso*) advertisement. ~**'nista** *mf* advertiser

insetti'cida *m* insecticide

in'setto *m* insect

insicu'rezza *f* insecurity. **insi'curo** *adj* insecure

in'sidi|a *f* trick; (*tranello*) snare. ~**'are** *vt/i* lay a trap for. ~**'oso** *adj* insidious

insi'eme *adv* together; (*contemporaneamente*) at the same time ● *prep* ~ **a** [together] with ● *m* whole; (*completo*) outfit; (*Theat*) ensemble; (*Math*) set; **nell'**~ as a whole; **tutto** ~ all together; (bere) at one go

in'signe *adj* renowned

insignifi'cante *adj* insignificant

insi'gnire *vt* decorate

insinda'cabile *adj* final

insinu'ante *adj* insinuating

insinu'a|re *vt* insinuate. ~**rsi** *vr* pene-

trate; **~rsi in** *fig* creep into
in'sipido *adj* insipid
insi'sten|te *adj* insistent. **~te'mente** *adv* repeatedly. **~za** *f* insistence. **in'sistere** *vi* insist; (*perseverare*) persevere
insoddisfa'cente *adj* unsatisfactory
insoddi'sfa|tto *adj* unsatisfied; (*scontento*) dissatisfied. **~zi'one** *f* dissatisfaction
insoffe'ren|te *adj* intolerant. **~za** *f* intolerance
insolazi'one *f* sunstroke
inso'len|te *adj* rude, insolent. **~za** *f* rudeness, insolence; (*commento*) insolent remark
in'solito *adj* unusual
inso'lubile *adj* insoluble
inso'luto *adj* unsolved; (*non pagato*) unpaid
insol'v|enza *f* insolvency
in'somma *adv* in short; **~!** well really!; (*così così*) so so
in'sonn|e *adj* sleepless. **~ia** *f* insomnia
insonno'lito *adj* sleepy
insonoriz'zato *adj* soundproofed
insoppor'tabile *adj* unbearable
insor'genza *f* onset
in'sorgere *vi* revolt, rise up; (*sorgere*) arise; (difficoltà) crop up
insormon'tabile *adj* (ostacolo, difficoltà) insurmountable
in'sorto *pp di* **insorgere** • *adj* rebellious • *m* rebel
insospet'tabile *adj* unsuspected
insospet'tir|e *vt* make suspicious • *vi*, **~si** *vr* become suspicious
insoste'nibile *adj* untenable; (*insopportabile*) unbearable
insostitu'ibile *adj* irreplaceable
inspe'ra|bile *adj* **una sua vittoria è ~bile** there is no hope of him winning. **~to** *adj* unhoped-for
inspie'gabile *adj* inexplicable
inspi'rare *vt* breathe in
in'stabil|e *adj* unstable; (tempo) changeable. **~ità** *f* instability; (*di tempo*) changeability
instal'la|re *vt* install. **~rsi** *vr* settle in. **~zi'one** *f* installation
instau'ra|re *vt* found. **~rsi** *vr* become established. **~zi'one** *f* foundation
instra'dare *vt* direct
insù *adv* **all'~** upwards
insuc'cesso *m* failure
insudici'ar|e *vt* dirty. **~si** *vr* get dirty
insuffici'en|te *adj* insufficient; (*inadeguato*) inadequate • *m* (*Sch*) fail. **~za** *f* insufficiency; (*inadeguatezza*) inadequacy; (*Sch*) fail. **~za cardiaca** heart failure. **~za di prove** lack of evidence
insu'lare *adj* insular
insu'lina *f* insulin
in'sulso *adj* insipid; (*sciocco*) silly
insul'tare *vt* insult. **in'sulto** *m* insult
insupe'rabile *adj* insuperable; (*eccezionale*) incomparable
insussi'stente *adj* groundless
intac'care *vt* nick; (*corrodere*) corrode; draw on (capitale); (*danneggiare*) damage
intagli'are *vt* carve. **in'taglio** *m* carving
intan'gibile *adj* untouchable
in'tanto *adv* meanwhile; (*per ora*) for the moment; (*avversativo*) but; **~ che** while
intarsi'a|re *vt* inlay. **~to** *adj* **~to di** inset with. **in'tarsio** *m* inlay
inta'sa|re *vt* clog; block (traffico). **~rsi** *vr* get blocked. **~to** *adj* blocked
inta'scare *vt* pocket
in'tatto *adj* intact
intavo'lare *vt* start
inte'gra|le *adj* whole; **edizione ~le** unabridged edition; **pane ~le** wholemeal bread. **~nte** *adj* integral. **'integro** *adj* complete; (*retto*) upright
inte'gra|re *vt* integrate; (*aggiungere*) supplement. **~rsi** *vr* integrate. **~'tivo** *adj* (corso) supplementary. **~zi'one** *f* integration
integrità *f* integrity
intelaia'tura *f* framework
intel'letto *m* intellect
intellettu'al|e *adj & mf* intellectual. **~'mente** *adv* intellectually
intelli'gen|te *adj* intelligent. **~te'mente** *adv* intelligently. **~za** *f* intelligence
intelli'gibile *adj* intelligible
intempe'ranza *f* intemperance

intem'perie *fpl* bad weather
inten'den|te *m* superintendent. **~za** *f* **~za di finanza** inland revenue office
in'tender|e *vt* (*comprendere*) understand; (*udire*) hear; (*avere intenzione*) intend; (*significare*) mean. **~sela con** have an understanding with; **~si** *vr* (*capirsi*) understand each other; **~si di** (*essere esperto*) have a good knowledge of
intendi|'mento *m* understanding; (*intenzione*) intention. **~'tore, ~'trice** *mf* connoisseur
intene'rir|e *vt* soften; (*commuovere*) touch. **~si** *vr* be touched
intensifi'car|e *vt*, **~si** *vr* intensify
intensità *f* intensity. **inten'sivo** *adj* intensive. **in'tenso** *adj* intense
inten'tare *vt* start up; **~ causa contro qcno** bring *o* institute proceedings against sb
in'tento *adj* engrossed (**a** in) ● *m* purpose
intenzio|'nale *adj* intentional. **intenzi'one** *f* intention; **senza ~ne** unintentionally; **avere ~ne di fare qcsa** intend to do sth, have the intention of doing sth.
intenzio'nato *adj* **essere ~ a fare qcsa** have the intention of doing sth
intera'gire *vi* interact
intera'mente *adv* completely
intera|t'tivo *adj* interactive. **~zi'one** *f* interaction
interca'lare[1] *m* stock phrase
interca'lare[2] *vt* insert
intercambi'abile *adj* interchangeable
interca'pedine *f* cavity
inter'ce|dere *vi* intercede. **~ssi'one** *f* intercession
intercet'ta|re *vt* intercept; tap (telefono). **~zi'one** *f* interception. **~zione telefonica** telephone tapping
inter'city *m inv* inter-city
intercontinen'tale *adj* intercontinental
inter'correre *vi* (tempo:) elapse; (*esistere*) exist
inter'detto *pp di* **interdire** ● *adj* astonished; (*proibito*) forbidden; **rimanere ~** be taken aback
inter'di|re *vt* forbid; (*Jur*) deprive of civil rights. **~zi'one** *f* prohibition
interessa'mento *m* interest
interes'sante *adj* interesting; **essere in stato ~** be pregnant
interes'sa|re *vt* interest; (*riguardare*) concern ● *vi* **~re a** matter to. **~rsi** *vr* **~rsi a** take an interest in. **~rsi di** take care of. **~to, -a** *mf* interested party ● *adj* interested; **essere ~to** *pej* have an interest
inte'resse *m* interest; **fare qcsa per ~** do sth out of self-interest
inter'faccia *f* (*Comput*) interface
interfe'renza *f* interference
interfe'r|ire *vi* interfere
interiezi'one *f* interjection
interi'ora *fpl* entrails
interi'ore *adj* interior
inter'ludio *m* interlude
intermedi'ario, -a *adj & mf* intermediary
inter'medio *adj* in-between
inter'mezzo *m* (*Mus, Theat*) intermezzo
intermit'ten|te *adj* intermittent; (luce) flashing. **~za** *f* **luce a ~za** flashing light
interna'mento *m* internment; (*in manicomio*) committal
inter'nare *vt* intern; (*in manicomio*) commit [to a mental institution]
internazio'nale *adj* international
'Internet *f* Internet, internet
in'terno *adj* internal; (*Geog*) inland; (*interiore*) inner; (politica) national; **alunno ~** boarder ● *m* interior; (*di condominio*) flat; (*Teleph*) extension; *Cinema* interior shot; **all'~** inside
in'tero *adj* whole, entire; (*intatto*) intact; (*completo*) complete; **per ~** in full
interpel'lare *vt* consult
inter'por|re *vt* place (ostacolo). **~si** *vr* come between
interpre'ta|re *vt* interpret; (*Mus*) perform. **~zi'one** *f* interpretation; (*Mus*) performance. **in'terprete** *mf* interpreter; (*Mus*) performer
inter'ra|re *vt* (*seppellire*) bury; plant (pianta). **~to** *m* basement
interro'ga|re *vt* question; (*Sch*) test; examine (studenti). **~'tivo** *adj* interrogative; (sguardo) questioning; **punto ~tivo** question mark ● *m* question.

~'torio *adj & m* questioning. **~zi'one** *f* question; (*Sch*) oral [test]

inter'romper|e *vt* interrupt; (*sospendere*) stop; cut off (collegamento). **~si** *vr* break off

interrut'tore *m* switch

interruzi'one *f* interruption; **senza ~** non-stop. **~ di gravidanza** termination of pregnancy

interse|'care *vt*, **~'carsi** *vr* intersect. **~zi'one** *f* intersection

interur'ban|a *f* long-distance call. **~o** *adj* inter-city; **telefonata ~a** long-distance call

interval'lare *vt* space out. **inter'vallo** *m* interval; (*spazio*) space; (*Sch*) break. **intervallo pubblicitario** commercial break

interve'nire *vi* intervene; (*Med: operare*) operate; **~ a** take part in. **inter'vento** *m* intervention; (*presenza*) presence; (*chirurgico*) operation; **pronto intervento** emergency services

inter'vista *f* interview

intervi'sta|re *vt* interview. **~'tore, ~'trice** *mf* interviewer

in'tes|a *f* understanding; **cenno d'~a** acknowledgement. **~o** *pp di* **intendere** • *adj* **resta ~o che...** needless to say,...; **~i!** agreed!; **~o a** meant to

inte'sta|re *vt* head; write one's name and address at the top of (lettera); (*Comm*) register. **~rsi** *vr* **~rsi a fare qcsa** take it into one's head to do sth. **~'tario, -a** *mf* holder. **~zi'one** *f* heading; (*su carta da lettere*) letterhead

inte'stino *adj* (lotte) internal • *m* intestine

intima'mente *adv* intimately

inti'ma|re *vt* order; **~re l'alt a qcno** order sb to stop. **~zi'one** *f* order

intimida|'torio *adj* threatening. **~zi'one** *f* intimidation

intimi'dire *vt* intimidate

intimità *f* cosiness. **'intimo** *adj* intimate; (*interno*) innermost; (amico) close • *m* (*amico*) close friend; (*dell'animo*) heart

intimo'ri|re *vt* frighten. **~rsi** *vr* get frightened. **~to** *adj* frightened

in'tingere *vt* dip

in'tingolo *m* sauce; (*pietanza*) stew

intiriz'zi|re *vt* numb. **~rsi** *vr* grow numb. **~to** *adj* **essere ~to** (*dal freddo*) be perished

intito'lar|e *vt* entitle; (*dedicare*) dedicate. **~si** *vr* be called

intolle'rabile *adj* intolerable

intona'care *vt* plaster. **in'tonaco** *m* plaster

into'na|re *vt* start to sing; tune (strumento); (*accordare*) match. **~rsi** *vr* match. **~to** *adj* (persona) able to sing in tune; (colore) matching

intonazi'one *f* (*inflessione*) intonation; (*ironica*) tone

inton'ti|re *vt* daze; (gas:) make dizzy • *vi* be dazed. **~to** *adj* dazed

intop'pare *vi* **~ in** run into

in'toppo *m* obstacle

in'torno *adv* around • *prep* **~ a** around; (*circa*) about

intorpi'di|re *vt* numb. **~rsi** *vr* become numb. **~to** *adj* torpid

intossi'ca|re *vt* poison. **~rsi** *vr* be poisoned. **~zi'one** *f* poisoning

intralci'are *vt* hamper

in'tralcio *m* hitch; **essere d'~** be a hindrance (**a** to)

intrallaz'zare *vi* intrigue. **intral'lazzo** *m* racket

intramon'tabile *adj* timeless

intransi'gen|te *adj* uncompromising. **~za** *f* intransigence

intransi'tivo *adj* intransitive

intrappo'lato *adj* **rimanere ~** be trapped

intrapren'den|te *adj* enterprising. **~za** *f* initiative

intra'prendere *vt* undertake

intrat'tabile *adj* very difficult

intratte'n|ere *vt* entertain. **~ersi** *vr* linger. **~i'mento** *m* entertainment

intrave'dere *vt* catch a glimpse of; (*presagire*) foresee

intrecci'ar|e *vt* interweave; plait (capelli, corda). **~si** *vr* intertwine; (*aggrovigliarsi*) become tangled; **~e le mani** clasp one's hands

in'treccio *m* (*trama*) plot

intri'cato *adj* tangled

intri'gante *adj* scheming; (*affascinante*) intriguing

intri'ga|re *vt* entangle; (*incuriosire*) intrigue • *vi* intrigue, scheme. **~rsi** *vr*

i

meddle. **in'trigo** *m* plot; **intrighi** *pl* intrigues

in'triso *adj* **~ di** soaked in

intri'stirsi *vr* grow sad

intro'du|rre *vt* introduce; (*inserire*) insert; **~rre a** (*iniziare a*) introduce to. **~rsi** *vr* get in (**in** to). **~t'tivo** *adj* (pagine, discorso) introductory. **~zi'one** *f* introduction

in'troito *m* income, revenue; (*incasso*) takings *pl*

intro'metter|e *vt* introduce. **~si** *vr* interfere; (*interporsi*) intervene. **intromissi'one** *f* intervention

intro'vabile *adj* that can't be found; (prodotto) unobtainable

intro'verso, -a *adj* introverted ● *mf* introvert

intrufo'larsi *vr* sneak in

in'truglio *m* concoction

intrusi'one *f* intrusion. **in'truso, -a** *mf* intruder

intu'i|re *vt* perceive

intui|'tivo *adj* intuitive. **in'tuito** *m* intuition. **~zi'one** *f* intuition

inuguagli'anza *f* inequality

inu'mano *adj* inhuman

inu'mare *vt* inter

inumi'dir|e *vt* dampen; moisten (labbra). **~si** *vr* become damp

i'nutil|e *adj* useless; (*superfluo*) unnecessary. **~ità** *f* uselessness

inutiliz'za|bile *adj* unusable. **~to** *adj* unused

inva'dente *adj* intrusive

in'vadere *vt* invade; (*affollare*) overrun

invali'd|are *vt* invalidate. **~ità** *f* disability; (*Jur*) invalidity. **in'valido, -a** *adj* invalid; (*handicappato*) disabled ● *mf* disabled person

in'vano *adv* in vain

invari'abile *adj* invariable

invari'ato *adj* unchanged

invasi'one *f* invasion. **in'vaso** *pp di* **invadere. inva'sore** *adj* invading ● *m* invader

invecchia'mento *m* (*di vino*) maturation

invecchi'are *vt/i* age

in'vece *adv* instead; (*anzi*) but; **~ di** instead of

inve'ire *vi* **~ contro** inveigh against

inven'd|ibile *adj* unsaleable. **~uto** *adj* unsold

inven'tare *vt* invent

inventari'are *vt* make an inventory of. **inven'tario** *m* inventory

inven|'tivo, -a *adj* inventive ● *f* inventiveness. **~-'tore, ~'trice** *mf* inventor. **~zi'one** *f* invention

inver'nale *adj* wintry. **in'verno** *m* winter

invero'simile *adj* improbable

inversi'one *f* inversion; (*Mech*) reversal. **in'verso** *adj* inverse; (*opposto*) opposite ● *m* opposite

inverte'brato *adj & m* invertebrate

inver'ti|re *vt* reverse; (*capovolgere*) turn upside down.

investi'ga|re *vt* investigate. **~'tore** *m* investigator. **~zi'one** *f* investigation

investi'mento *m* investment; (*incidente*) crash

inve'sti|re *vt* invest; (*urtare*) collide with; (*travolgere*) run over; **~re qcno di** invest sb with. **~'tura** *f* investiture

invi'a|re *vt* send. **~to, -a** *mf* envoy; (*di giornale*) correspondent

invidi|a *f* envy. **~'are** *vt* envy. **~'oso** *adj* envious

invigo'rir|e *vt* invigorate. **~si** *vr* become strong

invin'cibile *adj* invincible

in'vio *m* dispatch; (*Comput*) enter

invipe'ri|rsi *vr* get nasty. **~to** *adj* furious

invi'sibil|e *adj* invisible. **~ità** *f* invisibility

invi'tante *adj* (piatto, profumo) enticing

invi'ta|re *vt* invite. **~to, -a** *mf* guest. **in'vito** *m* invitation

invo'ca|re *vt* invoke; (*implorare*) beg. **~zi'one** *f* invocation

invogli'ar|e *vt* tempt; (*indurre*) induce. **~si** *vr* **~si di** take a fancy to

involon|taria'mente *adv* involuntarily. **~'tario** *adj* involuntary

invol'tino *m* (*Culin*) beef olive

in'volto *m* parcel; (*fagotto*) bundle

in'volucro *m* wrapping

invulne'rabile *adj* invulnerable

inzacche'rare *vt* splash with mud

inzup'par|e *vt* soak; (*intingere*) dip. **~si** *vr* get soaked

'io *pers pron* I; **chi è? – [sono] io** who is it? – [it's] me; **l'ho fatto io [stesso]** I did it myself ● *m* **l'~** the ego

i'odio *m* iodine

I'onio *m* **lo ~** the Ionian [Sea]

i'osa: **a ~** *adv* in abundance

iperat'tivo *adj* hyperactive

ipermer'cato *m* hypermarket

iper'metrope *adj* long-sighted

ipertensi'one *f* high blood pressure

ip'no|si *f* hypnosis. **~tico** *adj* hypnotic. **~'tismo** *m* hypnotism. **~tiz'zare** *vt* hypnotize

ipoca'lorico *adj* low-calorie

ipocon'driaco, -a *adj & mf* hypochondriac

ipocri'sia *f* hypocrisy. **i'pocrita** *adj* hypocritical ● *mf* hypocrite

ipo'te|ca *f* mortgage. **~'care** *vt* mortgage

i'potesi *f inv* hypothesis; (*caso, eventualità*) eventuality. **ipo'tetico** *adj* hypothetical. **ipotiz'zare** *vt* hypothesize

'ippico, -a *adj* horse *attrib* ● *f* riding

ippoca'stano *m* horse-chestnut

ip'podromo *m* racecourse

ippo'potamo *m* hippopotamus

'ira *f* anger. **~'scibile** *adj* irascible

i'rato *adj* irate

'iride *f* (*Anat*) iris; (*arcobaleno*) rainbow

Ir'lan|da *f* Ireland. **~da del Nord** Northern Ireland. **i~'dese** *adj* Irish ● *m* Irishman; (*lingua*) Irish ● *f* Irishwoman

iro'nia *f* irony. **i'ronico** *adj* ironic[al]

irradi'a|re *vt/i* radiate. **~zi'one** *f* radiation

irraggiun'gibile *adj* unattainable

irragio'nevole *adj* unreasonable; (speranza, timore) irrational; (*assurdo*) absurd

irrazio'nal|e *adj* irrational. **~ità** *adj* irrationality

irre'a|le *adj* unreal. **~'listico** *adj* unrealistic. **~liz'zabile** *adj* unattainable. **~ltà** *f* unreality

irrecupe'rabile *adj* irrecoverable

irrego'lar|e *adj* irregular. **~ità** *f inv* irregularity

irremo'vibile *adj fig* adamant

irrepa'rabile *adj* irreparable

irrepe'ribile *adj* not to be found; **sarò ~** I won't be contactable

irrepren'sibile *adj* irreproachable

irrepri'mibile *adj* irrepressible

irrequi'eto *adj* restless

irresi'stibile *adj* irresistible

irrespon'sabil|e *adj* irresponsible. **~ità** *f* irresponsibility

irrever'sibile *adj* irreversible

irricono'scibile *adj* unrecognizable

irri'ga|re *vt* irrigate; (fiume:) flow through. **~zi'one** *f* irrigation

irrigidi'mento *m* stiffening

irrigi'dir|e *vt*, **~si** *vr* stiffen

irrile'vante *adj* unimportant

irrimedi'abile *adj* irreparable

irripe'tibile *adj* unrepeatable

irri'sorio *adj* derisive; (differenza, particolare, somma) insignificant

irri'ta|bile *adj* irritable. **~nte** *adj* aggravating

irri'ta|re *vt* irritate. **~rsi** *vr* get annoyed. **~to** *adj* irritated; (gola) sore. **~zi'one** *f* irritation

irrobu'stir|e *vt* fortify. **~si** *vr* get stronger

ir'rompere *vi* burst (**in** into)

irro'rare *vt* sprinkle

irru'ente *adj* impetuous

irruzi'one *f* **fare ~ in** burst into

i'scritto, -a *pp di* **iscrivere** ● *adj* registered ● *mf* member; **per ~** in writing

i'scriver|e *vt* register. **~si** *vr* **~si a** register at, enrol at (scuola); join (circolo ecc). **iscrizi'one** *f* registration; (*epigrafe*) inscription

i'sla|mico *adj* Islamic. **~'mismo** *m* Islam

I'slan|da *f* Iceland. **i~'dese** *adj* Icelandic ● *mf* Icelander

'isola *f* island. **le isole britanniche** the British Isles. **~ pedonale** pedestrian precinct. **~ spartitraffico** traffic island

iso'lante *adj* insulating ● *m* insulator

iso'la|re *vt* isolate; (*Electr, Mech*) insulate; (*acusticamente*) soundproof. **~to** *adj* isolated ● *m* (*di appartamenti*) block

ispes'sir|e *vt*, **~si** *vr* thicken

ispetto'rato *m* inspectorate. **ispet'tore** *m* inspector. **ispezio'nare** *vt* inspect. **ispezi'one** *f* inspection

'ispido *adj* bristly

ispi'ra|re *vt* inspire; suggest (idea, soluzione). **~rsi** *vr* **~rsi a** be based on. **~to** *adj* inspired. **~zi'one** *f* inspiration; (*idea*) idea

Isra'el|e *m* Israel. **i~i'ano, -a** *agg & mf* Israeli

istan'taneo, -a *adj* instantaneous ● *f* snapshot

i'stante *m* instant; **all'~** instantly

i'stanza *f* petition

i'sterico *adj* hysterical. **iste'rismo** *m* hysteria

isti'ga|re *vt* instigate; **~re qcno al male** incite sb to evil. **~zi'one** *f* instigation

istin'tivo *adj* instinctive. **i'stinto** *m* instinct; **d'istinto** instinctively

istitu'ire *vt* institute; (*fondare*) found; initiate (manifestazione)

isti'tu|to *m* institute; (*universitario*) department; (*Sch*) secondary school. **~to di bellezza** beauty salon. **~'tore, ~'trice** *mf* (*insegnante*) tutor; (*fondatore*) founder

istituzio'nale *adj* institutional. **istituzi'one** *f* institution

'istrice *m* porcupine

istru'i|re *vt* instruct; (*addestrare*) train; (*informare*) inform; (*Jur*) prepare. **~to** *adj* educated

istrut't|ivo *adj* instructive. **~ore, ~rice** *mf* instructor; **giudice ~ore** examining magistrate. **~oria** *f* (*Jur*) investigation. **istruzi'one** *f* education; (*indicazione*) instruction

I'tali|a *f* Italy. **i~'ano, -a** *adj & mf* Italian

> **i**
>
> **Italo-** Descendants of those who emigrated from Italy are often referred to as *italo-americani*, *italo-brasiliani*, etc. Massive emigration started in the 1870s, mainly from the north of Italy to South America. Buenos Aires and Sao Paulo have the highest concentrations of Italians outside Italy. Subsequently more and more southern Italians emigrated to the United States.

itine'rario *m* route, itinerary

itte'rizia *f* jaundice

'ittico *adj* fishing *attrib*

I.V.A. *f abbr* (imposta sul valore aggiunto) VAT

jack *m inv* jack

jazz *m* jazz. **jaz'zista** *mf* jazz player

jeep *f inv* jeep

'jolly *m inv* (*carta da gioco*) joker

ju'niores *mfpl Sport* juniors

Kk

ka'jal *m inv* kohl

kara'oke *m inv* karaoke

kara'te *m* karate

kg *abbr* (chilogrammo) kg

km *abbr* (chilometro) km

l' *def art mf* (*before vowel*) the; ▷**IL**

la *def art f* the; ▷**IL** ● *pron* (*oggetto, riferito a persona*) her; (*riferito a cosa, animale*) it; (*forma di cortesia*) you ● *m inv* (*Mus*) A

là *adv* there; **di là** (*in quel luogo*) in there; (*da quella parte*) that way; **eccolo là!** there he is!; **farsi più in là** (*far largo*) make way; **là dentro** in there; **là fuori** out there; **[ma] va là!** come off it!; **più in là** (*nel tempo*) later on; (*nello spazio*) further on

'labbro *m* (*pl f* (*Anat*) **labbra**) lip

labi'rinto *m* labyrinth; (*di sentieri ecc*) maze

labora'torio *m* laboratory; (*di negozio, officina ecc*) workshop

labori'oso *adj* industrious; (*faticoso*) laborious

labu'rista *adj* Labour ● *mf* member of the Labour Party

'lacca *f* lacquer; (*per capelli*) hairspray. **lac'care** *vt* lacquer

'laccio *m* noose; (*lazo*) lasso; (*trappola*) snare; (*stringa*) lace

lace'rante *adj* (grido) earsplitting

lace'ra|re *vt* tear; lacerate (carne). **~rsi** *vr* tear. **~zi'one** *f* laceration. **'lacero** *adj* torn; (*cencioso*) ragged

'lacri|ma *f* tear; (*goccia*) drop. **~'mare** *vi* weep. **~'mevole** *adj* tear-jerking

lacri'mogeno *adj* **gas ~** tear gas

la'cuna *f* gap. **lacu'noso** *adj* (preparazione, resoconto) incomplete

la'custre *adj* lake *attrib*

> i
>
> **Ladino** Ladin (*ladino* in Italian) is a direct descendant of the Latin spoken in the valleys in north-eastern Italy. Western Ladin is spoken in Alto Adige alongside German, and Eastern Ladin (also called Friulian) in Friuli-Venezia Giulia. Numbers of speakers are shrinking as gradually German or Italian predominate.

'ladro, -a *mf* thief; **al ~!** stop thief!; **~'cinio** *m* theft. **la'druncolo** *m* petty thief

'lager *m inv* concentration camp

laggiù *adv* down there; (*lontano*) over there

'lagna *f* ([!]: *persona*) moaning Minnie; (*film*) bore

la'gna|nza *f* complaint. **~rsi** *vr* moan; (*protestare*) complain (**di** about)

'lago *m* lake

la'guna *f* lagoon

'laico, -a *adj* lay; (vita) secular ● *m* layman ● *f* laywoman

'lama *f* blade ● *m inv* llama

lambic'carsi *vr* **~ il cervello** rack one's brains

lam'bire *vt* lap

lamé *m inv* lamé

lamen'tar|e *vt* lament. **~si** *vr* moan. **~si di** complain about

lamen'te|la *f* complaint. **~vole** *adj* mournful; (*pietoso*) pitiful. **la'mento** *m* moan

la'metta *f* **~ [da barba]** razor blade

lami'era *f* sheet metal

'lamina *f* foil. **~ d'oro** gold leaf

lami'na|re *vt* laminate. **~to** *adj* laminated ● *m* laminate; (*tessuto*) lamé

'lampa|da *f* lamp. **~da abbronzante** sunlamp. **~da a pila** torch. **~'dario** *m* chandelier. **~'dina** *f* light bulb

lam'pante *adj* clear

lampeggi'a|re *vi* flash. **~'tore** *m* (*Auto*) indicator

lampi'one *m* street lamp

'lampo *m* flash of lightning; (*luce*) flash; **lampi** *pl* lightning *sg*. **~ di genio** stroke of genius. **[cerniera] ~** zip [fastener], zipper *Am*

lam'pone *m* raspberry

'lana *f* wool; **di ~** woollen. **~ d'acciaio** steel wool. **~ vergine** new wool. **~ di vetro** glass wool

lan'cetta *f* pointer; (*di orologio*) hand

'lancia *f* spear; (*Naut*) launch

lanci'ar|e *vt* throw; (*da un aereo*) drop; launch (missile, prodotto); give (grido); **~e uno sguardo a** glance at. **~si** *vr* fling oneself; (*intraprendere*) launch out

lanci'nante *adj* piercing

'lancio *m* throwing; (*da aereo*) drop; (*di missile, prodotto*) launch. **~ del disco** discus [throwing]. **~ del giavellotto** javelin [throwing]

'landa *f* heath

lani'ero *adj* wool

lani'ficio *m* woollen mill

lan'terna *f* lantern; (*faro*) lighthouse

la'nugine *f* down

lapi'dare *vt* stone; *fig* demolish

lapi'dario *adj* (*conciso*) terse

'lapide *f* tombstone; (*commemorativa*) memorial tablet

'lapis *m inv* pencil

'lapsus *m inv* lapse, error

'lardo *m* lard

larga'mente *adv* widely

lar'ghezza *f* breadth; *fig* liberality. **~ di vedute** broadmindedness

'largo *adj* wide; (*ampio*) broad; (abito) loose; (*liberale*) liberal; (*abbondante*) generous; **stare alla larga** keep away; **~**

di manica *fig* generous; **~ di spalle/ vedute** broad-shouldered/-minded ● *m* width; **andare al ~** (*Naut*) go out to sea; **fare ~** make room; **farsi ~** make one's way; **al ~ di** off the coast of

'larice *m* larch

la'ringe *f* larynx. **larin'gite** *f* laryngitis

'larva *f* larva; (*persona emaciata*) shadow

la'sagne *fpl* lasagna *sg*

lasciapas'sare *m inv* pass

lasci'ar|e *vt* leave; (*rinunciare*) give up; (*rimetterci*) lose; (*smettere di tenere*) let go [of]; (*concedere*) let; **~e di fare qcsa** (*smettere*) stop doing sth; **lascia perdere!** forget it!; **lascialo venire** let him come. **~si** *vr* (*reciproco*) leave each other; **~si andare** let oneself go

'lascito *m* legacy

'laser *adj & m inv* **[raggio] ~** laser [beam]

lassa'tivo *adj & m* laxative

'lasso *m* **~ di tempo** period of time

lassù *adv* up there

'lastra *f* slab; (*di ghiaccio*) sheet; (*Phot, di metallo*) plate; (*radiografia*) X-ray [plate]

lastri'ca|re *vt* pave. **~to, 'lastrico** *m* pavement

la'tente *adj* latent

late'rale *adj* side *attrib*; (*Med, Techn ecc*) lateral; **via ~** side street

late'rizi *mpl* bricks

lati'fondo *m* large estate

la'tino *adj & m* Latin

lati'tan|te *adj* in hiding ● *mf* fugitive [from justice]

lati'tudine *f* latitude

'lato *adj* (*ampio*) broad; **in senso ~** broadly speaking ● *m* side; (*aspetto*) aspect; **a ~ di** beside; **dal ~ mio** (*punto di vista*) for my part; **d'altro ~** *fig* on the other hand

la'tra|re *vi* bark. **~to** *m* barking

la'trina *f* latrine

'latta *f* tin, can

lat'taio, -a *m* milkman ● *f* milkwoman

lat'tante *adj* breast-fed ● *mf* suckling

'latt|e *m* milk. **~e acido** sour milk. **~e condensato** condensed milk. **~e detergente** cleansing milk. **~e in polvere** powdered milk. **~e scremato** skimmed milk. **~eo** *adj* milky. **~e'ria** *f* dairy. **~i'cini** *mpl* dairy products. **~i'era** *f* milk jug

lat'tina *f* can

lat'tuga *f* lettuce

'laure|a *f* degree; **prendere la ~a** graduate. **~'ando, -a** *mf* final-year student

laure'a|rsi *vr* graduate. **~to, -a** *agg & mf* graduate

'lauro *m* laurel

'lauto *adj* lavish; **~ guadagno** handsome profit

'lava *f* lava

la'vabile *adj* washable

la'vabo *m* wash-basin

la'vaggio *m* washing. **~ automatico** (*per auto*) carwash. **~ a secco** dry-cleaning

la'vagna *f* slate; (*Sch*) blackboard

la'van|da *f* wash; (*Bot*) lavender; **fare una ~da gastrica** have one's stomach pumped. **~'daia** *f* washerwoman. **~de'ria** *f* laundry. **~deria automatica** launderette

lavan'dino *m* sink; (*[!] persona*) bottomless pit

lavapi'atti *mf inv* dishwasher

la'var|e *vt* wash; **~e i piatti** wash up. **~si** *vr* wash, have a wash; **~si i denti** brush one's teeth; **~si le mani** wash one's hands

lava'secco *mf inv* dry-cleaner's

lavasto'viglie *f inv* dishwasher

la'vata *f* wash; **darsi una ~** have a wash; **~ di capo** *fig* scolding

lava'tivo, -a *mf* idler

lava'trice *f* washing-machine

lavo'rante *mf* worker

lavo'ra|re *vi* work ● *vt* work; knead (pasta ecc); till (la terra); **~re a maglia** knit. **~'tivo** *adj* working. **~to** *adj* (pietra, legno) carved; (cuoio) tooled; (metallo) wrought. **~'tore, ~'trice** *mf* worker ● *adj* working. **~zi'one** *f* manufacture; (*di terra*) working; (*artigianale*) workmanship; (*del terreno*) cultivation. **lavo'rio** *m* intense activity

la'voro *m* work; (*faticoso, sociale*) labour; (*impiego*) job; (*Theat*) play; **mettersi al ~** set to work (**su** on). **~ a maglia** knitting. **~ nero** moonlighting. **~ straordinario** overtime. **~ a tempo pieno** full-time job. **lavori** *pl* **di**

casa housework. **lavori** *pl* **in corso** roadworks. **lavori** *pl* **stradali** roadworks

le *def art fpl* the; ▷**IL** ● *pers pron* (*oggetto*) them; (*a lei*) her; (*forma di cortesia*) you

le'al|e *adj* loyal. **~'mente** *adv* loyally. **~tà** *f* loyalty

'lebbra *f* leprosy

'lecca 'lecca *m inv* lollipop

leccapi'edi *mf inv pej* bootlicker

lec'ca|re *vt* lick; *fig* suck up to. **~rsi** *vr* lick; (*fig: agghindarsi*) doll oneself up; **da ~rsi i baffi** mouth-watering. **~ta** *f* lick

leccor'nia *f* delicacy

'lecito *adj* lawful; (*permesso*) permissible

'ledere *vt* damage; (*Med*) injure

'lega *f* league; (*di metalli*) alloy; **far ~ con qcno** take up with sb

le'gaccio *m* string; (*delle scarpe*) shoelace

le'gal|e *adj* legal ● *m* lawyer. **~ità** *f* legality. **~iz'zare** *vt* authenticate; (*rendere legale*) legalize. **~'mente** *adv* legally

le'game *m* tie; (*amoroso*) liaison; (*connessione*) link

lega'mento *m* (*Med*) ligament

le'gar|e *vt* tie; tie up (persona); tie together (due cose); (*unire, rilegare*) bind; alloy (metalli); (*connettere*) connect ● *vi* (*far lega*) get on well. **~si** *vr* bind oneself; **~si a qcno** become attached to sb

le'gato *m* legacy; (*Relig*) legate

lega'tura *f* tying; (*di libro*) binding

le'genda *f* legend

'legge *f* law; (*parlamentare*) act; **a norma di ~** by law

leg'genda *f* legend; (*didascalia*) caption. **leggen'dario** *adj* legendary

'leggere *vt/i* read

legge'r|ezza *f* lightness; (*frivolezza*) frivolity; (*incostanza*) fickleness. **~'mente** *adv* slightly

leg'gero *adj* light; (bevanda) weak; (*lieve*) slight; (*frivolo*) frivolous; (*incostante*) fickle

leg'gibile *adj* (scrittura) legible; (stile) readable

leg'gio *m* lectern; (*Mus*) music stand

legife'rare *vi* legislate

legio'nario *m* legionary. **legi'one** *f* legion

legisla|'tivo *adj* legislative. **~'tore** *m* legislator. **~'tura** *f* legislature. **~zi'one** *f* legislation

legittimità *f* legitimacy. **le'gittimo** *adj* legitimate; (*giusto*) proper; **legittima difesa** self-defence

'legna *f* firewood

le'gname *m* timber

'legno *m* wood; **di ~** wooden. **~ compensato** plywood. **le'gnoso** *adj* woody

le'gume *m* pod

'lei *pers pron* (*soggetto*) she; (*oggetto, con prep*) her; (*forma di cortesia*) you; **lo ha fatto ~ stessa** she did it herself

'lembo *m* edge; (*di terra*) strip

'lena *f* vigour

le'nire *vt* soothe

lenta'mente *adv* slowly

'lente *f* lens. **~ a contatto** contact lens. **~ d'ingrandimento** magnifying glass

len'tezza *f* slowness

len'ticchia *f* lentil

len'tiggine *f* freckle

'lento *adj* slow; (*allentato*) slack; (abito) loose

'lenza *f* fishing-line

len'zuolo *m* (*pl f* **lenzuola**) *m* sheet

le'one *m* lion; (*Astr*) Leo

leo'pardo *m* leopard

'lepre *f* hare

'lercio *adj* filthy

'lesbica *f* lesbian

lesi'nare *vt* grudge ● *vi* be stingy

lesio'nare *vt* damage. **lesi'one** *f* lesion

'leso *pp di* **ledere** ● *adj* injured

les'sare *vt* boil

'lessico *m* vocabulary

'lesso *adj* boiled ● *m* boiled meat

'lesto *adj* quick; (mente) sharp

le'tale *adj* lethal

le'targ|ico *adj* lethargic. **~o** *m* lethargy; (*di animali*) hibernation

le'tizia *f* joy

'lettera *f* letter; **alla ~** literally; **~ maiuscola** capital letter; **~ minuscola** small letter; **lettere** *pl* (*letteratura*) literature *sg*; (*Univ*) Arts; **dottore in lettere** BA, Bachelor of Arts

lette'rale *adj* literal

lette'rario *adj* literary

lette'rato *adj* well-read

lettera'tura *f* literature

let'tiga *f* stretcher

let'tino *m* cot; (*Med*) couch

'letto *m* bed. **~ a castello** bunkbed. **~ a una piazza** single bed. **~ a due piazze** double bed. **~ matrimoniale** double bed

letto'rato *m* (*corso*) ≈ tutorial

let'tore, -'trice *mf* reader; (*Univ*) language assistant ● *m* (*Comput*) disk drive. **~ di CD-ROM** CD-Rom drive

let'tura *f* reading

leuce'mia *f* leukaemia

'leva *f* lever; (*Mil*) call-up; **far ~** lever. **~ del cambio** gear lever

le'vante *m* East; (*vento*) east wind

le'va|re *vt* (*alzare*) raise; (*togliere*) take away; (*rimuovere*) take off; (*estrarre*) pull out; **~re di mezzo qcsa** get sth out of the way. **~rsi** *vr* rise; (*da letto*) get up; **~rsi di mezzo, ~rsi dai piedi** get out of the way. **~ta** *f* rising; (*di posta*) collection

l

leva'taccia *f* **fare una ~** get up at the crack of dawn

leva'toio *adj* **ponte ~** drawbridge

levi'ga|re *vt* smooth; (*con carta vetro*) rub down. **~to** *adj* (superficie) polished

levri'ero *m* greyhound

lezi'one *f* lesson; (*Univ*) lecture; (*rimprovero*) rebuke

lezi'oso *adj* (stile, modi) affected

li *pers pron mpl* them

lì *adv* there; **fin lì** as far as there; **giù di lì** thereabouts; **lì per lì** there and then

Li'bano *m* Lebanon

'libbra *f* (*peso*) pound

li'beccio *m* south-west wind

li'bellula *f* dragon-fly

libe'rale *adj* liberal; (*generoso*) generous ● *mf* liberal

libe'ra|re *vt* free; release (prigioniero); vacate (stanza); (*salvare*) rescue. **~rsi** *vr* (stanza:) become vacant; (*Teleph*) become free; (*da impegno*) get out of it; **~rsi di** get rid of. **~'tore, ~'trice** *adj* liberating ● *mf* liberator. **~zi'one** *f* liberation; **la L~zione** Liberation Day

'liber|o *adj* free; (strada) clear. **~o docente** qualified university lecturer. **~o professionista** selfemployed person. **~tà** *f inv* freedom; (*di prigioniero*) release. **~tà provvisoria** (*Jur*) bail; **~tà** *pl* (*confidenze*) liberties

'liberty *m & adj inv* Art Nouveau

'Libi|a *f* Libya. **l~co, -a** *adj & mf* Libyan

libra'io *m* bookseller

libre'ria *f* (*negozio*) bookshop; (*mobile*) bookcase; (*biblioteca*) library

li'bretto *m* booklet; (*Mus*) libretto. **~ degli assegni** cheque book. **~ di circolazione** logbook. **~ d'istruzioni** instruction booklet. **~ di risparmio** bankbook. **~ universitario** *student record of exam results*

'libro *m* book. **~ giallo** thriller. **~ paga** payroll

lice'ale *mf* secondary-school student ● *adj* secondary-school *attrib*

li'cenza *f* licence; (*permesso*) permission; (*Mil*) leave; (*Sch*) school-leaving certificate; **essere in ~** be on leave

licenzia'mento *m* dismissal

licenzi'a|re *vt* dismiss, sack [!]. **~rsi** *vr* (*da un impiego*) resign; (*accomiatarsi*) take one's leave

li'ceo *m* secondary school. **~ classico** *secondary school emphasizing humanities*. **~ scientifico** *secondary school emphasizing science*

> *i*
>
> **Liceo** There are two main types of secondary school in Italy: the *licei*, which offer an academic syllabus, and the *istituti*, which have a more vocational syllabus, offering subjects like accountancy, electronics, and catering. *Licei* may specialize in particular subjects such as science, languages or classical studies.

'lido *m* beach

li'eto *adj* glad; (evento) happy; **molto ~!** pleased to meet you!

li'eve *adj* light; (*debole*) faint; (*trascurabile*) slight

lievi'tare *vi* rise ● *vt* leaven. **li'evito** *m* yeast. **lievito in polvere** baking powder

'lifting *m inv* face-lift

'ligio *adj* **essere ~ al dovere** have a sense of duty

'lilla¹ (*colore*) lilac

'lillà² *m inv* (*Bot*) lilac

'lima *f* file

limacci'oso *adj* slimy

li'mare *vt* file

li'metta *f* nail-file

limi'ta|re *m* threshold ● *vt* limit. **~rsi** *vr* **~rsi a fare qcsa** restrict oneself to doing sth; **~rsi in qcsa** cut down on sth. **~'tivo** *adj* limiting. **~zi'one** *f* limitation

'limite *m* limit; (*confine*) boundary. **~ di velocità** speed limit

li'mitrofo *adj* neighbouring

limo'nata *f* (*bibita*) lemonade; (*succo*) lemon juice

li'mone *m* lemon; (*albero*) lemon tree

'limpido *adj* clear; (occhi) limpid

'lince *f* lynx

linci'are *vt* lynch

'lindo *adj* neat; (*pulito*) clean

'linea *f* line; (*di autobus, aereo*) route; (*di metro*) line; (*di abito*) cut; (*di auto, mobile*) design; (*fisico*) figure; **è caduta la ~** I've been cut off; **in ~** (*Comput*) on line; **mantenere la ~** keep one's figure; **mettersi in ~** line up; **nave di ~** liner; **volo di ~** scheduled flight. **~ d'arrivo** finishing line. **~ continua** unbroken line

linea'menti *mpl* features

line'are *adj* linear; (discorso) to the point; (ragionamento) consistent

line'etta *f* (*tratto lungo*) dash; (*d'unione*) hyphen

lin'gotto *m* ingot

'lingu|a *f* tongue; (*linguaggio*) language. **~'accia** *f* (*persona*) backbiter. **~'aggio** *m* language. **~'etta** *f* (*di scarpa*) tongue; (*di strumento*) reed; (*di busta*) flap

lingu'ist|a *mf* linguist. **~ica** *f* linguistics *sg*. **~ico** *adj* linguistic

'lino *m* (*Bot*) flax; (*tessuto*) linen

li'noleum *m* linoleum

liofiliz'za|re *vt* freeze-dry. **~to** *adj* freeze-dried

liposuzi'one *f* liposuction

lique'far|e *vt*, **~si** *vr* liquefy; (*sciogliersi*) melt

liqui'da|re *vt* liquidate; settle (conto); pay off (debiti); clear (merce); (**[!]**: *uccidere*) get rid of. **~zi'one** *f* liquidation; (*di conti*) settling; (*di merce*) clearance sale

'liquido *adj & m* liquid

liqui'rizia *f* liquorice

li'quore *m* liqueur; **liquori** *pl* (*bevande alcooliche*) liquors

'lira *f* lira; (*Mus*) lyre

'lirico, -a *adj* lyrical; (poesia) lyric; (cantante, musica) opera *attrib* ● *f* lyric poetry; (*Mus*) opera

lisci'are *vt* smooth; (*accarezzare*) stroke. **'liscio** *adj* smooth; (capelli) straight; (liquore) neat; (acqua minerale) still; **passarla liscia** get away with it

'liso *adj* worn [out]

'lista *f* list; (*striscia*) strip. **~ di attesa** waiting list; **in ~ di attesa** (*Aeron*) stand-by. **~ elettorale** electoral register. **~ nera** blacklist. **~ di nozze** wedding list. **li'stare** *vt* edge; (*Comput*) list

li'stino *m* list. **~ prezzi** price list

Lit. *abbr* (lire italiane) Italian lire

'lite *f* quarrel; (*baruffa*) row; (*Jur*) lawsuit

liti'gare *vi* quarrel. **li'tigio** *m* quarrel. **litigi'oso** *adj* quarrelsome

lito'rale *adj* coastal ● *m* coast

'litro *m* litre

li'turgico *adj* liturgical

li'vella *f* level. **~ a bolla d'aria** spirit level

livel'lar|e *vt* level. **~si** *vr* level out

li'vello *m* level; **passaggio a ~** level crossing; **sotto/sul ~ del mare** below/above sea level

'livido *adj* livid; (*per il freddo*) blue; (*per una botta*) black and blue ● *m* bruise

Li'vorno *f* Leghorn

'lizza *f* lists *pl*; **essere in ~ per qcsa** be in the running for sth

lo *def art m* (*before s + consonant, gn, ps, z*) the; ▷IL ● *pron* (*riferito a persona*) him; (*riferito a cosa*) it; **non lo so** I don't know

'lobo *m* lobe

lo'cal|e *adj* local ● *m* (*stanza*) room; (*treno*) local train; **~i** *pl* (*edifici*) pre-

mises. **~e notturno** night-club. **~ità** *f inv* locality
localiz'zare *vt* localize; (*trovare*) locate
localizza'zione *f* localization
lo'cand|a *f* inn
locan'dina *f* bill, poster
loca|'tario, -a *mf* tenant. **~'tore, ~'trice** *m* landlord ● *f* landlady. **~zi'one** *f* tenancy
locomo|'tiva *f* locomotive. **~zi'one** *f* locomotion; **mezzi di ~zione** means of transport
'loculo *m* burial niche
lo'custa *f* locust
locuzi'one *f* expression
lo'dare *vt* praise. **'lode** *f* praise; **laurea con lode** first-class degree
'loden *m inv* (*cappotto*) loden coat
'lodola *f* lark
'loggia *f* loggia; (*massonica*) lodge
loggi'one *m* gallery, the gods
'logica *f* logic

l

logica'mente *adv* (*in modo logico*) logically; (*ovviamente*) of course
'logico *adj* logical
lo'gistica *f* logistics *sg*
logo'ra|re *vt* wear out; (*sciupare*) waste. **~rsi** *vr* wear out; (persona:) wear oneself out. **logo'rio** *m* wear and tear. **'logoro** *adj* worn-out
lom'baggine *f* lumbago
Lombar'dia *f* Lombardy
lom'bata *f* loin. **'lombo** *m* (*Anat*) loin
lom'brico *m* earthworm
'Londra *f* London
lon'gevo *adj* long-lived
longi'lineo *adj* tall and slim
longi'tudine *f* longitude
lontana'mente *adv* distantly; (*vagamente*) vaguely; **neanche ~** not for a moment
lonta'nanza *f* distance; (*separazione*) separation; **in ~** in the distance
lon'tano *adj* far; (*distante*) distant; (*nel tempo*) far-off, distant; (parente) distant; (*vago*) vague; (*assente*) absent; **più ~** further ● *adv* far [away]; **da ~** from a distance
'lontra *f* otter
lo'quace *adj* talkative
'lordo *adj* dirty; (somma, peso) gross
'loro[1] *pron pl* (*soggetto*) they; (*oggetto*) them; (*forma di cortesia*) you; **sta a ~** it is up to them
'loro[2] (**il ~** *m*, **la ~** *f*, **i ~** *mpl*, **le ~** *fpl*) *poss adj* their; (*forma di cortesia*) your; **un ~ amico** a friend of theirs; (*forma di cortesia*) a friend of yours ● *poss pron* theirs; (*forma di cortesia*) yours; **i ~** (*famiglia*) their folk
losanga *f* lozenge; **a losanghe** diamond-shaped
'losco *adj* suspicious
'lott|a *f* fight, struggle; (*contrasto*) conflict; *Sport* wrestling. **lot'tare** *vi* fight, struggle; *Sport, fig* wrestle. **~a'tore** *m* wrestler
lotte'ria *f* lottery
'lotto *m* [national] lottery; (*porzione*) lot; (*di terreno*) plot
lozi'one *f* lotion
lubrifi'ca|nte *adj* lubricating ● *m* lubricant. **~re** *vt* lubricate
luc'chetto *m* padlock
lucci'ca|nte *adj* sparkling. **~re** *vi* sparkle. **lucci'chio** *m* sparkle
'luccio *m* pike
'lucciola *f* glow-worm
'luce *f* light; **far ~ su** shed light on; **dare alla ~** give birth to. **~ della luna** moonlight. **luci** *pl* **di posizione** sidelights. **~ del sole** sunlight
lu'cen|te *adj* shining. **~'tezza** *f* shine
lucer'nario *m* skylight
lu'certola *f* lizard
lucida'labbra *m inv* lip gloss
luci'da|re *vt* polish. **~'trice** *f* [floor-]polisher. **'lucido** *adj* shiny; (pavimento, scarpe) polished; (*chiaro*) clear; (persona, mente) lucid; (occhi) watery ● *m* shine. **lucido [da scarpe]** [shoe] polish
lucra'tivo *adj* lucrative
'luglio *m* July
'lugubre *adj* gloomy
'lui *pron* (*soggetto*) he; (*oggetto, con prep*) him; **lo ha fatto ~ stesso** he did it himself
lu'maca *f* (*mollusco*) snail; *fig* slowcoach
'lume *m* lamp; (*luce*) light; **a ~ di candela** by candlelight
luminosità *f* brightness. **lumi'noso**

adj luminous; (stanza, cielo ecc) bright

'luna *f* moon; **chiaro di ~** moonlight. **~ di miele** honeymoon

luna park *m inv* fairground

lu'nario *m* almanac; **sbarcare il ~** make both ends meet

lu'natico *a* moody

lunedì *m inv* Monday

lu'netta *f* half-moon [shape]

lun'gaggine *f* slowness

lun'ghezza *f* length. **~ d'onda** wavelength

'lungi *adv* **ero [ben] ~ dall'immaginare che...** I never dreamt for a moment that...

lungimi'rante *adj* far-sighted

'lungo *adj* long; (*diluito*) weak; (*lento*) slow; **saperla lunga** be shrewd • *m* length; **di gran lunga** by far; **andare per le lunghe** drag on • *prep* (*durante*) throughout; (*per la lunghezza di*) along

lungofi'ume *m* riverside

lungo'lago *m* lakeside

lungo'mare *m* sea front

lungome'traggio *m* feature film

lu'notto *m* rear window

lu'ogo *m* place; (*punto preciso*) spot; (*passo d'autore*) passage; **aver ~** take place; **dar ~ a** give rise to; **del ~** (usanze) local. **~ pubblico** public place

luogote'nente *m* (*Mil*) lieutenant

lu'petto *m* Cub [Scout]

'lupo *m* wolf

'luppolo *m* hop

'lurido *adj* filthy. **luri'dume** *m* filth

lusin'g|are *vt* flatter. **~arsi** *vr* flatter oneself; (*illudersi*) fool oneself. **~hi'ero** *a* flattering

lus'sa|re *vt*, **~rsi** *vr* dislocate. **~zi'one** *f* dislocation

Lussem'burgo *m* Luxembourg

'lusso *m* luxury; **di ~** luxury *attrib*

lussu'oso *adj* luxurious

lus'suria *f* lust

lu'strare *vt* polish

'lustro *adj* shiny • *m* sheen; *fig* prestige; (*quinquennio*) five-year period

'lutt|o *m* mourning; **~o stretto** deep mourning. **~u'oso** *a* mournful

Mm

m *abbr* (metro) m

ma *conj* but; (*eppure*) yet; **ma!** (*dubbio*) I don't know; (*indignazione*) really!; **ma davvero?** really?; **ma sì!** why not!; (*certo che sì*) of course!

'macabro *adj* macabre

macché *int* of course not!

macche'roni *mpl* macaroni *sg*

macche'ronico *adj* (italiano) broken

'macchia[1] *f* stain; (*di diverso colore*) spot; (*piccola*) speck; **senza ~** spotless

'macchia[2] *f* (*boscaglia*) scrub

macchi'a|re *vt*, **~rsi** *vr* stain. **~to** *adj* (caffè) with a dash of milk; **~to di** (*sporco*) stained with

'macchina *f* machine; (*motore*) engine; (*automobile*) car. **~ da cucire** sewing machine. **~ da presa** cine camera. **~ da scrivere** typewriter. **~ fotografica (digitale)** (digital) camera

macchinal'mente *adv* mechanically

macchi'nare *vt* plot

macchi'nario *m* machinery

macchi'netta *f* (*per i denti*) brace

macchi'nista *m* (*Rail*) engine-driver; (*Naut*) engineer; (*Theat*) stagehand

macchi'noso *adj* complicated

mace'donia *f* fruit salad

Mace'donia *f* Macedonia

macel'la|io *m* butcher. **~re** *vt* slaughter, butcher. **macelle'ria** *f* butcher's [shop]. **ma'cello** *m* (*mattatoio*) slaughterhouse; *fig* shambles *sg*; **andare al macello** *fig* go to the slaughter

mace'rar|e *vt* macerate; *fig* distress. **~si** *vr* be consumed

ma'cerie *fpl* rubble *sg*; (*rottami*) debris *sg*

ma'cigno *m* boulder

'macina *f* millstone

macinacaffè *m inv* coffee mill

macina'pepe *m inv* pepper mill

maci'na|re *vt* mill. **~to** *adj* ground • *m* (*carne*) mince. **maci'nino** *m* mill; (*hum*) old banger

maciul'lare *vt* (*stritolare*) crush

macrobiotic|a *f* **negozio di ~a** health-food shop. **~o** *adj* macrobiotic
macu'lato *adj* spotted
'madido *adj* **~ di** moist with
Ma'donna *f* Our Lady
mador'nale *adj* gross
'madre *f* mother. **~'lingua** *adj inv* **inglese ~lingua** English native speaker. **~'patria** *f* native land. **~'perla** *f* mother-of-pearl
ma'drina *f* godmother
maestà *f* majesty
maestosità *f* majesty. **mae'stoso** *adj* majestic
mae'strale *m* northwest wind
mae'stranza *f* workers *pl*
mae'stria *f* mastery
ma'estro, -a *mf* teacher ● *m* master; (*Mus*) maestro. **~ di cerimonie** master of ceremonies ● *adj* (*principale*) chief; (*di grande abilità*) skilful
'mafi|a *f* Mafia. **~'oso** *adj* of the Mafia ● *m* member of the Mafia, Mafioso

m

Mafia The Mafia developed in Sicily in the nineteenth century, where it continues to wield considerable power in opposition to the authorities. Strictly speaking, the term Mafia applies only to Sicily, and its equivalents in other regions (*Camorra* in Naples and *'ndrangheta* in Calabria) are separate organizations, although often working in collaboration with each other.

ma'gagna *f* fault
ma'gari *adv* (*forse*) maybe ● *int* I wish! ● *conj* (*per esprimere desiderio*) if only; (*anche se*) even if
magazzini'ere *m* storesman, warehouseman. **magaz'zino** *m* warehouse; (*emporio*) shop; **grande magazzino** department store
'maggio *m* May
maggio'lino *m* May bug
maggio'rana *f* marjoram
maggio'ranza *f* majority
maggio'rare *vt* increase
maggior'domo *m* butler
maggi'ore *adj* (*di dimensioni, numero*) bigger, larger; (*superlativo*) biggest, largest; (*di età*) older; (*superlativo*) oldest; (*di importanza, musica*) major; (*superlativo*) greatest; **la maggior parte di** most; **la maggior parte del tempo** most of the time ● *pron* (*di dimensioni*) the bigger, the larger; (*superlativo*) the biggest, the largest; (*di età*) the older; (*superlativo*) the oldest; (*di importanza*) the major; (*superlativo*) the greatest ● *m* (*Mil*) major; (*Aeron*) squadron leader. **maggio'renne** *adj* of age ● *mf* adult
maggior|i'tario *adj* (sistema) first-past-the-post *attrib.* **~'mente** *adv* [all] the more; (*più di tutto*) most
'Magi *mpl* **i re ~** the Magi
ma'gia *f* magic; (*trucco*) magic trick. **magica'mente** *adv* magically. **'magico** *adj* magic
magi'stero *m* (*insegnamento*) teaching; (*maestria*) skill; **facoltà di ~** arts faculty
magi'stra|le *adj* masterly; **istituto ~e** teachers' training college
magi'stra|to *m* magistrate. **~'tura** *f* magistrature. **la ~tura** the Bench
'magli|a *f* stitch; (*lavoro ai ferri*) knitting; (*tessuto*) jersey; (*di rete*) mesh; (*di catena*) link; (*indumento*) vest; **fare la ~a** knit. **~a diritta** knit. **~a rosa** (*ciclismo*) ≈ yellow jersey. **~a rovescia** purl. **~e'ria** *f* knitwear. **~'etta** *f* **~etta [a maniche corte]** tee-shirt. **~'ficio** *m* knitwear factory. **ma'glina** *f* (*tessuto*) jersey
magli'one *m* sweater
'magma *m* magma
ma'gnanimo *adj* magnanimous
ma'gnate *m* magnate
ma'gnesi|a *f* magnesia. **~o** *m* magnesium
ma'gne|te *m* magnet. **~tico** *adj* magnetic. **~'tismo** *m* magnetism
magne'tofono *m* tape recorder
magnifi|ca'mente *adv* magnificently. **~'cenza** *f* magnificence; (*generosità*) munificence. **ma'gnifico** *adj* magnificent; (*generoso*) munificent
ma'gnolia *f* magnolia
ma'gone *m* **avere il ~** be down; **mi è venuto il ~** I've got a lump in my throat
'magr|a *f* low water. **ma'grezza** *f* thinness. **~o** *adj* thin; (carne) lean; (*scarso*) meagre
'mai *adv* never; (*inter, talvolta*) ever; **caso**

~ if anything; **caso ~ tornasse** in case he comes back; **come ~?** why?; **cosa ~?** what on earth?; **~ più** never again; **più che ~** more than ever; **quando ~?** whenever?; **quasi ~** hardly ever

mai'ale *m* pig; (*carne*) pork

mai'olica *f* majolica

maio'nese *f* mayonnaise

'mais *m* maize

mai'uscol|a *f* capital [letter]. **~o** *adj* capital

mal ▷**MALE**

'mala *f* **la ~** ☒ the underworld

mala'fede *f* bad faith

malaf'fare *m* **gente di ~** shady characters *pl*

mala'lingua *f* backbiter

mala'mente *adv* (ridotto) badly

malan'dato *adj* in bad shape; (*di salute*) in poor health

ma'lanimo *m* ill will

ma'lanno *m* misfortune; (*malattia*) illness; **prendersi un ~** catch something

mala'pena: **a ~** *adv* hardly

ma'laria *f* malaria

mala'ticcio *adj* sickly

ma'lato, -a *adj* ill, sick; (pianta) diseased ● *mf* sick person. **~ di mente** mentally ill person. **malat'tia** *f* disease, illness; **ho preso due giorni di malattia** I had two days off sick. **malattia venerea** venereal disease

malaugu'rato *adj* ill-omened. **malau'gurio** *m* bad *o* ill omen

mala'vita *f* underworld

mala'voglia *f* unwillingness; **di ~** unwillingly

malcapi'tato *adj* wretched

malce'lato *adj* ill-concealed

mal'concio *adj* battered

malcon'tento *m* discontent

malco'stume *m* immorality

mal'destro *adj* awkward; (*inesperto*) inexperienced

maldi'cen|te *adj* slanderous. **~za** *f* slander

maldi'sposto *adj* ill-disposed

'male *adv* badly; **funzionare ~** not work properly; **star ~** be ill; **star ~ a qcno** (vestito ecc:) not suit sb; **rimanerci ~** be hurt; **non c'è ~!** not bad at all! ● *m* evil; (*dolore*) pain; (*malattia*) illness; (*danno*) harm. **distinguere il bene dal ~** know right from wrong; **andare a ~** go off; **aver ~ a** have a pain in; **dove hai ~?** where does it hurt?; **far ~ a qcno** (*provocare dolore*) hurt sb; (cibo:) be bad for sb; **le cipolle mi fanno ~** onions don't agree with me; **mi fa ~ la schiena** my back is hurting; **mal d'auto** car-sickness. **mal di denti** toothache. **mal di gola** sore throat. **mal di mare** sea-sickness; **avere il mal di mare** be sea-sick. **mal di pancia** stomach ache. **mal di testa** headache

male'detto *adj* cursed; (*orribile*) awful

male'di|re *vt* curse. **~zi'one** *f* curse; **~zione!** damn!

maledu|'cato *adj* ill-mannered. **~cazi'one** *f* rudeness

male'fatta *f* misdeed

ma'lefico *adj* (azione) evil; (*nocivo*) harmful

maleodo'rante *adj* foul-smelling

ma'lessere *m* indisposition; *fig* uneasiness

ma'levolo *adj* malevolent

malfa'mato *adj* of ill repute

mal'fat|to *adj* badly done; (*malformato*) ill-shaped. **~'tore** *m* wrongdoer

mal'fermo *adj* unsteady; (salute) poor

malfor'ma|to *adj* misshapen. **~zi'one** *f* malformation

mal'grado *prep* in spite of ● *conj* although

ma'lia *f* spell

mali'gn|are *vi* malign. **~ità** *f* malice; (*Med*) malignancy. **ma'ligno** *adj* malicious; (*perfido*) evil; (*Med*) malignant

malinco'ni|a *f* melancholy. **malin'conico** *adj* melancholy

malincu'ore: **a ~** *adv* reluctantly

malinfor'mato *adj* misinformed

malintenzio'nato, -a *mf* miscreant

malin'teso *adj* mistaken ● *m* misunderstanding

ma'lizi|a *f* malice; (*astuzia*) cunning; (*espediente*) trick. **~'oso** *adj* malicious; (*birichino*) mischievous

malle'abile *adj* malleable

malme'nare *vt* ill-treat

m

mal'messo *adj* (*vestito male*) shabbily dressed; (casa) poorly furnished; (*fig: senza soldi*) hard up

malnu'tri|to *adj* undernourished. **~zi'one** *f* malnutrition

'malo *adj* **in ~ modo** badly

ma'locchio *m* evil eye

ma'lora *f* ruin; **della ~** awful; **andare in ~** go to ruin

ma'lore *m* illness; **essere colto da ~** be suddenly taken ill

malri'dotto *adj* (persona) in a sorry state

mal'sano *adj* unhealthy

'malta *f* mortar

mal'tempo *m* bad weather

'malto *m* malt

maltrat|ta'mento *m* ill-treatment. **~'tare** *vt* ill-treat

malu'more *m* bad mood; **di ~** in a bad mood

mal'vagi|o *adj* wicked. **~tà** *f* wickedness

malversazi'one *f* embezzlement

m

mal'visto *adj* unpopular (**da** with)

malvi'vente *m* criminal

malvolenti'eri *adv* unwillingly

malvo'lere *vt* **farsi ~** make oneself unpopular

'mamma *f* mummy, mum; **~ mia!** good gracious!

mam'mella *f* breast

mam'mifero *m* mammal

'mammola *f* violet

ma'nata *f* handful; (*colpo*) slap

'manca *f* ▷**MANCO**

manca'mento *m* **avere un ~** faint

man'can|te *adj* missing. **~za** *f* lack; (*assenza*) absence; (*insufficienza*) shortage; (*fallo*) fault; (*imperfezione*) defect; **sento la sua ~za** I miss him

man'care *vi* be lacking; (*essere assente*) be missing; (*venir meno*) fail; (*morire*) pass away; **~ di** be lacking in; **~ a** fail to keep (promessa); **mi manca casa** I miss home; **mi manchi** I miss you; **mi è mancato il tempo** I didn't have [the] time; **mi manca un euro** I'm one euro short; **quanto manca alla partenza?** how long before we leave?; **è mancata la corrente** there was a power failure; **sentirsi ~** feel faint; **sentirsi ~ il respiro** be unable to breathe [properly] ● *vt* miss (bersaglio); **è mancato poco che cadesse** he nearly fell

'manche *f inv* heat

man'chevole *adj* defective

'mancia *f* tip

manci'ata *f* handful

man'cino *adj* left-handed

'manco, -a *adj* left ● *f* left hand ● *adv* (*nemmeno*) not even

man'dante *mf* (*di delitto*) instigator

manda'rancio *m* clementine

man'dare *vt* send; (*emettere*) give off; utter (suono); **~ a chiamare** send for; **~ avanti la casa** run the house; **~ giù** (*ingoiare*) swallow

manda'rino *m* (*Bot*) mandarin

man'data *f* consignment; (*di serratura*) turn; **chiudere a doppia ~** double lock

man'dato *m* (*incarico*) mandate; (*Jur*) warrant; (*di pagamento*) money order. **~ di comparizione [in giudizio]** subpoena. **~ di perquisizione** search warrant

man'dibola *f* jaw

mando'lino *m* mandolin

'mandor|la *f* almond; **a ~la** (occhi) almond-shaped. **~'lato** *m* nut brittle (*type of nougat*). **~lo** *m* almond[-tree]

'mandria *f* herd

maneg'gevole *adj* easy to handle. **maneggi'are** *vt* handle

ma'neggio *m* handling; (*intrigo*) plot; (*scuola di equitazione*) riding school

ma'netta *f* hand lever; **manette** *pl* handcuffs

man'forte *m* **dare ~ a qcno** support sb

manga'nello *m* truncheon

manga'nese *m* manganese

mange'reccio *adj* edible

mangia'dischi® *m inv type of portable record player*

mangia'fumo *adj inv* **candela ~** *air-purifier in the form of candle*

mangia'nastri *m inv* cassette player

mangi'a|re *vt/i* eat; (*consumare*) eat up; (*corrodere*) eat away; take (scacchi, carte ecc) ● *m* eating; (*cibo*) food; (*pasto*) meal. **~rsi** *vr* **~rsi le parole**

mumble; **~rsi le unghie** bite one's nails

mangi'ata *f* big meal; **farsi una bella ~ di...** feast on...

man'gime *m* fodder

mangiucchi'are *vt* nibble

'mango *m* mango

ma'nia *f* mania. **~ di grandezza** delusions of grandeur ● *mf* maniac

'manica *f* sleeve; (🅘: *gruppo*) band; **a maniche lunghe** long-sleeved; **essere in maniche di camicia** be in shirt sleeves

'Manica *f* **la ~** the [English] Channel

manica'retto *m* tasty dish

mani'chetta *f* hose

mani'chino *m* dummy

'manico *m* handle; (*Mus*) neck

mani'comio *m* mental home; (🅘: *confusione*) tip

mani'cotto *m* muff; (*Mech*) sleeve

mani'cure *f* manicure ● *mf inv* (*persona*) manicurist

mani'e|ra *f* manner; **in ~ra che** so that. **~'rato** *adj* affected; (stile) mannered. **~'rismo** *m* mannerism

manifat'tura *f* manufacture; (*fabbrica*) factory

manife'stante *mf* demonstrator

manife'sta|re *vt* show; (*esprimere*) express ● *vi* demonstrate. **~rsi** *vr* show oneself. **~zi'one** *f* show; (*espressione*) expression; (*sintomo*) manifestation; (*dimostrazione pubblica*) demonstration

mani'festo *adj* evident ● *m* poster; (*dichiarazione pubblica*) manifesto

ma'niglia *f* handle; (*sostegno, in autobus ecc*) strap

manipo'la|re *vt* handle; (*massaggiare*) massage; (*alterare*) adulterate; *fig* manipulate. **~'tore, ~'trice** *mf* manipulator. **~zi'one** *f* handling; (*massaggio*) massage; (*alterazione*) adulteration; *fig* manipulation

mani'scalco *m* smith

man'naia *f* axe; (*da macellaio*) cleaver

man'naro *adj* **lupo** *m* **~** werewolf

'mano *f* hand; (*strato di vernice ecc*) coat; **alla ~** informal; **fuori ~** out of the way; **man ~** little by little; **man ~ che** as; **sotto ~** to hand

mano'dopera *f* labour

ma'nometro *m* gauge

mano'mettere *vt* tamper with; (*violare*) violate

ma'nopola *f* knob; (*guanto*) mitten; (*su pullman*) handle

mano'scritto *adj* handwritten ● *m* manuscript

mano'vale *m* labourer

mano'vella *f* handle; (*Techn*) crank

ma'no|vra *f* manoeuvre; (*Rail*) shunting; **fare le ~vre** (*Auto*) manoeuvre. **~'vrabile** *adj fig* easy to manipulate. **~'vrare** *vt* operate; *fig* manipulate (persona) ● *vi* manoeuvre

manro'vescio *m* slap

man'sarda *f* attic

mansi'one *f* task; (*dovere*) duty

mansu'eto *adj* meek; (animale) docile

man'tell|a *f* cape. **~o** *m* cloak; (*soprabito, di animale*) coat; (*di neve*) mantle

mante'ner|e *vt* keep; (*in buono stato, sostentare*) maintain. **~si** *vr* **~si in forma** keep fit. **manteni'mento** *m* maintenance

'mantice *m* bellows *pl*; (*di automobile*) hood

'manto *m* cloak; (*coltre*) mantle

manto'vana *f* (*di tende*) pelmet

manu'al|e *adj & m* manual. **~e d'uso** user manual. **~'mente** *adv* manually

ma'nubrio *m* handle; (*di bicicletta*) handlebars *pl*; (*per ginnastica*) dumb-bell

manu'fatto *adj* manufactured

manutenzi'one *f* maintenance

'manzo *m* steer; (*carne*) beef

'mappa *f* map

mappa'mondo *m* globe

mar ▷**MARE**

ma'rasma *m fig* decline

mara'to|na *f* marathon. **~'neta** *mf* marathon runner

'marca *f* mark; (*Comm*) brand; (*fabbricazione*) make; (*scontrino*) ticket. **~ da bollo** revenue stamp

mar'ca|re *vt* mark; *Sport* score. **~ta'mente** *adv* markedly. **~to** *adj* (tratto, accento) strong. **~'tore** *m* (*nel calcio*) scorer

mar'chese, -a *m* marquis ● *f* marchioness

marchi'are *vt* brand

'marchio *m* brand; (*caratteristica*) mark.

m

~ **di fabbrica** trademark. ~ **registrato** registered trademark

'marcia *f* march; (*Auto*) gear; *Sport* walk; **mettere in** ~ put into gear; **mettersi in** ~ start off; **fare** ~ **indietro** reverse; *fig* back-pedal. ~ **funebre** funeral march. ~ **nuziale** wedding march

marciapi'ede *m* pavement; (*di stazione*) platform

marci'a|re *vi* march; (*funzionare*) go, work. **~'tore, ~'trice** *mf* walker

'marcio *adj* rotten ● *m* rotten part; *fig* corruption. **mar'cire** *vi* go bad, rot

'marco *m* (*moneta*) mark

'mare *m* sea; (*luogo di mare*) seaside; **sul** ~ (casa) at the seaside; (città) on the sea; **in alto** ~ on the high seas. ~ **Adriatico** Adriatic Sea. **mar Ionio** Ionian Sea. **mar Mediterraneo** Mediterranean. **mar Tirreno** Tyrrhenian Sea

ma'rea *f* tide; **una** ~ **di** hundreds of; **alta** ~ high tide; **bassa** ~ low tide

mareggi'ata *f* [sea] storm

mare'moto *m* tidal wave, seaquake

maresci'allo *m* marshal; (*sottufficiale*) warrant officer

marga'rina *f* margarine

marghe'rita *f* marguerite. **margheri'tina** *f* daisy

margi'nale *adj* marginal

'margine *m* margin; (*orlo*) brink; (*bordo*) border. ~ **di errore** margin of error. ~ **di sicurezza** safety margin

ma'rina *f* navy; (*costa*) seashore; (*quadro*) seascape. ~ **mercantile** merchant navy. ~ **militare** navy

mari'naio *m* sailor

mari'na|re *vt* marinate. **~ta** *f* marinade. **~to** *adj* (*Culin*) marinated

ma'rino *adj* sea *attrib*, marine

mario'netta *f* puppet

ma'rito *m* husband

ma'rittimo *adj* maritime

mar'maglia *f* rabble

marmel'lata *f* jam; (*di agrumi*) marmalade

mar'mitta *f* pot; (*Auto*) silencer. ~ **catalitica** catalytic converter

'marmo *m* marble

mar'mocchio *m* [!] brat

mar'mor|eo *adj* marble. **~iz'zato** *adj* marbled

mar'motta *f* marmot

Ma'rocco *m* Morocco

ma'roso *m* breaker

mar'rone *adj* brown ● *m* brown; (*castagna*) chestnut; **marroni** *pl* **canditi** marrons glacés

mar'sina *f* tails *pl*

mar'supio *m* (*borsa*) bumbag

martedì *m inv* Tuesday. ~ **grasso** Shrove Tuesday

martel'la|re *vt* hammer ● *vi* throb. **~ta** *f* hammer blow

martel'letto *m* (*di giudice*) gavel

mar'tello *m* hammer; (*di battente*) knocker. ~ **pneumatico** pneumatic drill

marti'netto *m* (*Mech*) jack

'martire *mf* martyr. **mar'tirio** *m* martyrdom

'martora *f* marten

martori'are *vt* torment

mar'xis|mo *m* Marxism. **~ta** *agg & mf* Marxist

marza'pane *m* marzipan

marzi'ale *adj* martial

marzi'ano, -a *mf* Martian

'marzo *m* March

mascal'zone *m* rascal

ma'scara *m inv* mascara

mascar'pone *m full-fat cream cheese*

ma'scella *f* jaw

'mascher|a *f* mask; (*costume*) fancy dress; (*Cinema, Theat*) usher *m*, usherette *f*; (*nella commedia dell'arte*) stock character. **~a antigas** gas mask. **~a di bellezza** face pack. **~a ad ossigeno** oxygen mask. **~a'mento** *m* masking; (*Mil*) camouflage. **masche'rare** *vt* mask. **~arsi** *vr* put on a mask; **~arsi da** dress up as. **~ata** *f* masquerade

maschi'accio *m* tomboy

ma'schi|le *adj* masculine; (sesso) male ● *m* masculine [gender]. **~'lista** *adj* sexist. **'maschio** *adj* male; (*virile*) manly ● *m* male; (*figlio*) son. **masco'lino** *adj* masculine

ma'scotte *f inv* mascot

maso'chis|mo *m* masochism. **~ta** *adj & mf* masochist

'massa *f* mass; (*Electr*) earth, ground

Am; **comunicazioni di ~** mass media

massa'crare *vt* massacre. **mas'sacro** *m* massacre; *fig* mess

massaggi'a|re *vt* massage. **mas'saggio** *m* massage. **~'tore, ~'trice** *m* masseur ● *f* masseuse

mas'saia *f* housewife

masse'rizie *fpl* household effects

mas'siccio *adj* massive; (oro ecc) solid; (corporatura) heavy ● *m* massif

'massim|a *f* maxim; (*temperatura*) maximum. **~o** *adj* greatest; (quantità) maximum, greatest ● *m* **il ~o** the maximum; **al ~o** at [the] most, as a maximum

'masso *m* rock

mas'sone *m* [Free]mason. **~'ria** Freemasonry

ma'stello *m wooden box for the grape or olive harvest*

masteriz'zare *vt* (*Comput*) burn

masterizza'tore *m* (*Comput*) burner

masti'care *vt* chew; (*borbottare*) mumble

'mastice *m* mastic; (*per vetri*) putty

ma'stino *m* mastiff

masto'dontico *adj* gigantic

'mastro *m* master; **libro ~** ledger

mastur'ba|rsi *vr* masturbate. **~zi'one** *f* masturbation

ma'tassa *f* skein

mate'matic|a *f* mathematics, maths. **~o, -a** *adj* mathematical ● *mf* mathematician

materas'sino *m* **~ gonfiabile** air bed

mate'rasso *m* mattress. **~ a molle** spring mattress

ma'teria *f* matter; (*materiale*) material; (*di studio*) subject. **~ prima** raw material

materi'a|le *adj* material; (*grossolano*) coarse ● *m* material. **~'lismo** *m* materialism. **~'lista** *adj* materialistic ● *mf* materialist. **~liz'zarsi** *vr* materialize. **~l'mente** *adv* physically

maternità *f* motherhood; **ospedale di ~** maternity hospital

ma'terno *adj* maternal; **lingua materna** mother tongue

ma'tita *f* pencil

ma'trice *f* matrix; (*origini*) roots *pl*; (*Comm*) counterfoil

ma'tricola *f* (*registro*) register; (*Univ*) fresher

ma'trigna *f* stepmother

matrimoni'ale *adj* matrimonial; **vita ~** married life. **matri'monio** *m* marriage; (*cerimonia*) wedding

ma'trona *f* matron

'matta *f* (*nelle carte*) joker

matta'toio *m* slaughterhouse

matte'rello *m* rolling-pin

mat'ti|na *f* morning; **la ~na** in the morning. **~'nata** *f* morning; (*Theat*) matinée. **~no** *m* morning

'matto, -a *adj* mad, crazy; (*Med*) insane; (*falso*) false; (*opaco*) matt; **~ da legare** barking mad; **avere una voglia matta di** be dying for ● *mf* madman; madwoman

mat'tone *m* brick; (*libro*) bore

matto'nella *f* tile

mattu'tino *adj* morning *attrib*

matu'rare *vt* ripen. **maturità** *f* maturity; (*Sch*) school-leaving certificate. **ma'turo** *adj* mature; (frutto) ripe

m

> *i*
>
> **Maturità** The Italian secondary school-leaving exam is called the *Esame di Maturità*. Candidates are examined by a committee consisting of external examiners and their own teachers, and the exams may be oral or written, depending on the subject. Candidates are tested on a wide range of subjects, including philosophy and history of art.

mauso'leo *m* mausoleum

maxi+ *pref* maxi+

'mazza *f* club; (*martello*) hammer; (*da baseball, cricket*) bat. **~ da golf** golf-club. **maz'zata** *f* blow

maz'zetta *f* (*di banconote*) bundle

'mazzo *m* bunch; (*carte da gioco*) pack

me *pers pron* me; **me lo ha dato** he gave it to me; **fai come me** do as I do; **è più veloce di me** he is faster than me *o* faster than I am

me'andro *m* meander

M.E.C. *m abbr* (Mercato Comune Europeo) EEC

mec'canica *f* mechanics *sg*
meccanica'mente *adv* mechanically
mec'canico *adj* mechanical ● *m* mechanic. **mecca'nismo** *m* mechanism
mèche *fpl* **[farsi] fare le ~** have one's hair streaked
me'dagli|a *f* medal. **~'one** *m* medallion; (*gioiello*) locket
me'desimo *adj* same
'medi|a *f* average; (*Sch*) average mark; (*Math*) mean; **essere nella ~a** be in the mid-range. **~'ano** *adj* middle ● *m* (*calcio*) half-back
medi'ante *prep* by
medi'a|re *vt* act as intermediary in. **~'tore, ~'trice** *mf* mediator; (*Comm*) middleman
medica'mento *m* medicine
medi'ca|re *vt* treat; dress (ferita). **~zi'one** *f* medication; (*di ferita*) dressing
medi'c|ina *f* medicine. **~ina legale** forensic medicine. **~i'nale** *adj* medicinal ● *m* medicine
'medico *adj* medical ● *m* doctor. **~ generico** general practitioner. **~ legale** forensic scientist. **~ di turno** duty doctor
medie'vale *adj* medieval
'medio *adj* average; (punto) middle; (statura) medium ● *m* (*dito*) middle finger
medi'ocre *adj* mediocre; (*scadente*) poor
medio'evo *m* Middle Ages *pl*
medi'ta|re *vt* meditate; (*progettare*) plan; (*considerare attentamente*) think over ● *vi* meditate. **~zi'one** *f* meditation
mediter'raneo *adj* Mediterranean; **il [mar] M~** the Mediterranean [Sea]
me'dusa *f* jellyfish
me'gafono *m* megaphone
mega'lomane *mf* megalomaniac
me'gera *f* hag
'meglio *adv* better; **tanto ~, ~ così** so much the better ● *adj* better; (*superlativo*) best ● *mf* best ● *f* **avere la ~ su** have the better of; **fare qcsa alla [bell'e] ~** do sth as best one can ● *m* **fare del proprio ~** do one's best; **fare qcsa il ~ possibile** make an excellent job of sth; **al ~** to the best of one's ability
'mela *f* apple. **~ cotogna** quince
mela'grana *f* pomegranate
mela'nina *f* melanin
melan'zana *f* aubergine, eggplant *Am*
me'lassa *f* molasses *sg*
me'lenso *adj* (persona, film) dull
mel'lifluo *adj* (parole) honeyed; (voce) sugary
'melma *f* slime. **mel'moso** *adj* slimy
melo *m* apple[-tree]
melo'di|a *f* melody. **me'lodico** *adj* melodic. **~'oso** *adj* melodious
melo'dram|ma *m* melodrama. **~'matico** *adj* melodramatic
melo'grano *m* pomegranate tree
me'lone *m* melon
'membro *m* member; (*pl f* **membra** (*Anat*)) limb
memo'rabile *adj* memorable
'memore *adj* mindful; (*riconoscente*) grateful
me'mori|a *f* memory; (*oggetto ricordo*) souvenir. **imparare a ~a** learn by heart. **~a tampone** (*Comput*) buffer. **~a volatile** (*Comput*) volatile memory; **memorie** *pl* (*biografiche*) memoirs. **~'ale** *m* memorial. **~z'zare** *vt* memorize; (*Comput*) save, store
mena'dito: **a ~** *adv* perfectly
me'nare *vt* lead; (🅄: *picchiare*) hit
mendi'ca|nte *mf* beggar. **~re** *vt/i* beg
me'ningi *fpl* **spremersi le ~** rack one's brains
menin'gite *f* meningitis
'meno *adv* less; (*superlativo*) least; (*in operazioni, con temperatura*) minus; **far qcsa alla ~ peggio** do sth as best one can; **fare a ~ di qcsa** do without sth; **non posso fare a ~ di ridere** I can't help laughing; **~ male!** thank goodness!; **sempre ~** less and less; **venir ~** (*svenire*) faint; **venir ~ a qcno** (coraggio:) fail sb; **sono le tre ~ un quarto** it's a quarter to three; **che tu venga o ~** whether you're coming or not; **quanto ~** at least ● *adj inv* less; (*con nomi plurali*) fewer ● *m* least; (*Math*) minus sign; **il ~ possibile** as little as possible; **per lo ~** at least ● *prep* except [for] ● *conj* **a ~ che** unless
meno'ma|re *vt* (incidente:) maim. **~to** *adj* disabled

meno'pausa *f* menopause
'mensa *f* table; (*Mil*) mess; (*Sch, Univ*) refectory
men'sil|e *adj* monthly ● *m* (*stipendio*) [monthly] salary; (*rivista*) monthly. **~ità** *f inv* monthly salary. **~'mente** *adv* monthly
'mensola *f* bracket; (*scaffale*) shelf
'menta *f* mint. **~ peperita** peppermint
men'tal|e *adj* mental. **~ità** *f inv* mentality
'mente *f* mind; **a ~ fredda** in cold blood; **venire in ~ a qcno** occur to sb
men'tina *f* mint
men'tire *vi* lie
'mento *m* chin
'mentre *conj* (*temporale*) while; (*invece*) whereas
menu *m inv* menu. **~ fisso** set menu. **~ a tendina** (*Comput*) pulldown menu
menzio'nare *vt* mention. **menzi'one** *f* mention
men'zogna *f* lie
mera'viglia *f* wonder; **a ~** marvellously; **che ~!** how wonderful!; **con mia grande ~** much to my amazement; **mi fa ~ che...** I am surprised that...
meravigli'ar|e *vt* surprise. **~si** *vr* **~si di** be surprised at
meravigli'oso *adj* marvellous
mer'can|te *m* merchant. **~teggi'are** *vi* trade; (*sul prezzo*) bargain. **~'zia** *f* merchandise, goods *pl* ● *m* merchant ship
mer'cato *m* market; *Fin* market[-place]. **a buon ~** (comprare) cheap[ly]; (articolo) cheap. **~ dei cambi** foreign exchange market. **~ coperto** covered market. **~ libero** free market. **~ nero** black market
'merce *f* goods *pl*
mercé *f* **alla ~ di** at the mercy of
merce'nario *adj & m* mercenary
merce'ria *f* haberdashery; (*negozio*) haberdasher's
mercoledì *m inv* Wednesday. **~ delle Ceneri** Ash Wednesday
mer'curio *m* mercury
me'renda *f* afternoon snack; **far ~** have an afternoon snack
meridi'ana *f* sundial
meridi'ano *adj* midday ● *m* meridian
meridio'nale *adj* southern ● *mf* southerner. **meridi'one** *m* south
me'rin|ga *f* meringue. **~'gata** *f* meringue pie
meri'tare *vt* deserve. **meri'tevole** *adj* deserving
'meri|to *m* merit; (*valore*) worth; **in ~to a** as to; **per ~to di** thanks to. **~'torio** *adj* meritorious
mer'letto *m* lace
'merlo *m* blackbird
mer'luzzo *m* cod
'mero *adj* mere
meschine'ria *f* meanness. **me'schino** *adj* wretched; (*gretto*) mean ● *m* wretch
mesco|la'mento *m* mixing. **~'lanza** *f* mixture
mesco'la|re *vt* mix; shuffle (carte); (*confondere*) mix up; blend (tè, tabacco ecc). **~rsi** *vr* mix; (*immischiarsi*) meddle. **~ta** *f* (*a carte*) shuffle; (*Culin*) stir
'mese *m* month
me'setto *m* **un ~** about a month
'messa[1] *f* Mass
'messa[2] *f* (*il mettere*) putting. **~ in moto** (*Auto*) starting. **~ in piega** (*di capelli*) set. **~ a punto** adjustment. **~ in scena** production. **~ a terra** earthing, grounding *Am*
messag'gero *m* messenger. **mes'saggio** *m* message
'messe *f* harvest
Mes'sia *m* Messiah
messi'cano, -a *adj & mf* Mexican
'Messico *m* Mexico
messin'scena *f* staging; *fig* act
'messo *pp di* **mettere** ● *m* messenger
mesti'ere *m* trade; (*lavoro*) job; **essere del ~** be an expert
'mesto *adj* sad
'mestola *f* (*di cuoco*) ladle
mestru'a|le *adj* menstrual. **~zi'one** *f* menstruation. **~zi'oni** *pl* period
'meta *f* destination; *fig* aim
metà *f inv* half; (*centro*) middle; **a ~ strada** half-way; **fare a ~ con qcno** go halves with sb
metabo'lismo *m* metabolism
meta'done *m* methadone

me'tafora *f* metaphor. **meta'forico** *adj* metaphorical

me'talli|co *adj* metallic. **~z'zato** *adj* (grigio) metallic

me'tall|o *m* metal. **~ur'gia** *f* metallurgy

metalmec'canico *adj* engineering ● *m* engineering worker

me'tano *m* methane. **~'dotto** *m* methane pipeline

meta'nolo *m* methanol

me'teora *f* meteor. **meteo'rite** *m* meteorite

meteoro|lo'gia *f* meteorology. **~'logico** *adj* meteorological

me'ticcio, -a *mf* half-caste

metico'loso *adj* meticulous

me'tod|ico *adj* methodical. **'metodo** *m* method. **~olo'gia** *f* methodology

me'traggio *m* length (*in metres*)

'metrico, -a *adj* metric; (*in poesia*) metrical ● *f* metrics *sg*

'metro *m* metre; (*nastro*) tape measure ● *f inv* ([!]: *metropolitana*) tube *Br*, subway

m

me'tronomo *m* metronome

metro'notte *mf inv* night security guard

me'tropoli *f inv* metropolis. **~'tana** *f* subway, underground *Br*. **~'tano** *adj* metropolitan

'metter|e *vt* put; (*indossare*) put on; ([!]: *installare*) put in; **~e al mondo** bring into the world; **~e da parte** set aside; **~e fiducia** inspire trust; **~e qcsa in chiaro** make sth clear; **~e in mostra** display; **~e a posto** tidy up; **~e in vendita** put up for sale; **~e su** set up (casa, azienda); **ci ho messo un'ora** it took me an hour; **mettiamo che...** let's suppose that... **~si** *vr* (*indossare*) put on; (*diventare*) turn out; **~si a** start to; **~si con qcno** ([!]: *formare una coppia*) start to go out with sb; **~si a letto** go to bed; **~si a sedere** sit down; **~si in viaggio** set out

'mezza *f* **è la ~** it's half past twelve; **sono le quattro e ~** it's half past four

mezza'luna *f* half moon; (*simbolo islamico*) crescent; (*coltello*) two-handled chopping knife

mezza'manica *f* **a ~** (maglia) short-sleeved

mez'zano *adj* middle

mezza'notte *f* midnight

mezz'asta: **a ~** *adv* at half mast

'mezzo *adj* half; **di mezza età** middle-aged; **~ bicchiere** half a glass; **una mezza idea** a vague idea; **sono le quattro e ~** it's half past four. **mezz'ora** *f* half an hour. **mezza pensione** *f* half board. **mezza stagione** *f* **una giacca di mezza stagione** a spring/autumn jacket ● *adv* (*a metà*) half ● *m* (*metà*) half; (*centro*) middle; (*per raggiungere un fine*) means *sg*; **uno e ~** one and a half; **tre anni e ~** three and a half years; **in ~ a** in the middle of; **il giusto ~** the happy medium; **levare di ~** clear away; **per ~ di** by means of; **a ~ posta** by mail; **via di ~** *fig* halfway house; (*soluzione*) middle way. **mezzi** *pl* (*denaro*) means *pl*. **mezzi pubblici** public transport. **mezzi di trasporto** [means of] transport

mezzo'busto: **a ~** *adj* (foto, ritratto) half-length

mezzo'fondo *m* middle-distance running

mezzogi'orno *m* midday; (*sud*) South. **il M~** Southern Italy. **~ in punto** high noon

mi[1] *pers pron* me; (*refl*) myself; **mi ha dato un libro** he gave me a book; **mi lavo le mani** I wash my hands; **eccomi** here I am

mi[2] *m* (*Mus*) E

'mica[1] *f* mica

'mica[2] *adv* [!] (*per caso*) by any chance; **hai ~ visto Paolo?** have you seen Paul, by any chance?; **non è ~ bello** it is not at all nice; **~ male** not bad

'miccia *f* fuse

micidi'ale *adj* deadly

'micio *m* pussy-cat

'microbo *m* microbe

micro'cosmo *m* microcosm

micro'fiche *f inv* microfiche

micro'film *m inv* microfilm

mi'crofono *m* microphone

microorga'nismo *m* micro-organism

microproces'sore *m* microprocessor

micro'scopi|o *m* microscope

micro'solco *m* (*disco*) long-playing record
mi'dollo *m* (*pl f* **midolla**, (*Anat*)) marrow; **fino al ~** through and through. **~ spinale** spinal cord
mi'ele *m* honey
'mie, mi'ei ▷**MIO**
mi'et|ere *vt* reap. **~i'trice** *f* (*Mech*) harvester. **~i'tura** *f* harvest
migli'aio *m* (*pl f* **migliaia**) thousand. **a migliaia** in thousands
'miglio *m* (*Bot*) millet; (*misura*: *pl f* **miglia**) mile
migliora'mento *m* improvement
miglio'rare *vt/i* improve
migli'ore *adj* better; (*superlativo*) the best • *mf* **il**/**la ~** the best
'mignolo *m* little finger; (*del piede*) little toe
mi'gra|re *vi* migrate. **~zi'one** *f* migration
'mila ▷**MILLE**
Mi'lano *f* Milan
miliar'dario, -a *m* millionaire; (*plurimiliardario*) billionaire • *f* millionairess; billionairess. **mili'ardo** *m* billion
mili'are *adj* **pietra** *f* **~** milestone
milio'nario, -a *m* millionaire • *f* millionairess
mili'one *m* million
milio'nesimo *adj* millionth
mili'tante *adj & mf* militant
mili'tare *vi* **~ in** be a member of (partito ecc) • *adj* military • *m* soldier; **fare il ~** do one's military service. **~ di leva** national serviceman
'milite *m* soldier. **mil'izia** *f* militia
'mille *adj & m* (*pl f* **mila**) a *o* one thousand; **due**/**tre mila** two/three thousand; **~ grazie!** thanks a lot!
mille'foglie *m inv* (*Culin*) vanilla slice
mil'lennio *m* millennium
millepi'edi *m inv* centipede
mil'lesimo *adj & m* thousandth
milli'grammo *m* milligram
mil'limetro *m* millimetre
mi'mare *vt* mimic (persona) • *vi* mime
mi'metico *adj* camouflage *attrib*
mimetiz'zar|e *vt* camouflage. **~si** *vr* camouflage oneself
'mim|ica *f* mime. **~ico** *adj* mimic. **~o** *m* mime
mi'mosa *f* mimosa
'mina *f* mine; (*di matita*) lead
mi'naccia *f* threat
minacci|'are *vt* threaten. **~'oso** *adj* threatening
mi'nare *vt* mine; *fig* undermine
mina'tor|e *m* miner. **~io** *adj* threatening
mine'ra|le *adj & m* mineral. **~rio** *adj* mining *attrib*
mi'nestra *f* soup. **mine'strone** *m* vegetable soup; ([!]: *insieme confuso*) hotchpotch
mini+ *pref* mini+
minia'tura *f* miniature. **miniaturiz'zato** *adj* miniaturized
mini'era *f* mine
mini'golf *m* miniature golf
mini'gonna *f* miniskirt
minima'mente *adv* minimally
mini'market *m inv* minimarket
minimiz'zare *vt* minimize
'minimo *adj* least, slightest; (*il più basso*) lowest; (salario, quantità ecc) minimum • *m* minimum
mini'stero *m* ministry; (*governo*) government
mi'nistro *m* minister. **M~ del Tesoro** Finance Minister
mino'ranza *f* minority *attrib*

> **Minoranza linguistica** *Minoranze linguistiche* (linguistic minorities) are protected by the Italian constitution. As well as dialects of Italian, and the related languages Sardinian and Ladin, other languages are spoken. They include German in Alto Adige; French in Valdaosta; Greek, Albanian, and Serbo-Croat in the rural south; Slovenian in the north-east and Catalan in Alghero.

mino'rato, -a *adj* disabled • *mf* disabled person
mi'nore *adj* (gruppo, numero) smaller; (*superlativo*) smallest; (distanza) shorter; (*superlativo*) shortest; (prezzo) lower; (*superlativo*) lowest; (*di età*) younger; (*superlativo*) youngest; (*di importanza*) minor; (*superlativo*) least important • *mf* younger; (*superlativo*) youngest; (*Jur*) minor; **i minori di 14 anni** children

m

under 14. **mino'renne** *adj* under age ● *mf* minor
minori'tario *adj* minority *attrib*
minu'etto *m* minuet
mi'nuscolo, -a *adj* tiny ● *f* small letter
mi'nuta *f* rough copy
mi'nuto¹ *adj* minute; (*persona*) delicate; (*ricerca*) detailed; (*pioggia, neve*) fine; **al ~** (*Comm*) retail
mi'nuto² *m* (*di tempo*) minute; **spaccare il ~** be dead on time
mi'nuzi|a *f* trifle. **~'oso** *adj* detailed; (persona) meticulous
'mio (**il mio** *m*, **la mia** *f*, **i miei** *mpl*, **le mie** *fpl*) *adj poss* my; **questa macchina è mia** this car is mine; **~ padre** my father; **un ~ amico** a friend of mine ● *poss pron* mine; **i miei** (*genitori ecc*) my folks
'miope *adj* short-sighted. **mio'pia** *f* short-sightedness
'mira *f* aim; (*bersaglio*) target; **prendere la ~** take aim
mi'racolo *m* miracle. **~sa'mente** *adv* miraculously. **miraco'loso** *adj* miraculous
mi'raggio *m* mirage
mi'rar|e *vi* [take] aim. **~si** *vr* (*guardarsi*) look at oneself
mi'riade *f* myriad
mi'rino *m* sight; (*Phot*) view-finder
mir'tillo *m* blueberry
mi'santropo, -a *mf* misanthropist
mi'scela *f* mixture; (*di caffè, tabacco ecc*) blend. **~'tore** *m* (*di acqua*) mixer tap
miscel'lanea *f* miscellany
'mischia *f* scuffle; (*nel rugby*) scrum
mischi'ar|e *vt* mix; shuffle (carte da gioco). **~si** *vr* mix; (*immischiarsi*) interfere
misco'noscere *vt* not appreciate
mi'scuglio *m* mixture
mise'rabile *adj* wretched
misera'mente *adv* (finire) miserably; (vivere) in abject poverty
mi'seria *f* poverty; (*infelicità*) misery; **guadagnare una ~** earn a pittance; **porca ~!** hell!
miseri'cordi|a *f* mercy. **~'oso** *adj* merciful
'misero *adj* (*miserabile*) wretched; (*povero*) poor; (*scarso*) paltry
mi'sfatto *m* misdeed
mi'sogino *m* misogynist
mis'saggio *m* vision mixer
'missile *m* missile
missio'nario, -a *mf* missionary. **missi'one** *f* mission
misteri|'oso *adj* mysterious. **mi'stero** *m* mystery
'misti|ca *f* mysticism. **~'cismo** *m* mysticism. **~co** *adj* mystic[al] ● *m* mystic
mistifi'ca|re *vt* distort (verità). **~zi'one** *f* (*della verità*) distortion
'misto *adj* mixed; **scuola mista** mixed *or* co-educational school ● *m* mixture; **~ lana/cotone** wool/cotton mix
mi'sura *f* measure; (*dimensione*) measurement; (*taglia*) size; (*limite*) limit; **su ~** (abiti) made to measure; (mobile) custom-made; **a ~** (andare, calzare) perfectly. **~ di sicurezza** safety measure. **misu'rare** *vt* measure; try on (indumenti); (*limitare*) limit. **misu'rarsi** *vr* **misurarsi con** (*gareggiare*) compete with. **misu'rato** *adj* measured. **misu'rino** *m* measuring spoon
'mite *adj* mild; (prezzo) moderate
'mitico *adj* mythical
miti'gar|e *vt* mitigate. **~si** *vr* calm down; (clima:) become mild
'mito *m* myth. **~lo'gia** *f* mythology. **~'logico** *adj* mythological
'mitra *f* (*Relig*) mitre ● *m inv* (*Mil*) machine-gun
mitragli'a|re *vt* machine-gun; **~re di domande** fire questions at. **~'trice** *f* machine-gun
mit'tente *mf* sender
mo' *m* **a ~ di** by way of (esempio, consolazione)
'mobbing *m* harassment
'mobile¹ *adj* mobile; (*volubile*) fickle; (*che si può muovere*) movable; **beni mobili** personal estate; **squadra ~** flying squad
'mobi|le² *m* piece of furniture; **mobili** *pl* furniture *sg*. **mo'bilia** *f* furniture. **~li'ficio** *m* furniture factory
mo'bilio *m* furniture
mobilità *f* mobility
mobili'ta|re *vt* mobilize. **~zi'one** *f* mobilization

m

mocas'sino *m* moccasin

'moccolo *m* candle-end; (*moccio*) snot

'moda *f* fashion; **di ~** in fashion; **alla ~** (musica, vestiti) up-to-date; **fuori ~** unfashionable

modalità *f inv* formality; **~ d'uso** instruction

mo'della *f* model. **model'lare** *vt* model

model'li|no *m* model. **~sta** *mf* designer

mo'dello *m* model; (*stampo*) mould; (*di carta*) pattern; (*modulo*) form

'modem *m inv* modem

mode'ra|re *vt* moderate; (*diminuire*) reduce. **~rsi** *vr* control oneself. **~ta'mente** *adv* moderately **~to** *adj* moderate. **~'tore, ~'trice** *mf* (*in tavola rotonda*) moderator. **~zi'one** *f* moderation

modern|a'mente *adv* (*in modo moderno*) in a modern style. **~iz'zare** *vt* modernize. **mo'derno** *adj* modern

mo'dest|ia *f* modesty. **~o** *adj* modest

'modico *adj* reasonable

mo'difica *f* modification

modifi'ca|re *vt* modify. **~zi'one** *f* modification

mo'dista *f* milliner

'modo *m* way; (*garbo*) manners *pl*; (*occasione*) chance; (*Gram*) mood; **ad ogni ~** anyhow; **di ~ che** so that; **fare in ~ di** try to; **in che ~** (*inter*) how; **in qualche ~** somehow; **in questo ~** like this; **~ di dire** idiom; **per ~ di dire** so to speak

modu'la|re *vt* modulate. **~zi'one** *f* modulation. **~zione di frequenza** frequency modulation

'modulo *m* form; (*lunare, di comando*) module. **~ continuo** continuous paper

'mogano *m* mahogany

'mogio *adj* dejected

'moglie *f* wife

'mola *f* millstone; (*Mech*) grindstone

mo'lare *m* molar

'mole *f* mass; (*dimensione*) size

mo'lecola *f* molecule

mole'stare *vt* bother; (*più forte*) molest. **mo'lestia** *f* nuisance. **mo'lesto** *adj* bothersome

'molla *f* spring; **molle** *pl* tongs

mol'lare *vt* let go; ([!]: *lasciare*) leave; [!] give (ceffone); (*Naut*) cast off ● *vi* cease; **mollala!** [!] stop that!

'molle *adj* soft; (*bagnato*) wet

mol'letta *f* (*per capelli*) hair-grip; (*per bucato*) clothes-peg; **mollette** *pl* (*per ghiaccio ecc*) tongs

mol'lezz|a *f* softness; **~e** *pl fig* luxury

mol'lica *f* crumb

'molo *m* pier; (*banchina*) dock

mol'teplic|e *adj* manifold; (*numeroso*) numerous. **~ità** *f* multiplicity

moltipli'ca|re *vt*, **~rsi** *vr* multiply. **~'tore** *m* multiplier. **~'trice** *f* calculating machine. **~zi'one** *f* multiplication

molti'tudine *f* multitude

'molto

- *adj* a lot of; (*con negazione e interrogazione*) much, a lot of; (*con nomi plurali*) many, a lot of; **non ~ tempo** not much time, not a lot of time
- *adv* very; (*con verbi*) a lot; (*con avverbi*) much; **~ stupido** very stupid; **mangiare ~** eat a lot; **~ più veloce** much faster; **non mangiare ~** not eat much
- *pron* a lot; (*molto tempo*) a lot of time; (*con negazione e interrogazione*) much, a lot; (*plurale*) many; **non ne ho ~** I don't have much; **non ne ho molti** I don't have many, I don't have a lot; **non ci metterò ~** I won't be long; **fra non ~** before long; **molti** (*persone*) a lot of people; **eravamo in molti** there were a lot of us

momentanea'mente *adv* momentarily; **è ~ assente** he's not here at the moment. **momen'taneo** *adj* momentary

mo'mento *m* moment; **a momenti** (*a volte*) sometimes; (*fra un momento*) in a moment; **dal ~ che** since; **per il ~** for the time being; **da un ~ all'altro** (cambiare idea ecc) from one moment to the next; (aspettare qcno ecc) at any moment

'monac|a *f* nun. **~o** *m* monk

'Monaco *m* Monaco ● *f* (*di Baviera*) Munich

mo'narc|a *m* monarch. **monar'chia** *f* monarchy

mona'stero *m* (*di monaci*) monastery; (*di monache*) convent. **mo'nastico** *adj* monastic.

monche'rino *m* stump

'monco *adj* maimed; (*fig*: *troncato*) truncated; **~ di un braccio** one-armed

mon'dano *adj* worldly; **vita mondana** social life

mondi'ale *adj* world *attrib*; **di fama ~** world-famous

'mondo *m* world; **il bel ~** fashionable society; **un ~** (*molto*) a lot

mondovisi'one *f* **in ~** transmitted worldwide

mo'nello, -a *mf* urchin

mo'neta *f* coin; (*denaro*) money; (*denaro spicciolo*) [small] change. **~ estera** foreign currency. **~ legale** legal tender. **~ unica** single currency. **mone'tario** *adj* monetary

mongolfi'era *f* hot air balloon

mo'nile *m* jewel

'monito *m* warning

m

moni'tore *m* monitor

monoco'lore *adj* (*Pol*) one-party

mono'dose *adj inv* individually packaged

monogra'fia *f* monograph

mono'gramma *m* monogram

mono'kini *m inv* monokini

mono'lingue *adj* monolingual

monolo'cale *m* studio apartment

mo'nologo *m* monologue

mono'pattino *m* [child's] scooter

mono'poli|o *m* monopoly. **~o di Stato** state monopoly. **~z'zare** *vt* monopolize

mono'sci *m inv* monoski

monosil'labico *adj* monosyllabic. **mono'sillabo** *m* monosyllable

monoto'nia *f* monotony. **mo'notono** *adj* monotonous

mono'uso *adj* disposable

monsi'gnore *m* monsignor

mon'sone *m* monsoon

monta'carichi *m inv* hoist

mon'taggio *m* (*Mech*) assembly; *Cinema* editing; **catena di ~** production line

mon'ta|gna *f* mountain; (*zona*) mountains *pl*. **montagne** *pl* **russe** big dipper. **~'gnoso** *adj* mountainous. **~'naro, -a** *mf* highlander. **~no** *adj* mountain *attrib*

mon'tante *m* (*di finestra, porta*) upright

mon'ta|re *vt/i* mount; get on (veicolo); (*aumentare*) rise; (*Mech*) assemble; frame (quadro); (*Culin*) whip; edit (film); (*a cavallo*) ride; *fig* blow up; **~rsi la testa** get big-headed. **~to, -a** *mf* poser. **~'tura** *f* (*Mech*) assembling; (*di occhiali*) frame; (*di gioiello*) mounting; *fig* exaggeration

'monte *m* mountain; **a ~** up-stream; **andare a ~** be ruined; **mandare a ~ qcsa** ruin sth. **~ di pietà** pawnshop

Monte'negro *m* Montenegro

monte'premi *m inv* jackpot

mon'tone *m* ram; **carne di ~** mutton

montu'oso *adj* mountainous

monumen'tale *adj* monumental. **monu'mento** *m* monument

mo'quette *f* fitted carpet

'mora *f* (*del gelso*) mulberry; (*del rovo*) blackberry

mo'ral|e *adj* moral ● *f* morals *pl*; (*di storia*) moral ● *m* morale. **mora'lista** *mf* moralist. **~ità** *f* morality; (*condotta*) morals *pl*. **~iz'zare** *vt/i* moralize. **~'mente** *adv* morally

morbi'dezza *f* softness

'morbido *adj* soft

mor'billo *m* measles *sg*

'morbo *m* disease. **~sità** *f* (*qualità*) morbidity

mor'boso *adj* morbid

mor'dente *adj* biting. **'mordere** *vt* bite; (*corrodere*) bite into. **mordicchi'are** *vt* gnaw

mor'fina *f* morphine. **morfi'nomane** *mf* morphine addict

mori'bondo *adj* dying; (istituzione) moribund

morige'rato *adj* moderate

mo'rire *vi* die; *fig* die out; **fa un freddo da ~** it's freezing cold, it's perishing; **~ di noia** be bored to death

mor'mone *mf* Mormon

mormo'r|are *vt/i* murmur; (*brontolare*) mutter. **~io** *m* murmuring; (*lamentela*) grumbling

'moro *adj* dark ● *m* Moor

mo'roso *adj* in arrears

'morsa *f* vice; *fig* grip

'morse *adj* **alfabeto ~** Morse code

mor'setto *m* clamp

morsi'care *vt* bite. **'morso** *m* bite; (*di cibo, briglia*) bit; **i morsi della fame** hunger pangs

morta'della *f* mortadella (*type of salted pork*)

mor'taio *m* mortar

mor'tal|e *adj* mortal; (*simile a morte*) deadly; **di una noia ~e** deadly. **~ità** *f* mortality. **~'mente** *adv* (ferito) fatally; (offeso) mortally

morta'retto *m* firecracker

'morte *f* death

mortifi'ca|re *vt* mortify. **~rsi** *vr* be mortified. **~to** *adj* mortified. **~zi'one** *f* mortification

'morto, -a *pp di* **morire** ● *adj* dead; **~ di freddo** frozen to death; **stanco ~** dead tired ● *m* dead man ● *f* dead woman

mor'torio *m* funeral

mo'saico *m* mosaic

'mosca *f* fly. **~ cieca** blindman's buff

'Mosca *f* Moscow

mo'scato *adj* muscat; **noce moscata** nutmeg ● *m* muscatel

mosce'rino *m* midge

mo'schea *f* mosque

moschi'cida *adj* fly *attrib*

'moscio *adj* limp; **avere l'erre moscia** not be able to say one's r's properly

mo'scone *m* bluebottle; (*barca*) pedalo

'moss|a *f* movement; (*passo*) move. **~o** *pp di* **muovere** ● *adj* (mare) rough; (capelli) wavy; (fotografia) blurred

mo'starda *f* mustard

'mostra *f* show; (*d'arte*) exhibition; **far ~ di** pretend; **in ~** on show; **mettersi in ~** make oneself conspicuous

mo'stra|re *vt* show; (*indicare*) point out; (*spiegare*) explain. **~rsi** *vr* show oneself; (*apparire*) appear

'mostro *m* monster; (*fig: persona*) genius; **~ sacro** *fig* sacred cow

mostru|osa'mente *adv* tremendously. **~'oso** *adj* monstrous; (*incredibile*) enormous

mo'tel *m inv* motel

moti'va|re *vt* cause; (*Jur*) justify. **~to** *adj* (persona) motivated. **~zi'one** *f* motivation; (*giustificazione*) justification

mo'tivo *m* reason; (*movente*) motive; (*in musica, letteratura*) theme; (*disegno*) motif

'moto *m* motion; (*esercizio*) exercise; (*gesto*) movement; (*sommossa*) rising ● *f inv* (*motocicletta*) motor bike; **mettere in ~** start (motore)

moto'carro *m* three-wheeler

motoci'cl|etta *f* motor cycle. **~ismo** *m* motorcycling. **~ista** *mf* motor-cyclist

moto'cros|s *m* motocross. **~'sista** *mf* scrambler

moto'lancia *f* motor launch

moto'nave *f* motor vessel

mo'tore *adj* motor ● *m* motor, engine. **~ di ricerca** (*Comput*) search engine. **moto'retta** *f* motor scooter. **moto'rino** *m* moped. **motorino d'avviamento** starter

motoriz'za|to *adj* (*Mil*) motorized. **~zi'one** *f* (*ufficio*) vehicle licensing office

moto'scafo *m* motorboat

motove'detta *f* patrol vessel

'motto *m* motto; (*facezia*) witticism; (*massima*) saying

mouse *m inv* (*Comput*) mouse

mo'vente *m* motive

movimen'ta|re *vt* enliven. **~to** *adj* lively. **movi'mento** *m* movement; **essere sempre in movimento** be always on the go

mozi'one *f* motion

mozzafi'ato *adj inv* nail-biting

moz'zare *vt* cut off; dock (coda); **~ il fiato a qcno** take sb's breath away

mozza'rella *f* mozzarella (*mild, white cheese*)

mozzi'cone *m* (*di sigaretta*) stub

'mozzo *m* (*Mech*) hub; (*Naut*) ship's boy ● *adj* (coda) truncated; (testa) severed

'mucca *f* cow. **morbo della ~ pazza** mad cow disease

'mucchio *m* heap, pile; **un ~ di** *fig* lots of

'muco *m* mucus

'muffa *f* mould; **fare la ~** go mouldy. **muf'fire** *vi* go mouldy

muf'fole *fpl* mittens

mug'gi|re *vi* (mucca:) moo, low; (toro:) bellow
mu'ghetto *m* lily of the valley
mugo'lare *vi* whine; (persona:) moan. **mugo'lio** *m* whining
mulatti'era *f* mule track
mu'latto, -a *mf* mulatto
muli'nello *m* (*d'acqua*) whirl-pool; (*di vento*) eddy; (*giocattolo*) windmill
mu'lino *m* mill. **~ a vento** windmill
'mulo *m* mule
'multa *f* fine. **mul'tare** *vt* fine
multico'lore *adj* multicoloured
multi'lingue *adj* multilingual
multi'media *mpl* multimedia
multimedi'ale *adj* multimedia *attrib*
multimiliar'dario, -a *mf* multi-millionaire
multinazio'nale *f* multinational
'multiplo *adj & m* multiple
multiproprietà *f inv* time-share
multi'uso *adj* (utensile) all-purpose
'mummia *f* mummy
'mungere *vt* milk
munici'pal|e *adj* municipal. **~ità** *f inv* town council. **muni'cipio** *m* town hall
mu'nifico *adj* munificent
mu'nire *vt* fortify; **~ di** (*provvedere*) supply with
munizi'oni *fpl* ammunition *sg*
'munto *pp di* **mungere**
mu'over|e *vt* move; (*suscitare*) arouse. **~si** *vr* move
mura *fpl* (*cinta di città*) walls
mu'raglia *f* wall
mu'rale *adj* mural; (pittura) wall *attrib*
mur'a|re *vt* wall up. **~'tore** *m* bricklayer; (*con pietre*) mason; (*operaio edile*) builder. **~'tura** *f* (*di pietra*) masonry, stonework; (*di mattoni*) brickwork
mu'rena *f* moray eel
'muro *m* wall; (*di nebbia*) bank; **a ~** (armadio) built-in. **~ portante** load-bearing wall. **~ del suono** sound barrier
'muschio *m* (*Bot*) moss
musco'la|re *adj* muscular. **~'tura** *f* muscles *pl*. **'muscolo** *m* muscle
mu'seo *m* museum
museru'ola *f* muzzle
'musi|ca *f* music. **~cal** *m inv* musical. **~'cale** *adj* musical. **~'cista** *mf* musician.
'muso *m* muzzle; (*pej: di persona*) mug; (*di aeroplano*) nose; **fare il ~** sulk. **mu'sone, -a** *mf* sulker
'mussola *f* muslin
musul'mano, -a *mf* Moslem
'muta *f* (*cambio*) change; (*di penne*) moult; (*di cani*) pack; (*per immersione subacquea*) wetsuit
muta'mento *m* change
mu'tan|de *fpl* pants; (*da donna*) knickers. **~'doni** *mpl* (*da uomo*) long johns; (*da donna*) bloomers
mu'tare *vt* change
mu'tevole *adj* changeable
muti'la|re *vt* mutilate. **~to, -a** *mf* disabled person. **~to di guerra** disabled ex-serviceman
mu'tismo *m* dumbness; *fig* obstinate silence
'muto *adj* dumb; (*silenzioso*) silent; (*fonetica*) mute
'mutu|a *f* **[cassa** *f* **] ~** sickness benefit fund. **~'ato, -a** *mf* ≈ NHS patient
'mutuo¹ *adj* mutual
'mutuo² *m* loan; (*per la casa*) mortgage; **fare un ~** take out a mortgage. **~ ipotecario** mortgage

Nn

n° *abbr* (numero) No
'nacchera *f* castanet
'nafta *f* naphtha; (*per motori*) diesel oil
'naia *f* cobra; (☒: *servizio militare*) national service
'nailon *m* nylon
'nano, -a *adj & mf* dwarf
napole'tano, -a *adj & mf* Neapolitan
'Napoli *f* Naples
'nappa *f* tassel; (*pelle*) soft leather
nar'ciso *m* narcissus
nar'cotico *adj & m* narcotic
na'rice *f* nostril
nar'ra|re *vt* tell. **~'tivo, -a** *adj* narrative ● *f* fiction. **~'tore, ~'trice** *mf* nar-

rator. **~zi'one** *f* narration; (*racconto*) story

na'sale *adj* nasal

'nasc|ere *vi* (*venire al mondo*) be born; (*germogliare*) sprout; (*sorgere*) rise; **~ere da** *fig* arise from. **~ita** *f* birth. **~i'turo** *m* unborn child

na'sconder|e *vt* hide. **~si** *vr* hide

nascon'di|glio *m* hiding-place. **~no** *m* hide-and-seek. **na'scosto** *pp di* **nascondere** ● *adj* hidden; **di nascosto** secretly

na'sello *m* (*pesce*) hake

'naso *m* nose

'nastro *m* ribbon; (*di registratore ecc*) tape. **~ adesivo** adhesive tape. **~ isolante** insulating tape. **~ trasportatore** conveyor belt

na'tal|e *adj* (paese) of one's birth. **N~e** *m* Christmas; **~i** *pl* parentage. **~ità** *f* [number of] births. **nata'lizio** *adj* (*del Natale*) Christmas *attrib*; (*di nascita*) of one's birth

na'tante *adj* floating ● *m* craft

'natica *f* buttock

na'tio *adj* native

Natività *f* Nativity. **na'tivo, -a** *agg & mf* native

'nato *pp di* **nascere** ● *adj* born; **uno scrittore ~** a born writer; **nata Rossi** née Rossi

NATO *f* Nato, NATO

na'tura *f* nature; **pagare in ~** pay in kind. **~ morta** still life

natu'ra|le *adj* natural; **al ~le** (alimento) plain, natural; **~le!** naturally, of course. **~'lezza** *f* naturalness. **~liz'zare** *vt* naturalize. **~l'mente** *adv* naturally

natu'rista *mf* naturalist

naufra'gare *vi* be wrecked; (persona:) be shipwrecked. **nau'fragio** *m* shipwreck; *fig* wreck. **'naufrago, -a** *mf* survivor

'nause|a *f* nausea; **avere la ~a** feel sick. **~'ante** *adj* nauseating. **~'are** *vt* nauseate

'nautic|a *f* navigation. **~o** *adj* nautical

na'vale *adj* naval

na'vata *f* nave; (*laterale*) aisle

'nave *f* ship. **~ cisterna** tanker. **~ da guerra** warship. **~ spaziale** spaceship

na'vetta *f* shuttle

navicella *f* **~ spaziale** nose cone

navi'gabile *adj* navigable

navi'ga|re *vi* sail; **~re in Internet** surf the Net. **~'tore, ~'trice** *mf* navigator. **~zi'one** *f* navigation

na'viglio *m* fleet; (*canale*) canal

nazio'na|le *adj* national ● *f Sport* national team. **~'lismo** *m* nationalism. **~'lista** *mf* nationalist **~lità** *f inv* nationality.

nazionaliz'zare *vt* nationalize. **nazi'one** *f* nation

na'zista *adj & mf* Nazi

N.B. *abbr* (nota bene) N.B.

ne

! Spesso non si traduce: **Ne ho cinque** I've got five (of them)

● *pers pron* (*di lui*) about him; (*di lei*) about her; (*di loro*) about them; (*di ciò*) about it; (*da ciò*) from that; (*di un insieme*) of it; (*di un gruppo*) of them

····➤ **non ne conosco nessuno** I don't know any of them; **ne ho** I have some; **non ne ho più** I don't have any left

● *adv* from there; **ne vengo ora** I've just come from there; **me ne vado** I'm off

né *conj* **né... né...**neither... nor...; **non ne ho il tempo né la voglia** I don't have either the time or the inclination; **né tu né io vogliamo andare** neither you nor I want to go; **né l'uno né l'altro** neither [of them/us]

ne'anche *adv* (*neppure*) not even; (*senza neppure*) without even ● *conj* (*e neppure*) neither... nor; **non parlo inglese, e lui ~** I don't speak English, neither does he *o* and he doesn't either

'nebbi|a *f* mist; (*in città, su strada*) fog. **~'oso** *adj* misty; foggy

necessaria'mente *adv* necessarily. **neces'sario** *adj* necessary

necessità *f inv* necessity; (*bisogno*) need

necessi'tare *vi* **~ di** need; (*essere necessario*) be necessary

necro'logio *m* obituary

ne'fando *adj* wicked

ne'fasto *adj* ill-omened

ne'ga|re *vt* deny; (*rifiutare*) refuse; **essere ~to per qcsa** be no good at sth. **~'tivo, -a** *adj* negative ● *f* negative. **~zi'one** *f* negation; (*diniego*) denial; (*Gram*) negative

ne'gletto *adj* neglected

'negli = IN + GLI

negli'gen|te *adj* negligent. **~za** *f* negligence

negozi'abile *adj* negotiable

negozi'ante *mf* dealer; (*bottegaio*) shopkeeper

negozi'a|re *vt* negotiate ● *vi* **~re in** trade in. **~ti** *mpl* negotiations

ne'gozio *m* shop

'negro, -a *adj* black ● *mf* black; (*scrittore*) ghost writer

'nei = IN + I. **nel** = IN + IL. **'nella** = IN + LA. **'nelle** = IN + LE. **'nello** = IN + LO

'nembo *m* nimbus

ne'mico, -a *adj* hostile ● *mf* enemy

nem'meno *conj* not even

'nenia *f* dirge; (*per bambini*) lullaby; (*piagnucolio*) wail

n

'neo+ *pref* neo+

neofa'scismo *m* neofascism

neo'litico *adj* Neolithic

'neon *m* neon

neo'nato, -a *adj* newborn ● *mf* newborn baby

neozelan'dese *adj* New Zealand ● *mf* New Zealander

nep'pure *conj* not even

'nerb|o *m* (*forza*) strength; *fig* backbone. **~o'ruto** *adj* brawny

ne'retto *m* (*Typ*) bold [type]

'nero *adj* black; ([!]: *arrabbiato*) fuming ● *m* black; **mettere ~ su bianco** put in writing

nerva'tura *f* nerves *pl*; (*Bot*) veining; (*di libro*) band

'nervo *m* nerve; (*Bot*) vein; **avere i nervi** be bad-tempered; **dare ai nervi a qcno** get on sb's nerves. **~'sismo** *m* nerviness

ner'voso *adj* nervous; (*irritabile*) bad-tempered; **avere il ~** be irritable; **esaurimento** *m* **~** nervous breakdown

'nespol|a *f* medlar. **~o** *m* medlar[-tree]

'nesso *m* link

nes'suno *adj* no, not... any; (*qualche*) any; **non ho nessun problema** I don't have any problems, I have no problems; **non lo trovo da nessuna parte** I can't find it anywhere; **in nessun modo** on no account ● *pron* nobody, no one, not... anybody, not... anyone; (*qualcuno*) anybody, anyone; **hai delle domande? – nessuna** do you have any questions? – none; **~ di voi** none of you; **~ dei due** (*di voi due*) neither of you; **non ho visto ~ dei tuoi amici** I haven't seen any of your friends; **c'è ~?** is anybody there?

net'tare *vt* clean

net'tezza *f* cleanliness. **~ urbana** cleansing department

'netto *adj* clean; (*chiaro*) clear; (*Comm*) net; **di ~** just like that

nettur'bino *m* dustman

neu'tral|e *adj & m* neutral. **~ità** *f* neutrality. **~iz'zare** *vt* neutralize. **'neutro** *adj* neutral; (*Gram*) neuter ● *m* (*Gram*) neuter

neu'trone *m* neutron

'neve *f* snow

nevi|'care *vi* snow; **~ca** it is snowing. **~'cata** *f* snowfall. **ne'vischio** *m* sleet. **ne'voso** *adj* snowy

nevral'gia *f* neuralgia

ne'vro|si *f inv* neurosis. **~tico** *adj* neurotic

'nibbio *m* kite

'nicchia *f* niche

nicchi'are *vi* shilly-shally

'nichel *m* nickel

nichi'lista *adj & mf* nihilist

nico'tina *f* nicotine

nidi'ata *f* brood. **'nido** *m* nest; (*giardino d'infanzia*) crèche

ni'ente *pron* nothing, not... anything; (*qualcosa*) anything; **non ho fatto ~ di male** I didn't do anything wrong, I did nothing wrong; **grazie! – di ~!** thank you! – don't mention it!; **non serve a ~** it is no use; **vuoi ~?** do you want anything?; **da ~** (*poco importante*) minor; (*di poco valore*) worthless ● *adj inv* [!] **non ho ~ fame** I'm not the slightest bit hungry ● *adv* **non fa ~** (*non importa*) it doesn't matter; **per ~** at all; (litigare) over nothing; **~ affatto!** no way! ● *m* **un bel ~** absolutely nothing

nientedi'meno, **niente'meno** *adv* **~ che** no less than ● *int* fancy that!

'ninfa *f* nymph

nin'fea *f* water-lily

'ninnolo *m* plaything; (*fronzolo*) knick-knack

ni'pote *m* (*di zii*) nephew; (*di nonni*) grandson, grandchild ● *f* (*di zii*) niece; (*di nonni*) granddaughter, grandchild

'nitido *adj* neat; (*chiaro*) clear

ni'trato *m* nitrate

ni'tri|re *vi* neigh. **~to** *m* (*di cavallo*) neigh

no *adv* no; (*con congiunzione*) not; **dire di no** say no; **credo di no** I don't think so; **perché no?** why not?; **io no** not me; **fa freddo, no?** it's cold, isn't it?

'nobil|e *adj* noble ● *m* noble, nobleman ● *f* noble, noblewoman. **~i'are** *adj* noble. **~tà** *f* nobility

'nocca *f* knuckle

nocci'ol|a *f* hazelnut. **~o** *m* (*albero*) hazel

'nocciolo *m* stone; *fig* heart

'noce *f* walnut ● *m* (*albero, legno*) walnut. **~ moscata** nutmeg. **~'pesca** *f* nectarine

no'civo *adj* harmful

'nodo *m* knot; *fig* lump; (*Comput*) node; **fare il ~ della cravatta** do up one's tie. **no'doso** *adj* knotty

'noi *pers pron* (*soggetto*) we; (*oggetto, con prep*) us; **chi è? – siamo ~** who is it? – it's us

'noia *f* boredom; (*fastidio*) bother; (*persona*) bore; **dar ~** annoy

noi'altri *pers pron* we

noi'oso *adj* boring; (*fastidioso*) tiresome

noleggi'are *vt* hire; (*dare a noleggio*) hire out; charter (nave, aereo). **no'leggio** *m* hire; (*di nave, aereo*) charter. **'nolo** *m* hire; (*Naut*) freight; **a nolo** for hire

'nomade *adj* nomadic ● *mf* nomad

'nome *m* name; (*Gram*) noun; **a ~ di** in the name of; **di ~** by name. **~ di famiglia** surname. **~ da ragazza** maiden name. **no'mea** *f* reputation

nomencla'tura *f* nomenclature

no'mignolo *m* nickname

'nomina *f* appointment. **nomi'nale** *adj* nominal; (*Gram*) noun *attrib*

nomi'na|re *vt* name; (*menzionare*) mention; (*eleggere*) appoint. **~'tivo** *adj* nominative; (*Comm*) registered ● *m* nominative; (*nome*) name

non *adv* not; **~ ti amo** I do not love you; **~ c'è di che** not at all

> **!** Per formare il negativo dei verbi regolari si usa l'ausiliare *do*: **Non mi piace** I don' like it

nonché *conj* (*tanto meno*) let alone; (*e anche*) as well as

noncu'ran|te *adj* nonchalant; (*negligente*) indifferent. **~za** *f* nonchalance; (*negligenza*) indifference

nondi'meno *conj* nevertheless

'nonna *f* grandmother

'nonno *m* grandfather; **nonni** *pl* grandparents

non'nulla *m inv* trifle

'nono *adj & m* ninth

nono'stante *prep* in spite of ● *conj* although

nonvio'lento *adj* nonviolent

nord *m* north; **del ~** northern

nor'd-est *m* northeast; **a ~** northeasterly

'nordico *adj* northern

nordocciden'tale *adj* northwestern

nordorien'tale *adj* northeastern

nor'd-ovest *m* northwest; **a ~** northwesterly

'norma *f* rule; (*istruzione*) instruction; **a ~ di legge** according to law; **è buona ~** it's advisable

nor'mal|e *adj* normal. **~ità** *f* normality. **~iz'zare** *vt* normalize. **~'mente** *adv* normally

norve'gese *adj & mf* Norwegian. **Nor'vegia** *f* Norway

nossi'gnore *adv* no way

nostal'gia *f* (*di casa, patria*) homesickness; (*del passato*) nostalgia; **aver ~** be homesick; **aver ~ di qcno** miss sb. **no'stalgico, -a** *adj* nostalgic ● *mf* reactionary

no'strano *adj* local; (*fatto in casa*) home-made

'nostro (**il nostro** *m*, **la nostra** *f*, **i nostri** *mpl*, **le nostre** *fpl*) *poss adj* our; **quella macchina è nostra** that car is ours; **~ padre** our father; **un ~ amico** a friend of ours ● *poss pron* ours

'nota *f* (*segno*) sign; (*comunicazione, commento, musica*) note; (*conto*) bill; (*lista*) list; **degno di ~** noteworthy; **prendere ~** take note. **note** *pl* **caratteristiche** distinguishing marks

no'tabile *adj & m* notable

no'taio *m* notary

no'ta|re *vt* (*segnare*) mark; (*annotare*) note down; (*osservare*) notice; **far ~re qcsa** point sth out. **~zi'one** *f* marking; (*annotazione*) notation

'notes *m inv* notepad

no'tevole *adj* (*degno di nota*) remarkable; (*grande*) considerable

no'tifica *f* notification. **notifi'care** *vt* notify; (*Comm*) advise. **~zi'one** *f* notification

no'tizi|a *f* **una ~a** a piece of news; (*informazione*) a piece of information; **le ~e** the news *sg*. **~'ario** *m* news *sg*

'noto *adj* [well-]known; **rendere ~** (*far sapere*) announce

notorietà *f* fame; **raggiungere la ~** become famous. **no'torio** *adj* well-known; *pej* notorious

not'tambulo *m* night-bird

not'tata *f* night; **far ~** stay up all night

'notte *f* night; **di ~** at night; **~ bianca** sleepless night. **~'tempo** *adv* at night

not'turno *adj* nocturnal; (servizio ecc) night

no'vanta *adj & m* ninety

novan't|enne *adj & mf* ninety-year-old. **~esimo** *adj* ninetieth. **~ina** *f* about ninety. **'nove** *adj & m* nine. **nove'cento** *adj & m* nine hundred. **il Novecento** the twentieth century

no'vella *f* short story

novel'lino, -a *adj* inexperienced ● *mf* novice, beginner. **no'vello** *adj* new

no'vembre *m* November

novità *f inv* novelty; (*notizie*) news *sg*; **l'ultima ~** (*moda*) the latest fashion

novizi'ato *m* (*Relig*) novitiate; (*tirocinio*) apprenticeship

nozi'one *f* notion; **nozioni** *pl* rudiments

'nozze *fpl* marriage *sg*; (*cerimonia*) wedding *sg*. **~ d'argento** silver wedding [anniversary]. **~ d'oro** golden wedding [anniversary]

'nub|e *f* cloud. **~e tossica** toxic cloud. **~i'fragio** *m* cloudburst

'nubile *adj* unmarried ● *f* unmarried woman

'nuca *f* nape

nucle'are *adj* nuclear

'nucleo *m* nucleus; (*unità*) unit

nu'di|sta *mf* nudist. **~tà** *f inv* nudity

'nudo *adj* naked; (spoglio) bare; **a occhio ~** to the naked eye

'nugolo *m* large number

'nulla *pron* = NIENTE

nulla'osta *m inv* permit

nullità *f inv* (*persona*) nonentity

'nullo *adj* (*Jur*) null and void

nume'ra|bile *adj* countable. **~le** *adj & m* numeral

nume'ra|re *vt* number. **~zi'one** *f* numbering. **nu'merico** *adj* numerical

'numero *m* number; (*romano, arabo*) numeral; (*di scarpe ecc*) size; **dare i numeri** be off one's head. **~ cardinale** cardinal [number]. **~ decimale** decimal. **~ ordinale** ordinal [number]. **~ di telefono** phone number. **~ verde** Freephone®. **nume'roso** *adj* numerous

'nunzio *m* nuncio

nu'ocere *vi* **~ a** harm

nu'ora *f* daughter-in-law

nuo'ta|re *vi* swim; *fig* wallow. **nu'oto** *m* swimming. **~'tore, ~'trice** *mf* swimmer

nu'ov|a *f* (*notizia*) news *sg*. **~a'mente** *adv* again. **~o** *adj* new; **di ~o** again; **rimettere a ~o** give a new lease of life to

nutri|'ente *adj* nourishing. **~'mento** *m* nourishment

nu'tri|re *vt* nourish; harbour (sentimenti). **~rsi** eat; **~rsi di** *fig* live on. **~'tivo** *adj* nourishing. **~zi'one** *f* nutrition

'nuvola *f* cloud. **nuvo'loso** *adj* cloudy

nuzi'ale *adj* nuptial; (vestito, anello ecc) wedding *attrib*

Oo

o *conj* or; **~ l'uno ~ l'altro** one or the other, either
O *abbr* (ovest) W
'oasi *f inv* oasis
obbedi'ente ecc = **UBBIDIENTE** ecc
obbli'ga|re *vt* force, oblige; **~rsi** *vr* **~rsi a** undertake to. **~to** *adj* obliged. **~'torio** *adj* compulsory. **~zi'one** *f* obligation; (*Comm*) bond. **'obbligo** *m* obligation; (*dovere*) duty; **avere obblighi verso** be under an obligation to; **d'obbligo** obligatory
obbligatoria'mente *adv* **fare qcsa ~** be obliged to do sth
ob'bro|brio *m* disgrace. **~'brioso** *adj* disgraceful
obe'lisco *m* obelisk
obe'rare *vt* overburden
obesità *f* obesity. **o'beso** *adj* obese
obiet'tare *vt/i* object; **~ su** object to
obiettivi'tà *f* objectivity. **obiet'tivo** *adj* objective ● *m* objective; (*scopo*) object
obie|t'tore *m* objector. **~ttore di coscienza** conscientious objector. **~zi'one** *f* objection
obi'torio *m* mortuary
o'blio *m* oblivion
o'bliquo *adj* oblique; *fig* underhand
oblite'rare *vt* obliterate
oblò *m inv* porthole
'oboe *m* oboe
obso'leto *adj* obsolete
'oca *f* (*pl* **oche**) goose
occasio'nal|e *adj* occasional. **~'mente** *adv* occasionally
occasi'one *f* occasion; (*buon affare*) bargain; (*motivo*) cause; (*opportunità*) chance; **d'~** secondhand
occhi'aia *f* eye socket; **occhiaie** *pl* shadows under the eyes
occhi'ali *mpl* glasses, spectacles. **~ da sole** sunglasses. **~ da vista** glasses, spectacles
occhi'ata *f* look; **dare un'~ a** have a look at
occhieggi'are *vt* ogle ● *vi* peep
occhi'ello *m* buttonhole; (*asola*) eyelet
'occhio *m* eye; **~!** watch out!; **a quattr'occhi** in private; **tenere d'~ qcno** keep an eye on sb; **a ~ [e croce]** roughly; **chiudere un'~** turn a blind eye; **dare nell'~** attract attention; **pagare** *o* **spendere un ~** pay an arm and a leg. **~ nero** (*pesto*) black eye. **~ di pernice** (*callo*) corn. **~'lino** *m* **fare l'~lino a qcno** wink at sb
occiden'tale *adj* western ● *mf* westerner. **occi'dente** *m* west
oc'clu|dere *vt* obstruct. **~si'one** *f* occlusion
occor'ren|te *adj* necessary ● *m* the necessary. **~za** *f* need; **all'~za** if need be
oc'correre *vi* be necessary
occulta'mento *m* **~ di prove** concealment of evidence
occul't|are *vt* hide. **~ismo** *m* occult. **oc'culto** *adj* hidden; (*magico*) occult
occu'pante *mf* occupier; (*abusivo*) squatter
occu'pa|re *vt* occupy; spend (tempo); take up (spazio); (*dar lavoro a*) employ. **~rsi** *vr* occupy oneself; (*trovare lavoro*) find a job; **~rsi di** (*badare*) look after. **~to** *adj* engaged; (persona) busy; (posto) taken. **~zi'one** *f* occupation
o'ceano *m* ocean. **~ Atlantico** Atlantic [Ocean]. **~ Pacifico** Pacific [Ocean]
'ocra *f* ochre
ocu'lare *adj* ocular; (testimone, bagno) eye *attrib*
ocula'tezza *f* care. **ocu'lato** *adj* (scelta) wise
ocu'lista *mf* optician; (*per malattie*) ophthalmologist
od *conj* or
'ode *f* ode
odi'are *vt* hate
odi'erno *adj* of today; (*attuale*) present
'odi|o *m* hatred; **avere in ~o** hate. **~'oso** *adj* hateful
odo'ra|re *vt* smell; (*profumare*) perfume ● *vi* **~re di** smell of. **~to** *m* sense of smell. **o'dore** *m* smell; (*profumo*) scent; **c'è odore di...** there's a smell of...; **sentire odore di** smell; **odori** *pl* (*Culin*) herbs. **odo'roso** *adj* fragrant

of'fender|e *vt* offend; (*ferire*) injure. **~si** *vr* take offence

offen'siv|a *f* (*Mil*) offensive. **~o** *adj* offensive

offe'rente *mf* offerer; (*in aste*) bidder

of'fert|a *f* offer; (*donazione*) donation; (*Comm*) supply; (*nelle aste*) bid; **in ~a speciale** on special offer. **~o** *pp di* **offrire**

of'fes|a *f* offence. **~o** *pp di* **offendere** ● *adj* offended

offi'ciare *vt* officiate

offi'cina *f* workshop; **~ [meccanica]** garage

of'frir|e *vt* offer. **~si** *vr* offer oneself; (occasione:) present itself; **~si di fare qcsa** offer to do sth

offu'scar|e *vt* darken; *fig* dull (memoria, bellezza); blur (vista). **~si** *vr* darken; *fig*: (memoria, bellezza:) fade away; (vista:) become blurred

of'talmico *adj* ophthalmic

oggettività *f* objectivity. **ogget'tivo** *adj* objective

og'getto *m* object; (*argomento*) subject; **oggetti** *pl* **smarriti** lost property, lost and found *Am*

'oggi *adv & m* today; (*al giorno d'oggi*) nowadays; **da ~ in poi** from today on; **~ a otto** a week today; **dall'~ al domani** overnight; **al giorno d'~** nowadays. **~gi'orno** *adv* nowadays

'ogni *adj inv* every; (*qualsiasi*) any; **~ tre giorni** every three days; **ad ~ costo** at any cost; **ad ~ modo** anyway; **~ cosa** everything; **~ tanto** now and then; **~ volta che** whenever

o'gnuno *pron* everyone, everybody; **~ di voi** each of you

'ola *f inv* Mexican wave

O'lan|da *f* Holland. **o~'dese** *adj* Dutch ● *m* Dutchman; (*lingua*) Dutch ● *f* Dutchwoman

ole'andro *m* oleander

ole'at|o *adj* oiled; **carta ~a** greaseproof paper

oleo'dotto *m* oil pipeline. **ole'oso** *adj* oily

ol'fatto *m* sense of smell

oli'are *vt* oil

oli'era *f* cruet

olim'piadi *fpl* Olympic Games. **o'limpico** *adj* Olympic. **olim'pionico** *adj* (primato, squadra) Olympic

'olio *m* oil; **sott'~** in oil; **colori a ~** oils; **quadro a ~** oil painting. **~ di mais** corn oil. **~ d'oliva** olive oil. **~ di semi** vegetable oil. **~ solare** suntan oil

o'liv|a *f* olive. **oli'vastro** *adj* olive. **oli'veto** *m* olive grove. **~o** *m* olive tree

'olmo *m* elm

oltraggi'are *vt* offend. **ol'traggio** *m* offence

ol'tranza *f* **ad ~** to the bitter end

'oltre *adv* (*di luogo*) further; (*di tempo*) longer ● *prep* (*di luogo*) over; (*di tempo*) later than; (*più di*) more than; (*in aggiunta*) besides; **~ a** (*eccetto*) except, apart from; **per ~ due settimane** for more than two weeks. **~'mare** *adv* overseas. **~'modo** *adv* extremely

oltrepas'sare *vt* go beyond; (*eccedere*) exceed

o'maggio *m* homage; (*dono*) gift; **in ~ con** free with; **omaggi** *pl* (*saluti*) respects

ombeli'cale *adj* umbilical. **ombe'lico** *m* navel

'ombr|a *f* (*zona*) shade; (*immagine oscura*) shadow; **all'~a** in the shade. **~eggi'are** *vt* shade

om'brello *m* umbrella. **ombrel'lone** *m* beach umbrella

om'bretto *m* eye-shadow

om'broso *adj* shady

ome'lette *f inv* omelette

ome'lia *f* (*Relig*) sermon

omeopa'tia *f* homoeopathy. **omeo'patico** *adj* homoeopathic ● *m* homoeopath

omertà *f* conspiracy of silence

o'messo *pp di* **omettere**

o'mettere *vt* omit

OMG *m abbr* (organismo modificato geneticamente) GMO

omi'cid|a *adj* murderous ● *mf* murderer. **~io** *m* murder. **~io colposo** manslaughter

omissi'one *f* omission

omogeneiz'zato *adj* homogenized. **omo'geneo** *adj* homogeneous

omolo'gare *vt* approve

o'monimo, -a *mf* namesake ● *m* (*parola*) homonym

omosessu'al|e *adj & mf* homosexual.

~**ità** *f* homosexuality
On. *abbr* (onorevole) MP
'oncia *f* ounce
'onda *f* wave; **andare in ~** *Radio* go on the air. **onde** *pl* **corte** short wave. **onde** *pl* **lunghe** long wave. **onde** *pl* **medie** medium wave. **on'data** *f* wave
ondeggi'are *vi* wave; (barca:) roll
ondula|'torio *adj* undulating. **~zi'one** *f* undulation; (*di capelli*) wave
'oner|e *m* burden. **~'oso** *adj* onerous
onestà *f* honesty; (*rettitudine*) integrity. **o'nesto** *adj* honest; (*giusto*) just
'onice *f* onyx
onnipo'tente *adj* omnipotent
onnipre'sente *adj* ubiquitous; *Rel* omnipresent
ono'mastico *m* name-day
ono'ra|bile *adj* honourable. **~re** *vt* (*fare onore a*) be a credit to; honour (promessa). **~rio** *adj* honorary ● *m* fee. **~rsi** *vr* **~rsi di** be proud of
o'nore *m* honour; **in ~ di** (festa, ricevimento) in honour of; **fare ~ a** do justice to (pranzo); **farsi ~ in** excel in
ono'revole *adj* honourable ● *mf* Member of Parliament
onorifi'cenza *f* honour; (*decorazione*) decoration. **ono'rifico** *adj* honorary
O.N.U. *f abbr* (Organizzazione delle Nazioni Unite) UN
o'paco *adj* opaque; (colori ecc) dull; (fotografia, rossetto) matt
o'pale *f* opal
'opera *f* (*lavoro*) work; (*azione*) deed; (*Mus*) opera; (*teatro*) opera house; (*ente*) institution; **mettere in ~** put into effect; **mettersi all'~** get to work; **opere** *pl* **pubbliche** public works. **~ d'arte** work of art. **~ lirica** opera
ope'raio, -a *adj* working ● *mf* worker; **~ specializzato** skilled worker
ope'ra|re *vt* (*Med*) operate on; **farsi ~re** have an operation ● *vi* operate; (*agire*) work. **~'tivo, ~'torio** *adj* operating *attrib.* **~'tore, ~'trice** *mf* operator; (*TV*) cameraman. **~tore turistico** tour operator. **~zi'one** *f* operation; (*Comm*) transaction
ope'retta *f* operetta
ope'roso *adj* industrious
opini'one *f* opinion. **~ pubblica** public opinion, vox pop
'oppio *m* opium
oppo'nente *adj* opposing ● *mf* opponent
op'por|re *vt* oppose; (*obiettare*) object; **~re resistenza** offer resistance. **~si** *vr* **~si a** oppose
opportu'ni|smo *m* expediency. **~sta** *mf* opportunist. **~tà** *f inv* opportunity; (*l'essere opportuno*) timeliness. **oppor'tuno** *adj* opportune; (*adeguato*) appropriate; **il momento opportuno** the right moment
opposi|'tore *m* opposer. **~zi'one** *f* opposition; **d'~zione** (giornale, partito) opposition
op'posto *pp di* **opporre** ● *adj* opposite; (opinioni) opposing ● *m* opposite; **all'~** on the contrary
oppres|si'one *f* oppression. **~'sivo** *adj* oppressive. **op'presso** *pp di* **opprimere** ● *adj* oppressed. **~'sore** *m* oppressor
oppri'me|nte *adj* oppressive. **op'primere** *vt* oppress; (*gravare*) weigh down
op'pure *conj* otherwise, or [else]; **lunedì ~ martedì** Monday or Tuesday
op'tare *vi* **~ per** opt for
opu'lento *adj* opulent
o'puscolo *m* booklet; (*pubblicitario*) brochure
opzio'nale *adj* optional. **opzi'one** *f* option
'ora¹ *f* time; (*unità*) hour; **di buon'~** early; **che ~ è?, che ore sono?** what time is it?; **mezz'~** half an hour; **a ore** (lavorare, pagare) by the hour; **50 km all'~** 50 km an hour; **a un'~ di macchina** one hour by car. **~ d'arrivo** arrival time. **l'~ esatta** (*Teleph*) speaking clock. **~ legale** daylight saving time. **~ di punta, ore** *pl* **di punta** peak time; (*per il traffico*) rush hour
'ora² *adv* now; (*tra poco*) presently; **~ come ~** at the moment; **d'~ in poi** from now on; **per ~** for the time being, for now; **è ~ di finirla!** that's enough now! ● *conj* (*dunque*) now [then]; **~ che ci penso,...** now that I come to think about it,...
'orafo *m* goldsmith
o'rale *adj & m* oral; **per via ~** by mouth
ora'mai *adv* = **ORMAI**
o'rario *adj* (tariffa) hourly; (segnale)

time *attrib*; (velocità) per hour ● *m* time; (*tabella dell'orario*) timetable, schedule *Am*; **essere in ~** be on time; **in senso ~** clockwise. **~ di chiusura** closing time. **~ flessibile** flexitime. **~ di sportello** banking hours. **~ d'ufficio** business hours. **~ di visita** (*Med*) consulting hours

o'rata *f* gilthead

ora'tore, **-'trice** *mf* speaker

ora'torio, -a *adj* oratorical ● *m* (*Mus*) oratorio ● *f* oratory. **orazi'one** *f* (*Relig*) prayer

'orbita *f* orbit; (*Anat*) [eye-]socket

or'chestra *f* orchestra; (*parte del teatro*) pit

orche'stra|le *adj* orchestral ● *mf* member of an/the orchestra. **~re** *vt* orchestrate

orchi'dea *f* orchid

'orco *m* ogre

'orda *f* horde

or'digno *m* device; (*arnese*) tool. **~ esplosivo** explosive device

ordi'nale *adj & m* ordinal

ordina'mento *m* order; (*leggi*) rules *pl.*

ordi'nanza *f* bylaw; **d'~** (soldato) on duty

O

ordi'nare *vt* (*sistemare*) arrange; (*comandare*) order; (*prescrivere*) prescribe; (*Relig*) ordain

ordi'nario *adj* ordinary; (*grossolano*) common; (professore) with tenure; **di ordinaria amministrazione** routine ● *m* ordinary; (*Univ*) professor

ordi'nato *adj* (*in ordine*) tidy

ordinazi'one *f* order; **fare un'~** place an order

'ordine *m* order; (*di avvocati, medici*) association; **mettere in ~** put in order; **di prim'~** first-class; **di terz'~e** (film, albergo) third- rate; **di ~ pratico/economico** of a practical/economic nature; **fino a nuovo ~** until further notice; **parola d'~** password. **~ del giorno** agenda. **ordini sacri** *pl* Holy Orders

or'dire *vt* (*tramare*) plot

orec'chino *m* ear-ring

o'recchi|o *m* (*pl f* **orecchie**) ear; **avere ~o** have a good ear; **mi è giunto all'~o che...** I've heard that...;

~'oni *pl* (*Med*) mumps *sg*

o'refice *m* jeweller. **~'ria** *f* (*arte*) goldsmith's art; (*negozio*) goldsmith's [shop]

'orfano, -a *adj* orphan ● *mf* orphan. **~'trofio** *m* orphanage

orga'netto *m* barrel-organ; (*a bocca*) mouth-organ; (*fisarmonica*) accordion

or'ganico *adj* organic ● *m* personnel

orga'nismo *m* organism; (*corpo umano*) body

orga'nista *mf* organist

organiz'za|re *vt* organize. **~rsi** *vr* get organized. **~'tore, ~'trice** *mf* organizer. **~zi'one** *f* organization

'organo *m* organ

or'gasmo *m* orgasm

'orgia *f* orgy

or'goglì|o *m* pride. **~'oso** *adj* proud

orien'tale *adj* eastern; (*cinese ecc*) oriental

orienta'mento *m* orientation; **perdere l'~** lose one's bearings; **senso dell'~** sense of direction

orien'ta|re *vt* orientate. **~rsi** *vr* find one's bearings; (*tendere*) tend

ori'ente *m* east. **l'Estremo O~** the Far East. **il Medio O~** the Middle East

o'rigano *m* oregano

origi'na|le *adj* original; (*eccentrico*) odd ● *m* original. **~lità** *f* originality. **~re** *vt/i* originate. **~rio** *adj* (*nativo*) native

o'rigine *f* origin; **in ~** originally; **aver ~ da** originate from; **dare ~ a** give rise to

o'rina *f* urine. **ori'nale** *m* chamber-pot. **ori'nare** *vi* urinate

ori'undo *adj* native

orizzon'tale *adj* horizontal

orizzon'tare *vt* = **ORIENTARE**. **oriz'zonte** *m* horizon

or'la|re *vt* hem. **~'tura** *f* hem. **'orlo** *m* edge; (*di vestito ecc*) hem

'orma *f* track; (*di piede*) footprint; (*impronta*) mark

or'mai *adv* by now; (*passato*) by then; (*quasi*) almost

ormegg'iare *vt* moor

ormo'nale *adj* hormonal. **or'mone** *m* hormone

ornamen'tale *adj* ornamental. **orna'mento** *m* ornament

or'na|re *vt* decorate. **~rsi** *vr* deck oneself. **~to** *adj* (stile) ornate

ornitolo'gia *f* ornithology

'oro *m* gold; **d'~** gold; *fig* golden

orologi'aio, -a *mf* clockmaker, watchmaker

oro'logio *m* watch; (*da tavolo, muro ecc*) clock. **~ a pendolo** grandfather clock. **~ da polso** wrist-watch. **~ a sveglia** alarm clock

o'roscopo *m* horoscope

or'rendo *adj* awful, dreadful

or'ribile *adj* horrible

orripi'lante *adj* horrifying

or'rore *m* horror; **avere qcsa in ~** hate sth

orsacchi'otto *m* teddy bear

'orso *m* bear; (*persona scontrosa*) hermit. **~ bianco** polar bear

or'taggio *m* vegetable

or'tensia *f* hydrangea

or'tica *f* nettle

orticol'tura *f* horticulture. **'orto** *m* vegetable plot

orto'dosso *adj* orthodox

ortogo'nale *adj* perpendicular

orto|gra'fia *f* spelling. **~'grafico** *adj* spelling *attrib*

orto'lano *m* market gardener; (*negozio*) greengrocer's

orto|pe'dia *f* orthopaedics *sg*. **~'pedico** *adj* orthopaedic • *m* orthopaedist

orzai'olo *m* sty

or'zata *f* barley-water

o'sare *vt/i* dare; (*avere audacia*) be daring

oscenità *f inv* obscenity. **o'sceno** *adj* obscene

oscil'la|re *vi* swing; (prezzi ecc:) fluctuate; *Tech* oscillate; (*fig: essere indeciso*) vacillate. **~zi'one** *f* swinging; (*di prezzi*) fluctuation; *Tech* oscillation

oscura'mento *m* darkening; (*di vista, mente*) dimming; (*totale*) black-out

oscu'r|are *vt* darken; *fig* obscure. **~arsi** *vr* get dark. **~ità** *f* darkness. **o'scuro** *adj* dark; (*triste*) gloomy; (*incomprensibile*) obscure

ospe'dal|e *m* hospital. **~i'ero** *adj* hospital *attrib*

ospi'ta|le *adj* hospitable. **~lità** *f* hospitality. **~re** *vt* give hospitality to.

'ospite *m* (*chi ospita*) host; (*chi viene ospitato*) guest • *f* hostess; guest

o'spizio *m* [old people's] home

ossa'tura *f* bone structure; (*di romanzo*) structure, framework. **'osseo** *adj* bone *attrib*

ossequi|'are *vt* pay one's respects to. **os'sequio** *m* homage; **ossequi** *pl* respects. **~'oso** *adj* obsequious

osser'van|te *adj* (cattolico) practising. **~za** *f* observance

osser'va|re *vt* observe; (*notare*) notice; keep (ordine, silenzio). **~'tore, ~'trice** *mf* observer. **~'torio** *m* (*Astr*) observatory; (*Mil*) observation post. **~zi'one** *f* observation; (*rimprovero*) reproach

ossessio'na|nte *adj* haunting; (persona) nagging. **~re** *vt* obsess; (*infastidire*) nag. **ossessi'one** *f* obsession. **osses'sivo** *adj* obsessive. **os'sesso** *adj* obsessed

os'sia *conj* that is

ossi'dabile *adj* liable to tarnish

ossi'dar|e *vt*, **~si** *vr* oxidize

'ossido *m* oxide. **~ di carbonio** carbon monoxide

os'sidrico *adj* **fiamma ossidrica** blowlamp

ossige'nar|e *vt* oxygenate; (*decolorare*) bleach; *fig* put back on its feet (azienda). **~si** *vr* **~si i capelli** dye one's hair blonde. **os'sigeno** *m* oxygen

'osso *m* ((*Anat*): *pl f* **ossa**) bone; (*di frutto*) stone

osso'buco *m* marrowbone

os'suto *adj* bony

ostaco'lare *vt* hinder, obstruct. **o'stacolo** *m* obstacle; *Sport* hurdle

o'staggio *m* hostage; **prendere in ~** take hostage

o'stello *m* **~ della gioventù** youth hostel

osten'ta|re *vt* show off; **~re indifferenza** pretend to be indifferent. **~zi'one** *f* ostentation

oste'ria *f* inn

o'stetrico, -a *adj* obstetric • *mf* obstetrician

'ostia *f* host; (*cialda*) wafer

'ostico *adj* tough

o'stil|e *adj* hostile. **~ità** *f inv* hostility

osti'na|rsi *vr* persist (**a** in). **~to** *adj*

O

obstinate. **~zi'one** *f* obstinacy

'ostrica *f* oyster

ostru|'ire *vt* obstruct. **~zi'one** *f* obstruction

otorinolaringoi'atra *mf* ear, nose and throat specialist

ottago'nale *adj* octagonal. **ot'tagono** *m* octagon

ot'tan|ta *adj & m* eighty. **~'tenne** *adj & mf* eighty-year-old. **~'tesimo** *adj* eightieth. **~'tina** *f* about eighty

ot'tav|a *f* octave. **~o** *adj* eighth

otte'nere *vt* obtain; (*più comune*) get; (*conseguire*) achieve

'ottico, -a *adj* optic[al] ● *mf* optician ● *f* (*scienza*) optics *sg*; (*di lenti ecc*) optics *pl*

otti'ma|le *adj* optimum. **~'mente** *adv* very well

otti'mis|mo *m* optimism. **~ta** *mf* optimist. **~tico** *adj* optimistic

'ottimo *adj* very good ● *m* optimum

'otto *adj & m* eight

ot'tobre *m* October

otto'cento *adj & m* eight hundred; **l'O~** the nineteenth century

ot'tone *m* brass

ottu'ra|re *vt* block; fill (dente). **~rsi** *vr* clog. **~'tore** *m* (*Phot*) shutter. **~zi'one** *f* stopping; (*di dente*) filling

ot'tuso *pp di* **ottundere** ● *adj* obtuse

o'vaia *f* ovary

o'vale *adj & m* oval

o'vatta *f* cotton wool

ovazi'one *f* ovation

over'dose *f inv* overdose

'ovest *m* west

o'vi|le *m* sheep-fold. **~no** *adj* sheep *attrib*

ovo'via *f two-seater cable car*

ovulazi'one *f* ovulation

o'vunque *adv* = DOVUNQUE

ov'vero *conj* or; (*cioè*) that is

ovvia'mente *adv* obviously

ovvi'are *vi* **~ a qcsa** counter sth. **'ovvio** *adj* obvious

ozi'are *vi* laze around. **'ozio** *m* idleness. **ozi'oso** *adj* idle; (questione) pointless

o'zono *m* ozone; **buco nell'~** hole in the ozone layer

Pp

pa'ca|re *vt* quieten. **~to** *adj* quiet

pac'chetto *m* packet; (*postale*) parcel, package; (*di sigarette*) pack, packet. **~ software** software package

'pacchia *f* [!] bed of roses

pacchi'ano *adj* garish

'pacco *m* parcel; (*involto*) bundle. **~ regalo** gift-wrapped package

paccot'tiglia *f* junk, rubbish

'pace *f* peace; **darsi ~** forget it; **fare ~ con qcno** make it up with sb; **lasciare in ~ qcno** leave sb in peace

pachi'stano, -a *mf & adj* Pakistani

pacifi'ca|re *vt* reconcile; (*mettere pace*) pacify. **~zi'one** *f* reconciliation

pa'cifico *adj* pacific; (*calmo*) peaceful; **il P~** the Pacific

paci'fis|mo *m* pacifism. **~ta** *mf* pacifist

pa'dano *adj* **pianura padana** Po Valley

pa'del|la *f* frying-pan; (*per malati*) bedpan

padigli'one *m* pavilion

'padr|e *m* father; **~i** *pl* (*antenati*) forefathers. **pa'drino** *m* godfather. **~e'nostro** *m* **il ~enostro** the Lord's Prayer. **~e'terno** *m* God Almighty

padro'nanza *f* mastery. **~ di sé** self-control

pa'drone, -a *mf* master; mistress; (*datore di lavoro*) boss; (*proprietario*) owner. **~ggi'are** *vt* master

pae'sag|gio *m* scenery; (*pittura*) landscape. **~'gista** *mf* landscape architect

pae'sano, -a *adj* country ● *mf* villager

pa'ese *m* (*nazione*) country; (*territorio*) land; (*villaggio*) village; **il Bel P~** Italy; **va' a quel ~!** get lost!; **Paesi** *pl* **Bassi** Netherlands

paf'futo *adj* plump

'paga *f* pay, wages *pl*

pa'gabile *adj* payable

pa'gaia *f* paddle

paga'mento *m* payment; **a ~** (parcheggio) which you have to pay to use. **~ anticipato** (*Comm*) advance payment. **~ alla consegna** cash on delivery, COD

pa'gano, -a *adj & mf* pagan

pa'gare *vt/i* pay; **~ da bere a qcno** buy sb a drink

pa'gella *f* [school] report

'pagina *f* page. **Pagine** *pl* **Gialle®** Yellow Pages. **~ web** (*Comput*) web page

'paglia *f* straw

pagliac'cetto *m* (*per bambini*) rompers *pl*

pagliac'ciata *f* farce

pagli'accio *m* clown

pagli'aio *m* haystack

paglie'riccio *m* straw mattress

pagli'etta *f* (*cappello*) boater; (*per pentole*) steel wool

pagli'uzza *f* wisp of straw; (*di metallo*) particle

pa'gnotta *f* [round] loaf

pail'lette *f inv* sequin

'paio *m* (*pl f* **paia**) pair; **un ~** (*circa due*) a couple; **un ~ di** (scarpe, forbici) a pair of

'Pakistan *m* Pakistan

'pala *f* shovel; (*di remo, elica*) blade; (*di ruota*) paddle

pala'fitta *f* pile-dwelling

pala'sport *m inv* indoor sports arena

pa'late *fpl* **a ~** (fare soldi) hand over fist

pa'lato *m* palate

palaz'zetto *m* **~ dello sport** indoor sports arena

palaz'zina *f* villa

pa'lazzo *m* palace; (*edificio*) building. **~ delle esposizioni** exhibition centre. **~ di giustizia** law courts *pl*, courthouse. **~ dello sport** indoor sports arena

'palco *m* (*pedana*) platform; (*Theat*) box. **~['scenico]** *m* stage

pale'sar|e *vt* disclose. **~si** *vr* reveal oneself. **pa'lese** *adj* evident

Pale'sti|na *f* Palestine. **~'nese** *mf* Palestinian

pa'lestra *f* gymnasium, gym; (*ginnastica*) gymnastics *pl*

pa'letta *f* spade; (*per focolare*) shovel. **~ [della spazzatura]** dustpan

pa'letto *m* peg

'palio *m* (*premio*) prize. **il P~** horse-race held at Siena

paliz'zata *f* fence

'palla *f* ball; (*proiettile*) bullet; (!: *bugia*) porkie; **che palle!** ! this is a pain in the arse!. **~ di neve** snowball. **~ al piede** *fig* millstone round one's neck

pallaca'nestro *f* basketball

palla'mano *f* handball

pallanu'oto *f* water polo

palla'volo *f* volley-ball

palleggi'are *vi* (*calcio*) practise ball control; *Tennis* knock up

pallia'tivo *m* palliative

'pallido *adj* pale

pal'lina *f* (*di vetro*) marble

pal'lino *m* **avere il ~ del calcio** be crazy about football

pallon'cino *m* balloon; (*lanterna*) Chinese lantern; (!: *etilometro*) Breathalyzer®

pal'lone *m* ball; (*calcio*) football; (*aerostato*) balloon

pal'lore *m* pallor

pal'loso *adj* ✖ boring

pal'lottola *f* pellet; (*proiettile*) bullet

'palm|a *f* (*Bot*) palm. **~o** *m* (*Anat*) palm; (*misura*) hand's-breadth; **restare con un ~o di naso** feel disappointed

pal'mare *m* palmtop

'palo *m* pole; (*di sostegno*) stake; (*in calcio*) goalpost; **fare il ~** (ladro:) keep a lookout. **~ della luce** lamppost

palom'baro *m* diver

pal'pare *vt* feel

'palpebra *f* eyelid

palpi'ta|re *vi* throb; (*fremere*) quiver. **~zi'one** *f* palpitation. **'palpito** *m* throb; (*del cuore*) beat

pa'lude *f* marsh, swamp

palu'doso *adj* marshy

pa'lustre *adj* marshy; (piante, uccelli) marsh *attrib*

'pampino *m* vine leaf

'panca *f* bench; (*in chiesa*) pew

pancarré *m* sliced bread

pan'cetta *f* (*Culin*) bacon; (*di una certa età*) paunch

pan'chetto *m* [foot]stool

pan'china *f* garden seat; (*in calcio*) bench

'pancia *f* belly; **mal di ~** stomach-

p

ache; **metter su ~** develop a paunch; **a ~ in giù** lying face down
panci'olle: **stare in ~** lounge about
panci'one *m* (*persona*) pot belly
panci'otto *m* waistcoat
pande'monio *m* pandemonium
pan'doro *m* *sponge cake eaten at Christmas*
'pane *m* bread; (*pagnotta*) loaf; (*di burro*) block. **~ a cassetta** sliced bread. **pan grattato** breadcrumbs *pl.* **~ di segale** rye bread. **pan di Spagna** sponge cake. **~ tostato** toast
panett|e'ria *f* bakery; (*negozio*) baker's [shop]. **~i'ere, -a** *mf* baker
panet'tone *m* *kind of Christmas cake*
'panfilo *m* yacht
pan'forte *m* *nougat-like delicacy from Siena*
'panico *m* panic; **lasciarsi prendere dal ~** panic
pani'ere *m* basket; (*cesta*) hamper
pani'ficio *m* bakery; (*negozio*) baker's [shop]
pa'nino *m* [bread] roll. **~ imbottito** filled roll. **~ al prosciutto** ham roll. **~'teca** *f* sandwich bar
'panna *f* cream. **~ da cucina** [single] cream. **~ montata** whipped cream
'panne *f* (*Mech*) **in ~** broken down; **restare in ~** break down
pan'nello *m* panel. **~ solare** solar panel
'panno *m* cloth; **panni** *pl* (*abiti*) clothes
pan'nocchia *f* (*di granoturco*) cob
panno'lino *m* (*per bambini*) nappy; (*da donna*) sanitary towel
pano'ram|a *m* panorama; *fig* overview. **~ico** *adj* panoramic
pantacol'lant *mpl* leggings
pantalon'cini *mpl* **~ [corti]** shorts
panta'loni *mpl* trousers, pants *Am*
pan'tano *m* bog
pan'tera *f* panther; (*auto della polizia*) high-speed police car
pan'tofo|la *f* slipper
pan'zana *f* fib
pao'nazzo *adj* purple
'papa *m* Pope
papà *m inv* dad[dy]
pa'pale *adj* papal
papa'lina *f* skull-cap
papa'razzo *m* paparazzo
pa'pato *m* papacy
pa'pavero *m* poppy
'paper|a *f* (*errore*) slip of the tongue. **~o** *m* gosling
papil'lon *m inv* bow tie
pa'piro *m* papyrus
'pappa *f* (*per bambini*) pap
pappa'gallo *m* parrot
pappa'molle *mf* wimp
'para *f* **suole** *fpl* **di ~** crêpe soles
pa'rabola *f* parable; (*curva*) parabola. **~ satellitare** satellite dish
para'bolico *adj* parabolic
para'brezza *m inv* windscreen, windshield *Am*
paracadu'tar|e *vt* parachute. **~si** *vr* parachute
paraca'du|te *m inv* parachute. **~'tista** *mf* parachutist
para'carro *m* roadside post
paradi'siaco *adj* heavenly
para'diso *m* paradise. **~ terrestre** Eden, earthly paradise
parados'sale *adj* paradoxical. **para'dosso** *m* paradox
para'fango *m* mudguard
paraf'fina *f* paraffin
parafra'sare *vt* paraphrase
para'fulmine *m* lightning-conductor
pa'raggi *mpl* neighbourhood *sg*
parago'na|bile *adj* comparable (**a** to). **~re** *vt* compare. **para'gone** *m* comparison; **a paragone di** in comparison with
pa'ragrafo *m* paragraph
pa'ra|lisi *f inv* paralysis. **~'litico, -a** *adj & mf* paralytic. **~liz'zare** *vt* paralyse
paral'lel|a *f* parallel line. **~a'mente** *adv* in parallel. **~o** *agg & m* parallel; **~e** *pl* parallel bars. **~o'gramma** *m* parallelogram
para'lume *m* lampshade
para'medico *m* paramedic
pa'rametro *m* parameter
para'noia *f* paranoia
para'occhi *mpl* blinkers. **parao'recchie** *mpl* earmuffs
Paraolim'piadi *fpl* Paralympic Games
para'petto *m* parapet

para'piglia *m* turmoil

para'plegico, -a *adj & mf* paraplegic

pa'rar|e *vt* (*addobbare*) adorn; (*riparare*) shield; save (tiro, pallone); ward off, parry (schiaffo, pugno) ● *vi* (*mirare*) lead up to. **~si** *vr* (*abbigliarsi*) dress up; (*da pioggia, pugni*) protect oneself; **~si dinanzi a qcno** appear in front of sb

para'sole *m inv* parasol

paras'sita *adj* parasitic ● *m* parasite

parasta'tale *adj* government-controlled

pa'rata *f* parade; (*in calcio*) save; (*in scherma, pugilato*) parry

para'urti *m inv* (*Auto*) bumper, fender *Am*

para'vento *m* screen

par'cella *f* bill

parcheggi'a|re *vt* park. **par'cheggio** *m* parking; (*posteggio*) carpark, parking lot *Am*. **~'tore, ~'trice** *mf* parking attendant. **~tore abusivo** *person extorting money for guarding cars*

par'chimetro *m* parking-meter

'parco¹ *adj* sparing; (*moderato*) moderate

'parco² *m* park. **~ a tema** theme park. **~ di divertimenti** fun-fair. **~ giochi** playground. **~ naturale** wildlife park. **~ nazionale** national park. **~ regionale** [regional] wildlife park

pa'recchi *adj* a good many ● *pron* several

pa'recchio *adj* quite a lot of ● *pron* quite a lot ● *adv* rather; (*parecchio tempo*) quite a time

pareggi'are *vt* level; (*eguagliare*) equal; (*Comm*) balance ● *vi* draw

pa'reggio *m* (*Comm*) balance; *Sport* draw

paren'tado *m* relatives *pl*; (*vincolo di sangue*) relationship

pa'rente *mf* relative. **~ stretto** close relation

paren'tela *f* relatives *pl*; (*vincolo di sangue*) relationship

pa'rentesi *f inv* parenthesis; (*segno grafico*) bracket; (*fig: pausa*) break. **~** *pl* **graffe** curly brackets. **~ quadre** square brackets. **~ tonde** round brackets

pa'reo *m* sarong

pa'rere¹ *m* opinion; **a mio ~** in my opinion

pa'rere² *vi* seem; (*pensare*) think; **che te ne pare?** what do you think of it?; **pare di sì** it seems so

pa'rete *f* wall; (*in alpinismo*) face. **~ divisoria** partition wall

'pari *adj inv* equal; (numero) even; **andare di ~ passo** keep pace; **arrivare ~** draw; **~ ~** (copiare, ripetere) word for word ● *mf inv* equal; **ragazza alla ~** au pair [girl] ● *m* (*titolo nobiliare*) peer

Pa'rigi *f* Paris

pa'riglia *f* pair

pari|tà *f* equality; *Tennis* deuce. **~'tario** *adj* parity *attrib*

parlamen'tare *adj* parliamentary ● *mf* Member of Parliament ● *vi* discuss. **parla'mento** *m* Parliament. **il Parlamento europeo** the European Parliament

par'la|re *vt/i* speak, talk; (*confessare*) talk; **~ bene/male di qcno** speak well/ill of somebody; **non parliamone più** let's forget about it; **non se ne parla nemmeno!** don't even mention it!. **~to** *adj* (lingua) spoken. **~'torio** *m* parlour; (*in prigione*) visiting room

parlot'tare *vi* mutter. **parlot'tio** *m* muttering

parmigi'ano *m* Parmesan

paro'dia *f* parody

pa'rola *f* word; (*facoltà*) speech; **parole** *pl* (*di canzone*) words, lyrics; **rivolgere la ~ a** address; **dare a qcno la propria ~** give sb one's word; **in parole povere** crudely speaking. **parole** *pl* **incrociate** crossword [puzzle] *sg*. **~ d'ordine** password. **paro'laccia** *f* swear-word

par'quet *m inv* (*pavimento*) parquet flooring

par'rocchi|a *f* parish. **~'ale** *adj* parish *attrib*. **~'ano, -a** *mf* parishioner. **'parr'oco** *m* parish priest

par'rucca *f* wig

parrucchi'ere, -a *mf* hairdresser

parruc'chino *m* toupée, hairpiece

parsi'moni|a *f* thrift

'parso *pp di* **parere**

'parte *f* part; (*lato*) side; (*partito*) party; (*porzione*) share; **a ~** apart from; **in ~** in part; **la maggior ~ di** the majority

p

of; **d'altra ~** on the other hand; **da ~** aside; (*in disparte*) to one side; **farsi da ~** stand aside; **da ~ di** from; (*per conto di*) on behalf of; **è gentile da ~ tua** it is kind of you; **fare una brutta ~ a qcno** behave badly towards sb; **da che ~ è...?** whereabouts is...?; **da una ~..., dall'altra...** on the one hand..., on the other hand...; **dall'altra ~ di** on the other side of; **da nessuna ~** nowhere; **da tutte le parti** (*essere*) everywhere; **da questa ~** (*in questa direzione*) this way; **da un anno a questa ~** for about a year now; **essere dalla ~ di qcno** be on sb's side; **essere ~ in causa** be involved; **prendere ~ a** take part in. **~ civile** plaintiff

parteci'pante *mf* participant

parteci'pa|re *vi* **~re a** participate in, take part in; (*condividere*) share in. **~zi'one** *f* participation; (*annuncio*) announcement; *Fin* shareholding; (*presenza*) presence. **par'tecipe** *adj* participating

parteggi'are *vi* **~ per** side with

par'tenza *f* departure; *Sport* start; **in ~ per** leaving for

parti'cella *f* particle

parti'cipio *m* participle

partico'lar|e *adj* particular; (*privato*) private • *m* detail, particular; **fin nei minimi ~i** down to the smallest detail. **~eggi'ato** *adj* detailed. **~ità** *f inv* particularity; (*dettaglio*) detail

partigi'ano, -a *adj & mf* partisan

par'tire *vi* leave; (*aver inizio*) start; **a ~ da** [beginning] from

par'tita *f* game; (*incontro*) match; (*Comm*) lot; (*contabilità*) entry. **~ di calcio** football match. **~ a carte** game of cards

par'tito *m* party; (*scelta*) choice; (*occasione di matrimonio*) match

'parto *m* childbirth; **un ~ facile** an easy birth *o* labour; **dolori** *pl* **del ~** labour pains. **~ cesareo** Caesarian section. **~'rire** *vt* give birth to

par'venza *f* appearance

parzi'al|e *adj* partial. **~ità** *f* partiality. **~'mente** *adv* (*non completamente*) partially; **~mente scremato** semi-skimmed

pasco'lare *vt* graze. **'pascolo** *m* pasture

'Pasqua *f* Easter. **pa'squale** *adj* Easter *attrib*

'passa: **e ~** *adv* (*e oltre*) plus

pas'sabile *adj* passable

pas'saggio *m* passage; (*traversata*) crossing; *Sport* pass; (*su veicolo*) lift; **essere di ~** be passing through. **~ a livello** level crossing, grade crossing *Am*. **~ pedonale** pedestrian crossing

pas'sante *mf* passer-by • *m* (*di cintura*) loop • *adj Tennis* passing

passa'porto *m* passport

pas'sa|re *vi* pass; (*attraversare*) pass through; (*far visita*) call; (*andare*) go; (*essere approvato*) be passed; **~re alla storia** go down in history; **mi è ~to di mente** it slipped my mind; **~re per un genio/idiota** be taken for a genius/an idiot • *vt* (*far scorrere*) pass over; (*sopportare*) go through; (*al telefono*) put through; (*Culin*) strain; **~re di moda** go out of fashion; **le passo il signor Rossi** I'll put you through to Mr Rossi; **~rsela bene** be well off; **come te la passi?** how are you doing?. **~ta** *f* (*di vernice*) coat; (*spolverata*) dusting; (*occhiata*) look

passa'tempo *m* pastime

pas'sato *adj* past; **l'anno ~** last year; **sono le tre passate** it's past *o* after three o'clock • *m* past; (*Culin*) purée; (*Gram*) past tense. **~ prossimo** (*Gram*) present perfect. **~ remoto** (*Gram*) [simple] past. **~ di verdure** cream of vegetable soup

passaver'dure *m inv* food mill

passeg'gero, -a *adj* passing • *mf* passenger

passeggi'a|re *vi* walk, stroll. **~ta** *f* walk, stroll; (*luogo*) public walk; (*in bicicletta*) ride; **fare una ~ta** go for a walk

passeg'gino *m* pushchair, stroller *Am*

pas'seggio *m* walk; (*luogo*) promenade; **andare a ~** go for a walk; **scarpe da ~** walking shoes

passe-partout *m inv* master-key

passe'rella *f* gangway; (*Aeron*) boarding bridge; (*per sfilate*) catwalk

'passero *m* sparrow. **passe'rotto** *m* (*passero*) sparrow

pas'sibile *adj* **~ di** liable to

passio'nale *adj* passionate. **passi'one** *f* passion

pas'sivo *adj* passive ● *m* passive; (*Comm*) liabilities *pl*; **in ~** (bilancio) loss-making

pass magnetico *m inv* swipe card

'passo *m* step; (*orma*) footprint; (*andatura*) pace; (*brano*) passage; (*valico*) pass; **a due passi da qui** a stone's throw away; **a ~ d'uomo** at walking pace; **fare due passi** go for a stroll; **di pari ~** *fig* hand in hand. **~ carrabile, ~ carraio** driveway

'past|a *f* (*impasto per pane ecc*) dough; (*per dolci, pasticcino*) pastry; (*pastasciutta*) pasta; (*massa molle*) paste; *fig* nature. **~a frolla** shortcrust pastry. **pa'stella** *f* batter

> **Pasta** A popular myth says that Marco Polo brought pasta back from China. Italians like to make their own pasta for special occasions (*pasta fatta in casa*), usually with eggs and sometimes with various fillings. Traditional pasta varies enormously from region to region, and sometimes the same name can be used for different types.

pastasci'utta *f* pasta

pa'stello *m* pastel

pa'sticca *f* pastille; (!: *pastiglia*) pill

pasticc|e'ria *f* cake shop, patisserie; (*pasticcini*) pastries *pl*; (*arte*) confectionery

pasticci'are *vi* make a mess ● *vt* make a mess of

pasticci'ere, -a *mf* confectioner

pastic'cino *m* little cake

pa'sticci|o *m* (*Culin*) pie; (*lavoro disordinato*) mess. **~'one, -a** *mf* bungler ● *adj* bungling

pasti'ficio *m* pasta factory

pa'stiglia *f* (*Med*) pill, tablet; (*di menta*) sweet. **~ dei freni** brake pad

'pasto *m* meal

pasto'rale *adj* pastoral. **pa'store** *m* shepherd; (*Relig*) pastor. **pastore tedesco** German shepherd

pastoriz'za|re *vt* pasteurize. **~zi'one** *f* pasteurization

pa'stoso *adj* doughy; *fig* mellow

pa'stura *f* pasture; (*per pesci*) bait

pa'tacca *f* (*macchia*) stain; (*fig: oggetto senza valore*) piece of junk

pa'tata *f* potato. **patate** *pl* **fritte** chips *Br*, French fries. **pata'tine** *fpl* [potato] crisps, chips *Am*

pata'trac *m inv* (*crollo*) crash

pâté *m inv* pâté

pa'tella *f* limpet

pa'tema *m* anxiety

pa'tente *f* licence. **~ di guida** driving licence

pater'na|le *f* scolding. **~'lista** *m* paternalist

paternità *f* paternity. **pa'terno** *adj* paternal; (affetto ecc) fatherly

pa'tetico *adj* pathetic. **'pathos** *m* pathos

pa'tibolo *m* gallows *sg*

'patina *f* patina; (*sulla lingua*) coating

pa'ti|re *vt/i* suffer. **~to, -a** *adj* suffering ● *mf* fanatic. **~to della musica** music lover

patolo'gia *f* pathology. **pato'logico** *adj* pathological

'patria *f* native land

patri'arca *m* patriarch

pa'trigno *m* stepfather

patrimoni'ale *adj* property *attrib*. **pa-tri'monio** *m* estate

patri'o|ta *mf* patriot

pa'trizio, -a *adj & mf* patrician

patro|ci'nare *vt* support. **~'cinio** *m* support

patro'nato *m* patronage. **pa'trono** *m* (*Relig*) patron saint; (*Jur*) counsel

'patta[1] *f* (*di tasca*) flap

'patta[2] *f* (*pareggio*) draw

patteggi|a'mento *m* bargaining. **~'are** *vt/i* negotiate

patti'naggio *m* skating. **~ su ghiaccio** ice skating. **~ a rotelle** roller skating

patti'na|re *vi* skate; (auto:) skid. **~'tore, ~'trice** *mf* skater. **'pattino** *m* skate; (*Aeron*) skid. **pattino da ghiaccio** iceskate. **pattino a rotelle** roller skate; **pattini** *mpl* **in linea** roller blades®.

'patto *m* deal; (*Pol*) pact; **a ~ che** on condition that

pat'tuglia *f* patrol. **~ stradale** patrol car; highway patrol

pattu'ire *vt* negotiate

pattumi'era *f* dustbin, trashcan *Am*

pa'ura *f* fear; (*spavento*) fright; **aver ~** be afraid; **mettere ~ a** frighten. **pau'roso** *adj* (*che fa paura*) frightening; (*che ha paura*) fearful; ([!]: *enorme*) awesome

'pausa *f* pause; (*nel lavoro*) break; **fare una ~** pause; (*nel lavoro*) have a break

pavimen'ta|re *vt* pave (strada). **~zi'one** *f* (*operazione*) paving. **pavi'mento** *m* floor

pa'vone *m* peacock

pazien'tare *vi* be patient

pazi'ente *adj & mf* patient. **~'mente** *adv* patiently. **pazi'enza** *f* patience

'pazza *f* madwoman. **~'mente** *adv* madly

paz'z|esco *adj* foolish; (*esagerato*) crazy. **~ia** *f* madness; (*azione*) [act of] folly. **'pazzo** *adj* mad; *fig* crazy • *m* madman; **essere pazzo di/per** be crazy about; **darsi alla pazza gioia** live it up. **paz'zoide** *adj* whacky

'pecca *f* fault; **senza ~** flawless. **peccami'noso** *adj* sinful

pec'ca|re *vi* sin; **~re di** be guilty of (ingratitudine). **~to** *m* sin; **~to che...** it's a pity that...; **[che] ~to!** [what a] pity!. **~'tore, ~'trice** *mf* sinner

'pece *f* pitch

'peco|ra *f* sheep. **~ra nera** black sheep. **~'raio** *m* shepherd. **~'rella** *f* **cielo a ~relle** sky full of fluffy white clouds. **~'rino** *m* (*formaggio*) sheep's milk cheese

peculi'ar|e *adj* **~ di** peculiar to. **~ità** *f inv* peculiarity

pe'daggio *m* toll

pedago'gia *f* pedagogy. **peda'gogico** *adj* pedagogical

peda'lare *vi* pedal. **pe'dale** *m* pedal. **pedalò** *m inv* pedalo

pe'dana *f* footrest; *Sport* springboard

pe'dante *adj* pedantic. **~'ria** *f* pedantry. **pedan'tesco** *adj* pedantic

pe'data *f* (*in calcio*) kick; (*impronta*) footprint

pede'rasta *m* pederast

pe'destre *adj* pedestrian

pedi'atra *mf* paediatrician. **pedia'tria** *f* paediatrics *sg*

pedi'cure *mf inv* chiropodist, podiatrist *Am* • *m* pedicure

pedi'gree *m inv* pedigree

pe'dina *f* (*nella dama*) piece; *fig* pawn. **~'mento** *m* shadowing. **pedi'nare** *vt* shadow

pe'dofilo, -a *mf* paedophile

pedo'nale *adj* pedestrian. **pe'done, -a** *mf* pedestrian

peeling *m inv* exfoliation treatment

'peggio *adv* worse; **~ per te!** too bad!; **la persona ~ vestita** the worst-dressed person • *adj* worse; **niente di ~** nothing worse • *m* **il ~ è che...** the worst of it is that...; **pensare al ~** think the worst • *f* **alla ~** at worst; **avere la ~** get the worst of it; **alla meno ~** as best I can

peggiora'mento *m* worsening

peggio'ra|re *vt* make worse, worsen • *vi* get worse. **~'tivo** *adj* pejorative

peggi'ore *adj* worse; (*superlativo*) worst • *mf* **il/la ~** the worst

'pegno *m* pledge; (*nei giochi di società*) forfeit; *fig* token

pelan'drone *m* slob

pe'la|re *vt* (*spennare*) pluck; (*spellare*) skin; (*sbucciare*) peel; ([!]: *spillare denaro*) fleece. **~rsi** *vr* [!] lose one's hair. **~to** *adj* bald. **~ti** *mpl* (*pomodori*) peeled tomatoes

pel'lame *m* skins *pl*

'pelle *f* skin; (*cuoio*) leather; (*buccia*) peel; **avere la ~ d'oca** have gooseflesh

pellegri'naggio *m* pilgrimage. **pelle'grino, -a** *mf* pilgrim

pelle'rossa *mf* Red Indian

pellette'ria *f* leather goods *pl*

pelli'cano *m* pelican

pellicc|e'ria *f* furrier's [shop]. **pel'liccia** *f* fur; (*indumento*) fur coat. **~i'aio, -a** *mf* furrier

pel'licola *f* film. **~ [trasparente]** cling film

'pelo *m* hair; (*di animale*) coat; (*di lana*) pile; **per un ~** by the skin of one's teeth. **pe'loso** *adj* hairy

'peltro *m* pewter

pe'luche *m*: **giocattolo di ~** soft toy

pe'luria *f* down

'pelvico *adj* pelvic

'pena *f* (*punizione*) punishment; (*sofferenza*) pain; (*dispiacere*) sorrow; (*disturbo*) trouble; **a mala ~** hardly; **mi fa ~** I pity him; **vale la ~ andare** it is worth [while] going. **~ di morte** death sentence

pe'nal|e *adj* criminal; **diritto** *m* **~e** criminal law. **~ità** *f inv* penalty

penaliz'za|re *vt* penalize. **~zi'one** *f* (*penalità*) penalty

pe'nare *vi* suffer; (*faticare*) find it difficult

pen'daglio *m* pendant

pen'dant *m inv* **fare ~ [con]** match

pen'den|te *adj* hanging; (*Comm*) outstanding • *m* (*ciondolo*) pendant; **~ti** *pl* drop earrings. **~za** *f* slope; (*Comm*) outstanding account

'pendere *vi* hang; (superficie:) slope; (*essere inclinato*) lean

pen'dio *m* slope; **in ~** sloping

pendo'l|are *adj* pendulum • *mf* commuter. **~ino** *m* (*treno*) special, first class only, fast train

'pendolo *m* pendulum

'pene *m* penis

pene'trante *adj* penetrating; (freddo) biting

pene'tra|re *vt/i* penetrate; (*trafiggere*) pierce • *vt* (odore:) get into • *vi* (*entrare furtivamente*) steal in. **~zi'one** *f* penetration

penicil'lina *f* penicillin

pe'nisola *f* peninsula

peni'ten|te *adj & mf* penitent. **~za** *f* penitence; (*in gioco*) forfeit. **~zi'ario** *m* penitentiary

'penna *f* pen; (*di uccello*) feather. **~ a feltro** felt-tip[ped pen]. **~ a sfera** ball-point [pen]

pen'nacchio *m* plume

penna'rello *m* felt-tip[ped pen]

pennel'la|re *vt* paint. **~ta** *f* brushstroke. **pen'nello** *m* brush; **a pennello** (*alla perfezione*) perfectly

pen'nino *m* nib

pen'none *m* flagpole

pen'nuto *adj* feathered

pe'nombra *f* half-light

pe'noso *adj* (**!**: *pessimo*) painful

pen'sa|re *vi* think; **penso di sì** I think so; **~re a** think of; remember to (chiudere il gas ecc); **ci penso io** I'll take care of it; **~re di fare qcsa** think of doing sth; **~re tra sé e sé** think to oneself • *vt* think. **~ta** *f* idea

pensi'e|ro *m* thought; (*mente*) mind; (*preoccupazione*) worry; **stare in ~ro per** be anxious about. **~'roso** *adj* pensive

'pensi|le *adj* hanging; **giardino ~le** roof-garden • *m* (*mobile*) wall unit. **~'lina** *f* bus shelter

pensio'nante *mf* boarder; (*ospite pagante*) lodger

pensio'nato, -a *mf* pensioner • *m* (*per anziani*) [old folks'] home; (*per studenti*) hostel. **pensi'one** *f* pension; (*albergo*) boarding-house; (*vitto e alloggio*) board and lodging; **andare in pensione** retire; **mezza pensione** half board. **pensione completa** full board

pen'soso *adj* pensive

pen'tagono *m* pentagon

Pente'coste *f* Whitsun

pen'ti|rsi *vr* **~rsi di** repent of; (*rammaricarsi*) regret. **~'tismo** *m turning informant*. **~to** *m Mafioso turned informant*

'pentola *f* saucepan; (*contenuto*) potful. **~ a pressione** pressure cooker

pe'nultimo *adj* penultimate

pe'nuria *f* shortage

penzo'l|are *vi* dangle. **~oni** *adv* dangling

pe'pa|re *vt* pepper. **~to** *adj* peppery

'pepe *m* pepper; **grano di ~** peppercorn. **~ in grani** whole peppercorns. **~ macinato** ground pepper

pepero'n|ata *f peppers cooked in olive oil with onion, tomato and garlic*. **~'cino** *m* chilli pepper. **pepe'rone** *m* pepper. **peperone verde** green pepper

pe'pita *f* nugget

per *prep* for; (*attraverso*) through; (*stato in luogo*) in, on; (*distributivo*) per; (*mezzo, entro*) by; (*causa*) with; (*in qualità di*) as; **~ strada** on the street; **~ la fine del mese** by the end of the month; **in fila ~ due** in double file; **l'ho sentito ~ telefono** I spoke to him on the phone; **~ iscritto** in writing; **~ caso** by chance; **ho aspettato ~ ore** I've been waiting for hours; **~ tempo** in time; **~ sempre** forever; **~ scherzo** as a joke; **gridare ~ il dolore** scream with pain; **vendere ~ 10 milioni** sell for 10 million; **uno ~ volta** one at a time; **uno ~ uno** one by one; **venti ~ cento** twenty per cent; **~ fare**

qcsa [in order to] do sth; **stare ~** be about to

'pera *f* pear; **farsi una ~** ([✱]: *di eroina*) shoot up

per'cento *adv* per cent. **percentu'ale** *f* percentage

perce'pibile *adj* perceivable; (somma) payable

perce'pi|re *vt* perceive; (*riscuotere*) cash

perce|t'tibile *adj* perceptible. **~zi'one** *f* perception

perché *conj* (*in interrogazioni*) why; (*per il fatto che*) because; (*affinché*) so that; **~ non vieni?** why don't you come?; **dimmi ~** tell me why; **~ no/sì!** because!; **la ragione ~ l'ho fatto** the reason [that] I did it, the reason why I did it; **è troppo difficile ~ lo possa capire** it's too difficult for me to understand ● *m inv* reason [why]; **senza un ~** without any reason

perciò *conj* so

per'correre *vt* cover (distanza); (*viaggiare*) travel. **per'corso** *pp di* **percorrere** ● *m* (*distanza*) distance; (*viaggio*) journey

per'coss|a *f* blow. **~o** *pp di* **percuotere**. **percu'otere** *vt* strike

percussi'o|ne *f* percussion; **strumenti** *pl* **a ~ne** percussion instruments. **~'nista** *mf* percussionist

p

per'dente *mf* loser

'perder|e *vt* lose; (*sprecare*) waste; (*non prendere*) miss; *fig*: ruin; (vizio:) **~e tempo** waste time ● *vi* lose; (recipiente:) leak; **lascia ~e!** forget it!. **~si** *vr* get lost; (*reciproco*) lose touch

perdigi'orno *mf inv* idler

'perdita *f* loss; (*spreco*) waste; (*falla*) leak; **a ~ d'occhio** as far as the eye can see. **~ di tempo** waste of time. **perdi'tempo** *m* time-waster

perdo'nare *vt* forgive; (*scusare*) excuse. **per'dono** *m* forgiveness; (*Jur*) pardon

perdu'rare *vi* last; (*perseverare*) persist

perduta'mente *adv* hopelessly. **per'duto** *pp di* **perdere** ● *adj* lost; (*rovinato*) ruined

pe'renne *adj* everlasting; (*Bot*) perennial. **~'mente** *adv* perpetually

peren'torio *adj* peremptory

per'fetto *adj* perfect ● *m* (*Gram*) perfect [tense]

perfezio'nar|e *vt* perfect; (*migliorare*) improve. **~si** *vr* improve oneself; (*specializzarsi*) specialize

perfezi'o|ne *f* perfection; **alla ~ne** to perfection. **~'nista** *mf* perfectionist

per'fidia *f* wickedness; (*atto*) wicked act. **'perfido** *adj* treacherous; (*malvagio*) perverse

per'fino *adv* even

perfo'ra|re *vt* pierce; punch (schede); (*Mech*) drill. **~'tore, ~'trice** *mf* punch-card operator ● *m* perforator. **~zi'one** *f* perforation; (*di schede*) punching

per'formance *f inv* performance

perga'mena *f* parchment

perico'lante *adj* precarious; (azienda) shaky

pe'rico|lo *m* danger; (*rischio*) risk; **mettere in ~lo** endanger. **~'loso** *adj* dangerous

perife'ria *f* periphery; (*di città*) outskirts *pl*; *fig* fringes *pl*

peri'feric|a *f* peripheral; (*strada*) ring road. **~o** *adj* (quartiere) outlying

pe'rifrasi *f inv* circumlocution

pe'rimetro *m* perimeter

peri'odico *m* periodical ● *adj* periodical; (vento, mal di testa) (*Math*) recurring. **pe'riodo** *m* period; (*Gram*) sentence. **periodo di prova** trial period

peripe'zie *fpl* misadventures

pe'rire *vi* perish

pe'ri|to, -a *adj* skilled ● *mf* expert

perito'nite *f* peritonitis

pe'rizia *f* skill; (*valutazione*) survey

'perla *f* pearl. **per'lina** *f* bead

perlo'meno *adv* at least

perlu'stra|re *vt* patrol. **~zi'one** *f* patrol; **andare in ~zione** go on patrol

perma'loso *adj* touchy

perma'ne|nte *adj* permanent ● *f* perm; **farsi [fare] la ~nte** have a perm. **~nza** *f* permanence; (*soggiorno*) stay; **in ~nza** permanently. **~re** *vi* remain

perme'are *vt* permeate

per'messo *pp di* **permettere** ● *m* permission; (*autorizzazione*) permit; (*Mil*) leave; **[è] ~?** (*posso entrare?*) may I come in?; (*posso passare?*) excuse me. **~ di lavoro** work permit

per'mettere *vt* allow, permit; **potersi ~ qcsa** (*finanziariamente*) afford sth; **come si permette?** how dare you?
permutazi'one *f* exchange; (*Math*) permutation
per'nic|e *f* partridge. **~i'oso** *adj* pernicious
'perno *m* pivot
pernot'tare *vi* stay overnight
'pero *m* pear-tree
però *conj* but; (*tuttavia*) however
pero'rare *vt* plead
perpendico'lare *adj & f* perpendicular
perpe'trare *vt* perpetrate
perpetu'are *vt* perpetuate. **per'petuo** *adj* perpetual
perplessità *f inv* perplexity; (*dubbio*) doubt. **per'plesso** *adj* perplexed
perqui'si|re *vt* search. **~zi'one** *f* search. **~zione domiciliare** search of the premises
persecu|'tore, -'trice *mf* persecutor. **~zi'one** *f* persecution
persegu'ire *vt* pursue
persegui'tare *vt* persecute
perseve'ra|nza *f* perseverance. **~re** *vi* persevere
persi'ano, -a *adj* Persian ● *f* (*di finestra*) shutter. **'persico** *adj* Persian
per'sino *adv* = **PERFINO**
persi'sten|te *adj* persistent. **~za** *f* persistence. **per'sistere** *vi* persist
'perso *pp di* **perdere** ● *adj* lost; **a tempo ~** in one's spare time
per'sona *f* person; (*un tale*) somebody; **di ~, in ~** in person, personally; **per ~** per person, a head; **per interposta ~** through an intermediary; **persone** *pl* people
perso'naggio *m* personality; (*Theat*) character
perso'nal|e *adj* personal ● *m* staff. **~e di terra** ground crew. **~ità** *f inv* personality. **~iz'zare** *vt* customize (auto ecc); personalize (penna ecc)
personifi'ca|re *vt* personify. **~zi'one** *f* personification
perspi'cace *adj* shrewd
persua|'dere *vt* convince; impress (critici); **~dere qcno a fare qcsa** persuade sb to do sth. **~si'one** *f* persuasion. **~'sivo** *adj* persuasive. **persu'aso** *pp di* **persuadere**
per'tanto *conj* therefore
'pertica *f* pole
perti'nente *adj* relevant
per'tosse *f* whooping cough
pertur'ba|re *vt* perturb. **~rsi** *vr* be perturbed. **~zi'one** *f* disturbance. **~zione atmosferica** atmospheric disturbance
per'va|dere *vt* pervade. **~so** *pp di* **pervadere**
perven'ire *vi* reach; **far ~ qcsa a qcno** send sth to sb
pervers|i'one *f* perversion. **~ità** *f* perversity. **per'verso** *adj* perverse
perver'ti|re *vt* pervert. **~to** *adj* perverted ● *m* pervert
per'vinca *m* (*colore*) blue with a touch of purple
p.es. *abbr* (per esempio) e.g.
pesa *f* weighing; (*bilancia*) weighing machine; (*per veicoli*) weighbridge
pe'sante *adj* heavy; (stomaco) overfull ● *adv* (vestirsi) warmly. **~'mente** *adv* (cadere) heavily. **pesan'tezza** *f* heaviness
pe'sar|e *vt/i* weigh; **~e su** *fig* lie heavy on; **~e le parole** weigh one's words. **~si** *vr* weigh oneself
'pesca[1] *f* (*frutto*) peach
'pesca[2] *f* fishing; **andare a ~** go fishing. **~ subacquea** underwater fishing. **pe'scare** *vt* fish for; (*prendere*) catch; (*fig: trovare*) fish out. **~'tore** *m* fisherman
'pesce *m* fish. **~ d'aprile!** April Fool!. **~ grosso** *fig* big fish. **~ piccolo** *fig* small fry. **~ rosso** goldfish. **~ spada** swordfish. **Pesci** *pl* (*Astr*) Pisces
pesce'cane *m* shark
pesche'reccio *m* fishing boat
pesc|he'ria *f* fishmonger's [shop]. **~hi'era** *f* fish-pond. **~i'vendolo** *m* fishmonger
'pesco *m* peach-tree
'peso *m* weight; **essere di ~ per qcno** be a burden to sb; **di poco ~** (*senza importanza*) not very important
pessi'mis|mo *m* pessimism. **~ta** *mf* pessimist ● *adj* pessimistic. **'pessimo** *adj* very bad
pe'staggio *m* beating-up. **pe'stare** *vt*

tread on; (*schiacciare*) crush; (*picchiare*) beat; crush (aglio, prezzemolo)

'peste *f* plague; (*persona*) pest

pe'stello *m* pestle

pesti'cida *m* pesticide

pesti'len|za *f* pestilence; (*fetore*) stench. **~zi'ale** *adj* noxious

'pesto *adj* ground; **occhio ~** black eye ● *m basil and garlic sauce*

'petalo *m* petal

pe'tardo *m* banger

petizi'one *f* petition; **fare una ~** draw up a petition

petro|li'era *f* [oil] tanker. **~'lifero** *adj* oil-bearing. **pe'trolio** *m* oil

pettego|'lare *vi* gossip. **~'lezzo** *m* piece of gossip; **far ~lezzi** gossip

pet'tegolo, -a *adj* gossipy ● *mf* gossip

petti'na|re *vt* comb. **~rsi** *vr* comb one's hair. **~'tura** *f* combing; (*acconciatura*) hair-style. **'pettine** *m* comb

'petting *m* petting

petti'nino *m* (*fermaglio*) comb

petti'rosso *m* robin

'petto *m* chest; (*seno*) breast; **a doppio ~** double-breasted

petto|'rale *m* (*in gare sportive*) number. **~'rina** *f* (*di salopette*) bib. **~'ruto** *adj* (donna) full-breasted; (uomo) broad-chested

p

petu'lante *adj* impertinent

'pezza *f* cloth; (*toppa*) patch; (*rotolo di tessuto*) roll

pez'zente *mf* tramp; (*avaro*) miser

'pezzo *m* piece; (*parte*) part; **un ~** (*di tempo*) some time; (*di spazio*) a long way; **al ~** (costare) each; **fare a pezzi** tear to shreds. **~ grosso** bigwig

pia'cente *adj* attractive

pia'ce|re

● *m* pleasure; (*favore*) favour; **a ~re** as much as one likes; **per ~re!** please!; **~re [di conoscerla]**! pleased to meet you!; **con ~re** with pleasure

● *vi* **la Scozia mi piace** I like Scotland; **mi piacciono i dolci** I like sweets; **ti piace?** do you like it?; **faccio come mi pare e piace** I do as I please; **lo spettacolo è piaciuto** the show was a success.

! Nota che il soggetto in italiano corrisponde al complemento oggetto in inglese, mentre il complemento indiretto in italiano corrisponde al soggetto in inglese: **Non mi piace** I don't like it

pia|vole *adj* pleasant

piaci'mento *m* **a ~** as much as you like

pia'dina *f unleavened bread*

pi'aga *f* sore; scourge; (*persona noiosa*) pain; (*fig: ricordo doloroso*) wound

piagni'steo *m* whining

piagnuco'lare *vi* whimper

pi'alla *f* plane. **pial'lare** *vt* plane

pi'ana *f* plane. **pianeggi'ante** *adj* level

piane'rottolo *m* landing

pia'neta *m* planet

pi'angere *vi* cry; (*disperatamente*) weep ● *vt* (*lamentare*) lament; (*per un lutto*) mourn

pianifi'ca|re *vt* plan. **~zi'one** *f* planning

pia'nista *mf* (*Mus*) pianist

pi'ano *adj* flat; (*a livello*) flush; (*regolare*) smooth; (*facile*) easy ● *adv* slowly; (*con cautela*) gently; **andarci ~** go carefully ● *m* plain; (*di edificio*) floor; (*livello*) plane; (*progetto*) plan; (*Mus*) piano; **di primo ~** first-rate; **primo ~** (*Phot*) close-up; **in primo ~** in the foreground. **~ regolatore** town plan. **~ di studi** syllabus

piano'forte *m* piano. **~ a coda** grand piano

piano'terra *m inv* ground floor

pi'anta *f* plant; (*del piede*) sole; (*disegno*) plan; **di sana ~** (*totalmente*) entirely; **in ~ stabile** permanently. **~ stradale** road map. **~gi'one** *f* plantation

pian'tar|e *vt* plant; (*conficcare*) drive; (**!**: *abbandonare*) dump; **piantala!** **!** stop it!. **~si** *vr* plant oneself; (**!**: *lasciarsi*) leave each other

pianter'reno *m* ground floor

pi'anto *pp di* **piangere** ● *m* crying; (*disperato*) weeping; (*lacrime*) tears *pl*

pian|to'nare *vt* guard. **~'tone** *m* guard

pia'nura *f* plain

p'iastra *f* plate; (*lastra*) slab; (*Culin*) griddle. **~ elettronica** circuit board. **~ madre** (*Comput*) motherboard

pia'strella *f* tile

pia'strina *f* (*Mil*) identity disc; (*Med*) platelet; (*Comput*) chip

piatta'forma *f* platform. **~ di lancio** launch pad

piat'tino *m* saucer

pi'atto *adj* flat • *m* plate; (*da portata, vivanda*) dish; (*portata*) course; (*parte piatta*) flat; (*di giradischi*) turntable; **piatti** *pl* (*Mus*) cymbals; **lavare i piatti** do the washing-up. **~ fondo** soup plate. **~ piano** [ordinary] plate

pi'azza *f* square; (*Comm*) market; **letto a una ~** single bed; **letto a due piazze** double bed; **far ~ pulita** make a clean sweep. **~'forte** *m* stronghold. **piaz'zale** *m* large square. **~'mento** *m* (*in classifica*) placing

piaz'za|re *vt* place. **~rsi** *vr Sport* be placed; **~rsi secondo** come second. **~to** *adj* (cavallo) placed; **ben ~to** (*robusto*) well built

piaz'zista *m* salesman

piaz'zuola *f* **~ di sosta** pull-in

pic'cante *adj* hot; (*pungente*) sharp; (*salace*) spicy

pic'carsi *vr* (*risentirsi*) take offence; **~ di** (*vantarsi di*) claim to

'picche *fpl* (*in carte*) spades

picchet'tare *vt* stake; (scioperanti:) picket. **pic'chetto** *m* picket

picchi'a|re *vt* beat, hit • *vi* (*bussare*) knock; (*Aeron*) nosedive; **~re in testa** (motore:) knock. **~ta** *f* beating; (*Aeron*) nosedive; **scendere in ~ta** nosedive

picchiet'tare *vt* tap; (*punteggiare*) spot

'picchio *m* woodpecker

pic'cino *adj* tiny; (*gretto*) mean; (*di poca importanza*) petty • *m* little one, child

picci'one *m* pigeon

'picco *m* peak; **a ~** vertically; **colare a ~** sink

'piccolo, -a *adj* small, little; (*di età*) young; (*di statura*) short; (*gretto*) petty • *mf* child; **da ~** as a child

pic'co|ne *m* pickaxe. **~zza** *f* ice axe

pic'nic *m inv* picnic

pi'docchio *m* louse

piè *m inv* **a ~ di pagina** at the foot of the page; **saltare a ~ pari** skip

pi'ede *m* foot; **a piedi** on foot; **andare a piedi** walk; **a piedi nudi** barefoot; **a ~ libero** free; **in piedi** standing; **alzarsi in piedi** stand up; **ai piedi di** (montagna) at the foot of; **prendere ~** *fig* gain ground; (moda:) catch on; **mettere in piedi** (*allestire*) set up

piedi'stallo *m* pedestal

pi'ega *f* (*piegatura*) fold; (*di gonna*) pleat; (*di pantaloni*) crease; (*grinza*) wrinkle; (*andamento*) turn; **non fare una ~** (ragionamento:) be flawless

pie'ga|re *vt* fold; (*flettere*) bend • *vi* bend. **~rsi** *vr* bend. **~rsi a** *fig* yield to. **~'tura** *f* folding

pieghet'ta|re *vt* pleat. **~to** *adj* pleated. **pie'ghevole** *adj* pliable; (tavolo) folding • *m* leaflet

piemon'tese *adj* Piedmontese

pi'en|a *f* (*di fiume*) flood; (*folla*) crowd. **~o** *adj* full; (*massiccio*) solid; **in ~a estate** in the middle of summer; **a ~i voti** (diplomarsi) ≈ with A-grades, with first class honours • *m* (*colmo*) height; (*carico*) full load; **in ~o** (*completamente*) fully; **fare il ~o** (*di benzina*) fill up

pie'none *m* **c'era il ~** the place was packed

'piercing *m inv* body piercing

pietà *f* pity; (*misericordia*) mercy; **senza ~** (persona) pitiless; (*spietatamente*) pitilessly; **avere ~ di qcno** take pity on sb; **far ~** (*far pena*) be pitiful

pie'tanza *f* dish

pie'toso *adj* pitiful, merciful; (*pessimo*) terrible

pi'etr|a *f* stone. **~a dura** semi-precious stone. **~a preziosa** precious stone. **~a dello scandalo** cause of the scandal. **pie'trame** *m* stones *pl*. **~ifi'care** *vt* petrify. **pie'trina** *f* flint. **pie'troso** *adj* stony

pigi'ama *m* pyjamas *pl*

'pigia 'pigia *m inv* crowd, crush. **pigi'are** *vt* press

pigi'one *f* rent; **dare a ~** let, rent out; **prendere a ~** rent

pigli'are *vt* (**[!]**: *afferrare*) catch. **'piglio** *m* air

pig'mento *m* pigment
'pigna *f* cone
pi'gnolo *adj* pedantic
pigo'lare *vi* chirp. **pigo'lio** *m* chirping
pi'grizia *f* laziness. **'pigro** *adj* lazy; (intelletto) slow
'pila *f* pile; (*Electr*) battery; ([!]: *lampadina tascabile*) torch; (*vasca*) basin; **a pile** battery powered
pi'lastro *m* pillar
'pillola *f* pill; **prendere la ~** be on the pill
pi'lone *m* pylon; (*di ponte*) pier
pi'lota *mf* pilot ● *m* (*Auto*) driver. **pilo'tare** *vt* pilot; drive (auto)
pinaco'teca *f* art gallery
pi'neta *f* pine-wood
ping-'pong *m* table tennis, ping-pong [!]
'pingu|e *adj* fat. **~'edine** *f* fatness
pingu'ino *m* penguin; (*gelato*) choc ice on a stick
'pinna *f* fin; (*per nuotare*) flipper
'pino *m* pine[-tree]; **~ marittimo** cluster pine. **pi'nolo** *m* pine kernel
'pinta *f* pint
'pinza *f* pliers *pl*; (*Med*) forceps *pl*
pin'za|re *vt* (*con pinzatrice*) staple. **~'trice** *f* stapler
pin'zette *fpl* tweezers *pl*
pinzi'monio *m* sauce for crudités
'pio *adj* pious; (*benefico*) charitable
pi'oggia *f* rain; (*fig*: *di pietre, insulti*) hail, shower; **sotto la ~** in the rain. **~ acida** acid rain
pi'olo *m* (*di scala*) rung
piom'ba|re *vi* fall heavily; **~re su** fall upon ● *vt* fill (dente). **~'tura** *f* (*di dente*) filling. **piom'bino** *m* (*sigillo*) [lead] seal; (*da pesca*) sinker; (*in gonne*) weight
pi'ombo *m* lead; (*sigillo*) [lead] seal; **a ~** plumb; **senza ~** (benzina) lead-free
pioni'ere, -a *mf* pioneer
pi'oppo *m* poplar
pio'vano *adj* **acqua piovana** rainwater
pi'ov|ere *vi* rain; **~e** it's raining; **~ig-gi'nare** *vi* drizzle. **pio'voso** *adj* rainy
'pipa *f* pipe
pipì *f* **fare [la] ~** pee
pipi'strello *m* bat
pi'ramide *f* pyramid
pi'ranha *m inv* piranha
pi'rat|a *m* pirate. **~a della strada** road-hog ● *adj inv* pirate. **~e'ria** *f* piracy
pi'rofil|a *f* (*tegame*) oven-proof dish. **~o** *adj* heat-resistant
pi'romane *mf* pyromaniac
pi'roscafo *m* steamer. **~ di linea** liner
pi'scina *f* swimming pool. **~ coperta** indoor swimming pool. **~ scoperta** outdoor swimming pool
pi'sello *m* pea; ([!]: *pene*) willie
piso'lino *m* nap; **fare un ~** have a nap
'pista *f* track; (*Aeron*) runway; (*orma*) footprint; (*sci*) slope, piste. **~ d'atterraggio** airstrip. **~ da ballo** dance floor. **~ ciclabile** cycle track
pi'stacchio *m* pistachio
pi'stola *f* pistol; (*per spruzzare*) spray-gun. **~ a spruzzo** paint spray
pi'stone *m* piston
pi'tone *m* python
pit'to|re, -'trice *mf* painter. **~'resco** *adj* picturesque. **pit'torico** *adj* pictorial
pit'tu|ra *f* painting. **~'rare** *vt* paint

più

● *adv* more; (*superlativo*) most

> **!** Il comparativo e il superlativo di aggettivi di una sillaba o che terminano in *-y* si formano con i suffissi *-er* e *-est*: **più breve** shorter **il più giovane** the youngest

~ importante more important; **il ~ importante** the most important; **~ caro** more expensive; **il ~ caro** the most expensive; **di ~** more; **una coperta in ~** an extra blanket; **non ho ~ soldi** I don't have any more money; **non vive ~ a Milano** he doesn't live in Milan any longer; **~ o meno** more or less; **il ~ lentamente possibile** as slowly as possible; **per di ~** what's more; **mai ~!** never again!; **~ di** more than; **sempre ~** more and more; (*Math*) plus

● *adj* more; (*superlativo*) most; **~ tempo** more time; **la classe con**

p

~ **alunni** the class with most pupils; ~ **volte** several times
● *m* most; (*Math*) plus sign; **il ~ è fatto** the worst is over; **parlare del ~ e del meno** make small talk; **i ~** the majority

piuccheper'fetto *m* pluperfect
pi'uma *f* feather. **piu'maggio** *m* plumage. **piu'mino** *m* (*di cigni*) down; (*copriletto*) eiderdown; (*per cipria*) powder-puff; (*per spolverare*) feather duster; (*giacca*) down jacket. **piu'mone®** *m* duvet
piut'tosto *adv* rather; (*invece*) instead
pi'vello *m* [!] greenhorn
'pizza *f* pizza; *Cinema* reel.
pizzai'ola *f slices of beef in tomato sauce, oregano and anchovies*
pizze'ria *f* pizza restaurant
pizzi'c|are *vt* pinch; (*pungere*) sting; (*di sapore*) taste sharp; ([!]: *sorprendere*) catch; (*Mus*) pluck ● *vi* scratch; (cibo:) be spicy **'pizzico** *m*, **~otto** *m* pinch
'pizzo *m* lace; (*di montagna*) peak
pla'car|e *vt* placate; assuage (fame, dolore). **~si** *vr* calm down
'placca *f* plate; (*commemorativa, dentale*) plaque; (*Med*) patch
plac'ca|re *vt* plate. **~to** *adj* **~to d'argento** silver-plated. **~to d'oro** gold-plated. **~'tura** *f* plating
pla'centa *f* placenta
'placido *adj* placid
plagi'are *vt* plagiarize; pressure (persona). **'plagio** *m* plagiarism
plaid *m inv* tartan rug
pla'nare *vi* glide
'plancia *f* (*Naut*) bridge; (*passerella*) gangplank
pla'smare *vt* mould
'plastic|a *f* (*arte*) plastic art; (*Med*) plastic surgery; (*materia*) plastic. **~o** *adj* plastic ● *m* plastic model
'platano *m* plane[-tree]
pla'tea *f* stalls *pl*; (*pubblico*) audience
'platino *m* platinum
plau'sibil|e *adj* plausible. **~ità** *f* plausibility
ple'baglia *f pej* mob
pleni'lunio *m* full moon
'plettro *m* plectrum
pleu'rite *f* pleurisy
'plico *m* packet; **in ~ a parte** under separate cover
plissé *adj inv* plissé; (gonna) accordeon-pleated
plo'tone *m* platoon; (*di ciclisti*) group. **~ d'esecuzione** firing-squad
'plumbeo *adj* leaden
plu'ral|e *adj & m* plural; **al ~e** in the plural. **~ità** *f* majority
pluridiscipli'nare *adj* multidisciplinary
plurien'nale *adj* **~ esperienza** many years' experience
pluripar'titico *adj* (*Pol*) multi-party
plu'tonio *m* plutonium
pluvi'ale *adj* rain *attrib*
pneu'matico *adj* pneumatic ● *m* tyre
pneu'monia *f* pneumonia
po' ▹**POCO**
po'chette *f inv* clutch bag
po'chino *m* **un ~** a little bit

'poco
● *adj* little; (tempo) short; (*con nomi plurali*) few
● *adv* (*con verbi*) not much; (*con avverbi*) not very; **parla ~** he doesn't speak much; **lo conosco ~** I don't know him very well

! **poco** + aggettivo spesso si traduce con un aggettivo specifico: **~ probabile** unlikely, **~ profondo** shallow

● *pron* little; (*poco tempo*) a short time; (*plurale*) few
● *m* little; **un po'** a little [bit]; **un po' di** a little, some; **a ~ a ~** little by little; **fra ~** soon; **per ~** (*a poco prezzo*) cheap; (*quasi*) nearly; **~ fa** a little while ago; **sono arrivato da ~** I have just arrived; **un bel po'** quite a lot

po'dere *m* farm
pode'roso *adj* powerful
'podio *m* dais; (*Mus*) podium
po'dis|mo *m* walking. **~ta** *mf* walker
po'e|ma *m* poem. **~'sia** *f* poetry; (*componimento*) poem. **~ta** *m* poet. **~'tessa** *f* poetess. **~tico** *adj* poetic

P

poggiapi'edi *m inv* footrest

poggi'a|re *vt* lean; (*posare*) place • *vi* **~re su** be based on. **~'testa** *m inv* head-rest

poggi'olo *m* balcony

'poi *adv* (*dopo*) then; (*più tardi*) later [on]; (*finalmente*) finally. **d'ora in ~** from now on; **questa ~!** well!

poiché *conj* since

pois *m inv* **a ~** polka-dot

'poker *m* poker

po'lacco, -a *adj* Polish • *mf* Pole • *m* (*lingua*) Polish

po'lar|e *adj* polar. **~iz'zare** *vt* polarize

'polca *f* polka

po'lemi|ca *f* controversy. **~ca'mente** *adv* controversially. **~co** *adj* controversial. **~z'zare** *vi* engage in controversy

po'lenta *f cornmeal porridge*

poli'clinico *m* general hospital

poli'estere *m* polyester

polio[mie'lite] *f* polio[myelitis]

'polipo *m* polyp

polisti'rolo *m* polystyrene

poli'tecnico *m* polytechnic

po'litic|a *f* politics *sg*; (*linea di condotta*) policy; **fare ~a** be in politics. **~iz'zare** *vt* politicize. **~o, -a** *adj* political • *mf* politician

poliva'lente *adj* catch-all

p

poli'zi|a *f* police. **~a giudiziaria** ≈ Criminal Investigation Department. **~a stradale** traffic police. **~'esco** *adj* police *attrib*; (romanzo, film) detective *attrib*. **~'otto** *m* policeman

'polizza *f* policy

pol'la|io *m* chicken run; ([!]: *luogo chiassoso*) mad house. **~me** *m* poultry. **~'strello** *m* spring chicken. **~stro** *m* cockerel

'pollice *m* thumb; (*unità di misura*) inch

'polline *m* pollen; **allergia al ~** hay fever

polli'vendolo, -a *mf* poulterer

'pollo *m* chicken; ([!]: *semplicione*) simpleton

polmo|'nare *adj* pulmonary. **pol'mone** *m* lung. **~'nite** *f* pneumonia

'polo *m* pole; *Sport* polo; (*maglietta*) polo top. **~ nord** North Pole. **~ sud** South Pole

Po'lonia *f* Poland

'polpa *f* pulp

pol'paccio *m* calf

polpa'strello *m* fingertip

pol'pet|ta *f* meatball. **~'tone** *m* meat loaf

'polpo *m* octopus

pol'sino *m* cuff

'polso *m* pulse; (*Anat*) wrist; *fig* authority; **avere ~** be strict

pol'tiglia *f* mush

pol'trire *vi* lie around

pol'tron|a *f* armchair; (*Theat*) seat in the stalls. **~e** *adj* lazy

'polve|re *f* dust; (*sostanza polverizzata*) powder; **in ~re** powdered; **sapone in ~re** soap powder. **~'rina** *f* (*medicina*) powder. **~riz'zare** *vt* pulverize; (*nebulizzare*) atomize. **~'rone** *m* cloud of dust. **~'roso** *adj* dusty

po'mata *f* ointment, cream

po'mello *m* knob; (*guancia*) cheek

pomeridi'ano *adj* afternoon *attrib*; **alle tre pomeridiane** at three in the afternoon. **pome'riggio** *m* afternoon

'pomice *f* pumice

'pomo *m* (*oggetto*) knob. **~ d'Adamo** Adam's apple

pomo'doro *m* tomato

'pompa *f* pump; (*sfarzo*) pomp. **pompe** *pl* **funebri** (*funzione*) funeral. **pom'pare** *vt* pump; (*gonfiare d'aria*) pump up; (*fig: esagerare*) exaggerate; **pompare fuori** pump out

pom'pelmo *m* grapefruit

pompi'ere *m* fireman; **i pompieri** the fire brigade

pom'poso *adj* pompous

ponde'rare *vt* ponder

po'nente *m* west

'ponte *m* bridge; (*Naut*) deck; (*impalcatura*) scaffolding; **fare il ~** make a long weekend of it

pon'tefice *m* pontiff

pontifi'ca|re *vi* pontificate. **~to** *m* pontificate

ponti'ficio *adj* papal

pon'tile *m* jetty

popò *f inv* [!] pooh

popo'lano *adj* of the people

popo'la|re *adj* popular; (*comune*) common • *vt* populate. **~rsi** *vr* get crowded. **~rità** *f* popularity. **~zi'one** *f* population. **'popolo** *m* people. **popo'loso** *adj* populous

'poppa *f* (*Naut*) stern; (*mammella*) breast; **a ~** astern

pop'pa|re *vt* suck. **~ta** *f* (*pasto*) feed. **~'toio** *m* [feeding-]bottle

popu'lista *mf* populist

por'cata *f* load of rubbish; **porcate** *pl* (⚠: *cibo*) junk food

porcel'lana *f* porcelain

porcel'lino *m* piglet. **~ d'India** guinea-pig

porche'ria *f* dirt; (*cosa orrenda*) piece of filth; (*robaccia*) rubbish

por'ci|le *m* pigsty. **~no** *adj* pig *attrib* ● *m* (*fungo*) edible mushroom. **'porco** *m* pig; (*carne*) pork

'porgere *vt* give; (*offrire*) offer; **porgo distinti saluti** (*in lettera*) I remain, yours sincerely

porno|gra'fia *f* pornography. **~'grafico** *adj* pornographic

'poro *m* pore. **po'roso** *adj* porous

'porpora *f* purple

'por|re *vt* put; (*collocare*) place; (*supporre*) suppose; ask (domanda); present (candidatura); **poniamo il caso che...** let us suppose that...; **~re fine** *o* **termine a** put an end to. **~si** *vr* put oneself; **~si a sedere** sit down; **~si in cammino** set out

'porro *m* (*Bot*) leek; (*verruca*) wart

'porta *f* door; *Sport* goal; (*di città*) gate; (*Comput*) port. **~ a ~** door-to-door; **mettere alla ~** show sb the door. **~ di servizio** tradesmen's entrance

portaba'gagli *m inv* porter; (*di treno ecc*) luggage rack; (*Auto*) boot, trunk *Am*; (*sul tetto di un'auto*) roof rack

portabot'tiglie *m inv* bottle rack, wine rack

porta'cenere *m inv* ashtray

portachi'avi *m inv* keyring

porta'cipria *m inv* compact

portadocu'menti *m inv* document wallet

porta'erei *f inv* aircraft carrier

portafi'nestra *f* French window

porta'foglio *m* wallet; (*per documenti*) portfolio; (*ministero*) ministry

portafor'tuna *m inv* lucky charm ● *adj inv* lucky

portagi'oie *m inv* jewellery box

por'tale *m* door

portama'tite *m inv* pencil case

porta'mento *m* carriage; (*condotta*) behaviour

porta'mina *m inv* propelling pencil

portamo'nete *m inv* purse

portaom'brelli *m inv* umbrella stand

porta'pacchi *m inv* roof rack; (*su bicicletta*) luggage rack

porta'penne *m inv* pencil case

por'ta|re *vt* (*verso chi parla*) bring; (*lontano da chi parla*) take; (*sorreggere*) (*Math*) carry; (*condurre*) lead; (*indossare*) wear; (*avere*) bear. **~rsi** *vr* (*trasferirsi*) move; (*comportarsi*) behave; **~rsi bene/male gli anni** look young/old for one's age

portari'viste *m inv* magazine rack

porta'sci *m inv* ski rack

portasiga'rette *m inv* cigarette-case

por'ta|ta *f* (*di pranzo*) course; (*Auto*) carrying capacity; (*di arma*) range; (*fig: abilità*) capability; **a ~ta di mano** within reach. **por'tatile** *agg & m* portable. **~to** *adj* (indumento) worn; (*dotato*) gifted; **essere ~to per qcsa** have a gift for sth; **essere ~to a** (*tendere a*) be inclined to. **~'tore, ~'trice** *mf* bearer; **al ~tore** to the bearer. **~tore di handicap** disabled person

portatovagli'olo *m* napkin ring

portau'ovo *m inv* egg-cup

porta'voce *m inv* spokesman ● *f inv* spokeswoman

por'tento *m* marvel; (*persona dotata*) prodigy

'portico *m* portico

porti'er|a *f* door; (*tendaggio*) door curtain. **~e** *m* porter, doorman; *Sport* goalkeeper. **~e di notte** night porter

porti'n|aio, -a *mf* caretaker. **~e'ria** *f* concierge's room; (*di ospedale*) porter's lodge

'porto *pp di* **porgere** ● *m* harbour; (*complesso*) port; (*vino*) port [wine]; (*spesa di trasporto*) carriage; **andare in ~** succeed. **~ d'armi** gun licence

Porto'g|allo *m* Portugal. **p~hese** *adj & mf* Portuguese

por'tone *m* main door
portu'ale *m* docker
porzi'one *f* portion
'posa *f* laying; (*riposo*) rest; (*Phot*) exposure; (*atteggiamento*) pose; **mettersi in ~** pose
po'sa|re *vt* put; (*giù*) put [down] ● *vi* (*poggiare*) rest; (*per un ritratto*) pose. **~rsi** *vr* alight; (*sostare*) rest; (*Aeron*) land. **~ta** *f* piece of cutlery; **~te** *pl* cutlery *sg*. **~to** *adj* sedate
po'scritto *m* postscript
posi'tivo *adj* positive
posizio'nare *vt* position
posizi'one *f* position; **farsi una ~** get ahead
posolo'gia *f* dosage
po'spo|rre *vt* place after; (*posticipare*) postpone. **~sto** *pp di* **posporre**
posse'd|ere *vt* possess, own. **~i'mento** *m* possession
posses|'sivo *adj* possessive. **pos'sesso** *m* ownership; (*bene*) possession. **~'sore** *m* owner
pos'sibil|e *adj* possible; **il più presto ~e** as soon as possible ● *m* **fare [tutto] il ~e** do one's best. **~ità** *f inv* possibility; (*occasione*) chance ● *fpl* (*mezzi*) means
possi'dente *mf* land-owner
'posta *f* post, mail; (*ufficio postale*) post office; (*al gioco*) stake; **spese di ~** postage; **per ~** by post, by mail; **a bella ~** on purpose; **Poste e Telecomunicazioni** *pl* [Italian] Post Office. **~ elettronica** e-mail. **~ prioritaria** ≈ first-class mail. **~ vocale** voice-mail
posta'giro *m* postal giro
po'stale *adj* postal
postazi'one *f* position
postda'tare *vt* postdate (assegno)
posteggi'a|re *vt/i* park. **~'tore, ~'trice** *mf* parking attendant. **po'steggio** *m* car-park, parking lot *Am*; (*di taxi*) taxi-rank
'posteri *mpl* descendants. **~'ore** *adj* rear; (*nel tempo*) later **~tà** *f* posterity
po'sticcio *adj* artificial; (baffi, barba) false ● *m* hair-piece
postici'pare *vt* postpone
po'stilla *f* note; (*Jur*) rider
po'stino *m* postman, mailman *Am*
'posto *pp di* **porre** ● *m* place; (*spazio*) room; (*impiego*) job; (*Mil*) post; (*sedile*) seat; **a/fuori ~** in/out of place; **prendere ~** take up room; **sul ~** on-site; **essere a ~** (casa, libri) be tidy; **fare ~ a** make room for; **al ~ di** (*invece di*) in place of, instead of. **~ di blocco** checkpoint. **~ di guida** driving seat. **~ di lavoro** workstation. **posti** *pl* **in piedi** standing room. **~ di polizia** police station
post-'partum *adj* post-natal
'postumo *adj* posthumous ● *m* after-effect
po'tabile *adj* drinkable; **acqua ~** drinking water
po'tare *vt* prune
po'tassio *m* potassium
po'ten|te *adj* powerful; (*efficace*) potent. **~za** *f* power; (*efficacia*) potency. **~zi'ale** *adj & m* potential
po'tere *m* power; **al ~** in power ● *vi* can, be able to; **posso entrare?** may I come in?; **posso fare qualche cosa?** can I do something?; **che tu possa essere felice!** may you be happy!; **non ne posso più** (*sono stanco*) I can't go on; (*sono stufo*) I can't take any more; **può darsi** perhaps; **può darsi che sia vero** perhaps it's true; **potrebbe aver ragione** he could be right, he might be right; **avresti potuto telefonare** you could have phoned, you might have phoned; **spero di poter venire** I hope to be able to come
potestà *f inv* power
'pover|o, -a *adj* poor; (*semplice*) plain ● *m* poor man ● *f* poor woman; **i ~i** the poor. **~tà** *f* poverty
'pozza *f* pool. **poz'zanghera** *f* puddle
'pozzo *m* well; (*minerario*) pit. **~ petrolifero** oil-well
PP.TT. *abbr* (Poste e Telegrafi) [Italian] Post Office
prali'nato *adj* (mandorla, gelato) praline-coated
pram'matica *f* **essere di ~** be customary
pran'zare *vi* dine; (*a mezzogiorno*) lunch. **'pranzo** *m* dinner; (*a mezzogiorno*) lunch. **pranzo di nozze** wedding breakfast

Pranzo *Pranzo* is traditonally the day's main meal and school timetables and hours of business are geared to a break between one and four o'clock. It starts with a *primo* (usually pasta), followed by a *secondo* (main course). Gradually Italians, especially city-dwellers, are adopting a more northern European timetable and making less of *pranzo*.

'prassi *f* standard procedure

prate'ria *f* grassland

'prati|ca *f* practice; (*esperienza*) experience; (*documentazione*) file; **avere ~ca di qcsa** be familiar with sth; **far ~ca** gain experience. **~'cabile** *adj* practicable; (strada) passable. **~ca'mente** *adv* practically. **~'cante** *mf* apprentice; (*Relig*) [regular] church-goer

prati'ca|re *vt* practise; (*frequentare*) associate with; (*fare*) make

praticità *f* practicality. **'pratico** *adj* practical; (*esperto*) experienced; **essere pratico di qcsa** know about sth

'prato *m* meadow; (*di giardino*) lawn

pre'ambolo *m* preamble

preannunci'are *vt* give advance notice of

preavvi'sare *vt* forewarn. **preav'viso** *m* warning

pre'cario *adj* precarious

precauzi'one *f* precaution; (*cautela*) care

prece'den|te *adj* previous ● *m* precedent. **~te'mente** *adv* previously. **~za** *f* precedence; (*di veicoli*) right of way; **dare la ~za** give way. **pre'cedere** *vt* precede

pre'cetto *m* precept

precipi'ta|re *vt* **~re le cose** precipitate events ● *vi* fall headlong; (situazione, eventi:) come to a head. **~rsi** *vr* (*gettarsi*) throw oneself; (*affrettarsi*) rush; **~rsi a fare qcsa** rush to do sth. **~zi'one** *f* (*fretta*) haste; (*atmosferica*) precipitation. **precipi'toso** *adj* hasty; (*avventato*) reckless; (caduta) headlong

preci'pizio *m* precipice; **a ~** headlong

precisa'mente *adv* precisely

preci'sa|re *vt* specify; (*spiegare*) clarify. **~zi'one** *f* clarification

precisi'one *f* precision. **pre'ciso** *adj* precise; (ore) sharp; (*identico*) identical

pre'clu|dere *vt* preclude. **~so** *pp di* **precludere**

pre'coc|e *adj* precocious; (*prematuro*) premature

precon'cetto *adj* preconceived ● *m* prejudice

pre'corr|ere *vt* **~ere i tempi** be ahead of one's time

precur'sore *m* precursor

'preda *f* prey; (*bottino*) booty; **essere in ~ al panico** be panic-stricken; **in ~ alle fiamme** engulfed in flames. **pre'dare** *vt* plunder. **~'tore** *m* predator

predeces'sore *mf* predecessor

pre'del|la *f* platform. **~'lino** *m* step

predesti'na|re *vt* predestine. **~to** *adj* (*Relig*) predestined, preordained

predetermi'nato *adj* predetermined, preordained

pre'detto *pp di* **predire**

'predica *f* sermon; *fig* lecture

predi'care *vt* preach

predi'le|tto, -a *pp di* **prediligere** ● *adj* favourite ● *mf* pet. **~zi'one** *f* predilection. **predi'ligere** *vt* prefer

pre'dire *vt* foretell

predi'spo|rre *vt* arrange. **~rsi** *vr* **~rsi a** prepare oneself for. **~sizi'one** *f* predisposition; (*al disegno ecc*) bent (**a** for). **~sto** *pp di* **predisporre**

predizi'one *f* prediction

predomi'na|nte *adj* predominant. **~re** *vi* predominate. **predo'minio** *m* predominance

pre'done *m* robber

prefabbri'cato *adj* prefabricated ● *m* prefabricated building

prefazi'one *f* preface

prefe'renz|a *f* preference; **di ~a** preferably. **~i'ale** *adj* preferential; **corsia ~iale** bus and taxi lane

prefe'ribil|e *adj* preferable. **~'mente** *adv* preferably

prefe'ri|re *vt* prefer. **~to, -a** *agg & mf* favourite

pre'fet|to *m* prefect. **~'tura** *f* prefecture

pre'figgersi *vr* be determined

pre'fisso *pp di* **prefiggere** ● *m* prefix; (*Teleph*) [dialling] code

p

pre'gare *vt/i* pray; (*supplicare*) beg; **farsi ~** need persuading

pre'gevole *adj* valuable

preghi'era *f* prayer; (*richiesta*) request

pregi'ato *adj* esteemed; (*prezioso*) valuable. **'pregio** *m* esteem; (*valore*) value; (*di persona*) good point; **di pregio** valuable

pregiudi'ca|re *vt* prejudice; (*danneggiare*) harm. **~to** *adj* prejudiced ● *m* (*Jur*) previous offender

pregiu'dizio *m* prejudice; (*danno*) detriment

'prego *int* (*non c'è di che*) don't mention it!; (*per favore*) please; **~?** I beg your pardon?

pregu'stare *vt* look forward to

pre'lato *m* prelate

prela'vaggio *m* prewash

preleva'mento *m* withdrawal. **prele'vare** *vt* withdraw (denaro); collect (merci); (*Med*) take. **preli'evo** *m* (*di soldi*) withdrawal. **prelievo di sangue** blood sample

prelimi'nare *adj* preliminary ● *m* **preliminari** *pl* preliminaries

pre'ludio *m* prelude

prema'man *m inv* maternity dress ● *adj* maternity *attrib*

prema'turo, -a *adj* premature ● *mf* premature baby

premedi'ta|re *vt* premeditate. **~zi'one** *f* premeditation

'premere *vt* press; (*Comput*) hit (tasto) ● *vi* **~ a** (*importare*) matter to; **mi preme sapere** I need to know; **~ su** press on; push (pulsante)

pre'messa *f* introduction

pre'me|sso *pp di* **premettere. ~sso che** bearing in mind that. **~ttere** *vt* put forward; (*mettere prima*) put before.

premi'a|re *vt* give a prize to; (*ricompensare*) reward. **~zi'one** *f* prize giving

premi'nente *adj* pre-eminent

'premio *m* prize; (*ricompensa*) reward; (*Comm*) premium. **~ di consolazione** booby prize

premoni|'tore *adj* (sogno, segno) premonitory. **~zi'one** *f* premonition

premu'nir|e *vt* fortify. **~si** *vr* take protective measures; **~si di** provide oneself with; **~si contro** protect oneself against

pre'mu|ra *f* (*fretta*) hurry; (*cura*) care. **~'roso** *adj* thoughtful

prena'tale *adj* antenatal

'prender|e *vt* take; (*afferrare*) seize; catch (treno, malattia, ladro, pesce); have (cibo, bevanda); (*far pagare*) charge; (*assumere*) take on; (*ottenere*) get; (*occupare*) take up; **~e informazioni** make inquiries; **~e a calci/pugni** kick/punch; **quanto prende?** what do you charge?; **~e una persona per un'altra** mistake a person for someone else ● *vi* (*voltare*) turn; (*attecchire*) take root; (*rapprendersi*) set; **~e a destra/sinistra** turn right/left; **~e a fare qcsa** start doing sth. **~si** *vr* **~si a pugni** come to blows; **~si cura di** take care of (ammalato)

prendi'sole *m inv* sundress

preno'ta|re *vt* book, reserve. **~to** *adj* booked, reserved **~zi'one** *f* booking, reservation

preoccu'pante *adj* alarming

preoccu'pa|re *vt* worry. **~rsi** *vr* **~rsi** worry (**di** about); **~rsi di fare qcsa** take the trouble to do sth. **~to** *adj* (*ansioso*) worried. **~zi'one** *f* worry; (*apprensione*) concern

prepa'gato *adj* prepaid

prepa'ra|re *vt* prepare. **~rsi** *vr* get ready. **~'tivi** *mpl* preparations. **~to** *m* (*prodotto*) preparation. **~'torio** *adj* preparatory. **~zi'one** *f* preparation

prepensiona'mento *m* early retirement

preponde'ran|te *adj* predominant. **~za** *f* prevalence

pre'porre *vt* place before

preposizi'one *f* preposition

pre'posto *pp di* **preporre** ● *adj* **~ a** (*addetto a*) in charge of

prepo'ten|te *adj* overbearing ● *mf* bully

preroga'tiva *f* prerogative

'presa *f* taking; (*conquista*) capture; (*stretta*) hold; (*di cemento ecc*) setting; (*Electr*) socket; (*pizzico*) pinch; **essere alle prese con** be struggling with; **a ~ rapida** (cemento, colla) quick-setting; **fare ~ su qcno** influence sb. **~ d'aria** air vent. **~ multipla** adaptor

pre'sagio *m* omen. **presa'gire** *vt* foretell

'presbite *adj* long-sighted

presbi'terio *m* presbytery
pre'scelto *adj* selected
pre'scindere *vi* ~ **da** leave aside; **a ~ da** apart from
presco'lare *adj* **in età ~** pre-school
pre'scri|tto *pp di* **prescrivere**
pre'scri|vere *vt* prescribe. **~zi'one** *f* prescription; (*norma*) rule
preselezi'one *f* **chiamare qcno in ~** call sb via the operator
presen'ta|re *vt* present; (*far conoscere*) introduce; show (documento); (*inoltrare*) submit. **~rsi** *vr* present oneself; (*farsi conoscere*) introduce oneself; (*a ufficio*) attend; (*alla polizia ecc*) report; (*come candidato*) stand, run; (occasione:) occur; **~rsi bene/male** (persona:) make a good/bad impression; (situazione:) look good/bad. **~'tore, ~'trice** *mf* presenter; (*di notizie*) announcer. **~zi'one** *f* presentation; (*per conoscersi*) introduction
pre'sente *adj* present; (*attuale*) current; (*questo*) this; **aver ~** remember ● *m* present; **i presenti** those present ● *f* **allegato alla ~** (*in lettera*) enclosed
presenti'mento *m* foreboding
pre'senza *f* presence; (*aspetto*) appearance; **in ~ di, alla ~ di** in the presence of; **di bella ~** personable. **~ di spirito** presence of mind
presenzi'are *vi* **~ a** attend
pre'sepe *m*, **pre'sepio** *m* crib

> **Presepe** The *presepe* (also called *presepio*) is a traditional nativity scene made with ceramic or wooden figures. Most homes have small ones and large-scale models are assembled in churches during Advent. *Presepi* from Naples, sometimes made of porcelain, are particularly prized.

preser'va|re *vt* preserve; (*proteggere*) protect (**da** from). **~'tivo** *m* condom. **~zi'one** *f* preservation
'preside *m* headmaster; (*Univ*) dean ● *f* headmistress; (*Univ*) dean
presi'den|te *m* chairman; (*Pol*) president ● *f* chairwoman; (*Pol*) president. **~ del consiglio [dei ministri]** Prime Minister. **~ della repubblica** President of the Republic. **~za** *f* presidency; (*di assemblea*) chairmanship
presidi'are *vt* garrison. **pre'sidio** *m* garrison
presi'edere *vt* preside over
'preso *pp di* **prendere**
'pressa *f* (*Mech*) press
pres'sante *adj* urgent
pressap'poco *adv* about
pres'sare *vt* press
pressi'one *f* pressure. **~ del sangue** blood pressure
'presso *prep* near; (*a casa di*) with; (*negli indirizzi*) care of, c/o; (lavorare) for ● **pressi** *mpl*: **nei pressi di...** in the neighbourhood *o* vicinity of...
pressoché *adv* almost
pressuriz'za|re *vt* pressurize. **~to** *adj* pressurized
prestabi'li|re *vt* arrange in advance. **~to** *adj* agreed
prestam'pato *adj* printed ● *m* (*modulo*) form
pre'stante *adj* good-looking
pre'star|e *vt* lend; **~e attenzione** pay attention; **~e aiuto** lend a hand; **farsi ~e** borrow (**da** from). **~si** *vr* (frase:) lend itself; (persona:) offer
prestazi'one *f* performance; **prestazioni** *pl* (*servizi*) services
prestigia'tore, -'trice *mf* conjurer
pre'stigi|o *m* prestige; **gioco di ~o** conjuring trick. **~'oso** *m* prestigious
'prestito *m* loan; **dare in ~** lend; **prendere in ~** borrow
'presto *adv* soon; (*di buon'ora*) early; (*in fretta*) quickly; **a ~** see you soon; **al più ~** as soon as possible; **~ o tardi** sooner or later
pre'sumere *vt* presume; (*credere*) think
presu'mibile *adj* **è ~ che...** presumably,...
pre'sunto *adj* (colpevole) presumed
presun|tu'oso *adj* presumptuous. **~zi'one** *f* presumption
presup'po|rre *vt* suppose; (*richiedere*) presuppose. **~sizi'one** *f* presupposition. **~sto** *m* essential requirement
'prete *m* priest
preten'dente *mf* pretender ● *m* (*corteggiatore*) suitor
pre'ten|dere *vt* (*sostenere*) claim; (*esi-*

p

gere) demand ● *vi* **~dere a** claim to; **~dere di** (*esigere*) demand to. **~si'one** *f* pretension. **~zi'oso** *adj* pretentious

pre'tes|a *f* pretension; (*esigenza*) claim; **senza ~e** unpretentious. **~o** *pp di* **pretendere**

pre'testo *m* pretext

pre'tore *m* magistrate

pre'tura *f* magistrate's court

preva'le|nte *adj* prevalent. **~nte'mente** *adv* primarily. **~nza** *f* prevalence. **~re** *vi* prevail

pre'valso *pp di* **prevalere**

preve'dere *vt* foresee; forecast (tempo); (legge ecc:) provide for

preve'nire *vt* precede; (*evitare*) prevent; (*avvertire*) forewarn

preven|ti'vare *vt* estimate; (*aspettarsi*) budget for. **~'tivo** *adj* preventive ● *m* (*Comm*) estimate

preve'n|uto *adj* forewarned; (*mal disposto*) prejudiced. **~zi'one** *f* prevention; (*preconcetto*) prejudice

previ'den|te *adj* provident. **~za** *f* foresight. **~za sociale** social security, welfare *Am*. **~zi'ale** *adj* provident

'previo *adj* **~ pagamento** on payment

previsi'one *f* forecast; **in ~ di** in anticipation of

pre'visto *pp di* **prevedere** ● *adj* foreseen ● *m* **più/meno/prima del ~** more/less/earlier than expected

prezi'oso *adj* precious

prez'zemolo *m* parsley

'prezzo *m* price. **~ di fabbrica** factory price. **~ all'ingrosso** wholesale price. **[a] metà ~** half price

prigi'on|e *f* prison; (*pena*) imprisonment. **prigio'nia** *f* imprisonment. **~i'ero, -a** *adj* imprisoned ● *mf* prisoner

'prima *adv* before; (*più presto*) earlier; (*in primo luogo*) first; **~, finiamo questo** let's finish this first; **~ o poi** sooner or later; **quanto ~** as soon as possible ● *prep* **~ di** before; **~ d'ora** before now ● *conj* **~ che** before ● *f* first class; (*Theat*) first night; (*Auto*) first [gear]

pri'mario *adj* primary; (*principale*) principal

pri'mat|e *m* primate. **~o** *m* supremacy; *Sport* record

prima've|ra *f* spring. **~'rile** *adj* spring *attrib*

primeggi'are *vi* excel

primi'tivo *adj* primitive; (*originario*) original

pri'mizie *fpl* early produce *sg*

'primo *adj* first; (*fondamentale*) principal; (*precedente di due*) former; (*iniziale*) early; (*migliore*) best ● *m* first; **primi** *pl* (*i primi giorni*) the beginning; **in un ~ tempo** at first. **prima copia** master copy

> *i*
>
> **Primo** In Italy, lunch invariably includes a *primo*, or first course, before the main course. The most common *primi* are pasta (traditional in the Centre and South) and risotto (traditional in the North), but a *primo* may also consist of soup (often containing small pasta shapes) or *gnocchi* (potato dumplings).

primordi'ale *adj* primordial

'primula *f* primrose

princi'pale *adj* main ● *m* head, boss [!]

princi|'pato *m* principality. **'principe** *m* prince. **~'pessa** *f* princess

principi'ante *mf* beginner

prin'cipio *m* beginning; (*concetto*) principle; (*causa*) cause; **per ~** on principle

pri'ore *m* prior

priori|tà *f inv* priority. **~'tario** *adj* having priority

'prisma *m* prism

pri'va|re *vt* deprive. **~rsi** *vr* deprive oneself

privatizzazi'one *f* privatization. **pri'vato, -a** *adj* private ● *mf* private citizen

privazi'one *f* deprivation

privilegi'are *vt* privilege; (*considerare più importante*) favour. **privi'legio** *m* privilege

'privo *adj* **~ di** devoid of; (*mancante*) lacking in

pro *prep* for ● *m* advantage; **a che ~?** what's the point?

pro'babil|e *adj* probable. **~ità** *f inv* probability. **~'mente** *adv* probably

pro'ble|ma *m* problem. **~'matico** *adj* problematic

pro'boscide *f* trunk

p

procacci'ar|e *vt*, **~si** *vr* obtain
pro'cace *adj* (ragazza) provocative
pro'ced|ere *vi* proceed; (*iniziare*) start; **~ere contro** (*Jur*) start legal proceedings against. **~i'mento** *m* process; (*Jur*) proceedings *pl*. **proce'dura** *f* procedure
proces'sare *vt* (*Jur*) try
processi'one *f* procession
pro'cesso *m* process; (*Jur*) trial
proces'sore *m* processor
processu'ale *adj* trial
pro'cinto *m* **essere in ~ di** be about to
pro'clama *m* proclamation
procla'ma|re *vt* proclaim. **~zi'one** *f* proclamation
procreazi'one *f* procreation
pro'cura *f* power of attorney; **per ~** by proxy
procu'ra|re *vt/i* procure; (*causare*) cause; (*cercare*) try. **~'tore** *m* attorney. **P~tore Generale** Attorney General. **~tore legale** lawyer. **~tore della repubblica** public prosecutor
'prode *adj* brave. **pro'dezza** *f* bravery
prodi'gar|e *vt* lavish. **~si** *vr* do one's best
pro'digi|o *m* prodigy. **~'oso** *adj* prodigious
pro'dotto *pp di* **produrre** ● *m* product. **prodotti agricoli** farm produce *sg*. **~ derivato** by-product. **~ interno lordo** gross domestic product. **~ nazionale lordo** gross national product
pro'du|rre *vt* produce. **~rsi** *vr* (attore:) play; (*accadere*) happen. **~ttività** *f* productivity. **~t'tivo** *adj* productive. **~t'tore, ~t'trice** *mf* producer. **~zi'one** *f* production
Prof. *abbr* (Professore) Prof.
profa'na|re *vt* desecrate
profe'rire *vt* utter
Prof.essa *abbr* (Professoressa) Prof.
profes'sare *vt* profess; practise (professione)
professio'nale *adj* professional
professi'o|ne *f* profession; **libera ~ne** profession. **~'nismo** *m* professionalism. **~'nista** *mf* professional
profes'sor|e, -'essa *mf* (*Sch*) teacher; (*Univ*) lecturer; (*titolare di cattedra*) professor
pro'fe|ta *m* prophet
pro'ficuo *adj* profitable
profi'lar|e *vt* outline; (*ornare*) border; (*Aeron*) streamline. **~si** *vr* stand out
profi'lattico *adj* prophylactic ● *m* condom
pro'filo *m* profile; (*breve studio*) outline; **di ~** in profile
profit'tare *vi* **~ di** (*avvantaggiarsi*) profit by; (*approfittare*) take advantage of. **pro'fitto** *m* profit; (*vantaggio*) advantage
profond|a'mente *adv* deeply, profoundly. **~ità** *f inv* depth
pro'fondo *adj* deep; *fig* profound; (cultura) great
'profugo, -a *mf* refugee
profu'mar|e *vt* perfume. **~si** *vr* put on perfume
profu'mato *adj* (fiore) fragrant; (fazzoletto ecc) scented
profume'ria *f* perfumery. **pro'fumo** *m* perfume, scent
profusi'one *f* profusion; **a ~** in profusion. **pro'fuso** *pp di* **profondere** ● *adj* profuse
proget|'tare *vt* plan. **~'tista** *mf* designer. **pro'getto** *m* plan; (*di lavoro importante*) project. **progetto di legge** bill
prog'nosi *f inv* prognosis; **in ~ riservata** on the danger list
pro'gramma *m* programme; (*Comput*) program. **~ scolastico** syllabus
program'ma|re *vt* programme; (*Comput*) program. **~'tore, ~'trice** *mf* [computer] programmer. **~zi'one** *f* programming
progre'dire *vi* [make] progress
progres|'sione *f* progression. **~'sivo** *adj* progressive. **pro'gresso** *m* progress
proi'bi|re *vt* forbid. **~'tivo** *adj* prohibitive. **~to** *adj* forbidden. **~zi'one** *f* prohibition
proie|t'tare *vt* project; show (film). **~t'tore** *m* projector; (*Auto*) headlight
proi'ettile *m* bullet
proiezi'one *f* projection
'prole *f* offspring. **prole'tario** *agg & m* proletarian
prolife'rare *vi* proliferate. **pro'lifico** *adj* prolific
pro'lisso *adj* verbose, prolix

p

'**prologo** *m* prologue
pro'lunga *f* (*Electr*) extension
prolun'gar|e *vt* prolong; (*allungare*) lengthen; extend (contratto, scadenza). **~si** *vr* continue; **~si su** (*dilungarsi*) dwell upon
prome'moria *m* memo; (*per se stessi*) reminder, note; (*formale*) memorandum
pro'me|ssa *f* promise. **~sso** *pp di* **promettere. ~ttere** *vt/i* promise
promet'tente *adj* promising
promi'nente *adj* prominent
promiscuità *f* promiscuity. **pro'miscuo** *adj* promiscuous
promon'torio *m* promontory
pro'mo|sso *pp di* **promuovere** ● *adj* (*Sch*) who has gone up a year; (*Univ*) who has passed an exam. **~'tore, ~'trice** *mf* promoter
promozio'nale *adj* promotional. **promozi'one** *f* promotion
promul'gare *vt* promulgate
promu'overe *vt* promote; (*Sch*) move up a class
proni'pote *m* (*di bisnonno*) great-grandson; (*di prozio*) great-nephew ● *f* (*di bisnonno*) great-granddaughter; (*di prozio*) great-niece
pro'nome *m* pronoun
pronosti'care *vt* forecast. **pro'nostico** *m* forecast
pron'tezza *f* readiness; (*rapidità*) quickness
'**pronto** *adj* ready; (*rapido*) quick; **~!** (*Teleph*) hello!; **tenersi ~** be ready (**per** for); **pronti, via!** (*in gare*) ready! steady! go!. **~ soccorso** first aid; (*in ospedale*) accident and emergency
prontu'ario *m* handbook
pro'nuncia *f* pronunciation
pronunci'a|re *vt* pronounce; (*dire*) utter; deliver (discorso). **~rsi** *vr* (*su un argomento*) give one's opinion. **~to** *adj* pronounced; (*prominente*) prominent
pro'nunzia ecc = **PRONUNCIA** ecc
propa'ganda *f* propaganda
propa'ga|re *vt* propagate. **~rsi** *vr* spread. **~zi'one** *f* propagation
prope'deutico *adj* introductory
pro'pen|dere *vi* **~dere per** be in favour of. **~so** *pp di* **propendere** ● *adj* **essere ~so a fare qcsa** be inclined to do sth
propi'nare *vt* administer
pro'pizio *adj* favourable
proponi'mento *m* resolution
pro'por|re *vt* propose; (*suggerire*) suggest. **~si** *vr* set oneself (obiettivo, meta); **~si di** intend to
proporzio'na|le *adj* proportional. **~re** *vt* proportion. **proporzi'one** *f* proportion
pro'posito *m* purpose; **a ~** by the way; **a ~ di** with regard to; **di ~** (*apposta*) on purpose
proposizi'one *f* clause; (*frase*) sentence
pro'post|a *f* proposal. **~o** *pp di* **proporre**
proprietà *f inv* property; (*diritto*) ownership; (*correttezza*) propriety. **~ immobiliare** property. **~ privata** private property. **proprie'taria** *f* owner; (*di casa affittata*) landlady. **proprie'tario** *m* owner; (*di casa affittata*) landlord
'**proprio** *adj* one's [own]; (*caratteristico*) typical; (*appropriato*) proper ● *adv* just; (*veramente*) really; **non ~** not really, not exactly; (*affatto*) not... at all ● *pron* one's own ● *m* one's [own]; **lavorare in ~** be one's own boss; **mettersi in ~** set up on one's own
propul|si'one *f* propulsion. **~'sore** *m* propeller
'**proroga** *f* extension
proro'ga|bile *adj* extendable. **~re** *vt* extend
pro'rompere *vi* burst out
'**prosa** *f* prose. **pro'saico** *adj* prosaic
pro'scio|gliere *vt* release; (*Jur*) acquit. **~lto** *pp di* **prosciogliere**
prosciu'gar|e *vt* dry up; (*bonificare*) reclaim. **~si** *vr* dry up
prosci'utto *m* ham. **~ cotto** cooked ham. **~ crudo** Parma ham
pro'scri|tto, -a *pp di* **proscrivere** ● *mf* exile
prosecuzi'one *f* continuation
prosegui'mento *m* continuation; **buon ~!** (*viaggio*) have a good journey!; (*festa*) enjoy the rest of the party!
prosegu'ire *vt* continue ● *vi* go on, continue

prospe'r|are *vi* prosper. **~ità** *f* prosperity. **'prospero** *adj* prosperous; (*favorevole*) favourable. **~oso** *adj* flourishing; (ragazza) buxom

prospet'tar|e *vt* show. **~si** *vr* seem

prospet'tiva *f* perspective; (*panorama*) view; *fig* prospect. **pro'spetto** *m* (*vista*) view; (*facciata*) façade; (*tabella*) table

prospici'ente *adj* facing

prossima'mente *adv* soon

prossimità *f* proximity

'prossimo, -a *adj* near; (*seguente*) next; (*molto vicino*) close; **l'anno ~** next year ● *mf* neighbour

prosti'tu|ta *f* prostitute. **~zi'one** *f* prostitution

protago'nista *mf* protagonist

pro'teggere *vt* protect; (*favorire*) favour

prote'ina *f* protein

pro'tender|e *vt* stretch out. **~si** *vr* (*in avanti*) lean out. **pro'teso** *pp di* **protendere**

pro'te|sta *f* protest; (*dichiarazione*) protestation. **~'stante** *adj & mf* Protestant. **~'stare** *vt/i* protest

prote|t'tivo *adj* protective. **~tto** *pp di* **proteggere**. **~t'tore, ~t'trice** *mf* protector; (*sostenitore*) patron ● *m* (*di prostituta*) pimp. **~zi'one** *f* protection

protocol'lare *adj* (visita) protocol ● *vt* register

proto'collo *m* protocol; (*registro*) register; **carta ~** official stamped paper

pro'totipo *m* prototype

pro'tra|rre *vt* protract; (*differire*) postpone. **~rsi** *vr* go on, continue. **~tto** *pp di* **protrarre**

protube'ran|te *adj* protuberant. **~za** *f* protuberance

'prova *f* test; (*dimostrazione*) proof; (*tentativo*) try; (*di abito*) fitting; *Sport* heat; (*Theat*) rehearsal; (*bozza*) proof; **in ~** (*assumere*) for a trial period; **mettere alla ~** put to the test. **~ generale** dress rehearsal

pro'var|e *vt* test; (*dimostrare*) prove; (*tentare*) try; try on (abiti ecc); (*sentire*) feel; (*Theat*) rehearse. **~si** *vr* try

proveni'enza *f* origin. **prove'nire** *vi* **provenire da** come from

pro'vento *m* proceeds *pl*

prove'nuto *pp di* **provenire**

pro'verbio *m* proverb

pro'vetta *f* test-tube; **bambino in ~** test-tube baby

pro'vetto *adj* skilled

'provider *m inv* ISP, Internet Service Provider

pro'vinci|a *f* province; (*strada*) B road, secondary road. **~'ale** *adj* provincial; **strada ~ale** B road

pro'vino *m* specimen; *Cinema* screen test

provo'ca|nte *adj* provocative. **~re** *vt* provoke; (*causare*) cause. **~'tore, ~'trice** *mf* trouble-maker. **~'torio** *adj* provocative. **~zi'one** *f* provocation

provve'd|ere *vi* **~ere a** provide for. **~i'mento** *m* measure; (*previdenza*) precaution

provvi'denz|a *f* providence. **~i'ale** *adj* providential

provvigi'one *f* commission

provvi'sorio *adj* provisional

prov'vista *f* supply

pro'zio, -a *m* great-uncle ● *f* great-aunt

'prua *f* prow

pru'den|te *adj* prudent. **~za** *f* prudence; **per ~za** as a precaution

'prudere *vi* itch

'prugn|a *f* plum. **~a secca** prune. **~o** *m* plum[-tree]

pru'rito *m* itch.

pseu'donimo *m* pseudonym

psica'na|lisi *f* psychoanalysis. **~'lista** *mf* psychoanalyst. **~liz'zare** *vt* psychoanalyse

'psiche *f* psyche

psichi'a|tra *mf* psychiatrist. **~'tria** *f* psychiatry. **~trico** *adj* psychiatric

'psichico *adj* mental

psico|lo'gia *f* psychology. **~'lo-gico** *adj* psychological. **psi'cologo, -a** *mf* psychologist

psico'patico, -a *mf* psychopath

PT *abbr* (Posta e Telecomunicazioni) PO

pubbli'ca|re *vt* publish. **~zi'one** *f* publication. **~zioni** *pl* (*di matrimonio*) banns

pubbli'cista *mf Journ* correspondent

pubblicità *f inv* publicity; (*annuncio*)

p

advertisement, advert; **fare ~ a qcsa** advertise sth; **piccola ~** small advertisements. **pubblici'tario** *adj* advertising

'pubblico *adj* public; **scuola pubblica** state school ● *m* public; (*spettatori*) audience; **grande ~** general public. **Pubblica Sicurezza** Police. **~ ufficiale** civil servant

'pube *m* pubis

pubertà *f* puberty

pu'dico *adj* modest

pue'rile *adj* children's; *pej* childish

pugi'lato *m* boxing. **'pugile** *m* boxer

pugna'la|re *vt* stab. **~ta** *f* stab. **pu'gnale** *m* dagger

'pugno *m* fist; (*colpo*) punch; (*manciata*) fistful; (*numero limitato*) handful; **dare un ~ a** punch

'pulce *f* flea; (*microfono*) bug

pul'cino *m* chick; (*nel calcio*) junior

pu'ledra *f* filly

pu'ledro *m* colt

pu'li|re *vt* clean. **~re a secco** dry-clean. **~to** *adj* clean. **~'tura** *f* cleaning. **~'zia** *f* (*il pulire*) cleaning; (*l'essere pulito*) cleanliness; **~zie** *pl* housework; **fare le ~zie** do the cleaning

'pullman *m inv* bus, coach; (*urbano*) bus

pul'mino *m* minibus

'pulpito *m* pulpit

pul'sante *m* button; (*Electr*) [push-]button. **~ di accensione** on-/off switch

pul'sa|re *vi* pulsate. **~zi'one** *f* pulsation

pul'viscolo *m* dust

'puma *m inv* puma

pun'gente *adj* prickly; (insetto) stinging; (odore ecc) sharp

'punger|e *vt* prick; (insetto:) sting

pungigli'one *m* sting

pu'ni|re *vt* punish. **~'tivo** *adj* punitive. **~zi'one** *f* punishment; *Sport* free kick

'punta *f* point; (*estremità*) tip; (*di monte*) peak; (*un po'*) pinch; *Sport* forward; **doppie punte** (*di capelli*) split ends

pun'tare *vt* point; (*spingere con forza*) push; (*scommettere*) bet; ([!]: *appuntare*) fasten ● *vi* **~ su** *fig* rely on; **~ verso** (*dirigersi*) head for; **~ a** aspire to

punta'spilli *m inv* pincushion

pun'tat|a *f* (*di una storia*) instalment; (*televisiva*) episode; (*al gioco*) stake, bet; (*breve visita*) flying visit; **a ~e** serialized, in instalments

punteggia'tura *f* punctuation

pun'teggio *m* score

puntel'lare *vt* prop. **pun'tello** *m* prop

pun'tigli|o *m* spite; (*ostinazione*) obstinacy. **~'oso** *adj* punctilious, pernickety *pej*

pun'tin|a *f* (*da disegno*) drawing pin, thumb tack *Am*; (*di giradischi*) stylus. **~o** *m* dot; **a ~o** perfectly; (cotto) to a T

'punto *m* point; (*Med, in cucito,*) stitch; (*in punteggiatura*) full stop; **in che ~?** where, exactly?; **due punti** colon; **in ~** sharp; **mettere a ~** put right; *fig* fine tune; tune up (motore); **essere sul ~ di fare qcsa** be about to do sth, be on the point of doing sth. **~ esclamativo** exclamation mark. **~ interrogativo** question mark. **~ nero** (*Med*) blackhead. **~ di riferimento** landmark; (*per la qualità*) benchmark. **~ di vendita** point of sale. **~ e virgola** semicolon. **~ di vista** point of view

puntu'al|e *adj* punctual. **~ità** *f* punctuality. **~'mente** *adv* punctually

pun'tura *f* (*di insetto*) sting; (*di ago ecc*) prick; (*Med*) puncture; (*iniezione*) injection; (*fitta*) stabbing pain

punzecchi'are *vt* prick; *fig* tease

'pupa *f* doll. **pu'pazzo** *m* puppet. **pupazzo di neve** snowman

pup'illa *f* (*Anat*) pupil

pu'pillo, -a *mf* (*di professore*) favourite

purché *conj* provided

'pure *adv* too, also; (*concessivo*) **fate ~!** please do! ● *conj* (*tuttavia*) yet; (*anche se*) even if; **pur di** just to

purè *m inv* purée. **~ di patate** creamed potatoes

pu'rezza *f* purity

'purga *f* purge. **pur'gante** *m* laxative. **pur'gare** *vt* purge

purga'torio *m* purgatory

purifi'care *vt* purify

puri'tano, -a *adj & mf* Puritan

'puro *adj* pure; (vino ecc) undiluted; **per ~ caso** purely by chance

puro'sangue *adj & m* thoroughbred

pur'troppo *adv* unfortunately

pus *m* pus. **'pustola** *f* pimple
puti'ferio *m* uproar
putre'far|e *vi*, **~si** *vr* putrefy
'putrido *adj* putrid
'puzza *f* = **PUZZO**
puz'zare *vi* stink; **~ di bruciato** *fig* smell fishy
'puzzo *m* stink, bad smell. **~la** *f* polecat. **~'lente** *adj* stinking
p.zza *abbr* (piazza) Sq.

Qq

qua *adv* here; **da un anno in ~** for the last year; **da quando in ~?** since when?; **di ~** this way; **di ~ di** on this side of; **~ dentro** in here; **~ sotto** under here; **~ vicino** near here; **~ e là** here and there
qua'derno *m* exercise book; (*per appunti*) notebook
quadrango'lare *adj* (forma) quadrangular. **qua'drangolo** *m* quadrangle
qua'drante *m* quadrant; (*di orologio*) dial
qua'dra|re *vt* square; (*contabilità*) balance ● *vi* fit in. **~to** *adj* square; (*equilibrato*) level-headed ● *m* square; (*pugilato*) ring; **al ~to** squared
quadret'tato *adj* squared; (carta) graph *attrib*. **qua'dretto** *m* square; (*piccolo quadro*) small picture; **a quadretti** (tessuto) check
quadrien'nale *adj* (*che dura quattro anni*) four-year
quadri'foglio *m* four-leaf clover
quadri'latero *m* quadrilateral
quadri'mestre *m* four-month period
'quadro *m* picture, painting; (*quadrato*) square; (*fig: scena*) sight; (*tabella*) table; (*Theat*) scene; (*Comm*) executive **quadri** *pl* (*carte*) diamonds; **a quadri** (tessuto, giacca, motivo) check. **quadri** *pl* **direttivi** senior management
quaggiù *adv* down here
'quaglia *f* quail
'qualche *adj* (*alcuni*) a few, some; (*un certo*) some; (*in interrogazioni*) any; **ho ~ problema** I have a few problems, I have some problems; **~ tempo fa** some time ago; **hai ~ libro italiano?** have you any Italian books?; **posso pren-dere ~ libro?** can I take some books?; **in ~ modo** somehow; **in ~ posto** somewhere; **~ volta** sometimes; **~ cosa** = **QUALCOSA**
qual'cos|a *pron* something; (*in interrogazioni*) anything; **~'altro** something else; **vuoi ~'altro?** would you like anything else?; **~a di strano** something strange; **vuoi ~a da mangiare?** would you like something to eat?
qual'cuno *pron* someone, somebody; (*in interrogazioni*) anyone, anybody; (*alcuni*) some; (*in interrogazioni*) any; **c'è ~?** is anybody in?; **qualcun altro** someone else, somebody else; **c'è qualcun altro che aspetta?** is anybody else waiting?; **ho letto ~ dei suoi libri** I've read some of his books; **conosci ~ dei suoi amici?** do you know any of his friends?
'quale *adj* which; (*indeterminato*) what; (*come*) as, like; **~ macchina è la tua?** which car is yours?; **~ motivo avrà di parlare così?** what reason would he have to speak like that?; **~ onore!** what an honour!; **città quali Venezia** towns like Venice; **~ che sia la tua opinione** whatever you may think ● *pron inter* which [one]; **~ preferisci?** which [one] do you prefer? ● *pron rel* **il/la ~** (*persona*) who; (*animale, cosa*) that, which; (*oggetto: con prep*) whom; (*animale, cosa*) which; **ho incontrato tua madre, la ~ mi ha detto...** I met your mother, who told me...; **l'ufficio nel ~ lavoro** the office in which I work; **l'uomo con il ~ parlavo** the man to whom I was speaking ● *adv* (*come*) as
qua'lifica *f* qualification; (*titolo*) title
qualifi'ca|re *vt* qualify; (*definire*) define. **~rsi** *vr* be placed. **~'tivo** *adj* qualifying. **~to** *adj* (operaio) semi-skilled. **~zi'one** *f* qualification
qualità *f inv* quality; (*specie*) kind; **in ~ di** in one's capacity as. **qualita'tivo** *adj* qualitative
qua'lora *conj* in case
qual'siasi, qua'lunque *adj* any; (*non importa quale*) whatever; (*ordinario*) ordinary; **dammi una penna ~** give

me any pen [whatsoever]; **farei ~ cosa** I would do anything; **~ cosa io faccia** whatever I do; **~ persona** anyone; **in ~ caso** in any case; **uno ~** any one, whichever; **l'uomo qualunque** the man in the street

qualunqu'ismo *m* lack of political views

'quando *conj & adv* when; **da ~ ti ho visto** since I saw you; **da ~ esci con lui?** how long have you been going out with him?; **da ~ in qua?** since when?; **~... ~...** sometimes..., sometimes...

quantifi'care *vt* quantify

quantità *f inv* quantity; **una ~ di** (*gran numero*) a great deal of. **quantita'tivo** *m* amount ● *adj* quantitative

'quanto

● *adj inter* how much; (*con nomi plurali*) how many; (*in esclamazione*) what a lot of; **~ tempo?** how long?; **quanti anni hai?** how old are you?

● *adj rel* as much... as; (*con nomi plurali*) as many... as; **prendi ~ denaro ti serve** take as much money as you need; **prendi quanti libri vuoi** take as many books as you like

● *pron inter* how much; (*quanto tempo*) how long; (*plurale*) how many; **quanti ne abbiamo oggi?** what date is it today?, what's the date today?

● *pron rel* as much as; (*quanto tempo*) as long as; (*plurale*) as many as; **prendine ~/quanti ne vuoi** take as much/as many as you like; **stai ~ vuoi** stay as long as you like; **questo è ~** that's it

● *adv inter* how much; (*quanto tempo*) how long; **~ sei alto?** how tall are you?; **~ hai aspettato?** how long did you wait for?; **~ costa?** how much is it?; **~ mi dispiace!** I'm so sorry!; **~ è bello!** how nice!

● *adv rel* as much as; **lavoro ~ posso** I work as much as I can; **è tanto intelligente ~ bello** he's as intelligent as he's good-looking; **in ~** (*in qualità di*) as; (*poiché*) since; **in ~ a me** as far as I'm concerned; **per ~** however; **per ~ ne sappia** as far as I know; **per ~ mi riguarda** as far as I'm concerned; **~ a** as for; **~ prima** (*al più presto*) as soon as possible

quan'tunque *conj* although

qua'ranta *adj & m* forty

quaran'tena *f* quarantine

quaran'tenn|e *adj* forty-year-old. **~io** *m* period of forty years

quaran't|esimo *adj* fortieth. **~ina** *f* **una ~ina** about forty

qua'resima *f* Lent

quar'tetto *m* quartet

quarti'ere *m* district; (*Mil*) quarters *pl*. **~ generale** headquarters

quarto *adj* fourth ● *m* fourth; (*quarta parte*) quarter; **le sette e un ~** a quarter past seven. **quarti** *pl* **di finale** quarterfinals. **~ d'ora** quarter of an hour. **quar'tultimo, -a** *mf* fourth from the end

'quarzo *m* quartz

'quasi *adv* almost, nearly; **~ mai** hardly ever ● *conj* (*come se*) as if; **~ ~ sto a casa** I'm tempted to stay home

quassù *adv* up here

'quatto *adj* crouching; (*silenzioso*) silent

quat'tordici *adj & m* fourteen

quat'trini *mpl* money *sg*

'quattro *adj & m* four; **dirne ~ a qcno** give sb a piece of one's mind; **farsi in ~ (per qcno/per fare qcsa)** go to a lot of trouble (for sb/to do sth); **in ~ e quattr'otto** in a flash. **~ per ~** *m inv* (*Auto*) four-wheel drive [vehicle]

quat'trocchi: **a ~** *adv* in private

quattro|'cento *adj & m* four hundred; **il Q~cento** the fifteenth century

quattro'mila *adj & m* four thousand

'quell|o *adj* that (*pl* those); **quell'albero** that tree; **quegli alberi** those trees; **quel cane** that dog; **quei cani** those dogs ● *pron* that [one] (*pl* those [ones]); **~o lì** that one over there; **~o che** the one that; (*ciò che*) what; **quelli che** the ones that, those that; **~o a destra** the one on the right

'quercia *f* oak

que'rela *f* [legal] action

quere'lare *vt* bring an action against

que'sito *m* question

questio'nario *m* questionnaire

quest'ione *f* question; (*faccenda*) matter; (*litigio*) quarrel; **in ~** in doubt; **è fuori ~** it's out of the question

'quest|o *adj* this (*pl* these) • *pron* this [one] (*pl* these [ones]); **~o qui, ~o qua** this one here; **~o è quello che ha detto** that's what he said; **per ~o** for this *or* that reason. **quest'oggi** today

que'store *m* chief of police

que'stura *f* police headquarters

qui *adv* here; **da ~ in poi** from now on; **fin ~** (*di tempo*) up till now, until now; **~ dentro** in here; **~ sotto** under here; **~ vicino** near here • *m* **~ pro quo** misunderstanding

quie'scienza *f* **trattamento di ~** retirement package

quie'tanza *f* receipt

quie'tar|e *vt* calm. **~si** *vr* quieten down

qui'et|e *f* quiet; **disturbo della ~e pubblica** breach of the peace. **~o** *adj* quiet

'quindi *adv* then • *conj* therefore

'quindi|ci *adj & m* fifteen. **~'cina** *f* **una ~cina** about fifteen; **una ~cina di giorni** two weeks *pl*

quinquen'nale *adj* (*che dura cinque anni*) five-year. **quin'quennio** *m* [period of] five years

quin'tale *m* a hundred kilograms

'quinte *fpl* (*Theat*) wings

quin'tetto *m* quintet

'quinto *adj* fifth

quin'tuplo *adj* quintuple

'quota *f* quota; (*rata*) instalment; (*altitudine*) height; (*Aeron*) altitude, height; (*ippica*) odds *pl*; **perdere ~** lose altitude; **prendere ~** gain altitude. **~ di iscrizione** entry fee

quo'ta|re *vt* (*Comm*) quote. **~to** *adj* quoted; **essere ~to in Borsa** be quoted on the Stock Exchange. **~zi'one** *f* quotation

quotidi|ana'mente *adv* daily. **~'ano** *adj* daily; (*ordinario*) everyday • *m* daily [paper]

quozi'ente *m* quotient. **~ d'intelligenza** intelligence quotient, IQ

Rr

ra'barbaro *m* rhubarb

'rabbia *f* rage; (*ira*) anger; (*Med*) rabies *sg*; **che ~!** what a nuisance!; **mi fa ~** it makes me angry

rab'bino *m* rabbi

rabbiosa'mente *adv* furiously. **rabbi'oso** *adj* hot-tempered; (*Med*) rabid; (*violento*) violent

rabbo'nir|e *vt* pacify. **~si** *vr* calm down

rabbrivi'dire *vi* shudder; (*di freddo*) shiver

rabbui'arsi *vr* become dark

raccapez'zar|e *vt* put together. **~si** *vr* see one's way ahead

raccapricci'ante *adj* horrifying

raccatta'palle *m inv* ball boy • *f inv* ball girl

raccat'tare *vt* pick up

rac'chetta *f* racket. **~ da ping pong** table-tennis bat. **~ da sci** ski pole. **~ da tennis** tennis racket

racchi'udere *vt* contain

rac'cogli|ere *vt* pick; (*da terra*) pick up; (*mietere*) harvest; (*collezionare*) collect; (*radunare*) gather; win (voti ecc); (*dare asilo a*) take in. **~ersi** *vr* gather; (*concentrarsi*) collect one's thoughts. **~'mento** *m* concentration. **~'tore, ~'trice** *mf* collector • *m* (*cartella*) ring-binder

rac'colto, -a *pp di* **raccogliere** • *adj* (*rannicchiato*) hunched; (*intimo*) cosy; (*concentrato*) engrossed • *m* (*mietitura*) harvest • *f* collection; (*di scritti*) compilation; (*del grano ecc*) harvesting; (*adunata*) gathering

raccoman'dabile *adj* recommendable; **poco ~** (persona) shady

raccoman'da|re *vt* recommend; (*affidare*) entrust. **~rsi** *vr* (*implorare*) beg. **~ta** *f* registered letter; **~ta con ricevuta di ritorno** recorded delivery. **~-espresso** *f next-day delivery of recorded items*. **~zi'one** *f* recommendation

raccon'tare *vt* tell. **rac'conto** *m* story

raccorci'are *vt* shorten

raccor'dare *vt* join. **rac'cordo** *m* connection; (*stradale*) feeder. **raccordo anulare** ring road. **raccordo ferroviario** siding

ra'chitico *adj* rickety; (*poco sviluppato*) stunted

racimo'lare *vt* scrape together

'racket *m inv* racket

'radar *m inv* radar

raddol'cir|e *vt* sweeten; *fig* soften. **~si** *vr* become milder; (carattere:) mellow

raddoppi'are *vt* double. **rad'doppio** *m* doubling

raddriz'zare *vt* straighten

'rader|e *vt* shave; graze (muro); **~e al suolo** raze. **~si** *vr* shave

radi'are *vt* strike off; **~ dall'albo** strike off

radia|'tore *m* radiator. **~zi'one** *f* radiation

'radica *f* briar

radi'cale *adj* radical ● *m* (*Gram*) root; (*Pol*) radical

ra'dicchio *m* chicory

ra'dice *f* root

'radio *f inv* radio; **via ~** by radio. **~ a transistor** transistor radio ● *m* (*Chem*) radium.

radioama'tore, -'trice *mf* [radio] ham

radioascolta'tore, -'trice *mf* listener

radioat|tività *f* radioactivity. **~'tivo** *adj* radioactive

radio'cro|naca *f* radio commentary; **fare la ~naca di** commentate on. **~'nista** *mf* radio reporter

radiodiffusi'one *f* broadcasting

radio'fonico *adj* radio *attrib*

radiogra|'fare *vt* X-ray. **~'fia** *f* X-ray [photograph]; (*radiologia*) radiography; **fare una ~fia** (paziente:) have an X-ray; (dottore:) take an X-ray

radio'lina *f* transistor

radi'ologo, -a *mf* radiologist

radi'oso *adj* radiant

radio'sveglia *f* radio alarm

radio'taxi *m inv* radio taxi

radiote'lefono *m* radiotelephone; (*privato*) cordless [phone]

radiotelevi'sivo *adj* broadcasting *attrib*

'rado *adj* sparse; (*non frequente*) rare; **di ~** seldom

radu'nar|e *vt*, **~si** *vr* gather [together]. **ra'duno** *m* meeting; *Sport* rally

ra'dura *f* clearing

'rafano *m* horseradish

raf'fermo *adj* stale

'raffica *f* gust; (*di armi da fuoco*) burst; (*di domande*) barrage

raffigu'ra|re *vt* represent. **~zi'one** *f* representation

raffi'na|re *vt* refine. **~ta'mente** *adv* elegantly. **~to** *adj* refined. **raffine'ria** *f* refinery

rafforza|'mento *m* reinforcement; (*di muscolatura*) strengthening. **~re** *vt* reinforce. **~'tivo** *m* (*Gram*) intensifier

raffredda'mento *m* (*processo*) cooling

raffred'd|are *vt* cool. **~arsi** *vr* get cold; (*prendere un raffreddore*) catch a cold. **~ore** *m* cold. **~ore da fieno** hay fever

raf'fronto *m* comparison

'rafia *f* raffia

Rag. *abbr* **ragioniere**

ra'gaz|za *f* girl; (*fidanzata*) girlfriend. **~za alla pari** au pair [girl]. **~'zata** *f* prank. **~zo** *m* boy; (*fidanzato*) boyfriend

ragge'lar|e *vt fig* freeze. **~si** *vr fig* turn to ice

raggi'ante *adj* radiant; **~ di successo** flushed with success

raggi'era *f* **a ~** with a pattern like spokes radiating from a centre

'raggio *m* ray; (*Math*) radius; (*di ruota*) spoke; **~ d'azione** range. **~ laser** laser beam

raggi'rare *vt* trick. **rag'giro** *m* trick

raggi'un|gere *vt* reach; (*conseguire*) achieve. **~'gibile** *adj* (luogo) within reach

raggomito'lar|e *vt* wind. **~si** *vr* curl up

raggranel'lare *vt* scrape together

raggrin'zir|e *vt*, **~si** *vr* wrinkle

raggrup|pa'mento *m* (*gruppo*) group; (*azione*) grouping. **~'pare** *vt* group together

ragguagli'are *vt* compare; (*informare*) inform. **raggu'aglio** *m* comparison; (*informazione*) information

ragguar'devole *adj* considerable

'ragia *f* resin; **acqua ~** turpentine

ragiona'mento *m* reasoning; (*discussione*) discussion. **ragio'nare** *vi* reason; (*discutere*) discuss

ragi'one *f* reason; (*ciò che è giusto*) right; **a ~ o a torto** rightly or wrongly; **aver ~** be right; **perdere la ~** go out of one's mind

ragione'ria *f* accountancy

ragio'nevol|e *adj* reasonable. **~'mente** *adv* reasonably

ragioni'ere, -a *mf* accountant

ragli'are *vi* bray

ragna'tela *f* cobweb. **'ragno** *m* spider

ragù *m inv* meat sauce

RAI *f abbr* (Radio Audizioni Italiane) *Italian public broadcasting company*

ralle'gra|re *vt* gladden. **~rsi** *vr* rejoice; **~rsi con qcno** congratulate sb. **~'menti** *mpl* congratulations

rallenta'mento *m* slowing down

rallen'ta|re *vt/i* slow down; (*allentare*) slacken. **~rsi** *vr* slow down. **~'tore** *m* speed bump; **al ~tore** in slow motion

raman'zina *f* reprimand

ra'marro *m type of lizard*

ra'mato *adj* copper[-coloured]

'rame *m* copper

ramifi'ca|re *vi*, **~rsi** *vr* branch out; (strada:) branch. **~zi'one** *f* ramification

rammari'carsi *vr* **~ di** regret; (*lamentarsi*) complain (**di** about). **ram'marico** *m* regret

rammen'dare *vt* darn. **ram'mendo** *m* darning

rammen'tar|e *vt* remember; **~e qcsa a qcno** (*richiamare alla memoria*) remind sb of sth. **~si** *vr* remember

rammol'li|re *vt* soften. **~rsi** *vr* go soft. **~to, -a** *mf* wimp

'ramo *m* branch. **~'scello** *m* twig

'rampa *f* (*di scale*) flight. **~ d'accesso** slip road. **~ di lancio** launch[ing] pad

ram'pante *adj* **giovane ~** yuppie

rampi'cante *adj* climbing ● *m* (*Bot*) creeper

ram'pollo *m hum* brat; (*discendente*) descendant

ram'pone *m* harpoon; (*per scarpe*) crampon

'rana *f* frog; (*nel nuoto*) breaststroke; **uomo ~** frogman

ran'core *m* resentment

ran'dagio *adj* stray

'rango *m* rank

rannicchi'arsi *vr* huddle up

rannuvo'larsi *vr* cloud over

ra'nocchio *m* frog

ranto'lare *vi* wheeze. **'rantolo** *m* wheeze; (*di moribondo*) death rattle

'rapa *f* turnip

ra'pace *adj* rapacious; (uccello) predatory

ra'pare *vt* crop

'rapida *f* rapids *pl*. **~'mente** *adv* rapidly

rapidità *f* speed

'rapido *adj* swift ● *m* (*treno*) express [train]

rapi'mento *m* kidnapping

ra'pina *f* robbery; **~ a mano armata** armed robbery. **~ in banca** bank robbery. **rapi'nare** *vt* rob. **~'tore** *m* robber

ra'pi|re *vt* abduct; (*a scopo di riscatto*) kidnap; (*estasiare*) ravish. **~'tore, ~'trice** *mf* kidnapper

rappacifi'ca|re *vt* pacify. **~rsi** *vr* be reconciled. **~zi'one** *f* reconciliation

rappor'tare *vt* reproduce (disegno); (*confrontare*) compare

rap'porto *m* report; (*connessione*) relation; (*legame*) relationship; (*Math, Techn*) ratio; **rapporti** *pl* relationship; **essere in buoni rapporti** be on good terms. **~ di amicizia** friendship. **~ di lavoro** working relationship. **rapporti** *pl* **sessuali** sexual intercourse

rap'prendersi *vr* set; (latte:) curdle

rappre'saglia *f* reprisal

rappresen'tan|te *mf* representative. **~te di commercio** sales representative. **~za** *f* delegation; (*Comm*) agency; **spese** *pl* **di ~za** entertainment expenses; **di ~za** (appartamento ecc) company

rappresen'ta|re *vt* represent; (*Theat*) perform. **~'tivo** *adj* representative.

~zi'one *f* representation; (*spettacolo*) performance

rap'preso *pp di* **rapprendersi**

rapso'dia *f* rhapsody

'raptus *m inv* fit of madness

rara'mente *adv* rarely, seldom

rare'fa|re *vt*, **~rsi** *vr* rarefy. **~tto** *adj* rarefied

rarità *f inv* rarity. **'raro** *adj* rare

ra'sar|e *vt* shave; trim (siepe ecc). **~si** *vr* shave

raschi'are *vt* scrape; (*togliere*) scrape off

rasen'tare *vt* go close to. **ra'sente** *prep* very close to

'raso *pp di* **radere** ● *adj* smooth; (*colmo*) full to the brim; (barba) close-cropped; **~ terra** close to the ground; **un cucchiaio ~** a level spoonful ● *m* satin

ra'soio *m* razor

ras'segna *f* review; (*mostra*) exhibition; (*musicale, cinematografica*) festival; **passare in ~** review; (*Mil*) inspect

rasse'gna|re *vt* present. **~rsi** *vr* resign oneself. **~to** *adj* (persona, aria, tono) resigned. **~zi'one** *f* resignation

rassere'nar|e *vt* clear; *fig* cheer up. **~si** *vr* become clear; *fig* cheer up

rasset'tare *vt* tidy up; (*riparare*) mend

rassicu'ra|nte *adj* reassuring. **~re** *vt* reassure. **~zi'one** *f* reassurance

rasso'dare *vt* harden; *fig* strengthen

rassomigli'a|nza *f* resemblance. **~re** *vi* **~re a** resemble

r

rastrella'mento *m* (*di fieno*) raking; (*perlustrazione*) combing. **rastrel'lare** *vt* rake; (*perlustrare*) comb

rastrelli'era *f* rack; (*per biciclette*) bicycle rack; (*scolapiatti*) [plate] rack. **ra'strello** *m* rake

'rata *f* instalment; **pagare a rate** pay by instalments. **rate'ale** *adj* by instalments; **pagamento rateale** payment by instalments

rate'are, rateiz'zare *vt* divide into instalments

ra'tifica *f* (*Jur*) ratification

ratifi'care *vt* (*Jur*) ratify

'ratto *m* abduction; (*roditore*) rat

rattop'pare *vt* patch. **rat'toppo** *m* patch

rattrap'pir|e *vt* make stiff. **~si** *vr* become stiff

rattri'star|e *vt* sadden. **~si** *vr* become sad

rau'cedine *f* hoarseness. **'rauco** *adj* hoarse

rava'nello *m* radish

ravi'oli *mpl* ravioli *sg*

ravve'dersi *vr* mend one's ways

ravvicina'mento *m* reconciliation; (*Pol*) rapprochement

ravvici'nar|e *vt* bring closer; (*riconciliare*) reconcile. **~si** *vr* be reconciled

ravvi'sare *vt* recognize

ravvi'var|e *vt* revive; *fig* brighten up. **~si** *vr* revive

'rayon *m* rayon

razio'cinio *m* rational thought; (*buon senso*) common sense

razio'nal|e *adj* rational. **~ità** *f* (*raziocinio*) rationality; (*di ambiente*) functional nature. **~iz'zare** *vt* rationalize (programmi, metodi, spazio). **~'mente** *adv* rationally

razio'nare *vt* ration. **razi'one** *f* ration

'razza *f* race; (*di cani ecc*) breed; (*genere*) kind; **che ~ di idiota!** [!] what an idiot!

raz'zia *f* raid

razzi'ale *adj* racial

raz'zis|mo *m* racism. **~ta** *adj & mf* racist

'razzo *m* rocket. **~ da segnalazione** flare

razzo'lare *vi* (polli:) scratch about

re *m inv* king; (*Mus*) D

rea'gire *vi* react

re'ale *adj* real; (*di re*) royal

rea'lis|mo *m* realism. **~ta** *mf* realist; (*fautore del re*) royalist

realistica'mente *adv* realistically. **rea'listico** *adj* realistic

'reality tv *f* reality tv

realiz'zabile *adj* feasible

realiz'za|re *vt* (*attuare*) carry out, realize; (*Comm*) make; score (gol, canestro); (*rendersi conto di*) realize. **~rsi** *vr* come true; (*nel lavoro ecc*) fulfil oneself. **~zi'one** *f* realization; (*di sogno, persona*) fulfilment. **~zione scenica** production

rea'lizzo *m* (*vendita*) proceeds *pl*; (*riscossione*) yield

real'mente *adv* really
realtà *f inv* reality. ~ **virtuale** virtual reality
re'ato *m* crime
reat'tivo *adj* reactive
reat'tore *m* reactor; (*Aeron*) jet [aircraft]
reazio'nario, -a *adj & mf* reactionary
reazi'one *f* reaction. ~ **a catena** chain reaction
'rebus *m inv* rebus; (*enigma*) puzzle
recapi'tare *vt* deliver. **re'capito** *m* address; (*consegna*) delivery. **recapito a domicilio** home delivery. **recapito telefonico** contact telephone number
re'car|e *vt* bear; (*produrre*) cause. **~si** *vr* go
re'cedere *vi* recede; *fig* give up
recensi'one *f* review
recen's|ire *vt* review. **~ore** *m* reviewer
re'cente *adj* recent; **di** ~ recently. **~'mente** *adv* recently
recessi'one *f* recession
re'cesso *m* recess
re'cidere *vt* cut off
reci'divo, -a *adj* (*Med*) recurrent • *mf* repeat offender
recin|'tare *vt* close off. **re'cinto** *m* enclosure; (*per animali*) pen; (*per bambini*) play-pen. **~zi'one** *f* (*muro*) wall; (*rete*) wire fence; (*cancellata*) railings *pl*
recipi'ente *m* container
re'ciproco *adj* reciprocal
re'ciso *pp di* **recidere**
'recita *f* performance. **reci'tare** *vt* recite; (*Theat*) act; play (ruolo). **~zi'one** *f* recitation; (*Theat*) acting
recla'mare *vi* protest • *vt* claim
ré'clame *f inv* advertising; (*avviso pubblicitario*) advertisement
re'clamo *m* complaint; **ufficio reclami** complaints department
recli'na|bile *adj* reclining; **sedile ~bile** reclining seat. **~re** *vt* tilt (sedile); lean (capo)
reclusi'one *f* imprisonment. **re'cluso, -a** *adj* secluded • *mf* prisoner
'recluta *f* recruit
reclu|ta'mento *m* recruitment. **~'tare** *vt* recruit
'record *m inv* record • *adj inv* (cifra) record *attrib*
recrimi'na|re *vi* recriminate
recupe'rare *vt* recover. **re'cupero** *m* recovery; **corso di recupero** additional classes; **minuti di recupero** *Sport* injury time
redargu'ire *vt* rebuke
re'datto *pp di* **redigere**
redat'tore, -'trice *mf* editor; (*di testo*) writer
redazi'one *f* (*ufficio*) editorial office; (*di testi*) editing
reddi'tizio *adj* profitable
'reddito *m* income. ~ **imponibile** taxable income
re'den|to *pp di* **redimere. ~'tore** *m* redeemer. **~zi'one** *f* redemption
re'digere *vt* write; draw up (documento)
re'dimer|e *vt* redeem. **~si** *vr* redeem oneself
'redini *fpl* reins
'reduce *adj* ~ **da** back from • *mf* survivor
refe'rendum *m inv* referendum
refe'renza *f* reference
refet'torio *m* refectory
refrat'tario *adj* refractory; **essere ~ a** have no aptitude for
refrige'ra|re *vt* refrigerate. **~zi'o-ne** *f* refrigeration
refur'tiva *f* stolen goods *pl*
rega'lare *vt* give
re'galo *m* present, gift
re'gata *f* regatta
reg'gen|te *mf* regent. **~za** *f* regency
'regger|e *vt* (*sorreggere*) bear; (*tenere in mano*) hold; (*dirigere*) run; (*governare*) govern; (*Gram*) take • *vi* (*resistere*) hold out; (*durare*) last; *fig* stand. **~si** *vr* stand
'reggia *f* royal palace
reggi'calze *m inv* suspender belt
reggi'mento *m* regiment
reggi'petto, reggi'seno *m* bra
re'gia *f Cinema* direction; (*Theat*) production
re'gime *m* regime; (*dieta*) diet; (*Mech*) speed
re'gina *f* queen
'regio *adj* royal

regio'na|le *adj* regional. **~'lismo** *m* (*parola*) regionalism

regi'one *f* region

re'gista *mf* (*Cinema*) director; (*Theat, TV*) producer

regi'stra|re *vt* register; (*Comm*) enter; (*incidere su nastro*) tape, record; (*su disco*) record. **~'tore** *m* recorder; (*magnetofono*) tape-recorder. **~tore di cassa** cash register. **~zi'one** *f* registration; (*Comm*) entry; (*di programma*) recording

re'gistro *m* register; (*ufficio*) registry. **~ di cassa** ledger

re'gnare *vi* reign

'regno *m* kingdom; (*sovranità*) reign. **R~ Unito** United Kingdom

'regola *f* rule; **essere in ~** be in order; (persona:) have one's papers in order. **rego'labile** *adj* (meccanismo) adjustable. **~'mento** *m* regulation; (*Comm*) settlement

rego'lar|e *adj* regular • *vt* regulate; (*ridurre, moderare*) limit; (*sistemare*) settle. **~si** *vr* (*agire*) act; (*moderarsi*) control oneself. **~ità** *f* regularity. **~iz'zare** *vt* settle (debito)

rego'la|ta *f* **darsi una ~ta** pull oneself together. **~'tore, ~'trice** *adj* **piano ~tore** urban development plan

'regolo *m* ruler

regres'sivo *adj* regressive. **re'gresso** *m* decline

reinseri'mento *m* (*di persona*) reintegration

reinser'irsi *vr* (*in ambiente*) reintegrate

reinte'grare *vt* restore

relativa'mente *adv* relatively; **~ a** as regards. **rela'tivo** *adj* relative

rela'tore, -'trice *mf* (*in una conferenza*) speaker

re'lax *m* relaxation

relazi'one *f* relation[ship]; (*rapporto amoroso*) [love] affair; (*resoconto*) report; **pubbliche relazioni** *pl* public relations

rele'gare *vt* relegate

religi'o|ne *f* religion. **~so, -a** *adj* religious • *m* monk • *f* nun

re'liqui|a *f* relic. **~'ario** *m* reliquary

re'litto *m* wreck

re'ma|re *vi* row. **~'tore, ~'trice** *mf* rower

remini'scenza *f* reminiscence

remissi'one *f* remission; (*sottomissione*) submissiveness. **remis'sivo** *adj* submissive

'remo *m* oar

'remora *f* **senza remore** without hesitation

re'moto *adj* remote

remune'ra|re *vt* remunerate. **~zi'one** *f* remuneration

'render|e *vt* (*restituire*) return; (*esprimere*) render; (*fruttare*) yield; (*far diventare*) make. **~si** *vr* become; **~si conto di qcsa** realize sth; **~si utile** make oneself useful

rendi'conto *m* report

rendi'mento *m* rendering; (*produzione*) yield

'rendita *f* income; (*dello Stato*) revenue

'rene *m* kidney. **~ artificiale** kidney machine

'reni *fpl* (*schiena*) back

reni'tente *adj* **essere ~ a** (consigli di qcno) be unwilling to accept

'renna *f* reindeer (*pl inv*); (*pelle*) buckskin

'reo, -a *adj* guilty • *mf* offender

re'parto *m* department; (*Mil*) unit

repel'lente *adj* repulsive

repen'taglio *m* **mettere a ~** risk

repen'tino *adj* sudden

reper'ibile *adj* available; **non è ~** (*perduto*) it's not to be found

repe'rire *vt* trace (fondi)

re'perto *m* **~ archeologico** find

reper'torio *m* repertory; (*elenco*) index; **immagini** *pl* **di ~** archive footage

'replica *f* reply; (*obiezione*) objection; (*copia*) replica; (*Theat*) repeat performance. **repli'care** *vt* reply; (*Theat*) repeat

repor'tage *m inv* report

repres|si'one *f* repression. **~'si-vo** *adj* repressive. **re'presso** *pp di* **reprimere**. **re'primere** *vt* repress

re'pubbli|ca *f* republic. **~'cano, -a** *adj & mf* republican

repu'tare *vt* consider

reputazi'one *f* reputation

requi'sito *m* requirement

requisi'toria *f* (*arringa*) closing speech

'resa *f* surrender; (*Comm*) rendering. **~ dei conti** rendering of accounts

'residence *m inv* residential hotel

resi'den|te *adj & mf* resident. **~za** *f* residence; (*soggiorno*) stay. **~zi'ale** *adj* residential; **zona ~ziale** residential district

re'siduo *adj* residual • *m* remainder

'resina *f* resin

resi'sten|te *adj* resistant; **~te all'acqua** water-resistant. **~za** *f* resistance; (*fisica*) stamina; (*Electr*) resistor; **la R~za** the Resistance

re'sistere *vi* **~ [a]** resist; (*a colpi, scosse*) stand up to; **~ alla pioggia/al vento** be rain-/wind-resistant

'reso *pp di* **rendere**

reso'conto *m* report

re'spin|gere *vt* repel; (*rifiutare*) reject; (*bocciare*) fail. **~to** *pp di* **respingere**

respi'ra|re *vt/i* breathe. **~'tore** *m* respirator. **~tore [a tubo]** snorkel; **~'torio** *adj* respiratory. **~zi'one** *f* breathing; (*Med*) respiration. **~zione bocca a bocca** mouth-to-mouth resuscitation, kiss of life. **re'spiro** *m* breath; (*il respirare*) breathing; *fig* respite

respon'sabil|e *adj* responsible (**di** for); (*Jur*) liable • *mf* person responsible. **~e della produzione** production manager. **~ità** *f inv* responsibility; (*Jur*) liability. **~iz'zare** *vt* give responsibility to

re'sponso *m* response

'ressa *f* crowd

re'stante *adj* remaining • *m* remainder

re'stare *vi* = **RIMANERE**

restau'ra|re *vt* restore. **~'tore, ~'trice** *mf* restorer. **~zi'one** *f* restoration. **re'stauro** *m* (*riparazione*) repair

re'stio *adj* restive; **~ a** reluctant to

restitu|'ire *vt* return; (*reintegrare*) restore. **~zi'one** *f* return; (*Jur*) restitution

'resto *m* remainder; (*saldo*) balance; (*denaro*) change; **resti** *pl* (*avanzi*) remains; **del ~** besides

re'stringer|e *vt* contract; take in (vestiti); (*limitare*) restrict; shrink (stoffa). **~si** *vr* contract; (*farsi più vicini*) close up; (stoffa:) shrink. **restringi'mento** *m* (*di tessuto*) shrinkage

restri|t'tivo *adj* restrictive. **~zi'one** *f* restriction

resurrezi'one *f* resurrection

resusci'tare *vt/i* revive

re'tata *f* round-up

'rete *f* net; (*sistema*) network; (*televisiva*) channel; (*in calcio*) goal; *fig* trap; (*per la spesa*) string bag. **~ locale** (*Comput*) local [area] network. **~ stradale** road network. **~ televisiva** television channel

reti'cen|te *adj* reticent. **~za** *f* reticence

retico'lato *m* grid; (*rete metallica*) wire netting. **re'ticolo** *m* network

re'torico, -a *adj* rhetorical; **domanda retorica** rhetorical question • *f* rhetoric

retribu|'ire *vt* remunerate. **~zi'one** *f* remuneration

'retro *adv* behind; **vedi ~** see over • *m inv* back. **~ di copertina** outside back cover

retroat'tivo *adj* retroactive

retro'ce|dere *vi* retreat • *vt* (*Mil*) demote; *Sport* relegate. **~ssi'one** *f Sport* relegation

retroda'tare *vt* backdate

re'trogrado *adj* retrograde; *fig* old-fashioned; (*Pol*) reactionary

retrogu'ardia *f* (*Mil*) rearguard

retro'marcia *f* reverse [gear]

retro'scena *m inv* (*Theat*) backstage; *fig* background details *pl*

retrospet'tivo *adj* retrospective

retro'stante *adj* **il palazzo ~** the building behind

retrovi'sore *m* rear-view mirror

'retta[1] *f* (*Math*) straight line; (*di collegio, pensionato*) fee

'retta[2] *f* **dar ~ a qcno** take sb's advice

rettango'lare *adj* rectangular. **ret'tangolo** *m* rectangle

ret'tifi|ca *f* rectification. **~'care** *vt* rectify

'rettile *m* reptile

retti'lineo *adj* rectilinear; (*retto*) upright • *m Sport* back straight

'retto *pp di* **reggere** • *adj* straight; *fig* upright; (*giusto*) correct; **angolo ~** right angle

ret'tore *m* (*Relig*) rector; (*Univ*) principal, vice-chancellor

reu'matico *adj* rheumatic

reuma'tismi *mpl* rheumatism
reve'rendo *adj* reverend
rever'sibile *adj* reversible
revisio'nare *vt* revise; (*Comm*) audit; (*Auto*) overhaul. **revisi'one** *f* revision; (*Comm*) audit; (*Auto*) overhaul. **revi'sore** *m* (*di conti*) auditor; (*di bozze*) proofreader; (*di traduzioni*) revisor
re'vival *m inv* revival
'revoca *f* repeal. **revo'care** *vt* repeal
riabili'ta|re *vt* rehabilitate. **~zi'one** *f* rehabilitation
riabitu'ar|e *vt* reaccustom. **~si** *vr* reaccustom oneself
riac'cender|e *vt* rekindle (fuoco). **~si** *vr* (luce:) come back on
riacqui'stare *vt* buy back; regain (libertà, prestigio); recover (vista, udito)
riagganci'are *vt* replace (ricevitore); **~ la cornetta** hang up • *vi* hang up
riallac'ciare *vt* refasten; reconnect (corrente); renew (amicizia)
rial'zare *vt* raise • *vi* rise. **ri'alzo** *m* rise
riani'mar|e *vt* (*Med*) resuscitate; (*ridare forza a*) revive; (*ridare coraggio a*) cheer up. **~si** *vr* regain consciousness; (*riprendere forza*) revive; (*riprendere coraggio*) cheer up
riaper'tura *f* reopening
ria'prir|e *vt*, **~si** *vr* reopen
rias'sumere *vt* summarize
riassun'tivo *adj* summarizing. **rias'sunto** *pp di* **riassumere** • *m* summary
ria'ver|e *vt* get back; regain (salute, vista). **~si** *vr* recover
riavvicina'mento *m* reconciliation
riavvici'nar|e *vt* reconcile (paesi, persone). **~si** *vr* (*riconciliarsi*) be reconciled, make it up
riba'dire *vt* (*confermare*) reaffirm
ri'balta *f* flap; (*Theat*) footlights *pl*; *fig* limelight
ribal'tar|e *vt/i*, **~si** *vr* tip over; (*Naut*) capsize
ribas'sare *vt* lower • *vi* fall. **ri'basso** *m* fall; (*sconto*) discount
ri'battere *vt* (*a macchina*) retype; (*controbattere*) deny • *vi* answer back
ribel'l|arsi *vr* rebel. **ri'belle** *adj* rebellious • *mf* rebel. **~'ione** *f* rebellion
'ribes *m inv* (*rosso*) redcurrant; (*nero*) blackcurrant

r

ribol'lire *vi* ferment; *fig* seethe
ri'brezzo *m* disgust; **far ~ a** disgust
rica'dere *vi* fall back; (*nel peccato ecc*) lapse; (*pendere*) hang [down]; **~ su** (*riversarsi*) fall on. **rica'duta** *f* relapse
rical'care *vt* trace
rica'ma|re *vt* embroider. **~to** *adj* embroidered
ri'cambi *mpl* spare parts
ricambi'are *vt* return; reciprocate (sentimento); **~ qcsa a qcno** repay sb for sth. **ri'cambio** *m* replacement; (*Biol*) metabolism; **pezzo di ricambio** spare [part]
ri'camo *m* embroidery
ricapito'la|re *vt* sum up. **~zi'one** *f* summary, recap [!]
ri'carica *f* (*di sveglia*) rewinding; (*Teleph*) top-up card
ricari'care *vt* reload (macchina fotografica, fucile, camion); recharge (batteria); (*Comput*) reboot
ricat'ta|re *vt* blackmail. **~'tore, ~'trice** *mf* blackmailer. **ri'catto** *m* blackmail
rica'va|re *vt* get; (*ottenere*) obtain; (*dedurre*) draw. **~to** *m* proceeds *pl*. **ri'cavo** *m* proceeds *pl*
'ricca *f* rich woman. **~'mente** *adv* lavishly
ric'chezza *f* wealth; *fig* richness
'riccio *adj* curly • *m* curl; (*animale*) hedgehog. **~ di mare** sea-urchin. **~lo** *m* curl. **~'luto** *adj* curly. **ricci'uto** *adj* (barba) curly
'ricco *adj* rich • *m* rich man
ri'cerca *f* search; (*indagine*) investigation; (*scientifica*) research; (*Sch*) project
ricer'ca|re *vt* search for; (*fare ricerche su*) research. **~ta** *f* wanted woman. **~'tezza** *f* refinement. **~to** *adj* sought-after; (*raffinato*) refined; (*affettato*) affected • *m* (*dalla polizia*) wanted man
ricetrasmit'tente *f* transceiver
ri'cetta *f* prescription; (*Culin*) recipe
ricet'tacolo *m* receptacle
ricet'tario *m* (*di cucina*) recipe book
ricetta|'tore, -'trice *mf* fence, receiver of stolen goods. **~zi'one** *f* receiving [stolen goods]
rice'vente *adj* (apparecchio, stazione) receiving • *mf* receiver
ri'cev|ere *vt* receive; (*dare il benvenuto*)

welcome; (*di albergo*) accommodate. **~i'mento** *m* receiving; (*accoglienza*) welcome; (*trattenimento*) reception

ricevi'tor|e *m* receiver. **~'ia** *f* **~ia del lotto** *agency authorized to sell lottery tickets*

rice'vuta *f* receipt

ricezi'one *f* (*Radio, TV*) reception

richia'mare *vt* (*al telefono*) call back; (*far tornare*) recall; (*rimproverare*) rebuke; (*attirare*) draw; **~ alla mente** call to mind. **richi'amo** *m* recall; (*attrazione*) call

richi'edere *vt* ask for; (*di nuovo*) ask again for; **~ a qcno di fare qcsa** ask *o* request sb to do sth. **richi'esta** *f* request; (*Comm*) demand

ri'chiuder|e *vt* close again. **~si** *vr* (ferita:) heal

rici'claggio *m* recycling

rici'clare *vt* recycle (carta, vetro); launder (denaro sporco)

'ricino *m* **olio di ~** castor oil

ricognizi'one *f* reconnaissance

ri'colmo *adj* full

ricominci'are *vt/i* start again

ricompa'rire *vi* reappear

ricom'pen|sa *f* reward. **~'sare** *vt* reward

ricom'por|re *vt* (*riscrivere*) rewrite; (*ricostruire*) reform; (*Typ*) reset. **~si** *vr* regain one's composure

riconcili'a|re *vt* reconcile. **~rsi** *vr* be reconciled. **~zi'one** *f* reconciliation

ricono'scen|te *adj* grateful. **~za** *f* gratitude

rico'nosc|ere *vt* recognize; (*ammettere*) acknowledge. **~i'mento** *m* recognition; (*ammissione*) acknowledgement; (*per la polizia*) identification. **~i'uto** *adj* recognized

riconside'rare *vt* rethink

rico'prire *vt* re-cover; (*rivestire*) coat; (*di insulti*) shower (**di** with); hold (carica)

ricor'dar|e *vt* remember; (*richiamare alla memoria*) recall; (*far ricordare*) remind; (*rassomigliare*) look like. **~si** *vr* **~si [di]** remember. **ri'cordo** *m* memory; (*oggetto*) memento; (*di viaggio*) souvenir; **ricordi** *pl* (*memorie*) memoirs

ricor'ren|te *adj* recurrent. **~za** *f* recurrence; (*anniversario*) anniversary

ri'correre *vi* recur; (*accadere*) occur; (data:) fall; **~ a** have recourse to; (*rivolgersi a*) turn to. **ri'corso** *pp di* **ricorrere** ● *m* recourse; (*Jur*) appeal

ricostitu'ente *m* tonic

ricostitu'ire *vt* re-establish

ricostru|'ire *vt* reconstruct. **~zi'o-ne** *f* reconstruction

ricove'ra|re *vt* give shelter to; **~re in ospedale** admit to hospital, hospitalize. **~to, -a** *mf* hospital patient. **ri'covero** *m* shelter; (*ospizio*) home

ricre'a|re *vt* re-create; (*ristorare*) restore. **~rsi** *vr* amuse oneself. **~'tivo** *adj* recreational. **~zi'one** *f* recreation; (*Sch*) break

ri'credersi *vr* change one's mind

ricupe'rare *vt* recover; rehabilitate (tossicodipendente); **~ il tempo perduto** make up for lost time. **ri'cupero** *m* recovery; (*di tossicodipendente*) rehabilitation; (*salvataggio*) rescue; **[minuti** *mpl* **di] ricupero** injury time

ri'curvo *adj* bent

ri'dare *vt* give back, return

ri'dente *adj* (*piacevole*) pleasant

'ridere *vi* laugh; **~ di** (*deridere*) laugh at

ri'detto *pp di* **ridire**

ridicoliz'zare *vt* ridicule. **ri'dicolo** *adj* ridiculous

ridimensio'nare *vt* reshape; *fig* see in the right perspective

ri'dire *vt* repeat; (*criticare*) find fault with

ridon'dante *adj* redundant

ri'dotto *pp di* **ridurre** ● *m* (*Theat*) foyer ● *adj* reduced

ri'du|rre *vt* reduce. **~rsi** *vr* diminish. **~rsi a** be reduced to. **~t'tivo** *adj* reductive. **~zi'one** *f* reduction; (*per cinema, teatro*) adaptation

rieducazi'one *f* (*di malato*) rehabilitation

riem'pi|re *vt* fill [up]; fill in (moduli ecc). **~rsi** *vr* fill [up]. **~'tivo** *adj* filling ● *m* filler

rien'tranza *f* recess

rien'trare *vi* go/come back in; (*tornare*) return; (*piegare indentro*) recede; **~ in** (*far parte*) fall within. **ri'entro** *m* return; (*di astronave*) re-entry

riepilo'gare *vt* recapitulate. **rie'pilogo** *m* roundup

riesami'nare *vt* reappraise

riesu'mare *vt* exhume

rievo'ca|re *vt* commemorate. **~zi'one** *f* commemoration

rifaci'mento *m* remake

ri'fa|re *vt* do again; (*creare*) make again; (*riparare*) repair; (*imitare*) imitate; make (letto). **~rsi** *vr* (*rimettersi*) recover; (*vendicarsi*) get even; **~rsi una vita/carriera** make a new life/career for oneself; **~rsi di** make up for. **~tto** *pp di* **rifare**

riferi'mento *m* reference

rife'rir|e *vt* report; **~e a** attribute to • *vi* make a report. **~si** *vr* **~si a** refer to

rifi'lare *vt* (*tagliare a filo*) trim; ([!]: *affibbiare*) saddle

rifi'ni|re *vt* finish off. **~'tura** *f* finish

rifiu'tare *vt* refuse. **rifi'uto** *m* refusal; **rifiuti** *pl* (*immondizie*) rubbish *sg*. **rifiuti** *pl* **urbani** urban waste *sg*

riflessi'one *f* reflection; (*osservazione*) remark. **rifles'sivo** *adj* thoughtful; (*Gram*) reflexive

ri'flesso *pp di* **riflettere** • *m* (*luce*) reflection; (*Med*) reflex; **per ~** indirectly

ri'fletter|e *vt* reflect • *vi* think. **~si** *vr* be reflected

riflet'tore *m* reflector; (*proiettore*) searchlight

ri'flusso *m* ebb

rifocil'lar|e *vt* restore. **~si** *vr liter, hum* take some refreshment

ri'fondere *vt* refund

ri'forma *f* reform; (*Relig*) reformation; (*Mil*) medical exemption

rifor'ma|re *vt* re-form; (*migliorare*) reform; (*Mil*) declare unfit for military service. **~to** *adj* (chiesa) Reformed. **~'tore, ~'trice** *mf* reformer. **~'torio** *m* reformatory. **rifor'mista** *adj* reformist

riforni'mento *m* supply; (*scorta*) stock; (*di combustibile*) refuelling; **stazione** *f* **di ~** petrol station

rifor'nir|e *vt* **~e di** provide with. **~si** *vr* restock, stock up (**di** with)

ri'fra|ngere *vt* refract. **~tto** *pp di* **rifrangere. ~zi'one** *f* refraction

rifug'gire *vi* **~ da** *fig* shun

rifugi'a|rsi *vr* take refuge. **~to, -a** *mf* refugee. **~to economico** economic refugee

ri'fugio *m* shelter; (*nascondiglio*) hideaway

'riga *f* line; (*fila*) row; (*striscia*) stripe; (*scriminatura*) parting; (*regolo*) rule; **a righe** (stoffa) striped; (quaderno) ruled; **mettersi in ~** line up

ri'gagnolo *m* rivulet

ri'gare *vt* rule (foglio) • *vi* **~ dritto** behave well

rigatti'ere *m* junk dealer

rigene'rare *vt* regenerate

riget'tare *vt* throw back; (*respingere*) reject; (*vomitare*) throw up. **ri'getto** *m* rejection

ri'ghello *m* ruler

rigid|a'mente *adv* rigidly. **~ità** *f* rigidity; (*di clima*) severity; (*severità*) strictness. **'rigido** *adj* rigid; (*freddo*) severe; (*severo*) strict

rigi'rar|e *vt* turn again; (*ripercorrere*) go round; *fig* twist (argomentazione) • *vi* walk about. **~si** *vr* turn round; (*nel letto*) turn over. **ri'giro** *m* (*imbroglio*) trick

'rigo *m* line; (*Mus*) staff

ri'gogli|o *m* bloom. **~'oso** *adj* luxuriant

ri'gonfio *adj* swollen

ri'gore *m* rigours *pl*; **a ~** strictly speaking; **calcio di ~** penalty [kick]; **area di ~** penalty area; **essere di ~** be compulsory

rigo'roso *adj* (*severo*) strict; (*scrupoloso*) rigorous

riguada'gnare *vt* regain (quota, velocità)

riguar'dar|e *vt* look at again; (*considerare*) regard; (*concernere*) concern; **per quanto riguarda** with regard to. **~si** *vr* take care of oneself. **rigu'ardo** *m* care; (*considerazione*) consideration; **nei riguardi di** towards; **riguardo a** with regard to

ri'gurgito *m* regurgitation

rilanci'are *vt* throw back (palla); (*di nuovo*) throw again; increase (offerta); revive (moda); relaunch (prodotto) • *vi* (*a carte*) raise the stakes

rilasci'ar|e *vt* (*concedere*) grant; (*liberare*) release; issue (documento). **~si** *vr*

r

relax. **ri'lascio** *m* release; (*di documento*) issue

rilassa'mento *m* relaxation

rilas'sa|re *vt*, **~rsi** *vr* relax. **~to** *adj* (ambiente) relaxed

rile'ga|re *vt* bind (libro). **~to** *adj* bound. **~'tura** *f* binding

ri'leggere *vt* reread

ri'lento: **a ~** *adv* slowly

rileva'mento *m* survey; (*Comm*) buyout

rile'van|te *adj* considerable

rile'va|re *vt* (*trarre*) get; (*mettere in evidenza*) point out; (*notare*) notice; (*topografia*) survey; (*Comm*) take over; (*Mil*) relieve. **~zi'one** *f* (*statistica*) survey

rili'evo *m* relief; (*Geog*) elevation; (*topografia*) survey; (*importanza*) importance; (*osservazione*) remark; **mettere in ~ qcsa** point sth out

rilut'tan|te *adj* reluctant. **~za** *f* reluctance

'rima *f* rhyme

riman'dare *vt* (*posporre*) postpone; (*mandare indietro*) send back; (*mandare di nuovo*) send again; (*far ridare un esame*) make resit an examination. **ri'mando** *m* return; (*in un libro*) crossreference

rima'nen|te *adj* remaining ● *m* remainder. **~za** *f* remainder

rima'ne|re *vi* stay, remain; (*essere d'avanzo*) be left; (*venirsi a trovare*) be; (*restare stupito*) be astonished; (*restare d'accordo*) agree

rimar'chevole *adj* remarkable

ri'mare *vt/i* rhyme

rimargi'nar|e *vt*, **~si** *vr* heal

ri'masto *pp di* **rimanere**

rimbal'zare *vi* rebound; (proiettile:) ricochet; **far ~** bounce. **rim'balzo** *m* rebound; (*di proiettile*) ricochet

rimbam'bi|re *vi* be in one's dotage ● *vt* stun. **~to** *adj* in one's dotage

rimboc'care *vt* turn up; roll up (maniche); tuck in (coperte)

rimbom'bare *vi* resound

rimbor'sare *vt* reimburse, repay. **rim'borso** *m* reimbursement, repayment. **rimborso spese** reimbursement of expenses

rimedi'are *vi* **~ a** remedy; make up for (errore); (*procurare*) scrape up. **ri'medio** *m* remedy

rimesco'lare *vt* mix [up]; shuffle (carte); (*rivangare*) rake up

ri'messa *f* (*locale per veicoli*) garage; (*per aerei*) hangar; (*per autobus*) depot; (*di denaro*) remittance; (*di merci*) consignment

ri'messo *pp di* **rimettere**

ri'metter|e *vt* put back; (*restituire*) return; (*affidare*) entrust; (*perdonare*) remit; (*rimandare*) put off; (*vomitare*) bring up. **~si** *vr* (*ristabilirsi*) recover; (tempo:) clear up; **~si a** start again

'rimmel® *m inv* mascara

rimoder'nare *vt* modernize

rimon'tare *vt* (*risalire*) go up; (*Mech*) reassemble ● *vi* remount; **~ a** (*risalire*) go back to

rimorchi'a|re *vt* tow; [!] pick up (ragazza). **~'tore** *m* tug[boat]. **ri'morchio** *m* tow; (*veicolo*) trailer

ri'morso *m* remorse

rimo'stranza *f* complaint

rimozi'one *f* removal; (*da un incarico*) dismissal. **~ forzata** *illegally parked vehicles removed at owner's expense*

rim'pasto *m* (*Pol*) reshuffle

rimpatri'are *vt/i* repatriate. **rim'patrio** *m* repatriation

rim'pian|gere *vt* regret. **~to** *pp di* **rimpiangere** ● *m* regret

rimpiaz'zare *vt* replace

rimpiccio'lire *vi* become smaller

rimpinz'ar|e *vt* **~e di** stuff with. **~si** *vr* stuff oneself

rimprove'rare *vt* reproach; **~ qcsa a qcno** reproach sb for sth. **rim'provero** *m* reproach

rimune'ra|re *vt* remunerate. **~'tivo** *adj* remunerative. **~zi'one** *f* remuneration

ri'muovere *vt* remove

ri'nascere *vi* be reborn

rinascimen'tale *adj* Renaissance. **Rinasci'mento** *m* Renaissance

ri'nascita *f* rebirth

rincal'zare *vt* (*sostenere*) support; (*rimboccare*) tuck in. **rin'calzo** *m* support; **rincalzi** *pl* (*Mil*) reserves

rincantucci'arsi *vr* hide oneself away in a corner

rinca'rare *vt* increase the price of ● *vi* become more expensive. **rin'caro** *m* price increase

rinca'sare *vi* return home

rinchi'uder|e *vt* shut up. **~si** *vr* shut oneself up

rin'correre *vt* run after

rin'cors|a *f* run-up. **~o** *pp di* **rincorrere**

rin'cresc|ere *vi* **mi rincresce di non...** I'm sorry *o* I regret that I can't...; **se non ti ~e** if you don't mind. **~i'mento** *m* regret. **~i'uto** *pp di* **rincrescere**

rincreti'nire *vi* be stupid

rincu'lare *vi* (arma:) recoil; (cavallo:) shy. **rin'culo** *m* recoil

rincuo'rar|e *vt* encourage. **~si** *vr* take heart

rinfacci'are *vt* **~ qcsa a qcno** throw sth in sb's face

rinfor'zar|e *vt* strengthen; (*rendere più saldo*) reinforce. **~si** *vr* become stronger. **rin'forzo** *m* reinforcement; *fig* support

rinfran'care *vt* reassure

rinfre'scante *adj* cooling

rinfre'scar|e *vt* cool; (*rinnovare*) freshen up • *vi* get cooler. **~si** *vr* freshen [oneself] up. **rin'fresco** *m* light refreshment; (*ricevimento*) party

rin'fusa *f* **alla ~** at random

ringhi'era *f* railing; (*di scala*) banisters *pl*

ringiova'nire *vt* rejuvenate (pelle, persona); (vestito:) make look younger • *vi* become young again; (*sembrare*) look young again

r

ringrazi|a'mento *m* thanks *pl*. **~'are** *vt* thank

rinne'ga|re *vt* disown. **~to, -a** *mf* renegade

rinnova'mento *m* renewal; (*di edifici*) renovation

rinno'var|e *vt* renew; renovate (edifici). **~si** *vr* be renewed; (*ripetersi*) recur, happen again. **rin'novo** *m* renewal

rinoce'ronte *m* rhinoceros

rino'mato *adj* renowned

rinsal'dare *vt* consolidate

rinsa'vire *vi* come to one's senses

rinsec'chi|re *vi* shrivel up. **~to** *adj* shrivelled up

rinta'narsi *vr* hide oneself away; (animale:) retreat into its den

rintoc'care *vi* (campana:) toll; (orologio:) strike. **rin'tocco** *m* toll; (*di orologio*) stroke

rinton'ti|re *vt* stun. **~to** *adj* dazed

rintracci'are *vt* trace

rintro'nare *vt* stun • *vi* boom

ri'nuncia *f* renunciation

rinunci'a|re *vi* **~re a** renounce, give up. **~'tario** *adj* defeatist

ri'nunzia, rinunzi'are = **RINUNCIA, RINUNCIARE**

rinveni'mento *m* (*di reperti*) discovery; (*di refurtiva*) recovery. **rinve'nire** *vt* find • *vi* (*riprendere i sensi*) come round; (*ridiventare fresco*) revive

rinvi'are *vt* put off; (*mandare indietro*) return; (*in libro*) refer; **~ a giudizio** indict

rin'vio *m Sport* goal kick; (*in libro*) cross-reference; (*di appuntamento*) postponement; (*di merce*) return

rio'nale *adj* local. **ri'one** *m* district

riordi'nare *vt* tidy [up]; (*ordinare di nuovo*) reorder; (*riorganizzare*) reorganize

riorganiz'zare *vt* reorganize

ripa'gare *vt* repay

ripa'ra|re *vt* protect; (*aggiustare*) repair; (*porre rimedio*) remedy • *vi* **~re a** make up for. **~rsi** *vr* take shelter. **~to** *adj* (luogo) sheltered. **~zi'one** *f* repair; *fig* reparation. **ri'paro** *m* shelter; (*rimedio*) remedy

ripar'ti|re *vt* (*dividere*) divide • *vi* leave again. **~zi'one** *f* division

ripas'sa|re *vt* recross; (*rivedere*) revise • *vi* pass again. **ri'passo** *m* (*di lezione*) revision

ripensa'mento *m* second thoughts *pl*

ripen'sare *vi* change one's mind; **~ a** think of; **ripensaci!** think again!

riper'correre *vt* go back over

riper'cosso *pp di* **ripercuotere**

ripercu'oter|e *vt* strike again. **~si** *vr* (suono:) reverberate; **~si su** (*avere conseguenze*) impact on. **ripercussi'one** *f* repercussion

ripe'scare *vt* fish out (oggetti)

ripe'tente *mf student repeating a year*

ri'pet|ere *vt* repeat. **~ersi** *vr* (evento:) recur. **~izi'one** *f* repetition; (*di lezione*) revision; (*lezione privata*) private lesson. **~uta'mente** *adv* repeatedly

ri'piano *m* (*di scaffale*) shelf; (*terreno pianeggiante*) terrace

ri'picc|a *f* **fare qcsa per ~a** do sth out of spite. **~o** *m* spite

'ripido *adj* steep

ripie'gar|e *vt* refold; (*abbassare*) lower • *vi* (*indietreggiare*) retreat. **~si** *vr* bend; (sedile:) fold. **ripi'ego** *m* expedient; (*via d'uscita*) way out

ripi'eno *adj* full; (*Culin*) stuffed • *m* filling; (*Culin*) stuffing

ri'porre *vt* put back; (*mettere da parte*) put away; (*collocare*) place; repeat (domanda)

ripor'tar|e *vt* (*restituire*) bring/take back; (*riferire*) report; (*subire*) suffer; (*Math*) carry; win (vittoria); transfer (disegno). **~si** *vr* go back; (*riferirsi*) refer

ripo'sante *adj* (colore) restful, soothing

ripo'sa|re *vi* rest • *vt* put back. **~rsi** *vr* rest. **~to** *adj* (mente) fresh. **ri'poso** *m* rest; **andare a riposo** retire; **riposo!** (*Mil*) at ease!; **giorno di riposo** day off

ripo'stiglio *m* cupboard

ri'posto *pp di* **riporre**

ri'prender|e *vt* take again; (*prendere indietro*) take back; (*riconquistare*) recapture; (*ricuperare*) recover; (*ricominciare*) resume; (*rimproverare*) reprimand; take in (cucitura); *Cinema* shoot. **~si** *vr* recover; (*correggersi*) correct oneself

ri'presa *f* resumption; (*ricupero*) recovery; (*Theat*) revival; *Cinema* shot; (*Auto*) acceleration; (*Mus*) repeat. **~ aerea** bird's-eye view

ripresen'tar|e *vt* resubmit (domanda, certificato). **~si** *vr* go/come back again; (*come candidato*) run again; (occasione:) arise again

ri'preso *pp di* **riprendere**

ripristi'nare *vt* restore

ripro'dotto *pp di* **riprodurre**

ripro'du|rre *vt*, **~rsi** *vr* reproduce. **~t'tivo** *adj* reproductive. **~zi'one** *f* reproduction

ripro'mettersi *vr* intend

ri'prova *f* confirmation

ripudi'are *vt* repudiate

ripu'gnan|te *adj* repugnant. **~za** *f* disgust. **ripu'gnare** *vi* **ripugnare a** disgust

ripu'li|re *vt* clean [up]; *fig* polish

ripuls|i'one *f* repulsion. **~'ivo** *adj* repulsive

ri'quadro *m* square; (*pannello*) panel

ri'sacca *f* undertow

risa'lire *vt* go back up • *vi* **~ a** (*nel tempo*) go back to; (*essere datato a*) date back to, go back to

risal'tare *vi* stand out. **ri'salto** *m* prominence; (*rilievo*) relief

risa'nare *vt* heal; (*bonificare*) reclaim

risa'puto *adj* well-known

risarci'mento *m* compensation. **risar'cire** *vt* indemnify

ri'sata *f* laugh

riscalda'mento *m* heating. **~ autonomo** central heating (*for one flat*)

riscal'dar|e *vt* heat; warm (persona). **~si** *vr* warm up

riscat'tar|e *vt* ransom. **~si** *vr* redeem oneself. **ri'scatto** *m* ransom; (*morale*) redemption

rischia'rar|e *vt* light up; brighten (colore). **~si** *vr* light up; (cielo:) clear up

rischi|'are *vt* risk • *vi* run the risk. **'rischio** *m* risk. **~'oso** *adj* risky

risciac'quare *vt* rinse

riscon'trare *vt* (*confrontare*) compare; (*verificare*) check; (*rilevare*) find. **ri'scontro** *m* comparison; check; (*Comm: risposta*) reply

ri'scossa *f* revolt; (*riconquista*) recovery

riscossi'one *f* collection

ri'scosso *pp di* **riscuotere**

riscu'oter|e *vt* shake; (*percepire*) draw; (*ottenere*) gain; cash (assegno). **~si** *vr* rouse oneself

risen'ti|re *vt* hear again; (*provare*) feel • *vi* **~re di** feel the effect of. **~rsi** *vr* (*offendersi*) take offence. **~to** *adj* resentful

ri'serbo *m* reserve; **mantenere il ~** remain tight-lipped

ri'serva *f* reserve; (*di caccia, pesca*) preserve; *Sport* substitute, reserve. **~ di caccia** game reserve. **~ naturale** wildlife reserve

riser'va|re *vt* reserve; (*prenotare*) book; (*per occasione*) keep. **~rsi** *vr* (*ripromettersi*) plan for oneself (cambiamento). **~'tezza** *f* reserve. **~to** *adj* reserved

ri'siedere *vi* **~ a** live in/at

'riso[1] *m* (*cereale*) rice

'riso[2] *pp di* **ridere** • *m* (*pl f* **risa**) laugh-

r

ter; (*singolo*) laugh. **~'lino** *m* giggle

ri'solto *pp di* **risolvere**

risolu|'tezza *f* determination. **riso'luto** *adj* resolute, determined. **~zi'one** *f* resolution

ri'solver|e *vt* resolve; (*Math*) solve. **~si** *vr* (*decidersi*) decide; **~si in** turn into

riso'na|nza *f* resonance; **aver ~nza** arouse great interest. **~re** *vi* resound; (*rimbombare*) echo

ri'sorgere *vi* rise again

risorgi'mento *m* revival; (*storico*) Risorgimento

ri'sorsa *f* resource; (*espediente*) resort

ri'sorto *pp di* **risorgere**

ri'sotto *m* risotto

ri'sparmi *mpl* (*soldi*) savings

risparmi'a|re *vt* save; (*salvare*) spare. **~'tore, ~'trice** *mf* saver **ri'sparmio** *m* saving

rispecchi'are *vt* reflect

rispet'tabil|e *adj* respectable. **~ità** *f* respectability

rispet'tare *vt* respect; **farsi ~** command respect

rispet'tivo *adj* respective

ri'spetto *m* respect; **~ a** as regards; (*in confronto a*) compared to

rispet|tosa'mente *adv* respectfully. **~'toso** *adj* respectful

risplen'dente *adj* shining. **ri'splendere** *vi* shine

rispon'den|te *adj* **~te a** in keeping with. **~za** *f* correspondence

ri'spondere *vi* answer; (*rimbeccare*) answer back; (*obbedire*) respond; **~ a** reply to; **~ di** (*rendersi responsabile*) answer for

ri'spost|a *f* answer, reply; (*reazione*) response. **~o** *pp di* **rispondere**

'rissa *f* brawl. **ris'soso** *adj* pugnacious

ristabi'lir|e *vt* re-establish. **~si** *vr* (*in salute*) recover

rista'gnare *vi* stagnate; (sangue:) coagulate. **ri'stagno** *m* stagnation

ri'stampa *f* reprint; (*azione*) reprinting. **ristam'pare** *vt* reprint

risto'rante *m* restaurant

risto'ra|re *vt* refresh. **~rsi** *vr liter* take some refreshment; (*riposarsi*) take a rest. **~'tore, ~'trice** *mf* (*proprietario di ristorante*) restaurateur; (*fornitore*) caterer ● *adj* refreshing. **ri'storo** *m* refreshment; (*sollievo*) relief

ristret'tezza *f* narrowness; (*povertà*) poverty

ri'stretto *pp di* **restringere** ● *adj* narrow; (*condensato*) condensed; (*limitato*) restricted; **di idee ristrette** narrow-minded

ristruttu'rare *vt* restructure (ditta); refurbish (casa)

risucchi'are *vt* suck in. **ri'succhio** *m* whirlpool; (*di corrente*) undertow

risul'ta|re *vi* result; (*riuscire*) turn out. **~to** *m* result

risuo'nare *vi* echo; (*Phys*) resonate

risurrezi'one *f* resurrection

risusci'tare *vt* resuscitate; *fig* revive ● *vi* return to life

risvegli'ar|e *vt* reawaken (interesse). **~si** *vr* wake up; (natura:) awake; (desiderio:) be aroused. **ri'sveglio** *m* waking up; (*dell'interesse*) revival; (*del desiderio*) arousal

ri'svolto *m* lapel; (*di pantaloni*) turn-up, cuff *Am*; (*di manica*) cuff; (*di tasca*) flap; (*di libro*) inside flap

ritagli'are *vt* cut out. **ri'taglio** *m* cutting; (*di stoffa*) scrap

ritar'da|re *vi* be late; (orologio:) be slow ● *vt* delay; slow down (progresso); (*differire*) postpone. **~'tario, -a** *mf* late-comer

ri'tardo *m* delay; **essere in ~** be late; (volo:) be delayed

ri'tegno *m* reserve

rite'n|ere *vt* retain; deduct (somma); (*credere*) believe. **~uta** *f* deduction

riti'ra|re *vt* throw back (palla); (*prelevare*) withdraw; (*riscuotere*) draw; collect (pacco). **~rsi** *vr* withdraw; (stoffa:) shrink; (*da attività*) retire; (marea:) recede. **~ta** *f* retreat; (*WC*) toilet. **ri'tiro** *m* withdrawal; (*Relig*) retreat; (*da attività*) retirement. **ritiro bagagli** baggage reclaim

'ritmo *m* rhythm

'rito *m* rite; **di ~** customary

ritoc'care *vt* touch up

ritor'nare *vi* return; (*andare venire indietro*) go/come back; (*ricorrere*) recur; (*ridiventare*) become again

ritor'nello *m* refrain

r

ri'torno *m* return
ritorsi'one *f* retaliation
ri'trarre *vt* withdraw; (*distogliere*) turn away; (*rappresentare*) portray
ritrat'ta|re *vt* deal with again; retract (dichiarazione). **~zi'one** *f* withdrawal, retraction
ritrat'tista *mf* portrait painter. **ri'tratto** *pp di* **ritrarre** ● *m* portrait
ritro'sia *f* shyness. **ri'troso** *adj* backward; (*timido*) shy; **a ritroso** backwards; **ritroso a** reluctant to
ritro'va|re *vt* find [again]; regain (salute). **~rsi** *vr* meet; (*di nuovo*) meet again; (*capitare*) find oneself; (*raccapezzarsi*) see one's way. **~to** *m* discovery. **ri'trovo** *m* meeting-place; (*notturno*) night-club
'ritto *adj* upright; (*diritto*) straight
ritu'ale *adj & m* ritual
riunifi'ca|re *vt* reunify. **~rsi** *vr* be reunited. **~zi'one** *f* reunification
riuni'one *f* meeting; (*fra amici*) reunion
riu'nir|e *vt* (*unire*) join together; (*radunare*) gather. **~si** *vr* be re-united; (*adunarsi*) meet
riusc'i|re *vi* (*aver successo*) succeed; (*in matematica ecc*) be good (**in** at); (*aver esito*) turn out; **le è riuscito simpatico** she found him likeable. **~ta** *f* result; (*successo*) success
'riva *f* shore; (*di fiume*) bank
ri'val|e *mf* rival. **~ità** *f inv* rivalry
rivalutazi'one *f* revaluation
rive'dere *vt* see again; revise (lezione); (*verificare*) check
rive'la|re *vt* reveal. **~rsi** *vr* (*dimostrarsi*) turn out. **~'tore** *adj* revealing ● *m* (*Techn*) detector. **~zi'one** *f* revelation
ri'vendere *vt* resell
rivendi'ca|re *vt* claim. **~zi'one** *f* claim
ri'vendi|ta *f* (*negozio*) shop. **~'tore, ~'trice** *mf* retailer. **~tore autorizzato** authorized dealer
ri'verbero *m* reverberation; (*bagliore*) glare
rive'renza *f* reverence; (*inchino*) curtsy; (*di uomo*) bow
rive'rire *vt* respect; (*ossequiare*) pay one's respects to
river'sar|e *vt* pour. **~si** *vr* (fiume:) flow
rivesti'mento *m* covering
rive'sti|re *vt* (*rifornire di abiti*) clothe; (*ricoprire*) cover; (*internamente*) line; hold (carica). **~rsi** *vr* get dressed again; (*per una festa*) dress up
rivi'era *f* coast; **la ~ ligure** the Italian Riviera
ri'vincita *f Sport* return match; (*vendetta*) revenge
rivis'suto *pp di* **rivivere**
ri'vista *f* review; (*pubblicazione*) magazine; (*Theat*) revue; **passare in ~** review
ri'vivere *vi* come to life again; (*riprendere le forze*) revive ● *vt* relive
ri'volger|e *vt* turn; (*indirizzare*) address; **~e da** (*distogliere*) turn away from. **~si** *vr* turn round; **~si a** (*indirizzarsi*) turn to
ri'volta *f* revolt
rivol'tante *adj* disgusting
rivol'tar|e *vt* turn [over]; (*mettendo l'interno verso l'esterno*) turn inside out; (*sconvolgere*) upset. **~si** *vr* (*ribellarsi*) revolt
rivol'tella *f* revolver
ri'volto *pp di* **rivolgere**
rivoluzio'nar|e *vt* revolutionize. **~io, -a** *adj & mf* revolutionary. **rivoluzi'one** *f* revolution; (*fig: disordine*) chaos
riz'zar|e *vt* raise; (*innalzare*) erect; prick up (orecchie). **~si** *vr* stand up; (capelli:) stand on end; (orecchie:) prick up
'roaming *m inv* (*Teleph*) **~ [internazionale]** roaming
'roba *f* stuff; (*personale*) belongings *pl*, stuff; (*faccenda*) thing; (☒: *droga*) drugs *pl*. **~ da mangiare** things to eat
ro'baccia *f* rubbish
ro'bot *m inv* robot. **~ da cucina** food processor
robu'stezza *f* sturdiness, robustness; (*forza*) strength. **ro'busto** *adj* sturdy, robust; (*forte*) strong
'rocca *f* fortress. **~'forte** *f* stronghold
roc'chetto *m* reel
'roccia *f* rock
ro'da|ggio *m* running in. **~re** *vt* run in
'roder|e *vt* gnaw; (*corrodere*) corrode.

r

~si *vr* ~si da be consumed with. **ro·di'tore** *m* rodent

rodo'dendro *m* rhododendron

ro'gnone *m* (*Culin*) kidney

'rogo *m* (*supplizio*) stake; (*per cadaveri*) pyre

'Roma *f* Rome

Roma'nia *f* Romania

ro'manico *adj* Romanesque

ro'mano, -a *adj & mf* Roman

romanti'cismo *m* romanticism. **ro'mantico** *adj* romantic

ro'man|za *f* romance. **~'zato** *adj* romanticized. **~'zesco** *adj* fictional; (*stravagante*) wild, unrealistic. **~zi'ere** *m* novelist

ro'manzo *adj* Romance ● *m* novel. **~ giallo** thriller

'rombo *m* rumble; (*Math*) rhombus; (*pesce*) turbot

'romper|e *vt* break; break off (relazione); **non ~e [le scatole]!** ([!]: *seccare*) don't be a pain [in the neck]!. **~si** *vr* break; **~si una gamba** break one's leg

rompi'capo *m* nuisance; (*indovinello*) puzzle

rompi'collo *m* daredevil; **a ~** at breakneck speed

rompighi'accio *m* ice-breaker

rompi'scatole *mf inv* [!] pain

'ronda *f* rounds *pl*

ron'della *f* (*Mech*) washer

'rondine *f* swallow

ron'done *m* swift

ron'fare *vi* snore

ron'zino *m* jade

ron'zio *m* buzz

'rosa *f* rose. **~ dei venti** wind rose ● *adj & m* pink. **ro'saio** *m* rose-bush

ro'sario *m* rosary

ro'sato *adj* rosy ● *m* (*vino*) rosé

'roseo *adj* pink

ro'seto *m* rose garden

rosma'rino *m* rosemary

'roso *pp di* **rodere**

roso'lare *vt* brown

roso'lia *f* German measles

ro'sone *m* rosette; (*apertura*) rose-window

'rospo *m* toad

ros'setto *m* (*per labbra*) lipstick

'rosso *adj & m* red; **passare con il ~** jump a red light. **~ d'uovo** [egg] yolk. **ros'sore** *m* redness; (*della pelle*) flush

rosticce'ria *f shop selling cooked meat and other prepared food*

ro'tabile *adj* **strada ~** carriageway

ro'taia *f* rail; (*solco*) rut

ro'ta|re *vt/i* rotate. **~zi'one** *f* rotation

rote'are *vt/i* roll

ro'tella *f* small wheel; (*di mobile*) castor

roto'lar|e *vt/i* roll. **~si** *vr* roll [about]. **'rotolo** *m* roll; **andare a rotoli** go to rack and ruin

rotondità *f* roundness; **~** *pl* (*curve femminili*) curves. **ro'tondo, -a** *adj* round ● *f* (*spiazzo*) terrace

ro'tore *m* rotor

'rotta[1] *f* (*Naut*), (*Aeron*) course; **far ~ per** make course for; **fuori ~** off course

'rotta[2] *f* **a ~ di collo** at breakneck speed; **essere in ~ con** be on bad terms with

rot'tame *m* scrap; *fig* wreck

'rotto *pp di* **rompere** ● *adj* broken; (*stracciato*) torn

rot'tura *f* break

'rotula *f* kneecap

rou'lette *f inv* roulette

rou'lotte *f inv* caravan, trailer *Am*

rou'tine *f inv* routine; **di ~** (operazioni, controlli) routine

ro'vente *adj* scorching

'rovere *m* (*legno*) oak

rovesci'ar|e *vt* knock over; (*sottosopra*) turn upside down; (*rivoltare*) turn inside out; spill (liquido); overthrow (governo); reverse (situazione). **~si** *vr* (*capovolgersi*) overturn; (*riversarsi*) pour. **ro'vescio** *adj* (*contrario*) reverse; **alla rovescia** (*capovolto*) upside down; (*con l'interno all'esterno*) inside out ● *m* reverse; (*nella maglia*) purl; (*di pioggia*) downpour; *Tennis* backhand

ro'vina *f* ruin; (*crollo*) collapse

rovi'na|re *vt* ruin; (*guastare*) spoil ● *vi* crash. **~rsi** *vr* be ruined. **~to** *adj* (oggetto) ruined. **rovi'noso** *adj* ruinous

rovi'stare *vt* ransack
'rovo *m* bramble
'rozzo *adj* rough
R.R. *abbr* (ricevuta di ritorno) return receipt for registered mail
'ruba *f* **andare a ~** sell like hot cakes
ru'bare *vt* steal
rubi'netto *m* tap, faucet *Am*
ru'bino *m* ruby
ru'brica *f* column; (*in programma televisivo*) TV report; (*quaderno con indice*) address book. **~ telefonica** telephone and address book
'rude *adj* rough
'rudere *m* ruin
rudimen'tale *adj* rudimentary. **rudi'menti** *mpl* rudiments
ruffi'an|a *f* procuress. **~o** *m* pimp; (*adulatore*) bootlicker
'ruga *f* wrinkle
'ruggine *f* rust; **fare la ~** go rusty
rug'gi|re *vi* roar. **~to** *m* roar
rugi'ada *f* dew
ru'goso *adj* wrinkled
rul'lare *vi* roll; (*Aeron*) taxi
rul'lino *m* film
rul'lio *m* rolling; (*Aeron*) taxiing
rum *m inv* rum
ru'meno, -a *adj & mf* Romanian
ru'mor|e *m* noise; *fig* rumour. **~eggi'are** *vi* rumble. **rumo'roso** *adj* noisy; (*sonoro*) loud
ru'olo *m* roll; (*Theat*) role; **di ~** on the staff
ru'ota *f* wheel; **andare a ~ libera** free-wheel. **~ di scorta** spare wheel
'rupe *f* cliff
ru'rale *adj* rural
ru'scello *m* stream
'ruspa *f* bulldozer
rus'sare *vi* snore
'Russ|ia *f* Russia. **r~o, -a** *adj & mf* Russian; (*lingua*) Russian
'rustico *adj* rural; (carattere) rough
rut'tare *vi* belch. **'rutto** *m* belch
'ruvido *adj* coarse
ruzzo'l|are *vi* tumble down. **~one** *m* tumble; **cadere ruzzoloni** tumble down

Ss

'sabato *m* Saturday
'sabbi|a *f* sand. **~e** *pl* **mobili** quicksand. **~'oso** a sandy
sabo'ta|ggio *m* sabotage. **~re** *vt* sabotage. **~'tore, ~'trice** *mf* saboteur
'sacca *f* bag. **~ da viaggio** travelling-bag
sacca'rina *f* saccharin
sac'cente *adj* pretentious • *mf* know-all
saccheggi'a|re *vt* sack; *hum* raid (frigo)
sac'chetto *m* bag
'sacco *m* sack; (*Anat*) sac; **mettere nel ~** *fig* swindle; **un ~** (*moltissimo*) a lot; **un ~ di** (*gran quantità*) lots of. **~ a pelo** sleeping-bag
sacer'do|te *m* priest
sacra'mento *m* sacrament
sacrifi'ca|re *vt* sacrifice. **~rsi** *vr* sacrifice oneself. **~to** *adj* (*non valorizzato*) wasted. **sacri'ficio** *m* sacrifice
sa'crilego *adj* sacrilegious
'sacro *adj* sacred • *m* (*Anat*) sacrum
sacro'santo *adj* sacrosanct
'sadico, -a *adj* sadistic • *mf* sadist. **sa'dismo** *m* sadism
sa'etta *f* arrow
sa'fari *m inv* safari
'saga *f* saga
sa'gace *adj* shrewd
sag'gezza *f* wisdom
saggi'are *vt* test
'saggio[1] *m* (*scritto*) essay; (*prova*) proof; (*di metallo*) assay; (*campione*) sample; (*esempio*) example
'saggio[2] *adj* wise
sag'gistica *f* non-fiction
Sagit'tario *m* (*Astr*) Sagittarius
'sagoma *f* shape; (*profilo*) outline. **sago'mato** *adj* shaped
'sagra *f* festival
sagre|'stano *m* sacristan. **~'stia** *f* sacristy
'sala *f* hall; (*stanza*) room; (*salotto*) living room. **~ d'attesa** waiting room. **~**

da ballo ballroom. ~ **d'imbarco** departure lounge. ~ **macchine** engine room. ~ **operatoria** operating theatre. ~ **parto** delivery room. ~ **da pranzo** dining room

sa'lame *m* salami

sala'moia *f* brine

sa'lare *vt* salt

sa'lario *m* wages *pl*

sa'lasso *m* **essere un** ~ *fig* cost a fortune

sala'tini *mpl* savouries (*eaten with aperitifs*)

sa'lato *adj* salty; (*costoso*) dear

sal'ciccia *f* = SALSICCIA

sal'dar|e *vt* weld; set (osso); pay off (debito); settle (conto); **~e a stagno** solder. **~si** *vr* (*Med: osso:*) knit

salda'trice *f* welder; (*a stagno*) soldering iron

salda'tura *f* weld; (*azione*) welding; (*di osso*) knitting

'saldo *adj* firm; (*resistente*) strong • *m* settlement; (*svendita*) sale; (*Comm*) balance

'sale *m* salt. ~ **fine** table salt. ~ **grosso** cooking salt. **sali** *pl* **e tabacchi** tobacconist's shop

'salice *m* willow. ~ **piangente** weeping willow

sali'ente *adj* outstanding; **i punti salienti di un discorso** the main points of a speech

sali'era *f* salt-cellar

sa'lina *f* salt-works *sg*

sa'li|re *vi* go/come up; (*levarsi*) rise; (*su treno ecc*) get on; (*in macchina*) get in • *vt* go/come up (scale). **~ta** *f* climb; (*aumento*) rise; **in ~ta** uphill

sa'liva *f* saliva

'salma *f* corpse

'salmo *m* psalm

sal'mone *m & adj inv* salmon

sa'lone *m* hall; (*salotto*) living room; (*di parrucchiere*) salon. ~ **di bellezza** beauty parlour

salo'pette *f inv* dungarees *pl*

salot'tino *m* bower

sa'lotto *m* drawing room; (*soggiorno*) sitting room; (*mobili*) [three-piece] suite

sal'pare *vt/i* sail; ~ **l'ancora** weigh anchor

'salsa *f* sauce

sal'sedine *f* saltiness

sal'siccia *f* sausage

sal'ta|re *vi* jump; (*venir via*) come off; (*balzare*) leap; (*esplodere*) blow up; **~r fuori** spring from nowhere; (oggetto cercato:) turn up; **è ~to fuori che...** it emerged that...; **~re fuori con...** come out with...; **~re in mente** spring to mind • *vt* jump [over]; skip (pasti, lezioni); (*Culin*) sauté. **~to** *adj* (*Culin*) sautéed

saltel'lare *vi* hop; (*di gioia*) skip

saltim'banco *m* acrobat

'salto *m* jump; (*balzo*) leap; (*dislivello*) drop; (*omissione, lacuna*) gap; **fare un ~ da** drop in on. ~ **in alto** high jump. ~ **con l'asta** pole-vault. ~ **in lungo** long jump. ~ **pagina** (*Comput*) page down

saltuaria'mente *adv* occasionally. **saltu'ario** *adj* desultory; **lavoro saltuario** casual work

sa'lubre *adj* healthy

salume'ria *f* delicatessen. **sa'lumi** *mpl* cold cuts

salu'tare *vt* greet; (*congedandosi*) say goodbye to; (*portare i saluti a*) give one's regards to; (*Mil*) salute • *adj* healthy

sa'lute *f* health; **~!** (*dopo uno starnuto*) bless you!; (*a un brindisi*) your health!

sa'luto *m* greeting; (*di addio*) goodbye; (*Mil*) salute; **saluti** *pl* (*ossequi*) regards

'salva *f* salvo; **sparare a salve** fire blanks

salvada'naio *m* money box

salva'gente *m* lifebelt; (*a giubbotto*) life-jacket; (*ciambella*) rubber ring; (*spartitraffico*) traffic island

salvaguar'dare *vt* safeguard. **salvagu'ardia** *f* safeguard

sal'var|e *vt* save; (*proteggere*) protect. **~si** *vr* save oneself

salva'slip *m inv* panty-liner

salva|'taggio *m* rescue; (*Naut*) salvage; (*Comput*) saving; **battello di ~taggio** lifeboat

sal'vezza *f* safety; (*Relig*) salvation

'salvia *f* sage

salvi'etta *f* serviette

'salvo *adj* safe ●*prep* except [for] ●*conj* ~ **che** (*a meno che*) unless; (*eccetto che*) except that

samari'tano, -a *adj & mf* Samaritan

sam'buco *m* elder

san *m* **S~ Francesco** Saint Francis

sa'nare *vt* heal

sana'torio *m* sanatorium

san'cire *vt* sanction

'sandalo *m* sandal

'sangu|e *m* blood; **al ~e** (carne) rare; **farsi cattivo ~e per** worry about. **~e freddo** composure; **a ~e freddo** in cold blood. **~'igno** *adj* blood

sangui'naccio *m* (*Culin*) black pudding

sangui'nante *adj* bleeding

sangui'nar|e *vi* bleed. **~io** *adj* bloodthirsty

sangui'noso *adj* bloody

sangui'suga *f* leech

sanità *f* soundness; (*salute*) health. **~ mentale** mental health

sani'tario *adj* sanitary; **Servizio S~** Health Service

'sano *adj* sound; (*salutare*) healthy; **~ di mente** sane; **~ come un pesce** as fit as a fiddle

San Sil'vestro *m* New Year's Eve

santifi'care *vt* sanctify

'santo *adj* holy; (*con nome proprio*) saint ●*m* saint. **san'tone** *m* guru. **santu'ario** *m* sanctuary

sanzi'one *f* sanction

sa'pere *vt* know; (*essere capace di*) be able to; (*venire a sapere*) hear; **saperla lunga** know a thing or two ●*vi* **~ di** know about; (*aver sapore di*) taste of; (*aver odore di*) smell of; **saperci fare** have the know-how ●*m* knowledge

sapi'en|te *adj* wise; (*esperto*) expert ●*m* (*uomo colto*) sage. **~za** *f* wisdom

sa'pone *m* soap. **~ da bucato** washing soap. **sapo'netta** *f* bar of soap

sa'pore *m* taste. **saporita'mente** *adv* soundly. **sapo'rito** *adj* tasty

sapu'tello, -a *adj & m* ☒ know-all, know-it-all *Am*

saraci'nesca *f* roller shutter

sar'cas|mo *m* sarcasm. **~tico** *adj* sarcastic

Sar'degna *f* Sardinia

sar'dina *f* sardine

'sardo, -a *adj & mf* Sardinian

> *i*
> **Sardo** *Sardo* is Sardinia's traditional language. It is considered to be an independent language because of its many differences from Italian and its long independent history. Sardinian preserves many features derived from Latin which were lost in Italian, e.g. the k-sound in words like *chelu* (Italian *cielo*).

sar'donico *adj* sardonic

'sarto, -a *m* tailor ●*f* dressmaker. **~'ria** *f* tailor's; dressmaker's; (*arte*) couture

'sasso *m* stone; (*ciottolo*) pebble

sassofo'nista *mf* saxophonist. **sas'sofono** *m* saxophone

sas'soso *adj* stony

sa'tellite *adj inv & nm* satellite

sati'nato *adj* glossy

'satira *f* satire. **sa'tirico** *adj* satirical

satu'ra|re *vt* saturate. **~zi'one** *f* saturation. **'saturo** *adj* saturated; (*pieno*) full

'sauna *f* sauna

savoi'ardo *m* (*biscotto*) sponge finger

sazi'ar|e *vt* satiate. **~si** *vr* **~si di** *fig* grow tired of

sazietà *f* **mangiare a ~** eat one's fill. **'sazio** *adj* satiated

sbaciucchi'ar|e *vt* smother with kisses. **~si** *vr* kiss and cuddle

sbada'ta|ggine *f* carelessness; **è stata una ~ggine** it was careless. **~'mente** *adv* carelessly. **sba'dato** *adj* careless

sbadigli'are *vi* yawn. **sba'diglio** *m* yawn

sba'fa|re *vt* sponge

'sbafo *m* sponging; **a ~** without paying

sbagli'ar|e *vi* make a mistake; (*aver torto*) be wrong ●*vt* make a mistake in; **~e strada** go the wrong way; **~e numero** get the number wrong; (*Teleph*) dial a wrong number. **~si** *vr* make a mistake. **'sbaglio** *m* mistake; **per sbaglio** by mistake

sbal'l|are *vt* unpack; ⓘ screw up

S

(conti) • *vi* [!] go crazy. **~ato** *adj* (*squilibrato*) unbalanced
sballot'tare *vt* toss about
sbalor'di|re *vt* stun • *vi* be stunned. **~'tivo** *adj* amazing. **~to** *adj* stunned
sbal'zare *vt* throw; (*da una carica*) dismiss • *vi* bounce; (*saltare*) leap. **'sbalzo** *m* bounce; (*sussulto*) jolt; (*di temperatura*) sudden change; **a sbalzi** in spurts; **a sbalzo** (*lavoro a rilievo*) embossed
sban'care *vt* bankrupt; **~ il banco** break the bank
sbanda'mento *m* (*Auto*) skid; (*Naut*) list; *fig* going off the rails
sban'da|re *vi* (*Auto*) skid; (*Naut*) list. **~rsi** *vr* (*disperdersi*) disperse. **~ta** *f* skid; (*Naut*) list. **~to, -a** *adj* mixed-up • *mf* mixed-up person
sbandie'rare *vt* wave; *fig* display
sbarac'care *vt/i* clear up
sbaragli'are *vt* rout. **sba'raglio** *m* rout; **mettere allo sbaraglio** rout
sbaraz'zar|e *vt* clear. **~si** *vr* **~si di** get rid of
sbaraz'zino, -a *adj* mischievous • *mf* scamp
sbar'bar|e *vt*, **~si** *vr* shave
sbar'care *vt/i* disembark; **~ il lunario** make ends meet. **'sbarco** *m* landing; (*di merci*) unloading
'sbarra *f* bar; (*di passaggio a livello*) barrier. **~'mento** *m* barricade. **sbar'rare** *vt* bar; (*ostruire*) block; cross (assegno); (*spalancare*) open wide
sbatacchi'are *vt/i* [x] bang
'sbatter|e *vt* bang; slam, bang (porta); (*urtare*) knock; (*Culin*) beat; flap (ali); shake (tappeto) • *vi* bang; (porta:) slam, bang. **~si** *vr* [x] rush around; **~sene di qcsa** not give a damn about sth. **sbat'tuto** *adj* tossed; (*Culin*) beaten; *fig* run down
sba'va|re *vi* dribble; (colore:) smear. **~'tura** *f* smear; **senza ~ture** *fig* faultless
sbelli'carsi *vr* **~ dalle risa** split one's sides [with laughter]
'sberla *f* slap
sbia'di|re *vt/i*, **~rsi** *vr* fade. **~to** *adj* faded; *fig* colourless
sbian'car|e *vt/i*, **~si** *vr* whiten
sbi'eco *adj* slanting; **di ~** on the slant; (guardare) sidelong; **guardare qcno di ~** look askance at sb; **tagliare di ~** cut on the bias
sbigot'ti|re *vt* dismay • *vi*, **~rsi** *vr* be dismayed. **~to** *adj* dismayed
sbilanci'ar|e *vt* unbalance • *vi* (*perdere l'equilibrio*) overbalance. **~si** *vr* lose one's balance
sbizzar'rirsi *vr* satisfy one's whims
sbloc'care *vt* unblock; (*Mech*) release; decontrol (prezzi)
sboc'care *vi* **~ in** (fiume:) flow into; (strada:) lead to; (folla:) pour into
sboc'cato *adj* foul-mouthed
sbocci'are *vi* blossom
'sbocco *m* flowing; (*foce*) mouth; (*Comm*) outlet
sbolo'gnare *vt* [!] get rid of
'sbornia *f* **prendere una ~** get drunk
sbor'sare *vt* pay out
sbot'tare *vi* burst out
sbotto'nar|e *vt* unbutton. **~si** *vr* ([!]: *confidarsi*) open up; **~si la camicia** unbutton one's shirt
sbra'carsi *vr* put on something more comfortable; **~ dalle risate** [!] kill oneself laughing
sbracci'a|rsi *vr* wave one's arms. **~to** *adj* bare-armed; (abito) sleeveless
sbrai'tare *vi* bawl
sbra'nare *vt* tear to pieces
sbricio'lar|e *vt*, **~si** *vr* crumble
sbri'ga|re *vt* expedite; (*occuparsi di*) attend to. **~rsi** *vr* be quick. **~'tivo** *adj* quick
sbrindel'lare *vt* tear to shreds. **~to** *adj* in rags
sbrodo'l|are *vt* stain
'sbronz|a *f* **prendersi una ~a** get tight. **sbron'zarsi** *vr* get tight. **~o** *adj* (*ubriaco*) tight
sbruffo'nata *f* boast. **sbruf'fone, -a** *mf* boaster
sbu'care *vi* come out
sbucci'ar|e *vt* peel; shell (piselli). **~si** *vr* graze oneself
sbuf'fare *vi* snort; (*per impazienza*) fume. **'sbuffo** *m* puff
'scabbia *f* scabies *sg*
sca'broso *adj* rough; *fig* difficult; (scena) indecent
scacci'are *vt* chase away
'scacc|o *m* check; **~hi** *pl* (*gioco*) chess;

S

(*pezzi*) chessmen; **dare ~o matto a** checkmate; **a ~hi** (tessuto) checked. **~hi'era** *f* chess-board

sca'dente *adj* shoddy

sca'de|nza *f* expiry; (*Comm*) maturity; (*di progetto*) deadline; **a breve/lunga ~nza** short-/long-term. **~re** *vi* expire; (valore:) decline; (debito:) be due. **sca'duto** *adj* out-of-date

sca'fandro *m* diving suit; (*di astronauta*) spacesuit

scaf'fale *m* shelf; (*libreria*) bookshelf

sca'fista *m* motor-boat operator; (*pej*) refugee smuggler (using motorboat)

'scafo *m* hull

scagion'are *vt* exonerate

'scaglia *f* scale; (*di sapone*) flake; (*scheggia*) chip

scagli'ar|e *vt* fling. **~si** *vr* fling oneself; **~si contro** *fig* rail against

scagli|o'nare *vt* space out. **~'one** *m* group; **a ~oni** in groups. **~one di reddito** tax bracket

'scala *f* staircase; (*portatile*) ladder; (*Mus, misura, fig*) scale; **scale** *pl* stairs. **~ mobile** escalator; (*dei salari*) cost of living index

sca'la|re *vt* climb; layer (capelli); (*detrarre*) deduct. **~ta** *f* climb; (*dell'Everest ecc*) ascent; **fare delle ~te** go climbing. **~'tore, ~'trice** *mf* climber

scalca'gnato *adj* down at heel

scalci'are *vi* kick

scalci'nato *adj* shabby

scalda'bagno *m* water heater

scalda'muscoli *m inv* leg-warmer

scal'dar|e *vt* heat. **~si** *vr* warm up; (*eccitarsi*) get excited

scal'fi|re *vt* scratch. **~t'tura** *f* scratch

scali'nata *f* flight of steps. **sca'lino** *m* step; (*di scala a pioli*) rung

scalma'narsi *vr* get worked up

'scalo *m* slipway; (*Aeron, Naut*) port of call; **fare ~ a** call at; (*Aeron*) land at

sca'lo|gna *f* bad luck. **~'gnato** *adj* unlucky

scalop'pina *f* escalope

scal'pello *m* chisel

'scalpo *m* scalp

scal'pore *m* noise; **far ~** *fig* cause a sensation

scal'trezza *f* shrewdness. **'scaltro** *adj* shrewd

scal'zare *vt* bare the roots of (albero); *fig* undermine; (*da una carica*) oust

'scalzo *adj & adv* barefoot

scambi|'are *vt* exchange; **~are qcno per qualcun altro** mistake sb for somebody else. **~'evole** *adj* reciprocal

'scambio *m* exchange; (*Comm*) trade; **libero ~** free trade

scamosci'ato *adj* suede

scampa'gnata *f* trip to the country

scampa'nato *adj* (gonna) flared

scampanel'lata *f* [loud] ring

scam'pare *vt* save; (*evitare*) escape. **'scampo** *m* escape

'scampolo *m* remnant

scanala'tura *f* groove

scandagli'are *vt* sound

scanda'listico *adj* sensational

scandal|iz'zare *vt* scandalize. **~iz'zarsi** *vr* be scandalized

'scanda|lo *m* scandal. **~'loso** *adj* (somma) ecc scandalous; (fortuna) outrageous

Scandi'navia *f* Scandinavia. **scandi'navo, -a** *adj & mf* Scandinavian

scan'dire *vt* scan (verso); pronounce clearly (parole)

scan'nare *vt* slaughter

'scanner *m inv* scanner

scanneriz'zare *vt* (*Comput*) scan

scan'sar|e *vt* shift; (*evitare*) avoid. **~si** *vr* get out of the way

scansi'one *f* (*Comput*) scanning

'scanso *m* **a ~ di** in order to avoid; **a ~ di equivoci** to avoid any misunderstanding

S

scanti'nato *m* basement

scanto'nare *vi* turn the corner; (*svignarsela*) sneak off

scanzo'nato *adj* easy-going

scapacci'one *m* smack

scape'strato *adj* dissolute

'scapito *m* loss

'scapola *f* shoulder-blade

'scapolo *m* bachelor

scappa'mento *m* (*Auto*) exhaust

scap'pa|re *vi* escape; (*andarsene*) dash [off]; (*sfuggire*) slip; **mi ~ da ridere!** I want to burst out laughing. **~ta** *f* short visit. **~'tella** *f* escapade; (*infe-*

deltà) fling. **~'toia** *f* way out
scappel'lotto *m* cuff
scarabocchi'are *vt* scribble
scara'bocchio *m* scribble
scara'faggio *m* cockroach
scara'muccia *f* skirmish
scaraven'tare *vt* hurl
scarce'rare *vt* release [from prison]
scardi'nare *vt* unhinge
'scarica *f* discharge; (*di arma da fuoco*) volley; *fig* shower
scari'ca|re *vt* discharge; unload (arma, merci); (*Comput*) download; *fig* unburden. **~rsi** *vr* (fiume:) flow; (orologio, batteria:) run down; *fig* unwind. **~'tore** *m* loader; (*di porto*) docker. **'scarico** *adj* unloaded; (*vuoto*) empty; (orologio) run-down; (batteria) flat; *fig* untroubled ● *m* unloading; (*di rifiuti*) dumping; (*di acqua*) draining; (*di sostanze inquinanti*) discharge; (*luogo*) [rubbish] dump; (*Auto*) exhaust; (*idraulico*) drain; (*tubo*) waste pipe
scarlat'tina *f* scarlet fever
scar'latto *adj* scarlet
'scarno *adj* thin; (stile) bare
sca'ro|gna *f* [!] bad luck. **~'gnato** *adj* [!] unlucky
'scarpa *f* shoe. **scarpe** *pl* **da ginnastica** trainers, gym shoes
scar'pata *f* slope; (*burrone*) escarpment
scarpi'nare *vi* hike
scar'pone *m* boot. **scarponi** *pl* **da sci** ski boot. **scarponi** *pl* **da trekking** walking boots
scarroz'zare *vt/i* drive around
scarseggi'are *vi* be scarce; **~ di** (*mancare*) be short of
scar'sezza *f* scarcity, shortage. **scarsità** *f* shortage. **'scarso** *adj* scarce; (*manchevole*) short
scarta'mento *m* (*Rail*) gauge. **~ ridotto** narrow gauge
scar'tare *vt* discard; unwrap (pacco); (*respingere*) reject ● *vi* (*deviare*) swerve. **'scarto** *m* scrap; (*in carte*) discard; (*deviazione*) swerve; (*distacco*) gap
scas'sa|re *vt* break. **~to** *adj* [!] clapped out
scassi'nare *vt* force open
scassina'tore, -'trice *mf* burglar. **'scasso** *m* (*furto*) house-breaking

scate'na|re *vt fig* stir up. **~rsi** *vr* break out; *fig*: (temporale:) break; ([!]: *infiammarsi*) get excited. **~to** *adj* crazy
'scatola *f* box; (*di latta*) can, tin *Br*; **in ~** (cibo) canned, tinned *Br*
scat'tare *vi* go off; (*balzare*) spring up; (*adirarsi*) lose one's temper; take (foto). **'scatto** *m* (*balzo*) spring; (*d'ira*) outburst; (*di telefono*) unit; (*dispositivo*) release; **a scatti** jerkily; **di scatto** suddenly
scatu'rire *vi* spring
scaval'care *vt* jump over (muretto); climb over (muro); (*fig: superare*) overtake
sca'vare *vt* dig (buca); dig up (tesoro); excavate (città sepolta). **'scavo** *m* excavation
'scegliere *vt* choose, select
scelle'rato *adj* wicked
'scelt|a *f* choice; (*di articoli*) range; **...a ~a** (*in menu*) choice of...; **prendine uno a ~a** take your choice *o* pick; **di prima ~a** top-grade, choice. **~o** *pp di* **scegliere** ● *adj* select; (*merce ecc*) choice
sce'mare *vt/i* diminish
sce'menza *f* silliness; (*azione*) silly thing to do/say. **'scemo** *adj* silly
'scempio *m* havoc; (*fig: di paesaggio*) ruination; **fare ~ di** play havoc with
'scena *f* scene; (*palcoscenico*) stage; **entrare in ~** go/come on; *fig* enter the scene; **fare ~** put on an act; **fare una ~** make a scene; **andare in ~** (*Theat*) be staged, be put on. **sce'nario** *m* scenery
sce'nata *f* row, scene
'scendere *vi* go/come down; (*da treno, autobus*) get off; (*da macchina*) get out; (strada:) slope; (notte, prezzi:) fall ● *vt* go/come down (scale)
sceneggi'a|re *vt* dramatize. **~to** *m* television serial. **~'tura** *f* screenplay
'scenico *adj* scenic
scervel'la|rsi *vr* rack one's brains. **~to** *adj* brainless
'sceso *pp di* **scendere**
scetti'cismo *m* scepticism. **'scettico, -a** *adj* sceptical ● *mf* sceptic
'scheda *f* card. **~ elettorale** ballot-paper. **~ di espansione** (*Comput*) expansion card. **~ telefonica** phonecard. **sche'dare** *vt* file. **sche'dario** *m*

file; (*mobile*) filing cabinet

sche'dina *f* ≈ pools coupon; **giocare la** ~ do the pools

'scheggi|a *f* fragment; (*di legno*) splinter. **~'arsi** *vr* chip; (legno:) splinter

'scheletro *m* skeleton

'schema *m* diagram; (*abbozzo*) outline. **sche'matico** *adj* schematic

'scherma *f* fencing

scher'mirsi *vr* protect oneself

'schermo *m* screen; **grande** ~ big screen

scher'nire *vt* mock. **'scherno** *m* mockery

scher'zare *vi* joke; (*giocare*) play

'scherzo *m* joke; (*trucco*) trick; (*effetto*) play; (*Mus*) scherzo; **fare uno** ~ **a qcno** play a joke on sb. **scher'zoso** *adj* playful

schiaccia'noci *m inv* nutcrackers *pl*

schiacci'ante *adj* damning

schiacci'are *vt* crush; *Sport* smash; press (pulsante); crack (noce)

schiaffeggi'are *vt* slap. **schi'affo** *m* slap; **dare uno schiaffo a** slap

schiamaz'zare *vi* make a racket; (galline:) cackle

schian'tar|e *vt* break. **~si** *vr* crash ● *vi* **schianto dalla fatica** I'm wiped out. **'schianto** *m* crash; [!] knock-out; (*divertente*) scream

schia'rir|e *vt* clear; (*sbiadire*) fade ● *vi*, **~si** *vr* brighten up; **~si la gola** clear one's throat

schiavitù *f* slavery. **schi'avo, -a** *mf* slave

schi'ena *f* back; **mal di** ~ backache. **schie'nale** *m* (*di sedia*) back

schi'er|a *f* (*Mil*) rank; (*moltitudine*) crowd. **~a'mento** *m* lining up

schie'rar|e *vt* draw up. **~si** *vr* draw up; **~si con** (*parteggiare*) side with

schiet'tezza *f* frankness. **schi'etto** *adj* frank; (*puro*) pure

schi'fezza *f* **una** ~ rubbish. **schifil'toso** *adj* fussy. **'schifo** *m* disgust; **mi fa schifo** it makes me sick. **schi'foso** *adj* disgusting; (*di cattiva qualità*) rubbishy

schioc'care *vt* crack; snap (dita). **schi'occo** *m* (*di frusta*) crack; (*di bacio*) smack; (*di dita, lingua*) click

schi'uder|e *vt*, **~si** *vr* open

schi'u|ma *f* foam; (*di sapone*) lather; (*feccia*) scum. **~ma da barba** shaving foam. **~'mare** *vt* skim ● *vi* foam

schi'uso *pp di* **schiudere**

schi'vare *vt* avoid. **'schivo** *adj* bashful

schizo'frenico *adj* schizophrenic

schiz'zare *vt* squirt; (*inzaccherare*) splash; (*abbozzare*) sketch ● *vi* spurt; ~ **via** scurry away

schizzi'noso *adj* squeamish

'schizzo *m* squirt; (*di fango*) splash; (*abbozzo*) sketch

sci *m inv* ski; (*sport*) skiing. ~ **d'acqua** water-skiing

'scia *f* wake; (*di fumo ecc*) trail

sci'abola *f* sabre

scia'callo *m* jackal; *fig* profiteer

sciac'quar|e *vt* rinse. **~si** *vr* rinse oneself. **sci'acquo** *m* mouthwash

scia'gu|ra *f* disaster. **~'rato** *adj* unfortunate; (*scellerato*) wicked

scialac'quare *vt* squander

scia'lare *vi* squander

sci'albo *adj* pale; *fig* dull

sci'alle *m* shawl

scia'luppa *f* dinghy. ~ **di salvataggio** lifeboat

sci'ame *m* swarm

sci'ampo *m* shampoo

scian'cato *adj* lame

sci'are *vi* ski

sci'arpa *f* scarf

sci'atica *f* (*Med*) sciatica

scia'tore, -'trice *mf* skier

sci'atto *adj* slovenly; (stile) careless. **sciat'tone, -a** *mf* slovenly person

scienti'fico *adj* scientific

sci'enz|a *f* science; (*sapere*) knowledge. **~i'ato, -a** *mf* scientist

'scimmi|a *f* monkey. **~ot'tare** *vt* ape

scimpanzé *m inv* chimpanzee, chimp

scimu'nito *adj* idiotic

'scinder|e *vt*, **~si** *vr* split

scin'tilla *f* spark. **scintil'lante** *adj* sparkling. **scintil'lare** *vi* sparkle

scioc'ca|nte *adj* shocking. **~re** *vt* shock

scioc'chezza *f* foolishness; (*assurdità*) nonsense. **sci'occo** *adj* foolish

sci'oglier|e *vt* untie; (*liberare*) release; (*liquefare*) melt; dissolve (contratto, qcsa nell'acqua); loosen up (muscoli).

S

~si *vr* release oneself; (*liquefarsi*) melt; (contratto:) be dissolved; (pastiglia:) dissolve
sciogli'lingua *m inv* tongue-twister
scio'lina *f* wax
sciol'tezza *f* agility; (*disinvoltura*) ease
sci'olto *pp di* **sciogliere** ● *adj* loose; (*agile*) agile; (*disinvolto*) easy; **versi sciolti** blank verse *sg*
sciope'ra|nte *mf* striker. **~re** *vi* go on strike, strike. **sci'opero** *m* strike. **sciopero a singhiozzo** on-off strike
sciori'nare *vt fig* show off
sci'pito *adj* insipid
scip'pa|re *vt* ! snatch. **~'tore, ~'trice** *mf* bag snatcher. **'scippo** *m* bag-snatching
sci'rocco *m* sirocco
scirop'pato *adj* (frutta) in syrup. **sci'roppo** *m* syrup
'scisma *m* schism
scissi'one *f* division
'scisso *pp di* **scindere**
sciu'par|e *vt* spoil; (*sperperare*) waste. **~si** *vr* get spoiled; (*deperire*) wear oneself out. **sciu'pio** *m* waste
scivo'l|are *vi* slide; (*involontariamente*) slip. **'scivolo** *m* slide; (*Techn*) chute. **~oso** *adj* slippery
scoc'care *vt* shoot ● *vi* (scintilla:) shoot out; (ora:) strike
scocci'a|re *vt* (*dare noia a*) bother. **~rsi** *vr* be bothered. **~to** *adj* ! narked. **~'tore, ~'trice** *mf* bore. **~'tura** *f* nuisance
sco'della *f* bowl
S **scodinzo'lare** *vi* wag its tail
scogli'era *f* cliff; (*a fior d'acqua*) reef. **'scoglio** *m* rock; (*fig: ostacolo*) stumbling block
scoi'attolo *m* squirrel
scola|'pasta *m inv* colander. **~pi'atti** *m inv* dish drainer
sco'lara *f* schoolgirl
sco'lare *vt* drain; strain (pasta, verdura) ● *vi* drip
sco'la|ro *m* schoolboy. **~'resca** *f* pupils *pl.* **~stico** *adj* school *attrib*
scol'la|re *vt* cut away the neck of (abito); (*staccare*) unstick. **~to** *adj* low-necked. **~'tura** *f* neckline
'scolo *m* drainage

scolo'ri|re *vt*, **~rsi** *vr* fade. **~to** *adj* faded
scol'pire *vt* carve; (*imprimere*) engrave
scombi'nare *vt* upset
scombusso'lare *vt* muddle up
scom'mess|a *f* bet. **~o** *pp di* **scommettere. scom'mettere** *vt* bet
scomo'dar|e *vt*, **~si** *vr* trouble. **scomodità** *f* discomfort. **'scomodo** *adj* uncomfortable
scompa'rire *vi* disappear; (*morire*) pass on. **scom'parsa** *f* disappearance; (*morte*) passing, death. **scom'parso, -a** *pp di* **scomparire** ● *mf* departed
scomparti'mento *m* compartment. **scom'parto** *f* compartment
scom'penso *m* imbalance
scompigli'are *vt* disarrange. **scom'piglio** *m* confusion
scom'po|rre *vt* take to pieces; (*fig: turbare*) upset. **~rsi** *vr* get flustered. **~sto** *pp di* **scomporre** ● *adj* (*sguaiato*) unseemly; (*disordinato*) untidy
sco'muni|ca *f* excommunication. **~'care** *vt* excommunicate
sconcer'ta|re *vt* disconcert; (*rendere perplesso*) bewilder. **~to** *adj* disconcerted; bewildered
scon'cezza *f* obscenity. **'sconcio** *adj* dirty ● *m* **è uno sconcio che...** it's a disgrace that...
sconclusio'nato *adj* incoherent
scon'dito *adj* unseasoned; (*insalata*) with no dressing
sconfes'sare *vt* disown
scon'figgere *vt* defeat
sconfi'na|re *vi* cross the border; (*in proprietà privata*) trespass. **~to** *adj* unlimited
scon'fitt|a *f* defeat. **~o** *pp di* **sconfiggere**
scon'forto *m* dejection
sconge'lare *vt* thaw out (cibo), defrost
scongi|u'rare *vt* beseech; (*evitare*) avert. **~'uro** *m* **fare gli scongiuri** touch wood, knock on wood *Am*
scon'nesso *pp di* **sconnettere** ● *adj fig* incoherent. **scon'nettere** *vt* disconnect
sconosci'uto, -a *adj* unknown ● *mf* stranger
sconquas'sare *vt* smash; (*sconvolgere*) upset

sconside'rato *adj* inconsiderate

sconsigli'a|bile *adj* not advisable. **~re** *vt* advise against

sconso'lato *adj* disconsolate

scon'ta|re *vt* discount; (*dedurre*) deduct; (*pagare*) pay off; serve (pena). **~to** *adj* discount; (*ovvio*) expected; **~to del 10%** with 10% discount

scon'tento *adj* displeased ● *m* discontent

'sconto *m* discount; **fare uno ~** give a discount

scon'trarsi *vr* clash; (*urtare*) collide

scon'trino *m* ticket; (*di cassa*) receipt

'scontro *m* clash; (*urto*) collision

scon'troso *adj* unsociable

sconveni'ente *adj* unprofitable; (*scorretto*) unseemly

sconvol'gente *adj* mind-blowing

scon'vol|gere *vt* upset; (*mettere in disordine*) disarrange. **~gi'mento** *m* upheaval. **~to** *pp di* **sconvolgere** ● *adj* distraught

'scopa *f* broom. **sco'pare** *vt* sweep

scoperchi'are *vt* take the lid off (pentola); take the roof off (casa)

sco'pert|a *f* discovery. **~o** *pp di* **scoprire** ● *adj* uncovered; (*senza riparo*) exposed; (*conto*) overdrawn; (*spoglio*) bare

'scopo *m* aim; **allo ~ di** in order to

scoppi'are *vi* burst; *fig* break out. **scoppiet'tare** *vi* crackle. **'scoppio** *m* burst; (*di guerra*) outbreak; (*esplosione*) explosion

sco'prire *vt* discover; (*togliere la copertura a*) uncover

scoraggi'a|re *vt* discourage. **~rsi** *vr* lose heart

scor'butico *adj* peevish

scorcia'toia *f* short cut

'scorcio *m* (*di epoca*) end; (*di cielo*) patch; (*in arte*) foreshortening; **di ~** (vedere) from an angle. **~ panoramico** panoramic view

scor'da|re *vt*, **~rsi** *vr* forget. **~to** *adj* (*Mus*) out of tune

'scorgere *vt* make out; (*notare*) notice

'scoria *f* waste; (*di metallo, carbone*) slag; **scorie** *pl* **radioattive** radioactive waste

scor'nato *adj fig* hangdog. **'scorno** *m* humiliation

scorpi'one *m* scorpion; (*Astr*) **S ~** Scorpio

scorraz'zare *vi* run about

'scorrere *vt* (*dare un'occhiata*) glance through ● *vi* run; (*scivolare*) slide; (*fluire*) flow; (*Comput*) scroll. **scor'revole** *adj* **porta scorrevole** sliding door

scorre'ria *f* raid

scorret'tezza *f* (*mancanza di educazione*) bad manners *pl*. **scor'retto** *adj* incorrect; (*sconveniente*) improper

scorri'banda *f* raid; *fig* excursion

'scors|a *f* glance. **~o** *pp di* **scorrere** ● *adj* last

scor'soio *adj* **nodo ~** noose

'scor|ta *f* escort; (*provvista*) supply. **~'tare** *vt* escort

scor'te|se *adj* discourteous. **~'sia** *f* discourtesy

scorti'ca|re *vt* skin. **~'tura** *f* graze

'scorto *pp di* **scorgere**

'scorza *f* peel; (*crosta*) crust; (*corteccia*) bark

sco'sceso *adj* steep

'scossa *f* shake; (*Electr, fig*) shock; **prendere la ~** get an electric shock. **~ elettrica** electric shock. **~ sismica** earth tremor

'scosso *pp di* **scuotere** ● *adj* shaken; (*sconvolto*) upset

sco'stante *adj* off-putting

sco'sta|re *vt* push away. **~rsi** *vr* stand aside

scostu'mato *adj* dissolute; (*maleducato*) ill-mannered

scot'tante *adj* dangerous

scot'ta|re *vt* scald ● *vi* burn; (bevanda:) be too hot; (sole, pentola:) be very hot. **~rsi** *vr* burn oneself; (*al sole*) get sunburnt; *fig* get one's fingers burnt. **~'tura** *f* burn; (*da liquido*) scald; **~tura solare** sunburn; *fig* painful experience

'scotto *adj* overcooked

sco'vare *vt* (*scoprire*) discover

'Scoz|ia *f* Scotland. **~'zese** *adj* Scottish ● *mf* Scot

scredi'tare *vt* discredit

scre'mare *vt* skim

screpo'la|re *vt*, **~rsi** *vr* crack. **~to** *adj* (labbra) chapped. **~'tura** *f* crack

screzi'ato *adj* speckled

'screzio *m* disagreement
scribac|chi'are *vt* scribble. **~'chino, -a** *mf* scribbler; (*impiegato*) penpusher
scricchio'l|are *vi* creak. **~io** *m* creaking
'scricciolo *m* wren
'scrigno *m* casket
scrimina'tura *f* parting
'scrit|ta *f* writing; (*su muro*) graffiti. **~to** *pp di* **scrivere** ● *adj* written ● *m* writing; (*lettera*) letter. **~'toio** *m* writing-desk. **~'tore, ~'trice** *mf* writer. **~'tura** *f* writing; (*Relig*) scripture
scrittu'rare *vt* engage
scriva'nia *f* desk
'scrivere *vt* write; (*descrivere*) write about; **~ a macchina** type
scroc'c|are *vt* **~are a** sponge off. **'scrocco** *m* [!] **a scrocco** [!] without paying. **~one, -a** *mf* sponger
'scrofa *f* sow
scrol'lar|e *vt* shake; **~e le spalle** shrug one's shoulders. **~si** *vr* shake oneself; **~si qcsa di dosso** shake sth off
scrosci'are *vi* roar; (pioggia:) pelt down. **'scroscio** *m* roar; (*di pioggia*) pelting
scro'star|e *vt* scrape. **~si** *vr* peel off
'scrupo|lo *m* scruple; (*diligenza*) care; **senza scrupoli** unscrupulous, without scruples. **~'loso** *adj* scrupulous
scru'ta|re *vt* scan; (*indagare*) search. **~'tore** *m* (*alle elezioni*) returning officer
scruti'nare *vt* scrutinize. **scru'tinio** *m* (*di voti alle elezioni*) poll; (*Sch*) assessment of progress
scu'cire *vt* unstitch
scude'ria *f* stable
scu'detto *m Sport* championship shield
'scudo *m* shield
sculacci|'are *vt* spank. **~'ata** *f* spanking. **~'one** *m* spanking
sculet'tare *vi* wiggle one's hips
scul|'tore, -'trice *m* sculptor ● *f* sculptress. **~'tura** *f* sculpture
scu'ola *f* school. **~ elementare** primary school. **~ guida** driving school. **~ materna** day nursery. **~ media [inferiore]** secondary school (*10-13*). **~ [media] superiore** secondary school (*13-18*)
scu'oter|e *vt* shake. **~si** *vr* (*destarsi*) rouse oneself; **~si di dosso** shake off
'scure *f* axe
scu'reggia *f* [!] fart. **scureggi'are** *vi* [!] fart
scu'rire *vt/i* darken
'scuro *adj* dark ● *m* darkness; (*imposta*) shutter
'scusa *f* excuse; (*giustificazione*) apology; **chiedere ~** apologize; **chiedo ~!** I'm sorry!
scu'sar|e *vt* excuse. **~si** *vr* **~si** apologize (**di** for); **[mi] scusi!** excuse me!; (*chiedendo perdono*) [I'm] sorry!
sdebi'tarsi *vr* repay a kindness
sde'gna|re *vt* despise. **~rsi** *vr* get angry. **~to** *adj* indignant. **'sdegno** *m* disdain. **sde'gnoso** *adj* disdainful
sdolci'nato *adj* sentimental
sdoppi'are *vt* halve
sdrai'arsi *vr* lie down. **'sdraio** *m* **[sedia a] sdraio** deckchair
sdrammatiz'zare *vi* provide some comic relief
sdruccio'levole *adj* slippery

se

● *conj* if; (*interrogativo*) whether, if; **se mai** (*caso mai*) if need be; **se mai telefonasse,...** should he call,..., if he calls,...; **se no** otherwise, or else; **se non altro** at least, if nothing else; **se pure** (*sebbene*) even though; (*anche se*) even if; **non so se sia vero** I don't know whether it's true, I don't know if it's true; **come se** as if; **se lo avessi saputo prima!** if only I had known before!; **e se andassimo fuori a cena?** how about going out for dinner?

● *m inv* if

sé *pers pron* oneself; (*lui*) himself; (*lei*) herself; (*esso, essa*) itself; (*loro*) themselves; **l'ha fatto da sé** he did it himself; **ha preso i soldi con sé** he took the money with him; **si sono tenuti le notizie per sé** they kept the news to themselves
seb'bene *conj* although
'secca *f* shallows *pl*; **in ~** (nave) aground
sec'cante *adj* annoying

sec'ca|re *vt* dry; (*importunare*) annoy ● *vi* dry up. **~rsi** *vr* dry up; (*irritarsi*) get annoyed; (*annoiarsi*) get bored. **~'tore, ~'trice** *mf* nuisance. **~'tura** *f* bother

secchi'ello *m* pail

'secchio *m* bucket. **~ della spazzatura** rubbish bin, trash can *Am*

'secco, -a *adj* dry; (*disseccato*) dried; (*magro*) thin; (*brusco*) curt; (*preciso*) sharp ● *m* (*siccità*) drought; **lavare a ~** dry-clean

secessi'one *f* secession

seco'lare *adj* age-old; (*laico*) secular. **'secolo** *m* century; (*epoca*) age

se'cond|a *f* (*Rail, Sch*) second class; (*Auto*) second [gear]. **~o** *adj* second ● *m* second; (*secondo piatto*) main course ● *prep* according to; **~o me** in my opinion

secrezi'one *f* secretion

'sedano *m* celery

seda'tivo *adj & m* sedative

'sede *f* seat; (*centro*) centre; (*Relig*) see; (*Comm*) head office. **~ sociale** registered office

seden'tario *adj* sedentary

se'der|e *vi* sit. **~si** *vr* sit down ● *m* (*deretano*) bottom

'sedia *f* chair. **~ a dondolo** rocking chair. **~ a rotelle** wheelchair

sedi'cente *adj* self-styled

'sedici *adj & m* sixteen

se'dile *m* seat

sedizi'o|ne *f* sedition. **~so** *adj* seditious

se'dotto *pp di* **sedurre**

sedu'cente *adj* seductive

se'durre *vt* seduce

se'duta *f* session; (*di posa*) sitting. **~ stante** *adv* here and now

seduzi'one *f* seduction

'sega *f* saw

'segala *f* rye

se'gare *vt* saw

'seggio *m* seat. **~ elettorale** polling station

seg'gio|la *f* chair. **~'lino** *m* seat; (*da bambino*) child's seat. **~'lone** *m* (*per bambini*) high chair

seggio'via *f* chair lift

seghe'ria *f* sawmill

se'ghetto *m* hacksaw

seg'mento *m* segment

segna'lar|e *vt* signal; (*annunciare*) announce; (*indicare*) point out. **~si** *vr* distinguish oneself

se'gna|le *m* signal; (*stradale*) sign. **~le acustico** beep. **~le orario** time signal. **~'letica** *f* signals *pl*. **~letica stradale** road signs *pl*

se'gnar|e *vt* mark; (*prendere nota*) note; (*indicare*) indicate; *Sport* score. **~si** *vr* cross oneself. **'segno** *m* sign; (*traccia, limite*) mark; (*bersaglio*) target; **far segno** (*col capo*) nod; (*con la mano*) beckon. **segno zodiacale** birth sign

segre'ga|re *vt* segregate. **~zi'one** *f* segregation

segretari'ato *m* secretariat

segre'tario, -a *mf* secretary. **~ comunale** town clerk

segrete'ria *f* [administrative] office; (*segretariato*) secretariat. **~ telefonica** answering machine

segre'tezza *f* secrecy

se'greto *adj & m* secret; **in ~** in secret

segu'ace *mf* follower

segu'ente *adj* following, next

se'gugio *m* bloodhound

segu'ire *vt/i* follow; (*continuare*) continue

segui'tare *vt/i* continue

'seguito *m* retinue; (*sequela*) series; (*continuazione*) continuation; **di ~** in succession; **in ~** later on; **in ~ a** following; **al ~** owing to; **fare ~ a** follow up

'sei *adj & m* six. **sei'cento** *adj & m* six hundred; **il Seicento** the seventeenth century. **sei'mila** *adj & m* six thousand

sel'ciato *m* paving

selet'tivo *adj* selective. **selezio'nare** *vt* select. **selezi'one** *f* selection

'sella *f* saddle. **sel'lare** *vt* saddle

seltz *m* soda water

'selva *f* forest

selvag'gina *f* game

sel'vaggio, -a *adj* wild; (*primitivo*) savage ● *mf* savage

sel'vatico *adj* wild

se'maforo *m* traffic lights *pl*

se'mantica *f* semantics *sg*

sem'brare *vi* seem; (*assomigliare*) look like; **che te ne sembra?** what do you

think?; **mi sembra che...** I think...
'seme *m* seed; (*di mela*) pip; (*di carte*) suit; (*sperma*) semen
se'mestre *m* half-year
semi'cerchio *m* semicircle
semifi'nale *f* semifinal
semi'freddo *m ice cream and sponge dessert*
'semina *f* sowing
semi'nare *vt* sow; [!] shake off (inseguitori)
semi'nario *m* seminar; (*Relig*) seminary
seminter'rato *m* basement
se'mitico *adj* Semitic
sem'mai *conj* in case ● *adv* **è lui, ~, che...** if anyone, it's him who...
'semola *f* bran. **semo'lino** *m* semolina
'sempli|ce *adj* simple; **in parole semplici** in plain words. **~'cemente** *adv* simply. **~cità** *f* simplicity. **~fi'care** *vt* simplify
'sempre *adv* always; (*ancora*) still; **per ~** for ever
sempre'verde *adj & m* evergreen
'senape *f* mustard
se'nato *m* senate. **sena'tore** *m* senator
se'nil|e *adj* senile. **~ità** *f* senility
'senno *m* sense
'seno *m* breast; (*Math*) sine
sen'sato *adj* sensible
sensazi|o'nale *adj* sensational. **~'one** *f* sensation
sen'sibil|e *adj* sensitive; (*percepibile*) perceptible; (*notevole*) considerable. **~ità** *f* sensitivity. **~iz'zare** *vt* make more aware (**a** of)
sensi'tivo, -a *adj* sensory ● *mf* sensitive person; (*medium*) medium
'senso *m* sense; (*significato*) meaning; (*direzione*) direction; **non ha ~** it doesn't make sense; **perdere i sensi** lose consciousness. **~ dell'umorismo** sense of humour. **~ unico** (strada) one-way; **~ vietato** no entry
sensu'al|e *adj* sensual. **~ità** *f* sensuality
sen'tenz|a *f* sentence; (*massima*) saying. **~i'are** *vi* pass judgment
senti'ero *m* path
sentimen'tale *adj* sentimental. **senti'mento** *m* feeling
senti'nella *f* sentry
sen'ti|re *vt* feel; (*udire*) hear; (*ascoltare*) listen to; (*gustare*) taste; (*odorare*) smell ● *vi* feel; (*udire*) hear; **~re caldo/freddo** feel hot/cold. **~rsi** *vr* feel; **~rsi di fare qcsa** feel like doing sth; **~rsi bene** feel well; **~rsi poco bene** feel unwell. **~to** *adj* sincere
sen'tore *m* inkling
'senza *prep* without; **~ correre** without running; **senz'altro** certainly; **~ ombrello** without an umbrella
senza'tetto *m inv* **i ~** the homeless
sepa'ra|re *vt* separate. **~rsi** *vr* separate; (amici:) part; **~rsi da** be separated from. **~ta'mente** *adv* separately. **~zi'one** *f* separation
se'pol|cro *m* sepulchre. **~to** *pp di* **seppellire**. **~'tura** *f* burial
seppel'lire *vt* bury
'seppia *f* cuttle fish; **nero di ~** sepia
sep'pure *conj* even if
se'quenza *f* sequence
seque'strare *vt* (*rapire*) kidnap; (*Jur*) impound; (*confiscare*) confiscate. **se'questro** *m* impounding; (*di persona*) kidnap[ping]
'sera *f* evening; **di ~** in the evening. **se'rale** *adj* evening. **se'rata** *f* evening; (*ricevimento*) party
ser'bare *vt* keep; harbour (odio); cherish (speranza)
serba'toio *m* tank. **~ d'acqua** water tank; (*per una città*) reservoir
'Serbia *f* Serbia
'serbo, -a *adj & mf* Serbian ● *m* (*lingua*) Serbian
sere'nata *f* serenade
serenità *f* serenity. **se'reno** *adj* serene; (cielo) clear
ser'gente *m* sergeant
seria'mente *adv* seriously
'serie *f inv* series; (*complesso*) set; *Sport* division; **fuori ~** custom-built; **produzione in ~** mass production; **di ~ B** second-rate
serietà *f* seriousness. **'serio** *adj* serious; (*degno di fiducia*) reliable; **sul serio** seriously; (*davvero*) really
ser'mone *m* sermon
'serpe *f liter* viper. **~ggi'are** *vi* meander; (*diffondersi*) spread
ser'pente *m* snake

S

'serra *f* greenhouse; **effetto ~** greenhouse effect
ser'randa *f* shutter
ser'ra|re *vt* shut; (*stringere*) tighten; (*incalzare*) press on. **~'tura** *f* lock
'server *m inv* (*Comput*) server
ser'vir|e *vt* serve; (*al ristorante*) wait on • *vi* serve; (*essere utile*) be of use; **non serve** it's no good. **~si** *vr* (*di cibo*) help oneself; **~si da** buy from; **~si di** use
servitù *f* servitude; (*personale di servizio*) servants *pl*
ser'vizio *m* service; (*da caffè ecc*) set; (*di cronaca, sportivo*) report; **servizi** *pl* bathroom; **essere di ~** be on duty; **fare ~** (autobus ecc:) run; **fuori ~** (bus) not in service; (ascensore) out of order; **~ compreso** service charge included. **~ in camera** room service. **~ civile** *civilian duties done instead of national service*. **~ militare** military service. **~ pubblico** utility company. **~ al tavolo** waiter service
'servo, -a *mf* servant
servo'sterzo *m* power steering
ses'san|ta *adj & m* sixty. **~'tina** *f* **una ~tina** about sixty
sessi'one *f* session
'sesso *m* sex
sessu'al|e *adj* sexual. **~ità** *f* sexuality
'sesto[1] *adj* sixth
'sesto[2] *m* (*ordine*) order
'seta *f* silk
setacci'are *vt* sieve. **se'taccio** *m* sieve
'sete *f* thirst; **avere ~** be thirsty
'setta *f* sect
set'tan|ta *adj & m* seventy. **~'tina** *f* **una ~tina** about seventy
'sette *adj & m* seven. **~'cento** *agg & m* seven hundred; **il S~cento** the eighteenth century
set'tembre *m* September
settentri|o'nale *adj* northern • *mf* northerner. **~'one** *m* north
setti'ma|na *f* week. **~'nale** *agg & m* weekly
'settimo *adj* seventh
set'tore *m* sector
severità *f* severity. **se'vero** *adj* severe; (*rigoroso*) strict
se'vizi|a *f* torture; **se'vizie** *pl* torture *sg*. **~'are** *vt* torture
sezio'nare *vt* divide; (*Med*) dissect. **sezi'one** *f* section; (*reparto*) department; (*Med*) dissection
sfaccen'dato *adj* idle
sfacchi'na|re *vi* toil. **~ta** *f* drudgery
sfacci|a'taggine *f* insolence. **~'ato** *adj* cheeky, fresh *Am*
sfa'celo *m* ruin; **in ~** in ruins
sfal'darsi *vr* flake off
sfa'mar|e *vt* feed. **~si** *vr* satisfy one's hunger
sfar'zoso *adj* sumptuous
sfa'sato *adj* [!] confused; (motore) which needs tuning
sfasci'a|re *vt* unbandage; (*fracassare*) smash. **~rsi** *vr* fall to pieces. **~to** *adj* beat-up
sfa'tare *vt* explode
sfati'cato *adj* lazy
sfavil'lare *vi* sparkle
sfavo'revole *adj* unfavourable
sfavo'rire *vt* disadvantage
'sfer|a *f* sphere. **~ico** *adj* spherical
sfer'rare *vt* unshoe (cavallo); (*scagliare*) land
sfer'zare *vt* whip
sfian'carsi *vr* wear oneself out
sfi'bra|re *vt* exhaust. **~to** *adj* exhausted
'sfida *f* challenge. **sfi'dare** *vt* challenge
sfi'duci|a *f* mistrust. **~'ato** *adj* discouraged
sfigu'rare *vt* disfigure • *vi* (*far cattiva figura*) look out of place
sfilacci'ar|e *vt*, **~si** *vr* fray
sfi'la|re *vt* unthread; (*togliere di dosso*) take off • *vi* (truppe:) march past; (*in parata*) parade. **~rsi** *vr* come unthreaded; (collant:) ladder; take off (pantaloni). **~ta** *f* parade; (*sfilza*) series. **~ta di moda** fashion show
'sfilza *f* (*di errori*) string
'sfinge *f* sphinx
sfi'nito *adj* worn out
sfio'rare *vt* skim; touch on (argomento)
sfio'rire *vi* wither; (bellezza:) fade
'sfitto *adj* vacant
'sfizio *m* whim, fancy; **togliersi uno ~** satisfy a whim
sfo'cato *adj* out of focus
sfoci'are *vi* **~ in** flow into

sfode'ra|re *vt* draw (pistola, spada). **~to** *adj* unlined

sfo'gar|e *vt* vent. **~si** *vr* give vent to one's feelings

sfoggi'are *vt/i* show off. **'sfoggio** *m* show, display; **fare sfoggio di** show off

'sfoglia *f* sheet of pastry; **pasta ~** puff pastry

sfogli'are *vt* leaf through

'sfogo *m* outlet; *fig* outburst; (*Med*) rash; **dare ~ a** give vent to

sfolgo'rare *vi* blaze

sfol'lare *vt* clear ● *vi* (*Mil*) be evacuated

sfol'tire *vt* thin [out]

sfon'dare *vt* break down ● *vi* (*aver successo*) make a name for oneself

'sfondo *m* background

sfor'ma|re *vt* pull out of shape (tasche). **~rsi** *vr* lose its shape; (persona:) lose one's figure. **~to** *m* (*Culin*) flan

sfor'nito *adj* **~ di** (negozio) out of

sfor'tuna *f* bad luck. **~ta'mente** *adv* unfortunately. **sfortu'nato** *adj* unlucky

sfor'zar|e *vt* force. **~si** *vr* try hard. **'sforzo** *m* effort; (*tensione*) strain

'sfottere *vt* ⊠ tease

sfracel'larsi *vr* smash

sfrat'tare *vt* evict. **'sfratto** *m* eviction

sfrecci'are *vi* flash past

sfregi'a|re *vt* slash. **~to** *adj* scarred

'sfregio *m* slash

sfre'na|rsi *vr* run wild. **~to** *adj* wild

sfron'tato *adj* shameless

S **sfrutta'mento** *m* exploitation. **sfrut'tare** *vt* exploit

sfug'gente *adj* elusive; (mento) receding

sfug'gi|re *vi* escape; **~re a** escape [from]; **mi sfugge** it escapes me; **mi è sfuggito di mano** I lost hold of it ● *vt* avoid. **~ta** *f* **di ~ta** in passing

sfu'ma|re *vi* (*svanire*) vanish; (colore:) shade off ● *vt* soften (colore). **~'tura** *f* shade

sfuri'ata *f* outburst [of anger]

sga'bello *m* stool

sgabuz'zino *m* cupboard

sgambet'tare *vi* kick one's legs; (*camminare*) trot. **sgam'betto** *m* **fare lo sgambetto a qcno** trip sb up

sganasci'arsi *vr* **~ dalle risa** roar with laughter

sganci'ar|e *vt* unhook; (*Rail*) uncouple; drop (bombe); ⓘ cough up (denaro). **~si** *vr* become unhooked; *fig* get away

sganghe'rato *adj* ramshackle

sgar'bato *adj* rude. **'sgarbo** *m* discourtesy

sgargi'ante *adj* garish

sgar'rare *vi* be wrong; (*da regola*) stray from the straight and narrow. **'sgarro** *m* mistake, slip

sgattaio'lare *vi* sneak away; **~ via** decamp

sghignaz'zare *vi* laugh scornfully, sneer

sgoccio'lare *vi* drip

sgo'larsi *vr* shout oneself hoarse

sgomb[e]'rare *vt* clear [out]. **'sgombro** *adj* clear ● *m* (*trasloco*) removal; (*pesce*) mackerel

sgomen'tar|e *vt* dismay. **~si** *vr* be dismayed. **sgo'mento** *m* dismay

sgomi'nare *vt* defeat

sgom'mata *f* screech of tyres

sgonfi'ar|e *vt* deflate. **~si** *vr* go down. **'sgonfio** *adj* flat

'sgorbio *m* scrawl; (*fig: vista sgradevole*) sight

sgor'gare *vi* gush [out] ● *vt* flush out, unblock (lavandino)

sgoz'zare *vt* **~ qcno** cut sb's throat

sgra'd|evole *adj* disagreeable. **~ito** *adj* unwelcome

sgrammati'cato *adj* ungrammatical

sgra'nare *vt* shell (piselli); open wide (occhi)

sgran'chir|e *vt*, **~si** *vr* stretch

sgranocchi'are *vt* munch

sgras'sare *vt* remove the grease from

sgrazi'ato *adj* ungainly

sgreto'lar|e *vt*, **~si** *vr* crumble

sgri'da|re *vt* scold. **~ta** *f* scolding

sgros'sare *vt* rough-hew (marmo); *fig* polish

sguai'ato *adj* coarse

sgual'cire *vt* crumple

sgu'ardo *m* look; (*breve*) glance

sguaz'zare *vi* splash; (*nel fango*) wallow

sguinzagli'are *vt* unleash
sgusci'are *vt* shell ● *vi* (*sfuggire*) slip away; ~ **fuori** slip out
shake'rare *vt* shake

si
● *pers pron* (*riflessivo*) oneself; (*lui*) himself; (*lei*) herself; (*esso, essa*) itself; (*loro*) themselves; (*reciproco*) each other; (*tra più di due*) one another; (*impersonale*) you, one; **lavarsi** wash [oneself]; **si è lavata** she washed [herself]; **lavarsi le mani** wash one's hands; **si è lavata le mani** she washed her hands; **si è mangiato un pollo intero** he ate an entire chicken by himself; **incontrarsi** meet each other; **la gente si aiuta a vicenda** people help one another; **non si sa mai** you never know, one never knows *fml*; **queste cose si dimenticano facilmente** these things are easily forgotten
● *m* (*chiave, nota*) B

sì *adv* yes
'sia[1] ▸**ESSERE**
'sia[2] *conj* **~...~...** (*entrambi*) both... and...; (*o l'uno o l'altro*) either...or...; **~ che venga, ~ che non venga** whether he comes or not; **scegli ~ questo ~ quello** choose either this one or that one; **voglio ~ questo che quello** I want both this one and that one
sia'mese *adj* Siamese
sibi'lare *vi* hiss
si'cario *m* hired killer
sicché *conj* (*perciò*) so [that]; (*allora*) then
siccità *f* drought
sic'come *conj* as
Si'cili|a *f* Sicily. **s~'ano, -a** *adj & mf* Sicilian
si'cura *f* safety catch; (*di portiera*) childproof lock. **~'mente** *adv* definitely
sicu'rezza *f* certainty; (*salvezza*) safety; **uscita di ~** emergency exit. **~ delle frontiere** homeland security
si'curo *adj* safe; (*certo*) sure; (saldo) steady; (*Comm*) sound ● *adv* certainly ● *m* safety; **al ~** safe; **andare sul ~** play [it] safe; **di ~** definitely; **di ~, sarà arrivato** he must have arrived
siderur'gia *f* iron and steel industry
'sidro *m* cider
si'epe *f* hedge
si'ero *m* serum
sieroposi'tivo *adj* HIV positive
si'esta *f* afternoon nap
si'fone *m* siphon
Sig. *abbr* (signore) Mr
Sig.a *abbr* (signora) Mrs, Ms
siga'retta *f* cigarette
'sigaro *m* cigar
Sigg. *abbr* (signori) Messrs
sigil'lare *vt* seal. **si'gillo** *m* seal
'sigla *f* initials *pl*. **~ musicale** signature tune. **si'glare** *vt* initial
Sig.na *abbr* (signorina) Miss, Ms
signifi'ca|re *vt* mean. **~'tivo** *adj* significant. **~to** *m* meaning
si'gnora *f* lady; (*davanti a nome proprio*) Mrs; (*non sposata*) Miss; (*in lettere ufficiali*) Dear Madam; **il signor Vené e ~** Mr and Mrs Vené
si'gnore *m* gentleman; (*Relig*) lord; (*davanti a nome proprio*) Mr; (*in lettere ufficiali*) Dear Sir. **signo'rile** *adj* gentlemanly; (*di lusso*) luxury
signo'rina *f* young lady; (*seguito da nome proprio*) Miss
silenzia'tore *m* silencer
si'lenzi|o *m* silence. **~'oso** *adj* silent
silhou'ette *f* silhouette
si'licio *m* **piastrina di ~** silicon chip
sili'cone *m* silicone
'sillaba *f* syllable
silu'rare *vt* torpedo. **si'luro** *m* torpedo
simboleggi'are *vt* symbolize
sim'bolico *adj* symbolic[al]
'simbolo *m* symbol
similarità *f inv* similarity
'simil|e *adj* similar; (*tale*) such; **~e a** like ● *m* (*il prossimo*) fellow man. **~'mente** *adv* similarly. **~'pelle** *f* Leatherette®
simme'tria *f* symmetry. **sim'metrico** *adj* symmetric[al]
simpa'ti|a *f* liking; (*compenetrazione*) sympathy; **prendere qcno in ~a** take a liking to sb. **sim'patico** *adj* nice. **~iz'zante** *mf* well-wisher. **~iz'zare** *vt* **~izzare con** take a liking to; **~izzare per qcsa/qcno** lean towards sth/sb

S

sim'posio *m* symposium
simu'la|re *vt* simulate; feign (amicizia, interesse). **~zi'one** *f* simulation
simul'taneo *adj* simultaneous
sina'goga *f* synagogue
sincerità *f* sincerity. **sin'cero** *adj* sincere
'sincope *f* syncopation; (*Med*) fainting fit
sincron'ia *f* synchronization
sincroniz'zare *vt* synchronize
sinda'ca|le *adj* [trade] union, [labor] union *Am*. **~'lista** *mf* trade unionist, labor union member *Am*. **~re** *vt* inspect. **~to** *m* [trade] union, [labor] union *Am*; (*associazione*) syndicate
'sindaco *m* mayor
'sindrome *f* syndrome
sinfo'nia *f* symphony. **sin'fonico** *adj* symphonic
singhi|oz'zare *vi* (*di pianto*) sob. **~'ozzo** *m* hiccup; (*di pianto*) sob
singo'lar|e *adj* singular ● *m* singular. **~'mente** *adv* individually; (*stranamente*) peculiarly
'singolo *adj* single ● *m* individual; *Tennis* singles *pl*
si'nistra *f* left; **a ~** on the left; **girare a ~** turn to the left; **con la guida a ~** (auto) with left-hand drive
sini'strato *adj* injured
si'nistr|o, -a *adj* left[-hand]; (*avverso*) sinister ● *m* accident ● *f* left [hand]; (*Pol*) left [wing]
'sino *prep* = FINO[1]
si'nonimo *adj* synonymous ● *m* synonym
sin'tassi *f* syntax
'sintesi *f inv* synthesis; (*riassunto*) summary
sin'teti|co *adj* synthetic; (*conciso*) summary. **~z'zare** *vt* summarize
sintetizza'tore *m* synthesizer
sinto'matico *adj* symptomatic. **'sintomo** *m* symptom
sinto'nia *f* tuning; **in ~** on the same wavelength
sinu'oso *adj* (*strada*) winding
si'pario *m* curtain
si'rena *f* siren
'Siri|a *f* Syria. **s~'ano, -a** *adj & mf* Syrian
si'ringa *f* syringe
'sismico *adj* seismic
si'stem|a *m* system. **~a operativo** (*Comput*) operating system
siste'ma|re *vt* (*mettere*) put; tidy up (casa, camera); (*risolvere*) sort out; (*procurare lavoro a*) fix up with a job; (*trovare alloggio a*) find accommodation for; (*sposare*) marry off; ([!]: *punire*) sort out. **~rsi** *vr* settle down; (*trovare un lavoro*) find a job; (*trovare alloggio*) find accommodation; (*sposarsi*) marry. **~tico** *adj* systematic. **~zi'one** *f* arrangement; (*di questione*) settlement; (*lavoro*) job; (*alloggio*) accommodation; (*matrimonio*) marriage
'sito *m* site. **~ web** web site
situ'are *vt* place
situazi'one *f* situation
ski-'lift *m inv* ski tow
slacci'are *vt* unfasten
slanci'a|rsi *vr* hurl oneself. **~to** *adj* slender. **'slancio** *m* impetus; (*impulso*) impulse
sla'vato *adj* fair
'slavo *adj* Slav[onic]
sle'al|e *adj* disloyal. **~tà** *f* disloyalty
sle'gare *vt* untie
'slitta *f* sledge, sleigh. **~'mento** *m* (*di macchina*) skid; (*fig: di riunione*) postponement
slit'ta|re *vi* (*Auto*) skid; (riunione:) be put off. **~ta** *f* skid
slit'tino *m* toboggan
'slogan *m inv* slogan
slo'ga|re *vt* dislocate. **~rsi** *vr* **~rsi una caviglia** sprain one's ankle. **~'tura** *f* dislocation
sloggi'are *vi* move out
Slo'vacchia *f* Slovakia
Slo'venia *f* Slovenia
smacchi'a|re *vt* clean. **~'tore** *m* stain remover
'smacco *m* humiliating defeat
smagli'ante *adj* dazzling
smagli'a|rsi *vr* (calza:) run. **~'tura** *f* run
smalizi'ato *adj* cunning
smal'ta|re *vt* enamel; glaze (ceramica); varnish (unghie). **~to** *adj* enamelled
smalti'mento *m* disposal; (*di merce*)

S

selling off. ~ **rifiuti** waste disposal; (*di grassi*) burning off

smal'tire *vt* burn off; (*merce*) sell off; *fig* get through (corrispondenza); ~ **la sbornia** sober up

'smalto *m* enamel; (*di ceramica*) glaze; (*per le unghie*) nail varnish

smantel|la'mento *m* dismantling. **~'lare** *vt* dismantle

smarri'mento *m* loss; (*psicologico*) bewilderment

smar'ri|re *vt* lose; (*temporaneamente*) mislay. **~rsi** *vr* get lost; (*turbarsi*) be bewildered

smasche'rar|e *vt* unmask. **~si** *vr* (*tradirsi*) give oneself away

smemo'rato, -a *adj* forgetful ● *mf* scatterbrain

smen'ti|re *vt* deny. **~ta** *f* denial

sme'raldo *m & adj* emerald

smerci'are *vt* sell off

smerigli'ato *adj* emery; **vetro ~** frosted glass. **sme'riglio** *m* emery

'smesso *pp di* **smettere** ● *adj* (abiti) cast-off

'smett|ere *vt* stop; stop wearing (abiti); **~ila!** stop it!

smidol'lato *adj* spineless

sminu'ir|e *vt* diminish. **~si** *vr fig* belittle oneself

sminuz'zare *vt* crumble; (*fig: analizzare*) analyse in detail

smista'mento *m* clearing; (*postale*) sorting. **smi'stare** *vt* sort; (*Mil*) post

smisu'rato *adj* boundless; (*esorbitante*) excessive

smobili'ta|re *vt* demobilize. **~zi'one** *f* demobilization

smo'dato *adj* immoderate

smog *m* smog

'smoking *m inv* dinner jacket, tuxedo *Am*

smon'tar|e *vt* take to pieces; (*scoraggiare*) dishearten ● *vi* (*da veicolo*) get off; (*da cavallo*) dismount; (*dal servizio*) go off duty. **~si** *vr* lose heart

'smorfi|a *f* grimace; (*moina*) simper; **fare ~e** make faces. **~'oso** *adj* affected

'smorto *adj* pale; (colore) dull

smor'zare *vt* dim (luce); tone down (colori); deaden (suoni); quench (sete)

'smosso *pp di* **smuovere**

smotta'mento *m* landslide

sms *m inv* (short message service) text message

'smunto *adj* emaciated

smu'over|e *vt* shift; (*commuovere*) move. **~si** *vr* move; (*commuoversi*) be moved

smus'sar|e *vt* round off; (*fig: attenuare*) tone down. **~si** *vr* go blunt

snatu'rato *adj* inhuman

snel'lir|e *vt* slim down. **~si** *vr* slim [down]. **'snello** *adj* slim

sner'va|re *vt* enervate. **~rsi** *vr* get exhausted

sni'dare *vt* drive out

snif'fare *vt* snort

snob'bare *vt* snub. **sno'bismo** *m* snobbery

snoccio'lare *vt* stone; *fig* blurt out

sno'da|re *vt* untie; (*sciogliere*) loosen. **~rsi** *vr* come untied; (strada:) wind. **~to** *adj* (persona) double-jointed; (dita) flexible

so'ave *adj* gentle

sobbal'zare *vi* jerk; (*trasalire*) start. **sob'balzo** *m* jerk; (*trasalimento*) start

sobbar'carsi *vr* ~ **a** undertake

sob'borgo *m* suburb

sobil'la|re *vt* stir up

'sobrio *adj* sober

soc'chiu|dere *vt* half-close. **~so** *pp di* **socchiudere** ● *adj* (occhi) half-closed; (porta) ajar

soc'cor|rere *vt* assist. **~so** *pp di* **soccorrere** ● *m* assistance; **soccorsi** *pl* rescuers; (*dopo disastro*) relief workers. **~so stradale** breakdown service

socialdemo'cra|tico, -a *adj* Social Democratic ● *mf* Social Democrat. **~'zia** *f* Social Democracy

soci'ale *adj* social

socia'li|smo *m* Socialism. **~sta** *agg & mf* Socialist. **~z'zare** *vi* socialize

società *f inv* society; (*Comm*) company. ~ **per azioni** plc. ~ **a responsabilità limitata** limited liability company

soci'evole *adj* sociable

'socio, -a *mf* member; (*Comm*) partner

sociolo'gia *f* sociology. **socio'logico** *adj* sociological

'soda *f* soda

soddisfa'cente *adj* satisfactory
soddi'sfa|re *vt/i* satisfy; meet (richiesta); make amends for (offesa). **~tto** *pp di* **soddisfare** ● *adj* satisfied. **~zi'one** *f* satisfaction
'sodo *adj* hard; *fig* firm; (uovo) hard-boiled ● *adv* hard; **dormire ~** sleep soundly
sofà *m inv* sofa
soffe'ren|te *adj* ill
soffer'marsi *vr* pause; **~ su** dwell on
sof'ferto *pp di* **soffrire**
soffi'a|re *vt* blow; reveal (segreto); (*rubare*) pinch [!] ● *vi* blow. **~ta** *f fig* [✖] tip-off
'soffice *adj* soft
'soffio *m* puff; (*Med*) murmur
sof'fitt|a *f* attic. **~o** *m* ceiling
soffo|ca'mento *m* suffocation
soffo'ca|nte *adj* suffocating. **~re** *vt/i* suffocate; (*con cibo*) choke; *fig* stifle
sof'friggere *vt* fry lightly
sof'frire *vt/i* suffer; (*sopportare*) bear; **~ di** suffer from
sof'fritto *pp di* **soffriggere**
sof'fuso *adj* (luce) soft
sofisti'ca|re *vt* (*adulterare*) adulterate ● *vi* (*sottilizzare*) quibble. **~to** *adj* sophisticated
sogget'tivo *adj* subjective
sog'getto *m* subject ● *adj* subject; **essere ~ a** be subject to
soggezi'one *f* subjection; (*rispetto*) awe
sogghi'gnare *vi* sneer
soggio'gare *vt* subdue
soggior'nare *vi* stay. **soggi'orno** *m* stay; (*stanza*) living room
soggi'ungere *vt* add
'soglia *f* threshold
'sogliola *f* sole
so'gna|re *vt/i* dream; **~re a occhi aperti** daydream. **~'tore, ~'trice** *mf* dreamer. **'sogno** *m* dream; **fare un sogno** have a dream; **neanche per sogno!** not at all!
'soia *f* soya
sol *m* (*Mus*) G
so'laio *m* attic
sola'mente *adv* only
so'lar|e *adj* (energia, raggi) solar; (crema) sun *attrib*. **~ium** *m inv* solarium
sol'care *vt* plough. **'solco** *m* furrow; (*di ruota*) track; (*di nave*) wake; (*di disco*) groove
sol'dato *m* soldier
'soldo *m* **non ha un ~** he hasn't got a penny; **senza un ~** penniless; **soldi** *pl* (*denaro*) money *sg*
'sole *m* sun; (*luce del sole*) sun[light]; **al ~** in the sun; **prendere il ~** sunbathe
soleggi'ato *adj* sunny
so'lenn|e *adj* solemn. **~ità** *f* solemnity
so'lere *vi* be in the habit of; **come si suol dire** as they say
sol'fato *m* sulphate
soli'da|le *adj* in agreement. **~rietà** *f* solidarity
solidifi'car|e *vt/i*, **~si** *vr* solidify
solidità *f* solidity; (*di colori*) fastness. **'solido** *adj* solid; (*robusto*) sturdy; (colore) fast ● *m* solid
so'lista *adj* solo ● *mf* soloist
solita'mente *adv* usually
soli'tario *adj* solitary; (*isolato*) lonely ● *m* (*brillante*) solitaire; (*gioco di carte*) patience, solitaire
'solito *adj* usual; **essere ~ fare qcsa** be in the habit of doing sth ● *m* usual; **di ~** usually
soli'tudine *f* solitude
solleci'ta|re *vt* speed up; urge (persona). **~zi'one** *f* (*richiesta*) request; (*preghiera*) entreaty
sol'leci|to *adj* prompt ● *m* reminder. **~'tudine** *f* promptness; (*interessamento*) concern
solle'one *m* noonday sun; (*periodo*) dog days of summer
solleti'care *vt* tickle
solleva'mento *m* **~ pesi** weightlifting
solle'var|e *vt* lift; (*elevare*) raise; (*confortare*) comfort. **~si** *vr* rise; (*riaversi*) recover
solli'evo *m* relief
'solo, -a *adj* alone; (*isolato*) lonely; (*unico*) only; (*Mus*) solo; **da ~** by myself/yourself/himself etc ● *mf* **il ~, la sola** the only one ● *m* (*Mus*) solo ● *adv* only
sol'stizio *m* solstice
sol'tanto *adv* only
so'lubile *adj* soluble; (caffè) instant

soluzi'one *f* solution; (*Comm*) payment

sol'vente *adj & m* solvent; **~ per unghie** nail polish remover

so'maro *m* ass; (*Sch*) dunce

so'matico *adj* somatic

somigli'an|te *adj* similar. **~za** *f* resemblance

somigli'ar|e *vi* **~e a** resemble. **~si** *vr* be alike

'somma *f* sum; (*Math*) addition

som'mare *vt* add; (*totalizzare*) add up

som'mario *adj & m* summary

som'mato *adj* **tutto ~** all things considered

sommeli'er *m inv* wine waiter

som'mer|gere *vt* submerge. **~'gibile** *m* submarine. **~so** *pp di* **sommergere**

som'messo *adj* soft

sommini'stra|re *vt* administer. **~zi'one** *f* administration

sommità *f inv* summit

'sommo *adj* highest; *fig* supreme ● *m* summit

som'mossa *f* rising

sommozza'tore *m* frogman

so'naglio *m* bell

so'nata *f* sonata; *fig* [!] beating

'sonda *f* (*Mech*) drill; (*Med, spaziale*). **son'daggio** *m* drilling; (*Med, spaziale*) probe; (*indagine*) survey. **sondaggio d'opinioni** opinion poll. **son'dare** *vt* sound; (*investigare*) probe

sonnambu'lismo *m* sleepwalking. **son'nambulo, -a** *mf* sleepwalker

sonnecchi'are *vi* doze

son'nifero *m* sleeping-pill

'sonno *m* sleep; **aver ~** be sleepy. **~'lenza** *f* sleepiness

so'noro *adj* resonant; (*rumoroso*) loud; (onde, scheda) sound *attrib*

sontu'oso *adj* sumptuous

sopo'rifero *adj* soporific

sop'palco *m* platform

soppe'rire *vi* **~ a qcsa** provide for sth

soppe'sare *vt* weigh up

soppor'ta|re *vt* support; (*tollerare*) stand; bear (dolore)

soppressi'one *f* removal; (*di legge*) abolition; (*di diritti, pubblicazione*) suppression; (*annullamento*) cancellation. **sop'presso** *pp di* **sopprimere**

sop'primere *vt* get rid of; abolish (legge); suppress (diritti, pubblicazione); (*annullare*) cancel

'sopra *adv* on top; (*più in alto*) higher [up]; (*al piano superiore*) upstairs; (*in testo*) above; **mettilo lì ~** put it up there; **di ~** upstairs; **pensarci ~** think about it; **vedi ~** see above ● *prep* **~ [a]** on; (*senza contatto, oltre*) over; (*riguardo a*) about; **è ~ al tavolo, è ~ il tavolo** it's on the table; **il quadro è appeso ~ al camino** the picture is hanging over the fireplace; **il ponte passa ~ all'autostrada** the bridge crosses over the motorway; **è caduto ~ il tetto** it fell on the roof; **l'uno ~ l'altro** one on top of the other; (*senza contatto*) one above the other; **abita ~ di me** he lives upstairs from me; **i bambini ~ i dieci anni** children over ten; **20° ~ lo zero** 20° above zero; **~ il livello del mare** above sea level; **rifletti ~ quello che è successo** think about what happened ● *m* **il [di] ~** the top

so'prabito *m* overcoat

soprac'ciglio *m* (*pl f* **sopracciglia**) eyebrow

sopracco'per|ta *f* bedspread; (*di libro*) [dust-]jacket. **~'tina** *f* book jacket

soprad'detto *adj* above-mentioned

sopraele'vata *f* elevated railway

sopraf'fa|re *vt* overwhelm. **~tto** *pp di* **sopraffare**. **~zi'one** *f* abuse of power

sopraf'fino *adj* excellent; (gusto, udito) highly refined

sopraggi'ungere *vi* (persona:) turn up; (*accadere*) happen

sopralluo'ogo *m* inspection

sopram'mobile *m* ornament

soprannatu'rale *adj & m* supernatural

sopran'nome *m* nickname

so'prano *mf* soprano

soprappensi'ero *adv* lost in thought

sopras'salto *m* **di ~** with a start

soprasse'dere *vi* **~ a** postpone

soprat'tutto *adv* above all

sopravvalu'tare *vt* overvalue

soprav|ve'nire *vi* turn up; (*accadere*) happen. **~'vento** *m fig* upper hand

sopravvi|s'suto *pp di* **sopravvivere**. **~'venza** *f* survival. **soprav'vivere** *vi* survive; **sopravvivere a** outlive (persona)

soprinten'den|te *mf* supervisor; (*di museo ecc*) keeper. **~za** *f* supervision; (*ente*) board

so'pruso *m* abuse of power

soq'quadro *m* **mettere a ~** turn upside down

sor'betto *m* sorbet

'sordido *adj* sordid; (*avaro*) stingy

sor'dina *f* mute; **in ~** on the quiet

sordità *f* deafness. **'sordo, -a** *adj* deaf; (rumore, dolore) dull ● *mf* deaf person. **sordo'muto, -a** *adj* deaf-and-dumb

so'rel|la *f* sister. **~'lastra** *f* stepsister

sor'gente *f* spring; (*fonte*) source

'sorgere *vi* rise; *fig* arise

sormon'tare *vt* surmount

sorni'one *adj* sly

sorpas'sa|re *vt* surpass; (*eccedere*) exceed; overtake (veicolo). **~to** *adj* old-fashioned. **sor'passo** *m* overtaking

sorpren'dente *adj* surprising; (*straordinario*) remarkable

sor'prendere *vt* surprise; (*cogliere in flagrante*) catch

sor'pres|a *f* surprise; **di ~a** by surprise. **~o** *pp di* **sorprendere**

sor're|ggere *vt* support; (*tenere*) hold up. **~ggersi** *vr* support oneself. **~tto** *pp di* **sorreggere**

sor'ri|dere *vi* smile. **~so** *pp di* **sorridere** ● *m* smile

sorseggi'are *vt* sip. **'sorso** *m* sip; (*piccola quantità*) drop

'sorta *f* sort; **di ~** whatever; **ogni ~ di** all sorts of

'sorte *f* fate; (*caso imprevisto*) chance; **tirare a ~** draw lots. **sor'teggio** *m* draw

sorti'legio *m* witchcraft

sor'ti|re *vi* come out. **~ta** *f* (*Mil*) sortie; (*battuta*) witticism

'sorto *pp di* **sorgere**

sorvegli'an|te *mf* keeper; (*controllore*) overseer. **~za** *f* watch; (*Mil ecc*) surveillance

sorvegli'are *vt* watch over; (*controllare*) oversee; (polizia:) keep under surveillance

sorvo'lare *vt* fly over; *fig* skip

'sosia *m inv* double

so'spen|dere *vt* hang; (*interrompere*) stop; (*privare di una carica*) suspend. **~si'one** *f* suspension

so'speso *pp di* **sospendere** ● *adj* (impiegato, alunno) suspended; **~ a** hanging from; **~ a un filo** *fig* hanging by a thread ● *m* **in ~** pending; (*emozionato*) in suspense

sospet|'tare *vt* suspect. **so'spetto** *adj* suspicious; **persona sospetta** suspicious person ● *m* suspicion; (*persona*) suspect. **~'toso** *adj* suspicious

so'spin|gere *vt* drive. **~to** *pp di* **sospingere**

sospi'rare *vi* sigh ● *vt* long for. **so'spiro** *m* sigh

'sosta *f* stop; (*pausa*) pause; **senza ~** non-stop; **"divieto di ~"** "no parking"

sostan'tivo *m* noun

so'stanz|a *f* substance; **~e** *pl* (*patrimonio*) property *sg*. **~i'oso** *adj* substantial; (cibo) nourishing

so'stare *vi* stop; (*fare una pausa*) pause

so'stegno *m* support

soste'ner|e *vt* support; (*sopportare*) bear; (*resistere*) withstand; (*affermare*) maintain; (*nutrire*) sustain; sit (esame); **~e le spese** meet the costs. **~si** *vr* support oneself

sosteni'tore, -'trice *mf* supporter

sostenta'mento *m* maintenance

soste'nuto *adj* (stile) formal; (prezzi, velocità) high

sostitu'ir|e *vt* substitute (**a** for), replace (**con** with). **~si** *vr* **~si a** replace

sosti'tu|to, -ta *mf* replacement, stand-in ● *m* (*surrogato*) substitute. **~zi'one** *f* substitution

sot'tana *f* petticoat; (*di prete*) cassock

sotter'raneo *adj* underground ● *m* cellar

sotter'rare *vt* bury

sottigli'ezza *f* slimness; *fig* subtlety

sot'til|e *adj* thin; (udito, odorato) keen; (osservazione, distinzione) subtle. **~iz'zare** *vi* split hairs

sottin'te|ndere *vt* imply. **~so** *pp di* **sottintendere** ● *m* allusion; **senza ~si** openly ● *adj* implied

'sotto *adv* below; (*più in basso*) lower [down]; (*al di sotto*) underneath; (*al piano di sotto*) downstairs; **è lì ~** it's underneath; **~ ~** deep down; (*di nascosto*) on the quiet; **di ~** downstairs; **mettersi ~** *fig* get down to it; **mettere ~** (🅸: *investire*) knock down ● *prep* **~ [a]** under; (*al di sotto di*) under[neath]; **abita ~ di me** he lives downstairs from me; **i bambini ~ i dieci anni** children under ten; **20° ~ zero** 20° below zero; **~ il livello del mare** below sea level; **~ la pioggia** in the rain; **~ calmante** under sedation; **~ condizione che...** on condition that...; **~ giuramento** under oath; **~ sorveglianza** under surveillance; **~ Natale/gli esami** around Christmas/exam time; **al di ~ di** under; **andare ~ i 50 all'ora** do less than 50km an hour ● *m* **il [di] ~** the bottom

sotto'banco *adv* under the counter

sottobicchi'ere *m* coaster

sotto'bosco *m* undergrowth

sotto'braccio *adv* arm in arm

sotto'fondo *m* background

sottoline'are *vt* underline; *fig* stress

sot'tolio *adv* in oil

sotto'mano *adv* within reach

sottoma'rino *adj & m* submarine

sotto'messo *pp di* **sottomettere**

sotto'metter|e *vt* submit; subdue (popolo). **~si** *vr* submit. **sottomissi'one** *f* submission

sottopas'saggio *m* underpass; (*pedonale*) subway

sotto'por|re *vt* submit; (*costringere*) subject. **~si** *vr* submit oneself; **~si a** undergo. **sotto'posto** *pp di* **sottoporre**

sotto'scala *m* cupboard under the stairs

sotto'scritto *pp di* **sottoscrivere** ● *m* undersigned

sotto'scri|vere *vt* sign; (*approvare*) sanction, subscribe to. **~zi'one** *f* (*petizione*) petition; (*approvazione*) sanction; (*raccolta di denaro*) appeal

sotto'sopra *adv* upside down

sotto'stante *adj* **la strada ~** the road below

sottosu'olo *m* subsoil

sottosvilup'pato *adj* underdeveloped

sotto'terra *adv* underground

sotto'titolo *m* subtitle

sottovalu'tare *vt* underestimate

sotto'veste *f* slip

sotto'voce *adv* in a low voice

sottovu'oto *adj* vacuum-packed

sot'tra|rre *vt* remove; embezzle (fondi); (*Math*) subtract. **~rsi** *vr* **~rsi a** escape from; avoid (responsabilità). **~tto** *pp di* **sottrarre. ~zi'one** *f* removal; (*di fondi*) embezzlement; (*Math*) subtraction

sottuffici'ale *m* non-commissioned officer; (*Naut*) petty officer

sou'brette *f inv* showgirl

so'vietico, -a *adj & mf* Soviet

sovraccari'care *vt* overload. **sovrac'carico** *adj* overloaded (**di** with) ● *m* overload

sovrannatu'rale *adj & m* = **SOPRANNATURALE**

so'vrano, -a *adj* sovereign; *fig* supreme ● *mf* sovereign

sovrap'por|re *vt* superimpose. **~si** *vr* overlap

sovra'stare *vt* dominate; *fig*: (pericolo:) hang over

sovrinten'den|te, ~za = **SOPRINTENDENTE, SOPRINTENDENZA**

sovru'mano *adj* superhuman

sovvenzi'one *f* subsidy

sovver'sivo *adj* subversive

'sozzo *adj* filthy

S.p.A. *abbr* (società per azioni) plc

spac'ca|re *vt* split; chop (legna). **~rsi** *vr* split. **~'tura** *f* split

spacci'a|re *vt* deal in, push (droga); **~re qcsa per qcsa** pass sth off as sth. **~rsi** *vr* **~rsi per** pass oneself off as. **~'tore, ~'trice** *mf* (*di droga*) pusher; (*di denaro falso*) distributor of forged bank notes. **'spaccio** *m* (*di droga*) dealing; (*negozio*) shop

'spacco *m* split

spac'cone, -a *mf* boaster

'spada *f* sword. **~c'cino** *m* swordsman

spae'sato *adj* disorientated

spa'ghetti *mpl* spaghetti *sg*

spa'ghetto *m* (🅸: *spavento*) fright

'Spagna *f* Spain

spa'gnolo, -a *adj* Spanish ● *mf* Spaniard ● *m* (*lingua*) Spanish

S

'spago *m* string; **dare ~ a qcno** encourage sb

spai'ato *adj* odd

spalan'ca|re *vt*, **~rsi** *vr* open wide. **~to** *adj* wide open

spa'lare *vt* shovel

'spall|a *f* shoulder; (*di comico*) straight man; **~e** *pl* (*schiena*) back; **alle ~e di qcno** (ridere) behind sb's back. **~eggi'are** *vt* back up

spal'letta *f* parapet

spalli'era *f* back; (*di letto*) headboard; (*ginnastica*) wall bars *pl*

spal'lina *f* strap; (*imbottitura*) shoulder pad

spal'mare *vt* spread

'spander|e *vt* spread; (*versare*) spill. **~si** *vr* spread

spappo'lare *vt* crush

spa'ra|re *vt/i* shoot; **~rle grosse** talk big. **~'toria** *f* shooting

sparecchi'are *vt* clear

spa'reggio *m* (*Comm*) deficit; *Sport* play-off

'sparg|ere *vt* scatter; (*diffondere*) spread; shed (lacrime, sangue). **~ersi** *vr* spread. **~i'mento** *m* scattering; **~imento di sangue** bloodshed

spa'ri|re *vi* disappear; **~sci!** get lost!. **~zi'one** *f* disappearance

spar'lare *vi* **~ di** run down

'sparo *m* shot

sparpagli'ar|e *vt*, **~si** *vr* scatter

'sparso *pp di* **spargere** ● *adj* scattered; (*sciolto*) loose

spar'tire *vt* share out; (*separare*) separate

sparti'traffico *m inv* traffic island; (*di autostrada*) central reservation, median strip *Am*

spartizi'one *f* division

spa'ruto *adj* gaunt; (gruppo) small; (peli, capelli) sparse

sparvi'ero *m* sparrow-hawk

'spasimo *m* spasm

spa'smodico *adj* spasmodic

spas'sar|si *vr* amuse oneself; **~sela** have a good time

spassio'nato *adj* dispassionate

'spasso *m* fun; **essere uno ~** be hilarious; **andare a ~** go for a walk. **spas'soso** *adj* hilarious

'spatola *f* spatula

spau'racchio *m* scarecrow; *fig* bugbear. **spau'rire** *vt* frighten

spa'valdo *adj* defiant

spaventa'passeri *m inv* scarecrow

spaven'tar|e *vt* frighten. **~si** *vr* be frightened. **spa'vento** *m* fright. **spaven'toso** *adj* frightening; ([!]: *enorme*) incredible

spazi'ale *adj* spatial; (*cosmico*) space *attrib*

spazi'are *vt* space out ● *vi* range

spazien'tirsi *vr* lose patience

'spazi|o *m* space. **~'oso** *adj* spacious

spaz'z|are *vt* sweep; **~are via** sweep away; ([!]: *mangiare*) devour. **~a'tura** *f* rubbish. **~ino** *m* road sweeper; (*netturbino*) dustman

'spazzo|la *f* brush; (*di tergicristallo*) blade. **~'lare** *vt* brush. **~'lino** *m* small brush. **~lino da denti** toothbrush. **~'lone** *m* scrubbing brush

specchi'arsi *vr* look at oneself in the mirror; (*riflettersi*) be mirrored; **~ in qcno** model oneself on sb

specchi'etto *m* **~ retrovisore** driving mirror

'specchio *m* mirror

speci'a|le *adj* special ● *m* (*TV*) special [programme]. **~'lista** *mf* specialist. **~lità** *f inv* specialty

specializ'za|re *vt*, **~rsi** *vr* specialize. **~to** *adj* skilled

special'mente *adv* especially

'specie *f inv* species; (*tipo*) kind; **fare ~ a** surprise

specifi'care *vt* specify. **spe'cifico** *adj* specific

specu'lare[1] *vi* speculate; **~ su** (*indagare*) speculate on; (*Fin*) speculate in

specu'lare[2] *adj* mirror *attrib*

specula|'tore, -'trice *mf* speculator. **~zi'one** *f* speculation

spe'di|re *vt* send. **~to** *pp di* **spedire** ● *adj* quick; (parlata) fluent. **~zi'one** *f* dispatch; (*Comm*) consignment; (*scientifica*) expedition

'spegner|e *vt* put out; turn off (gas, luce); switch off (motore); slake (sete). **~si** *vr* go out; (*morire*) pass away

S

spelacchi'ato *adj* (tappeto) threadbare; (cane) mangy
spe'lar|e *vt* skin (coniglio). **~si** *vr* (cane:) moult
speleolo'gia *f* potholing
spel'lar|e *vt* skin; *fig* fleece. **~si** *vr* peel off
spe'lonca *f* cave; *fig* hole
spendacci'one, -a *mf* spendthrift
'spendere *vt* spend; **~ fiato** waste one's breath
spen'nare *vt* pluck; [!] fleece (cliente)
spennel'lare *vt* brush
spensie|ra'tezza *f* lightheartedness. **~'rato** *adj* carefree
'spento *pp di* **spegnere** • *adj* off; (gas) out; (*smorto*) dull
spe'ranza *f* hope; **pieno di ~** hopeful; **senza ~** hopeless
spe'rare *vt* hope for; (*aspettarsi*) expect • *vi* **~ in** trust in; **spero di sì** I hope so
'sper|dersi *vr* get lost. **~'duto** *adj* lost; (*isolato*) secluded
spergi'uro, -a *mf* perjurer • *m* perjury
sperimen'ta|le *adj* experimental. **~re** *vt* experiment with; test (resistenza, capacità, teoria). **~zi'one** *f* experimentation
'sperma *m* sperm
spe'rone *m* spur
sperpe'rare *vt* squander. **'sperpero** *m* waste
'spes|a *f* expense; (*acquisto*) purchase; **andare a far ~e** go shopping; **fare la ~a** do the shopping; **fare le ~e di** pay for. **~e** *pl* **bancarie** bank charges. **~e a carico del destinatario** carriage forward. **spe'sato** *adj* all-expenses-paid. **~o** *pp di* **spendere**
'spesso[1] *adj* thick
'spesso[2] *adv* often
spes'sore *m* thickness; (*fig: consistenza*) substance
spet'tabile *adj* (*Comm*) *abbr* (**Spett.**) **S~ ditta Rossi** Messrs Rossi
spettaco|'lare *adj* spectacular. **spet'tacolo** *m* spectacle; (*rappresentazione*) show. **~'loso** *adj* spectacular
spet'tare *vi* **~ a** be up to; (diritto:) be due to
spetta'tore, -'trice *mf* spectator; **spettatori** *pl* audience *sg*
spettego'lare *vi* gossip
spet'trale *adj* ghostly. **'spettro** *m* ghost; (*Phys*) spectrum
'spezie *fpl* spices
spez'zar|e *vt*, **~si** *vr* break
spezza'tino *m* stew
spez'zato *m* coordinated jacket and trousers
spezzet'tare *vt* break into small pieces
'spia *f* spy; (*della polizia*) informer; (*di porta*) peep-hole; **fare la ~** sneak. **~ [luminosa]** light. **~ dell'olio** oil [warning] light
spiacci'care *vt* squash
spia'ce|nte *adj* sorry. **~vole** *adj* unpleasant
spi'aggia *f* beach
spia'nare *vt* level; (*rendere liscio*) smooth; roll out (pasta); raze to the ground (edificio)
spian'tato *adj fig* penniless
spi'are *vt* spy on; wait for (occasione ecc)
spiattel'lare *vt* blurt out; shove (oggetto)
spi'azzo *m* (*radura*) clearing
spic'ca|re *vt* **~re un salto** jump; **~re il volo** take flight • *vi* stand out. **~to** *adj* marked
'spicchio *m* (*di agrumi*) segment; (*di aglio*) clove
spicci'a|rsi *vr* hurry up. **~'tivo** *adj* speedy
'spicciolo *adj* (*comune*) banal; (denaro, 5 euro) in change. **spiccioli** *pl* change *sg*
'spicco *m* relief; **fare ~** stand out
'spider *f inv* open-top sports car
spie'dino *m* kebab. **spi'edo** *m* spit; **allo spiedo** on a spit, spit-roasted
spie'ga|re *vt* explain; open out (cartina); unfurl (vele). **~rsi** *vr* explain oneself; (vele, bandiere:) unfurl. **~zi'one** *f* explanation
spiegaz'zato *adj* crumpled
spie'tato *adj* ruthless
spiffe'rare *vt* blurt out • *vi* (vento:)

whistle. '**spiffero** *m* draught
'**spiga** *f* spike; (*Bot*) ear
spigli'ato *adj* self-possessed
'**spigolo** *m* edge; (*angolo*) corner
'**spilla** *f* brooch. ~ **da balia** safety pin. ~ **di sicurezza** safety pin
spil'lare *vt* tap
'**spillo** *m* pin. ~ **di sicurezza** safety pin; (*in arma*) safety catch
spi'lorcio *adj* stingy
'**spina** *f* thorn; (*di pesce*) bone; (*Electr*) plug. ~ **dorsale** spine
spi'naci *mpl* spinach
spi'nale *adj* spinal
spi'nato *adj* (filo) barbed; (pianta) thorny
spi'nello *m* [!] joint
'**spinger|e** *vt* push; *fig* drive. ~**si** *vr* (*andare*) proceed
spi'noso *adj* thorny
'**spint|a** *f* push; (*violenta*) thrust; *fig* spur. ~**o** *pp di* **spingere**
spio'naggio *m* espionage
spio'vente *adj* sloping
spi'overe *vi liter* stop raining; (*ricadere*) fall; (*scorrere*) flow down
'**spira** *f* coil
spi'raglio *m* small opening; (*soffio d'aria*) breath of air; (*raggio di luce*) gleam of light
spi'rale *adj* spiral ● *f* spiral; (*negli orologi*) hairspring; (*anticoncezionale*) coil
spi'rare *vi* (*soffiare*) blow; (*morire*) pass away
S
spiri't|ato *adj* possessed; (espressione) wild. '**spirito** *m* spirit; (*arguzia*) wit; (*intelletto*) mind; **fare dello spirito** be witty; **sotto spirito** in brandy. ~**o'saggine** *f* witticism. **spiri'toso** *adj* witty
spiritu'ale *adj* spiritual
'**splen|dere** *vi* shine. ~**dido** *adj* splendid. ~**'dore** *m* splendour
'**spoglia** *f* (*di animale*) skin; **spoglie** *pl* (*salma*) mortal remains; (*bottino*) spoils
spogli'a|re *vt* strip; (*svestire*) undress; (*fare lo spoglio di*) go through. ~**'rello** *m* strip-tease. ~**rsi** *vr* strip, undress. ~**'toio** *m* dressing room; *Sport* changing room; (*guardaroba*) cloakroom, checkroom *Am*. '**spoglio** *adj* undressed; (albero, muro) bare ● *m* (*scrutinio*) perusal
'**spola** *f* shuttle; **fare la** ~ shuttle
spol'pare *vt* flesh; *fig* fleece
spolve'rare *vt* dust; [!] devour (cibo)
'**sponda** *f* shore; (*di fiume*) bank; (*bordo*) edge
sponsoriz'zare *vt* sponsor
spon'taneo *adj* spontaneous
spopo'lar|e *vt* depopulate ● *vi* (*avere successo*) draw the crowds. ~**si** *vr* become depopulated
sporadica'mente *adv* sporadically. **spo'radico** *adj* sporadic
spor'c|are *vt* dirty; (*macchiare*) soil. ~**arsi** *vr* get dirty. ~**izia** *f* dirt. '**sporco** *adj* dirty; **avere la coscienza sporca** have a guilty conscience ● *m* dirt
spor'gen|te *adj* jutting. ~**za** *f* projection
'**sporger|e** *vt* stretch out; ~**e querela contro** take legal action against ● *vi* jut out. ~**si** *vr* lean out
sport *m inv* sport
'**sporta** *f* shopping basket
spor'tello *m* door; (*di banca ecc*) window. ~ **automatico** cash dispenser
spor'tivo, -a *adj* sports *attrib*; (persona) sporty ● *m* sportsman ● *f* sportswoman
'**sporto** *pp di* **sporgere**
'**sposa** *f* bride. ~**'lizio** *m* wedding
spo'sa|re *vt* marry; *fig* espouse. ~**rsi** *vr* get married; (vino:) go (**con** with). ~**to** *adj* married. '**sposo** *m* bridegroom; **sposi** *pl* **[novelli]** newlyweds
spossa'tezza *f* exhaustion. **spos'sato** *adj* exhausted, worn out
spo'sta|re *vt* move; (*differire*) postpone; (*cambiare*) change. ~**rsi** *vr* move. ~**to, -a** *adj* ill-adjusted ● *mf* (*disadattato*) misfit
'**spranga** *f* bar. **spran'gare** *vt* bar
'**sprazzo** *m* (*di colore*) splash; (*di luce*) flash; *fig* glimmer
spre'care *vt* waste. '**spreco** *m* waste
spre'g|evole *adj* despicable. ~**ia'tivo** *adj* pejorative. '**spregio** *m* contempt
spregiudi'cato *adj* unscrupulous

'spremer|e *vt* squeeze. **~si** *vr* **~si le meningi** rack one's brains

spremia'grumi *m* lemon squeezer

spre'muta *f* juice. **~ d'arancia** fresh orange [juice]

sprez'zante *adj* contemptuous

sprigio'nar|e *vt* emit. **~si** *vr* burst out

spriz'zare *vt/i* spurt; be bursting with (salute, gioia)

sprofon'dar|e *vi* sink; (*crollare*) collapse. **~si** *vr* **~si in** sink into; *fig* be engrossed in

'sprone *m* spur; (*sartoria*) yoke

sproporzi|o'nato *adj* disproportionate. **~'one** *f* disproportion

sproposi'tato *adj* full of blunders; (*enorme*) huge. **spro'posito** *m* blunder; (*eccesso*) excessive amount

sprovve'duto *adj* unprepared; **~ di** lacking in

sprov'visto *adj* **~ di** out of; lacking in (fantasia, pazienza); **alla sprovvista** unexpectedly

spruz'za|re *vt* sprinkle; (*vaporizzare*) spray; (*inzaccherare*) spatter. **~'tore** *m* spray; **'spruzzo** *m* spray; (*di fango*) splash

spudo|ra'tezza *f* shamelessness. **~'rato** *adj* shameless

'spugna *f* sponge; (*tessuto*) towelling. **spu'gnoso** *adj* spongy

'spuma *f* foam; (*schiuma*) froth; (*Culin*) mousse. **spu'mante** *m* sparkling wine. **spumeggi'are** *vi* foam

spun'ta|re *vt* break the point of; trim (capelli); **~rla** *fig* win ● *vi* (pianta:) sprout; (capelli:) begin to grow; (*sorgere*) rise; (*apparire*) appear. **~rsi** *vr* get blunt. **~ta** *f* trim

spun'tino *m* snack

'spunto *m* cue; *fig* starting point; **dare ~ a** give rise to

spur'gar|e *vt* purge. **~si** *vr* (*Med*) expectorate

spu'tare *vt/i* spit; **~ sentenze** pass judgment. **'sputo** *m* spit

'squadra *f* team, squad; (*di polizia ecc*) squad; (*da disegno*) square. **squa'drare** *vt* square; (*guardare*) look up and down

squa'dr|iglia *f*, **~one** *m* squadron

squagli'ar|e *vt*, **~si** *vr* melt; **~sela** ([!]: *svignarsela*) steal out

squa'lifi|ca *f* disqualification. **~'care** *vt* disqualify

'squallido *adj* squalid. **squal'lore** *m* squalor

'squalo *m* shark

'squama *f* scale; (*di pelle*) flake

squa'm|are *vt* scale. **~arsi** *vr* (pelle:) flake off. **~'moso** *adj* scaly; (pelle) flaky

squarcia'gola: **a ~** *adv* at the top of one's voice

squarci'are *vt* rip. **'squarcio** *m* rip; (*di ferita, in nave*) gash; (*di cielo*) patch

squattri'nato *adj* penniless

squilib'ra|re *vt* unbalance. **~to, -a** *adj* unbalanced ● *mf* lunatic. **squi'librio** *m* imbalance

squil'la|nte *adj* shrill. **~re** *vi* (campana:) peal; (tromba:) blare; (telefono:) ring. **'squillo** *m* blare; (*Teleph*) ring ● *f* (*ragazza*) call girl

squi'sito *adj* exquisite

sradi'care *vt* uproot; eradicate (vizio, male)

sragio'nare *vi* rave

srego'lato *adj* inordinate; (*dissoluto*) dissolute

s.r.l. *abbr* (società a responsabilità limitata) Ltd

sroto'lare *vt* uncoil

SS *abbr* (strada statale) national road

'stabile *adj* stable; (*permanente*) lasting; (saldo) steady; **compagnia ~** (*Theat*) repertory company ● *m* (*edificio*) building

stabili'mento *m* factory; (*industriale*) plant; (*edificio*) establishment. **~ balneare** lido

stabi'li|re *vt* establish; (*decidere*) decide. **~rsi** *vr* settle. **~tà** *f* stability

stabiliz'za|re *vt* stabilize. **~rsi** *vr* stabilize. **~'tore** *m* stabilizer

stac'car|e *vt* detach; pronounce clearly (parole); (*separare*) separate; turn off (corrente) ● *vi* ([!]: *finire di lavorare*) knock off. **~si** *vr* come off; **~si da** break away from (partito, famiglia)

staccio'nata *f* fence

'stacco *m* gap

'stadio *m* stadium
'staffa *f* stirrup
staf'fetta *f* dispatch rider
stagio'nale *adj* seasonal
stagio'na|re *vt* season (legno); mature (formaggio). **~to** *adj* (legno) seasoned; (formaggio) matured
stagi'one *f* season; **alta/bassa ~** high/low season
stagli'arsi *vr* stand out
sta'gna|nte *adj* stagnant. **~re** *vt* (*saldare*) solder; (*chiudere ermeticamente*) seal ● *vi* stagnate. **'stagno** *adj* watertight ● *m* pond; (*metallo*) tin
sta'gnola *f* tinfoil
'stall|a *f* stable; (*per buoi*) cowshed. **~i'ere** *m* groom
stal'lone *m* stallion
sta'mani, **stamat'tina** *adv* this morning
stam'becco *m* ibex
stam'berga *f* hovel
'stampa *f* (*Typ*) printing; (*giornali, giornalisti*) press; (*riproduzione*) print
stam'pa|nte *f* printer. **~nte laser** laser printer. **~re** *vt* print. **~'tello** *m* block letters *pl*
stam'pella *f* crutch
'stampo *m* mould; **di vecchio ~** (*persona*) of the old school
sta'nare *vt* drive out
stan'car|e *vt* tire; (*annoiare*) bore. **~si** *vr* get tired
stan'chezza *f* tiredness. **'stanco** *adj* tired; **stanco di** fed up with. **stanco morto** dead tired, exhausted
'standard *adj & m inv* standard. **~iz'zare** *vt* standardize
'stan|ga *f* bar; (*persona*) beanpole. **~'gata** *f fig* blow; ([!]: *nel calcio*) big kick. **stan'ghetta** *f* (*di occhiali*) leg
sta'notte *adv* tonight; (*la notte scorsa*) last night
'stante *prep* on account of; **a se ~** separate
stan'tio *adj* stale
stan'tuffo *m* piston
'stanza *f* room; (*metrica*) stanza
stanzi'are *vt* allocate
stap'pare *vt* uncork

'stare

● *vi* (*rimanere*) stay; (*abitare*) live; (*con gerundio*) be; **sto solo cinque minuti** I'll stay only five minutes; **sto in piazza Peyron** I live in Peyron Square; **sta dormendo** he's sleeping; **~ a** (*attenersi*) keep to; (*spettare*) be up to; **~ bene** (*economicamente*) be well off; (*di salute*) be well; (*addirsi*) suit; **~ dietro a** (*seguire*) follow; (*sorvegliare*) keep an eye on; (*corteggiare*) run after; **~ in piedi** stand; **~ per** be about to; **come stai/sta?** how are you?; **lasciar ~** leave alone; **starci** (*essere contenuto*) go into; (*essere d'accordo*) agree; **il 3 nel 12 ci sta 4 volte** 3 into 12 goes 4; **non sa ~ agli scherzi** he can't take a joke; **~ sulle proprie** keep oneself to oneself.

● **starsene** *vr* (*rimanere*) stay

starnu'tire *vi* sneeze. **star'nuto** *m* sneeze
sta'sera *adv* this evening, tonight
sta'tale *adj* state *attrib* ● *mf* state employee ● *f* main road
'statico *adj* static
sta'tista *m* statesman
sta'tistic|a *f* statistics *sg*. **~o** *adj* statistical
'stato *pp di* **essere, stare** ● *m* state; (*posizione sociale*) position; (*Jur*) status. **~ d'animo** frame of mind. **~ civile** marital status. **S~ Maggiore** (*Mil*) General Staff. **Stati** *pl* **Uniti [d'America]** United States [of America]
'statua *f* statue
statuni'tense *adj* United States *attrib*, US *attrib* ● *mf* citizen of the United States, US citizen
sta'tura *f* height; **di alta ~** tall; **di bassa ~** short
sta'tuto *m* statute
stazio'nario *adj* stationary
stazi'one *f* station; (*città*) resort. **~ balneare** seaside resort. **~ ferroviaria** train station. **~ di servizio** service station. **~ termale** spa
'stecca *f* stick; (*di ombrello*) rib; (*da biliardo*) cue; (*Med*) splint; (*di sigarette*) carton; (*di reggiseno*) stiffener

S

stec'cato *m* fence
stec'chito *adj* skinny; (*rigido*) stiff; (*morto*) stone cold dead
'stella *f* star; **salire alle stelle** (prezzi:) rise sky-high. **~ alpina** edelweiss. **~ cadente** shooting star. **~ filante** streamer. **~ di mare** starfish
stel'lare *adj* stellar
'stelo *m* stem; **lampada** *f* **a ~** standard lamp
'stemma *m* coat of arms
stempi'ato *adj* bald at the temples
sten'dardo *m* standard
'stender|e *vt* spread out; (*appendere*) hang out; (*distendere*) stretch [out]; (*scrivere*) write down. **~si** *vr* stretch out
stendibianche'ria *m inv*, **stendi'toio** *m* clothes horse
stenodatti|logra'fia *f* shorthand typing
stenogra'f|are *vt* take down in shorthand. **~ia** *f* shorthand
sten'ta|re *vi* **~re a** find it hard to. **~to** *adj* laboured. **'stento** *m* effort; **a stento** with difficulty; **stenti** *pl* hardships, privations
'sterco *m* dung
'stereo['fonico] *adj* stereo[phonic]
stereoti'pato *adj* stereotyped; (sorriso) insincere. **stere'otipo** *m* stereotype
'steril|e *adj* sterile; (terreno) barren. **~ità** *f* sterility. **~iz'zare** *vt* sterilize. **~izzazi'one** *f* sterilization
ster'lina *f* pound; **lira ~** [pound] sterling
stermi'nare *vt* exterminate
stermi'nato *adj* immense
ster'minio *m* extermination
ste'roide *m* steroid
ster'zare *vi* steer. **'sterzo** *m* steering
'steso *pp di* **stendere**
'stesso *adj* same; **io ~** myself; **tu ~** yourself; **me ~** myself; **se ~** himself; **in quel momento ~** at that very moment; **dalla stessa regina** by the Queen herself; **coi miei stessi occhi** with my own eyes ● *pron* **lo ~** the same one; (*la stessa cosa*) the same; **fa lo ~** it's all the same; **ci vado lo ~** I'll go just the same
ste'sura *f* drawing up; (*documento*) draft
stick *m* **colla a ~** glue stick; **deodorante a ~** stick deodorant
'stigma *m* stigma. **~te** *fpl* stigmata
sti'lare *vt* draw up
'stil|e *m* style. **sti'lista** *mf* stylist. **~iz'zato** *adj* stylized
stil'lare *vi* ooze
stilo'grafic|a *f* fountain pen. **~o** *adj* **penna ~a** fountain pen
'stima *f* esteem; (*valutazione*) estimate. **sti'mare** *vt* esteem; (*valutare*) estimate; (*ritenere*) consider
stimo'la|nte *adj* stimulating ● *m* stimulant. **~re** *vt* stimulate; (*incitare*) incite
'stimolo *m* stimulus; (*fitta*) pang
'stinco *m* shin
'stinger|e *vt/i* fade. **~si** *vr* fade. **'stinto** *pp di* **stingere**
sti'par|e *vt* cram. **~si** *vr* crowd together
stipendi'ato *adj* salaried ● *m* salaried worker. **sti'pendio** *m* salary
'stipite *m* doorpost
stipu'la|re *vt* stipulate. **~zi'one** *f* stipulation; (*accordo*) agreement
stira'mento *m* sprain
sti'ra|re *vt* iron; (*distendere*) stretch. **~rsi** *vr* (*distendersi*) stretch; pull (muscolo). **~'tura** *f* ironing. **'stiro** *m* **ferro da stiro** iron
'stirpe *f* stock
stiti'chezza *f* constipation. **'stitico** *adj* constipated
'stiva *f* (*Naut*) hold
sti'vale *m* boot. **stivali** *pl* **di gomma** Wellington boots
'stizza *f* anger
stiz'zi|re *vt* irritate. **~rsi** *vr* become irritated. **~to** *adj* irritated. **stiz'zoso** *adj* peevish
stocca'fisso *m* stockfish
stoc'cata *f* stab; (*battuta pungente*) gibe
'stoffa *f* material; *fig* stuff
'stola *f* stole
'stolto *adj* foolish
stoma'chevole *adj* revolting
'stomaco *m* stomach; **mal di ~** stomach-ache
sto'na|re *vt/i* sing/play out of tune ● *vi*

(*non intonarsi*) clash. **~to** *adj* out of tune; (*discordante*) clashing; (*confuso*) bewildered. **~'tura** *f* false note; (*discordanza*) clash

'stoppia *f* stubble

stop'pino *m* wick

stop'poso *adj* tough

'storcer|e *vt*, **~si** *vr* twist

stor'di|re *vt* stun; (*intontire*) daze. **~rsi** *vr* dull one's senses. **~to** *adj* stunned; (*intontito*) dazed; (*sventato*) heedless

'storia *f* history; (*racconto, bugia*) story; (*pretesto*) excuse; **fare [delle] storie** make a fuss

'storico, -a *adj* historical; (*di importanza storica*) historic ● *mf* historian

stori'one *m* sturgeon

'stormo *m* flock

'storno *m* starling

storpi'a|re *vt* cripple; mangle (parole). **~'tura** *f* deformation. **'storpio, -a** *adj* crippled ● *mf* cripple

'stort|a *f* (*distorsione*) sprain; **prendere una ~a alla caviglia** sprain one's ankle. **~o** *pp di* **storcere** ● *adj* crooked; (*ritorto*) twisted; (gambe) bandy; *fig* wrong

sto'viglie *fpl* crockery *sg*

'strabico *adj* cross-eyed

strabili'ante *adj* astonishing

stra'bismo *m* squint

straboc'care *vi* overflow

stra'carico *adj* overloaded

stracci|'are *vt* tear; (⊡: *vincere*) thrash. **~'ato** *adj* torn; (persona) in rags; (prezzi) slashed; **a un prezzo ~ato** dirt cheap. **'straccio** *adj* torn ● *m* rag; (*strofinaccio*) cloth. **~'one** *m* tramp

stra'cotto *adj* overdone; (⊡: *innamorato*) head over heels ● *m* stew

'strada *f* road; (*di città*) street; **essere fuori ~** be on the wrong track; **fare ~** lead the way; **farsi ~** make one's way. **~ maestra** main road. **~ a senso unico** one-way street. **~ senza uscita** blind alley. **stra'dale** *adj* road *attrib*

strafalci'one *m* blunder

stra'fare *vi* overdo things

stra'foro: **di ~** *adv* on the sly

strafot'ten|te *adj* arrogant. **~za** *f* arrogance

'strage *f* slaughter

'stralcio *m* (*parte*) extract

stralu'na|re *vt* **~re gli occhi** open one's eyes wide. **~to** *adj* (occhi) staring; (persona) distraught

stramaz'zare *vi* fall heavily

strambe'ria *f* oddity. **'strambo** *adj* strange

strampa'lato *adj* odd

stra'nezza *f* strangeness

strango'lare *vt* strangle

strani'ero, -a *adj* foreign ● *mf* foreigner

'strano *adj* strange

straordi|naria'mente *adv* extraordinarily. **~'nario** *adj* extraordinary; (*notevole*) remarkable; (edizione) special; **lavoro ~nario** overtime; **treno ~nario** special train

strapaz'zar|e *vt* ill-treat; scramble (uova). **~si** *vr* tire oneself out. **stra'pazzo** *m* strain; **da strapazzo** *fig* worthless

strapi'eno *adj* overflowing

strapi'ombo *m* projection; **a ~** sheer

strap'par|e *vt* tear; (*per distruggere*) tear up; pull out (dente, capelli); (*sradicare*) pull up; (*estorcere*) wring. **~si** *vr* get torn; (*allontanarsi*) tear oneself away. **'strappo** *m* tear; (*strattone*) jerk; (⊡: *passaggio*) lift; **fare uno strappo alla regola** make an exception to the rule. **~ muscolare** muscle strain

strapun'tino *m* folding seat

strari'pare *vi* flood

strasci'c|are *vt* trail; shuffle (piedi); drawl (parole). **'strascico** *m* train; *fig* after-effect

strass *m inv* rhinestone

strata'gemma *m* stratagem

strate'gia *f* strategy. **stra'tegico** *adj* strategic

'strato *m* layer; (*di vernice ecc*) coat; (*roccioso, sociale*) stratum. **~'sfera** *f* stratosphere. **~'sferico** *adj* stratospheric

stravac'carsi *vr* ⊡ slouch

strava'gan|te *adj* extravagant; (*eccentrico*) eccentric. **~za** *f* extravagance; (*eccentricità*) eccentricity

stra'vecchio *adj* ancient

strave'dere *vt* **~ per** worship

stravizi'are *vi* indulge oneself. **stra'vizio** *m* excess

stra'volg|ere *vt* twist; (*turbare*) upset. **~i'mento** *m* twisting. **stra'volto** *adj* distraught; ([!]: *stanco*) done in

strazi'a|nte *adj* heartrending; (dolore) agonizing. **~re** *vt* grate on (orecchie); break (cuore). **'strazio** *m* agony; **che strazio!** [!] it's awful!

'strega *f* witch. **stre'gare** *vt* bewitch. **stre'gone** *m* wizard

'stregua *f* **alla ~ di** like

stre'ma|re *vt* exhaust. **~to** *adj* exhausted

'strenuo *adj* strenuous

strepi|'tare *vi* make a din. **'strepito** *m* noise. **~'toso** *adj* noisy; *fig* resounding

stres'sa|nte *adj* (lavoro, situazione) stressful. **~to** *adj* stressed [out]

'stretta *f* grasp; (*dolore*) pang; **essere alle strette** be in dire straits. **~ di mano** handshake

stret'tezza *f* narrowness; **stret'tezze** *pl* (*difficoltà finanziarie*) financial difficulties

'stret|to *pp di* **stringere** ● *adj* narrow; (*serrato*) tight; (*vicino*) close; (dialetto) broad; (*rigoroso*) strict; **lo ~to necessario** the bare minimum ● *m* (*Geog*) strait. **~'toia** *f* bottleneck; ([!]: *difficoltà*) tight spot

stri'a|to *adj* striped. **~'tura** *f* streak

stri'dente *adj* strident

'stridere *vi* squeak; *fig* clash. **stri'dore** *m* screech

'stridulo *adj* shrill

strigli'a|re *vt* groom. **~ta** *f* grooming; *fig* dressing down

stril'l|are *vi t* scream. **'strillo** *m* scream

strimin'zito *adj* skimpy; (*magro*) skinny

strimpel'lare *vt* strum

'strin|ga *f* lace; (*Comput*) string. **~'gato** *adj fig* terse

'stringer|e *vt* press; (*serrare*) squeeze; (*tenere stretto*) hold tight; take in (abito); (*comprimere*) be tight; (*restringere*) tighten; **~e la mano a** shake hands with ● *vi* (*premere*) press. **~si** *vr* (*accostarsi*) draw close (**a** to); (*avvicinarsi*) squeeze up

'striscia *f* strip; (*riga*) stripe. **strisce** *pl* **[pedonali]** zebra crossing *sg*

strisci'ar|e *vi* crawl; (*sfiorare*) graze ● *vt* drag (piedi). **~si** *vr* **~si a** rub against. **'striscio** *m* graze; (*Med*) smear; **colpire di striscio** graze

strisci'one *m* banner

strito'lare *vt* grind

striz'zare *vt* squeeze; (*torcere*) wring [out]; **~ l'occhio** wink

'strofa *f* strophe

strofi'naccio *m* cloth; (*per spolverare*) duster

strofi'nare *vt* rub

strombaz'zare *vt* boast about ● *vi* hoot

strombaz'zata *f* hoot

stron'care *vt* cut off; (*reprimere*) crush; (*criticare*) tear to shreds

stropicci'are *vt* rub; crumple (vestito)

stroz'za|re *vt* strangle. **~'tura** *f* strangling; (*di strada*) narrowing

strozzi'naggio *m* loan-sharking

stroz'zino *m pej* usurer; (*truffatore*) shark

strug'gente *adj* all-consuming

strumen'tale *adj* instrumental

strumentaliz'zare *vt* make use of

stru'mento *m* instrument; (*arnese*) tool. **~ a corda** string instrument. **~ musicale** musical instrument

strusci'are *vt* rub

'strutto *m* lard

strut'tura *f* structure. **struttu'rale** *adj* structural

struttu'rare *vt* structure

strutturazi'one *f* structuring

'struzzo *m* ostrich

stuc'ca|re *vt* stucco

stuc'chevole *adj* nauseating

'stucco *m* stucco

stu'den|te, -t'essa *mf* student; (*di scuola*) schoolboy; schoolgirl. **~'tesco** *adj* student; (*di scolaro*) school *attrib*

studi'ar|e *vt* study. **~si** *vr* **~si di** try to

'studi|o *m* studying; (*stanza, ricerca*) study; (*di artista, TV ecc*) studio; (*di professionista*) office. **~'oso, -a** *adj* studious ● *mf* scholar

'stufa *f* stove. **~ elettrica** electric fire

stu'fa|re *vt* (*Culin*) stew; (*dare fastidio*)

S

bore. **~rsi** *vr* get bored. **~to** *m* stew

'stufo *adj* bored; **essere ~ di** be fed up with

stu'oia *f* mat

stupefa'cente *adj* amazing ● *m* drug

stu'pendo *adj* stupendous

stupi'd|aggine *f* (*azione*) stupid thing; (*cosa da poco*) nothing. **~ata** *f* stupid thing. **~ità** *f* stupidity. **'stupido** *adj* stupid

stu'pir|e *vt* astonish ● *vi*, **~si** *vr* be astonished. **stu'pore** *m* amazement

stu'pra|re *vt* rape. **~'tore** *m* rapist. **'stupro** *m* rape

sturalavan'dini *m inv* plunger

stu'rare *vt* uncork; unblock (lavandino)

stuzzi'care *vt* prod [at]; pick (denti); poke (fuoco); (*molestare*) tease; whet (appetito)

stuzzi'chino *m* (*Culin*) appetizer

su *prep* on; (*senza contatto*) over; (*riguardo a*) about; (*circa, intorno a*) about, around; **le chiavi sono sul tavolo** the keys are on the table; **il quadro è appeso sul camino** the picture is hanging over the fireplace; **un libro sull'antico Egitto** a book on *o* about Ancient Egypt; **costa sui 25 euro** it costs about 25 euros; **decidere sul momento** decide at the time; **su commissione** on commission; **su due piedi** on the spot; **uno su dieci** one out of ten ● *adv* (*sopra*) up; (*al piano di sopra*) upstairs; (*addosso*) on; **ho su il cappotto** I've got my coat on; **in su** (guardare) up; **dalla vita in su** from the waist up; **su!** come on!

su'bacqueo *adj* underwater

subaffit'tare *vt* sublet. **subaf'fitto** *m* sublet

subal'terno *adj & m* subordinate

sub'buglio *m* turmoil

sub'conscio *adj & m* subconscious

'subdolo *adj* devious

suben'trare *vi* (circostanze:) come up; **~ a** take the place of

su'bire *vt* undergo; (*patire*) suffer

subis'sare *vt fig* **~ di** overwhelm with

'subito *adv* at once; **~ dopo** straight after

su'blime *adj* sublime

subodo'rare *vt* suspect

subordi'nato, -a *adj & mf* subordinate

subur'bano *adj* suburban

suc'ceder|e *vi* (*accadere*) happen; **~e a** succeed; (*venire dopo*) follow; **~e al trono** succeed to the throne. **~si** *vr* happen one after the other

successi'one *f* succession; **in ~** in succession

succes|siva'mente *adv* subsequently. **~'sivo** *adj* successive

suc'ces|so *pp di* **succedere** ● *m* success; (*esito*) outcome; (*disco ecc*) hit

succes'sore *m* successor

succhi'are *vt* suck [up]

suc'cinto *adj* (*conciso*) concise; (abito) scanty

'succo *m* juice; *fig* essence; **~ di frutta** fruit juice. **suc'coso** *adj* juicy

succu'lento *adj* succulent

succur'sale *f* branch [office]

sud *m* south; **del ~** southern

su'da|re *vi* sweat; (*faticare*) sweat blood; **~re freddo** be in a cold sweat. **~ta** *f* sweat. **~'ticcio** *adj* sweaty. **~to** *adj* sweaty

sud'detto *adj* above-mentioned

'suddito, -a *mf* subject

suddi'vi|dere *vt* subdivide. **~si'o-ne** *f* subdivision

su'd-est *m* southeast

'sudici|o *adj* filthy. **~'ume** *m* filth

su'dore *m* sweat; *fig* sweat

su'd-ovest *m* southwest

suffici'en|te *adj* sufficient; (*presuntuoso*) conceited ● *m* bare essentials *pl*; (*Sch*) pass mark. **~za** *f* sufficiency; (*presunzione*) conceit; (*Sch*) pass; **a ~za** enough

suf'fisso *m* suffix

suf'fragio *m* vote. **~ universale** universal suffrage

suggeri'mento *m* suggestion

sugge'ri|re *vt* suggest; (*Theat*) prompt. **~'tore, ~'trice** *mf* (*Theat*) prompter

suggestiona'bile *adj* suggestible

suggestio'na|re *vt* influence **suggesti'one** *f* influence

sugge'stivo *adj* suggestive; (musica ecc) evocative

'sughero *m* cork

'sugli = **SU + GLI**

'sugo *m* (*di frutta*) juice; (*di carne*) gravy; (*salsa*) sauce; (*sostanza*) substance

'sui = **SU + I**

sui'cid|a *adj* suicidal ● *mf* suicide. **sui-ci'darsi** *vr* commit suicide. **~io** *m* suicide

su'ino *adj* **carne suina** pork ● *m* swine

sul = **SU + IL**. **'sullo** = **SU + LO**. **'sulla** = **SU + LA**. **'sulle** = **SU + LE**

sul'ta|na *f* sultana. **~'nina** *adj* **uva ~nina** sultana. **~no** *m* sultan

'sunto *m* summary

'suo, -a *poss adj* **il ~, i suoi** his; (*di cosa, animale*) its; (*forma di cortesia*) your; **la sua, le sue** her; (*di cosa, animale*) its; (*forma di cortesia*) your; **questa macchina è sua** this car is his/hers; **~ padre** his/her/your father; **un ~ amico** a friend of his/hers/yours ● *poss pron* **il ~, i suoi** his; (*di cosa, animale*) its; (*forma di cortesia*) yours; **la sua, le sue** hers; (*di cosa animale*) its; (*forma di cortesia*) yours; **i suoi** his/her folk

su'ocera *f* mother-in-law

su'ocero *m* father-in-law

su'ola *f* sole

su'olo *m* ground; (*terreno*) soil

suo'na|re *vt/i* (*Mus*) play; ring (campanello); sound (allarme, clacson); (orologio:) strike. **~'tore, ~'trice** *mf* player. **suone'ria** *f* alarm. **su'ono** *m* sound

su'ora *f* nun; **Suor Maria** Sister Maria

superal'colico *m* spirit ● *adj* **bevande** *pl* **superalcoliche** spirits

supera'mento *m* (*di timidezza*) overcoming; (*di esame*) success (**di** in)

supe'rare *vt* surpass; (*eccedere*) exceed; (*vincere*) overcome; overtake (veicolo); pass (esame)

su'perbo *adj* haughty; (*magnifico*) superb

superdo'tato *adj* highly gifted

superfici'al|e *adj* superficial ● *mf* superficial person. **~ità** *f* superficiality. **super'ficie** *f* surface; (*area*) area

su'perfluo *adj* superfluous

superi'or|e *adj* superior; (*di grado*) senior; (*più elevato*) higher; (*sovrastante*) upper; (*al di sopra*) above ● *mf* superior. **~ità** *f* superiority

superla'tivo *adj & m* superlative

supermer'cato *m* supermarket

super'sonico *adj* supersonic

su'perstite *adj* surviving ● *mf* survivor

superstizi'o|ne *f* superstition. **~so** *adj* superstitious

super'strada *f* toll-free motorway

supervi|si'one *f* supervision. **~'sore** *m* supervisor

su'pino *adj* supine

suppel'lettili *fpl* furnishings

suppergiù *adv* about

supplemen'tare *adj* supplementary

supple'mento *m* supplement; **~ rapido** express train supplement

sup'plen|te *adj* temporary ● *mf* (*Sch*) supply teacher. **~za** *f* temporary post

'suppli|ca *f* plea; (*domanda*) petition. **~'care** *vt* beg

sup'plire *vt* replace ● *vi* **~ a** (*compensare*) make up for

sup'plizio *m* torture

sup'porre *vt* suppose

sup'porto *m* support

supposizi'one *f* supposition

sup'posta *f* suppository

sup'posto *pp di* **supporre**

suprema'zia *f* supremacy. **su'premo** *adj* supreme

sur'fare *vi* **~ in Internet** surf the Net

surge'la|re *vt* deep-freeze. **~ti** *mpl* frozen food *sg*. **~to** *adj* frozen

surrea'lis|mo *m* surrealism. **~ta** *mf* surrealist

surriscal'dare *vt* overheat

surro'gato *m* substitute

suscet'tibil|e *adj* touchy. **~ità** *f* touchiness

susci'tare *vt* stir up; arouse (ammirazione ecc)

su'sin|a *f* plum. **~o** *m* plumtree

su'spense *f* suspense

sussegu|'ente *adj* subsequent. **~'irsi** *vr* follow one after the other

sussidi'ar|e *vt* subsidize. **~io** *adj* subsidiary. **sus'sidio** *m* subsidy; (*aiuto*) aid. **sussidio di disoccupazione** unemployment benefit

sussi'ego *m* haughtiness

sussi'stenza *f* subsistence. **sus'sistere** *vi* subsist; (*essere valido*) hold good

sussul'tare *vi* start. **sus'sulto** *m* start

sussur'rare *vt* whisper. **sus'surro** *m* whisper

sva'gar|e *vt* amuse. **~si** *vr* amuse oneself. **'svago** *m* relaxation; (*divertimento*) amusement

svaligi'are *vt* rob; burgle (casa)

svalu'ta|re *vt* devalue; *fig* underestimate. **~rsi** *vr* lose value. **~zi'one** *f* devaluation

svam'pito *adj* absent-minded

sva'nire *vi* vanish

svantaggi|'ato *adj* at a disadvantage; (bambino, paese) disadvantaged. **svan'taggio** *m* disadvantage; **essere in svantaggio** *Sport* be losing; **~'oso** *adj* disadvantageous

svapo'rare *vi* evaporate

svari'ato *adj* varied

sva'sato *adj* flared

'svastica *f* swastika

sve'dese *adj & m* (*lingua*) Swedish • *mf* Swede

'sveglia *f* (*orologio*) alarm [clock]; **~!** get up!; **mettere la ~** set the alarm [clock]

svegli'ar|e *vt* wake up; *fig* awaken. **~si** *vr* wake up. **'sveglio** *adj* awake; (*di mente*) quick-witted

S

sve'lare *vt* reveal

svel'tezza *f* speed; *fig* quick-wittedness

svel'tir|e *vt* quicken. **~si** *vr* (persona:) liven up. **'svelto** *adj* quick; (*slanciato*) svelte; **alla svelta** quickly

'svend|ere *vt* undersell. **~ita** *f* [clearance] sale

sve'nire *vi* faint

sven'ta|re *vt* foil. **~to** *adj* thoughtless • *mf* thoughtless person

'sventola *f* slap

svento'lare *vt/i* wave

sven'trare *vt* disembowel; *fig* demolish (edificio)

sven'tura *f* misfortune. **sventu'rato** *adj* unfortunate

sve'nuto *pp di* **svenire**

svergo'gnato *adj* shameless

sver'nare *vi* winter

sve'stir|e *vt* undress

'Svezia *f* Sweden

svez'zare *vt* wean

svi'ar|e *vt* divert; (*corrompere*) lead astray. **~si** *vr fig* go astray

svico'lare *vi* turn down a side street; (*dalla questione ecc*) evade the issue; (*da una persona*) dodge out of the way

svi'gnarsela *vr* slip away

svi'lire *vt* debase

svilup'par|e *vt*, **~si** *vr* develop. **svi'luppo** *m* development; **paese in via di sviluppo** developing country

svinco'lar|e *vt* release; clear (merce). **~si** *vr* free oneself. **'svincolo** *m* clearance; (*di autostrada*) exit

svisce'ra|re *vt* gut; *fig* dissect. **~to** *adj* passionate; (*ossequioso*) obsequious

'svista *f* oversight

svi'ta|re *vt* unscrew. **~to** *adj* (**!**: *matto*) cracked, nutty

'Svizzer|a *f* Switzerland. **s~o, -a** *adj & mf* Swiss

i

Svizzera Italian is one of the four national languages of Switzerland, but is spoken widely only in the canton of Ticino in the south of the country, and to a lesser extent in Grisons. Around half a million people in Switzerland have Italian as their first language. Their language rights are protected by the Swiss constitution.

svogli|a'tezza *f* half-heartedness. **~'ato** *adj* lazy

svolaz'za|nte *adj* (capelli) windswept. **~re** *vi* flutter

'svolger|e *vt* unwind; unwrap (pacco); (*risolvere*) solve; (*portare a termine*) carry out; (*sviluppare*) develop. **~si** *vr* (*accadere*) take place. **svolgi'mento** *m* course; (*sviluppo*) development

'svolta *f* turning; *fig* turning-point. **svol'tare** *vi* turn

'svolto *pp di* **svolgere**

svuo'tare *vt* empty [out]

Tt

tabac'c|aio, -a *mf* tobacconist. **~he'ria** *f* tobacconist's. **ta'bacco** *m* tobacco

> **Tabaccheria** By law, cigarettes and other tobacco products can be sold only in *tabaccherie*, which must be licensed by the State. They can be recognized by a sign with a large T. As well as tobacco, *tabaccherie* have a monopoly on postage stamps, lottery tickets, and other items controlled by the State.

ta'bel|la *f* table; (*lista*) list. **~la dei prezzi** price list. **~'lina** *f* (*Math*) multiplication table. **~'lone** *m* wall chart. **~lone del canestro** backboard

taber'nacolo *m* tabernacle

tabù *adj & m inv* taboo

tabu'lato *m* [data] printout

'tacca *f* notch; **di mezza ~** (attore, giornalista) second-rate

tac'cagno *adj* [!] stingy

tac'cheggio *m* shoplifting

tac'chetto *m Sport* stud

tac'chino *m* turkey

tacci'are *vt* **~ qcno di qcsa** accuse sb of sth

'tacco *m* heel; **alzare i tacchi** take to one's heels; **scarpe senza ~** flat shoes. **tacchi** *pl* **a spillo** stiletto heels

taccu'ino *m* notebook

ta'cere *vi* be silent • *vt* say nothing about; **mettere a ~ qcsa** (scandalo) hush sth up

ta'chimetro *m* speedometer

'tacito *adj* silent; (*inespresso*) tacit. **taci'turno** *adj* taciturn

ta'fano *m* horsefly

taffe'ruglio *m* scuffle

'taglia *f* (*riscatto*) ransom; (*ricompensa*) reward; (*statura*) height; (*misura*) size. **~ unica** one size

taglia'carte *m inv* paperknife

taglia'erba *m inv* lawn-mower

tagliafu'oco *adj inv* **porta ~** fire door; **striscia ~** fire break

tagli'ando *m* coupon; **fare il ~** ≈ put one's car in for its MOT

tagli'ar|e *vt* cut; (*attraversare*) cut across; (*interrompere*) cut off; (*togliere*) cut out; carve (carne); mow (erba); **farsi ~e i capelli** have a haircut • *vi* cut. **~si** *vr* cut oneself; **~si i capelli** have a haircut

taglia'telle *fpl* tagliatelle *sg*, *thin, flat strips of egg pasta*

taglieggi'are *vt* extort money from

tagli'e|nte *adj* sharp • *m* cutting edge. **~re** *m* chopping board

'taglio *m* cut; (*il tagliare*) cutting; (*di stoffa*) length; (*parte tagliente*) edge. **~ cesareo** Caesarean section

tagli'ola *f* trap

tagliuz'zare *vt* cut

tail'leur *m inv* [lady's] suit

'talco *m* talcum powder

'tale *adj* such a; (*con nomi plurali*) such; **c'è un ~ disordine** there is such a mess; **non accetto tali scuse** I won't accept such excuses; **il rumore era ~ che non si sentiva nulla** there was so much noise you couldn't hear yourself think; **il ~ giorno** on such and such a day; **quel tal signore** that gentleman; **~ quale** just like • *pron* **un ~** someone; **quel ~** that man; **il tal dei tali** such and such a person

ta'lento *m* talent

tali'smano *m* talisman

tallo'nare *vt* be hot on the heels of

tallon'cino *m* coupon

tal'lone *m* heel

tal'mente *adv* so

ta'lora *adv* = TALVOLTA

'talpa *f* mole

tal'volta *adv* sometimes

tamburel'lare *vi* (*con le dita*) drum; (pioggia:) beat, drum. **tambu'rello** *m* tambourine. **tambu'rino** *m* drummer. **tam'buro** *m* drum

tampona'mento *m* (*Auto*) collision; (*di ferita*) dressing; (*di falla*) plugging. **~ a catena** pile-up. **tampo'nare** *vt* (*urtare*) crash into; (*otturare*) plug. **tam'pone** *m* swab; (*per timbri*) pad; (*per mestruazioni*) tampon; (*Comput*) (*per treni*) buffer

'tana *f* den

'tanfo *m* stench

'tanga *m inv* tanga

tan'gen|te *adj* tangent ●*f* tangent; (*somma*) bribe. **~'topoli** *f widespread corruption in Italy in the early 90s*. **~zi'ale** *f* orbital road

tan'gibile *adj* tangible

'tango *m* tango

tan'tino: **un** ~ *adv* a little [bit]

'tanto *adj* [so] much; (*con nomi plurali*) [so] many, [such] a lot of; **~ tempo** [such] a long time; **non ha tanta pazienza** he doesn't have much patience; **~ tempo quanto ti serve** as much time as you need; **non è ~ intelligente quanto suo padre** he's not as intelligent as his father; **tanti amici quanti parenti** as many friends as relatives ●*pron* much; (*plurale*) many; (*tanto tempo*) a long time; **è un uomo come tanti** he's just an ordinary man; **tanti** (*molte persone*) many people; **non ci vuole così ~** it doesn't take that long; **~ quanto** as much as; **tanti quanti** as many as ●*conj* (*comunque*) anyway, in any case ●*adv* (*così*) so; (*con verbi*) so much; **~ debole** so weak; **è ~ ingenuo da crederle** he's naive enough to believe her; **di ~ in ~** every now and then; **~ l'uno come l'altro** both; **~ quanto** as much as; **tre volte ~** three times as much; **una volta ~** once in a while; **tant'è** so much so; **~ per cambiare** for a change

'tappa *f* stop; (*parte di viaggio*) stage

tappa'buchi *m inv* stopgap

tap'par|e *vt* plug; cork (bottiglia); **~e la bocca a qcno** [!] shut sb up. **~si** *vr* **~si gli occhi** cover one's eyes; **~si il naso** hold one's nose

tappa'rella *f* [!] roller blind

tappe'tino *m* mat; (*Comput*) mouse mat

tap'peto *m* carpet; (*piccolo*) rug; **mandare qcno al ~** knock sb down

tappez'z|are *vt* paper (pareti); (*rivestire*) cover. **~e'ria** *f* tapestry; (*di carta*) wallpaper; (*arte*) upholstery. **~i'ere** *m* upholsterer; (*imbianchino*) decorator

'tappo *m* plug; (*di sughero*) cork; (*di metallo, per penna*) top; ([!]: *persona piccola*) dwarf. **~ di sughero** cork

'tara *f* (*difetto*) flaw; (*ereditaria*) hereditary defect; (*peso*) tare

ta'rantola *f* tarantula

ta'ra|re *vt* calibrate (strumento). **~to** *adj* (*Comm*) discounted; (*Techn*) calibrated; (*Med*) with a hereditary defect; [!] crazy

tarchi'ato *adj* stocky

tar'dare *vi* be late ●*vt* delay

'tard|i *adv* late; **al più ~i** at the latest; **più ~i** later [on]; **sul ~i** late in the day; **far ~i** (*essere in ritardo*) be late; (*con gli amici*) stay up late; **a più ~i** see you later. **tar'divo** *adj* late; (bambino) retarded. **~o** *adj* slow; (*tempo*) late

'targ|a *f* plate; (*Auto*) numberplate. **~a di circolazione** numberplate. **tar'gato** *adj* **un'auto targata...** a car with the registration number.... **~'hetta** *f* (*su porta*) nameplate; (*sulla valigia*) name tag

ta'rif|fa *f* rate, tariff. **~'fario** *m* price list

'tarlo *m* woodworm

'tarma *f* moth

ta'rocco *m* tarot; **ta'rocchi** *pl* tarot

tartagli'are *vi* stutter

'tartaro *adj & m* tartar

tarta'ruga *f* tortoise; (*di mare*) turtle; (*per pettine ecc*) tortoiseshell

tartas'sare *vt* harass

tar'tina *f* canapé

tar'tufo *m* truffle

'tasca *f* pocket; (*in borsa*) compartment; **da ~** pocket *attrib.* **~ da pasticciere** icing bag

ta'scabile *adj* pocket *attrib* ●*m* paperback

tasca'pane *m inv* haversack

ta'schino *m* breast pocket

'tassa *f* tax; (*d'scrizione ecc*) fee; (*doganale*) duty. **~ di circolazione** road tax. **~ d'iscrizione** registration fee

tas'sametro *m* taximeter

tas'sare *vt* tax

tassa|tiva'mente *adv* without question

tassazi'one *f* taxation

tas'sello *m* wedge; (*di stoffa*) gusset

tassì *m inv* taxi. **tas'sista** *mf* taxi driver

'tasso¹ *m* yew; (*animale*) badger

'tasso² *m* rate. **~ di cambio** exchange rate. **~ di interesse** interest rate

ta'stare *vt* feel; (*sondare*) sound; ~ **il terreno** *fig* test the water

tasti'e|ra *f* keyboard. ~**'rista** *mf* keyboarder

'tasto *m* key; (*tatto*) touch. ~ **delicato** *fig* touchy subject. ~ **funzione** (*Comput*) function key. ~ **tabulatore** tab key

'tattica *f* tactics *pl*

'tattico *adj* tactical

'tatto *m* (*senso*) touch; (*accortezza*) tact; **aver** ~ be tactful

tatu'a|ggio *m* tattoo. ~**re** *vt* tattoo

'tavola *f* table; (*illustrazione*) plate; (*asse*) plank. ~ **calda** snackbar

tavo'lato *m* boarding; (*pavimento*) wood floor

tavo'letta *f* bar; (*medicinale*) tablet; **andare a** ~ (*Auto*) drive flat out

tavo'lino *m* small table

'tavolo *m* table. ~ **operatorio** (*Med*) operating table

tavo'lozza *f* palette

'tazza *f* cup; (*del water*) bowl. ~ **da caffè/tè** coffee-cup/teacup

taz'zina *f* ~ **da caffè** espresso coffee cup

T.C.I. *abbr* (Touring Club Italiano) Italian Touring Club

te *pers pron* you; **te l'ho dato** I gave it to you

tè *m inv* tea

tea'trale *adj* theatrical

te'atro *m* theatre. ~ **all'aperto** open-air theatre. ~ **di posa** *Cinema* set. ~ **tenda** *marquee for theatre performances*

'tecnico, -a *adj* technical • *mf* technician • *f* technique

tec'nigrafo *m* drawing board

tecno|lo'gia *f* technology. ~**'logico** *adj* technological

te'desco, -a *adj & mf* German

'tedioso *adj* tedious

te'game *m* saucepan

'teglia *f* baking tin

'tegola *f* tile; *fig* blow

tei'era *f* teapot

tek *m* teak

'tela *f* cloth; (*per quadri, vele*) canvas; (*Theat*) curtain. ~ **cerata** oilcloth. ~ **di lino** linen

te'laio *m* (*di bicicletta, finestra*) frame; (*Auto*) chassis; (*per tessere*) loom

tele'camera *f* television camera

teleco|man'dato *adj* remote-controlled, remote control *attrib*. ~**'mando** *m* remote control

Telecom Italia *f* Italian State telephone company

telecomunicazi'oni *fpl* telecommunications

tele'cro|naca *f* [television] commentary. ~**naca diretta** live [television] coverage. ~**'nista** *mf* television commentator

tele'ferica *f* cableway

telefo'na|re *vt/i* [tele]phone, ring. ~**ta** *f* call. ~**ta interurbana** long-distance call

telefonica'mente *adv* by [tele-]phone

tele'fo|nico *adj* [tele]phone *attrib*. ~**'nino** *m* mobile [phone]. ~**'nista** *mf* operator

te'lefono *m* [tele]phone. ~ **senza filo** cordless [phone]. ~ **interno** internal telephone. ~ **satellitare** satphone. ~ **a schede** cardphone

telegior'nale *m* television news *sg*

tele'grafico *adj* telegraphic; (risposta) monosyllabic; **sii telegrafico** keep it brief

tele'gramma *m* telegram

telela'voro *m* teleworking

tele'matica *f* data communications, telematics

teleno'vela *f* soap opera

teleobiet'tivo *m* telephoto lens

telepa'tia *f* telepathy

telero'manzo *m* television serial

tele'scopio *m* telescope

teleselezi'one *f* subscriber trunk dialling, STD; **chiamare in** ~ dial direct

telespetta'tore, -'trice *mf* viewer

tele'text® *m* Teletext®

televisi'one *f* television; **guardare la** ~ watch television

televi'sivo *adj* television *attrib*; **operatore** ~ television cameraman; **apparecchio** ~ television set

televi'sore *m* television [set]

'tema *m* theme; (*Sch*) essay. **te'matica** *f* main theme

teme'rario *adj* reckless
te'mere *vt* be afraid of, fear ● *vi* be afraid, fear
temperama'tite *m inv* pencil-sharpener
tempera'mento *m* temperament
tempe'ra|re *vt* temper; sharpen (matita). **~to** *adj* temperate. **~'tura** *f* temperature. **~tura ambiente** room temperature
tempe'rino *m* penknife
tem'pe|sta *f* storm. **~sta di neve** snowstorm. **~sta di sabbia** sandstorm
tempe|stiva'mente *adv* quickly. **~'stivo** *adj* timely. **~'stoso** *adj* stormy
'tempia *f* (*Anat*) temple
'tempio *m* (*Relig*) temple
tem'pismo *m* timing
'tempo *m* time; (*atmosferico*) weather; (*Mus*) tempo; (*Gram*) tense; (*di film*) part; (*di partita*) half; **a suo ~** in due course; **~ fa** some time ago; **un ~** once; **ha fatto il suo ~** it's superannuated. **~ supplementare** *Sport* extra time, overtime *Am*. **~'rale** *adj* temporal ● *m* [thunder]storm. **~ranea'mente** *adv* temporarily. **~'raneo** *adj* temporary. **~reggi'are** *vi* play for time
tem'prare *vt* temper
te'nac|e *adj* tenacious. **~ia** *f* tenacity
te'naglia *f* pincers *pl*
'tenda *f* curtain; (*per campeggio*) tent; (*tendone*) awning. **~ a ossigeno** oxygen tent
ten'denz|a *f* tendency. **~ial'mente** *adv* by nature
'tendere *vt* (*allargare*) stretch [out]; (*tirare*) tighten; (*porgere*) hold out; *fig* lay (trappola) ● *vi* **~ a** aim at; (*essere portato a*) tend to
'tendine *m* tendon
ten'do|ne *m* awning; (*di circo*) tent. **~poli** *f inv* tent city
tene'broso *adj* gloomy
te'nente *m* lieutenant
tenera'mente *adv* tenderly
te'ner|e *vt* hold; (*mantenere*) keep; (*gestire*) run; (*prendere*) take; (*seguire*) follow; (*considerare*) consider ● *vi* hold; **~ci a, ~e a** be keen on; **~e per** support (squadra). **~si** *vr* hold on (**a** to); (*in una condizione*) keep oneself; (*seguire*) stick to; **~si indietro** stand back
tene'rezza *f* tenderness. **'tenero** *adj* tender
'tenia *f* tapeworm
'tennis *m* tennis. **~ da tavolo** table tennis. **ten'nista** *mf* tennis player
te'nore *m* standard; (*Mus*) tenor; **a ~ di legge** by law. **~ di vita** standard of living
tensi'one *f* tension; (*Electr*) voltage; **alta ~** high voltage
ten'tacolo *m* tentacle
ten'ta|re *vt* attempt; (*sperimentare*) try; (*indurre in tentazione*) tempt. **~'tivo** *m* attempt. **~zi'one** *f* temptation
tenten'nare *vi* waver
'tenue *adj* fine; (*debole*) weak; (*esiguo*) small; (*leggero*) slight
te'nuta *f* (*capacità*) capacity; (*Sport: resistenza*) stamina; (*possedimento*) estate; (*divisa*) uniform; (*abbigliamento*) clothes *pl*; **a ~ d'aria** airtight. **~ di strada** road holding
teolo'gia *f* theology. **teo'logico** *adj* theological. **te'ologo** *m* theologian
teo'rema *m* theorem
teo'ria *f* theory
teorica'mente *adv* theoretically. **te'orico** *adj* theoretical
te'pore *m* warmth
'teppa *f* mob. **tep'pismo** *m* hooliganism. **tep'pista** *m* hooligan
tera'peutico *adj* therapeutic. **tera'pia** *f* therapy
tergicri'stallo *m* windscreen wiper, windshield wiper *Am*
tergilu'notto *m* rear windscreen wiper
tergiver'sare *vi* hesitate
'tergo *m* **a ~** behind
ter'male *adj* thermal; **stazione ~** spa. **'terme** *fpl* thermal baths
'termico *adj* thermal
termi'na|le *adj & m* terminal; **malato ~le** terminally ill person. **~re** *vt/i* finish, end. **'termine** *m* (*limite*) limit; (*fine*) end; (*condizione, espressione*) term
terminolo'gia *f* terminology
'termite *f* termite
termoco'perta *f* electric blanket
ter'mometro *m* thermometer
'termos *m inv* thermos®

termosi'fone *m* radiator; (*sistema*) central heating

ter'mostato *m* thermostat

'terra *f* earth; (*regione*) land; (*terreno*) ground; (*argilla*) clay; (*cosmetico*) dark face powder (*for impression of tan*); **a ~** (*sulla costa*) ashore; (installazioni) onshore; **per ~** on the ground; **sotto ~** underground. **~'cotta** *f* terracotta; **vasellame di ~cotta** earthenware. **~pi'eno** *m* embankment

ter'razz|a *f*, **~o** *m* balcony

terremo'tato, -a *adj* (zona) affected by an earthquake ● *mf* earthquake victim. **terre'moto** *m* earthquake

ter'reno *adj* earthly ● *m* ground; (*suolo*) soil; (*proprietà terriera*) land; **perdere/guadagnare ~** lose/gain ground. **~ di gioco** playing field

ter'restre *adj* terrestrial; **esercito ~** land forces *pl*

ter'ribil|e *adj* terrible. **~'mente** *adv* terribly

ter'riccio *m* potting compost

terrifi'cante *adj* terrifying

territori'ale *adj* territorial. **terri'torio** *m* territory

ter'rore *m* terror

terro'ris|mo *m* terrorism. **~ta** *mf* terrorist

terroriz'zare *vt* terrorize

'terso *adj* clear

ter'zetto *m* trio

terzi'ario *adj* tertiary

'terzo *adj* third; **di terz'ordine** (locale, servizio) third-rate; **la terza età** the third age ● *m* third; **terzi** *pl* (*Jur*) third party *sg*. **ter'zultimo, -a** *agg & mf* third from last

'tesa *f* brim

'teschio *m* skull

'tesi *f inv* thesis

'teso *pp di* **tendere** ● *adj* taut; *fig* tense

tesor|e'ria *f* treasury. **~i'ere** *m* treasurer

te'soro *m* treasure; (*tesoreria*) treasury

'tessera *f* card; (*abbonamento all'autobus*) season ticket

'tessere *vt* weave; hatch (complotto)

tesse'rino *m* travel card

'tessile *adj* textile. **tessili** *mpl* textiles; (*operai*) textile workers

tessi|'tore, -'trice *mf* weaver

tes'suto *m* fabric; (*Anat*) tissue

'testa *f* head; (*cervello*) brain; **essere in ~ a** be ahead of; **in ~** *Sport* in the lead; **~ o croce?** heads or tails?

'testa-'coda *m inv* **fare un ~** spin right round

testa'mento *m* will; **T~** (*Relig*) Testament

testar'daggine *f* stubbornness. **te'stardo** *adj* stubborn

te'stata *f* head; (*intestazione*) heading; (*colpo*) butt

'teste *mf* witness

te'sticolo *m* testicle

testi'mon|e *mf* witness. **~e oculare** eye witness

testi'monial *mf inv celebrity promoting brand of cosmetics*

testimoni|'anza *f* testimony. **~'are** *vt* testify to ● *vi* give evidence

'testo *m* text; **far ~** be an authority

te'stone, -a *mf* blockhead

testu'ale *adj* textual

'tetano *m* tetanus

'tetro *adj* gloomy

tetta'rella *f* teat

'tetto *m* roof. **~ apribile** sunshine roof. **tet'toia** *f* roofing. **tet'tuccio** *m* **tettuccio apribile** sun-roof

'Tevere *m* Tiber

ti *pers pron* you; (*riflessivo*) yourself; **ti ha dato un libro** he gave you a book; **lavati le mani** wash your hands; **eccoti!** here you are!; **sbrigati!** hurry up!

ti'ara *f* tiara

ticchet't|are *vi* tick. **~io** *m* ticking

'ticchio *m* tic; (*ghiribizzo*) whim

'ticket *m inv* (*per farmaco, esame*) *amount paid by National Health patients*

tiepida'mente *adv* half-heartedly. **ti'epido** *adj* lukewarm

ti'fare *vi* **~ per** shout for. **'tifo** *m* (*Med*) typhus; **fare il tifo per** *fig* be a fan of

tifoi'dea *f* typhoid

ti'fone *m* typhoon

ti'foso, -a *mf* fan

'tiglio *m* lime

ti'grato *adj* **gatto ~** tabby [cat]

'tigre *f* tiger

'tilde *mf* tilde

tim'ballo *m* (*Culin*) pie

t

tim'brare *vt* stamp; ~ **il cartellino** clock in/out

'timbro *m* stamp; (*di voce*) tone

timida'mente *adv* timidly, shyly. **ti-mi'dezza** *f* timidity, shyness. **'timido** *adj* timid, shy

'timo *m* thyme

ti'mon|e *m* rudder. **~i'ere** *m* helmsman

ti'more *m* fear; (*soggezione*) awe

'timpano *m* eardrum; (*Mus*) kettle-drum

ti'nello *m* dining-room

'tinger|e *vt* dye; (*macchiare*) stain. **~si** *vi* (viso, cielo:) be tinged (**di** with); **~si i capelli** have one's hair dyed; (*da solo*) dye one's hair

'tino *m*, **ti'nozza** *f* tub

'tint|a *f* dye; (*colore*) colour; **in ~a unita** plain. **~a'rella** *f* [!] suntan

tintin'nare *vi* tinkle

'tinto *pp di* **tingere**. **~'ria** *f* (*negozio*) cleaner's. **tin'tura** *f* dyeing; (*colorante*) dye.

'tipico *adj* typical

'tipo *m* type; (*individuo*) guy

tipogra'fia *f* printery; (*arte*) typography. **tipo'grafico** *adj* typographic[al]. **ti'pografo** *m* printer

tip tap *m* tap dancing

ti'raggio *m* draught

tiramisù *m inv dessert made of coffee-soaked sponge, eggs, Marsala, cream and cocoa powder*

tiran'nia *f* tyranny. **ti'ranno, -a** *adj* tyrannical ● *mf* tyrant

ti'rar|e *vt* pull; (*gettare*) throw; kick (palla); (*sparare*) fire; (*tracciare*) draw; (*stampare*) print ● *vi* pull; (vento:) blow; (abito:) be tight; (*sparare*) fire; **~e avanti** get by; **~e su** (*crescere*) bring up; (*da terra*) pick up. **~si** *vr* **~si indietro** *fig* back out

tiras'segno *m* target shooting; (*alla fiera*) rifle range

ti'rata *f* tug; **in una ~** in one go

tira'tore *m* shot. **~ scelto** marksman

tira'tura *f* printing; (*di giornali*) circulation; (*di libri*) [print] run

'tirchio *adj* mean

tiri'tera *f* spiel

'tiro *m* (*traino*) draught; (*lancio*) throw; (*sparo*) shot; (*scherzo*) trick. **~ con l'arco** archery. **~ alla fune** tug-of-war. **~ a segno** rifle-range

tiro'cinio *m* apprenticeship

ti'roide *f* thyroid

Tir'reno *m* **il [mar] ~** the Tyrrhenian Sea

ti'sana *f* herb[al] tea

tito'lare *adj* regular ● *mf* principal; (*proprietario*) owner; (*calcio*) regular player

'titolo *m* title; (*accademico*) qualification; (*Comm*) security; **a ~ di** as; **a ~ di favore** as a favour. **titoli** *pl* **di studio** qualifications

titu'ba|nte *adj* hesitant. **~nza** *f* hesitation. **~re** *vi* hesitate

tivù *f inv* [!] TV, telly

'tizio *m* fellow

tiz'zone *m* brand

toc'cante *adj* touching

toc'ca|re *vt* touch; touch on (argomento); (*tastare*) feel; (*riguardare*) concern ● *vi* **~re a** (*capitare*) happen to; **mi tocca aspettare** I'll have to wait; **tocca a te** it's your turn; (*pagare da bere*) it's your round

tocca'sana *m inv* cure-all

'tocco *m* touch; (*di pennello, orologio*) stroke; (*di pane ecc*) chunk ● *adj* [!] crazy, touched

'toga *f* toga; (*accademica, di magistrato*) gown

'toglier|e *vt* take off (coperta); take away (bambino da scuola, sete) (*Math*); take out, remove (dente); **~e qcsa di mano a qcno** take sth away from sb; **~e qcno dei guai** get sb out of trouble; **ciò non toglie che...** nevertheless... **~si** *vr* take off (abito); **~si la vita** take one's [own] life

toilette *f inv*, **to'letta** *f* toilet; (*mobile*) dressing table

tolle'ra|nte *adj* tolerant. **~nza** *f* tolerance. **~re** *vt* tolerate

'tolto *pp di* **togliere**

to'maia *f* upper

'tomba *f* grave, tomb

tom'bino *m* manhole cover

'tombola *f* bingo; (*caduta*) tumble

'tomo *m* tome

'tonaca *f* habit

tonalità *f inv* (*Mus*) tonality

t

'tondo *adj* round ● *m* circle
'tonico *adj & m* tonic
tonifi'care *vt* brace
tonnel'la|ggio *m* tonnage. **~ta** *f* ton
'tonno *m* tuna [fish]
'tono *m* tone
ton'sil|la *f* tonsil. **~'lite** *f* tonsillitis
'tonto *adj* [!] thick
top *m inv* (*indumento*) sun-top
to'pazio *m* topaz
'topless *m inv* **in ~** topless
'topo *m* mouse. **~ di biblioteca** *fig* bookworm
to'ponimo *m* place name
'toppa *f* patch; (*serratura*) keyhole
to'race *m* chest
'torba *f* peat
'torbido *adj* cloudy; *fig* troubled
'torcer|e *vt* twist; wring [out] (biancheria). **~si** *vr* twist
'torchio *m* press
'torcia *f* torch
torci'collo *m* stiff neck
'tordo *m* thrush
to'rero *m* bullfighter
To'rino *f* Turin
tor'menta *f* snowstorm
tormen'tare *vt* torment. **tor'mento** *m* torment
torna'conto *m* benefit
tor'nado *m* tornado
tor'nante *m* hairpin bend
tor'nare *vi* return, go/come back; (*ridiventare*) become again; (conto:) add up; **~ a sorridere** become happy again
tor'neo *m* tournament
'tornio *m* lathe
'torno *m* **togliersi di ~** get out of the way
'toro *m* bull; (*Astr*) **T~**Taurus
tor'pedin|e *f* torpedo
tor'pore *m* torpor
'torre *f* tower; (*scacchi*) castle. **~ di controllo** control tower
torrefazi'one *f* roasting
tor'ren|te *m* torrent, mountain stream; (*fig*: *di lacrime*) flood. **~zi'ale** *adj* torrential
tor'retta *f* turret
'torrido *adj* torrid
torri'one *m* keep
tor'rone *m* nougat
'torso *m* torso; (*di mela, pera*) core; **a ~ nudo** bare-chested
'torsolo *m* core
'torta *f* cake; (*crostata*) tart
tortel'lini *mpl* tortellini, *small packets of pasta stuffed with pork, ham, Parmesan and nutmeg*
torti'era *f* baking tin
tor'tino *m* pie
'torto *pp di* **torcere** ● *adj* twisted ● *m* wrong; (*colpa*) fault; **aver ~** be wrong; **a ~** wrongly
'tortora *f* turtle-dove
tortu'oso *adj* winding; (*ambiguo*) tortuous
tor'tu|ra *f* torture. **~'rare** *vt* torture
'torvo *adj* grim
to'sare *vt* shear
tosa'tura *f* shearing
To'scana *f* Tuscany
'tosse *f* cough
'tossico *adj* toxic ● *m* poison. **tossi'comane** *mf* drug addict
tos'sire *vi* cough
tosta'pane *m inv* toaster
to'stare *vt* toast (pane); roast (caffè)
'tosto *adv* (*subito*) soon ● *adj* [!] cool
tot *adj inv* **una cifra ~** such and such a figure ● *m* **un ~** so much
to'tal|e *adj & m* total. **~ità** *f* entirety; **la ~ità dei presenti** all those present
totali'tario *adj* totalitarian
totaliz'zare *vt* total; score (punti)
total'mente *adv* totally
'totano *m* squid
toto'calcio *m* ≈ [football] pools *pl*
tournée *f inv* tour
to'vagli|a *f* tablecloth. **~'etta** *f* **~etta [all'americana]** place mat. **~'olo** *m* napkin
'tozzo *adj* squat
tra = **FRA**
trabal'la|nte *adj* staggering; (sedia) rickety. **~re** *vi* stagger; (veicolo:) jolt
tra'biccolo *m* [!] contraption; (*auto*) jalopy
traboc'care *vi* overflow
traboc'chetto *m* trap
tracan'nare *vt* gulp down

t

'tracci|a *f* track; (*orma*) footstep; (*striscia*) trail; (*residuo*) trace; *fig* sign. **~'are** *vt* trace; sketch out (schema); draw (linea). **~'ato** *m* (*schema*) layout

tra'chea *f* windpipe

tra'colla *f* shoulder-strap; **borsa a ~** shoulder-bag

tra'collo *m* collapse

tradi'mento *m* betrayal

tra'di|re *vt* betray; be unfaithful to (moglie, marito). **~'tore, ~'trice** *mf* traitor

tradizio'na|le *adj* traditional. **~'lista** *mf* traditionalist. **~l'mente** *adv* traditionally. **tradizi'one** *f* tradition

tra'dotto *pp di* **tradurre**

tra'du|rre *vt* translate. **~t'tore, ~t'trice** *mf* translator. **~ttore elettronico** electronic phrasebook. **~zi'one** *f* translation

tra'ente *mf* (*Comm*) drawer

trafe'lato *adj* breathless

traffi'ca|nte *mf* dealer. **~nte di droga** [drug] pusher. **~re** *vi* (*affaccendarsi*) busy oneself; **~re in** *pej* traffic in. **'traffico** *m* traffic; (*Comm*) trade

tra'figgere *vt* stab; (*straziare*) pierce

tra'fila *f fig* rigmarole

trafo'rare *vt* bore, drill. **tra'foro** *m* boring; (*galleria*) tunnel

trafu'gare *vt* steal

tra'gedia *f* tragedy

traghet'tare *vt* ferry. **tra'ghetto** *m* ferrying; (*nave*) ferry

tragica'mente *adv* tragically. **'tragico** *adj* tragic

tra'gitto *m* journey; (*per mare*) crossing

tragu'ardo *m* finishing post; (*meta*) goal

traiet'toria *f* trajectory

trai'nare *vt* drag; (*rimorchiare*) tow

tralasci'are *vt* interrupt; (*omettere*) leave out

'tralcio *m* (*Bot*) shoot

tra'liccio *m* trellis

tram *m inv* tram, streetcar *Am*

'trama *f* weft; (*di film ecc*) plot

traman'dare *vt* hand down

tra'mare *vt* weave; (*macchinare*) plot

tram'busto *m* turmoil

trame'stio *m* bustle

tramez'zino *m* sandwich

tra'mezzo *m* partition

'tramite *prep* through ● *m* link; **fare da ~** act as go-between

tramon'tana *f* north wind

tramon'tare *vi* set; (*declinare*) decline. **tra'monto** *m* sunset; (*declino*) decline

tramor'tire *vt* stun ● *vi* faint

trampo'lino *m* springboard; (*per lo sci*) ski-jump

'trampolo *m* stilt

tramu'tare *vt* transform

'trancia *f* shears *pl*; (*fetta*) slice

tra'nello *m* trap

trangugi'are *vt* gulp down

'tranne *prep* except

tranquilla'mente *adv* peacefully

tranquil'lante *m* tranquillizer

tranquilli|tà *f* calm; (*di spirito*) tranquillity. **~z'zare** *vt* reassure. **tran'quillo** *adj* quiet; (*pacifico*) peaceful; (*coscienza*) easy

transat'lantico *adj* transatlantic ● *m* ocean liner

tran'sa|tto *pp di* **transigere**. **~zi'one** *f* (*Comm*) transaction

tran'senna *f* (*barriera*) barrier

trans'genico *adj* genetically modified, transgenic

tran'sigere *vi* reach an agreement; (*cedere*) yield

transi'ta|bile *adj* passable. **~re** *vi* pass

transi'tivo *adj* transitive

'transi|to *m* transit; **diritto di ~to** right of way; **"divieto di ~to"** "no thoroughfare". **~'torio** *adj* transitory. **~zi'one** *f* transition

tranvi'ere *m* tram driver

'trapano *m* drill

trapas'sare *vt* go [right] through ● *vi* (*morire*) pass away

tra'passo *m* passage

tra'pezio *m* trapeze; (*Math*) trapezium

trapi|an'tare *vt* transplant. **~'anto** *m* transplant

'trappola *f* trap

tra'punta *f* quilt

'trarre *vt* draw; (*ricavare*) obtain; **~ in inganno** deceive

trasa'lire *vi* start

trasan'dato *adj* shabby

trasbor'dare *vt* transfer; (*Naut*) tran[s]ship ● *vi* change. **tra'sbordo** *m* trans[s]hipment

tra'scendere *vt* transcend ● *vi* (*eccedere*) go too far

trasci'nar|e *vt* drag; (entusiasmo:) carry away. **~si** *vr* drag oneself

tra'scorrere *vt* spend ● *vi* pass

tra'scri|tto *pp di* **trascrivere**. **~vere** *vt* transcribe. **~zi'one** *f* transcription

trascu'ra|bile *adj* negligible. **~re** *vt* neglect; (*non tenere conto di*) disregard. **~'tezza** *f* negligence. **~to** *adj* negligent; (*curato male*) neglected; (*nel vestire*) slovenly

traseco'lato *adj* amazed

trasferi'mento *m* transfer; (*trasloco*) move

trasfe'ri|re *vt* transfer. **~rsi** *vr* move

tra'sferta *f* transfer; (*indennità*) subsistence allowance; *Sport* away match; **giocare in ~** play away

trasfigu'rare *vt* transfigure

trasfor'ma|re *vt* transform; (*in rugby*) convert. **~'tore** *m* transformer. **~zi'one** *f* transformation; (*in rugby*) conversion

trasfor'mista *mf* quick-change artist

trasfusi'one *f* transfusion

trasgre'dire *vt* disobey; (*Jur*) infringe

trasgredi'trice *f* transgressor

trasgres|si'one *f* infringement. **~'sore** *m* transgressor

tra'slato *adj* metaphorical

traslo'car|e *vt* move ● *vi*, **~si** *vr* move house. **tra'sloco** *m* removal

tra'smesso *pp di* **trasmettere**

tra'smett|ere *vt* pass on; (*Radio, TV*) broadcast; (*Med, Techn*) transmit. **~i'tore** *m* transmitter

trasmis'si|bile *adj* transmissible. **~'one** *f* transmission; (*Radio, TV*) programme

trasmit'tente *m* transmitter ● *f* broadcasting station

traso'gna|re *vi* day-dream

traspa'ren|te *adj* transparent. **~za** *f* transparency; **in ~za** against the light. **traspa'rire** *vi* show [through]

traspi'ra|re *vi* perspire; *fig* transpire. **~zi'one** *f* perspiration

tra'sporre *vt* transpose

traspor'tare *vt* transport; **lasciarsi ~ da** get carried away by. **tra'sporto** *m* transport; (*passione*) passion

trastul'lar|e *vt* amuse. **~si** *vr* amuse oneself

trasu'dare *vt* ooze with ● *vi* sweat

trasver'sale *adj* transverse

trasvo'la|re *vt* fly over ● *vi* **~re su** *fig* skim over. **~ta** *f* crossing [by air]

'tratta *f* illegal trade; (*Comm*) draft

trat'tabile *adj* or near offer

tratta'mento *m* treatment. **~ di riguardo** special treatment

trat'ta|re *vt* treat; (*commerciare in*) deal in; (*negoziare*) negotiate ● *vi* **~re di** deal with. **~rsi** *vr* **di che si tratta?** what is it about?; **si tratta di...** it's about.... **~'tive** *fpl* negotiations. **~to** *m* treaty; (*opera scritta*) treatise

tratteggi'are *vt* outline; (*descrivere*) sketch

tratte'ner|e *vt* (*far restare*) keep; hold (respiro, in questura); hold back (lacrime, riso); (*frenare*) restrain; (*da paga*) withhold; **sono stato trattenuto** (*ritardato*) I got held up. **~si** *vr* restrain oneself; (*fermarsi*) stay; **~si su** (*indugiare*) dwell on. **tratteni'mento** *m* entertainment; (*ricevimento*) party

tratte'nuta *f* deduction

trat'tino *m* dash; (*in parole composte*) hyphen

'tratto *pp di* **trarre** ● *m* (*di spazio, tempo*) stretch; (*di penna*) stroke; (*linea*) line; (*brano*) passage; **tratti** *pl* features; **a tratti** at intervals; **ad un ~** suddenly

trat'tore *m* tractor

tratto'ria *f* restaurant

'trauma *m* trauma. **trau'matico** *adj* traumatic

tra'vaglio *m* labour; (*angoscia*) anguish

trava'sare *vt* decant

'trave *f* beam

tra'versa *f* crossbar; **è una ~ di Via Roma** it's off Via Roma

traver'sa|re *vt* cross. **~ta** *f* crossing

traver'sie *fpl* misfortunes

traver'sina *f* (*Rail*) sleeper

tra'vers|o *adj* crosswise ● *adv* **di ~o** crossways; **andare di ~o** (cibo:) go down the wrong way; **camminare di ~o** not walk in a straight line. **~one** *m* (*in calcio*) cross

t

travesti'mento *m* disguise
trave'sti|re *vt* disguise. **~rsi** *vr* disguise oneself. **~to** *adj* disguised ● *m* transvestite
travi'are *vt* lead astray
travi'sare *vt* distort
tra'vol|gere *vt* sweep away; (*sopraffare*) overwhelm. **~to** *pp di* **travolgere**
trazi'one *f* traction. **~ anteriore/ posteriore** front-/rear-wheel drive
tre *adj & m* three
trebbi'a|re *vt* thresh
'treccia *f* plait, braid
tre'cento *adj & m* three hundred; **il T~** the fourteenth century
tredi'cesima *f Christmas bonus of one month's pay*
'tredici *adj & m* thirteen
'tregua *f* truce; *fig* respite
tre'mare *vi* tremble; (*di freddo*) shiver
tremenda'mente *adv* terribly. **tre'mendo** *adj* terrible; **ho una fame tremenda** I'm very hungry
tremen'tina *f* turpentine
tre'mila *adj & m* three thousand
'tremito *m* tremble
tremo'lare *vi* shake; (luce:) flicker. **tre'more** *m* trembling
tre'nino *m* miniature railway
'treno *m* train
'tren|ta *adj & m* thirty; **~ta e lode** top marks. **~tatré giri** *m inv* LP. **~'tenne** *adj & mf* thirty-year-old. **~'tesimo** *adj & m* thirtieth. **~'tina** *f* **una ~tina di** about thirty
trepi'dare *vi* be anxious. **'trepido** *adj* anxious
treppi'ede *m* tripod
'tresca *f* intrigue; (*amorosa*) affair
tri'angolo *m* triangle
tri'bale *adj* tribal
tribo'la|re *vi* suffer; (*fare fatica*) go through trials and tribulations. **~zi'one** *f* tribulation
tribù *f inv* tribe
tri'buna *f* tribune; (*per uditori*) gallery; *Sport* stand. **~ coperta** stand
tribu'nale *m* court
tribu'tare *vt* bestow
tribu'tario *adj* tax *attrib*. **tri'buto** *m* tribute; (*tassa*) tax
tri'checo *m* walrus
tri'ciclo *m* tricycle
trico'lore *adj* three-coloured ● *m* (*bandiera*) tricolour
tri'dente *m* trident
trien'nale *adj* (*ogni tre anni*) three-yearly; (*lungo tre anni*) three-year. **tri'ennio** *m* three-year period
tri'foglio *m* clover
trifo'lato *adj sliced and cooked with olive oil, parsley and garlic*
'triglia *f* mullet
trigonome'tria *f* trigonometry
tri'mestre *m* quarter; (*Sch*) term
'trina *f* lace
trin'ce|a *f* trench
trincia'pollo *m inv* poultry shears *pl*
trinci'are *vt* cut up
Trinità *f* Trinity
'trio *m* trio
trion'fa|le *adj* triumphal. **~nte** *adj* triumphant. **~re** *vi* triumph; **~re su** triumph over. **tri'onfo** *m* triumph
tripli'care *vt* triple. **'triplice** *adj* triple; **in triplice [copia]** in triplicate. **'triplo** *adj* treble ● *m* **il triplo (di)** three times as much (as)
'trippa *f* tripe; (!: *pancia*) belly
'trist|e *adj* sad; (luogo) gloomy. **tri'stezza** *f* sadness. **~o** *adj* wicked; (*meschino*) miserable
trita'carne *m inv* mincer
tri'ta|re *vt* mince. **'trito** *adj* **trito e ritrito** well-worn, trite
'trittico *m* triptych
tritu'rare *vt* chop finely
triumvi'rato *m* triumvirate
tri'vella *f* drill. **trivel'lare** *vt* drill
trivi'ale *adj* vulgar
tro'feo *m* trophy
'trogolo *m* (*per maiali*) trough
'troia *f* sow; (⊠ *donna*) whore
'tromba *f* trumpet; (*Auto*) horn; (*delle scale*) well. **~ d'aria** whirlwind
trom'b|etta *m* toy trumpet. **~one** *m* trombone
trom'bosi *f* thrombosis
tron'care *vt* sever; truncate (parola)
'tronco *adj* truncated; **licenziare in ~** fire on the spot ● *m* trunk; (*di strada*) section. **tron'cone** *m* stump
troneggi'are *vi* **~ su** tower over

'trono *m* throne

tropi'cale *adj* tropical. **'tropico** *m* tropic

'troppo *adj* too much; (*con nomi plurali*) too many ● *pron* too much; (*plurale*) too many; (*troppo tempo*) too long; **troppi** (*troppa gente*) too many people ● *adv* too; (*con verbi*) too much; **~ stanco** too tired; **ho mangiato ~** I ate too much; **hai fame? - non ~** are you hungry? - not very

'trota *f* trout

trot'tare *vi* trot. **trotterel'lare** *vi* trot along; (bimbo:) toddle

'trotto *m* trot; **andare al ~** trot

'trottola *f* [spinning] top; (*movimento*) spin

troupe *f inv* **~ televisiva** camera crew

tro'va|re *vt* find; (*scoprire*) find out; (*incontrare*) meet; (*ritenere*) think; **andare a ~re** go and see. **~rsi** *vr* find oneself; (luogo:) be; (*sentirsi*) feel. **~ta** *f* bright idea. **~ta pubblicitaria** advertising gimmick

truc'ca|re *vt* make up; (*falsificare*) fix ⊠. **~rsi** *vr* make up

'trucco *m* (*cosmetico*) make-up; (*imbroglio*) trick

'truce *adj* fierce; (delitto) appalling

truci'dare *vt* slay

'truciolo *m* shaving

trucu'lento *adj* truculent

'truffa *f* fraud. **truf'fare** *vt* swindle. **~'tore, ~trice** *mf* swindler

'truppa *f* troops *pl*; (*gruppo*) group

tu *pers pron* you; **sei tu?** is that you?; **l'hai fatto tu?** did you do it yourself?; **a tu per tu** in private; **darsi del tu** *use the familiar tu*

'tuba *f* tuba; (*cappello*) top hat

tuba'tura *f* piping

tubazi'oni *fpl* piping *sg*, pipes

tuberco'losi *f* tuberculosis

tu'betto *m* tube

tu'bino *m* (*vestito*) shift

'tubo *m* pipe; (*Anat*) canal; **non ho capito un ~** ⊡ I understood zilch. **~ di scappamento** exhaust [pipe]

tuf'fa|re *vt* plunge. **~rsi** *vr* dive. **~'tore, ~'trice** *mf* diver

'tuffo *m* dive; (*bagno*) dip; **ho avuto un ~ al cuore** my heart missed a beat. **~ di testa** dive

'tufo *m* tufa

tu'gurio *m* hovel

tuli'pano *m* tulip

'tulle *m* tulle

tume'fa|tto *adj* swollen. **~zi'one** *f* swelling. **'tumido** *adj* swollen

tu'more *m* tumour

tumulazi'one *f* burial

tu'mult|o *m* turmoil; (*sommossa*) riot. **~u'oso** *adj* uproarious

'tunica *f* tunic

Tuni'sia *f* Tunisia

'tunnel *m inv* tunnel

'tuo (**il ~** *m*, **la tua** *f*, **i ~i** *mpl*, **le tue** *fpl*) *poss adj* your; **è tua questa macchina?** is this car yours?; **un ~ amico** a friend of yours; **~ padre** your father ● *poss pron* yours; **i tuoi** your folks

tuo'nare *vi* thunder. **tu'ono** *m* thunder

tu'orlo *m* yolk

tu'racciolo *m* stopper; (*di sughero*) cork

tu'rar|e *vt* stop; cork (bottiglia). **~si** *vr* become blocked; **~si il naso** hold one's nose

turba'mento *m* disturbance; (*sconvolgimento*) upsetting. **~ della quiete pubblica** breach of the peace

tur'bante *m* turban

tur'ba|re *vt* upset. **~rsi** *vr* get upset. **~to** *adj* upset

tur'bina *f* turbine

turbi'nare *vi* whirl. **'turbine** *m* whirl. **turbine di vento** whirlwind

turbo'lenza *f* turbulence

turboreat'tore *m* turbo-jet

tur'chese *adj & mf* turquoise

Tur'chia *f* Turkey

tur'chino *adj & m* deep blue

'turco, -a *adj* Turkish ● *mf* Turk ● *m* (*lingua*) Turkish; *fig* double Dutch; **fumare come un ~** smoke like a chimney

tu'ris|mo *m* tourism. **~ culturale** heritage tourism. **~ta** *mf* tourist. **~tico** *adj* tourist *attrib*

'turno *m* turn; **a ~** in turn; **di ~** on duty; **fare a ~** take turns. **~ di notte** night shift

'turp|e *adj* base

'tuta *f* overalls *pl*; *Sport* tracksuit. **~ da**

lavoro overalls *pl*. ~ **mimetica** camouflage. ~ **spaziale** spacesuit. ~ **subacquea** wetsuit

tu'tela *f* (*Jur*) guardianship; (*protezione*) protection. **tute'lare** *vt* protect

tu'tina *f* sleepsuit; (*da danza*) leotard

tu'tore, -'trice *mf* guardian

'tutta *f* **mettercela** ~ **per fare qcsa** go flat out for sth

tutta'via *conj* nevertheless

'tutto *adj* whole; (*con nomi plurali*) all; (*ogni*) every; **tutta la classe** the whole class, all the class; **tutti gli alunni** all the pupils; **a tutta velocità** at full speed; **ho aspettato** ~ **il giorno** I waited all day [long]; **in** ~ **il mondo** all over the world; **noi tutti** all of us; **era tutta contenta** she was delighted; **tutti e due** both; **tutti e tre** all three ● *pron* all; (*tutta la gente*) everybody; (*tutte le cose*) everything; (*qualunque cosa*) anything; **l'ho mangiato** ~ I ate it all; **le ho lavate tutte** I washed them all; **raccontami** ~ tell me everything; **lo sanno tutti** everybody knows; **è capace di** ~ he's capable of anything; ~ **compreso** all in; **del** ~ quite; **in** ~ altogether ● *adv* completely; **tutt'a un tratto** all at once; **tutt'altro** not at all; **tutt'altro che** anything but ● *m* whole. ~**'fare** *adj inv & nmf* **[impiegato]** ~ general handyman; **donna** ~ general maid

tut'tora *adv* still

tutù *m inv* tutu, ballet dress

tv *f inv* TV

Uu

ubbidi'en|te *adj* obedient. ~**za** *f* obedience. **ubbi'dire** *vi* ~ **(a)** obey

ubi'ca|to *adj* located. ~**zi'one** *f* location

ubria'car|e *vt* get drunk. ~**si** *vr* get drunk; ~**si di** *fig* become intoxicated with

ubria'chezza *f* drunkenness; **in stato di** ~ inebriated

ubri'aco, -a *adj* drunk ● *mf* drunk

ubria'cone *m* drunkard

uccelli'era *f* aviary. **uc'cello** *m* bird; (☒: *pene*) cock

uc'cider|e *vt* kill. ~**si** *vr* kill oneself

ucci|si'one *f* killing. **uc'ciso** *pp di* **uccidere**. ~**'sore** *m* killer

u'dente *adj* **i non udenti** the hearing-impaired

u'dibile *adj* audible

udi'enza *f* audience; (*colloquio*) interview; (*Jur*) hearing

u'di|re *vt* hear. ~**'tivo** *adj* auditory. ~**to** *m* hearing. ~**'tore,** ~**'trice** *mf* listener; (*Sch*) unregistered student (*allowed to attend lectures*). ~**'torio** *m* audience

uffici'al|e *adj* official ● *m* officer; (*funzionario*) official; **pubblico** ~**e** public official. ~**iz'zare** *vt* make official

uf'ficio *m* office; (*dovere*) duty. ~ **di collocamento** employment office. ~ **informazioni** information office. ~ **del personale** personnel department. ~**sa'mente** *adv* unofficially

uffici'oso *adj* unofficial

'ufo[1] *m inv* ufo

'ufo[2]: **a** ~ *adv* without paying

uggi'oso *adj* boring

uguagli'a|nza *f* equality. ~**re** *vt* make equal; (*essere uguale*) equal; (*livellare*) level. ~**rsi** *vr* ~**rsi a** compare oneself to

ugu'al|e *adj* equal; (*lo stesso*) the same; (*simile*) like. ~**'mente** *adv* equally; (*malgrado tutto*) all the same

'ulcera *f* ulcer

uli'veto *m* olive grove

ulteri'or|e *adj* further. ~**'mente** *adv* further

ultima'mente *adv* lately

ulti'ma|re *vt* complete. ~**tum** *m inv* ultimatum

ulti'missime *fpl* stop press *sg*

'ultimo *adj* last; (*notizie ecc*) latest; (*più lontano*) farthest; *fig* ultimate ● *m* last; **fino all'**~ to the last; **per** ~ at the end; **l'**~ **piano** the top floor

ultrà *mf inv Sport* fanatical supporter

ultramo'derno *adj* ultramodern

ultra'rapido *adj* extra-fast

ultrasen'sibile *adj* ultrasensitive

ultra's|onico *adj* ultrasonic. **~u'ono** *m* ultrasound

ultravio'letto *adj* ultraviolet

ulu'la|re *vi* howl. **~to** *m* howling

umana'mente *adv* (trattare) humanely; **~ impossibile** not humanly possible

uma'nesimo *m* humanism

umanità *f* humanity. **umani'tario** *adj* humanitarian. **u'mano** *adj* human; (*benevolo*) humane

umidifica'tore *m* humidifier

umidità *f* dampness; (*di clima*) humidity. **'umido** *adj* damp; (clima) humid; (mani, occhi) moist ● *m* dampness; **in umido** (*Culin*) stewed

'umile *adj* humble

umili'a|nte *adj* humiliating. **~re** *vt* humiliate. **~rsi** *vr* humble oneself. **~zi'one** *f* humiliation. **umil'mente** *adv* humbly. **umilità** *f* humility

u'more *m* humour; (*stato d'animo*) mood; **di cattivo/buon ~** in a bad/good mood

umo'ris|mo *m* humour. **~ta** *mf* humorist. **~tico** *adj* humorous

un *in def art*

> **!** **Un/una** si traduce con *one* quando si tratta di un numero

a;

····➤ (*davanti a vocale o h muta*) an; ▷**UNO**

una *indef art f* a; ▷**UN**

u'nanim|e *adj* unanimous. **~e'mente** *adv* unanimously. **~ità** *f* unanimity; **all'~ità** unanimously

unci'nato *adj* hooked; (parentesi) angle

un'cino *m* hook

'undici *adj & m* eleven

'unger|e *vt* grease; (*sporcare*) get greasy; (*Relig*) anoint; (*blandire*) flatter. **~si** *vr* (*con olio solare*) oil oneself; **~si le mani** get one's hands greasy

unghe'rese *adj & mf* Hungarian. **Unghe'ria** *f* Hungary

'unghi|a *f* nail; (*di animale*) claw. **~'ata** *f* (*graffio*) scratch

ungu'ento *m* ointment

unica'mente *adv* only. **'unico** *adj* only; (*singolo*) single; (*incomparabile*) unique

unifi'ca|re *vt* unify. **~zi'one** *f* unification

unifor'mar|e *vt* level. **~si** *vr* conform (**a** to)

uni'form|e *adj & f* uniform. **~ità** *f* uniformity

unilate'rale *adj* unilateral

uni'one *f* union; (*armonia*) unity. **U~ Europea** European Union. **U~ Monetaria Europea** European Monetary Union. **~ sindacale** trade union

u'ni|re *vt* unite; (*collegare*) join; blend (colori ecc). **~rsi** *vr* unite; (*collegarsi*) join

'unisex *adj inv* unisex

unità *f inv* unity; (*Math, Mil*) unit; (*Comput*) drive. **~rio** *adj* unitary

u'nito *adj* united; (tinta) plain

univer'sal|e *adj* universal. **~'mente** *adv* universally

università *f inv* university. **~rio, -a** *adj* university *attrib* ● *mf* (*insegnante*) university lecturer; (*studente*) undergraduate

> **i** **Università** Italy's first university was founded in Bologna in 1088, and they are still run on traditional lines. Oral exams are the norm. Students study for a number of exams, which can be taken in a flexible order. For this reason Italian students often combine study with a job. The drop-out rate is high.

uni'verso *m* universe

uno, -a *indef art* (*before s + consonant, gn, ps, z*) a

● *pron* one; **a ~ a ~** one by one; **l'~ e l'altro** both [of them]; **né l'~ né l'altro** neither [of them]; **~ di noi** one of us; **~ fa quello che può** you do what you can

● *adj* a, one

● *m* (*numerale*) one; (*un tale*) some man;

● *f* some woman

'unt|o *pp di* **ungere** ● *adj* greasy ● *m* grease. **~u'oso** *adj* greasy. **unzi'one** *f* **l'Estrema Unzione** Extreme Unction

u'omo *m* (*pl* **uomini**) man. **~ d'affari** business man. **~ di fiducia** right-hand man. **~ di Stato** statesman
u'ovo *m* (*pl f* **uova**) egg. **~ in camicia** poached egg. **~ alla coque** boiled egg. **~ di Pasqua** Easter egg. **~ sodo** hard-boiled egg. **~ strapazzato** scrambled egg
ura'gano *m* hurricane
u'ranio *m* uranium
urba'n|esimo *m* urbanization. **~ista** *mf* town planner. **~istica** *f* town planning. **~istico** *adj* urban. **urbanizza'zi'one** *f* urbanization. **ur'bano** *adj* urban; (*cortese*) urbane
ur'gen|te *adj* urgent. **~te'mente** *adv* urgently. **~za** *f* urgency; **in caso d'~za** in an emergency; **d'~za** (misura, chiamata) emergency
'urgere *vi* be urgent
u'rina *f* urine. **uri'nare** *vi* urinate
ur'lare *vi* yell; (cane, vento:) howl. **'urlo** *m* (*pl m* **urli,** *f* **urla**) shout; (*di cane, vento*) howling
'urna *f* urn; (*elettorale*) ballot box; **andare alle urne** go to the polls
urrà *int* hurrah!
ur'tar|e *vt* knock against; (*scontrarsi*) bump into; *fig* irritate. **~si** *vr* collide; *fig* clash
'urto *m* knock; (*scontro*) crash; (*contrasto*) conflict; *fig* clash; **d'~** (misure, terapia) shock
usa e getta *adj inv* (rasoio, siringa) disposable
u'sanza *f* custom; (*moda*) fashion
u'sa|re *vt* use; (*impiegare*) employ; (*esercitare*) exercise; **~re fare qcsa** be in the habit of doing sth • *vi* (*essere di moda*) be fashionable; **non si usa più** it is out of fashion; it's not used any more. **~to** *adj* used; (*non nuovo*) second-hand
u'scente *adj* (presidente) outgoing
usci'ere *m* usher. **'uscio** *m* door
u'sci|re *vi* come out; (*andare fuori*) go out; (*sfuggire*) get out; (*essere sorteggiato*) come up; (giornale:) come out; **~re da** (*Comput*) exit from, quit; **~re di strada** leave the road. **~ta** *f* exit, way out; (*spesa*) outlay; (*di autostrada*) junction; (*battuta*) witty remark; **essere in libera ~ta** be off duty. **~ta di servizio** back door. **~ta di sicurezza** emergency exit
usi'gnolo *m* nightingale
'uso *m* use; (*abitudine*) custom; (*usanza*) usage; **fuori ~** out of use; **per ~ esterno** for external use only
U.S.S.L. *f abbr* (Unità Socio-Sanitaria Locale) local health centre
ustio'na|rsi *vr* burn oneself • **~to** *adj* burnt. **usti'one** *f* burn
usu'ale *adj* usual
usufru'ire *vi* **~ di** take advantage of
u'sura *f* usury
usur'pare *vt* usurp
u'tensile *m* tool; (*Culin*) utensil; **cassetta degli utensili** tool box
u'tente *mf* user. **~ finale** end user
u'tenza *f* use; (*utenti*) users *pl*. **~ finale** end users
ute'rino *adj* uterine. **'utero** *m* womb
'util|e *adj* useful • *m* (*Comm*) profit. **~ità** *f* usefulness; (*Comput*) utility. **~i'taria** *f* (*Auto*) small car. **~i'tario** *adj* utilitarian
utiliz'za|re *vt* utilize. **~zi'one** *f* utilization. **uti'lizzo** *m* use
uto'pistico *adj* Utopian
'uva *f* grapes *pl*; **chicco d'~** grape. **~ passa** raisins *pl*. **~ sultanina** currants *pl*

Vv

va'cante *adj* vacant
va'canza *f* holiday; (*posto vacante*) vacancy. **essere in ~** be on holiday
'vacca *f* cow. **~ da latte** dairy cow
vacc|i'nare *vt* vaccinate. **~inazi'one** *f* vaccination. **vac'cino** *m* vaccine
vacil'la|nte *adj* tottering; (oggetto) wobbly; (luce) flickering; *fig* wavering. **~re** *vi* totter; (oggetto:) wobble; (luce:) flicker; *fig* waver
'vacuo *adj* (*vano*) vain; *fig* empty • *m* vacuum
vagabon'dare *vi* wander. **vaga'bondo, -a** *adj* (cane) stray; **gente vagabonda** tramps *pl* • *mf* tramp

va'gare *vi* wander
vagheggi'are *vt* long for
va'gi|na *f* vagina. **~'nale** *adj* vaginal
va'gi|re *vi* whimper
'vaglia *m inv* money order. **~ bancario** bank draft. **~ postale** postal order
vagli'are *vt* sift; *fig* weigh
'vago *adj* vague
vagon'cino *m* (*di funivia*) car
va'gone *m* (*per passeggeri*) carriage; (*per merci*) wagon. **~ letto** sleeper. **~ ristorante** restaurant car
vai'olo *m* smallpox
va'langa *f* avalanche
va'lente *adj* skilful
va'ler|e *vi* be worth; (*contare*) count; (regola:) apply (**per** to); (*essere valido*) be valid; **far ~e i propri diritti** assert one's rights; **farsi ~e** assert oneself; **non vale!** that's not fair! ● *vt* **~re qcsa a qcno** (*procurare*) earn sb sth; **~ne la pena** be worth it; **vale la pena di vederlo** it's worth seeing; **~si di** avail oneself of
valeri'ana *f* valerian
va'levole *adj* valid
vali'care *vt* cross. **'valico** *m* pass
validità *f* validity; **con ~ illimitata** valid indefinitely
'valido *adj* valid; (*efficace*) efficient; (contributo) valuable
valige'ria *f* (*fabbrica*) leather factory; (*negozio*) leather goods shop
va'ligia *f* suitcase; **fare le valigie** pack one's bags. **~ diplomatica** diplomatic bag
val'lata *f* valley. **'valle** *f* valley; **a valle** downstream
val'lett|a *f* (*TV*) assistant. **~o** *m* valet; (*TV*) assistant
val'lone *m* (*valle*) deep valley
va'lor|e *m* value; (*merito*) merit; (*coraggio*) valour; **~i** *pl* (*Comm*) securities; **di ~e** (oggetto) valuable; **oggetti** *pl* **di ~e** valuables; **senza ~e** worthless. **~iz'zare** *vt* (*mettere in valore*) use to advantage; (*aumentare di valore*) increase the value of; (*migliorare l'aspetto di*) enhance
valo'roso *adj* courageous
'valso *pp di* **valere**
va'luta *f* currency. **~ estera** foreign currency
valu'ta|re *vt* value; weigh up (situazione). **~rio** *adj* (mercato, norme) currency. **~zi'one** *f* valuation
'valva *f* valve. **'valvola** *f* valve; (*Electr*) fuse
vam'pata *f* blaze; (*di calore*) blast; (*al viso*) flush
vam'piro *m* vampire
vana'mente *adv* in vain
van'da|lico *adj* **atto ~lico** act of vandalism. **~'lismo** *m* vandalism. **'vandalo** *m* vandal
vaneggi'are *vi* rave
'vanga *f* spade. **van'gare** *vt* dig
van'gelo *m* Gospel; (🅸: *verità*) gospel [truth]
vanifi'care *vt* nullify
va'nigli|a *f* vanilla. **~'ato** *adj* (zucchero) vanilla *attrib*
vanità *f* vanity. **vani'toso** *adj* vain
'vano *adj* vain ● *m* (*stanza*) room; (*spazio vuoto*) hollow
van'taggi|o *m* advantage; *Sport* lead; *Tennis* advantage; **trarre ~o da qcsa** derive benefit from sth. **~'oso** *adj* advantageous
van't|are *vt* praise; (*possedere*) boast. **~arsi** *vr* boast. **~e'ria** *f* boasting. **'vanto** *m* boast
'vanvera *f* **a ~** at random; **parlare a ~** talk nonsense
va'por|e *m* steam; (*di benzina, cascata*) vapour; **a ~e** steam *attrib*; **al ~e** (*Culin*) steamed. **~e acqueo** steam, water vapour; **battello a ~e** steamboat. **vapo'retto** *m* ferry. **~i'era** *f* steam engine
vaporiz'za|re *vt* vaporize. **~'tore** *m* spray
vapo'roso *adj* (vestito) filmy; **capelli vaporosi** big hair *sg*
va'rare *vt* launch
var'care *vt* cross. **'varco** *m* passage; **aspettare al varco** lie in wait
vari'abil|e *adj* variable ● *f* variable. **~ità** *f* variability
vari'a|nte *f* variant. **~re** *vt/i* vary; **~re di umore** change one's mood. **~zi'one** *f* variation
va'rice *f* varicose vein
vari'cella *f* chickenpox
vari'coso *adj* varicose
varie'gato *adj* variegated

varietà *f inv* variety ●*m inv* variety show

'vario *adj* varied; (*al pl, parecchi*) various; **vari** *pl* (*molti*) several; **varie ed eventuali** any other business

vario'pinto *adj* multicoloured

'varo *m* launch

va'saio *m* potter

'vasca *f* tub; (*piscina*) pool; (*lunghezza*) length. **~ da bagno** bath

va'scello *m* vessel

va'schetta *f* tub

vase'lina *f* Vaseline®

vasel'lame *m* china. **~ d'oro/d'argento** gold/silver plate

'vaso *m* pot; (*da fiori*) vase; (*Anat*) vessel; (*per cibi*) jar. **~ da notte** chamber pot

vas'soio *m* tray

vastità *f* vastness. **'vasto** *adj* vast; **di vaste vedute** broad-minded

Vati'cano *m* Vatican

ve *pers pron* you; **ve l'ho dato** I gave it to you

vecchia *f* old woman. **vecchi'aia** *f* old age. **'vecchio** *adj* old ●*mf* old man; **i vecchi** old people

'vece *f* **in ~ di** in place of; **fare le veci di qcno** take sb's place

ve'dente *adj* **i non vedenti** the visually handicapped

ve'der|e *vt/i* see; **far ~e** show; **farsi ~e** show one's face; **non vedo l'ora di...** I can't wait to.... **~si** *vr* see oneself; (*reciproco*) see each other

ve'detta *f* lookout; (*Naut*) patrol vessel

'vedovo, -a *m* widower ●*f* widow

ve'duta *f* view

vee'mente *adj* vehement

vege'ta|le *adj & m* vegetable. **~li'ano** *adj & mf* vegan. **~re** *vi* vegetate. **~ri'ano, -a** *adj & mf* vegetarian. **~zi'one** *f* vegetation

'vegeto *adj* ▷**VIVO**

veg'gente *mf* clairvoyant

'veglia *f* watch; **fare la ~** keep watch. **~ funebre** vigil

vegli|'are *vi* be awake; **~are su** watch over. **~'one** *m* **~one di Capodanno** New Year's Eve celebration

ve'icolo *m* vehicle

'vela *f* sail; (*Sport*) sailing; **far ~** set sail

ve'la|re *vt* veil; (*fig: nascondere*) hide. **~rsi** *vr* (vista:) mist over; (voce:) go husky. **~ta'mente** *adv* indirectly. **~to** *adj* veiled; (occhi) misty; (collant) sheer

'velcro® *m* velcro®

veleggi'are *vi* sail

ve'leno *m* poison. **vele'noso** *adj* poisonous

veli'ero *m* sailing ship

ve'lina *f* **(carta) ~** tissue paper; (*copia*) carbon copy

ve'lista *m* yachtsman ●*f* yachtswoman

ve'livolo *m* aircraft

vellei'tario *adj* unrealistic

'vello *m* fleece

vellu'tato *adj* velvety. **vel'luto** *m* velvet. **velluto a coste** corduroy

'velo *m* veil; (*di zucchero, cipria*) dusting; (*tessuto*) voile

ve'loc|e *adj* fast. **~e'mente** *adv* quickly. **velo'cista** *mf* (*Sport*) sprinter. **~ità** *f inv* speed; (*Auto: marcia*) gear. **~iz'zare** *vt* speed up

ve'lodromo *m* cycle track

'vena *f* vein; **essere in ~ di** be in the mood for

ve'nale *adj* venal; (persona) mercenary, venal

ve'nato *adj* grainy

vena'torio *adj* hunting *attrib*

vena'tura *f* (*di legno*) grain; (*di foglia, marmo*) vein

ven'demmi|a *f* grape harvest. **~'are** *vt* harvest

'vender|e *vt* sell. **~si** *vr* sell oneself; **"vendesi"** "for sale"

ven'detta *f* revenge

vendi'ca|re *vt* avenge. **~rsi** *vr* get one's revenge. **~'tivo** *adj* vindictive

'vendi|ta *f* sale; **in ~ta** on sale. **~ta all'asta** sale by auction. **~ta al dettaglio** retailing. **~ta all'ingrosso** wholesaling. **~ta al minuto** retailing. **~'tore, ~'trice** *mf* seller. **~tore ambulante** hawker, pedlar

vene'ra|bile, ~ndo *adj* venerable

vene'ra|re *vt* revere

venerdì *m inv* Friday. **V~ Santo** Good Friday

'Venere *f* Venus. **ve'nereo** *adj* venereal

Ve'nezi|a *f* Venice. **v~'ano, -a** *agg & mf* Venetian ●*f* (*persiana*) Venetian blind; (*Culin*) sweet bun

V

veni'ale *adj* venial

ve'nire *vi* come; (*riuscire*) turn out; (*costare*) cost; (*in passivi*) be; **~ a sapere** learn; **~ in mente** occur; **~ meno** (*svenire*) faint; **~ meno a un contratto** go back on a contract; **~ via** come away; (*staccarsi*) come off; **vieni a prendermi** come and pick me up

ven'taglio *m* fan

ven'tata *f* gust [of wind]; *fig* breath

ven'te|nne *adj & mf* twenty-year-old. **~simo** *adj & m* twentieth. **'venti** *adj & m* twenty

venti'la|re *vt* air. **~'tore** *m* fan. **~zi'one** *f* ventilation

ven'tina *f* **una ~** (*circa venti*) about twenty

ventiquat'trore *f inv* (*valigia*) overnight case

'vento *m* wind; **farsi ~** fan oneself

ven'tosa *f* sucker

ven'toso *adj* windy

'ventre *m* stomach. **ven'triloquo** *m* ventriloquist

ven'tura *f* fortune

ven'turo *adj* next

ve'nuta *f* coming

vera'mente *adv* really

ve'randa *f* veranda

ver'bal|e *adj* verbal ● *m* (*di riunione*) minutes *pl*. **~'mente** *adv* verbally

'verbo *m* verb. **~ ausiliare** auxiliary [verb]

'verde *adj* green ● *m* green; (*vegetazione*) greenery; (*semaforo*) green light. **~ oliva** olive green. **~'rame** *m* verdigris

ver'detto *m* verdict

ver'dura *f* vegetables *pl*; **una ~** a vegetable

'verga *f* rod

vergi'n|ale *adj* virginal. **'vergine** *f* virgin; (*Astr*) **V~** Virgo ● *adj* virgin; (cassetta) blank. **~ità** *f* virginity

ver'gogna *f* shame; (*timidezza*) shyness

vergo'gn|arsi *vr* feel ashamed; (*essere timido*) feel shy. **~oso** *adj* ashamed; (*timido*) shy; (*disonorevole*) shameful

ve'rifica *f* check. **verifi'cabile** *adj* verifiable

verifi'car|e *vt* check. **~si** *vr* come true

ve'rismo *m* realism

verit|à *f* truth. **~i'ero** *adj* truthful

'verme *m* worm. **~ solitario** tapeworm

ver'miglio *adj & m* vermilion

'vermut *m inv* vermouth

ver'nacolo *m* vernacular

ver'nic|e *f* paint; (*trasparente*) varnish; (*pelle*) patent leather; *fig* veneer; **"vernice fresca"** "wet paint". **~i'are** *vt* paint; (*con vernice trasparente*) varnish. **~ia'tura** *f* painting; (*strato*) paintwork; *fig* veneer

'vero *adj* true; (*autentico*) real; (*perfetto*) perfect; **è ~?** is that so?; **sei stanca, ~?** you're tired, aren't you ● *m* truth; (*realtà*) life

verosimigli'anza *f* probability. **vero'simile** *adj* probable

ver'ruca *f* wart; (*sotto la pianta del piede*) verruca

versa'mento *m* payment; (*in banca*) deposit

ver'sante *m* slope

ver'sa|re *vt* pour; (*spargere*) shed; (*rovesciare*) spill; pay (denaro). **~rsi** *vr* spill; (*sfociare*) flow

ver'satil|e *adj* versatile. **~ità** *f* versatility

ver'setto *m* verse

versi'one *f* version; (*traduzione*) translation; **"~ integrale"** "unabridged version"

'verso[1] *m* verse; (*grido*) cry; (*gesto*) gesture; (*senso*) direction; (*modo*) manner; **non c'è ~ di** there is no way of

'verso[2] *prep* towards; (*nei pressi di*) round about; **~ dove?** which way?

'vertebra *f* vertebra

'vertere *vi* **~ su** focus on

verti'cal|e *adj* vertical; (*in parole crociate*) down ● *m* vertical ● *f* handstand. **~'mente** *adv* vertically

'vertice *m* summit; (*Math*) vertex; **conferenza al ~** summit conference

ver'tigine *f* dizziness; (*Med*) vertigo. **vertigini** *pl* giddy spells

vertigi|nosa'mente *adv* dizzily. **~'noso** *adj* dizzy; (velocità) breakneck; (prezzi) sky-high; (scollatura) plunging

ve'scica *f* bladder; (*sulla pelle*) blister

'vescovo *m* bishop

'vespa *f* wasp

vespasi'ano *m* urinal
'vespro *m* vespers *pl*
ves'sillo *m* standard
ve'staglia *f* dressing gown
'vest|e *f* dress; (*rivestimento*) covering; **in ~e di** in the capacity of. **~i'ario** *m* clothing
ve'stibolo *m* hall
ve'stigio *m* (*pl m* **vestigi**, *pl f* **vestigia**) trace
ve'sti|re *vt* dress. **~rsi** *vr* get dressed. **~ti** *pl* clothes. **~to** *adj* dressed ● *m* (*da uomo*) suit; (*da donna*) dress
vete'rano, -a *adj & mf* veteran
veteri'naria *f* veterinary science
veteri'nario *adj* veterinary ● *m* veterinary surgeon
'veto *m inv* veto
ve'tra|io *m* glazier. **~ta** *f* big window; (*in chiesa*) stained-glass window; (*porta*) glass door. **~to** *adj* glazed. **vetre'ria** *f* glass works
ve'tri|na *f* [shop-]window; (*mobile*) display cabinet. **~'nista** *mf* window dresser
vetri'olo *m* vitriol
'vetro *m* glass; (*di finestra, porta*) pane. **~'resina** *f* fibreglass
'vetta *f* peak
vet'tore *m* vector
vetto'vaglie *fpl* provisions
vet'tura *f* coach; (*ferroviaria*) carriage; (*Auto*) car. **vettu'rino** *m* coachman
vezzeggi'a|re *vt* fondle. **~'tivo** *m* pet name. **'vezzo** *m* habit; (*attrattiva*) charm; **vezzi** *pl* (*moine*) affectation *sg*. **vez'zoso** *adj* charming; *pej* affected
vi *pers pron* you; (*riflessivo*) yourselves; (*reciproco*) each other; (*tra più persone*) one another; **vi ho dato un libro** I gave you a book; **lavatevi le mani** wash your hands; **eccovi!** here you are! ● *adv* = **ci**
V
'via¹ *f* street, road; *fig* way; (*Anat*) tract; **in ~ di** in the course of; **per ~ di** on account of; **~ ~ che** as; **per ~ aerea** by airmail
'via² *adv* away; (*fuori*) out; **andar ~** go away; **e così ~** and so on; **e ~ dicendo** and whatnot ● *int* **~!** go away!; *Sport* go!; (*andiamo*) come on! ● *m* starting signal
viabilità *f* road conditions *pl*; (*rete*) road network; (*norme*) road and traffic laws *pl*
via'card *f inv* motorway card
viaggi'a|re *vi* travel. **~'tore, ~'trice** *mf* traveller
vi'aggio *m* journey; (*breve*) trip; **buon ~!** safe journey!, have a good trip!; **fare un ~** go on a journey. **~ di nozze** honeymoon
vi'ale *m* avenue; (*privato*) drive
vi'bra|nte *adj* vibrant. **~re** *vi* vibrate; (*fremere*) quiver. **~zi'one** *f* vibration
vi'cario *m* vicar
'vice *mf* deputy. **~diret'tore** *m* assistant manager
vi'cenda *f* event; **a ~** (*fra due*) each other; (*a turno*) in turn[s]
vice'versa *adv* vice versa
vici'na|nza *f* nearness; **~nze** *pl* (*paraggi*) neighbourhood. **~to** *m* neighbourhood; (*vicini*) neighbours *pl*
vi'cino, -a *adj* near; (*accanto*) next ● *adv* near, close. **~ a** *prep* near [to] ● *mf* neighbour. **~ di casa** nextdoor neighbour
'vicolo *m* alley
'video *m* video. **~'camera** *f* camcorder. **~cas'setta** *f* video cassette
videoci'tofono *m* video entry phone
video'clip *m inv* video clip
videogi'oco *m* video game
videoregistra'tore *m* videorecorder
video'teca *f* video library
video'tel® *m* ≈ Videotex®
videote'lefono *m* videophone
videotermi'nale *m* visual display unit, VDU
vidi'mare *vt* authenticate
vie'ta|re *vt* forbid; **sosta ~ta** no parking; **~to fumare** no smoking
vi'gente *adj* in force. **'vigere** *vi* be in force
vigi'la|nte *adj* vigilant. **~nza** *f* vigilance. **~re** *vt* keep an eye on ● *vi* keep watch
'vigile *adj* watchful ● *m* **~ [urbano]** policeman. **~ del fuoco** fireman
vi'gilia *f* eve
vigliacche'ria *f* cowardice. **vi'gliacco, -a** *adj* cowardly ● *mf* coward
'vigna *f*, **vi'gneto** *m* vineyard

vi'gnetta *f* cartoon

vi'gore *m* vigour; **entrare in ~** come into force. **vigo'roso** *adj* vigorous

'vile *adj* cowardly; (*abietto*) vile

'villa *f* villa

vil'laggio *m* village. **~ turistico** holiday village

vil'lano *adj* rude ● *m* boor; (*contadino*) peasant

villeggi'a|nte *mf* holiday-maker. **~re** *vi* spend one's holidays. **~'tura** *f* holiday[s] [*pl*]

vil'l|etta *f* small detached house. **~ino** *m* detached house

viltà *f* cowardice

'vimine *m* wicker

'vinc|ere *vt* win; (*sconfiggere*) beat; (*superare*) overcome. **~ita** *f* win; (*somma vinta*) winnings *pl*. **~i'tore, ~i'trice** *mf* winner

vinco'la|nte *adj* binding. **~re** *vt* bind; (*Comm*) tie up. **'vincolo** *m* bond

vi'nicolo *adj* wine *attrib*

vinil'pelle® *f* Leatherette®

'vino *m* wine. **~ spumante** sparkling wine. **~ da taglio** blending wine. **~ da tavola** table wine

'vinto *pp di* **vincere**

vi'ola *f* (*Bot*) violet; (*Mus*) viola. **viola** *adj & m inv* purple

vio'la|re *vt* violate. **~zi'one** *f* violation. **~zione di domicilio** breaking and entering

violen'tare *vt* rape

vio'len|to *adj* violent. **~za** *f* violence. **~za carnale** rape

vio'letta *f* violet

vio'letto *adj & m* (*colore*) violet

violi'nista *mf* violinist. **vio'lino** *m* violin. **violon'cello** *m* cello

vi'ottolo *m* path

'vipera *f* viper

vi'ra|ggio *m* (*Phot*) toning; (*Aeron, Naut*) turn. **~re** *vi* turn

'virgol|a *f* comma. **~ette** *fpl* inverted commas

vi'ril|e *adj* virile; (*da uomo*) manly. **~ità** *f* virility; manliness

virtù *f inv* virtue; **in ~ di** (legge) under. **virtu'ale** *adj* virtual. **virtu'oso** *adj* virtuous ● *m* virtuoso

viru'lento *adj* virulent

'virus *m inv* virus

visa'gista *mf* beautician

visce'rale *adj* visceral; (odio) deep-seated; (reazione) gut

'viscere *m* internal organ ● *fpl* guts

'vischi|o *m* mistletoe. **~'oso** *adj* viscous; (*appiccicoso*) sticky

vi'scont|e *m* viscount. **~'essa** *f* viscountess

vi'scoso *adj* viscous

vi'sibile *adj* visible

visi'bilio *m* profusion; **andare in ~** go into ecstasies

visibilità *f* visibility

visi'era *f* (*di elmo*) visor; (*di berretto*) peak

visio'nare *vt* examine; *Cinema* screen. **visi'one** *f* vision; **prima visione** *Cinema* first showing

'visit|a *f* visit; (*breve*) call; (*Med*) examination. **~a di controllo** (*Med*) checkup. **visi'tare** *vt* visit; (*brevemente*) call on; (*Med*) examine; **~a'tore, ~a'trice** *mf* visitor

vi'sivo *adj* visual

'viso *m* face

vi'sone *m* mink

'vispo *adj* lively

vis'suto *pp di* **vivere** ● *adj* experienced

'vist|a *f* sight; (*veduta*) view; **a ~a d'occhio** (crescere) visibly; (estendersi) as far as the eye can see; **in ~a di** in view of. **~o** *pp di* **vedere** ● *m* visa. **vi'stoso** *adj* showy; (*notevole*) considerable

visu'al|e *adj* visual. **~izza'tore** *m* (*Comput*) display, VDU. **~izzazi'one** *f* (*Comput*) display

'vita *f* life; (*durata della vita*) lifetime; (*Anat*) waist; **a ~** for life; **essere in ~** be alive

vi'tal|e *adj* vital. **~ità** *f* vitality

vita'lizio *adj* life *attrib* ● *m* [life] annuity

vita'min|a *f* vitamin. **~iz'zato** *adj* vitamin-enriched

'vite *f* (*Mech*) screw; (*Bot*) vine

vi'tello *m* calf; (*Culin*) veal; (*pelle*) calfskin

vi'ticcio *m* tendril

viticol't|ore *m* wine grower. **~ura** *f* wine growing

'vitreo *adj* vitreous; (sguardo) glassy

'vittima *f* victim

'vitto *m* food; (*pasti*) board. **~ e alloggio** board and lodging
vit'toria *f* victory
vittori'oso *adj* victorious
vi'uzza *f* narrow lane
'viva *int* hurrah!; **~ la Regina!** long live the Queen!
vi'vac|e *adj* vivacious; (mente) lively; (colore) bright. **~ità** *f* vivacity; (*di mente*) liveliness; (*di colore*) brightness. **~iz'zare** *vt* liven up
vi'vaio *m* nursery; (*per pesci*) pond; *fig* breeding ground
viva'mente *adv* (ringraziare) warmly
vi'vanda *f* food; (*piatto*) dish
vi'vente *adj* living ● *mpl* **i viventi** the living
'vivere *vi* live; **~ di** live on ● *vt* (*passare*) go through ● *m* life
'viveri *mpl* provisions
'vivido *adj* vivid
vivisezi'one *f* vivisection
'vivo *adj* alive; (*vivente*) living; (*vivace*) lively; (colore) bright; **~ e vegeto** alive and kicking; **farsi ~** keep in touch; (*arrivare*) turn up ● *m* **dal ~** (trasmissione) live; (disegnare) from life; **i vivi** the living
vizi|'are *vt* spoil (bambino ecc); (*guastare*) vitiate. **~'ato** *adj* spoilt; (aria) stale. **'vizio** *m* vice; (*cattiva abitudine*) bad habit; (*difetto*) flaw. **~'oso** *adj* dissolute; (*difettoso*) faulty; **circolo ~oso** vicious circle
vocabo'lario *m* dictionary; (*lessico*) vocabulary. **vo'cabolo** *m* word
vo'cale *adj* vocal ● *f* vowel. **vo'calico** *adj* (corde) vocal; (suono) vowel *attrib*
vocazi'one *f* vocation
'voce *f* voice; (*diceria*) rumour; (*di bilancio, dizionario*) entry
voci'are *vi* (*spettegolare*) gossip ● *m* buzz of conversation
V **vocife'rare** *vi* shout
'vog|a *f* rowing; (*lena*) enthusiasm; (*moda*) vogue; **essere in ~a** be in fashion. **vo'gare** *vi* row. **~a'tore** *m* oarsman; (*attrezzo*) rowing machine
'vogli|a *f* desire; (*volontà*) will; (*della pelle*) birthmark; **aver ~a di fare qcsa** feel like doing sth
'voi *pers pron* you; **siete ~?** is that you?; **l'avete fatto ~?** did you do it yourself?. **~a'ltri** *pers pron* you
vo'lano *m* shuttlecock; (*Mech*) flywheel
vo'lante *adj* flying; (foglio) loose ● *m* steering-wheel
volan'tino *m* leaflet
vo'la|re *vi* fly. **~ta** *f Sport* final sprint; **di ~ta** in a rush
vo'latile *adj* (liquido) volatile ● *m* bird
volée *f inv Tennis* volley
vo'lente *adj* **~ o nolente** whether you like it or not
volenti'eri *adv* willingly; **~!** with pleasure!
vo'lere *vt* want; (*chiedere di*) ask for; (*aver bisogno di*) need; **vuole che lo faccia io** he wants me to do it; **fai come vuoi** do as you like; **se tuo padre vuole, ti porto al cinema** if your father agrees, I'll take you to the cinema; **vorrei un caffè** I'd like a coffee; **la vuoi smettere?** will you stop that!; **senza ~** without meaning to; **voler bene/male a qcno** love/have something against sb; **voler dire** mean; **ci vuole il latte** we need milk; **ci vuole tempo/pazienza** it takes time/patience; **volerne a** have a grudge against; **vuoi ... vuoi...** either... or... ● *m* will; **voleri** *pl* wishes
vol'gar|e *adj* vulgar; (*popolare*) common. **~ità** *f inv* vulgarity. **~iz'zare** *vt* popularize. **~'mente** *adv* (*grossolanamente*) vulgarly, coarsely; (*comunemente*) commonly
'volger|e *vt/i* turn. **~si** *vr* turn [round]; **~si a** (*dedicarsi*) take up
voli'era *f* aviary
voli'tivo *adj* strong-minded
'volo *m* flight; **al ~** (fare qcsa) quickly; (prendere qcsa) in mid-air; **alzarsi in ~** (uccello:) take off; **in ~** airborne. **~ di linea** scheduled flight. **~ nazionale** domestic flight. **~ a vela** gliding.
volontà *f inv* will; (*desiderio*) wish; **a ~** (mangiare) as much as you like. **volontaria'mente** *adv* voluntarily. **volon'tario** *adj* voluntary ● *m* volunteer
volonte'roso *adj* willing
'volpe *f* fox
volt *m inv* volt
'volta *f* time; (*turno*) turn; (*curva*) bend; (*Archit*) vault; **4 volte 4** 4 times 4; **a volte** sometimes; **c'era una ~...** once

upon a time, there was...; **una ~** once; **due volte** twice; **tre/quattro volte** three/four times; **una ~ per tutte** once and for all; **uno per ~** one at a time; **uno alla ~** one at a time; **alla ~ di** in the direction of

volta'faccia *m inv* volte-face

vol'taggio *m* voltage

vol'ta|re *vt/i* turn; (*rigirare*) turn round; (*rivoltare*) turn over. **~rsi** *vr* turn [round]

volta'stomaco *m* nausea

volteggi'are *vi* circle; (*ginnastica*) vault

'volto *pp di* **volgere** ● *m* face; **mi ha mostrato il suo vero ~** he revealed his true colours

vo'lubile *adj* fickle

vo'lum|e *m* volume. **~i'noso** *adj* voluminous

voluta'mente *adv* deliberately

voluttu|osità *f* voluptuousness. **~'oso** *adj* voluptuous

vomi'tare *vt* vomit, be sick. **'vomito** *m* vomit

'vongola *f* clam

vo'race *adj* voracious

vo'ragine *f* abyss

'vortice *m* whirl; (*gorgo*) whirlpool; (*di vento*) whirlwind

'vostro (**il ~** *m*, **la vostra** *f*, **i vostri** *mpl*, **le vostre** *fpl*) *poss adj* your; **è vostra questa macchina?** is this car yours?; **un ~ amico** a friend of yours; **~ padre** your father ● *poss pron* yours; **i vostri** your folks

vo'ta|nte *mf* voter. **~re** *vi* vote. **~zi'one** *f* voting; (*Sch*) marks *pl*. **'voto** *m* vote; (*Sch*) mark; (*Relig*) vow

vs. *abbr* (*Comm*) (vostro) yours

vul'canico *adj* volcanic. **vul'cano** *m* volcano

vulne'rabil|e *adj* vulnerable. **~ità** *f* vulnerability

vuo'tare *vt*, **vuo'tarsi** *vr* empty

vu'oto *adj* empty; (*non occupato*) vacant; **~ di** (*sprovvisto*) devoid of ● *m* empty space; (*Phys*) vacuum; *fig* void; **assegno a ~** dud cheque; **sotto ~** (prodotto) vacuum-packed; **~ a perdere** no deposit. **~ d'aria** air pocket

Ww

W *abbr* (viva) long live

'wafer *m inv* (*biscotto*) wafer

walkie-'talkie *m inv* walkie-talkie

watt *m inv* watt

WC *m* WC

'Web *m inv* Web

'webmaster *m* webmaster

'western *adj inv* cowboy *attrib* ● *m Cinema* western

X, x *adj* **raggi** *pl* **X** X-rays; **il giorno X** D-day

xenofo'bia *f* xenophobia. **xe'nofobo, -a** *adj* xenophobic ● *mf* xenophobe

xi'lofono *m* xylophone

yacht *m inv* yacht

yen *m inv Fin* yen

'yoga *m* yoga; (*praticante*) yogi

'yogurt *m inv* yoghurt. **~i'era** *f* yoghurt-maker

Zz

zaba[gl]i'one *m* zabaglione (*dessert made from eggs, wine or marsala and sugar*)

zaf'fata *f* whiff; (*di fumo*) cloud

zaffe'rano *m* saffron

zaf'firo *m* sapphire

'zaino *m* rucksack
'zampa *f* leg; **a quattro zampe** (animale) four-legged; (*carponi*) on all fours
zampil'la|nte *adj* spurting. **~re** *vi* spurt. **zam'pillo** *m* spurt
zam'pogna *f* bagpipe
zam'pone *fpl stuffed pig's trotter with lentils*
'zanna *f* fang; (*di elefante*) tusk
zan'zar|a *f* mosquito. **~i'era** *f* (*velo*) mosquito net; (*su finestra*) insect screen
'zappa *f* hoe. **zap'pare** *vt* hoe
'zattera *f* raft
zatte'roni *mpl* (*scarpe*) wedge shoes
za'vorra *f* ballast; *fig* dead wood
'zazzera *f* mop of hair
'zebra *f* zebra; **zebre** *pl* (*passaggio pedonale*) zebra crossing
'zecca[1] *f* mint; **nuovo di ~** brand-new
'zecca[2] *f* (*parassita*) tick
zec'chino *m* sequin; **oro ~** pure gold
ze'lante *adj* zealous. **'zelo** *m* zeal
'zenit *m* zenith
'zenzero *m* ginger
'zeppa *f* wedge
'zeppo *adj* packed full; **pieno ~ di** crammed *o* packed with
zer'bino *m* doormat
'zero *m* zero, nought; (*in calcio*) nil; *Tennis* love; **due a ~** (*in partite*) two nil
'zeta *f* zed, zee *Am*
'zia *f* aunt
zibel'lino *m* sable
'zigomo *m* cheek-bone
zig'zag *m inv* zigzag; **andare a ~** zigzag
zim'bello *m* decoy; (*oggetto di scherno*) laughing-stock
'zinco *m* zinc
'zingaro, -a *mf* gypsy
'zio *m* uncle
zi'tel|la *f* spinster; *pej* old maid. **~'lona** *f pej* old maid
zit'tire *vi* fall silent ● *vt* silence. **'zitto** *adj* silent; **sta' zitto!** keep quiet!
ziz'zania *f* (*discordia*) discord
'zoccolo *m* clog; (*di cavallo*) hoof; (*di terra*) clump; (*di parete*) skirting board, baseboard *Am*; (*di colonna*) base
zodia'cale *adj* of the zodiac. **zo'diaco** *m* zodiac
'zolfo *m* sulphur
'zolla *f* clod; (*di zucchero*) lump
zol'letta *f* sugar lump
'zombi *mf inv fig* zombie
'zona *f* zone; (*area*) area. **~ di depressione** area of low pressure. **~ disco** area for parking discs only. **~ pedonale** pedestrian precinct. **~ verde** green belt
'zonzo *adv* **andare a ~** stroll about
zoo *m inv* zoo
zoolo'gia *f* zoology. **zoo'logico** *adj* zoological. **zo'ologo, -a** *mf* zoologist
zoo sa'fari *m inv* safari park
zoppi'ca|nte *adj* limping; *fig* shaky. **~re** *vi* limp; (*essere debole*) be shaky. **'zoppo, -a** *adj* lame ● *mf* cripple
zoti'cone *m* boor
'zucca *f* marrow; ([!]: *testa*) head; ([!]: *persona*) thickie
zucche'r|are *vt* sugar. **~i'era** *f* sugar bowl. **~i'ficio** *m* sugar refinery. **zucche'rino** *adj* sugary ● *m* sugar lump
'zucchero *m* sugar. **~ di canna** cane sugar. **~ vanigliato** vanilla sugar. **~ a velo** icing sugar. **zucche'roso** *adj* honeyed
zuc'chin|a *f*, **~o** *m* courgette, zucchini *Am*
'zuffa *f* scuffle
zufo'lare *vt/i* whistle
zu'mare *vi* zoom
'zuppa *f* soup. **~ inglese** trifle
zup'petta *f* **fare ~ [con]** dunk
zuppi'era *f* soup tureen
'zuppo *adj* soaked

Aa

a /ə/, accentato /eɪ/ *indef art; davanti a una vocale* **an**

- ····➤ un *m*, una *f*; (*before s + consonant, gn, ps and z*) uno; (*before feminine noun starting with a vowel*) un'; **a tiger is a feline** la tigre è un felino; **a knife and fork** un coltello e una forchetta; **a Mr Smith is looking for you** un certo signor Smith ti sta cercando
- ····➤ (*each*) a; **£2 a kilo/a head** due sterline al chilo/a testa

! when *a* refers to professions, it is not translated: **I am a lawyer** sono avvocato

A /eɪ/ *n* (*Mus*) la *m inv*

aback /ə'bæk/ *adv* **be taken ~** essere preso in contropiede

abandon /ə'bændən/ *vt* abbandonare; (*give up*) rinunciare a ● *n* abbandono *m*. **~ed** *adj* abbandonato

abashed /ə'bæʃt/ *adj* imbarazzato

abate /ə'beɪt/ *vi* calmarsi

abattoir /'æbətwɑ:(r)/ *n* mattatoio *m*

abbey /'æbɪ/ *n* abbazia *f*

abbreviat|e /ə'bri:vɪeɪt/ *vt* abbreviare. **~ion** *n* abbreviazione *f*

abdicat|e /'æbdɪkeɪt/ *vi* abdicare ● *vt* rinunciare a. **~ion** *n* abdicazione *f*

abdom|en /'æbdəmən/ *n* addome *m*. **~inal** *adj* addominale

abduct /əb'dʌkt/ *vt* rapire. **~ion** *n* rapimento *m*

abhor /əb'hɔ:(r)/ *vt* (*pt/pp* **abhorred**) aborrire. **~rence** *n* orrore *m*

abid|e /ə'baɪd/ *vt* (*pt/pp* **abided**) (*tolerate*) sopportare ● **abide by** *vi* rispettare. **~ing** *adj* perpetuo

ability /ə'bɪlətɪ/ *n* capacità *f inv*

abject /'æbdʒekt/ *adj* (poverty) degradante; (apology) umile; (coward) abietto

ablaze /ə'bleɪz/ *adj* in fiamme; **be ~ with light** risplendere di luci

able /'eɪbl/ *adj* capace, abile; **be ~ to do sth** poter fare qcsa; **were you ~ to...?** sei riuscito a...? **~-'bodied** *adj* robusto; (*Mil*) abile

ably /'eɪblɪ/ *adv* abilmente

abnormal /æb'nɔ:ml/ *adj* anormale. **~ity** *n* anormalità *f inv*. **~ly** *adv* in modo anormale

aboard /ə'bɔ:d/ *adv & prep* a bordo

abol|ish /ə'bɒlɪʃ/ *vt* abolire. **~ition** *n* abolizione *f*

abomina|ble /ə'bɒmɪnəbl/ *adj* abominevole

abort /ə'bɔ:t/ *vt* fare abortire; *fig* annullare. **~ion** *n* aborto *m*; **have an ~ion** abortire. **~ive** *adj* (attempt) infruttuoso

abound /ə'baʊnd/ *vi* abbondare; **~ in** abbondare di

about /ə'baʊt/ *adv* (*here and there*) [di] qua e [di] là; (*approximately*) circa; **be ~** (illness, tourists:) essere in giro; **be up and ~** essere alzato; **leave sth lying ~** lasciare in giro qcsa ● *prep* (*concerning*) su; (*in the region of*) intorno a; (*here and there in*) per; **what is the book/the film ~?** di cosa parla il libro/il film?; **he wants to see you - what ~?** ti vuole vedere - a che proposito?; **talk/know ~** parlare/sapere di; **I know nothing ~ it** non ne so niente; **~ 5 o'clock** intorno alle 5; **travel ~ the world** viaggiare per il mondo; **be ~ to do sth** stare per fare qcsa; **how ~ going to the cinema?** e se andassimo al cinema?

about: ~-'face *n*, **~-'turn** *n* dietro front *m inv*

above /ə'bʌv/ *adv & prep* sopra; **~ all** soprattutto

above: ~-'board *adj* onesto. **~-'mentioned** *adj* suddetto

abrasive /ə'breɪsɪv/ *adj* abrasivo; (remark) caustico ● *n* abrasivo *m*

abreast /ə'brest/ *adv* fianco a fianco; **come ~ of** allinearsi con; **keep ~ of** tenersi al corrente di

abroad /ə'brɔ:d/ *adv* all'estero

abrupt /ə'brʌpt/ *adj* brusco

abscess /'æbsɪs/ *n* ascesso *m*

a

abscond /əb'skɒnd/ *vi* fuggire

absence /'æbsəns/ *n* assenza *f*; (*lack*) mancanza *f*

absent¹ /'æbsənt/ *adj* assente

absent² /æb'sent/ *vt* ~ **oneself** essere assente

absentee /æbsən'ti:/ *n* assente *mf*

absent-minded /æbsənt'maɪndɪd/ *adj* distratto

absolute /'æbsəlu:t/ *adj* assoluto; **an ~ idiot** un perfetto idiota. **~ly** *adv* assolutamente; ([!]: *indicating agreement*) esattamente

absolve /əb'zɒlv/ *vt* assolvere

absorb /əb'sɔ:b/ *vt* assorbire; **~ed in** assorto in. **~ent** *adj* assorbente

absorption /əb'sɔ:pʃn/ *n* assorbimento *m*; (*in activity*) concentrazione *f*

abstain /əb'steɪn/ *vi* astenersi (**from** da)

abstemious /əb'sti:mɪəs/ *adj* moderato

abstention /əb'stenʃn/ *n* (*Pol*) astensione *f*

abstract /'æbstrækt/ *adj* astratto • *n* astratto *m*; (*summary*) estratto *m*

absurd /əb'sɜ:d/ *adj* assurdo. **~ity** *n* assurdità *f inv*

abundan|ce /ə'bʌndəns/ *n* abbondanza *f*. **~t** *adj* abbondante

abuse¹ /ə'bju:z/ *vt* (*misuse*) abusare di; (*insult*) insultare; (*ill-treat*) maltrattare

abus|e² /ə'bju:s/ *n* abuso *m*; (*verbal*) insulti *mpl*; (*ill-treatment*) maltrattamento *m*. **~ive** *adj* offensivo

abysmal /ə'bɪzml/ *adj* [!] pessimo; (ignorance) abissale

abyss /ə'bɪs/ *n* abisso *m*

academic /ækə'demɪk/ *adj* teorico; (qualifications, system) scolastico; **be ~** (person:) avere predisposizione allo studio • *n* docente *mf* universitario, -a

academy /ə'kædəmɪ/ *n* accademia *f*; (*of music*) conservatorio *m*

accelerat|e /ək'seləreɪt/ *vt/i* accelerare. **~ion** *n* accelerazione *f*. **~or** *n* (*Auto*) acceleratore *m*

accent /'æksənt/ *n* accento *m*

accept /ək'sept/ *vt* accettare. **~able** *adj* accettabile. **~ance** *n* accettazione *f*

access /'ækses/ *n* accesso *m*. **~ible** *adj* accessibile

accession /ək'seʃn/ *n* (*to throne*) ascesa *f* al trono

accessory /ək'sesərɪ/ *n* accessorio *m*; (*Jur*) complice *mf*

accident /'æksɪdənt/ *n* incidente *m*; (*chance*) caso *m*; **by ~** per caso; (*unintentionally*) senza volere; **I'm sorry, it was an ~** mi dispiace, non l'ho fatto apposta. **~al** *adj* (meeting) casuale; (death) incidentale; (*unintentional*) involontario. **~ally** *adv* per caso; (*unintentionally*) inavvertitamente

acclaim /ə'kleɪm/ *n* acclamazione *f* • *vt* acclamare (**as** come)

accolade /'ækəleɪd/ *n* riconoscimento *m*

accommodat|e /ə'kɒmədeɪt/ *vt* ospitare; (*oblige*) favorire. **~ing** *adj* accomodante. **~ion** *n* (*place to stay*) sistemazione *f*

accompan|iment /ə'kʌmpənɪmənt/ *n* accompagnamento *m*. **~ist** *n* (*Mus*) accompagnatore, -trice *mf*

accompany /ə'kʌmpənɪ/ *vt* (*pt/pp* **-ied**) accompagnare

accomplice /ə'kʌmplɪs/ *n* complice *mf*

accomplish /ə'kʌmplɪʃ/ *vt* (*achieve*) concludere; realizzare (aim). **~ed** *adj* dotato; (fact) compiuto. **~ment** *n* realizzazione *f*; (*achievement*) risultato *m*; (*talent*) talento *m*

accord /ə'kɔ:d/ *n* (*treaty*) accordo *m*; **with one ~** tutti d'accordo; **of his own ~** di sua spontanea volontà. **~ance** *n* **in ~ance with** in conformità di *o* a

according /ə'kɔ:dɪŋ/ *adv* **~ to** secondo. **~ly** *adv* di conseguenza

accordion /ə'kɔ:dɪən/ *n* fisarmonica *f*

accost /ə'kɒst/ *vt* abbordare

account /ə'kaʊnt/ *n* conto *m*; (*report*) descrizione *f*; (*of eye-witness*) resoconto *m*; **~s** *pl* (*Comm*) conti *mpl*; **on ~ of** a causa di; **on no ~** per nessun motivo; **on this ~** per questo motivo; **on my ~** per causa mia; **of no ~** di nessuna importanza; **take into ~** tener conto di • **account for** *vi* (*explain*) spiegare; (person:) render conto di; (*constitute*) costituire. **~ability** *n* responsabilità *f inv*. **~able** *adj* responsabile (**for** di)

accountant /ə'kaʊntənt/ *n* (*book-*

keeper) contabile *mf*; (*consultant*) commercialista *mf*

accumulat|e /ə'kju:mjʊleɪt/ *vt* accumulare ● *vi* accumularsi. **~ion** *n* accumulazione *f*

accura|cy /'ækʊrəsɪ/ *n* precisione *f*. **~te** *adj* preciso. **~tely** *adv* con precisione

accusation /ækjʊ'zeɪʃn/ *n* accusa *f*

accuse /ə'kju:z/ *vt* accusare; **~ sb of doing sth** accusare qcno di fare qcsa. **~d** *n* **the ~d** l'accusato *m*, l'accusata *f*

accustom /ə'kʌstəm/ *vt* abituare (**to** a); **grow** *or* **get ~ed to** abituarsi a. **~ed** *adj* abituato

ace /eɪs/ *n* (*Cards*) asso *m*; (*tennis*) ace *m inv*

ache /eɪk/ *n* dolore *m* ● *vi* dolere, far male; **~ all over** essere tutto indolenzito

achieve /ə'tʃi:v/ *vt* ottenere (success); realizzare (goal, ambition). **~ment** *n* (*feat*) successo *m*

acid /'æsɪd/ *adj* acido ● *n* acido *m*. **~ity** *n* acidità *f*. **~ 'rain** *n* pioggia *f* acida

acknowledge /ək'nɒlɪdʒ/ *vt* riconoscere; rispondere a (greeting); far cenno di aver notato (sb's presence); **~ receipt of** accusare ricevuta di. **~ment** *n* riconoscimento *m*; **send an ~ment of a letter** confermare il ricevimento di una lettera

acne /'æknɪ/ *n* acne *f*

acorn /'eɪkɔ:n/ *n* ghianda *f*

acoustic /ə'ku:stɪk/ *adj* acustico. **~s** *npl* acustica *fsg*

acquaint /ə'kweɪnt/ *vt* **~ sb with** metter qcno al corrente di; **be ~ed with** conoscere (person); essere a conoscenza di (fact). **~ance** *n* (*person*) conoscente *mf*; **make sb's ~ance** fare la conoscenza di qcno

acquiesce /ækwɪ'es/ *vi* acconsentire (**to, in** a). **~nce** *n* acquiescenza *f*

acquire /ə'kwaɪə(r)/ *vt* acquisire

acquisit|ion /ækwɪ'zɪʃn/ *n* acquisizione *f*. **~ive** *adj* avido

acquit /ə'kwɪt/ *vt* (*pt/pp* **acquitted**) assolvere; **~ oneself well** cavarsela bene. **~tal** *n* assoluzione *f*

acre /'eɪkə(r)/ *n* acro *m* (= *4 047 m²*)

acrid /'ækrɪd/ *adj* acre

acrimon|ious /ækrɪ'məʊnɪəs/ *adj* aspro. **~y** *n* asprezza *f*

acrobat /'ækrəbæt/ *n* acrobata *mf*. **~ic** *adj* acrobatico

across /ə'krɒs/ *adv* dall'altra parte; (*wide*) in larghezza; (*not lengthwise*) attraverso; (*in crossword*) orizzontale; **come ~ sth** imbattersi in qcsa; **go ~** attraversare ● *prep* (*crosswise*) di traverso su; (*on the other side of*) dall'altra parte di

act /ækt/ *n* atto *m*; (*in variety show*) numero *m*; **put on an ~** [!] fare scena ● *vi* agire; (*behave*) comportarsi; (*Theat*) recitare; (*pretend*) fingere; **~ as** fare da ● *vt* recitare (role). **~ing** *adj* (deputy) provvisorio ● *n* (*Theat*) recitazione *f*; (*profession*) teatro *m*. **~ing profession** *n* professione *f* dell'attore

action /'ækʃn/ *n* azione *f*; (*Mil*) combattimento *m*; (*Jur*) azione *f* legale; **out of ~** (machine:) fuori uso; **take ~** agire. **~ 'replay** *n* replay *m inv*

activ|e /'æktɪv/ *adj* attivo. **~ely** *adv* attivamente. **~ity** *n* attività *f inv*

act|or /'æktə(r)/ *n* attore *m*. **~ress** *n* attrice *f*

actual /'æktʃʊəl/ *adj* (*real*) reale. **~ly** *adv* in realtà

acute /ə'kju:t/ *adj* acuto; (shortage, hardship) estremo

ad /æd/ *n* [!] pubblicità *f inv*

AD *abbr* (Anno Domini) d.C.

adapt /ə'dæpt/ *vt* adattare (play) ● *vi* adattarsi. **~ability** *n* adattabilità *f*. **~able** *adj* adattabile

adaptation /ædæp'teɪʃn/ *n* (*Theat*) adattamento *m*

adapter, **adaptor** /ə'dæptə(r)/ *n* adattatore *m*; (*two-way*) presa *f* multipla

add /æd/ *vt* aggiungere; (*Math*) addizionare ● *vi* addizionare; **~ to** (*fig: increase*) aggravare. □ **~ up** *vt* addizionare (figures) ● *vi* addizionare; **~ up to** ammontare a; **it doesn't ~ up** *fig* non quadra

adder /'ædə(r)/ *n* vipera *f*

addict /'ædɪkt/ *n* tossicodipendente *mf*; *fig* fanatico, -a *mf*

addict|ed /ə'dɪktɪd/ *adj* assuefatto (**to** a); **~ed to drugs** tossicodipendente; **he's ~ed to television** è videodipendente. **~ion** *n* dipendenza *f*; (*to drugs*) tossicodipendenza *f*. **~ive** *adj* **be ~ive** dare assuefazione

addition /ə'dɪʃn/ *n* (*Math*) addizione *f*;

(*thing added*) aggiunta *f*; **in ~** in aggiunta. **~al** *adj* supplementare. **~ally** *adv* in più

additive /'ædɪtɪv/ *n* additivo *m*

address /ə'dres/ *n* indirizzo *m*; (*speech*) discorso *m*; **form of ~** formula *f* di cortesia ● *vt* indirizzare; (*speak to*) rivolgersi a (person); tenere un discorso a (meeting). **~ee** *n* destinatario, -a *mf*

adept /'ædept/ *adj & n* esperto, -a *mf* (**at** in)

adequate /'ædɪkwət/ *adj* adeguato. **~ly** *adv* adeguatamente

adhere /əd'hɪə(r)/ *vi* aderire; **~ to** attenersi a (principles, rules)

adhesive /əd'hi:sɪv/ *adj* adesivo ● *n* adesivo *m*

adjacent /ə'dʒeɪsənt/ *adj* adiacente

adjective /'ædʒɪktɪv/ *n* aggettivo *m*

adjourn /ə'dʒɜ:n/ *vt/i* aggiornare (**until** a). **~ment** *n* aggiornamento *m*

adjust /ə'dʒʌst/ *vt* modificare; regolare (focus, sound etc) ● *vi* adattarsi. **~able** *adj* regolabile. **~ment** *n* adattamento *m*; (*Techn*) regolamento *m*

administer /əd'mɪnɪstə(r)/ *vt* amministrare; somministrare (medicine)

administrat|ion /ədmɪnɪ'streɪʃn/ *n* amministrazione *f*; (*Pol*) governo *m*. **~or** *n* amministratore, -trice *mf*

admirable /'ædmərəbl/ *adj* ammirevole

admiral /'ædmərəl/ *n* ammiraglio *m*

admiration /ædmə'reɪʃn/ *n* ammirazione *f*

admire /əd'maɪə(r)/ *vt* ammirare. **~r** *n* ammiratore, -trice *mf*

admission /əd'mɪʃn/ *n* ammissione *f*; (*to hospital*) ricovero *m*; (*entry*) ingresso *m*

admit /əd'mɪt/ *vt* (*pt/pp* **admitted**) (*let in*) far entrare; (*to hospital*) ricoverare; (*acknowledge*) ammettere ● *vi* **~ to sth** ammettere qcsa. **~tance** *n* ammissione *f*; **'no ~tance'** 'vietato l'ingresso'. **~tedly** *adv* bisogna riconoscerlo

admonish /əd'mɒnɪʃ/ *vt* ammonire

ado /ə'du:/ *n* **without more ~** senza ulteriori indugi

adolescen|ce /ædə'lesns/ *n* adolescenza *f*. **~t** *adj & n* adolescente *mf*

adopt /ə'dɒpt/ *vt* adottare; (*Pol*) scegliere (candidate). **~ion** *n* adozione *f*. **~ive** *adj* adottivo

ador|able /ə'dɔ:rəbl/ *adj* adorabile. **~ation** *n* adorazione *f*

adore /ə'dɔ:(r)/ *vt* adorare

adrenalin /ə'drenəlɪn/ *n* adrenalina *f*

Adriatic /eɪdrɪ'ætɪk/ *adj & n* **the ~ [Sea]** il mare Adriatico, l'Adriatico *m*

adrift /ə'drɪft/ *adj* alla deriva; **be ~** andare alla deriva; **come ~** staccarsi

adult /'ædʌlt/ *n* adulto, -a *mf*

adultery /ə'dʌltərɪ/ *n* adulterio *m*

advance /əd'vɑ:ns/ *n* avanzamento *m*; (*Mil*) avanzata *f*; (*payment*) anticipo *m*; **in ~** in anticipo ● *vi* avanzare; (*make progress*) fare progressi ● *vt* avanzare (theory); promuovere (cause); anticipare (money). **~ booking** *n* prenotazione *f* [in anticipo]. **~d** *adj* avanzato. **~ment** *n* promozione *f*

advantage /əd'vɑ:ntɪdʒ/ *n* vantaggio *m*; **take ~ of** approfittare di. **~ous** *adj* vantaggioso

advent /'ædvent/ *n* avvento *m*

adventur|e /əd'ventʃə(r)/ *n* avventura *f*. **~ous** *adj* avventuroso

adverb /'ædvɜ:b/ *n* avverbio *m*

adversary /'ædvəsərɪ/ *n* avversario, -a *mf*

advers|e /'ædvɜ:s/ *adj* avverso. **~ity** *n* avversità *f*

advert /'ædvɜ:t/ *n* [!] = **advertisement**

advertise /'ædvətaɪz/ *vt* reclamizzare; mettere un annuncio per (job, flat) ● *vi* fare pubblicità; (*for job, flat*) mettere un annuncio

advertisement /əd'vɜ:tɪsmənt/ *n* pubblicità *f inv*; (*in paper*) inserzione *f*, annuncio *m*

advertis|er /'ædvətaɪzə(r)/ *n* (*in newspaper*) inserzionista *mf*. **~ing** *n* pubblicità *f* ● *attrib* pubblicitario

advice /əd'vaɪs/ *n* consigli *mpl*; **piece of ~** consiglio *m*

advisable /əd'vaɪzəbl/ *adj* consigliabile

advis|e /əd'vaɪz/ *vt* consigliare; (*inform*) avvisare; **~e sb to do sth** consigliare a qcno di fare qcsa; **~e sb against sth** sconsigliare qcsa a qcno. **~er** *n* consulente *mf*. **~ory** *adj* consultivo

advocate[1] /ˈædvəkət/ *n* (*supporter*) fautore, -trice *mf*
advocate[2] /ˈædvəkeɪt/ *vt* propugnare
aerial /ˈeərɪəl/ *adj* aereo ● *n* antenna *f*
aerobics /eəˈrəʊbɪks/ *n* aerobica *fsg*
aero|drome /ˈeərədrəʊm/ *n* aerodromo *m*. **~plane** *n* aeroplano *m*
aerosol /ˈeərəsɒl/ *n* bomboletta *f* spray
aesthetic /iːsˈθetɪk/ *adj* estetico
afar /əˈfɑː(r)/ *adv* **from ~** da lontano
affable /ˈæfəbl/ *adj* affabile
affair /əˈfeə(r)/ *n* affare *m*; (*scandal*) caso *m*; (*sexual*) relazione *f*
affect /əˈfekt/ *vt* influire su; (*emotionally*) colpire; (*concern*) riguardare. **~ation** *n* affettazione *f*. **~ed** *adj* affettato
affection /əˈfekʃn/ *n* affetto *m*. **~ate** *adj* affettuoso
affirm /əˈfɜːm/ *vt* affermare; (*Jur*) dichiarare solennemente
affirmative /əˈfɜːmətɪv/ *adj* affermativo ● *n* **in the ~** affermativamente
afflict /əˈflɪkt/ *vt* affliggere. **~ion** *n* afflizione *f*
affluen|ce /ˈæflʊəns/ *n* agiatezza *f*. **~t** *adj* agiato
afford /əˈfɔːd/ *vt* **be able to ~ sth** potersi permettere qcsa. **~able** *adj* abbordabile
affront /əˈfrʌnt/ *n* affronto *m*
afield /əˈfiːld/ *adv* **further ~** più lontano
afloat /əˈfləʊt/ *adj* a galla
afraid /əˈfreɪd/ *adj* **be ~** aver paura; **I'm ~ not** purtroppo no; **I'm ~ so** temo di sì; **I'm ~ I can't help you** mi dispiace, ma non posso esserle d'aiuto
afresh /əˈfreʃ/ *adv* da capo
Africa /ˈæfrɪkə/ *n* Africa *f*. **~n** *adj & n* africano, -a *mf*
after /ˈɑːftə(r)/ *adv* dopo; **the day ~** il giorno dopo; **be ~** cercare ● *prep* dopo; **~ all** dopotutto; **the day ~ tomorrow** dopodomani ● *conj* dopo che
after: ~-effect *n* conseguenza *f*. **~math** /-mɑːθ/ *n* conseguenze *fpl*; **the ~math of war** il dopoguerra; **in the ~math of** nel periodo successivo a. **~'noon** *n* pomeriggio *m*; **good ~noon!** buon giorno!. **~shave** *n* [lozione *f*] dopobarba *m inv*. **~thought** *n* **added as an ~thought** aggiunto in un secondo momento; **~wards** *adv* in seguito
again /əˈgeɪn/ *adv* di nuovo; [**then**] **~** (*besides*) inoltre; (*on the other hand*) d'altra parte; **~ and ~** continuamente
against /əˈgeɪnst/ *prep* contro
age /eɪdʒ/ *n* età *f inv*; (*era*) era *f*; **~s** ⊡ secoli; **what ~ are you?** quanti anni hai?; **be under ~** non avere l'età richiesta; **he's two years of ~** ha due anni ● *vt/i* (*pres p* **ageing**) invecchiare
aged[1] /eɪdʒd/ *adj* **~ two** di due anni
aged[2] /ˈeɪdʒɪd/ *adj* anziano ● *n* **the ~** *pl* gli anziani
agency /ˈeɪdʒənsɪ/ *n* agenzia *f*; **have the ~ for** essere un concessionario di
agenda /əˈdʒendə/ *n* ordine *m* del giorno; **on the ~** all'ordine del giorno; *fig* in programma
agent /ˈeɪdʒənt/ *n* agente *mf*
aggravat|e /ˈægrəveɪt/ *vt* aggravare; (*annoy*) esasperare. **~ion** *n* aggravamento *m*; (*annoyance*) esasperazione *f*
aggress|ion /əˈgreʃn/ *n* aggressione *f*. **~ive** *adj* aggressivo. **~iveness** *n* aggressività *f*. **~or** *n* aggressore *m*
aghast /əˈgɑːst/ *adj* inorridito
agil|e /ˈædʒaɪl/ *adj* agile. **~ity** *n* agilità *f*
agitat|e /ˈædʒɪteɪt/ *vt* mettere in agitazione; (*shake*) agitare ● *vi fig* **~e for** creare delle agitazioni per. **~ed** *adj* agitato. **~ion** *n* agitazione *f*. **~or** *n* agitatore, -trice *mf*
ago /əˈgəʊ/ *adv* fa; **a long time/a month ~** molto tempo/un mese fa
agoniz|e /ˈægənaɪz/ *vi* angosciarsi (**over** per). **~ing** *adj* angosciante
agony /ˈægənɪ/ *n* agonia *f*; (*mental*) angoscia *f*; **be in ~** avere dei dolori atroci
agree /əˈgriː/ *vt* accordarsi su; **~ to do sth** accettare di fare qcsa; **~ that** essere d'accordo [sul fatto] che ● *vi* essere d'accordo; (figures:) concordare; (*reach agreement*) mettersi d'accordo; (*get on*) andare d'accordo; (*consent*) acconsentire (**to** a); **it doesn't ~ with me** mi fa male; **~ with sth** (*approve of*) approvare qcsa
agreeable /əˈgriːəbl/ *adj* gradevole; (*willing*) d'accordo
agreed /əˈgriːd/ *adj* convenuto

a

agreement /ə'gri:mənt/ *n* accordo *m*; **in ~** d'accordo

agricultur|al /ægrɪ'kʌltʃərəl/ *adj* agricolo. **~e** *n* agricoltura *f*

aground /ə'graʊnd/ *adv* **run ~** (ship:) arenarsi

ahead /ə'hed/ *adv* avanti; **be ~ of** essere davanti a; *fig* essere avanti rispetto a; **draw ~** passare davanti (**of** a); **get ~** (*in life*) riuscire; **go ~!** fai pure!; **look ~** pensare all'avvenire; **plan ~** fare progetti per l'avvenire

aid /eɪd/ *n* aiuto *m*; **in ~ of** a favore di ● *vt* aiutare

Aids /eɪdz/ *n* AIDS *m*

aim /eɪm/ *n* mira *f*; *fig* scopo *m*; **take ~** prendere la mira ● *vt* puntare (gun) (**at** contro) ● *vi* mirare; **~ to do sth** aspirare a fare qcsa. **~less** *adj*, **~lessly** *adv* senza scopo

air /eə(r)/ *n* aria *f*; **be on the ~** (programme:) essere in onda; **put on ~s** darsi delle arie; **by ~** in aereo; (*airmail*) per via aerea ● *vt* arieggiare; far conoscere (views)

air: ~-conditioned *adj* con aria condizionata. **~-conditioning** *n* aria *f* condizionata. **~craft** *n* aereo *m*. **~craft carrier** *n* portaerei *f inv*. **~field** *n* campo *m* d'aviazione. **~ force** *n* aviazione *f*. **~ freshener** *n* deodorante *m* per l'ambiente. **~gun** *n* fucile *m* pneumatico. **~ hostess** *n* hostess *f inv*. **~line** *n* compagnia *f* aerea. **~mail** *n* posta *f* aerea. **~plane** *n Am* aereo *m*. **~port** *n* aeroporto *m*. **~tight** *adj* ermetico. **~-traffic controller** *n* controllore *m* di volo

airy /'eərɪ/ *adj* (**-ier, -iest**) arieggiato; (manner) noncurante

aisle /aɪl/ *n* corridoio *m*; (*in supermarket*) corsia *f*; (*in church*) navata *f*

ajar /ə'dʒɑ:(r)/ *adj* socchiuso

alarm /ə'lɑ:m/ *n* allarme *m*; **set the ~** (*of alarm clock*) mettere la sveglia ● *vt* allarmare. **~ clock** *n* sveglia *f*

Albania /æl'beɪnɪə/ *n* Albania *f*

album /'ælbəm/ *n* album *m inv*

alcohol /'ælkəhɒl/ *n* alcol *m*. **~ic** *adj* alcolico ● *n* alcolizzato, -a *mf*. **~ism** *n* alcolismo *m*

alcove /'ælkəʊv/ *n* alcova *f*

alert /ə'lɜ:t/ *adj* sveglio; (*watchful*) vigile ● *n* segnale *m* d'allarme; **be on the ~** stare allerta ● *vt* allertare

algebra /'ældʒɪbrə/ *n* algebra *f*

Algeria /æl'dʒɪərɪə/ *n* Algeria *f*. **~n** *adj & n* algerino, -a *mf*

alias /'eɪlɪəs/ *n* pseudonimo *m* ● *adv* alias

alibi /'ælɪbaɪ/ *n* alibi *m inv*

alien /'eɪlɪən/ *adj* straniero; *fig* estraneo ● *n* straniero, -a *mf*; (*from space*) alieno, -a *mf*

alienat|e /'eɪlɪəneɪt/ *vt* alienare. **~ion** *n* alienazione *f*

alight¹ /ə'laɪt/ *vi* scendere; (bird:) posarsi

alight² *adj* **be ~** essere in fiamme; **set ~** dar fuoco a

align /ə'laɪn/ *vt* allineare. **~ment** *n* allineamento *m*; **out of ~ment** non allineato

alike /ə'laɪk/ *adj* simile; **be ~** rassomigliarsi ● *adv* in modo simile; **look ~** rassomigliarsi; **summer and winter ~** sia d'estate che d'inverno

alimony /'ælɪmənɪ/ *n* alimenti *mpl*

alive /ə'laɪv/ *adj* vivo; **~ with** brulicante di; **~ to** sensibile a; **~ and kicking** vivo e vegeto

alkali /'ælkəlaɪ/ *n* alcali *m*

all /ɔ:l/

● *adj* tutto; **~ the children, ~ children** tutti i bambini; **~ day** tutto il giorno; **he refused ~ help** ha rifiutato qualsiasi aiuto; **for ~ that** (*nevertheless*) ciononostante; **in ~ sincerity** in tutta sincerità; **be ~ for** essere favorevole a

● *pron* tutto; **~ of you/them** tutti voi/loro; **~ of it** tutto; **~ of the town** tutta la città; **in ~** in tutto; **~ in ~** tutto sommato; **most of ~** più di ogni altra cosa; **once and for ~** una volta per tutte

● *adv* completamente; **~ but** quasi; **~ at once** (*at the same time*) tutto in una volta; **~ at once, ~ of a sudden** all'improvviso; **~ too soon** troppo presto; **~ the same** (*nevertheless*) ciononostante; **~ the better** meglio ancora; **she's not ~ that good an actress** non è poi così brava come attrice; **~ in** in tutto; [!] esausto; **thirty/three** ~ (*in sport*) trenta/tre pari; **~ over** (*finished*) tutto finito; (*everywhere*) dappertutto; **it's ~ right** (*I don't mind*) non fa niente; **I'm ~ right** (*not hurt*) non ho niente; **~ right!** va bene!

allay /ə'leɪ/ *vt* placare (suspicions, anger)

allegation /ælɪ'geɪʃn/ *n* accusa *f*

allege /ə'ledʒ/ *vt* dichiarare. **~d** *adj* presunto. **~dly** *adv* a quanto si dice

allegiance /ə'li:dʒəns/ *n* fedeltà *f*

allerg|ic /ə'lɜ:dʒɪk/ *adj* allergico. **~y** *n* allergia *f*

alleviate /ə'li:vɪeɪt/ *vt* alleviare

alley /'ælɪ/ *n* vicolo *m*; (*for bowling*) corsia *f*

alliance /ə'laɪəns/ *n* alleanza *f*

alligator /'ælɪgeɪtə(r)/ *n* alligatore *m*

allocat|e /'æləkeɪt/ *vt* assegnare; distribuire (resources). **~ion** *n* assegnazione *f*; (*of resources*) distribuzione *f*

allot /ə'lɒt/ *vt* (*pt/pp* **allotted**) distribuire. **~ment** *n* distribuzione *f*; (*share*) parte *f*; (*land*) piccolo lotto *m* di terreno

allow /ə'laʊ/ *vt* permettere; (*grant*) accordare; (*reckon on*) contare; (*agree*) ammettere; **~ for** tener conto di; **~ sb to do sth** permettere a qcno di fare qcsa; **you are not ~ed to...** è vietato...

allowance /ə'laʊəns/ *n* sussidio *m*; (*Am: pocket money*) paghetta *f*; (*for petrol etc*) indennità *f inv*; (*of luggage, duty free*) limite *m*; **make ~s for** essere indulgente verso (sb); tener conto di (sth)

alloy /'ælɔɪ/ *n* lega *f*

allusion /ə'lu:ʒn/ *n* allusione *f*

ally¹ /'ælaɪ/ *n* alleato, -a *mf*

ally² /ə'laɪ/ *vt* (*pt/pp* **-ied**) alleare; **~ oneself with** allearsi con

almighty /ɔ:l'maɪtɪ/ *adj* ([!]: *big*) mega *inv* ● *n* **the A~** l'Onnipotente *m*

almond /'ɑ:mənd/ *n* mandorla *f*; (*tree*) mandorlo *m*

almost /'ɔ:lməʊst/ *adv* quasi

alone /ə'ləʊn/ *adj* solo; **leave me ~!** lasciami in pace!; **let ~** (*not to mention*) figurarsi ● *adv* da solo

along /ə'lɒŋ/ *prep* lungo ● *adv* **~ with** assieme a; **all ~** tutto il tempo; **come ~!** (*hurry up*) vieni qui!; **I'll be ~ in a minute** arrivo tra un attimo; **move ~** spostarsi; **move ~!** circolare!

along'side *adv* lungo bordo ● *prep* lungo; **work ~ sb** lavorare fianco a fianco con qcno

aloof /ə'lu:f/ *adj* distante

aloud /ə'laʊd/ *adv* ad alta voce

alphabet /'ælfəbet/ *n* alfabeto *m*. **~ical** *adj* alfabetico

Alps /ælps/ *npl* Alpi *fpl*

already /ɔ:l'redɪ/ *adv* già

Alsatian /æl'seɪʃn/ *n* (*dog*) pastore *m* tedesco

also /'ɔ:lsəʊ/ *adv* anche; **~, I need...** [e] inoltre, ho bisogno di...

altar /'ɔ:ltə(r)/ *n* altare *m*

alter /'ɔ:ltə(r)/ *vt* cambiare; aggiustare (clothes) ● *vi* cambiare. **~ation** *n* modifica *f*

alternate¹ /'ɔ:ltəneɪt/ *vi* alternarsi ● *vt* alternare

alternate² /ɔ:l'tɜ:nət/ *adj* alterno; **on ~ days** a giorni alterni

alternative /ɔ:l'tɜ:nətɪv/ *adj* alternativo ● *n* alternativa *f*. **~ly** *adv* alternativamente

although /ɔ:l'ðəʊ/ *conj* benché, sebbene

altitude /'æltɪtju:d/ *n* altitudine *f*

altogether /ɔ:ltə'geðə(r)/ *adv* (*in all*) in tutto; (*completely*) completamente; **I'm not ~ sure** non sono del tutto sicuro

aluminium /æljʊ'mɪnɪəm/ *n*, *Am* **aluminum** /ə'lu:mɪnəm/ *n* alluminio *m*

always /'ɔ:lweɪz/ *adv* sempre

am /æm/ ▷**BE**

a.m. *abbr* (ante meridiem) del mattino

amalgamate /ə'mælgəmeɪt/ *vt* fondere ● *vi* fondersi

amass /ə'mæs/ *vt* accumulare

amateur /'æmətə(r)/ *n* non professionista *mf*; *pej* dilettante *mf* ● *attrib* dilettante; **~ dramatics** filodrammatica *f*. **~ish** *adj* dilettantesco

amaze /ə'meɪz/ *vt* stupire. **~d** *adj* stupito. **~ment** *n* stupore *m*

amazing /ə'meɪzɪŋ/ *adj* incredibile

ambassador /æm'bæsədə(r)/ *n* ambasciatore, -trice *mf*

a

ambigu|ity /æmbɪ'gju:ətɪ/ *n* ambiguità *f inv*. **~ous** *adj* ambiguo

ambiti|on /æm'bɪʃn/ *n* ambizione *f*; (*aim*) aspirazione *f*. **~ous** *adj* ambizioso

ambivalent /æm'bɪvələnt/ *adj* ambivalente

amble /'æmbl/ *vi* camminare senza fretta

ambulance /'æmbjʊləns/ *n* ambulanza *f*

ambush /'æmbʊʃ/ *n* imboscata *f* ● *vt* tendere un'imboscata a

amend /ə'mend/ *vt* modificare. **~ment** *n* modifica *f*. **~s** *npl* **make ~s** fare ammenda (**for** di, per)

amenities /ə'mi:nətɪz/ *npl* comodità *fpl*

America /ə'merɪkə/ *n* America *f*. **~n** *adj & n* americano, -a *mf*

> **American dream** Il cosiddetto 'sogno americano' è la convinzione che negli Stati Uniti chiunque sia disposto a lavorare sodo possa migliorare la propria posizione economica e sociale. Per gli immigrati e le minoranze il concetto di *American dream* significa anche libertà e uguaglianza di diritti.

amiable /'eɪmɪəbl/ *adj* amabile

amicable /'æmɪkəbl/ *adj* amichevole

ammonia /ə'məʊnɪə/ *n* ammoniaca *f*

ammunition /æmjʊ'nɪʃn/ *n* munizioni *fpl*

amnesty /'æmnəstɪ/ *n* amnistia *f*

among[st] /ə'mʌŋ[st]/ *prep* tra, fra

amount /ə'maʊnt/ *n* quantità *f inv*; (*sum of money*) importo *m* ● *vi* **~ to** ammontare a; *fig* equivalere a

amphibi|an /æm'fɪbɪən/ *n* anfibio *m*. **~ous** *adj* anfibio

amphitheatre /'æmfɪ-/ *n* anfiteatro *m*

ampl|e /'æmpl/ *adj* (*large*) grande; (*proportions*) ampio; (*enough*) largamente sufficiente

amplif|ier /'æmplɪfaɪə(r)/ *n* amplificatore *m*. **~y** *vt* (*pt/pp* **-ied**) amplificare (sound)

amputat|e /'æmpjʊteɪt/ *vt* amputare. **~ion** *n* amputazione *f*

amuse /ə'mju:z/ *vt* divertire. **~ment** *n* divertimento *m*. **~ment arcade** *n* sala *f* giochi

amusing /ə'mju:zɪŋ/ *adj* divertente

an /ən/, *accentato* /æn/ ▷**A**

anaem|ia /ə'ni:mɪə/ *n* anemia *f*. **~ic** *adj* anemico

anaesthetic /ænəs'θetɪk/ *n* anestesia *f*

anaesthet|ist /ə'ni:sθətɪst/ *n* anestesista *mf*

analogy /ə'nælədʒɪ/ *n* analogia *f*

analyse /'ænəlaɪz/ *vt* analizzare

analysis /ə'næləsɪs/ *n* analisi *f inv*

analyst /'ænəlɪst/ *n* analista *mf*

analytical /ænə'lɪtɪkl/ *adj* analitico

anarch|ist /'ænəkɪst/ *n* anarchico, -a *mf*. **~y** *n* anarchia *f*

anatom|ical /ænə'tɒmɪkl/ *adj* anatomico. **~ically** *adv* anatomicamente. **~y** *n* anatomia *f*

ancest|or /'ænsestə(r)/ *n* antenato, -a *mf*. **~ry** *n* antenati *mpl*

anchor /'æŋkə(r)/ *n* ancora *f* ● *vi* gettar l'ancora ● *vt* ancorare

anchovy /'æntʃəvɪ/ *n* acciuga *f*

ancient /'eɪnʃənt/ *adj* antico; [!] vecchio

ancillary /æn'sɪlərɪ/ *adj* ausiliario

and /ənd/, *accentato* /ænd/ *conj* e; **two ~ two** due più due; **six hundred ~ two** seicentodue; **more ~ more** sempre più; **nice ~ warm** bello caldo; **try ~ come** cerca di venire; **go ~ get** vai a prendere

anecdote /'ænɪkdəʊt/ *n* aneddoto *m*

anew /ə'nju:/ *adv* di nuovo

angel /'eɪndʒl/ *n* angelo *m*. **~ic** *adj* angelico

anger /'æŋgə(r)/ *n* rabbia *f* ● *vt* far arrabbiare

angle[1] /'æŋgl/ *n* angolo *m*; *fig* angolazione *f*; **at an ~** storto

angle[2] *vi* pescare con la lenza; **~ for** *fig* cercare di ottenere. **~r** *n* pescatore, -trice *mf*

Anglican /'æŋglɪkən/ *adj & n* anglicano, -a *mf*

angr|y /'æŋgrɪ/ *adj* (**-ier, -iest**) arrabbiato; **get ~y** arrabbiarsi; **~y with** *or* **at sb** arrabbiato con qcno; **~y at** *or* **about sth** arrabbiato per qcsa. **~ily** *adv* rabbiosamente

anguish /ˈæŋgwɪʃ/ *n* angoscia *f*
animal /ˈænɪml/ *adj & n* animale *m*
animate[1] /ˈænɪmət/ *adj* animato
animat|e[2] /ˈænɪmeɪt/ *vt* animare. **~ed** *adj* animato; (person) vivace. **~ion** *n* animazione *f*
animosity /ænɪˈmɒsətɪ/ *n* animosità *f inv*
ankle /ˈæŋkl/ *n* caviglia *f*
annihilat|e /əˈnaɪəleɪt/ *vt* annientare. **~ion** *n* annientamento *m*
anniversary /ænɪˈvɜːsərɪ/ *n* anniversario *m*
announce /əˈnaʊns/ *vt* annunciare. **~ment** *n* annuncio *m*. **~r** *n* annunciatore, -trice *mf*
annoy /əˈnɔɪ/ *vt* dare fastidio a; **get ~ed** essere infastidito. **~ance** *n* seccatura *f*; (*anger*) irritazione *f*. **~ing** *adj* fastidioso
annual /ˈænjʊəl/ *adj* annuale; (income) annuo ● *n* (*Bot*) pianta *f* annua; (*children's book*) almanacco *m*
annul /əˈnʌl/ *vt* (*pt/pp* **annulled**) annullare
anonymous /əˈnɒnɪməs/ *adj* anonimo
anorak /ˈænəræk/ *n* giacca *f* a vento
another /əˈnʌðə(r)/ *adj & pron*; **~ [one]** un altro, un'altra; **in ~ way** diversamente; **one ~** l'un l'altro
answer /ˈɑːnsə(r)/ *n* risposta *f*; (*solution*) soluzione *f* ● *vt* rispondere a (person, question, letter); esaudire (prayer); **~ the door** aprire la porta; **~ the telephone** rispondere al telefono ● *vi* rispondere; **~ back** ribattere; **~ for** rispondere di. **~able** *adj* responsabile; **be ~able to sb** rispondere a qcno. **~ing machine** *n* (*Teleph*) segreteria *f* telefonica
ant /ænt/ *n* formica *f*
antagonis|m /ænˈtægənɪzm/ *n* antagonismo *m*. **~tic** *adj* antagonistico
antagonize /ænˈtægənaɪz/ *vt* provocare l'ostilità di
Antarctic /ænˈtɑːktɪk/ *n* Antartico *m* ● *adj* antartico
antenatal /æntɪˈneɪtl/ *adj* prenatale
antenna /ænˈtenə/ *n* antenna *f*
anthem /ˈænθəm/ *n* inno *m*
anthology /ænˈθɒlədʒɪ/ *n* antologia *f*
anthropology /ænθrəˈpɒlədʒɪ/ *n* antropologia *f*
anti-ˈaircraft /æntɪ-/ *adj* antiaereo
antibiotic /æntɪbaɪˈɒtɪk/ *n* antibiotico *m*
anticipat|e /ænˈtɪsɪpeɪt/ *vt* prevedere; (*forestall*) anticipare. **~ion** *n* anticipo *m*; (*excitement*) attesa *f*
antiˈclimax *n* delusione *f*
antiˈclockwise *adj & adv* in senso antiorario
antidote /ˈæntɪdəʊt/ *n* antidoto *m*
ˈantifreeze *n* antigelo *m*
antiquated /ˈæntɪkweɪtɪd/ *adj* antiquato
antique /ænˈtiːk/ *adj* antico ● *n* antichità *f inv*. **~ dealer** *n* antiquario, -a *mf*
antiquity /ænˈtɪkwətɪ/ *n* antichità *f*
antiˈseptic *adj & n* antisettico *m*
antiˈsocial *adj* (behaviour) antisociale; (person) asociale
antlers /ˈæntləz/ *npl* corna *fpl*
anus /ˈeɪnəs/ *n* ano *m*
anxiety /æŋˈzaɪətɪ/ *n* ansia *f*
anxious /ˈæŋkʃəs/ *adj* ansioso. **~ly** *adv* con ansia

any /ˈenɪ/

● *adj* (*no matter which*) qualsiasi, qualunque; **~ colour/number you like** qualsiasi colore/numero ti piaccia; **we don't have ~ wine/biscuits** non abbiamo vino/biscotti; **for ~ reason** per qualsiasi ragione

! **any** is often not translated: **have we ~ wine/biscuits?** abbiamo del vino/dei biscotti?

● *pron* (*some*) ne; (*no matter which*) uno qualsiasi; **I don't want ~ [of it]** non ne voglio [nessuno]; **there aren't ~** non ce ne sono; **have we ~?** ne abbiamo?; **have you read ~ of her books?** hai letto qualcuno dei suoi libri?

● *adv* **I can't go ~ quicker** non posso andare più in fretta; **is it ~ better?** va un po' meglio?; **would you like ~ more?** ne vuoi ancora?; **I can't eat ~ more** non posso mangiare più niente

'anybody *pron* chiunque; (*after negative*) nessuno; **I haven't seen ~** non ho visto nessuno

'anyhow *adv* ad ogni modo, comunque; (*badly*) non importa come

'anyone *pron* = **anybody**

'anything *pron* qualche cosa, qualcosa; (*no matter what*) qualsiasi cosa; (*after negative*) niente; **take/buy ~ you like** prendi/compra quello che vuoi; **I don't remember ~** non mi ricordo niente; **he's ~ but stupid** è tutto, ma non stupido; **I'll do ~ but that** farò qualsiasi cosa, tranne quello

'anyway *adv* ad ogni modo, comunque

'anywhere *adv* dovunque; (*after negative*) da nessuna parte; **put it ~** mettilo dove vuoi; **I can't find it ~** non lo trovo da nessuna parte; **~ else** da qualch'altra parte; (*after negative*) da nessun'altra parte; **I don't want to go ~ else** non voglio andare da nessun'altra parte

apart /ə'pɑ:t/ *adv* lontano; **live ~** vivere separati; **100 miles ~** lontani 100 miglia; **~ from** a parte; **you can't tell them ~** non si possono distinguere; **joking ~** scherzi a parte

apartment /ə'pɑ:tmənt/ *n* (*Am: flat*) appartamento *m*; **in my ~** a casa mia

apathy /'æpəθɪ/ *n* apatia *f*

ape /eɪp/ *n* scimmia *f* ● *vt* scimmiottare

aperitif /ə'perəti:f/ *n* aperitivo *m*

aperture /'æpətʃə(r)/ *n* apertura *f*

apex /'eɪpeks/ *n* vertice *m*

apologetic /əpɒlə'dʒetɪk/ *adj* (air, remark) di scusa; **be ~** essere spiacente

apologize /ə'pɒlədʒaɪz/ *vi* scusarsi (**for** per)

apology /ə'pɒlədʒɪ/ *n* scusa *f*; *fig* **an ~ for a dinner** una sottospecie di cena

apostle /ə'pɒsl/ *n* apostolo *m*

apostrophe /ə'pɒstrəfɪ/ *n* apostrofo *m*

appal /ə'pɔ:l/ *vt* (*pt/pp* **appalled**) sconvolgere. **~ling** *adj* sconvolgente

apparatus /æpə'reɪtəs/ *n* apparato *m*

apparent /ə'pærənt/ *adj* evidente; (*seeming*) apparente. **~ly** *adv* apparentemente

apparition /æpə'rɪʃn/ *n* apparizione *f*

appeal /ə'pi:l/ *n* appello *m*; (*attraction*) attrattiva *f* ● *vi* fare appello; **~ to** (*be attractive to*) attrarre. **~ing** *adj* attraente

appear /ə'pɪə(r)/ *vi* apparire; (*seem*) sembrare; (publication:) uscire; (*Theat*) esibirsi. **~ance** *n* apparizione *f*; (*look*) aspetto *m*; **to all ~ances** a giudicare dalle apparenze; **keep up ~ances** salvare le apparenze

appease /ə'pi:z/ *vt* placare

appendicitis /əpendɪ'saɪtɪs/ *n* appendicite *f*

appendix /ə'pendɪks/ *n* (*pl* **-ices** /-ɪsi:z/) (*of book*) appendice *f*; (*pl* **-es**) (*Anat*) appendice *f*

appetite /'æpɪtaɪt/ *n* appetito *m*

applau|d /ə'plɔ:d/ *vt/i* applaudire. **~se** *n* applauso *m*

apple /'æpl/ *n* mela *f*. **~-tree** *n* melo *m*

appliance /ə'plaɪəns/ *n* attrezzo *m*; **[electrical] ~** elettrodomestico *m*

applicable /'æplɪkəbl/ *adj* **be ~ to** essere valido per; **not ~** (*on form*) non applicabile

applicant /'æplɪkənt/ *n* candidato, -a *mf*

application /æplɪ'keɪʃn/ *n* applicazione *f*; (*request*) domanda *f*; (*for job*) candidatura *f*. **~ form** *n* modulo *m* di domanda

applied /ə'plaɪd/ *adj* applicato

apply /ə'plaɪ/ *vt* (*pt/pp* **-ied**) applicare; **~ oneself** applicarsi ● *vi* applicarsi; (law:) essere applicabile; **~ to** (*ask*) rivolgersi a; **~ for** fare domanda per (job etc)

appoint /ə'pɔɪnt/ *vt* nominare; fissare (time). **~ment** *n* appuntamento *m*; (*to job*) nomina *f*; (*job*) posto *m*

appraisal /ə'preɪz(ə)l/ *n* valutazione *f*

appreciable /ə'pri:ʃəbl/ *adj* sensibile

appreciat|e /ə'pri:ʃɪeɪt/ *vt* apprezzare; (*understand*) comprendere ● *vi* (*increase in value*) aumentare di valore. **~ion** *n* (*gratitude*) riconoscenza *f*; (*enjoyment*) apprezzamento *m*; (*understanding*) comprensione *f*; (*in value*) aumento *m*. **~ive** *adj* riconoscente

apprehens|ion /æprɪ'henʃn/ *n* arresto *m*; (*fear*) apprensione *f*. **~ive** *adj* apprensivo

apprentice /ə'prentɪs/ *n* apprendista *mf*. **~ship** *n* apprendistato *m*

approach /ə'prəʊtʃ/ *n* avvicinamento

m; (*to problem*) approccio *m*; (*access*) accesso *m*; **make ~es to** fare degli approcci con ● *vi* avvicinarsi ● *vt* avvicinarsi a; (*with request*) rivolgersi a; affrontare (problem). **~able** *adj* accessibile

appropriate[1] /ə'prəʊprɪət/ *adj* appropriato

appropriate[2] /ə'prəʊprɪeɪt/ *vt* appropriarsi di

approval /ə'pru:vl/ *n* approvazione *f*; **on ~** in prova

approv|e /ə'pru:v/ *vt* approvare ● *vi* **~e of** approvare (sth); avere una buona opinione di (sb). **~ing** *adj* (smile, nod) d'approvazione

approximate /ə'prɒksɪmət/ *adj* approssimativo. **~ly** *adv* approssimativamente

approximation /əprɒksɪ'meɪʃn/ *n* approssimazione *f*

apricot /'eɪprɪkɒt/ *n* albicocca *f*

April /'eɪprəl/ *n* aprile *m*; **~ Fool's Day** il primo d'aprile

apron /'eɪprən/ *n* grembiule *m*

apt /æpt/ *adj* appropriato; **be ~ to do sth** avere tendenza a fare qcsa

aptitude /'æptɪtju:d/ *n* disposizione *f*. **~ test** *n* test *m inv* attitudinale

aquarium /ə'kweərɪəm/ *n* acquario *m*

Aquarius /ə'kweərɪəs/ *n* (*Astr*) Acquario *m*

aquatic /ə'kwætɪk/ *adj* acquatico

Arab /'ærəb/ *adj & n* arabo, -a *mf*. **~ian** *adj* arabo

Arabic /'ærəbɪk/ *adj* arabo; **~ numerals** numeri *mpl* arabici ● *n* arabo *m*

arable /'ærəbl/ *adj* coltivabile

arbitrary /'ɑ:bɪtrərɪ/ *adj* arbitrario

arbitrat|e /'ɑ:bɪtreɪt/ *vi* arbitrare. **~ion** *n* arbitraggio *m*

arc /ɑ:k/ *n* arco *m*

arcade /ɑ:'keɪd/ *n* portico *m*; (*shops*) galleria *f*

arch /ɑ:tʃ/ *n* arco *m*; (*of foot*) dorso *m* del piede

archaeological /ɑ:kɪə'lɒdʒɪkl/ *adj* archeologico

archaeolog|ist /ɑ:kɪ'ɒlədʒɪst/ *n* archeologo, -a *mf*. **~y** *n* archeologia *f*

archaic /ɑ:'keɪɪk/ *adj* arcaico

arch'bishop /ɑ:tʃ-/ *n* arcivescovo *m*

architect /'ɑ:kɪtekt/ *n* architetto *m*. **~ural** *adj* architettonico

architecture /'ɑ:kɪtektʃə(r)/ *n* architettura *f*

archives /'ɑ:kaɪvz/ *npl* archivi *mpl*

archway /'ɑ:tʃweɪ/ *n* arco *m*

Arctic /'ɑ:ktɪk/ *adj* artico ● *n* **the ~** l'Artico

ardent /'ɑ:dənt/ *adj* ardente

arduous /'ɑ:djʊəs/ *adj* arduo

are /ɑ:(r)/ ▷**BE**

area /'eərɪə/ *n* area *f*; (*region*) zona *f*; (*fig: field*) campo *m*. **~ code** *n* prefisso *m* [telefonico]

arena /ə'ri:nə/ *n* arena *f*

Argentina /ɑ:dʒən'ti:nə/ *n* Argentina *f*

Argentinian /-'tɪnɪən/ *adj & n* argentino, -a *mf*

argue /'ɑ:gju:/ *vi* litigare (**about** su); (*debate*) dibattere; **don't ~!** non discutere! ● *vt* (*debate*) dibattere; (*reason*) **~ that** sostenere che

argument /'ɑ:gjʊmənt/ *n* argomento *m*; (*reasoning*) ragionamento *m*; **have an ~** litigare. **~ative** *adj* polemico

arid /'ærɪd/ *adj* arido

Aries /'eəri:z/ *n* (*Astr*) Ariete *m*

arise /ə'raɪz/ *vi* (*pt* **arose**, *pp* **arisen**) (opportunity, need, problem:) presentarsi; (*result*) derivare

aristocracy /ærɪ'stɒkrəsɪ/ *n* aristocrazia *f*

aristocrat /'ærɪstəkræt/ *n* aristocratico, -a *mf*. **~ic** *adj* aristocratico

arithmetic /ə'rɪθmətɪk/ *n* aritmetica *f*

arm /ɑ:m/ *n* braccio *m*; (*of chair*) bracciolo *m*; **~s** *pl* (*weapons*) armi *fpl*; **~ in ~** a braccetto; **up in ~s** [!] furioso (**about** per) ● *vt* armare

'armchair *n* poltrona *f*

armed /ɑ:md/ *adj* armato; **~ forces** forze *fpl* armate; **~ robbery** rapina *f* a mano armata

armour /'ɑ:mə(r)/ *n* armatura *f*. **~ed** *adj* (vehicle) blindato

'armpit *n* ascella *f*

army /'ɑ:mɪ/ *n* esercito *m*; **join the ~** arruolarsi

aroma /ə'rəʊmə/ *n* aroma *f*. **~tic** *adj* aromatico

arose /ə'rəʊz/ ▷**ARISE**

around /ə'raʊnd/ *adv* intorno; **all ~**

a

tutt'intorno; **I'm not from ~ here** non sono di qui; **he's not ~** non c'è ● *prep* intorno a; in giro per (room, shops, world)

arouse /ə'raʊz/ *vt* svegliare; (*sexually*) eccitare

arrange /ə'reɪndʒ/ *vt* sistemare (furniture, books); organizzare (meeting); fissare (date, time); **~ to do sth** combinare di fare qcsa. **~ment** *n* (*of furniture*) sistemazione *f*; (*Mus*) arrangiamento *m*; (*agreement*) accordo; (*of flowers*) composizione *f*; **make ~ments** prendere disposizioni

arrears /ə'rɪəz/ *npl* arretrati *mpl*; **be in ~** essere in arretrato; **paid in ~** pagato a lavoro eseguito

arrest /ə'rest/ *n* arresto *m*; **under ~** in stato d'arresto ● *vt* arrestare

arrival /ə'raɪvl/ *n* arrivo *m*; **new ~s** *pl* nuovi arrivati *mpl*

arrive /ə'raɪv/ *vi* arrivare; **~ at** *fig* raggiungere

arrogan|ce /'ærəgəns/ *n* arroganza *f*. **~t** *adj* arrogante

arrow /'ærəʊ/ *n* freccia *f*

arse /ɑːs/ *n* [!] culo *m*

arsenic /'ɑːsənɪk/ *n* arsenico *m*

arson /'ɑːsn/ *n* incendio *m* doloso. **~ist** *n* incendiario, -a *mf*

art /ɑːt/ *n* arte *f*; **~s and crafts** *pl* artigianato *m*; **the A~s** *pl* l'arte *f*; **A~s degree** (*Univ*) laurea *f* in Lettere

artery /'ɑːtərɪ/ *n* arteria *f*

'art gallery *n* galleria *f* d'arte

arthritis /ɑː'θraɪtɪs/ *n* artrite *f*

artichoke /'ɑːtɪtʃəʊk/ *n* carciofo *m*

article /'ɑːtɪkl/ *n* articolo *m*; **~ of clothing** capo *m* d'abbigliamento

articulate[1] /ɑː'tɪkjʊlət/ *adj* (speech) chiaro; **be ~** esprimersi bene

articulate[2] /ɑː'tɪkjʊleɪt/ *vt* scandire (words). **~d lorry** *n* autotreno *m*

artificial /ɑːtɪ'fɪʃl/ *adj* artificiale. **~ly** *adv* artificialmente; (smile) artificiosamente

artillery /ɑː'tɪlərɪ/ *n* artiglieria *f*

artist /'ɑːtɪst/ *n* artista *mf*

as /æz/ *conj* come; (*since*) siccome; (*while*) mentre; **as he grew older** diventando vecchio; **as you get to know her** conoscendola meglio; **young as she is** per quanto sia giovane ● *prep* come; **as a friend** come amico; **as a child** da bambino; **as a foreigner** in quanto straniero; **disguised as** travestito da ● *adv* **as well** (*also*) anche; **as soon as I get home** [non] appena arrivo a casa; **as quick as you** veloce quanto te; **as quick as you can** più veloce che puoi; **as far as** (*distance*) fino a; **as far as I'm concerned** per quanto mi riguarda; **as long as** finché; (*provided that*) purché

asbestos /æz'bestɒs/ *n* amianto *m*

ascend /ə'send/ *vi* salire ● *vt* salire a (throne)

Ascension /ə'senʃn/ *n* (*Relig*) Ascensione *f*

ascent /ə'sent/ *n* ascesa *f*

ascertain /æsə'teɪn/ *vt* accertare

ash[1] /æʃ/ *n* (*tree*) frassino *m*

ash[2] *n* cenere *f*

ashamed /ə'ʃeɪmd/ *adj* **be/feel ~** vergognarsi

ashore /ə'ʃɔː(r)/ *adv* a terra; **go ~** sbarcare

ash: ~tray *n* portacenere *m*. **A~ 'Wednesday** *n* mercoledì *m inv* delle Ceneri

Asia /'eɪʒə/ *n* Asia *f*. **~n** *adj & n* asiatico, -a *mf*. **~tic** *adj* asiatico

aside /ə'saɪd/ *adv* **take sb ~** prendere qcno a parte; **put sth ~** mettere qcsa da parte; **~ from you** *Am* a parte te

ask /ɑːsk/ *vt* fare (question); (*invite*) invitare; **~ sb sth** domandare *or* chiedere qcsa a qcno; **~ sb to do sth** domandare *or* chiedere a qcno di fare qcsa ● *vi* **~ about sth** informarsi su qcsa; **~ after** chiedere [notizie] di; **~ for** chiedere (sth); chiedere di (sb); **~ for trouble** [!] andare in cerca di guai. □ **~ in** *vt* **~ sb in** invitare qcno ad entrare. □ **~ out** *vt* **~ sb out** chiedere a qcno di uscire

askew /ə'skjuː/ *adj & adv* di traverso

asleep /ə'sliːp/ *adj* **be ~** dormire; **fall ~** addormentarsi

asparagus /ə'spærəgəs/ *n* asparagi *mpl*

aspect /'æspekt/ *n* aspetto *m*

asphalt /'æsfælt/ *n* asfalto *m*

aspire /ə'spaɪə(r)/ *vi* **~ to** aspirare a

ass /æs/ *n* asino *m*

assassin /ə'sæsɪn/ *n* assassino, -a *mf*.

~ate *vt* assassinare. **~ation** *n* assassinio *m*

assault /ə'sɔ:lt/ *n* (*Mil*) assalto *m*; (*Jur*) aggressione *f* ● *vt* aggredire

assemble /ə'sembl/ *vi* radunarsi ● *vt* radunare; (*Techn*) montare

assembly /ə'semblɪ/ *n* assemblea *f*; (*Sch*) *assemblea f giornaliera di alunni e professori di una scuola*; (*Techn*) montaggio *m*. **~ line** *n* catena *f* di montaggio

assent /ə'sent/ *n* assenso *m* ● *vi* acconsentire

assert /ə'sɜ:t/ *vt* asserire; far valere (one's rights); **~ oneself** farsi valere. **~ion** *n* asserzione *f*. **~ive** *adj* **be ~ive** farsi valere

assess /ə'ses/ *vt* valutare; (*for tax purposes*) stabilire l'imponibile di. **~ment** *n* valutazione *f*; (*of tax*) accertamento *m*

asset /'æset/ *n* (*advantage*) vantaggio *m*; (*person*) elemento *m* prezioso. **~s** *pl* beni *mpl*; (*on balance sheet*) attivo *msg*

assign /ə'saɪn/ *vt* assegnare. **~ment** *n* (*task*) incarico *m*

assimilate /ə'sɪmɪleɪt/ *vt* assimilare; integrare (person)

assist /ə'sɪst/ *vt/i* assistere; **~ sb to do sth** assistere qcno nel fare qcsa. **~ance** *n* assistenza *f*. **~ant** *adj* **~ant manager** vicedirettore, -trice *mf* ● *n* assistente *mf*; (*in shop*) commesso, -a *mf*

associat|e¹ /ə'səʊʃɪeɪt/ *vt* associare (**with** a); **be ~ed with sth** (*involved in*) essere coinvolto in qcsa ● *vi* **~e with** frequentare. **~ion** *n* associazione *f*. **A~ion 'Football** *n* [gioco *m* del] calcio *m*

associate² /ə'səʊʃɪət/ *adj* associato ● *n* collega *mf*; (*member*) socio, -a *mf*

assort|ed /ə'sɔ:tɪd/ *adj* assortito. **~ment** *n* assortimento *m*

assum|e /ə'sju:m/ *vt* presumere; assumere (control); **~e office** entrare in carica; **~ing that you're right,...** ammettendo che tu abbia ragione,...

assumption /ə'sʌmpʃn/ *n* supposizione *f*; **on the ~ that** partendo dal presupposto che; **the A~** (*Relig*) l'Assunzione *f*

assurance /ə'ʃʊərəns/ *n* assicurazione *f*; (*confidence*) sicurezza *f*

assure /ə'ʃʊə(r)/ *vt* assicurare. **~d** *adj* sicuro

asterisk /'æstərɪsk/ *n* asterisco *m*

asthma /'æsmə/ *n* asma *f*. **~tic** *adj* asmatico

astonish /ə'stɒnɪʃ/ *vt* stupire. **~ing** *adj* stupefacente. **~ment** *n* stupore *m*

astound /ə'staʊnd/ *vt* stupire

astray /ə'streɪ/ *adv* **go ~** smarrirsi; (*morally*) uscire dalla retta via; **lead ~** traviare

astronaut /'æstrənɔ:t/ *n* astronauta *mf*

astronom|er /ə'strɒnəmə(r)/ *n* astronomo, -a *mf*. **~ical** *adj* astronomico. **~y** *n* astronomia *f*

astute /ə'stju:t/ *adj* astuto

asylum /ə'saɪləm/ *n* **[political] ~** asilo *m* politico; **[lunatic] ~** manicomio *m*

at /ət/, *accentato* /æt/ *prep* a; **at the station/the market** alla stazione/al mercato; **at the office/the bank** in ufficio/banca; **at the beginning** all'inizio; **at John's** da John; **at the hairdresser's** dal parrucchiere; **at home** a casa; **at work** al lavoro; **at school** a scuola; **at a party/wedding** a una festa/un matrimonio; **at 1 o'clock** all'una; **at 50 km an hour** ai 50 all'ora; **at Christmas/Easter** a Natale/Pasqua; **at times** talvolta; **two at a time** due alla volta; **good at languages** bravo nelle lingue; **at sb's request** su richiesta di qcno; **are you at all worried?** sei preoccupato?

ate /et/ ▷EAT

atheist /'eɪθɪɪst/ *n* ateo, -a *mf*

athlet|e /'æθli:t/ *n* atleta *mf*. **~ic** *adj* atletico. **~ics** *n* atletica *fsg*

Atlantic /ət'læntɪk/ *adj & n* **the ~ [Ocean]** l'[Oceano *m*] Atlantico *m*

atlas /'ætləs/ *n* atlante *m*

atmospher|e /'ætməsfɪə(r)/ *n* atmosfera *f*. **~ic** *adj* atmosferico

atom /'ætəm/ *n* atomo *m*. **~ bomb** *n* bomba *f* atomica

atomic /ə'tɒmɪk/ *adj* atomico

atrocious /ə'trəʊʃəs/ *adj* atroce; (meal, weather) abominevole

atrocity /ə'trɒsətɪ/ *n* atrocità *f inv*

attach /ə'tætʃ/ *vt* attaccare; attribuire (importance); **be ~ed to** *fig* essere attaccato a

attachment /ə'tætʃmənt/ *n* (*affection*)

attaccamento *m*; (*accessory*) accessorio *m*

attack /ə'tæk/ *n* attacco *m*; (*physical*) aggressione *f* ● *vt* attaccare; (*physically*) aggredire. **~er** *n* assalitore, -trice *mf*; (*critic*) detrattore, -trice *mf*

attain /ə'teɪn/ *vt* realizzare (ambition); raggiungere (success, age, goal)

attempt /ə'tempt/ *n* tentativo *m* ● *vt* tentare

attend /ə'tend/ *vt* essere presente a; (*go regularly to*) frequentare; (doctor:) avere in cura ● *vi* essere presente; (*pay attention*) prestare attenzione. □ **~ to** *vt* occuparsi di; (*in shop*) servire. **~ance** *n* presenza *f*. **~ant** *n* guardiano, -a *mf*

attention /ə'tenʃn/ *n* attenzione *f*; **~!** (*Mil*) attenti!; **pay ~** prestare attenzione; **need ~** aver bisogno di attenzioni; (skin, hair, plant:) dover essere curato; (car, tyres:) dover essere riparato; **for the ~ of** all'attenzione di

attentive /ə'tentɪv/ *adj* (pupil, audience) attento

attic /'ætɪk/ *n* soffitta *f*

attitude /'ætɪtju:d/ *n* atteggiamento *m*

attorney /ə'tɜ:nɪ/ *n* (*Am: lawyer*) avvocato *m*; **power of ~** delega *f*

attract /ə'trækt/ *vt* attirare. **~ion** *n* attrazione *f*; (*feature*) attrattiva *f*. **~ive** *adj* (person) attraente; (proposal, price) allettante

attribute¹ /'ætrɪbju:t/ *n* attributo *m*

attribute² /ə'trɪbju:t/ *vt* attribuire

aubergine /'əʊbəʒi:n/ *n* melanzana *f*

auction /'ɔ:kʃn/ *n* asta *f* ● *vt* vendere all'asta. **~eer** *n* banditore *m*

audaci|ous /ɔ:'deɪʃəs/ *adj* sfacciato; (*daring*) audace. **~ty** *n* sfacciataggine *f*; (*daring*) audacia *f*

audible /'ɔ:dəbl/ *adj* udibile

audience /'ɔ:dɪəns/ *n* (*Theat*) pubblico *m*; (*TV*) telespettatori *mpl*; (*Radio*) ascoltatori *mpl*; (*meeting*) udienza *f*

audit /'ɔ:dɪt/ *n* verifica *f* del bilancio ● *vt* verificare

audition /ɔ:'dɪʃn/ *n* audizione *f* ● *vi* fare un'audizione

auditor /'ɔ:dɪtə(r)/ *n* revisore *m* di conti

auditorium /ɔ:dɪ'tɔ:rɪəm/ *n* sala *f*

augment /ɔ:g'ment/ *vt* aumentare

augur /'ɔ:gə(r)/ *vi* **~ well/ill** essere di buon/cattivo augurio

August /'ɔ:gəst/ *n* agosto *m*

aunt /ɑ:nt/ *n* zia *f*

au pair /əʊ'peə(r)/ *n* **~ [girl]** ragazza *f* alla pari

aura /'ɔ:rə/ *n* aura *f*

auster|e /ɒ'stɪə(r)/ *adj* austero. **~ity** *n* austerità *f*

Australia /ɒ'streɪlɪə/ *n* Australia *f*. **~n** *adj & n* australiano, -a *mf*

Austria /'ɒstrɪə/ *n* Austria *f*. **~n** *adj & n* austriaco, -a *mf*

authentic /ɔ:'θentɪk/ *adj* autentico. **~ate** *vt* autenticare. **~ity** *n* autenticità *f*

author /'ɔ:θə(r)/ *n* autore *m*

authoritative /ɔ:'θɒrɪtətɪv/ *adj* autorevole; (manner) autoritario

authority /ɔ:'θɒrətɪ/ *n* autorità *f*; (*permission*) autorizzazione *f*; **be in ~ over** avere autorità su

authorization /ɔ:θəraɪ'zeɪʃn/ *n* autorizzazione *f*

authorize /'ɔ:θəraɪz/ *vt* autorizzare

autobi'ography /ɔ:tə-/ *n* autobiografia *f*

autograph /'ɔ:tə-/ *n* autografo *m*

automate /'ɔ:təmeɪt/ *vt* automatizzare

automatic /ɔ:tə'mætɪk/ *adj* automatico ● *n* (*car*) macchina *f* col cambio automatico; (*washing machine*) lavatrice *f* automatica. **~ally** *adv* automaticamente

automation /ɔ:tə'meɪʃn/ *n* automazione *f*

automobile /'ɔ:təməbi:l/ *n* automobile *f*

autonom|ous /ɔ:'tɒnəməs/ *adj* autonomo. **~y** *n* autonomia *f*

autopsy /'ɔtɒpsɪ/ *n* autopsia *f*

autumn /'ɔ:təm/ *n* autunno *m*. **~al** *adj* autunnale

auxiliary /ɔ:g'zɪlɪərɪ/ *adj* ausiliario ● *n* ausiliare *m*

avail /ə'veɪl/ *n* **to no ~** invano ● *vi* **~ oneself of** approfittare di

available /ə'veɪləbl/ *adj* disponibile; (book, record etc) in vendita

avalanche /'ævəlɑ:nʃ/ *n* valanga *f*

avarice /'ævərɪs/ *n* avidità *f*

avenue /'ævənju:/ *n* viale *m*; *fig* strada *f*

average /'ævərɪdʒ/ *adj* medio; (*mediocre*) mediocre ● *n* media *f*; **on ~** in media ● *vt* (sales, attendance) *etc*: raggiungere una media di. □ **~ out at** *vt* risultare in media

avers|e /ə'vɜ:s/ *adj* **not be ~e to sth** non essere contro qcsa. **~ion** *n* avversione *f* (**to** per)

avert /ə'vɜ:t/ *vt* evitare (crisis); distogliere (eyes)

aviation /eɪvɪ'eɪʃn/ *n* aviazione *f*

avid /'ævɪd/ *adj* avido (**for** di); (reader) appassionato

avocado /ævə'kɑ:dəʊ/ *n* avocado *m*

avoid /ə'vɔɪd/ *vt* evitare. **~able** *adj* evitabile

await /ə'weɪt/ *vt* attendere

awake /ə'weɪk/ *adj* sveglio; **wide ~** completamente sveglio ● *vi* (*pt* **awoke**, *pp* **awoken**) svegliarsi

awaken /ə'weɪkn/ *vt* svegliare. **~ing** *n* risveglio *m*

award /ə'wɔ:d/ *n* premio *m*; (*medal*) riconoscimento *m*; (*of prize*) assegnazione *f* ● *vt* assegnare; (*hand over*) consegnare

aware /ə'weə(r)/ *adj* **be ~ of** (*sense*) percepire; (*know*) essere conscio di; **become ~ of** accorgersi di; (*learn*) venire a sapere di; **be ~ that** rendersi conto che. **~ness** *n* percezione *f*; (*knowledge*) consapevolezza *f*

awash /ə'wɒʃ/ *adj* inondato (**with** di)

away /ə'weɪ/ *adv* via; **go/stay ~** andare/stare via; **he's ~ from his desk/the office** non è alla sua scrivania/in ufficio; **far ~** lontano; **four kilometres ~** a quattro chilometri; **play ~** (*Sport*) giocare fuori casa. **~ game** *n* partita *f* fuori casa

awe /ɔ:/ *n* soggezione *f*

awful /'ɔ:fl/ *adj* terribile. **~ly** *adv* terribilmente; (pretty) estremamente

awkward /'ɔ:kwəd/ *adj* (movement) goffo; (moment, situation) imbarazzante; (time) scomodo. **~ly** *adv* (move) goffamente; (say) con imbarazzo

awning /'ɔ:nɪŋ/ *n* tendone *m*

awoke(n) /ə'wəʊk (ən)/ ▷ **AWAKE**

axe /æks/ *n* scure *f* ● *vt* (*pres p* **axing**) fare dei tagli a (budget); sopprimere (jobs); annullare (project)

axis /'æksɪs/ *n* (*pl* **axes** /-si:z/) asse *m*

axle /'æksl/ *n* (*Techn*) asse *m*

Bb

BA *n abbr* Bachelor of Arts

babble /'bæbl/ *vi* farfugliare; (stream:) gorgogliare

baby /'beɪbɪ/ *n* bambino, -a *mf*; (❗: *darling*) tesoro *m*

baby: ~ carriage *n Am* carrozzina *f*. **~ish** *adj* bambinesco. **~-sit** *vi* fare da baby-sitter. **~-sitter** *n* baby-sitter *mf*

bachelor /'bætʃələ(r)/ *n* scapolo *m*; **B~ of Arts/Science** laureato, -a *mf* in lettere/in scienze

back /bæk/ *n* schiena *f*; (*of horse, hand*) dorso *m*; (*of chair*) schienale *m*; (*of house, cheque, page*) retro *m*; (*in football*) difesa *f*; **at the ~** in fondo; **in the ~** (*Auto*) dietro; **~ to front** (sweater) il davanti di dietro; **at the ~ of beyond** in un posto sperduto ● *adj* posteriore; (taxes, payments) arretrato ● *adv* indietro; (*returned*) di ritorno; **turn/move ~** tornare/spostarsi indietro; **put it ~ here/there** rimettilo qui/là; **~ at home** di ritorno a casa; **I'll be ~ in five minutes** torno fra cinque minuti; **I'm just ~** sono appena tornato; **when do you want the book ~?** quando rivuoi il libro?; **pay ~** ripagare (sb); restituire (money); **~ in power** di nuovo al potere ● *vt* (*support*) sostenere; (*with money*) finanziare; puntare su (horse); (*cover the back of*) rivestire il retro di ● *vi* (*Auto*) fare retromarcia. □ **~ down** *vi* battere in ritirata. □ **~ in** *vi* (*Auto*) entrare in retromarcia; (person:) entrare camminando all'indietro. □ **~ out** *vi* (*Auto*) uscire in retromarcia; (person:) uscire camminando all'indietro; *fig* tirarsi indietro (**of** da). □ **~ up** *vt* sostenere; confermare (person's alibi); (*Comput*) fare una copia di salvataggio di; **be ~ed up** (traffic:) essere congestionato ● *vi* (*Auto*) fare retromarcia

b

back: ~ache *n* mal *m* di schiena. **~bone** *n* spina *f* dorsale. **~date** *vt* retrodatare (cheque). **~ 'door** *n* porta *f* di servizio

backer /'bækə(r)/ *n* sostenitore, -trice *mf*; (*with money*) finanziatore, -trice *mf*

back: ~'fire *vi* (*Auto*) avere un ritorno di fiamma; (fig: plan) fallire. **~ground** *n* sfondo *m*; (*environment*) ambiente *m*. **~hand** *n* (*tennis*) rovescio *m*

backing /'bækɪŋ/ *n* (*support*) supporto *m*; (*material*) riserva *f*; (*Mus*) accompagnamento *m*; **~ group** gruppo *m* d'accompagnamento

back: ~lash *n fig* reazione *f* opposta. **~log** *n* **~log of work** lavoro *m* arretrato. **~side** *n* [!] fondoschiena *m inv*. **~slash** *n* (*Typ*) barra *f* retroversa. **~stage** *adj & adv* dietro le quinte. **~stroke** *n* dorso *m*. **~-up** *n* rinforzi *mpl*; (*Comput*) riserva *f*

backward /'bækwəd/ *adj* (step) indietro; (child) lento nell'apprendimento; (country) arretrato ● *adv* **~s** (*also Am:* **~**) indietro; (fall, walk) all'indietro; **~s and forwards** avanti e indietro

back: ~water *n fig* luogo *m* allo scarto. **~ 'yard** *n* cortile *m*

bacon /'beɪkn/ *n* ≈ pancetta *f*

bacteria /bæk'tɪərɪə/ *npl* batteri *mpl*

bad /bæd/ *adj* (**worse, worst**) cattivo; (weather, habit, news, accident) brutto; (apple etc) marcio; **the light is ~** non c'è una buona luce; **use ~ language** dire delle parolacce; **feel ~** sentirsi male; (*feel guilty*) sentirsi in colpa; **have a ~ back** avere dei problemi alla schiena; **smoking is ~ for you** fumare fa male; **go ~** andare a male; **that's just too ~!** pazienza!; **not ~** niente male

bade /bæd/ ▷BID

badge /bædʒ/ *n* distintivo *m*

badger /'bædʒə(r)/ *n* tasso *m* ● *vt* tormentare

badly /'bædlɪ/ *adv* male; (hurt) gravemente; **~ off** povero; **~ behaved** maleducato; **need ~** aver estremamente bisogno di

bad-'mannered *adj* maleducato

badminton /'bædmɪntən/ *n* badminton *m*

bad-'tempered *adj* irascibile

baffle /'bæfl/ *vt* confondere

bag /bæg/ *n* borsa *f*; (*of paper*) sacchetto *m*; **old ~** [✖] megera *f*; **~s under the eyes** occhiaie *fpl*; **~s of** [!] un sacco di

baggage /'bægɪdʒ/ *n* bagagli *mpl*

baggy /'bægɪ/ *adj* (clothes) ampio

'bagpipes *npl* cornamusa *fsg*

bail /beɪl/ *n* cauzione *f*; **on ~** su cauzione ● **bail out** *vt* (*Naut*) aggottare; **~ sb out** (*Jur*) pagare la cauzione per qcno ● *vi* (*Aeron*) paracadutarsi

bait /beɪt/ *n* esca *f* ● *vt* innescare; (*fig: torment*) tormentare

bake /beɪk/ *vt* cuocere al forno; (*make*) fare ● *vi* cuocersi al forno

baker /'beɪkə(r)/ *n* fornaio, -a *mf*, pasticciere, -a *mf*; **~'s [shop]** panetteria *f*. **~y** *n* panificio *m*, forno *m*

balance /'bæləns/ *n* equilibrio *m*; (*Comm*) bilancio *m*; (*outstanding sum*) saldo *m*; **[bank] ~** saldo *m*; **be** *or* **hang in the ~** *fig* essere in sospeso ● *vt* bilanciare; equilibrare (budget); (*Comm*) fare il bilancio di (books) ● *vi* bilanciarsi; (*Comm*) essere in pareggio. **~d** *adj* equilibrato. **~ sheet** *n* bilancio *m* [d'esercizio]

balcony /'bælkənɪ/ *n* balcone *m*

bald /bɔːld/ *adj* (person) calvo; (tyre) liscio; (statement) nudo e crudo; **go ~** perdere i capelli

bale /beɪl/ *n* balla *f*

ball[1] /bɔːl/ *n* palla *f*; (*football*) pallone *m*; (*of yarn*) gomitolo *m*; **on the ~** [!] sveglio

ball[2] *n* (*dance*) ballo *m*

ballad /'bæləd/ *n* ballata *f*

ballast /'bæləst/ *n* zavorra *f*

ball-'bearing *n* cuscinetto *m* a sfera

ballerina /bælə'riːnə/ *n* ballerina *f* [classica]

ballet /'bæleɪ/ *n* balletto *m*; (*art form*) danza *f*; **~ dancer** *n* ballerino, -a *mf* [classico, -a]

balloon /bə'luːn/ *n* pallone *m*; (*Aeron*) mongolfiera *f*

ballot /'bælət/ *n* votazione *f*. **~-box** *n* urna *f*. **~-paper** *n* scheda *f* di votazione

ball: ~-point ['pen] *n* penna *f* a sfera. **~room** *n* sala *f* da ballo

Baltic /'bɔːltɪk/ *adj & n* **the ~ [Sea]** il [mar] Baltico

bamboo /bæm'bu:/ *n* bambù *m inv*

ban /bæn/ *n* proibizione *f* ● *vt* (*pt/pp* **banned**) proibire; ~ **from** espellere da (club); **she was ~ned from driving** le hanno ritirato la patente

banal /bə'nɑ:l/ *adj* banale. **~ity** *n* banalità *f inv*

banana /bə'nɑ:nə/ *n* banana *f*

band /bænd/ *n* banda *f*; (*stripe*) nastro *m*; (*Mus: pop group*) complesso *m*; (*Mus: brass* ~) banda *f*; (*Mil*) fanfara *f* ● **band together** *vi* riunirsi

bandage /'bændɪdʒ/ *n* benda *f* ● *vt* fasciare (limb)

b. & b. *abbr* bed and breakfast

bandit /'bændɪt/ *n* bandito *m*

band: ~stand *n* palco *m* coperto [dell'orchestra]. **~wagon** *n* **jump on the ~wagon** *fig* seguire la corrente

bandy[1] /'bændɪ/ *vt* (*pt/pp* **-ied**) scambiarsi (words). □ ~ **about** *vt* far circolare

bandy[2] *adj* (**-ier, -iest**) **be** ~ avere le gambe storte

bang /bæŋ/ *n* (*noise*) fragore *m*; (*of gun, firework*) scoppio *m*; (*blow*) colpo *m* ● *adv* ~ **in the middle of** [!] proprio nel mezzo di; **go** ~ (gun:) sparare; (balloon:) esplodere ● *int* bum! ● *vt* battere (fist); battere su (table); sbattere (door, head) ● *vi* scoppiare; (door:) sbattere

banger /'bæŋə(r)/ *n* (*firework*) petardo *m*; ([!]: *sausage*) salsiccia *f*; **old** ~ ([!]: *car*) macinino *m*

bangle /'bæŋgl/ *n* braccialetto *m*

banish /'bænɪʃ/ *vt* bandire

banisters /'bænɪstəz/ *npl* ringhiera *fsg*

bank[1] /bæŋk/ *n* (*of river*) sponda *f*; (*slope*) scarpata *f* ● *vi* (*Aeron*) inclinarsi in virata

bank[2] *n* banca *f* ● *vt* depositare in banca ● *vi* ~ **with** avere un conto [bancario] presso. □ ~ **on** *vt* contare su

'bank card *n* carta *f* assegno.

banker /'bæŋkə(r)/ *n* banchiere *m*

bank: ~ 'holiday *n* giorno *m* festivo. **~ing** *n* bancario *m*. **~note** *n* banconota *f*

bankrupt /'bæŋkrʌpt/ *adj* fallito; **go** ~ fallire ● *n* persona *f* che ha fatto fallimento ● *vt* far fallire. **~cy** *n* bancarotta *f*

banner /'bænə(r)/ *n* stendardo *m*; (*of demonstrators*) striscione *m*

banquet /'bæŋkwɪt/ *n* banchetto *m*

banter /'bæntə(r)/ *n* battute *fpl* di spirito

baptism /'bæptɪzm/ *n* battesimo *m*

Baptist /'bæptɪst/ *adj & n* battista *mf*

baptize /bæp'taɪz/ *vt* battezzare

bar /bɑ:(r)/ *n* sbarra *f*; (*Jur*) ordine *m* degli avvocati; (*of chocolate*) tavoletta *f*; (*café*) bar *m inv*; (*counter*) banco *m*; (*Mus*) battuta *f*; (*fig: obstacle*) ostacolo *m*; ~ **of soap/gold** saponetta *f*/lingotto *m*; **behind ~s** [!] dietro le sbarre ● *vt* (*pt/pp* **barred**) sbarrare (way); sprangare (door); escludere (person) ● *prep* tranne; ~ **none** in assoluto

barbarian /bɑ:'beərɪən/ *n* barbaro, -a *mf*

barbar|ic /bɑ:'bærɪk/ *adj* barbarico. **~ity** *n* barbarie *f inv*. **~ous** *adj* barbaro

barbecue /'bɑ:bɪkju:/ *n* barbecue *m inv*; (*party*) grigliata *f*, barbecue *m inv* ● *vt* arrostire sul barbecue

barber /'bɑ:bə(r)/ *n* barbiere *m*

bare /beə(r)/ *adj* nudo; (tree, room) spoglio; (floor) senza moquette ● *vt* scoprire; mostrare (teeth)

bare: ~back *adv* senza sella. **~faced** *adj* sfacciato. **~foot** *adv* scalzo. **~'headed** *adj* a capo scoperto

barely /'beəlɪ/ *adv* appena

bargain /'bɑ:gɪn/ *n* (*agreement*) patto *m*; (*good buy*) affare *m*; **into the** ~ per di più ● *vi* contrattare; (*haggle*) trattare. □ ~ **for** *vt* (*expect*) aspettarsi

barge /bɑ:dʒ/ *n* barcone *m* ● **barge in** *vi* [!] (*to room*) piombare dentro; (*into conversation*) interrompere bruscamente. ~ **into** *vt* piombare dentro a (room); venire addosso a (person)

baritone /'bærɪtəʊn/ *n* baritono *m*

bark[1] /bɑ:k/ *n* (*of tree*) corteccia *f*

bark[2] *n* abbaiamento *m* ● *vi* abbaiare

barley /'bɑ:lɪ/ *n* orzo *m*

bar: ~maid *n* barista *f*. **~man** *n* barista *m*

barmy /'bɑ:mɪ/ *adj* [!] strampalato

barn /bɑ:n/ *n* granaio *m*

barometer /bə'rɒmɪtə(r)/ *n* barometro *m*

b

b

baron /ˈbærn/ *n* barone *m*. **~ess** *n* baronessa *f*

baroque /bəˈrɒk/ *adj & n* barocco *m*

barracks /ˈbærəks/ *npl* caserma *fsg*

barrage /ˈbærɑːʒ/ *n* (*Mil*) sbarramento *m*; (*fig: of criticism*) sfilza *f*

barrel /ˈbærl/ *n* barile *m*, botte *f*; (*of gun*) canna *f*. **~-organ** *n* organetto *m* [a cilindro]

barren /ˈbærən/ *adj* sterile; (landscape) brullo

barricade /bærɪˈkeɪd/ *n* barricata *f* • *vt* barricare

barrier /ˈbærɪə(r)/ *n* barriera *f*; (*Rail*) cancello *m*; *fig* ostacolo *m*

barrister /ˈbærɪstə(r)/ *n* avvocato *m*

barter /ˈbɑːtə(r)/ *vi* barattare (**for** con)

base /beɪs/ *n* base *f* • *adj* vile • *vt* basare; **be ~d on** basarsi su

base: ~ball *n* baseball *m*. **~ment** *n* seminterrato *m*

bash /bæʃ/ *n* colpo *m* [violento] • *vt* colpire [violentemente]; (*dent*) ammaccare; **~ed in** ammaccato

bashful /ˈbæʃfl/ *adj* timido

basic /ˈbeɪsɪk/ *adj* di base; (condition, requirement) basilare; (living conditions) povero; **my Italian is pretty ~** il mio italiano è abbastanza rudimentale; **the ~s** (*of language, science*) i rudimenti; (*essentials*) l'essenziale *m*. **~ally** *adv* fondamentalmente

basil /ˈbæzɪl/ *n* basilico *m*

basin /ˈbeɪsn/ *n* bacinella *f*; (*wash-hand* ~) lavabo *m*; (*for food*) recipiente *m*; (*Geog*) bacino *m*

basis /ˈbeɪsɪs/ *n* (*pl* **-ses** /-siːz/) base *f*

bask /bɑːsk/ *vi* crogiolarsi

basket /ˈbɑːskɪt/ *n* cestino *m*. **~ball** *n* pallacanestro *f*

bass /beɪs/ *adj* basso; **~ voice** voce *f* di basso • *n* basso *m*

bastard /ˈbɑːstəd/ *n* (*illegitimate child*) bastardo, -a *mf*; ⊠ figlio *m* di puttana

bat¹ /bæt/ *n* mazza *f*; (*for table tennis*) racchetta *f*; **off one's own ~** [!] tutto da solo • *vt* (*pt/pp* **batted**) battere; **she didn't ~ an eyelid** *fig* non ha battuto ciglio

bat² *n* (*Zool*) pipistrello *m*

batch /bætʃ/ *n* gruppo *m*; (*of goods*) partita *f*; (*of bread*) infornata *f*

bated /ˈbeɪtɪd/ *adj* **with ~ breath** col fiato sospeso

bath /bɑːθ/ *n* (*pl* **~s** /bɑːðz/) bagno *m*; (*tub*) vasca *f* da bagno; **~s** *pl* piscina *f*; **have a ~** fare un bagno • *vt* fare il bagno a

bathe /beɪð/ *n* bagno *m* • *vi* fare il bagno • *vt* lavare (wound). **~r** *n* bagnante *mf*

bathing /ˈbeɪðɪŋ/ *n* bagni *mpl*. **~-cap** *n* cuffia *f*. **~-costume** *n* costume *m* da bagno

bathroom *n* bagno *m*

battalion /bəˈtælɪən/ *n* battaglione *m*

batter /ˈbætə(r)/ *n* (*Culin*) pastella *f*; **~ed** *adj* (car) malandato; (wife, baby) maltrattato

battery /ˈbætərɪ/ *n* batteria *f*; (*of torch, radio*) pila *f*

battle /ˈbætl/ *n* battaglia *f*; *fig* lotta *f* • *vi fig* lottare

battle: ~field *n* campo *m* di battaglia. **~ship** *n* corazzata *f*

bawl /bɔːl/ *vt/i* urlare

bay¹ /beɪ/ *n* (*Geog*) baia *f*

bay² *n* **keep at ~** tenere a bada

bay³ *n* (*Bot*) alloro *m*. **~-leaf** *n* foglia *f* d'alloro

bayonet /ˈbeɪənɪt/ *n* baionetta *f*

bay ˈwindow *n* bay window *f inv* (*grande finestra sporgente*)

bazaar /bəˈzɑː(r)/ *n* bazar *m inv*

BC *abbr* (before Christ) a.C.

be /biː/

• *vi* (*pres* **am, are, is, are**; *pt* **was, were**; *pp* **been**) essere; **he is a teacher** è insegnante, fa l'insegnante; **what do you want to be?** cosa vuoi fare?; **be quiet!** sta' zitto!; **I am cold/hot** ho freddo/caldo; **it's cold/hot, isn't it?** fa freddo/caldo, vero?; **how are you?** come stai?; **I am well** sto bene; **there is** c'è; **there are** ci sono; **I have been to Venice** sono stato a Venezia; **has the postman been?** è passato il postino?; **you're coming too, aren't you?** vieni anche tu, no?; **it's yours, is it?** è tuo, vero?; **was John there? – yes, he was** c'era John? – sì;

John wasn't there – yes he was! John non c'era – sì che c'era!; **three and three are six** tre più tre fanno sei; **he is five** ha cinque anni; **that will be £10, please** fanno 10 sterline, per favore; **how much is it?** quanto costa?; **that's £5 you owe me** mi devi 5 sterline

● *v aux* **I am coming/reading** sto venendo/leggendo; **I'm staying** (*not leaving*) resto; **I am being lazy** sono pigro; **I was thinking of you** stavo pensando a te; **you are not to tell him** non devi dirgielo; **you are to do that immediately** devi farlo subito

● *passive* essere; **I have been robbed** sono stato derubato

beach /biːtʃ/ *n* spiaggia *f*. **~wear** *n* abbigliamento *m* da spiaggia

bead /biːd/ *n* perlina *f*

beak /biːk/ *n* becco *m*

beaker /ˈbiːkə(r)/ *n* coppa *f*

beam /biːm/ *n* trave *f*; (*of light*) raggio *m* ● *vi* irradiare; (person:) essere raggiante. **~ing** *adj* raggiante

bean /biːn/ *n* fagiolo *m*; (*of coffee*) chicco *m*

bear¹ /beə(r)/ *n* orso *m*

bear² *v* (*pt* **bore**, *pp* **borne**) ● *vt* (*endure*) sopportare; mettere al mondo (child); (*carry*) portare; **~ in mind** tenere presente ● *vi* **~ left/right** andare a sinistra/a destra. □ **~ with** *vt* aver pazienza con. **~able** *adj* sopportabile

beard /bɪəd/ *n* barba *f*. **~ed** *adj* barbuto

bearer /ˈbeərə(r)/ *n* portatore, -trice *mf*; (*of passport*) titolare *mf*

bearing /ˈbeərɪŋ/ *n* portamento *m*; (*Techn*) cuscinetto *m* [a sfera]; **have a ~ on** avere attinenza con; **get one's ~s** orientarsi

beast /biːst/ *n* bestia *f*; (**!**: *person*) animale *m*

beat /biːt/ *n* battito *m*; (*rhythm*) battuta *f*; (*of policeman*) giro *m* d'ispezione ● *v* (*pt* **beat**, *pp* **beaten**) ● *vt* battere; picchiare (person); **~ it! !** darsela a gambe!; **it ~s me why... !** non capisco proprio perché... **beat up** *vt* picchiare

beating /ˈbiːtɪŋ/ *n* bastonata *f*; **get a ~ing** (*with fists*) essere preso a pugni; (team, player:) prendere una batosta

beautician /bjuːˈtɪʃn/ *n* estetista *mf*

beauti|ful /ˈbjuːtɪfl/ *adj* bello. **~fully** *adv* splendidamente

beauty /ˈbjuːtɪ/ *n* bellezza *f*. **~ parlour** *n* istituto *m* di bellezza. **~ spot** *n* neo *m*; (*place*) luogo *m* pittoresco

beaver /ˈbiːvə(r)/ *n* castoro *m*

became /bɪˈkeɪm/ ▷**BECOME**

because /bɪˈkɒz/ *conj* perché; **~ you didn't tell me, I...** poiché non me lo hai detto,... ● *adv* **~ of** a causa di

beckon /ˈbekn/ *vt/i* **~ [to]** chiamare con un cenno

becom|e /bɪˈkʌm/ *v* (*pt* **became**, *pp* **become**) ● *vt* diventare ● *vi* diventare; **what has ~e of her?** che ne è di lei? **~ing** *adj* (clothes) bello

bed /bed/ *n* letto *m*; (*of sea, lake*) fondo *m*; (*layer*) strato *m*; (*of flowers*) aiuola *f*; **in ~** a letto; **go to ~** andare a letto; **~ and breakfast** *pensione f familiare in cui il prezzo della camera comprende la prima colazione*. **~clothes** *npl* lenzuola *fpl* e coperte *fpl*. **~ding** *n biancheria f per il letto, materasso e guanciali*

bed: ~room *n* camera *f* da letto. **~'sitter** *n* = camera *f* ammobiliata fornita di cucina. **~spread** *n* copriletto *m*. **~time** *n* l'ora *f* di andare a letto

bee /biː/ *n* ape *f*

beech /biːtʃ/ *n* faggio *m*

beef /biːf/ *n* manzo *m*. **~burger** *n* hamburger *m inv*

bee: ~hive *n* alveare *m*. **~-line** *n* **make a ~line for !** precipitarsi verso

been /biːn/ ▷**BE**

beer /bɪə(r)/ *n* birra *f*

beetle /ˈbiːtl/ *n* scarafaggio *m*

beetroot /ˈbiːtruːt/ *n* barbabietola *f*

before /bɪˈfɔː(r)/ *prep* prima di; **the day ~ yesterday** ieri l'altro; **~ long** fra poco ● *adv* prima; **never ~ have I seen...** non ho mai visto prima...; **~ that** prima; **~ going** prima di andare ● *conj* (*time*) prima che; **~ you go** prima che tu vada. **~hand** *adv* in anticipo

befriend /bɪˈfrend/ *vt* trattare da amico

beg /beg/ *v* (*pt/pp* **begged**) ● *vi* mendi-

b

care ● *vt* pregare; chiedere (favour, forgiveness)

began /bɪ'gæn/ ▷**BEGIN**

beggar /'begə(r)/ *n* mendicante *mf*; **poor ~!** povero cristo!

begin /bɪ'gɪn/ *vt/i* (*pt* **began**, *pp* **begun**, *pres p* **beginning**) cominciare. **~ner** *n* principiante *mf*. **~ning** *n* principio *m*

begrudge /bɪ'grʌdʒ/ *vt* (*envy*) essere invidioso di; dare malvolentieri (money)

begun /bɪ'gʌn/ ▷**BEGIN**

behalf /bɪ'hɑːf/ *n* **on ~ of** a nome di; **on my ~** a nome mio

behave /bɪ'heɪv/ *vi* comportarsi; **~ [oneself]** comportarsi bene

behaviour /bɪ'heɪvjə(r)/ *n* comportamento *m*; (*of prisoner, soldier*) condotta *f*

behead /bɪ'hed/ *vt* decapitare

behind /bɪ'haɪnd/ *prep* dietro; **be ~ sth** *fig* stare dietro qcsa ● *adv* dietro, indietro; (*late*) in ritardo; **a long way ~** molto indietro ● *n* 🅸 didietro *m*. **~hand** *adv* indietro

beige /beɪʒ/ *adj & n* beige *m inv*

being /'biːɪŋ/ *n* essere *m*; **come into ~** nascere

belated /bɪ'leɪtɪd/ *adj* tardivo

belch /beltʃ/ *vi* ruttare ● *vt* **~ [out]** eruttare (smoke)

belfry /'belfrɪ/ *n* campanile *m*

Belgian /'beldʒən/ *adj & n* belga *mf*

Belgium /'beldʒəm/ *n* Belgio *m*

belief /bɪ'liːf/ *n* fede *f*; (*opinion*) convinzione *f*

believe /bɪ'liːv/ *vt/i* credere. **~r** *n* (*Relig*) credente *mf*; **be a great ~r in** credere fermamente in

belittle /bɪ'lɪtl/ *vt* sminuire (person, achievements)

bell /bel/ *n* campana *f*; (*on door*) campanello *m*

belligerent /bɪ'lɪdʒərənt/ *adj* belligerante; (*aggressive*) bellicoso

bellow /'beləʊ/ *vi* gridare a squarciagola; (animal:) muggire

bellows /'beləʊz/ *npl* (*for fire*) soffietto *msg*

belly /'belɪ/ *n* pancia *f*

belong /bɪ'lɒŋ/ *vi* appartenere (**to** a); (*be member*) essere socio (**to** di). **~ings** *npl* cose *fpl*

beloved /bɪ'lʌvɪd/ *adj & n* amato, -a *mf*

below /bɪ'ləʊ/ *prep* sotto; (*with numbers*) al di sotto di ● *adv* sotto, di sotto; (*Naut*) sotto coperta; **see ~** guardare qui di seguito

belt /belt/ *n* cintura *f*; (*area*) zona *f*; (*Techn*) cinghia *f* ● *vi* **~ along** (🅸: *rush*) filare velocemente ● *vt* (🅸: *hit*) picchiare

bench /bentʃ/ *n* panchina *f*; (*work~*) piano *m* da lavoro; **the B~** (*Jur*) la magistratura

bend /bend/ *n* curva *f*; (*of river*) ansa *f* ● *v* (*pt/pp* **bent**) ● *vt* piegare ● *vi* piegarsi; (road:) curvare; **~ [down]** chinarsi. □ **~ over** *vi* inchinarsi

beneath /bɪ'niːθ/ *prep* sotto, al di sotto di; **he thinks it's ~ him** *fig* pensa che sia sotto al suo livello ● *adv* giù

beneficial /benɪ'fɪʃl/ *adj* benefico

beneficiary /benɪ'fɪʃərɪ/ *n* beneficiario, -a *mf*

benefit /'benɪfɪt/ *n* vantaggio *m*; (*allowance*) indennità *f inv* ● *v* (*pt/pp* **-fited**, *pres p* **-fiting**) ● *vt* giovare a ● *vi* trarre vantaggio (**from** da)

benign /bɪ'naɪn/ *adj* benevolo; (*Med*) benigno

bent /bent/ ▷**BEND** ● *adj* (person) ricurvo; (*distorted*) curvato; (🅸: *dishonest*) corrotto; **be ~ on doing sth** essere ben deciso a fare qcsa ● *n* predisposizione *f*

bereave|d /bɪ'riːvd/ *n* **the ~d** *pl* i familiari del defunto. **~ment** *n* lutto *m*

beret /'bereɪ/ *n* berretto *m*

berry /'berɪ/ *n* bacca *f*

berserk /bə'sɜːk/ *adj* **go ~** diventare una belva

berth /bɜːθ/ *n* (*bed*) cuccetta *f*; (*anchorage*) ormeggio *m* ● *vi* ormeggiare

beside /bɪ'saɪd/ *prep* accanto a; **~ oneself** fuori di sé

besides /bɪ'saɪdz/ *prep* oltre a ● *adv* inoltre

besiege /bɪ'siːdʒ/ *vt* assediare

best /best/ *adj* migliore; **the ~ part of a year** la maggior parte dell'anno; **~ before** (*Comm*) preferibilmente prima di ● *n* **the ~** il meglio; (*person*) il/la migliore; **at ~** tutt'al più; **all the ~!** tanti auguri!; **do one's ~** fare del proprio meglio; **to the ~ of my knowledge** per quel che ne so; **make the ~ of it** cogliere il lato buono della cosa ● *adv* meglio, nel modo migliore; **as ~ I could** meglio che potevo. **~ 'man** *n* testimone *m*

bestow /bɪ'stəʊ/ *vt* conferire (**on** a)

best'seller *n* bestseller *m inv*

bet /bet/ *n* scommessa *f* ● *vt/i* (*pt/pp* **bet** *or* **betted**) scommettere

betray /bɪ'treɪ/ *vt* tradire. **~al** *n* tradimento *m*

better /'betə(r)/ *adj* migliore, meglio; **get ~** migliorare; (*after illness*) rimettersi ● *adv* meglio; **~ off** meglio; (*wealthier*) più ricco; **all the ~** tanto meglio; **the sooner the ~** prima è, meglio è; **I've thought ~ of it** ci ho ripensato; **you'd ~ stay** faresti meglio a restare; **I'd ~ not** è meglio che non lo faccia ● *vt* migliorare; **~ oneself** migliorare le proprie condizioni

between /bɪ'twi:n/ *prep* fra, tra; **~ you and me** detto fra di noi; **~ us** (*together*) tra me e te ● *adv* **[in] ~** in mezzo; (*time*) frattempo

beverage /'bevərɪdʒ/ *n* bevanda *f*

beware /bɪ'weə(r)/ *vi* guardarsi (**of** da); **~ of the dog!** attenti al cane!

bewilder /bɪ'wɪldə(r)/ *vt* disorientare; **~ed** perplesso. **~ment** *n* perplessità *f*

beyond /bɪ'jɒnd/ *prep* oltre; **~ reach** irraggiungibile; **~ doubt** senza alcun dubbio; **~ belief** da non credere; **it's ~ me** [!] non riesco proprio a capire ● *adv* più in là

bias /'baɪəs/ *n* (*preference*) preferenza *f*; *pej* pregiudizio *m* ● *vt* (*pt/pp* **biased**) (*influence*) influenzare. **~ed** *adj* parziale

bib /bɪb/ *n* bavaglino *m*

Bible /'baɪbl/ *n* Bibbia *f*

biblical /'bɪblɪkl/ *adj* biblico

biceps /'baɪseps/ *n* bicipite *m*

bicker /'bɪkə(r)/ *vi* litigare

bicycle /'baɪsɪkl/ *n* bicicletta *f* ● *vi* andare in bicicletta

bid¹ /bɪd/ *n* offerta *f*; (*attempt*) tentativo *m* ● *vt/i* (*pt/pp* **bid**, *pres p* **bidding**) offrire; (*in cards*) dichiarare

bid² *vt* (*pt* **bade** *or* **bid**, *pp* **bidden** *or* **bid**, *pres p* **bidding**) *liter* (*command*) comandare; **~ sb welcome** dare il benvenuto a qcno

bidder /'bɪdə(r)/ *n* offerente *mf*

bide /baɪd/ *vt* **~ one's time** aspettare il momento buono

bifocals /baɪ'fəʊklz/ *npl* occhiali *mpl* bifocali

big /bɪg/ *adj* (**bigger, biggest**) grande; (brother, sister) più grande; ([!]: *generous*) generoso ● *adv* **talk ~** [!] spararle grosse

bigam|ist /'bɪgəmɪst/ *n* bigamo, -a *mf*. **~y** *n* bigamia *f*

big-'headed *adj* [!] gasato

bigot /'bɪgət/ *n* fanatico, -a *mf*. **~ed** *adj* di mentalità ristretta

bike /baɪk/ *n* [!] bici *f inv*

bikini /bɪ'ki:nɪ/ *n* bikini *m inv*

bile /baɪl/ *n* bile *f*

bilingual /baɪ'lɪŋgwəl/ *adj* bilingue

bill¹ /bɪl/ *n* fattura *f*; (*in restaurant etc*) conto *m*; (*poster*) manifesto *m*; (*Pol*) progetto *m* di legge; (*Am: note*) biglietto *m* di banca ● *vt* fatturare

bill² *n* (*beak*) becco *m*

'billfold *n Am* portafoglio *m*

billiards /'bɪljədz/ *n* biliardo *m*

billion /'bɪljən/ *n* (*thousand million*) miliardo *m*; (*old-fashioned Br: million million*) mille miliardi *mpl*

bin /bɪn/ *n* bidone *m*

bind /baɪnd/ *vt* (*pt/pp* **bound**) legare (**to** a); (*bandage*) fasciare; (*Jur*) obbligare. **~ing** *adj* (promise, contract) vincolante ● *n* (*of book*) rilegatura *f*; (*on ski*) attacco *m* [di sicurezza]

binge /bɪndʒ/ *n* [!] **have a ~** fare baldoria; (*eat a lot*) abbuffarsi ● *vi* abbuffarsi (**on** di)

binoculars /bɪ'nɒkjʊləz/ *npl* **[pair of] ~** binocolo *msg*

biograph|er /baɪ'ɒgrəfə(r)/ *n* biografo, -a *mf*. **~y** *n* biografia *f*

biological /baɪə'lɒdʒɪkl/ *adj* biologico

biolog|ist /baɪ'ɒlədʒɪst/ *n* biologo, -a *mf*. **~y** *n* biologia *f*

birch /bɜ:tʃ/ *n* (*tree*) betulla *f*

bird /bɜ:d/ *n* uccello *m*; ([!]: *girl*) ragazza *f*

Biro® /'baɪrəʊ/ *n* biro® *f inv*

birth /bɜ:θ/ *n* nascita *f*

birth: ~ certificate *n* certificato *m* di nascita. **~-control** *n* controllo *m* delle nascite. **~day** *n* compleanno *m*.

~**mark** *n* voglia *f*. ~**-rate** *n* natalità *f*

biscuit /'bɪskɪt/ *n* biscotto *m*

bisect /baɪ'sekt/ *vt* dividere in due [parti]

bishop /'bɪʃəp/ *n* vescovo *m*; (*in chess*) alfiere *m*

bit¹ /bɪt/ *n* pezzo *m*; (*smaller*) pezzetto *m*; (*for horse*) morso *m*; (*Comput*) bit *m inv*; **a ~ of** un pezzo di (cheese, paper); un po' di (time, rain, silence); **~ by ~** poco a poco; **do one's ~** fare la propria parte

bit² ▷BITE

bitch /bɪtʃ/ *n* cagna *f*; ☒ stronza *f*. ~**y** *adj* velenoso

bit|e /baɪt/ *n* morso *m*; (*insect* ~) puntura *f*; (*mouthful*) boccone *m* ● *vt* (*pt* **bit**, *pp* **bitten**) mordere; (insect:) pungere; **~e one's nails** mangiarsi le unghie ● *vi* mordere; (insect:) pungere. ~**ing** *adj* (wind, criticism) pungente; (remark) mordace

bitter /'bɪtə(r)/ *adj* amaro ● *n Br* birra *f* amara. ~**ly** *adv* amaramente; **it's ~ly cold** c'è un freddo pungente. ~**ness** *n* amarezza *f*

bizarre /bɪ'zɑ:(r)/ *adj* bizzarro

black /blæk/ *adj* nero; **be ~ and blue** essere pieno di lividi ● *n* negro, -a *mf* ● *vt* boicottare (goods). ▫ **~ out** *vt* cancellare ● *vi* (*lose consciousness*) perdere coscienza

black: ~berry *n* mora *f*. ~**bird** *n* merlo *m*. ~**board** *n* (*Sch*) lavagna *f*. ~**'currant** *n* ribes *m inv* nero; **~ 'eye** *n* occhio *m* nero. **~ 'ice** *n* ghiaccio *m* (*sulla strada*). ~**leg** *n Br* crumiro *m*. ~**list** *vt* mettere sulla lista nera. ~**mail** *n* ricatto *m* ● *vt* ricattare. ~**mailer** *n* ricattatore, -trice *mf*. ~**-out** *n* blackout *m inv*; **have a ~-out** (*Med*) perdere coscienza. ~**smith** *n* fabbro *m*

bladder /'blædə(r)/ *n* (*Anat*) vescica *f*

blade /bleɪd/ *n* lama *f*; (*of grass*) filo *m*

blame /bleɪm/ *n* colpa *f* ● *vt* dare la colpa a; **~ sb for doing sth** dare la colpa a qcno per aver fatto qcsa; **no one is to ~** non è colpa di nessuno. ~**less** *adj* innocente

bland /blænd/ *adj* (food) insipido; (person) insulso

blank /blæŋk/ *adj* bianco; (look) vuoto ● *n* spazio *m* vuoto; (*cartridge*) a salve. **~ 'cheque** *n* assegno *m* in bianco

blanket /'blæŋkɪt/ *n* coperta *f*

blare /bleə(r)/ *vi* suonare a tutto volume. ▫ **~ out** *vt* far risuonare ● *vi* (music, radio:) strillare

blaspheme /blæs'fi:m/ *vi* bestemmiare

blasphem|ous /'blæsfəməs/ *adj* blasfemo. ~**y** *n* bestemmia *f*

blast /blɑ:st/ *n* (*gust*) raffica *f*; (*sound*) scoppio *m* ● *vt* (*with explosive*) far saltare ● *int* ☒ maledizione!. ~**ed** *adj* ☒ maledetto

blast-off *n* (*of missile*) lancio *m*

blatant /'bleɪtənt/ *adj* sfacciato

blaze /bleɪz/ *n* incendio *m*; **a ~ of colour** un'esplosione *f* di colori ● *vi* ardere

blazer /'bleɪzə(r)/ *n* blazer *m inv*

bleach /bli:tʃ/ *n* decolorante *m*; (*for cleaning*) candeggina *f* ● *vt* sbiancare; ossigenare (hair)

bleak /bli:k/ *adj* desolato; (*fig*: prospects, future) tetro

bleat /bli:t/ *vi* belare ● *n* belato *m*

bleed /bli:d/ *v* (*pt/pp* **bled**) ● *vi* sanguinare ● *vt* spurgare (brakes, radiator)

bleep /bli:p/ *n* bip *m* ● *vi* suonare ● *vt* chiamare (*col cercapersone*) (doctor). ~**er** *n* cercapersone *m inv*

blemish /'blemɪʃ/ *n* macchia *f*

blend /blend/ *n* (*of tea, coffee, whisky*) miscela *f*; (*of colours*) insieme *m* ● *vt* mescolare ● *vi* (colours, sounds:) fondersi (**with** con). ~**er** *n* (*Culin*) frullatore *m*

bless /bles/ *vt* benedire. ~**ed** *adj also* ☒ benedetto. ~**ing** *n* benedizione *f*

blew /blu:/ ▷BLOW²

blight /blaɪt/ *n* (*Bot*) ruggine *f* ● *vt* far avvizzire (plants)

blind¹ /blaɪnd/ *adj* cieco; **the ~** *npl* i ciechi *mpl*; **~ man/woman** cieco/cieca ● *vt* accecare

blind² *n* **[roller] ~** avvolgibile *m*; **[Venetian] ~** veneziana *f*

blind: ~ 'alley *n* vicolo *m* cieco. ~**fold** *adj* **be ~fold** avere gli occhi bendati ● *n* benda *f* ● *vt* bendare gli occhi a. ~**ly** *adv* ciecamente. ~**ness** *n* cecità *f*

blink /blɪŋk/ *vi* sbattere le palpebre; (light:) tremolare

blinkers /ˈblɪŋkəz/ *npl* paraocchi *mpl*

bliss /blɪs/ *n* (*Rel*) beatitudine *f*; (*happiness*) felicità *f*. **~ful** *adj* beato; (*happy*) meraviglioso

blister /ˈblɪstə(r)/ *n* (*Med*) vescica *f*; (*in paint*) bolla *f* ● *vi* (paint:) formare una bolla/delle bolle

blizzard /ˈblɪzəd/ *n* tormenta *f*

bloated /ˈbləʊtɪd/ *adj* gonfio

blob /blɒb/ *n* goccia *f*

bloc /blɒk/ *n* (*Pol*) blocco *m*

block /blɒk/ *n* blocco *m*; (*building*) isolato *m*; (*building ~*) cubo *m* (*per giochi di costruzione*); **~ of flats** palazzo *m* ● *vt* bloccare. □ **~ up** *vt* bloccare

blockade /blɒˈkeɪd/ *n* blocco *m* ● *vt* bloccare

blockage /ˈblɒkɪdʒ/ *n* ostruzione *f*

block: ~head *n* [!] testone, -a *mf*. **~ ˈletters** *npl* stampatello *m*

bloke /bləʊk/ *n* [!] tizio *m*

blonde /blɒnd/ *adj* biondo ● *n* bionda *f*

blood /blʌd/ *n* sangue *m*

blood: ~ bath *n* bagno *m* di sangue. **~ group** *n* gruppo *m* sanguigno. **~hound** *n* segugio *m*. **~ pressure** *n* pressione *f* del sangue. **~shed** *n* spargimento *m* di sangue. **~shot** *adj* iniettato di sangue. **~stream** *n* sangue *m*. **~thirsty** *adj* assetato di sangue

bloody /ˈblʌdɪ/ *adj* (**-ier, -iest**) insanguinato; [x] maledetto ● *adv* [x] **~ easy/difficult** facile/difficile da matti. **~-ˈminded** *adj* scorbutico

bloom /blu:m/ *n* fiore *m*; **in ~** (flower:) sbocciato; (tree:) in fiore ● *vi* fiorire; *fig* essere in forma smagliante

blossom /ˈblɒsəm/ *n* fiori *mpl* (*d'albero*); (*single one*) fiore *m* ● *vi* sbocciare

blot /blɒt/ *n also fig* macchia *f* ● **blot out** *vt* (*pt/pp* **blotted**) *fig* cancellare

blotch /blɒtʃ/ *n* macchia *f*. **~y** *adj* chiazzato

ˈblotting-paper *n* carta *f* assorbente

blouse /blaʊz/ *n* camicetta *f*

blow¹ /bləʊ/ *n* colpo *m*

blow² *v* (*pt* **blew**, *pp* **blown**) ● *vi* (wind:) soffiare; (fuse:) saltare ● *vt* ([!]: *squander*) sperperare; **~ one's nose** soffiarsi il naso. □ **~ away** *vt* far volar via (papers) ● *vi* (papers:) volare via. □ **~ down** *vt* abbattere ● *vi* abbattersi al suolo. □ **~ out** *vt* (*extinguish*) spegnere. □ **~ over** *vi* (storm:) passare; (fuss, trouble:) dissiparsi. □ **~ up** *vt* (*inflate*) gonfiare; (*enlarge*) ingrandire (photograph); (*by explosion*) far esplodere ● *vi* esplodere

blow: ~-dry *vt* asciugare col fon. **~lamp** *n* fiamma *f* ossidrica

ˈblowtorch *n* fiamma *f* ossidrica

blue /blu:/ *adj* (*pale*) celeste; (*navy*) blu *inv*; (*royal*) azzurro; **~ with cold** livido per il freddo ● *n* blu *m inv*; **have the ~s** essere giù [di tono]; **out of the ~** inaspettatamente

blue: ~bell *n* giacinto *m* di bosco. **~berry** *n* mirtillo *m*. **~bottle** *n* moscone *m*. **~ film** *n* film *m inv* a luci rosse. **~print** *n fig* riferimento *m*

bluff /blʌf/ *n* bluff *m inv* ● *vi* bluffare

blunder /ˈblʌndə(r)/ *n* gaffe *f inv* ● *vi* fare una/delle gaffe

blunt /blʌnt/ *adj* spuntato; (person) reciso. **~ly** *adv* schiettamente

blur /blɜ:(r)/ *n* **it's all a ~** *fig* è tutto un insieme confuso ● *vt* (*pt/pp* **blurred**) rendere confuso. **~red** *adj* (vision, photo) sfocato

blurb /blɜ:b/ *n* soffietto *m* editoriale

blurt /blɜ:t/ *vt* **~ out** spifferare

blush /blʌʃ/ *n* rossore *m* ● *vi* arrossire

boar /bɔ:(r)/ *n* cinghiale *m*

board /bɔ:d/ *n* tavola *f*; (*for notices*) tabellone *m*; (*committee*) assemblea *f*; (*of directors*) consiglio *m*; **full ~** *Br* pensione *f* completa; **half ~** *Br* mezza pensione *f*; **~ and lodging** vitto e alloggio *m*; **go by the ~** [!] andare a monte ● *vt* (*Naut, Aeron*) salire a bordo di ● *vi* (passengers:) salire a bordo. □ **~ up** *vt* sbarrare con delle assi. □ **~ with** *vt* stare a pensione da.

boarder /ˈbɔ:də(r)/ *n* pensionante *mf*; (*Sch*) convittore, -trice *mf*

board: ~ing-house *n* pensione *f*. **~ing-school** *n* collegio *m*

boast /bəʊst/ *vi* vantarsi (**about** di). **~ful** *adj* vanaglorioso

boat /bəʊt/ *n* barca *f*; (*ship*) nave *f*. **~er** *n* (*hat*) paglietta *f*

bob /bɒb/ *n* (*hairstyle*) caschetto *m* ● *vi* (*pt/pp* **bobbed**) (*also* **~ up and down**) andare su e giù

ˈbob-sleigh *n* bob *m inv*

b

bode /bəʊd/ *vi* ~ **well/ill** essere di buono/cattivo augurio

bodily /ˈbɒdɪlɪ/ *adj* fisico ● *adv* (*forcibly*) fisicamente

body /ˈbɒdɪ/ *n* corpo *m*; (*organization*) ente *m*; (*amount: of poems etc*) quantità *f*. **~guard** *n* guardia *f* del corpo. **~ part** *n* pezzo *m* del corpo. **~work** *n* (*Auto*) carrozzeria *f*

bog /bɒg/ *n* palude *f* ● *vt* (*pt/pp* **bogged**) **get ~ged down** impantanarsi

boggle /ˈbɒgl/ *vi* **the mind ~s** non posso neanche immaginarlo

bogus /ˈbəʊgəs/ *adj* falso

boil[1] /bɔɪl/ *n* (*Med*) foruncolo *m*

boil[2] *n* **bring/come to the ~** portare/arrivare ad ebollizione ● *vt* [far] bollire ● *vi* bollire; (*fig: with anger*) ribollire; **the water** *or* **kettle's ~ing** l'acqua bolle. **boil down to** *vt fig* ridursi a. □ **~ over** *vi* straboccare (*bollendo*). □ **~ up** *vt* far bollire

boiler /ˈbɔɪlə(r)/ *n* caldaia *f*. **~suit** *n* tuta *f*

boisterous /ˈbɔɪstərəs/ *adj* chiassoso

bold /bəʊld/ *adj* audace ● *n* (*Typ*) neretto *m*. **~ness** *n* audacia *f*

bolster /ˈbəʊlstə(r)/ *n* cuscino *m* (*lungo e rotondo*) ● *vt* **~ [up]** sostenere

bolt /bəʊlt/ *n* (*for door*) catenaccio *m*; (*for fixing*) bullone *m* ● *vt* fissare (*con i bulloni*) (**to** a); chiudere col chiavistello (door); ingurgitare (food) ● *vi* svignarsela; (horse:) scappar via ● *adv* **~ upright** diritto come un fuso

bomb /bɒm/ *n* bomba *f* ● *vt* bombardare

bombard /bɒmˈbɑːd/ *vt also fig* bombardare

bomb|er /ˈbɒmə(r)/ *n* (*Aeron*) bombardiere *m*; (*person*) dinamitardo *m*. **~er jacket** giubbotto *m*, bomber *m inv*. **~shell** *n* (*fig: news*) bomba *f*

bond /bɒnd/ *n fig* legame *m*; (*Comm*) obbligazione *f* ● *vt* (glue:) attaccare

bondage /ˈbɒndɪdʒ/ *n* schiavitù *f*

bone /bəʊn/ *n* osso *m*; (*of fish*) spina *f* ● *vt* disossare (meat); togliere le spine da (fish). **~-'dry** *adj* secco

bonfire /ˈbɒn-/ *n* falò *m inv*. **~ night** *festa celebrata la notte del 5 novembre con fuochi d'artificio e falò*

bonnet /ˈbɒnɪt/ *n* cuffia *f*; (*of car*) cofano *m*

bonus /ˈbəʊnəs/ *n* (*individual*) gratifica *f*; (*production ~*) premio *m*; (*life insurance*) dividendo *m*; **a ~** *fig* qualcosa in più

bony /ˈbəʊnɪ/ *adj* (**-ier, -iest**) ossuto; (fish) pieno di spine

boo /buː/ *interj* (*to surprise or frighten*) bu! ● *vt/i* fischiare

boob /buːb/ *n* [!] (*mistake*) gaffe *f inv*; (*breast*) tetta *f* ● *vi* [!] fare una gaffe

book /bʊk/ *n* libro *m*; (*of tickets*) blocchetto *m*; **keep the ~s** (*Comm*) tenere la contabilità; **be in sb's bad/good ~s** essere nel libro nero/nelle grazie di qcno ● *vt* (*reserve*) prenotare; (*for offence*) multare ● *vi* (*reserve*) prenotare

book: ~case *n* libreria *f*. **~ing-office** *n* biglietteria *f*. **~keeping** *n* contabilità *f*. **~let** *n* opuscolo *m*. **~maker** *n* allibratore *m*. **~mark** *n* segnalibro *m*. **~seller** *n* libraio, -a *mf*. **~shop** *n* libreria *f*. **~worm** *n* topo *m* di biblioteca

boom /buːm/ *n* (*Comm*) boom *m inv*; (*upturn*) impennata *f*; (*of thunder, gun*) rimbombo *m* ● *vi* (thunder, gun:) rimbombare; *fig* prosperare

boost /buːst/ *n* spinta *f* ● *vt* stimolare (sales); sollevare (morale); far crescere (hopes). **~er** *n* (*Med*) dose *f* supplementare

boot /buːt/ *n* stivale *m*; (*up to ankle*) stivaletto *m*; (*football*) scarpetta *f*; (*climbing*) scarpone *m*; (*Auto*) portabagagli *m inv* ● *vt* (*Comput*) inizializzare

booth /buːð/ *n* (*telephone, voting*) cabina *f*; (*at market*) bancarella *f*

booze /buːz/ [!] *n* alcolici *mpl*. **~-up** *n* bella bevuta *f*

border /ˈbɔːdə(r)/ *n* bordo *m*; (*frontier*) frontiera *f*; (*in garden*) bordura *f* ● *vi* **~ on** confinare con; *fig* essere ai confini di (madness). **~line** *n* linea *f* di demarcazione; **~line case** caso *m* dubbio

bore[1] /bɔː(r)/ ▸**BEAR**[2]

bore[2] *vt* (*Techn*) forare

bor|e[3] *n* (*of gun*) calibro *m*; (*person*) seccatore, -trice *mf*; (*thing*) seccatura *f* ● *vt* annoiare. **~edom** *n* noia *f*. **be ~ed (to tears** *or* **to death)** annoiarsi (da morire). **~ing** *adj* noioso

born /bɔːn/ *pp* **be ~** nascere; **I was ~**

in 1966 sono nato nel 1966 ● *adj* nato; **a ~ liar/actor** un bugiardo/attore nato

borne /bɔːn/ ▷**BEAR²**

borough /ˈbʌrə/ *n* municipalità *f inv*

borrow /ˈbɒrəʊ/ *vt* prendere a prestito (**from** da); **can I ~ your pen?** mi presti la tua penna?

boss /bɒs/ *n* direttore, -trice *mf* ● *vt* (*also* **~ about**) comandare a bacchetta. **~y** *adj* autoritario

botanical /bəˈtænɪkl/ *adj* botanico

botan|ist /ˈbɒtənɪst/ *n* botanico, -a *mf*. **~y** *n* botanica *f*

both /bəʊθ/ *adj & pron* tutti e due, entrambi ● *adv* **~ men and women** entrambi uomini e donne; **~ [of] the children** tutti e due i bambini; **they are ~ dead** sono morti entrambi; **~ of them** tutti e due

bother /ˈbɒðə(r)/ *n* preoccupazione *f*; (*minor trouble*) fastidio *m*; **it's no ~** non c'è problema ● *int* 🅸 che seccatura! ● *vt* (*annoy*) dare fastidio a; (*disturb*) disturbare ● *vi* preoccuparsi (**about** di); **don't ~** lascia perdere

bottle /ˈbɒtl/ *n* bottiglia *f*; (*baby's*) biberon *m inv* ● *vt* imbottigliare. □ **~ up** *vt fig* reprimere

bottle: ~-neck *n fig* ingorgo *m*. **~-opener** *n* apribottiglie *m inv*

bottom /ˈbɒtm/ *adj* ultimo; **the ~ shelf** l'ultimo scaffale in basso ● *n* (*of container*) fondo *m*; (*of river*) fondale *m*; (*of hill*) piedi *mpl*; (*buttocks*) sedere *m*; **at the ~ of the page** in fondo alla pagina; **get to the ~ of** *fig* vedere cosa c'è sotto. **~less** *adj* senza fondo

bough /baʊ/ *n* ramoscello *m*

bought /bɔːt/ ▷**BUY**

boulder /ˈbəʊldə(r)/ *n* masso *m*

bounce /baʊns/ *vi* rimbalzare; (🅸: cheque:) essere respinto ● *vt* far rimbalzare (ball)

bound¹ /baʊnd/ *n* balzo *m* ● *vi* balzare

bound² ▷**BIND** ● *adj* **~ for** (ship) diretto a; **be ~ to do** (*likely*) dovere fare per forza; (*obliged*) essere costretto a fare

boundary /ˈbaʊndərɪ/ *n* limite *m*

bouquet /bʊˈkeɪ/ *n* mazzo *m* di fiori; (*of wine*) bouquet *m*

bout /baʊt/ *n* (*Med*) attacco *m*; (*Sport*) incontro *m*

bow¹ /bəʊ/ *n* (*weapon*) arco *m*; (*Mus*) archetto *m*; (*knot*) nodo *m*

bow² /baʊ/ *n* inchino *m* ● *vi* inchinarsi ● *vt* piegare (head)

bow³ /baʊ/ *n* (*Naut*) prua *f*

bowl¹ /bəʊl/ *n* (*for soup, cereal*) scodella *f*; (*of pipe*) fornello *m*

bowl² *n* (*ball*) boccia *f* ● *vt* lanciare ● *vi* (*Cricket*) servire; (*in bowls*) lanciare. □ **~ over** *vt* buttar giù; (*fig: leave speechless*) lasciar senza parole

bowler¹ /ˈbəʊlə(r)/ *n* (*Cricket*) lanciatore *m*; (*Bowls*) giocatore *m* di bocce

bowler² *n* **~ [hat]** bombetta *f*

bowling /ˈbəʊlɪŋ/ *n* gioco *m* delle bocce. **~-alley** *n* pista *f* da bowling

bow-ˈtie /bəʊ-/ *n* cravatta *f* a farfalla

box¹ /bɒks/ *n* scatola *f*; (*Theat*) palco *m*

box² *vi* (*Sport*) fare il pugile ● *vt* **~ sb's ears** dare uno scappaccione a qcno

box|er /ˈbɒksə(r)/ *n* pugile *m*. **~ing** *n* pugilato *m*. **B~ing Day** *n* [giorno *m* di] Santo Stefano *m*

box: ~-office *n* (*Theat*) botteghino *m*. **~-room** *n Br* sgabuzzino *m*

boy /bɔɪ/ *n* ragazzo *m*; (*younger*) bambino *m*

ˈboy band *n* boy band *f inv*

boycott /ˈbɔɪkɒt/ *n* boicottaggio *m* ● *vt* boicottare

boy: ~friend *n* ragazzo *m*. **~ish** *adj* da ragazzino

bra /brɑː/ *n* reggiseno *m*

brace /breɪs/ *n* sostegno *m*; (*dental*) apparecchio *m*; **~s** *npl* bretelle *fpl* ● *vt* **~ oneself** *fig* farsi forza (**for** per affrontare)

bracelet /ˈbreɪslɪt/ *n* braccialetto *m*

bracken /ˈbrækn/ *n* felce *f*

bracket /ˈbrækɪt/ *n* mensola *f*; (*group*) categoria *f*; (*Typ*) parentesi *f inv* ● *vt* mettere fra parentesi

brag /bræg/ *vi* (*pt/pp* **bragged**) vantarsi (**about** di)

braid /breɪd/ *n* (*edging*) passamano *m*

brain /breɪn/ *n* cervello *m*; **~s** *pl fig* testa *fsg*

brain: ~child *n* invenzione *f* personale. **~wash** *vt* fare il lavaggio del cervello a. **~wave** *n* lampo *m* di genio

brainy /ˈbreɪnɪ/ *adj* (**-ier, -iest**) intelligente

brake /breɪk/ *n* freno *m* ● *vi* frenare. **~-light** *n* stop *m inv*

bramble /ˈbræmbl/ *n* rovo *m*; (*fruit*) mora *f*

bran /bræn/ *n* crusca *f*

branch /brɑːntʃ/ *n also fig* ramo *m*; (*Comm*) succursale *f* ● *vi* (road:) biforcarsi. □ **~ off** *vi* biforcarsi. □ **~ out** *vi* **~ out into** allargare le proprie attività nel ramo di

brand /brænd/ *n* marca *f*; (*on animal*) marchio *m* ● *vt* marcare (animal); *fig* tacciare (**as** di)

brandish /ˈbrændɪʃ/ *vt* brandire

brandy /ˈbrændɪ/ *n* brandy *m inv*

brash /bræʃ/ *adj* sfrontato

brass /brɑːs/ *n* ottone *m*; **the ~** (*Mus*) gli ottoni *mpl*; **top ~** [!] pezzi *mpl* grossi. **~ band** *n* banda *f* (*di soli ottoni*)

brassiere /ˈbræzɪə(r)/ *n fml, Am* reggipetto *m*

brat /bræt/ *n pej* marmocchio, -a *mf*

bravado /brəˈvɑːdəʊ/ *n* bravata *f*

brave /breɪv/ *adj* coraggioso ● *vt* affrontare. **~ry** *n* coraggio *m*

brawl /brɔːl/ *n* rissa *f* ● *vi* azzuffarsi

brazen /ˈbreɪzn/ *adj* sfrontato

Brazil /brəˈzɪl/ *n* Brasile *m*. **~ian** *adj & n* brasiliano, -a *mf*. **~ nut** *n* noce *f* del Brasile

breach /briːtʃ/ *n* (*of law*) violazione *f*; (*gap*) breccia *f*; (*fig: in party*) frattura *f*; **~ of contract** inadempienza *f* di contratto; **~ of the peace** violazione *f* della quiete pubblica ● *vt* recedere (contract)

bread /bred/ *n* pane *m*; **a slice of ~ and butter** una fetta di pane imburrato

breadcrumbs *npl* briciole *fpl*; (*Culin*) pangrattato *m*

breadth /bredθ/ *n* larghezza *f*

ˈbread-winner *n* quello, -a *mf* che porta i soldi a casa

break /breɪk/ *n* rottura *f*; (*interval*) intervallo *m*; (*interruption*) interruzione *f*; ([!]*: chance*) opportunità *f inv* ● *v* (*pt* **broke**, *pp* **broken**) ● *vt* rompere; (*interrupt*) interrompere; **~ one's arm** rompersi un braccio ● *vi* rompersi; (day:) spuntare; (storm:) scoppiare; (news:) diffondersi; (boy's voice:) cambiare. □ **~ away** *vi* scappare; *fig* chiudere (**from** con). □ **~ down** *vi* (machine, car:) guastarsi; (*emotionally*) cedere (*psicologicamente*) ● *vt* sfondare (door); ripartire (figures). □ **~ into** *vt* introdursi (*con la forza*) in; forzare (car). □ **~ off** *vt* rompere (engagement) ● *vi* (part of whole:) rompersi. □ **~ out** *vi* (fight, war:) scoppiare. □ **~ up** *vt* far cessare (fight); disperdere (crowd) ● *vi* (crowd:) disperdersi; (couple:) separarsi; (*Sch*) iniziare le vacanze

ˈbreak|able /ˈbreɪkəbl/ *adj* fragile. **~age** *n* rottura *f*. **~down** *n* (*of car, machine*) guasto *m*; (*Med*) esaurimento *m* nervoso; (*of figures*) analisi *f inv*. **~er** *n* (*wave*) frangente *m*

breakfast /ˈbrekfəst/ *n* [prima] colazione *f*

break: ~through *n* scoperta *f*. **~water** *n* frangiflutti *m inv*

breast /brest/ *n* seno *m*. **~-feed** *vt* allattare [al seno]. **~-stroke** *n* nuoto *m* a rana

breath /ˈbreθ/: **~less** *adj* senza fiato. **~-taking** *adj* mozzafiato. **~ test** *n* prova [etilica] *f* del palloncino

breathalyse /ˈbreθəlaɪz/ *vt* sottoporre alla prova [etilica] del palloncino. **~r®** *n Br* alcoltest *m inv*

breathe /briːð/ *vt/i* respirare. □ **~ in** *vi* inspirare ● *vt* respirare (scent, air). □ **~ out** *vt/i* espirare

breath|er /ˈbriːðə(r)/ *n* pausa *f*. **~ing** *n* respirazione *f*

bred /bred/ ▷**BREED**

breed /briːd/ *n* razza *f* ● *v* (*pt/pp* **bred**) ● *vt* allevare; (*give rise to*) generare ● *vi* riprodursi. **~er** *n* allevatore, -trice *mf*. **~ing** *n* allevamento *m*; *fig* educazione *f*

breez|e /briːz/ *n* brezza *f*. **~y** *adj* ventoso

brew /bruː/ *n* infuso *m* ● *vt* mettere in infusione (tea); produrre (beer) ● *vi fig* (trouble:) essere nell'aria. **~er** *n* birraio *m*. **~ery** *n* fabbrica *f* di birra

bribe /braɪb/ *n* (*money*) bustarella *f*; (*large sum of money*) tangente *f* ● *vt* corrompere. **~ry** *n* corruzione *f*

brick /brɪk/ *n* mattone *m*. **ˈ~layer** *n* muratore *m* ● **brick up** *vt* murare

bridal /ˈbraɪdl/ *adj* nuziale

bride /braɪd/ *n* sposa *f*. **~groom** *n*

sposo *m*. **~smaid** *n* damigella *f* d'onore

bridge¹ /brɪdʒ/ *n* ponte *m*; (*of nose*) dorso *m*; (*of spectacles*) ponticello *m* ● *vt fig* colmare (gap)

bridge² *n* (*Cards*) bridge *m*

bridle /'braɪdl/ *n* briglia *f*

brief¹ /bri:f/ *adj* breve

brief² *n* istruzioni *fpl*; (*Jur: case*) causa *f* ● *vt* dare istruzioni a; (*Jur*) affidare la causa a. **~case** *n* cartella *f*

briefs /bri:fs/ *npl* slip *m inv*

brigad|e /brɪ'geɪd/ *n* brigata *f*. **~ier** *n* generale *m* di brigata

bright /braɪt/ *adj* (metal, idea) brillante; (day, room, future) luminoso; (*clever*) intelligente; **~ red** rosso *m* acceso

bright|en /'braɪtn/ *v* **~en [up]** ● *vt* ravvivare; rallegrare (person) ● *vi* (weather:) schiarirsi; (face:) illuminarsi; (person:) rallegrarsi. **~ly** *adv* (shine) intensamente; (smile) allegramente. **~ness** *n* luminosità *f*; (*intelligence*) intelligenza *f*

brilliance /'brɪljəns/ *n* luminosità *f*; (*of person*) genialità *f*

brilliant /'brɪljənt/ *adj* (*very good*) eccezionale; (*very intelligent*) brillante; (sunshine) splendente

brim /brɪm/ *n* bordo *m*; (*of hat*) tesa *f* ● **brim over** *vi* (*pt/pp* **brimmed**) traboccare

brine /braɪn/ *n* salamoia *f*

bring /brɪŋ/ *vt* (*pt/pp* **brought**) portare (person, object). □ **~ about** *vt* causare. □ **~ along** *vt* portare [con sé]. □ **~ back** *vt* restituire (sth borrowed); reintrodurre (hanging); fare ritornare in mente (memories). □ **~ down** *vt* portare giù; fare cadere (government); fare abbassare (price). □ **~ off** *vt* **~ sth off** riuscire a fare qcsa. □ **~ on** *vt* (*cause*) provocare. □ **~ out** *vt* (*emphasize*) mettere in evidenza; pubblicare (book). □ **~ round** *vt* portare; (*persuade*) convincere; far rinvenire (unconscious person). □ **~ up** *vt* (*vomit*) rimettere; allevare (children); tirare fuori (question, subject)

brink /brɪŋk/ *n* orlo *m*

brisk /brɪsk/ *adj* svelto; (person) sbrigativo; (trade, business) redditizio; (walk) a passo spedito

brist|le /'brɪsl/ *n* setola *f* ● *vi* **~ling with** pieno di. **~ly** *adj* (chin) ispido

Brit|ain /'brɪtn/ *n* Gran Bretagna *f*. **~ish** *adj* britannico; (ambassador) della Gran Bretagna ● *npl* **the ~ish** il popolo britannico. **~on** *n* cittadino, -a britannico, -a *mf*

brittle /'brɪtl/ *adj* fragile

broach /brəʊtʃ/ *vt* toccare (subject)

broad /brɔ:d/ *adj* ampio; (hint) chiaro; (accent) marcato. **two metres ~** largo due metri; **in ~ daylight** in pieno giorno. **~ band** *n* banda *f* larga. **~ beans** *npl* fave *fpl*

'broadcast *n* trasmissione *f* ● *vt/i* (*pt/pp* **-cast**) trasmettere. **~er** *n* giornalista *mf* radiotelevisivo, -a. **~ing** *n* diffusione *f* radiotelevisiva; **be in ~ing** lavorare per la televisione/radio

broaden /'brɔ:dn/ *vt* allargare ● *vi* allargarsi

broadly /'brɔ:dlɪ/ *adv* largamente; **~ [speaking]** generalmente

broad'minded *adj* di larghe vedute

broccoli /'brɒkəlɪ/ *n inv* broccoli *mpl*

brochure /'brəʊʃə(r)/ *n* opuscolo *m*; (*travel* **~**) dépliant *m inv*

broke /brəʊk/ ▶**BREAK** ● *adj* [!] al verde

broken /'brəʊkn/ ▶**BREAK** ● *adj* rotto; (fig: marriage) fallito. **~ English** inglese *m* stentato. **~-hearted** *adj* affranto

broker /'brəʊkə(r)/ *n* broker *m inv*

brolly /'brɒlɪ/ *n* [!] ombrello *m*

bronchitis /brɒŋ'kaɪtɪs/ *n* bronchite *f*

bronze /brɒnz/ *n* bronzo *m* ● *attrib* di bronzo

brooch /brəʊtʃ/ *n* spilla *f*

brood /bru:d/ *n* covata *f*; (*hum: children*) prole *f* ● *vi fig* rimuginare

brook /brʊk/ *n* ruscello *m*

broom /bru:m/ *n* scopa *f*. **~stick** *n* manico *m* di scopa

broth /brɒθ/ *n* brodo *m*

brothel /'brɒθl/ *n* bordello *m*

brother /'brʌðə(r)/ *n* fratello *m*

brother: ~-in-law *n* (*pl* **~s-in-law**) cognato *m*. **~ly** *adj* fraterno

brought /brɔ:t/ ▶**BRING**

brow /braʊ/ *n* fronte *f*; (*of hill*) cima *f*

b

'browbeat *vt* (*pt* **-beat**, *pp* **-beaten**) intimidire

brown /braʊn/ *adj* marrone; castano (hair) ● *n* marrone *m* ● *vt* rosolare (meat) ● *vi* (meat:) rosolarsi. **~ 'paper** *n* carta *f* da pacchi

browse /braʊz/ *vi* (*read*) leggicchiare; (*in shop*) curiosare

bruise /bru:z/ *n* livido *m*; (*on fruit*) ammaccatura *f* ● *vt* ammaccare (fruit); **~ one's arm** farsi un livido sul braccio. **~d** *adj* contuso

brunette /bru:'net/ *n* bruna *f*

brunt /brʌnt/ *n* **bear the ~ of sth** subire maggiormente qcsa

brush /brʌʃ/ *n* spazzola *f*; (*with long handle*) spazzolone *m*; (*for paint*) pennello *m*; (*bushes*) boscaglia *f*; (*fig: conflict*) breve scontro *m* ● *vt* spazzolare (hair); lavarsi (teeth); scopare (stairs, floor). □ **~ against** *vt* sfiorare. □ **~ aside** *vt fig* ignorare. □ **~ off** *vt* spazzolare; (*with hands*) togliere; ignorare (criticism). □ **~ up** *vt/i fig* **~ up [on]** rinfrescare

brusque /brʊsk/ *adj* brusco

Brussels /'brʌslz/ *n* Bruxelles *f*. **~ sprouts** *npl* cavoletti *mpl* di Bruxelles

brutal /'bru:tl/ *adj* brutale. **~ity** *n* brutalità *f inv*

brute /bru:t/ *n* bruto *m*. **~ force** *n* forza *f* bruta

BSc *n abbr* Bachelor of Science

BSE *n abbr* (bovine spongiform encephalitis) encefalite *f* bovina spongiforme

bubble /'bʌbl/ *n* bolla *f*; (*in drink*) bollicina *f*

buck¹ /bʌk/ *n* maschio *m* del cervo; (*rabbit*) maschio *m* del coniglio ● *vi* (horse:) saltare a quattro zampe. □ **~ up** *vi* [!] tirarsi su; (*hurry*) sbrigarsi

buck² *n Am* [!] dollaro *m*

buck³ *n* **pass the ~** scaricare la responsabilità

bucket /'bʌkɪt/ *n* secchio *m*

buckle /'bʌkl/ *n* fibbia *f* ● *vt* allacciare ● *vi* (shelf:) piegarsi; (wheel:) storcersi

bud /bʌd/ *n* bocciolo *m*

Buddhis|m /'bʊdɪzm/ *n* buddismo *m*. **~t** *adj & n* buddista *mf*

buddy /'bʌdɪ/ *n* [!] amico, -a *mf*

budge /bʌdʒ/ *vt* spostare ● *vi* spostarsi

budgerigar /'bʌdʒərɪgɑ:(r)/ *n* cocorita *f*

budget /'bʌdʒɪt/ *n* bilancio *m*; (*allotted to specific activity*) budget *m inv* ● *vi* (*pt/pp* **budgeted**) prevedere le spese; **~ for sth** includere qcsa nelle spese previste

buffalo /'bʌfələʊ/ *n* (*inv or pl* **-es**) bufalo *m*

buffer /'bʌfə(r)/ *n* (*Rail*) respingente *m*; **old ~** [!] vecchio bacucco *m*; **~ zone** *n* zona *f* cuscinetto

buffet¹ /'bʊfeɪ/ *n* buffet *m inv*

buffet² /'bʌfɪt/ *vt* (*pt/pp* **buffeted**) sferzare

bug /bʌg/ *n* (*insect*) insetto *m*; (*Comput*) bug *m inv*; ([!]*: device*) cimice *f* ● *vt* (*pt/pp* **bugged**) [!] installare delle microspie in (room); mettere sotto controllo (telephone); ([!]*: annoy*) scocciare

buggy /'bʌgɪ/ *n* **[baby] ~** passeggino *m*

bugle /'bju:gl/ *n* tromba *f*

build /bɪld/ *n* (*of person*) corporatura *f* ● *vt/i* (*pt/pp* **built**) costruire. □ **~ on** *vt* aggiungere (extra storey); sviluppare (previous work). □ **~ up** *vt* **~ up one's strength** rimettersi in forza ● *vi* (pressure, traffic:) aumentare; (excitement, tension:) crescere

builder /'bɪldə(r)/ *n* (*company*) costruttore *m*; (*worker*) muratore *m*

building /'bɪldɪŋ/ *n* edificio *m*. **~ site** *n* cantiere *m* [di costruzione]. **~ society** *n* istituto *m* di credito immobiliare

'build-up *n* (*of gas etc*) accumulo *m*; *fig* battage *m inv* pubblicitario

built /bɪlt/ ▷**BUILD**. **~-in** *adj* (unit) a muro; (fig: feature) incorporato. **~-up area** *n* (*Auto*) centro *m* abitato

bulb /bʌlb/ *n* bulbo *m*; (*Electr*) lampadina *f*

Bulgaria /bʌl'geərɪə/ *n* Bulgaria *f*

bulg|e /bʌldʒ/ *n* rigonfiamento *m* ● *vi* esser gonfio (**with** di); (stomach, wall:) sporgere; (eyes, with surprise:) uscire dalle orbite. **~ing** *adj* gonfio; (eyes) sporgente

bulk /bʌlk/ *n* volume *m*; (*greater part*) grosso *m*; **in ~** in grande quantità; (*loose*) sfuso. **~y** *adj* voluminoso

bull /bʊl/ *n* toro *m*

'bulldog *n* bulldog *m inv*

bulldozer /'bʊldəʊzə(r)/ *n* bulldozer *m inv*

bullet /'bʊlɪt/ *n* pallottola *f*

bulletin /ˈbʊlɪtɪn/ *n* bollettino *m*. ~ **board** *n* (*Comput*) bacheca *f* elettronica
ˈbullet-proof *adj* antiproiettile *inv*; (vehicle) blindato
ˈbullfight *n* corrida *f*. **~er** *n* torero *m*
bull: **~ring** *n* arena *f*. **~'s-eye** *n* centro *m* del bersaglio; **score a ~'s-eye** fare centro
bully /ˈbʊlɪ/ *n* prepotente *mf* ● *vt* fare il/la prepotente con. **~ing** *n* prepotenze *fpl*
bum¹ /bʌm/ *n* ☒ sedere *m*
bum² *n Am* ! vagabondo, -a *mf* ● **bum around** *vi* ! vagabondare
bumble-bee /ˈbʌmbl-/ *n* calabrone *m*
bump /bʌmp/ *n* botta *f*; (*swelling*) bozzo *m*, gonfiore *m*; (*in road*) protuberanza *f* ● *vt* sbattere. □ **~ into** *vt* sbattere contro; (*meet*) imbattersi in. □ **~ off** *vt* ! far fuori
bumper /ˈbʌmpə(r)/ *n* (*Auto*) paraurti *m inv* ● *adj* abbondante
bun /bʌn/ *n* focaccina *f* (*dolce*); (*hair*) chignon *m inv*
bunch /bʌntʃ/ *n* (*of flowers, keys*) mazzo *m*; (*of bananas*) casco *m*; (*of people*) gruppo *m*; **~ of grapes** grappolo *m* d'uva
bundle /ˈbʌndl/ *n* fascio *m*; (*of money*) mazzetta *f*; **a ~ of nerves** ! un fascio di nervi ● *vt* **~ [up]** affastellare
bungalow /ˈbʌŋgələʊ/ *n* bungalow *m inv*
bungle /ˈbʌŋgl/ *vt* fare un pasticcio di
bunk /bʌŋk/ *n* cuccetta *f*. **~-beds** *npl* letti *mpl* a castello
bunny /ˈbʌnɪ/ *n* ! coniglietto *m*
buoy /bɔɪ/ *n* boa *f*
burden /ˈbɜːdn/ *n* carico *m* ● *vt* caricare. **~some** *adj* gravoso
bureau /ˈbjʊərəʊ/ *n* (*pl* **-x** /-əʊz/ *or* **~s**) (*desk*) scrivania *f*; (*office*) ufficio *m*
bureaucracy /bjʊəˈrɒkrəsɪ/ *n* burocrazia *f*
bureaucrat /ˈbjʊərəkræt/ *n* burocrate *mf*. **~ic** *adj* burocratico
burger /ˈbɜːgə(r)/ *n* hamburger *m inv*
burglar /ˈbɜːglə(r)/ *n* svaligiatore, -trice *mf*. **~ alarm** *n* antifurto *m inv*
burgle /ˈbɜːgl/ *vt* svaligiare
burial /ˈberɪəl/ *n* sepoltura *f*. **~ ground** cimitero *m*
burly /ˈbɜːlɪ/ *adj* (**-ier, -iest**) corpulento
burn /bɜːn/ *n* bruciatura *f* ● *v* (*pt/pp* **burnt** *or* **burned**) ● *vt* bruciare ● *vi* bruciare. □ **~ down** *vt/i* bruciare. □ **~ out** *vi fig* esaurirsi. **~er** *n* ● (*on stove*) bruciatore *m* ● (*Comput*) masterizzatore *m*
burnt /bɜːnt/ ▷**BURN**
burp /bɜːp/ *n* ! rutto *m* ● *vi* ! ruttare
burrow /ˈbʌrəʊ/ *n* tana *f* ● *vt* scavare (hole)
bursar /ˈbɜːsə(r)/ *n* economo, -a *mf*. **~y** *n* borsa *f* di studio
burst /bɜːst/ *n* (*of gunfire, energy, laughter*) scoppio *m*; (*of speed*) scatto *m* ● *v* (*pt/pp* **burst**) ● *vt* far scoppiare ● *vi* scoppiare; **~ into tears** scoppiare in lacrime; **she ~ into the room** ha fatto irruzione nella stanza. □ **~ out** *vi* **~ out laughing/crying** scoppiare a ridere/piangere
bury /ˈberɪ/ *vt* (*pt/pp* **-ied**) seppellire; (*hide*) nascondere
bus /bʌs/ *n* autobus *m inv*, pullman *m inv*; (*long distance*) pullman *m inv*, corriera *f*
bush /bʊʃ/ *n* cespuglio *m*; (*land*) boscaglia *f*. **~y** *adj* (**-ier, -iest**) folto
business /ˈbɪznɪs/ *n* affare *m*; (*Comm*) affari *mpl*; (*establishment*) attività *f* di commercio; **on ~** per affari; **he has no ~ to** non ha alcun diritto di; **mind one's own ~** farsi gli affari propri; **that's none of your ~** non sono affari tuoi. **~-like** *adj* efficiente. **~man** *n* uomo *m* d'affari. **~woman** *n* donna *f* d'affari
busker /ˈbʌskə(r)/ *n* suonatore, -trice *mf* ambulante
ˈbus station *n* stazione *f* degli autobus
ˈbus-stop *n* fermata *f* d'autobus
bust¹ /bʌst/ *n* busto *m*; (*chest*) petto *m*
bust² *adj* ! rotto; **go ~** fallire ● *v* (*pt/pp* **busted** *or* **bust**) ! ● *vt* far scoppiare ● *vi* scoppiare
ˈbust-up *n* ! lite *f*
busy /ˈbɪzɪ/ *adj* (**-ier, -iest**) occupato; (day, time) intenso; (street) affollato; (*with traffic*) pieno di traffico; **be ~ doing** essere occupato a fare ● *vt* **~ oneself** darsi da fare
ˈbusybody *n* ficcanaso *mf inv*
but /bʌt/, *atono* /bət/ *conj* ma ● *prep* eccetto, tranne; **nobody ~ you** nessuno

b
c

tranne te; ~ **for** (*without*) se non fosse stato per; **the last** ~ **one** il penultimo; **the next** ~ **one** il secondo ● *adv* (*only*) soltanto; **there were** ~ **two** ce n'erano soltanto due

butcher /'bʊtʃə(r)/ *n* macellaio *m*; ~**'s [shop]** macelleria *f* ● *vt* macellare; *fig* massacrare

butler /'bʌtlə(r)/ *n* maggiordomo *m*

butt /bʌt/ *n* (*of gun*) calcio *m*; (*of cigarette*) mozzicone *m*; (*for water*) barile *m*; (*fig: target*) bersaglio *m* ● *vt* dare una testata a; (goat:) dare una cornata a. □ ~ **in** *vi* interrompere

butter /'bʌtə(r)/ *n* burro *m* ● *vt* imburrare. □ ~ **up** *vt* [!] arruffianarsi

butter: ~**cup** *n* ranuncolo *m*. ~**fingers** *nsg* [!] **be a** ~**fingers** avere le mani di pasta frolla. ~**fly** *n* farfalla *f*

button /'bʌtn/ *n* bottone *m* ● *vt* ~ **[up]** abbottonare ● *vi* abbottonarsi. ~**hole** *n* occhiello *m*, asola *f*

buy /baɪ/ *n* **good/bad** ~ buon/cattivo acquisto *m* ● *vt* (*pt/pp* **bought**) comprare; ~ **sb a drink** pagare da bere a qcno; **I'll** ~ **this one** (*drink*) questo, lo offro io. ~**er** *n* compratore, -trice *mf*

buzz /bʌz/ *n* ronzio *m*; **give sb a** ~ [!] (*on phone*) dare un colpo di telefono a qcno; (*excite*) mettere in fermento qcno ● *vi* ronzare ● *vt* ~ **sb** chiamare qcno col cicalino. □ ~ **off** *vi* [!] levarsi di torno

buzzer /'bʌzə(r)/ *n* cicalino *m*

by /baɪ/

● *prep* (*near, next to*) vicino a; (*at the latest*) per; **by Mozart** di Mozart; **he was run over by a bus** è stato investito da un autobus; **by oneself** da solo; **by the sea** al mare; **by sea** via mare; **by car/bus** in macchina/autobus; **by day/night** di giorno/notte; **by the hour/metre** a ore/metri; **six metres by four** sei metri per quattro; **he won by six metres** ha vinto di sei metri; **I missed the train by a minute** ho perso il treno per un minuto; **I'll be home by six** sarò a casa per le sei; **by this time next week** a quest'ora tra una settimana; **he rushed by me** mi è passato accanto di corsa

● *adv* **she'll be here by and by** sarà qui fra poco; **by and large** in complesso

bye[-bye] /baɪ['baɪ]/ *int* [!] ciao

by: ~**-election** *n elezione f straordinaria indetta per coprire una carica rimasta vacante in Parlamento.* ~**-law** *n* legge *f* locale. ~**pass** *n* circonvallazione *f*; (*Med*) by-pass *m inv* ● *vt* evitare. ~**-product** *n* sottoprodotto *m*. ~**stander** *n* spettatore, -trice *mf*

Cc

cab /kæb/ *n* taxi *m inv*; (*of lorry, train*) cabina *f*

cabaret /'kæbəreɪ/ *n* cabaret *m inv*

cabbage /'kæbɪdʒ/ *n* cavolo *m*

cabin /'kæbɪn/ *n* (*of plane, ship*) cabina *f*; (*hut*) capanna *f*

cabinet /'kæbɪnɪt/ *n* armadietto *m*; **[display]** ~ vetrina *f*; **C**~ (*Pol*) consiglio *m* dei ministri. ~**-maker** *n* ebanista *mf*

cable /'keɪbl/ *n* cavo *m*. ~ **'railway** *n* funicolare *f*. ~ **'television** *n* televisione *f* via cavo

cackle /'kækl/ *vi* ridacchiare

cactus /'kæktəs/ *n* (*pl* **-ti** /-taɪ/ *or* **-tuses**) cactus *m inv*

caddie /'kædɪ/ *n* portabastoni *m inv*

caddy /'kædɪ/ *n* **[tea-]**~ barattolo *m* del tè

cadet /kə'det/ *n* cadetto *m*

cadge /kædʒ/ *vt/i* [!] scroccare

café /'kæfeɪ/ *n* caffè *m inv*

cafeteria /kæfə'tɪərɪə/ *n* tavola *f* calda

caffeine /'kæfi:n/ *n* caffeina *f*

cage /keɪdʒ/ *n* gabbia *f*

cake /keɪk/ *n* torta *f*; (*small*) pasticcino *m*. ~**d** *adj* incrostato (**with** di)

calamity /kə'læmətɪ/ *n* calamità *f inv*

calcium /'kælsɪəm/ *n* calcio *m*

calculat|e /'kælkjʊleɪt/ *vt* calcolare. ~**ing** *adj fig* calcolatore. ~**ion** *n* calcolo *m*. ~**or** *n* calcolatrice *f*

calendar /ˈkælɪndə(r)/ *n* calendario *m*
calf¹ /kɑːf/ *n* (*pl* **calves**) vitello *m*
calf² *n* (*pl* **calves**) (*Anat*) polpaccio *m*
calibre /ˈkælɪbə(r)/ *n* calibro *m*
call /kɔːl/ *n* grido *m*; (*Teleph*) telefonata *f*; (*visit*) visita *f*; **be on ~** (doctor:) essere di guardia ● *vt* chiamare; indire (strike); **be ~ed** chiamarsi ● *vi* chiamare; **~ [in** *or* **round]** passare. □ **~ back** *vt/i* richiamare. □ **~ for** *vt* (*ask for*) chiedere; (*require*) richiedere; (*fetch*) passare a prendere. □ **~ off** *vt* richiamare (dog); disdire (meeting); revocare (strike). □ **~ on** *vt* chiamare; (*appeal to*) fare un appello a; (*visit*) visitare. □ **~ out** *vt* chiamare ad alta voce (names) ● *vi* chiamare ad alta voce. □ **~ together** *vt* riunire. □ **~ up** *vt* (*Mil*) chiamare alle armi; (*Teleph*) chiamare
call: ~-box *n* cabina *f* telefonica. **~ centre** *n* call centre *m inv*. **~er** *n* visitatore, -trice *mf*; (*Teleph*) *persona f che telefona*. **~ing** *n* vocazione *f*
callous /ˈkæləs/ *adj* insensibile
calm /kɑːm/ *adj* calmo ● *n* calma *f*. □ **~ down** *vt* calmare ● *vi* calmarsi. **~ly** *adv* con calma
calorie /ˈkælərɪ/ *n* caloria *f*
calves /kɑːvz/ *npl see* **calf**1 &2
camcorder /ˈkæmkɔːdə(r)/ *n* videocamera *f*
came /keɪm/ ▷COME
camel /ˈkæml/ *n* cammello *m*
camera /ˈkæmərə/ *n* macchina *f* fotografica; (*TV*) telecamera *f*. **~man** *n* operatore *m* [televisivo], cameraman *m inv*
camouflage /ˈkæməflɑːʒ/ *n* mimetizzazione *f* ● *vt* mimetizzare
camp /kæmp/ *n* campeggio *f*; (*Mil*) campo *m* ● *vi* campeggiare; (*Mil*) accamparsi
campaign /kæmˈpeɪn/ *n* campagna *f* ● *vi* fare una campagna
camp: ~-bed *n* letto *m* da campo. **~er** *n* campeggiatore, -trice *mf*; (*Auto*) camper *m inv*. **~ing** *n* campeggio *m*. **~site** *n* campeggio *m*
campus /ˈkæmpəs/ *n* (*pl* **-puses**) (*Univ*) città *f* universitaria, campus *m inv*
can¹ /kæn/ *n* (*for petrol*) latta *f*; (*tin*) scatola *f*; **~ of beer** lattina *f* di birra ● *vt* mettere in scatola

> **can²** /kæn/, *atono* /kən/ *v aux* (*pres* **can**; *pt* **could**) (*be able to*) potere; (*know how to*) sapere; **I cannot** *or* **can't go** non posso andare; **he could not** *or* **couldn't go** non poteva andare; **she can't swim** non sa nuotare; **I ~ smell something burning** sento odor di bruciato

Canad|a /ˈkænədə/ *n* Canada *m*. **~ian** *adj & n* canadese *mf*
canal /kəˈnæl/ *n* canale *m*
Canaries /kəˈneərɪz/ *npl* Canarie *fpl*
canary /kəˈneərɪ/ *n* canarino *m*
cancel /ˈkænsl/ *v* (*pt/pp* **cancelled**) ● *vt* disdire (meeting, newspaper); revocare (contract, order); annullare (reservation, appointment, stamp). **~lation** *n* (*of meeting, contract*) revoca *f*; (*in hotel, restaurant, for flight*) cancellazione *f*
cancer /ˈkænsə(r)/ *n* cancro *m*; **C~** (*Astr*) Cancro *m*. **~ous** *adj* canceroso
candid /ˈkændɪd/ *adj* franco
candidate /ˈkændɪdət/ *n* candidato, -a *mf*
candle /ˈkændl/ *n* candela *f*. **~stick** *n* portacandele *m inv*
candour /ˈkændə(r)/ *n* franchezza *f*
candy /ˈkændɪ/ *n Am* caramella *f*; **a [piece of] ~** una caramella. **~floss** *n* zucchero *m* filato
cane /keɪn/ *n* (*stick*) bastone *m*; (*Sch*) bacchetta *f* ● *vt* prendere a bacchettate (pupil)
canister /ˈkænɪstə(r)/ *n* barattolo *m* (*di metallo*)
cannabis /ˈkænəbɪs/ *n* cannabis *f*
cannibal /ˈkænɪbl/ *n* cannibale *mf*. **~ism** *n* cannibalismo *m*
cannon /ˈkænən/ *n inv* cannone *m*. **~-ball** *n* palla *f* di cannone
cannot /ˈkænɒt/ ▷CAN²
canoe /kəˈnuː/ *n* canoa *f* ● *vi* andare in canoa
ˈcan-opener *n* apriscatole *m inv*
canopy /ˈkænəpɪ/ *n* baldacchino *f*; (*of parachute*) calotta *f*
cantankerous /kænˈtæŋkərəs/ *adj* stizzoso
canteen /kænˈtiːn/ *n* mensa *f*; **~ of**

cutlery servizio *m* di posate
canter /'kæntə(r)/ *vi* andare a piccolo galoppo
canvas /'kænvəs/ *n* tela *f*; (*painting*) dipinto *m* su tela
canvass /'kænvəs/ *vi* (*Pol*) fare propaganda elettorale. **~ing** *n* sollecitazione *f* di voti
canyon /'kænjən/ *n* canyon *m inv*
cap /kæp/ *n* berretto *m*; (*nurse's*) cuffia *f*; (*top, lid*) tappo *m* ● *vt* (*pt/pp* **capped**) (*fig: do better than*) superare
capability /keɪpə'bɪlətɪ/ *n* capacità *f*
capabl|e /'keɪpəbl/ *adj* capace; (*skilful*) abile; **be ~e of doing sth** essere capace di fare qcsa. **~y** *adv* con abilità
capacity /kə'pæsətɪ/ *n* capacità *f*; (*function*) qualità *f*; **in my ~ as** in qualità di
cape[1] /keɪp/ *n* (*cloak*) cappa *f*
cape[2] *n* (*Geog*) capo *m*
capital /'kæpɪtl/ *n* (*town*) capitale *f*; (*money*) capitale *m*; (*letter*) lettera *f* maiuscola. **~ city** *n* capitale *f*
capital|ism /'kæpɪtəlɪzm/ *n* capitalismo *m*. **~ist** *adj & n* capitalista *mf*. **~ize** *vi* **~ize on** *fig* trarre vantaggio da. **~ 'letter** *n* lettera *f* maiuscola. **~ 'punishment** *n* pena *f* capitale

> *i* **Capitol** Situato su Capitol Hill, nella città di Washington, il Campidoglio (*the Capitol*) è la sede del Congresso (*Congress*) degli Stati Uniti d'America e per estensione indica il Congresso stesso.

capitulat|e /kə'pɪtjʊleɪt/ *vi* capitolare. **~ion** *n* capitolazione *f*
Capricorn /'kæprɪkɔːn/ *n* (*Astr*) Capricorno *m*
capsize /kæp'saɪz/ *vi* capovolgersi ● *vt* capovolgere
capsule /'kæpsjʊl/ *n* capsula *f*
captain /'kæptɪn/ *n* capitano *m* ● *vt* comandare (team)
caption /'kæpʃn/ *n* intestazione *f*; (*of illustration*) didascalia *f*
captivate /'kæptɪveɪt/ *vt* incantare
captiv|e /'kæptɪv/ *adj* prigionero; **hold/take ~e** tenere/fare prigioniero ● *n* prigioniero, -a *mf*. **~ity** *n* prigionia *f*; (*animals*) cattività *f*
capture /'kæptʃə(r)/ *n* cattura *f* ● *vt* catturare; attirare (attention)
car /kɑː(r)/ *n* macchina *f*; **by ~** in macchina
carafe /kə'ræf/ *n* caraffa *f*
caramel /'kærəmel/ *n* (*sweet*) caramella *f* al mou; (*Culin*) caramello *m*
caravan /'kærəvæn/ *n* roulotte *f inv*; (*horse-drawn*) carovana *f*
carbohydrate /kɑːbə'haɪdreɪt/ *n* carboidrato *m*
carbon /'kɑːbən/ *n* carbonio *m*
carbon di'oxide *n* anidride *f* carbonica
carburettor /kɑːbjʊ'retə(r)/ *n* carburatore *m*
carcass /'kɑːkəs/ *n* carcassa *f*
card /kɑːd/ *n* (*for birthday, Christmas etc*) biglietto *m* di auguri; (*playing ~*) carta *f* [da gioco]; (*membership ~*) tessera *f*; (*business ~*) biglietto *m* da visita; (*credit ~*) carta *f* di credito; (*Comput*) scheda *f*
'cardboard *n* cartone *m*. **~ 'box** *n* scatola *f* di cartone; (*large*) scatolone *m*
cardigan /'kɑːdɪgən/ *n* cardigan *m inv*
cardinal /'kɑːdɪnl/ *adj* cardinale; **~ number** numero *m* cardinale ● *n* (*Relig*) cardinale *m*
care /keə(r)/ *n* cura *f*; (*caution*) attenzione *f*; (*worry*) preoccupazione *f*; **~ of** (*on letter abbr* **c/o**) presso; **take ~** (*be cautious*) fare attenzione; **bye, take ~** ciao, stammi bene; **take ~ of** occuparsi di; **be taken into ~** essere preso in custodia da un ente assistenziale ● *vi* **~ about** interessarsi di; **~ for** (*feel affection for*) volere bene a; (*look after*) aver cura di; **I don't ~ for chocolate** non mi piace il cioccolato; **I don't ~** non me ne importa; **who ~s?** chi se ne frega?
career /kə'rɪə(r)/ *n* carriera *f*; (*profession*) professione *f* ● *vi* andare a tutta velocità
care: ~free *adj* spensierato. **~ful** *adj* attento; (driver) prudente. **~fully** *adv* con attenzione. **~less** *adj* irresponsabile; (*in work*) trascurato; (work) fatto con poca cura; (driver) distratto. **~lessly** *adv* negligentemente. **~lessness** *n* trascuratezza *f*. **~r** *n persona f che accudisce a un anziano o a un malato*
caress /kə'res/ *n* carezza *f* ● *vt* accarezzare

'caretaker *n* custode *mf*; (*in school*) bidello *m*

'car ferry *n* traghetto *m* (*per il trasporto di auto*)

cargo /'kɑːɡəʊ/ *n* (*pl* **-es**) carico *m*

Caribbean /kærɪ'biːən/ *n* **the ~** (*sea*) il Mar dei Caraibi ● *adj* caraibico

caricature /'kærɪkətjʊə(r)/ *n* caricatura *f*

carnage /'kɑːnɪdʒ/ *n* carneficina *f*

carnation /kɑː'neɪʃn/ *n* garofano *m*

carnival /'kɑːnɪvl/ *n* carnevale *m*

carol /'kærəl/ *n* **[Christmas] ~** canzone *f* natalizia

carp¹ /kɑːp/ *n inv* carpa *f*

carp² *vi* **~ at** trovare da ridire su

'car park *n* parcheggio *m*

carpent|er /'kɑːpɪntə(r)/ *n* falegname *m*. **~ry** *n* falegnameria *f*

carpet /'kɑːpɪt/ *n* tappeto *m*; (*wall-to-wall*) moquette *f inv* ● *vt* mettere la moquette in (room)

carriage /'kærɪdʒ/ *n* carrozza *f*; (*of goods*) trasporto *m*; (*cost*) spese *fpl* di trasporto; (*bearing*) portamento *m*; **~way** *n* strada *f* carrozzabile; **northbound ~way** carreggiata *f* nord

carrier /'kærɪə(r)/ *n* (*company*) impresa *f* di trasporti; (*Aeron*) compagnia *f* di trasporto aereo; (*of disease*) portatore *m*. **~ bag** *n* borsa *f* [per la spesa]

carrot /'kærət/ *n* carota *f*

carry /'kærɪ/ *v* (*pt/pp* **-ied**) ● *vt* portare; (*transport*) trasportare; **get carried away** [!] lasciarsi prender la mano ● *vi* (sound:) trasmettersi. □ **~ off** *vt* portare via; vincere (prize). □ **~ on** *vi* continuare; ([!]: *make scene*) fare delle storie; **~ on with sth** continuare qcsa; **~ on with sb** [!] intendersela con qcno ● *vt* mantenere (business). □ **~ out** *vt* portare fuori; eseguire (instructions, task); mettere in atto (threat); effettuare (experiment, survey)

'carry-cot *n* porte-enfant *m inv*

cart /kɑːt/ *n* carretto *m* ● *vt* ([!]: *carry*) portare

carton /'kɑːtn/ *n* scatola *f* di cartone; (*for drink*) cartone *m*; (*of cream, yoghurt*) vasetto *m*; (*of cigarettes*) stecca *f*

cartoon /kɑː'tuːn/ *n* vignetta *f*; (*strip*) vignette *fpl*; (*film*) cartone *m* animato; (*in art*) bozzetto *m*. **~ist** *n* vignettista *mf*; (*for films*) disegnatore, -trice *mf* di cartoni animati

cartridge /'kɑːtrɪdʒ/ *n* cartuccia *f*; (*for film*) bobina *f*; (*of record player*) testina *f*

carve /kɑːv/ *vt* scolpire; tagliare (meat)

C

case¹ /keɪs/ *n* caso *m*; **in any ~** in ogni caso; **in that ~** in questo caso; **just in ~** per sicurezza; **in ~ he comes** nel caso in cui venisse

case² *n* (*container*) scatola *f*; (*crate*) cassa *f*; (*for spectacles*) astuccio *m*; (*suitcase*) valigia *f*; (*for display*) vetrina *f*

cash /kæʃ/ *n* denaro *m* contante; ([!]: *money*) contanti *mpl*; **pay [in] ~** pagare in contanti; **~ on delivery** pagamento alla consegna ● *vt* incassare (cheque). **~ desk** *n* cassa *f*

cashier /kæ'ʃɪə(r)/ *n* cassiere, -a *mf*

casino /kə'siːnəʊ/ *n* casinò *m inv*

casket /'kɑːskɪt/ *n* scrigno *m*; (*Am: coffin*) bara *f*

casserole /'kæsərəʊl/ *n* casseruola *f*; (*stew*) stufato *m*

cassette /kə'set/ *n* cassetta *f*. **~ recorder** *n* registratore *m* (*a cassette*)

cast /kɑːst/ *n* (*mould*) forma *f*; (*Theat*) cast *m inv*; **[plaster] ~** (*Med*) ingessatura *f* ● *vt* (*pt/pp* **cast**) dare (vote); (*Theat*) assegnare le parti di (play); fondere (metal); (*throw*) gettare; **~ an actor as** dare ad un attore il ruolo di; **~ a glance at** lanciare uno sguardo a. □ **~ off** *vi* (*Naut*) sganciare gli ormeggi ● *vt* (*in knitting*) diminuire. □ **~ on** *vt* (*in knitting*) avviare

castaway /'kɑːstəweɪ/ *n* naufrago, -a *mf*

caster /'kɑːstə(r)/ *n* (*wheel*) rotella *f*. **~ sugar** *n* zucchero *m* raffinato

cast 'iron *n* ghisa *f*

cast-'iron *adj* di ghisa; *fig* solido

castle /'kɑːsl/ *n* castello *m*; (*in chess*) torre *f*

'cast-offs *npl* abiti *mpl* smessi

castrat|e /kæ'streɪt/ *vt* castrare. **~ion** *n* castrazione *f*

casual /'kæʒʊəl/ *adj* (*chance*) casuale; (remark) senza importanza; (glance) di sfuggita; (attitude, approach) disinvolto; (chat) informale; (clothes) casual *inv*; (work) saltuario; **~ wear** abbigliamento *m* casual. **~ly** *adv* (dress) casual; (meet) casualmente

casualty /ˈkæʒʊəltɪ/ *n* (*injured person*) ferito *m*; (*killed*) vittima *f*. ~ **[department]** *n* pronto soccorso *m*

cat /kæt/ *n* gatto *m*; *pej* arpia *f*

catalogue /ˈkætəlɒg/ *n* catalogo *m* • *vt* catalogare

catalyst /ˈkætəlɪst/ *n* (*Chem*) & *fig* catalizzatore *m*

catapult /ˈkætəpʌlt/ *n* catapulta *f*; (*child's*) fionda *f* • *vt fig* catapultare

catarrh /kəˈtɑː(r)/ *n* catarro *m*

catastroph|e /kəˈtæstrəfɪ/ *n* catastrofe *f*. **~ic** *adj* catastrofico

catch /kætʃ/ *n* (*of fish*) pesca *f*; (*fastener*) fermaglio *m*; (*on door*) fermo *m*; (*on window*) gancio *m*; ([!]: *snag*) tranello *m* • *v* (*pt/pp* **caught**) • *vt* acchiappare (ball); (*grab*) afferrare; prendere (illness, fugitive, train); ~ **a cold** prendersi un raffreddore; ~ **sight of** scorgere; **I caught him stealing** l'ho sorpreso mentre rubava; ~ **one's finger in the door** chiudersi il dito nella porta; ~ **sb's eye** *or* **attention** attirare l'attenzione di qcno • *vi* (fire:) prendere; (*get stuck*) impigliarsi. □ ~ **on** *vi* [!] (*understand*) afferrare; (*become popular*) diventare popolare. □ ~ **up** *vt* raggiungere • *vi* recuperare; (runner:) riguadagnare terreno; ~ **up with** raggiungere (sb); mettersi in pari con (work)

catching /ˈkætʃɪŋ/ *adj* contagioso

catchphrase *n* tormentone *m*

catchy /ˈkætʃɪ/ *adj* (**-ier, -iest**) orecchiabile

categor|ical /kætɪˈgɒrɪkl/ *adj* categorico. **~y** *n* categoria *f*

cater /ˈkeɪtə(r)/ *vi* ~ **for** provvedere a (needs); *fig* venire incontro alle esigenze di. **~ing** *n* (*trade*) ristorazione *f*; (*food*) rinfresco *m*

caterpillar /ˈkætəpɪlə(r)/ *n* bruco *m*

cathedral /kəˈθiːdrl/ *n* cattedrale *f*

Catholic /ˈkæθəlɪk/ *adj* & *n* cattolico, -a *mf*. **~ism** *n* cattolicesimo *m*

cat's eyes *npl* catarifrangente *msg* (*inserito nell'asfalto*)

cattle /ˈkætl/ *npl* bestiame *msg*

catwalk /ˈkætwɔːk/ *n* passerella *f*

caught /kɔːt/ ▷CATCH

cauliflower /ˈkɒlɪ-/ *n* cavolfiore *m*

cause /kɔːz/ *n* causa *f* • *vt* causare; ~ **sb to do sth** far fare qcsa a qcno

caution /ˈkɔːʃn/ *n* cautela *f*; (*warning*) ammonizione *f* • *vt* mettere in guardia; (*Jur*) ammonire

cautious /ˈkɔːʃəs/ *adj* cauto

cavalry /ˈkævəlrɪ/ *n* cavalleria *f*

cave /keɪv/ *n* caverna *f* • **cave in** *vi* (roof:) crollare; (*fig: give in*) capitolare

cavern /ˈkævən/ *n* caverna *f*

caviare /ˈkævɪɑː(r)/ *n* caviale *m*

cavity /ˈkævətɪ/ *n* cavità *f inv*; (*in tooth*) carie *f inv*

CD *n* CD *m inv*. ~ **player** *n* lettore *m* [di] compact

CD-Rom /siːdiːˈrɒm/ *n* CD-Rom *m inv*. ~ **drive** *n* lettore *m* [di] CD-Rom

cease /siːs/ *n* **without** ~ incessantemente • *vt/i* cessare. **~-fire** *n* cessate il fuoco *m inv*. **~less** *adj* incessante

cedar /ˈsiːdə(r)/ *n* cedro *m*

ceiling /ˈsiːlɪŋ/ *n* soffitto *m*; *fig* tetto *m* [massimo]

celebrat|e /ˈselɪbreɪt/ *vt* festeggiare (birthday, victory) • *vi* far festa. **~ed** *adj* celebre (**for** per). **~ion** *n* celebrazione *f*

celebrity /sɪˈlebrətɪ/ *n* celebrità *f inv*

celery /ˈselərɪ/ *n* sedano *m*

cell /sel/ *n* cella *f*; (*Biol*) cellula *f*

cellar /ˈselə(r)/ *n* scantinato *m*; (*for wine*) cantina *f*

cello /ˈtʃeləʊ/ *n* violoncello *m*

Cellophane® /ˈseləfeɪn/ *n* cellofan *m inv*

cellphone /ˈselfəʊn/ *n* cellulare *m*

cellular phone /seljʊləˈfəʊn/ *n* [telefono *m*] cellulare *m*

celluloid /ˈseljʊlɔɪd/ *n* celluloide *f*

Celsius /ˈselsɪəs/ *adj* Celsius

cement /sɪˈment/ *n* cemento *m*; (*adhesive*) mastice *m* • *vt* cementare; *fig* consolidare

cemetery /ˈsemətrɪ/ *n* cimitero *m*

censor /ˈsensə(r)/ *n* censore *m* • *vt* censurare. **~ship** *n* censura *f*

censure /ˈsenʃə(r)/ *vt* biasimare

census /ˈsensəs/ *n* censimento *m*

cent /sent/ *n* (*of dollar*) centesimo *m*; (*of euro*) cent *m inv*, centesimo *m*

centenary /senˈtiːnərɪ/ *n*, *Am* **centennial** /senˈtenɪəl/ *n* centenario *m*

center /ˈsentə(r)/ *n Am* = **centre**

centi|grade /ˈsentɪ-/ *adj* centigrado.

~metre *n* centimetro *m*. **~pede** *n* centopiedi *m inv*

central /'sentrəl/ *adj* centrale. **~ 'heating** *n* riscaldamento *m* autonomo. **~ize** *vt* centralizzare. **~ly** *adv* al centro; **~ly heated** con riscaldamento autonomo. **~ reser'vation** *n* (*Auto*) banchina *f* spartitraffico

centre /'sentə(r)/ *n* centro *m* ● *v* (*pt/pp* **centred**) ● *vt* centrare ● *vi* **~ on** *fig* incentrarsi su. **~-'forward** *n* centravanti *m inv*

century /'sentʃərɪ/ *n* secolo *m*

cereal /'sɪərɪəl/ *n* cereale *m*

ceremon|ial /serɪ'məʊnɪəl/ *adj* da cerimonia ● *n* cerimoniale *m*. **~ious** *adj* cerimonioso

ceremony /'serɪmənɪ/ *n* cerimonia *f*

certain /'sɜ:tn/ *adj* certo; **for ~** di sicuro; **make ~** accertarsi ; **he is ~ to win** è certo di vincere; **it's not ~ whether he'll come** non è sicuro che venga. **~ly** *adv* certamente; **~ly not!** no di certo! **~ty** *n* certezza *f*; **it's a ~ty** è una cosa certa

certificate /sə'tɪfɪkət/ *n* certificato *m*

certify /'sɜ:tɪfaɪ/ *vt* (*pt/pp* **-ied**) certificare; (*declare insane*) dichiarare malato di mente

chafe /tʃeɪf/ *vt* irritare

chain /tʃeɪn/ *n* catena *f* ● *vt* incatenare (prisoner); attaccare con la catena (dog) (**to** a). □ **~ up** *vt* legare alla catena (dog)

chain: ~ re'action *n* reazione *f* a catena. **~-smoker** *n* fumatore, -trice *mf* accanito, -a. **~ store** *n* negozio *m* appartenente a una catena

chair /tʃeə(r)/ *n* sedia *f*; (*Univ*) cattedra *f* ● *vt* presiedere. **~-lift** *n* seggiovia *f*. **~man** *n* presidente *m*

chalet /'ʃæleɪ/ *n* chalet *m inv*; (*in holiday camp*) bungalow *m inv*

chalk /tʃɔ:k/ *n* gesso *m*. **~y** *adj* gessoso

challeng|e /'tʃælɪndʒ/ *n* sfida *f*; (*Mil*) intimazione *f* ● *vt* sfidare; (*Mil*) intimare il chi va là a; *fig* mettere in dubbio (statement). **~er** *n* sfidante *mf*. **~ing** *adj* (job) impegnativo

chamber /'tʃeɪmbə(r)/ *n* **C~ of Commerce** camera *f* di commercio

chambermaid *n* cameriera *f* [d'albergo]

champagne /ʃæm'peɪn/ *n* champagne *m inv*

champion /'tʃæmpɪən/ *n* (*Sport*) campione *m*; (*of cause*) difensore, difenditrice *mf* ● *vt* (*defend*) difendere; (*fight for*) lottare per. **~ship** *n* (*Sport*) campionato *m*

chance /tʃɑ:ns/ *n* caso *m*; (*possibility*) possibilità *f inv*; (*opportunity*) occasione *f*; **by ~** per caso; **take a ~** provarci; **give sb a second ~** dare un'altra possibilità a qcno ● *attrib* fortuito ● *vt* **I'll ~ it** [!] corro il rischio

chancellor /'tʃɑ:nsələ(r)/ *n* cancelliere *m*; (*Univ*) rettore *m*; **C~ of the Exchequer** ≈ ministro *m* del tesoro

chandelier /ʃændə'lɪə(r)/ *n* lampadario *m*

change /tʃeɪndʒ/ *n* cambiamento *m*; (*money*) resto *m*; (*small coins*) spiccioli *mpl*; **for a ~** tanto per cambiare; **a ~ of clothes** un cambio di vestiti; **the ~ [of life]** la menopausa ● *vt* cambiare; (*substitute*) scambiare (**for** con); **~ one's clothes** cambiarsi [i vestiti]; **~ trains** cambiare treno ● *vi* cambiare; (*~ clothes*) cambiarsi; **all ~!** stazione terminale!

changeable /'tʃeɪndʒəbl/ *adj* mutevole; (weather) variabile

'changing-room *n* camerino *m*; (*for sports*) spogliatoio *m*

channel /'tʃænl/ *n* canale *m*; **the [English] C~** la Manica; **the C~ Islands** le Isole del Canale ● *vt* (*pt/pp* **channelled**) **~ one's energies into sth** convogliare le proprie energie in qcsa

chant /tʃɑ:nt/ *n* cantilena *f*; (*of demonstrators*) slogan *m inv* di protesta ● *vt* cantare; (demonstrators:) gridare

chao|s /'keɪɒs/ *n* caos *m*. **~tic** *adj* caotico

chap /tʃæp/ *n* [!] tipo *m*

chapel /'tʃæpl/ *n* cappella *f*

chaperon /'ʃæpərəʊn/ *n* chaperon *f inv* ● *vt* fare da chaperon a (sb)

chapter /'tʃæptə(r)/ *n* capitolo *m*

char¹ /tʃɑ:(r)/ *n* [!] donna *f* delle pulizie

char² *vt* (*pt/pp* **charred**) (*burn*) carbonizzare

character /'kærɪktə(r)/ *n* carattere *m*; (*in novel, play*) personaggio *m*; **quite a**

C

~ [!] un tipo particolare

characteristic /kærɪktə'rɪstɪk/ *adj* caratteristico ● *n* caratteristica *f*. **~ally** *adv* tipicamente

C

characterize /'kærɪktəraɪz/ *vt* caratterizzare

charade /ʃə'rɑ:d/ *n* farsa *f*

charcoal /'tʃɑ:-/ *n* carbonella *f*

charge /tʃɑ:dʒ/ *n* (*cost*) prezzo *m*; (*Electr, Mil*) carica *f*; (*Jur*) accusa *f*; **free of ~** gratuito; **be in ~** essere responsabile (**of** di); **take ~** assumersi la responsabilità; **take ~ of** occuparsi di ● *vt* far pagare (fee); far pagare a (person); (*Electr, Mil*) caricare; (*Jur*) accusare (**with** di); **~ sb for sth** far pagare qcsa a qcno; **~ it to my account** lo addebiti sul mio conto ● *vi* (*attack*) caricare

charitable /'tʃærɪtəbl/ *adj* caritatevole; (*kind*) indulgente

charity /'tʃærətɪ/ *n* carità *f*; (*organization*) associazione *f* di beneficenza; **concert given for ~** concerto *m* di beneficenza; **live on ~** vivere di elemosina

charm /tʃɑ:m/ *n* fascino *m*; (*object*) ciondolo *m* ● *vt* affascinare. **~ing** *adj* affascinante

chart /tʃɑ:t/ *n* carta *f* nautica; (*table*) tabella *f*

charter /'tʃɑ:tə(r)/ *n* **~ [flight]** [volo *m*] charter *m inv* ● *vt* noleggiare. **~ed accountant** *n* commercialista *mf*

chase /tʃeɪs/ *n* inseguimento *m* ● *vt* inseguire. **chase away** *or* **off** *vt* cacciare via

chassis /'ʃæsɪ/ *n* (*pl* **chassis** /-sɪz/) telaio *m*

chastity /'tʃæstətɪ/ *n* castità *f*

chat /tʃæt/ *n* chiacchierata *f*; **have a ~ with** fare quattro chiacchere con ● *vi* (*pt/pp* **chatted**) chiacchierare; (*Comput*) chattare. **~ show** *n* talk show *m inv*

chatter /'tʃætə(r)/ *n* chiacchiere *fpl* ● *vi* chiacchierare; (teeth:) battere. **~box** *n* [!] chiacchierone, -a *mf*

chauffeur /'ʃəʊfə(r)/ *n* autista *mf*

chauvin|ism /'ʃəʊvɪnɪzm/ *n* sciovinismo *m*. **~ist** *n* sciovinista *mf*. **male ~ist** *n* [!] maschilista *m*

cheap /tʃi:p/ *adj* a buon mercato; (rate) economico; (*vulgar*) grossolano; (*of poor quality*) scadente ● *adv* a buon mercato. **~ly** *adv* a buon mercato

cheat /tʃi:t/ *n* imbroglione, -a *mf*; (*at cards*) baro *m* ● *vt* imbrogliare; **~ sb out of sth** sottrarre qcsa a qcno con l'inganno ● *vi* imbrogliare; (*at cards*) barare. □ **~ on** *vt* [!] tradire (wife)

check¹ /tʃek/ *adj* (pattern) a quadri ● *n* disegno *m* a quadri

check² *n* verifica *f*; (*of tickets*) controllo *m*; (*in chess*) scacco *m*; (*Am: bill*) conto *m*; (*Am: cheque*) assegno *m*; (*Am: tick*) segnetto *m*; **keep a ~ on** controllare; **keep in ~** tenere sotto controllo ● *vt* verificare; controllare (tickets); (*restrain*) contenere; (*stop*) bloccare ● *vi* controllare; **~ on sth** controllare qcsa. □ **~ in** *vi* registrarsi all'arrivo (*in albergo*); (*Aeron*) fare il check-in ● *vt* registrare all'arrivo (*in albergo*). □ **~ out** *vi* (*of hotel*) saldare il conto ● *vt* ([!]: *investigate*) controllare. □ **~ up** *vi* accertarsi; **~ up on** prendere informazioni su

check: ~-in *n* (*in airport: place*) banco *m* accettazione, check-in *m inv*; **~mate** *int* scacco matto! **~-out** *n* (*in supermarket*) cassa *f*. **~-up** *n* (*Med*) visita *f* di controllo, check-up *m inv*

cheek /tʃi:k/ *n* guancia *f*; (*impudence*) sfacciataggine *f*. **~y** *adj* sfacciato

cheep /tʃi:p/ *vi* pigolare

cheer /tʃɪə(r)/ *n* evviva *m inv*; **three ~s** tre urrà; **~s!** salute!; (*goodbye*) arrivederci!; (*thanks*) grazie! ● *vt/i* acclamare. □ **~ up** *vt* tirare su [di morale] ● *vi* tirarsi su [di morale]; **~ up!** su con la vita!. **~ful** *adj* allegro. **~fulness** *n* allegria *f*. **~ing** *n* acclamazione *f*

cheerio /tʃɪərɪ'əʊ/ *int* [!] arrivederci

'cheerless *adj* triste, tetro

cheese /tʃi:z/ *n* formaggio *m*. **~cake** *n* dolce *m* al formaggio

chef /ʃef/ *n* cuoco, -a *mf*, chef *mf inv*

chemical /'kemɪkl/ *adj* chimico ● *n* prodotto *m* chimico

chemist /'kemɪst/ *n* (*pharmacist*) farmacista *mf*; (*scientist*) chimico, -a *mf*; **~'s [shop]** farmacia *f*. **~ry** *n* chimica *f*

cheque /tʃek/ *n* assegno *m*. **~-book** *n* libretto *m* degli assegni. **~ card** *n* carta *f* assegni

cherish /'tʃerɪʃ/ *vt* curare teneramente; (*love*) avere caro; nutrire (hope)

cherry /'tʃerɪ/ *n* ciliegia *f*; (*tree*) ciliegio *m*

chess /tʃes/ *n* scacchi *mpl*

chessboard *n* scacchiera *f*
chest /tʃest/ *n* petto *m*; (*box*) cassapanca *f*
chestnut /'tʃesnʌt/ *n* castagna *f*; (*tree*) castagno *m*
chest of 'drawers *n* cassettone *m*
chew /tʃu:/ *vt* masticare. **~inggum** *n* gomma *f* da masticare
chic /ʃi:k/ *adj* chic *inv*
chick /tʃɪk/ *n* pulcino *m*; (**!**: *girl*) ragazza *f*
chicken /'tʃɪkn/ *n* pollo *m* ● *adj attrib* (soup) di pollo ● **chicken out** *vi* **!** **he ~ed out** gli è venuta fifa. **~pox** *n* varicella *f*
chicory /'tʃɪkərɪ/ *n* cicoria *f*
chief /tʃi:f/ *adj* principale ● *n* capo *m*. **~ly** *adv* principalmente
chilblain /'tʃɪlbleɪn/ *n* gelone *m*
child /tʃaɪld/ *n* (*pl* **~ren**) bambino, -a *mf*; (*son/daughter*) figlio, -a *mf*
child: ~birth *n* parto *m*. **~hood** *n* infanzia *f*. **~ish** *adj* infantile. **~less** *adj* senza figli. **~like** *adj* ingenuo
Chile /'tʃɪlɪ/ *n* Cile *m*. **~an** *adj & n* cileno, -a *mf*
chill /tʃɪl/ *n* freddo *m*; (*illness*) infreddatura *f* ● *vt* raffreddare
chilli /'tʃɪlɪ/ *n* (*pl* **-es**) **~ [pepper]** peperoncino *m*
chilly /'tʃɪlɪ/ *adj* freddo
chime /tʃaɪm/ *vi* suonare
chimney /'tʃɪmnɪ/ *n* camino *m*. **~-pot** *n* comignolo *m*. **~-sweep** *n* spazzacamino *m*
chimpanzee /tʃɪmpæn'zi:/ *n* scimpanzé *m inv*
chin /tʃɪn/ *n* mento *m*
china /'tʃaɪnə/ *n* porcellana *f*
Chin|a *n* Cina *f*. **~ese** *adj & n* cinese *mf*; (*language*) cinese *m*; **the ~ese** *pl* i cinesi
chink[1] /tʃɪŋk/ *n* (*slit*) fessura *f*
chink[2] *n* (*noise*) tintinnio *m*
chip /tʃɪp/ *n* (*fragment*) scheggia *f*; (*in china, paintwork*) scheggiatura *f*; (*Comput*) chip *m inv*; (*in gambling*) fiche *f inv*; **~s** *pl* *Br* (*Culin*) patatine *fpl* fritte; *Am* (*Culin*) patatine *fpl* ● *vt* (*pt/pp* **chipped**) (*damage*) scheggiare. ▫ **~ in** *vi* **!** intromettersi; (*with money*) contribuire. **~ped** *adj* (*damaged*) scheggiato
chiropod|ist /kɪ'rɒpədɪst/ *n* podiatra *mf inv*. **~y** *n* podiatria *f*
chirp /tʃɜ:p/ *vi* cinguettare; (cricket:) fare cri cri. **~y** *adj* **!** pimpante
chisel /'tʃɪzl/ *n* scalpello *m*
chival|rous /'ʃɪvlrəs/ *adj* cavalleresco. **~ry** *n* cavalleria *f*
chives /tʃaɪvz/ *npl* erba *f* cipollina
chlorine /'klɔ:ri:n/ *n* cloro *m*
chock-a-block /tʃɒkə'blɒk/, **chock-full** /tʃɒk'fʊl/ *adj* pieno zeppo
chocolate /'tʃɒkələt/ *n* cioccolato *m*; (*drink*) cioccolata *f*; **a ~** un cioccolatino
choice /tʃɔɪs/ *n* scelta *f* ● *adj* scelto
choir /'kwaɪə(r)/ *n* coro *m*. **~boy** *n* corista *m*
choke /tʃəʊk/ *n* (*Auto*) aria *f* ● *vt/i* soffocare
cholera /'kɒlərə/ *n* colera *m*
cholesterol /kə'lestərɒl/ *n* colesterolo *m*
choose /tʃu:z/ *vt/i* (*pt* **chose**, *pp* **chosen**) scegliere; **as you ~** come vuoi
chop /tʃɒp/ *n* (*blow*) colpo *m* (*d'ascia*); (*Culin*) costata *f* ● *vt* (*pt/pp* **chopped**) tagliare. ▫ **~ down** *vt* abbattere (tree). ▫ **~ off** *vt* spaccare
chop|per /'tʃɒpə(r)/ *n* accetta *f*; **!** elicottero *m*. **~py** *adj* increspato
chord /kɔ:d/ *n* (*Mus*) corda *f*
chore /tʃɔ:(r)/ *n* corvé *f inv*; **[household] ~s** faccende *fpl* domestiche
chorus /'kɔ:rəs/ *n* coro *m*; (*of song*) ritornello *m*
chose, chosen /tʃəʊz/, /'tʃəʊzn/ ▷CHOOSE
Christ /kraɪst/ *n* Cristo *m*
christen /'krɪsn/ *vt* battezzare. **~ing** *n* battesimo *m*
Christian /'krɪstʃən/ *adj & n* cristiano, -a *mf*. **~ity** *n* cristianesimo *m*. **~ name** *n* nome *m* di battesimo
Christmas /'krɪsməs/ *n* Natale *m* ● *attrib* di Natale. **'~ card** *n* biglietto *m* d'auguri di Natale. **~ 'Day** *n* il giorno di Natale. **~ 'Eve** *n* la vigilia di Natale. **'~ present** *n* regalo *m* di Natale. **~ 'pudding** *dolce m natalizio a base di frutta candita e liquore*. **'~ tree** *n* albero *m* di Natale
chrome /krəʊm/ *n*, **chromium** /'krəʊmɪəm/ *n* cromo *m*

C

chromosome /'krəʊməsəʊm/ *n* cromosoma *m*
chronic /'krɒnɪk/ *adj* cronico
chronicle /'krɒnɪkl/ *n* cronaca *f*
chronological /krɒnə'lɒdʒɪkl/ *adj* cronologico. **~ly** *adv* (ordered) in ordine cronologico
chubby /'tʃʌbɪ/ *adj* (**-ier, -iest**) paffuto
chuck /tʃʌk/ *vt* [!] buttare. □ **~ out** *vt* [!] buttare via (object); buttare fuori (person)
chuckle /'tʃʌkl/ *vi* ridacchiare
chug /tʃʌg/ *vi* (*pt/pp* **chugged**) **the train ~ged out of the station** il treno è uscito dalla stazione sbuffando
chum /tʃʌm/ *n* amico, -a *mf*. **~my** *adj* [!] **be ~my with** essere amico di
chunk /tʃʌŋk/ *n* grosso pezzo *m*
church /tʃɜ:tʃ/ *n* chiesa *f*. **~yard** *n* cimitero *m*
churn /tʃɜ:n/ *vt* **churn out** sfornare
chute /ʃu:t/ *n* scivolo *m*; (*for rubbish*) canale *m* di scarico
cider /'saɪdə(r)/ *n* sidro *m*
cigar /sɪ'gɑ:(r)/ *n* sigaro *m*
cigarette /sɪgə'ret/ *n* sigaretta *f*
cine-camera /'sɪnɪ-/ *n* cinepresa *f*
cinema /'sɪnɪmə/ *n* cinema *m inv*
cinnamon /'sɪnəmən/ *n* cannella *f*
circle /'sɜ:kl/ *n* cerchio *m*; (*Theat*) galleria *f*; **in a ~** in cerchio ● *vt* girare intorno a; cerchiare (mistake) ● *vi* descrivere dei cerchi
circuit /'sɜ:kɪt/ *n* circuito *m*; (*lap*) giro *m*; **~ board** *n* circuito *m* stampato. **~ous** *adj* **~ous route** percorso *m* lungo e indiretto
circular /'sɜ:kjʊlə(r)/ *adj* circolare ● *n* circolare *f*
circulat|e /'sɜ:kjʊleɪt/ *vt* far circolare ● *vi* circolare. **~ion** *n* circolazione *f*; (*of newspaper*) tiratura *f*
circumcis|e /'sɜ:kəmsaɪz/ *vt* circoncidere. **~ion** *n* circoncisione *f*
circumference /ʃə'kʌmfərəns/ *n* conconferenza *f*
circumstance /'sɜ:kəmstəns/ *n* circostanza *f*; **~s** *pl* (*financial*) condizioni *fpl* finanziarie
circus /'sɜ:kəs/ *n* circo *m*
cistern /'sɪstən/ *n* (*tank*) cisterna *f*; (*of WC*) serbatoio *m*
cite /saɪt/ *vt* citare
citizen /'sɪtɪzn/ *n* cittadino, -a *mf*; (*of town*) abitante *mf*. **~ship** *n* cittadinanza *f*
citrus /'sɪtrəs/ *n* **~ [fruit]** agrume *m*
city /'sɪtɪ/ *n* città *f inv*; **the C~** la City (*di Londra*)

> **City** La *City* è quella parte del centro di Londra dove un tempo si trovava l'antica città. Oggi è il centro finanziario della capitale britannica dove numerose banche e istituti finanziari hanno la propria sede centrale; molto spesso *the City* indica infatti le istituzioni finanziarie oltre che la zona della città.

civic /'sɪvɪk/ *adj* civico
civil /'ʃɪvl/ *adj* civile
civilian /sɪ'vɪljən/ *adj* civile; **in ~ clothes** in borghese ● *n* civile *mf*
civiliz|ation /sɪvɪlaɪ'zeɪʃn/ *n* civiltà *f inv*. **~e** *vt* civilizzare
civil: ~ 'servant *n* impiegato, -a *mf* statale. **C~ 'Service** *n* pubblica amministrazione *f*
clad /klæd/ *adj* vestito (**in** di)
claim /kleɪm/ *n* richiesta *f*; (*right*) diritto *m*; (*assertion*) dichiarazione *f*; **lay ~ to sth** rivendicare qcsa ● *vt* richiedere; reclamare (lost property); rivendicare (ownership); **~ that** sostenere che. **~ant** *n* richiedente *mf*
clairvoyant /kleə'vɔɪənt/ *n* chiaroveggente *mf*
clam /klæm/ *n* (*Culin*) vongola *f* ● **clam up** *vi* (*pt/pp* **clammed**) zittirsi
clamber /'klæmbə(r)/ *vi* arrampicarsi
clammy /'klæmɪ/ *adj* (**-ier, -iest**) appiccicaticcio
clamour /'klæmə(r)/ *n* (*protest*) rimostranza *f* ● *vi* **~ for** chiedere a gran voce
clamp /klæmp/ *n* morsa *f* ● *vt* ammorsare; (*Auto*) mettere i ceppi bloccaruote a. □ **~ down** *vi* [!] essere duro; **~ down on** reprimere
clan /klæn/ *n* clan *m inv*
clang /klæŋ/ *n* suono *m* metallico. **~er** *n* [!] gaffe *f inv*
clap /klæp/ *n* **give sb a ~** applaudire qcno; **~ of thunder** tuono *m* ● *vt/i* (*pt/pp* **clapped**) applaudire; **~ one's**

hands applaudire. **~ping** *n* applausi *mpl*

clari|fication /klærɪfɪ'keɪʃn/ *n* chiarimento *m*. **~fy** *vt/i* (*pt/pp* **-ied**) chiarire

clarinet /klærɪ'net/ *n* clarinetto *m*

clarity /'klærətɪ/ *n* chiarezza *f*

clash /klæʃ/ *n* scontro *m*; (*noise*) fragore *m* ● *vi* scontrarsi; (colours:) stonare; (events:) coincidere

clasp /klɑːsp/ *n* chiusura *f* ● *vt* agganciare; (*hold*) stringere

class /klɑːs/ *n* classe *f*; (*lesson*) corso *m* ● *vt* classificare

classic /'klæsɪk/ *adj* classico ● *n* classico *m*; **~s** *pl* (*Univ*) lettere *fpl* classiche. **~al** *adj* classico

classi|fication /klæsɪfɪ'keɪʃn/ *n* classificazione *f*. **~fy** *vt* (*pt/pp* **-ied**) classificare

classroom *n* aula *f*

classy /'klɑːsɪ/ *adj* (**-ier, -iest**) [!] d'alta classe

clatter /'klætə(r)/ *n* fracasso *m* ● *vi* far fracasso

clause /klɔːz/ *n* clausola *f*; (*Gram*) proposizione *f*

claustrophob|ia /klɔːstrə'fəʊbɪə/ *n* claustrofobia *f*

claw /klɔː/ *n* artiglio *m*; (*of crab, lobster &* (*Techn*)) tenaglia *f* ● *vt* (cat:) graffiare

clay /kleɪ/ *n* argilla *f*

clean /kliːn/ *adj* pulito, lindo ● *adv* completamente ● *vt* pulire (shoes, windows); **~ one's teeth** lavarsi i denti; **have a coat ~ed** portare un cappotto in lavanderia. **clean up** *vt* pulire ● *vi* far pulizia

cleaner /'kliːnə(r)/ *n* uomo *m*/donna *f* delle pulizie; (*substance*) detersivo *m*; [**dry**] **~'s** lavanderia *f*, tintoria *f*

cleanliness /'klenlɪnɪs/ *n* pulizia *f*

cleanse /klenz/ *vt* pulire. **~r** *n* detergente *m*

cleansing cream /'klenz-/ *n* latte *m* detergente

clear /klɪə(r)/ *adj* chiaro; (conscience) pulito; (road) libero; (profit, advantage, majority) netto; (sky) sereno; (water) limpido; (glass) trasparente; **make sth ~** mettere qcsa in chiaro; **have I made myself ~?** mi sono fatto capire?; **five ~ days** cinque giorni buoni ● *adv* **stand ~ of** allontanarsi da; **keep ~ of** tenersi alla larga da ● *vt* sgombrare (room, street); sparecchiare (table); (*acquit*) scagionare; (*authorize*) autorizzare; scavalcare senza toccare (fence, wall); guadagnare (sum of money); passare (Customs); **~ one's throat** schiarirsi la gola ● *vi* (face, sky:) rasserenarsi; (fog:) dissiparsi. □ **~ away** *vt* metter via. □ **~ off** *vi* [!] filar via. □ **~ out** *vt* sgombrare ● *vi* [!] filar via. □ **~ up** *vt* (*tidy*) mettere a posto; chiarire (mystery) ● *vi* (weather:) schiarirsi

clearance /'klɪərəns/ *n* (*space*) spazio *m* libero; (*authorization*) autorizzazione *f*; (*Customs*) sdoganamento *m*. **~ sale** *n* liquidazione *f*

clear|ing /'klɪərɪŋ/ *n* radura *f*. **~ly** *adv* chiaramente. **~way** *n* (*Auto*) strada *f* con divieto di sosta

cleavage /'kliːvɪdʒ/ *n* (*woman's*) décolleté *m inv*

clench /klentʃ/ *vt* serrare

clergy /'klɜːdʒɪ/ *npl* clero *m*. **~man** *n* ecclesiastico *m*

cleric /'klerɪk/ *n* ecclesiastico *m*. **~al** *adj* impiegatizio; (*Relig*) clericale

clerk /klɑːk/, *Am* /klɜːk/ *n* impiegato, -a *mf*; (*Am: shop assistant*) commesso, -a *mf*

clever /'klevə(r)/ *adj* intelligente; (*skilful*) abile

cliché /'kliːʃeɪ/ *n* cliché *m inv*

click /klɪk/ *vi* scattare; (*Comput*) cliccare ● *n* (*Comput*) click *m*. **click on** *vt* (*Comput*) cliccare su

client /'klaɪənt/ *n* cliente *mf*

cliff /klɪf/ *n* scogliera *f*

climat|e /'klaɪmət/ *n* clima *f*. **~ic** *adj* climatico

climax /'klaɪmæks/ *n* punto *m* culminante

climb /klaɪm/ *n* salita *f* ● *vt* scalare (mountain); arrampicarsi su (ladder, tree) ● *vi* arrampicarsi; (*rise*) salire; (road:) salire. □ **~ down** *vi* scendere; (*from ladder, tree*) scendere; *fig* tornare sui propri passi

climber /'klaɪmə(r)/ *n* alpinista *mf*; (*plant*) rampicante *m*

clinch /klɪntʃ/ *vt* [!] concludere (deal) ● *n* (*in boxing*) clinch *m inv*

cling /klɪŋ/ *vi* (*pt/pp* **clung**) aggrap-

C

parsi; (*stick*) aderire. **~ film** *n* pellicola *f* trasparente

clinic /'klɪnɪk/ *n* ambulatorio *m*. **~al** *adj* clinico

clink /klɪŋk/ *n* tintinnio *m*; ([!]: *prison*) galera *f* ● *vi* tintinnare

clip¹ /klɪp/ *n* fermaglio *m*; (*jewellery*) spilla *f* ● *vt* (*pt/pp* **clipped**) attaccare

clip² *n* (*extract*) taglio *m* ● *vt* obliterare (ticket). **~board** *n* fermabloc *m inv*. **~pers** *npl* (*for hair*) rasoio *m*; (*for hedge*) tosasiepi *m inv*; (*for nails*) tronchesina *f*. **~ping** *n* (*from newspaper*) ritaglio *m*

cloak /kləʊk/ *n* mantello *m*. **~room** *n* guardaroba *m inv*; (*toilet*) bagno *m*

clock /klɒk/ *n* orologio *m*; ([!]: *speedometer*) tachimetro *m* □ **~ in** *vi* attaccare. □ **~ out** *vi* staccare

clock: ~wise *adj & adv* in senso orario. **~work** *n* meccanismo *m*

clog /klɒg/ *n* zoccolo *m* ● *vt* (*pt/pp* **clogged**) **~ [up]** intasare (drain); inceppare (mechanism) ● *vi* (drain:) intasarsi

cloister /'klɔɪstə(r)/ *n* chiostro *m*

clone /kləʊn/ *n* clone *m*

close¹ /kləʊs/ *adj* vicino; (friend) intimo; (weather) afoso; **have a ~ shave** [!] scamparla bella; **be ~ to sb** essere unito a qcno ● *adv* vicino; **~ by** vicino; **~ on five o'clock** quasi le cinque

close² /kləʊz/ *n* fine *f* ● *vt* chiudere ● *vi* chiudersi; (shop:) chiudere. □ **~ down** *vt* chiudere ● *vi* (TV station:) interrompere la trasmissione; (factory:) chiudere

closely /'kləʊslɪ/ *adv* da vicino; (watch, listen) attentamente

closet /'klɒzɪt/ *n Am* armadio *m*

close-up /'kləʊs-/ *n* primo piano *m*

closure /'kləʊʒə(r)/ *n* chiusura *f*

clot /klɒt/ *n* grumo *m*; ([!]: *idiot*) tonto, -a *mf* ● *vi* (*pt/pp* **clotted**) (blood:) coagularsi

cloth /klɒθ/ *n* (*fabric*) tessuto *m*; (*duster etc*) straccio *m*

clothe /kləʊð/ *vt* vestire

clothes /kləʊðz/ *npl* vestiti *mpl*, abiti *mpl*. **~-brush** *n* spazzola *f* per abiti. **~-line** *n* corda *f* stendibiancheria

clothing /'kləʊðɪŋ/ *n* abbigliamento *m*

cloud /klaʊd/ *n* nuvola *f* ● **cloud over** *vi* rannuvolarsi. **~burst** *n* acquazzone *m*

cloudy /'klaʊdɪ/ *adj* (**-ier, -iest**) nuvoloso; (liquid) torbido

clout /klaʊt/ *n* [!] colpo *m*; (*influence*) impatto *m* (**with** su) ● *vt* [!] colpire

clove /kləʊv/ *n* chiodo *m* di garofano; **~ of garlic** spicchio *m* d'aglio

clover /'kləʊvə(r)/ *n* trifoglio *m*

clown /klaʊn/ *n* pagliaccio *m* ● *vi* **~ [about]** fare il pagliaccio

club /klʌb/ *n* club *m inv*; (*weapon*) clava *f*; (*Sport*) mazza *f*; **~s** *pl* (*Cards*) fiori *mpl* ● *v* (*pt/pp* **clubbed**) ● *vt* bastonare. □ **~ together** *vi* unirsi

cluck /klʌk/ *vi* chiocciare

clue /klu:/ *n* indizio *m*; (*in crossword*) definizione *f*; **I haven't a ~** [!] non ne ho idea

clump /klʌmp/ *n* gruppo *m*

clumsiness /'klʌmzɪnɪs/ *n* goffaggine *f*

clumsy /'klʌmzɪ/ *adj* (**-ier, -iest**) maldestro; (tool) scomodo; (remark) senza tatto

clung /klʌŋ/ ▷CLING

cluster /'klʌstə(r)/ *n* gruppo *m* ● *vi* raggrupparsi (**round** intorno a)

clutch /klʌtʃ/ *n* stretta *f*; (*Auto*) frizione *f*; **be in sb's ~es** essere in balia di qcno ● *vt* stringere; (*grab*) afferrare ● *vi* **~ at** afferrare

clutter /'klʌtə(r)/ *n* caos *m* ● *vt* **~ [up]** ingombrare

coach /kəʊtʃ/ *n* pullman *m inv*; (*Rail*) vagone *m*; (*horse-drawn*) carrozza *f*; (*Sport*) allenatore, -trice *mf* ● *vt* fare esercitare; (*Sport*) allenare

coal /kəʊl/ *n* carbone *m*

coalition /kəʊə'lɪʃn/ *n* coalizione *f*

coarse /kɔ:s/ *adj* grossolano; (joke) spinto

coast /kəʊst/ *n* costa *f* ● *vi* (*freewheel*) scendere a ruota libera **~al** *adj* costiero. **~er** *n* (*mat*) sottobicchiere *m inv*

coast: ~guard *n* guardia *f* costiera. **~line** *n* litorale *m*

coat /kəʊt/ *n* cappotto *m*; (*of animal*) manto *m*; (*of paint*) mano *f*; **~ of arms** stemma *f* ● *vt* coprire; (*with paint*) ricoprire. **~-hanger** *n* gruccia *f*. **~-hook** *n* gancio *m* [appendiabiti]

coating /'kəʊtɪŋ/ *n* rivestimento *m*; (*of paint*) stato *m*

coax /kəʊks/ *vt* convincere con le moine

cobweb /'kɒb-/ *n* ragnatela *f*

cocaine /kə'keɪn/ *n* cocaina *f*

cock /kɒk/ *n* gallo *m*; (*any male bird*) maschio *m* ● *vt* sollevare il grilletto di (gun); ~ **its ears** (animal:) drizzare le orecchie

cockerel /'kɒkərəl/ *n* galletto *m*

cock-'eyed *adj* [!] storto; (*absurd*) assurdo

cockney /'kɒknɪ/ *n* (*dialect*) dialetto *m* londinese; (*person*) abitante *mf* dell'est di Londra

cock: ~**pit** *n* (*Aeron*) cabina *f*. ~**roach** /-rəʊtʃ/ *n* scarafaggio *m*. ~**tail** *n* cocktail *m inv*. ~**-up** *n* [✱] **make a ~-up** fare un casino (**of** con)

cocky /'kɒkɪ/ *adj* (**-ier, -iest**) [!] presuntuoso

cocoa /'kəʊkəʊ/ *n* cacao *m*

coconut /'kəʊkənʌt/ *n* noce *f* di cocco

cocoon /kə'ku:n/ *n* bozzolo *m*

cod /kɒd/ *n inv* merluzzo *m*

COD *abbr* (cash on delivery) pagamento *m* alla consegna

code /kəʊd/ *n* codice *m*. ~**d** *adj* codificato

coedu'cational /kəʊ-/ *adj* misto

coerc|e /kəʊ'3:s/ *vt* costringere. ~**ion** *n* coercizione *f*

coffee /'kɒfɪ/ *n* caffè *m inv*

coffeepot *n* caffettiera *f*

coffin /'kɒfɪn/ *n* bara *f*

cog /kɒg/ *n* (*Techn*) dente *m* (*di ruota*)

coherent /kəʊ'hɪərənt/ *adj* coerente; (*when speaking*) logico

coil /kɔɪl/ *n* rotolo *m*; (*Electr*) bobina *f*; ~**s** *pl* spire *fpl* ● *vt* ~ **[up]** avvolgere

coin /kɔɪn/ *n* moneta *f* ● *vt* coniare (word)

coincide /kəʊɪn'saɪd/ *vi* coincidere

coinciden|ce /kəʊ'ɪnsɪdəns/ *n* coincidenza *f*. ~**tal** *adj* casuale. ~**tally** *adv* casualmente

coke /kəʊk/ *n* [carbone *m*] coke *m*

Coke® *n* Coca[-cola]® *f*

cold /kəʊld/ *adj* freddo; **I'm** ~ ho freddo ● *n* freddo *m*; (*Med*) raffreddore *m*

cold-'blooded *adj* spietato

coleslaw /'kəʊlslɔ:/ *n insalata f di cavolo crudo, cipolle e carote in maionese*

collaborat|e /kə'læbəreɪt/ *vi* collaborare; ~**e on sth** collaborare in qcsa. ~**ion** *n* collaborazione *f*; (*with enemy*) collaborazionismo *m*. ~**or** *n* collaboratore, -trice *mf*; (*with enemy*) collaborazionista *mf*

collaps|e /kə'læps/ *n* crollo *m* ● *vi* (person:) svenire; (roof, building:) crollare. ~**ible** *adj* pieghevole

collar /'kɒlə(r)/ *n* colletto *m*; (*for animal*) collare *m*. ~**-bone** *n* clavicola *f*

colleague /'kɒli:g/ *n* collega *mf*

collect /kə'lekt/ *vt* andare a prendere (person); ritirare (parcel, tickets); riscuotere (taxes); raccogliere (rubbish); (*as hobby*) collezionare ● *vi* riunirsi ● *adv* **call** ~ *Am* telefonare a carico del destinatario. ~**ed** *adj* controllato

collection /kə'lekʃn/ *n* collezione *f*; (*in church*) questua *f*; (*of rubbish*) raccolta *f*; (*of post*) levata *f*

collector /kə'lektə(r)/ *n* (*of stamps etc*) collezionista *mf*

college /'kɒlɪdʒ/ *n* istituto *m* parauniversitario; **C~ of...** Scuola *f* di...

collide /kə'laɪd/ *vi* scontrarsi

collision /kə'lɪʒn/ *n* scontro *m*

colloquial /kə'ləʊkwɪəl/ *adj* colloquiale. ~**ism** *n* espressione *f* colloquiale

colon /'kəʊlən/ *n* due punti *mpl*; (*Anat*) colon *m inv*

colonel /'k3:nl/ *n* colonnello *m*

colonial /kə'ləʊnɪəl/ *adj* coloniale

colon|ize /'kɒlənaɪz/ *vt* colonizzare. ~**y** *n* colonia *f*

colossal /kə'lɒsl/ *adj* colossale

colour /'kʌlə(r)/ *n* colore *m*; (*complexion*) colorito *m*; ~**s** *pl* (*flag*) bandiera *fsg*; **off** ~ [!] giù di tono ● *vt* colorare; ~ **[in]** colorare ● *vi* (*blush*) arrossire

colour: ~**-blind** *adj* daltonico. ~**ed** *adj* colorato; (person) di colore ● *n* (*person*) persona *f* di colore. ~**ful** *adj* pieno di colore. ~**less** *adj* incolore

column /'kɒləm/ *n* colonna *f*. ~**ist** *n giornalista mf che cura una rubrica*

coma /'kəʊmə/ *n* coma *m inv*

comb /kəʊm/ *n* pettine *m*; (*for wearing*) pettinino *m* ● *vt* pettinare; (*fig: search*) setacciare; ~ **one's hair** pettinarsi i capelli

combat /ˈkɒmbæt/ *n* combattimento *m* ● *vt* (*pt/pp* **combated**) combattere

C

combination /kɒmbɪˈneɪʃn/ *n* combinazione *f*

combine¹ /kəmˈbaɪn/ *vt* unire; ~ **a job with being a mother** conciliare il lavoro con il ruolo di madre ● *vi* (chemical elements:) combinarsi

combine² /ˈkɒmbaɪn/ *n* (*Comm*) associazione *f*. ~ **harvester** *n* mietitrebbia *f*

combustion /kəmˈbʌstʃn/ *n* combustione *f*

come /kʌm/ *vi* (*pt* **came**, *pp* **come**) venire; **where do you** ~ **from?** da dove vieni?; ~ **to** (*reach*) arrivare a; **that** ~**s to £10** fanno 10 sterline; ~ **into money** ricevere dei soldi; ~ **true/open** verificarsi/aprirsi; ~ **first** arrivare primo; *fig* venire prima di tutto; ~ **in two sizes** esistere in due misure; **the years to** ~ gli anni a venire; **how** ~**?** [!] come mai? **come about** *vi* succedere. □ ~ **across** *vi* ~ **across as being** [!] dare l'impressione di essere ● *vt* (*find*) imbattersi in. □ ~ **along** *vi* venire; (job, opportunity:) presentarsi; (*progress*) andare bene. □ ~ **apart** *vi* smontarsi; (*break*) rompersi. □ ~ **away** *vi* venir via; (button, fastener:) staccarsi. □ ~ **back** *vi* ritornare. □ ~ **by** *vi* passare ● *vt* (*obtain*) avere. □ ~ **down** *vi* scendere; ~ **down to** (*reach*) arrivare a. **come in** *vi* entrare; (*in race*) arrivare; (tide:) salire. □ ~ **in for** *vt* ~ **in for criticism** essere criticato. □ ~ **off** *vi* staccarsi; (*take place*) esserci; (*succeed*) riuscire. □ ~ **on** *vi* (*make progress*) migliorare; ~ **on!** (*hurry*) dai!; (*indicating disbelief*) ma va là!. □ ~ **out** *vi* venir fuori; (book, sun:) uscire; (stain:) andar via. □ ~ **over** *vi* venire. □ ~ **round** *vi* venire; (*after fainting*) riaversi; (*change one's mind*) farsi convincere. □ ~ **to** *vi* (*after fainting*) riaversi. □ ~ **up** *vi* salire; (sun:) sorgere; (plant:) crescere; **something came up** (*I was prevented*) ho avuto un imprevisto. □ ~ **up with** *vt* tirar fuori

ˈ**come-back** *n* ritorno *m*

comedian /kəˈmiːdɪən/ *n* comico *m*

comedy /ˈkɒmədɪ/ *n* commedia *f*

comet /ˈkɒmɪt/ *n* cometa *f*

comfort /ˈkʌmfət/ *n* benessere *m*; (*consolation*) conforto *m* ● *vt* confortare

comfortabl|e /ˈkʌmfətəbl/ *adj* comodo; **be** ~**e** (person:) stare comodo; (*fig: in situation*) essere a proprio agio; (*financially*) star bene. ~**y** *adv* comodamente

ˈ**comfort station** *n Am* bagno *m* pubblico

comic /ˈkɒmɪk/ *adj* comico ● *n* comico, -a *mf*; (*periodical*) fumetto *m*. ~**al** *adj* comico. ~ **strip** *n* striscia *f* di fumetti

coming /ˈkʌmɪŋ/ *n* venuta *f*; ~**s and goings** viavai *m*

comma /ˈkɒmə/ *n* virgola *f*

command /kəˈmɑːnd/ *n* comando *m*; (*order*) ordine *m*; (*mastery*) padronanza *f* ● *vt* ordinare; comandare (army)

commandeer /kɒmənˈdɪə(r)/ *vt* requisire

command|er /kəˈmɑːndə(r)/ *n* comandante *m*. ~**ing** *adj* (view) imponente; (lead) dominante. ~**ing officer** *n* comandante *m*. ~**ment** *n* comandamento *m*

commemorat|e /kəˈmeməreɪt/ *vt* commemorare. ~**ion** *n* commemorazione *f*. ~**ive** *adj* commemorativo

commence /kəˈmens/ *vt/i* cominciare. ~**ment** *n* inizio *m*

commend /kəˈmend/ *vt* complimentarsi con (**on** per); (*recommend*) raccomandare (**to** a). ~**able** *adj* lodevole

comment /ˈkɒment/ *n* commento *m* ● *vi* fare commenti (**on** su)

commentary /ˈkɒməntrɪ/ *n* commento *m*; [**running**] ~ (*on radio*, (*TV*)) cronaca *f* diretta

commentat|e /ˈkɒmənteɪt/ *vt* ~**e on** (*TV, Radio*) fare la cronaca di. ~**or** *n* cronista *mf*

commerce /ˈkɒmɜːs/ *n* commercio *m*

commercial /kəˈmɜːʃl/ *adj* commerciale ● *n* (*TV*) pubblicità *f inv*. ~**ize** *vt* commercializzare

commiserate /kəˈmɪzəreɪt/ *vi* esprimere il proprio rincrescimento (**with** a)

commission /kəˈmɪʃn/ *n* commissione *f*; **receive one's** ~ (*Mil*) essere promosso ufficiale; **out of** ~ fuori uso ● *vt* commissionare

commissionaire /kəmɪʃə'neə(r)/ *n* portiere *m*

commit /kə'mɪt/ *vt* (*pt/pp* **committed**) commettere; (*to prison, hospital*) affidare (**to** a); impegnare (funds); ~ **oneself** impegnarsi. **~ment** *n* impegno *m*; (*involvement*) compromissione *f*. **~ted** *adj* impegnato

committee /kə'mɪtɪ/ *n* comitato *m*

commodity /kə'mɒdətɪ/ *n* prodotto *m*

common /'kɒmən/ *adj* comune; (*vulgar*) volgare ● *n* prato *m* pubblico; **have in ~** avere in comune; **House of C~s** Camera *f* dei Comuni. **~er** *n persona f non nobile*

common: ~'law *n* diritto *m* consuetudinario. **~ly** *adv* comunemente. **C~ 'Market** *n* Mercato *m* Comune. **~place** *adj* banale. **~-room** *n* sala *f* dei professori/degli studenti. **~ 'sense** *n* buon senso *m*

> **Commonwealth** Il *Commonwealth*, fondato nel 1931, è l'insieme delle ex colonie e possedimenti dell'ex impero britannico. I paesi membri, oggi stati indipendenti, sono legati da legami economici e culturali. I vari capi di stato si incontrano con scadenza biennale, e progetti educativi internazionali vengono promossi regolarmente. Ogni quattro anni, inoltre, si tengono i *Commonwealth Games*, manifestazioni sportive cui partecipano atleti dei vari paesi.

commotion /kə'məʊʃn/ *n* confusione *f*

communicate /kə'mju:nɪkeɪt/ *vt/i* comunicare

communication /kəmju:nɪ'keɪʃn/ *n* comunicazione *f*; (*of disease*) trasmissione *f*; **be in ~ with sb** essere in contatto con qcno; **~s** *pl* (*technology*) telecomunicazioni *fpl*. **~ cord** *n* fermata *f* d'emergenza

communicative /kə'mju:nɪkətɪv/ *adj* comunicativo

Communion /kə'mju:nɪən/ *n* [**Holy**] **~** comunione *f*

Communis|m /'kɒmjʊnɪzm/ *n* comunismo *m*. **~t** *adj & n* comunista *mf*

community /kə'mju:nətɪ/ *n* comunità *f*. **~ centre** *n* centro *m* sociale

commute /kə'mju:t/ *vi* fare il pendolare ● *vt* (*Jur*) commutare. **~r** *n* pendolare *mf*

compact¹ /kəm'pækt/ *adj* compatto

compact² /'kɒmpækt/ *n* portacipria *m inv*. **~ disc** *n* compact disc *m inv*

companion /kəm'pænjən/ *n* compagno, -a *mf*. **~ship** *n* compagnia *f*

company /'kʌmpənɪ/ *n* compagnia *f*; (*guests*) ospiti *mpl*. **~ car** *n* macchina *f* della ditta

comparable /'kɒmpərəbl/ *adj* paragonabile

comparative /kəm'pærətɪv/ *adj* comparativo; (*relative*) relativo ● *n* (*Gram*) comparativo *m*. **~ly** *adv* relativamente

compare /kəm'peə(r)/ *vt* paragonare (**with/to** a) ● *vi* essere paragonato

comparison /kəm'pærɪsn/ *n* paragone *m*

compartment /kəm'pɑ:tmənt/ *n* compartimento *m*; (*Rail*) scompartimento *m*

compass /'kʌmpəs/ *n* bussola *f*. **~es** *npl*, **pair of ~es** compasso *msg*

compassion /kəm'pæʃn/ *n* compassione *f*. **~ate** *adj* compassionevole

compatible /kəm'pætəbl/ *adj* compatibile

compel /kəm'pel/ *vt* (*pt/pp* **compelled**) costringere. **~ling** *adj* (reason) inconfutabile

compensat|e /'kɒmpənseɪt/ *vt* risarcire ● *vi* **~e for** *fig* compensare di. **~ion** *n* risarcimento *m*; (*fig: comfort*) consolazione *f*

compère /'kɒmpeə(r)/ *n* presentatore, -trice *mf*

compete /kəm'pi:t/ *vi* competere; (*take part*) gareggiare

competen|ce /'kɒmpɪtəns/ *n* competenza *f*. **~t** *adj* competente

competition /kɒmpə'tɪʃn/ *n* concorrenza *f*; (*contest*) gara *f*

competitive /kəm'petɪtɪv/ *adj* competitivo; **~ prices** prezzi *mpl* concorrenziali

competitor /kəm'petɪtə(r)/ *n* concorrente *mf*

complacen|cy /kəm'pleɪsənsɪ/ *n* compiacimento *m*. **~t** *adj* compiaciuto

C

complain /kəm'pleɪn/ *vi* lamentarsi (**about** di); (*formally*) reclamare; ~ **of** (*Med*) accusare. ~**t** *n* lamentela *f*; (*formal*) reclamo *m*; (*Med*) disturbo *m*

complement¹ /'kɒmplɪmənt/ *n* complemento *m*

complement² /'kɒmplɪment/ *vt* complementare; ~ **each other** complementarsi a vicenda. ~**ary** *adj* complementare

complete /kəm'pli:t/ *adj* completo; (*utter*) finito ● *vt* completare; compilare (form). ~**ly** *adv* completamente

completion /kəm'pli:ʃn/ *n* fine *f*

complex /'kɒmpleks/ *adj* complesso ● *n* complesso *m*

complexion /kəm'plekʃn/ *n* carnagione *f*

complexity /kəm'pleksətɪ/ *n* complessità *f inv*

complicat|e /'kɒmplɪkeɪt/ *vt* complicare. ~**ed** *adj* complicato. ~**ion** *n* complicazione *f*

compliment /'kɒmplɪmənt/ *n* complimento *m*; ~**s** *pl* omaggi *mpl* ● *vt* complimentare. ~**ary** *adj* complimentoso; (*given free*) in omaggio

comply /kəm'plaɪ/ *vi* (*pt/pp* **-ied**) ~ **with** conformarsi a

component /kəm'pəʊnənt/ *adj* & *n* ~ [**part**] componente *m*

compose /kəm'pəʊz/ *vt* comporre; ~ **oneself** ricomporsi; **be** ~**d of** essere composto da. ~**d** *adj* (*calm*) composto. ~**r** *n* compositore, -trice *mf*

composition /kɒmpə'zɪʃn/ *n* composizione *f*; (*essay*) tema *m*

compost /'kɒmpɒst/ *n* composta *f*

composure /kəm'pəʊʒə(r)/ *n* calma *f*

compound /'kɒmpaʊnd/ *adj* composto. ~ **fracture** *n* frattura *f* esposta. ~ '**interest** *n* interesse *m* composto ● *n* (*Chem*) composto *m*; (*Gram*) parola *f* composta; (*enclosure*) recinto *m*

comprehen|d /kɒmprɪ'hend/ *vt* comprendere. ~**sible** *adj* comprensibile. ~**sion** *n* comprensione *f*

comprehensive /kɒmprɪ'hensɪv/ *adj* & *n* comprensivo; ~ [**school**] *scuola f media in cui gli allievi hanno capacità d'apprendimento diverse*. ~ **insurance** *n* (*Auto*) polizza *f* casco

compress¹ /'kɒmpres/ *n* compressa *f*

compress² /kəm'pres/ *vt* comprimere; ~**ed air** aria *f* compressa

comprise /kəm'praɪz/ *vt* comprendere; (*form*) costituire

compromise /'kɒmprəmaɪz/ *n* compromesso *m* ● *vt* compromettere ● *vi* fare un compromesso

compuls|ion /kəm'pʌlʃn/ *n* desiderio *m* irresistibile. ~**ive** *adj* (*Psych*) patologico. ~**ive eating** voglia *f* ossessiva di mangiare. ~**ory** *adj* obbligatorio

compute /kəm'pju:t/ *vt* calcolare

comput|er /kəm'pju:tə(r)/ *n* computer *m inv*. ~**erize** *vt* computerizzare. ~**ing** *n* informatica *f*

comrade /'kɒmreɪd/ *n* camerata *m*; (*Pol*) compagno, -a *mf*. ~**ship** *n* cameratismo *m*

con¹ /kɒn/ ▷**PRO**

con² *n* [!] fregatura *f* ● *vt* (*pt/pp* **conned**) [!] fregare

concave /'kɒnkeɪv/ *adj* concavo

conceal /kən'si:l/ *vt* nascondere

concede /kən'si:d/ *vt* (*admit*) ammettere; (*give up*) rinunciare a; lasciar fare (goal)

conceit /kən'si:t/ *n* presunzione *f*. ~**ed** *adj* presuntuoso

conceivable /kən'si:vəbl/ *adj* concepibile

conceive /kən'si:v/ *vt* (*Biol*) concepire ● *vi* aver figli. □ ~ **of** *vt fig* concepire

concentrat|e /'kɒnsəntreɪt/ *vt* concentrare ● *vi* concentrarsi. ~**ion** *n* concentrazione *f*. ~**ion camp** *n* campo *m* di concentramento

concept /'kɒnsept/ *n* concetto *m*. ~**ion** *n* concezione *f*; (*idea*) idea *f*

concern /kən'sɜ:n/ *n* preoccupazione *f*; (*Comm*) attività *f inv* ● *vt* (*be about, affect*) riguardare; (*worry*) preoccupare; **be** ~**ed about** essere preoccupato per; ~ **oneself with** preoccuparsi di; **as far as I am** ~**ed** per quanto mi riguarda. ~**ing** *prep* riguardo a

concert /'kɒnsət/ *n* concerto *m*. ~**ed** *adj* collettivo

concertina /kɒnsə'ti:nə/ *n* piccola fisarmonica *f*

concerto /kən'tʃeətəʊ/ *n* concerto *m*

concession /kən'seʃn/ *n* concessione *f*; (*reduction*) sconto *m*. ~**ary** *adj* (*reduced*) scontato

concise /kən'saɪs/ *adj* conciso
conclu|de /kən'klu:d/ *vt* concludere ● *vi* concludersi. **~ding** *adj* finale
conclusion /kən'klu:ʒn/ *n* conclusione *f*; **in ~** per concludere
conclusive /kən'klu:sɪv/ *adj* definitivo. **~ly** *adv* in modo definitivo
concoct /kən'kɒkt/ *vt* confezionare; *fig* inventare. **~ion** *n* mistura *f*; (*drink*) intruglio *m*
concrete /'kɒŋkri:t/ *adj* concreto ● *n* calcestruzzo *m*
concussion /kən'kʌʃn/ *n* commozione *f* cerebrale
condemn /kən'dem/ *vt* condannare; dichiarare inagibile (building). **~ation** *n* condanna *f*
condensation /kɒnden'seɪʃn/ *n* condensazione *f*
condense /kən'dens/ *vt* condensare; (*Phys*) condensare ● *vi* condensarsi. **~d milk** *n* latte *m* condensato
condescend /kɒndɪ'send/ *vi* degnarsi. **~ing** *adj* condiscendente
condition /kən'dɪʃn/ *n* condizione *f*; **on ~ that** a condizione che ● *vt* (*Psych*) condizionare. **~al** *adj* (acceptance) condizionato; (*Gram*) condizionale ● *n* (*Gram*) condizionale *m*. **~er** *n* balsamo *m*; (*for fabrics*) ammorbidente *m*
condolences /kən'dəʊlənsɪz/ *npl* condoglianze *fpl*
condom /'kɒndəm/ *n* preservativo *m*
condo[minium] /'kɒndə ('mɪnɪəm)/ *n Am* condominio *m*
condone /kən'dəʊn/ *vt* passare sopra a
conduct¹ /'kɒndʌkt/ *n* condotta *f*
conduct² /kən'dʌkt/ *vt* condurre; dirigere (orchestra). **~or** *n* direttore *m* d'orchestra; (*of bus*) bigliettaio *m*; (*Phys*) conduttore *m*. **~ress** *n* bigliettaia *f*
cone /kəʊn/ *n* cono *m*; (*Bot*) pigna *f*; (*Auto*) birillo *m* ● **cone off** *vt* **be ~d off** (*Auto*) essere chiuso da birilli
confederation /kənfedə'reɪʃn/ *n* confederazione *f*
conference /'kɒnfərəns/ *n* conferenza *f*
confess /kən'fes/ *vt* confessare ● *vi* confessare; (*Relig*) confessarsi. **~ion** *n* confessione *f*. **~ional** *n* confessionale *m*. **~or** *n* confessore *m*
confetti /kən'fetɪ/ *n* coriandoli *mpl*
confide /kən'faɪd/ *vt* confidare. □ **~ in** *vt* **~ in sb** fidarsi di qcno

C

confidence /'kɒnfɪdəns/ *n* (*trust*) fiducia *f*; (*self-assurance*) sicurezza *f* di sé; (*secret*) confidenza *f*; **in ~** in confidenza. **~ trick** *n* truffa *f*
confident /'kɒnfɪdənt/ *adj* fiducioso; (*self-assured*) sicuro di sé. **~ly** *adv* con aria fiduciosa
confidential /kɒnfɪ'denʃl/ *adj* confidenziale
configur|ation /kənfɪɡə'reɪʃn/ *n* configurazione *f*. **~e** *vt* configurare
confine /kən'faɪn/ *vt* rinchiudere; (*limit*) limitare; **be ~d to bed** essere confinato a letto. **~d** *adj* (space) limitato. **~ment** *n* detenzione *f*; (*Med*) parto *m*
confirm /kən'fɜ:m/ *vt* confermare; (*Relig*) cresimare. **~ation** *n* conferma *f*; (*Relig*) cresima *f*. **~ed** *adj* incallito; **~ed bachelor** scapolo *m* impenitente
confiscat|e /'kɒnfɪskeɪt/ *vt* confiscare. **~ion** *n* confisca *f*
conflict¹ /'kɒnflɪkt/ *n* conflitto *m*
conflict² /kən'flɪkt/ *vi* essere in contraddizione. **~ing** *adj* contraddittorio
conform /kən'fɔ:m/ *vi* (person:) conformarsi; (thing:) essere conforme (**to** a). **~ist** *n* conformista *mf*
confounded /kən'faʊndɪd/ *adj* [!] maledetto
confront /kən'frʌnt/ *vt* affrontare; **the problems ~ing us** i problemi che dobbiamo affrontare. **~ation** *n* confronto *m*
confus|e /kən'fju:z/ *vt* confondere. **~ing** *adj* che confonde. **~ion** *n* confusione *f*
congeal /kən'dʒi:l/ *vi* (blood:) coagularsi
congest|ed /kən'dʒestɪd/ *adj* congestionato. **~ion** *n* congestione *f*
congratulat|e /kən'ɡrætjʊleɪt/ *vt* congratularsi con (**on** per). **~ions** *npl* radunarsi.
congregat|e /'kɒŋɡrɪɡeɪt/ *vi* radunarsi. **~ion** *n* (*Relig*) assemblea *f*
congress /'kɒŋɡres/ *n* congresso *m*. **~man** *n Am* (*Pol*) membro *m* del congresso

C

conifer /'kɒnɪfə(r)/ *n* conifera *f*

conjugat|e /'kɒndʒʊgeɪt/ *vt* coniugare. **~ion** *n* coniugazione *f*

conjunction /kən'dʒʌŋkʃn/ *n* congiunzione *f*; **in ~ with** insieme a

conjur|e /'kʌndʒə(r)/ *vi* **~ing tricks** *npl* giochi *mpl* di prestigio. **~or** *n* prestigiatore, -trice *mf*. □ **~ up** *vt* evocare (image); tirar fuori dal nulla (meal)

conk /kɒŋk/ *vi* **~ out** [!] (machine:) guastarsi; (person:) crollare

'con-man *n* [!] truffatore *m*

connect /kə'nekt/ *vt* collegare; **be ~ed with** avere legami con; (*be related to*) essere imparentato con; **be well ~ed** aver conoscenze influenti ● *vi* essere collegato (**with** a); (train:) fare coincidenza

connection /kə'nekʃn/ *n* (*between ideas*) nesso *m*; (*in travel*) coincidenza *f*; (*Electr*) collegamento *m*; **in ~ with** con riferimento a. **~s** *pl* (*people*) conoscenze *fpl*

connoisseur /kɒnə'sɜ:(r)/ *n* intenditore, -trice *mf*

conquer /'kɒŋkə(r)/ *vt* conquistare; *fig* superare (fear). **~or** *n* conquistatore *m*

conquest /'kɒŋkwest/ *n* conquista *f*

conscience /'kɒnʃəns/ *n* coscienza *f*

conscientious /kɒnʃɪ'enʃəs/ *adj* coscienzioso. **~ ob'jector** *n* obiettore *m* di coscienza

conscious /'kɒnʃəs/ *adj* conscio; (decision) meditato; [**fully**] **~** cosciente; **be/become ~ of sth** rendersi conto di qcsa. **~ly** *adv* consapevolmente. **~ness** *n* consapevolezza *f*; (*Med*) conoscenza *f*

conscript¹ /'kɒnskrɪpt/ *n* coscritto *m*

conscript² /kən'skrɪpt/ *vt* (*Mil*) chiamare alle armi. **~ion** *n* coscrizione *f*, leva *f*

consecrat|e /'kɒnsɪkreɪt/ *vt* consacrare. **~ion** *n* consacrazione *f*

consecutive /kən'sekjʊtɪv/ *adj* consecutivo

consensus /kən'sensəs/ *n* consenso *m*

consent /kən'sent/ *n* consenso *m* ● *vi* acconsentire

consequen|ce /'kɒnsɪkwəns/ *n* conseguenza *f*; (*importance*) importanza *f*. **~t** *adj* conseguente. **~tly** *adv* di conseguenza

conservation /kɒnsə'veɪʃn/ *n* conservazione *f*. **~ist** *n* fautore, -trice *mf* della tutela ambientale

conservative /kən'sɜ:vətɪv/ *adj* conservativo; (estimate) ottimistico. **C~** (*Pol*) *adj* conservatore ● *n* conservatore, -trice *mf*

conservatory /kən'sɜ:vətrɪ/ *n spazio m chiuso da vetrate adiacente alla casa*

conserve /kən'sɜ:v/ *vt* conservare

consider /kən'sɪdə(r)/ *vt* considerare; **~ doing sth** considerare la possibilità di fare qcsa. **~able** *adj* considerevole. **~ably** *adv* considerevolmente

consider|ate /kən'sɪdərət/ *adj* pieno di riguardo. **~ately** *adv* con riguardo. **~ation** *n* considerazione *f*; (*thoughtfulness*) attenzione *f*; (*respect*) riguardo *m*; (*payment*) compenso *m*; **take sth into ~ation** prendere qcsa in considerazione. **~ing** *prep* considerando

consign /kən'saɪn/ *vt* affidare. **~ment** *n* consegna *f*

consist /kən'sɪst/ *vi* **~ of** consistere di

consisten|cy /kən'sɪstənsɪ/ *n* coerenza *f*; (*density*) consistenza *f*. **~t** *adj* coerente; (loyalty) costante. **~tly** *adv* coerentemente; (late, loyal) costantemente

consolation /kɒnsə'leɪʃn/ *n* consolazione *f*. **~ prize** *n* premio *m* di consolazione

console /kən'səʊl/ *vt* consolare

consolidate /kən'sɒlɪdeɪt/ *vt* consolidare

consonant /'kɒnsənənt/ *n* consonante *f*

conspicuous /kən'spɪkjʊəs/ *adj* facilmente distinguibile

conspiracy /kən'spɪrəsɪ/ *n* cospirazione *f*

conspire /kən'spaɪə(r)/ *vi* cospirare

constable /'kʌnstəbl/ *n* agente *m* [di polizia]

constant /'kɒnstənt/ *adj* costante. **~ly** *adv* costantemente

constellation /kɒnstə'leɪʃn/ *n* costellazione *f*

consternation /kɒnstə'neɪʃn/ *n* costernazione *f*

constipat|ed /'kɒnstɪpeɪtɪd/ *adj* stitico. **~ion** *n* stitichezza *f*

constituency /kən'stɪtjʊənsɪ/ *n area f*

elettorale di un deputato nel Regno Unito

constituent /kən'stɪtjʊənt/ *n* costituente *m*; (*Pol*) elettore, -trice *mf*

constitut|e /'kɒnstɪtju:t/ *vt* costituire. **~ion** *n* costituzione *f*. **~ional** *adj* costituzionale

construct /kən'strʌkt/ *vt* costruire. **~ion** *n* costruzione *f*; **under ~ion** in costruzione. **~ive** *adj* costruttivo

consul /'kɒnsl/ *n* console *m*. **~ar** *adj* consolare. **~ate** *n* consolato *m*

consult /kən'sʌlt/ *vt* consultare. **~ant** *n* consulente *mf*; (*Med*) specialista *mf*. **~ation** *n* consultazione *f*; (*Med*) consulto *m*

consume /kən'sju:m/ *vt* consumare. **~r** *n* consumatore, -trice *mf*. **~r goods** *npl* beni *mpl* di consumo. **~er organization** *n* organizzazione *f* per la tutela dei consumatori

consummate /'kɒnsəmeɪt/ *vt* consumare

consumption /kən'sʌmpʃn/ *n* consumo *m*

contact /'kɒntækt/ *n* contatto *m*; (*person*) conoscenza *f* • *vt* mettersi in contatto con. **~ 'lenses** *npl* lenti *fpl* a contatto

contagious /kən'teɪdʒəs/ *adj* contagioso

contain /kən'teɪn/ *vt* contenere; **~ oneself** controllarsi. **~er** *n* recipiente *m*; (*for transport*) container *m inv*

contaminat|e /kən'tæmɪneɪt/ *vt* contaminare. **~ion** *n* contaminazione *f*

contemplat|e /'kɒntəmpleɪt/ *vt* contemplare; (*consider*) considerare; **~e doing sth** considerare di fare qcsa. **~ion** *n* contemplazione *f*

contemporary /kən'tempərərɪ/ *adj & n* contemporaneo, -a *mf*

contempt /kən'tempt/ *n* disprezzo *m*; **beneath ~** più che vergognoso; **~ of court** oltraggio *m* alla Corte. **~ible** *adj* spregevole. **~uous** *adj* sprezzante

contend /kən'tend/ *vi* **~ with** occuparsi di • *vt* (*assert*) sostenere. **~er** *n* concorrente *mf*

content[1] /'kɒntent/ *n* contenuto *m*

content[2] /kən'tent/ *adj* soddisfatto • *vt* **~ oneself** accontentarsi (**with** di). **~ed** *adj* soddisfatto. **~edly** *adv* con aria soddisfatta

contentment /kən'tentmənt/ *n* soddisfazione *f*

contents /'kɒntents/ *npl* contenuto *m*

contest[1] /'kɒntest/ *n* gara *f*

contest[2] /kən'test/ *vt* contestare (statement); impugnare (will); (*Pol*) (candidates:) contendersi; (one candidate:) aspirare a. **~ant** *n* concorrente *mf*

context /'kɒntekst/ *n* contesto *m*

continent /'kɒntɪnənt/ *n* continente *m*; **the C~** l'Europa *f* continentale

continental /kɒntɪ'nentl/ *adj* continentale. **~ breakfast** *n prima colazione f a base di pane, burro, marmellata, croissant, ecc.* **~ quilt** *n* piumone *m*

contingency /kən'tɪndʒənsɪ/ *n* eventualità *f inv*

continual /kən'tɪnjʊəl/ *adj* continuo

continuation /kəntɪnjʊ'eɪʃn/ *n* continuazione *f*

continue /kən'tɪnju:/ *vt* continuare; **~ doing** *or* **to do sth** continuare a fare qcsa; **to be ~d** continua • *vi* continuare. **~d** *adj* continuo

continuity /kɒntɪ'nju:ətɪ/ *n* continuità *f*

continuous /kən'tɪnjʊəs/ *adj* continuo

contort /kən'tɔ:t/ *vt* contorcere. **~ion** *n* contorsione *f*. **~ionist** *n* contorsionista *mf*

contour /'kɒntʊə(r)/ *n* contorno *m*; (*line*) curva *f* di livello

contraband /'kɒntrəbænd/ *n* contrabbando *m*

contracep|tion /kɒntrə'sepʃn/ *n* contraccezione *f*. **~tive** *n* contraccettivo *m*

contract[1] /'kɒntrækt/ *n* contratto *m*

contract[2] /kən'trækt/ *vi* (*get smaller*) contrarsi • *vt* contrarre (illness). **~ion** *n* contrazione *f*. **~or** *n* imprenditore, -trice *mf*

contradict /kɒntrə'dɪkt/ *vt* contraddire. **~ion** *n* contraddizione *f*. **~ory** *adj* contradditorio

contraption /kən'træpʃn/ *n* [!] aggeggio *m*

contrary[1] /'kɒntrərɪ/ *adj* contrario • *adv* **~ to** contrariamente a • *n* contrario *m*; **on the ~** al contrario

C

contrary[2] /kən'treərɪ/ *adj* disobbediente

contrast[1] /'kɒntrɑːst/ *n* contrasto *m*

contrast[2] /kən'trɑːst/ *vt* confrontare ● *vi* contrastare. **~ing** *adj* contrastante

contraven|e /kɒntrə'viːn/ *vt* trasgredire. **~tion** *n* trasgressione *f*

contribut|e /kən'trɪbjuːt/ *vt/i* contribuire. **~ion** *n* contribuzione *f*; (*what is contributed*) contributo *m*. **~or** *n* contributore, -trice *mf*

contrive /kən'traɪv/ *vt* escogitare; **~ to do sth** riuscire a fare qcsa

control /kən'trəʊl/ *n* controllo *m*; **~s** *pl* (*of car, plane*) comandi *mpl*; **get out of ~** sfuggire al controllo ● *vt* (*pt/pp* **controlled**) controllare; **~ oneself** controllarsi

controvers|ial /kɒntrə'vɜːʃl/ *adj* controverso. **~y** *n* controversia *f*

convalesce /kɒnvə'les/ *vi* essere in convalescenza

convector /kən'vektə(r)/ *n* **~ [heater]** convettore *m*

convene /kən'viːn/ *vt* convocare ● *vi* riunirsi

convenience /kən'viːnɪəns/ *n* convenienza *f*; **[public] ~** gabinetti *mpl* pubblici; **with all modern ~s** con tutti i comfort

convenient /kən'viːnɪənt/ *adj* comodo; **be ~ for sb** andar bene per qcno; **if it is ~ [for you]** se ti va bene. **~ly** *adv* comodamente; **~ly located** in una posizione comoda

convent /'kɒnvənt/ *n* convento *m*

convention /kən'venʃn/ *n* convenzione *f*; (*assembly*) convegno *m*. **~al** *adj* convenzionale

converge /kən'vɜːdʒ/ *vi* convergere

conversation /kɒnvə'seɪʃn/ *n* conversazione *f*. **~al** *adj* di conversazione. **~alist** *n* conversatore, -trice *mf*

converse[1] /kən'vɜːs/ *vi* conversare

converse[2] /'kɒnvɜːs/ *n* inverso *m*. **~ly** *adv* viceversa

conversion /kən'vɜːʃn/ *n* conversione *f*

convert[1] /'kɒnvɜːt/ *n* convertito, -a *mf*

convert[2] /kən'vɜːt/ *vt* convertire (**into** in); sconsacrare (church). **~ible** *adj* convertibile ● *n* (*Auto*) macchina *f* decappottabile

convex /'kɒnveks/ *adj* convesso

convey /kən'veɪ/ *vt* portare; trasmettere (idea, message). **~or belt** *n* nastro *m* trasportatore

convict[1] /'kɒnvɪkt/ *n* condannato, -a *mf*

convict[2] /kən'vɪkt/ *vt* giudicare colpevole. **~ion** *n* condanna *f*; (*belief*) convinzione *f*; **previous ~ion** precedente *m* penale

convinc|e /kən'vɪns/ *vt* convincere. **~ing** *adj* convincente

convoluted /'kɒnvəluːtɪd/ *adj* contorto

convoy /'kɒnvɔɪ/ *n* convoglio *m*

convuls|e /kən'vʌls/ *vt* sconvolgere; **be ~ed with laughter** contorcersi dalle risa. **~ion** *n* convulsione *f*

coo /kuː/ *vi* tubare

cook /kʊk/ *n* cuoco, -a *mf* ● *vt* cucinare; **is it ~ed?** è cotto?; **~ the books** [!] truccare i libri contabili ● *vi* (food:) cuocere; (person:) cucinare. **~book** *n* libro *m* di cucina

cooker /'kʊkə(r)/ *n* cucina *f*; (*apple*) mela *f* da cuocere. **~y** *n* cucina *f*. **~y book** *n* libro *m* di cucina

cookie /'kʊkɪ/ *n Am* biscotto *m*

cool /kuːl/ *adj* fresco; (*calm*) calmo; (*unfriendly*) freddo ● *n* fresco *m* ● *vt* rinfrescare ● *vi* rinfrescarsi. **~-box** *n* borsa *f* termica. **~ness** *n* freddezza *f*

coop /kuːp/ *n* stia *f* ● *vt* **~ up** rinchiudere

co-operat|e /kəʊ'ɒpəreɪt/ *vi* cooperare. **~ion** *n* cooperazione *f*

co-operative /kəʊ'ɒpərətɪv/ *adj* cooperativo ● *n* cooperativa *f*

co-opt /kəʊ'ɒpt/ *vt* eleggere

co-ordinat|e /kəʊ'ɔːdɪneɪt/ *vt* coordinare. **~ion** *n* coordinazione *f*

cop /kɒp/ *n* [!] poliziotto *m*

cope /kəʊp/ *vi* [!] farcela; **can she ~ by herself?** ce la fa da sola?; **~ with** farcela con

copious /'kəʊpɪəs/ *adj* abbondante

copper[1] /'kɒpə(r)/ *n* rame *m*; **~s** *pl* *monete fpl da uno o due pence* ● *attrib* di rame

copper[2] *n* [!] poliziotto *m*

copy /'kɒpɪ/ *n* copia *f* ● *vt* (*pt/pp* **-ied**) copiare

copyright *n* diritti *mpl* d'autore

coral /ˈkɒrəl/ *n* corallo *m*
cord /kɔːd/ *n* corda *f*; (*thinner*) cordoncino *m*; (*fabric*) velluto *m* a coste; **~s** *pl* pantaloni *mpl* di velluto a coste
cordial /ˈkɔːdɪəl/ *adj* cordiale ● *n* analcolico *m*
cordon /ˈkɔːdn/ *n* cordone *m* (*di persone*) ● **cordon off** *vt* mettere un cordone (*di persone*) intorno a
core /kɔː(r)/ *n* (*of apple, pear*) torsolo *m*; (*fig: of organization*) cuore *m*; (*of problem, theory*) nocciolo *m*
cork /kɔːk/ *n* sughero *m*; (*for bottle*) turacciolo *m*. **~screw** *n* cavatappi *m inv*
corn¹ /kɔːn/ *n* grano *m*; (*Am: maize*) granturco *m*
corn² *n* (*Med*) callo *m*
corned beef /kɔːndˈbiːf/ *n* manzo *m* sotto sale
corner /ˈkɔːnə(r)/ *n* angolo *m*; (*football*) calcio *m* d'angolo, corner *m inv* ● *vt fig* bloccare; (*Comm*) accaparrarsi (market)
cornet /ˈkɔːnɪt/ *n* (*Mus*) cornetta *f*; (*for ice-cream*) cono *m*
corn: ~flour *n*, *Am* **~starch** *n* farina *f* di granturco
corny /ˈkɔːnɪ// *adj* (-ier, -iest) ([!]: joke, film) scontato; (person) banale; (*sentimental*) sdolcinato
coronary /ˈkɒrənərɪ/ *adj* coronario ● *n* **~ [thrombosis]** trombosi *f* coronarica
coronation /kɒrəˈneɪʃn/ *n* incoronazione *f*
coroner /ˈkɒrənə(r)/ *n* coroner *m inv* (*nel diritto britannico, ufficiale incaricato delle indagini su morti sospette*)
corporal¹ /ˈkɔːpərəl/ *n* (*Mil*) caporale *m*
corporal² *adj* corporale; **~ punishment** punizione *f* corporale
corporate /ˈkɔːpərət/ *adj* (decision, policy, image) aziendale; **~ life** la vita in un'azienda
corporation /kɔːpəˈreɪʃn/ *n* ente *m*; (*of town*) consiglio *m* comunale
corps /kɔː(r)/ *n* (*pl* **corps** /kɔːz/) corpo *m*
corpse /kɔːps/ *n* cadavere *m*
corpulent /ˈkɔːpjʊlənt/ *adj* corpulento
correct /kəˈrekt/ *adj* corretto; **be ~** (person:) aver ragione; **~!** esatto! ● *vt* correggere. **~ion** *n* correzione *f*. **~ly** *adv* correttamente
correspond /kɒrɪˈspɒnd/ *vi* corrispondere (**to** a); (two things:) corrispondere; (*write*) scriversi. **~ence** *n* corrispondenza *f*. **~ent** *n* corrispondente *mf*. **~ing** *adj* corrispondente. **~ingly** *adv* in modo corrispondente
corridor /ˈkɒrɪdɔː(r)/ *n* corridoio *m*
corro|de /kəˈrəʊd/ *vt* corrodere ● *vi* corrodersi. **~sion** *n* corrosione *f*
corrugated /ˈkɒrəgeɪtɪd/ *adj* ondulato. **~ iron** *n* lamiera *f* ondulata
corrupt /kəˈrʌpt/ *adj* corrotto ● *vt* corrompere. **~ion** *n* corruzione *f*
corset /ˈkɔːsɪt/ *n* & **-s** *pl* busto *m*
Corsica /ˈkɔːsɪkə/ *n* Corsica *f*. **~n** *adj & n* corso, -a *mf*
cosmetic /kɒzˈmetɪk/ *adj* cosmetico ● *n* **~s** *pl* cosmetici *mpl*
cosmic /ˈkɒzmɪk/ *adj* cosmico
cosmopolitan /kɒzməˈpɒlɪtən/ *adj* cosmopolita
cosmos /ˈkɒzmɒs/ *n* cosmo *m*
cosset /ˈkɒsɪt/ *vt* coccolare
cost /kɒst/ *n* costo *m*; **~s** *pl* (*Jur*) spese *fpl* processuali; **at all ~s** a tutti i costi; **I learnt to my ~** ho imparato a mie spese ● *vt* (*pt/pp* **cost**) costare; **it ~ me £20** mi è costato 20 sterline ● *vt* (*pt/pp* **costed**) **~ [out]** stabilire il prezzo di
costly /ˈkɒstlɪ/ *adj* (**-ier, -iest**) costoso
costume /ˈkɒstjuːm/ *n* costume *m*. **~ jewellery** *n* bigiotteria *f*
cosy /ˈkəʊzɪ/ *adj* (**-ier, -iest**) (pub, chat) intimo; **it's nice and ~ in here** si sta bene qui
cot /kɒt/ *n* lettino *m*; (*Am: camp-bed*) branda *f*
cottage /ˈkɒtɪdʒ/ *n* casetta *f*. **~ ˈcheese** *n* fiocchi *mpl* di latte
cotton /ˈkɒtn/ *n* cotone *m* ● *attrib* di cotone ● **cotton on** *vi* [!] capire
cotton ˈwool *n* cotone *m* idrofilo
couch /kaʊtʃ/ *n* divano *m*. **~ potato** *n* pantofolaio, -a *mf*
cough /kɒf/ *n* tosse *f* ● *vi* tossire. □ **~ up** *vt/i* sputare; ([!]: *pay*) sborsare
ˈcough mixture *n* sciroppo *m* per la tosse

C

could /kʊd/, *atono* /kəd/ *v aux* (*see also* **can²**) **~ I have a glass of water?** potrei avere un bicchier d'acqua?; **I ~n't do it even if I wanted to** non potrei farlo nemmeno se lo volessi; **I ~n't care less** non potrebbe importarmene di meno; **he ~n't have done it without help** non avrebbe potuto farlo senza aiuto; **you ~ have phoned** avresti potuto telefonare

council /'kaʊnsl/ *n* consiglio *m*. **~ house** *n* casa *f* popolare

councillor /'kaʊnsələ(r)/ *n* consigliere, -a *mf*

counsel /'kaʊnsl/ *n* consigli *mpl*; (*Jur*) avvocato *m* ● *vt* (*pt/pp* **counselled**) consigliare a (person). **~lor** *n* consigliere, -a *mf*

count¹ /kaʊnt/ *n* (*nobleman*) conte *m*

count² *n* conto *m*; **keep ~** tenere il conto ● *vt/i* contare. □ **~ on** *vt* contare su

countdown /'kaʊntdaʊn/ *n* conto *m* alla rovescia

counter¹ /'kaʊntə(r)/ *n* banco *m*; (*in games*) gettone *m*

counter² *adv* **~ to** contro, in contrasto a; **go ~ to sth** andare contro qcsa ● *vt/i* opporre (measure, effect); parare (blow)

counter'act *vt* neutralizzare

'counter-attack *n* contrattacco *m*

'counterfeit /-fɪt/ *adj* contraffatto ● *n* contraffazione *f* ● *vt* contraffare

'counterfoil *n* matrice *f*

counter-pro'ductive *adj* controproduttivo

countess /'kaʊntɪs/ *n* contessa *f*

countless /'kaʊntlɪs/ *adj* innumerevole

country /'kʌntrɪ/ *n* nazione *f*, paese *m*; (*native land*) patria *f*; (*countryside*) campagna *f*; **in the ~** in campagna; **go to the ~** andare in campagna; (*Pol*) indire le elezioni politiche. **~man** *n* uomo *m* di campagna; (*fellow ~man*) compatriota *m*. **~side** *n* campagna *f*

county /'kaʊntɪ/ *n* contea *f* (*unità amministrativa britannica*)

coup /kuː/ *n* (*Pol*) colpo *m* di stato

couple /'kʌpl/ *n* coppia *f*; **a ~ of** un paio di

coupon /'kuːpɒn/ *n* tagliando *m*; (*for discount*) buono *m* sconto

courage /'kʌrɪdʒ/ *n* coraggio *m*. **~ous** *adj* coraggioso

courgette /kʊə'ʒet/ *n* zucchino *m*

courier /'kʊrɪə(r)/ *n* corriere *m*; (*for tourists*) guida *f*

course /kɔːs/ *n* (*Sch*) corso *m*; (*Naut*) rotta *f*; (*Culin*) portata *f*; (*for golf*) campo *m*; **~ of treatment** (*Med*) serie *f inv* di cure; **of ~** naturalmente; **in the ~ of** durante; **in due ~** a tempo debito

court /kɔːt/ *n* tribunale *m*; (*Sport*) campo *m*; **take sb to ~** citare qcno in giudizio ● *vt* fare la corte a (woman); sfidare (danger); **~ing couples** coppiette *fpl*

courteous /'kɜːtɪəs/ *adj* cortese

courtesy /'kɜːtəsɪ/ *n* cortesia *f*

court: ~ 'martial *n* (*pl* **~s martial**) corte *f* marziale **~-martial** *vt* (*pt* **~-martialled**) portare davanti alla corte marziale; **~yard** *n* cortile *m*

cousin /'kʌzn/ *n* cugino, -a *mf*

cove /kəʊv/ *n* insenatura *f*

cover /'kʌvə(r)/ *n* copertura *f*; (*of cushion, to protect sth*) fodera *f*; (*of book, magazine*) copertina *f*; **take ~** mettersi al riparo; **under separate ~** a parte ● *vt* coprire; foderare (cushion); (*Journ*) fare un servizio su. □ **~ up** *vt* coprire; *fig* soffocare (scandal)

coverage /'kʌvərɪdʒ/ *n* (*Journ*) **it got a lot of ~** i media gli hanno dedicato molto spazio

cover: ~ charge *n* coperto *m*. **~ing** *n* copertura *f*; (*for floor*) rivestimento *m*; **~ing letter** lettera *f* d'accompagnamento

covet /'kʌvɪt/ *vt* bramare

cow /kaʊ/ *n* vacca *f*, mucca *f*

coward /'kaʊəd/ *n* vigliacco, -a *mf*. **~ice** *n* vigliaccheria *f*. **~ly** *adj* da vigliacco

'cowboy *n* cowboy *m inv*; [!] buffone *m*

cower /'kaʊə(r)/ *vi* acquattarsi

coy /kɔɪ/ *adj* falsamente timido; (*flirtatiously*) civettuolo; **be ~ about sth** essere evasivo su qcsa

crab /kræb/ *n* granchio *m*

crack /kræk/ *n* (*in wall*) crepa *f*; (*in china, glass, bone*) incrinatura *f*; (*noise*) scoppio *m*; ([!]: *joke*) battuta *f*; **have a ~** (*try*) fare un tentativo ● *adj* ([!]: *best*) di prim'ordine ● *vt* incrinare (china, glass); schiacciare (nut); decifrare (code); [!] risolvere (problem); **~ a joke** [!] fare una battuta ● *vi* (china, glass:) incrinarsi; (whip:) schioccare. □ **~ down** *vi* [!] prendere seri provvedimenti. □ **~ down on** *vt* [!] prendere seri provvedimenti contro

cracker /ˈkrækə(r)/ *n* (*biscuit*) cracker *m inv*; (*firework*) petardo *m*; **[Christmas] ~** *tubo m di cartone colorato contenente una sorpresa*

crackle /ˈkrækl/ *vi* crepitare

cradle /ˈkreɪdl/ *n* culla *f*

craft¹ /krɑːft/ *n inv* (*boat*) imbarcazione *f*

craft² *n* mestiere *m*; (*technique*) arte *f*. **~sman** *n* artigiano *m*

crafty /ˈkrɑːftɪ/ *adj* (**-ier, -iest**) astuto

cram /kræm/ *v* (*pt/pp* **crammed**) ● *vt* stipare (**into** in) ● *vi* (*for exams*) sgobbare

cramp /kræmp/ *n* crampo *m*. **~ed** *adj* (room) stretto; (handwriting) appiccicato

cranberry /ˈkrænbərɪ/ *n* (*Culin*) mirtillo *m* rosso

crane /kreɪn/ *n* (*at docks, bird*) gru *f inv* ● *vt* **~ one's neck** allungare il collo

crank¹ /kræŋk/ *n* tipo, -a *mf* strampalato, -a

crank² *n* (*Techn*) manovella *f*. **~shaft** *n* albero *m* a gomiti

cranky /ˈkræŋkɪ/ *adj* strampalato; (*Am: irritable*) irritabile

cranny /ˈkrænɪ/ *n* fessura *f*

crash /kræʃ/ *n* (*noise*) fragore *m*; (*Aeron, Auto*) incidente *m*; (*Comm*) crollo *m* ● *vi* schiantarsi (**into** contro); (plane:) precipitare ● *vt* schiantare (car)

crash: ~ course *n* corso *m* intensivo. **~-helmet** *n* casco *m*

crate /kreɪt/ *n* (*for packing*) cassa *f*

crater /ˈkreɪtə(r)/ *n* cratere *m*

crav|e /kreɪv/ *vt* morire dalla voglia di. **~ing** *n* voglia *f* smodata

crawl /krɔːl/ *n* (*swimming*) stile *m* libero; **do the ~** nuotare a stile libero; **at a ~** a passo di lumaca ● *vi* andare carponi; **~ with** brulicare di. **~er lane** *n* (*Auto*) corsia *f* riservata al traffico lento

crayon /ˈkreɪən/ *n* pastello *m* a cera; (*pencil*) matita *f* colorata

craze /kreɪz/ *n* mania *f*

crazy /ˈkreɪzɪ/ *adj* (**-ier, -iest**) matto; **be ~ about** andar matto per

creak /kriːk/ *n* scricchiolio *m* ● *vi* scricchiolare

cream /kriːm/ *n* crema *f*; (*fresh*) panna *f* ● *adj* (*colour*) [bianco] panna *inv* ● *vt* (*Culin*) sbattere. **~ 'cheese** *n* formaggio *m* cremoso. **~y** *adj* cremoso

crease /kriːs/ *n* piega *f* ● *vt* stropicciare ● *vi* stropicciarsi. **~-resistant** *adj* che non si stropiccia

creat|e /kriːˈeɪt/ *vt* creare. **~ion** *n* creazione *f*. **~ive** *adj* creativo. **~or** *n* creatore, -trice *mf*

creature /ˈkriːtʃə(r)/ *n* creatura *f*

crèche /kreʃ/ *n* asilo *m* nido

credibility /kredəˈbɪlətɪ/ *n* credibilità *f*

credible /ˈkredəbl/ *adj* credibile

credit /ˈkredɪt/ *n* credito *m*; (*honour*) merito *m*; **take the ~ for** prendersi il merito di ● *vt* (*pt/pp* **credited**) accreditare; **~ sb with sth** (*Comm*) accreditare qcsa a qcno; *fig* attribuire qcsa a qcno. **~able** *adj* lodevole

credit: ~ card *n* carta *f* di credito. **~or** *n* creditore, -trice *mf*

creed /kriːd/ *n* credo *m inv*

creek /kriːk/ *n* insenatura *f*; (*Am: stream*) torrente *m*

creep /kriːp/ *vi* (*pt/pp* **crept**) muoversi furtivamente ● *n* [!] tipo *m* viscido. **~er** *n* pianta *f* rampicante. **~y** *adj* che fa venire i brividi

cremat|e /krɪˈmeɪt/ *vt* cremare. **~ion** *n* cremazione *f*

crematorium /kreməˈtɔːrɪəm/ *n* crematorio *m*

crept /krept/ ▷**CREEP**

crescent /ˈkresənt/ *n* mezzaluna *f*

crest /krest/ *n* cresta *f*; (*coat of arms*) cimiero *m*

Crete /kriːt/ *n* Creta *f*

crevice /ˈkrevɪs/ *n* crepa *f*

crew /kruː/ *n* equipaggio *m*; (*gang*) équipe *f inv*. **~ cut** *n* capelli *mpl* a spazzola. **~ neck** *n* girocollo *m*

C

crib¹ /krɪb/ *n* (*for baby*) culla *f*
crib² *vt/i* (*pt/pp* **cribbed**) [!] copiare
crick /krɪk/ *n* ~ **in the neck** torcicollo *m*
cricket¹ /'krɪkɪt/ *n* (*insect*) grillo *m*
cricket² *n* cricket *m*. ~**er** *n* giocatore *m* di cricket
crime /kraɪm/ *n* crimine *m*; (*criminality*) criminalità *f*
criminal /'krɪmɪnl/ *adj* criminale; (law, court) penale ● *n* criminale *mf*
crimson /'krɪmzn/ *adj* cremisi *inv*
cringe /krɪndʒ/ *vi* (*cower*) acquattarsi; (*at bad joke etc*) fare una smorfia
crinkle /'krɪŋkl/ *vt* spiegazzare ● *vi* spiegazzarsi
cripple /'krɪpl/ *n* storpio, -a *mf* ● *vt* storpiare; *fig* danneggiare. ~**d** *adj* (person) storpio; (ship) danneggiato
crisis /'kraɪsɪs/ *n* (*pl* **-ses** /-si:z/) crisi *f inv*
crisp /krɪsp/ *adj* croccante; (air) frizzante; (style) incisivo. ~**bread** *n* crostini *mpl* di pane. ~**s** *npl* patatine *fpl*
criterion /kraɪ'tɪərɪən/ *n* (*pl* **-ria** /-rɪə/) criterio *m*
critic /'krɪtɪk/ *n* critico, -a *mf*. ~**al** *adj* critico. ~**ally** *adv* in modo critico; ~**ally ill** gravemente malato
criticism /'krɪtɪsɪzm/ *n* critica *f*; **he doesn't like** ~ non ama le critiche
criticize /'krɪtɪsaɪz/ *vt* criticare
croak /krəʊk/ *vi* gracchiare; (frog:) gracidare
Croatia /krəʊ'eɪʃə/ *n* Croazia *f*
crochet /'krəʊʃeɪ/ *n* lavoro *m* all'uncinetto ● *vt* fare all'uncinetto. ~**-hook** *n* uncinetto *m*
crockery /'krɒkərɪ/ *n* terrecotte *fpl*
crocodile /'krɒkədaɪl/ *n* coccodrillo *m*. ~ **tears** lacrime *fpl* di coccodrillo
crocus /'krəʊkəs/ *n* (*pl* **-es**) croco *m*
crook /krʊk/ *n* ([!]: *criminal*) truffatore, -trice *mf*
crooked /'krʊkɪd/ *adj* storto; (limb) storpiato; ([!]: *dishonest*) disonesto
crop /krɒp/ *n* raccolto *m*; *fig* quantità *f inv* ● *v* (*pt/pp* **cropped**) ● *vt* coltivare. □ ~ **up** *vi* [!] presentarsi
croquet /'krəʊkeɪ/ *n* croquet *m*
croquette /krəʊ'ket/ *n* crocchetta *f*
cross /krɒs/ *adj* (*annoyed*) arrabbiato; **talk at** ~ **purposes** fraintendersi ● *n* croce *f*; (*Bot, Zool*) incrocio *m* ● *vt* sbarrare (cheque); incrociare (road, animals); ~ **oneself** farsi il segno della croce; ~ **one's arms** incrociare le braccia; ~ **one's legs** accavallare le gambe; **keep one's fingers** ~**ed for sb** tenere le dita incrociate per qcno; **it** ~**ed my mind** mi è venuto in mente ● *vi* (*go across*) attraversare; (lines:) incrociarsi. □ ~ **out** *vt* depennare
cross: ~**bar** *n* (*of goal*) traversa *f*; (*on bicycle*) canna *f*. ~**ex'amine** *vt* sottoporre a controinterrogatorio. ~**-'eyed** *adj* strabico. ~**fire** *n* fuoco *m* incrociato. ~**ing** *n* (*for pedestrians*) passaggio *m* pedonale; (*sea journey*) traversata *f*. ~**-'reference** *n* rimando *m*. ~**roads** *n* incrocio *m*. ~**-'section** *n* sezione *f*; (*of community*) campione *m*. ~**word** *n* ~**word [puzzle]** parole *fpl* crociate
crouch /kraʊtʃ/ *vi* accovacciarsi
crow /krəʊ/ *n* corvo *m*; **as the** ~ **flies** in linea d'aria ● *vi* cantare. ~**bar** *n* piede *m* di porco
crowd /kraʊd/ *n* folla *f* ● *vt* affollare ● *vi* affollarsi. ~**ed** *adj* affollato
crown /kraʊn/ *n* corona *f* ● *vt* incoronare; incapsulare (tooth)
crucial /'kru:ʃl/ *adj* cruciale
crucifix /'kru:sɪfɪks/ *n* crocifisso *m*
crucif|ixion /kru:sɪ'fɪkʃn/ *n* crocifissione *f*. ~**y** *vt* (*pt/pp* **-ied**) crocifiggere
crude /kru:d/ *adj* (oil) greggio; (language) crudo; (person) rozzo
cruel /kru:əl/ *adj* (**crueller, cruellest**) crudele (**to** verso). ~**ly** *adv* con crudeltà. ~**ty** *n* crudeltà *f*
cruis|e /kru:z/ *n* crociera *f* ● *vi* fare una crociera; (car:) andare a velocità di crociera. ~**er** *n* (*Mil*) incrociatore *m*; (*motor boat*) motoscafo *m*. ~**ing speed** *n* velocità *m inv* di crociera
crumb /krʌm/ *n* briciola *f*
crumb|le /'krʌmbl/ *vt* sbriciolare ● *vi* sbriciolarsi; (building, society:) sgretolarsi. ~**ly** *adj* friabile
crumple /'krʌmpl/ *vt* spiegazzare ● *vi* spiegazzarsi
crunch /krʌntʃ/ *n* [!] **when it comes to the** ~ quando si viene al dunque ● *vt* sgranocchiare ● *vi* (snow:) scricchiolare

crusade /kru:'seɪd/ *n* crociata *f*. **~r** *n* crociato *m*

crush /krʌʃ/ *n* (*crowd*) calca *f*; **have a ~ on sb** essersi preso una cotta per qcno ● *vt* schiacciare; sgualcire (clothes)

crust /krʌst/ *n* crosta *f*

crutch /krʌtʃ/ *n* gruccia *f*; (*Anat*) inforcatura *f*

crux /krʌks/ *n fig* punto *m* cruciale

cry /kraɪ/ *n* grido *m*; **have a ~** farsi un pianto; **a far ~ from** *fig* tutta un'altra cosa rispetto a ● *vi* (*pt/pp* **cried**) (*weep*) piangere; (*call*) gridare

crypt /krɪpt/ *n* cripta *f*. **~ic** *adj* criptico

crystal /'krɪstl/ *n* cristallo *m*; (*glassware*) cristalli *mpl*. **~lize** *vi* (*become clear*) concretizzarsi

cub /kʌb/ *n* (*animal*) cucciolo *m*; **C~** [**Scout**] lupetto *m*

Cuba /'kju:bə/ *n* Cuba *f*

cubby-hole /'kʌbɪ-/ *n* (*compartment*) scomparto *m*; (*room*) ripostiglio *m*

cub|e /kju:b/ *n* cubo *m*. **~ic** *adj* cubico

cubicle /'kju:bɪkl/ *n* cabina *f*

cuckoo /'kʊku:/ *n* cuculo *m*. **~ clock** *n* orologio *m* a cucù

cucumber /'kju:kʌmbə(r)/ *n* cetriolo *m*

cuddl|e /'kʌdl/ *vt* coccolare ● *vi* **~e up to** starsene accoccolato insieme a ● *n* **have a ~e** (child:) farsi coccolare; (lovers:) abbracciarsi. **~y** *adj* tenerone; (*wanting cuddles*) coccolone. **~y 'toy** *n* peluche *m inv*

cue[1] /kju:/ *n* segnale *m*; (*Theat*) battuta *f* d'entrata

cue[2] *n* (*in billiards*) stecca *f*. **~ ball** *n* pallino *m*

cuff /kʌf/ *n* polsino *m*; (*Am: turn-up*) orlo *m*; (*blow*) scapaccione *m*; **off the ~** improvvisando ● *vt* dare una pacca a. **~-link** *n* gemello *m*

cul-de-sac /'kʌldəsæk/ *n* vicolo *m* cieco

culinary /'kʌlɪnərɪ/ *adj* culinario

cull /kʌl/ *vt* scegliere (flowers); (*kill*) selezionare e uccidere

culminat|e /'kʌlmɪneɪt/ *vi* culminare. **~ion** *n* culmine *m*

culprit /'kʌlprɪt/ *n* colpevole *mf*

cult /kʌlt/ *n* culto *m*

cultivate /'kʌltɪveɪt/ *vt* coltivare; *fig* coltivarsi (person)

cultural /'kʌltʃərəl/ *adj* culturale

culture /'kʌltʃə(r)/ *n* cultura *f*. **~d** *adj* colto

cumbersome /'kʌmbəsəm/ *adj* ingombrante

cunning /'kʌnɪŋ/ *adj* astuto ● *n* astuzia *f*

cup /kʌp/ *n* tazza *f*; (*prize, of bra*) coppa *f*

cupboard /'kʌbəd/ *n* armadio *m*. **~love** [!] amore *m* interessato

curator /kjʊə'reɪtə(r)/ *n* direttore, -trice *mf* (*di museo*)

curb /kɜ:b/ *vt* tenere a freno

curdle /'kɜ:dl/ *vi* coagularsi

cure /kjʊə(r)/ *n* cura *f* ● *vt* curare; (*salt*) mettere sotto sale; (*smoke*) affumicare

curfew /'kɜ:fju:/ *n* coprifuoco *m*

curiosity /kjʊərɪ'ɒsətɪ/ *n* curiosità *f*

curious /'kjʊərɪəs/ *adj* curioso. **~ly** *adv* (*strangely*) curiosamente

curl /kɜ:l/ *n* ricciolo *m* ● *vt* arricciare ● *vi* arricciarsi. □ **~ up** *vi* raggomitolarsi

curler /'kɜ:lə(r)/ *n* bigodino *m*

curly /'kɜ:lɪ/ *adj* (**-ier, -iest**) riccio

currant /'kʌrənt/ *n* (*dried*) uvetta *f*

currency /'kʌrənsɪ/ *n* valuta *f*; (*of word*) ricorrenza *f*; **foreign ~** valuta *f* estera

current /'kʌrənt/ *adj* corrente ● *n* corrente *f*. **~ affairs** *or* **events** *npl* attualità *fsg*. **~ly** *adv* attualmente

curriculum /kə'rɪkjʊləm/ *n* programma *m* di studi. **~ vitae** *n* curriculum vitae *m inv*

curry /'kʌrɪ/ *n* curry *m inv*; (*meal*) piatto *m* cucinato nel curry ● *vt* (*pt/pp* **-ied**) **~ favour with sb** cercare d'ingraziarsi qcno

curse /kɜ:s/ *n* maledizione *f*; (*oath*) imprecazione *f* ● *vt* maledire ● *vi* imprecare

cursory /'kɜ:sərɪ/ *adj* sbrigativo

curt /kɜ:t/ *adj* brusco

curtain /'kɜ:tn/ *n* tenda *f*; (*Theat*) sipario *m*

curtsy /'kɜ:tsɪ/ *n* inchino *m* ● *vi* (*pt/pp* **-ied**) fare l'inchino

curve /kɜ:v/ *n* curva *f* ● *vi* curvare; **~ to the right/left** curvare a destra/

sinistra. **~d** *adj* curvo
cushion /ˈkʊʃn/ *n* cuscino *m* ● *vt* attutire; (*protect*) proteggere
cushy /ˈkʊʃɪ/ *adj* (**-ier, -iest**) [!] facile
custard /ˈkʌstəd/ *n* (*liquid*) crema *f* pasticciera
custody /ˈkʌstədɪ/ *n* (*of child*) custodia *f*; (*imprisonment*) detenzione *f* preventiva
custom /ˈkʌstəm/ *n* usanza *f*; (*Jur*) consuetudine *f*; (*Comm*) clientela *f*. **~ary** *adj* (*habitual*) abituale; **it's ~ary to...** è consuetudine.... **~er** *n* cliente *mf*
customs /ˈkʌstəmz/ *npl* dogana *f*. **~ officer** *n* doganiere *m*
cut /kʌt/ *n* (*with knife etc, of clothes*) taglio *m*; (*reduction*) riduzione *f*; (*in public spending*) taglio *m* ● *vt/i* (*pt/pp* **cut**, *pres p* **cutting**) tagliare; (*reduce*) ridurre; **~ one's finger** tagliarsi il dito; **~ sb's hair** tagliare i capelli a qcno ● *vi* (*with cards*) alzare. □ **~ back** *vt* tagliare (hair); potare (hedge); (*reduce*) ridurre. □ **~ down** *vt* abbattere (tree); (*reduce*) ridurre. □ **~ off** *vt* tagliar via; (*disconnect*) interrompere; *fig* isolare; **I was ~ off** (*Teleph*) la linea è caduta. □ **~ out** *vt* ritagliare; (*delete*) eliminare; **be ~ out for** [!] essere tagliato per; **~ it out!** [!] dacci un taglio!. □ **~ up** *vt* (*slice*) tagliare a pezzi
cute /kju:t/ *adj* [!] (*in appearance*) carino; (*clever*) acuto
cutlery /ˈkʌtlərɪ/ *n* posate *fpl*
cutlet /ˈkʌtlɪt/ *n* cotoletta *f*
ˈcut-price *adj* a prezzo ridotto; (shop) che fa prezzi ridotti
ˈcut-throat *adj* spietato
cutting /ˈkʌtɪŋ/ *adj* (remark) tagliente ● *n* (*from newspaper*) ritaglio *m*; (*of plant*) talea *f*
CV *n abbr* curriculum vitae
cycl|e /ˈsaɪkl/ *n* ciclo *m*; (*bicycle*) bicicletta *f*, bici *f inv* [!] ● *vi* andare in bicicletta. **~ing** *n* ciclismo *m*. **~ist** *n* ciclista *mf*
cylind|er /ˈsɪlɪndə(r)/ *n* cilindro *m*. **~rical** *adj* cilindrico
cynic /ˈsɪnɪk/ *n* cinico, -a *mf*. **~al** *adj* cinico. **~ism** *n* cinismo *m*
Cyprus /ˈsaɪprəs/ *n* Cipro *m*
Czech /tʃek/ *adj* ceco; **~ Republic** Repubblica *f* Ceca ● *n* ceco, -a *mf*

Dd

dab /dæb/ *n* colpetto *m*; **a ~ of** un pochino di ● *vt* (*pt/pp* **dabbed**) toccare leggermente (eyes). □ **~ on** *vt* mettere un po' di (paint etc)
dad[dy] /ˈdæd[ɪ]/ *n* [!] papà *m inv*, babbo *m*
daddy-ˈlong-legs *n* zanzarone *m* [dei boschi]; (*Am: spider*) ragno *m*
daffodil /ˈdæfədɪl/ *n* giunchiglia *f*
daft /dɑ:ft/ *adj* sciocco
dagger /ˈdægə(r)/ *n* stiletto *m*

> **Dáil Éireann** Dáil Éireann è la camera bassa del Parlamento della Reppubblica di Irlanda. È composto di 166 deputati (o TD) in rappresentanza di 41 collegi elettorali. I deputati sono infatti eletti col sistema proporzionale e la Costituzione ne prevede uno per ogni 20.000-30.000 cittadini.

daily /ˈdeɪlɪ/ *adj* giornaliero ● *adv* giornalmente ● *n* (*newspaper*) quotidiano *m*; ([!]: *cleaner*) donna *f* delle pulizie
dainty /ˈdeɪntɪ/ *adj* (**-ier, -iest**) grazioso; (movement) delicato
dairy /ˈdeərɪ/ *n* caseificio *m*; (*shop*) latteria *f*. **~ cow** *n* mucca *f* da latte. **~ products** *npl* latticini *mpl*
daisy /ˈdeɪzɪ/ *n* margheritina *f*; (*larger*) margherita *f*
dam /dæm/ *n* diga *f* ● *vt* (*pt/pp* **dammed**) costruire una diga su
damag|e /ˈdæmɪdʒ/ *n* danno *m* (**to** a); **~es** *pl* (*Jur*) risarcimento *msg* ● *vt* danneggiare; *fig* nuocere a. **~ing** *adj* dannoso
dame /deɪm/ *n liter* dama *f*; *Am* [✖] donna *f*
damn /dæm/ *adj* [!] maledetto ● *adv* (lucky, late) maledettamente ● *n* **I don't give a ~** [!] non me ne frega un accidente ● *vt* dannare. **~ation** *n* dannazione *f* ● *int* [!] accidenti!
damp /dæmp/ *adj* umido ● *n* umidità *f* ● *vt* inumidire
dance /dɑ:ns/ *n* ballo *m* ● *vt/i* ballare.

~**-hall** *n* sala *f* da ballo. ~ **music** *n* musica *f* da ballo

dancer /ˈdɑːnsə(r)/ *n* ballerino, -a *mf*

dandelion /ˈdændɪlaɪən/ *n* dente *m* di leone

dandruff /ˈdændrʌf/ *n* forfora *f*

Dane /deɪn/ *n* danese *mf*; **Great** ~ danese *m*

danger /ˈdeɪndʒə(r)/ *n* pericolo *m*; **in/out of** ~ in/fuori pericolo. ~**ous** *adj* pericoloso. ~**ously** *adv* pericolosamente; ~**ously ill** in pericolo di vita

dangle /ˈdæŋgl/ *vi* penzolare ● *vt* far penzolare

Danish /ˈdeɪnɪʃ/ *adj & n* danese *m*. ~ **ˈpastry** *n dolce m a base di pasta sfoglia contenente pasta di mandorle, mele ecc*

dare /deə(r)/ *vt/i* osare; (*challenge*) sfidare (**to** a); ~ **[to] do sth** osare fare qcsa; **I** ~ **say!** molto probabilmente! ● *n* sfida *f*. ~**devil** *n* spericolato, -a *mf*

daring /ˈdeərɪŋ/ *adj* audace ● *n* audacia *f*

dark /dɑːk/ *adj* buio; ~ **blue/brown** blu/marrone scuro; **it's getting** ~ sta cominciando a fare buio; ~ **horse** *fig* (*in race, contest*) vincitore *m* imprevisto; (*not much known about*) misterioso *m*; **keep sth** ~ *fig* tenere qcsa nascosto ● *n* **after** ~ col buio; **in the** ~ al buio; **keep sb in the** ~ *fig* tenere qcno all'oscuro

dark|en /ˈdɑːkn/ *vt* oscurare ● *vi* oscurarsi. ~**ness** *n* buio *m*

ˈdark-room *n* camera *f* oscura

darling /ˈdɑːlɪŋ/ *adj* adorabile; **my** ~ **Joan** carissima Joan ● *n* tesoro *m*

darn /dɑːn/ *vt* rammendare. ~**ing-needle** *n* ago *m* da rammendo

dart /dɑːt/ *n* dardo *m*; (*in sewing*) pince *f inv*; ~**s** *sg* (*game*) freccette *fpl* ● *vi* lanciarsi

dartboard /ˈdɑːtbɔːd/ *n* bersaglio *m* [per freccette]

dash /dæʃ/ *n* (*Typ*) trattino *m*; (*in Morse*) linea *f*; **a** ~ **of milk** un goccio di latte; **make a** ~ **for** lanciarsi verso ● *vi* **I must** ~ devo scappare ● *vt* far svanire (hopes). □ ~ **off** *vi* scappar via ● *vt* (*write quickly*) buttare giù. □ ~ **out** *vi* uscire di corsa

ˈdashboard *n* cruscotto *m*

data /ˈdeɪtə/ *npl & sg* dati *mpl*. ~**base** *n* base [di] dati *f*, database *m inv*. ~**comms** *n* telematica *f*. ~ **processing** *n* elaborazione *f* [di] dati

date[1] /deɪt/ *n* (*fruit*) dattero *m*

date[2] *n* data *f*; (*meeting*) appuntamento *m*; **to** ~ fino ad oggi; **out of** ~ (*not fashionable*) fuori moda; (*expired*) scaduto; (information) non aggiornato; **make a** ~ **with sb** dare un appuntamento a qcno; **be up to** ~ essere aggiornato ● *vt/i* datare; (*go out with*) uscire con. □ ~ **back to** *vi* risalire a

dated /ˈdeɪtɪd/ *adj* fuori moda; (language) antiquato

daub /dɔːb/ *vt* imbrattare (walls)

daughter /ˈdɔːtə(r)/ *n* figlia *f*. ~**-in-law** *n* (*pl* ~**s-in-law**) nuora *f*

dawdle /ˈdɔːdl/ *vi* bighellonare; (*over work*) cincischiarsi

dawn /dɔːn/ *n* alba *f*; **at** ~ all'alba ● *vi* albeggiare; **it** ~**ed on me** *fig* mi è apparso chiaro

day /deɪ/ *n* giorno *m*; (*whole day*) giornata *f*; (*period*) epoca *f*; **these** ~**s** oggigiorno; **in those** ~**s** a quei tempi; **it's had its** ~ [!] ha fatto il suo tempo

day: ~**break** *n* **at** ~**break** allo spuntar del giorno. ~**-dream** *n* sogno *m* ad occhi aperti ● *vi* sognare ad occhi aperti. ~**light** *n* luce *f* del giorno. ~**time** *n* giorno *m*; **in the** ~**time** di giorno

daze /deɪz/ *n* **in a** ~ stordito; *fig* sbalordito. ~**d** *adj* stordito; *fig* sbalordito

dazzle /ˈdæzl/ *vt* abbagliare

dead /ded/ *adj* morto; (*numb*) intorpidito; ~ **body** morto *m*; ~ **centre** pieno centro *m* ● *adv* ~ **tired** stanco morto; ~ **slow/easy** lentissimo/facilissimo; **you're** ~ **right** hai perfettamente ragione; **stop** ~ fermarsi di colpo; **be** ~ **on time** essere in perfetto orario ● *n* **the** ~ *pl* i morti; **in the** ~ **of night** nel cuore della notte

deaden /ˈdedn/ *vt* attutire (sound); calmare (pain)

dead: ~ **ˈend** *n* vicolo *m* cieco. ~**line** *n* scadenza *f*. ~**lock** *n* **reach** ~**lock** *fig* giungere a un punto morto

deadly /ˈdedlɪ/ *adj* (**-ier, -iest**) mortale; ([!]: *dreary*) barboso; ~ **sins** peccati *mpl* capitali

deaf /def/ *adj* sordo; ~ **and dumb** sor-

d

domuto. **~-aid** *n* apparecchio *m* acustico

deaf|en /'defn/ *vt* assordare; (*permanently*) render sordo. **~ening** *adj* assordante. **~ness** *n* sordità *f*

deal /di:l/ *n* (*agreement*) patto *m*; (*in business*) accordo *m*; **whose ~?** (*in cards*) a chi tocca dare le carte?; **a good** *or* **great ~** molto; **get a raw ~** [!] ricevere un trattamento ingiusto ● *vt* (*pt/pp* **dealt** /delt/) (*in cards*) dare; **~ sb a blow** dare un colpo a qcno. □ **~ in** *vt* trattare in. □ **~ out** *vt* (hand out) distribuire. □ **~ with** *vt* (*handle*) occuparsi di; trattare con (company); (*be about*) trattare di; **that's been ~t with** è stato risolto

deal|er /'di:lə(r)/ *n* commerciante *mf*; (*in drugs*) spacciatore, -trice *mf*. **~ings** *npl* **have ~ings with** avere a che fare con

dean /di:n/ *n* decano *m*; (*Univ*) ≈ preside *mf* di facoltà

dear /dɪə(r)/ *adj* caro; (*in letter*) Caro; (*formal*) Gentile ● *n* caro, -a *mf* ● *int* **oh ~!** Dio mio!. **~ly** *adv* (love) profondamente; (pay) profumatamente

death /deθ/ *n* morte *f*. **~ certificate** *n* certificato *m* di morte. **~ duty** *n* tassa *f* di successione

death trap *n* trappola *f* mortale

debatable /dɪ'beɪtəbl/ *adj* discutibile

debate /dɪ'beɪt/ *n* dibattito *m* ● *vt* discutere; (*in formal debate*) dibattere ● *vi* **~ whether to...** considerare se...

debauchery /dɪ'bɔ:tʃərɪ/ *n* dissolutezza *f*

debit /'debɪt/ *n* debito *m* ● *vt* (*pt/pp* **debited**) (*Comm*) addebitare (sum)

debris /'debri:/ *n* macerie *fpl*

debt /det/ *n* debito *m*; **be in ~** avere dei debiti. **~or** *n* debitore, -trice *mf*

decade /'dekeɪd/ *n* decennio *m*

decaden|ce /'dekədəns/ *n* decadenza *f*. **~t** *adj* decadente

decay /dɪ'keɪ/ *n* (*also fig*) decadenza *f*; (*rot*) decomposizione *f*; (*of tooth*) carie *f inv* ● *vi* imputridire; (*rot*) decomporsi; (tooth:) cariarsi

deceased /dɪ'si:st/ *adj* defunto ● *n* **the ~d** il defunto; la defunta

deceit /dɪ'si:t/ *n* inganno *m*. **~ful** *adj* falso

deceive /dɪ'si:v/ *vt* ingannare

December /dɪ'sembə(r)/ *n* dicembre *m*

decency /'di:sənsɪ/ *n* decenza *f*

decent /'di:sənt/ *adj* decente; (*respectable*) rispettabile; **very ~ of you** molto gentile da parte tua. **~ly** *adv* decentemente; (*kindly*) gentilmente

decept|ion /dɪ'sepʃn/ *n* inganno *m*. **~ive** *adj* ingannevole. **~ively** *adv* ingannevolmente; **it looks ~ively easy** sembra facile, ma non lo è

decibel /'desɪbel/ *n* decibel *m inv*

decide /dɪ'saɪd/ *vt* decidere ● *vi* decidere (**on** di)

decided /dɪ'saɪdɪd/ *adj* risoluto. **~ly** *adv* risolutamente; (*without doubt*) senza dubbio

decimal /'desɪml/ *adj* decimale ● *n* numero *m* decimale. **~ 'point** *n* virgola *f*

decipher /dɪ'saɪfə(r)/ *vt* decifrare

decision /dɪ'sɪʒn/ *n* decisione *f*

decisive /dɪ'saɪsɪv/ *adj* decisivo

deck¹ /dek/ *vt* abbigliare

deck² *n* (*Naut*) ponte *m*; **on ~** in coperta; **top ~** (*of bus*) piano *m* di sopra; **~ of cards** mazzo *m*. **~-chair** *n* [sedia *f* a] sdraio *f inv*

declaration /deklə'reɪʃn/ *n* dichiarazione *f*

declare /dɪ'kleə(r)/ *vt* dichiarare; **anything to ~?** niente da dichiarare?

decline /dɪ'klaɪn/ *n* declino *m* ● *vt also* (*Gram*) declinare ● *vi* (*decrease*) diminuire; (health:) deperire; (*say no*) rifiutare

decode /di:'kəʊd/ *vt* decifrare; (*Comput*) decodificare

decompose /di:kəm'pəʊz/ *vi* decomporsi

décor /'deɪkɔ:(r)/ *n* decorazione *f*; (*including furniture*) arredamento *m*

decorat|e /'dekəreɪt/ *vt* decorare; (*paint*) pitturare; (*wallpaper*) tappezzare. **~ion** *n* decorazione *f*. **~ive** *adj* decorativo. **~or** *n* **painter and ~or** imbianchino *m*

decoy¹ /'di:kɔɪ/ *n* esca *f*

decoy² /dɪ'kɔɪ/ *vt* adescare

decrease¹ /'di:kri:s/ *n* diminuzione *f*

decrease² /dɪ'kri:s/ *vt/i* diminuire

decree /dɪ'kri:/ *n* decreto *m* ● *vt* (*pt/pp* **decreed**) decretare

decrepit /dɪ'krepɪt/ *adj* decrepito
dedicat|e /'dedɪkeɪt/ *vt* dedicare. **~ed** *adj* (person) scrupoloso. **~ion** *n* dedizione *f*; (*in book*) dedica *f*
deduce /dɪ'dju:s/ *vt* dedurre (**from** da)
deduct /dɪ'dʌkt/ *vt* dedurre
deduction /dɪ'dʌkʃn/ *n* deduzione *f*
deed /di:d/ *n* azione *f*; (*Jur*) atto *m* di proprietà
deem /di:m/ *vt* ritenere
deep /di:p/ *adj* profondo; **go off the ~ end** [!] arrabbiarsi
deepen /'di:pn/ *vt* approfondire; scavare più profondamente (trench) ● *vi* approfondirsi; (fig: mystery:) infittirsi
deep-'freeze *n* congelatore *m*
deeply /'di:plɪ /*adv* profondamente
deer /dɪə(r)/ *n inv* cervo *m*
deface /dɪ'feɪs/ *vt* sfigurare (picture); deturpare (monument)
default /dɪ'fɔ:lt/ *n* (*non-payment*) morosità *f*; (*failure to appear*) contumacia *f*; **win by ~** (*Sport*) vincere per abbandono dell'avversario; **in ~ of** per mancanza di ● *adj* **~ drive** (*Comput*) lettore *m* di default ● *vi* (*not pay*) venir meno a un pagamento
defeat /dɪ'fi:t/ *n* sconfitta *f* ● *vt* sconfiggere; (*frustrate*) vanificare (attempts); **that ~s the object** questo fa fallire l'obiettivo
defect¹ /dɪ'fekt/ *vi* (*Pol*) fare defezione
defect² /'di:fekt/ *n* difetto *m*. **~ive** *adj* difettoso
defence /dɪ'fens/ *n* difesa *f*. **~less** *adj* indifeso
defend /dɪ'fend/ *vt* difendere; (*justify*) giustificare. **~ant** *n* (*Jur*) imputato, -a *mf*
defensive /dɪ'fensɪv/ *adj* difensivo ● *n* difensiva *f*; **on the ~** sulla difensiva
defer /dɪ'fɜ:(r)/ *v* (*pt/pp* **deferred**) ● *vt* (*postpone*) rinviare ● *vi* **~ to sb** rimettersi a qcno
deferen|ce /'defərəns/ *n* deferenza *f*. **~tial** *adj* deferente
defian|ce /dɪ'faɪəns/ *n* sfida *f*; **in ~ce of** sfidando. **~t** *adj* (person) ribelle; (gesture, attitude) di sfida. **~tly** *adv* con aria di sfida
deficien|cy /dɪ'fɪʃənsɪ/ *n* insufficienza *f*. **~t** *adj* insufficiente; **be ~t in** mancare di
deficit /'defɪsɪt/ *n* deficit *m inv*
define /dɪ'faɪn/ *vt* definire
definite /'defɪnɪt/ *adj* definito; (*certain*) (answer, yes) definitivo; (improvement, difference) netto; **he was ~ about it** è stato chiaro in proposito. **~ly** *adv* sicuramente
definition /defɪ'nɪʃn/ *n* definizione *f*
definitive /dɪ'fɪnətɪv/ *adj* definitivo
deflat|e /dɪ'fleɪt/ *vt* sgonfiare. **~ion** *n* (*Comm*) deflazione *f*
deflect /dɪ'flekt/ *vt* deflettere
deform|ed /dɪ'fɔ:md/ *adj* deforme. **~ity** *n* deformità *f inv*
defrost /di:'frɒst/ *vt* sbrinare (fridge); scongelare (food)
deft /deft/ *adj* abile
defuse /di:'fju:z/ *vt* disinnescare; calmare (situation)
defy /dɪ'faɪ/ *vt* (*pt/pp* **-ied**) (*challenge*) sfidare; resistere a (attempt); (*not obey*) disobbedire a
degenerate¹ /dɪ'dʒenəreɪt/ *vi* degenerare; **~ into** *fig* degenerare in
degenerate² /dɪ'dʒenərət/ *adj* degenerato
degree /dɪ'gri:/ *n* grado *m*; (*Univ*) laurea *f*; **20 ~s** 20 gradi; **not to the same ~** non allo stesso livello
deign /deɪn/ *vi* **~ to do sth** degnarsi di fare qcsa
deity /'di:ɪtɪ/ *n* divinità *f inv*
dejected /dɪ'dʒektɪd/ *adj* demoralizzato
delay /dɪ'leɪ/ *n* ritardo *m*; **without ~** senza indugio ● *vt* ritardare; **be ~ed** (person:) essere trattenuto; (train, aircraft:) essere in ritardo ● *vi* indugiare
delegate¹ /'delɪgət/ *n* delegato, -a *mf*
delegat|e² /'delɪgeɪt/ *vt* delegare. **~ion** *n* delegazione *f*
delet|e /dɪ'li:t/ *vt* cancellare. **~ion** *n* cancellatura *f*
deliberate¹ /dɪ'lɪbərət/ *adj* deliberato; (*slow*) posato. **~ly** *adv* deliberatamente; (*slowly*) in modo posato
deliberat|e² /dɪ'lɪbəreɪt/ *vt/i* deliberare. **~ion** *n* deliberazione *f*
delicacy /'delɪkəsɪ/ *n* delicatezza *f*; (*food*) prelibatezza *f*
delicate /'delɪkət/ *adj* delicato
delicatessen /delɪkə'tesn/ *n* negozio *m* di specialità gastronomiche

delicious /dɪˈlɪʃəs/ *adj* delizioso

delight /dɪˈlaɪt/ *n* piacere *m* ● *vt* deliziare ● *vi* ~ **in** dilettarsi con. **~ed** *adj* lieto. **~ful** *adj* delizioso

deli|rious /dɪˈlɪrɪəs/ *adj* **be ~rious** delirare; (*fig: very happy*) essere pazzo di gioia. **~rium** *n* delirio *m*

deliver /dɪˈlɪvə(r)/ *vt* consegnare; recapitare (post, newspaper); tenere (speech); dare (message); tirare (blow); (*set free*) liberare; **~ a baby** far nascere un bambino. **~ance** *n* liberazione *f*. **~y** *n* consegna *f*; (*of post*) distribuzione *f*; (*Med*) parto *m*; **cash on ~y** pagamento *m* alla consegna

delude /dɪˈluːd/ *vt* ingannare; **~ oneself** illudersi

deluge /ˈdeljuːdʒ/ *n* diluvio *m* ● *vt* (*fig: with requests etc*) inondare

delusion /dɪˈluːʒn/ *n* illusione *f*

de luxe /dəˈlʌks/ *adj* di lusso

delve /delv/ *vi* **~ into** (*into pocket etc*) frugare in; (*into notes, the past*) fare ricerche in

demand /dɪˈmɑːnd/ *n* richiesta *f*; (*Comm*) domanda *f*; **in ~** richiesto; **on ~** a richiesta ● *vt* esigere (**of/from** da). **~ing** *adj* esigente

demented /dɪˈmentɪd/ *adj* demente

demister /diːˈmɪstə(r)/ *n* (*Auto*) sbrinatore *m*

demo /ˈdeməʊ/ *n* (*pl* **~s**) [!] manifestazione *f*; **~ disk** (*Comput*) demodisk *m inv*

democracy /dɪˈmɒkrəsɪ/ *n* democrazia *f*

democrat /ˈdeməkræt/ *n* democratico, -a *mf*. **~ic** *adj* democratico

demo|lish /dɪˈmɒlɪʃ/ *vt* demolire. **~lition** *n* demolizione *f*

demon /ˈdiːmən/ *n* demonio *m*

demonstrat|e /ˈdemənstreɪt/ *vt* dimostrare; fare una dimostrazione sull'uso di (appliance) ● *vi* (*Pol*) manifestare. **~ion** *n* dimostrazione *f*; (*Pol*) manifestazione *f*

demonstrator /ˈdemənstreɪtə(r)/ *n* (*Pol*) manifestante *mf*; (*for product*) dimostratore, -trice *mf*

demoralize /dɪˈmɒrəlaɪz/ *vt* demoralizzare

demote /dɪˈməʊt/ *vt* retrocedere di grado; (*Mil*) degradare

demure /dɪˈmjʊə(r)/ *adj* schivo

den /den/ *n* tana *f*; (*room*) rifugio *m*

denial /dɪˈnaɪəl/ *n* smentita *f*

denim /ˈdenɪm/ *n* [tessuto *m*] jeans *m*; **~s** *pl* [blue]jeans *mpl*

Denmark /ˈdenmɑːk/ *n* Danimarca *f*

denounce /dɪˈnaʊns/ *vt* denunciare

dens|e /dens/ *adj* denso; (crowd, forest) fitto; (*stupid*) ottuso. **~ely** *adv* (populated) densamente; **~ely wooded** fittamente ricoperto di alberi. **~ity** *n* densità *f inv*; (*of forest*) fittezza *f*

dent /dent/ *n* ammaccatura *f* ● *vt* ammaccare; **~ed** *adj* ammaccato

dental /ˈdentl/ *adj* dei denti; (treatment) dentistico; (hygiene) dentale. **~ surgeon** *n* odontoiatra *mf*, medico *m* dentista

dentist /ˈdentɪst/ *n* dentista *mf*. **~ry** *n* odontoiatria *f*

dentures /ˈdentʃəz/ *npl* dentiera *fsg*

deny /dɪˈnaɪ/ *vt* (*pt/pp* **-ied**) negare; (*officially*) smentire; **~ sb sth** negare qcsa a qcno

deodorant /diːˈəʊdərənt/ *n* deodorante *m*

depart /dɪˈpɑːt/ *vi* (plane, train:) partire; (liter: person) andare via; (*deviate*) allontanarsi (**from** da)

department /dɪˈpɑːtmənt/ *n* reparto *m*; (*Pol*) ministero *m*; (*of company*) sezione *f*; (*Univ*) dipartimento *m*. **~ store** *n* grande magazzino *m*

departure /dɪˈpɑːtʃə(r)/ *n* partenza *f*; (*from rule*) allontanamento *m*; **new ~** svolta *f*

depend /dɪˈpend/ *vi* dipendere (**on** da); (*rely*) contare (**on** su); **it all ~s** dipende; **~ing on what he says** a seconda di quello che dice. **~able** *adj* fidato. **~ant** *n* persona *f* a carico. **~ence** *n* dipendenza *f*. **~ent** *adj* dipendente (**on** da)

depict /dɪˈpɪkt/ *vt* (*in writing*) dipingere; (*with picture*) rappresentare

deplete /dɪˈpliːt/ *vt* ridurre; **totally ~d** completamente esaurito

deplor|able /dɪˈplɔːrəbl/ *adj* deplorevole. **~e** *vt* deplorare

deploy /dɪˈplɔɪ/ *vt* (*Mil*) spiegare ● *vi* schierarsi

deport /dɪˈpɔːt/ *vt* deportare. **~ation** *n* deportazione *f*

depose /dɪ'pəʊz/ *vt* deporre

deposit /dɪ'pɒzɪt/ *n* deposito *m*; (*against damage*) cauzione *f*; (*first instalment*) acconto *m* ● *vt* (*pt/pp* **deposited**) depositare. ~ **account** *n* libretto *m* di risparmio; (*without instant access*) conto *m* vincolato

depot /'depəʊ/ *n* deposito *m*; *Am* (*Rail*) stazione *f* ferroviaria

depress /dɪ'pres/ *vt* deprimere; (*press down*) premere. **~ed** *adj* depresso; **~ed area** zona *f* depressa. **~ing** *adj* deprimente. **~ion** *n* depressione *f*

deprivation /deprɪ'veɪʃn/ *n* privazione *f*

deprive /dɪ'praɪv/ *vt* ~ **sb of sth** privare qcno di qcsa. **~d** *adj* (area, childhood) disagiato

depth /depθ/ *n* profondità *f inv*; **in** ~ (study, analyse) in modo approfondito; **in the ~s of winter** in pieno inverno; **be out of one's** ~ (*in water*) non toccare il fondo; *fig* sentirsi in alto mare

deputize /'depjʊtaɪz/ *vi* ~ **for** fare le veci di

deputy /'depjʊtɪ/ *n* vice *mf*; (*temporary*) sostituto, -a *mf* ● *attrib* ~ **leader** ≈ vicesegretario, -a *mf*; ~ **chairman** vicepresidente *mf*

derail /dɪ'reɪl/ *vt* **be ~ed** (train:) essere deragliato. **~ment** *n* deragliamento *m*

derelict /'derəlɪkt/ *adj* abbandonato

deri|de /dɪ'raɪd/ *vt* deridere. **~sion** *n* derisione *f*

derisory /dɪ'raɪsərɪ/ *adj* (laughter) derisorio; (offer) irrisorio

derivation /derɪ'veɪʃn/ *n* derivazione *f*

derivative /dɪ'rɪvətɪv/ *adj* derivato ● *n* derivato *m*

derive /dɪ'raɪv/ *vt* (*obtain*) derivare; **be ~d from** (word:) derivare da

derogatory /dɪ'rɒgətrɪ/ *adj* (comments) peggiorativo

descend /dɪ'send/ *vi* scendere ● *vt* scendere da; **be ~ed from** discendere da. **~ant** *n* discendente *mf*

descent /dɪ'sent/ *n* discesa *f*; (*lineage*) origine *f*

describe /dɪ'skraɪb/ *vt* descrivere

descrip|tion /dɪ'skrɪpʃn/ *n* descrizione *f*; **they had no help of any ~tion** non hanno avuto proprio nessun aiuto. **~tive** *adj* descrittivo; (*vivid*) vivido

desecrat|e /'desɪkreɪt/ *vt* profanare. **~ion** *n* profanazione *f*

desert¹ /'dezət/ *n* deserto *m* ● *adj* deserto; ~ **island** isola *f* deserta

desert² /dɪ'zɜːt/ *vt* abbandonare ● *vi* disertare. **~ed** *adj* deserto. **~er** *n* (*Mil*) disertore *m*. **~ion** *n* (*Mil*) diserzione *f*; (*of family*) abbandono *m*

deserts /dɪ'zɜːts/ *npl* **get one's just** ~ ottenere ciò che ci si merita

deserv|e /dɪ'zɜːv/ *vt* meritare. **~ing** *adj* meritevole; **~ing cause** opera *f* meritoria

design /dɪ'zaɪn/ *n* progettazione *f*; (*fashion ~, appearance*) design *m inv*; (*pattern*) modello *m*; (*aim*) proposito *m* ● *vt* progettare; disegnare (clothes, furniture, model); **be ~ed for** essere fatto per

designat|e /'dezɪgneɪt/ *vt* designare. **~ion** *n* designazione *f*

designer /dɪ'zaɪnə(r)/ *n* progettista *mf*; (*of clothes*) stilista *mf*; (*Theat: of set*) scenografo, -a *mf*

desirable /dɪ'zaɪərəbl/ *adj* desiderabile

desire /dɪ'zaɪə(r)/ *n* desiderio *m* ● *vt* desiderare

desk /desk/ *n* scrivania *f*; (*in school*) banco *m*; (*in hotel*) reception *f inv*; (*cash* ~) cassa *f*. **~top 'publishing** *n* desktop publishing *m*, editoria *f* da tavolo

desolat|e /'desələt/ *adj* desolato. **~ion** *n* desolazione *f*

despair /dɪ'speə(r)/ *n* disperazione *f*; **in** ~ disperato; (say) per disperazione ● *vi* **I** ~ **of that boy** quel ragazzo mi fa disperare

desperat|e /'despərət/ *adj* disperato; **be ~e** (criminal:) essere un disperato; **be ~e for sth** morire dalla voglia di. **~ely** *adv* disperatamente; **he said ~ely** ha detto, disperato. **~ion** *n* disperazione *f*; **in ~ion** per disperazione

despicable /dɪ'spɪkəbl/ *adj* disprezzevole

despise /dɪ'spaɪz/ *vt* disprezzare

despite /dɪ'spaɪt/ *prep* malgrado

despondent /dɪ'spɒndənt/ *adj* abbattuto

despot /'despɒt/ *n* despota *m*

d

dessert /dɪ'zɜːt/ *n* dolce *m*. **~ spoon** *n* cucchiaio *m* da dolce

destination /destɪ'neɪʃn/ *n* destinazione *f*

destiny /'destɪnɪ/ *n* destino *m*

destitute /'destɪtjuːt/ *adj* bisognoso

destroy /dɪ'strɔɪ/ *vt* distruggere. **~er** *n* (*Naut*) cacciatorpediniere *m*

destruc|tion /dɪ'strʌkʃn/ *n* distruzione *f*. **~tive** *adj* distruttivo; (fig: criticism) negativo

detach /dɪ'tætʃ/ *vt* staccare. **~able** *adj* separabile. **~ed** *adj fig* distaccato; **~ed house** villetta *f*

detachment /dɪ'tætʃmənt/ *n* distacco *m*; (*Mil*) distaccamento *m*

detail /'diːteɪl/ *n* particolare *m*, dettaglio *m*; **in ~** particolareggiatamente ● *vt* esporre con tutti i particolari; (*Mil*) assegnare. **~ed** *adj* particolareggiato, dettagliato

detain /dɪ'teɪn/ *vt* (police:) trattenere; (*delay*) far ritardare. **~ee** *n* detenuto, -a *mf*

detect /dɪ'tekt/ *vt* individuare; (*perceive*) percepire. **~ion** *n* scoperta *f*

detective /dɪ'tektɪv/ *n* investigatore, -trice *mf*. **~ story** *n* racconto *m* poliziesco

detector /dɪ'tektə(r)/ *n* (*for metal*) metal detector *m inv*

detention /dɪ'tenʃn/ *n* detenzione *f*; (*Sch*) punizione *f*

deter /dɪ'tɜː(r)/ *vt* (*pt/pp* **deterred**) impedire; **~ sb from doing sth** impedire a qcno di fare qcsa

detergent /dɪ'tɜːdʒənt/ *n* detersivo *m*

deteriorat|e /dɪ'tɪərɪəreɪt/ *vi* deteriorarsi. **~ion** *n* deterioramento *m*

determination /dɪtɜːmɪ'neɪʃn/ *n* determinazione *f*

determine /dɪ'tɜːmɪn/ *vt* (*ascertain*) determinare; **~ to** (*resolve*) decidere di. **~d** *adj* deciso

deterrent /dɪ'terənt/ *n* deterrente *m*

detest /dɪ'test/ *vt* detestare. **~able** *adj* detestabile

detonat|e /'detəneɪt/ *vt* far detonare ● *vi* detonare. **~or** *n* detonatore *m*

detour /'diːtʊə(r)/ *n* deviazione *f*

detract /dɪ'trækt/ *vi* **~ from** sminuire (merit); rovinare (pleasure, beauty)

detriment /'detrɪmənt/ *n* **to the ~ of** a danno di. **~al** *adj* dannoso

de'value *vt* svalutare (currency)

devastat|e /'devəsteɪt/ *vt* devastare. **~ed** *adj* [!] sconvolto. **~ing** *adj* devastante; (news) sconvolgente. **~ion** *n* devastazione *f*

develop /dɪ'veləp/ *vt* sviluppare; contrarre (illness); (*add to value of*) valorizzare (area) ● *vi* svilupparsi; **~ into** divenire. **~er** *n* **[property] ~er** imprenditore, -trice *mf* edile

development /dɪ'veləpmənt/ *n* sviluppo *m*; (*of vaccine etc*) messa *f* a punto

deviant /'diːvɪənt/ *adj* deviato

deviat|e /'diːvɪeɪt/ *vi* deviare. **~ion** *n* deviazione *f*

device /dɪ'vaɪs/ *n* dispositivo *m*

devil /'devl/ *n* diavolo *m*

devious /'diːvɪəs/ *adj* (person) subdolo; (route) tortuoso

devise /dɪ'vaɪz/ *vt* escogitare

devoid /dɪ'vɔɪd/ *adj* **~ of** privo di

devolution /diːvə'luːʃn/ *n* (*of power*) decentramento *m*

devot|e /dɪ'vəʊt/ *vt* dedicare. **~ed** *adj* (daughter etc) affezionato; **be ~ed to sth** consacrarsi a qcsa. **~ee** *n* appassionato, -a *mf*

devotion /dɪ'vəʊʃn/ *n* dedizione *f*; **~s** *pl* (*Relig*) devozione *fsg*

devour /dɪ'vaʊə(r)/ *vt* divorare

devout /dɪ'vaʊt/ *adj* devoto

dew /djuː/ *n* rugiada *f*

dexterity /dek'sterətɪ/ *n* destrezza *f*

diabet|es /daɪə'biːtiːz/ *n* diabete *m*. **~ic** *adj* diabetico ● *n* diabetico, -a *mf*

diabolical /daɪə'bɒlɪkl/ *adj* diabolico

diagnose /daɪəg'nəʊz/ *vt* diagnosticare

diagnosis /daɪəg'nəʊsɪs/ *n* (*pl* **-oses** /-siːz/) diagnosi *f inv*

diagonal /daɪ'ægənl/ *adj* diagonale ● *n* diagonale *f*

diagram /'daɪəgræm/ *n* diagramma *m*

dial /'daɪəl/ *n* (*of clock, machine*) quadrante *m*; (*Teleph*) disco *m* combinatore ● *v* (*pt/pp* **dialled**) ● *vi* (*Teleph*) fare il numero; **~ direct** chiamare in teleselezione ● *vt* fare (number)

dialect /'daɪəlekt/ *n* dialetto *m*

dialling: ~ code *n* prefisso *m*. **~**

tone *n* segnale *m* di linea libera
dialogue /ˈdaɪəlɒg/ *n* dialogo *m*
ˈ**dial tone** *n Am* (*Teleph*) segnale *m* di linea libera
diameter /daɪˈæmɪtə(r)/ *n* diametro *m*
diamond /ˈdaɪəmənd/ *n* diamante *m*, brillante *m*; (*shape*) losanga *f*; **~s** *pl* (*in cards*) quadri *mpl*
diaper /ˈdaɪəpə(r)/ *n Am* pannolino *m*
diaphragm /ˈdaɪəfræm/ *n* diaframma *m*
diarrhoea /daɪəˈri:ə/ *n* diarrea *f*
diary /ˈdaɪərɪ/ *n* (*for appointments*) agenda *f*; (*for writing in*) diario *m*
dice /daɪs/ *n inv* dadi *mpl* ● *vt* (*Culin*) tagliare a dadini
dictat|e /dɪkˈteɪt/ *vt/i* dettare. **~ion** *n* dettato *m*
dictator /dɪkˈteɪtə(r)/ *n* dittatore *m*. **~ial** *adj* dittatoriale. **~ship** *n* dittatura *f*
dictionary /ˈdɪkʃənrɪ/ *n* dizionario *m*
did /dɪd/ ⊳**DO**
didn't /ˈdɪdnt/ = **did not**
die /daɪ/ *vi* (*pres p* **dying**) morire (**of** di); **be dying to do sth** [!] morire dalla voglia di fare qcsa. □ **~ down** *vi* calmarsi; (fire, flames:) spegnersi. □ **~ out** *vi* estinguersi; (custom:) morire
diesel /ˈdi:zl/ *n* diesel *m*
diet /ˈdaɪət/ *n* regime *m* alimentare; (*restricted*) dieta *f*; **be on a ~** essere a dieta ● *vi* essere a dieta
differ /ˈdɪfə(r)/ *vi* differire; (*disagree*) non essere d'accordo
difference /ˈdɪfrəns/ *n* differenza *f*; (*disagreement*) divergenza *f*
different /ˈdɪfrənt/ *adj* diverso, differente; (*various*) diversi; **be ~ from** essere diverso da
differently /ˈdɪfrəntlɪ/ *adv* in modo diverso; **~ from** diversamente da
difficult /ˈdɪfɪkəlt/ *adj* difficile. **~y** *n* difficoltà *f inv*
diffuse[1] /dɪˈfju:s/ *adj* diffuso; (*wordy*) prolisso
diffuse[2] /dɪˈfju:z/ *vt* (*Phys*) diffondere
dig /dɪg/ *n* (*poke*) spinta *f*; (*remark*) frecciata *f*; (*Archaeol*) scavo *m*; **~s** *pl* [!] camera *fsg* ammobiliata ● *vt/i* (*pt/pp* **dug**, *pres p* **digging**) scavare (hole); vangare (garden); (*thrust*) conficcare; **~ sb in the ribs** dare una gomitata a qcno. □ **~ out** *vt fig* tirar fuori. □ **~ up** *vt* scavare (garden, street, object); sradicare (plant); (*fig: find*) scovare
digest[1] /ˈdaɪdʒest/ *n* compendio *m*
digest[2] /daɪˈdʒest/ *vt* digerire. **~ible** *adj* digeribile. **~ion** *n* digestione *f*
digger /ˈdɪgə(r)/ *n* (*Techn*) scavatrice *f*
digit /ˈdɪdʒɪt/ *n* cifra *f*; (*finger*) dito *m*
digital /ˈdɪdʒɪtl/ *adj* digitale; **~ camera** fotocamera *f* digitale. **~ clock** orologio *m* digitale
digitize /ˈdɪdʒɪtaɪz/ *vt* digitalizzare
dignified /ˈdɪgnɪfaɪd/ *adj* dignitoso
dignitary /ˈdɪgnɪtərɪ/ *n* dignitario *m*
dignity /ˈdɪgnɪtɪ/ *n* dignità *f*
digress /daɪˈgres/ *vi* divagare. **~ion** *n* digressione *f*
dike /daɪk/ *n* diga *f*
dilapidated /dɪˈlæpɪdeɪtɪd/ *adj* cadente
dilate /daɪˈleɪt/ *vi* dilatarsi
dilemma /dɪˈlemə/ *n* dilemma *m*
dilute /daɪˈlu:t/ *vt* diluire
dim /dɪm/ *adj* (**dimmer, dimmest**) debole (light); (*dark*) scuro; (prospect, chance) scarso; (*indistinct*) impreciso; ([!]: *stupid*) tonto ● *vt/i* (*pt/pp* **dimmed**) affievolire. **~ly** *adv* (see, remember) indistintamente; (shine) debolmente
dime /daɪm/ *n Am* moneta *f* da dieci centesimi
dimension /daɪˈmenʃn/ *n* dimensione *f*
diminish /dɪˈmɪnɪʃ/ *vt/i* diminuire
dimple /ˈdɪmpl/ *n* fossetta *f*
din /dɪn/ *n* baccano *m*
dine /daɪn/ *vi* pranzare. **~r** *n* (*Am: restaurant*) tavola *f* calda; **the last ~r in the restaurant** l'ultimo cliente nel ristorante
dinghy /ˈdɪŋgɪ/ *n* dinghy *m*; (*inflatable*) canotto *m* pneumatico
dingy /ˈdɪndʒɪ/ *adj* (**-ier, -iest**) squallido e tetro
dinner /ˈdɪnə(r)/ *n* cena *f*; (*at midday*) pranzo *m*. **~-jacket** *n* smoking *m inv*
dinosaur /ˈdaɪnəsɔ:(r)/ *n* dinosauro *m*
dint /dɪnt/ *n* **by ~ of** a forza di
dip /dɪp/ *n* (*in ground*) inclinazione *f*; (*Culin*) salsina *f*; **go for a ~** andare a fare una nuotata ● *v* (*pt/pp* **dipped**) ● *vt* (*in liquid*) immergere; abbassare

(head, headlights) ● *vi* (land:) formare un avvallamento. □ ~ **into** *vt* scorrere (book)

diphthong /ˈdɪfθɒŋ/ *n* dittongo *m*

diploma /dɪˈpləʊmə/ *n* diploma *m*

diplomacy /dɪˈpləʊməsɪ/ *n* diplomazia *f*

diplomat /ˈdɪpləmæt/ *n* diplomatico, -a *mf*. **~ic** *adj* diplomatico. **~ically** *adv* con diplomazia

ˈdip-stick *n* (*Auto*) astina *f* dell'olio

dire /ˈdaɪə(r)/ *adj* (situation, consequences) terribile

direct /dɪˈrekt/ *adj* diretto ● *adv* direttamente ● *vt* (*aim*) rivolgere (attention, criticism); (*control*) dirigere; fare la regia di (film, play); ~ **sb** (*show the way*) indicare la strada a qcno; ~ **sb to do sth** ordinare a qcno di fare qcsa. ~ **ˈcurrent** *n* corrente *m* continua

direction /dɪˈrekʃn/ *n* direzione *f*; (*of play, film*) regia *f*; **~s** *pl* indicazioni *fpl*

directly /dɪˈrektlɪ/ *adv* direttamente; (*at once*) immediatamente ● *conj* [non] appena

director /dɪˈrektə(r)/ *n* (*Comm*) direttore, -trice *mf*; (*of play, film*) regista *mf*

directory /dɪˈrektərɪ/ *n* elenco *m*; (*Teleph*) elenco *m* [telefonico]; (*of streets*) stradario *m*

dirt /dɜːt/ *n* sporco *m*; ~ **cheap** [!] a [un] prezzo stracciato

dirty /ˈdɜːtɪ/ *adj* (**-ier, -iest**) sporco; ~ **trick** brutto scherzo *m*; ~ **word** parolaccia *f* ● *vt* (*pt/pp* **-ied**) sporcare

dis|aˈbility /dɪs-/ *n* infermità *f inv*. **~abled** *adj* invalido

disadˈvan|tage *n* svantaggio *m*; **at a ~tage** in una posizione di svantaggio. **~taged** *adj* svantaggiato. **~ˈtageous** *adj* svantaggioso

disaˈgree *vi* non essere d'accordo; ~ **with** (food:) far male a

disaˈgreeable *adj* sgradevole

disaˈgreement *n* disaccordo *m*; (*quarrel*) dissidio *m*

disapˈpear *vi* scomparire. **~ance** *n* scomparsa *f*

disapˈpoint *vt* deludere; **I'm ~ed** sono deluso. **~ing** *adj* deludente. **~ment** *n* delusione *f*

disapˈproval *n* disapprovazione *f*

disapˈprove *vi* disapprovare; ~ **of sb/sth** disapprovare qcno/qcsa

disˈarm *vt* disarmare ● *vi* (*Mil*) disarmarsi. **~ament** *n* disarmo *m*. **~ing** *adj* (frankness etc) disarmante

disarˈray *n* **in** ~ in disordine

disast|er /dɪˈzɑːstə(r)/ *n* disastro *m*. **~rous** *adj* disastroso

disˈband *vt* scogliere; smobilitare (troops) ● *vi* scogliersi; (regiment:) essere smobilitato

disbeˈlief *n* incredulità *f*; **in** ~ con incredulità

disc /dɪsk/ *n* disco *m*; (*CD*) compact disc *m inv*

discard /dɪˈskɑːd/ *vt* scartare; (*throw away*) eliminare; scaricare (boyfriend)

discern /dɪˈsɜːn/ *vt* discernere. **~ible** *adj* discernibile. **~ing** *adj* perspicace

ˈdischarge¹ *n* (*Electr*) scarica *f*; (*dismissal*) licenziamento *m*; (*Mil*) congedo *m*; (*Med: of blood*) emissione *f*; (*of cargo*) scarico *m*

disˈcharge² *vt* scaricare (battery, cargo); (*dismiss*) licenziare; (*Mil*) congedare; (*Jur*) assolvere (accused); dimettere (patient) ● *vi* (*Electr*) scaricarsi

disciple /dɪˈsaɪpl/ *n* discepolo *m*

disciplinary /ˈdɪsɪplɪnərɪ/ *adj* disciplinare

discipline /ˈdɪsɪplɪn/ *n* disciplina *f* ● *vt* disciplinare; (*punish*) punire

ˈdisc jockey *n* disc jockey *m inv*

disˈclaim *vt* disconoscere. **~er** *n* rifiuto *m*

disˈclos|e *vt* svelare. **~ure** *n* rivelazione *f*

disco /ˈdɪskəʊ/ *n* discoteca *f*

disˈcolour *vt* scolorire ● *vi* scolorirsi

disˈcomfort *n* scomodità *f*; *fig* disagio *m*

disconcert /dɪskənˈsɜːt/ *vt* sconcertare

disconˈnect *vt* disconnettere

disconsolate /dɪsˈkɒnsələt/ *adj* sconsolato

disconˈtent *n* scontentezza *f*. **~ed** *adj* scontento

disconˈtinue *vt* cessare, smettere; (*Comm*) sospendere la produzione di; **~d line** fine *f* serie

ˈdiscord *n* discordia *f*; (*Mus*) dissonanza *f*. **~ant** *adj* **~ant note** nota *f* discordante

'discount¹ *n* sconto *m*

dis'count² *vt* (*not believe*) non credere a; (*leave out of consideration*) non tener conto di

dis'courage *vt* scoraggiare; (*dissuade*) dissuadere

dis'courteous *adj* scortese

discover /dɪ'skʌvə(r)/ *vt* scoprire. **~y** *n* scoperta *f*

dis'credit *n* discredito *m* ● *vt* (*pt/pp* **discredited**) screditare

discreet /dɪ'skriːt/ *adj* discreto

discrepancy /dɪ'skrepənsɪ/ *n* discrepanza *f*

discretion /dɪ'skreʃn/ *n* discrezione *f*

discriminat|e /dɪ'skrɪmɪneɪt/ *vi* discriminare (**against** contro); **~e between** distinguere tra. **~ing** *adj* esigente. **~ion** *n* discriminazione *f*; (*quality*) discernimento *m*

discus /'dɪskəs/ *n* disco *m*

discuss /dɪ'skʌs/ *vt* discutere; (*examine critically*) esaminare. **~ion** *n* discussione *f*

disdain /dɪs'deɪn/ *n* sdegno *f* ● *vt* sdegnare. **~ful** *adj* sdegnoso

disease /dɪ'ziːz/ *n* malattia *f*. **~d** *adj* malato

disem'bark *vi* sbarcare

disen'tangle *vt* districare

dis'figure *vt* deformare

dis'grace *n* vergogna *f*; **I am in ~** sono caduto in disgrazia; **it's a ~** è una vergogna ● *vt* disonorare. **~ful** *adj* vergognoso

disgruntled /dɪs'grʌntld/ *adj* malcontento

disguise /dɪs'gaɪz/ *n* travestimento *m*; **in ~** travestito ● *vt* contraffare (voice); dissimulare (emotions); **~d as** travestito da

disgust /dɪs'gʌst/ *n* disgusto *m*; **in ~** con aria disgustata ● *vt* disgustare. **~ing** *adj* disgustoso

dish /dɪʃ/ *n* piatto *m*; **do the ~es** lavare i piatti ● **dish out** *vt* (*serve*) servire; (*distribute*) distribuire. □ **~ up** *vt* servire

'dishcloth *n* strofinaccio *m*

dis'honest *adj* disonesto. **~y** *n* disonestà *f*

dis'honour *n* disonore *m* ● *vt* disonorare (family); non onorare (cheque). **~able** *adj* disonorevole. **~ably** *adv* in modo disonorevole

'dishwasher *n* lavapiatti *f inv*

disil'lusion *vt* disilludere. **~ment** *n* disillusione *f*

disin'fect *vt* disinfettare. **~ant** *n* disinfettante *m*

dis'integrate *vi* disintegrarsi

dis'interested *adj* disinteressato

dis'jointed *adj* sconnesso

disk /dɪsk/ *n* (*Comput*) disco *m*; (*diskette*) dischetto *m*

dis'like *n* avversione *f*; **your likes and ~s** i tuoi gusti ● *vt* **I ~ him/it** non mi piace; **I don't ~ him/it** non mi dispiace

dislocate /'dɪsləkeɪt/ *vt* slogare; **~ one's shoulder** slogarsi una spalla

dis'lodge *vt* sloggiare

dis'loyal *adj* sleale. **~ty** *n* slealtà *f*

dismal /'dɪzməl/ *adj* (person) abbacchiato; (news, weather) deprimente; (performance) mediocre

dismantle /dɪs'mæntl/ *vt* smontare (tent, machine); *fig* smantellare

dis'may *n* sgomento *m*. **~ed** *adj* sgomento

dis'miss *vt* licenziare (employee); (*reject*) scartare (idea, suggestion). **~al** *n* licenziamento *m*

dis'mount *vi* smontare

diso'bedien|ce *n* disubbidienza *f*. **~t** *adj* disubbidiente

diso'bey *vt* disubbidire a (rule) ● *vi* disubbidire

dis'order *n* disordine *m*; (*Med*) disturbo *m*. **~ly** *adj* disordinato; (crowd) turbolento; **~ly conduct** turbamento *m* della quiete pubblica

dis'organized *adj* disorganizzato

dis'orientate *vt* disorientare

dis'own *vt* disconoscere

disparaging /dɪ'spærɪdʒɪŋ/ *adj* sprezzante

dispatch /dɪ'spætʃ/ *n* (*Comm*) spedizione *f*; (*Mil, report*) dispaccio *m*; **with ~** con prontezza ● *vt* spedire; (*kill*) spedire al creatore

d

dispel /dɪ'spel/ *vt* (*pt/pp* **dispelled**) dissipare

dispensable /dɪ'spensəbl/ *adj* dispensabile

dispense /dɪ'spens/ *vt* distribuire; ~ **with** fare a meno di; **dispensing chemist** farmacista *mf*; (*shop*) farmacia *f*. ~**r** *n* (*device*) distributore *m*

dispers|al /dɪ'spɜ:sl/ *n* disperzione *f*. ~**e** *vt* disperdere ● *vi* disperdersi

dispirited /dɪ'spɪrɪtɪd/ *adj* scoraggiato

display /dɪ'spleɪ/ *n* mostra *f*; (*Comm*) esposizione *f*; (*of feelings*) manifestazione *f*; *pej* ostentazione *f*; (*Comput*) display *m inv* ● *vt* mostrare; esporre (goods); manifestare (feeling); (*Comput*) visualizzare

dis'please *vt* non piacere a; **be ~d with** essere scontento di

dis'pleasure *n* malcontento *m*

disposable /dɪ'spəʊzəbl/ *adj* (*throw-away*) usa e getta; (income) disponibile

disposal /dɪ'spəʊzl/ *n* (*getting rid of*) eliminazione *f*; **be at sb's ~** essere a disposizione di qcno

disproportionate /dɪsprə'pɔ:ʃənət/ *adj* sproporzionato

dis'prove *vt* confutare

dispute /dɪ'spju:t/ *n* disputa *f*; (*industrial*) contestazione *f* ● *vt* contestare (statement)

disqualifi'cation *n* squalifica *f*; (*from driving*) ritiro *m* della patente

dis'qualify *vt* (*pt/pp* **-ied**) escludere; (*Sport*) squalificare; **~ sb from driving** ritirare la patente a qcno

disre'gard *n* mancanza *f* di considerazione ● *vt* ignorare

dis'reputable *adj* malfamato

disre'spect *n* mancanza *f* di rispetto. ~**ful** *adj* irrispettoso

disrupt /dɪs'rʌpt/ *vt* creare scompiglio in; sconvolgere (plans). ~**ion** *n* scompiglio *m*; (*of plans*) sconvolgimento *m*. ~**ive** *adj* (person, behaviour) indisciplinato

dissatis'faction *n* malcontento *m*

dis'satisfied *adj* scontento

dissect /dɪ'sekt/ *vt* sezionare. ~**ion** *n* dissezione *f*

dissent /dɪ'sent/ *n* dissenso *m* ● *vi* dissentire

dissertation /dɪsə'teɪʃn/ *n* tesi *f inv*

dissident /'dɪsɪdənt/ *n* dissidente *mf*

dis'similar *adj* dissimile (**to** da)

dissolute /'dɪsəlu:t/ *adj* dissoluto

dissolve /dɪ'zɒlv/ *vt* dissolvere ● *vi* dissolversi

dissuade /dɪ'sweɪd/ *vt* dissuadere

distance /'dɪstəns/ *n* distanza *f*; **it's a short ~ from here to the station** la stazione non è lontana da qui; **in the ~** in lontananza; **from a ~** da lontano

distant /'dɪstənt/ *adj* distante; (relative) lontano

dis'taste *n* avversione *f*. ~**ful** *adj* spiacevole

distil /dɪ'stɪl/ *vt* (*pt/pp* **distilled**) distillare. ~**lation** *n* distillazione *f*. ~**lery** *n* distilleria *f*

distinct /dɪ'stɪŋkt/ *adj* chiaro; (*different*) distinto. ~**ion** *n* distinzione *f*; (*Sch*) massimo *m* dei voti. ~**ive** *adj* caratteristico. ~**ly** *adv* chiaramente

distinguish /dɪ'stɪŋgwɪʃ/ *vt/i* distinguere; **~ oneself** distinguersi. ~**ed** *adj* rinomato; (appearance) distinto; (career) brillante

distort /dɪ'stɔ:t/ *vt* distorcere. ~**ion** *n* distorsione *f*

distract /dɪ'strækt/ *vt* distrarre. ~**ed** *adj* assente; ([!]: *worried*) preoccupato. ~**ing** *adj* che distoglie. ~**ion** *n* distrazione *f*; (*despair*) disperazione *f*; **drive sb to ~** portare qcno alla disperazione

distraught /dɪ'strɔ:t/ *adj* sconvolto

distress /dɪ'stres/ *n* angoscia *f*; (*pain*) sofferenza *f*; (*danger*) difficoltà *f* ● *vt* sconvolgere; (*sadden*) affliggere. ~**ing** *adj* penoso; (*shocking*) sconvolgente. **~ signal** *n* segnale *m* di richiesta di soccorso

distribut|e /dɪ'strɪbju:t/ *vt* distribuire. ~**ion** *n* distribuzione *f*. ~**or** *n* distributore *m*

district /'dɪstrɪkt/ *n* regione *f*; (*Admin*) distretto *m*. **~ nurse** *n* infermiere, -a *mf* che fa visite a domicilio

dis'trust *n* sfiducia *f* ● *vt* non fidarsi di. ~**ful** *adj* diffidente

disturb /dɪ'stɜ:b/ *vt* disturbare; (*emotionally*) turbare; spostare (papers).

~ance *n* disturbo *m*; ~ances (*pl: rioting etc*) disordini *mpl*. ~ed *adj* turbato; [mentally] ~ed malato di mente. ~ing *adj* inquietante

dis'used *adj* non utilizzato

ditch /dɪtʃ/ *n* fosso *m* ● *vt* ([!]: *abandon*) abbandonare (plan, car); piantare (lover)

dither /'dɪðə(r)/ *vi* titubare

divan /dɪ'væn/ *n* divano *m*

dive /daɪv/ *n* tuffo *m*; (*Aeron*) picchiata *f*; ([!]: *place*) bettola *f* ● *vi* tuffarsi; (*when in water*) immergersi; (*Aeron*) scendere in picchiata; ([!]: *rush*) precipitarsi

diver /'daɪvə(r)/ *n* (*from board*) tuffatore, -trice *mf*; (*scuba*) sommozzatore, -trice *mf*; (*deep sea*) palombaro *m*

diver|ge /daɪ'vɜ:dʒ/ *vi* divergere. ~**gent** *adj* divergente

diverse /daɪ'vɜ:s/ *adj* vario

diversify /daɪ'vɜ:sɪfaɪ/ *vt/i* (*pt/pp* **-ied**) diversificare

diversion /daɪ'vɜ:ʃn/ *n* deviazione *f*; (*distraction*) diversivo *m*

diversity /daɪ'vɜ:sətɪ/ *n* varietà *f*

divert /daɪ'vɜ:t/ *vt* deviare (traffic); distogliere (attention)

divide /dɪ'vaɪd/ *vt* dividere (**by** per); **six ~d by two** sei diviso due ● *vi* dividersi

dividend /'dɪvɪdend/ *n* dividendo *m*; **pay ~s** *fig* ripagare

divine /dɪ'vaɪn/ *adj* divino

diving /'daɪvɪŋ/ *n* (*from board*) tuffi *mpl*; (*scuba*) immersione *f*. **~-board** *n* trampolino *m*. **~ mask** *n* maschera *f* [subacquea]. **~-suit** *n* muta *f*; (*deep sea*) scafandro *m*

division /dɪ'vɪʒn/ *n* divisione *f*; (*in sports league*) serie *f*

divorce /dɪ'vɔ:s/ *n* divorzio *m* ● *vt* divorziare da. **~d** *adj* divorziato; **get ~d** divorziare

divorcee /dɪvɔ:'si:/ *n* divorziato, -a *mf*

divulge /daɪ'vʌldʒ/ *vt* rendere pubblico

DIY *n abbr* do-it-yourself

dizziness /'dɪzɪnɪs/ *n* giramenti *mpl* di testa

dizzy /'dɪzɪ/ *adj* (**-ier, -iest**) vertiginoso; **I feel ~** mi gira la testa

do¹ /du:/

> ! *3 sing pres tense* **does**; *past tense* **did**; *past participle* **done**

● *vt* fare; ([!]: *cheat*) fregare; **be done** (*Culin*) essere cotto; **well done** bravo; (*Culin*) ben cotto; **do the flowers** sistemare i fiori; **do the washing up** lavare i piatti; **do one's hair** farsi i capelli

● *vi* (*be suitable*) andare; (*be enough*) bastare; **this will do** questo va bene; **that will do!** basta così!; **do well/badly** cavarsela bene/male; **how is he doing?** come sta?

● *v aux* (*used to form questions and negatives; often not translated*) **do you speak Italian?** parli italiano?; **you don't like him, do you?** non ti piace, vero?; (*expressing astonishment*) non dirmi che ti piace!; **yes, I do** sì; (*emphatic*) invece sì; **no, I don't** no; **I don't smoke** non fumo; **don't you/doesn't he?** vero?; **so do I** anch'io; **do come in, John** entra, John; **how do you do?** piacere. □ **~ away with** *vt* abolire (rule). □ **~ for** *vt* **done for** [!] rovinato. □ **~ in** *vt* ([!]: *kill*) uccidere; farsi male a (back); **done in** [!] esausto. □ **~ up** *vt* (*fasten*) abbottonare; (*renovate*) rimettere a nuovo; (*wrap*) avvolgere. □ **~ with** *vt* **I could do with a spanner** mi ci vorrebbe una chiave inglese. □ **~ without** *vt* fare a meno di

do² /du:/ *n* (*pl* **dos** *or* **do's**) [!] festa *f*

docile /'dəʊsaɪl/ *adj* docile

dock¹ /dɒk/ *n* (*Jur*) banco *m* degli imputati

dock² *n* (*Naut*) bacino *m* ● *vi* entrare in porto; (spaceship:) congiungersi. **~er** *n* portuale *m*. **~s** *npl* porto *m*. **~yard** *n* cantiere *m* navale

doctor /'dɒktə(r)/ *n* dottore *m*, dottoressa *f* ● *vt* alterare (drink); castrare (cat). **~ate** *n* dottorato *m*

doctrine /'dɒktrɪn/ *n* dottrina *f*

document /'dɒkjʊmənt/ *n* documento *m*. **~ary** *adj* documentario ● *n* documentario *m*

dodge /dɒdʒ/ *n* [!] trucco *m* ● *vt* schivare (blow); evitare (person) ● *vi* scansarsi; ~ **out of the way** scansarsi

dodgems /'dɒdʒəmz/ *npl* autoscontro *msg*

dodgy /'dɒdʒɪ/ *adj* (**-ier, -iest**) (🄸: *dubious*) sospetto

doe /dəʊ/ *n* femmina *f* (*di daino, renna, lepre*); (*rabbit*) coniglia *f*

d

does /dʌz/ ▷DO

doesn't /'dʌznt/ = **does not**

dog /dɒg/ *n* cane *m* ● *vt* (*pt/pp* **dogged**) (illness, bad luck:) perseguitare

dogged /'dɒgɪd/ *adj* ostinato

'**dog house** *n* **in the** ~ 🄸 in disgrazia

dogma /'dɒgmə/ *n* dogma *m*. ~**tic** *adj* dogmatico

do-it-yourself /du:ɪtjə'self/ *n* fai da te *m*, bricolage *m*. ~ **shop** *n* negozio *m* di bricolage

dole /dəʊl/ *n* sussidio *m* di disoccupazione; **be on the** ~ essere disoccupato ● **dole out** *vt* distribuire

doleful /'dəʊlfl/ *adj* triste

doll /dɒl/ *n* bambola *f* ● **doll oneself up** *vt* 🄸 mettersi in ghingheri

dollar /'dɒlə(r)/ *n* dollaro *m*

dollop /'dɒləp/ *n* 🄸 cucchiaiata *f*

dolphin /'dɒlfɪn/ *n* delfino *m*

dome /dəʊm/ *n* cupola *f*

domestic /də'mestɪk/ *adj* domestico; (*Pol*) interno; (*Comm*) nazionale

domesticated /də'mestɪkeɪtɪd/ *adj* (animal) addomesticato

domestic flight *n* volo *m* nazionale

dominant /'dɒmɪnənt/ *adj* dominante

dominat|e /'dɒmɪneɪt/ *vt/i* dominare. ~**ion** *n* dominio *m*

domineering /dɒmɪ'nɪərɪŋ/ *adj* autoritario

dominion /də'mɪnjən/ *n Br* (*Pol*) dominion *m inv*

donat|e /dəʊ'neɪt/ *vt* donare. ~**ion** *n* donazione *f*

done /dʌn/ ▷DO

donkey /'dɒŋkɪ/ *n* asino *m*; ~**'s years** 🄸 secoli *mpl*. ~**-work** *n* sgobbata *f*

donor /'dəʊnə(r)/ *n* donatore, -trice *mf*

doodle /'du:dl/ *vi* scarabocchiare

doom /du:m/ *n* fato *m*; (*ruin*) rovina *f* ● *vt* **be** ~**ed [to failure]** essere destinato al fallimento; ~**ed** (ship) destinato ad affondare

door /dɔ:(r)/ *n* porta *f*; (*of car*) portiera *f*; **out of** ~**s** all'aperto

door: ~**mat** *n* zerbino *m*. ~**step** *n* gradino *m* della porta. ~**way** *n* vano *m* della porta

dope /dəʊp/ *n* 🄸 (*drug*) droga *f* leggera; (*information*) indiscrezioni *fpl*; (*idiot*) idiota *mf* ● *vt* drogare; (*Sport*) dopare

dormant /'dɔ:mənt/ *adj* latente; (volcano) inattivo

dormitory /'dɔ:mɪtərɪ/ *n* dormitorio *m*

dormouse /'dɔ:-/ *n* ghiro *m*

dosage /'dəʊsɪdʒ/ *n* dosaggio *m*

dose /dəʊs/ *n* dose *f*

dot /dɒt/ *n* punto *m*; **at 8 o'clock on the** ~ alle 8 in punto

dot-com /dɒt'kɒm/ *n* azienda *f* legata a Internet

dote /dəʊt/ *vi* ~ **on** stravedere per

dotty /'dɒtɪ/ *adj* (**-ier, -iest**) 🄸 tocco; (idea) folle

double /'dʌbl/ *adj* doppio ● *adv* **cost** ~ costare il doppio; **see** ~ vedere doppio; ~ **the amount** la quantità doppia ● *n* doppio *m*; (*person*) sosia *m inv*; ~**s** *pl* (*Tennis*) doppio *m*; **at the** ~ di corsa ● *vt* raddoppiare; (*fold*) piegare in due ● *vi* raddoppiare. □ ~ **back** *vi* (*go back*) fare dietro front. □ ~ **up** *vi* (*bend*) piegarsi in due (**with** per); (*share*) dividere una stanza

double: ~**-'bass** *n* contrabbasso *m*. ~ '**bed** *n* letto *m* matrimoniale. ~ '**chin** *n* doppio mento *m*. ~**-'click** *vt/i* cliccare due volte, fare doppio clic (**on** su). ~**-'cross** *vt* ingannare. ~**-'decker** *n* autobus *m inv* a due piani. ~ '**Dutch** *n* 🄸 ostrogoto *m*. ~ '**glazing** *n* doppiovetro *m*

doubly /'dʌblɪ/ *adv* doppiamente

doubt /daʊt/ *n* dubbio *m* ● *vt* dubitare di. ~**ful** *adj* dubbio; (*having doubts*) in dubbio. ~**fully** *adv* con aria dubbiosa. ~**less** *adv* indubbiamente

dough /dəʊ/ *n* pasta *f*; (*for bread*) impasto *m*; (🄸: *money*) quattrini *mpl*. ~**nut** *n* bombolone *m*, krapfen *m inv*

dove /dʌv/ *n* colomba *f*. ~**tail** *n* (*Techn*) incastro *m* a coda di rondine

down¹ /daʊn/ *n* (*feathers*) piumino *m*

down² *adv* giù; **go/come** ~ scendere; ~ **there** laggiù; **sales are** ~ le vendite sono diminuite; **£50 ~** 50 sterline d'acconto; **~ 10%** ridotto del 10%; **~ with...!** abbasso...! ● *prep* **walk ~ the road** camminare per strada; **~ the stairs** giù per le scale; **fall ~ the stairs** cadere giù dalle scale; **get that ~ you!** [!] butta giù!; **be ~ the pub** [!] essere al pub ● *vt* bere tutto d'un fiato (drink)

down: ~-and-'out *n* spiantato, -a *mf*. **~cast** *adj* abbattuto. **~fall** *n* caduta *f*; (*of person*) rovina *f*. **~-'hearted** *adj* scoraggiato. **~'hill** *adv* in discesa; **go ~hill** essere in declino. **~'load** *vt* scaricare. **~ payment** *n* deposito *m*. **~pour** *n* acquazzone *m*. **~right** *adj* (*absolute*) totale; (lie) bell'e buono; (idiot) perfetto ● *adv* (*completely*) completamente. **~'stairs** *adv* al piano di sotto ● *adj* del piano di sotto. **~'stream** *adv* a valle. **~-to-'earth** *adj* (person) con i piedi per terra. **~town** *adv Am* in centro. **~ward[s]** *adj* verso il basso; (slope) in discesa ● *adv* verso il basso

> *i*
>
> **Downing Street** È una via del centro di Londra, nel quartiere di Westminster. Al numero 10 si trova la residenza ufficiale del Primo Ministro britannico e al numero 11 quella del *Chancellor of the Exchequer* (il Cancelliere dello Scacchiere, equivalente del Ministro delle Finanze e del Tesoro). Le espressioni *Downing Street* e *Number 10* sono spesso usate dalla stampa per indicare il Primo Ministro.

dowry /'daʊrɪ/ *n* dote *f*

doze /dəʊz/ *n* sonnellino *m* ● *vi* sonnecchiare. □ **~ off** *vi* assopirsi

dozen /'dʌzn/ *n* dozzina *f*; **~s of books** libri a dozzine

Dr *abbr* doctor

drab /dræb/ *adj* spento

draft¹ /drɑːft/ *n* abbozzo *m*; (*Comm*) cambiale *f*; *Am* (*Mil*) leva *f* ● *vt* abbozzare; *Am* (*Mil*) arruolare

draft² *n Am* = **draught**

drag /dræg/ *n* [!] scocciatura *f*; **in ~** [!] (man) travestito da donna ● *vt* (*pt*/*pp* **dragged**) trascinare; dragare (river). □ **~ on** *vi* (time, meeting:) trascinarsi

dragon /'drægən/ *n* drago *m*. **~-fly** *n* libellula *f*

drain /dreɪn/ *n* tubo *m* di scarico; (*grid*) tombino *m*; **the ~s** *pl* le fognature; **be a ~ on sb's finances** prosciugare le finanze di qcno ● *vt* drenare (land, wound); scolare (liquid, vegetables); svuotare (tank, glass, person) ● *vi* **~ [away]** andar via

drama /'drɑːmə/ *n* arte *f* drammatica; (*play*) opera *f* teatrale; (*event*) dramma *m*

dramatic /drə'mætɪk/ *adj* drammatico

dramat|ist /'dræmətɪst/ *n* drammaturgo, -a *mf*. **~ize** *vt* adattare per il teatro; *fig* drammatizzare

drank /dræŋk/ ▷**DRINK**

drape /dreɪp/ *n Am* tenda *f* ● *vt* appoggiare (**over** su)

drastic /'dræstɪk/ *adj* drastico; **~ally** *adv* drasticamente

draught /drɑːft/ *n* corrente *f* [d'aria]; **~s** *sg* (*game*) [gioco *m* della] dama *fsg*

draught beer *n* birra *f* alla spina

draughty /'drɑːftɪ/ *adj* pieno di correnti d'aria; **it's ~** c'è corrente

draw /drɔː/ *n* (*attraction*) attrazione *f*; (*Sport*) pareggio *m*; (*in lottery*) sorteggio *m* ● *v* (*pt* **drew**, *pp* **drawn**) ● *vt* tirare; (*attract*) attirare; disegnare (picture); tracciare (line); ritirare (money); **~ lots** tirare a sorte ● *vi* (tea:) essere in infusione; (*Sport*) pareggiare; **~ near** avvicinarsi. □ **~ back** *vt* tirare indietro; ritirare (hand); tirare (curtains) ● *vi* (*recoil*) tirarsi indietro. □ **~ in** *vt* ritrarre (claws etc) ● *vi* (train:) arrivare; (days:) accorciarsi. □ **~ out** *vt* (*pull out*) tirar fuori; ritirare (money) ● *vi* (train:) partire; (days:) allungarsi. □ **~ up** *vt* redigere (document); accostare (chair); **~ oneself up to one's full height** farsi grande ● *vi* (*stop*) fermarsi

draw: ~back *n* inconveniente *m*. **~bridge** *n* ponte *m* levatoio

drawer /drɔː(r)/ *n* cassetto *m*

drawing /'drɔːɪŋ/ *n* disegno *m*

drawing: ~ pin *n* puntina *f*. **~ room** *n* salotto *m*

drawl /drɔːl/ *n* pronuncia *f* strascicata

drawn /drɔːn/ ▷**DRAW**

dread /dred/ *n* terrore *m* ● *vt* aver il terrore di

dreadful /'dredfʊl/ *adj* terribile. **~ly** *adv* terribilmente

dream /dri:m/ *n* sogno *m* ● *attrib* di sogno ● *vt/i* (*pt/pp* **dreamt** /dremt/ *or* **dreamed**) sognare (**about**/**of** di)

dreary /'drɪərɪ/ *adj* (**-ier, -iest**) tetro; (*boring*) monotono

dredge /dredʒ/ *vt/i* dragare

dregs /dregz/ *npl* feccia *fsg*

drench /drentʃ/ *vt* **get ~ed** inzupparsi; **~ed** zuppo

dress /dres/ *n* (*woman's*) vestito *m*; (*clothing*) abbigliamento *m* ● *vt* vestire; (*decorate*) adornare; (*Culin*) condire; (*Med*) fasciare; **~ oneself, get ~ed** vestirsi ● *vi* vestirsi. □ **~ up** *vi* mettersi elegante; (*in disguise*) travestirsi (**as** da)

dress circle *n* (*Theat*) prima galleria *f*

dressing /'dresɪŋ/ *n* (*Culin*) condimento *m*; (*Med*) fasciatura *f*

dressing: ~-gown *n* vestaglia *f*. **~-room** *n* (*in gym*) spogliatoio *m*; (*Theat*) camerino *m*. **~-table** *n* toilette *f inv*

dress: ~maker *n* sarta *f*. **~ rehearsal** *n* prova *f* generale

drew /dru:/ ▷DRAW

dribble /'drɪbl/ *vi* gocciolare; (baby:) sbavare; (*Sport*) dribblare

dried /draɪd/ *adj* (food) essiccato

drier /'draɪə(r)/ *n* asciugabiancheria *m inv*

drift /drɪft/ *n* movimento *m* lento; (*of snow*) cumulo *m*; (*meaning*) senso *m* ● *vi* (*off course*) andare alla deriva; (snow:) accumularsi; (fig: person:) procedere senza meta. □ **~ apart** *vi* (people:) allontanarsi l'uno dall'altro

drill /drɪl/ *n* trapano *m*; (*Mil*) esercitazione *f* ● *vt* trapanare; (*Mil*) fare esercitare ● *vi* (*Mil*) esercitarsi; **~ for oil** trivellare in cerca di petrolio

drink /drɪŋk/ *n* bevanda *f*; (*alcoholic*) bicchierino *m*; **have a ~** bere qualcosa; **a ~ of water** un po' d'acqua ● *vt/i* (*pt* **drank**, *pp* **drunk**) bere. □ **~ up** *vt* finire ● *vi* finire il bicchiere

drink|able /'drɪŋkəbl/ *adj* potabile. **~er** *n* bevitore, -trice *mf*

'drinking-water *n* acqua *f* potabile

drip /drɪp/ *n* gocciolamento *m*; (*drop*) goccia *f*; (*Med*) flebo *f inv*; ([!]: *person*) mollaccione, -a *mf* ● *vi* (*pt/pp* **dripped**) gocciolare. **~-'dry** *adj* che non si stira. **~ping** *n* (*from meat*) grasso *m* d'arrosto ● *adj* **~ping [wet]** fradicio

drive /draɪv/ *n* (*in car*) giro *m*; (*entrance*) viale *m*; (*energy*) grinta *f*; (*Psych*) pulsione *f*; (*organized effort*) operazione *f*; (*Techn*) motore *m*; (*Comput*) lettore *m* ● *v* (*pt* **drove**, *pp* **driven**) ● *vt* portare (person by car); guidare (car); (*Sport: hit*) mandare; (*Techn*) far funzionare; **~ sb mad** far diventare matto qcno ● *vi* guidare. □ **~ at** *vt* **what are you driving at?** dove vuoi arrivare? **drive away** *vt* portare via in macchina; (*chase*) cacciare ● *vi* andare via in macchina. □ **~ in** *vt* piantare (nail) ● *vi* arrivare [in macchina]. □ **~ off** *vt* portare via in macchina; (*chase*) cacciare ● *vi* andare via in macchina. □ **~ on** *vi* proseguire (*in macchina*). □ **~ up** *vi* arrivare (*in macchina*)

drivel /'drɪvl/ *n* [!] sciocchezze *fpl*

driver /'draɪvə(r)/ *n* guidatore, -trice *mf*; (*of train*) conducente *mf*

driving /'draɪvɪŋ/ *adj* (rain) violento; (force) motore ● *n* guida *f*

driving: ~ licence *n* patente *f* di guida. **~ test** *n* esame *m* di guida

drizzle /'drɪzl/ *n* pioggerella *f* ● *vi* piovigginare

drone /drəʊn/ *n* (*bee*) fuco *m*; (*sound*) ronzio *m*

droop /dru:p/ *vi* abbassarsi; (flowers:) afflosciarsi

drop /drɒp/ *n* (*of liquid*) goccia *f*; (*fall*) caduta *f*; (*in price, temperature*) calo *m* ● *v* (*pt/pp* **dropped**) ● *vt* far cadere; sganciare (bomb); (*omit*) omettere; (*give up*) abbandonare ● *vi* cadere; (price, temperature, wind:) calare; (ground:) essere in pendenza. □ **~ in** *vi* passare. □ **~ off** *vt* depositare (person) ● *vi* cadere; (*fall asleep*) assopirsi. □ **~ out** *vi* cadere; (*of race, society*) ritirarsi; **~ out of school** lasciare la scuola

'drop-out *n* persona *f* contro il sistema sociale

drought /draʊt/ *n* siccità *f*

drove /drəʊv/ ▷DRIVE

drown /draʊn/ *vi* annegare ● *vt* annegare; coprire (noise); **he was ~ed** è annegato

drowsy /'draʊzɪ/ *adj* sonnolento

drudgery /'drʌdʒərɪ/ *n* lavoro *m* pesante e noioso

drug /drʌg/ *n* droga *f*; (*Med*) farmaco *m*; **take ~s** drogarsi • *vt* (*pt/pp* **drugged**) drogare

drug: ~ addict *n* tossicomane, -a *mf*. **~ dealer** *n* spacciatore, -trice *mf* [di droga]. **~gist** *n Am* farmacista *mf*. **~store** *n Am negozio m di generi vari, inclusi medicinali, che funge anche da bar*; (*dispensing*) farmacia *f*

drum /drʌm/ *n* tamburo *m*; (*for oil*) bidone *m*; **~s** (*pl: in pop-group*) batteria *f* • *v* (*pt/pp* **drummed**) • *vi* suonare il tamburo; (*in pop-group*) suonare la batteria • *vt* **~ sth into sb** ripetere qcsa a qcno cento volte. **~mer** *n* percussionista *mf*; (*in pop-group*) batterista *mf*. **~stick** *n* bacchetta *f*; (*of chicken, turkey*) coscia *f*

drunk /drʌŋk/ ▷**DRINK** • *adj* ubriaco; **get ~** ubriacarsi • *n* ubriaco, -a *mf*

drunk|ard /'drʌŋkəd/ *n* ubriacone, -a *mf*. **~en** *adj* ubriaco; **~en driving** guida *f* in stato di ebbrezza

dry /draɪ/ *adj* (**drier, driest**) asciutto; (climate, country) secco • *vt/i* (*pt/pp* **dried**) asciugare; **~ one's eyes** asciugarsi le lacrime. □ **~ up** *vi* seccarsi; (fig: source:) prosciugarsi; (🅘: *be quiet*) stare zitto; (*do dishes*) asciugare i piatti

dry: ~-'clean *vt* pulire a secco. **~-'cleaner's** *n* (*shop*) tintoria *f*. **~ness** *n* secchezza *f*

DTD *n abbr* (digital type definition) DTD *f*

dual /'dju:əl/ *adj* doppio

dual 'carriageway *n* strada *f* a due carreggiate

dub /dʌb/ *vt* (*pt/pp* **dubbed**) doppiare (film); (*name*) soprannominare

dubious /'dju:bɪəs/ *adj* dubbio; **be ~ about** avere dei dubbi riguardo

duchess /'dʌtʃɪs/ *n* duchessa *f*

duck /dʌk/ *n* anatra *f* • *vt* (*in water*) immergere; **~ one's head** abbassare la testa • *vi* abbassarsi. **~ling** *n* anatroccolo *m*

duct /dʌkt/ *n* condotto *m*; (*Anat*) dotto *m*

dud /dʌd/ 🅘 *adj* (*Mil*) disattivato; (coin) falso; (cheque) a vuoto • *n* (*banknote*) banconota *f* falsa

due /dju:/ *adj* dovuto; **be ~** (train:) essere previsto; **the baby is ~ next week** il bambino dovrebbe nascere la settimana prossima; **~ to** (*owing to*) a causa di; **be ~ to** (*causally*) essere dovuto a; **I'm ~ to...** dovrei...; **in ~ course** a tempo debito • *adv* **~ north** direttamente a nord

duel /'dju:əl/ *n* duello *m*

dues /dju:z/ *npl* quota *f* [di iscrizione]

duet /dju:'et/ *n* duetto *m*

dug /dʌg/ ▷**DIG**

duke /dju:k/ *n* duca *m*

dull /dʌl/ *adj* (*overcast, not bright*) cupo; (*not shiny*) opaco; (sound) soffocato; (*boring*) monotono; (*stupid*) ottuso • *vt* intorpidire (mind); attenuare (pain)

dumb /dʌm/ *adj* muto; (🅘: *stupid*) ottuso. **~founded** *adj* sbigottito. □ **~ down** *vt* semplificare il livello di

dummy /'dʌmɪ/ *n* (*tailor's*) manichino *m*; (*for baby*) succhiotto *m*; (*model*) riproduzione *f*

dump /dʌmp/ *n* (*for refuse*) scarico *m*; (🅘: *town*) mortorio *m*; **be down in the ~s** 🅘 essere depresso • *vt* scaricare; (🅘: *put down*) lasciare; (🅘: *get rid of*) liberarsi di

dumpling /'dʌmplɪŋ/ *n* gnocco *m*

dunce /dʌns/ *n* zuccone, -a *mf*

dung /dʌŋ/ *n* sterco *m*

dungarees /dʌŋgə'ri:z/ *npl* tuta *fsg*

dungeon /'dʌndʒən/ *n* prigione *f* sotterranea

duplicate¹ /'dju:plɪkət/ *adj* doppio • *n* duplicato *m*; (*document*) copia *f*; **in ~** in duplicato

duplicat|e² /'dju:plɪkeɪt/ *vt* fare un duplicato di; (research:) essere una ripetizione di (work)

durable /'djʊərəbl/ *adj* resistente; durevole (basis, institution)

duration /djʊə'reɪʃn/ *n* durata *f*

duress /djʊə'res/ *n* costrizione *f*; **under ~** sotto minaccia

during /'djʊərɪŋ/ *prep* durante

dusk /dʌsk/ *n* crepuscolo *m*

dust /dʌst/ *n* polvere *f* • *vt* spolverare; (*sprinkle*) cospargere (cake) (**with** di) • *vi* spolverare

dust: ~bin *n* pattumiera *f*. **~er** *n* strofinaccio *m*. **~-jacket** *n* sopraccoperta *f*. **~man** *n* spazzino *m*. **~pan** *n* paletta *f* per la spazzatura

dusty /'dʌstɪ/ *adj* (**-ier, -iest**) polveroso
Dutch /dʌtʃ/ *adj* olandese; **go ~** [!] fare alla romana ● *n* (*language*) olandese *m*; **the ~** *pl* gli olandesi. **~man** *n* olandese *m*
duty /'dju:tɪ/ *n* dovere *m*; (*task*) compito *m*; (*tax*) dogana *f*; **be on ~** essere di servizio. **~-free** *adj* esente da dogana
duvet /'du:veɪ/ *n* piumone *m*
dwarf /dwɔ:f/ *n* (*pl* **-s** *or* **dwarves**) nano, -a *mf* ● *vt* rimpicciolire
dwell /dwel/ *vi* (*pt/pp* **dwelt**) *liter* dimorare. □ **~ on** *vt fig* soffermarsi su. **~ing** *n* abitazione *f*
dwindle /'dwɪndl/ *vi* diminuire
dye /daɪ/ *n* tintura *f* ● *vt* (*pres p* **dyeing**) tingere
dying /'daɪɪŋ/ ▷**DIE²**
dynamic /daɪ'næmɪk/ *adj* dinamico
dynamite /'daɪnəmaɪt/ *n* dinamite *f*
dynamo /'daɪnəməʊ/ *n* dinamo *f inv*
dynasty /'dɪnəstɪ/ *n* dinastia *f*

Ee

each /i:tʃ/ *adj* ogni ● *pron* ognuno; **£1 ~** una sterlina ciascuno; **they love/hate ~ other** si amano/odiano; **we lend ~ other money** ci prestiamo i soldi
eager /'i:gə(r)/ *adj* ansioso (**to do** di fare); (pupil) avido di sapere. **~ly** *adv* (wait) ansiosamente; (offer) premurosamente. **~ness** *n* premura *f*
eagle /'i:gl/ *n* aquila *f*
ear¹ /ɪə(r)/ *n* (*of corn*) spiga *f*
ear² *n* orecchio *m*. **~ache** *n* mal *m* d'orecchi. **~-drum** *n* timpano *m*
earl /ɜ:l/ *n* conte *m*
early /'ɜ:lɪ/ *adj* (**-ier, -iest**) (*before expected time*) in anticipo; (spring) prematuro; (reply) pronto; (works, writings) primo; **be here ~!** sii puntuale!; **you're ~!** sei in anticipo!; **~ morning walk** passeggiata *f* mattutina; **in the ~ morning** la mattina presto; **in the ~ spring** all'inizio della primavera; **~ retirement** prepensionamento *m* ● *adv* presto; (*ahead of time*) in anticipo; **~ in the morning** la mattina presto
earn /ɜ:n/ *vt* guadagnare; (*deserve*) meritare
earnest /'ɜ:nɪst/ *adj* serio ● *n* **in ~** sul serio. **~ly** *adv* con aria seria
earnings /'ɜ:nɪŋz/ *npl* guadagni *mpl*; (*salary*) stipendio *m*
ear: ~phones *npl* cuffia *fsg*. **~-ring** *n* orecchino *m*. **~shot** *n* **within ~shot** a portata d'orecchio; **he is out of ~shot** non può sentire
earth /ɜ:θ/ *n* terra *f*; **where/what on ~?** dove/che diavolo? ● *vt* (*Electr*) mettere a terra
'earthquake *n* terremoto *m*
earwig /'ɪəwɪg/ *n* forbicina *f*
ease /i:z/ *n* **at ~** a proprio agio; **at ~!** (*Mil*) riposo!; **ill at ~** a disagio; **with ~** con facilità ● *vt* calmare (pain); alleviare (tension, shortage); (*slow down*) rallentare; (*loosen*) allentare ● *vi* (pain, situation, wind:) calmarsi
easel /'i:zl/ *n* cavalletto *m*
easily /'i:zɪlɪ/ *adv* con facilità; **~ the best** certamente il meglio
east /i:st/ *n* est *m*; **to the ~ of** a est di ● *adj* dell'est ● *adv* verso est
Easter /'i:stə(r)/ *n* Pasqua *f*. **~ egg** *n* uovo *m* di Pasqua
east|erly /'i:stəlɪ/ *adj* da levante. **~ern** *adj* orientale. **~ward[s]** /-wəd[z]/ *adv* verso est
easy /'i:zɪ/ *adj* (**-ier, -iest**) facile; **take it** *or* **things ~** prendersela con calma; **take it ~!** (*don't get excited*) calma!; **go ~ with** andarci piano con
easy: ~ chair *n* poltrona *f*. **~'going** *adj* conciliante; **too ~going** troppo accomodante
eat /i:t/ *vt/i* (*pt* **ate**, *pp* **eaten**) mangiare. □ **~ into** *vt* intaccare. □ **~ up** *vt* mangiare tutto (food); *fig* inghiottire (profits)
eaves /i:vz/ *npl* cornicione *msg*. **~drop** *vi* (*pt/pp* **~dropped**) origliare; **~drop on** ascoltare di nascosto
ebb /eb/ *n* (*tide*) riflusso *m*; **at a low ~** *fig* a terra ● *vi* rifluire; *fig* declinare
ebony /'ebənɪ/ *n* ebano *m*
eccentric /ɪk'sentrɪk/ *adj & n* eccentrico, -a *mf*

echo /ˈekəʊ/ *n* (*pl* **-es**) eco *f or m* ● *v* (*pt/pp* **echoed**, *pres p* **echoing**) ● *vt* echeggiare; ripetere (words) ● *vi* risuonare (**with** di)

eclipse /ɪˈklɪps/ *n* (*Astr*) eclissi *f inv* ● *vt fig* eclissare

ecolog|ical /iːkəˈlɒdʒɪkl/ *adj* ecologico. **~y** *n* ecologia *f*

e-commerce /ˈiːˈkɒmɜːs/ *n* e-commerce *m inv*, commercio *m* elettronico

economic /iːkəˈnɒmɪk/ *adj* economico; **~ refugee** rifugiato, -a *mf* economico, -a. **~al** *adj* economico. **~ally** *adv* economicamente; (*thriftily*) in economia. **~s** *n* economia *f*

economist /ɪˈkɒnəmɪst/ *n* economista *mf*

economize /ɪˈkɒnəmaɪz/ *vi* economizzare (**on** su)

economy /ɪˈkɒnəmɪ/ *n* economia *f*

ecstasy /ˈekstəsɪ/ *n* estasi *f inv*; (*drug*) ecstasy *f*

eczema /ˈeksɪmə/ *n* eczema *m*

edge /edʒ/ *n* bordo *m*; (*of knife*) filo *m*; (*of road*) ciglio *m*; **on ~** con i nervi tesi; **have the ~ on** [!] avere un vantaggio su ● *vt* bordare. ▫ **~ forward** *vi* avanzare lentamente

edgeways /ˈedʒweɪz/ *adv* di fianco; **I couldn't get a word in ~** non ho potuto infilare neanche mezza parola nel discorso

edgy /ˈedʒɪ/ *adj* nervoso

edible /ˈedɪbl/ *adj* commestibile; **this pizza's not ~** questa pizza è immangiabile

> **Edinburgh Festival** La più importante manifestazione culturale britannica, fondata nel 1947 e tenuta annualmente nella capitale scozzese, in agosto. Il festival offre spettacoli di musica, teatro, danza, ecc. e attira ogni anno moltissimi visitatori. Un settore sempre molto interessante è quello del cosiddetto *Fringe*, ossia gli eventi fuori dal programma ufficiale.

edit /ˈedɪt/ *vt* (*pt/pp* **edited**) far la revisione di (text); curare l'edizione di (anthology, dictionary); dirigere (newspaper); montare (film); editare (tape); **~ed by** (book) a cura di

edition /ɪˈdɪʃn/ *n* edizione *f*

editor /ˈedɪtə(r)/ *n* (*of anthology, dictionary*) curatore, -trice *mf*; (*of newspaper*) redattore, -trice *mf*; (*of film*) responsabile *mf* del montaggio

editorial /edɪˈtɔːrɪəl/ *adj* redazionale ● *n* (*Journ*) editoriale *m*

educate /ˈedjʊkeɪt/ *vt* istruire; educare (public, mind); **be ~d at Eton** essere educato a Eton. **~d** *adj* istruito

education /edjʊˈkeɪʃn/ *n* istruzione *f*; (*culture*) cultura *f*, educazione *f*. **~al** *adj* istruttivo; (visit) educativo; (publishing) didattico

eel /iːl/ *n* anguilla *f*

eerie /ˈɪərɪ/ *adj* (**-ier, -iest**) inquietante

effect /ɪˈfekt/ *n* effetto *m*; **in ~** in effetti; **take ~** (law:) entrare in vigore; (medicine:) fare effetto ● *vt* effettuare

effective /ɪˈfektɪv/ *adj* efficace; (*striking*) che colpisce; (*actual*) di fatto; **~ from** in vigore a partire da. **~ly** *adv* efficacemente; (*actually*) di fatto. **~ness** *n* efficacia *f*

effeminate /ɪˈfemɪnət/ *adj* effeminato

efficiency /ɪˈfɪʃənsɪ/ *n* efficienza *f*; (*of machine*) rendimento *m*

efficient /ɪˈfɪʃənt/ *adj* efficiente. **~ly** *adv* efficientemente

effort /ˈefət/ *n* sforzo *m*; **make an ~** sforzarsi. **~less** *adj* facile. **~lessly** *adv* con facilità

e.g. *abbr* (exempli gratia) per es.

egg[1] /eg/ *vt* **~ on** [!] incitare

egg[2] *n* uovo *m*. **~-cup** *n* portauovo *m inv*. **~head** *n* [!] intellettuale *mf*. **~shell** *n* guscio *m* d'uovo. **~timer** *n clessidra f per misurare il tempo di cottura delle uova*

ego /ˈiːgəʊ/ *n* ego *m*. **~centric** *adj* egocentrico. **~ism** *n* egoismo *m*. **~ist** *n* egoista *mf*. **~tism** *n* egotismo *m*. **~tist** *n* egotista *mf*

Egypt /ˈiːdʒɪpt/ *n* Egitto *m*. **~ian** *adj & n* egiziano, -a *mf*

eiderdown /ˈaɪdə-/ *n* (*quilt*) piumino *m*

eigh|t /eɪt/ *adj* otto ● *n* otto *m*. **~ˈteen** *adj* diciotto. **~ˈteenth** *adj* diciottesimo

eighth /eɪtθ/ *adj* ottavo ● *n* ottavo *m*

eightieth /ˈeɪtɪɪθ/ *adj* ottantesimo

eighty /ˈeɪtɪ/ *adj* ottanta

either /ˈaɪðə(r)/ *adj & pron* ~ **[of them]** l'uno o l'altro; **I don't like ~ [of them]** non mi piace né l'uno né l'altro; **on ~ side** da tutte e due le parti ● *adv* **I don't ~** nemmeno io; **I don't like John or his brother ~** non mi piace John e nemmeno suo fratello ● *conj* **~ John or his brother will be there** ci saranno o John o suo fratello; **I don't like ~ John or his brother** non mi piacciono né John né suo fratello; **~ you go to bed or else...** o vai a letto o altrimenti ...

e

eject /ɪˈdʒekt/ *vt* eiettare (pilot); espellere (tape, drunk)
eke /iːk/ *vt* **~ out** far bastare; (*increase*) arrotondare; **~ out a living** arrangiarsi
elaborate¹ /ɪˈlæbərət/ *adj* elaborato
elaborate² /ɪˈlæbəreɪt/ *vi* entrare nei particolari (**on** di)
elapse /ɪˈlæps/ *vi* trascorrere
elastic /ɪˈlæstɪk/ *adj* elastico ● *n* elastico *m*. **~ 'band** *n* elastico *m*
elated /ɪˈleɪtɪd/ *adj* esultante
elbow /ˈelbəʊ/ *n* gomito *m*
elder¹ /ˈeldə(r)/ *n* (*tree*) sambuco *m*
eld|er² *adj* maggiore ● *n* **the ~** il/la maggiore. **~erly** *adj* anziano. **~est** *adj* maggiore ● *n* **the ~est** il/la maggiore
elect /ɪˈlekt/ *adj* **the president ~** il futuro presidente ● *vt* eleggere; **~ to do sth** decidere di fare qcsa. **~ion** *n* elezione *f*
elector /ɪˈlektə(r)/ *n* elettore, -trice *mf*. **~al** *adj* elettorale; **~al roll** liste *fpl* elettorali. **~ate** *n* elettorato *m*
electric /ɪˈlektrɪk/ *adj* elettrico
electrical /ɪˈlektrɪkl/ *adj* elettrico; **~ engineering** elettrotecnica *f*
electric 'blanket *n* termocoperta *f*
electrician /ɪlekˈtrɪʃn/ *n* elettricista *m*
electricity /ɪlekˈtrɪsətɪ/ *n* elettricità *f*
electrify /ɪˈlektrɪfaɪ/ *vt* (*pt/pp* **-ied**) elettrificare; *fig* elettrizzare. **~ing** *adj fig* elettrizzante
electrocute /ɪˈlektrəkjuːt/ *vt* fulminare; (*execute*) giustiziare sulla sedia elettrica
electrode /ɪˈlektrəʊd/ *n* elettrodo *m*
electron /ɪˈlektrɒn/ *n* elettrone *m*
electronic /ɪlekˈtrɒnɪk/ *adj* elettronico. **~ mail** *n* posta *f* elettronica. **~s** *n* elettronica *f*
elegance /ˈelɪgəns/ *n* eleganza *f*
elegant /ˈelɪgənt/ *adj* elegante
element /ˈelɪmənt/ *n* elemento *m*. **~ary** *adj* elementare
elephant /ˈelɪfənt/ *n* elefante *m*
elevat|e /ˈelɪveɪt/ *vt* elevare. **~ion** *n* elevazione *f*; (*height*) altitudine *f*; (*angle*) alzo *m*
elevator /ˈelɪveɪtə(r)/ *n Am* ascensore *m*
eleven /ɪˈlevn/ *adj* undici ● *n* undici *m*. **~th** *adj* undicesimo; **at the ~th hour** [!] all'ultimo momento
elf /elf/ *n* (*pl* **elves**) elfo *m*
eligible /ˈelɪdʒəbl/ *adj* eleggibile; **be ~ for** aver diritto a
eliminate /ɪˈlɪmɪneɪt/ *vt* eliminare
élite /eɪˈliːt/ *n* fior fiore *m*
ellip|se /ɪˈlɪps/ *n* ellisse *f*. **~tical** *adj* ellittico
elm /elm/ *n* olmo *m*
elope /ɪˈləʊp/ *vi* fuggire [per sposarsi]
eloquen|ce /ˈeləkwəns/ *n* eloquenza *f*. **~t** *adj* eloquente. **~tly** *adv* con eloquenza
else /els/ *adv* altro; **who ~?** e chi altro?; **he did of course, who ~?** l'ha fatto lui e chi, se no?; **nothing ~** nient'altro; **or ~** altrimenti; **someone ~** qualcun altro; **somewhere ~** da qualche altra parte; **anyone ~** chiunque altro; (*as question*) nessun'altro?; **anything ~** qualunque altra cosa; (*as question*) altro?. **~where** *adv* altrove
elude /ɪˈluːd/ *vt* eludere; (*avoid*) evitare; **the name ~s me** il nome mi sfugge
elusive /ɪˈluːsɪv/ *adj* elusivo
emaciated /ɪˈmeɪsɪeɪtɪd/ *adj* emaciato
e-mail /ˈiːmeɪl/ *n* posta *f* elettronica ● *vt* spedire via posta elettronica. **~ address** *n* indirizzo *m* e-mail
embankment /ɪmˈbæŋkmənt/ *n* argine *m*; (*Rail*) massicciata *f*
embargo /emˈbɑːgəʊ/ *n* (*pl* **-es**) embargo *m*
embark /ɪmˈbɑːk/ *vi* imbarcarsi; **~ on** intraprendere. **~ation** *n* imbarco *m*
embarrass /emˈbærəs/ *vt* imbarazzare. **~ed** *adj* imbarazzato. **~ing** *adj* imbarazzante. **~ment** *n* imbarazzo *m*
embassy /ˈembəsɪ/ *n* ambasciata *f*

embedded /ɪm'bedɪd/ *adj* (*in concrete*) cementato; (traditions, feelings) radicato

embellish /ɪm'belɪʃ/ *vt* abbellire

embers /'embəz/ *npl* braci *fpl*

embezzle /ɪm'bezl/ *vt* appropriarsi indebitamente di. **~ment** *n* appropriazione *f* indebita

emblem /'embləm/ *n* emblema *m*

embrace /ɪm'breɪs/ *n* abbraccio *m* ● *vt* abbracciare ● *vi* abbracciarsi

embroider /ɪm'brɔɪdə(r)/ *vt* ricamare (design); *fig* abbellire. **~y** *n* ricamo *m*

embryo /'embrɪəʊ/ *n* embrione *m*

emerald /'emərəld/ *n* smeraldo *m*

emer|ge /ɪ'mɜːdʒ/ *vi* emergere; (*come into being: nation*) nascere; (sun, flowers) spuntare fuori. **~gence** *n* emergere *m*; (*of new country*) nascita *f*

emergency /ɪ'mɜːdʒənsɪ/ *n* emergenza *f*; **in an ~** in caso di emergenza. **~ exit** *n* uscita *f* di sicurezza

emigrant /'emɪgrənt/ *n* emigrante *mf*

emigrat|e /'emɪgreɪt/ *vi* emigrare. **~ion** *n* emigrazione *f*

eminent /'emɪnənt/ *adj* eminente. **~ly** *adv* eminentemente

emission /ɪ'mɪʃn/ *n* emissione *f*; (*of fumes*) esalazione *f*

emit /ɪ'mɪt/ *vt* (*pt/pp* **emitted**) emettere; esalare (fumes)

emotion /ɪ'məʊʃn/ *n* emozione *f*. **~al** *adj* denso di emozione; (person, reaction) emotivo; **become ~al** avere una reazione emotiva

emotive /ɪ'məʊtɪv/ *adj* emotivo

emperor /'empərə(r)/ *n* imperatore *m*

emphasis /'emfəsɪs/ *n* enfasi *f*; **put the ~ on sth** accentuare qcsa

emphasize /'emfəsaɪz/ *vt* accentuare (word, syllable); sottolineare (need)

emphatic /ɪm'fætɪk/ *adj* categorico

empire /'empaɪə(r)/ *n* impero *m*

empirical /em'pɪrɪkl/ *adj* empirico

employ /em'plɔɪ/ *vt* impiegare; *fig* usare (tact). **~ee** *n* impiegato, -a *mf*. **~er** *n* datore *m* di lavoro. **~ment** *n* occupazione *f*; (*work*) lavoro *m*. **~ment agency** *n* ufficio *m* di collocamento

empower /ɪm'paʊə(r)/ *vt* autorizzare; (*enable*) mettere in grado

empress /'emprɪs/ *n* imperatrice *f*

empty /'emptɪ/ *adj* vuoto; (promise, threat) vano ● *v* (*pt/pp* **-ied**) ● *vt* vuotare (container) ● *vi* vuotarsi

emulate /'emjʊleɪt/ *vt* emulare

emulsion /ɪ'mʌlʃn/ *n* emulsione *f*

enable /ɪ'neɪbl/ *vt* **~ sb to** mettere qcno in grado di

enact /ɪ'nækt/ *vt* (*Theat*) rappresentare; decretare (law)

enamel /ɪ'næml/ *n* smalto *m* ● *vt* (*pt/pp* **enamelled**) smaltare

enchant /ɪn'tʃɑːnt/ *vt* incantare. **~ing** *adj* incantevole. **~ment** *n* incanto *m*

encircle /ɪn'sɜːkl/ *vt* circondare

enclave /'enkleɪv/ *n* enclave *f inv*; *fig* territorio *m*

enclos|e /ɪn'kləʊz/ *vt* circondare (land); (*in letter*) allegare (**with** a). **~ed** *adj* (space) chiuso; (*in letter*) allegato. **~ure** *n* (*at zoo*) recinto *m*; (*in letter*) allegato *m*

encore /'ɒŋkɔː(r)/ *n & int* bis *m inv*

encounter /ɪn'kaʊntə(r)/ *n* incontro *m*; (*battle*) scontro *m* ● *vt* incontrare

encourag|e /ɪn'kʌrɪdʒ/ *vt* incoraggiare; promuovere (the arts, independence). **~ement** *n* incoraggiamento *m*; (*of the arts*) promozione *f*. **~ing** *adj* incoraggiante; (smile) di incoraggiamento

encroach /ɪn'krəʊtʃ/ *vt* **~ on** invadere (land, privacy); abusare di (time); interferire con (rights)

encyclop[a]ed|ia /ɪnsaɪklə'piːdɪə/ *n* enciclopedia *f*. **~ic** *adj* enciclopedico

end /end/ *n* fine *f*; (*of box, table, piece of string*) estremità *f*; (*of town, room*) parte *f*; (*purpose*) fine *m*; **in the ~** alla fine; **at the ~ of May** alla fine di maggio; **at the ~ of the street/garden** in fondo alla strada/al giardino; **on ~** (*upright*) in piedi; **for days on ~** per giorni e giorni; **for six days on ~** per sei giorni di fila; **put an ~ to sth** mettere fine a qcsa; **make ~s meet** ! sbarcare il lunario; **no ~ of** ! un sacco di ● *vt/i* finire. □ **~ up** *vi* finire; **~ up doing sth** finire col fare qcsa

endanger /ɪn'deɪndʒə(r)/ *vt* rischiare (one's life); mettere a repentaglio (sb else, success of sth)

endear|ing /ɪn'dɪərɪŋ/ *adj* accattivante. **~ment** *n* **term of ~ment** vezzeggiativo *m*

e

endeavour /ɪn'devə(r)/ *n* tentativo *m* ● *vi* sforzarsi (**to** di)

ending /'endɪŋ/ *n* fine *f*; (*Gram*) desinenza *f*

endless /'endlɪs/ *adj* interminabile; (patience) infinito. **~ly** *adv* continuamente; (patient) infinitamente

endorse /en'dɔ:s/ *vt* girare (cheque); (sports personality:) fare pubblicità a (product); approvare (plan). **~ment** *n* (*of cheque*) girata *f*; (*of plan*) conferma *f*; (*on driving licence*) registrazione *f* su patente di un'infrazione

endur|e /ɪn'djʊə(r)/ *vt* sopportare ● *vi* durare. **~ing** *adj* duraturo

enemy /'enəmɪ/ *n* nemico, -a *mf* ● *attrib* nemico

energetic /enə'dʒetɪk/ *adj* energico

energy /'enədʒɪ/ *n* energia *f*

enforce /ɪn'fɔ:s/ *vt* far rispettare (law). **~d** *adj* forzato

engage /ɪn'geɪdʒ/ *vt* assumere (staff); (*Theat*) ingaggiare; (*Auto*) ingranare (gear) ● *vi* (*Techn*) ingranare; **~ in** impegnarsi in. **~d** *adj* (*in use, busy*) occupato; (person) impegnato; (*to be married*) fidanzato; **get ~d** fidanzarsi (**to** con); **~d tone** (*Teleph*) segnale *m* di occupato. **~ment** *n* fidanzamento *m*; (*appointment*) appuntamento *m*; (*Mil*) combattimento *m*; **~ment ring** anello *m* di fidanzamento

engine /'endʒɪn/ *n* motore *m*; (*Rail*) locomotrice *f*. **~-driver** *n* macchinista *m*

engineer /endʒɪ'nɪə(r)/ *n* ingegnere *m*; (*service, installation*) tecnico *m*; (*Naut*), *Am* (*Rail*) macchinista *m* ● *vt fig* architettare. **~ing** *n* ingegneria *f*

England /'ɪŋglənd/ *n* Inghilterra *f*

English /'ɪŋglɪʃ/ *adj* inglese; **the ~ Channel** la Manica ● *n* (*language*) inglese *m*; **the ~** *pl* gli inglesi. **~man** *n* inglese *m*. **~woman** *n* inglese *f*

engrav|e /ɪn'greɪv/ *vt* incidere. **~ing** *n* incisione *f*

engulf /ɪn'gʌlf/ *vt* (fire, waves:) inghiottire

enhance /ɪn'hɑ:ns/ *vt* accrescere (beauty, reputation); migliorare (performance)

enigma /ɪ'nɪgmə/ *n* enigma *m*. **~tic** *adj* enigmatico

enjoy /ɪn'dʒɔɪ/ *vt* godere di (good health); **~ oneself** divertirsi; **I ~ cooking/painting** mi piace cucinare/dipingere; **~ your meal** buon appetito. **~able** *adj* piacevole. **~ment** *n* piacere *m*

enlarge /ɪn'lɑ:dʒ/ *vt* ingrandire ● *vi* **~ upon** dilungarsi su. **~ment** *n* ingrandimento *m*

enlighten /ɪn'laɪtn/ *vt* illuminare. **~ed** *adj* progressista. **~ment** *n* **The E~ment** l'Illuminismo *m*

enlist /ɪn'lɪst/ *vt* (*Mil*) reclutare; **~ sb's help** farsi aiutare da qcno ● *vi* (*Mil*) arruolarsi

enliven /ɪn'laɪvn/ *vt* animare

enormity /ɪ'nɔ:mətɪ/ *n* enormità *f*

enormous /ɪ'nɔ:məs/ *adj* enorme. **~ly** *adv* estremamente; (grateful) infinitamente

enough /ɪ'nʌf/ *adj & n* abbastanza; **I didn't bring ~ clothes** non ho portato abbastanza vestiti; **have you had ~?** (*to eat/drink*) hai mangiato/bevuto abbastanza?; **I've had ~!** [!] ne ho abbastanza!; **is that ~?** basta?; **that's ~!** basta così!; **£50 isn't ~** 50 sterline non sono sufficienti ● *adv* abbastanza; **you're not working fast ~** non lavori abbastanza in fretta; **funnily ~** stranamente

enquir|e /ɪn'kwaɪə(r)/ *vi* domandare; **~e about** chiedere informazioni su. **~y** *n* domanda *f*; (*investigation*) inchiesta *f*

enrage /ɪn'reɪdʒ/ *vt* fare arrabbiare

enrol /ɪn'rəʊl/ *vi* (*pt/pp* **-rolled**) (*for exam, in club*) iscriversi (**for, in** a). **~ment** *n* iscrizione *f*

ensu|e /ɪn'sju:/ *vi* seguire; **the ~ing discussion** la discussione che ne è seguita

ensure /ɪn'ʃʊə(r)/ *vt* assicurare; **~ that** (person:) assicurarsi che; (measure:) garantire che

entail /ɪn'teɪl/ *vt* comportare; **what does it ~?** in che cosa consiste?

entangle /ɪn'tæŋgl/ *vt* **get ~d in** rimanere impigliato in; *fig* rimanere coinvolto in

enter /'entə(r)/ *vt* entrare in; iscrivere (horse, runner in race); cominciare (university); partecipare a (competition); (*Comput*) immettere (data); (*write down*) scrivere ● *vi* entrare; (*Theat*) entrare in scena; (*register as competitor*) iscriversi; (*take part*) partecipare (**in** a)

enterpris|e /ˈentəpraɪz/ *n* impresa *f*; (*quality*) iniziativa *f*. **~ing** *adj* intraprendente

entertain /entəˈteɪn/ *vt* intrattenere; (*invite*) ricevere; nutrire (ideas, hopes); prendere in considerazione (possibility) ● *vi* intrattenersi; (*have guests*) ricevere. **~er** *n* artista *mf*. **~ing** *adj* (person) di gradevole compagnia; (evening, film, play) divertente. **~ment** *n* (*amusement*) intrattenimento *m*

enthral /ɪnˈθrɔːl/ *vt* (*pt/pp* **enthralled**) **be ~led** essere affascinato (**by** da)

enthusias|m /ɪnˈθjuːzɪæzm/ *n* entusiasmo *m*. **~t** *n* entusiasta *mf*. **~tic** *adj* entusiastico

entice /ɪnˈtaɪs/ *vt* attirare. **~ment** *n* (*incentive*) incentivo *m*

entire /ɪnˈtaɪə(r)/ *adj* intero. **~ly** *adv* del tutto; **I'm not ~ly satisfied** non sono completamente soddisfatto. **~ty** *n* **in its ~ty** nell'insieme

entitlement /ɪnˈtaɪtlmənt/ *n* diritto *m*

entity /ˈentətɪ/ *n* entità *f*

entrance[1] /ˈentrəns/ *n* entrata *f*; (*Theat*) entrata *f* in scena; (*right to enter*) ammissione *f*; **'no ~'** 'ingresso vietato'. **~ examination** *n* esame *m* di ammissione. **~ fee** *n* **how much is the ~ fee?** quanto costa il biglietto di ingresso?

entrance[2] /ɪnˈtrɑːns/ *vt* estasiare

entrant /ˈentrənt/ *n* concorrente *mf*

entreat /ɪnˈtriːt/ *vt* supplicare

entrenched /ɪnˈtrentʃt/ *adj* (ideas, views) radicato

entrust /ɪnˈtrʌst/ *vt* **~ sb with sth, ~ sth to sb** affidare qcsa a qcno

entry /ˈentrɪ/ *n* ingresso *m*; (*way in*) entrata *f*; (*in directory etc*) voce *f*; (*in appointment diary*) appuntamento *m*; **no ~** ingresso vietato; (*Auto*) accesso vietato. **~ form** *n* modulo *m* di ammissione. **~ visa** *n* visto *m* di ingresso

enumerate /ɪˈnjuːməreɪt/ *vt* enumerare

envelop /ɪnˈveləp/ *vt* (*pt/pp* **enveloped**) avviluppare

envelope /ˈenvələʊp/ *n* busta *f*

enviable /ˈenvɪəbl/ *adj* invidiabile

envious /ˈenvɪəs/ *adj* invidioso. **~ly** *adv* con invidia

environment /ɪnˈvaɪrənmənt/ *n* ambiente *m*

environmental /ɪnvaɪrənˈmentl/ *adj* ambientale. **~ist** *n* ambientalista *mf*. **~ly** *adv* **~ly friendly** che rispetta l'ambiente

envisage /ɪnˈvɪzɪdʒ/ *vt* prevedere

envoy /ˈenvɔɪ/ *n* inviato, -a *mf*

envy /ˈenvɪ/ *n* invidia *f* ● *vt* (*pt/pp* **-ied**) **~ sb sth** invidiare qcno per qcsa

enzyme /ˈenzaɪm/ *n* enzima *m*

epic /ˈepɪk/ *adj* epico ● *n* epopea *f*

epidemic /epɪˈdemɪk/ *n* epidemia *f*

epilep|sy /ˈepɪlepsɪ/ *n* epilessia *f*. **~tic** *adj & n* epilettico, -a *mf*

epilogue /ˈepɪlɒg/ *n* epilogo *m*

episode /ˈepɪsəʊd/ *n* episodio *m*

epitaph /ˈepɪtɑːf/ *n* epitaffio *m*

epitom|e /ɪˈpɪtəmɪ/ *n* epitome *f*. **~ize** *vt* essere il classico esempio di

epoch /ˈiːpɒk/ *n* epoca *f*

equal /ˈiːkwl/ *adj* (parts, amounts) uguale; **of ~ height** della stessa altezza; **be ~ to the task** essere a l'altezza del compito ● *n* pari *m inv* ● *vt* (*pt/pp* **equalled**) (*be same in quantity as*) essere pari a; (*rival*) uguagliare; **5 plus 5 ~s 10** 5 più 5 [è] uguale a 10. **~ity** *n* uguaglianza *f*

equalize /ˈiːkwəlaɪz/ *vi* (*Sport*) pareggiare. **~r** *n* (*Sport*) pareggio *m*

equally /ˈiːkwəlɪ/ *adv* (divide) in parti uguali; **~ intelligent** della stessa intelligenza; **~,...** allo stesso tempo...

equator /ɪˈkweɪtə(r)/ *n* equatore *m*

equilibrium /iːkwɪˈlɪbrɪəm/ *n* equilibrio *m*

equinox /ˈiːkwɪnɒks/ *n* equinozio *m*

equip /ɪˈkwɪp/ *vt* (*pt/pp* **equipped**) equipaggiare; attrezzare (kitchen, office). **~ment** *n* attrezzatura *f*

equivalent /ɪˈkwɪvələnt/ *adj* equivalente; **be ~ to** equivalere a ● *n* equivalente *m*

equivocal /ɪˈkwɪvəkl/ *adj* equivoco

era /ˈɪərə/ *n* età *f*; (*geological*) era *f*

eradicate /ɪˈrædɪkeɪt/ *vt* eradicare

erase /ɪˈreɪz/ *vt* cancellare. **~r** *n* gomma *f* [da cancellare]; (*for blackboard*) cancellino *m*

e

erect /ɪˈrekt/ *adj* eretto ● *vt* erigere. **~ion** *n* erezione *f*

ero|de /ɪˈrəʊd/ *vt* (water:) erodere; (acid:) corrodere. **~sion** *n* erosione *f*; (*by acid*) corrosione *f*

erotic /ɪˈrɒtɪk/ *adj* erotico.

err /ɜː(r)/ *vi* errare; (*sin*) peccare

errand /ˈerənd/ *n* commissione *f*

erratic /ɪˈrætɪk/ *adj* irregolare; (person, moods) imprevedibile; (exchange rate) incostante

erroneous /ɪˈrəʊnɪəs/ *adj* erroneo

error /ˈerə(r)/ *n* errore *m*; **in ~** per errore

erudit|e /ˈerʊdaɪt/ *adj* erudito. **~ion** *n* erudizione *f*

erupt /ɪˈrʌpt/ *vi* eruttare; (spots:) spuntare; (*fig: in anger*) dare in escandescenze. **~ion** *n* eruzione *f*; *fig* scoppio *m*

escalat|e /ˈeskəleɪt/ *vi* intensificarsi ● *vt* intensificare. **~ion** *n* escalation *f inv*. **~or** *n* scala *f* mobile

escapade /ˈeskəpeɪd/ *n* scappatella *f*

escape /ɪˈskeɪp/ *n* fuga *f*; (*from prison*) evasione *f*; **have a narrow ~** cavarsela per un pelo ● *vi* (prisoner:) evadere (**from** da); sfuggire (**from sb** alla sorveglianza di qcno); (animal:) scappare; (gas:) fuoriuscire ● *vt* **~ notice** passare inosservato; **the name ~s me** mi sfugge il nome

escapism /ɪˈskeɪpɪzm/ *n* evasione *f* [dalla realtà]

escort¹ /ˈeskɔːt/ *n* accompagnatore, -trice *mf*; (*Mil etc*) scorta *f*

escort² /ɪˈskɔːt/ *vt* accompagnare; (*Mil etc*) scortare

Eskimo /ˈeskɪməʊ/ *n* esquimese *mf*

especial /ɪˈspeʃl/ *adj* speciale. **~ly** *adv* specialmente; (kind) particolarmente

espionage /ˈespɪənɑːʒ/ *n* spionaggio *m*

essay /ˈeseɪ/ *n* saggio *m*; (*Sch*) tema *f*

essence /ˈesns/ *n* essenza *f*; **in ~** in sostanza

essential /ɪˈsenʃl/ *adj* essenziale ● *npl* **the ~s** l'essenziale *m*. **~ly** *adv* essenzialmente

establish /ɪˈstæblɪʃ/ *vt* stabilire (contact, lead); fondare (firm); (*prove*) accertare; **~ oneself as** affermarsi come. **~ment** *n* (*firm*) azienda *f*; **the E~ment** l'ordine *m* costituito

estate /ɪˈsteɪt/ *n* tenuta *f*; (*possessions*) patrimonio *m*; (*housing*) quartiere *m* residenziale. **~ agent** *n* agente *m* immobiliare. **~ car** *n* giardiniera *f*

esteem /ɪˈstiːm/ *n* stima *f* ● *vt* stimare; (*consider*) giudicare

estimate¹ /ˈestɪmət/ *n* valutazione *f*; (*Comm*) preventivo *m*; **at a rough ~** a occhio e croce

estimat|e² /ˈestɪmeɪt/ *vt* stimare. **~ion** *n* (*esteem*) stima *f*; **in my ~ion** (*judgement*) a mio giudizio

estuary /ˈestjʊərɪ/ *n* estuario *m*

etc /etˈsetərə/ *abbr* (et cetera) ecc

etching /ˈetʃɪŋ/ *n* acquaforte *f*

eternal /ɪˈtɜːnl/ *adj* eterno

eternity /ɪˈθɜːnətɪ/ *n* eternità *f*

ethic /ˈeθɪk/ *n* etica *f*. **~al** *adj* etico. **~s** *n* etica *f*

ethnic /ˈeθnɪk/ *adj* etnico

etiquette /ˈetɪket/ *n* etichetta *f*

EU *n abbr* (European Union) UE *f*

euphemis|m /ˈjuːfəmɪzm/ *n* eufemismo *m*. **~tic** *adj* eufemistico

euphoria /juːˈfɔːrɪə/ *n* euforia *f*

euro /ˈjʊərəʊ/ *n* euro *m inv*

Euro- /ˈjʊərəʊ-/ *pref* **~cheque** *n* eurochèque *m inv*. **~dollar** *n* eurodollaro *m*

Europe /ˈjʊərəp/ *n* Europa *f*

European /jʊərəˈpɪən/ *adj* europeo; **~ Union** Unione *f* Europea ● *n* europeo, -a *mf*

Euro-sceptic /jʊərəʊˈskeptɪk/ *adj* euroscettico ● *n* euroscettico, -a *mf*

evacuat|e /ɪˈvækjʊeɪt/ *vt* evacuare (building, area). **~ion** *n* evacuazione *f*

evade /ɪˈveɪd/ *vt* evadere (taxes); evitare (the enemy, authorities); **~ the issue** evitare l'argomento

evaluat|e /ɪˈvæljʊeɪt/ *vt* valutare. **~ion** /-ˈeɪʃn/ *n* valutazione *f*

evange|lical /iːvænˈdʒelɪkl/ *adj* evangelico. **~list** *n* evangelista *m*

evaporat|e /ɪˈvæpəreɪt/ *vi* evaporare; *fig* svanire. **~ion** *n* evaporazione *f*

evasion /ɪˈveɪʒn/ *n* evasione *f*

evasive /ɪˈveɪsɪv/ *adj* evasivo

eve /iːv/ *n liter* vigilia *f*

even /ˈiːvn/ *adj* (*level*) piatto; (*same, equal*) uguale; (*regular*) regolare; (number) pari; **get ~ with** vendicarsi di;

now we're ~ adesso siamo pari ● *adv* anche, ancora; ~ **if** anche se; ~ **so** con tutto ciò; **not** ~ nemmeno; ~ **bigger/hotter** ancora più grande/caldo ● *vt* ~ **the score** (*Sport*) pareggiare. □ ~ **out** *vi* livellarsi. □ ~ **up** *vt* livellare

evening /'i:vnɪŋ/ *n* sera *f*; (*whole evening*) serata *f*; **this** ~ stasera; **in the** ~ la sera. ~ **class** *n* corso *m* serale. ~ **dress** *n* abito *m* scuro; (*woman's*) abito *m* da sera

event /ɪ'vent/ *n* avvenimento *m*; (*function*) manifestazione *f*; (*Sport*) gara *f*; **in the** ~ **of** nell'eventualità di; **in the** ~ alla fine. ~**ful** *adj* movimentato

eventual /ɪ'ventjʊəl/ *adj* **the** ~ **winner was...** alla fine il vincitore è stato.... ~**ity** *n* eventualità *f*. ~**ly** *adv* alla fine; ~**ly!** finalmente!

ever /'evə(r)/ *adv* mai; **I haven't** ~... non ho mai...; **for** ~ per sempre; **hardly** ~ quasi mai; ~ **since** da quando; (*since that time*) da allora; ~ **so** [!] veramente

'evergreen *n* sempreverde *m*

ever'lasting *adj* eterno

every /'evrɪ/ *adj* ogni; ~ **one** ciascuno; ~ **other day** un giorno si un giorno no

every: ~**body** *pron* tutti *pl*. ~**day** *adj* quotidiano, di ogni giorno. ~**one** *pron* tutti *pl*; ~**thing** *pron* tutto; ~**where** *adv* dappertutto; (*wherever*) dovunque

evict /ɪ'vɪkt/ *vt* sfrattare. ~**ion** *n* sfratto *m*

eviden|ce /'evɪdəns/ *n* evidenza *f*; (*Jur*) testimonianza *f*; **give** ~**ce** testimoniare. ~**t** *adj* evidente. ~**tly** *adv* evidentemente

evil /'i:vl/ *adj* cattivo ● *n* male *m*

evocative /ɪ'vɒkətɪv/ *adj* evocativo; **be** ~ **of** evocare

evoke /ɪ'vəʊk/ *vt* evocare

evolution /i:və'lu:ʃn/ *n* evoluzione *f*

evolve /ɪ'vɒlv/ *vt* evolvere ● *vi* evolversi

ewe /ju:/ *n* pecora *f*

exact /ɪg'zækt/ *adj* esatto ● *vt* esigere. ~**ing** *adj* esigente. ~**itude** *n* esattezza *f*. ~**ly** *adv* esattamente; **not** ~**ly** non proprio. ~**ness** *n* precisione *f*

exaggerat|e /ɪg'zædʒəreɪt/ *vt/i* esagerare. ~**ion** *n* esagerazione *f*

exam /ɪg'zæm/ *n* esame *m*

examination /ɪgzæmɪ'neɪʃn/ *n* esame *m*; (*of patient*) visita *f*

examine /ɪg'zæmɪn/ *vt* esaminare; visitare (patient). ~**r** *n* (*Sch*) esaminatore, -trice *mf*

example /ɪg'zɑ:mpl/ *n* esempio *m*; **for** ~ per esempio; **make an** ~ **of sb** punire qcno per dare un esempio; **be an** ~ **to sb** dare il buon esempio a qcno

exasperat|e /ɪg'zæspəreɪt/ *vt* esasperare. ~**ion** *n* esasperazione *f*

excavat|e /'ekskəveɪt/ *vt* scavare; (*Archaeol*) fare gli scavi di. ~**ion** *n* scavo *m*

exceed /ɪk'si:d/ *vt* eccedere. ~**ingly** *adv* estremamente

excel /ɪk'sel/ *v* (*pt/pp* **excelled**) ● *vi* eccellere ● *vt* ~ **oneself** superare se stessi

excellen|ce /'eksələns/ *n* eccellenza *f*. **E**~**cy** *n* (*title*) Eccellenza *f*. ~**t** *adj* eccellente

except /ɪk'sept/ *prep* eccetto, tranne; ~ **for** eccetto, tranne; ~ **that...** eccetto che... ● *vt* eccettuare. ~**ing** *prep* eccetto, tranne

exception /ɪk'sepʃn/ *n* eccezione *f*; **take** ~ **to** fare obiezioni a. ~**al** *adj* eccezionale. ~**ally** *adv* eccezionalmente

excerpt /'eksɜ:pt/ *n* estratto *m*

excess /ɪk'ses/ *n* eccesso *m*; **in** ~ **of** oltre. ~ **baggage** *n* bagaglio *m* in eccedenza. ~ **'fare** *n* supplemento *m*

excessive /ɪk'sesɪv/ *adj* eccessivo. ~**ly** *adv* eccessivamente

exchange /ɪks'tʃeɪndʒ/ *n* scambio *m*; (*Teleph*) centrale *f*; (*Comm*) cambio *m*; **in** ~ in cambio (**for** di) ● *vt* scambiare (**for** con); cambiare (money). ~ **rate** *n* tasso *m* di cambio

excise[1] /'eksaɪz/ *n* dazio *m*; ~ **duty** dazio *m*

excise[2] /ek'saɪz/ *vt* recidere

excitable /ɪk'saɪtəbl/ *adj* eccitabile

excit|e /ɪk'saɪt/ *vt* eccitare. ~**ed** *adj* eccitato; **get** ~**ed** eccitarsi. ~**edly** *adv* tutto eccitato. ~**ement** *n* eccitazione *f*. ~**ing** *adj* eccitante; (story, film) appassionante; (holiday) entusiasmante

exclaim /ɪk'skleɪm/ *vt/i* esclamare

exclamation /eksklə'meɪʃn/ *n* esclamazione *f*. ~ **mark** *n*, *Am* ~ **point** *n* punto *m* esclamativo

exclu|de /ɪk'skluːd/ *vt* escludere. **~ding** *pron* escluso. **~sion** *n* esclusione *f*

exclusive /ɪk'skluːsɪv/ *adj* (rights, club) esclusivo; (interview) in esclusiva; **~ of...** ...escluso. **~ly** *adv* esclusivamente

excruciating /ɪk'skruːʃɪeɪtɪŋ/ *adj* atroce (pain); ([!]: *very bad*) spaventoso

excursion /ɪk'skɜːʃn/ *n* escursione *f*

excusable /ɪk'skjuːzəbl/ *adj* perdonabile

excuse[1] /ɪk'skjuːs/ *n* scusa *f*

excuse[2] /ɪk'skjuːz/ *vt* scusare; **~ from** esonerare da; **~ me!** (*to get attention*) scusi!; (*to get past*) permesso!, scusi!; (*indignant*) come ha detto?

ex-di'rectory *adj* **be ~** non figurare sull'elenco telefonico

execute /'eksɪkjuːt/ *vt* eseguire; (*put to death*) giustiziare; attuare (plan)

execution /eksɪ'kjuːʃn/ *n* esecuzione *f*; (*of plan*) attuazione *f*. **~er** *n* boia *m inv*

executive /ɪg'zekjʊtɪv/ *adj* esecutivo • *n* dirigente *mf*; (*Pol*) esecutivo *m*

executor /ɪg'zekjʊtə(r)/ *n* (*Jur*) esecutore, -trice *mf*

exempt /ɪg'zempt/ *adj* esente • *vt* esentare (**from** da). **~ion** *n* esenzione *f*

exercise /'eksəsaɪz/ *n* esercizio *m*; (*Mil*) esercitazione *f*; **physical ~s** ginnastica *f*; **take ~** fare del moto • *vt* esercitare (muscles, horse); portare a spasso (dog); mettere in pratica (skills) • *vi* esercitarsi. **~ book** *n* quaderno *m*

exert /ɪg'zɜːt/ *vt* esercitare; **~ oneself** sforzarsi. **~ion** *n* sforzo *m*

exhale /eks'heɪl/ *vt/i* esalare

exhaust /ɪg'zɔːst/ *n* (*Auto*) scappamento *m*; (*pipe*) tubo *m* di scappamento; **~ fumes** fumi *mpl* di scarico *m* • *vt* esaurire. **~ed** *adj* esausto. **~ing** *adj* estenuante; (climate, person) sfibrante. **~ion** *n* esaurimento *m*. **~ive** *adj fig* esauriente

exhibit /ɪg'zɪbɪt/ *n* oggetto *m* esposto; (*Jur*) reperto *m* • *vt* esporre; *fig* dimostrare

exhibition /eksɪ'bɪʃn/ *n* mostra *f*; (*of strength, skill*) dimostrazione *f*. **~ist** *n* esibizionista *mf*

exhibitor /ɪg'zɪbɪtə(r)/ *n* espositore, -trice *mf*

exhort /ɪg'zɔːt/ *vt* esortare

exile /'eksaɪl/ *n* esilio *m*; (*person*) esule *mf* • *vt* esiliare

exist /ɪg'zɪst/ *vi* esistere. **~ence** *n* esistenza *f*; **in ~** esistente; **be in ~ence** esistere. **~ing** *adj* attuale

exit /'eksɪt/ *n* uscita *f*; (*Theat*) uscita *f* di scena • *vi* (*Theat*) uscire di scena; (*Comput*) uscire

exorbitant /ɪg'zɔːbɪtənt/ *adj* esorbitante

exotic /ɪg'zɒtɪk/ *adj* esotico

expand /ɪk'spænd/ *vt* espandere • *vi* espandersi; (*Comm*) svilupparsi; (metal:) dilatarsi; **~ on** (*fig: explain better*) approfondire

expans|e /ɪk'spæns/ *n* estensione *f*. **~ion** *n* espansione *f*; (*Comm*) sviluppo *m*; (*of metal*) dilatazione *f*. **~ive** *adj* espansivo

expatriate /eks'pætrɪət/ *n* espatriato, -a *mf*

expect /ɪk'spekt/ *vt* aspettare (letter, baby); (*suppose*) pensare; (*demand*) esigere; **I ~ so** penso di sì; **be ~ing** essere in stato interessante

expectan|cy /ɪk'spektənsɪ/ *n* aspettativa *f*. **~t** *adj* in attesa; **~t mother** donna *f* incinta. **~tly** *adv* con impazienza

expectation /ekspek'teɪʃn/ *n* aspettativa *f*, speranza *f*

expedient /ɪk'spiːdɪənt/ *adj* conveniente • *n* espediente *m*

expedition /ekspɪ'dɪʃn/ *n* spedizione *f*. **~ary** *adj* (*Mil*) di spedizione

expel /ɪk'spel/ *vt* (*pt/pp* **expelled**) espellere

expend /ɪk'spend/ *vt* consumare. **~able** *adj* sacrificabile

expenditure /ɪk'spendɪtʃə(r)/ *n* spesa *f*

expense /ɪk'spens/ *n* spesa *f*; **business ~s** *pl* spese *fpl*; **at my ~** a mie spese; **at the ~ of** *fig* a spese di

expensive /ɪk'spensɪv/ *adj* caro, costoso. **~ly** *adv* costosamente

experience /ɪk'spɪərɪəns/ *n* esperienza *f* • *vt* provare (sensation); avere

(problem). **~d** *adj* esperto
experiment /ɪk'sperɪmənt/ *n* esperimento ● *vi* sperimentare. **~al** *adj* sperimentale
expert /'ekspɜːt/ *adj & n* esperto, -a *mf*. **~ly** *adv* abilmente
expertise /ekspɜː'tiːz/ *n* competenza *f*
expire /ɪk'spaɪə(r)/ *vi* scadere
expiry /ɪk'spaɪərɪ/ *n* scadenza *f*. **~ date** *n* data *f* di scadenza
explain /ɪk'spleɪn/ *vt* spiegare
explana|tion /eksplə'neɪʃn/ *n* spiegazione *f*. **~tory** *adj* esplicativo
explicit /ɪk'splɪsɪt/ *adj* esplicito. **~ly** *adv* esplicitamente
explode /ɪk'spləʊd/ *vi* esplodere ● *vt* fare esplodere
exploit[1] /'eksplɔɪt/ *n* impresa *f*
exploit[2] /ɪk'splɔɪt/ *vt* sfruttare. **~ation** *n* sfruttamento *m*
explora|tion /eksplə'reɪʃn/ *n* esplorazione *f*. **~tory** *adj* esplorativo
explore /ɪk'splɔː(r)/ *vt* esplorare; *fig* studiare (implications). **~r** *n* esploratore, -trice *mf*
explos|ion /ɪk'spləʊʒn/ *n* esplosione *f*. **~ive** *adj & n* esplosivo *m*
export /'ekspɔːt/ *n* esportazione *f* ● *vt* /-'spɔːt/ esportare. **~er** *n* esportatore, -trice *mf*
expos|e /ɪk'spəʊz/ *vt* esporre; (*reveal*) svelare; smascherare (traitor etc). **~ure** *n* esposizione *f*; (*Med*) esposizione *f* prolungata al freddo/caldo; (*of crimes*) smascheramento *m*; **24 ~ures** (*Phot*) 24 pose
express /ɪk'spres/ *adj* espresso ● *adv* (send) per espresso ● *n* (*train*) espresso *m* ● *vt* esprimere; **~ oneself** esprimersi. **~ion** *n* espressione *f*. **~ive** *adj* espressivo. **~ly** *adv* espressamente
expulsion /ɪk'spʌlʃn/ *n* espulsione *f*
exquisite /ek'skwɪzɪt/ *adj* squisito
extend /ɪk'stend/ *vt* prolungare (visit, road); prorogare (visa, contract); ampliare (building, knowledge); (*stretch out*) allungare; tendere (hand) ● *vi* (garden, knowledge:) estendersi
extension /ɪk'stenʃn/ *n* prolungamento *m*; (*of visa, contract*) proroga *f*; (*of treaty*) ampliamento *m*; (*part of building*) annesso *m*; (*length of cable*) prolunga *f*; (*Teleph*) interno *m*; **~ 226** interno 226
extensive /ɪk'stensɪv/ *adj* ampio, vasto. **~ly** *adv* ampiamente
extent /ɪk'stent/ *n* (*scope*) portata *f*; **to a certain ~** fino a un certo punto; **to such an ~ that...** fino al punto che...
exterior /ɪk'stɪərɪə(r)/ *adj & n* esterno *m*
exterminat|e /ɪk'stɜːmɪneɪt/ *vt* sterminare. **~ion** *n* sterminio *m*
external /ɪk'stɜːnl/ *adj* esterno; **for ~ use only** (*Med*) per uso esterno. **~ly** *adv* esternamente
extinct /ɪk'stɪŋkt/ *adj* estinto. **~ion** *n* estinzione *f*
extinguish /ɪk'stɪŋgwɪʃ/ *vt* estinguere. **~er** *n* estintore *m*
extort /ɪk'stɔːt/ *vt* estorcere. **~ion** *n* estorsione *f*
extortionate /ɪk'stɔːʃənət/ *adj* esorbitante
extra /'ekstrə/ *adj* in più; (train) straordinario; **an ~ £10** 10 sterline extra, 10 sterline in più ● *adv* in più; (*especially*) più; **pay ~** pagare in più, pagare extra; **~ strong/busy** fortissimo/occupatissimo ● *n* (*Theat*) comparsa *f*; **~s** *pl* extra *mpl*
extract[1] /'ekstrækt/ *n* estratto *m*
extract[2] /ɪk'strækt/ *vt* estrarre (tooth, oil); strappare (secret); ricavare (truth). **~or [fan]** *n* aspiratore *m*
extradit|e /'ekstrədaɪt/ *vt* (*Jur*) estradare. **~ion** *n* estradizione *f*
extraordinar|y /ɪk'strɔːdɪnərɪ/ *adj* straordinario. **~ily** *adv* straordinariamente
extravagan|ce /ɪk'strævəgəns/ *n* (*with money*) prodigalità *f*; (*of behaviour*) stravaganza *f*. **~t** *adj* spendaccione; (*bizarre*) stravagante; (claim) esagerato
extrem|e /ɪk'striːm/ *adj* estremo ● *n* estremo *m*; **in the ~e** al massimo. **~ely** *adv* estremamente. **~ist** *n* estremista *mf*
extricate /'ekstrɪkeɪt/ *vt* districare
extrovert /'ekstrəvɜːt/ *n* estroverso, -a *mf*
exuberant /ɪg'zjuːbərənt/ *adj* esuberante
exude /ɪg'zjuːd/ *vt also fig* trasudare
exult /ɪg'zʌlt/ *vi* esultare
eye /aɪ/ *n* occhio *m*; (*of needle*) cruna *f*; **keep an ~ on** tener d'occhio; **see ~**

to ~ aver le stesse idee • *vt* (*pt/pp* **eyed**, *pres p* **ey[e]ing**) guardare

eye: **~ball** *n* bulbo *m* oculare. **~ brow** *n* sopracciglio *m* (*pl* sopracciglia *f*). **~lash** *n* ciglio *m* (*pl* ciglia *f*). **~lid** *n* palpebra *f*. **~-opener** *n* rivelazione *f*. **~-shadow** *n* ombretto *m*. **~sight** *n* vista *f*. **~sore** *n* [!] pugno *m* nell'occhio. **~witness** *n* testimone *mf* oculare

e

f

Ff

fable /ˈfeɪbl/ *n* favola *f*

fabric /ˈfæbrɪk/ *n also fig* tessuto *m*

fabulous /ˈfæbjʊləs/ *adj* [!] favoloso

façade /fəˈsɑːd/ *n* (*of building, person*) facciata *f*

face /feɪs/ *n* faccia *f*, viso *m*; (*grimace*) smorfia *f*; (*surface*) faccia *f*; (*of clock*) quadrante *m*; **pull ~s** far boccacce; **in the ~ of** di fronte a; **on the ~ of it** in apparenza • *vt* essere di fronte a; (*confront*) affrontare; **~ north** (house:) dare a nord; **~ the fact that** arrendersi al fatto che. □ **~ up to** *vt* accettare (facts); affrontare (person)

face: **~-flannel** *n* ≈ guanto *m* di spugna. **~less** *adj* anonimo. **~-lift** *n* plastica *f* facciale

facetious /fəˈsiːʃəs/ *adj* spiritoso. **~ remarks** spiritosaggini *mpl*

facial /ˈfeɪʃl/ *adj* facciale • *n* trattamento *m* di bellezza al viso

facile /ˈfæsaɪl/ *adj* semplicistico

facilitate /fəˈsɪlɪteɪt/ *vt* rendere possibile; (*make easier*) facilitare

facilit|y /fəˈsɪlətɪ/ *n* facilità *f*; **~ies** *pl* (*of area, in hotel etc*) attrezzature *fpl*

fact /fækt/ *n* fatto *m*; **in ~** infatti

faction /ˈfækʃn/ *n* fazione *f*

factor /ˈfæktə(r)/ *n* fattore *m*

factory /ˈfæktərɪ/ *n* fabbrica *f*

factual /ˈfæktʃʊəl/ *adj* **be ~** attenersi ai fatti. **~ly** *adv* (inaccurate) dal punto di vista dei fatti

faculty /ˈfækəltɪ/ *n* facoltà *f inv*

fad /fæd/ *n* capriccio *m*

fade /feɪd/ *vi* sbiadire; (sound, light:) affievolirsi; (flower:) appassire. □ **~ in** *vt* cominciare in dissolvenza (picture). □ **~ out** *vt* finire in dissolvenza (picture)

fag /fæg/ *n* (*chore*) fatica *f*; ([!]: *cigarette*) sigaretta *f*; (*Am* [✱]: *homosexual*) frocio *m*. **~ end** *n* [!] cicca *f*

Fahrenheit /ˈfærənhaɪt/ *adj* Fahrenheit

fail /feɪl/ *n* **without ~** senz'altro • *vi* (attempt:) fallire; (eyesight, memory:) indebolirsi; (engine, machine:) guastarsi; (marriage:) andare a rotoli; (*in exam*) essere bocciato; **~ to do sth** non fare qcsa; **I tried but I ~ed** ho provato ma non ci sono riuscito • *vt* non superare (exam); bocciare (candidate); (*disappoint*) deludere; **words ~ me** mi mancano le parole

failing /ˈfeɪlɪŋ/ *n* difetto *m* • *prep* **~ that** altrimenti

failure /ˈfeɪljə(r)/ *n* fallimento *m*; (*mechanical*) guasto *m*; (*person*) incapace *mf*

faint /feɪnt/ *adj* leggero; (memory) vago; **feel ~** sentirsi mancare • *n* svenimento *m* • *vi* svenire

faint: **~-'hearted** *adj* timido. **~ly** *adv* (*slightly*) leggermente

fair¹ /feə(r)/ *n* fiera *f*

fair² *adj* (hair, person) biondo; (skin) chiaro; (weather) bello; (*just*) giusto; (*quite good*) discreto; (*Sch*) abbastanza bene; **a ~ amount** abbastanza • *adv* **play ~** fare un gioco pulito. **~ly** *adv* con giustizia; (*rather*) discretamente, abbastanza. **~ness** *n* giustizia *f*. **~ play** *n* fair play *m inv*

fairy /ˈfeərɪ/ *n* fata *f*; **~ story, ~-tale** *n* fiaba *f*

faith /feɪθ/ *n* fede *f*; (*trust*) fiducia *f*; **in good/bad ~** in buona/mala fede

faithful /ˈfeɪθfl/ *adj* fedele. **~ly** *adv* fedelmente; **yours ~ly** distinti saluti. **~ness** *n* fedeltà *f*

fake /feɪk/ *adj* falso • *n* falsificazione *f*; (*person*) impostore *m* • *vt* falsificare; (*pretend*) fingere

falcon /ˈfɔːlkən/ *n* falcone *m*

fall /fɔːl/ *n* caduta *f*; (*in prices*) ribasso *m*; (*Am: autumn*) autunno *m*; **have a ~** fare una caduta • *vi* (*pt* **fell**, *pp* **fallen**) cadere; (night:) scendere; **~ in love** innamorarsi. □ ~ **about** *vi* (*with laughter*) morire dal ridere. □ ~ **back on** *vt* ritornare su. □ ~ **for** *vt* [!] innamorarsi di (person); cascarci (sth, trick). □ ~ **down** *vi* cadere; (building:) crollare. □ ~ **in** *vi* caderci dentro; (*collapse*) crollare; (*Mil*) mettersi in riga; ~ **in with** concordare con (suggestion, plan). □ ~ **off** *vi* cadere; (*diminish*) diminuire. □ ~ **out** *vi* (*quarrel*) litigare; **his hair is ~ing out** perde i capelli. □ ~ **over** *vi* cadere. □ ~ **through** *vi* (plan:) andare a monte

fallacy /'fæləsɪ/ *n* errore *m*

fallible /'fæləbl/ *adj* fallibile

'fall-out *n* pioggia *f* radioattiva

false /fɔ:ls/ *adj* falso; ~ **bottom** doppio fondo *m*; ~ **start** (*Sport*) falsa partenza *f*. **~hood** *n* menzogna *f*. **~ness** *n* falsità *f*

false 'teeth *npl* dentiera *f*

falsify /'fɔ:lsɪfaɪ/ *vt* (*pt/pp* **-ied**) falsificare

falter /'fɔ:ltə(r)/ *vi* vacillare; (*making speech*) esitare

fame /feɪm/ *n* fama *f*

familiar /fə'mɪljə(r)/ *adj* familiare; **be ~ with** (*know*) conoscere. **~ity** *n* familiarità *f*. **~ize** *vt* familiarizzare; **~ize oneself with** familiarizzarsi con

family /'fæməlɪ/ *n* famiglia *f*

family: ~ **'planning** *n* pianificazione *f* familiare. ~ **'tree** *n* albero *m* genealogico

famine /'fæmɪn/ *n* carestia *f*

famished /'fæmɪʃt/ *adj* **be ~** [!] avere una fame da lupo

famous /'feɪməs/ *adj* famoso

fan[1] /fæn/ *n* ventilatore *m*; (*handheld*) ventaglio *m* ● *vt* (*pt/pp* **fanned**) far vento a; ~ **oneself** sventagliarsi; *fig* ~ **the flames** soffiare sul fuoco. □ ~ **out** *vi* spiegarsi a ventaglio

fan[2] *n* (*admirer*) ammiratore, -trice *mf*; (*Sport*) tifoso *m*; (*of Verdi etc*) appassionato, -a *mf*

fanatic /fə'nætɪk/ *n* fanatico, -a *mf*. **~al** *adj* fanatico. **~ism** *n* fanatismo *m*

'fan belt *n* cinghia *f* per ventilatore

fanciful /'fænsɪfl/ *adj* fantasioso

fancy /'fænsɪ/ *n* fantasia *f*; **I've taken a real ~ to him** mi è molto simpatico; **as the ~ takes you** come ti pare ● *adj* [a] fantasia ● *vt* (*pt/pp* **-ied**) (*believe*) credere; ([!]: *want*) aver voglia di; **he fancies you** [!] gli piaci; ~ **that!** ma guarda un po'! ~ **'dress** *n* costume *m* (*per maschera*)

fanfare /'fænfeə(r)/ *n* fanfara *f*

fang /fæŋ/ *n* zanna *f*; (*of snake*) dente *m*

fantas|ize /'fæntəsaɪz/ *vi* fantasticare. **~tic** *adj* fantastico. **~y** *n* fantasia *f*

far /fɑ:(r)/ *adv* lontano; (*much*) molto; **by ~** di gran lunga; ~ **away** lontano; **as ~ as the church** fino alla chiesa; **how ~ is it from here?** quanto dista da qui?; **as ~ as I know** per quanto io sappia ● *adj* (end, side) altro; **the F~ East** l'Estremo Oriente *m*

farc|e /fɑ:s/ *n* farsa *f*. **~ical** *adj* ridicolo

fare /feə(r)/ *n* tariffa *f*; (*food*) vitto *m*. **~-dodger** *n* passeggero, -a *mf* senza biglietto

farewell /feə'wel/ *int liter* addio! ● *n* addio *m*

far-'fetched *adj* improbabile

farm /fɑ:m/ *n* fattoria *f* ● *vi* fare l'agricoltore ● *vt* coltivare (land). **~er** *n* agricoltore *m*

farm: **~house** *n* casa *f* colonica. **~ing** *n* agricoltura *f*. **~yard** *n* aia *f*

far: **~-'reaching** *adj* di larga portata. **~-'sighted** *adj fig* prudente; (*Am: long-sighted*) presbite

farther /'fɑ:ðə(r)/ *adv* più lontano ● *adj* **at the ~ end of** all'altra estremità di

fascinat|e /'fæsɪneɪt/ *vt* affascinare. **~ing** *adj* affascinante. **~ion** *n* fascino *m*

fascis|m /'fæʃɪzm/ *n* fascismo *m*. **~t** *n* fascista *mf* ● *adj* fascista

fashion /'fæʃn/ *n* moda *f*; (*manner*) maniera *f* ● *vt* modellare. **~able** *adj* di moda; **be ~able** essere alla moda. **~ably** *adv* alla moda

fast[1] /fɑ:st/ *adj* veloce; (colour) indelebile; **be ~** (clock:) andare avanti ● *adv* velocemente; (*firmly*) saldamente; **~er!** più in fretta!; **be ~ asleep** dormire profondamente

fast[2] *n* digiuno *m* ● *vi* digiunare

fasten /'fɑ:sn/ *vt* allacciare; chiudere (window); (*stop flapping*) mettere un fermo a ● *vi* allacciarsi. **~er** *n*, **~ing** *n* chiusura *f*

fat /fæt/ *adj* (**fatter, fattest**) (person,

f

cheque) grasso ● *n* grasso *m*

fatal /'feɪtl/ *adj* mortale; (error) fatale. **~ism** *n* fatalismo *m*. **~ist** *n* fatalista *mf*. **~ity** *n* morte *f*. **~ly** *adv* mortalmente

fate /feɪt/ *n* destino *m*. **~ful** *adj* fatidico

father /'fɑ:ðə(r)/ *n* padre *m*; **F~ Christmas** Babbo *m* Natale ● *vt* generare (child)

father: ~hood *n* paternità *f*. **~-in-law** *n* (*pl* **~s-in-law**) suocero *m*. **~ly** *adj* paterno

fathom /'fæð(ə)m/ *n* (*Naut*) braccio *m* ● *vt* **~ [out]** comprendere

fatigue /fə'ti:g/ *n* fatica *f*

fatten /'fætn/ *vt* ingrassare (animal). **~ing** *adj* **cream is ~ing** la panna fa ingrassare

fatty /'fætɪ/ *adj* grasso ● *n* [!] ciccione, -a *mf*

fatuous /'fætjʊəs/ *adj* fatuo

faucet /'fɔ:sɪt/ *n Am* rubinetto *m*

fault /fɔ:lt/ *n* difetto *m*; (*Geol*) faglia *f*; (*Tennis*) fallo *m*; **be at ~** avere torto; **find ~ with** trovare da ridire su; **it's your ~** è colpa tua ● *vt* criticare. **~less** *adj* impeccabile

faulty /'fɔ:ltɪ/ *adj* difettoso

favour /'feɪvə(r)/ *n* favore *m*; **be in ~ of sth** essere a favore di qcsa; **do sb a ~** fare un piacere a qcno ● *vt* (*prefer*) preferire. **~able** *adj* favorevole

favourit|e /'feɪv(ə)rɪt/ *adj* preferito ● *n* preferito, -a *mf*; (*Sport*) favorito, -a *mf*. **~ism** *n* favoritismo *m*

fawn /fɔ:n/ *adj* fulvo ● *n* (*animal*) cerbiatto *m*

fax /fæks/ *n* (*document, machine*) fax *m inv*; **by ~** per fax ● *vt* faxare. **~ machine** *n* fax *m inv*. **~-modem** *n* modem-fax *m inv*, fax-modem *m inv*

fear /fɪə(r)/ *n* paura *f*; **no ~!** [!] vai tranquillo! ● *vt* temere ● *vi* **~ for sth** temere per qcsa

fear|ful /'fɪəfl/ *adj* pauroso; (*awful*) terribile. **~less** *adj* impavido. **~some** *adj* spaventoso

feas|ibility /fi:zɪ'bɪlɪtɪ/ *n* praticabilità *f*. **~ible** *adj* fattibile; (*possible*) probabile

feast /fi:st/ *n* festa *f*; (*banquet*) banchetto *m* ● *vi* banchettare; **~ on** godersi

feat /fi:t/ *n* impresa *f*

feather /'feðə(r)/ *n* piuma *f*

feature /'fi:tʃə(r)/ *n* (*quality*) caratteristica *f*; (*Journ*) articolo *m*; **~s** (*pl: of face*) lineamenti *mpl* ● *vt* (film:) avere come protagonista ● *vi* (*on a list etc*) comparire. **~ film** *n* lungometraggio *m*

February /'febrʊərɪ/ *n* febbraio *m*

fed /fed/ ▷**FEED** ● *adj* **be ~ up** [!] essere stufo (**with** di)

federal /'fed(ə)rəl/ *adj* federale

federation /fedə'reɪʃn/ *n* federazione *f*

fee /fi:/ *n* tariffa *f*; (*lawyer's, doctor's*) onorario *m*; (*for membership, school*) quota *f*

feeble /'fi:bl/ *adj* debole; (excuse) fiacco

feed /fi:d/ *n* mangiare *m*; (*for baby*) pappa *f* ● *v* (*pt/pp* **fed**) ● *vt* dar da mangiare a (animal); (*support*) nutrire; **~ sth into sth** inserire qcsa in qcsa ● *vi* mangiare

'feedback *n* controreazione *f*; (*of information*) reazione *f*, feedback *m*

feel /fi:l/ *v* (*pt/pp* **felt**) ● *vt* sentire; (*experience*) provare; (*think*) pensare; (*touch: searching*) tastare; (*touch: for texture*) toccare ● *vi* **~ soft/hard** essere duro/morbido al tatto; **~ hot/hungry** aver caldo/fame; **~ ill** sentirsi male; **I don't ~ like it** non ne ho voglia; **how do you ~ about it?** (*opinion*) che te ne pare?; **it doesn't ~ right** non mi sembra giusto. **~er** *n* (*of animal*) antenna *f*; **put out ~ers** *fig* tastare il terreno. **~ing** *n* sentimento *m*; (*awareness*) sensazione *f*

feet /fi:t/ ▷**FOOT**

feign /feɪn/ *vt* simulare

fell[1] /fel/ *vt* (*knock down*) abbattere

fell[2] ▷**FALL**

fellow /'feləʊ/ *n* (*of society*) socio *m*; ([!]*: man*) tipo *m*

fellow 'countryman *n* compatriota *m*

felony /'felənɪ/ *n* delitto *m*

felt[1] /felt/ ▷**FEEL**

felt[2] *n* feltro *m*. **~[-tipped] 'pen** /[-tɪpt]/ *n* pennarello *m*

female /'fi:meɪl/ *adj* femminile; **the ~ antelope** l'antilope femmina ● *n* femmina *f*

femin|ine /ˈfemɪnɪn/ *adj* femminile ● *n* (*Gram*) femminile *m*. **~inity** *n* femminilità *f*. **~ist** *adj & n* femminista *mf*

fenc|e /fens/ *n* recinto *m*; (🅸: *person*) ricettatore *m* ● *vi* (*Sport*) tirar di scherma. ▫ **~ in** *vt* chiudere in un recinto. **~er** *n* schermidore *m*. **~ing** *n* steccato *m*; (*Sport*) scherma *f*

fend /fend/ *vi* **~ for oneself** badare a se stesso. ▫ **~ off** *vt* parare; difendersi da (criticisms)

fender /ˈfendə(r)/ *n* parafuoco *m inv*; (*Am: on car*) parafango *m*

fennel /ˈfenl/ *n* finocchio *m*

ferment¹ /ˈfɜːment/ *n* fermento *m*

ferment² /fəˈment/ *vi* fermentare ● *vt* far fermentare. **~ation** *n* fermentazione *f*

fern /fɜːn/ *n* felce *f*

feroc|ious /fəˈrəʊʃəs/ *adj* feroce. **~ity** *n* ferocia *f*

ferret /ˈferɪt/ *n* furetto *m* ● **ferret out** *vt* scovare

ferry /ˈferɪ/ *n* traghetto *m* ● *vt* traghettare

fertil|e /ˈfɜːtaɪl/ *adj* fertile. **~ity** *n* fertilità *f*

fertilize /ˈfɜːtɪlaɪz/ *vt* fertilizzare (land, ovum). **~r** *n* fertilizzante *m*

fervent /ˈfɜːvənt/ *adj* fervente

fervour /ˈfɜːvə(r)/ *n* fervore *m*

fester /ˈfestə(r)/ *vi* suppurare

festival /ˈfestɪvl/ *n* (*Mus, Theat*) festival *m*; (*Relig*) festa *f*

festiv|e /ˈfestɪv/ *adj* festivo; **~e season** periodo *m* delle feste natalizie. **~ities** *npl* festeggiamenti *m*

fetch /fetʃ/ *vt* andare/venire a prendere; (*be sold for*) raggiungere [il prezzo di]

fetching /ˈfetʃɪŋ/ *adj* attraente

fête /feɪt/ *n* festa *f* ● *vt* festeggiare

fetish /ˈfetɪʃ/ *n* feticcio *m*

fetter /ˈfetə(r)/ *vt* incatenare

feud /fjuːd/ *n* faida *f*

feudal /ˈfjuːdl/ *adj* feudale

fever /ˈfiːvə(r)/ *n* febbre *f*. **~ish** *adj* febbricitante; *fig* febbrile

few /fjuː/ *adj* pochi; **every ~ days** ogni due o tre giorni; **a ~ people** alcuni; **~er reservations** meno prenotazioni; **the ~est number** il numero più basso ● *pron* pochi; **~ of us** pochi di noi; **a ~** alcuni; **quite a ~** parecchi; **~er than last year** meno dell'anno scorso

fiancé /fɪˈɒnseɪ/ *n* fidanzato *m*. **~e** *n* fidanzata *f*

fiasco /fɪˈæskəʊ/ *n* fiasco *m*

fib /fɪb/ *n* storia *f*; **tell a ~** raccontare una storia

fibre /ˈfaɪbə(r)/ *n* fibra *f*. **~glass** *n* fibra *f* di vetro

fickle /ˈfɪkl/ *adj* incostante

fiction /ˈfɪkʃn/ *n* [**works of**] **~** narrativa *f*; (*fabrication*) finzione *f*. **~al** *adj* immaginario

fictitious /fɪkˈtɪʃəs/ *adj* fittizio

fiddle /ˈfɪdl/ *n* 🅸 violino *m*; (*cheating*) imbroglio *m* ● *vi* gingillarsi (**with** con) ● *vt* 🅸 truccare (accounts)

fidget /ˈfɪdʒɪt/ *vi* agitarsi. **~y** *adj* agitato

field /fiːld/ *n* campo *m*

field: ~-glasses *npl* binocolo *msg*. **F~ 'Marshal** *n* feldmaresciallo *m*. **~work** *n* ricerche *fpl* sul terreno

fiend /fiːnd/ *n* demonio *m*

fierce /fɪəs/ *adj* feroce. **~ness** *n* ferocia *f*

fiery /ˈfaɪərɪ/ *adj* (**-ier, -iest**) focoso

fifteen /fɪfˈtiːn/ *adj & n* quindici *m*. **~th** *adj* quindicesimo

fifth /fɪfθ/ *adj* quinto

fiftieth /ˈfɪftɪɪθ/ *adj* cinquantesimo

fifty /ˈfɪftɪ/ *adj* cinquanta

fig /fɪg/ *n* fico *m*

fight /faɪt/ *n* lotta *f*; (*brawl*) zuffa *f*; (*argument*) litigio *m*; (*boxing*) incontro *m* ● *v* (*pt/pp* **fought**) ● *vt also fig* combattere ● *vi* combattere; (*brawl*) azzuffarsi; (*argue*) litigare. **~er** *n* combattente *mf*; (*Aeron*) caccia *m inv*. **~ing** *n* combattimento *m*

figment /ˈfɪgmənt/ *n* **it's a ~ of your imagination** questo è tutta una tua invenzione

figurative /ˈfɪgjərətɪv/ *adj* (sense) figurato; (art) figurativo

figure /ˈfɪgə(r)/ *n* (*digit*) cifra *f*; (*carving, sculpture, illustration, form*) figura *f*; (*body shape*) linea *f*; **~ of speech** modo *m* di dire ● *vi* (*appear*) figurare ● *vt* (*Am: think*) pensare. ▫ **~ out** *vt* dedurre; capire (person)

f

figurehead *n* figura *f* simbolica

file¹ /faɪl/ *n* scheda *f*; (*set of documents*) incartamento *m*; (*folder*) cartellina *f*; (*Comput*) file *m inv* ● *vt* archiviare (documents)

file² *n* (*line*) fila *f*; **in single ~** in fila

file³ *n* (*Techn*) lima *f* ● *vt* limare

filing cabinet /ˈfaɪlɪŋkæbɪnət/ *n* schedario *m*, classificatore *m*

fill /fɪl/ *n* **eat one's ~** mangiare a sazietà ● *vt* riempire; otturare (tooth) ● *vi* riempirsi. □ **~ in** *vt* compilare (form). □ **~ out** *vt* compilare (form). □ **~ up** *vi* (room, tank:) riempirsi; (*Auto*) far il pieno ● *vt* riempire

f

fillet /ˈfɪlɪt/ *n* filetto *m* ● *vt* (*pt/pp* **filleted**) disossare

filling /ˈfɪlɪŋ/ *n* (*Culin*) ripieno *m*; (*of tooth*) piombatura *f*. **~ station** *n* stazione *f* di rifornimento

film /fɪlm/ *n* (*Cinema*) film *m inv*; (*Phot*) pellicola *f*; [**cling**] **~** pellicola *f* per alimenti ● *vt/i* filmare. **~ star** *n* star *f inv*, divo, -a *mf*

filter /ˈfɪltə(r)/ *n* filtro *m* ● *vt* filtrare. □ **~ through** *vi* (news:) trapelare. **~ tip** *n* filtro *m*; (*cigarette*) sigaretta *f* col filtro

filth /fɪlθ/ *n* sudiciume *m*. **~y** *adj* (**-ier, -iest**) sudicio; (word) sconcio

fin /fɪn/ *n* pinna *f*

final /ˈfaɪnl/ *adj* finale; (*conclusive*) decisivo ● *n* (*Sport*) finale *f*; **~s** *pl* (*Univ*) esami *mpl* finali

finale /fɪˈnɑːlɪ/ *n* finale *m*

final|ist /ˈfaɪnəlɪst/ *n* finalista *mf*. **~ity** *n* finalità *f*

final|ize /ˈfaɪnəlaɪz/ *vt* mettere a punto (text); definire (agreement). **~ly** *adv* (*at last*) finalmente; (*at the end*) alla fine; (*to conclude*) per finire

finance /ˈfaɪnæns/ *n* finanza *f* ● *vt* finanziare

financial /faɪˈnænʃl/ *adj* finanziario

find /faɪnd/ *n* scoperta *f* ● *vt* (*pt/pp* **found**) trovare; (*establish*) scoprire; **~ sb guilty** (*Jur*) dichiarare qcno colpevole. □ **~ out** *vt* scoprire ● *vi* (*enquire*) informarsi

findings /ˈfaɪndɪŋz/ *npl* conclusioni *fpl*

fine¹ /faɪn/ *n* (*penalty*) multa *f* ● *vt* multare

fine² *adj* bello; (*slender*) fine; **he's ~** (*in health*) sta bene. **~ arts** *npl* belle arti *fpl*. ● *adv* bene; **that's cutting it ~** non ci lascia molto tempo ● *int* [va] bene. **~ly** *adv* (cut) finemente

finger /ˈfɪŋgə(r)/ *n* dito *m* (*pl* dita *f*) ● *vt* tastare

finger: ~nail *n* unghia *f*. **~print** *n* impronta *f* digitale. **~tip** *n* punta *f* del dito; **have sth at one's ~tips** sapere qcsa a menadito; (*close at hand*) avere qcsa a portata di mano

finish /ˈfɪnɪʃ/ *n* fine *f*; (*finishing line*) traguardo *m*; (*of product*) finitura *f*; **have a good ~** (runner:) avere un buon finale ● *vt* finire; **~ reading** finire di leggere ● *vi* finire

finite /ˈfaɪnaɪt/ *adj* limitato

Finland /ˈfɪnlənd/ *n* Finlandia *f*

Finn /fɪn/ *n* finlandese *mf*. **~ish** *adj* finlandese ● *n* (*language*) finnico *m*

fiord /fjɔːd/ *n* fiordo *m*

fir /fɜː(r)/ *n* abete *m*

fire /ˈfaɪə(r)/ *n* fuoco *m*; (*forest, house*) incendio *m*; **be on ~** bruciare; **catch ~** prendere fuoco; **set ~ to** dar fuoco a; **under ~** sotto il fuoco ● *vt* cuocere (pottery); sparare (shot); tirare (gun); (*[!]: dismiss*) buttar fuori ● *vi* sparare (**at** a)

fire: ~ alarm *n* allarme *m* antincendio. **~arm** *n* arma *f* da fuoco. **~ brigade** *n* vigili *mpl* del fuoco. **~-engine** *n* autopompa *f*. **~-escape** *n* uscita *f* di sicurezza. **~ extinguisher** *n* estintore *m*. **~man** *n* pompiere *m*, vigile *m* del fuoco. **~place** *n* caminetto *m*. **~side** *n* **by** *or* **at the ~side** accanto al fuoco. **~wood** *n* legna *f* (*da ardere*). **~work** *n* fuoco *m* d'artificio

firm¹ /fɜːm/ *n* ditta *f*, azienda *f*

firm² *adj* fermo; (soil) compatto; (*stable, properly fixed*) solido; (*resolute*) risoluto. **~ly** *adv* (hold) stretto; (say) con fermezza

first /fɜːst/ *adj & n* primo, -a *mf*; **at ~** all'inizio; **who's ~?** chi è il primo?; **from the ~** [fin] dall'inizio ● *adv* (arrive, leave) per primo; (*beforehand*) prima; (*in listing*) prima di tutto, innanzitutto

first: ~ 'aid *n* pronto soccorso *m*. **~-'aid kit** *n* cassetta *f* di pronto soccorso. **~-class** *adj* di prim'ordine; (*Rail*) di prima classe ● *adv* (travel) in prima classe. ~ '**floor** *n* primo piano *m*; (*Am: ground floor*) pianterreno *m*. ~**ly** *adv* in primo luogo. ~ **name** *n* nome *m* di battesimo. ~**-rate** *adj* ottimo

fish /fɪʃ/ *n* pesce *m* ● *vt/i* pescare. □ ~ **out** *vt* tirar fuori

fish: ~**erman** *n* pescatore *m*. ~ '**finger** *n* bastoncino *m* di pesce

fishing /'fɪʃɪŋ/ *n* pesca *f*. ~ **boat** *n* peschereccio *m*. ~**-rod** *n* canna *f* da pesca

fish: ~**monger** /-mʌŋgə(r)/ *n* pescivendolo *m*. ~**y** *adj* ([!]: *suspicious*) sospetto

fission /'fɪʃn/ *n* (*Phys*) fissione *f*

fist /fɪst/ *n* pugno *m*

fit[1] /fɪt/ *n* (*attack*) attacco *m*; (*of rage*) accesso *m*; (*of generosity*) slancio *m*

fit[2] *adj* (**fitter, fittest**) (*suitable*) adatto; (*healthy*) in buona salute; (*Sport*) in forma; **be ~ to do sth** essere in grado di fare qcsa; ~ **to eat** buono da mangiare; **keep ~** tenersi in forma

fit[3] *n* (*of clothes*) taglio *m*; **it's a good ~** (coat) *etc*: ti/le sta bene ● *v* (*pt/pp* **fitted**) ● *vi* (*be the right size*) andare bene; **it won't ~** (*no room*) non ci sta ● *vt* (*fix*) applicare (**to** a); (*install*) installare; **it doesn't ~ me** (coat *etc*:) non mi va bene; ~ **with** fornire di. □ ~ **in** *vi* (person:) adattarsi; **it won't ~ in** (*no room*) non ci sta ● *vt* (*in schedule, vehicle*) trovare un buco per

fit|ful /'fɪtfl/ *adj* irregolare. ~**fully** *adv* (sleep) a sprazzi. ~**ments** *npl* (*in house*) impianti *mpl* fissi. ~**ness** *n* (*suitability*) capacità *f*; [**physical**] ~**ness** forma *f*, fitness *m*

fitting /'fɪtɪŋ/ *adj* appropriato ● *n* (*of clothes*) prova *f*; (*Techn*) montaggio *m*; ~**s** *pl* accessori *mpl*. ~ **room** *n* camerino *m*

five /faɪv/ *adj & n* cinque *m*. ~**r** *n* [!] biglietto *m* da cinque sterline

fix /fɪks/ *n* ([✖]: *drugs*) pera *f*; **be in a ~** [!] essere nei guai ● *vt* fissare; (*repair*) aggiustare; preparare (meal). □ ~ **up** *vt* fissare (meeting)

fixed /fɪkst/ *adj* fisso

fixture /'fɪkstʃə(r)/ *n* (*Sport*) incontro *m*; ~**s and fittings** impianti *mpl* fissi

fizz /fɪz/ *vi* frizzare

fizzle /'fɪzl/ *vi* ~ **out** finire in nulla

fizzy /'fɪzɪ/ *adj* gassoso. ~ **drink** *n* bibita *f* gassata

flabbergasted /'flæbəgɑ:stɪd/ *adj* **be ~** rimanere a bocca aperta

flabby /'flæbɪ/ *adj* floscio

flag[1] /flæg/ *n* bandiera *f* ● **flag down** *vt* (*pt/pp* **flagged**) far segno di fermarsi a (taxi)

flag[2] *vi* (*pt/pp* **flagged**) cedere

'**flag-pole** *n* asta *f* della bandiera

flagrant /'fleɪgrənt/ *adj* flagrante

flair /fleə(r)/ *n* (*skill*) talento *m*; (*style*) stile *m*

flake /fleɪk/ *n* fiocco *m* ● *vi* ~ [**off**] cadere in fiocchi

flaky /'fleɪkɪ/ *adj* a scaglie. ~ **pastry** *n* pasta *f* sfoglia

flamboyant /flæm'bɔɪənt/ *adj* (personality) brillante; (tie) sgargiante

flame /fleɪm/ *n* fiamma *f*

flammable /'flæməbl/ *adj* infiammabile

flan /flæn/ *n* [**fruit**] ~ crostata *f*

flank /flæŋk/ *n* fianco *m* ● *vt* fiancheggiare

flannel /'flæn(ə)l/ *n* flanella *f*; (*for washing*) ≈ guanto *m* di spugna; ~**s** (*trousers*) pantaloni *mpl* di flanella

flap /flæp/ *n* (*of pocket, envelope*) risvolto *m*; (*of table*) ribalta *f*; **in a ~** [!] in grande agitazione ● *v* (*pt/pp* **flapped**) ● *vi* sbattere; [!] agitarsi ● *vt* ~ **its wings** battere le ali

flare /fleə(r)/ *n* fiammata *f*; (*device*) razzo *m* ● **flare up** *vi* (rash:) venire fuori; (fire:) fare una fiammata; (person, situation:) esplodere. ~**d** *adj* (garment) svasato

flash /flæʃ/ *n* lampo *m*; **in a ~** [!] in un attimo ● *vi* lampeggiare; ~ **past** passare come un bolide ● *vt* lanciare (smile); ~ **one's head-lights** lampeggiare; ~ **a torch at** puntare una torcia su

flash: ~**back** *n* scena *f* retrospettiva. ~**light** *n* (*Phot*) flash *m inv*; (*Am: torch*) torcia *f* [elettrica]. ~**y** *adj* vistoso

flask /flɑ:sk/ *n* fiasco *m*; (*vacuum ~*) termos *m inv*

flat /flæt/ *adj* (**flatter, flattest**) piatto; (refusal) reciso; (beer) sgassato; (battery) scarico; (tyre) a terra; **A ~** (*Mus*) la bemolle ● *n* appartamento *m*; (*Mus*)

bemolle *m*; (*puncture*) gomma *f* a terra
flat: ~ly *adv* (refuse) categoricamente. **~ rate** *n* tariffa *f* unica
flatten /'flætn/ *vt* appiattire
flatter /'flætə(r)/ *vt* adulare. **~ing** *adj* (comments) lusinghiero; (colour, dress) che fa sembrare più bello. **~y** *n* adulazione *f*
flaunt /flɔ:nt/ *vt* ostentare
flavour /'fleɪvə(r)/ *n* sapore *m* ● *vt* condire; **chocolate ~ed** al sapore di cioccolato. **~ing** *n* condimento *m*
flaw /flɔ:/ *n* difetto *m*. **~less** *adj* perfetto
flea /fli:/ *n* pulce *m*. **~ market** *n* mercato *m* delle pulci
fleck /flek/ *n* macchiolina *f*
fled /fled/ ▷**FLEE**
flee /fli:/ *vt/i* (*pt/pp* **fled**) fuggire (**from** da)
fleec|e /fli:s/ *n* pelliccia *f* ● *vt* [!] spennare. **~y** *adj* (lining) felpato
fleet /fli:t/ *n* flotta *f*; (*of cars*) parco *m*
fleeting /'fli:tɪŋ/ *adj* **catch a ~ glance of sth** intravedere qcsa; **for a ~ moment** per un attimo
flesh /fleʃ/ *n* carne *f*; **in the ~** in persona. **~y** *adj* carnoso
flew /flu:/ ▷**FLY²**
flex¹ /fleks/ *vt* flettere (muscle)
flex² *n* (*Electr*) filo *m*
flexib|ility /fleksɪ'bɪlətɪ/ *n* flessibilità *f*. **~le** *adj* flessibile
'flexitime /'fleksɪ-/ *n* orario *m* flessibile
flick /flɪk/ *vt* dare un buffetto a; **~ sth off sth** togliere qcsa da qcsa con un colpetto. ▫ **~ through** *vt* sfogliare
flicker /'flɪkə(r)/ *vi* tremolare
flight¹ /flaɪt/ *n* (*fleeing*) fuga *f*; **take ~** darsi alla fuga
flight² *n* (*flying*) volo *m*; **~ of stairs** rampa *f*
flight recorder *n* registratore *m* di volo
flimsy /'flɪmzɪ/ *adj* (**-ier, -iest**) (material) leggero; (shelves) poco robusto; (excuse) debole
flinch /flɪntʃ/ *vi* (*wince*) sussultare; (*draw back*) ritirarsi; **~ from a task** *fig* sottrarsi a un compito
fling /flɪŋ/ *n* **have a ~** ([!]: *affair*) aver un'avventura ● *vt* (*pt/pp* **flung**) gettare
flint /flɪnt/ *n* pietra *f* focaia; (*for lighter*) pietrina *f*
flip /flɪp/ *v* (*pt/pp* **flipped**) ● *vt* dare un colpetto a; buttare in aria (coin) ● *vi* [!] uscire dai gangheri; (*go mad*) impazzire. ▫ **~ through** *vt* sfogliare
flippant /'flɪpənt/ *adj* irriverente
flipper /'flɪpə(r)/ *n* pinna *f*
flirt /flɜ:t/ *n* civetta *f* ● *vi* flirtare
flit /flɪt/ *vi* (*pt/pp* **flitted**) volteggiare
float /fləʊt/ *n* galleggiante *m*; (*in procession*) carro *m*; (*money*) riserva *f* di cassa ● *vi* galleggiare; (*Fin*) fluttuare
flock /flɒk/ *n* gregge *m*; (*of birds*) stormo *m* ● *vi* affollarsi
flog /flɒg/ *vt* (*pt/pp* **flogged**) bastonare; ([!]: *sell*) vendere
flood /flʌd/ *n* alluvione *f*; (*of river*) straripamento *m*; (*fig: of replies, letters, tears*) diluvio *m*; **be in ~** (river:) essere straripato ● *vt* allagare ● *vi* (river:) straripare
'floodlight *n* riflettore *m* ● *vt* (*pt/pp* **floodlit**) illuminare con riflettori
floor /flɔ:(r)/ *n* pavimento *m*; (*storey*) piano *m*; (*for dancing*) pista *f* ● *vt* (*baffle*) confondere; (*knock down*) stendere (person)
floor polish *n* cera *f* per il pavimento
flop /flɒp/ *n* [!] (*failure*) tonfo *m*; (*Theat*) fiasco *m* ● *vi* (*pt/pp* **flopped**) ([!]: *fail*) far fiasco. ▫ **~ down** *vi* accasciarsi
floppy /'flɒpɪ/ *adj* floscio. **~ 'disk** *n* floppy disk *m inv*. **~ [disk] drive** *n* lettore di floppy *m*
floral /'flɔ:rəl/ *adj* floreale
florid /'flɒrɪd/ *adj* (complexion) florido; (style) troppo ricercato
florist /'flɒrɪst/ *n* fioraio, -a *mf*
flounder¹ /'flaʊndə(r)/ *vi* dibattersi; (speaker:) impappinarsi
flounder² *n* (*fish*) passera *f* di mare
flour /'flaʊə(r)/ *n* farina *f*
flourish /'flʌrɪʃ/ *n* gesto *m* drammatico; (*scroll*) ghirigoro *m* ● *vi* prosperare ● *vt* brandire
flout /flaʊt/ *vt* fregarsene di (rules)
flow /fləʊ/ *n* flusso *m* ● *vi* scorrere; (*hang loosely*) ricadere
flower /'flaʊə(r)/ *n* fiore *m* ● *vi* fiorire
flower: ~-bed *n* aiuola *f*. **~y** *adj* fiorito

flown /fləʊn/ ▷**FLY²**

flu /flu:/ *n* influenza *f*

fluctuat|e /'flʌktjʊeɪt/ *vi* fluttuare. **~ion** *n* fluttuazione *f*

fluent /'flu:ənt/ *adj* spedito; **speak ~ Italian** parlare correntemente l'italiano. **~ly** *adv* speditamente

fluff /flʌf/ *n* peluria *f*. **~y** *adj* (**-ier, -iest**) vaporoso; (toy) di peluche

fluid /'flu:ɪd/ *adj* fluido ● *n* fluido *m*

flung /flʌŋ/ ▷**FLING**

fluorescent /flʊə'resnt/ *adj* fluorescente

flush /flʌʃ/ *n* (*blush*) [vampata *f* di] rossore *m* ● *vi* arrossire ● *vt* lavare con un getto d'acqua; **~ the toilet** tirare l'acqua ● *adj* a livello (**with** di); ([!]: *affluent*) a soldi

flute /flu:t/ *n* flauto *m*

flutter /'flʌtə(r)/ *n* battito *m* ● *vi* svolazzare

flux /flʌks/ *n* **in a state of ~** in uno stato di flusso

fly¹ /flaɪ/ *n* (*pl* **flies**) mosca *f*

fly² *v* (*pt* **flew**, *pp* **flown**) ● *vi* volare; (*go by plane*) andare in aereo; (flag:) sventolare; (*rush*) precipitarsi; **~ open** spalancarsi ● *vt* pilotare (plane); trasportare [in aereo] (troops, supplies); volare con (Alitalia etc)

fly³ *n* & **flies** *pl* (*on trousers*) patta *f*

flying /'flaɪɪŋ/: **~ 'buttress** *n* arco *m* rampante. **~ 'colours: with ~ colours** a pieni voti. **~ 'saucer** *n* disco *m* volante. **~ 'start** *n* **get off to a ~ start** fare un'ottima partenza. **~ 'visit** *n* visita *f* lampo

fly: ~ leaf *n* risguardo *m*. **~over** *n* cavalcavia *m inv*

foal /fəʊl/ *n* puledro *m*

foam /fəʊm/ *n* schiuma *f*; (*synthetic*) gommapiuma® *f* ● *vi* spumare; **~ at the mouth** far la bava alla bocca. **~ 'rubber** *n* gommapiuma® *f*

fob /fɒb/ *vt* (*pt/pp* **fobbed**) **~ sth off** affibbiare qcsa (**on sb** a qcno); **~ sb off** liquidare qcno

focal /'fəʊkl/ *adj* focale

focus /'fəʊkəs/ *n* fuoco *m*; **in ~** a fuoco; **out of ~** sfocato ● *v* (*pt/pp* **focused** *or* **focussed**) ● *vt fig* concentrare (**on** su) ● *vi* (*Phot*) **~ on** mettere a fuoco; *fig* concentrarsi (**on** su)

fodder /'fɒdə(r)/ *n* foraggio *m*

foe /fəʊ/ *n* nemico, -a *mf*

foetus /'fi:təs/ *n* (*pl* **-tuses**) feto *m*

fog /fɒg/ *n* nebbia *f*

foggy /'fɒgɪ/ *adj* (**foggier, foggiest**) nebbioso; **it's ~** c'è nebbia

'fog-horn *n* sirena *f* da nebbia

foil¹ /fɔɪl/ *n* lamina *f* di metallo

foil² *vt* (*thwart*) frustrare

foil³ *n* (*sword*) fioretto *m*

foist /fɔɪst/ *vt* appioppare (**on sb** a qcno)

fold¹ /fəʊld/ *n* (*for sheep*) ovile *m*

fold² *n* piega *f* ● *vt* piegare; **~ one's arms** incrociare le braccia ● *vi* piegarsi; (*fail*) crollare. □ **~ up** *vt* ripiegare (chair) ● *vi* essere pieghevole; (business:) collassare

fold|er /'fəʊldə(r)/ *n* cartella *f*. **~ing** *adj* pieghevole

folk /fəʊk/ *npl* gente *f*; **my ~s** (*family*) i miei; **hello there ~s** ciao a tutti

folklore *n* folclore *m*

follow /'fɒləʊ/ *vt/i* seguire; **it doesn't ~** non è necessariamente così; **~ suit** *fig* fare lo stesso; **as ~s** come segue. □ **~ up** *vt* fare seguito a (letter)

follow|er /'fɒləʊə(r)/ *n* seguace *mf*. **~ing** *adj* seguente ● *n* seguito *m*; (*supporters*) seguaci *mpl* ● *prep* in seguito a

folly /'fɒlɪ/ *n* follia *f*

fond /fɒnd/ *adj* affezionato; (hope) vivo; **be ~ of** essere appassionato di (music); **I'm ~ of...** (food, person) mi piace moltissimo...

fondle /'fɒndl/ *vt* coccolare

fondness /'fɒndnɪs/ *n* affetto *m*; (*for things*) amore *m*

font /fɒnt/ *n* fonte *f* battesimale; (*Typ*) carattere *m* di stampa

food /fu:d/ *n* cibo *m*; (*for animals, groceries*) mangiare *m*; **let's buy some ~** compriamo qualcosa da mangiare

food processor *n* tritatutto *m inv* elettrico

fool¹ /fu:l/ *n* sciocco, -a *mf*; **she's no ~** non è una stupida; **make a ~ of oneself** rendersi ridicolo ● *vt* prendere in giro ● *vi* **~ around** giocare; (husband, wife:) avere l'amante

fool² *n* (*Culin*) crema *f*

'fool|hardy *adj* temerario. **~ish** *adj* stolto. **~ishly** *adv* scioccamente.

~ishness *n* sciocchezza *f*. **~proof** *adj* facilissimo

foot /fʊt/ *n* (*pl* **feet**) piede *m*; (*of animal*) zampa *f*; (*measure*) piede *m* (= *30,48 cm*); **on ~** a piedi; **on one's feet** in piedi; **put one's ~ in it** 🅘 fare una gaffe

foot: ~-and-'mouth disease *n* afta *f* epizootica. **~ball** *n* calcio *m*; (*ball*) pallone *m*. **~baller** *n* giocatore *m* di calcio. **~-bridge** *n* passerella *f*. **~hills** *npl* colline *fpl* pedemontane. **~hold** *n* punto *m* d'appoggio. **~ing** *n* **lose one's ~ing** perdere l'appiglio; **on an equal ~ing** in condizioni di parità. **~man** *n* valletto *m*. **~note** *n* nota *f* a piè di pagina. **~path** *n* sentiero *m*. **~print** *n* orma *f*. **~step** *n* passo *m*; **follow in sb's ~steps** *fig* seguire l'esempio di qcno. **~wear** *n* calzature *fpl*

f

for /fə(r)/, *accentato* /fɔː(r)/

- *prep* per; **~ this reason** per questa ragione; **I have lived here ~ ten years** vivo qui da dieci anni; **~ supper** per cena; **~ all that** nonostante questo; **what ~?** a che scopo?; **send ~ a doctor** chiamare un dottore; **fight ~ a cause** lottare per una causa; **go ~ a walk** andare a fare una passeggiata; **there's no need ~ you to go** non c'è bisogno che tu vada; **it's not ~ me to say** non sta a me dirlo; **now you're ~ it** ora sei nei pasticci
- *conj* poiché, perché

forage /'fɒrɪdʒ/ *n* foraggio *m* • *vi* **~ for** cercare

forbade /fə'bæd/ ▷ FORBID

forbear|ance /fɔː'beərəns/ *n* pazienza *f*. **~ing** *adj* tollerante

forbid /fə'bɪd/ *vt* (*pt* **forbade**, *pp* **forbidden**) proibire. **~ding** *adj* (prospect) che spaventa; (*stern*) severo

force /fɔːs/ *n* forza *f*; **in ~** in vigore; (*in large numbers*) in massa; **come into ~** entrare in vigore; **the** [**armed**] **~s** *pl* le forze armate • *vt* forzare; **~ sth on sb** (decision) imporre qcsa a qcno; (drink) costringere qcno a fare qcsa

forced /fɔːst/ *adj* forzato

force: ~-'feed *vt* (*pt/pp* **-fed**) nutrire a forza. **~ful** *adj* energico

forceps /'fɔːseps/ *npl* forcipe *m*

forcible /'fɔːsɪbl/ *adj* forzato

ford /fɔːd/ *n* guado *m* • *vt* guadare

fore /fɔː(r)/ *n* **to the ~** in vista; **come to the ~** salire alla ribalta

fore: ~arm *n* avambraccio *m*. **~boding** /-'bəʊdɪŋ/ *n* presentimento *m*. **~cast** *n* previsione *f* • *vt* (*pt/pp* **~cast**) prevedere. **~court** *n* cortile *m* anteriore. **~finger** *n* [dito *m*] indice *m*. **~front** *n* **be in the ~front** essere all'avanguardia. **~gone** *adj* **be a ~gone conclusion** essere una cosa scontata. **~ground** *n* primo piano *m*. **~head** /'fɔːhed/, /'fɒrɪd/ *n* fronte *f*

foreign /'fɒrən/ *adj* straniero; (trade) estero; (*not belonging*) estraneo; **he is ~** è uno straniero. **~ currency** *n* valuta *f* estera. **~er** *n* straniero, -a *mf*. **~ language** *n* lingua *f* straniera

fore: ~man *n* caporeparto *m*. **~most** *adj* principale • *adv* **first and ~most** in primo luogo

'forerunner *n* precursore *m*

fore'see *vt* (*pt* **-saw**, *pp* **-seen**) prevedere. **~able** *adj* **in the ~able future** in futuro per quanto si possa prevedere

'foresight *n* previdenza *f*

forest /'fɒrɪst/ *n* foresta *f*. **~er** *n* guardia *f* forestale

fore'stall *vt* prevenire

forestry /'fɒrɪstrɪ/ *n* silvicoltura *f*

'foretaste *n* pregustazione *f*

fore'tell *vt* (*pt/pp* **-told**) predire

forever /fə'revə(r)/ *adv* per sempre; **he's ~ complaining** si lamenta sempre

fore'warn *vt* avvertire

foreword /'fɔːwɜːd/ *n* prefazione *f*

forfeit /'fɔːfɪt/ *n* (*in game*) pegno *m*; (*Jur*) penalità *f* • *vt* perdere

forgave /fə'geɪv/ ▷ FORGIVE

forge[1] /fɔːdʒ/ *vi* **~ ahead** (runner:) lasciarsi indietro gli altri; *fig* farsi strada

forge[2] *n* fucina *f* • *vt* fucinare; (*counterfeit*) contraffare. **~r** *n* contraffattore *m*. **~ry** *n* contraffazione *f*

forget /fə'get/ *vt/i* (*pt* **-got**, *pp* **-gotten**, *pres p* **-getting**) dimenticare; dimenticarsi di (language, skill). **~ful** *adj* smemorato. **~fulness** *n* smemoratezza *f*. **~-me-not** *n* non-ti-scordar-dimé *m inv*. **~table** *adj* (day, film) da dimenticare

forgive /fə'gɪv/ *vt* (*pt* **-gave**, *pp* **-given**) **~ sb for sth** perdonare qcno per qcsa. **~ness** *n* perdono *m*

forgo /fɔː'gəʊ/ *vt* (*pt* **-went**, *pp* **-gone**) rinunciare a

forgot(ten) /fə'gɒt(n)/ ▷**FORGET**

fork /fɔːk/ *n* forchetta *f*; (*for digging*) forca *f*; (*in road*) bivio *m* ● *vi* (road:) biforcarsi; **~ right** prendere a destra. ◻ **~ out** *vt* 🄸 sborsare

fork-lift 'truck *n* elevatore *m*

forlorn /fə'lɔːn/ *adj* (look) perduto; (place) derelitto; **~ hope** speranza *f* vana

form /fɔːm/ *n* forma *f*; (*document*) modulo *m*; (*Sch*) classe *f* ● *vt* formare; formulare (opinion) ● *vi* formarsi

formal /'fɔːml/ *adj* formale. **~ity** *n* formalità *f inv*. **~ly** *adv* in modo formale; (*officially*) ufficialmente

format /'fɔːmæt/ *n* formato *m* ● *vt* formattare (disk, page)

formation /fɔː'meɪʃn/ *n* formazione *f*

former /'fɔːmə(r)/ *adj* precedente; (PM, colleague) ex; **the ~, the latter** il primo, l'ultimo. **~ly** *adv* precedentemente; (*in olden times*) in altri tempi

formidable /'fɔːmɪdəbl/ *adj* formidabile

formula /'fɔːmjʊlə/ *n* (*pl* **-ae** /-liː/ *or* **-s**) formula *f*

formulate /'fɔːmjʊleɪt/ *vt* formulare

forsake /fə'seɪk/ *vt* (*pt* **-sook** /-sʊk/, *pp* **-saken**) abbandonare

fort /fɔːt/ *n* (*Mil*) forte *m*

forth /fɔːθ/ *adv* **back and ~** avanti e indietro; **and so ~** e così via

forth: ~'coming *adj* prossimo; (*communicative*) communicativo; **no response was ~** non arrivava nessuna risposta. **~right** *adj* schietto. **~'with** *adv* immediatamente

fortieth /'fɔːtɪɪθ/ *adj* quarantesimo

fortnight /'fɔːt-/ *Br n* quindicina *f*. **~ly** *adj* bimensile ● *adv* ogni due settimane

fortress /'fɔːtrɪs/ *n* fortezza *f*

fortunate /'fɔːtʃənət/ *adj* fortunato; **that's ~**! meno male!. **~ly** *adv* fortunatamente

fortune /'fɔːtʃuːn/ *n* fortuna *f*. **~-teller** *n* indovino, -a *mf*

forty /'fɔːtɪ/ *adj & n* quaranta *m*

forum /'fɔːrəm/ *n* foro *m*

forward /'fɔːwəd/ *adv* avanti; (*towards the front*) in avanti ● *adj* in avanti; (*presumptuous*) sfacciato ● *n* (*Sport*) attaccante *m* ● *vt* inoltrare (letter); spedire (goods). **~s** *adv* avanti

fossil /'fɒsl/ *n* fossile *m*. **~ized** *adj* fossile; (ideas) fossilizzato

foster /'fɒstə(r)/ *vt* allevare (child). **~-child** *n* figlio, -a *mf* in affidamento. **~-mother** *n* madre *f* affidataria

fought /fɔːt/ ▷**FIGHT**

foul /faʊl/ *adj* (smell, taste) cattivo; (air) viziato; (language) osceno; (mood, weather) orrendo; **~ play** (*Jur*) delitto *m* ● *n* (*Sport*) fallo *m* ● *vt* inquinare (water); (*Sport*) commettere un fallo contro; (nets, rope:) impigliarsi in. **~-smelling** *adj* puzzo

found¹ /faʊnd/ ▷**FIND**

found² *vt* fondare

foundation /faʊn'deɪʃn/ *n* (*basis*) fondamento *m*; (*charitable*) fondazione *f*; **~s** *pl* (*of building*) fondamenta *fpl*; **lay the ~-stone** porre la prima pietra

founder¹ /'faʊndə(r)/ *n* fondatore, -trice *mf*

founder² *vi* (ship:) affondare

fountain /'faʊntɪn/ *n* fontana *f*. **~-pen** *n* penna *f* stilografica

four /fɔː(r)/ *adj & n* quattro *m*

four: ~some /'fɔːsəm/ *n* quartetto *m*. **~'teen** *adj & n* quattordici *m*. **~'teenth** *adj* quattordicesimo

fourth /fɔːθ/ *adj* quarto

fowl /faʊl/ *n* pollame *m*

fox /fɒks/ *n* volpe *f* ● *vt* (*puzzle*) ingannare

foyer /'fɔɪeɪ/ *n* (*Theat*) ridotto *m*; (*in hotel*) salone *m* d'ingresso

fraction /'frækʃn/ *n* frazione *f*

fracture /'fræktʃə(r)/ *n* frattura *f* ● *vt* fratturare ● *vi* fratturarsi

fragile /'frædʒaɪl/ *adj* fragile

fragment /'frægmənt/ *n* frammento *m*. **~ary** *adj* frammentario

fragran|ce /'freɪgrəns/ *n* fragranza *f*. **~t** *adj* fragrante

frail /freɪl/ *adj* gracile

frame /freɪm/ *n* (*of picture, door, window*)

cornice *f*; (*of spectacles*) montatura *f*; (*Anat*) ossatura *f*; (*structure, of bike*) telaio *m*; ~ **of mind** stato *m* d'animo ● *vt* incorniciare (picture); *fig* formulare; (☒: *incriminate*) montare. ~**work** *n* struttura *f*

France /frɑːns/ *n* Francia *f*

frank¹ /fræŋk/ *vt* affrancare (letter)

frank² *adj* franco. ~**ly** *adv* francamente

frantic /ˈfræntɪk/ *adj* frenetico; **be ~ with worry** essere agitatissimo. ~**ally** *adv* freneticamente

fraternal /frəˈtɜːnl/ *adj* fraterno

fraud /frɔːd/ *n* frode *f*; (*person*) impostore *m*. ~**ulent** *adj* fraudolento

fraught /frɔːt/ *adj* ~ **with** pieno di

fray¹ /freɪ/ *n* mischia *f*

fray² *vi* sfilacciarsi

freak /friːk/ *n* fenomeno *m*; (*person*) scherzo *m* di natura; (!: *weird person*) tipo *m* strambo ● *adj* anormale. ~**ish** *adj* strambo

freckle /ˈfrekl/ *n* lentiggine *f*. ~**d** *adj* lentigginoso

free /friː/ *adj* (**freer, freest**) libero; (ticket, copy) gratuito; (*lavish*) generoso; ~ **of charge** gratuito; **set** ~ liberare ● *vt* (*pt/pp* **freed**) liberare

free: ~**dom** *n* libertà *f*. ~**hold** *n* proprietà *f* [fondiaria] assoluta. ~ ˈ**kick** *n* calcio *m* di punizione. ~**lance** *adj & adv* indipendente. ~**ly** *adv* liberamente; (*generously*) generosamente; **I ~ly admit that...** devo ammettere che.... **f~mason** *n* massone *m*. ~**-range** *adj* ~**-range egg** uovo *m* di gallina ruspante. ~**style** *n* stile *m* libero. ~**way** *n Am* autostrada *f*

freez|e /friːz/ *vt* (*pt* **froze**, *pp* **frozen**) gelare; bloccare (wages) ● *vi* (water:) gelare; **it's ~ing** si gela; **my hands are ~ing** ho le mani congelate

freez|er /ˈfriːzə(r)/ *n* freezer *m inv*, congelatore *m*. ~**ing** *adj* gelido ● *n* **below ~ing** sotto zero

freight /freɪt/ *n* carico *m*. ~**er** *n* nave *f* da carico. ~ **train** *n Am* treno *m* merci

French /frentʃ/ *adj* francese ● *n* (*language*) francese *m*; **the** ~ *pl* i francesi *mpl*

French: ~ ˈ**fries** *npl* patate *fpl* fritte. ~**man** *n* francese *m*. ~ ˈ**window** *n* porta-finestra *f*. ~**woman** *n* francese *f*

frenzied /ˈfrenzɪd/ *adj* frenetico

frenzy /ˈfrenzɪ/ *n* frenesia *f*

frequency /ˈfriːkwənsɪ/ *n* frequenza *f*

frequent¹ /ˈfriːkwənt/ *adj* frequente. ~**ly** *adv* frequentemente

frequent² /frɪˈkwent/ *vt* frequentare

fresh /freʃ/ *adj* fresco; (*new*) nuovo; (*Am: cheeky*) sfacciato. ~**ly** *adv* di recente

freshen /ˈfreʃn/ *vi* (wind:) rinfrescare. □ ~ **up** *vt* dare una rinfrescata a ● *vi* rinfrescarsi

freshness /ˈfreʃnɪs/ *n* freschezza *f*

fret /fret/ *vi* (*pt/pp* **fretted**) inquietarsi. ~**ful** *adj* irritabile

friction /ˈfrɪkʃn/ *n* frizione *f*

Friday /ˈfraɪdeɪ/ *n* venerdì *m inv*

fridge /frɪdʒ/ *n* frigo *m*

fried /fraɪd/ ▷FRY ● *adj* fritto; ~ **egg** uovo *m* fritto

friend /frend/ *n* amico, -a *mf*. ~**ly** *adj* (**-ier, -iest**) (relations, meeting, match) amichevole; (neighbourhood, smile) piacevole; (software) di facile uso; **be ~ly with** essere amico di. ~**ship** *n* amicizia *f*

frieze /friːz/ *n* fregio *m*

fright /fraɪt/ *n* paura *f*; **take** ~ spaventarsi

frighten /ˈfraɪtn/ *vt* spaventare. ~**ed** *adj* spaventato; **be ~ed** aver paura (**of** di). ~**ing** *adj* spaventoso

frightful /ˈfraɪtfl/ *adj* terribile

frigid /ˈfrɪdʒɪd/ *adj* frigido. ~**ity** *n* freddezza *f*; (*Psych*) frigidità *f*

frill /frɪl/ *n* volant *m inv*. ~**y** *adj* (dress) con tanti volant

fringe /frɪndʒ/ *n* frangia *f*; (*of hair*) frangetta *f*; (*fig: edge*) margine *m*. ~ **benefits** *npl* benefici *mpl* supplementari

fritter /ˈfrɪtə(r)/ *n* frittella *f* ● **fritter away** *vt* sprecare

frivol|ity /frɪˈvɒlətɪ/ *n* frivolezza *f*. ~**ous** *adj* frivolo

fro /frəʊ/ ▷TO

frock /frɒk/ *n* abito *m*

frog /frɒg/ *n* rana *f*. ~**man** *n* uomo *m* rana

frolic /ˈfrɒlɪk/ *vi* (*pt/pp* **frolicked**)

(lambs:) sgambettare; (people:) folleggiare

from /frɒm/ *prep* da; **~ Monday** da lunedì; **~ that day** da quel giorno; **he's ~ London** è di Londra; **this is a letter ~ my brother** questa è una lettera di mio fratello; **documents ~ the 16th century** documenti del XVI secolo; **made ~** fatto con; **she felt ill ~ fatigue** si sentiva male dalla stanchezza; **~ now on** d'ora in poi

front /frʌnt/ *n* parte *f* anteriore; (*fig: organization etc*) facciata *f*; (*of garment*) davanti *m*; (*sea~*) lungomare *m*; (*Mil, Pol, Meteorol*) fronte *m*; **in ~ of** davanti a; **in** *or* **at the ~** davanti; **to the ~** avanti ● *adj* davanti; (page, row, wheel) anteriore

frontal /ˈfrʌntl/ *adj* frontale

front ˈdoor *n* porta *f* d'entrata

frontier /ˈfrʌntɪə(r)/ *n* frontiera *f*

frost /frɒst/ *n* gelo *m*; (*hoar~*) brina *f*. **~bite** *n* congelamento *m*. **~bitten** *adj* congelato

frost|ed /ˈfrɒstɪd/ *adj* **~ed glass** vetro *m* smerigliato. **~ily** *adv* gelidamente. **~ing** *n Am* (*Culin*) glassa *f*. **~y** *adj also fig* gelido

froth /frɒθ/ *n* schiuma *f* ● *vi* far schiuma. **~y** *adj* schiumoso

frown /fraʊn/ *n* cipiglio *m* ● *vi* aggrottare le sopraciglia. □ **~ on** *vt* disapprovare

froze /frəʊz/ ▹FREEZE

frozen /ˈfrəʊzn/ ▹FREEZE ● *adj* (corpse, hand) congelato; (wastes) gelido; (*Culin*) surgelato; **I'm ~** sono gelato. **~ food** *n* surgelati *mpl*

frugal /ˈfruːgl/ *adj* frugale

fruit /fruːt/ *n* frutto *m*; (*collectively*) frutta *f*; **eat more ~** mangia più frutta. **~ cake** *n dolce m con frutta candita*

fruition /fruːˈɪʃn/ *n* **come to ~** dare dei frutti

fruit: ~less *adj* infruttuoso. **~ ˈsalad** *n* macedonia *f* [di frutta]

frustrat|e /frʌˈstreɪt/ *vt* frustrare; rovinare (plans). **~ing** *adj* frustrante. **~ion** *n* frustrazione *f*

fry¹ *vt/i* (*pt/pp* **fried**) friggere

fry² /fraɪ/ *n inv* **small ~** *fig* pesce *m* piccolo

frying pan *n* padella *f*

fudge /fʌdʒ/ *n caramella f a base di zucchero, burro e latte*

fuel /ˈfjuːəl/ *n* carburante *m*; *fig* nutrimento *m* ● *vt fig* alimentare

fugitive /ˈfjuːdʒɪtɪv/ *n* fuggiasco, -a *mf*

fulfil /fʊlˈfɪl/ *vt* (*pt/pp* **-filled**) soddisfare (conditions, need); realizzare (dream, desire); **~ oneself** realizzarsi. **~ling** *adj* soddisfacente. **~ment** *n* **sense of ~ment** senso *m* di appagamento

f

full /fʊl/ *adj* pieno (**of** di); (*detailed*) esauriente; (bus, hotel) completo; (skirt) ampio; **at ~ speed** a tutta velocità; **in ~ swing** in pieno fervore ● *n* **in ~** per intero

full: ~ ˈmoon *n* luna *f* piena. **~-scale** *adj* (model) in scala reale; (alert) di massima gravità. **~ ˈstop** *n* punto *m*. **~-time** *adj & adv* a tempo pieno

fully /ˈfʊlɪ/ *adv* completamente; (*in detail*) dettagliatamente; **~ booked** (hotel, restaurant) tutto prenotato

fumble /ˈfʌmbl/ *vi* **~ in** rovistare in; **~ with** armeggiare con; **~ for one's keys** rovistare alla ricerca delle chiavi

fume /fjuːm/ *vi* (*be angry*) essere furioso

fumes /fjuːmz/ *npl* fumi *mpl*; (*from car*) gas *mpl* di scarico

fumigate /ˈfjuːmɪgeɪt/ *vt* suffumicare

fun /fʌn/ *n* divertimento *m*; **for ~** per ridere; **make ~ of** prendere in giro; **have ~** divertirsi

function /ˈfʌŋkʃn/ *n* funzione *f*; (*event*) cerimonia *f* ● *vi* funzionare; **~ as** (*serve as*) funzionare da. **~al** *adj* funzionale

fund /fʌnd/ *n* fondo *m*; *fig* pozzo *m*; **~s** *pl* fondi *mpl* ● *vt* finanziare

fundamental /fʌndəˈmentl/ *adj* fondamentale

funeral /ˈfjuːnərəl/ *n* funerale *m*

funeral directors *n* impresa *f* di pompe funebri

ˈfunfair *n* luna park *m inv*

fungus /ˈfʌŋgəs/ *n* (*pl* **-gi** /-gaɪ/) fungo *m*

funnel /ˈfʌnl/ *n* imbuto *m*; (*on ship*) ciminiera *f*

funnily /ˈfʌnɪlɪ/ *adv* comicamente; (*oddly*) stranamente; **~ enough** strano a dirsi

funny /ˈfʌnɪ/ *adj* (**-ier, -iest**) buffo;

(*odd*) strano. ~ **business** *n* affare *m* losco

fur /fɜː(r)/ *n* pelo *m*; (*for clothing*) pelliccia *f*; (*in kettle*) deposito *m*. ~ **'coat** *n* pelliccia *f*

furious /'fjʊərɪəs/ *adj* furioso

furnace /'fɜːnɪs/ *n* fornace *f*

furnish /'fɜːnɪʃ/ *vt* ammobiliare (flat); fornire (supplies). **~ed** *adj* **~ed room** stanza *f* ammobiliata. **~ings** *npl* mobili *mpl*

furniture /'fɜːnɪtʃə(r)/ *n* mobili *mpl*

furrow /'fʌrəʊ/ *n* solco *m*

furry /'fɜːrɪ/ *adj* (animal) peloso; (toy) di peluche

further /'fɜːðə(r)/ *adj* (*additional*) ulteriore; **at the ~ end** all'altra estremità; **until ~ notice** fino a nuovo avviso ● *adv* più lontano; **~,...** inoltre,...; **~ off** più lontano ● *vt* promuovere

further'more *adv* per di più

furthest /'fɜːðɪst/ *adj* più lontano ● *adv* più lontano

furtive /'fɜːtɪv/ *adj* furtivo

fury /'fjʊərɪ/ *n* furore *m*

fuse[1] /fjuːz/ *n* (*of bomb*) detonatore *m*; (*cord*) miccia *f*

fuse[2] *n* (*Electr*) fusibile *m* ● *vt* fondere; (*Electr*) far saltare ● *vi* fondersi; (*Electr*) saltare; **the lights have ~d** sono saltate le luci. **~-box** *n* scatola *f* dei fusibili

fuselage /'fjuːzəlɑːʒ/ *n* (*Aeron*) fusoliera *f*

fusion /'fjuːʒn/ *n* fusione *f*

fuss /fʌs/ *n* storie *fpl*; **make a ~** fare storie; **make a ~ of** colmare di attenzioni ● *vi* fare storie

fussy /'fʌsɪ/ *adj* (**-ier, -iest**) (person) difficile da accontentare; (clothes etc) pieno di fronzoli

futil|e /'fjuːtaɪl/ *adj* inutile. **~ity** *n* futilità *f*

future /'fjuːtʃə(r)/ *adj & n* futuro; **in ~** in futuro. **~ perfect** futuro *m* anteriore

futuristic /fjuːtʃə'rɪstɪk/ *adj* futuristico

fuzz /fʌz/ *n* **the ~** (☒: *police*) la pula

fuzzy /'fʌzɪ/ *adj* (**-ier, -iest**) (hair) crespo; (photo) sfuocato

Gg

gab /gæb/ *n* ! **have the gift of the ~** avere la parlantina

gabble /'gæb(ə)l/ *vi* parlare troppo in fretta

gad /gæd/ *vi* (*pt/pp* **gadded**) **~ about** andarsene in giro

gadget /'gædʒɪt/ *n* aggeggio *m*

Gaelic /'geɪlɪk/ *adj & n* gaelico *m*

gaffe /gæf/ *n* gaffe *f inv*

gag /gæg/ *n* bavaglio *m*; (*joke*) battuta *f* ● *vt* (*pt/pp* **gagged**) imbavagliare

gaily /'geɪlɪ/ *adv* allegramente

gain /geɪn/ *n* guadagno *m*; (*increase*) aumento *m* ● *vt* acquisire; **~ weight** aumentare di peso; **~ access** accedere ● *vi* (clock:) andare avanti. **~ful** *adj* **~ful employment** lavoro *m* remunerativo

gait /geɪt/ *n* andatura *f*

gala /'gɑːlə/ *n* gala *f*; **swimming ~** manifestazione *f* di nuoto ● *attrib* di gala

galaxy /'gæləksɪ/ *n* galassia *f*

gale /geɪl/ *n* bufera *f*

gall /gɔːl/ *n* (*impudence*) impudenza *f*

gallant /'gælənt/ *adj* coraggioso; (*chivalrous*) galante. **~ry** *n* coraggio *m*

'gall-bladder *n* cistifellea *f*

gallery /'gælərɪ/ *n* galleria *f*

galley /'gælɪ/ *n* (*ship's kitchen*) cambusa *f*; **~ [proof]** bozza *f* in colonna

gallivant /'gælɪvænt/ *vi* ! andare in giro

gallon /'gælən/ *n* gallone *m* (= *4,5 l*; *Am = 3,7 l*)

gallop /'gæləp/ *n* galoppo *m* ● *vi* galoppare

gallows /'gæləʊz/ *n* forca *f*

galore /gə'lɔː(r)/ *adv* a bizzeffe

galvanize /'gælvənaɪz/ *vt* (*Techn*) galvanizzare; *fig* stimolare (**into** a)

gambl|e /'gæmbl/ *n* (*risk*) azzardo *m* ● *vi* giocare; (*on Stock Exchange*) speculare; **~e on** (*rely*) contare su. **~er** *n* giocatore, -trice *mf* [d'azzardo]. **~ing** *n* gioco *m* [d'azzardo]

game /geɪm/ *n* gioco *m*; (*match*) partita *f*; (*animals, birds*) selvaggina *f*; **~s** (*Sch*) ≈ ginnastica *f* ● *adj* (*brave*) coraggioso; **are you ~?** ti va?; **be ~ for** essere pronto per. **~keeper** *n* guardacaccia *m inv*

gammon /'gæmən/ *n coscia f di maiale*

gamut /'gæmət/ *n fig* gamma *f*

gander /'gændə(r)/ *n* oca *f* maschio

gang /gæŋ/ *n* banda *f*; (*of workmen*) squadra *f* ● **gang up** *vi* far comunella (**on** contro)

gangling /'gæŋglɪŋ/ *adj* spilungone

gangmaster /'gæŋmɑ:stə(r)/ *n* caporale *m* (*di manodopera abusiva*)

gangrene /'gæŋgri:n/ *n* cancrena *f*

gangster /'gæŋstə(r)/ *n* gangster *m inv*

gangway /'gæŋweɪ/ *n* passaggio *m*; (*Aeron, Naut*) passerella *f*

gaol /dʒeɪl/ *n* carcere *m* ● *vt* incarcerare. **~er** *n* carceriere *m*

gap /gæp/ *n* spazio *m*; (*in ages, between teeth*) scarto *m*; (*in memory*) vuoto *m*; (*in story*) punto *m* oscuro

gap|e /geɪp/ *vi* stare a bocca aperta; (*be wide open*) spalancarsi; **~e at** guardare a bocca aperta. **~ing** *adj* aperto

> *i* **gap year** In Gran Bretagna il *gap year* è l'anno di intervallo che gli studenti si prendono tra la fine della scuola secondaria e l'università. Molti studenti utilizzano questo periodo sabbatico per intraprendere attività completamente diverse da ciò che hanno studiato o che studieranno e alcuni lo utilizzano per lavorare e mettere da parte qualche risparmio. Altri, infine, ne approfittano per viaggiare all'estero e conoscere il mondo.

garage /'gærɑ:ʒ/ *n* garage *m inv*; (*for repairs*) meccanico *m*; (*for petrol*) stazione *f* di servizio

garbage /'gɑ:bɪdʒ/ *n* immondizia *f*; (*nonsense*) idiozie *fpl*. **~ can** *n Am* bidone *m* dell'immondizia

garden /'gɑ:dn/ *n* giardino *m*; [**public**] **~s** *pl* giardini *mpl* pubblici ● *vi* fare giardinaggio. **~ centre** *n negozio m di piante e articoli da giardinaggio.* **~er** *n* giardiniere, -a *mf*. **~ing** *n* giardinaggio *m*

gargle /'gɑ:gl/ *n* gargarismo *m* ● *vi* fare gargarismi

gargoyle /'gɑ:gɔɪl/ *n* gargouille *f inv*

garish /'geərɪʃ/ *adj* sgargiante

garland /'gɑ:lənd/ *n* ghirlanda *f*

garlic /'gɑ:lɪk/ *n* aglio *m*. **~ bread** *n* pane *m* condito con aglio

garment /'gɑ:mənt/ *n* indumento *m*

garnish /'gɑ:nɪʃ/ *n* guarnizione *f* ● *vt* guarnire

garrison /'gærɪsn/ *n* guarnigione *f*

garter /'gɑ:tə(r)/ *n* giarrettiera *f*; (*for socks*) reggicalze *m inv* da uomo

gas /gæs/ *n* gas *m inv*; (*Am* [!]: *petrol*) benzina *f* ● *v* (*pt/pp* **gassed**) ● *vt* asfissiare ● *vi* [!] blaterare. **~ cooker** *n* cucina *f* a gas. **~ 'fire** *n* stufa *f* a gas

gash /gæʃ/ *n* taglio *m* ● *vt* tagliare

gasket /'gæskɪt/ *n* (*Techn*) guarnizione *f*

gas: ~ mask *n* maschera *f* antigas. **~-meter** *n* contatore *m* del gas

gasoline /'gæsəli:n/ *n Am* benzina *f*

gasp /gɑ:sp/ *vi* avere il fiato mozzato

'gas station *n Am* distributore *m* di benzina

gastric /'gæstrɪk/ *adj* gastrico. **~ 'flu** *n* influenza *f* gastro-intestinale. **~ 'ulcer** *n* ulcera *f* gastrica

gate /geɪt/ *n* cancello *m*; (*at airport*) uscita *f*

gate: ~crash *vt* entrare senza invito a. **~crasher** *n* intruso, -a *mf*. **~way** *n* ingresso *m*

gather /'gæðə(r)/ *vt* raccogliere; (*conclude*) dedurre; (*in sewing*) arricciare; **~ speed** acquistare velocità; **~ together** radunare (people, belongings); (*obtain gradually*) acquistare ● *vi* (people:) radunarsi. **~ing** *n* **family ~ing** ritrovo *m* di famiglia

gaudy /'gɔ:dɪ/ *adj* (**-ier, -iest**) pacchiano

gauge /geɪdʒ/ *n* calibro *m*; (*Rail*) scartamento *m*; (*device*) indicatore *m* ● *vt* misurare; *fig* stimare

gaunt /gɔ:nt/ *adj* (*thin*) smunto

gauze /gɔ:z/ *n* garza *f*

gave /geɪv/ ▷GIVE

gawky /'gɔ:kɪ/ *adj* (**-ier, -iest**) sgraziato

g

gawp /gɔ:p/ *vi* ~ [at] [!] guardare con aria da ebete

gay /geɪ/ *adj* gaio; (*homosexual*) omosessuale; (bar, club) gay

gaze /geɪz/ *n* sguardo *m* fisso ● *vi* guardare; ~ **at** fissare

GB *abbr* (Great Britain) GB

gear /gɪə(r)/ *n* equipaggiamento *m*; (*Techn*) ingranaggio *m*; (*Auto*) marcia *f*; **in** ~ con la marcia innestata; **change** ~ cambiare marcia ● *vt* finalizzare (**to** a)

g

gearbox *n* (*Auto*) scatola *f* del cambio

geese /gi:s/ ▷**GOOSE**

gel /dʒel/ *n* gel *m inv*

gelatine /ˈdʒelətɪn/ *n* gelatina *f*

gelignite /ˈdʒelɪgnaɪt/ *n* gelatina esplosiva *f*

gem /dʒem/ *n* gemma *f*

Gemini /ˈdʒemɪnaɪ/ *n* (*Astr*) Gemelli *mpl*

gender /ˈdʒendə(r)/ *n* (*Gram*) genere *m*

gene /dʒi:n/ *n* gene *m*

genealogy /dʒi:nɪˈælədʒɪ/ *n* genealogia *f*

general /ˈdʒenrəl/ *adj* generale ● *n* generale *m*; **in** ~ in generale. ~ **e'lection** *n* elezioni *fpl* politiche

generaliz|ation /dʒenrəlaɪˈzeɪʃn/ *n* generalizzazione *f*. ~**e** *vi* generalizzare

generally /ˈdʒenrəlɪ/ *adv* generalmente

general prac'titioner *n* medico *m* generico

generate /ˈdʒenəreɪt/ *vt* generare

generation /dʒenəˈreɪʃn/ *n* generazione *f*

generator /ˈdʒenəreɪtə(r)/ *n* generatore *m*

generosity /dʒenəˈrɒsɪtɪ/ *n* generosità *f*

generous /ˈdʒenərəs/ *adj* generoso. ~**ly** *adv* generosamente

genetic /dʒɪˈnetɪk/ *adj* genetico. ~ **engineering** *n* ingegneria *f* genetica. ~**s** *n* genetica *f*

Geneva /dʒɪˈni:və/ *n* Ginevra *f*

genial /ˈdʒi:nɪəl/ *adj* gioviale

genitals /ˈdʒenɪtlz/ *npl* genitali *mpl*

genitive /ˈdʒenɪtɪv/ *adj & n* ~ **[case]** genitivo *m*

genius /ˈdʒi:nɪəs/ *n* (*pl* **-uses**) genio *m*

genocide /ˈdʒenəsaɪd/ *n* genocidio *m*

genre /ˈʒæɪg.rə/ *n* genere *m* [letterario]

gent /dʒent/ *n* [!] signore *m*; **the** ~**s** *sg* il bagno per uomini

genteel /dʒenˈti:l/ *adj* raffinato

gentle /ˈdʒentl/ *adj* delicato; (breeze, tap, slope) leggero

gentleman /ˈdʒentlmən/ *n* signore *m*; (*well-mannered*) gentiluomo *m*

gent|leness /ˈdʒentlnɪs/ *n* delicatezza *f*. ~**ly** *adv* delicatamente

genuine /ˈdʒenjʊɪn/ *adj* genuino. ~**ly** *adv* (sorry) sinceramente

geograph|ical /dʒɪəˈgræfɪkl/ *adj* geografico. ~**y** *n* geografia *f*

geological /dʒɪəˈlɒdʒɪkl/ *adj* geologico

geolog|ist /dʒɪˈɒlədʒɪst/ *n* geologo, -a *mf*. ~**y** *n* geologia *f*

geranium /dʒəˈreɪnɪəm/ *n* geranio *m*

geriatric /dʒerɪˈætrɪk/ *adj* geriatrico; ~ **ward** *n* reparto *m* geriatria. ~**s** *n* geriatria *f*

germ /dʒɜ:m/ *n* germe *m*; ~**s** *pl* microbi *mpl*

German /ˈdʒɜ:mən/ *n & adj* tedesco, -a *mf*; (*language*) tedesco *m*

Germanic /dʒəˈmænɪk/ *adj* germanico

German 'measles *n* rosolia *f*

Germany /ˈdʒɜ:mənɪ/ *n* Germania *f*

germinate /ˈdʒɜ:mɪneɪt/ *vi* germogliare

gesticulate /dʒeˈstɪkjʊleɪt/ *vi* gesticolare

gesture /ˈdʒestʃə(r)/ *n* gesto *m*

get /get/ *verb*

> **!** *past tense/past participle* **got**, *past participle Am* **gotten**, *pres participle* **getting**)

● *vt* (*receive*) ricevere; (*obtain*) ottenere; trovare (job); (*buy, catch, fetch*) prendere; (*transport, deliver to airport etc*) portare; (*reach on telephone*) trovare; ([!]: *understand*) comprendere; preparare (meal); ~ **sb to do sth** far fare qcsa a qcno

● *vi* (*become*) ~ **tired**/**bored**/**angry** stancarsi/annoiarsi/arrabbiarsi; **I'm** ~**ting hungry** mi sta venendo fame; ~ **dressed**/**married** vestirsi/sposarsi; ~ **sth ready** preparare qcsa; ~ **nowhere** non concludere nulla; **this is ~ting us nowhere** questo non ci è di nessun aiuto; ~ **to** (*reach*) arrivare a. □ ~ **at** *vi* (*criticize*) criticare; **I see what you're ~ting at** ho capito cosa vuoi dire; **what are you ~ting at?** dove vuoi andare a parare?. □ ~ **away** *vi* (*leave*) andarsene; (*escape*) scappare. □ ~ **back** *vi* tornare ● *vt* (*recover*) riavere; ~ **one's own back** rifarsi. □ ~ **by** *vi* passare; (*manage*) cavarsela. □ ~ **down** *vi* scendere; ~ **down to work** mettersi al lavoro ● *vt* (*depress*) buttare giù. □ ~ **in** *vi* entrare ● *vt* mettere dentro (washing); far venire (plumber). □ ~ **off** *vi* scendere; (*from work*) andarsene; (*Jur*) essere assolto; ~ **off the bus/one's bike** scendere dal pullman/dalla bici ● *vt* (*remove*) togliere. □ ~ **on** *vi* salire; (*be on good terms*) andare d'accordo; (*make progress*) andare avanti; (*in life*) riuscire; ~ **on the bus/one's bike** salire sul pullman/sulla bici; **how are you ~ting on?** come va?. □ ~ **out** *vi* uscire; (*of car*) scendere; ~ **out!** fuori!; ~ **out of** (*avoid doing*) evitare ● *vt* togliere (cork, stain). □ ~ **over** *vi* andare al di là ● *vt fig* riprendersi da (illness). □ ~ **round** *vt* aggirare (rule); rigirare (person) ● *vi* **I never ~ round to it** non mi sono mai deciso a farlo. □ ~ **through** *vi* (*on telephone*) prendere la linea. □ ~ **up** *vi* alzarsi; (*climb*) salire; ~ **up a hill** salire su una collina

geyser /ˈgiːzə(r)/ *n* scaldabagno *m*; (*Geol*) geyser *m inv*

ghastly /ˈgɑːstlɪ/ *adj* (**-ier, -iest**) terribile; **feel** ~ sentirsi da cani

gherkin /ˈgɜːkɪn/ *n* cetriolino *m*

ghetto /ˈgetəʊ/ *n* ghetto *m*

ghost /gəʊst/ *n* fantasma *m*. **~ly** *adj* spettrale

giant /ˈdʒaɪənt/ *n* gigante *m* ● *adj* gigante

gibberish /ˈdʒɪbərɪʃ/ *n* stupidaggini *fpl*

gibe /dʒaɪb/ *n* malignità *f inv*

giblets /ˈdʒɪblɪts/ *npl* frattaglie *fpl*

giddiness /ˈgɪdɪnɪs/ *n* vertigini *fpl*

giddy /ˈgɪdɪ/ *adj* (**-ier, -iest**) vertiginoso; **feel** ~ avere le vertigini

gift /gɪft/ *n* dono *m*; (*to charity*) donazione *f*. **~ed** *adj* dotato. **~-wrap** *vt* impacchettare in carta da regalo

gig /gɪg/ *n* (*Mus*) [!] concerto *m*

gigantic /dʒaɪˈgæntɪk/ *adj* gigantesco

giggle /ˈgɪgl/ *n* risatina *f* ● *vi* ridacchiare

gild /gɪld/ *vt* dorare

gills /gɪlz/ *npl* branchia *fsg*

gilt /gɪlt/ *adj* dorato ● *n* doratura *f*. **~-edged stock** *n* investimento *m* sicuro

gimmick /ˈgɪmɪk/ *n* trovata *f*

gin /dʒɪn/ *n* gin *m inv*

ginger /ˈdʒɪndʒə(r)/ *adj* rosso fuoco *inv*; (cat) rosso ● *n* zenzero *m*. ~ **ale** *n*, ~ **beer** *n bibita f allo zenzero*. **~bread** *n* panpepato *m*

gipsy /ˈdʒɪpsɪ/ *n* = **gypsy**

giraffe /dʒɪˈrɑːf/ *n* giraffa *f*

girder /ˈgɜːdə(r)/ *n* (*Techn*) trave *f*

girl /gɜːl/ *n* ragazza *f*; (*female child*) femmina *f*. ~ **band** *n* girl band *f inv*. **~friend** *n* amica *f*; (*of boy*) ragazza *f*. **~ish** *adj* da ragazza

giro /ˈdʒaɪərəʊ/ *n* bancogiro *m*; (*cheque*) sussidio *m* di disoccupazione

girth /gɜːθ/ *n* circonferenza *f*

gist /dʒɪst/ *n* **the** ~ la sostanza

give /gɪv/ *n* elasticità *f* ● *v* (*pt* **gave**, *pp* **given**) ● *vt* dare; (*as present*) regalare (**to** a); fare (lecture, present, shriek); donare (blood); ~ **birth** partorire ● *vi* (*to charity*) fare delle donazioni; (*yield*) cedere. □ ~ **away** *vt* dar via; (*betray*) tradire; (*distribute*) assegnare; ~ **away the bride** portare la sposa all'altare. □ ~ **back** *vt* restituire. □ ~ **in** *vt* consegnare ● *vi* (*yield*) arrendersi. □ ~ **off** *vt* emanare. □ ~ **over** *vi* ~ **over!** piantala!. □ ~ **up** *vt* rinunciare a; ~ **oneself up** arrendersi ● *vi* rinunciare. □ ~ **way** *vi* cedere; (*Auto*) dare la precedenza; (*collapse*) crollare

given /ˈgɪvn/ ▷GIVE ● *adj* ~ **name** nome *m* di battesimo

glacier /ˈglæsɪə(r)/ *n* ghiacciaio *m*

glad /glæd/ *adj* contento (**of** di). **~den** *vt* rallegrare

gladly /ˈglædlɪ/ *adv* volentieri

glamour /ˈglæmə(r)/ *n* fascino *m*

glance /glɑːns/ *n* sguardo *m* ● *vi* **~ at** dare un'occhiata a. □ **~ up** *vi* alzare gli occhi
gland /glænd/ *n* glandola *f*
glare /gleə(r)/ *n* bagliore *m*; (*look*) occhiataccia *f* ● *vi* **~ at** dare un'occhiataccia a
glaring /ˈgleərɪŋ/ *adj* sfolgorante; (mistake) madornale
glass /glɑːs/ *n* vetro *m*; (*for drinking*) bicchiere *m*; **~es** (*pl: spectacles*) occhiali *mpl*. **~y** *adj* vitreo
g
glaze /gleɪz/ *n* smalto *m* ● *vt* mettere i vetri a (door, window); smaltare (pottery); (*Culin*) spennellare. **~d** *adj* (eyes) vitreo
gleam /gliːm/ *n* luccichio *m* ● *vi* luccicare
glean /gliːn/ *vt* racimolare (information)
glee /gliː/ *n* gioia *f*. **~ful** *adj* gioioso
glib /glɪb/ *adj pej* insincero
glid|e /glaɪd/ *vi* scorrere; (*through the air*) planare. **~er** *n* aliante *m*
glimmer /ˈglɪmə(r)/ *n* barlume *m* ● *vi* emettere un barlume
glimpse /glɪmps/ *n* **catch a ~ of** intravedere ● *vt* intravedere
glint /glɪnt/ *vi* luccicare
glisten /ˈglɪsn/ *vi* luccicare
glitter /ˈglɪtə(r)/ *vi* brillare
gloat /gləʊt/ *vi* gongolare (**over** su)
global /ˈgləʊbl/ *adj* mondiale. **~ization** *n* globalizzazione *f*
globe /gləʊb/ *n* globo *m*; (*map*) mappamondo *m*
gloom /gluːm/ *n* oscurità *f*; (*sadness*) tristezza *f*. **~ily** *adv* (*sadly*) con aria cupa
gloomy /ˈgluːmɪ/ *adj* (**-ier, -iest**) cupo
glorif|y /ˈglɔːrɪfaɪ/ *vt* (*pt/pp* **-ied**) glorificare; **a ~ied waitress** niente più che una cameriera
glorious /ˈglɔːrɪəs/ *adj* splendido; (deed, hero) glorioso
glory /ˈglɔːrɪ/ *n* gloria *f*; (*splendour*) splendore *m*; (*cause for pride*) vanto *m* ● *vi* (*pt/pp* **-ied**) **~ in** vantarsi di
gloss /glɒs/ *n* lucentezza *f*. **~ paint** *n* vernice *f* lucida ● **gloss over** *vt* sorvolare su
glossary /ˈglɒsərɪ/ *n* glossario *m*
glossy /ˈglɒsɪ/ *adj* (**-ier, -iest**) lucido; **~ [magazine]** rivista *f* femminile
glove /glʌv/ *n* guanto *m*. **~ compartment** *n* (*Auto*) cruscotto *m*
glow /gləʊ/ *n* splendore *m*; (*in cheeks*) rossore *m*; (*of candle*) luce *f* soffusa ● *vi* risplendere; (candle:) brillare; (person:) avvampare. **~ing** *adj* ardente; (account) entusiastico. **~-worm** *n* lucciola *f*
glucose /ˈgluːkəʊs/ *n* glucosio *m*
glue /gluː/ *n* colla *f* ● *vt* (*pres p* **gluing**) incollare
glum /glʌm/ *adj* (**glummer, glummest**) tetro
glutton /ˈglʌtən/ *n* ghiottone, -a *mf*. **~ous** *adj* ghiotto. **~y** *n* ghiottoneria *f*
gnarled /nɑːld/ *adj* nodoso
gnash /næʃ/ *vt* **~ one's teeth** digrignare i denti
gnaw /nɔː/ *vt* rosicchiare
go¹ /gəʊ/ *n* (*pl* **goes**) energia *f*; (*attempt*) tentativo *m*; **on the go** in movimento; **at one go** in una sola volta; **it's your go** tocca a te; **make a go of it** riuscire

go² /gəʊ/

> **!** *3 sing pres tense* **goes**, *past tense* **went**, *past participle* **gone**

● *vi* andare; (*leave*) andar via; (*vanish*) sparire; (*become*) diventare; (*be sold*) vendersi; **go and see** andare a vedere; **go swimming/shopping** andare a nuotare/fare spese; **where's the time gone?** come ha fatto il tempo a volare così?; **it's all gone** è finito; **be going to do** stare per fare; **I'm not going to** non ne ho nessuna intenzione; **to go** (**!** hamburgers etc) da asporto; **a coffee to go** un caffè da portar via. □ **~ about** *vi* andare in giro. □ **~ away** *vi* andarsene. □ **~ back** *vi* ritornare. □ **~ by** *vi* passare. □ **~ down** *vi* scendere; (sun:) tramontare; (ship:) affondare; (swelling:) diminuire. □ **~ for** *vt* andare a prendere; andare a cercare (doctor); (*choose*) optare per; (**!**: *attack*) aggredire; **he's not the kind I go for** non è il genere che mi attira. □ **~ in** *vi* entrare. □ **~ in for** *vt* partecipare a (competition); darsi a (tennis). □ **~ off** *vi* andarsene; (alarm:) scattare; (gun, bomb:) esplodere; (food, milk:) andare a male; **go off well** riuscire. ▫ **~ on** *vi* andare avanti; **what's going on?** cosa succede? **go on at** *vt* [!] scocciare. ▫ **~ out** *vi* uscire; (light, fire:) spegnersi. ▫ **~ over** *vi* andare ● *vt* (*check*) controllare. ▫ **~ round** *vi* andare in giro; (*visit*) andare; (*turn*) girare; **is there enough to go round?** ce n'è abbastanza per tutti? **go through** *vi* (bill, proposal:) passare ● *vt* (*suffer*) subire; (*check*) controllare; (*read*) leggere. ▫ **~ under** *vi* passare sotto; (ship, swimmer:) andare sott'acqua; (*fail*) fallire. ▫ **~ up** *vi* salire; (*Theat: curtain:*) aprirsi. ▫ **~ with** *vt* accompagnare. ▫ **~ without** *vt* fare a meno di (supper, sleep) ● *vi* fare senza

goad /gəʊd/ *vt* spingere (**into** a); (*taunt*) spronare

'go-ahead *adj* (person, company) intraprendente ● *n* okay *m*

goal /gəʊl/ *n* porta *f*; (*point scored*) gol *m inv*; (*in life*) obiettivo *m*; **score a ~** segnare. **~ie** [!], **~keeper** *n* portiere *m*. **~-post** *n* palo *m*

goat /gəʊt/ *n* capra *f*

gobble /'gɒbl/ *vt* **~ [down, up]** trangugiare

God, god /gɒd/ *n* Dio *m*, dio *m*

god: ~child *n* figlioccio, -a *mf*. **~-daughter** *n* figlioccia *f*. **~dess** *n* dea *f*. **~father** *n* padrino *m*. **~-forsaken** *adj* dimenticato da Dio. **~mother** *n* madrina *f*. **~send** *n* manna *f*. **~son** *n* figlioccio *m*

going /'gəʊɪŋ/ *adj* (price, rate) corrente; **~ concern** azienda *f* florida ● *n* **it's hard ~** è una faticaccia; **while the ~ is good** finché si può. **~s-'on** *npl* avvenimenti *mpl*

gold /gəʊld/ *n* oro *m* ● *adj* d'oro

golden /'gəʊldn/ *adj* dorato. **~ 'handshake** *n* buonuscita *f* (*al termine di un rapporto di lavoro*). **~ mean** *n* giusto mezzo *m*. **~ 'wedding** *n* nozze *fpl* d'oro

gold: ~fish *n inv* pesce *m* rosso. **~-mine** *n* miniera *f* d'oro. **~-plated** *adj* placcato d'oro. **~smith** *n* orefice *m*

golf /gɒlf/ *n* golf *m*

golf: ~-club *n* circolo *m* di golf; (*implement*) mazza *f* da golf. **~-course** *n* campo *m* di golf. **~er** *n* giocatore, -trice *mf* di golf

gondo|la /'gɒndələ/ *n* gondola *f*. **~lier** *n* gondoliere *m*

gone /gɒn/ ▸**GO**

gong /gɒŋ/ *n* gong *m inv*

good /gʊd/ *adj* (**better, best**) buono; (child, footballer, singer) bravo; (holiday, film) bello; **~ at** bravo in; **a ~ deal of anger** molta rabbia; **as ~ as** (*almost*) quasi; **~ morning, ~ afternoon** buon giorno; **~ evening** buona sera; **~ night** buonanotte; **have a ~ time** divertirsi ● *n* bene *m*; **for ~** per sempre; **do ~** far del bene; **do sb ~** far bene a qcno; **it's no ~** è inutile; **be up to no ~** combinare qualcosa

goodbye /gʊd'baɪ/ *int* arrivederci

good: ~-for-nothing *n* buono, -a *mf* a nulla. **G~ 'Friday** *n* Venerdì *m* Santo

good-'looking *adj* bello

goodness /'gʊdnɪs/ *n* bontà *f*; **my ~!** santo cielo!; **thank ~!** grazie al cielo!

goods /gʊdz/ *npl* prodotti *mpl*. **~ train** *n* treno *m* merci

good'will *n* buona volontà *f*; (*Comm*) avviamento *m*

goody /'gʊdɪ/ *n* ([!]*: person*) buono *m*. **~-goody** *n* santarellino, -a *mf*

gooey /'gu:ɪ/ *adj* [!] appiccicaticcio; *fig* sdolcinato

google /'gu:gl/ *vt/i* googlare

goose /gu:s/: **~-flesh** *n*, **~-pimples** *npl* pelle *fsg* d'oca

gooseberry /'gʊzbərɪ/ *n* uva *f* spina

gore[1] /gɔ:(r)/ *n* sangue *m*

gore[2] *vt* incornare

gorge /gɔ:dʒ/ *n* (*Geog*) gola *f* ● *vt* **~ oneself** ingozzarsi

gorgeous /'gɔ:dʒəs/ *adj* stupendo

gorilla /gə'rɪlə/ *n* gorilla *m inv*

gorse /gɔ:s/ *n* ginestrone *m*

gory /'gɔ:rɪ/ *adj* (**-ier, -iest**) cruento

gosh /gɒʃ/ *int* [!] caspita

gospel /'gɒspl/ *n* vangelo *m*. **~ truth** *n* sacrosanta verità *f*

gossip /'gɒsɪp/ *n* pettegolezzi *mpl*; (*per-*

son) pettegolo, -a *mf* ● *vi* pettegolare. **~y** *adj* pettegolo

got /gɒt/ ▷GET; **have ~** avere; **have ~ to do sth** dover fare qcsa

gotten /'gɒtn/ *Am see* **get**

gouge /gaʊdʒ/ *vt* **~ out** cavare

gourmet /'gʊəmeɪ/ *n* buongustaio, -a *mf*

govern /'gʌv(ə)n/ *vt/i* governare; (*determine*) determinare

government /'gʌvnmənt/ *n* governo *m*. **~al** *adj* governativo

g

governor /'gʌvənə(r)/ *n* governatore *m*; (*of school*) membro *m* del consiglio di istituto; (*of prison*) direttore, -trice *mf*; ([!]: *boss*) capo *m*

gown /gaʊn/ *n* vestito *m*; (*Jur, Univ*) toga *f*

GP *n abbr* general practitioner

GPS *abbr* (Global Positioning System) GPS *m*

grab /græb/ *vt* (*pt/pp* **grabbed**) **~ [hold of]** afferrare

grace /greɪs/ *n* grazia *f*; (*before meal*) benedicite *m inv*; **with good ~** volentieri; **three days' ~** tre giorni di proroga. **~ful** *adj* aggraziato. **~fully** *adv* con grazia

gracious /'greɪʃəs/ *adj* cortese; (*elegant*) lussuoso

grade /greɪd/ *n* livello *m*; (*Comm*) qualità *f*; (*Sch*) voto *m*; (*Am Sch: class*) classe *f*; *Am* = **gradient** ● *vt* (*Comm*) classificare; (*Sch*) dare il voto a. **~ crossing** *n Am* passaggio *m* a livello

gradient /'greɪdɪənt/ *n* pendenza *f*

gradual /'grædʒʊəl/ *adj* graduale. **~ly** *adv* gradualmente

graduate[1] /'grædʒʊət/ *n* laureato, -a *mf*

graduate[2] /'grædʒʊeɪt/ *vi* (*Univ*) laurearsi

graduation /grædʒʊ'eɪʃn/ *n* laurea *f*

graffiti /grə'fi:tɪ/ *npl* graffiti *mpl*

graft /grɑ:ft/ *n* (*Bot, Med*) innesto *m*; (*Med: organ*) trapianto *m*; ([!]: *hard work*) duro lavoro *m*; ([!]: *corruption*) corruzione *f* ● *vt* innestare; trapiantare (organ)

grain /greɪn/ *n* (*of sand, salt*) granello *m*; (*of rice*) chicco *m*; (*cereals*) cereali *mpl*; (*in wood*) venatura *f*; **it goes against the ~** *fig* è contro la mia/sua natura

gram /græm/ *n* grammo *m*

grammar /'græmə(r)/ *n* grammatica *f*. **~ school** *n* ≈ liceo *m*

grammatical /grə'mætɪkl/ *adj* grammaticale

grand /grænd/ *adj* grandioso; [!] eccellente

'grandchild *n* nipote *mf*

'granddaughter *n* nipote *f*

grandeur /'grændʒə(r)/ *n* grandiosità *f*

'grandfather *n* nonno *m*. **~ clock** *n* pendolo *m* (*che poggia a terra*)

grandiose /'grændɪəʊs/ *adj* grandioso

grand: ~mother *n* nonna *f*. **~parents** *npl* nonni *mpl*. **~ pi'ano** *n* pianoforte *m* a coda. **~son** *n* nipote *m*. **~stand** *n* tribuna *f*

granite /'grænɪt/ *n* granito *m*

granny /'grænɪ/ *n* [!] nonna *f*

grant /grɑ:nt/ *n* (*money*) sussidio *m*; (*Univ*) borsa *f* di studio ● *vt* accordare; (*admit*) ammettere; **take sth for ~ed** dare per scontato qcsa

granule /'grænju:l/ *n* granello *m*

grape /greɪp/ *n* acino *m*; **~s** *pl* uva *fsg*

grapefruit /'greɪp-/ *n inv* pompelmo *m*

graph /grɑ:f/ *n* grafico *m*

graphic /'græfɪk/ *adj* grafico; (*vivid*) vivido. **~s** *n* grafica *f*

grapple /'græpl/ *vi* **~ with** *also fig* essere alle prese con

grasp /grɑ:sp/ *n* stretta *f*; (*understanding*) comprensione *f* ● *vt* afferrare. **~ing** *adj* avido

grass /grɑ:s/ *n* erba *f*; **at the ~ roots** alla base. **~hopper** *n* cavalletta *f*. **~land** *n* prateria *f*

grassy /'grɑ:sɪ/ *adj* erboso

grate[1] /greɪt/ *n* grata *f*

grate[2] *vt* (*Culin*) grattugiare ● *vi* stridere

grateful /'greɪtfl/ *adj* grato. **~ly** *adv* con gratitudine

grater /'greɪtə(r)/ *n* (*Culin*) grattugia *f*

gratif|y /'grætɪfaɪ/ *vt* (*pt/pp* **-ied**) appagare. **~ied** *adj* appagato. **~ying** *adj* appagante

grating /'greɪtɪŋ/ *n* grata *f*

gratitude /'grætɪtju:d/ *n* gratitudine *f*

gratuitous /grə'tju:ɪtəs/ *adj* gratuito

gratuity /grə'tju:ɪtɪ/ *n* gratifica *f*

grave[1] /greɪv/ *adj* grave

grave[2] *n* tomba *f*

gravel /'grævl/ *n* ghiaia *f*

grave: ~stone *n* lapide *f.* **~yard** *n* cimitero *m*

gravitate /'grævɪteɪt/ *vi* gravitare

gravity /'grævɪtɪ/ *n* gravità *f*

gravy /'greɪvɪ/ *n* sugo *m* della carne

gray /greɪ/ *adj Am* = **grey**

graze[1] /greɪz/ *vi* (animal:) pascolare

graze[2] *n* escoriazione *f* ● *vt* (*touch lightly*) sfiorare; (*scrape*) escoriare; sbucciarsi (knee)

grease /gri:s/ *n* grasso *m* ● *vt* ungere. **~-proof 'paper** *n* carta *f* oleata

greasy /'gri:sɪ/ *adj* (**-ier, -iest**) untuoso; (hair, skin) grasso

great /greɪt/ *adj* grande; ([!]: *marvellous*) eccezionale

great: G~ 'Britain *n* Gran Bretagna *f.* **~-'grandfather** *n* bisnonno *m.* **~-'grandmother** *n* bisnonna *f*

great|ly /'greɪtlɪ/ *adv* enormemente. **~ness** *n* grandezza *f*

Greece /gri:s/ *n* Grecia *f*

greed /gri:d/ *n* avidità *f*; (*for food*) ingordigia *f*

greedy /'gri:dɪ/ *adj* (**-ier, -iest**) avido; (*for food*) ingordo

Greek /gri:k/ *adj & n* greco, -a *mf*; (*language*) greco *m*

green /gri:n/ *adj* verde; (*fig: inexperienced*) immaturo ● *n* verde *m*; **~s** *pl* verdura *f*; **the G~s** *pl* (*Pol*) i verdi. **~ belt** *n zona f verde intorno a una città.* **~ card** *n* (*Auto*) carta *f* verde

> **Green Card** Negli Stati Uniti è un documento ufficiale che concede a qualsiasi persona priva della cittadinanza americana il permesso di risiedere e lavorare indefinitivamente negli Stati Uniti. Nel Regno Unito, invece, è un documento che i conducenti o proprietari di autoveicoli devono richiedere alla propria compagnia di assicurazione per convalidare la polizza in occasione di viaggi all'estero.

greenery /'gri:nərɪ/ *n* verde *m*

green: ~grocer *n* fruttivendolo, -a *mf.* **~house** *n* serra *f.* **~house effect** *n* effetto *m* serra. **~ light** *n* [!] verde *m*

greet /gri:t/ *vt* salutare; (*welcome*) accogliere. **~ing** *n* saluto *m*; (*welcome*) accoglienza *f.* **~ings card** *n* biglietto *m* d'auguri

gregarious /grɪ'geərɪəs/ *adj* gregario; (*person*) socievole

grenade /grɪ'neɪd/ *n* granata *f*

grew /gru:/ ▷GROW

grey /greɪ/ *adj* grigio; (hair) bianco ● *n* grigio *m.* **~hound** *n* levriero *m*

grid /grɪd/ *n* griglia *f*; (*on map*) reticolato *m*; (*Electr*) rete *f*

grief /gri:f/ *n* dolore *m*; **come to ~** (plans:) naufragare

grievance /'gri:vəns/ *n* lamentela *f*

grieve /gri:v/ *vt* addolorare ● *vi* essere addolorato

grill /grɪl/ *n* graticola *f*; (*for grilling*) griglia *f*; **mixed ~** grigliata *f* mista ● *vt/i* cuocere alla griglia; (*interrogate*) sottoporre al terzo grado

grille /grɪl/ *n* grata *f*

grim /grɪm/ *adj* (**grimmer, grimmest**) arcigno; (determination) accanito

grimace /grɪ'meɪs/ *n* smorfia *f* ● *vi* fare una smorfia

grime /graɪm/ *n* sudiciume *m*

grimy /'graɪmɪ/ *adj* (**-ier, -iest**) sudicio

grin /grɪn/ *n* sorriso *m* ● *vi* (*pt/pp* **grinned**) fare un gran sorriso

grind /graɪnd/ *n* ([!]: *hard work*) sfacchinata *f* ● *vt* (*pt/pp* **ground**) macinare; affilare (knife); (*Am: mince*) tritare; **~ one's teeth** digrignare i denti

grip /grɪp/ *n* presa *f*; *fig* controllo *m*; (*bag*) borsone *m*; **get a ~ on oneself** controllarsi ● *vt* (*pt/pp* **gripped**) afferrare; (tyres:) far presa su; tenere avvinto (attention)

grisly /'grɪzlɪ/ *adj* (**-ier, -iest**) raccapricciante

gristle /'grɪsl/ *n* cartilagine *f*

grit /grɪt/ *n* graniglia *f*; (*for roads*) sabbia *f*; (*courage*) coraggio *m* ● *vt* (*pt/pp* **gritted**) spargere sabbia su (road); **~ one's teeth** serrare i denti

groan /grəʊn/ *n* gemito *m* ● *vi* gemere

grocer /'grəʊsə(r)/ *n* droghiere, -a *mf*; **~'s [shop]** drogheria *f.* **~ies** *npl* generi *mpl* alimentari

groggy /'grɒgɪ/ *adj* (-ier, -iest) stordito; (*unsteady*) barcollante

groin /grɔɪn/ *n* (*Anat*) inguine *m*

groom /gru:m/ *n* sposo *m*; (*for horse*) stalliere *m* ● *vt* strigliare (horse); *fig* preparare; **well-~ed** ben curato

groove /gru:v/ *n* scanalatura *f*

grope /grəʊp/ *vi* brancolare; **~ for** cercare a tastoni

gross /grəʊs/ *adj* obeso; (*coarse*) volgare; (*glaring*) grossolano; (salary, weight) lordo ● *n inv* grossa *f*. **~ly** *adv* (*very*) enormemente

grotesque /grəʊ'tesk/ *adj* grottesco

ground¹ /graʊnd/ ▷GRIND

ground² *n* terra *f*; (*Sport*) terreno *m*; (*reason*) ragione *f*; **~s** *pl* (*park*) giardini *mpl*; (*of coffee*) fondi *mpl* ● *vi* (ship:) arenarsi ● *vt* bloccare a terra (aircraft); *Am* (*Electr*) mettere a terra

ground: ~ floor *n* pianterreno *m*. **~ing** *n* base *f*. **~less** *adj* infondato. **~sheet** *n* telone *m* impermeabile. **~work** *n* lavoro *m* di preparazione

group /gru:p/ *n* gruppo *m* ● *vt* raggruppare ● *vi* raggrupparsi

grouse¹ /graʊs/ *n inv* gallo *m* cedrone

grouse² *vi* [!] brontolare

grovel /'grɒvl/ *vi* (*pt/pp* **grovelled**) strisciare. **~ling** *adj* leccapiedi *inv*

grow /grəʊ/ *v* (*pt* **grew**, *pp* **grown**) ● *vi* crescere; (*become*) diventare; (unemployment, fear:) aumentare; (town:) ingrandirsi ● *vt* coltivare; **~ one's hair** farsi crescere i capelli. □ **~ up** *vi* crescere; (town:) svilupparsi

growl /graʊl/ *n* grugnito *m* ● *vi* ringhiare

grown /grəʊn/ ▷GROW ● *adj* adulto. **~-up** *adj & n* adulto, -a *mf*

growth /grəʊθ/ *n* crescita *f*; (*increase*) aumento *m*; (*Med*) tumore *m*

grub /grʌb/ *n* larva *f*; ([!]: *food*) mangiare *m*

grubby /'grʌbɪ/ *adj* (**-ier, -iest**) sporco

grudg|e /grʌdʒ/ *n* rancore *m*; **bear sb a ~e** portare rancore a qcno ● *vt* dare a malincuore. **~ing** *adj* riluttante. **~ingly** *adv* a malincuore

gruelling /'gru:əlɪŋ/ *adj* estenuante

gruesome /'gru:səm/ *adj* macabro

gruff /grʌf/ *adj* burbero

grumble /'grʌmbl/ *vi* brontolare (**at** contro)

grumpy /'grʌmpɪ/ *adj* (**-ier, -iest**) scorbutico

grunt /grʌnt/ *n* grugnito *m* ● *vi* fare un grugnito

guarant|ee /gærən'ti:/ *n* garanzia *f* ● *vt* garantire. **~or** *n* garante *mf*

guard /gɑ:d/ *n* guardia *f*; (*security*) guardiano *m*; (*on train*) capotreno *m*; (*Techn*) schermo *m* protettivo; **be on ~** essere di guardia ● *vt* sorvegliare; (*protect*) proteggere. □ **~ against** *vt* guardarsi da. **~-dog** *n* cane *m* da guardia

guarded /'gɑ:dɪd/ *adj* guardingo

guardian /'gɑ:dɪən/ *n* (*of minor*) tutore, -trice *mf*

guerrilla /gə'rɪlə/ *n* guerrigliero, -a *mf*. **~ warfare** *n* guerriglia *f*

guess /ges/ *n* supposizione *f* ● *vt* indovinare ● *vi* indovinare; (*Am: suppose*) supporre. **~work** *n* supposizione *f*

guest /gest/ *n* ospite *mf*; (*in hotel*) cliente *mf*. **~-house** *n* pensione *f*

guffaw /gʌ'fɔ:/ *n* sghignazzata *f* ● *vi* sghignazzare

guidance /'gaɪdəns/ *n* guida *f*; (*advice*) consigli *mpl*

guide /gaɪd/ *n* guida *f*; **[Girl] G~** giovane esploratrice *f* ● *vt* guidare. **~book** *n* guida *f* turistica

guide: ~-dog *n* cane *m* per ciechi. **~lines** *npl* direttive *fpl*

guild /gɪld/ *n* corporazione *f*

guile /gaɪl/ *n* astuzia *f*

guillotine /'gɪləti:n/ *n* ghigliottina *f*; (*for paper*) taglierina *f*

guilt /gɪlt/ *n* colpa *f*. **~ily** *adv* con aria colpevole

guilty /'gɪltɪ/ *adj* (**-ier, -iest**) colpevole; **have a ~ conscience** avere la coscienza sporca

guinea-pig /'gɪnɪ-/ *n* porcellino *m* d'India; (*fig: used for experiments*) cavia *f*

guitar /gɪ'tɑ:(r)/ *n* chitarra *f*. **~ist** *n* chitarrista *mf*

gulf /gʌlf/ *n* (*Geog*) golfo *m*; *fig* abisso *m*

gull /gʌl/ *n* gabbiano *m*

gullet /'gʌlɪt/ *n* esofago *m*; (*throat*) gola *f*

gullible /'gʌlɪbl/ *adj* credulone

gully /'gʌlɪ/ *n* burrone *m*; (*drain*) canale *m* di scolo

gulp /gʌlp/ *n* azione *f* di deglutire; (*of food*) boccone *m*; (*of liquid*) sorso *m* ● *vi* deglutire. □ ~ **down** *vt* trangugiare (food); scolarsi (liquid)

gum¹ /gʌm/ *n* (*Anat*) gengiva *f*

gum² *n* gomma *f*; (*chewing gum*) gomma *f* da masticare, chewing gum *m inv* ● *vt* (*pt/pp* **gummed**) ingommare (**to** a)

gun /gʌn/ *n* pistola *f*; (*rifle*) fucile *m*; (*cannon*) cannone *m* ● **gun down** *vt* (*pt/pp* **gunned**) freddare

gun: ~fire *n* spari *mpl*; (*of cannon*) colpi *mpl* [di cannone]. **~man** uomo *m* armato

gun: ~powder *n* polvere *f* da sparo. **~shot** *n* colpo *m* [di pistola]

gurgle /'gɜːgl/ *vi* gorgogliare; (baby:) fare degli urletti

gush /gʌʃ/ *vi* sgorgare; (*enthuse*) parlare con troppo entusiasmo (**over** di). □ ~ **out** *vi* sgorgare. **~ing** *adj* eccessivamente entusiastico

gust /gʌst/ *n* (*of wind*) raffica *f*

gusto /'gʌstəʊ/ *n* **with ~** con trasporto

gusty /'gʌstɪ/ *adj* ventoso

gut /gʌt/ *n* intestino *m*; **~s** *pl* pancia *f*; (!: *courage*) fegato *m* ● *vt* (*pt/pp* **gutted**) (*Culin*) svuotare delle interiora; **~ted by fire** sventrato da un incendio

gutter /'gʌtə(r)/ *n* canale *m* di scolo; (*on roof*) grondaia *f*; *fig* bassifondi *mpl*

guttural /'gʌtərəl/ *adj* gutturale

guy /gaɪ/ *n* ! tipo *m*, tizio *m*

guzzle /'gʌzl/ *vt* ingozzarsi con (food); **he's ~d the lot** si è sbafato tutto

gym /dʒɪm/ *n* ! palestra *f*; (*gymnastics*) ginnastica *f*

gymnasium /dʒɪm'neɪzɪəm/ *n* palestra *f*

gymnast /'dʒɪmnæst/ *n* ginnasta *mf*. **~ics** *n* ginnastica *f*

gymslip *n* (*Sch*) ≈ grembiule *m* (*da bambina*)

gynaecolog|ist /gaɪnɪ'kɒlədʒɪst/ *n* ginecologo, -a *mf*. **~y** *n* ginecologia *f*

gypsy /'dʒɪpsɪ/ *n* zingaro, -a *mf*

gyrate /dʒaɪ'reɪt/ *vi* roteare

Hh

haberdashery /hæbə'dæʃərɪ/ *n* merceria *f*; *Am* negozio *m* d'abbigliamento da uomo

habit /'hæbɪt/ *n* abitudine *f*; (*Relig: costume*) tonaca *f*; **be in the ~ of doing sth** avere l'abitudine di fare qcsa

habitable /'hæbɪtəbl/ *adj* abitabile

habitat /'hæbɪtæt/ *n* habitat *m inv*

habitation /hæbɪ'teɪʃn/ *n* **unfit for human ~** inagibile

habitual /hə'bɪtjʊəl/ *adj* abituale; (smoker, liar) inveterato. **~ly** *adv* regolarmente

hack¹ /hæk/ *n* (*writer*) scribacchino, -a *mf*

hack² *vt* tagliare; **~ to pieces** tagliare a pezzi

hackneyed /'hæknɪd/ *adj* trito [e ritrito]

had /hæd/ ▸ **HAVE**

haddock /'hædək/ *n inv* eglefino *m*

haemorrhage /'hemərɪdʒ/ *n* emorragia *f*

haemorrhoids /'hemərɔɪdz/ *npl* emorroidi *fpl*

hag /hæg/ *n* **old ~** vecchia befana *f*

haggard /'hægəd/ *adj* sfatto

hail¹ /heɪl/ *vt* salutare; far segno a (taxi) ● *vi* **~ from** provenire da

hail² *n* grandine *f* ● *vi* grandinare. **~stone** *n* chicco *m* di grandine. **~storm** *n* grandinata *f*

hair /heə(r)/ *n* capelli *mpl*; (*on body, of animal*) pelo *m*

hair: ~brush *n* spazzola *f* per capelli. **~cut** *n* taglio *m* di capelli; **have a ~cut** farsi tagliare i capelli. **~-do** *n* ! pettinatura *f*. **~dresser** *n* parrucchiere, -a *mf*. **~-dryer** *n* fon *m inv*; (*with hood*) casco *m* [asciugacapelli]. **~-grip** *n* molletta *f*. **~pin** *n* forcina *f*. **~pin 'bend** *n* tornante *m*, curva *f* a gomito. **~-raising** *adj* terrificante. **~-style** *n* acconciatura *f*

hairy /'heərɪ/ *adj* (**-ier, -iest**) peloso; (!: *frightening*) spaventoso

half /hɑːf/ *n* (*pl* **halves**) metà *f inv*; **cut**

in ~ tagliare a metà; **one and a ~** uno e mezzo; **~ a dozen** mezza dozzina; **~ an hour** mezz'ora ● *adj* mezzo; [**at**] **~ price** [a] metà prezzo ● *adv* a metà; **~ past two** le due e mezza

half: ~-'hearted *adj* esitante. **~ 'mast** *n* **at ~ mast** a mezz'asta. **~-'term** *n* vacanza *f* di metà trimestre. **~-'time** *n* (*Sport*) intervallo *m*. **~'way** *adj* **the ~way mark/stage** il livello intermedio ● *adv* a metà strada; **get ~way** *fig* arrivare a metà

hall /hɔːl/ *n* (*entrance*) ingresso *m*; (*room*) sala *f*; (*mansion*) residenza *f* di campagna; **~ of residence** (*Univ*) casa *f* dello studente

h

'hallmark *n* marchio *m* di garanzia; *fig* marchio *m*

hallo /hə'ləʊ/ *int* ciao!; (*on telephone*) pronto!; **say ~ to** salutare

Hallowe'en /hæləʊ'iːn/ *n vigilia f d'Ognissanti e notte delle streghe, celebrata soprattutto dai bambini*

hallucination /həluːsɪ'neɪʃn/ *n* allucinazione *f*

halo /'heɪləʊ/ *n* (*pl* **-es**) aureola *f*; (*Astr*) alone *m*

halt /hɔːlt/ *n* alt *m inv*; **come to a ~** fermarsi; (traffic:) bloccarsi ● *vi* fermarsi; **~!** alt! ● *vt* fermare. **~ing** *adj* esitante

halve /hɑːv/ *vt* dividere a metà; (*reduce*) dimezzare

ham /hæm/ *n* prosciutto *m*; (*Theat*) attore, -trice *mf* da strapazzo

hamburger /'hæmbɜːgə(r)/ *n* hamburger *m inv*

hammer /'hæmə(r)/ *n* martello *m* ● *vt* martellare ● *vi* **~ at/on** picchiare a

hammock /'hæmək/ *n* amaca *f*

hamper[1] /'hæmpə(r)/ *n* cesto *m*; [**gift**] **~** cestino *m*

hamper[2] *vt* ostacolare

hamster /'hæmstə(r)/ *n* criceto *m*

hand /hænd/ *n* mano *f*; (*of clock*) lancetta *f*; (*writing*) scrittura *f*; (*worker*) manovale *m*; **at ~, to ~** a portata di mano; **on the one ~** da un lato; **on the other ~** d'altra parte; **out of ~** incontrollabile; (*summarily*) su due piedi; **give sb a ~** dare una mano a qcno ● *vt* porgere. □ **~ down** *vt* tramandare. □ **~ in** *vt* consegnare. □ **~ out** *vt* distribuire. □ **~ over** *vt* passare; (*to police*) consegnare

hand: ~bag *n* borsa *f* (*da signora*). **~brake** *n* freno *m* a mano. **~cuffs** *npl* manette *fpl*. **~ful** *n* manciata *f*; **be [quite] a ~ful** 🅸 essere difficile da tenere a freno

handicap /'hændɪkæp/ *n* handicap *m inv*. **~ped** *adj* **mentally/physically ~ped** mentalmente/fisicamente handicappato

handi|craft /'hændɪkrɑːft/ *n* artigianato *m*. **~work** *n* opera *f*

handkerchief /'hæŋkətʃɪf/ *n* (*pl* **~s** & **-chieves**) fazzoletto *m*

handle /'hændl/ *n* manico *m*; (*of door*) maniglia *f*; **fly off the ~** 🅸 perdere le staffe ● *vt* maneggiare; occuparsi di (problem, customer); prendere (difficult person); trattare (subject). **~bars** *npl* manubrio *m*

hand: ~-out *n* (*at lecture*) foglio *m* informativo; (🅸: *money*) elemosina *f*. **~shake** *n* stretta *f* di mano

handsome /'hænsəm/ *adj* bello; (*fig: generous*) generoso

handwriting *n* calligrafia *f*

handy /'hændɪ/ *adj* (**-ier, -iest**) utile; (person) abile; **have/keep ~** avere/tenere a portata di mano. **~man** *n* tuttofare *m inv*

hang /hæŋ/ *vt* (*pt/pp* **hung**) appendere (picture); (*pt/pp* **hanged**) impiccare (criminal); **~ oneself** impiccarsi ● *vi* (*pt/pp* **hung**) pendere; (hair:) scendere ● *n* **get the ~ of it** 🅸 afferrare. □ **~ about** *vi* gironzolare. □ **~ on** *vi* tenersi stretto; (🅸: *wait*) aspettare; (*Teleph*) restare in linea. □ **~ on to** *vt* tenersi stretto a; (*keep*) tenere. □ **~ out** *vi* spuntare; **where does he usually ~ out?** 🅸 dove bazzica di solito? ● *vt* stendere (washing). □ **~ up** *vt* appendere; (*Teleph*) riattaccare ● *vi* essere appeso; (*Teleph*) riattaccare

hangar /'hæŋə(r)/ *n* (*Aeron*) hangar *m inv*

hanger /'hæŋə(r)/ *n* gruccia *f*. **~-on** *n* leccapiedi *mf*

hang: ~-glider *n* deltaplano *m*. **~over** *n* 🅸 postumi *mpl* da sbornia. **~-up** *n* 🅸 complesso *m*

hanky /'hæŋkɪ/ *n* [!] fazzoletto *m*

haphazard /hæp'hæzəd/ *adj* a casaccio

happen /'hæpn/ *vi* capitare, succedere; **as it ~s** per caso; **I ~ed to meet him** mi è capitato di incontrarlo; **what has ~ed to him?** cosa gli è capitato?; (*become of*) che fine ha fatto? **~ing** *n* avvenimento *m*

happi|ly /'hæpɪlɪ/ *adv* felicemente; (*fortunately*) fortunatamente. **~ness** *n* felicità *f*

happy /'hæpɪ/ *adj* (**-ier, -iest**) contento, felice. **~-go-'lucky** *adj* spensierato

harass /'hærəs/ *vt* perseguitare. **~ed** *adj* stressato. **~ment** *n* persecuzione *f*; **sexual ~ment** molestie *fpl* sessuali

harbour /'hɑ:bə(r)/ *n* porto *m* • *vt* dare asilo a; nutrire (grudge)

hard /hɑ:d/ *adj* duro; (question, problem) difficile; **~ of hearing** duro d'orecchi; **be ~ on sb** (person:) essere duro con qcno • *adv* (work) duramente; (pull, hit, rain, snow) forte; **~ hit by unemployment** duramente colpito dalla disoccupazione; **take sth ~** non accettare qcsa; **think ~!** pensaci bene!; **try ~** mettercela tutta; **try ~er** metterci più impegno; **~ done by** [!] trattato ingiustamente

hard: hard-boiled *adj* (egg) sodo. **~ disk** *n* hard disk *m inv*, disco *m* rigido

harden /'hɑ:dn/ *vi* indurirsi

hard: ~-'headed *adj* (businessman) dal sangue freddo. **~line** *adj* duro

hard|ly /'hɑ:dlɪ/ *adv* appena; **~ly ever** quasi mai. **~ness** *n* durezza *f*. **~ship** *n* avversità *f inv*

hard: ~ 'shoulder *n* (*Auto*) corsia *f* d'emergenza. **~ware** *n* ferramenta *fpl*; (*Comput*) hardware *m inv*. **~-'working** *adj* **be ~-working** essere un gran lavoratore

hardy /'hɑ:dɪ/ *adj* (**-ier, -iest**) dal fisico resistente; (plant) che sopporta il gelo

hare /heə(r)/ *n* lepre *f*. **~-brained** *adj* [!] (scheme) da scervellati

hark /hɑ:k/ *vi* **~ back to** *fig* ritornare su

harm /hɑ:m/ *n* male *m*; (*damage*) danni *mpl*; **out of ~'s way** in un posto sicuro; **it won't do any ~** non farà certo male • *vt* far male a; (*damage*) danneggiare. **~ful** *adj* dannoso. **~less** *adj* innocuo

harmonica /hɑ:'mɒnɪkə/ *n* armonica *f* [a bocca]

harmonious /hɑ:'məʊnɪəs/ *adj* armonioso. **~ly** *adv* in armonia

harness /'hɑ:nɪs/ *n* finimenti *mpl*; (*of parachute*) imbracatura *f* • *vt* bardare (horse); sfruttare (resources)

harp /hɑ:p/ *n* arpa *f* • **harp on** *vi* [!] insistere (**about** su). **~ist** *n* arpista *mf*

harpoon /hɑ:'pu:n/ *n* arpione *m*

harpsichord /'hɑ:psɪkɔ:d/ *n* clavicembalo *m*

h

harrowing /'hærəʊɪŋ/ *adj* straziante

harsh /hɑ:ʃ/ *adj* duro; (light) abbagliante. **~ness** *n* durezza *f*

harvest /'hɑ:vɪst/ *n* raccolta *f*; (*of grapes*) vendemmia *f*; (*crop*) raccolto *m* • *vt* raccogliere

has /hæz/ ▷**HAVE**

hassle /'hæsl/ [!] *n* rottura *f* • *vt* rompere le scatole a

haste /heɪst/ *n* fretta *f*

hast|y /'heɪstɪ/ *adj* (**-ier, -iest**) frettoloso; (decision) affrettato. **~ily** *adv* frettolosamente

hat /hæt/ *n* cappello *m*

hatch¹ /hætʃ/ *n* (*for food*) sportello *m* passavivande; (*Naut*) boccaporto *m*

hatch² *vi* **~[out]** rompere il guscio; (egg:) schiudersi • *vt* covare; tramare (plot)

'hatchback *n* tre/cinque porte *m inv*; (*door*) porta *f* del bagagliaio

hatchet /'hætʃɪt/ *n* ascia *f*

hate /heɪt/ *n* odio *m* • *vt* odiare. **~ful** *adj* odioso

hatred /'heɪtrɪd/ *n* odio *m*

haught|y /'hɔ:tɪ/ *adj* (**-ier, -iest**) altezzoso. **~ily** *adv* altezzosamente

haul /hɔ:l/ *n* (*fish*) pescata *f*; (*loot*) bottino *m*; (*pull*) tirata *f* • *vt* tirare; trasportare (goods) • *vi* **~ on** tirare. **~age** *n* trasporto *m*. **~ier** *n* autotrasportatore *m*

haunt /hɔ:nt/ *n* ritrovo *m* • *vt* frequentare; (*linger in the mind*) perseguitare; **this house is ~ed** questa casa è abitata da fantasmi

have /hæv/

- *vt* (*3 sg pres tense* **has**; *pt/pp* **had**) avere; fare (breakfast, bath, walk etc); **~ a drink** bere qualcosa; **~ lunch/dinner** pranzare/cenare; **~ a rest** riposarsi; **I had my hair cut** mi sono tagliata i capelli; **we had the house painted** abbiamo fatto tinteggiare la casa; **I had it made** l'ho fatto fare; **~ to do sth** dover fare qcsa; **~ him telephone me tomorrow** digli di telefonarmi domani; **he has** *or* **he's got two houses** ha due case; **you've got the money, ~n't you?** hai i soldi, no?
- *v aux* avere; (*with verbs of motion & some others*) essere; **I ~ seen him** l'ho visto; **he has never been there** non ci è mai stato. □ **~ on** *vt* (*be wearing*) portare; (*dupe*) prendere in giro; **I've got something on tonight** ho un impegno stasera. □ **~ out** *vt* **~ it out with sb** chiarire le cose con qcno
- *npl* **the ~s and the ~-nots** i ricchi e i poveri

h

haven /ˈheɪvn/ *n fig* rifugio *m*
haversack /ˈhævə-/ *n* zaino *m*
havoc /ˈhævək/ *n* strage *f*; **play ~ with** *fig* scombussolare
hawk /hɔːk/ *n* falco *m*
hay /heɪ/ *n* fieno *m*. **~ fever** *n* raffreddore *m* da fieno. **~stack** *n* pagliaio *m*
ˈ**haywire** *adj* 🅸 **go ~** dare i numeri; (plans:) andare all'aria
hazard /ˈhæzəd/ *n* (*risk*) rischio *m* ● *vt* rischiare; **~ a guess** azzardare un'ipotesi. **~ous** *adj* rischioso. **~ [warning] lights** *npl* (*Auto*) luci *fpl* d'emergenza
haze /heɪz/ *n* foschia *f*
hazel /ˈheɪz(ə)l/ *n* nocciolo *m*; (*colour*) [color *m*] nocciola *m*. **~-nut** *n* nocciola *f*
hazy /ˈheɪzɪ/ *adj* (**-ier, -iest**) nebbioso; (fig: person) confuso; (memories) vago
he /hiː/ *pron* lui; **he's tired** è stanco; **I'm going but he's not** io vengo, ma lui no
head /hed/ *n* testa *f*; (*of firm*) capo *m*; (*of primary school*) direttore, -trice *mf*; (*of secondary school*) preside *mf*; (*on beer*) schiuma *f*; **be off one's ~** essere fuori di testa; **have a good ~ for business** avere il senso degli affari; **have a good ~ for heights** non soffrire di vertigini; **10 pounds a ~** 10 sterline a testa; **20 ~ of cattle** 20 capi di bestiame; **~ first** a capofitto; **~ over heels in love** innamorato pazzo; **~s or tails?** testa o croce? ● *vt* essere a capo di; essere in testa a (list); colpire di testa (ball) ● *vi* **~ for** dirigersi verso.
head: ~ache *n* mal *m* di testa. **~er** /ˈhedə(r)/ *n* rinvio *m* di testa; (*dive*) tuffo *m* di testa. **~ing** *n* (*in list etc*) titolo *m*. **~lamp** *n* (*Auto*) fanale *m*. **~land** *n* promontorio *m*. **~line** *n* titolo *m*. **~long** *adj & adv* a capofitto. **~ˈmaster** *n* (*of primary school*) direttore *m*; (*of secondary school*) preside *m*. **~ˈmistress** *n* (*of primary school*) direttrice *f*; (*of secondary school*) preside *f*. **~-on** *adj* (collision) frontale ● *adv* frontalmente. **~phones** *npl* cuffie *fpl*. **~quarters** *npl* sede *fsg*; (*Mil*) quartier *m* generale *msg*. **~strong** *adj* testardo
heady /ˈhedɪ/ *adj* che dà alla testa
heal /hiːl/ *vt/i* guarire
health /helθ/ *n* salute *f*
health|y /ˈhelθɪ/ *adj* (**-ier, -iest**) sano. **~ily** *adv* in modo sano
heap /hiːp/ *n* mucchio *m*; **~s of** 🅸 un sacco di ● *vt* **~ [up]** ammucchiare; **~ed teaspoon** un cucchiaino abbondante
hear /hɪə(r)/ *vt/i* (*pt/pp* **heard**) sentire; **~, ~!** bravo! **~ from** *vi* aver notizie di. □ **~ of** *vi* sentir parlare di; **he would not ~ of it** non ne ha voluto sentir parlare
hearing /ˈhɪərɪŋ/ *n* udito *m*; (*Jur*) udienza *f*. **~-aid** *n* apparecchio *m* acustico
ˈ**hearsay** *n* **from ~** per sentito dire
hearse /hɜːs/ *n* carro *m* funebre
heart /hɑːt/ *n* cuore *m*; **~s** *pl* (*in cards*) cuori *mpl*; **by ~** a memoria
heart: ~ache *n* pena *f*. **~ attack** *n* infarto *m*. **~-break** *n* afflizione *f*. **~-breaking** *adj* straziante. **~burn** *n* mal *m* di stomaco. **~felt** *adj* di cuore
hearth /hɑːθ/ *n* focolare *m*
heart|ily /ˈhɑːtɪlɪ/ *adv* di cuore; (eat) con appetito; **be ~ily sick of sth** non poterne più di qcsa. **~less** *adj* spie-

tato. **~-searching** *n* esame *m* di coscienza. **~-to-~** *n* conversazione *f* a cuore aperto ● *adj* a cuore aperto. **~y** *adj* caloroso; (meal) copioso; (person) gioviale

heat /hi:t/ *n* calore *m*; (*Sport*) prova *f* eliminatoria ● *vt* scaldare ● *vi* scaldarsi. **~ed** *adj* (swimming pool) riscaldato; (discussion) animato. **~er** *n* (*for room*) stufa *f*; (*for water*) boiler *m inv*; (*Auto*) riscaldamento *m*

heath /hi:θ/ *n* brughiera *f*

heathen /'hi:ðn/ *adj & n* pagano, -a *mf*

heather /'heðə(r)/ *n* erica *f*

heating /'hi:tɪŋ/ *n* riscaldamento *m*

heat: ~-stroke *n* colpo *m* di sole. **~ wave** *n* ondata *f* di calore

heave /hi:v/ *vt* tirare; (*lift*) tirare su; (*[!]: throw*) gettare; emettere (sigh) ● *vi* tirare

heaven /'hev(ə)n/ *n* paradiso *m*; **~ help you if...** Dio ti scampi se...; **H~s!** santo cielo!. **~ly** *adj* celeste; [!] delizioso

heav|y /'hevɪ/ *adj* (**-ier, -iest**) pesante; (traffic) intenso; (rain, cold) forte; **be a ~y smoker/drinker** essere un gran fumatore/bevitore. **~ily** *adv* pesantemente; (smoke, drink etc) molto. **~yweight** *n* peso *m* massimo

Hebrew /'hi:bru:/ *adj* ebreo

heckle /'hekl/ *vt* interrompere di continuo. **~r** *n* disturbatore, -trice *mf*

hectic /'hektɪk/ *adj* frenetico

hedge /hedʒ/ *n* siepe *f* ● *vi fig* essere evasivo. **~hog** *n* riccio *m*

heed /hi:d/ *n* **pay ~ to** prestare ascolto a ● *vt* prestare ascolto a. **~less** *adj* noncurante

heel¹ /hi:l/ *n* tallone *m*; (*of shoe*) tacco *m*; **take to one's ~s** [!] darsela a gambe

heel² *vi* **~ over** (*Naut*) inclinarsi

hefty /'heftɪ/ *adj* (**-ier, -iest**) massiccio

heifer /'hefə(r)/ *n* giovenca *f*

height /haɪt/ *n* altezza *f*; (*of plane*) altitudine *f*; (*of season, fame*) culmine *m*. **~en** *vt fig* accrescere

heir /eə(r)/ *n* erede *mf*. **~ess** *n* ereditiera *f*. **~loom** *n* cimelio *m* di famiglia

held /held/ ▷**HOLD²**

helicopter /'helɪkɒptə(r)/ *n* elicottero *m*

hell /hel/ *n* inferno *m*; **go to ~!** [✖] va' al diavolo! ● *int* porca miseria!

hello /hə'ləʊ/ *int & n* = **hallo**

helm /helm/ *n* timone *m*; **at the ~** *fig* al timone

helmet /'helmɪt/ *n* casco *m*

help /help/ *n* aiuto *m*; (*employee*) aiuto *m* domestico; **that's no ~** non è d'aiuto ● *vt* aiutare; **~ oneself to sth** servirsi di qcsa; **~ yourself** (*at table*) serviti pure; **I could not ~ laughing** non ho potuto trattenermi dal ridere; **it cannot be ~ed** non c'è niente da fare; **I can't ~ it** non ci posso far niente ● *vi* aiutare

help|er /'helpə(r)/ *n* aiutante *mf*. **~ful** *adj* (person) di aiuto; (advice) utile. **~ing** *n* porzione *f*. **~less** *adj* (*unable to manage*) incapace; (*powerless*) impotente

hem /hem/ *n* orlo *m* ● *vt* (*pt/pp* **hemmed**) orlare. □ **~ in** *vt* intrappolare

hemisphere /'hemɪ-/ *n* emisfero *m*

hen /hen/ *n* gallina *f*; (*any female bird*) femmina *f*

hence /hens/ *adv* (*for this reason*) quindi. **~'forth** *adv* d'ora innanzi

henpecked *adj* tiranneggiato dalla moglie

her /hɜ:(r)/ *poss adj* il suo *m*, la sua *f*, i suoi *mpl*, le sue *fpl*; **~ mother/father** sua madre/suo padre ● *pers pron* (*direct object*) la; (*indirect object*) le; (*after prep*) lei; **I know ~** la conosco; **give ~ the money** dalle i soldi; **give it to ~** daglielo; **I came with ~** sono venuto con lei; **it's ~** è lei; **I've seen ~** l'ho vista; **I've seen ~, but not him** ho visto lei, ma non lui

herb /hɜ:b/ *n* erba *f*

herbal /'hɜ:b(ə)l/ *adj* alle erbe; **~ tea** tisana *f*

herd /hɜ:d/ *n* gregge *m* ● *vt* (*tend*) sorvegliare; (*drive*) far muovere; *fig* ammassare

here /hɪə(r)/ *adv* qui, qua; **in ~** qui dentro; **come/bring ~** vieni/porta qui; **~ is..., ~ are...** ecco...; **~ you are!** ecco qua!. **~'after** *adv* in futuro. **~'by** *adv* con la presente

heredit|ary /hə'redɪtərɪ/ *adj* ereditario. **~y** *n* eredità *f*

here|sy /'herəsɪ/ *n* eresia *f*. **~tic** *n* eretico, -a *mf*

h

here'with *adv* (*Comm*) con la presente
heritage /'herɪtɪdʒ/ *n* eredità *f.* ~ **'tourism** *n* turismo *m* culturale
hernia /'hɜːnɪə/ *n* ernia *f*
hero /'hɪərəʊ/ *n* (*pl* **-es**) eroe *m*
heroic /hɪ'rəʊɪk/ *adj* eroico
heroin /'herəʊɪn/ *n* eroina *f* (*droga*)
hero|ine /'herəʊɪn/ *n* eroina *f.* **~ism** *n* eroismo *m*
heron /'herən/ *n* airone *m*
herring /'herɪŋ/ *n* aringa *f*
hers /hɜːz/ *poss pron* il suo *m*, la sua *f*, i suoi *mpl*, le sue *fpl*; **a friend of ~** un suo amico; **friends of ~** dei suoi amici; **that is ~** quello è suo; (*as opposed to mine*) quello è il suo
her'self *pers pron* (*reflexive*) si; (*emphatic*) lei stessa; (*after prep*) sé, se stessa; **she poured ~ a drink** si è versata da bere; **she told me so ~** me lo ha detto lei stessa; **she's proud of ~** è fiera di sé; **by ~** da sola
hesitant /'hezɪtənt/ *adj* esitante. **~ly** *adv* con esitazione
hesitat|e /'hezɪteɪt/ *vi* esitare. **~ion** *n* esitazione *f*
hetero'sexual /hetərəʊ-/ *adj* eterosessuale
hexagon /'heksəgən/ *n* esagono *m.* **~al** *adj* esagonale
hey /heɪ/ *int* ehi
heyday /'heɪ-/ *n* tempi *mpl* d'oro
hi /haɪ/ *int* ciao!
hibernat|e /'haɪbəneɪt/ *vi* andare in letargo. **~ion** *n* letargo *m*
hiccup /'hɪkʌp/ *n* singhiozzo *m*; ([!]: *hitch*) intoppo *m* ● *vi* fare un singhiozzo
hide[1] /haɪd/ *n* (*leather*) pelle *f* (*di animale*)
hide[2] *vt* (*pt* **hid**, *pp* **hidden**) nascondere ● *vi* nascondersi. **~-and-'seek** *n* **play ~-and-seek** giocare a nascondino
hideous /'hɪdɪəs/ *adj* orribile
'hide-out *n* nascondiglio *m*
hiding[1] /'haɪdɪŋ/ *n* ([!]: *beating*) bastonata *f*; (*defeat*) batosta *f*
hiding[2] *n* **go into ~** sparire dalla circolazione
hierarchy /'haɪərɑːkɪ/ *n* gerarchia *f*
hieroglyphics /haɪərə'glɪfɪks/ *npl* geroglifici *mpl*
hi-fi /'haɪfaɪ/ *n* [!] stereo *m*, hi-fi *m inv* ● *adj* [!] ad alta fedeltà

high /haɪ/ *adj* alto; (meat) che comincia ad andare a male; (wind) forte; (*on drugs*) fatto; **it's ~ time we did something about it** è ora di fare qualcosa in proposito ● *adv* in alto; **~ and low** in lungo e in largo ● *n* massimo *m*; (*temperature*) massima *f*; **be on a ~** [!] essere fatto
high: ~er education *n* formazione *f* universitaria. **~'-handed** *adj* dispotico. **~ heels** *npl* tacchi *mpl* alti
highlight /'haɪlaɪt/ *n fig* momento *m* clou; **~s** *pl* (*in hair*) mèche *fpl* ● *vt* (*emphasize*) evidenziare. **~er** *n* (*marker*) evidenziatore *m*
highly /'haɪlɪ/ *adv* molto; **speak ~ of** lodare; **think ~ of** avere un'alta opinione di. **~-'strung** *adj* nervoso
high: ~-rise *adj* (building) molto alto ● *n* edificio *m* molto alto. **~ school** *n* ≈ scuola *f* superiore. **~ street** *n* strada *f* principale. **~way code** *n* codice *m* stradale

> *i*
> **High School** Negli Stati Uniti indica la scuola superiore, generalmente per studenti di età compresa tra i 14 e i 18 anni. In Gran Bretagna il termine è usato solo nella denominazione di alcune scuole.

hijack /'haɪdʒæk/ *vt* dirottare ● *n* dirottamento *m.* **~er** *n* dirottatore, -trice *mf*
hike /haɪk/ *n* escursione *f* a piedi ● *vi* fare un'escursione a piedi. **~r** *n* escursionista *mf*
hilarious /hɪ'leərɪəs/ *adj* esilarante
hill /hɪl/ *n* collina *f*; (*mound*) collinetta *f*; (*slope*) altura *f*
hill: ~side *n* pendio *m.* **~y** *adj* collinoso
hilt /hɪlt/ *n* impugnatura *f*; **to the ~** (support) fino in fondo; (mortgaged) fino al collo
him /hɪm/ *pers pron* (*direct object*) lo; (*indirect object*) gli; (*with prep*) lui; **I know ~** lo conosco; **give ~ the money** dagli i soldi; **give it to ~** daglielo; **I spoke to ~** gli ho parlato; **it's ~** è lui; **she loves ~** lo ama; **she loves ~, not you** ama lui, non te. **~'self** *pers pron* (*reflexive*) si; (*emphatic*) lui stesso; (*after prep*) sé, se stesso; **he poured ~ a drink** si è versato da bere; **he told me**

so ~**self** me lo ha detto lui stesso; **he's proud of ~self** è fiero di sé; **by ~self** da solo

hind|er /ˈhɪndə(r)/ *vt* intralciare. **~rance** *n* intralcio *m*

hindsight /ˈhaɪnd-/ *n* **with ~** con il senno del poi

Hindu /ˈhɪndu:/ *n* indù *mf inv* ● *adj* indù. **~ism** *n* induismo *m*

hinge /hɪndʒ/ *n* cardine *m* ● *vi* **~ on** *fig* dipendere da

hint /hɪnt/ *n* (*clue*) accenno *m*; (*advice*) suggerimento *m*; (*indirect suggestion*) allusione *f*; (*trace*) tocco *m* ● *vt* **~ that...** far capire che... ● *vi* **~ at** alludere a

hip /hɪp/ *n* fianco *m*

hippie /ˈhɪpɪ/ *n* hippy *mf inv*

hippopotamus /hɪpəˈpɒtəməs/ *n* (*pl* **-muses** *or* **-mi** /-maɪ/) ippopotamo *m*

hire /ˈhaɪə(r)/ *vt* affittare; assumere (person); **~ [out]** affittare ● *n* noleggio *m*; **'for ~'** 'affittasi'. **~ car** *n* macchina *f* a noleggio. **~ purchase** *n* acquisto *m* rateale

his /hɪz/ *poss adj* il suo *m*, la sua *f*, i suoi *mpl*, le sue *fpl*; **~ mother/father** sua madre/suo padre ● *poss pron* il suo *m*, la sua *f*, i suoi *mpl*, le sue *fpl*; **a friend of ~** un suo amico; **friends of ~** dei suoi amici; **that is ~** questo è suo; (*as opposed to mine*) questo è il suo

hiss /hɪs/ *n* sibilo *m*; (*of disapproval*) fischio *m* ● *vt* fischiare ● *vi* sibilare; (*in disapproval*) fischiare

historian /hɪˈstɔ:rɪən/ *n* storico, -a *mf*

history /ˈhɪstərɪ/ *n* storia *f*; **make ~** passare alla storia

hit /hɪt/ *n* (*blow*) colpo *m*; ([!]: *success*) successo *m*; **score a direct ~** (missile:) colpire in pieno ● *vt/i* (*pt/pp* **hit**, *pres p* **hitting**) colpire; **~ one's head on the table** battere la testa contro il tavolo; **the car ~ the wall** la macchina ha sbattuto contro il muro; **~ the roof** [!] perdere le staffe. □ **~ off** *vt* **~ it off** andare d'accordo. □ **~ on** *vt fig* trovare

hitch /hɪtʃ/ *n* intoppo *m*; **technical ~** problema *m* tecnico ● *vt* attaccare; **~ a lift** chiedere un passaggio. □ **~ up** *vt* tirarsi su (trousers). **~-hike** *vi* fare l'autostop. **~-hiker** *n* autostoppista *mf*

hither /ˈhɪðə(r)/ *adv* **~ and thither** di qua e di là. **~'to** *adv* finora

hit-or-'miss *adj* **on a very ~ basis** all'improvvisata

hive /haɪv/ *n* alveare *m*; **~ of industry** fucina *f* di lavoro ● **hive off** *vt* (*Comm*) separare

hoard /hɔ:d/ *n* provvista *f*; (*of money*) gruzzolo *m* ● *vt* accumulare

hoarding /ˈhɔ:dɪŋ/ *n* palizzata *f*; (*with advertisements*) tabellone *m* per manifesti pubblicitari

hoarse /hɔ:s/ *adj* rauco. **~ly** *adv* con voce rauca. **~ness** *n* raucedine *f*

hoax /həʊks/ *n* scherzo *m*; (*false alarm*) falso allarme *m*. **~er** *n* burlone, -a *mf*

hob /hɒb/ *n* piano *m* di cottura

hobble /ˈhɒbl/ *vi* zoppicare

hobby /ˈhɒbɪ/ *n* hobby *m inv*. **~-horse** *n fig* fissazione *f*

hockey /ˈhɒkɪ/ *n* hockey *m*

hoe /həʊ/ *n* zappa *f*

hog /hɒg/ *n* maiale *m* ● *vt* (*pt/pp* **hogged**) [!] monopolizzare

hoist /hɔɪst/ *n* montacarichi *m inv*; ([!]: *push*) spinta *f* in su ● *vt* sollevare; innalzare (flag); levare (anchor)

hold[1] /həʊld/ *n* (*Aeron, Naut*) stiva *f*

hold[2] *n* presa *f*; (*fig: influence*) ascendente *m*; **get ~ of** trovare; procurarsi (information) ● *v* (*pt/pp* **held**) ● *vt* tenere; (container:) contenere; essere titolare di (licence, passport); trattenere (breath, suspect); mantenere vivo (interest); (civil servant etc:) occupare (position); (*retain*) mantenere; **~ sb's hand** tenere qcno per mano; **~ one's tongue** tenere la bocca chiusa; **~ sb responsible** considerare qcno responsabile; **~ that** (*believe*) ritenere che ● *vi* tenere; (weather, luck:) durare; (offer:) essere valido; (*Teleph*) restare in linea; **I don't ~ with the idea that...** [!] non sono d'accordo sul fatto che... □ **~ back** *vt* rallentare ● *vi* esitare. □ **~ down** *vt* tenere a bada (sb). □ **~ on** *vi* (*wait*) attendere; (*Teleph*) restare in linea. □ **~ on to** *vt* aggrapparsi a; (*keep*) tenersi. □ **~ out** *vt* porgere (hand); *fig* offrire (possibility) ● *vi* (*resist*) resistere. □ **~ up** *vt* tenere su; (*delay*) rallentare; (*rob*) assalire; **~ one's head up** *fig* tenere la testa alta

'hold: ~all *n* borsone *m*. **~er** *n* titolare *mf*; (*of record*) detentore, -trice *mf*; (*container*) astuccio *m*. **~-up** *n* ritardo

m; (*attack*) rapina *f* a mano armata
hole /həʊl/ *n* buco *m*
holiday /'hɒlɪdeɪ/ *n* vacanza *f*; (*public*) giorno *m* festivo; (*day off*) giorno *m* di ferie; **go on ~** andare in vacanza ● *vi* andare in vacanza. **~-maker** *n* vacanziere *mf*
holiness /'həʊlɪnɪs/ *n* santità *f*; **Your H~** Sua Santità
Holland /'hɒlənd/ *n* Olanda *f*
hollow /'hɒləʊ/ *adj* cavo; (promise) a vuoto; (voice) assente; (cheeks) infossato ● *n* cavità *f inv*; (*in ground*) affossamento *m*
holly /'hɒlɪ/ *n* agrifoglio *m*
holocaust /'hɒləkɔ:st/ *n* olocausto *m*
holster /'həʊlstə(r)/ *n* fondina *f*
holy /'həʊlɪ/ *adj* (**-ier, -est**) santo; (water) benedetto. **H~ Ghost** *or* **Spirit** *n* Spirito *m* Santo. **H~ Scriptures** *npl* sacre scritture *fpl*. **H~ Week** *n* settimana *f* santa
homage /'hɒmɪdʒ/ *n* omaggio *m*; **pay ~ to** rendere omaggio a
home /həʊm/ *n* casa *f*; (*for children*) istituto *m*; (*for old people*) casa *f* di riposo; (*native land*) patria *f* ● *adv* **at ~** a casa; (*football*) in casa; **feel at ~** sentirsi a casa propria; **come**/**go ~** venire/andare a casa; **drive a nail ~** piantare un chiodo a fondo ● *adj* domestico; (movie, video) casalingo; (team) ospitante; (*Pol*) nazionale
home: ~ ad'dress *n* indirizzo *m* di casa. **~land** *n* patria *f*; **~land se'curity** *n* sicurezza *f* delle frontiere. **~less** *adj* senza tetto
homely /'həʊmlɪ/ *adj* (**-ier, -iest**) semplice; (atmosphere) familiare; (*Am: ugly*) bruttino
home: ~-'made *adj* fatto in casa. **H~ Office** *n Br* ministero *m* degli interni. **~sick** *adj* **be ~sick** avere nostalgia (**for** di). **~ 'town** *n* città *f inv* natia. **~work** *n* (*Sch*) compiti *mpl*
homicide /'hɒmɪsaɪd/ *n* (*crime*) omicidio *m*
homoeopath|ic /həʊmɪə'pæθɪk/ *adj* omeopatico. **~y** *n* omeopatia *f*
homogeneous /hɒmə'dʒi:nɪəs/ *adj* omogeneo
homo'sexual *adj & n* omosessuale *mf*
honest /'ɒnɪst/ *adj* onesto; (frank) sincero. **~ly** *adv* onestamente; (*frankly*) sinceramente; **~ly!** ma insomma!. **~y** *n* onestà *f*; (*frankness*) sincerità *f*
honey /'hʌnɪ/ *n* miele *m*; (🅘: *darling*) tesoro *m*
honey: ~comb *n* favo *m*. **~moon** *n* luna *f* di miele. **~suckle** *n* caprifoglio *m*
honorary /'ɒnərərɪ/ *adj* onorario
honour /'ɒnə(r)/ *n* onore *m* ● *vt* onorare. **~able** *adj* onorevole. **~ably** *adv* con onore. **~s degree** *n* ≈ diploma *m* di laurea
hood /hʊd/ *n* cappuccio *m*; (*of pram*) tettuccio *m*; (*over cooker*) cappa *f*; *Am* (*Auto*) cofano *m*
hoodlum /'hu:dləm/ *n* teppista *m*
'hoodwink *vt* 🅘 infinocchiare
hoof /hu:f/ *n* (*pl* **~s** *or* **hooves**) zoccolo *m*
hook /hʊk/ *n* gancio *m*; (*for fishing*) amo *m*; **off the ~** (*Teleph*) staccato; *fig* fuori pericolo ● *vt* agganciare ● *vi* agganciarsi
hook|ed /hʊkt/ *adj* (nose) adunco **~ed on** (🅘: *drugs*) dedito a; **be ~ed on skiing** essere un fanatico dello sci. **~er** *n Am* ☒ battona *f*
hookey /'hʊkɪ/ *n* **play ~** *Am* 🅘 marinare la scuola
hooligan /'hu:lɪgən/ *n* teppista *mf*. **~ism** *n* teppismo *m*
hoop /hu:p/ *n* cerchio *m*
hooray /hʊ'reɪ/ *int & n* = **hurrah**
hoot /hu:t/ *n* colpo *m* di clacson; (*of siren*) ululato *m*; (*of owl*) grido *m* ● *vi* (owl:) gridare; (car:) clacsonare; (siren:) ululare; (*jeer*) fischiare. **~er** *n* (*of factory*) sirena *f*; (*Auto*) clacson *m inv*
hoover® /'hu:və(r)/ *n* aspirapolvere *m inv* ● *vt* passare l'aspirapolvere su (carpet); passare l'aspirapolvere in (room)
hop /hɒp/ *n* saltello *m* ● *vi* (*pt*/*pp* **hopped**) saltellare; **~ it!** 🅘 tela!. □ **~ in** *vi* 🅘 saltar su
hope /həʊp/ *n* speranza *f* ● *vi* sperare (**for** in); **I ~ so**/**not** spero di sì/no ● *vt* **~ that** sperare che
hope|ful /'həʊpfl/ *adj* pieno di speranza; (*promising*) promettente; **be ~ful that** avere buone speranze che. **~fully** *adv* con speranza; (*it is hoped*) se tutto va bene. **~less** *adj* senza spe-

ranze; (*useless*) impossibile; (*incompetent*) incapace. **~lessly** *adv* disperatamente; (inefficient, lost) completamente. **~lessness** *n* disperazione *f*

horde /hɔːd/ *n* orda *f*

horizon /həˈraɪzn/ *n* orizzonte *m*

horizontal /hɒrɪˈzɒntl/ *adj* orizzontale

hormone /ˈhɔːməʊn/ *n* ormone *m*

horn /hɔːn/ *n* corno *m*; (*Auto*) clacson *m inv*

horoscope /ˈhɒrəskəʊp/ *n* oroscopo *m*

horribl|e /ˈhɒrɪbl/ *adj* orribile. **~y** *adv* spaventosamente

horrid /ˈhɒrɪd/ *adj* orrendo

horrific /həˈrɪfɪk/ *adj* raccapricciante; (accident, prices, story) terrificante

horrify /ˈhɒrɪfaɪ/ *vt* (*pt*/*pp* **-ied**) far inorridire; **I was horrified** ero sconvolto. **~ing** *adj* terrificante

horror /ˈhɒrə(r)/ *n* orrore *m*. **~ film** *n* film *m* dell'orrore

horse /hɔːs/ *n* cavallo *m*

horse: ~back *n* **on ~back** a cavallo. **~power** *n* cavallo *m* [vapore]. **~-racing** *n* corse *fpl* di cavalli. **~shoe** *n* ferro *m* di cavallo

horti'cultural /hɔːtɪ-/ *adj* di orticoltura

'horticulture *n* orticoltura *f*

hose /həʊz/ *n* (*pipe*) manichetta *f* ● **hose down** *vt* lavare con la manichetta

hospice /ˈhɒspɪs/ *n* (*for the terminally ill*) ospedale *m* per i malati in fase terminale

hospitabl|e /hɒˈspɪtəbl/ *adj* ospitale. **~y** *adv* con ospitalità

hospital /ˈhɒspɪtl/ *n* ospedale *m*

hospitality /hɒspɪˈtælətɪ/ *n* ospitalità *f*

host[1] /həʊst/ *n* **a ~ of** una moltitudine di

host[2] *n* ospite *m*

host[3] *n* (*Relig*) ostia *f*

hostage /ˈhɒstɪdʒ/ *n* ostaggio *m*; **hold sb ~** tenere qcno in ostaggio

hostel /ˈhɒstl/ *n* ostello *m*

hostess /ˈhəʊstɪs/ *n* padrona *f* di casa; (*Aeron*) hostess *f inv*

hostile /ˈhɒstaɪl/ *adj* ostile

hostilit|y /hɒˈstɪlətɪ/ *n* ostilità *f*; **~ies** *pl* ostilità *fpl*

hot /hɒt/ *adj* (**hotter, hottest**) caldo; (*spicy*) piccante; **I am** *or* **feel ~** ho caldo; **it is ~** fa caldo

'hotbed *n fig* focolaio *m*

hotchpotch /ˈhɒtʃpɒtʃ/ *n* miscuglio *m*

'hot-dog *n* hot dog *m inv*

hotel /həʊˈtel/ *n* albergo *m*. **~ier** *n* albergatore, -trice *mf*

hot: ~house *n* serra *f*. **~plate** *n* piastra *f* riscaldante **~-'water bottle** *n* borsa *f* dell'acqua calda

hound /haʊnd/ *n* cane *m* da caccia ● *vt fig* perseguire

hour /ˈaʊə(r)/ *n* ora *f*. **~ly** *adj* ad ogni ora; (pay, rate) a ora ● *adv* ogni ora

house /haʊs/: **~boat** *n* casa *f* galleggiante. **~breaking** *n* furto *m* con scasso. **~hold** *n* casa *f*, famiglia *f*. **~holder** *n* capo *m* di famiglia. **~keeper** *n* governante *f* di casa. **~keeping** *n* governo *m* della casa; (*money*) soldi *mpl* per le spese di casa. **~-plant** *n* pianta *f* da appartamento. **~-trained** *adj* che non sporca in casa. **~-warming party** *n* festa *f* di inaugurazione della nuova casa. **~wife** *n* casalinga *f*. **~work** *n* lavoro *m* domestico

house[1] /haʊs/ *n* casa *f*; (*Pol*) camera *f*; (*Theat*) sala *f*; **at my ~** a casa mia, da me

house[2] /haʊz/ *vt* alloggiare (person)

housing /ˈhaʊzɪŋ/ *n* alloggio *m*. **~ estate** *n* zona *f* residenziale

hovel /ˈhɒvl/ *n* tugurio *m*

hover /ˈhɒvə(r)/ *vi* librarsi; (*linger*) indugiare. **~craft** *n* hovercraft *m inv*

how /haʊ/ *adv* come; **~ are you?** come stai?; **~ about a coffee/going on holiday?** che ne diresti di un caffè/di andare in vacanza?; **~ do you do?** molto lieto!; **~ old are you?** quanti anni hai?; **~ long** quanto tempo; **~ many** quanti; **~ much** quanto; **~ often** ogni quanto; **and ~!** eccome!; **~ odd!** che strano!

how'ever *adv* (*nevertheless*) comunque; **~ small** per quanto piccolo

howl /haʊl/ *n* ululato *m* ● *vi* ululare; (*cry, with laughter*) singhiozzare. **~er** *n* [!] strafalcione *m*

h

HP *n abbr* hire purchase; *n abbr* (horse power) C.V.
hub /hʌb/ *n* mozzo *m*; *fig* centro *m*
'hub-cap *n* coprimozzo *m*
huddle /'hʌdl/ *vi* ~ **together** rannicchiarsi
hue[1] /hju:/ *n* colore *m*
hue[2] *n* ~ **and cry** clamore *m*
huff /hʌf/ *n* **be in/go into a** ~ fare il broncio
hug /hʌg/ *n* abbraccio *m* ● *vt* (*pt/pp* **hugged**) abbracciare; (*keep close to*) tenersi vicino a
huge /hju:dʒ/ *adj* enorme
hull /hʌl/ *n* (*Naut*) scafo *m*
hullo /hə'ləʊ/ *int* = **hallo**
hum /hʌm/ *n* ronzio *m* ● *v* (*pt/pp* **hummed**) ● *vt* canticchiare ● *vi* (motor:) ronzare; *fig* fervere (*di attività*); ~ **and haw** esitare
human /'hju:mən/ *adj* umano ● *n* essere *m* umano. ~ **'being** *n* essere *m* umano
humane /hju:'meɪn/ *adj* umano
humanitarian /hju:mænɪ'teərɪən/ *adj & n* umanitario, -a *mf*
humanit|y /hju:'mænətɪ/ *n* umanità *f*; ~**ies** *pl* (*Univ*) dottrine *fpl* umanistiche
humbl|e /'hʌmbl/ *adj* umile ● *vt* umiliare
'humdrum *adj* noioso
humid /'hju:mɪd/ *adj* umido. ~**ifier** *n* umidificatore *m*. ~**ity** /-'mɪdətɪ/ *n* umidità *f*
humiliat|e /hju:'mɪlɪeɪt/ *vt* umiliare. ~**ion** *n* umiliazione *f*
humility /hju:'mɪlətɪ/ *n* umiltà *f*
humorous /'hju:mərəs/ *adj* umoristico. ~**ly** *adv* con spirito
humour /'hju:mə(r)/ *n* umorismo *m*; (*mood*) umore *m*; **have a sense of** ~ avere il senso dell'umorismo ● *vt* compiacere
hump /hʌmp/ *n* protuberanza *f*; (*of camel, hunchback*) gobba *f*
hunch /hʌntʃ/ *n* (*idea*) intuizione *f*
'hunch|back *n* gobbo, -a *mf*. ~**ed** *adj* ~**ed up** incurvato
hundred /'hʌndrəd/ *adj* **one/a** ~ cento ● *n* cento *m*; ~**s of** centinaia di. ~**th** *adj* centesimo ● *n* centesimo *m*. ~**weight** *n* cinquanta chili *m*
hung /hʌŋ/ ▷**HANG**
Hungarian /hʌŋ'geərɪən/ *n & adj* ungherese *mf*; (*language*) ungherese *m*
Hungary /'hʌŋgərɪ/ *n* Ungheria *f*
hunger /'hʌŋgə(r)/ *n* fame *f*. ~**-strike** *n* sciopero *m* della fame *m*
hungr|y /'hʌŋgrɪ/ *adj* (**-ier, -iest**) affamato; **be** ~**y** aver fame. ~**ily** *adv* con appetito
hunk /hʌŋk/ *n* [grosso] pezzo *m*
hunt /hʌnt/ *n* caccia *f* ● *vt* andare a caccia di (animal); dare la caccia a (criminal) ● *vi* andare a caccia; ~ **for** cercare. ~**er** *n* cacciatore *m*. ~**ing** *n* caccia *f*
hurl /hɜ:l/ *vt* scagliare
hurrah /hʊ'rɑ:/, **hurray** /hʊ'reɪ/ *int* urrà! ● *n* urrà *m*
hurricane /'hʌrɪkən/ *n* uragano *m*
hurried /'hʌrɪd/ *adj* affrettato; (job) fatto in fretta. ~**ly** *adv* in fretta
hurry /'hʌrɪ/ *n* fretta *f*; **be in a** ~ aver fretta ● *vi* (*pt/pp* **-ied**) affrettarsi. □ ~ **up** *vi* sbrigarsi ● *vt* fare sbrigare (person); accelerare (things)
hurt /hɜ:t/ *v* (*pt/pp* **hurt**) ● *vt* far male a; (*offend*) ferire ● *vi* far male; **my leg** ~**s** mi fa male la gamba. ~**ful** *adj fig* offensivo
hurtle /'hɜ:tl/ *vi* ~ **along** andare a tutta velocità
husband /'hʌzbənd/ *n* marito *m*
hush /hʌʃ/ *n* silenzio *m* ● **hush up** *vt* mettere a tacere. ~**ed** *adj* (voice) sommesso. ~**-'hush** *adj* [!] segretissimo
husky /'hʌskɪ/ *adj* (**-ier, -iest**) (voice) rauco
hustle /'hʌsl/ *vt* affrettare ● *n* attività *f* incessante; ~ **and bustle** trambusto *m*
hut /hʌt/ *n* capanna *f*
hybrid /'haɪbrɪd/ *adj* ibrido ● *n* ibrido *m*
hydrant /'haɪdrənt/ *n* [**fire**] ~ idrante *m*
hydraulic /haɪ'drɔ:lɪk/ *adj* idraulico
hydroe'lectric /haɪdrəʊ-/ *adj* idroelettrico
hydrofoil /'haɪdrə-/ *n* aliscafo *m*
hydrogen /'haɪdrədʒən/ *n* idrogeno *m*
hyena /haɪ'i:nə/ *n* iena *f*
hygien|e /'haɪdʒi:n/ *n* igiene *f*. ~**ic** *adj* igienico

hymn /hɪm/ *n* inno *m*. **~-book** *n* libro *m* dei canti
hypermarket /ˈhaɪpəmɑːkɪt/ *n* ipermercato *m*
hyphen /ˈhaɪfn/ *n* lineetta *f*. **~ate** *vt* unire con lineetta
hypno|sis /hɪpˈnəʊsɪs/ *n* ipnosi *f*. **~tic** *adj* ipnotico
hypno|tism /ˈhɪpnətɪzm/ *n* ipnotismo *m*. **~tist** *n* ipnotizzatore, -trice *mf*. **~tize** *vt* ipnotizzare
hypochondriac /haɪpəˈkɒndrɪæk/ *adj* ipocondriaco ● *n* ipocondriaco, -a *mf*
hypocrisy /hɪˈpɒkrəsɪ/ *n* ipocrisia *f*
hypocrit|e /ˈhɪpəkrɪt/ *n* ipocrita *mf*. **~ical** *adj* ipocrita
hypodermic /haɪpəˈdɜːmɪk/ *adj* & *n* **~ [syringe]** siringa *f* ipodermica
hypothe|sis /haɪˈpɒθəsɪs/ *n* ipotesi *f inv*. **~tical** *adj* ipotetico. **~tically** *adv* in teoria; (speak) per ipotesi
hyster|ia /hɪˈstɪərɪə/ *n* isterismo *m*. **~ical** *adj* isterico. **~ically** *adv* istericamente; **~ically funny** da morir dal ridere. **~ics** *npl* attacco *m* isterico

Ii

I /aɪ/ *pron* io; **I'm tired** sono stanco; **he's going, but I'm not** lui va, ma io no
ice /aɪs/ *n* ghiaccio *m* ● *vt* glassare (cake). □ **~ over/up** *vi* ghiacciarsi
ice: ~-axe *n* piccozza *f* per il ghiaccio. **~berg** /-bɜːg/ *n* iceberg *m inv*. **~box** *n* *Am* frigorifero *m*. **~-'cream** *n* gelato *m*. **~-cube** *n* cubetto *m* di ghiaccio
Iceland /ˈaɪslənd/ *n* Islanda *f*. **~er** *n* islandese *mf*; **~ic** /-ˈlændɪk/ *adj* & *n* islandese *m*
ice: ~'lolly *n* ghiacciolo *m*. **~ rink** *n* pista *f* di pattinaggio. **~ skater** pattinatore, -trice *mf* sul ghiaccio. **~ skating** pattinaggio *m* su ghiaccio
icicle /ˈaɪsɪkl/ *n* ghiacciolo *m*
icing /ˈaɪsɪŋ/ *n* glassa *f*. **~ sugar** *n* zucchero *m* a velo
icon /ˈaɪkɒn/ *n* icona *f*
ic|y /ˈaɪsɪ/ *adj* (**-ier, -iest**) ghiacciato; *fig* gelido. **~ily** *adv* gelidamente
idea /aɪˈdɪə/ *n* idea *f*; **I've no ~!** non ne ho idea!
ideal /aɪˈdɪəl/ *adj* ideale ● *n* ideale *m*. **~ism** *n* idealismo *m*. **~ist** *n* idealista *mf*. **~istic** *adj* idealistico. **~ize** *vt* idealizzare. **~ly** *adv* idealmente
identical /aɪˈdentɪkl/ *adj* identico
identi|fication /aɪdentɪfɪˈkeɪʃn/ *n* identificazione *f*; (*proof of identity*) documento *m* di riconoscimento. **~fy** *vt* (*pt/pp* **-ied**) identificare
identity /aɪˈdentətɪ/ *n* identità *f inv*. **~ card** *n* carta *f* d'identità. **~ theft** *n* furto *m* d'identità
ideolog|ical /aɪdɪəˈlɒdʒɪkl/ *adj* ideologico. **~y** *n* ideologia *f*
idiom /ˈɪdɪəm/ *n* idioma *f*. **~atic** *adj* idiomatico
idiot /ˈɪdɪət/ *n* idiota *mf*. **~ic** *adj* idiota
idl|e /ˈaɪd(ə)l/ *adj* (*lazy*) pigro, ozioso; (*empty*) vano; (machine) fermo ● *vi* oziare; (engine:) girare a vuoto. **~eness** *n* ozio *m*. **~y** *adv* oziosamente
idol /ˈaɪdl/ *n* idolo *m*. **~ize** *vt* idolatrare
idyllic /ɪˈdɪlɪk/ *adj* idillico
i.e. *abbr* (id est) cioè
if /ɪf/ *conj* se; **as if** come se
ignite /ɪgˈnaɪt/ *vt* dar fuoco a ● *vi* prender fuoco
ignition /ɪgˈnɪʃn/ *n* (*Auto*) accensione *f*. **~ key** *n* chiave *f* d'accensione
ignoramus /ɪgnəˈreɪməs/ *n* ignorante *mf*
ignoran|ce /ˈɪgnərəns/ *n* ignoranza *f*. **~t** *adj* (*lacking knowledge*) ignaro; (*rude*) ignorante
ignore /ɪgˈnɔː(r)/ *vt* ignorare
ill /ɪl/ *adj* ammalato; **feel ~ at ease** sentirsi a disagio ● *adv* male ● *n* male *m*. **~-advised** *adj* avventato. **~-bred** *adj* maleducato
illegal /ɪˈliːgl/ *adj* illegale
illegibl|e /ɪˈledʒɪbl/ *adj* illeggibile
illegitima|cy /ɪlɪˈdʒɪtɪməsɪ/ *n* illegittimità *f*. **~te** *adj* illegittimo
illitera|cy /ɪˈlɪtərəsɪ/ *n* analfabetismo *m*. **~te** *adj* & *n* analfabeta *mf*
illness /ˈɪlnɪs/ *n* malattia *f*
illogical /ɪˈlɒdʒɪkl/ *adj* illogico
illuminat|e /ɪˈluːmɪneɪt/ *vt* illuminare. **~ing** *adj* chiarificatore. **~ion** *n* illuminazione *f*

illusion /ɪ'lu:ʒn/ *n* illusione *f*; **be under the ~ that** avere l'illusione che

illustrat|e /'ɪləstreɪt/ *vt* illustrare. **~ion** *n* illustrazione *f*. **~or** *n* illustratore, -trice *mf*

illustrious /ɪ'lʌstrɪəs/ *adj* illustre

ill 'will *n* malanimo *m*

image /'ɪmɪdʒ/ *n* immagine *f*; (*exact likeness*) ritratto *m*

imagin|able /ɪ'mædʒɪnəbl/ *adj* immaginabile. **~ary** *adj* immaginario

imaginat|ion /ɪmædʒɪ'neɪʃn/ *n* immaginazione *f*, fantasia *f*; **it's your ~ion** è solo una tua idea. **~ive** *adj* fantasioso. **~ively** *adv* con fantasia *or* immaginazione

i

imagine /ɪ'mædʒɪn/ *vt* immaginare; (*wrongly*) inventare

im'balance *n* squilibrio *m*

imbecile /'ɪmbəsi:l/ *n* imbecille *mf*

imitat|e /'ɪmɪteɪt/ *vt* imitare. **~ion** *n* imitazione *f*. **~or** *n* imitatore, -trice *mf*

immaculate /ɪ'mækjʊlət/ *adj* immacolato. **~ly** *adv* immacolatamente

imma'ture *adj* immaturo

immediate /ɪ'mi:dɪət/ *adj* immediato; (relative) stretto; **in the ~ vicinity** nelle immediate vicinanze. **~ly** *adv* immediatamente; **~ly next to** subito accanto a ● *conj* [non] appena

immense /ɪ'mens/ *adj* immenso

immers|e /ɪ'mɜ:s/ *vt* immergere; **be ~ed in** *fig* essere immerso in. **~ion** *n* immersione *f*. **~ion heater** *n* scaldabagno *m* elettrico

immigrant /'ɪmɪgrənt/ *n* immigrante *mf*

imminent /'ɪmɪnənt/ *adj* imminente

immobil|e /ɪ'məʊbaɪl/ *adj* immobile. **~ize** *vt* immobilizzare

immoderate /ɪ'mɒdərət/ *adj* smodato

immoral /ɪ'mɒrəl/ *adj* immorale. **~ity** *n* immoralità *f*

immortal /ɪ'mɔ:tl/ *adj* immortale. **~ity** *n* immortalità *f*. **~ize** *vt* immortalare

immune /ɪ'mju:n/ *adj* immune (**to/from** da). **~ system** *n* sistema *m* immunitario

immunity /ɪ'mju:nətɪ/ *n* immunità *f*

immuniz|e /'ɪmjʊnaɪz/ *vt* immunizzare

imp /ɪmp/ *n* diavoletto *m*

impact /'ɪmpækt/ *n* impatto *m*

impair /ɪm'peə(r)/ *vt* danneggiare

impale /ɪm'peɪl/ *vt* impalare

impart /ɪm'pɑ:t/ *vt* impartire

im'parti|al *adj* imparziale. **~'ality** *n* imparzialità *f*

im'passable *adj* impraticabile

im'passive *adj* impassibile

im'patien|ce *n* impazienza *f*. **~t** *adj* impaziente. **~tly** *adv* impazientemente

impeccabl|e /ɪm'pekəbl/ *adj* impeccabile. **~y** *adv* in modo impeccabile

impede /ɪm'pi:d/ *vt* impedire

impediment /ɪm'pedɪmənt/ *n* impedimento *m*; (*in speech*) difetto *m*

impending /ɪm'pendɪŋ/ *adj* imminente

impenetrable /ɪm'penɪtrəbl/ *adj* impenetrabile

imperative /ɪm'perətɪv/ *adj* imperativo ● *n* (*Gram*) imperativo *m*

imper'ceptible *adj* impercettibile

im'perfect *adj* imperfetto; (*faulty*) difettoso ● *n* (*Gram*) imperfetto *m*. **~ion** *n* imperfezione *f*

imperial /ɪm'pɪərɪəl/ *adj* imperiale. **~ism** *n* imperialismo *m*. **~ist** *n* imperialista *mf*

im'personal *adj* impersonale

impersonat|e /ɪm'pɜ:səneɪt/ *vt* impersonare. **~or** *n* imitatore, -trice *mf*

impertinen|ce /ɪm'pɜ:tɪnəns/ *n* impertinenza *f*. **~t** *adj* impertinente

impervious /ɪm'pɜ:vɪəs/ *adj* **~ to** *fig* indifferente a

impetuous /ɪm'petjʊəs/ *adj* impetuoso. **~ly** *adv* impetuosamente

impetus /'ɪmpɪtəs/ *n* impeto *m*

implacable /ɪm'plækəbl/ *adj* implacabile

im'plant[1] *vt* trapiantare; *fig* inculcare

'implant[2] *n* trapianto *m*

implement[1] /'ɪmplɪmənt/ *n* attrezzo *m*

implement[2] /'ɪmplɪment/ *vt* mettere in atto. **~ation** /-'eɪʃn/ *n* attuazione *f*

implicat|e /'ɪmplɪkeɪt/ *vt* implicare. **~ion** *n* implicazione *f*; **by ~ion** implicitamente

implicit /ɪm'plɪsɪt/ *adj* implicito; (*absolute*) assoluto

implore /ɪm'plɔ:(r)/ *vt* implorare
imply /ɪm'plaɪ/ *vt* (*pt/pp* **-ied**) implicare; **what are you ~ing?** che cosa vorresti insinuare?
impo'lite *adj* sgarbato
import¹ /'ɪmpɔ:t/ *n* (*Comm*) importazione *f*
import² /ɪm'pɔ:t/ *vt* importare
importan|ce /ɪm'pɔ:təns/ *n* importanza *f*. **~t** *adj* importante
importer /ɪm'pɔ:tə(r)/ *n* importatore, -trice *mf*
impos|e /ɪm'pəʊz/ *vt* imporre (**on** a) ● *vi* imporsi; **~e on** abusare di. **~ing** *adj* imponente. **~ition** *n* imposizione *f*
impossi'bility *n* impossibilità *f*
im'possibl|e *adj* impossibile
impostor /ɪm'pɒstə(r)/ *n* impostore, -trice *mf*
impoten|ce /'ɪmpətəns/ *n* impotenza *f*. **~t** *adj* impotente
impound /ɪm'paʊnd/ *vt* confiscare
impoverished /ɪm'pɒvərɪʃt/ *adj* impoverito
im'practical *adj* non pratico
impregnable /ɪm'pregnəbl/ *adj* imprendibile
impregnate /'ɪmpregneɪt/ *vt* impregnare (**with** di); (*Biol*) fecondare
im'press *vt* imprimere; *fig* colpire (*positivamente*); **~ sth on sb** fare capire qcsa a qcno
impression /ɪm'preʃn/ *n* impressione *f*; (*imitation*) imitazione *f*. **~able** *adj* (child, mind) influenzabile. **~ism** *n* impressionismo *m*. **~ist** *n* imitatore, -trice *mf*; (*artist*) impressionista *mf*
impressive /ɪm'presɪv/ *adj* imponente
'imprint¹ *n* impressione *f*
im'print² *vt* imprimere; **~ed on my mind** impresso nella mia memoria
im'prison *vt* incarcerare. **~ment** *n* reclusione *f*
im'probable *adj* improbabile
impromptu /ɪm'prɒmptju:/ *adj* improvvisato
im'proper *adj* (use) improprio; (behaviour) scorretto. **~ly** *adv* scorrettamente
improve /ɪm'pru:v/ *vt/i* migliorare. **improve on** *vt* perfezionare. **~ment** *n* miglioramento *m*
improvis|e /'ɪmprəvaɪz/ *vt/i* improvvisare
impuden|ce /'ɪmpjʊdəns/ *n* sfrontatezza *f*. **~t** *adj* sfrontato
impuls|e /'ɪmpʌls/ *n* impulso *m*; **on [an] ~e** impulsivamente. **~ive** *adj* impulsivo
im'pur|e *adj* impuro. **~ity** *n* impurità *f inv*; **~ities** *pl* impurità *fpl*
in /ɪn/ *prep* in; (*with names of towns*) a; **in the garden** in giardino; **in the street** in *or* per strada; **in bed/hospital** a letto/all'ospedale; **in the world** nel mondo; **in the rain** sotto la pioggia; **in the sun** al sole; **in this heat** con questo caldo; **in summer/winter** in estate/inverno; **in 1995** nel 1995; **in the evening** la sera; **he's arriving in two hours time** arriva fra due ore; **deaf in one ear** sordo da un orecchio; **in the army** nell'esercito; **in English/Italian** in inglese/italiano; **in ink/pencil** a penna/matita; **in red** (dressed, circled) di rosso; **the man in the raincoat** l'uomo con l'impermeabile; **in a soft/loud voice** a voce bassa/alta; **one in ten people** una persona su dieci; **in doing this, he...** nel far questo,...; **in itself** in sé; **in that** in quanto ● *adv* (*at home*) a casa; (*indoors*) dentro; **he's not in yet** non è ancora arrivato; **in there/here** lì/qui dentro; **ten in all** dieci in tutto; **day in, day out** giorno dopo giorno; **have it in for sb** [!] avercela con qcno; **send him in** fallo entrare; **come in** entrare; **bring in the washing** portare dentro i panni ● *adj* ([!]: *in fashion*) di moda ● *n* **the ins and outs** i dettagli
ina'bility *n* incapacità *f*
inac'cessible *adj* inaccessibile
in'accura|cy *n* inesattezza *f*. **~te** *adj* inesatto
in'ac|tive *adj* inattivo. **~'tivity** *n* inattività *f*
in'adequate *adj* inadeguato. **~ly** *adv* inadeguatamente
inadvertently /ɪnəd'vɜ:təntlɪ/ *adv* inavvertitamente
inad'visable *adj* sconsigliabile
inane /ɪ'neɪn/ *adj* stupido
in'animate *adj* esanime
inap'propriate *adj* inadatto
inar'ticulate *adj* inarticolato

inat'tentive *adj* disattento
in'audibl|e *adj* impercettibile
inaugurat|e /ɪ'nɔ:gjʊreɪt/ *vt* inaugurare. **~ion** *n* inaugurazione *f*
inborn /'ɪnbɔ:n/ *adj* innato
inbred /ɪn'bred/ *adj* congenito
incalculable /ɪn'kælkjʊləbl/ *adj* incalcolabile
in'capable *adj* incapace
incapacitate /ɪnkə'pæsɪteɪt/ *vt* rendere incapace
incarnat|e /ɪn'kɑ:nət/ *adj* **the devil ~e** il diavolo in carne e ossa
incendiary /ɪn'sendɪərɪ/ *adj* incendiario
incense¹ /'ɪnsens/ *n* incenso *m*
incense² /ɪn'sens/ *vt* esasperare
incentive /ɪn'sentɪv/ *n* incentivo *m*
incessant /ɪn'sesənt/ *adj* incessante
incest /'ɪnsest/ *n* incesto *m*
inch /ɪntʃ/ *n* pollice *m* (= *2.54 cm*) ● *vi* **~ forward** avanzare gradatamente
inciden|ce /'ɪnsɪdəns/ *n* incidenza *f*. **~t** *n* incidente *m*
incidental /ɪnsɪ'dentl/ *adj* incidentale; **~ expenses** spese *fpl* accessorie. **~ly** *adv* incidentalmente; (*by the way*) a proposito
incinerat|e /ɪn'sɪnəreɪt/ *vt* incenerire. **~or** *n* inceneritore *m*
incision /ɪn'sɪʒn/ *n* incisione *f*
incite /ɪn'saɪt/ *vt* incitare. **~ment** *n* incitamento *m*
inclination /ɪnklɪ'neɪʃn/ *n* inclinazione *f*
incline¹ /ɪn'klaɪn/ *vt* inclinare; **be ~d to do sth** essere propenso a fare qcsa
incline² /'ɪnklaɪn/ *n* pendio *m*
inclu|de /ɪn'klu:d/ *vt* includere. **~ding** *prep* incluso. **~sion** *n* inclusione *f*
inclusive /ɪn'klu:sɪv/ *adj* incluso; **~ of** comprendente; **be ~ of** comprendere ● *adv* incluso
incognito /ɪnkɒg'ni:təʊ/ *adv* incognito
inco'herent *adj* incoerente; (*because drunk etc*) incomprensibile
income /'ɪnkʌm/ *n* reddito *m*. **~ tax** *n* imposta *f* sul reddito
'incoming *adj* in arrivo. **~ tide** *n* marea *f* montante
in'comparable *adj* incomparabile
incom'patible *adj* incompatibile
in'competen|ce *n* incompetenza *f*. **~t** *adj* incompetente
incom'plete *adj* incompleto
incompre'hensible *adj* incomprensibile
incon'ceivable *adj* inconcepibile
incon'clusive *adj* inconcludente
incongruous /ɪn'kɒŋgrʊəs/ *adj* contrastante
incon'siderate *adj* trascurabile
incon'sistency *n* incoerenza *f*
incon'sistent *adj* incoerente; **be ~ with** non essere coerente con. **~ly** *adv* in modo incoerente
incon'spicuous *adj* non appariscente. **~ly** *adv* modestamente
incon'venien|ce *n* scomodità *f*; (*drawback*) inconveniente *m*; **put sb to ~ce** dare disturbo a qcno. **~t** *adj* scomodo; (time, place) inopportuno. **~tly** *adv* in modo inopportuno
incorporate /ɪn'kɔ:pəreɪt/ *vt* incorporare; (*contain*) comprendere
incor'rect *adj* incorretto. **~ly** *adv* scorrettamente
increase¹ /'ɪnkri:s/ *n* aumento *m*; **on the ~** in aumento
increas|e² /ɪn'kri:s/ *vt/i* aumentare. **~ing** *adj* (impatience etc) crescente; (numbers) in aumento. **~ingly** *adv* sempre più
in'credible *adj* incredibile
incredulous /ɪn'kredjʊləs/ *adj* incredulo
incriminate /ɪn'krɪmɪneɪt/ *vt* (*Jur*) incriminare
incubat|e /'ɪŋkjʊbeɪt/ *vt* incubare. **~ion** *n* incubazione *f*. **~ion period** *n* (*Med*) periodo *m* di incubazione. **~or** *n* (*for baby*) incubatrice *f*
incur /ɪn'kɜ:(r)/ *vt* (*pt/pp* **incurred**) incorrere; contrarre (debts)
in'curable *adj* incurabile
indebted /ɪn'detɪd/ *adj* obbligato (**to** verso)
in'decent *adj* indecente
inde'cision *n* indecisione *f*
inde'cisive *adj* indeciso. **~ness** *n* indecisione *f*
indeed /ɪn'di:d/ *adv* (*in fact*) difatti; **yes ~!** sì, certamente!; **~ I am/do** veramente!; **very much ~** moltissimo;

thank you very much ~ grazie infinite; **~?** davvero?
inde'finable *adj* indefinible
in'definite *adj* indefinito. **~ly** *adv* indefinitamente; (postpone) a tempo indeterminato
indelible /ɪn'delɪbl/ *adj* indelebile
indemnity /ɪn'demnɪtɪ/ *n* indennità *f inv*
indent¹ /'ɪndent/ *n* (*Typ*) rientranza *f* dal margine
indent² /ɪn'dent/ *vt* (*Typ*) fare rientrare dal margine. **~ation** *n* (*notch*) intaccatura *f*
inde'penden|ce *n* indipendenza *f*. **~t** *adj* indipendente. **~tly** *adv* indipendentemente
indescribable /ɪndɪ'skraɪbəbl/ *adj* indescrivibile
indestructible /ɪndɪ'strʌktəbl/ *adj* indistruttibile
indeterminate /ɪndɪ'tɜːmɪnət/ *adj* indeterminato
index /'ɪndeks/ *n* indice *m*
index: ~ finger *n* dito *m* indice. **~-'linked** *adj* (pension) legato al costo della vita
India /'ɪndɪə/ *n* India *f*. **~n** *adj* indiano; (*American*) indiano [d'America] ● *n* indiano, -a *mf*; (*American*) indiano, -a *mf* [d'America]
indicat|e /'ɪndɪkeɪt/ *vt* indicare; (*register*) segnare ● *vi* (*Auto*) mettere la freccia. **~ion** *n* indicazione *f*
indicative /ɪn'dɪkətɪv/ *adj* **be ~ of** essere indicativo di ● *n* (*Gram*) indicativo *m*
indicator /'ɪndɪkeɪtə(r)/ *n* (*Auto*) freccia *f*
indict /ɪn'daɪt/ *vt* accusare. **~ment** *n* accusa *f*
in'differen|ce *n* indifferenza *f*. **~t** *adj* indifferente; (*not good*) mediocre
indi'gest|ible *adj* indigesto. **~ion** *n* indigestione *f*
indigna|nt /ɪn'dɪgnənt/ *adj* indignato. **~ntly** *adv* con indignazione. **~tion** *n* indignazione *f*
indi'rect *adj* indiretto. **~ly** *adv* indirettamente
indi'screet *adj* indiscreto
indis'cretion *n* indiscrezione *f*
indiscriminate /ɪndɪ'skrɪmɪnət/ *adj* indiscriminato. **~ly** *adv* senza distinzione
indi'spensable *adj* indispensabile
indisposed /ɪndɪ'spəʊzd/ *adj* indisposto
indisputable /ɪndɪ'spjuːtəbl/ *adj* indisputabile
indistinguishable /ɪndɪ'stɪŋgwɪʃəbl/ *adj* indistinguibile
individual /ɪndɪ'vɪdjʊəl/ *adj* individuale ● *n* individuo *m*. **~ity** *n* individualità *f*
indoctrinate /ɪn'dɒktrɪneɪt/ *vt* indottrinare
indomitable /ɪn'dɒmɪtəbl/ *adj* indomito
indoor /'ɪndɔː(r)/ *adj* interno; (shoes) per casa; (plant) da appartamento; (swimming pool etc) coperto. **~s** *adv* dentro
induce /ɪn'djuːs/ *vt* indurre (**to** a); (*produce*) causare. **~ment** *n* (*incentive*) incentivo *m*
indulge /ɪn'dʌldʒ/ *vt* soddisfare; viziare (child) ● *vi* **~ in** concedersi. **~nce** *n* lusso *m*; (*leniency*) indulgenza *f*. **~nt** *adj* indulgente
industrial /ɪn'dʌstrɪəl/ *adj* industriale; **take ~ action** scioperare. **~ist** *n* industriale *mf*. **~ized** *adj* industrializzato
industr|ious /ɪn'dʌstrɪəs/ *adj* industrioso. **~y** *n* industria *f*; (*zeal*) operosità *f*
inebriated /ɪ'niːbrɪeɪtɪd/ *adj* ebbro
in'edible *adj* immangiabile
inef'fective *adj* inefficace
ineffectual /ɪnɪ'fektʃʊəl/ *adj* inutile; (person) inconcludente
inef'ficien|cy *n* inefficienza *f*. **~t** *adj* inefficiente
in'eligible *adj* inadatto
inept /ɪ'nept/ *adj* inetto
ine'quality *n* ineguaglianza *f*
inert /ɪ'nɜːt/ *adj* inerte. **~ia** *n* inerzia *f*
inescapable /ɪnɪ'skeɪpəbl/ *adj* inevitabile
inevitabl|e /ɪn'evɪtəbl/ *adj* inevitabile. **~y** *adv* inevitabilmente
ine'xact *adj* inesatto
inex'cusable *adj* imperdonabile
inex'pensive *adj* poco costoso

inex'perience *n* inesperienza *f.* **~d** *adj* inesperto

inexplicable /ɪnɪk'splɪkəbl/ *adj* inesplicabile

in'fallible *adj* infallibile

infam|ous /'ɪnfəməs/ *adj* infame; (person) famigerato. **~y** *n* infamia *f*

infan|cy /'ɪnfənsɪ/ *n* infanzia *f*; **in its ~cy** *fig* agli inizi. **~t** *n* bambino, -a *mf* piccolo, -a. **~tile** *adj* infantile

infantry /'ɪnfəntrɪ/ *n* fanteria *f*

infatuat|ed /ɪn'fætʃʊeɪtɪd/ *adj* infatuato (**with** di). **~ion** *n* infatuazione *f*

infect /ɪn'fekt/ *vt* infettare; **become ~ed** (wound:) infettarsi. **~ion** *adj* infettivo

infer /ɪn'fɜ:(r)/ *vt* (*pt/pp* **inferred**) dedurre (**from** da); (*imply*) implicare. **~ence** *n* deduzione *f*

inferior /ɪn'fɪərɪə(r)/ *adj* inferiore; (goods) scadente; (*in rank*) subalterno ● *n* inferiore *mf*; (*in rank*) subalterno, -a *mf*

inferiority /ɪnfɪərɪ'ɒrətɪ/ *n* inferiorità *f.* **~ complex** *n* complesso *m* di inferiorità

in'fer|tile *adj* sterile. **~'tility** *n* sterilità *f*

infest /ɪn'fest/ *vt* **be ~ed with** essere infestato di

infi'delity *n* infedeltà *f*

infiltrate /'ɪnfɪltreɪt/ *vt* infiltrare; (*Pol*) infiltrarsi in

infinite /'ɪnfɪnət/ *adj* infinito

infinitive /ɪn'fɪnətɪv/ *n* (*Gram*) infinito *m*

infinity /ɪn'fɪnətɪ/ *n* infinità *f*

infirm /ɪn'fɜ:m/ *adj* debole. **~ary** *n* infermeria *f.* **~ity** *n* debolezza *f*

inflame /ɪn'fleɪm/ *vt* infiammare. **~d** *adj* infiammato; **become ~d** infiammarsi

in'flammable *adj* infiammabile

inflammation /ɪnflə'meɪʃn/ *n* infiammazione *f*

inflat|e /ɪn'fleɪt/ *vt* gonfiare. **~ion** *n* inflazione *f.* **~ionary** *adj* inflazionario

in'flexible *adj* inflessibile

inflict /ɪn'flɪkt/ *vt* infliggere (**on** a)

influen|ce /'ɪnflʊəns/ *n* influenza *f* ● *vt* influenzare. **~tial** *adj* influente

influenza /ɪnflʊ'enzə/ *n* influenza *f*

influx /'ɪnflʌks/ *n* affluenza *f*

inform /ɪn'fɔ:m/ *vt* informare; **keep sb ~ed** tenere qcno al corrente ● *vi* **~ against** denunziare

in'for|mal *adj* informale; (agreement) ufficioso. **~mally** *adv* in modo informale. **~'mality** *n* informalità *f inv*

informat|ion /ɪnfə'meɪʃn/ *n* informazioni *fpl*; **a piece of ~ion** un'informazione. **~ion highway** *n* autostrada *f* telematica. **~ion technology** *n* informatica *f.* **~ive** *adj* informativo; (film, book) istruttivo

informer /ɪn'fɔ:mə(r)/ *n* informatore, -trice *mf*; (*Pol*) delatore, -trice *mf*

infra-'red /ɪnfrə-/ *adj* infrarosso

infringe /ɪn'frɪndʒ/ *vt* **~ on** usurpare. **~ment** *n* violazione *f*

infuriat|e /ɪn'fjʊərɪeɪt/ *vt* infuriare. **~ing** *adj* esasperante

ingenious /ɪn'dʒi:nɪəs/ *adj* ingegnoso

ingenuity /ɪndʒɪ'nju:ətɪ/ *n* ingegnosità *f*

ingot /'ɪŋgət/ *n* lingotto *m*

ingrained /ɪn'greɪnd/ *adj* (*in person*) radicato; (dirt) incrostato

ingratiate /ɪn'greɪʃɪeɪt/ *vt* **~ oneself with sb** ingraziarsi qcno

in'gratitude *n* ingratitudine *f*

ingredient /ɪn'gri:dɪənt/ *n* ingrediente *m*

ingrowing /'ɪngrəʊɪŋ/ *adj* (nail) incarnito

inhabit /ɪn'hæbɪt/ *vt* abitare. **~ant** *n* abitante *mf*

inhale /ɪn'heɪl/ *vt* aspirare; (*Med*) inalare ● *vi* inspirare; (*when smoking*) aspirare. **~r** *n* (*device*) inalatore *m*

inherent /ɪn'hɪərənt/ *adj* inerente

inherit /ɪn'herɪt/ *vt* ereditare. **~ance** *n* eredità *f inv*

inhibit /ɪn'hɪbɪt/ *vt* inibire. **~ed** *adj* inibito. **~ion** *n* inibizione *f*

inho'spitable *adj* inospitale

initial /ɪ'nɪʃl/ *adj* iniziale ● *n* iniziale *f* ● *vt* (*pt/pp* **initialled**) siglare. **~ly** *adv* all'inizio

initiat|e /ɪ'nɪʃɪeɪt/ *vt* iniziare. **~ion** *n* iniziazione *f*

initiative /ɪ'nɪʃətɪv/ *n* iniziativa *f*

inject /ɪn'dʒekt/ *vt* iniettare. **~ion** *n* iniezione *f*

injur|e /'ɪndʒə(r)/ *vt* ferire; (*wrong*) nuocere. **~y** *n* ferita *f*; (*wrong*) torto *m*

in'justice *n* ingiustizia *f*; **do sb an ~** giudicare qcno in modo sbagliato

ink /ɪŋk/ *n* inchiostro *m*

inland /'ɪnlənd/ *adj* interno ● *adv* all'interno. **I~ Revenue** *n* fisco *m*

in-laws /'ɪnlɔ:z/ *npl* ! parenti *mpl* acquisiti

inlay /'ɪnleɪ/ *n* intarsio *m*

inlet /'ɪnlet/ *n* insenatura *f*; (*Techn*) entrata *f*

inmate /'ɪnmeɪt/ *n* (*of hospital*) degente *mf*; (*of prison*) carcerato, -a *mf*

inn /ɪn/ *n* locanda *f*

innate /ɪ'neɪt/ *adj* innato

inner /'ɪnə(r)/ *adj* interno. **~most** *adj* il più profondo. **~ tube** camera *f* d'aria

innocen|ce /'ɪnəsəns/ *n* innocenza *f*. **~t** *adj* innocente

innocuous /ɪ'nɒkjʊəs/ *adj* innocuo

innovat|e /'ɪnəveɪt/ *vi* innovare. **~ion** *n* innovazione *f*. **~ive** *adj* innovativo. **~or** *n* innovatore, -trice *mf*

innuendo /ɪnjʊ'endəʊ/ *n* (*pl* **-es**) insinuazione *f*

innumerable /ɪ'nju:mərəbl/ *adj* innumerevole

inoculat|e /ɪ'nɒkjʊleɪt/ *vt* vaccinare. **~ion** *n* vaccinazione *f*

inof'fensive *adj* inoffensivo

in'opportune *adj* inopportuno

input /'ɪnpʊt/ *n* input *m inv*, ingresso *m*

inquest /'ɪnkwest/ *n* inchiesta *f*

inquir|e /ɪn'kwaɪə(r)/ *vi* informarsi (**about** su); **~e into** far indagini su ● *vt* domandare. **~y** *n* domanda *f*; (*investigation*) inchiesta *f*

inquisitive /ɪn'kwɪzətɪv/ *adj* curioso

in'sane *adj* pazzo; *fig* insensato

in'sanity *n* pazzia *f*

insatiable /ɪn'seɪʃəbl/ *adj* insaziabile

inscri|be /ɪn'skraɪb/ *vt* iscrivere. **~ption** *n* iscrizione *f*

inscrutable /ɪn'skru:təbl/ *adj* impenetrabile

insect /'ɪnsekt/ *n* insetto *m*. **~icide** *n* insetticida *m*

inse'cur|e *adj* malsicuro; (fig: person) insicuro. **~ity** *n* mancanza *f* di sicurezza

in'sensitive *adj* insensibile

in'separable *adj* inseparabile

insert¹ /'ɪnsɜ:t/ *n* inserto *m*

insert² /ɪn'sɜ:t/ *vt* inserire. **~ion** *n* inserzione *f*

inside /ɪn'saɪd/ *n* interno *m*. **~s** *npl* ! pancia *f* ● *attrib* (*Auto*) **~ lane** *n* corsia *f* interna ● *adv* dentro; **~ out** a rovescio; (*thoroughly*) a fondo ● *prep* dentro; (*of time*) entro

insight /'ɪnsaɪt/ *n* intuito *m* (**into** per); **an ~ into** un quadro di

insig'nificant *adj* insignificante

insin'cer|e *adj* poco sincero. **~ity** *n* mancanza *f* di sincerità

insinuat|e /ɪn'sɪnjʊeɪt/ *vt* insinuare. **~ion** *n* insinuazione *f*

insipid /ɪn'sɪpɪd/ *adj* insipido

insist /ɪn'sɪst/ *vi* insistere (**on** per) ● *vt* **~ that** insistere che. **~ence** *n* insistenza *f*. **~ent** *adj* insistente

insolen|ce /'ɪnsələns/ *n* insolenza *f*. **~t** *adj* insolente

in'soluble *adj* insolubile

insomnia /ɪn'sɒmnɪə/ *n* insonnia *f*

inspect /ɪn'spekt/ *vt* ispezionare; controllare (ticket). **~ion** *n* ispezione *f*; (*of ticket*) controllo *m*. **~or** *n* ispettore, -trice *mf*; (*of tickets*) controllore *m*

inspiration /ɪnspə'reɪʃn/ *n* ispirazione *f*

inspire /ɪn'spaɪə(r)/ *vt* ispirare

insta'bility *n* instabilità *f*

install /ɪn'stɔ:l/ *vt* installare. **~ation** *n* installazione *f*

instalment /ɪn'stɔ:lmənt/ *n* (*Comm*) rata *f*; (*of serial*) puntata *f*; (*of publication*) fascicolo *m*

instance /'ɪnstəns/ *n* (*case*) caso *m*; (*example*) esempio *m*; **in the first ~** in primo luogo; **for ~** per esempio

instant /'ɪnstənt/ *adj* immediato; (*Culin*) espresso ● *n* istante *m*. **~aneous** *adj* istantaneo

instead /ɪn'sted/ *adv* invece; **~ of doing** anziché fare; **~ of me** al mio posto; **~ of going** invece di andare

instigat|e /'ɪnstɪgeɪt/ *vt* istigare. **~ion** *n* istigazione *f*; **at his ~ion** dietro suo suggerimento. **~or** *n* istigatore, -trice *mf*

instinct /'ɪnstɪŋkt/ *n* istinto *m*. **~ive** *adj* istintivo

institut|e /'ɪnstɪtju:t/ *n* istituto *m* ● *vt* istituire (scheme); iniziare (search); intentare (legal action). **~ion** *n* istituzione *f*; (*home for elderly*) istituto *m* per anziani; (*for mentally ill*) istituto *m* per malati di mente

instruct /ɪn'strʌkt/ *vt* istruire; (*order*) ordinare. **~ion** *n* istruzione *f*; **~s** (*orders*) ordini *mpl*. **~ive** *adj* istruttivo. **~or** *n* istruttore, -trice *mf*

instrument /'ɪnstrʊmənt/ *n* strumento *m*. **~al** *adj* strumentale; **be ~al in** contribuire a. **~alist** *n* strumentista *mf*

insu'bordi|nate *adj* insubordinato. **~nation** *n* insubordinazione *f*

in'sufferable *adj* insopportabile

insuf'ficient *adj* insufficiente

insular /'ɪnsjʊlə(r)/ *adj fig* gretto

i

insulat|e /'ɪnsjʊleɪt/ *vt* isolare. **~ing tape** *n* nastro *m* isolante. **~ion** *n* isolamento *m*

insulin /'ɪnsjʊlɪn/ *n* insulina *f*

insult[1] /'ɪnsʌlt/ *n* insulto *m*

insult[2] /ɪn'sʌlt/ *vt* insultare

insur|ance /ɪn'ʃʊərəns/ *n* assicurazione *f*. **~e** *vt* assicurare

intact /ɪn'tækt/ *adj* intatto

integral /'ɪntɪgrəl/ *adj* integrale

integrat|e /'ɪntɪgreɪt/ *vt* integrare • *vi* integrarsi. **~ion** *n* integrazione *f*

integrity /ɪn'tegrətɪ/ *n* integrità *f*

intellect /'ɪntəlekt/ *n* intelletto *m*. **~ual** *adj & n* intellettuale *mf*

intelligen|ce /ɪn'telɪdʒəns/ *n* intelligenza *f*; (*Mil*) informazioni *fpl*. **~t** *adj* intelligente

intelligible /ɪn'telɪdʒəbl/ *adj* intelligibile

intend /ɪn'tend/ *vt* destinare; (*have in mind*) aver intenzione di; **be ~ed for** essere destinato a. **~ed** *adj* (effect) voluto • *n* **my ~ed** [!] il mio/la mia fidanzato, -a

intense /ɪn'tens/ *adj* intenso; (person) dai sentimenti intensi. **~ly** *adv* intensamente; (*very*) estremamente

intensity /ɪn'tensətɪ/ *n* intensità *f*

intensive /ɪn'tensɪv/ *adj* intensivo. **~ care** (*for people in coma*) rianimazione *f*; **~ care [unit]** terapia *f* intensiva

intent /ɪn'tent/ *adj* intento; **~ on** (*absorbed in*) preso da; **be ~ on doing sth** essere intento a fare qcsa • *n* intenzione *f*; **to all ~s and purposes** a tutti gli effetti. **~ly** *adv* attentamente

intention /ɪn'tenʃn/ *n* intenzione *f*. **~al** *adj* intenzionale. **~ally** *adv* intenzionalmente

inter'acti|on *n* cooperazione *f*. **~ve** *adj* interattivo

intercept /ɪntə'sept/ *vt* intercettare

'interchange *n* scambio *m*; (*Auto*) raccordo *m* [autostradale]

inter'changeable *adj* interscambiabile

'intercourse *n* (*sexual*) rapporti *mpl* [sessuali]

interest /'ɪntrəst/ *n* interesse *m*; **have an ~ in** (*Comm*) essere cointeressato in; **be of ~** essere interessante; **~ rate** *n* tasso *m* di interesse • *vt* interessare. **~ed** *adj* interessato. **~ing** *adj* interessante

interface /'ɪntəfeɪs/ *n* interfaccia *f* • *vt* interfacciare • *vi* interfacciarsi

interfere /ɪntə'fɪə(r)/ *vi* interferire; **~ with** interferire con. **~nce** *n* interferenza *f*

interior /ɪn'tɪərɪə(r)/ *adj* interiore • *n* interno *m*. **~ designer** *n* arredatore, -trice *mf*

interlude /'ɪntəlu:d/ *n* intervallo *m*

intermediary /ɪntə'mi:dɪərɪ/ *n* intermediario, -a *mf*

interminable /ɪn'tɜ:mɪnəbl/ *adj* interminabile

intermittent /ɪntə'mɪtənt/ *adj* intermittente

intern /ɪn'tɜ:n/ *vt* internare

internal /ɪn'tɜ:nl/ *adj* interno. **I~ 'Revenue** (*Am*) *n* fisco *m*. **~ly** *adv* internamente; (deal with) all'interno

inter'national *adj* internazionale • *n* (*game*) incontro *m* internazionale; (*player*) competitore, -trice *mf* in gare internazionali. **~ly** *adv* internazionalmente

Internet /'ɪntənet/ *n* Internet *m*

interpret /ɪn'tɜ:prɪt/ *vt* interpretare • *vi* fare l'interprete. **~ation** *n* interpretazione *f*. **~er** *n* interprete *mf*

interrogat|e /ɪn'terəgeɪt/ *vt* interrogare. **~ion** *n* interrogazione *f*; (*by police*) interrogatorio *m*

interrogative /ɪntə'rɒgətɪv/ *adj & n* **~ [pronoun]** interrogativo *m*

interrupt /ɪntə'rʌpt/ *vt/i* interrompere. **~ion** *n* interruzione *f*

intersect /ɪntə'sekt/ *vi* intersecarsi ● *vt* intersecare. **~ion** *n* intersezione *f*; (*of street*) incrocio *m*

inter'twine *vi* attorcigliarsi

interval /'ɪntəvl/ *n* intervallo *m*; **bright ~s** *pl* schiarite *fpl*

interven|e /ɪntə'vi:n/ *vi* intervenire. **~tion** *n* intervento *m*

interview /'ɪntəvju:/ *n* (*Journ*) intervista *f*; (*for job*) colloquio *m* [di lavoro] ● *vt* intervistare. **~er** *n* intervistatore, -trice *mf*

intestin|e /ɪn'testɪn/ *n* intestino *m*. **~al** *adj* intestinale

intimacy /'ɪntɪməsɪ/ *n* intimità *f*

intimate[1] /'ɪntɪmət/ *adj* intimo. **~ly** *adv* intimamente

intimate[2] /'ɪntɪmeɪt/ *vt* far capire; (*imply*) suggerire

intimidat|e /ɪn'tɪmɪdeɪt/ *vt* intimidire. **~ion** *n* intimidazione *f*

into /'ɪntə/, *di fronte a una vocale* /'ɪntʊ/ *prep* dentro, in; **go ~ the house** andare dentro [casa] *o* in casa; **be ~** ([!]: *like*) essere appassionato di; **I'm not ~ that** questo non mi piace; **7 ~ 21 goes 3** il 7 nel 21 ci sta 3 volte; **translate ~ French** tradurre in francese; **get ~ trouble** mettersi nei guai

in'tolerable *adj* intollerabile

in'toleran|ce *n* intolleranza *f*. **~t** *adj* intollerante

intoxicat|ed /ɪn'tɒksɪkeɪtɪd/ *adj* inebriato. **~ion** *n* ebbrezza *f*

in'transitive *adj* intransitivo

intravenous /ɪntrə'vi:nəs/ *adj* endovenoso. **~ly** *adv* per via endovenosa

intrepid /ɪn'trepɪd/ *adj* intrepido

intricate /'ɪntrɪkət/ *adj* complesso

intrigu|e /ɪn'tri:g/ *n* intrigo *m* ● *vt* intrigare ● *vi* tramare. **~ing** *adj* intrigante

intrinsic /ɪn'trɪnsɪk/ *adj* intrinseco

introduce /ɪntrə'dju:s/ *vt* presentare; (*bring in, insert*) introdurre

introduct|ion /ɪntrə'dʌkʃn/ *n* introduzione *f*; (*to person*) presentazione *f*; (*to book*) prefazione *f*. **~ory** *adj* introduttivo

introvert /'ɪntrəvɜ:t/ *n* introverso, -a *mf*

intru|de /ɪn'tru:d/ *vi* intromettersi. **~der** *n* intruso, -a *mf*. **~sion** *n* intrusione *f*

intuit|ion /ɪntjʊ'ɪʃn/ *n* intuito *m*. **~ive** *adj* intuitivo

inundate /'ɪnəndeɪt/ *vt* (flood) inondare (**with** di)

invade /ɪn'veɪd/ *vt* invadere. **~r** *n* invasore *m*

invalid[1] /'ɪnvəlɪd/ *n* invalido, -a *mf*

invalid[2] /ɪn'vælɪd/ *adj* non valido. **~ate** *vt* invalidare

in'valuable *adj* prezioso; (*priceless*) inestimabile

in'variabl|e *adj* invariabile. **~y** *adv* invariabilmente

invasion /ɪn'veɪʒn/ *n* invasione *f*

invent /ɪn'vent/ *vt* inventare. **~ion** *n* invenzione *f*. **~ive** *adj* inventivo. **~or** *n* inventore, -trice *mf*

inventory /'ɪnvəntrɪ/ *n* inventario *m*

invest /ɪn'vest/ *vt* investire ● *vi* fare investimenti; **~ in** ([!]: *buy*) comprarsi

investigat|e /ɪn'vestɪgeɪt/ *vt* investigare. **~ion** *n* investigazione *f*

invest|ment /ɪn'vestmənt/ *n* investimento *m*. **~or** *n* investitore, -trice *mf*

inveterate /ɪn'vetərət/ *adj* inveterato

invidious /ɪn'vɪdɪəs/ *adj* ingiusto; (position) antipatico

invincible /ɪn'vɪnsəbl/ *adj* invincibile

in'visible *adj* invisibile

invitation /ɪnvɪ'teɪʃn/ *n* invito *m*

invit|e /ɪn'vaɪt/ *vt* invitare; (*attract*) attirare. **~ing** *adj* invitante

invoice /'ɪnvɔɪs/ *n* fattura *f* ● *vt* **~ sb** emettere una fattura a qcno

in'voluntar|y *adj* involontario

involve /ɪn'vɒlv/ *vt* comportare; (*affect, include*) coinvolgere; (*entail*) implicare; **get ~d with sb** legarsi a qcno; (*romantically*) legarsi sentimentalmente a qcno. **~d** *adj* complesso. **~ment** *n* coinvolgimento *m*

inward /'ɪnwəd/ *adj* interno; (thoughts etc) interiore; **~ investment** (*Comm*) investimento *m* straniero. **~ly** *adv* interiormente. **~[s]** *adv* verso l'interno

iodine /'aɪədi:n/ *n* iodio *m*

iota /aɪ'əʊtə/ *n* briciolo *m*

IOU *n abbr* (I owe you) pagherò *m inv*

IQ *n abbr* (intelligence quotient) Q.I.

Iran /ɪ'rɑ:n/ *n* Iran *m*. **~ian** *adj & n* iraniano, -a *mf*

Iraq /ɪ'rɑ:k/ *n* Iraq *m*. **~i** *adj & n* iracheno, -a *mf*

irate /aɪ'reɪt/ *adj* adirato

Ireland /'aɪələnd/ *n* Irlanda *f*

iris /'aɪrɪs/ *n* (*Anat*) iride *f*; (*Bot*) iris *f inv*

Irish /'aɪrɪʃ/ *adj* irlandese ● *n* **the ~** *pl* gli irlandesi *mpl*. **~man** *n* irlandese *m*. **~woman** *n* irlandese *f*

iron /'aɪən/ *adj* di ferro. **I~ Curtain** *n* cortina *f* di ferro ● *n* ferro *m*; (*appliance*) ferro *m* [da stiro] ● *vt/i* stirare. □ **~ out** *vt* eliminare stirando; *fig* appianare

i

'ironmonger /-mʌŋgə(r)/ *n* **~'s** [**shop**] negozio *m* di ferramenta

irony /'aɪrənɪ/ *n* ironia *f*

irrational /ɪ'ræʃənl/ *adj* irrazionale

irrefutable /ɪrɪ'fju:təbl/ *adj* irrefutabile

irregular /ɪ'regjʊlə(r)/ *adj* irregolare. **~ity** *n* irregolarità *f inv*

irrelevant /ɪ'reləvənt/ *adj* non pertinente

irreparabl|e /ɪ'repərəbl/ *adj* irreparabile. **~y** *adv* irreparabilmente

irreplaceable /ɪrɪ'pleɪsəbl/ *adj* insostituibile

irresistible /ɪrɪ'zɪstəbl/ *adj* irresistibile

irrespective /ɪrɪ'spektɪv/ *adj* **~ of** senza riguardo per

irresponsible /ɪrɪ'spɒnsɪbl/ *adj* irresponsabile

irreverent /ɪ'revərənt/ *adj* irreverente

irrevocabl|e /ɪ'revəkəbl/ *adj* irrevocabile. **~y** *adv* irrevocabilmente

irrigat|e /'ɪrɪgeɪt/ *vt* irrigare. **~ion** *n* irrigazione *f*

irritable /'ɪrɪtəbl/ *adj* irritabile

irritat|e /'ɪrɪteɪt/ *vt* irritare. **~ing** *adj* irritante. **~ion** *n* irritazione *f*

is /ɪz/ ▷**BE**

Islam /'ɪzlɑ:m/ *n* Islam *m*. **~ic** *adj* islamico

island /'aɪlənd/ *n* isola *f*; (*in road*) isola *f* spartitraffico. **~er** *n* isolano, -a *mf*

isolat|e /'aɪsəleɪt/ *vt* isolare. **~ed** *adj* isolato. **~ion** *n* isolamento *m*

Israel /'ɪzreɪl/ *n* Israele *m*. **~i** *adj & n* israeliano, -a *mf*

issue /'ɪʃu:/ *n* (*outcome*) risultato *m*; (*of magazine*) numero *m*; (*of stamps etc*) emissione *f*; (*offspring*) figli *mpl*; (*matter, question*) questione *f*; **at ~** in questione; **take ~ with sb** prendere posizione contro qcno ● *vt* distribuire (supplies); rilasciare (passport); emettere (stamps, order); pubblicare (book); **be ~d with sth** ricevere qcsa ● *vi* **~ from** uscire da

it /ɪt/ *pron* (*direct object*) lo *m*, la *f*; (*indirect object*) gli *m*, le *f*; **it's broken** è rotto/rotta; **will it be enough?** basterà?; **it's hot** fa caldo; **it's raining** piove; **it's me** sono io; **who is it?** chi è?; **it's two o'clock** sono le due; **I doubt it** ne dubito; **take it with you** prendilo con te; **give it a wipe** dagli una pulita

Italian /ɪ'tæljən/ *adj & n* italiano, -a *mf*; (*language*) italiano *m*

Italy /'ɪtəlɪ/ *n* Italia *f*

itch /ɪtʃ/ *n* prurito *m* ● *vi* avere prurito, prudere; **be ~ing to** [!] avere una voglia matta di. **~y** *adj* che prude; **my foot is ~y** ho prurito al piede

item /'aɪtəm/ *n* articolo *m*; (*on agenda, programme*) punto *m*; (*on invoice*) voce *f*; **~** [**of news**] notizia *f*. **~ize** *vt* dettagliare (bill)

itinerary /aɪ'tɪnərərɪ/ *n* itinerario *m*

itself /ɪt'self/ *pron* (*reflexive*) si; (*emphatic*) essa stessa; **the baby looked at ~ in the mirror** il bambino si è guardato nello specchio; **by ~** da solo; **the machine in ~ is simple** la macchina di per sé è semplice

ITV *n abbr* (Independent Television) *stazione f televisiva privata britannica*

ivory /'aɪvərɪ/ *n* avorio *m*

ivy /'aɪvɪ/ *n* edera *f*

> *i*
>
> **The Ivy League** Il gruppo delle più antiche e rinomate università statunitensi, situate nel nordest del paese: Harvard, Yale, Columbia University, Cornell University, Dartmouth College, Brown University, Princeton University e la University of Pennsylvania. L'espressione deriva dall'edera che cresce sugli antichi edifici universitari.

Jj

jab /dʒæb/ *n* colpo *m* secco; ([!]: *injection*) puntura *f* ● *vt* (*pt/pp* **jabbed**) punzecchiare

jack /dʒæk/ *n* (*Auto*) cric *m inv*; (*in cards*) fante *m*, jack *m inv* ● **jack up** *vt* (*Auto*) sollevare [con il cric]

jackdaw /ˈdʒækdɔ:/ *n* taccola *f*

jacket /ˈdʒækɪt/ *n* giacca *f*; (*of book*) sopraccoperta *f*. **~ poˈtato** *n patata f cotta al forno con la buccia*

ˈjackpot *n* premio *m* (*di una lotteria*); **win the ~** vincere alla lotteria; **hit the ~** *fig* fare un colpo grosso

jade /dʒeɪd/ *n* giada *f* ● *attrib* di giada

jagged /ˈdʒægɪd/ *adj* dentellato

jail /dʒeɪl/ = **gaol**

jam¹ /dʒæm/ *n* marmellata *f*

jam² *n* (*Auto*) ingorgo *m*; ([!]: *difficulty*) guaio *m* ● *v* (*pt/pp* **jammed**) ● *vt* (*cram*) pigiare; disturbare (broadcast); inceppare (mechanism, drawer etc); **be ~med** (roads:) essere congestionato ● *vi* (mechanism:) incepparsi; (window, drawer:) incastrarsi

Jamaica /dʒəˈmeɪkə/ *n* Giamaica *f*. **~n** *adj & n* giamaicano, -a *mf*

jangle /ˈdʒæŋgl/ *vt* far squillare ● *vi* squillare

janitor /ˈdʒænɪtə(r)/ *n* (*caretaker*) custode *m*; (*in school*) bidello, -a *mf*

January /ˈdʒænjʊərɪ/ *n* gennaio *m*

Japan /dʒəˈpæn/ *n* Giappone *m*. **~ese** *adj & n* giapponese *mf*; (*language*) giapponese *m*

jar¹ /dʒɑ:(r)/ *n* (*glass*) barattolo *m*

jar² *vi* (*pt/pp* **jarred**) (sound:) stridere

jargon /ˈdʒɑ:gən/ *n* gergo *m*

jaundice /ˈdʒɔ:ndɪs/ *n* itterizia *f*. **~d** *adj fig* inacidito

jaunt /dʒɔ:nt/ *n* gita *f*

jaunty /ˈdʒɔ:ntɪ/ *adj* (**-ier, -iest**) sbarazzino

jaw /dʒɔ:/ *n* mascella *f*; (*bone*) mandibola *f*

jay-walker /ˈdʒeɪwɔ:kə(r)/ *n* pedone *m* distratto

jazz /dʒæz/ *n* jazz *m* ● **jazz up** *vt* ravvivare. **~y** *adj* vistoso

jealous /ˈdʒeləs/ *adj* geloso. **~y** *n* gelosia *f*

jeans /dʒi:nz/ *npl* [blue] jeans *mpl*

jeep /dʒi:p/ *n* jeep *f inv*

jeer /dʒɪə(r)/ *n* scherno *m* ● *vi* schernire; **~ at** prendersi gioco di ● *vt* (*boo*) fischiare

jelly /ˈdʒelɪ/ *n* gelatina *f*. **~fish** *n* medusa *f*

jeopar|dize /ˈdʒepədaɪz/ *vt* mettere in pericolo. **~dy** *n* **in ~dy** in pericolo

jerk /dʒɜ:k/ *n* scatto *m*, scossa *f* ● *vt* scattare ● *vi* sobbalzare; (limb, muscle:) muoversi a scatti. **~ily** *adv* a scatti. **~y** *adj* traballante

jersey /ˈdʒɜ:zɪ/ *n* maglia *f*; (*Sport*) maglietta *f*; (*fabric*) jersey *m*

jest /dʒest/ *n* scherzo *m*; **in ~** per scherzo ● *vi* scherzare

Jesus /ˈdʒi:zəs/ *n* Gesù *m*

jet¹ /dʒet/ *n* (*stone*) giaietto *m*

jet² *n* (*of water*) getto *m*; (*nozzle*) becco *m*; (*plane*) aviogetto *m*, jet *m inv*

jet: ~-ˈblack *adj* nero ebano. **~lag** *n* scombussolamento *m* da fuso orario. **~-proˈpelled** *adj* a reazione

jettison /ˈdʒetɪsn/ *vt* gettare a mare; *fig* abbandonare

jetty /ˈdʒetɪ/ *n* molo *m*

Jew /dʒu:/ *n* ebreo *m*

jewel /ˈdʒu:əl/ *n* gioiello *m*. **~ler** *n* gioielliere *m*; **~ler's [shop]** gioielleria *f*. **~lery** *n* gioielli *mpl*

jiffy /ˈdʒɪfɪ/ *n* [!] **in a ~** in un batter d'occhio

jigsaw /ˈdʒɪgsɔ:/ *n* **~ [puzzle]** puzzle *m inv*

jilt /dʒɪlt/ *vt* piantare

jingle /ˈdʒɪŋgl/ *n* (*rhyme*) canzoncina *f* pubblicitaria ● *vi* tintinnare

job /dʒɒb/ *n* lavoro *m*; **this is going to be quite a ~** [!] [questa] non sarà un'impresa facile; **it's a good ~ that...** meno male che.... **~ centre** *n* ufficio *m* statale di collocamento. **~less** *adj* senza lavoro

jockey /ˈdʒɒkɪ/ *n* fantino *m*

jocular /ˈdʒɒkjʊlə(r)/ *adj* scherzoso

jog /dʒɒg/ *n* colpetto *m*; **at a ~** in un balzo; (*Sport*) **go for a ~** andare a fare jogging ● *v* (*pt/pp* **jogged**) ● *vt* (*hit*) urtare; ~ **sb's memory** farlo ritornare in mente a qcno ● *vi* (*Sport*) fare jogging. ~**ging** *n* jogging *m*

join /dʒɔɪn/ *n* giuntura *f* ● *vt* raggiungere, unire; raggiungere (person); (*become member of*) iscriversi a; entrare in (firm) ● *vi* (roads:) congiungersi. □ ~ **in** *vi* partecipare. □ ~ **up** *vi* (*Mil*) arruolarsi ● *vt* unire

joiner /ˈdʒɔɪnə(r)/ *n* falegname *m*

joint /dʒɔɪnt/ *adj* comune ● *n* articolazione *f*; (*in wood, brickwork*) giuntura *f*; (*Culin*) arrosto *m*; ([!]: *bar*) bettola *f*; ([✖]:*drug*) spinello *m*. ~**ly** *adv* unitamente

joist /dʒɔɪst/ *n* travetto *m*

jok|e /dʒəʊk/ *n* (*trick*) scherzo *m*; (*funny story*) barzelletta *f* ● *vi* scherzare. ~**er** *n* burlone, -a *mf*; (*in cards*) jolly *m inv*. ~**ing** *n* ~**ing apart** scherzi a parte. ~**ingly** *adv* per scherzo

jolly /ˈdʒɒlɪ/ *adj* (**-ier, -iest**) allegro ● *adv* [!] molto

jolt /dʒəʊlt/ *n* scossa *f*, sobbalzo *m* ● *vt* far sobbalzare ● *vi* sobbalzare

jostle /ˈdʒɒsl/ *vt* spingere

jot /dʒɒt/ *n* nulla *f* ● **jot down** *vt* (*pt/pp* **jotted**) annotare. ~**ter** *n* taccuino *m*

journal /ˈdʒɜːnl/ *n* giornale *m*; (*diary*) diario *m*. ~**ese** *n* gergo *m* giornalistico. ~**ism** *n* giornalismo *m*. ~**ist** *n* giornalista *mf*

journey /ˈdʒɜːnɪ/ *n* viaggio *m*

jovial /ˈdʒəʊvɪəl/ *adj* gioviale

joy /dʒɔɪ/ *n* gioia *f*. ~**ful** *adj* gioioso. ~**ride** *n* [!] giro *m* con una macchina rubata. ~**stick** *n* (*Comput*) joystick *m inv*

jubil|ant /ˈdʒuːbɪlənt/ *adj* giubilante. ~**ation** *n* giubilo *m*

jubilee /ˈdʒuːbɪliː/ *n* giubileo *m*

judge /dʒʌdʒ/ *n* giudice *m* ● *vt* giudicare; (*estimate*) valutare; (*consider*) ritenere ● *vi* giudicare (**by** da). ~**ment** *n* giudizio *m*; (*Jur*) sentenza *f*

judic|ial /dʒuːˈdɪʃl/ *adj* giudiziario. ~**iary** *n* magistratura *f*. ~**ious** *adj* giudizioso

judo /ˈdʒuːdəʊ/ *n* judo *m*

jug /dʒʌg/ *n* brocca *f*; (*small*) bricco *m*

juggernaut /ˈdʒʌgənɔːt/ *n* [!] grosso autotreno *m*

juggle /ˈdʒʌgl/ *vi* fare giochi di destrezza. ~**r** *n* giocoliere, -a *mf*

juice /dʒuːs/ *n* succo *m*

juicy /ˈdʒuːsɪ/ *adj* (**-ier, -iest**) succoso; ([!]: *story*) piccante

juke-box /ˈdʒuːk-/ *n* juke-box *m inv*

July /dʒʊˈlaɪ/ *n* luglio *m*

jumble /ˈdʒʌmbl/ *n* accozzaglia *f* ● *vt* ~ **[up]** mischiare. ~ **sale** *n* vendita *f* di beneficenza

jumbo /ˈdʒʌmbəʊ/ *n* ~ **[jet]** jumbo jet *m inv*

jump /dʒʌmp/ *n* salto *m*; (*in prices*) balzo *m*; (*in horse racing*) ostacolo *m* ● *vi* saltare; (*with fright*) sussultare; (prices:) salire rapidamente; ~ **to conclusions** saltare alle conclusioni ● *vt* saltare; ~ **the gun** *fig* precipitarsi; ~ **the queue** non rispettare la fila. □ ~ **at** *vt fig* accettare con entusiasmo (offer). □ ~ **up** *vi* rizzarsi in piedi

jumper /ˈdʒʌmpə(r)/ *n* (*sweater*) golf *m inv*

jumpy /ˈdʒʌmpɪ/ *adj* nervoso

junction /ˈdʒʌŋkʃn/ *n* (*of roads*) incrocio *m*; (*of motorway*) uscita *f*; (*Rail*) nodo *m* ferroviario

June /dʒuːn/ *n* giugno *m*

jungle /ˈdʒʌŋgl/ *n* giungla *f*

junior /ˈdʒuːnɪə(r)/ *adj* giovane; (*in rank*) subalterno; (*Sport*) junior *inv* ● *n* **the** ~**s** (*Sch*) i più giovani. ~ **school** *n* scuola *f* elementare

junk /dʒʌŋk/ *n* cianfrusaglie *fpl*. ~ **food** *n* [!] cibo *m* poco sano, porcherie *fpl*. ~ **mail** posta *f* spazzatura

junkie /ˈdʒʌŋkɪ/ *n* [✖] tossico, -a *mf*

ˈjunk-shop *n* negozio *m* di rigattiere

jurisdiction /dʒʊərɪsˈdɪkʃn/ *n* giurisdizione *f*

juror /ˈdʒʊərə(r)/ *n* giurato, -a *mf*

jury /ˈdʒʊərɪ/ *n* giuria *f*

just /dʒʌst/ *adj* giusto ● *adv* (*barely*) appena; (*simply*) solo; (*exactly*) esattamente; ~ **as tall** altrettanto alto; ~ **as I was leaving** proprio quando stavo andando via; **I've** ~ **seen her** l'ho appena vista; **it's** ~ **as well** meno male; ~ **at that moment** proprio in quel momento; ~ **listen!** ascolta!; **I'm** ~ **going** sto andando proprio ora

justice /ˈdʒʌstɪs/ *n* giustizia *f*; **do** ~ **to**

rendere giustizia a; **J~ of the Peace** giudice *m* conciliatore

justifiabl|e /ˈdʒʌstɪfaɪəbl/ *adj* giustificabile

justi|fication /dʒʌstɪfɪˈkeɪʃn/ *n* giustificazione *f*. **~fy** *vt* (*pt/pp* **-ied**) giustificare

jut /dʒʌt/ *vi* (*pt/pp* **jutted**) **~ out** sporgere

juvenile /ˈdʒu:vənaɪl/ *adj* giovanile; (*childish*) infantile; (*for the young*) per i giovani ● *n* giovane *mf*. **~ delinquency** *n* delinquenza *f* giovanile

Kk

kangaroo /kæŋgəˈru:/ *n* canguro *m*

karate /kəˈrɑ:tɪ/ *n* karate *m*

keel /ki:l/ *n* chiglia *f* ● **keel over** *vi* capovolgersi

keen /ki:n/ *adj* (*intense*) acuto; (interest) vivo; (*eager*) entusiastico; (competition) feroce; (wind, knife) tagliente; **~ on** entusiasta di; **she's ~ on him** le piace molto; **be ~ to do sth** avere voglia di fare qcsa. **~ness** *n* entusiasmo *m*

keep /ki:p/ *n* (*maintenance*) mantenimento *m*; (*of castle*) maschio *m*; **for ~s** per sempre ● *v* (*pt/pp* **kept**) ● *vt* tenere; (*not throw away*) conservare; (*detain*) trattenere; mantenere (family, promise); avere (shop); allevare (animals); rispettare (law, rules); **~ sth hot** tenere qcsa in caldo; **~ sb from doing sth** impedire a qcno di fare qcsa; **~ sb waiting** far aspettare qcno; **~ sth to oneself** tenere qcsa per sè; **~ sth from sb** tenere nascosto qcsa a qcno ● *vi* (*remain*) rimanere; (food:) conservarsi; **~ calm** rimanere calmo; **~ left/right** tenere la destra/la sinistra; **~ [on] doing sth** continuare a fare qcsa. □ **~ back** *vt* trattenere (person); **~ sth back from sb** tenere nascosto qcsa a qcno ● *vi* tenersi indietro. □ **~ in with** *vt* mantenersi in buoni rapporti con. □ **~ on** *vi* [!] assillare (**at sb** qcno). □ **~ up** *vi* stare al passo ● *vt* (*continue*) continuare

kennel /ˈkenl/ *n* canile *m*; **~s** *pl* (*boarding*) canile *m*; (*breeding*) allevamento *m* di cani

Kenya /ˈkenjə/ *n* Kenia *m*. **~n** *adj & n* keniota *mf*

kept /kept/ ▷**KEEP**

kerb /kɜ:b/ *n* bordo *m* del marciapiede

kerosene /ˈkerəsi:n/ *n Am* cherosene *m*

ketchup /ˈketʃʌp/ *n* ketchup *m*

kettle /ˈket(ə)l/ *n* bollitore *m*; **put the ~ on** mettere l'acqua a bollire

key /ki:/ *n also* (*Mus*) chiave *f*; (*of piano, typewriter*) tasto *m* ● *vt* **~ [in]** digitare (character); **could you ~ this?** puoi battere questo?

key: ~board *n* (*Comput, Mus*) tastiera *f*. **~hole** *n* buco *m* della serratura. **~-ring** *n* portachiavi *m inv*

khaki /ˈkɑ:kɪ/ *adj* cachi *inv* ● *n* cachi *m*

kick /kɪk/ *n* calcio *m*; ([!]: *thrill*) piacere *m*; **for ~s** [!] per spasso ● *vt* dar calci a; **~ the bucket** [!] crepare ● *vi* (animal:) scalciare; (person:) dare calci. □ **~ off** *vi* (*Sport*) dare il calcio d'inizio; [!] iniziare. □ **~ up** *vt* **~ up a row** fare une scenata

ˈkick-off *n* (*Sport*) calcio *m* d'inizio

kid /kɪd/ *n* capretto *m*; ([!]: *child*) ragazzino, -a *mf* ● *v* (*pt/pp* **kidded**) ● *vt* [!] prendere in giro ● *vi* [!] scherzare

kidnap /ˈkɪdnæp/ *vt* (*pt/pp* **-napped**) rapire, sequestrare. **~per** *n* sequestratore, -trice *mf*, rapitore, -trice *mf*. **~ping** *n* rapimento *m*, sequestro *m* [di persona]

kidney /ˈkɪdnɪ/ *n* rene *m*; (*Culin*) rognone *m*. **~ machine** *n* rene *m* artificiale

kill /kɪl/ *vt* uccidere; *fig* metter fine a; ammazzare (time). **~er** *n* assassino, -a *mf*. **~ing** *n* uccisione *f*; (*murder*) omicidio *m*; **make a ~ing** *fig* fare un colpo grosso

kiln /kɪln/ *n* fornace *f*

kilo /ˈkɪlə/: **~byte** *n* kilobyte *m inv*. **~gram** *n* chilogrammo *m*. **~metre** *n* chilometro *m*. **~watt** *n* chilowatt *m inv*

kilt /kɪlt/ *n* kilt *m inv* (*gonnellino degli scozzesi*)

kin /kɪn/ *n* congiunti *mpl*; **next of ~** parente *m* stretto; parenti *mpl* stretti

kind¹ /kaɪnd/ *n* genere *m*, specie *f*; (*brand, type*) tipo *m*; **~ of** [!] alquanto; **two of a ~** due della stessa specie

kind² *adj* gentile, buono; **~ to animals** amante degli animali; **~ regards** cordiali saluti

kindergarten /ˈkɪndəgɑːtn/ *n* asilo *m* infantile

kindle /ˈkɪndl/ *vt* accendere

kind|ly /ˈkaɪndlɪ/ *adj* (**-ier, -iest**) benevolo ● *adv* gentilmente; (*if you please*) per favore. **~ness** *n* gentilezza *f*

king /kɪŋ/ *n* re *m inv*. **~dom** *n* regno *m*

king: ~fisher *n* martin *m inv* pescatore. **~-sized** *adj* (cigarette) king-size *inv*, lungo; (bed) matrimoniale grande

kink /kɪŋk/ *n* nodo *m*. **~y** *adj* [!] bizzarro

kiosk /ˈkiːɒsk/ *n* chiosco *m*; (*Teleph*) cabina *f* telefonica

kipper /ˈkɪpə(r)/ *n* aringa *f* affumicata

kiss /kɪs/ *n* bacio *m*; **~ of life** respirazione *f* bocca a bocca ● *vt* baciare ● *vi* baciarsi

kit /kɪt/ *n* equipaggiamento *m*, kit *m inv*; (*tools*) attrezzi *mpl*; (*construction ~*) pezzi *mpl* da montare, kit *m inv* ● **kit out** *vt* (*pt/pp* **kitted**) equipaggiare. **~bag** *n* sacco *m* a spalla

kitchen /ˈkɪtʃɪn/ *n* cucina *f* ● *attrib* di cucina. **~ette** *n* cucinino *m*

kitchen towel Scottex® *m inv*

kite /kaɪt/ *n* aquilone *m*

kitten /ˈkɪtn/ *n* gattino *m*

knack /næk/ *n* tecnica *f*; **have the ~ for doing sth** avere la capacità di fare qcsa

knead /niːd/ *vt* impastare

knee /niː/ *n* ginocchio *m*. **~cap** *n* rotula *f*

kneel /niːl/ *vi* (*pt/pp* **knelt**) **~ [down]** inginocchiarsi; **be ~ing** essere inginocchiato

knelt /nelt/ ▷**KNEEL**

knew /njuː/ ▷**KNOW**

knickers /ˈnɪkəz/ *npl* mutandine *fpl*

knife /naɪf/ *n* (*pl* **knives**) coltello *m* ● *vt* [!] accoltellare

knight /naɪt/ *n* cavaliere *m*; (*in chess*) cavallo *m* ● *vt* nominare cavaliere

knit /nɪt/ *vt/i* (*pt/pp* **knitted**) lavorare a maglia; **~ one, purl one** un diritto, un rovescio. **~ting** *n* lavorare *m* a maglia; (*work*) lavoro *m* a maglia. **~ting-needle** *n* ferro *m* da calza. **~wear** *n* maglieria *f*

knives /naɪvz/ ▷**KNIFE**

knob /nɒb/ *n* pomello *m*; (*of stick*) pomo *m*; (*of butter*) noce *f*. **~bly** *adj* nodoso; (*bony*) spigoloso

knock /nɒk/ *n* colpo *m*; **there was a ~ at the door** hanno bussato alla porta ● *vt* bussare a (door); ([!]: *criticize*) denigrare; **~ a hole in sth** fare un buco in qcsa; **~ one's head** battere la testa (**on** contro) ● *vi* (*at door*) bussare. □ **~ about** *vt* malmenare ● *vi* [!] girovagare. □ **~ down** *vt* far cadere; (*with fist*) stendere con un pugno; (*in car*) investire; (*demolish*) abbattere; ([!]: *reduce*) ribassare (price). □ **~ off** *vt* ([!]: *steal*) fregare; ([!]: *complete quickly*) fare alla bell'e meglio ● *vi* ([!]: *cease work*) staccare. □ **~ out** *vt* eliminare; (*make unconscious*) mettere K.O.; ([!]: *anaesthetize*) addormentare. □ **~ over** *vt* rovesciare; (*in car*) investire

knock: ~er *n* battente *m*. **~-kneed** /-ˈniːd/ *adj* con gambe storte. **~-out** *n* (*in boxing*) knock-out *m inv*

knot /nɒt/ *n* nodo *m* ● *vt* (*pt/pp* **knotted**) annodare

know /nəʊ/ *v* (*pt* **knew**, *pp* **known**) ● *vt* sapere; conoscere (person, place); (*recognize*) riconoscere; **get to ~ sb** conoscere qcno; **~ how to swim** sapere nuotare ● *vi* sapere; **did you ~ about this?** lo sapevi? ● *n* **in the ~** [!] al corrente

know: ~-all *n* [!] sapientone, -a *mf*. **~-how** *n* abilità *f*. **~ingly** *adv* (*intentionally*) consapevolmente; (smile etc) con un'aria d'intesa

knowledge /ˈnɒlɪdʒ/ *n* conoscenza *f*. **~able** *adj* ben informato

known /nəʊn/ ▷**KNOW** ● *adj* noto

knuckle /ˈnʌkl/ *n* nocca *f* ● **knuckle down** *vi* darci sotto (**to** con). □ **~ under** *vi* sottomettersi

Koran /kəˈrɑːn/ *n* Corano *m*

Korea /kəˈrɪə/ *n* Corea *f*. **~n** *adj & n* coreano, -a *mf*

kosher /ˈkəʊʃə(r)/ *adj* kasher *inv*

kudos /ˈkjuːdɒs/ *n* [!] gloria *f*

Ll

lab /læb/ *n* laboratorio *m*

label /ˈleɪbl/ *n* etichetta *f* ● *vt* (*pt/pp* **labelled**) mettere un'etichetta a; *fig* etichettare (person)

laboratory /ləˈbɒrətrɪ/ *n* laboratorio *m*

laborious /ləˈbɔːrɪəs/ *adj* laborioso

labour /ˈleɪbə(r)/ *n* lavoro *m*; (*workers*) manodopera *f*; (*Med*) doglie *fpl*; **be in ~** avere le doglie; **L~** (*Pol*) partito *m* laburista ● *attrib* (*Pol*) laburista ● *vi* lavorare ● *vt* **~ the point** *fig* ribadire il concetto. **~er** *n* manovale *m*

lace /leɪs/ *n* pizzo *m*; (*of shoe*) laccio *m* ● *attrib* di pizzo ● *vt* allacciare (shoes); correggere (drink)

lacerate /ˈlæsəreɪt/ *vt* lacerare

lack /læk/ *n* mancanza *f* ● *vt* mancare di; **I ~ the time** mi manca il tempo ● *vi* **be ~ing** mancare; **be ~ing in sth** mancare di qcsa

lad /læd/ *n* ragazzo *m*

ladder /ˈlædə(r)/ *n* scala *f*; (*in tights*) sfilatura *f*

laden /ˈleɪdn/ *adj* carico (**with** di)

ladle /ˈleɪdl/ *n* mestolo *m* ● *vt* **~ [out]** versare (*col mestolo*)

lady /ˈleɪdɪ/ *n* signora *f*; (*title*) Lady; **ladies [room]** bagno *m* per donne

lady: ~bird *n*, *Am* **~bug** *n* coccinella *f*. **~like** *adj* signorile

lag¹ /læg/ *vi* (*pt/pp* **lagged**) **~ behind** restare indietro

lag² *vt* (*pt/pp* **lagged**) isolare (pipes)

lager /ˈlɑːgə(r)/ *n* birra *f* chiara

lagoon /ləˈguːn/ *n* laguna *f*

laid /leɪd/ ▸LAY³

lain /leɪn/ ▸LIE²

lair /leə(r)/ *n* tana *f*

lake /leɪk/ *n* lago *m*

lamb /læm/ *n* agnello *m*

lame /leɪm/ *adj* zoppo; *fig* (argument) zoppicante; (excuse) traballante

lament /ləˈment/ *n* lamento *m* ● *vt* lamentare ● *vi* lamentarsi

lamentable /ˈlæməntəbl/ *adj* deplorevole

lamp /læmp/ *n* lampada *f*; (*in street*) lampione *m*. **~post** *n* lampione *m*. **~shade** *n* paralume *m*

lance /lɑːns/ *n* fiocina *f* ● *vt* (*Med*) incidere. **~-ˈcorporal** *n* appuntato *m*

land /lænd/ *n* terreno *m*; (*country*) paese *m*; (*as opposed to sea*) terra *f*; **plot of ~** pezzo *m* di terreno ● *vt* (*Naut*) sbarcare; (*fam*: obtain) assicurarsi; **be ~ed with sth** [!] ritrovarsi fra capo e collo qcsa ● *vi* (*Aeron*) atterrare; (*fall*) cadere. □ **~ up** *vi* [!] finire

landing /ˈlændɪŋ/ *n* (*Naut*) sbarco *m*; (*Aeron*) atterraggio *m*; (*top of stairs*) pianerottolo *m*. **~-stage** *n* pontile *m* da sbarco. **~ strip** *n* pista *f* d'atterraggio di fortuna

land: ~lady *n* proprietaria *f*; (*of flat*) padrona *f* di casa. **~lord** *n* proprietario *m*; (*of flat*) padrone *m* di casa. **~mark** *n* punto *m* di riferimento; *fig* pietra *f* miliare. **~scape** /-skeɪp/ *n* paesaggio *m*. **~slide** *n* frana *f*; (*Pol*) valanga *f* di voti

lane /leɪn/ *n* sentiero *m*; (*Auto, Sport*) corsia *f*

language /ˈlæŋgwɪdʒ/ *n* lingua *f*; (*speech, style*) linguaggio *m*. **~ laboratory** *n* laboratorio *m* linguistico

lank /læŋk/ *adj* (hair) diritto

lanky /ˈlæŋkɪ/ *adj* (**-ier, -iest**) allampanato

lantern /ˈlæntən/ *n* lanterna *f*

lap¹ /læp/ *n* grembo *m*

lap² *n* (*of journey*) tappa *f*; (*Sport*) giro *m* ● *v* (*pt/pp* **lapped**) ● *vi* (water:) **~ against** lambire ● *vt* (*Sport*) doppiare

lap³ *vt* (*pt/pp* **lapped**) **~ up** bere avidamente; bersi completamente (lies); credere ciecamente a (praise)

lapel /ləˈpel/ *n* bavero *m*

lapse /læps/ *n* sbaglio *m*; (*moral*) sbandamento *m* [morale]; (*of time*) intervallo *m* ● *vi* (*expire*) scadere; (*morally*) scivolare; **~ into** cadere in

laptop /ˈlæptɒp/ *n* **~ [computer]** computer *m inv* portabile, laptop *m inv*

lard /lɑːd/ *n* strutto *m*

larder /ˈlɑːdə(r)/ *n* dispensa *f*

large /lɑːdʒ/ *adj* grande; (number, amount) grande, grosso; **by and ~** in complesso; **at ~** in libertà; (*in general*) ampiamente. **~ly** *adv* ampiamente; **~ly because of** in gran parte a causa di

lark¹ /lɑ:k/ *n* (*bird*) allodola *f*

lark² *n* (*joke*) burla *f* ● **lark about** *vi* giocherellare

larva /'lɑ:və/ *n* (*pl* **-vae** /-vi:/) larva *f*

laser /'leɪzə(r)/ *n* laser *m inv*. **~ printer** *n* stampante *f* laser

lash /læʃ/ *n* frustata *f*; (*eyelash*) ciglio *m* ● *vt* (*whip*) frustare; (*tie*) legare fermamente. ▫ **~ out** *vi* attaccare; (*spend*) sperperare (**on** in)

lashings /'læʃɪŋz/ *npl* **~ of** 🅸 una marea di

lass /læs/ *n* ragazzina *f*

lasso /lə'su:/ *n* lazo *m*

last /lɑ:st/ *adj* (*final*) ultimo; (*recent*) scorso; **~ year** l'anno scorso; **~ night** ieri sera; **at ~** alla fine; **at ~!** finalmente!; **that's the ~ straw** 🅸 questa è l'ultima goccia ● *n* ultimo, -a *mf*; **the ~ but one** il penultimo ● *adv* per ultimo; (*last time*) l'ultima volta ● *vi* durare. **~ing** *adj* durevole. **~ly** *adv* infine

late /leɪt/ *adj* (*delayed*) in ritardo; (*at a late hour*) tardo; (*deceased*) defunto; **it's ~** (*at night*) è tardi; **in ~ November** alla fine di Novembre ● *adv* tardi; **stay up ~** stare alzati fino a tardi. **~comer** *n* ritardatario, -a *mf*; (*to political party etc*) nuovo, -a arrivato, -a *mf*. **~ly** *adv* recentemente. **~ness** *n* ora *f* tarda; (*delay*) ritardo *m*

latent /'leɪtnt/ *adj* latente

later /'leɪtə(r)/ *adj* (train) che parte più tardi; (edition) più recente ● *adv* più tardi; **~ on** più tardi, dopo

lateral /'lætərəl/ *adj* laterale

latest /'leɪtɪst/ *adj* ultimo; (*most recent*) più recente; **the ~ [news]** le ultime notizie ● *n* **six o'clock at the ~** alle sei al più tardi

lathe /leɪð/ *n* tornio *m*

lather /'lɑ:ðə(r)/ *n* schiuma *f* ● *vt* insaponare ● *vi* far schiuma

Latin /'lætɪn/ *adj* latino ● *n* latino *m*. **~ A'merica** *n* America *f* Latina. **~ A'merican** *adj & n* latino-americano, -a *mf*

latitude /'lætɪtju:d/ *n* (*Geog*) latitudine *f*; *fig* libertà *f* d'azione

latter /'lætə(r)/ *adj* ultimo ● *n* **the ~** quest'ultimo. **~ly** *adv* ultimamente

Latvia /'lætvɪə/ *n* Lettonia *f*. **~n** *adj & n* lettone *mf*

laugh /lɑ:f/ *n* risata *f* ● *vi* ridere (**at**/**about** di); **~ at sb** (*mock*) prendere in giro qcno. **~able** *adj* ridicolo. **~ingstock** *n* zimbello *m*

laughter /'lɑ:ftə(r)/ *n* risata *f*

launch¹ /lɔ:ntʃ/ *n* (*boat*) varo *m*

launch² *n* lancio *m*; (*of ship*) varo *m* ● *vt* lanciare (rocket, product); varare (ship); sferrare (attack)

launder /'lɔ:ndə(r)/ *vt* lavare e stirare; **~ money** *fig* riciclare denaro sporco. **~ette** *n* lavanderia *f* automatica

laundry /'lɔ:ndrɪ/ *n* lavanderia *f*; (*clothes*) bucato *m*

lava /'lɑ:və/ *n* lava *f*

lavatory /'lævətrɪ/ *n* gabinetto *m*

lavish /'lævɪʃ/ *adj* copioso; (*wasteful*) prodigo; **on a ~ scale** su vasta scala ● *vt* **~ sth on sb** ricoprire qcno di qcsa. **~ly** *adv* copiosamente

law /lɔ:/ *n* legge *f*; **study ~** studiare giurisprudenza, studiare legge; **~ and order** ordine *m* pubblico

lawcourt *n* tribunale *m*

lawn /lɔ:n/ *n* prato *m* [all'inglese]. **~-mower** *n* tosaerbe *m inv*

'law suit *n* causa *f*

lawyer /'lɔ:jə(r)/ *n* avvocato *m*

lax /læks/ *adj* negligente; (morals etc) lassista

laxative /'læksətɪv/ *n* lassativo *m*

lay¹ /leɪ/ *adj* laico; *fig* profano

lay² ▷LIE²

lay³ *vt* (*pt/pp* **laid**) porre, mettere; apparecchiare (table) ● *vi* (hen:) fare le uova. ▫ **~ down** *vt* posare; stabilire (rules, conditions). ▫ **~ off** *vt* licenziare (workers) ● *vi* (🅸: *stop*) **~ off!** smettila! **lay out** *vt* (*display, set forth*) esporre; (*plan*) pianificare (garden); (*spend*) sborsare; (*Typ*) impaginare

lay: ~about *n* fannullone, -a *mf*. **~-by** *n* corsia *f* di sosta

layer /'leɪə(r)/ *n* strato *m*

lay: ~man *n* profano *m*. **~out** *n* disposizione *f*; (*Typ*) impaginazione *f*, layout *m inv*

laze /leɪz/ *vi* **~ [about]** oziare

laziness /'leɪzɪnɪs/ *n* pigrizia *f*

lazy /ˈleɪzɪ/ *adj* (**-ier, -iest**) pigro. **~-bones** *n* poltrone, -a *mf*

lead¹ /led/ *n* piombo *m*; (*of pencil*) mina *f*

lead² /liːd/ *n* guida *f*; (*leash*) giunzaglio *m*; (*flex*) filo *m*; (*clue*) indizio *m*; (*Theat*) parte *f* principale; (*distance ahead*) distanza *f* (**over** su); **in the ~** in testa ● *v* (*pt/pp* **led**) ● *vt* condurre; dirigere (expedition, party etc); (*induce*) indurre; **~ the way** mettersi in testa ● *vi* (*be in front*) condurre; (*in race, competition*) essere in testa; (*at cards*) giocare (*per primo*). □ **~ away** *vt* portar via. □ **~ to** *vt* portare a. □ **~ up to** *vt* preludere; **what's this ~ing up to?** dove porta questo?

leader /ˈliːdə(r)/ *n* capo *m*; (*of orchestra*) primo violino *m*; (*in newspaper*) articolo *m* di fondo. **~ship** *n* direzione *f*, leadership *f inv*; **show ~ship** mostrare capacità di comando

leading /ˈliːdɪŋ/ *adj* principale; **~ lady/man** attrice *f*/attore *m* principale; **~ question** domanda *f* tendenziosa

leaf /liːf/ *n* (*pl* **leaves**) foglia *f*; (*of table*) asse *f* ● **leaf through** *vt* sfogliare. **~let** *n* dépliant *m inv*; (*advertising*) dépliant *m inv* pubblicitario; (*political*) manifestino *m*

league /liːg/ *n* lega *f*; (*Sport*) campionato *m*; **be in ~ with** essere in combutta con

leak /liːk/ *n* (*hole*) fessura *f*; (*Naut*) falla *f*; (*of gas & fig*) fuga *f* ● *vi* colare; (ship:) fare acqua; (liquid, gas:) fuoriuscire ● *vt* **~ sth to sb** *fig* far trapelare qcsa a qcno. **~y** *adj* che perde; (*Naut*) che fa acqua

lean¹ /liːn/ *adj* magro

lean² *v* (*pt/pp* **leaned** *or* **leant** /lent/) ● *vt* appoggiare (**against**/**on** contro/su) ● *vi* appoggiarsi (**against**/**on** contro/su); (*not be straight*) pendere; **be ~ing against** essere appoggiato contro; **~ on sb** (*depend on*) appoggiarsi a qcno; ([!]: *exert pressure on*) stare alle calcagne di qcno. □ **~ back** *vi* sporgersi indietro. □ **~ forward** *vi* piegarsi in avanti. □ **~ out** *vi* sporgersi. □ **~ over** *vi* piegarsi

leaning /ˈliːnɪŋ/ *adj* pendente; **the L~ Tower of Pisa** la torre di Pisa, la torre pendente ● *n* tendenza *f*

leap /liːp/ *n* salto *m* ● *vi* (*pt/pp* **leapt** /lept/ *or* **leaped**) saltare; **he leapt at it** [!] l'ha preso al volo. **~-frog** *n* cavallina *f*. **~ year** *n* anno *m* bisestile

learn /lɜːn/ *v* (*pt/pp* **learnt** *or* **learned**) ● *vt* imparare; **~ to swim** imparare a nuotare; **I have ~ed that...** (*heard*) sono venuto a sapere che... ● *vi* imparare

learn|ed /ˈlɜːnɪd/ *adj* colto. **~er** *n also* (*Auto*) principiante *mf*. **~ing** *n* cultura *f*. **~ing curve** *n* curva *f* d'apprendimento

lease /liːs/ *n* contratto *m* d'affitto; (*rental*) affitto *m* ● *vt* affittare

leash /liːʃ/ *n* guinzaglio *m*

least /liːst/ *adj* più piccolo; (amount) minore; **you've got ~ luggage** hai meno bagagli di tutti ● *n* **the ~** il meno; **at ~** almeno; **not in the ~** niente affatto ● *adv* meno; **the ~ expensive wine** il vino meno caro

leather /ˈleðə(r)/ *n* pelle *f*; (*of soles*) cuoio *m* ● *attrib* di pelle/cuoio. **~y** *adj* (meat, skin) duro

leave /liːv/ *n* (*holiday*) congedo *m*; (*Mil*) licenza *f*; **on ~** in congedo/licenza ● *v* (*pt/pp* **left**) ● *vt* lasciare; uscire da (house, office); (*forget*) dimenticare; **there is nothing left** non è rimasto niente ● *vi* andare via; (train, bus:) partire. □ **~ behind** *vt* lasciare; (*forget*) dimenticare. □ **~ out** *vt* omettere; (*not put away*) lasciare fuori

leaves /liːvz/ ▷LEAF

Leban|on /ˈlebənən/ *n* Libano *m* **~ese** /-ˈniːz/ *adj & n* libanese *mf*

lecture /ˈlektʃə(r)/ *n* conferenza *f*; (*Univ*) lezione *f*; (*reproof*) ramanzina *f* ● *vi* fare una conferenza (**on** su); (*Univ*) insegnare (**on sth** qcsa) ● *vt* **~ sb** rimproverare qcno. **~r** *n* conferenziere, -a *mf*; (*Univ*) docente *mf* universitario, -a

led /led/ ▷LEAD²

ledge /ledʒ/ *n* cornice *f*; (*of window*) davanzale *m*

leek /liːk/ *n* porro *m*

leer /lɪə(r)/ *n* sguardo *m* libidinoso ● *vi* **~ [at]** guardare in modo libidinoso

left¹ /left/ ▷LEAVE

left² *adj* sinistro ● *adv* a sinistra ● *n also* (*Pol*) sinistra *f*; **on the ~** a sinistra;

left: ~-'handed *adj* mancino. **~-'luggage office** *n* deposito *m* bagagli. **~overs** *npl* rimasugli *mpl*. **~-'wing** *adj* (*Pol*) di sinistra

leg /leg/ *n* gamba *f*; (*of animal*) zampa *f*; (*of journey*) tappa *f*; (*Culin: of chicken*) coscia *f*; (*: of lamb*) cosciotto *m*

legacy /ˈlegəsɪ/ *n* lascito *m*

legal /ˈliːgl/ *adj* legale; **take ~ action** intentare un'azione legale. **~ly** *adv* legalmente

legality /lɪˈgælətɪ/ *n* legalità *f*

legalize /ˈliːgəlaɪz/ *vt* legalizzare

legend /ˈledʒənd/ *n* leggenda *f*. **~ary** *adj* leggendario

legib|le /ˈledʒəbl/ *adj* leggibile. **~ly** *adv* in modo leggibile

legislat|e /ˈledʒɪsleɪt/ *vi* legiferare. **~ion** *n* legislazione *f*

legitima|te /lɪˈdʒɪtɪmət/ *adj* legittimo; (excuse) valido

leisure /ˈleʒə(r)/ *n* tempo *m* libero; **at your ~** con comodo. **~ly** *adj* senza fretta

lemon /ˈlemən/ *n* limone *m*. **~ade** *n* limonata *f*

lend /lend/ *vt* (*pt/pp* **lent**) prestare; **~ a hand** *fig* dare una mano. **~ing library** *n* biblioteca *f* per il prestito

length /leŋθ/ *n* lunghezza *f*; (*piece*) pezzo *m*; (*of wallpaper*) parte *f*; (*of visit*) durata *f*; **at ~** a lungo; (*at last*) alla fine

length|en /ˈleŋθən/ *vt* allungare ● *vi* allungarsi. **~ways** *adv* per lungo

lengthy /ˈleŋθɪ/ *adj* (**-ier, -iest**) lungo

lens /lenz/ *n* lente *f*; (*Phot*) obiettivo *m*; (*of eye*) cristallino *m*

lent /lent/ ▷**LEND**

Lent *n* Quaresima *f*

Leo /ˈliːəʊ/ *n* (*Astr*) Leone *m*

leopard /ˈlepəd/ *n* leopardo *m*

leotard /ˈliːətɑːd/ *n* body *m inv*

lesbian /ˈlezbɪən/ *adj* lesbico ● *n* lesbica *f*

less /les/ *adj* meno di; **~ and ~** sempre meno ● *adv & prep* meno ● *n* meno *m*

lessen /ˈlesn/ *vt/i* diminuire

lesson /ˈlesn/ *n* lezione *f*

lest /lest/ *conj liter* per timore che

let /let/ *vt* (*pt/pp* **let**, *pres p* **letting**) lasciare, permettere; (*rent*) affittare; **~ alone** (*not to mention*) tanto meno; **'to ~'** 'affittasi'; **~ us go** andiamo; **~ sb do sth** lasciare fare qcsa a qcno, permettere a qcno di fare qcsa; **~ me know** fammi sapere; **just ~ him try!** che ci provi solamente!; **~ oneself in for sth** [!] impelagarsi in qcsa. □ **~ down** *vt* sciogliersi (hair); abbassare (blinds); (*lengthen*) allungare; (*disappoint*) deludere; **don't ~ me down** conto su di te. □ **~ in** *vt* far entrare. □ **~ off** *vt* far partire; (*not punish*) perdonare; **~ sb off doing sth** abbonare qcsa a qcno. □ **~ out** *vt* far uscire; (*make larger*) allargare; emettere (scream, groan). □ **~ through** *vt* far passare. □ **~ up** *vi* [!] diminuire

'let-down *n* delusione *f*

lethal /ˈliːθl/ *adj* letale

letharg|ic /lɪˈθɑːdʒɪk/ *adj* apatico. **~y** *n* apatia *f*

letter /ˈletə(r)/ *n* lettera *f*. **~-box** *n* buca *f* per le lettere. **~-head** *n* carta *f* intestata. **~ing** *n* caratteri *mpl*

lettuce /ˈletɪs/ *n* lattuga *f*

'let-up *n* [!] pausa *f*

leukaemia /luːˈkiːmɪə/ *n* leucemia *f*

level /ˈlevl/ *adj* piano; (*in height, competition*) allo stesso livello; (spoonful) raso; **draw ~ with sb** affiancare qcno ● *n* livello *m*; **on the ~** [!] giusto ● *vt* (*pt/pp* **levelled**) livellare; (*aim*) puntare (**at** su)

level 'crossing *n* passaggio *m* a livello

lever /ˈliːvə(r)/ *n* leva *f* ● **lever up** *vt* sollevare (*con una leva*). **~age** *n* azione *f* di una leva; *fig* influenza *f*

levy /ˈlevɪ/ *vt* (*pt/pp* **levied**) imporre (tax)

lewd /ljuːd/ *adj* osceno

liabilit|y /laɪəˈbɪlətɪ/ *n* responsabilità *f*; ([!]: *burden*) peso *m*; **~ies** *pl* debiti *mpl*

liable /ˈlaɪəbl/ *adj* responsabile (**for** di); **be ~ to** (rain, break etc) rischiare di; (*tend to*) tendere a

liaise /lɪˈeɪz/ *vi* [!] essere in contatto

liaison /lɪˈeɪzɒn/ *n* contatti *mpl*; (*Mil*) collegamento *m*; (*affair*) relazione *f*

liar /ˈlaɪə(r)/ *n* bugiardo, -a *mf*

libel /ˈlaɪbl/ *n* diffamazione *f* ● *vt* (*pt/pp* **libelled**) diffamare. **~lous** *adj* diffamatorio

liberal /ˈlɪb(ə)rəl/ *adj* (*tolerant*) di larghe vedute; (*generous*) generoso. **L~** *adj* (*Pol*) liberale ● *n* liberale *mf*

liberat|e /ˈlɪbəreɪt/ *vt* liberare. **~ed** *adj* (woman) emancipata. **~ion** *n* liberazione *f*; (*of women*) emancipazione *f*. **~or** *n* liberatore, -trice *mf*

liberty /ˈlɪbətɪ/ *n* libertà *f*; **take the ~ of doing sth** prendersi la libertà di fare qcsa; **be at ~ to do sth** essere libero di fare qcsa

Libra /ˈliːbrə/ *n* (*Astr*) Bilancia *f*

librarian /laɪˈbreərɪən/ *n* bibliotecario, -a *mf*

library /ˈlaɪbrərɪ/ *n* biblioteca *f*

Libya /ˈlɪbɪə/ *n* Libia *f*. **~n** *adj & n* libico, -a *mf*

lice /laɪs/ ▷**LOUSE**

licence /ˈlaɪsns/ *n* licenza *f*; (*for* (*TV*)) canone *m* televisivo; (*for driving*) patente *f*; (*freedom*) sregolatezza *f*. **~-plate** *n* targa *f*

license /ˈlaɪsns/ *vt* autorizzare; **be ~d** (car:) avere il bollo; (restaurant:) essere autorizzato alla vendita di alcolici

lick /lɪk/ *n* leccata *f*; **a ~ of paint** una passata leggera di pittura ● *vt* leccare; ([!]: *defeat*) battere; leccarsi (lips)

lid /lɪd/ *n* coperchio *m*; (*of eye*) palpebra *f*

lie¹ /laɪ/ *n* bugia *f*; **tell a ~** mentire ● *vi* (*pt*/*pp* **lied**, *pres p* **lying**) mentire

lie² *vi* (*pt* **lay**, *pp* **lain**, *pres p* **lying**) (person:) sdraiarsi; (object:) stare; (*remain*) rimanere; **leave sth lying about** *or* **around** lasciare qcsa in giro. □ **~ down** *vi* sdraiarsi

lie-in *n* [!] **have a ~** restare a letto fino a tardi

lieutenant /lefˈtenənt/ *n* tenente *m*

life /laɪf/ *n* (*pl* **lives**) vita *f*

life: ~belt *n* salvagente *m*. **~-boat** *n* lancia *f* di salvataggio; (*on ship*) scialuppa *f* di salvataggio. **~buoy** *n* salvagente *m*. **~ coach** *n* life coach *m*/*f inv*. **~-guard** *n* bagnino *m*. **~-jacket** *n* giubbotto *m* di salvataggio. **~less** *adj* inanimato. **~like** *adj* realistico. **~long** *adj* di tutta la vita. **~-size[d]** *adj* in grandezza naturale. **~time** *n* vita *f*; **the chance of a ~time** un'occasione unica

lift /lɪft/ *n* ascensore *m*; (*Auto*) passaggio *m* ● *vt* sollevare; revocare (restrictions); ([!]: *steal*) rubare ● *vi* (fog:) alzarsi. □ **~ up** *vt* sollevare

ˈlift-off *n* decollo *m* (*di razzo*)

light¹ /laɪt/ *adj* (*not dark*) luminoso; **~ green** verde chiaro ● *n* luce *f*; (*lamp*) lampada *f*; **in the ~ of** *fig* alla luce di; **have you got a ~?** ha da accendere?; **come to ~** essere rivelato ● *vt* (*pt*/*pp* **lit** *or* **lighted**) accendere; (*illuminate*) illuminare. □ **~ up** *vi* (face:) illuminarsi

light² *adj* (*not heavy*) leggero ● *adv* **travel ~** viaggiare con poco bagaglio

ˈlight-bulb *n* lampadina *f*

lighten¹ /ˈlaɪtn/ *vt* illuminare

lighten² *vt* alleggerire (load)

lighter /ˈlaɪtə(r)/ *n* accendino *m*

light: ~-ˈhearted *adj* spensierato. **~house** *n* faro *m*. **~ly** *adv* leggermente; (accuse) con leggerezza; (*without concern*) senza dare importanza alla cosa; **get off ~ly** cavarsela a buon mercato

lightning /ˈlaɪtnɪŋ/ *n* lampo *m*, fulmine *m*. **~-conductor** *n* parafulmine *m*

lightweight *adj* leggero ● *n* (*in boxing*) peso *m* leggero

like¹ /laɪk/ *adj* simile ● *prep* come; **~ this/that** così; **what's he ~?** com'è? ● *conj* ([!]: *as*) come; (*Am: as if*) come se

like² *vt* piacere, gradire; **I should/would ~** vorrei, gradirei; **I ~ him** mi piace; **I ~ this car** mi piace questa macchina; **I ~ dancing** mi piace ballare; **I ~ that!** [!] questa mi è piaciuta! ● *n* **~s and dislikes** *pl* gusti *mpl*

like|able /ˈlaɪkəbl/ *adj* simpatico. **~lihood** *n* probabilità *f*. **~ly** *adj* (**-ier, -iest**) probabile ● *adv* probabilmente; **not ~ly!** [!] neanche per sogno!

liken /ˈlaɪkən/ *vt* paragonare (**to** a)

like|ness /ˈlaɪknɪs/ *n* somiglianza *f*. **ˈ~wise** *adv* lo stesso

liking /ˈlaɪkɪŋ/ *n* gusto *m*; **is it to your ~?** è di suo gusto?; **take a ~ to sb** prendere qcno in simpatia

lilac /ˈlaɪlək/ *n* lillà *m* ● *adj* color lillà

lily /ˈlɪlɪ/ *n* giglio *m*. **~ of the valley** *n* mughetto *m*

limb /lɪm/ *n* arto *m*

lime¹ /laɪm/ *n* (*fruit*) cedro *m*; (*tree*) tiglio *m*

lime² *n* calce *f*. **ˈ~light** *n* **be in the**

~light essere molto in vista. '**~stone** *n* calcare *m*

limit /ˈlɪmɪt/ *n* limite *m*; **that's the ~!** ⓘ questo è troppo! ● *vt* limitare (**to** a). **~ation** *n* limite *m*. **~ed** *adj* ristretto; **~ed company** società *f* anonima

limousine /ˈlɪməziːn/ *n* limousine *f inv*

limp¹ /lɪmp/ *n* andatura *f* zoppicante; **have a ~** zoppicare ● *vi* zoppicare

limp² *adj* floscio

line¹ /laɪn/ *n* linea *f*; (*length of rope, cord*) filo *m*; (*of writing*) riga *f*; (*of poem*) verso *m*; (*row*) fila *f*; (*wrinkle*) ruga *f*; (*of business*) settore *m*; (*Am: queue*) coda *f*; **in ~ with** in conformità con ● *vt* segnare; fiancheggiare (street). □ **~ up** *vi* allinearsi ● *vt* allineare

line² *vt* foderare (garment)

lined¹ /laɪnd/ *adj* (face) rugoso; (paper) a righe

lined² *adj* (garment) foderato

linen /ˈlɪnɪn/ *n* lino *m*; (*articles*) biancheria *f* ● *attrib* di lino

liner /ˈlaɪnə(r)/ *n* nave *f* di linea

linger /ˈlɪŋgə(r)/ *vi* indugiare

lingerie /ˈlæia.ʒərɪ/ *n* biancheria *f* intima (*da donna*)

linguist /ˈlɪŋgwɪst/ *n* linguista *mf*

linguistic /lɪŋˈgwɪstɪk/ *adj* linguistico. **~s** *n* linguistica *fsg*

lining /ˈlaɪnɪŋ/ *n* (*of garment*) fodera *f*; (*of brakes*) guarnizione *f*

link /lɪŋk/ *n* (*of chain*) anello *m*; *fig* legame *m* ● *vt* collegare. □ **~ up** *vi* unirsi (**with** a); (*TV*) collegarsi

lino /ˈlaɪnəʊ/ *n*, **linoleum** /lɪˈnəʊlɪəm/ *n* linoleum *m*

lint /lɪnt/ *n* garza *f*

lion /ˈlaɪən/ *n* leone *m*. **~ess** *n* leonessa *f*

lip /lɪp/ *n* labbro *m* (*pl* labbra *f*); (*edge*) bordo *m*

lip: ~-read *vi* leggere le labbra; **~-service** *n* **pay ~-service to** approvare soltanto a parole. **~salve** *n* burro *m* [di] cacao. **~stick** *n* rossetto *m*

liqueur /lɪˈkjʊə(r)/ *n* liquore *m*

liquid /ˈlɪkwɪd/ *n* liquido *m* ● *adj* liquido

liquidat|e /ˈlɪkwɪdeɪt/ *vt* liquidare. **~ion** *n* liquidazione *f*; (*Comm*) **go into ~ion** andare in liquidazione

liquidize /ˈlɪkwɪdaɪz/ *vt* rendere liquido. **~r** *n* (*Culin*) frullatore *m*

liquor /ˈlɪkə(r)/ *n* bevanda *f* alcoolica

liquorice /ˈlɪkərɪs/ *n* liquirizia *f*

liquor store *n Am* negozio *m* di alcolici

lisp /lɪsp/ *n* pronuncia *f* con la lisca ● *vi* parlare con la lisca

list¹ /lɪst/ *n* lista *f* ● *vt* elencare

list² *vi* (ship:) inclinarsi

listen /ˈlɪsn/ *vi* ascoltare; **~ to** ascoltare. **~er** *n* ascoltatore, -trice *mf*

listless /ˈlɪstlɪs/ *adj* svogliato

lit /lɪt/ ▷**LIGHT¹**

literacy /ˈlɪtərəsɪ/ *n* alfabetizzazione *f*

literal /ˈlɪtərəl/ *adj* letterale. **~ly** *adv* letteralmente

literary /ˈlɪtərərɪ/ *adj* letterario

literate /ˈlɪtərət/ *adj* **be ~** saper leggere e scrivere

literature /ˈlɪtrətʃə(r)/ *n* letteratura *f*

Lithuania /lɪθjʊˈeɪnɪə/ *n* Lituania *f*. **~n** *adj & n* lituano, -a *mf*

litre /ˈliːtə(r)/ *n* litro *m*

litter /ˈlɪtə(r)/ *n* immondizie *fpl*; (*Zool*) figliata *f* ● *vt* **be ~ed with** essere ingombrato di. **~-bin** *n* bidone *m* della spazzatura

little /ˈlɪtl/ *adj* piccolo; (*not much*) poco ● *adv & n* poco *m*; **a ~** un po'; **a ~ water** un po' d'acqua; **a ~ better** un po' meglio; **~ by ~** a poco a poco

live¹ /laɪv/ *adj* vivo; (ammunition) carico; **~ broadcast** trasmissione *f* in diretta; **be ~** (*Electr*) essere sotto tensione; **~ wire** *n fig* persona *f* dinamica ● *adv* (broadcast) in diretta

live² /lɪv/ *vi* vivere; (*reside*) abitare; **~ with** convivere con. □ **~ down** *vt* far dimenticare. □ **~ off** *vt* vivere alle spalle di. □ **~ on** *vt* vivere di ● *vi* sopravvivere. □ **~ up** *vt* **~ it up** far la bella vita. □ **~ up to** *vt* essere all'altezza di

liveli|hood /ˈlaɪvlɪhʊd/ *n* mezzi *mpl* di sostentamento. **~ness** *n* vivacità *f*

lively /ˈlaɪvlɪ/ *adj* (**-ier, -iest**) vivace

liver /ˈlɪvə(r)/ *n* fegato *m*

lives /laɪvz/ ▷**LIFE**

livestock /ˈlaɪv-/ *n* bestiame *m*

livid /ˈlɪvɪd/ *adj* ⓘ livido

living /ˈlɪvɪŋ/ *adj* vivo ● *n* **earn one's**

~ guadagnarsi da vivere; **the ~** *pl* i vivi. **~-room** *n* soggiorno *m*

lizard /ˈlɪzəd/ *n* lucertola *f*

load /ləʊd/ *n* carico *m*; **~s of** [!] un sacco di • *vt* caricare. **~ed** *adj* carico; ([!]: *rich*) ricchissimo

loaf[1] /ləʊf/ *n* (*pl* **loaves**) pagnotta *f*

loaf[2] *vi* oziare

loan /ləʊn/ *n* prestito *m*; **on ~** in prestito • *vt* prestare

loath|e /ləʊð/ *vt* detestare. **~ing** *n* disgusto *m*. **~some** *adj* disgustoso

lobby /ˈlɒbɪ/ *n* atrio *m*; (*Pol*) gruppo *m* di pressione, lobby *m inv*

lobster /ˈlɒbstə(r)/ *n* aragosta *f*

local /ˈləʊkl/ *adj* locale; **I'm not ~** non sono del posto • *n* abitante *mf* del luogo; ([!]: *public house*) pub *m* locale. **~ auˈthority** *n* autorità *f* locale. **~ call** *n* (*Teleph*) telefonata *f* urbana. **~ government** *n* autorità *f inv* locale

locality /ləʊˈkælətɪ/ *n* zona *f*

local|ization /ləʊklaɪˈzeɪʃn/ *n* localizzazione *f*. **~|ized** *adj* localizzato

locally /ˈləʊkəlɪ/ *adv* localmente; (live, work) nei paraggi

locat|e /ləʊˈkeɪt/ *vt* situare; trovare (person); **be ~ed** essere situato. **~ion** *n* posizione *f*; **filmed on ~ion** girato in esterni

lock[1] /lɒk/ *n* (*hair*) ciocca *f*

lock[2] *n* (*on door*) serratura *f*; (*on canal*) chiusa *f* • *vt* chiudere a chiave; bloccare (wheels) • *vi* chiudersi. □ **~ in** *vt* chiudere dentro. □ **~ out** *vt* chiudere fuori. □ **~ up** *vt* (*in prison*) mettere dentro • *vi* chiudere

locker /ˈlɒkə(r)/ *n* armadietto *m*

locket /ˈlɒkɪt/ *n* medaglione *m*

lock: ~-out *n* serrata *f*. **~smith** *n* fabbro *m*

locomotive /ləʊkəˈməʊtɪv/ *n* locomotiva *f*

lodge /lɒdʒ/ *n* (*porter's*) portineria *f*; (*masonic*) loggia *f* • *vt* presentare (claim, complaint); (*with bank, solicitor*) depositare; **be ~d** essersi conficcato • *vi* essere a pensione (**with** da); (*become fixed*) conficcarsi. **~r** *n* inquilino, -a *mf*

lodgings /ˈlɒdʒɪŋz/ *npl* camere *fpl* in affitto

loft /lɒft/ *n* soffitta *f*

lofty /ˈlɒftɪ/ *adj* (**-ier, -iest**) alto; (*haughty*) altezzoso

log /lɒg/ *n* ceppo *m*; (*Auto*) libretto *m* di circolazione; (*Naut*) giornale *m* di bordo • *vt* (*pt* **logged**) registrare. □ **~ on to** *vt* (*Comput*) connettersi a

logarithm /ˈlɒgərɪðm/ *n* logaritmo *m*

ˈlog-book *n* (*Naut*) giornale *m* di bordo; (*Auto*) libretto *m* di circolazione

loggerheads /ˈlɒgə-/ *npl* **be at ~** [!] essere in totale disaccordo

logic /ˈlɒdʒɪk/ *n* logica *f*. **~al** *adj* logico. **~ally** *adv* logicamente

logistics /ləˈdʒɪstɪks/ *npl* logistica *f*

logo /ˈləʊgəʊ/ *n* logo *m inv*

loin /lɔɪn/ *n* (*Culin*) lombata *f*

loiter /ˈlɔɪtə(r)/ *vi* gironzolare

loll|ipop /ˈlɒlɪpɒp/ *n* lecca-lecca *m inv*. **~y** *n* lecca-lecca *m*; ([!]: *money*) quattrini *mpl*

London /ˈlʌndən/ *n* Londra *f* • *attrib* londinese, di Londra. **~er** *n* londinese *mf*

lone /ləʊn/ *adj* solitario. **~liness** *n* solitudine *f*

lonely /ˈləʊnlɪ/ *adj* (**-ier, -iest**) solitario; (person) solo

lone|r /ˈləʊnə(r)/ *n* persona *f* solitaria. **~some** *adj* solo

long[1] /lɒŋ/ *adj* lungo; **a ~ time** molto tempo; **a ~ way** distante; **in the ~ run** a lungo andare; (*in the end*) alla fin fine • *adv* a lungo, lungamente; **how ~ is?** quanto è lungo?; (*in time*) quanto dura?; **all day ~** tutto il giorno; **not ~ ago** non molto tempo fa; **before ~** fra breve; **he's no ~er here** non è più qui; **as** *or* **so ~as** finché; (*provided that*) purché; **so ~!** [!] ciao!; **will you be ~?** [ti] ci vuole molto?

long[2] *vi* **~ for** desiderare ardentemente

long-ˈdistance *adj* a grande distanza; (*Sport*) di fondo; (*call*) interurbano

longing /ˈlɒŋɪŋ/ *adj* desideroso • *n* brama *f*. **~ly** *adv* con desiderio

longitude /ˈlɒŋgɪtju:d/ *n* (*Geog*) longitudine *f*

long: ~ jump *n* salto *m* in lungo. **~-range** *adj* (*Aeron, Mil*) a lunga portata; (forecast) a lungo termine. **~-sighted** *adj* presbite. **~-term** *adj* a lunga scadenza. **~-winded** /-ˈwɪndɪd/ *adj* prolisso

loo /luː/ *n* [!] gabinetto *m*

look /lʊk/ *n* occhiata *f*; (*appearance*) aspetto *m*; [**good**] **~s** *pl* bellezza *f*; **have a ~ at** dare un'occhiata a ● *vi* guardare; (*seem*) sembrare; **~ here!** mi ascolti bene!; **~ at** guardare; **~ for** cercare; **~ like** (*resemble*) assomigliare a. □ **~ after** *vt* badare a. □ **~ down** *vi* guardare in basso; **~ down on sb** *fig* guardare dall'alto in basso qcno. □ **~ forward to** *vt* essere impaziente di. □ **~ in on** *vt* passare da. □ **~ into** *vt* (*examine*) esaminare. □ **~ on to** *vt* (room:) dare su. □ **~ out** *vi* guardare fuori; (*take care*) fare attenzione; **~ out for** cercare; **~ out!** attento! **look round** *vi* girarsi; (*in shop, town etc*) dare un'occhiata. □ **~ through** *vt* dare un'occhiata a (script, notes). □ **~ up** *vi* guardare in alto; **~ up to sb** *fig* rispettare qcno ● *vt* cercare [nel dizionario] (word); (*visit*) andare a trovare

ˈlook-out *n* guardia *f*; (*prospect*) prospettiva *f*; **be on the ~ for** tenere gli occhi aperti per

loom /luːm/ *vi* apparire; *fig* profilarsi

loony /ˈluːnɪ/ *adj & n* [!] matto, -a *mf*. **~ bin** *n* manicomio *m*

loop /luːp/ *n* cappio *m*; (*on garment*) passante *m*. **~hole** *n* (*in the law*) scappatoia *f*

loose /luːs/ *adj* libero; (knot) allentato; (page) staccato; (clothes) largo; (morals) dissoluto; (*inexact*) vago; **be at a ~ end** non sapere cosa fare; **come ~** (knot:) sciogliersi; **set ~** liberare. **~ ˈchange** *n* spiccioli *mpl*. **~ly** *adv* scorrevolmente; (defined) vagamente

loosen /ˈluːsn/ *vt* sciogliere

loot /luːt/ *n* bottino *m* ● *vt/i* depredare. **~er** *n* predatore, -trice *mf*. **~ing** *n* saccheggio *m*

lop /lɒp/ **~ off** *vt* (*pt/pp* **lopped**) potare

lopˈsided *adj* sbilenco

lord /lɔːd/ *n* signore *m*; (*title*) Lord *m*; **House of L~s** Camera *f* dei Lords; **the L~'s Prayer** il Padrenostro; **good L~!** Dio mio!

lorry /ˈlɒrɪ/ *n* camion *m inv*; **~ driver** camionista *mf*

lose /luːz/ *v* (*pt/pp* **lost**) ● *vt* perdere ● *vi* perdere; (clock:) essere indietro; **get lost** perdersi; **get lost!** [!] va a quel paese! **~r** *n* perdente *mf*

loss /lɒs/ *n* perdita *f*; (*Comm*) **~es** perdite *fpl*; **be at a ~** essere perplesso; **be at a ~ for words** non trovare le parole

lost /lɒst/ ▷**LOSE** ● *adj* perduto. **~ ˈproperty office** *n* ufficio *m* oggetti smarriti

lot[1] /lɒt/ (*at auction*) lotto *m*; **draw ~s** tirare a sorte

lot[2] *n* **the ~** il tutto; **a ~ of, ~s of** molto/i; **the ~ of you** tutti voi; **it has changed a ~** è cambiato molto

lotion /ˈləʊʃn/ *n* lozione *f*

lottery /ˈlɒtərɪ/ *n* lotteria *f*. **~ ticket** *n* biglietto *m* della lotteria

loud /laʊd/ *adj* sonoro, alto; (colours) sgargiante ● *adv* forte; **out ~** ad alta voce. **~ ˈhailer** *n* megafono *m*. **~ly** *adv* forte. **~ ˈspeaker** *n* altoparlante *m*

lounge /laʊndʒ/ *n* salotto *m*; (*in hotel*) salone *m* ● *vi* poltrire. **~ suit** *n* vestito *m* da uomo, completo *m* da uomo

louse /laʊs/ *n* (*pl* **lice**) pidocchio *m*

lousy /ˈlaʊzɪ/ *adj* (**-ier, -iest**) [!] schifoso

lout /laʊt/ *n* zoticone *m*. **~ish** *adj* rozzo

lovable /ˈlʌvəbl/ *adj* adorabile

love /lʌv/ *n* amore *m*; (*Tennis*) zero *m*; **in ~** innamorato (**with** di) ● *vt* amare (person, country); **I ~ watching tennis** mi piace molto guardare il tennis. **~-affair** *n* relazione *f* [sentimentale]. **~ letter** *n* lettera *f* d'amore

lovely /ˈlʌvlɪ/ *adj* (**-ier, -iest**) bello; (*in looks*) bello, attraente; (*in character*) piacevole; (meal) delizioso; **have a ~ time** divertirsi molto

lover /ˈlʌvə(r)/ *n* amante *mf*

loving /ˈlʌvɪŋ/ *adj* affettuoso

low /ləʊ/ *adj* basso; (*depressed*) giù *inv* ● *adv* basso; **feel ~** sentirsi giù ● *n* minimo *m*; (*Meteorol*) depressione *f*; **at an all-time ~** (prices etc) al livello minimo

lower /ˈləʊə(r)/ *adj & adv* ▷**LOW** ● *vt* abbassare; **~ oneself** abbassarsi

loyal /ˈlɔɪəl/ *adj* leale. **~ty** *n* lealtà *f*; **~ card** carta *f* fedeltà

lozenge /ˈlɒzɪndʒ/ *n* losanga *f*; (*tablet*) pastiglia *f*

LP *n abbr* long-playing record
Ltd *abbr* (Limited) s.r.l.
lubricat|e /'lu:brɪkeɪt/ *vt* lubrificare. **~ion** *n* lubrificazione *f*
lucid /'lu:sɪd/ *adj* (explanation) chiaro; (*sane*) lucido. **~ity** *n* lucidità *f*; (*of explanation*) chiarezza *f*
luck /lʌk/ *n* fortuna *f*; **bad ~** sfortuna *f*; **good ~!** buona fortuna! **~ily** *adv* fortunatamente
lucky /'lʌkɪ/ *adj* (**-ier, -iest**) fortunato; **be ~** essere fortunato; (thing:) portare fortuna. **~ 'charm** *n* portafortuna *m inv*
lucrative /'lu:krətɪv/ *adj* lucrativo
ludicrous /'lu:dɪkrəs/ *adj* ridicolo. **~ly** *adv* (expensive, complex) eccessivamente
lug /lʌg/ *vt* (*pt/pp* **lugged**) [!] trascinare
luggage /'lʌgɪdʒ/ *n* bagaglio *m*; **~-rack** *n* portabagagli *m inv*. **~ trolley** *n* carrello *m* portabagagli. **~-van** *n* bagagliaio *m*
lukewarm /'lu:k-/ *adj* tiepido; *fig* poco entusiasta
lull /lʌl/ *n* pausa *f* ● *vt* **~ to sleep** cullare
lullaby /'lʌləbaɪ/ *n* ninna nanna *f*
lumber /'lʌmbə(r)/ *n* cianfrusaglie *fpl*; (*Am: timber*) legname *m* ● *vt* [!] **~ sb with sth** affibbiare qcsa a qcno. **~ jack** *n* tagliaboschi *m inv*
luminous /'lu:mɪnəs/ *adj* luminoso
lump¹ /lʌmp/ *n* (*of sugar*) zolletta *f*; (*swelling*) gonfiore *m*; (*in breast*) nodulo *m*; (*in sauce*) grumo *m* ● *vt* **~ together** ammucchiare
lump² *vt* **~ it** [!] **you'll just have to ~ it** che ti piaccia o no è così
lump sum *n* somma *f* globale
lumpy /'lʌmpɪ/ *adj* (**-ier, -iest**) grumoso
lunacy /'lu:nəsɪ/ *n* follia *f*
lunar /'lu:nə(r)/ *adj* lunare
lunatic /'lu:nətɪk/ *n* pazzo, -a *mf*
lunch /lʌntʃ/ *n* pranzo *m* ● *vi* pranzare
luncheon /'lʌntʃn/ *n* (*formal*) pranzo *m*. **~ meat** *n carne f in scatola*. **~ voucher** *n* buono *m* pasto
lung /lʌŋ/ *n* polmone *m*. **~ cancer** *n* cancro *m* al polmone
lunge /lʌndʒ/ *vi* lanciarsi (**at** su)
lurch¹ /lɜ:tʃ/ *n* **leave in the ~** [!] lasciare nei guai
lurch² *vi* barcollare
lure /lʊə(r)/ *n* esca *f*; *fig* lusinga *f* ● *vt* adescare
lurid /'lʊərɪd/ *adj* (*gaudy*) sgargiante; (*sensational*) sensazionalistico
lurk /lɜ:k/ *vi* appostarsi
luscious /'lʌʃəs/ *adj* saporito; *fig* sexy *inv*
lush /lʌʃ/ *adj* lussureggiante
lust /lʌst/ *n* lussuria *f* ● *vi* **~ after** desiderare [fortemente]. **~ful** *adj* lussurioso
lute /lu:t/ *n* liuto *m*
luxuriant /lʌg'ʒʊərɪənt/ *adj* lussureggiante
luxurious /lʌg'ʒʊərɪəs/ *adj* lussuoso
luxury /'lʌkʃərɪ/ *n* lusso *m* ● *attrib* di lusso
lying /'laɪɪŋ/ ▷LIE¹ & ² ● *n* mentire *m*
lynch /lɪntʃ/ *vt* linciare
lyric /'lɪrɪk/ *adj* lirico. **~al** *adj* lirico; ([!]: *enthusiastic*) entusiasta. **~s** *npl* parole *fpl*

Mm

mac /mæk/ *n* [!] impermeabile *m*
macaroni /mækə'rəʊnɪ/ *n* maccheroni *mpl*
mace¹ /meɪs/ *n* (*staff*) mazza *f*
mace² *n* (*spice*) macis *m o f*
machine /mə'ʃi:n/ *n* macchina *f* ● *vt* (*sew*) cucire a macchina; (*Techn*) lavorare a macchina. **~-gun** *n* mitragliatrice *f*
machinery /mə'ʃi:nərɪ/ *n* macchinario *m*
mackerel /'mækr(ə)l/ *n inv* sgombro *m*
mackintosh /'mækɪntɒʃ/ *n* impermeabile *m*
mad /mæd/ *adj* (**madder, maddest**) pazzo, matto; ([!]: *angry*) furioso (**at** con); **like ~** [!] come un pazzo; **be ~ about sb/sth** ([!]: *keen on*) andare matto per qcno/qcsa
madam /'mædəm/ *n* signora *f*

mad cow disease *n* morbo *m* della mucca pazza

madden /'mædən/ *vt* (*make angry*) far diventare matto

made /meɪd/ ▷**MAKE**; **~ to measure** [fatto] su misura

mad|ly /'mædlɪ/ *adv* [!] follemente; **~ly in love** innamorato follemente. **~man** *n* pazzo *m*. **~ness** *n* pazzia *f*

madonna /mə'dɒnə/ *n* madonna *f*

magazine /mægə'zi:n/ *n* rivista *f*; (*Mil, Phot*) magazzino *m*

maggot /'mægət/ *n* verme *m*

magic /'mædʒɪk/ *n* magia *f*; (*tricks*) giochi *mpl* di prestigio ● *adj* magico; (trick) di prestigio. **~al** *adj* magico

magician /mə'dʒɪʃn/ *n* mago, -a *mf*; (*entertainer*) prestigiatore, -trice *mf*

magistrate /'mædʒɪstreɪt/ *n* magistrato *m*

magnet /'mægnɪt/ *n* magnete *m*, calamita *f*. **~ic** *adj* magnetico. **~ism** *n* magnetismo *m*

magnification /mægnɪfɪ'keɪʃn/ *n* ingrandimento *m*

m

magnificen|ce /mæg'nɪfɪsəns/ *n* magnificenza *f*. **~t** *adj* magnifico

magnify /'mægnɪfaɪ/ *vt* (*pt/pp* **-ied**) ingrandire; (*exaggerate*) ingigantire. **~ing glass** *n* lente *f* d'ingrandimento

magnitude /'mægnɪtju:d/ *n* grandezza *f*; (*importance*) importanza *f*

magpie /'mægpaɪ/ *n* gazza *f*

mahogany /mə'hɒgənɪ/ *n* mogano *m* ● *attrib* di mogano

maid /meɪd/ *n* cameriera *f*; **old ~** *pej* zitella *f*

maiden /'meɪdn/ *n* (*liter*) fanciulla *f* ● *adj* (speech, voyage) inaugurale. **~ 'aunt** *n* zia *f* zitella. **~ name** *n* nome *m* da ragazza

mail /meɪl/ *n* posta *f* ● *vt* impostare. **~-bag** *n* sacco *m* postale. **~box** *n Am* cassetta *f* delle lettere; (*e-mail*) casella *f* di posta elettronica. **~ing list** *n* elenco *m* d'indirizzi per un mailing. **~man** *n Am* postino *m*. **~ order** *n* vendita *f* per corrispondenza. **~-order firm** *n* ditta *f* di vendita per corrispondenza. **~shot** *n* mailing *m inv*

maim /meɪm/ *vt* menomare

main[1] /meɪn/ *n* (*water, gas, electricity*) conduttura *f* principale

main[2] *adj* principale; **the ~ thing is to...** la cosa essenziale è di... ● *n* **in the ~** in complesso

main: ~land /-lənd/ *n* continente *m*. **~ly** *adv* principalmente. **~ street** *n* via *f* principale

maintain /meɪn'teɪn/ *vt* mantenere; (*keep in repair*) curare la manutenzione di; (*claim*) sostenere

maintenance /'meɪntənəns/ *n* mantenimento *m*; (*care*) manutenzione *f*; (*allowance*) alimenti *mpl*

maisonette /meɪzə'net/ *n* appartamento *m* a due piani

majestic /mə'dʒestɪk/ *adj* maestoso

majesty /'mædʒəstɪ/ *n* maestà *f*; **His/Her M~** Sua Maestà

major /'meɪdʒə(r)/ *adj* maggiore; **~ road** strada *f* con diritto di precedenza ● *n* (*Mil, Mus*) maggiore *m* ● *vi Am* **~ in** specializzarsi in

Majorca /mə'jɔ:kə/ *n* Maiorca *f*

majority /mə'dʒɒrətɪ/ *n* maggioranza *f*; **be in the ~** avere la maggioranza

make /meɪk/ *n* (*brand*) marca *f* ● *v* (*pt/pp* **made**) ● *vt* fare; (*earn*) guadagnare; rendere (happy, clear); prendere (decision); **~ sb laugh** far ridere qcno; **~ sb do sth** far fare qcsa a qcno; **~ it** (*to party, top of hill etc*) farcela; **what time do you ~ it?** che ore fai? ● *vi* **~ as if to** fare per. □ **~ do** *vi* arrangiarsi. □ **~ for** *vt* dirigersi verso. □ **~ off** *vi* fuggire. □ **~ out** *vt* (*distinguish*) distinguere; (*write out*) rilasciare (cheque); compilare (list); (*claim*) far credere. □ **~ over** *vt* cedere. □ **~ up** *vt* (*constitute*) comporre; (*complete*) completare; (*invent*) inventare; (*apply cosmetics to*) truccare; fare (parcel); **~ up one's mind** decidersi; **~ it up** (*after quarrel*) riconciliarsi ● *vi* (*after quarrel*) fare la pace; **~ up for** compensare; **~ up for lost time** recuperare il tempo perso

'make-believe *n* finzione *f*

maker /'meɪkə(r)/ *n* fabbricante *mf*; **M~** Creatore *m*

make: ~ shift *adj* di fortuna ● *n* espediente *m*. **~-up** *n* trucco *m*; (*character*) natura *f*

making /'meɪkɪŋ/ *n* **have the ~s of** aver la stoffa di

maladjust|ed /mælə'dʒʌstɪd/ *adj* disadattato

malaria /mə'leərɪə/ *n* malaria *f*
Malaysia /mə'leɪzɪə/ *n* Malesia *f*
male /meɪl/ *adj* maschile ● *n* maschio *m*. **~ nurse** *n* infermiere *m*
malfunction /mæl'fʌŋkʃn/ *n* funzionamento *m* imperfetto ● *vi* funzionare male
malice /'mælɪs/ *n* malignità *f*; **bear sb ~** voler del male a qcno
malicious /mə'lɪʃəs/ *adj* maligno
mallet /'mælɪt/ *n* martello *m* di legno
malnu'trition /mæl-/ *n* malnutrizione *f*
mal'practice *n* negligenza *f*
malt /mɔ:lt/ *n* malto *m*
Malta /'mɔ:ltə/ *n* Malta *f*. **~ese** *adj & n* maltese *mf*
mammal /'mæml/ *n* mammifero *m*
mammoth /'mæməθ/ *adj* mastodontico ● *n* mammut *m inv*
man /mæn/ *n* (*pl* **men**) uomo *m*; (*chess, draughts*) pedina *f* ● *vt* (*pt/pp* **manned**) equipaggiare; essere di servizio a (counter, telephones)
manage /'mænɪdʒ/ *vt* dirigere; gestire (shop, affairs); (*cope with*) farcela; **~ to do sth** riuscire a fare qcsa ● *vi* riuscire; (*cope*) farcela (**on** con). **~able** *adj* (hair) docile; (size) maneggevole. **~ment** *n* gestione *f*; **the ~ment** la direzione
manager /'mænɪdʒə(r)/ *n* direttore *m*; (*of shop, bar*) gestore *m*; (*Sport*) manager *m inv*. **~ess** *n* direttrice *f*. **~ial** *adj* **~ial staff** personale *m* direttivo
mandat|e /'mændeɪt/ *n* mandato *m*. **~ory** *adj* obbligatorio
mane /meɪn/ *n* criniera *f*
mangle /'mæŋgl/ *vt* (*damage*) maciullare
man: ~'handle *vt* malmenare. **~hole** *n* botola *f*. **~hood** *n* età *f* adulta; (*quality*) virilità *f*. **~-hour** *n* ora *f* lavorativa. **~-hunt** *n* caccia *f* all'uomo
man|ia /'meɪnɪə/ *n* mania *f*. **~iac** *n* maniaco, -a *mf*
manicure /'mænɪkjʊə(r)/ *n* manicure *f* ● *vt* fare la manicure a
manifest /'mænɪfest/ *adj* manifesto ● *vt* **~ itself** manifestarsi. **~ly** *adv* palesemente
manifesto /mænɪ'festəʊ/ *n* manifesto *m*
manipulat|e /mə'nɪpjuleɪt/ *vt* manipolare. **~ion** *n* manipolazione *f*
man'kind *n* genere *m* umano
manly /'mænlɪ/ *adj* virile
'man-made *adj* artificiale. **~ fibre** *n* fibra *f* sintetica
manner /'mænə(r)/ *n* maniera *f*; **in this ~** in questo modo; **have no ~s** avere dei pessimi modi; **good/bad ~s** buone/cattive maniere *fpl*. **~ism** *n* affettazione *f*
manor /'mænə(r)/ *n* maniero *m*
'manpower *n* manodopera *f*
mansion /'mænʃn/ *n* palazzo *m*
'manslaughter *n* omicidio *m* colposo
mantelpiece /'mæntl-/ *n* mensola *f* di caminetto
manual /'mænjʊəl/ *adj* manuale ● *n* manuale *m*
manufacture /mænjʊ'fæktʃə(r)/ *vt* fabbricare ● *n* manifattura *f*. **~r** *n* fabbricante *m*
manure /mə'njʊə(r)/ *n* concime *m*
manuscript /'mænjʊskrɪpt/ *n* manoscritto *m*
many /'menɪ/ *adj & pron* molti; **there are as ~ boys as girls** ci sono tanti ragazzi quante ragazze; **as ~ as 500** ben 500; **as ~ as that** così tanti; **as ~** altrettanti; **very ~, a good/great ~** moltissimi; **~ a time** molte volte
map /mæp/ *n* carta *f* geografica; (*of town*) mappa *f* ● **map out** *vt* (*pt/pp* **mapped**) *fig* programmare
mar /mɑ:(r)/ *vt* (*pt/pp* **marred**) rovinare
marathon /'mærəθən/ *n* maratona *f*
marble /'mɑ:bl/ *n* marmo *m*; (*for game*) pallina *f* ● *attrib* di marmo
march *n* marcia *f*; (*protest*) dimostrazione *f* ● *vi* marciare ● *vt* far marciare; **~ sb off** scortare qcno fuori
March /mɑ:tʃ/ *n* marzo *m*
mare /meə(r)/ *n* giumenta *f*
margarine /mɑ:dʒə'ri:n/ *n* margarina *f*
margin /'mɑ:dʒɪn/ *n* margine *m*. **~al** *adj* marginale. **~ally** *adv* marginalmente
marijuana /mærʊ'wɑ:nə/ *n* marijuana *f*
marina /mə'ri:nə/ *n* porticciolo *m*
marine /mə'ri:n/ *adj* marino ● *n* (*sailor*)

soldato *m* di fanteria marina
marionette /mærɪə'net/ *n* marionetta *f*
mark¹ /mɑ:k/ *n* (*currency*) marco *m*
mark² *n* (*stain*) macchia *f*; (*sign, indication*) segno *m*; (*Sch*) voto *m* ● *vt* segnare; (*stain*) macchiare; (*Sch*) correggere; (*Sport*) marcare; **~ time** (*Mil*) segnare il passo; *fig* non far progressi; **~ my words** ricordati quello che dico. □ **~ out** *vt* delimitare; *fig* designare
marked /mɑ:kt/ *adj* marcato. **~ly** *adv* notevolmente
marker /'mɑ:kə(r)/ *n* (*for highlighting*) evidenziatore *m*; (*Sport*) marcatore *m*; (*of exam*) esaminatore, -trice *mf*
market /'mɑ:kɪt/ *n* mercato *m* ● *vt* vendere al mercato; (*launch*) commercializzare; **on the ~** sul mercato. **~ing** *n* marketing *m*. **~ re'search** *n* ricerca *f* di mercato
marksman /'mɑ:ksmən/ *n* tiratore *m* scelto
marmalade /'mɑ:məleɪd/ *n* marmellata *f* d'arance

m

maroon /mə'ru:n/ *adj* marrone rossastro
marquee /mɑ:'ki:/ *n* tendone *m*
marriage /'mærɪdʒ/ *n* matrimonio *m*
married /'mærɪd/ *adj* sposato; (life) coniugale
marrow /'mærəʊ/ *n* (*Anat*) midollo *m*; (*vegetable*) zucca *f*
marr|y /'mærɪ/ *vt* (*pt/pp* **married**) sposare; **get ~ied** sposarsi ● *vi* sposarsi
marsh /mɑ:ʃ/ *n* palude *f*
marshal /'mɑ:ʃl/ *n* (*steward*) cerimoniere *m* ● *vt* (*pt/pp* **marshalled**) *fig* organizzare (arguments)
marshy /'mɑ:ʃɪ/ *adj* paludoso
martial /'mɑ:ʃl/ *adj* marziale
martyr /'mɑ:tə(r)/ *n* martire *mf* ● *vt* martoriare. **~dom** *n* martirio *m*. **~ed** *adj* [!] da martire
marvel /'mɑ:vl/ *n* meraviglia *f* ● *vi* (*pt/pp* **marvelled**) meravigliarsi (**at** di). **~lous** *adj* meraviglioso
Marxis|m /'mɑ:ksɪzm/ *n* marxismo *m*. **~t** *adj & n* marxista *mf*
marzipan /'mɑ:zɪpæn/ *n* marzapane *m*
mascara /mæ'skɑ:rə/ *n* mascara *m inv*
mascot /'mæskət/ *n* mascotte *f inv*
masculin|e /'mæskjʊlɪn/ *adj* maschile ● *n* (*Gram*) maschile *m*. **~ity** *n* mascolinità *f*
mash /mæʃ/ *vt* impastare. **~ed potatoes** *npl* purè *m inv* di patate
mask /mɑ:sk/ *n* maschera *f* ● *vt* mascherare
masochis|m /'mæsəkɪzm/ *n* masochismo *m*. **~t** *n* masochista *mf*
mason /'meɪsn/ *n* muratore *m*
Mason *n* massone *m*. **~ic** *adj* massonico
masonry /'meɪsnrɪ/ *n* massoneria *f*
masquerade /mæskə'reɪd/ *n fig* mascherata *f* ● *vi* **~ as** (*pose*) farsi passare per
mass¹ /mæs/ *n* (*Relig*) messa *f*
mass² *n* massa *f*; **~es of** [!] un sacco di ● *vi* ammassarsi
massacre /'mæsəkə(r)/ *n* massacro *m* ● *vt* massacrare
massage /'mæsɑ:ʒ/ *n* massaggio *m* ● *vt* massaggiare; *fig* manipolare (statistics)
masseu|r /mæ'sɜ:(r)/ *n* massaggiatore *m*. **~se** *n* massaggiatrice *f*
massive /'mæsɪv/ *adj* enorme
mass: ~ media *npl* mezzi *mpl* di comunicazione di massa, mass media *mpl*. **~-pro'duce** *vt* produrre in serie
mast /mɑ:st/ *n* (*Naut*) albero *m*; (*for radio*) antenna *f*
master /'mɑ:stə(r)/ *n* maestro *m*, padrone *m*; (*teacher*) professore *m*; (*of ship*) capitano *m*; **M~** (*boy*) signorino *m*
master: ~-key *n* passe-partout *m inv*. **~-mind** *n* cervello *m* ● *vt* ideare e dirigere. **~piece** *n* capolavoro *m*. **~-stroke** *n* colpo *m* da maestro. **~y** *n* (*of subject*) padronanza *f*
masturbat|e /'mæstəbeɪt/ *vi* masturbarsi. **~ion** *n* masturbazione *f*
mat /mæt/ *n* stuoia *f*; (*on table*) sottopiatto *m*
match¹ /mætʃ/ *n* (*Sport*) partita *f*; (*equal*) uguale *mf*; (*marriage*) matrimonio *m*; (*person to marry*) partito *m*; **be a good ~** (colours:) intonarsi bene; **be no ~ for** non essere dello stesso livello di ● *vt* (*equal*) uguagliare; (*be like*) andare bene con ● *vi* intonarsi
match² *n* fiammifero *m*. **~box** *n* scatola *f* di fiammiferi

matching /ˈmætʃɪŋ/ *adj* intonato

mate[1] /meɪt/ *n* compagno, -a *mf*; (*assistant*) aiuto *m*; (*Naut*) secondo *m*; ([!]: *friend*) amico, -a *mf* ● *vi* accoppiarsi ● *vt* accoppiare

mate[2] *n* (*in chess*) scacco *m* matto

material /məˈtɪərɪəl/ *n* materiale *m*; (*fabric*) stoffa *f*; **raw ~s** materie *fpl* prime ● *adj* materiale

maternal /məˈtɜːnl/ *adj* materno

maternity /məˈtɜːnətɪ/ *n* maternità *f*. **~ clothes** *npl* abiti *mpl* premaman. **~ ward** *n* maternità *f inv*

mathematic|al /mæθəˈmætɪkl/ *adj* matematico. **~ian** *n* matematico, -a *mf*

mathematics /mæθˈmætɪks/ *n* matematica *fsg*

maths /mæθs/ *n* [!] matematica *fsg*

matinée /ˈmætɪneɪ/ *n* (*Theat*) matinée *m*

matriculat|e /məˈtrɪkjʊleɪt/ *vi* immatricolarsi. **~ion** *n* immatricolazione *f*

matrix /ˈmeɪtrɪks/ *n* (*pl* **matrices** /-siːz/) *n* matrice *f*

matted /ˈmætɪd/ *adj* **~ hair** capelli *mpl* tutti appiccicati tra loro

matter /ˈmætə(r)/ *n* (*affair*) faccenda *f*; (*question*) questione *f*; (*pus*) pus *m*; (*phys: substance*) materia *f*; **as a ~ of fact** a dire la verità; **what is the ~?** che cosa c'è? ● *vi* importare; **~ to sb** essere importante per qcno; **it doesn't ~** non importa. **~-of-fact** *adj* pratico

mattress /ˈmætrɪs/ *n* materasso *m*

matur|e /məˈtʃʊə(r)/ *adj* maturo; (*Comm*) in scadenza ● *vi* maturare ● *vt* far maturare. **~ity** *n* maturità *f*; (*Fin*) maturazione *f*

maul /mɔːl/ *vt* malmenare

mauve /məʊv/ *adj* malva

maxim /ˈmæksɪm/ *n* massima *f*

maximum /ˈmæksɪməm/ *adj* massimo; **ten minutes ~** dieci minuti al massimo ● *n* (*pl* **-ima**) massimo *m*

may /meɪ/ *v aux* (*solo al presente*) potere; **~ I come in?** posso entrare?; **if I ~ say so** se mi posso permettere; **~ you both be very happy** siate felici; **I ~ as well stay** potrei anche rimanere; **it ~ be true** potrebbe esser vero; **she ~ be old, but...** sarà anche vecchia, ma...

May /meɪ/ *n* maggio *m*

maybe /ˈmeɪbiː/ *adv* forse, può darsi

ˈMay Day *n* il primo maggio

mayonnaise /meɪəˈneɪz/ *n* maionese *f*

mayor /ˈmeə(r)/ *n* sindaco *m*. **~ess** *n* sindaco *m*; (*wife of mayor*) moglie *f* del sindaco

maze /meɪz/ *n* labirinto *m*

me /miː/ *pron* (*object*) mi; (*with preposition*) me; **she called me** mi ha chiamato; **she called me, not you** ha chiamato me, non te; **give me the money** dammi i soldi; **give it to me** dammelo; **he gave it to me** me lo ha dato; **it's ~** sono io

meadow /ˈmedəʊ/ *n* prato *m*

meagre /ˈmiːgə(r)/ *adj* scarso

meal[1] /miːl/ *n* pasto *m*

meal[2] *n* (*grain*) farina *f*

mean[1] /miːn/ *adj* avaro; (*unkind*) meschino

mean[2] *adj* medio ● *n* (*average*) media *f*; **Greenwich ~ time** ora *f* media di Greenwich

mean[3] *vt* (*pt/pp* **meant**) voler dire; (*signify*) significare; (*intend*) intendere; **I ~ it** lo dico seriamente; **~ well** avere buone intenzioni; **be meant for** (present:) essere destinato a; (remark:) essere riferito a

meander /mɪˈændə(r)/ *vi* vagare

meaning /ˈmiːnɪŋ/ *n* significato *m*. **~ful** *adj* significativo. **~less** *adj* senza senso

means /miːnz/ *n* mezzo *m*; **~ of transport** mezzo *m* di trasporto; **by ~ of** per mezzo di; **by all ~!** certamente!; **by no ~** niente affatto ● *npl* (*resources*) mezzi *mpl*

meant /ment/ ▷**MEAN**[3]

ˈmeantime *n* **in the ~** nel frattempo ● *adv* intanto

ˈmeanwhile *adv* intanto

measles /ˈmiːzlz/ *n* morbillo *m*

measly /ˈmiːzlɪ/ *adj* [!] misero

measure /ˈmeʒə(r)/ *n* misura *f* ● *vt/i* misurare. □ **~ up to** *vt fig* essere all'altezza di. **~d** *adj* misurato. **~ment** *n* misura *f*

meat /miːt/ *n* carne *f*. **~ ball** *n* (*Culin*) polpetta *f* di carne. **~ loaf** *n* polpettone *m*

mechan|ic /mɪ'kænɪk/ *n* meccanico *m*. **~ical** *adj* meccanico; **~ical engineering** ingegneria *f* meccanica. **~ically** *adv* meccanicamente. **~ics** *n* meccanica *f* ● *npl* meccanismo *msg*

mechan|ism /'mekənɪzm/ *n* meccanismo *m*. **~ize** *vt* meccanizzare

medal /'medl/ *n* medaglia *f*

medallist /'medəlɪst/ *n* vincitore, -trice *mf* di una medaglia

meddle /'medl/ *vi* immischiarsi (**in** di); (*tinker*) armeggiare (**with** con)

media /'mi:dɪə/ ▷**MEDIUM** ● *npl* **the ~** i mass media

mediat|e /'mi:dɪeɪt/ *vi* fare da mediatore. **~ion** *n* mediazione *f*. **~or** *n* mediatore, -trice *mf*

medical /'medɪkl/ *adj* medico ● *n* visita *f* medica. **~ insurance** *n* assicurazione *f* sanitaria. **~ student** *n* studente, -essa *mf* di medicina

medicat|ed /'medɪkeɪtɪd/ *adj* medicato. **~ion** *n* (*drugs*) medicinali *mpl*

medicinal /mɪ'dɪsɪnl/ *adj* medicinale

medicine /'medsən/ *n* medicina *f*

m

medieval /medɪ'i:vl/ *adj* medievale

mediocr|e /mi:dɪ'əʊkə(r)/ *adj* mediocre. **~ity** *n* mediocrità *f*

meditat|e /'medɪteɪt/ *vi* meditare (**on** su). **~ion** *n* meditazione *f*

Mediterranean /medɪtə'reɪnɪən/ *n* **the ~ [Sea]** il [mare *m*] Mediterraneo *m* ● *adj* mediterraneo

medium /'mi:dɪəm/ *adj* medio; (*Culin*) di media cottura ● *n* (*pl* **media**) mezzo *m*; (*pl* **-s**) (*person*) medium *mf inv*

medium-sized *adj* di taglia media

medley /'medlɪ/ *n* miscuglio *m*; (*Mus*) miscellanea *f*

meek /mi:k/ *adj* mite, mansueto. **~ly** *adv* docilmente

meet /mi:t/ *v* (*pt/pp* **met**) ● *vt* incontrare; (*at station, airport*) andare incontro a; (*for first time*) far la conoscenza di; pagare (bill); soddisfare (requirements) ● *vi* incontrarsi; (committee:) riunirsi; **~ with** incontrare (problem); incontrarsi con (person) ● *n* raduno *m* [sportivo]

meeting /'mi:tɪŋ/ *n* riunione *f*, meeting *m inv*; (*large*) assemblea *f*; (*by chance*) incontro *m*

megabyte /'megəbaɪt/ *n* megabyte *m*

megaphone /'megəfəʊn/ *n* megafono *m*

melancholy /'melənkəlɪ/ *adj* malinconico ● *n* malinconia *f*

mellow /'meləʊ/ *adj* (wine) generoso; (sound, colour) caldo; (person) dolce ● *vi* (person:) addolcirsi

melodrama /'melə-/ *n* melodramma *m*. **~tic** *adj* melodrammatico

melody /'melədɪ/ *n* melodia *f*

melon /'melən/ *n* melone *m*

melt /melt/ *vt* sciogliere ● *vi* sciogliersi. □ **~ down** *vt* fondere. **~ing-pot** *n fig* crogiuolo *m*

member /'membə(r)/ *n* membro *m*; **~ countries** paesi *mpl* membri; **M~ of Parliament** deputato, -a *mf*; **M~ of the European Parliament** eurodeputato, -a *mf*. **~ship** *n* iscrizione *f*; (*members*) soci *mpl*

membrane /'membreɪn/ *n* membrana *f*

memo /'meməʊ/ *n* promemoria *m inv*

memorable /'memərəbl/ *adj* memorabile

memorandum /memə'rændəm/ *n* promemoria *m inv*

memorial /mɪ'mɔ:rɪəl/ *n* monumento *m*. **~ service** *n* funzione *f* commemorativa

memorize /'meməraɪz/ *vt* memorizzare

memory /'memərɪ/ *n also* (*Comput*) memoria *f*; (*thing remembered*) ricordo *m*; **from ~** a memoria; **in ~ of** in ricordo di

men /men/ ▷**MAN**

menac|e /'menəs/ *n* minaccia *f*; (*nuisance*) piaga *f* ● *vt* minacciare. **~ing** *adj* minaccioso

mend /mend/ *vt* riparare; (*darn*) rammendare ● *n* **on the ~** in via di guarigione

'menfolk *n* uomini *mpl*

menial /'mi:nɪəl/ *adj* umile

meningitis /menɪn'dʒaɪtɪs/ *n* meningite *f*

menopause /'menə-/ *n* menopausa *f*

menstruat|e /'menstrʊeɪt/ *vi* mestruare. **~ion** *n* mestruazione *f*

mental /'mentl/ *adj* mentale; (**!**: *mad*) pazzo. **~ a'rithmetic** *n* calcolo *m* mentale. **~ 'illness** *n* malattia *f* mentale

mental|ity /men'tæləti/ *n* mentalità *f inv*. **~ly** *adv* mentalmente; **~ly ill** malato di mente

mention /'menʃn/ *n* menzione *f* ● *vt* menzionare; **don't ~ it** non c'è di che

menu /'menju:/ *n* menu *m inv*

MEP *n abbr* Member of the European Parliament

mercenary /'mɜ:sɪnərɪ/ *adj* mercenario ● *n* mercenario *m*

merchandise /'mɜ:tʃəndaɪz/ *n* merce *f*

merchant /'mɜ:tʃənt/ *n* commerciante *mf*. **~ bank** *n* banca *f* d'affari. **~ 'navy** *n* marina *f* mercantile

merci|ful /'mɜ:sɪfl/ *adj* misericordioso. **~fully** *adv* [!] grazie a Dio. **~less** *adj* spietato

mercury /'mɜ:kjʊrɪ/ *n* mercurio *m*

mercy /'mɜ:sɪ/ *n* misericordia *f*; **be at sb's ~** essere alla mercè di qcno, essere in balia di qcno

mere /mɪə(r)/ *adj* solo. **~ly** *adv* solamente

merge /mɜ:dʒ/ *vi* fondersi

merger /'mɜ:dʒə(r)/ *n* fusione *f*

meringue /mə'ræŋ/ *n* meringa *f*

merit /'merɪt/ *n* merito *m*; (*advantage*) qualità *f inv* ● *vt* meritare

mermaid /'mɜ:meɪd/ *n* sirena *f*

merri|ly /'merɪlɪ/ *adv* allegramente. **~ment** *n* baldoria *f*

merry /'merɪ/ *adj* (**-ier, -iest**) allegro; **~ Christmas!** Buon Natale!

merry: ~-go-round *n* giostra *f*. **~-making** *n* festa *f*

mesh /meʃ/ *n* maglia *f*

mesmerize /'mezməraɪz/ *vt* ipnotizzare. **~d** *adj fig* ipnotizzato

mess /mes/ *n* disordine *m*, casino *m* [!]; (*trouble*) guaio *m*; (*something spilt*) sporco *m*; (*Mil*) mensa *f*; **make a ~ of** (*botch*) fare un pasticcio di ● **mess about** *vi* perder tempo; **~ about with** armeggiare con ● *vt* prendere in giro (*person*). □ **~ up** *vt* mettere in disordine, incasinare [!]; (*botch*) mandare all'aria

message /'mesɪdʒ/ *n* messaggio *m*

messenger /'mesɪndʒə(r)/ *n* messaggero *m*

Messiah /mɪ'saɪə/ *n* Messia *m*

Messrs /'mesəz/ *npl* (*on letter*) **~ Smith** Spett. ditta Smith

messy /'mesɪ/ *adj* (**-ier, -iest**) disordinato; (*in dress*) sciatto

met /met/ ▹**MEET**

metal /'metl/ *n* metallo *m* ● *adj* di metallo. **~lic** *adj* metallico

metaphor /'metəfə(r)/ *n* metafora *f*. **~ical** *adj* metaforico

meteor /'mi:tɪə(r)/ *n* meteora *f*. **~ic** *adj fig* fulmineo

meteorological /mi:tɪərə'lɒdʒɪkl/ *adj* meteorologico

meteo|rologist /mi:tɪə'rɒlədʒɪst/ *n* meteorologo, -a *mf*. **~rology** *n* meteorologia *f*

meter[1] /'mi:tə(r)/ *n* contatore *m*

meter[2] *n Am* = **metre**

method /'meθəd/ *n* metodo *m*

methodical /mɪ'θɒdɪkl/ *adj* metodico. **~ly** *adv* metodicamente

methylated /'meθɪleɪtɪd/ *adj* **~ spirit[s]** alcol *m* denaturato

meticulous /mɪ'tɪkjʊləs/ *adj* meticoloso. **~ly** *adv* meticolosamente

metre /'mi:tə(r)/ *n* metro *m*

metric /'metrɪk/ *adj* metrico

metropolis /mɪ'trɒpəlɪs/ *n* metropoli *f inv*

mew /mju:/ *n* miao *m* ● *vi* miagolare

Mexican /'meksɪkən/ *adj & n* messicano, -a *mf*. **'Mexico** *n* Messico *m*

miaow /mɪ'aʊ/ *n* miao *m* ● *vi* miagolare

mice /maɪs/ ▹**MOUSE**

mickey /'mɪkɪ/ *n* **take the ~ out of** prendere in giro

micro /'maɪkrəʊ/: **~chip** *n* microchip *m*. **~computer** *n* microcomputer *m*. **~film** *n* microfilm *m*. **~phone** microfono *m*. **~processor** *n* microprocessore *m*. **~scope** *n* microscopio *m*. **~scopic** *adj* microscopico. **~wave** *n* microonda *f*; (*oven*) forno *m* a microonde

microbe /'maɪkrəʊb/ *n* microbo *m*

mid /mɪd/ *adj* **~ May** metà maggio; **in ~ air** a mezz'aria

midday /mɪd'deɪ/ *n* mezzogiorno *m*

middle /'mɪdl/ *adj* di centro; **the M~ Ages** il medioevo; **the ~ class[es]** la classe media; **the M~ East** il Medio Oriente ● *n* mezzo *m*; **in the ~ of** (room, floor etc) in mezzo a; **in the ~**

m

of the night nel pieno della notte, a notte piena

middle: ~-aged *adj* di mezza età. **~-class** *adj* borghese. **~man** *n* (*Comm*) intermediario *m*

middling /ˈmɪdlɪŋ/ *adj* discreto

midge /mɪdʒ/ *n* moscerino *m*

midget /ˈmɪdʒɪt/ *n* nano, -a *mf*

Midlands /ˈmɪdləndz/ *npl* **the ~** l'Inghilterra *fsg* centrale

ˈmidnight *n* mezzanotte *f*

midriff /ˈmɪdrɪf/ *n* diaframma *m*

midst /mɪdst/ *n* **in the ~ of** in mezzo a; **in our ~** fra di noi, in mezzo a noi

mid: ~summer *n* mezza estate *f* **~way** *adv* a metà strada. **~wife** *n* ostetrica *f*. **~ˈwinter** *n* pieno inverno *m*

might¹ /maɪt/ *v aux* **I ~** potrei; **will you come? - I ~** vieni? - può darsi; **it ~ be true** potrebbe essere vero; **I ~ as well stay** potrei anche restare; **you ~ have drowned** avresti potuto affogare; **you ~ have said so!** avresti potuto dirlo!

m

might² *n* potere *m*

mighty /ˈmaɪtɪ/ *adj* (**-ier, -iest**) potente • *adv* [!] molto

migraine /ˈmiːgreɪn/ *n* emicrania *f*

migrant /ˈmaɪgrənt/ *adj* migratore • *n* (*bird*) migratore, -trice *mf*; (*person: for work*) emigrante *mf*

migrat|e /maɪˈgreɪt/ *vi* migrare. **~ion** *n* migrazione *f*

Milan /mɪˈlæn/ *n* Milano *f*

mild /maɪld/ *adj* (weather) mite; (person) dolce; (flavour) delicato; (illness) leggero

mildew /ˈmɪldjuː/ *n* muffa *f*

mild|ly /ˈmaɪldlɪ/ *adv* moderatamente; (say) dolcemente; **to put it ~ly** a dir poco, senza esagerazione. **~ness** *n* (*of person, words*) dolcezza *f*; (*of weather*) mitezza *f*

mile /maɪl/ *n* miglio *m* (= *1,6 km*); **~s nicer** [!] molto più bello

mile|age /-ɪdʒ/ *n* chilometraggio *m*. **~stone** *n* pietra *f* miliare

militant /ˈmɪlɪtənt/ *adj & n* militante *mf*

military /ˈmɪlɪtrɪ/ *adj* militare. **~ service** *n* servizio *m* militare

militia /mɪˈlɪʃə/ *n* milizia *f*

milk /mɪlk/ *n* latte *m* • *vt* mungere

milk: ~man *n* lattaio *m*. **~ shake** *n* frappé *m inv*

milky /ˈmɪlkɪ/ *adj* (**-ier, -iest**) latteo; (tea etc) con molto latte. **M~ Way** *n* (*Astr*) Via *f* Lattea

mill /mɪl/ *n* mulino *m*; (*factory*) fabbrica *f*; (*for coffee etc*) macinino *m* • *vt* macinare (grain). **mill about, mill around** *vi* brulicare

millennium /mɪˈlenɪəm/ *n* millennio *m*

miller /ˈmɪlə(r)/ *n* mugnaio *m*

million /ˈmɪljən/ *n* milione *m*; **a ~ pounds** un milione di sterline. **~aire** *n* miliardario, -a *mf*

ˈmillstone *n fig* peso *m*

mime /maɪm/ *n* mimo *m* • *vt* mimare

mimic /ˈmɪmɪk/ *n* imitatore, -trice *mf* • *vt* (*pt/pp* **mimicked**) imitare. **~ry** *n* mimetismo *m*

mince /mɪns/ *n* carne *f* tritata • *vt* (*Culin*) tritare; **not ~ one's words** parlare senza mezzi termini

mince ˈpie *n pasticcino m a base di frutta secca*

mincer /ˈmɪnsə(r)/ *n* tritacarne *m inv*

mind /maɪnd/ *n* mente *f*; (*sanity*) ragione *f*; **to my ~** a mio parere; **give sb a piece of one's ~** dire chiaro e tondo a qcno quello che si pensa; **make up one's ~** decidersi; **have sth in ~** avere qcsa in mente; **bear sth in ~** tenere presente qcsa; **have something on one's ~** essere preoccupato; **have a good ~ to** avere una grande voglia di; **I have changed my ~** ho cambiato idea; **in two ~s** indeciso; **are you out of your ~?** sei diventato matto? • *vt* (*look after*) occuparsi di; **I don't ~ the noise** il rumore non mi dà fastidio; **I don't ~ what we do** non mi importa quello che facciamo; **~ the step!** attenzione al gradino! • *vi* **I don't ~** non mi importa; **never ~!** non importa!; **do you ~ if...?** ti dispiace se...? **mind out** *vi* **~ out!** [fai] attenzione!

mind|ful *adj* **~ful of** attento a. **~less** *adj* noncurante

mine¹ /maɪn/ *poss pron* il mio *m*, la mia *f*, i miei *mpl*, le mie *fpl*; **a friend of ~** un mio amico; **friends of ~** dei miei amici; **that is ~** questo è mio; (*as opposed to yours*) questo è il mio

mine² *n* miniera *f*; (*explosive*) mina *f* ● *vt* estrarre; (*Mil*) minare. **~ detector** *n* rivelatore *m* di mine. **~field** *n* campo *m* minato

mineral /'mɪnərəl/ *n* minerale *m* ● *adj* minerale. **~ water** *n* acqua *f* minerale

mingle /'mɪŋgl/ *vi* **~ with** mescolarsi a

mini /'mɪnɪ/ *n* (*skirt*) mini *f*

miniature /'mɪnɪtʃə(r)/ *adj* in miniatura ● *n* miniatura *f*

mini|bus /'mɪnɪ-/ *n* minibus *m*, pulmino *m*. **~cab** *n* taxi *m inv*

minim|al /'mɪnɪməl/ *adj* minimo. **~ize** *vt* minimizzare. **~um** *n* (*pl* **-ima**) minimo *m* ● *adj* minimo; **ten minutes ~um** minimo dieci minuti

mining /'maɪnɪŋ/ *n* estrazione *f* ● *adj* estrattivo

miniskirt /'mɪnɪ-/ *n* minigonna *f*

minist|er /'mɪnɪstə(r)/ *n* ministro *m*; (*Relig*) pastore *m*. **~erial** *adj* ministeriale

ministry /'mɪnɪstrɪ/ *n* (*Pol*) ministero *m*; **the ~** (*Relig*) il ministero sacerdotale

mink /mɪŋk/ *n* visone *m*

minor /'maɪnə(r)/ *adj* minore ● *n* minorenne *mf*

minority /maɪ'nɒrətɪ/ *n* minoranza *f*; (*age*) minore età *f*

mint¹ /mɪnt/ *n* [!] patrimonio *m* ● *adj* **in ~ condition** in condizione perfetta

mint² *n* (*herb*) menta *f*

minus /'maɪnəs/ *prep* meno; ([!]: *without*) senza ● *n* **~ [sign]** meno *m*

minute¹ /'mɪnɪt/ *n* minuto *m*; **in a ~** (*shortly*) in un minuto; **~s** *pl* (*of meeting*) verbale *msg*

minute² /maɪ'nju:t/ *adj* minuto; (*precise*) minuzioso

mirac|le /'mɪrəkl/ *n* miracolo *m*. **~ulous** *adj* miracoloso

mirage /'mɪrɑ:ʒ/ *n* miraggio *m*

mirror /'mɪrə(r)/ *n* specchio *m* ● *vt* rispecchiare

mirth /mɜ:θ/ *n* ilarità *f*

misappre'hension *n* malinteso *m*; **be under a ~** avere frainteso

misbe'have *vi* comportarsi male

mis'calcu|late *vt/i* calcolare male. **~'lation** *n* calcolo *m* sbagliato

'miscarriage *n* aborto *m* spontaneo; **~ of justice** errore *m* giudiziario. **mis'carry** *vi* abortire

miscellaneous /mɪsə'leɪnɪəs/ *adj* assortito

mischief /'mɪstʃɪf/ *n* malefatta *f*; (*harm*) danno *m*

mischievous /'mɪstʃɪvəs/ *adj* (*naughty*) birichino; (*malicious*) dannoso

miscon'ception *n* concetto *m* erroneo

mis'conduct *n* cattiva condotta *f*

misde'meanour *n* reato *m*

miser /'maɪzə(r)/ *n* avaro *m*

miserabl|e /'mɪzrəbl/ *adj* (*unhappy*) infelice; (*wretched*) miserabile; (fig: weather) deprimente. **~y** *adv* (live, fail) miseramente; (say) tristemente

miserly /'maɪzəlɪ/ *adj* avaro; (amount) ridicolo

misery /'mɪzərɪ/ *n* miseria *f*; ([!]: *person*) piagnone, -a *mf*

mis'fire *vi* (gun:) far cilecca; (plan etc:) non riuscire

'misfit *n* disadattato, -a *mf*

mis'fortune *n* sfortuna *f*

mis'guided *adj* fuorviato

mishap /'mɪshæp/ *n* disavventura *f*

misin'terpret *vt* fraintendere

mis'judge *vt* giudicar male; (*estimate wrongly*) valutare male

mis'lay *vt* (*pt/pp* **-laid**) smarrire

mis'lead *vt* (*pt/pp* **-led**) fuorviare. **~ing** *adj* fuorviante

mis'manage *vt* amministrare male. **~ment** *n* cattiva amministrazione *f*

'misprint *n* errore *m* di stampa

miss /mɪs/ *n* colpo *m* mancato ● *vt* (*fail to hit or find*) mancare; perdere (train, bus, class); (*feel the loss of*) sentire la mancanza di; **I ~ed that part** (*failed to notice*) mi è sfuggita quella parte ● *vi* **but he ~ed** (*failed to hit*) ma l'ha mancato. □ **~ out** *vt* saltare, omettere

Miss *n* (*pl* **-es**) signorina *f*

misshapen /mɪs'ʃeɪpən/ *adj* malformato

missile /'mɪsaɪl/ *n* missile *m*

missing /'mɪsɪŋ/ *adj* mancante; (person) scomparso; (*Mil*) disperso; **be ~** essere introvabile

mission /'mɪʃn/ *n* missione *f*

m

missionary /ˈmɪʃənrɪ/ *n* missionario, -a *mf*
mist /mɪst/ *n* (*fog*) foschia *f* ● **mist up** *vi* appannarsi, annebbiarsi
mistake /mɪˈsteɪk/ *n* sbaglio *m*; **by ~** per sbaglio ● *vt* (*pt* **mistook**, *pp* **mistaken**) sbagliare (road, house); fraintendere (meaning, words); **~ for** prendere per
mistaken /mɪˈsteɪkən/ *adj* sbagliato; **be ~** sbagliarsi; **~ identity** errore *m* di persona. **~ly** *adv* erroneamente
mistletoe /ˈmɪsltəʊ/ *n* vischio *m*
mistress /ˈmɪstrɪs/ *n* padrona *f*; (*teacher*) maestra *f*; (*lover*) amante *f*
misˈtrust *n* sfiducia *f* ● *vt* non aver fiducia in
misty /ˈmɪstɪ/ *adj* (**-ier, -iest**) nebbioso
misunderˈstand *vt* (*pt/pp* **-stood**) fraintendere. **~ing** *n* malinteso *m*
misuse¹ /mɪsˈjuːz/ *vt* usare male
misuse² /mɪsˈjuːs/ *n* cattivo uso *m*
mite /maɪt/ *n* (*child*) piccino, -a *mf*
mitten /ˈmɪtn/ *n* manopola *f*, muffola *m*

m

mix /mɪks/ *n* (*combination*) mescolanza *f*; (*Culin*) miscuglio *m*; (*ready-made*) preparato *m* ● *vt* mischiare ● *vi* mischiarsi; (person:) inserirsi; **~ with** (*associate with*) frequentare. □ **~ up** *vt* mescolare (papers); (*confuse, mistake for*) confondere
mixed /mɪkst/ *adj* misto; **~ up** (person) confuso
mixer /ˈmɪksə(r)/ *n* (*Culin*) frullatore *m*, mixer *m inv*; **he's a good ~** è un tipo socievole
mixture /ˈmɪkstʃə(r)/ *n* mescolanza *f*; (*medicine*) sciroppo *m*; (*Culin*) miscela *f*
ˈmix-up *n* (*confusion*) confusione *f*; (*mistake*) pasticcio *m*
moan /məʊn/ *n* lamento *m* ● *vi* lamentarsi; (*complain*) lagnarsi
moat /məʊt/ *n* fossato *m*
mob /mɒb/ *n* folla *f*; (*rabble*) gentaglia *f*; ([!]*: gang*) banda *f* ● *vt* (*pt/pp* **mobbed**) assalire
mobile /ˈməʊbaɪl/ *adj* mobile ● *n* composizione *f* mobile. **~ ˈhome** *n* casa *f* roulotte. **~ [phone]** *n* [telefono *m*] cellulare *m*, telefonino *m*
mock /mɒk/ *adj* finto ● *vt* canzonare. **~ery** *n* derisione *f*
model /ˈmɒdl/ *n* modello *m*; **[fashion] ~** indossatore, -trice *mf*, modello, -a *mf* ● *adj* (yacht, plane) in miniatura; (pupil, husband) esemplare, modello ● *v* (*pt/pp* **modelled**) ● *vt* indossare (clothes) ● *vi* fare l'indossatore, -trice *mf*; (*for artist*) posare
modem /ˈməʊdem/ *n* modem *m inv*
moderate¹ /ˈmɒdəreɪt/ *vt* moderare ● *vi* moderarsi
moderate² /ˈmɒdərət/ *adj* moderato ● *n* (*Pol*) moderato, -a *mf*. **~ly** *adv* (drink, speak etc) moderatamente; (good, bad etc) relativamente
moderation /mɒdəˈreɪʃn/ *n* moderazione *f*; **in ~** con moderazione
modern /ˈmɒdn/ *adj* moderno. **~ize** *vt* modernizzare
modest /ˈmɒdɪst/ *adj* modesto. **~y** *n* modestia *f*
modif|ication /mɒdɪfɪˈkeɪʃn/ *n* modificazione *f*. **~y** *vt* (*pt/pp* **-fied**) modificare
module /ˈmɒdjuːl/ *n* modulo *m*
moist /mɔɪst/ *adj* umido
moisten /ˈmɔɪsn/ *vt* inumidire
moistur|e /ˈmɔɪstʃə(r)/ *n* umidità *f*. **~izer** *n* [crema *f*] idratante *m*
mole¹ /məʊl/ *n* (*on face etc*) neo *m*
mole² *n* (*Zool*) talpa *f*
molecule /ˈmɒlɪkjuːl/ *n* molecola *f*
molest /məˈlest/ *vt* molestare
mollycoddle /ˈmɒlɪkɒdl/ *vt* tenere nella bambagia
molten /ˈməʊltən/ *adj* fuso
mom /mɒm/ *n Am* [!] mamma *f*
moment /ˈməʊmənt/ *n* momento *m*; **at the ~** in questo momento. **~arily** *adv* momentaneamente. **~ary** *adj* momentaneo
momentous /məˈmentəs/ *adj* molto importante
momentum /məˈmentəm/ *n* impeto *m*
monarch /ˈmɒnək/ *n* monarca *m*. **~y** *n* monarchia *f*
monast|ery /ˈmɒnəstrɪ/ *n* monastero *m*. **~ic** *adj* monastico
Monday /ˈmʌndeɪ/ *n* lunedì *m inv*
money /ˈmʌnɪ/ *n* denaro *m*
money-box *n* salvadanaio *m*
mongrel /ˈmʌŋgrəl/ *n* bastardo *m*

monitor /'mɒnɪtə(r)/ *n* (*Techn*) monitor *m inv* ● *vt* controllare
monk /mʌŋk/ *n* monaco *m*
monkey /'mʌŋkɪ/ *n* scimmia *f*. **~-nut** *n* nocciolina *f* americana. **~-wrench** *n* chiave *f* inglese a rullino
mono /'mɒnəʊ/ *n* mono *m*
monologue /'mɒnəlɒg/ *n* monologo *m*
monopol|ize /mə'nɒpəlaɪz/ *vt* monopolizzare. **~y** *n* monopolio *m*
monotone /'mɒnətəʊn/ *n* **speak in a ~** parlare con tono monotono
monoton|ous /mə'nɒtənəs/ *adj* monotono. **~y** *n* monotonia *f*
monsoon /mɒn'su:n/ *n* monsone *m*
monster /'mɒnstə(r)/ *n* mostro *m*
monstrous /'mɒnstrəs/ *adj* mostruoso
Montenegro /'mɒntɪ'ni:grəʊ/ *n* Montenegro *m*
month /mʌnθ/ *n* mese *m*. **~ly** *adj* mensile ● *adv* mensilmente ● *n* (*periodical*) mensile *m*
monument /'mɒnjʊmənt/ *n* monumento *m*. **~al** *adj fig* monumentale
moo /mu:/ *n* muggito *m* ● *vi* (*pt/pp* **mooed**) muggire
mood /mu:d/ *n* umore *m*; **be in a good/bad ~** essere di buon/cattivo umore; **be in the ~ for** essere in vena di
moody /'mu:dɪ/ *adj* (**-ier, -iest**) (*variable*) lunatico; (*bad-tempered*) di malumore
moon /mu:n/ *n* luna *f*; **over the ~** [!] al settimo cielo
moon: ~light *n* chiaro *m* di luna ● *vi* [!] lavorare in nero. **~lit** *adj* illuminato dalla luna
moor[1] /mʊə(r)/ *n* brughiera *f*
moor[2] *vt* (*Naut*) ormeggiare
mop /mɒp/ *n* straccio *m* (*per i pavimenti*); **~ of hair** zazzera *f* ● *vt* (*pt/pp* **mopped**) lavare con lo straccio. □ **~ up** *vt* (*dry*) asciugare con lo straccio; (*clean*) pulire con lo straccio
mope /məʊp/ *vi* essere depresso
moped /'məʊped/ *n* ciclomotore *m*
moral /'mɒrəl/ *adj* morale ● *n* morale *f*. **~ly** *adv* moralmente. **~s** *pl* moralità *f*
morale /mə'rɑ:l/ *n* morale *m*
morality /mə'rælətɪ/ *n* moralità *f*
more /mɔ:(r)/ *adj* più; **a few ~ books** un po' più di libri; **some ~ tea?** ancora un po' di tè?; **there's no ~ bread** non c'è più pane; **there are no ~ apples** non ci sono più mele; **one ~ word and...** ancora una parola e... ● *pron* di più; **would you like some ~?** ne vuoi ancora?; **no ~, thank you** non ne voglio più, grazie ● *adv* più; **~ interesting** più interessante; **~ and ~ quickly** sempre più veloce; **~ than** più di; **I don't love him any ~** non lo amo più; **once ~** ancora una volta; **~ or less** più o meno; **the ~ I see him, the ~ I like him** più lo vedo, più mi piace
moreover /mɔ:r'əʊvə(r)/ *adv* inoltre
morgue /mɔ:g/ *n* obitorio *m*
morning /'mɔ:nɪŋ/ *n* mattino *m*, mattina *f*; **in the ~** del mattino; (*tomorrow*) domani mattina
Morocc|o /mə'rɒkəʊ/ *n* Marocco *m* ● *adj* **~an** *adj & n* marocchino, -a *mf*
moron /'mɔ:rɒn/ *n* [!] deficiente *mf*
morose /mə'rəʊs/ *adj* scontroso
Morse /mɔ:s/ *n* **~ [code]** [codice *m*] Morse *m*
morsel /'mɔ:sl/ *n* (*food*) boccone *m*
mortal /'mɔ:tl/ *adj & n* mortale *mf*. **~ity** *n* mortalità *f*. **~ly** *adv* (wounded, offended) a morte; (afraid) da morire
mortar /'mɔ:tə(r)/ *n* mortaio *m*
mortgage /'mɔ:gɪdʒ/ *n* mutuo *m*; (*on property*) ipoteca *f* ● *vt* ipotecare
mortuary /'mɔ:tjʊərɪ/ *n* camera *f* mortuaria
mosaic /məʊ'zeɪɪk/ *n* mosaico *m*
Moslem /'mʊzlɪm/ *adj & n* musulmano, -a *mf*
mosque /mɒsk/ *n* moschea *f*
mosquito /mɒs'ki:təʊ/ *n* (*pl* **-es**) zanzara *f*
moss /mɒs/ *n* muschio *m*. **~y** *adj* muschioso
most /məʊst/ *adj* (*majority*) la maggior parte di; **for the ~ part** per lo più ● *adv* più, maggiormente; (*very*) estremamente, molto; **the ~ interesting day** la giornata più interessante; **a ~ interesting day** una giornata estremamente interessante; **the ~ beautiful woman in the world** la donna più bella del mondo; **~ unlikely** veramente improbabile ● *pron* **~ of them**

m

la maggior parte di loro; **at** [**the**] **~** al massimo; **make the ~ of** sfruttare al massimo; **~ of the time** la maggior parte del tempo. **~ly** *adv* per lo più

MOT *n* revisione *f* obbligatoria di autoveicoli

motel /məʊ'tel/ *n* motel *m inv*

moth /mɒθ/ *n* falena *f*; [**clothes-**] **~** tarma *f*

mother /'mʌðə(r)/ *n* madre *f*; **M~'s Day** la festa della mamma ● *vt* fare da madre a

mother: ~-in-law *n* (*pl* **~s-in-law**) suocera *f*. **~ly** *adj* materno. **~-of-pearl** *n* madreperla *f*. **~-to-be** *n* futura mamma *f*. **~ tongue** *n* madrelingua *f*

motif /məʊ'ti:f/ *n* motivo *m*

motion /'məʊʃn/ *n* moto *m*; (*proposal*) mozione *f*; (*gesture*) gesto *m* ● *vt/i* **~** [**to**] **sb to come in** fare segno a qcno di entrare. **~less** *adj* immobile. **~lessly** *adv* senza alcun movimento

motivat|e /'məʊtɪveɪt/ *vt* motivare. **~ion** *n* motivazione *f*

m

motive /'məʊtɪv/ *n* motivo *m*

motley /'mɒtlɪ/ *adj* disparato

motor /'məʊtə(r)/ *n* motore *m*; (*car*) macchina *f* ● *adj* a motore; (*Anat*) motore ● *vi* andare in macchina

motor: ~ bike *n* 🄸 moto *f inv*. **~ boat** *n* motoscafo *m*. **~ car** *n* automobile *f*. **~ cycle** *n* motocicletta *f*. **~-cyclist** *n* motociclista *mf*. **~ing** *n* automobilismo *m*. **~ist** *n* automobilista *mf*. **~way** *n* autostrada *f*

motto /'mɒtəʊ/ *n* (*pl* **-es**) motto *m*

mould¹ /məʊld/ *n* (*fungus*) muffa *f*

mould² *n* stampo *m* ● *vt* foggiare; *fig* formare. **~ing** *n* (*Archit*) cornice *f*

mouldy /'məʊldɪ/ *adj* ammuffito; (🄸: *worthless*) ridicolo

moult /məʊlt/ *vi* (bird:) fare la muta; (animal:) perdere il pelo

mound /maʊnd/ *n* mucchio *m*; (*hill*) collinetta *f*

mount /maʊnt/ *n* (*horse*) cavalcatura *f*; (*of jewel, photo, picture*) montatura *f* ● *vt* montare a (horse); salire su (bicycle); incastonare (jewel); incorniciare (photo, picture) ● *vi* aumentare. □ **~ up** *vi* aumentare

mountain /'maʊntɪn/ *n* montagna *f*; **~ bike** *n* mountain bike *f inv*

mountaineer /maʊntɪ'nɪə(r)/ *n* alpinista *mf*. **~ing** *n* alpinismo *m*

mountainous /'maʊntɪnəs/ *adj* montagnoso

mourn /mɔ:n/ *vt* lamentare ● *vi* **~ for** piangere la morte di. **~er** *n* persona *f* che participa a un funerale. **~ful** *adj* triste. **~ing** *n* **in ~ing** in lutto

mouse /maʊs/ *n* (*pl* **mice**) topo *m*; (*Comput*) mouse *m inv*. **~trap** *n* trappola *f* [per topi]

mousse /mu:s/ *n* (*Culin*) mousse *f inv*

moustache /mə'stɑ:ʃ/ *n* baffi *mpl*

mouth¹ /maʊð/ *vt* **~ sth** dire qcsa silenziosamente muovendo solamente le labbra

mouth² /maʊθ/ *n* bocca *f*; (*of river*) foce *f*

mouth: ~ful *n* boccone *m*. **~-organ** *n* armonica *f* [a bocca]. **~wash** *n* acqua *f* dentifricia

move /mu:v/ *n* mossa *f*; (*moving house*) trasloco *m*; **on the ~** in movimento; **get a ~ on** 🄸 darsi una mossa ● *vt* muovere; (*emotionally*) commuovere; spostare (car, furniture); (*transfer*) trasferire; (*propose*) proporre; **~ house** traslocare ● *vi* muoversi; (*move house*) traslocare. □ **~ along** *vi* andare avanti ● *vt* muovere in avanti. □ **~ away** *vi* allontanarsi; (*move house*) trasferirsi ● *vt* allontanare. □ **~ forward** *vi* avanzare ● *vt* spostare avanti. □ **~ in** *vi* (*to a house*) trasferirsi. □ **~ off** *vi* (vehicle:) muoversi. □ **~ out** *vi* (*of house*) andare via. □ **~ over** *vi* spostarsi ● *vt* spostare. □ **~ up** *vi* muoversi; (*advance, increase*) avanzare

movement /'mu:vmənt/ *n* movimento *m*

movie /'mu:vɪ/ *n* film *m inv*; **go to the ~s** andare al cinema

moving /'mu:vɪŋ/ *adj* mobile; (*touching*) commovente

mow /məʊ/ *vt* (*pt* **mowed**, *pp* **mown** *or* **mowed**) tagliare (lawn). □ **~ down** *vt* (*destroy*) sterminare

mower /'məʊə(r)/ *n* tosaerbe *m inv*

MP *n abbr* Member of Parliament

Mr /'mɪstə(r)/ *n* (*pl* **Messrs**) Signor *m*

Mrs /'mɪsɪz/ *n* Signora *f*

Ms /mɪz/ *n* Signora *f* (*modo m formale di*

rivolgersi ad una donna quando non si vuole connotarla come sposata o nubile)

much /mʌtʃ/ *adj, adv & pron* molto; **~ as** per quanto; **I love you just as ~ as before/him** ti amo quanto prima/lui; **as ~ as £5 million** ben cinque milioni di sterline; **as ~ as that** così tanto; **very ~** tantissimo, moltissimo; **~ the same** quasi uguale

muck /mʌk/ *n* (*dirt*) sporcizia *f*; (*farming*) letame *m*; ([!]: *filth*) porcheria *f*. □ **~ about** *vi* [!] perder tempo; **~ about with** trafficare con. □ **~ up** *vt* [!] rovinare; (*make dirty*) sporcare

mud /mʌd/ *n* fango *m*

muddle /'mʌdl/ *n* disordine *m*; (*mix-up*) confusione *f* ● *vt* **~ [up]** confondere (dates)

muddy /'mʌdɪ/ *adj* (**-ier, -iest**) (path) fangoso; (shoes) infangato

muesli /'mu:zlɪ/ *n* muesli *m inv*

muffle /'mʌfl/ *vt* smorzare (sound). **muffle up** *vt* (*for warmth*) imbacuccare

muffler /'mʌflə(r)/ *n* sciarpa *f*; *Am* (*Auto*) marmitta *f*

mug¹ /mʌg/ *n* tazza *f*; (*for beer*) boccale *m*; ([!]: *face*) muso *m*; ([!]: *simpleton*) pollo *m*

mug² *vt* (*pt/pp* **mugged**) aggredire e derubare. **~ger** *n* assalitore, -trice *mf*. **~ging** *n* aggressione *f* per furto

muggy /'mʌgɪ/ *adj* (**-ier, -iest**) afoso

mule /mju:l/ *n* mulo *m*

mull /mʌl/ *vt* **~ over** rimuginare su

multiple /'mʌltɪpl/ *adj* multiplo

multiplication /mʌltɪplɪ'keɪʃn/ *n* moltiplicazione *f*

multiply /'mʌltɪplaɪ/ *v* (*pt/pp* **-ied**) ● *vt* moltiplicare (**by** per) ● *vi* moltiplicarsi

mum¹ /mʌm/ *adj* **keep ~** [!] non aprire bocca

mum² *n* [!] mamma *f*

mumble /'mʌmbl/ *vt/i* borbottare

mummy¹ /'mʌmɪ/ *n* [!] mamma *f*

mummy² *n* (*Archaeol*) mummia *f*

mumps /mʌmps/ *n* orecchioni *mpl*

munch /mʌntʃ/ *vt/i* sgranocchiare

mundane /mʌn'deɪn/ *adj* (*everyday*) banale

municipal /mjʊ'nɪsɪpl/ *adj* municipale

mural /'mjʊərəl/ *n* dipinto *m* murale

murder /'mɜ:də(r)/ *n* assassinio *m* ● *vt* assassinare; ([!]: *ruin*) massacrare. **~er** *n* assassino, -a *mf*. **~ous** *adj* omicida

murky /'mɜ:kɪ/ *adj* (**-ier, -iest**) oscuro

murmur /'mɜ:mə(r)/ *n* mormorio *m* ● *vt/i* mormorare

muscle /'mʌsl/ *n* muscolo *m* ● **muscle in** *vi* [✖] intromettersi (**on** in)

muscular /'mʌskjʊlə(r)/ *adj* muscolare; (*strong*) muscoloso

muse /mju:z/ *vi* meditare (**on** su)

museum /mju:'zɪəm/ *n* museo *m*

mushroom /'mʌʃrʊm/ *n* fungo *m* ● *vi fig* spuntare come funghi

music /'mju:zɪk/ *n* musica *f*; (*written*) spartito *m*.

musical /'mju:zɪkl/ *adj* musicale; (person) dotato di senso musicale ● *n* commedia *f* musicale. **~ box** *n* carillon *m inv*. **~ instrument** *n* strumento *m* musicale

musician /mju:'zɪʃn/ *n* musicista *mf*

Muslim /'mʊzlɪm/ *adj & n* musulmano, -a *mf*

mussel /'mʌsl/ *n* cozza *f*

must /mʌst/ *v aux* (*solo al presente*) dovere; **you ~ not be late** non devi essere in ritardo; **she ~ have finished by now** (*probability*) deve aver finito ormai ● *n* **a ~** [!] una cosa da non perdere

mustard /'mʌstəd/ *n* senape *f*

musty /'mʌstɪ/ *adj* (**-ier, -iest**) stantio

mutation /mju:'teɪʃn/ *n* (*Biol*) mutazione *f*

mute /mju:t/ *adj* muto

mutilat|e /'mju:tɪleɪt/ *vt* mutilare. **~ion** *n* mutilazione *f*

mutter /'mʌtə(r)/ *vt/i* borbottare

mutton /'mʌtn/ *n* carne *f* di montone

mutual /'mju:tjʊəl/ *adj* reciproco; ([!]: *common*) comune. **~ly** *adv* reciprocamente

muzzle /'mʌzl/ *n* (*of animal*) muso *m*; (*of firearm*) bocca *f*; (*for dog*) museruola *f* ● *vt fig* mettere il bavaglio a

my /maɪ/ *adj* il mio *m*, la mia *f*, i miei *mpl*, le mie *fpl*; **my mother/father** mia madre/mio padre

myself /maɪ'self/ *pron* (*reflexive*) mi; (*emphatic*) me stesso; (*after prep*) me; **I've seen it ~** l'ho visto io stesso; **by ~** da solo; **I thought to ~** ho pensato tra me e me; **I'm proud of ~** sono fiero di me

mysterious /mɪˈstɪərɪəs/ *adj* misterioso. **~ly** *adv* misteriosamente

mystery /ˈmɪstərɪ/ *n* mistero *m*; **~ [story]** racconto *m* del mistero

mysti|c[al] /ˈmɪstɪk[l]/ *adj* mistico. **~cism** *n* misticismo *m*

mystify /ˈmɪstɪfaɪ/ *vt* (*pt/pp* **-ied**) disorientare

mystique /mɪˈstiːk/ *n* mistica *f*

myth /mɪθ/ *n* mito *m*. **~ical** *adj* mitico

mythology /mɪˈθɒlədʒɪ/ *n* mitologia *f*

Nn

nab /næb/ *vt* (*pt/pp* **nabbed**) [!] beccare

nag¹ /næg/ *n* (*horse*) ronzino *m*

nag² (*pt/pp* **nagged**) *vt* assillare ● *vi* essere insistente ● *n* (*person*) brontolone, -a *mf*. **~ging** *adj* (pain) persistente

nail /neɪl/ *n* chiodo *m*; (*of finger, toe*) unghia *f* ● **nail down** *vt* inchiodare; **~ sb down to a time/price** far fissare a qcno un'ora/un prezzo

nail polish *n* smalto *m* [per unghie]

naked /ˈneɪkɪd/ *adj* nudo; **with the ~ eye** a occhio nudo

name /neɪm/ *n* nome *m*; **what's your ~?** come ti chiami?; **my ~ is Matthew** mi chiamo Matthew; **I know her by ~** la conosco di nome; **by the ~ of Bates** di nome Bates; **call sb ~s** [!] insultare qcno ● *vt* (*to position*) nominare; chiamare (baby); (*identify*) citare; **be ~d after** essere chiamato col nome di. **~less** *adj* senza nome. **~ly** *adv* cioè

namesake *n* omonimo, -a *mf*

nanny /ˈnænɪ/ *n* bambinaia *f*. **~-goat** *n* capra *f*

nap /næp/ *n* pisolino *m*; **have a ~** fare un pisolino ● *vi* (*pt/pp* **napped**) **catch sb ~ping** cogliere qcno alla sprovvista

napkin /ˈnæpkɪn/ *n* tovagliolo *m*

Naples /ˈneɪplz/ *n* Napoli *f*

nappy /ˈnæpɪ/ *n* pannolino *m*

narcotic /nɑːˈkɒtɪk/ *adj & n* narcotico *m*

narrat|e /nəˈreɪt/ *vt* narrare. **~ion** *n* narrazione *f*

narrative /ˈnærətɪv/ *adj* narrativo ● *n* narrazione *f*

narrator /nəˈreɪtə(r)/ *n* narratore, -trice *mf*

narrow /ˈnærəʊ/ *adj* stretto; (fig: views) ristretto; (margin, majority) scarso ● *vi* restringersi. **~ly** *adv* **~ly escape death** evitare la morte per un pelo. **~-ˈminded** *adj* di idee ristrette

nasal /ˈneɪzl/ *adj* nasale

nasty /ˈnɑːstɪ/ *adj* (**-ier, -iest**) (smell, person, remark) cattivo; (injury, situation, weather) brutto; **turn ~** (person:) diventare cattivo

nation /ˈneɪʃn/ *n* nazione *f*

national /ˈnæʃənl/ *adj* nazionale ● *n* cittadino, -a *mf*

national ˈanthem *n* inno *m* nazionale

nationalism /ˈnæʃənəlɪzm/ *n* nazionalismo *m*

nationality /næʃəˈnælətɪ/ *n* nazionalità *f inv*

> *i* **National Trust** Fondazione britannica il cui scopo è la conservazione dei luoghi di interesse storico e la bellezza del paesaggio. Finanziato da donazioni e sovvenzioni private, il National Trust è il maggiore proprietario terriero britannico; nel corso degli anni ha acquisito enormi estensioni di terre e litorali, come pure edifici e borghi, molti dei quali vengono aperti al pubblico in certi periodi dell'anno. In Scozia esiste una fondazione analoga ma indipendente, il *National Trust for Scotland*.

ˈnation-wide *adj* su scala nazionale

native /ˈneɪtɪv/ *adj* nativo; (*innate*) innato ● *n* nativo, -a *mf*; (*local inhabitant*) abitante *mf* del posto; (*outside Europe*) indigeno, -a *mf*; **she's a ~ of Venice** è originaria di Venezia

native: ~ ˈland *n* paese *m* nativo. **~ ˈlanguage** *n* lingua *f* madre

Nativity /nəˈtɪvətɪ/ *n* **the ~** la Natività *f.* ~ **play** *n rappresentazione f sulla nascita di Gesù*

natter /ˈnætə(r)/ *vi* [!] chiacchierare

natural /ˈnætʃrəl/ *adj* naturale

natural ˈhistory *n* storia *f* naturale

naturalist /ˈnætʃ(ə)rəlɪst/ *n* naturalista *mf*

naturally /ˈnætʃ(ə)rəlɪ/ *adv* (*of course*) naturalmente; (*by nature*) per natura

nature /ˈneɪtʃə(r)/ *n* natura *f*; **by ~** per natura. **~ reserve** *n* riserva *f* naturale

naughty /ˈnɔːtɪ/ *adj* (**-ier, -iest**) monello; (*slightly indecent*) spinto

nausea /ˈnɔːzɪə/ *n* nausea *f*

nautical /ˈnɔːtɪkl/ *adj* nautico. **~ mile** *n* miglio *m* marino

naval /ˈneɪvl/ *adj* navale

nave /neɪv/ *n* navata *f* centrale

navel /ˈneɪvl/ *n* ombelico *m*

navigable /ˈnævɪgəbl/ *adj* navigabile

navigat|e /ˈnævɪgeɪt/ *vi* navigare; (*Auto*) fare da navigatore ● *vt* navigare su (river). **~ion** *n* navigazione *f.* **~or** *n* navigatore *m*

navy /ˈneɪvɪ/ *n* marina *f* ● **~ [blue]** *adj* blu marine *inv* ● *n* blu *m inv* marine

Neapolitan /nɪəˈpɒlɪtən/ *adj & n* napoletano, -a *mf*

near /nɪə(r)/ *adj* vicino; (future) prossimo; **the ~est bank** la banca più vicina ● *adv* vicino; **draw ~** avvicinarsi; **~ at hand** a portata di mano ● *prep* vicino a; **he was ~ to tears** aveva le lacrime agli occhi ● *vt* avvicinarsi a

near: ~ˈby *adj & adv* vicino. **~ly** *adv* quasi; **it's not ~ly enough** non è per niente sufficiente. **~-sighted** *adj Am* miope

neat /niːt/ *adj* (*tidy*) ordinato; (*clever*) efficace; (*undiluted*) liscio. **~ly** *adv* ordinatamente; (*cleverly*) efficacemente. **~ness** *n* (*tidiness*) ordine *m*

necessarily /nesəˈserɪlɪ/ *adv* necessariamente

necessary /ˈnesəsərɪ/ *adj* necessario

necessit|ate /nɪˈsesɪteɪt/ *vt* rendere necessario. **~y** *n* necessità *f inv*

neck /nek/ *n* collo *m*; (*of dress*) colletto *m*; **~ and ~** testa a testa

necklace /ˈneklɪs/ *n* collana *f*

neckline *n* scollatura *f*

need /niːd/ *n* bisogno *m*; **be in ~ of** avere bisogno di; **if ~ be** se ce ne fosse bisogno; **there is a ~ for** c'è bisogno di; **there is no ~ for that** non ce n'è bisogno; **there is no ~ for you to go** non c'è bisogno che tu vada ● *vt* aver bisogno di; **I ~ to know** devo saperlo; **it ~s to be done** bisogna farlo ● *v aux* **you ~ not go** non c'è bisogno che tu vada; **~ I come?** devo [proprio] venire?

needle /ˈniːdl/ *n* ago *m*; (*for knitting*) ferro *m* (da maglia); (*of record player*) puntina *f* ● *vt* ([!]: *annoy*) punzecchiare

needless /ˈniːdlɪs/ *adj* inutile

ˈneedlework *n* cucito *m*

needy /ˈniːdɪ/ *adj* (**-ier, -iest**) bisognoso

negative /ˈnegətɪv/ *adj* negativo ● *n* negazione *f*; (*Phot*) negativo *m*; **in the ~** (*Gram*) alla forma negativa

neglect /nɪˈglekt/ *n* trascuratezza *f*; **state of ~** stato *m* di abbandono ● *vt* trascurare; **he ~ed to write** non si è curato di scrivere. **~ed** *adj* trascurato. **~ful** *adj* negligente; **be ~ful of** trascurare

negligen|ce /ˈneglɪdʒəns/ *n* negligenza *f.* **~t** *adj* negligente

negligible /ˈneglɪdʒəbl/ *adj* trascurabile

negotiable /nɪˈgəʊʃəbl/ *adj* (road) transitabile; (*Comm*) negoziabile; **not ~** (cheque) non trasferibile

negotiat|e /nɪˈgəʊʃɪeɪt/ *vt* negoziare; (*Auto*) prendere (bend) ● *vi* negoziare. **~ion** *n* negoziato *m.* **~or** *n* negoziatore, -trice *mf*

neigh /neɪ/ *vi* nitrire

neighbour /ˈneɪbə(r)/ *n* vicino, -a *mf.* **~hood** *n* vicinato *m*; **in the ~hood of** nei dintorni di; *fig* circa. **~ing** *adj* vicino. **~ly** *adj* amichevole

neither /ˈnaɪðə(r)/ *adj & pron* nessuno dei due, né l'uno né l'altro ● *adv* **~... nor** né... né ● *conj* nemmeno, neanche; **~ do/did I** nemmeno io

neon /ˈniːɒn/ *n* neon *m.* **~ light** *n* luce *f* al neon

nephew /ˈnevjuː/ *n* nipote *m*

nerve /nɜːv/ *n* nervo *m*; ([!]: *courage*) coraggio *m*; ([!]: *impudence*) faccia *f* tosta; **lose one's ~** perdersi d'animo. **~-racking** *adj* logorante

nervous /ˈnɜːvəs/ *adj* nervoso; **he**

n

makes me ~ mi mette in agitazione; **be a ~ wreck** avere i nervi a pezzi. ~ **'breakdown** *n* esaurimento *m* nervoso. **~ly** *adv* nervosamente. **~ness** *n* nervosismo *m*; (*before important event*) tensione *f*

nervy /'nɜːvɪ/ *adj* (**-ier, -iest**) nervoso; (*Am: impudent*) sfacciato

nest /nest/ *n* nido *m* • *vi* fare il nido. **~-egg** *n* gruzzolo *m*

nestle /'nesl/ *vi* accoccolarsi

net¹ /net/ *n* rete *f* • *vt* (*pt/pp* **netted**) (*catch*) prendere (*con la rete*)

net² *adj* netto • *vt* (*pt/pp* **netted**) incassare un utile netto di

'netball *n sport m inv femminile, simile a pallacanestro*

Netherlands /'neðələndz/ *npl* **the ~** i Paesi *mpl* Bassi

netting /'netɪŋ/ *n* [**wire**] ~ reticolato *m*

nettle /'netl/ *n* ortica *f*

'network *n* rete *f*

neur|osis /njʊə'rəʊsɪs/ *n* (*pl* **-oses** /-siːz/) nevrosi *f inv*. **~otic** *adj* nevrotico

neuter /'njuːtə(r)/ *adj* (*Gram*) neutro • *n* (*Gram*) neutro *m* • *vt* sterilizzare

neutral /'njuːtrəl/ *adj* neutro; (*country, person*) neutrale • *n* **in ~** (*Auto*) in folle. **~ity** *n* neutralità *f*. **~ize** *vt* neutralizzare

never /'nevə(r)/ *adv* [non...] mai; (*[!]: expressing disbelief*) ma va; **~ again** mai più; **well I ~!** chi l'avrebbe detto!. **~-ending** *adj* interminabile

nevertheless /nevəðə'les/ *adv* tuttavia

new /njuː/ *adj* nuovo

new: ~born *adj* neonato. **~comer** *n* nuovo, -a arrivato, -a *mf*. **~fangled** /-'fæŋgld/ *adj pej* modernizzante

'newly *adv* (*recently*) di recente; **~-built** costruito di recente. **~-weds** *npl* sposini *mpl*

news /njuːz/ *n* notizie *fpl*; (*TV*) telegiornale *m*; (*Radio*) giornale *m* radio; **piece of ~** notizia *f*

news: ~agent *n* giornalaio, -a *mf*. **~caster** *n* giornalista *mf* televisivo, -a/radiofonico, -a. **~flash** *n* notizia *f* flash. **~letter** *n* bollettino *m* d'informazione. **~paper** *n* giornale *m*; (*material*) carta *f* di giornale. **~reader** *n* giornalista *mf* televisivo, -a/radiofonico, -a

new: ~ year *n* (*next year*) anno *m* nuovo; **N~ Year's Day** *n* Capodanno *m*. **N~ Year's 'Eve** *n* vigilia *f* di Capodanno. **N~ Zealand** /'ziːlənd/ *n* Nuova Zelanda *f*

next /nekst/ *adj* prossimo; (*adjoining*) vicino; **who's ~?** a chi tocca?; **~ door** accanto; **~ to nothing** quasi niente; **the ~ day** il giorno dopo; **~ week** la settimana prossima; **the week after ~** fra due settimane • *adv* dopo; **when will you see him ~?** quando lo rivedi la prossima volta?; **~ to** accanto a • *n* seguente *mf*; **~ of kin** parente *m* prossimo

nib /nɪb/ *n* pennino *m*

nibble /'nɪbl/ *vt/i* mordicchiare

nice /naɪs/ *adj* (day, weather, holiday) bello; (person) gentile, simpatico; (food) buono; **it was ~ meeting you** è stato un piacere conoscerla. **~ly** *adv* gentilmente; (*well*) bene. **~ties** *n pl* sottigliezze *f pl*

niche /niːʃ/ *n* nicchia *f*

nick /nɪk/ *n* tacca *f*; (*on chin etc*) taglietto *m*; (*[!]: prison*) galera *f*; (*[!]: police station*) centrale *f* [di polizia]; **in the ~ of time** [!] appena in tempo • *vt* intaccare; (*[!]: steal*) fregare; (*[!]: arrest*) beccare; **~ one's chin** farsi un taglietto nel mento

nickel /'nɪkl/ *n* nichel *m*; *Am* moneta *f* da cinque centesimi

'nickname *n* soprannome *m* • *vt* soprannominare

nicotine /'nɪkətiːn/ *n* nicotina *f*

niece /niːs/ *n* nipote *f*

niggling /'nɪglɪŋ/ *adj* (detail) insignificante; (pain) fastidioso; (doubt) persistente

night /naɪt/ *n* notte *f*; (*evening*) sera *f*; **at ~** la notte, di notte; (*in the evening*) la sera, di sera; **Monday ~** lunedì notte/sera • *adj* di notte

night: ~cap *n* papalina *f*; (*drink*) bicchierino *m* bevuto prima di andare a letto. **~-club** *n* locale *m* notturno, night[-club] *m inv*. **~-dress** *n* camicia *f* da notte. **~fall** *n* crepuscolo *m*. **~-gown**, [!] **~ie** /'naɪtɪ/ *n* camicia *f* da notte

night: ~-life *n* vita *f* notturna. **~ly** *adj*

di notte, di sera ● *adv* ogni notte, ogni sera. **~mare** *n* incubo *m*. **~-school** scuola *f* serale. **~-time** *n* **at ~-time** di notte, la notte. **~-'watchman** *n* guardiano *m* notturno

nil /nɪl/ *n* nulla *m*; (*Sport*) zero *m*

nimbl|e /'nɪmbl/ *adj* agile. **~y** *adv* agilmente

nine /naɪn/ *adj* nove *inv* ● *n* nove *m*. **~'teen** *adj* diciannove *inv* ● *n* diciannove. **~'teenth** *adj & n* diciannovesimo, -a *mf*

ninetieth /'naɪntɪɪθ/ *adj & n* novantesimo, -a *mf*

ninety /'naɪntɪ/ *adj* novanta *inv* ● *n* novanta *m*

ninth /naɪnθ/ *adj & n* nono, -a *mf*

nip /nɪp/ *n* pizzicotto *m*; (*bite*) morso *m* ● *vt* pizzicare; (*bite*) mordere; **~ in the bud** *fig* stroncare sul nascere ● *vi* (🄸: *run*) fare un salto

nipple /'nɪpl/ *n* capezzolo *m*; (*Am: on bottle*) tettarella *f*

nippy /'nɪpɪ/ *adj* (**-ier, -iest**) 🄸 (*cold*) pungente; (*quick*) svelto

nitrogen /'naɪtrədʒn/ *n* azoto *m*

no /nəʊ/ *adv* no ● *n* (*pl* **noes**) no *m inv* ● *adj* nessuno; **I have no time** non ho tempo; **in no time** in un baleno; **'no parking'** 'sosta vietata'; **'no smoking'** 'vietato fumare'; **no one** nessuno *v.* **nobody**

noble /'nəʊbl/ *adj* nobile. **~man** *n* nobile *m*

nobody /'nəʊbədɪ/ *pron* nessuno; **he knows ~** non conosce nessuno ● *n* **he's a ~** non è nessuno

nocturnal /nɒk'tɜːnl/ *adj* notturno

nod /nɒd/ *n* cenno *m* del capo ● *vi* (*pt/pp* **nodded**) fare un cenno col capo; (*in agreement*) fare di sì col capo ● *vt* **~ one's head** fare di sì col capo. □ **~ off** *vi* assopirsi

noise /nɔɪz/ *n* rumore *m*; (*loud*) rumore *m*, chiasso *m*. **~less** *adj* silenzioso. **~lessly** *adv* silenziosamente

noisy /'nɔɪzɪ/ *adj* (**-ier, -iest**) rumoroso

nomad /'nəʊmæd/ *n* nomade *mf*. **~ic** *adj* nomade

nominat|e /'nɒmɪneɪt/ *vt* proporre come candidato; (*appoint*) designare. **~ion** *n* nomina *f*; (*person nominated*) candidato, -a *mf*

nonchalant /'nɒnʃələnt/ *adj* disinvolto

non-com'mittal *adj* che non si sbilancia

nondescript /'nɒndɪskrɪpt/ *adj* qualunque

none /nʌn/ *pron* (*person*) nessuno; (*thing*) niente; **~ of us** nessuno di noi; **~ of this** niente di questo; **there's ~ left** non ce n'è più ● *adv* **she's ~ too pleased** non è per niente soddisfatta; **I'm ~ the wiser** non ne so più di prima

nonentity /nɒ'nentətɪ/ *n* nullità *f*

non-ex'istent *adj* inesistente

nonplussed /nɒn'plʌst/ *adj* perplesso

nonsens|e /'nɒnsəns/ *n* sciocchezze *fpl*. **~ical** *adj* assurdo

non-'smoker *n* non fumatore, -trice *mf*; (*compartment*) scompartimento *m* non fumatori

non-'stop *adj* **~ 'flight** volo *m* diretto ● *adv* senza sosta; (fly) senza scalo

noodles /'nuːdlz/ *npl* taglierini *mpl*

nook /nʊk/ *n* cantuccio *m*

noon /nuːn/ *n* mezzogiorno *m*; **at ~** a mezzogiorno

noose /nuːs/ *n* nodo *m* scorsoio

nor /nɔː(r)/ *adv & conj* né; **~ do I** neppure io

norm /nɔːm/ *n* norma *f*

normal /'nɔːml/ *adj* normale. **~ity** *n* normalità *f*. **~ly** *adv* (*usually*) normalmente

north /nɔːθ/ *n* nord *m*; **to the ~ of** a nord di ● *adj* del nord, settentrionale ● *adv* a nord

north: N~ America *n* America *f* del Nord. **~-east** *adj* di nord-est, nordorientale ● *n* nord-est *m* ● *adv* a nord-est; (travel) verso nord-est

norther|ly /'nɔːðəlɪ/ *adj* (direction) nord; (wind) del nord. **~n** *adj* del nord, settentrionale. **N~n Ireland** *n* Irlanda *f* del Nord

north: N~ 'Sea *n* Mare *m* del Nord. **~ward[s]** /-wəd[z]/ *adv* verso nord. **~-west** *adj* di nord-ovest, nordoccidentale ● *n* nord-ovest *m* ● *adv* a nord-ovest; (travel) verso nord-ovest

Nor|way /'nɔːweɪ/ *n* Norvegia *f*. **~wegian** *adj & n* norvegese *mf*

nose /nəʊz/ *n* naso *m*

nose: **~bleed** *n* emorragia *f* nasale. **~dive** *n* (*Aeron*) picchiata *f*

nostalg|ia /nɒ'stældʒɪə/ *n* nostalgia *f*. **~ic** *adj* nostalgico

nostril /'nɒstrəl/ *n* narice *f*

nosy /'nəʊzɪ/ *adj* (**-ier, -iest**) ⓘ ficcanaso *inv*

not /nɒt/ *adv* non; **he is ~ Italian** non è italiano; **I hope ~** spero di no; **~ all of us have been invited** non siamo stati tutti invitati; **if ~** se no; **~ at all** niente affatto; **~ a bit** per niente; **~ even** neanche; **~ yet** non ancora; **~ only... but also...** non solo... ma anche...

notabl|e /'nəʊtəbl/ *adj* (*remarkable*) notevole. **~y** *adv* (*in particular*) in particolare

notary /'nəʊtərɪ/ *n* notaio *m*; **~ 'public** notaio *m*

notch /nɒtʃ/ *n* tacca *f* ● **notch up** *vt* (*score*) segnare

note /nəʊt/ *n* nota *f*; (*short letter, banknote*) biglietto *m*; (*memo, written comment etc*) appunto *m*; **of ~** (person) di spicco; (comments, event) degno di nota; **make a ~ of** prendere nota di; **take ~ of** (*notice*) prendere nota di ● *vt* (*notice*) notare; (*write*) annotare. □ **~ down** *vt* annotare

'notebook *n* taccuino *m*; (*Comput*) notebook *m inv*

noted /'nəʊtɪd/ *adj* noto, celebre (**for** per)

notepaper *n* carta *f* da lettere

nothing /'nʌθɪŋ/ *pron* niente, nulla ● *adv* niente affatto. **for ~** (*free, in vain*) per niente; (*with no reason*) senza motivo; **~ but** nient'altro che; **~ much** poco o nulla; **~ interesting** niente di interessante; **it's ~ to do with you** non ti riguarda

notice /'nəʊtɪs/ *n* (*on board*) avviso *m*; (*review*) recensione *f*; (*termination of employment*) licenziamento *m*; **[advance] ~** preavviso *m*; **two months ~** due mesi di preavviso; **at short ~** con breve preavviso; **until further ~** fino nuovo avviso; **hand in one's ~** (employee:) dare le dimissioni; **give an employee ~** dare il preavviso a un impiegato; **take no ~ of** non fare caso a; **take no ~!** non farci caso! ● *vt* notare. **~able** *adj* evidente. **~ably** *adv* sensibilmente. **~-board** *n* bacheca *f*

noti|fication /nəʊtɪfɪ'keɪʃn/ *n* notifica *f*. **~fy** *vt* (*pt/pp* **-ied**) notificare

notion /'nəʊʃn/ *n* idea *f*, nozione *f*; **~s** *pl* (*Am: haberdashery*) merceria *f*

notorious /nəʊ'tɔːrɪəs/ *adj* famigerato; **be ~ for** essere tristemente famoso per

notwith'standing *prep* malgrado ● *adv* ciononostante

nougat /'nuːgɑː/ *n* torrone *m*

nought /nɔːt/ *n* zero *m*

noun /naʊn/ *n* nome *m*, sostantivo *m*

nourish /'nʌrɪʃ/ *vt* nutrire. **~ing** *adj* nutriente. **~ment** *n* nutrimento *m*

novel /'nɒvl/ *adj* insolito ● *n* romanzo *m*. **~ist** *n* romanziere, -a *mf*. **~ty** *n* novità *f*; **~ties** *pl* (*objects*) oggettini *mpl*

November /nəʊ'vembə(r)/ *n* novembre *m*

novice /'nɒvɪs/ *n* novizio, -a *mf*

now /naʊ/ *adv* ora, adesso; **by ~** ormai; **just ~** proprio ora; **right ~** subito; **~ and again, ~ and then** ogni tanto; **~, ~!** su! ● *conj* **~ [that]** ora che, adesso che

'nowadays *adv* oggigiorno

nowhere /'nəʊ-/ *adv* in nessun posto, da nessuna parte

nozzle /'nɒzl/ *n* bocchetta *f*

nuance /'njuːæia.s/ *n* sfumatura *f*

nuclear /'njuːklɪə(r)/ *adj* nucleare

nucleus /'njuːklɪəs/ *n* (*pl* **-lei** /-lɪaɪ/) nucleo *m*

nude /njuːd/ *adj* nudo ● *n* nudo *m*; **in the ~** nudo

nudge /nʌdʒ/ *n* colpetto *m* di gomito ● *vt* dare un colpetto col gomito a

nudism /'njuːdɪzm/ *n* nudismo *m*

nud|ist /'njuːdɪst/ *n* nudista *mf*. **~ity** *n* nudità *f*

nuisance /'njuːsns/ *n* seccatura *f*; (*person*) piaga *f*; **what a ~!** che seccatura!

null /nʌl/ *adj* **~ and void** nullo

numb /nʌm/ *adj* intorpidito; **~ with cold** intirizzito dal freddo

number /'nʌmbə(r)/ *n* numero *m*; **a ~ of people** un certo numero di persone ● *vt* numerare; (*include*) annoverare. **~-plate** *n* targa *f*

numeral /ˈnjuːmərəl/ *n* numero *m*, cifra *f*

numerical /njuːˈmerɪkl/ *adj* numerico; **in ~ order** in ordine numerico

numerous /ˈnjuːmərəs/ *adj* numeroso

nun /nʌn/ *n* suora *f*

nurse /nɜːs/ *n* infermiere, -a *mf*; **children's ~** bambinaia *f* ● *vt* curare

nursery /ˈnɜːsərɪ/ *n* stanza *f* dei bambini; (*for plants*) vivaio *m*; [**day**] **~** asilo *m*. **~ rhyme** *n* filastrocca *f*. **~ school** *n* scuola *f* materna

nut /nʌt/ *n* noce *f*; (*Techn*) dado *m*; ([!]: *head*) zucca *f*; **~s** *npl* frutta *f* secca; **be ~s** [!] essere svitato. **~crackers** *npl* schiaccianoci *m inv*. **~meg** *n* noce *f* moscata

nutrit|ion /njuːˈtrɪʃn/ *n* nutrizione *f*. **~ious** *adj* nutriente

ˈnutshell *n* **in a ~** *fig* in parole povere

nylon /ˈnaɪlɒn/ *n* nailon *m*; **~s** *pl* calze *fpl* di nailon ● *attrib* di nailon

oaf /əʊf/ *n* (*pl* **oafs**) zoticone, -a *mf*

oak /əʊk/ *n* quercia *f* ● *attrib* di quercia

OAP *n abbr* (old-age pensioner) pensionato, -a *mf*

oar /ɔː(r)/ *n* remo *m*. **~sman** *n* vogatore *m*

oasis /əʊˈeɪsɪs/ *n* (*pl* **oases** /-siːz/) oasi *f inv*

oath /əʊθ/ *n* giuramento *m*; (*swear-word*) bestemmia *f*

oatmeal /ˈəʊt-/ *n* farina *f* d'avena

oats /əʊts/ *npl* avena *fsg*; (*Culin*) [**rolled**] **~** fiocchi *mpl* di avena

obedien|ce /əˈbiːdɪəns/ *n* ubbidienza *f*. **~t** *adj* ubbidiente

obes|e /əˈbiːs/ *adj* obeso. **~ity** *n* obesità *f*

obey /əˈbeɪ/ *vt* ubbidire a; osservare (instructions, rules) ● *vi* ubbidire

obituary /əˈbɪtjʊərɪ/ *n* necrologio *m*

object¹ /ˈɒbdʒɪkt/ *n* oggetto *m*; (*Gram*) complemento *m* oggetto; **money is no ~** i soldi non sono un problema

object² /əbˈdʒekt/ *vi* (*be against*) opporsi (**to** a); **~ that...** obiettare che...

objection /əbˈdʒekʃn/ *n* obiezione *f*; **have no ~** non avere niente in contrario. **~able** *adj* discutibile; (person) sgradevole

objectiv|e /əbˈdʒektɪv/ *adj* oggettivo ● *n* obiettivo *m*. **~ely** *adv* obiettivamente. **~ity** *n* oggettività *f*

obligation /ɒblɪˈgeɪʃn/ *n* obbligo *m*; **be under an ~** avere un obbligo; **without ~** senza impegno

obligatory /əˈblɪgətrɪ/ *adj* obbligatorio

oblig|e /əˈblaɪdʒ/ *vt* (*compel*) obbligare; **much ~ed** grazie mille. **~ing** *adj* disponibile

oblique /əˈbliːk/ *adj* obliquo; *fig* indiretto ● *n* **~** [**stroke**] barra *f*

obliterate /əˈblɪtəreɪt/ *vt* obliterare

oblivion /əˈblɪvɪən/ *n* oblio *m*

oblivious /əˈblɪvɪəs/ *adj* **be ~** essere dimentico (**of, to** di)

oblong /ˈɒblɒŋ/ *adj* oblungo ● *n* rettangolo *m*

obnoxious /əbˈnɒkʃəs/ *adj* detestabile

oboe /ˈəʊbəʊ/ *n* oboe *m inv*

obscen|e /əbˈsiːn/ *adj* osceno; (profits, wealth) vergognoso. **~ity** *n* oscenità *f inv*

obscur|e /əbˈskjʊə(r)/ *adj* oscuro ● *vt* oscurare; (*confuse*) mettere in ombra. **~ity** *n* oscurità *f*

obsequious /əbˈsiːkwɪəs/ *adj* ossequioso

observatory /əbˈzɜːvətrɪ/ *n* osservatorio *m*

observe /əbˈzɜːv/ *vt* osservare; (*notice*) notare; (*keep, celebrate*) celebrare. **~r** *n* osservatore, -trice *mf*

obsess /əbˈses/ *vt* **be ~ed by** essere fissato con. **~ion** *n* fissazione *f*. **~ive** *adj* ossessivo

obsolete /ˈɒbsəliːt/ *adj* obsoleto; (word) desueto

obstacle /ˈɒbstəkl/ *n* ostacolo *m*

obstina|cy /ˈɒbstɪnəsɪ/ *n* ostinazione *f*. **~te** *adj* ostinato

obstruct /əbˈstrʌkt/ *vt* ostruire; (*hinder*) ostacolare. **~ion** *n* ostruzione *f*; (*obstacle*) ostacolo *m*. **~ive** *adj* **be ~ive** (person:) creare dei problemi

n

o

obtain /əb'teɪn/ *vt* ottenere. **~able** *adj* ottenibile

obtrusive /əb'truːsɪv/ *adj* (object) stonato

obtuse /əb'tjuːs/ *adj* ottuso

obvious /'ɒbvɪəs/ *adj* ovvio. **~ly** *adv* ovviamente

occasion /ə'keɪʒn/ *n* occasione *f*; (*event*) evento *m*; **on ~** talvolta; **on the ~ of** in occasione di

occasional /ə'keɪʒənl/ *adj* saltuario; **he has the ~ glass of wine** ogni tanto beve un bicchiere di vino. **~ly** *adv* ogni tanto

occult /ɒ'kʌlt/ *adj* occulto

occupant /'ɒkjʊpənt/ *n* occupante *mf*; (*of vehicle*) persona *f* a bordo

occupation /ɒkjʊ'peɪʃn/ *n* occupazione *f*; (*job*) professione *f* **~al** *adj* professionale

occupier /'ɒkjʊpaɪə(r)/ *n* residente *mf*

occupy /'ɒkjʊpaɪ/ *vt* (*pt*/*pp* **occupied**) occupare; (*keep busy*) tenere occupato

occur /ə'kɜː(r)/ *vi* (*pt*/*pp* **occurred**) accadere; (*exist*) trovarsi; **it ~red to me that** mi è venuto in mente che. **~rence** *n* (*event*) fatto *m*

ocean /'əʊʃn/ *n* oceano *m*

octave /'ɒktɪv/ *n* (*Mus*) ottava *f*

October /ɒk'təʊbə(r)/ *n* ottobre *m*

octopus /'ɒktəpəs/ *n* (*pl* **-puses**) polpo *m*

odd /ɒd/ *adj* (number) dispari; (*not of set*) scompagnato; (*strange*) strano; **forty ~** quaranta e rotti; **~ jobs** lavoretti *mpl*; **the ~ one out** l'eccezione; **at ~ moments** a tempo perso; **have the ~ glass of wine** avere un bicchiere di vino ogni tanto

odd|ity /'ɒdɪtɪ/ *n* stranezza *f*. **~ly** *adv* stranamente; **~ly enough** stranamente. **~ment** *n* (*of fabric*) scampolo *m*

odds /ɒdz/ *npl* (*chances*) probabilità *fpl*; **at ~** in disaccordo; **~ and ends** cianfrusaglie *fpl*; **it makes no ~** non fa alcuna differenza

odour /'əʊdə(r)/ *n* odore *m*. **~less** *adj* inodore

of /ɒv/, /əv/ *prep* di; **a cup of tea/coffee** una tazza di tè/caffè; **the hem of my skirt** l'orlo della mia gonna; **the summer of 1989** l'estate del 1989; **the two of us** noi due; **made of** di; **that's very kind of you** è molto gentile da parte tua; **a friend of mine** un mio amico; **a child of three** un bambino di tre anni; **the fourth of January** il quattro gennaio; **within a year of their divorce** a circa un anno dal loro divorzio; **half of it** la metà; **the whole of the room** tutta la stanza

off /ɒf/ *prep* da; (*distant from*) lontano da; **take £10 ~ the price** ridurre il prezzo di 10 sterline; **~ the coast** presso la costa; **a street ~ the main road** una traversa della via principale; (*near*) una strada vicino alla via principale; **get ~ the ladder** scendere dalla scala; **get off the bus** uscire dall'autobus; **leave the lid ~ the saucepan** lasciare la pentola senza il coperchio ● *adv* (button, handle) staccato; (light, machine) spento; (brake) tolto; (tap) chiuso; **'off'** (*on appliance*) 'off'; **2 kilometres ~** a due chilometri di distanza; **a long way ~** molto distante; (*time*) lontano; **~ and on** di tanto in tanto; **with his hat/coat ~** senza il cappello/cappotto; **with the light ~** a luce spenta; **20% ~** 20% di sconto; **be ~** (*leave*) andar via; (*Sport*) essere partito; (food:) essere andato a male; (*all gone*) essere finito; (wedding, engagement:) essere cancellato; **I'm ~ alcohol** ho smesso di bere; **be ~ one's food** non avere appetito; **she's ~ today** (*on holiday*) è in ferie oggi; (*ill*) è malata oggi; **I'm ~ home** vado a casa; **you'd be better ~ doing...** faresti meglio a fare...; **have a day ~** avere un giorno di vacanza; **drive/sail ~** andare via

'off-beat *adj* insolito

'off-chance *n* possibilità *f* remota

offence /ə'fens/ *n* (*illegal act*) reato *m*; **give ~** offendere; **take ~** offendersi (**at** per)

offend /ə'fend/ *vt* offendere. **~er** *n* (*Jur*) colpevole *mf*

offensive /ə'fensɪv/ *adj* offensivo ● *n* offensiva *f*

offer /'ɒfə(r)/ *n* offerta *f* ● *vt* offrire; opporre (resistance); **~ sb sth** offrire qcsa a qcno; **~ to do sth** offrirsi di fare qcsa. **~ing** *n* offerta *f*

off'hand *adj* (*casual*) spiccio ● *adv* su due piedi

office /'ɒfɪs/ *n* ufficio *m*; (*post, job*) carica *f*. **~ hours** *pl* orario *m* d'ufficio

officer /'ɒfɪsə(r)/ *n* ufficiale *m*; (*police*) agente *m* [di polizia]

official /ə'fɪʃl/ *adj* ufficiale ● *n* funzionario, -a *mf*; (*Sport*) dirigente *m*. **~ly** *adv* ufficialmente

'offing *n* **in the ~** in vista

'off-licence *n* negozio *m* per la vendita di alcolici

'off-putting *adj* [!] scoraggiante

'offset *vt* (*pt/pp* **-set**, *pres p* **-setting**) controbilanciare

'offshore ● *adj* (wind) di terra; (company, investment) offshore. ● *adv* (sail) al largo; (relocate) all'estero (*in paesi dove la manodopera costa meno*); **to move jobs ~** delocalizzare gli impieghi. **~ rig** *n* piattaforma *f* petrolifera, offshore *m inv*

off'side *adj* (*Sport*) [in] fuori gioco; (wheel etc) (*left*) sinistro; (*right*) destro

'offspring *n* prole *m*

off'stage *adv* dietro le quinte

off-'white *adj* bianco sporco

often /'ɒfn/ *adv* spesso; **how ~** ogni quanto; **every so ~** una volta ogni tanto

ogle /'əʊgl/ *vt* mangiarsi con gli occhi

oh /əʊ/ *int* oh!; **~ dear** oh Dio!

oil /ɔɪl/ *n* olio *m*; (*petroleum*) petrolio *m*; (*for heating*) nafta *f* ● *vt* oliare

oil: ~field *n* giacimento *m* di petrolio. **~-painting** *n* pittura *f* a olio. **~ refinery** *n* raffineria *f* di petrolio. **~ rig** piattaforma *f* per trivellazione subacquea

oily /'ɔɪlɪ/ *adj* (**-ier, -iest**) unto; *fig* untuoso

ointment /'ɔɪntmənt/ *n* pomata *f*

OK /əʊ'keɪ/ *int* va bene, o.k. ● *adj* **if that's OK with you** se ti va bene; **she's OK** (*well*) sta bene; **is the milk still OK?** il latte è ancora buono? ● *adv* (*well*) bene ● *vt* (*anche* **okay**) (*pt/pp* **okayed**) dare l'o.k.

old /əʊld/ *adj* vecchio; (girlfriend) ex; **how ~ is she?** quanti anni ha?; **she is ten years ~** ha dieci anni

old: ~ 'age *n* vecchiaia *f*. **~'fashioned** *adj* antiquato

olive /'ɒlɪv/ *n* (*fruit, colour*) oliva *f*; (*tree*) olivo *m* ● *adj* d'oliva; (*colour*) olivastro. **~ branch** *n fig* ramoscello *m* d'olivo. **~ 'oil** *n* olio *m* di oliva

Olympic /ə'lɪmpɪk/ *adj* olimpico; **~s, ~ Games** Olimpiadi *fpl*

omelette /'ɒmlɪt/ *n* omelette *f inv*

omen /'əʊmən/ *n* presagio *m*

omission /ə'mɪʃn/ *n* omissione *f*

omit /ə'mɪt/ *vt* (*pt/pp* **omitted**) omettere; **~ to do sth** tralasciare di fare qcsa

once /wʌns/ *adv* una volta; (*formerly*) un tempo; **~ upon a time there was** c'era una volta; **at ~** subito; (*at the same time*) contemporaneamente; **~ and for all** una volta per tutte ● *conj* [non] appena. **~-over** *n* [!] **give sb/sth the ~-over** (*look, check*) dare un'occhiata veloce a qcno/qcsa

one /wʌn/
- ● *adj* uno, una; **not ~ person** nemmeno una persona
- ● *n* uno *m*
- ● *pron* uno; (*impersonal*) si; **~ another** l'un l'altro; **~ by ~** [a] uno a uno; **~ never knows** non si sa mai

one: ~self *pron* (*reflexive*) si; (*emphatic*) sé, se stesso; **by ~self** da solo; **be proud of ~self** essere fieri di sé. **~-way** *adj* (street) a senso unico; (ticket) di sola andata

onion /'ʌnjən/ *n* cipolla *f*

on-'line *adj/adv* su Internet; **you are now ~** ora sei in linea

'onlooker *n* spettatore, -trice *mf*

only /'əʊnlɪ/ *adj* solo; **~ child** figlio, -a *mf* unico, -a ● *adv & conj* solo, solamente; **~ just** appena

'onset *n* (*beginning*) inizio *m*

'on-shore *adj* (*on land*) di terra; (*breeze*) di mare

onslaught /'ɒnslɔ:t/ *n* attacco *m*

onus /'əʊnəs/ *n* **the ~ is on me** spetta a me la responsabilità (**to** di)

ooze /u:z/ *vi* fluire

opaque /əʊ'peɪk/ *adj* opaco

open /'əʊpən/ *adj* aperto; (*free to all*) pubblico; (job) vacante; **in the ~ air** all'aperto ● *n* **in the ~** all'aperto; *fig* alla luce del sole ● *vt* aprire ● *vi* aprirsi; (shop:) aprire; (flower:) sbocciare. □ **~ up** *vt* aprire ● *vi* aprirsi

opening /'əʊpənɪŋ/ *n* apertura *f*; (*be-*

O

ginning) inizio *m*; (*job*) posto *m* libero; ~ **hours** *npl* orario *m* d'apertura

openly /'əʊpənlɪ/ *adv* apertamente

open: ~-'minded *adj* aperto; (*broad-minded*) di vedute larghe. **~-plan** *adj* a pianta aperta

Open University Fondata nel 1969, è il sistema di università a distanza del Regno Unito. L'insegnamento viene impartito con vari mezzi: per corrispondenza, attraverso programmi radiotelevisivi trasmessi dalla BBC e anche via Internet. Gli studenti inviano per posta i compiti svolti a un tutore. Generalmente si seguono corsi part time della durata di quattro o cinque anni, anche se non ci sono limiti di tempo per completare gli studi.

opera /'ɒpərə/ *n* opera *f*

opera-house *n* teatro *m* lirico

operate /'ɒpəreɪt/ *vt* far funzionare (machine, lift); azionare (lever, brake); mandare avanti (business) ● *vi* (*Techn*) funzionare; (*be in action*) essere in funzione; (*Mil, fig*) operare; ~ **on** (*Med*) operare

operatic /ɒpə'rætɪk/ *adj* lirico, operistico

operation /ɒpə'reɪʃn/ *n* operazione *f*; (*Techn*) funzionamento *m*; **in** ~ (*Techn*) in funzione; **come into** ~ *fig* entrare in funzione; (law:) entrare in vigore; **have an** ~ (*Med*) subire un'operazione. **~al** *adj* operativo; (law etc) in vigore

operative /'ɒpərətɪv/ *adj* operativo

operator /'ɒpəreɪtə(r)/ *n* (*user*) operatore, -trice *mf*; (*Teleph*) centralinista *mf*

opinion /ə'pɪnjən/ *n* opinione *f*; **in my** ~ secondo me. **~ated** *adj* dogmatico

opponent /ə'pəʊnənt/ *n* avversario, -a *mf*

opportun|e /'ɒpətju:n/ *adj* opportuno. **~ist** *n* opportunista *mf*. **~istic** *adj* opportunistico

opportunity /ɒpə'tju:nətɪ/ *n* opportunità *f inv*

oppos|e /ə'pəʊz/ *vt* opporsi a; **be ~ed to sth** esssere contrario a qcsa; **as ~ed to** al contrario di. **~ing** *adj* avversario; (*opposite*) opposto

opposite /'ɒpəzɪt/ *adj* opposto; (house) di fronte; ~ **number** *fig* controparte *f*; **the** ~ **sex** l'altro sesso ● *n* contrario *m* ● *adv* di fronte ● *prep* di fronte a

opposition /ɒpə'zɪʃn/ *n* opposizione *f*

oppress /ə'pres/ *vt* opprimere. **~ion** *n* oppressione *f*. **~ive** *adj* oppressivo; (heat) opprimente. **~or** *n* oppressore *m*

opt /ɒpt/ *vi* ~ **for** optare per; ~ **out** dissociarsi (**of** da)

optical /'ɒptɪkl/ *adj* ottico; ~ **illusion** illusione *f* ottica

optician /ɒp'tɪʃn/ *n* ottico, -a *mf*

optimis|m /'ɒptɪmɪzm/ *n* ottimismo *m*. **~t** *n* ottimista *mf*. **~tic** *adj* ottimistico

option /'ɒpʃn/ *n* scelta *f*; (*Comm*) opzione *f*. **~al** *adj* facoltativo; **~al extras** *pl* optional *m inv*

or /ɔ:(r)/ *conj* o, oppure; (*after negative*) né; **or [else]** se no; **in a year or two** fra un anno o due

oral /'ɔ:rəl/ *adj* orale ● *n* [!] esame *m* orale. **~ly** *adv* oralmente

orange /'ɒrɪndʒ/ *n* arancia *f*; (*colour*) arancione *m* ● *adj* arancione. **~ade** *n* aranciata *f*. ~ **juice** *n* succo *m* d'arancia

orbit /'ɔ:bɪt/ *n* orbita *f* ● *vt* orbitare. **~al** *adj* **~al road** tangenziale *f*

orchard /'ɔ:tʃəd/ *n* frutteto *m*

orches|tra /'ɔ:kɪstrə/ *n* orchestra *f*. **~tral** *adj* orchestrale. **~trate** *vt* orchestrare

orchid /'ɔ:kɪd/ *n* orchidea *f*

ordain /ɔ:'deɪn/ *vt* decretare; (*Relig*) ordinare

ordeal /ɔ:'di:l/ *n fig* terribile esperienza *f*

order /'ɔ:də(r)/ *n* ordine *m*; (*Comm*) ordinazione *f*; **out of** ~ (machine) fuori servizio; **in** ~ **that** affinché; **in** ~ **to** per ● *vt* ordinare

orderly /'ɔ:dəlɪ/ *adj* ordinato ● *n* (*Mil*) attendente *m*; (*Med*) inserviente *m*

ordinary /'ɔ:dɪnərɪ/ *adj* ordinario

ore /ɔ:(r)/ *n* minerale *m* grezzo

organ /'ɔ:gən/ *n* (*Anat, Mus*) organo *m*

organic /ɔ:'gænɪk/ *adj* organico; (*without chemicals*) biologico. **~ally** *adv* organicamente; **~ally grown** coltivato biologicamente

organism /'ɔ:gənɪzm/ *n* organismo *m*

organist /'ɔ:gənɪst/ *n* organista *mf*

organization /ɔ:gənaɪ'zeɪʃn/ *n* organizzazione *f*

organize /'ɔ:gənaɪz/ *vt* organizzare. **~r** *n* organizzatore, -trice *mf*

orgasm /'ɔ:gæzm/ *n* orgasmo *m*

orgy /'ɔ:dʒɪ/ *n* orgia *f*

Orient /'ɔ:rɪənt/ *n* Oriente *m*. **o~al** *adj* orientale ● *n* orientale *mf*

orient|ate /'ɔ:rɪenteɪt/ *vt* **~ate oneself** orientarsi. **~ation** *n* orientamento *m*

origin /'ɒrɪdʒɪn/ *n* origine *f*

original /ə'rɪdʒɪn(ə)l/ *adj* originario; (*not copied, new*) originale ● *n* originale *m*; **in the ~** in versione originale. **~ity** *n* originalità *f*. **~ly** *adv* originariamente

originat|e /ə'rɪdʒɪneɪt/ *vi* **~e in** avere origine in. **~or** *n* ideatore, -trice *mf*

ornament /'ɔ:nəmənt/ *n* ornamento *m*; (*on mantelpiece etc*) soprammobile *m*. **~al** *adj* ornamentale. **~ation** *n* decorazione *f*

ornate /ɔ:'neɪt/ *adj* ornato

orphan /'ɔ:fn/ *n* orfano, -a *mf* ● *vt* rendere orfano; **be ~ed** rimanere orfano. **~age** *n* orfanotrofio *m*

orthodox /'ɔ:θədɒks/ *adj* ortodosso

oscillate /'ɒsɪleɪt/ *vi* oscillare

osteopath /'ɒstɪəpæθ/ *n* osteopata *mf*

ostracize /'ɒstrəsaɪz/ *vt* bandire

ostrich /'ɒstrɪtʃ/ *n* struzzo *m*

other /'ʌðə(r)/ *adj, pron & n* altro, -a *mf*; **the ~ [one]** l'altro, -a *mf*; **the ~ two** gli altri due; **two ~s** altri due; **~ people** gli altri; **any ~ questions?** altre domande?; **every ~ day** (*alternate days*) a giorni alterni; **the ~ day** l'altro giorno; **the ~ evening** l'altra sera; **someone/something or ~** qualcuno/qualcosa ● *adv* **~ than him** tranne lui; **somehow or ~** in qualche modo; **somewhere or ~** da qualche parte

'otherwise *adv* altrimenti; (*differently*) diversamente

otter /'ɒtə(r)/ *n* lontra *f*

ouch /aʊtʃ/ *int* ahi!

ought /ɔ:t/ *v aux* **I/we ~ to stay** dovrei/dovremmo rimanere; **he ~ not to have done it** non avrebbe dovuto farlo; **that ~ to be enough** questo dovrebbe bastare

ounce /aʊns/ *n* oncia *f* (*= 28,35 g*)

our /'aʊə(r)/ *adj* il nostro *m*, la nostra *f*, i nostri *mpl*, le nostre *fpl*; **~ mother/father** nostra madre/nostro padre

ours /'aʊəz/ *poss pron* il nostro *m*, la nostra *f*, i nostri *mpl*, le nostre *fpl*; **a friend of ~** un nostro amico; **friends of ~** dei nostri amici; **that is ~** quello è nostro; (*as opposed to yours*) quello è il nostro

ourselves /aʊə'selvz/ *pron* (*reflexive*) ci; (*emphatic*) noi, noi stessi; **we poured ~ a drink** ci siamo versati da bere; **we heard it ~** l'abbiamo sentito noi stessi; **we are proud of ~** siamo fieri di noi; **by ~** da soli

out /aʊt/ *adv* fuori; (*not alight*) spento; **be ~** (flower:) essere sbocciato; (workers:) essere in sciopero; (calculation:) essere sbagliato; (*Sport*) essere fuori; (*unconscious*) aver perso i sensi; (*fig: not feasible*) fuori questione; **the sun is ~** è uscito il sole; **~ and about** in piedi; **get ~!** [!] fuori!; **you should get ~ more** dovresti uscire più spesso; **~ with it!** [!] sputa il rospo!; ● *prep* **~ of** fuori da; **~ of date** non aggiornato; (passport) scaduto; **~ of order** guasto; **~ of print/stock** esaurito; **~ of bed/the room** fuori dal letto/dalla stanza; **~ of breath** senza fiato; **~ of danger** fuori pericolo; **~ of work** disoccupato; **nine ~ of ten** nove su dieci; **be ~ of sugar/bread** rimanere senza zucchero/pane; **go ~ of the room** uscire dalla stanza

'outbreak *n* (*of war*) scoppio *m*; (*of disease*) insorgenza *f*

'outburst *n* esplosione *f*

'outcome *n* risultato *m*

'outcry *n* protesta *f*

out'dated *adj* sorpassato

out'do *vt* (*pt* **-did**, *pp* **-done**) superare

'outdoor *adj* (life, sports) all'aperto; **~ clothes** *pl* vestiti per uscire; **~ swimming pool** piscina *f* scoperta

out'doors *adv* all'aria aperta; **go ~** uscire [all'aria aperta]

'outer *adj* esterno

'outfit *n* equipaggiamento *m*; (*clothes*) completo *m*; ([!]*: organization*) organizza-

O

zione. **~ter** *n* **men's ~ter's** negozio *m* di abbigliamento maschile

'outgoing *adj* (*president*) uscente; (mail) in partenza; (*sociable*) estroverso. **~s** *npl* uscite *fpl*

out'grow *vi* (*pt* **-grew**, *pp* **-grown**) diventare troppo grande per

outing /'aʊtɪŋ/ *n* gita *f*

outlandish /aʊt'lændɪʃ/ *adj* stravagante

'outlaw *n* fuorilegge *mf inv* ● *vt* dichiarare illegale

'outlay *n* spesa *f*

'outlet *n* sbocco *m*; *fig* sfogo *m*; (*Comm*) punto *m* [di] vendita

'outline *n* contorno *m*; (*summary*) sommario *m* ● *vt* tracciare il contorno di; (*describe*) descrivere

out'live *vt* sopravvivere a

'outlook *n* vista *f*; (*future prospect*) prospettiva *f*; (*attitude*) visione *f*

'outlying *adj* **~ areas** *pl* zone *fpl* periferiche

out'number *vt* superare in numero

'out-patient *n* paziente *mf* esterno, -a; **~s' department** ambulatorio *m*

'output *n* produzione *f*

'outright¹ *adj* completo; (refusal) netto

O

out'right² *adv* completamente; (*at once*) immediatamente; (*frankly*) francamente

'outset *n* inizio *m*; **from the ~** fin dall'inizio

'outside¹ *adj* esterno ● *n* esterno *m*; **from the ~** dall'esterno; **at the ~** al massimo

out'side² *adv* all'esterno, fuori; (*out of doors*) fuori; **go ~** andare fuori ● *prep* fuori da; (*in front of*) davanti a

'outskirts *npl* sobborghi *mpl*

out'spoken *adj* schietto

out'standing *adj* eccezionale; (landmark) prominente; (*not settled*) in sospeso

out'stretched *adj* allungato

out'strip *vt* (*pt/pp* **-stripped**) superare

'outward /-wəd/ *adj* esterno; (*journey*) di andata ● *adv* verso l'esterno. **~ly** *adv* esternamente. **~s** *adv* verso l'esterno

out'weigh *vt* aver maggior peso di

out'wit *vt* (*pt/pp* **-witted**) battere in astuzia

oval /'əʊvl/ *adj* ovale ● *n* ovale *m*

ovary /'əʊvərɪ/ *n* (*Anat*) ovaia *f*

ovation /əʊ'veɪʃn/ *n* ovazione *f*

oven /'ʌvn/ *n* forno *m*. **~-ready** *adj* pronto da mettere in forno

over /'əʊvə(r)/ *prep* sopra; (*across*) al di là di; (*during*) durante; (*more than*) più di; **~ the phone** al telefono; **~ the page** alla pagina seguente; **all ~ Italy** in tutta [l']Italia; (travel) per l'Italia ● *adv* (*Math*) col resto di; (*ended*) finito; **~ again** un'altra volta; **~ and ~** più volte; **~ and above** oltre a; **~ here/there** qui/là; **all ~** (*everywhere*) dappertutto; **it's all ~** è tutto finito; **I ache all ~** ho male dappertutto; **come/bring ~** venire/portare; **turn ~** girare

over- *pref* (*too*) troppo

overall¹ /'əʊvərɔːl/ *n* grembiule *m*; **~s** *pl* tuta *fsg* [da lavoro]

overall² /əʊvər'ɔːl/ *adj* complessivo; (*general*) generale ● *adv* complessivamente

over'balance *vi* perdere l'equilibrio

over'bearing *adj* prepotente

'overboard *adv* (*Naut*) in mare

'overcast *adj* coperto

over'charge *vt* **~ sb** far pagare più del dovuto a qcno ● *vi* far pagare più del dovuto

'overcoat *n* cappotto *m*

over'come *vt* (*pt* **-came**, *pp* **-come**) vincere; **be ~ by** essere sopraffatto da

over'crowded *adj* sovraffollato

over'do *vt* (*pt* **-did**, *pp* **-done**) esagerare; (*cook too long*) stracuocere; **~ it** ([!]: *do too much*) strafare

'overdose *n* overdose *f inv*

'overdraft *n* scoperto *m*; **have an ~** avere il conto scoperto

over'draw *vt* (*pt* **-drew**, *pp* **-drawn**) **~ one's account** andare allo scoperto; **be ~n by** (account:) essere [allo] scoperto di

over'due *adj* in ritardo

over'estimate *vt* sopravvalutare

'overflow¹ *n* (*water*) acqua *f* che deborda; (*people*) pubblico *m* in eccesso; (*outlet*) scarico *m*; **~ car park** parcheggio *m* supplementare

over'flow² *vi* debordare

over'grown *adj* (garden) coperto di erbacce
'overhaul[1] *n* revisione *f*
over'haul[2] *vt* (*Techn*) revisionare
over'head[1] *adv* in alto
'overhead[2] *adj* aereo; (railway) sopraelevato; (lights) da soffitto. **~s** *npl* spese *fpl* generali
over'hear *vt* (*pt/pp* **-heard**) sentire per caso (conversation)
over'joyed *adj* felicissimo
'overland *adj & adv* via terra; **~ route** via *f* terrestre
over'lap *v* (*pt/pp* **-lapped**) ● *vi* sovrapporsi ● *vt* sovrapporre
over'leaf *adv* sul retro
over'load *vt* sovraccaricare
over'look *vt* dominare; (*fail to see, ignore*) lasciarsi sfuggire
over'night[1] *adv* per la notte; **stay ~** fermarsi a dormire
'overnight[2] *adj* notturno; **~ bag** piccola borsa *f* da viaggio; **~ stay** sosta *f* per la notte
'overpass *n* cavalcavia *m inv*
over'pay *vt* (*pt/pp* **-paid**) strapagare
over'power *vt* sopraffare. **~ing** *adj* insostenibile
over'priced *adj* troppo caro
overre'act *vi* avere una reazione eccessiva. **~ion** *n* reazione *f* eccessiva
over'rid|e *vt* (*pt* **-rode**, *pp* **-ridden**) passare sopra a. **~ing** *adj* prevalente
over'rule *vt* annullare (decision)
over'run *vt* (*pt* **-ran**, *pp* **-run**, *pres p* **-running**) invadere; oltrepassare (time); **be ~ with** essere invaso da
over'seas[1] *adv* oltremare
'overseas[2] *adj* d'oltremare
over'see *vt* (*pt* **-saw**, *pp* **-seen**) sorvegliare
over'shadow *vt* adombrare
over'shoot *vt* (*pt/pp* **-shot**) oltrepassare
'oversight *n* disattenzione *f*; **an ~** una svista
over'sleep *vi* (*pt/pp* **-slept**) svegliarsi troppo tardi
over'step *vt* (*pt/pp* **-stepped**) **~ the mark** oltrepassare ogni limite
overt /əʊ'vɜ:t/ *adj* palese
over'tak|e *vt/i* (*pt* **-took**, *pp* **-taken**) sorpassare. **~ing** *n* sorpasso *m*; **no ~ing** divieto di sorpasso
'overthrow[1] *n* (*Pol*) rovesciamento *m*
over'throw[2] *vt* (*pt* **-threw**, *pp* **-thrown**) (*Pol*) rovesciare
'overtime *n* lavoro *m* straordinario ● *adv* **work ~** fare lo straordinario
overture /'əʊvətjʊə(r)/ *n* (*Mus*) preludio *m*; **~s** *pl fig* approccio *msg*
over'turn *vt* ribaltare ● *vi* ribaltarsi
over'weight *adj* sovrappeso
overwhelm /-'welm/ *vt* sommergere (**with** di); (*with emotion*) confondere. **~ing** *adj* travolgente; (victory, majority) schiacciante
over'work *n* lavoro *m* eccessivo ● *vt* far lavorare eccessivamente ● *vi* lavorare eccessivamente
ow|e /əʊ/ *vt also fig* dovere (**[to] sb** a qcno); **~e sb sth** dovere qcsa a qcno. **~ing** *adj* **be ~ing** (money:) essere da pagare ● *prep* **~ing to** a causa di
owl /aʊl/ *n* gufo *m*
own[1] /əʊn/ *adj* proprio ● *pron* **a car of my ~** una macchina per conto mio; **on one's ~** da solo; **hold one's ~ with** tener testa a; **get one's ~ back** [!] prendersi una rivincita
own[2] *vt* possedere; (*confess*) ammettere; **I don't ~ it** non mi appartiene. □ **~ up** *vi* confessare (**to sth** qcsa)
owner /'əʊnə(r)/ *n* proprietario, -a *mf*. **~ship** *n* proprietà *f*
oxygen /'ɒksɪdʒən/ *n* ossigeno *m*; **~ mask** maschera *f* a ossigeno
oyster /'ɔɪstə(r)/ *n* ostrica *f*
ozone /'əʊzəʊn/ *n* ozono *m*. **~-'friendly** *adj* che non danneggia l'ozono. **~ layer** *n* fascia *f* d'ozono

Pp

pace /peɪs/ *n* passo *m*; (*speed*) ritmo *m*; **keep ~ with** camminare di pari passo con ● *vi* **~ up and down** camminare avanti e indietro. **~-maker** *n* (*Med*) pacemaker *m*; (*runner*) battistrada *m*
Pacific /pə'sɪfɪk/ *adj & n* **the ~**

[**Ocean**] l'oceano *m* Pacifico, il Pacifico

pacifist /'pæsɪfɪst/ *n* pacifista *mf*

pacify /'pæsɪfaɪ/ *vt* (*pt/pp* **-ied**) placare (person); pacificare (country)

pack /pæk/ *n* (*of cards*) mazzo *m*; (*of hounds*) muta *f*; (*of wolves, thieves*) branco *m*; (*of cigarettes etc*) pacchetto *m*; **a ~ of lies** un mucchio di bugie ● *vt* impacchettare (article); fare (suitcase); mettere in valigia (swimsuit etc); (*press down*) comprimere; **~ed [out]** (*crowded*) pieno zeppo ● *vi* fare i bagagli; **send sb ~ing** 🅘 mandare qcno a stendere. ▫ **~ up** *vt* impacchettare ● *vi* 🅘 (machine:) piantare in asso

package /'pækɪdʒ/ *n* pacco *m* ● *vt* impacchettare. **~ deal** offerta *f* tutto compreso. **~ holiday** *n* vacanza *f* organizzata. **~ tour** viaggio *m* organizzato

packet /'pækɪt/ *n* pacchetto *m*; **cost a ~** 🅘 costare un sacco

pact /pækt/ *n* patto *m*

pad¹ /pæd/ *n* imbottitura *f*; (*for writing*) bloc-notes *m*, taccuino *m*; (🅘: *home*) [piccolo] appartamento *m* ● *vt* (*pt/pp* **padded**) imbottire. ▫ **~ out** *vt* gonfiare

pad² *vi* (*pt/pp* **padded**) camminare con passo felpato

paddle¹ /'pæd(ə)l/ *n* pagaia *f* ● *vt* (*row*) spingere remando

paddle² *vi* (*wade*) sguazzare

paddock /'pædək/ *n* recinto *m*

padlock /'pædlɒk/ *n* lucchetto *m* ● *vt* chiudere con lucchetto

paediatrician /pi:dɪə'trɪʃn/ *n* pediatra *mf*

page¹ /peɪdʒ/ *n* pagina *f*

page² *n* (*boy*) paggetto *m*; (*in hotel*) fattorino *m* ● *vt* far chiamare (person)

pager /'peɪdʒə(r)/ *n* cercapersone *m inv*

paid /peɪd/ ▷**PAY** ● *adj* **~ employment** lavoro *m* remunerato; **put ~ to** mettere un termine a

pail /peɪl/ *n* secchio *m*

pain /peɪn/ *n* dolore *m*; **be in ~** soffrire; **take ~s** darsi un gran d'affare; **~ in the neck** 🅘 spina *f* nel fianco

pain: ~ful *adj* doloroso; (*laborious*) penoso. **~-killer** *n* calmante *m*. **~less** *adj* indolore

painstaking /'peɪnzteɪkɪŋ/ *adj* minuzioso

paint /peɪnt/ *n* pittura *f*; **~s** colori *mpl* ● *vt/i* pitturare; (artist:) dipingere. **~brush** *n* pennello *m*. **~er** *n* pittore, -trice *mf*; (*decorator*) imbianchino *m*. **~ing** *n* pittura *f*; (*picture*) dipinto *m*. **~work** *n* pittura *f*

pair /peə(r)/ *n* paio *m*; (*of people*) coppia *f*; **~ of trousers** paio *m* di pantaloni; **~ of scissors** paio *m* di forbici

pajamas /pə'dʒɑ:məz/ *npl Am* pigiama *msg*

Pakistan /pɑ:kɪ'stɑ:n/ *n* Pakistan *m*. **~i** *adj* pakistano ● *n* pakistano, -a *mf*

pal /pæl/ *n* 🅘 amico, -a *mf*

palace /'pælɪs/ *n* palazzo *m*

palatable /'pælətəbl/ *adj* gradevole (*al gusto*)

palate /'pælət/ *n* palato *m*

pale /peɪl/ *adj* pallido

Palestin|e /'pælɪstaɪn/ *n* Palestina *f*. **~ian** *adj* palestinese ● *n* palestinese *mf*

palette /'pælɪt/ *n* tavolozza *f*

palm /pɑ:m/ *n* palmo *m*; (*tree*) palma *f*; **P~ 'Sunday** *n* Domenica *f* delle Palme ● **palm off** *vt* **~ sth off on sb** rifilare qcsa a qcno

palpable /'pælpəbl/ *adj* palpabile; (*perceptible*) tangibile

palpitat|e /'pælpɪteɪt/ *vi* palpitare. **~ions** *npl* palpitazioni *fpl*

pamper /'pæmpə(r)/ *vt* viziare

pamphlet /'pæmflɪt/ *n* opuscolo *m*

pan /pæn/ *n* tegame *m*, pentola *f*; (*for frying*) padella *f*; (*of scales*) piatto *m* ● *vt* (*pt/pp* **panned**) (🅘: *criticize*) stroncare

'pancake *n* crêpe *f inv*, frittella *f*

panda /'pændə/ *n* panda *m inv*. **~ car** *n* macchina *f* della polizia

pandemonium /pændɪ'məʊnɪəm/ *n* pandemonio *m*

pander /'pændə(r)/ *vi* **~ to sb** compiacere qcno

pane /peɪn/ *n* **~ [of glass]** vetro *m*

panel /'pænl/ *n* pannello *m*; (*group of people*) giuria *f*; **~ of experts** gruppo *m* di esperti. **~ling** *n* pannelli *mpl*

pang /pæŋ/ *n* **~s of hunger** morsi *mpl* della fame; **~s of conscience** rimorsi *mpl* di coscienza

panic /'pænɪk/ *n* panico *m* ● *vi* (*pt/pp* **panicked**) lasciarsi prendere dal panico. **~-stricken** *adj* in preda al panico

panoram|a /pænə'rɑːmə/ *n* panorama *m*. **~ic** *adj* panoramico

pansy /'pænzɪ/ *n* viola *f* del pensiero; ([!]: *effeminate man*) finocchio *m*

pant /pænt/ *vi* ansimare

panther /'pænθə(r)/ *n* pantera *f*

panties /'pæntɪz/ *npl* mutandine *fpl*

pantomime /'pæntəmaɪm/ *n* pantomima *f*

pantry /'pæntrɪ/ *n* dispensa *f*

pants /pænts/ *npl* (*underwear*) mutande *fpl*; (*woman's*) mutandine *fpl*; (*trousers*) pantaloni *mpl*

'pantyhose *n Am* collant *m inv*

paper /'peɪpə(r)/ *n* carta *f*; (*wallpaper*) carta *f* da parati; (*newspaper*) giornale *m*; (*exam*) esame *m*; (*treatise*) saggio *m*; **~s** *pl* (*documents*) documenti *mpl*; (*for identification*) documento *m* [d'identità]; **on ~** in teoria; **put down on ~** mettere per iscritto ● *attrib* di carta ● *vt* tappezzare

paper: ~back *n* edizione *f* economica. **~-clip** *n* graffetta *f*. **~weight** *n* fermacarte *m inv*. **~work** *n* lavoro *m* d'ufficio

parable /'pærəbl/ *n* parabola *f*

parachut|e /'pærəʃuːt/ *n* paracadute *m* ● *vi* lanciarsi col paracadute. **~ist** *n* paracadutista *mf*

parade /pə'reɪd/ *n* (*military*) parata *f* militare ● *vi* sfilare ● *vt* (*show off*) far sfoggio di

paradise /'pærədaɪs/ *n* paradiso *m*

paraffin /'pærəfɪn/ *n* paraffina *f*

paragraph /'pærəgrɑːf/ *n* paragrafo *m*

parallel /'pærəlel/ *adj & adv* parallelo. **~ bars** *npl* parallele *fpl*. **~ port** *n* (*Comput*) porta *f* parallela ● *n* (*Geog*), *fig* parallelo *m*; (*line*) parallela *f* ● *vt* essere paragonabile a

Paralympics /pærə'lɪmpɪks/ *npl* **the P~** le Paraolimpiadi *fpl*

paralyse /'pærəlaɪz/ *vt also fig* paralizzare

paralysis /pə'ræləsɪs/ *n* (*pl* **-ses** /-siːz/ paralisi *f inv*

paramedic /pærə'medɪk/ *n* paramedico, -a *mf*

parameter /pə'ræmɪtə(r)/ *n* parametro *m*

paranoia /pærə'nɔɪə/ *n* paranoia *f*

paraphernalia /pærəfə'neɪlɪə/ *n* armamentario *m*

paraplegic /pærə'pliːdʒɪk/ *adj* paraplegico ● *n* paraplegico, -a *mf*

parasite /'pærəsaɪt/ *n* parassita *mf*

paratrooper /'pærətruːpə(r)/ *n* paracadutista *m*

parcel /'pɑːsl/ *n* pacco *m*

parch /pɑːtʃ/ *vt* disseccare; **be ~ed** (*person*:) morire dalla sete

pardon /'pɑːdn/ *n* perdono *m*; (*Jur*) grazia *f*; **~?** prego?; **I beg your ~?** *fml* chiedo scusa?; **I do beg your ~** (*sorry*) chiedo scusa! ● *vt* perdonare; (*Jur*) graziare

parent /'peərənt/ *n* genitore, -trice *mf*; **~s** *pl* genitori *mpl*. **~al** *adj* dei genitori

parenthesis /pə'renθəsɪs/ *n* (*pl* **-ses** /-siːz/) parentesi *m inv*

Paris /'pærɪs/ *n* Parigi *f*

parish /'pærɪʃ/ *n* parrocchia *f*. **~ioner** *n* parrocchiano, -a *mf*

park /pɑːk/ *n* parco *m* ● *vt/i* (*Auto*) posteggiare, parcheggiare; **~ oneself** [!] installarsi

park-and-'ride *n* park and ride *m inv*

parking /'pɑːkɪŋ/ *n* parcheggio *m*, posteggio *m*; **'no ~'** 'divieto di sosta'. **~-lot** *n Am* posteggio *m*, parcheggio *m*. **~-meter** *n* parchimetro *m*. **~ space** *n* posteggio *m*, parcheggio *m*

parliament /'pɑːləmənt/ *n* parlamento *m*. **~ary** *adj* parlamentare

P

> *i* **Parliament** Il Parlamento britannico è l'organo legislativo del paese, suddiviso in due Camere: *House of Commons* e *House of Lords*. La prima è composta di 646 parlamentari, o *MPs* (*Members of Parliament*), eletti a suffragio popolare; la seconda è formata da circa 730 membri, tra i quali esponenti dell'aristocrazia, ex primi ministri e cittadini che si sono in qualche modo distinti. Ogni anno è il capo della monarchia ad aprire ufficialmente il Parlamento e l'anno legislativo.

parlour /'pɑːlə(r)/ *n* salotto *m*

parochial /pə'rəʊkɪəl/ *adj* parrocchiale; *fig* ristretto

parody /ˈpærədɪ/ *n* parodia *f* ● *vt* (*pt/pp* **-ied**) parodiare

parole /pəˈrəʊl/ *n* **on ~** in libertà condizionale ● *vt* mettere in libertà condizionale

parrot /ˈpærət/ *n* pappagallo *m*

parsley /ˈpɑːslɪ/ *n* prezzemolo *m*

parsnip /ˈpɑːsnɪp/ *n* pastinaca *f*

part /pɑːt/ *n* parte *f*; (*of machine*) pezzo *m*; **for my ~** per quanto mi riguarda; **on the ~ of** da parte di; **take sb's ~** prendere le parti di qcno; **take ~ in** prendere parte a ● *adv* in parte ● *vt* **~ one's hair** farsi la riga ● *vi* (people:) separare; **~ with** separarsi da

partial /ˈpɑːʃl/ *adj* parziale; **be ~ to** aver un debole per. **~ly** *adv* parzialmente

particip|ant /pɑːˈtɪsɪpənt/ *n* partecipante *mf*. **~ate** *vi* partecipare (**in** a). **~ation** *n* partecipazione *f*

particle /ˈpɑːtɪkl/ *n* (*Gram, Phys*) particella *f*

particular /pəˈtɪkjʊlə(r)/ *adj* particolare; (*precise*) meticoloso; *pej* noioso; **in ~** in particolare. **~ly** *adv* particolarmente. **~s** *npl* particolari *mpl*

parting /ˈpɑːtɪŋ/ *n* separazione *f*; (*in hair*) scriminatura *f* ● *attrib* di commiato

partisan /pɑːtɪˈzæn/ *n* partigiano, -a *mf*

partition /pɑːˈtɪʃn/ *n* (*wall*) parete *f* divisoria; (*Pol*) divisione *f* ● *vt* dividere (*in parti*). □ **~ off** *vt* separare

partly /ˈpɑːtlɪ/ *adv* in parte

partner /ˈpɑːtnə(r)/ *n* (*Comm*) socio, -a *mf*; (*sport, in relationship*) compagno, -a *mf*. **~ship** *n* (*Comm*) società *f*

partridge /ˈpɑːtrɪdʒ/ *n* pernice *f*

part-ˈtime *adj & adv* part time; **be** *or* **work ~** lavorare part time

party /ˈpɑːtɪ/ *n* ricevimento *m*, festa *f*; (*group*) gruppo *m*; (*Pol*) partito *m*; (*Jur*) parte *f* [in causa]; **be ~ to** essere parte attiva in

pass /pɑːs/ *n* lasciapassare *m inv*; (*in mountains*) passo *m*; (*Sport*) passaggio *m*; (*Sch: mark*) [voto *m*] sufficiente *m*; **make a ~ at** [!] fare delle avances a ● *vt* passare; (*overtake*) sorpassare; (*approve*) far passare; fare (remark); (*Jur*) pronunciare (sentence); **~ the time** passare il tempo ● *vi* passare; (*in exam*) essere promosso. □ **~ away** *vi* mancare. □ **~ down** *vt* passare; *fig* trasmettere. □ **~ out** *vi* [!] svenire. □ **~ round** *vt* far passare. □ **~ through** *vt* attraversare. □ **~ up** *vt* passare; ([!]: *miss*) lasciarsi scappare

passable /ˈpɑːsəbl/ *adj* (road) praticabile; (*satisfactory*) passabile

passage /ˈpæsɪdʒ/ *n* passaggio *m*; (*corridor*) corridoio *m*; (*voyage*) traversata *f*

passenger /ˈpæsɪndʒə(r)/ *n* passeggero, -a *mf*. **~ seat** *n* posto *m* accanto al guidatore

passer-by /pɑːsəˈbaɪ/ *n* (*pl* **~sby**) passante *mf*

passion /ˈpæʃn/ *n* passione *f*. **~ate** *adj* appassionato

passive /ˈpæsɪv/ *adj* passivo ● *n* passivo *m*. **~ness** *n* passività *f*

Passover /ˈpɑːsəʊvə(r)/ *n* Pasqua *f* ebraica

pass: ~port *n* passaporto *m*. **~word** *n* parola *f* d'ordine

past /pɑːst/ *adj* passato; (*former*) ex; **in the ~ few days** nei giorni scorsi; **that's all ~** tutto questo è passato; **the ~ week** la settimana scorsa ● *n* passato *m* ● *prep* oltre; **at ten ~ two** alle due e dieci ● *adv* oltre; **go/come ~** passare

pasta /ˈpæstə/ *n* pasta[sciutta] *f*

paste /peɪst/ *n* pasta *f*; (*dough*) impasto *m*; (*adhesive*) colla *f* ● *vt* incollare

pastel /ˈpæstl/ *n* pastello *m* ● *attrib* pastello

pasteurize /ˈpɑːstʃəraɪz/ *vt* pastorizzare

pastime /ˈpɑːstaɪm/ *n* passatempo *m*

pastr|y /ˈpeɪstrɪ/ *n* pasta *f*; **~ies** pasticcini *mpl*

pasture /ˈpɑːstʃə(r)/ *n* pascolo *m*

pasty[1] /ˈpæstɪ/ *n* ≈ pasticcio *m*

pasty[2] /ˈpeɪstɪ/ *adj* smorto

pat /pæt/ *n* buffetto *m*; (*of butter*) pezzetto *m* ● *adv* **have sth off ~** conoscere qcsa a menadito ● *vt* (*pt/pp* **patted**) dare un buffetto a; **~ sb on the back** *fig* congratularsi con qcno

patch /pætʃ/ *n* toppa *f*; (*spot*) chiazza *f*; (*period*) periodo *m*; **not a ~ on** [!] molto inferiore a ● *vt* mettere una toppa su. □ **~ up** *vt* riparare alla bell'e meglio; appianare (quarrel)

pâté /ˈpæteɪ/ *n* pâté *m inv*

patent /'peɪtnt/ *adj* palese ● *n* brevetto *m* ● *vt* brevettare. ~ **leather shoes** *npl* scarpe *fpl* di vernice. **~ly** *adv* in modo palese

patern|al /pə'tɜ:nl/ *adj* paterno. **~ity** *n* paternità *f inv*

path /pɑ:θ/ *n* (*pl* **~s** /pɑ:ðz/) sentiero *m*; (*orbit*) traiettoria *m*; *fig* strada *f*

pathetic /pə'θetɪk/ *adj* patetico; (🄸: *very bad*) penoso

patience /'peɪʃns/ *n* pazienza *f*; (*game*) solitario *m*

patient /'peɪʃnt/ *adj* paziente ● *n* paziente *mf*. **~ly** *adv* pazientemente

patio /'pætɪəʊ/ *n* terrazza *f*

patriot /'pætrɪət/ *n* patriota *mf*. **~ic** *adj* patriottico. **~ism** *n* patriottismo *m*

patrol /pə'trəʊl/ *n* pattuglia *f* ● *vt/i* pattugliare. ~ **car** *n* autopattuglia *f*

patron /'peɪtrən/ *n* patrono *m*; (*of charity*) benefattore, -trice *mf*; (*of the arts*) mecenate *mf*; (*customer*) cliente *mf*

patroniz|e /'pætrənaɪz/ *vt* frequentare abitualmente; *fig* trattare con condiscendenza. **~ing** *adj* condiscendente. **~ingly** *adv* con condiscendenza

pattern /'pætn/ *n* disegno *m* (*stampato*); (*for knitting, sewing*) modello *m*

paunch /pɔ:ntʃ/ *n* pancia *f*

pause /pɔ:z/ *n* pausa *f* ● *vi* fare una pausa

pave /peɪv/ *vt* pavimentare; ~ **the way** preparare la strada (**for** a). **~ment** *n* marciapiede *m*

paw /pɔ:/ *n* zampa *f* ● *vt* 🄸 mettere le zampe addosso a

pawn¹ /pɔ:n/ *n* (*in chess*) pedone *m*; *fig* pedina *f*

pawn² *vt* impegnare ● *n* **in** ~ in pegno. **~broker** *n* prestatore, -trice *mf* su pegno. **~shop** *n* monte *m* di pietà

pay /peɪ/ *n* paga *f*; **in the** ~ **of** al soldo di ● *v* (*pt/pp* **paid**) ● *vt* pagare; prestare (attention); fare (compliment, visit); ~ **cash** pagare in contanti ● *vi* pagare; (*be profitable*) rendere; **it doesn't** ~ **to...** *fig* è fatica sprecata...; ~ **for sth** pagare per qcsa. □ ~ **back** *vt* ripagare. □ ~ **in** *vt* versare. □ ~ **off** *vt* saldare (debt) ● *vi fig* dare dei frutti. □ ~ **up** *vi* pagare

payable /'peɪəbl/ *adj* pagabile; **make** ~ **to** intestare a

payment /'peɪmənt/ *n* pagamento *m*

PC *n abbr* (personal computer) PC *m inv*

pea /pi:/ *n* pisello *m*

peace /pi:s/ *n* pace *f*; ~ **of mind** tranquillità *f*

peach /pi:tʃ/ *n* pesca *f*; (*tree*) pesco *m*

peacock /'pi:kɒk/ *n* pavone *m*

peak /pi:k/ *n* picco *m*; *fig* culmine *m*. **~ed 'cap** *n* berretto *m* a punta. ~ **hours** *npl* ore *fpl* di punta

peal /pi:l/ *n* (*of bells*) scampanio *m*; **~s of laughter** fragore *m* di risate

'peanut *n* nocciolina *f* [americana]; **~s** 🄸 miseria *f*

pear /peə(r)/ *n* pera *f*; (*tree*) pero *m*

pearl /pɜ:l/ *n* perla *f*

peasant /'peznt/ *n* contadino, -a *mf*

pebble /'pebl/ *n* ciottolo *m*

peck /pek/ *n* beccata *f*; (*kiss*) bacetto *m* ● *vt* beccare; (*kiss*) dare un bacetto a. **~ing order** *n* gerarchia *f*. □ ~ **at** *vt* beccare

peculiar /pɪ'kju:lɪə(r)/ *adj* strano; (*special*) particolare; ~ **to** tipico di. **~ity** *n* stranezza *f*; (*feature*) particolarità *f inv*

pedal /'pedl/ *n* pedale *m* ● *vi* pedalare. ~ **bin** *n* pattumiera *f* a pedale

pedantic /pɪ'dæntɪk/ *adj* pedante

pedestal /'pedɪstl/ *n* piedistallo *m*

pedestrian /pɪ'destrɪən/ *n* pedone *m* ● *adj fig* scadente. ~ **'crossing** *n* passaggio *m* pedonale. ~ **'precinct** *n* zona *f* pedonale

pedigree /'pedɪgri:/ *n* pedigree *m inv*; (*of person*) lignaggio *m* ● *attrib* (animal) di razza, con pedigree

peek /pi:k/ *vi* 🄸 sbirciare

peel /pi:l/ *n* buccia *f* ● *vt* sbucciare ● *vi* (nose) *etc*: spellarsi; (paint:) staccarsi

peep /pi:p/ *n* sbirciata *f* ● *vi* sbirciare

peer¹ /pɪə(r)/ *vi* ~ **at** scrutare

peer² *n* nobile *m*; **his ~s** *pl* (*in rank*) i suoi pari *mpl*; (*in age*) i suoi coetanei *mpl*. **~age** *n* nobiltà *f*

peg /peg/ *n* (*hook*) piolo *m*; (*for tent*) picchetto *m*; (*for clothes*) molletta *f*; **off the** ~ 🄸 prêt-à-porter

pejorative /pɪ'dʒɒrətɪv/ *adj* peggiorativo

pelican /'pelɪkən/ *n* pellicano *m*

pellet /'pelɪt/ *n* pallottola *f*

pelt /pelt/ *vt* bombardare ● *vi* (🄸: *run*

fast) catapultarsi; ~ **down** (rain:) venir giù a fiotti

pelvis /'pelvɪs/ *n* (*Anat*) bacino *m*

pen¹ /pen/ *n* (*for animals*) recinto *m*

pen² *n* penna *f*; (*ball-point*) penna *f* a sfera

penal /'pi:nl/ *adj* penale. **~ize** *vt* penalizzare

penalty /'penltɪ/ *n* sanzione *f*; (*fine*) multa *f*; (*in football*) ~ **[kick]** [calcio *m* di] rigore *m*; ~ **area** *or* **box** area *f* di rigore

penance /'penəns/ *n* penitenza *f*

pence /pens/ ▷**PENNY**

pencil /'pensl/ *n* matita *f*. **~-sharpener** *n* temperamatite *m inv*

pendulum /'pendjʊləm/ *n* pendolo *m*

penetrat|e /'penɪtreɪt/ *vt/i* penetrare. **~ing** *adj* acuto; (*sound, stare*) penetrante. **~ion** *n* penetrazione *f*

penguin /'peŋgwɪn/ *n* pinguino *m*

penicillin /penɪ'sɪlɪn/ *n* penicillina *f*

peninsula /pɪ'nɪnsjʊlə/ *n* penisola *f*

penis /'pi:nɪs/ *n* pene *m*

pen: ~knife *n* temperino *m*. **~-name** *n* pseudonimo *m*

penniless /'penɪlɪs/ *adj* senza un soldo

penny /'penɪ/ *n* (*pl* **pence**; *single coins* **pennies**) penny *m*; *Am* centesimo *m*; **spend a ~** [!] andare in bagno

pension /'penʃn/ *n* pensione *f*. **~er** *n* pensionato, -a *mf*

pensive /'pensɪv/ *adj* pensoso

Pentecost /'pentɪkɒst/ *n* Pentecoste *f*

pent-up /'pentʌp/ *adj* represso

penultimate /pɪ'nʌltɪmət/ *adj* penultimo

people /'pi:pl/ *npl* persone *fpl*, gente *fsg*; (*citizens*) popolo *msg*; **a lot of ~** una marea di gente; **the ~** la gente; **English ~** gli inglesi; **~ say** si dice; **for four ~** per quattro ● *vt* popolare

pepper /'pepə(r)/ *n* pepe *m*; (*vegetable*) peperone *m* ● *vt* (*season*) pepare

pepper: ~corn *n* grano *m* di pepe. **~ mill** macinapepe *m inv*. **~mint** *n* menta *f* peperita; (*sweet*) caramella *f* alla menta. **~pot** *n* pepiera *f*

per /pɜ:(r)/ *prep* per; **~ annum** all'anno; **~ cent** percento

perceive /pə'si:v/ *vt* percepire; (*interpret*) interpretare

percentage /pə'sentɪdʒ/ *n* percentuale *f*

perceptible /pə'septəbl/ *adj* percettibile; (difference) sensibile

percept|ion /pə'sepʃn/ *n* percezione *f*. **~ive** *adj* perspicace

perch /pɜ:tʃ/ *n* pertica *f* ● *vi* (bird:) appollaiarsi

percolator /'pɜ:kəleɪtə(r)/ *n* caffettiera *f* a filtro

percussion /pə'kʌʃn/ *n* percussione *f*. **~ instrument** *n* strumento *m* a percussione

perfect¹ /'pɜ:fɪkt/ *adj* perfetto ● *n* (*Gram*) passato *m* prossimo

perfect² /pə'fekt/ *vt* perfezionare. **~ion** *n* perfezione *f*; **to ~ion** alla perfezione. **~ionist** *n* perfezionista *mf*

perfectly /'pɜ:fɪktlɪ/ *adv* perfettamente

perform /pə'fɔ:m/ *vt* compiere, fare; eseguire (operation, sonata); recitare (role); mettere in scena (play) ● *vi* (*Theat*) recitare; (*Techn*) funzionare. **~ance** *n* esecuzione *f*; (*at theatre, cinema*) rappresentazione *f*; (*Techn*) rendimento *m*. **~er** *n* artista *mf*

perfume /'pɜ:fju:m/ *n* profumo *m*

perhaps /pə'hæps/ *adv* forse

peril /'perɪl/ *n* pericolo *m*. **~ous** *adj* pericoloso

perimeter /pə'rɪmɪtə(r)/ *n* perimetro *m*

period /'pɪərɪəd/ *n* periodo *m*; (*menstruation*) mestruazioni *fpl*; (*Sch*) ora *f* di lezione; (*full stop*) punto *m* fermo ● *attrib* (costume) d'epoca; (furniture) in stile. **~ic** *adj* periodico. **~ical** *n* periodico *m*, rivista *f*

peripher|al /pə'rɪfərəl/ *adj* periferico. **~y** *n* periferia *f*

perish /'perɪʃ/ *vi* (*rot*) deteriorarsi; (*die*) perire. **~able** *adj* deteriorabile

perjur|e /'pɜ:dʒə(r)/ *vt* **~e oneself** spergiurare. **~y** *n* spergiuro *m*

perk /pɜ:k/ *n* [!] vantaggio *m*

perm /pɜ:m/ *n* permanente *f* ● *vt* **~ sb's hair** fare la permanente a qno

permanent /'pɜ:mənənt/ *adj* permanente; (job, address) stabile. **~ly** *adv* stabilmente

permissible /pəˈmɪsəbl/ *adj* ammissibile

permission /pəˈmɪʃn/ *n* permesso *m*

permit¹ /pəˈmɪt/ *vt* (*pt/pp* **-mitted**) permettere; ~ **sb to do sth** permettere a qcno di fare qcsa

permit² /ˈpɜːmɪt/ *n* autorizzazione *f*

perpendicular /pɜːpənˈdɪkjʊlə(r)/ *adj* perpendicolare ● *n* perpendicolare *f*

perpetual /pəˈpetjʊəl/ *adj* perenne. **~ly** *adv* perennemente

perpetuate /pəˈpetjʊeɪt/ *vt* perpetuare

perplex /pəˈpleks/ *vt* lasciare perplesso. **~ed** *adj* perplesso. **~ity** *n* perplessità *f inv*

persecut|e /ˈpɜːsɪkjuːt/ *vt* perseguitare. **~ion** *n* persecuzione *f*

perseverance /pɜːsɪˈvɪərəns/ *n* perseveranza *f*

persever|e /pɜːsɪˈvɪə(r)/ *vi* perseverare. **~ing** *adj* assiduo

Persian /ˈpɜːʃn/ *adj* persiano

persist /pəˈsɪst/ *vi* persistere; ~ **in doing sth** persistere nel fare qcsa. **~ence** *n* persistenza *f*. **~ent** *adj* persistente. **~ently** *adv* persistentemente

person /ˈpɜːsn/ *n* persona *f*; **in** ~ di persona

personal /ˈpɜːsənl/ *adj* personale. ~ **ˈhygiene** *n* igiene *f* personale. ~ **organizer** *n* (*Comput*) agenda *f* elettronica. **~ly** *adv* personalmente.

personality /pɜːsəˈnælətɪ/ *n* personalità *f inv*; (*on* (*TV*)) personaggio *m*

personnel /pɜːsəˈnel/ *n* personale *m*

perspective /pəˈspektɪv/ *n* prospettiva *f*

persp|iration /pɜːspɪˈreɪʃn/ *n* sudore *m*. **~ire** *vi* sudare

persua|de /pəˈsweɪd/ *vt* persuadere. **~sion** *n* persuasione *f*; (*belief*) convinzione *f*

persuasive /pəˈsweɪsɪv/ *adj* persuasivo. **~ly** *adv* in modo persuasivo

pertinent /ˈpɜːtɪnənt/ *adj* pertinente (**to** a)

perturb /pəˈtɜːb/ *vt* perturbare

peruse /pəˈruːz/ *vt* leggere

pervers|e /pəˈvɜːs/ *adj* irragionevole. **~ion** *n* perversione *f*

pervert /ˈpɜːvɜːt/ *n* pervertito, -a *mf*

pessimis|m /ˈpesɪmɪzm/ *n* pessimismo *m*. **~t** *n* pessimista *mf*. **~tic** *adj* pessimistico. **~tically** *adv* in modo pessimistico

pest /pest/ *n* piaga *f*; (❗: *person*) peste *f*

pester /ˈpestə(r)/ *vt* molestare

pesticide /ˈpestɪsaɪd/ *n* pesticida *m*

pet /pet/ *n* animale *m* domestico; (*favourite*) cocco, -a *mf* ● *adj* prediletto ● *v* (*pt/pp* **petted**) ● *vt* coccolare ● *vi* (couple:) praticare il petting

petal /ˈpetl/ *n* petalo *m*

petition /pəˈtɪʃn/ *n* petizione *f*

pet ˈname *n* vezzeggiativo *m*

petrol /ˈpetrəl/ *n* benzina *f*

petroleum /pɪˈtrəʊlɪəm/ *n* petrolio *m*

petrol: **~-pump** *n* pompa *f* di benzina. ~ **station** *n* stazione *f* di servizio. ~ **tank** *n* serbatoio *m* della benzina

petticoat /ˈpetɪkəʊt/ *n* sottoveste *f*

petty /ˈpetɪ/ *adj* (**-ier, -iest**) insignificante; (*mean*) meschino. ~ **ˈcash** *n* cassa *f* per piccole spese

petulant /ˈpetjʊlənt/ *adj* petulante

pew /pjuː/ *n* banco *m* (*di chiesa*)

phantom /ˈfæntəm/ *n* fantasma *m*

pharmaceutical /fɑːməˈsjuːtɪkl/ *adj* farmaceutico

pharmac|ist /ˈfɑːməsɪst/ *n* farmacista *mf*. **~y** *n* farmacia *f*

phase /feɪz/ *n* fase *f* ● *vt* **phase in/out** introdurre/eliminare gradualmente

pheasant /ˈfeznt/ *n* fagiano *m*

phenomen|al /fɪˈnɒmɪnl/ *adj* fenomenale; (*incredible*) incredibile. **~ally** *adv* incredibilmente. **~on** *n* (*pl* **-na**) fenomeno *m*

philistine /ˈfɪlɪstaɪn/ *n* filisteo, -a *mf*

philosoph|er /fɪˈlɒsəfə(r)/ *n* filosofo, -a *mf*. **~ical** *adj* filosofico. **~ically** *adv* con filosofia. **~y** *n* filosofia *f*

phlegm /flem/ *n* (*Med*) flemma *f*

phlegmatic /flegˈmætɪk/ *adj* flemmatico

phobia /ˈfəʊbɪə/ *n* fobia *f*

phone /fəʊn/ *n* telefono *m*; **be on the** ~ avere il telefono; (*be phoning*) essere al telefono ● *vt* telefonare a ● *vi* telefonare. □ ~ **back** *vt/i* richiamare. ~ **book** *n* guida *f* del telefono. ~ **box** *n* cabina *f* telefonica. ~ **call** telefonata *f*. ~ **card** *n* scheda *f* telefonica. **~-in** *n* trasmissione *f* con chiamate in diretta.

p

~ **number** *n* numero *m* telefonico
phonetic /fəˈnetɪk/ *adj* fonetico. **~s** *n* fonetica *f*
phoney /ˈfəʊnɪ/ *adj* (**-ier, -iest**) fasullo
phosphorus /ˈfɒsfərəs/ *n* fosforo *m*
photo /ˈfəʊtəʊ/ *n* foto *f*; **~ album** album *m inv* di fotografie. **~copier** *n* fotocopiatrice *f*. **~copy** *n* fotocopia *f* ● *vt* fotocopiare
photogenic /fəʊtəʊˈdʒenɪk/ *adj* fotogenico
photograph /ˈfəʊtəgrɑːf/ *n* fotografia *f* ● *vt* fotografare
photograph|er /fəˈtɒgrəfə(r)/ *n* fotografo, -a *mf*. **~ic** *adj* fotografico. **~y** *n* fotografia *f*
phrase /freɪz/ *n* espressione *f* ● *vt* esprimere. **~-book** *n* libro *m* di fraseologia
physical /ˈfɪzɪkl/ *adj* fisico. **~ eduˈcation** *n* educazione *f* fisica. **~ly** *adv* fisicamente
physician /fɪˈzɪʃn/ *n* medico *m*
physic|ist /ˈfɪzɪsɪst/ *n* fisico, -a *mf*. **~s** *n* fisica *f*
physiology /fɪzɪˈɒlədʒɪ/ *n* fisiologia *f*
physioˈtherap|ist /fɪzɪəʊ-/ *n* fisioterapista *mf*. **~y** *n* fisioterapia *f*
physique /fɪˈziːk/ *n* fisico *m*
pianist /ˈpɪənɪst/ *n* pianista *mf*
p **piano** /pɪˈænəʊ/ *n* piano *m*
pick[1] /pɪk/ *n* (*tool*) piccone *m*
pick[2] *n* scelta *f*; **take your ~** prendi quello che vuoi ● *vt* (*select*) scegliere; cogliere (flowers); scassinare (lock); borseggiare (pockets); **~ and choose** fare il difficile; **~ one's nose** mettersi le dita nel naso; **~ a quarrel** attaccar briga; **~ holes in** [!] criticare; **~ at one's food** spilluzzicare. □ **~ on** *vt* ([!]: *nag*) assillare; **he always ~s on me** ce l'ha con me. □ **~ out** *vt* (*identify*) individuare. □ **~ up** *vt* sollevare; (*off the ground, information*) raccogliere; prendere in braccio (baby); (*learn*) imparare; prendersi (illness); (*buy*) comprare; captare (signal); (*collect*) andare/venire a prendere; prendere (passengers, habit); (police:) arrestare (criminal); [!] rimorchiare (girl); **~ oneself up** riprendersi ● *vi* (*improve*) recuperare; (weather:) rimettersi
ˈpickaxe *n* piccone *m*
picket /ˈpɪkɪt/ *n* picchettista *mf* ● *vt* picchettare. **~ line** *n* picchetto *m*
pickle /ˈpɪkl/ *n* **~s** *pl* sottaceti *mpl*; **in a ~** *fig* nei pasticci ● *vt* mettere sottaceto
pick: ~pocket *n* borsaiolo *m*. **~-up** *n* (*truck*) furgone *m*; (*on record-player*) pickup *m inv*
picnic /ˈpɪknɪk/ *n* picnic *m* ● *vi* (*pt/pp* **-nicked**) fare un picnic
picture /ˈpɪktʃə(r)/ *n* (*painting*) quadro *m*; (*photo*) fotografia *f*; (*drawing*) disegno *m*; (*film*) film *m inv*; **put sb in the ~** *fig* mettere qcno al corrente; **the ~s** il cinema ● *vt* (*imagine*) immaginare. **~sque** *adj* pittoresco
pie /paɪ/ *n* torta *f*
piece /piːs/ *n* pezzo *m*; (*in game*) pedina *f*; **a ~ of bread/paper** un pezzo di pane/carta; **a ~ of news/advice** una notizia/un consiglio; **take to ~s** smontare. **~meal** *adv* un po' alla volta. **~-work** *n* lavoro *m* a cottimo ● **piece together** *vt* montare; *fig* ricostruire
pier /pɪə(r)/ *n* molo *m*; (*pillar*) pilastro *m*
pierc|e /pɪəs/ *vt* perforare; **~e a hole in sth** fare un buco in qcsa. **~ing** *n* [**body**] **~** piercing *m inv* ● *adj* penetrante
pig /pɪg/ *n* maiale *m*
pigeon /ˈpɪdʒɪn/ *n* piccione *m*. **~-hole** *n* casella *f*
piggy /ˈpɪgɪ/ **~back** *n* **give sb a ~back** portare qcno sulle spalle. **~ bank** *n* salvadanaio *m*
pigˈheaded *adj* [!] cocciuto
pigtail *n* (*plait*) treccina *f*
pile *n* (*heap*) pila *f* ● *vt* **~ sth on to sth** appilare qcsa su qcsa. □ **~ up** *vt* accatastare ● *vi* ammucchiarsi
piles /paɪlz/ *npl* emorroidi *fpl*
ˈpile-up *n* tamponamento *m* a catena
pilgrim /ˈpɪlgrɪm/ *n* pellegrino, -a *mf*. **~age** *n* pellegrinaggio *m*
pill /pɪl/ *n* pillola *f*
pillar /ˈpɪlə(r)/ *n* pilastro *m*. **~-box** *n* buca *f* delle lettere
pillow /ˈpɪləʊ/ *n* guanciale *m*. **~case** *n* federa *f*
pilot /ˈpaɪlət/ *n* pilota *mf* ● *vt* pilotare. **~-light** *n* fiamma *f* di sicurezza
pimple /ˈpɪmpl/ *n* foruncolo *m*

pin /pɪn/ *n* spillo *m*; (*Electr*) spinotto *m*; (*Med*) chiodo *m*; **I have ~s and needles in my leg** [!] mi formicola una gamba ● *vt* (*pt/pp* **pinned**) appuntare (**to/on** su); (*sewing*) fissare con gli spilli; (*hold down*) immobilizzare; **~ sb down to a date** ottenere un appuntamento da qcno; **~ sth on sb** [!] addossare a qcno la colpa di qcsa. □ **~ up** *vt* appuntare; (*on wall*) affiggere
pinafore /ˈpɪnəfɔː(r)/ *n* grembiule *m*. **~ dress** *n* scamiciato *m*
pincers /ˈpɪnsəz/ *npl* tenaglie *fpl*
pinch /pɪntʃ/ *n* pizzicotto *m*; (*of salt*) presa *f*; **at a ~** [!] in caso di bisogno ● *vt* pizzicare; ([!]: *steal*) fregare ● *vi* (shoe:) stringere
pine¹ /paɪn/ *n* (*tree*) pino *m*
pine² *vi* **she is pining for you** le manchi molto. □ **~ away** *vi* deperire
pineapple /ˈpaɪn-/ *n* ananas *m inv*
ˈping-pong *n* ping-pong *m*
pink /pɪŋk/ *adj* rosa *m*
pinnacle /ˈpɪnəkl/ *n* guglia *f*
PIN number *n* codice *m* segreto
pin: ~point *vt* definire con precisione. **~stripe** *adj* gessato
pint /paɪnt/ *n* pinta *f* (= *0,571*, *Am: 0,47 l*); **a ~** [!] una birra media
pioneer /paɪəˈnɪə(r)/ *n* pioniere, -a *mf* ● *vt* essere un pioniere di
pious /ˈpaɪəs/ *adj* pio
pip /pɪp/ *n* (*seed*) seme *m*
pipe /paɪp/ *n* tubo *m*; (*for smoking*) pipa *f*; **the ~s** (*Mus*) la cornamusa ● *vt* far arrivare con tubature (water, gas etc). □ **~ down** *vi* [!] abbassare la voce
pipe: ~-dream *n* illusione *f*. **~line** *n* conduttura *f*; **in the ~line** [!] in cantiere
piping /ˈpaɪpɪŋ/ *adj* **~ hot** bollente
pirate /ˈpaɪrət/ *n* pirata *m*
Pisces /ˈpaɪsiːz/ *n* (*Astr*) Pesci *mpl*
piss /pɪs/ *vi* [✖] pisciare
pistol /ˈpɪstl/ *n* pistola *f*
piston /ˈpɪstn/ *n* (*Techn*) pistone *m*
pit /pɪt/ *n* fossa *f*; (*mine*) miniera *f*; (*for orchestra*) orchestra *f* ● *vt* (*pt/pp* **pitted**) *fig* opporre (**against** a)
pitch¹ /pɪtʃ/ *n* (*tone*) tono *m*; (*level*) altezza *f*; (*in sport*) campo *m*; (*fig: degree*) grado *m* ● *vt* montare (tent). □ **~ in** *vi* [!] mettersi sotto
pitch² *n* **~-ˈblack** *adj* nero come la pece. **~-ˈdark** *adj* buio pesto
ˈpitfall *n fig* trabocchetto *m*
pith /pɪθ/ *n* (*of lemon, orange*) interno *m* della buccia
piti|ful /ˈpɪtɪfl/ *adj* pietoso. **~less** *adj* spietato
pittance /ˈpɪtns/ *n* miseria *f*
pity /ˈpɪtɪ/ *n* pietà *f*; **what a ~!** che peccato!; **take ~ on** avere compassione di ● *vt* aver pietà di
pivot /ˈpɪvət/ *n* perno *m*; *fig* fulcro *m* ● *vi* imperniarsi (**on** su)
pizza /ˈpiːtsə/ *n* pizza *f*
placard /ˈplækɑːd/ *n* cartellone *m*
placate /pləˈkeɪt/ *vt* placare
place /pleɪs/ *n* posto *m*; ([!]: *house*) casa *f*; (*in book*) segno *m*; **feel out of ~** sentirsi fuori posto; **take ~** aver luogo; **all over the ~** dappertutto ● *vt* collocare; (*remember*) identificare; **~ an order** fare un'ordinazione; **be ~d** (*in race*) piazzarsi. **~-mat** *n* sottopiatto *m*
placid /ˈplæsɪd/ *adj* placido
plague /pleɪg/ *n* peste *f*
plaice /pleɪs/ *n inv* platessa *f*
plain /pleɪn/ *adj* chiaro; (*simple*) semplice; (*not pretty*) scialbo; (*not patterned*) normale; (chocolate) fondente; **in ~ clothes** in borghese ● *adv* (*simply*) semplicemente ● *n* pianura *f*. **~ly** *adv* francamente; (*simply*) semplicemente; (*obviously*) chiaramente
plaintiff /ˈpleɪntɪf/ *n* (*Jur*) parte *f* lesa
plait /plæt/ *n* treccia *f* ● *vt* intrecciare
plan /plæn/ *n* progetto *m*, piano *m* ● *vt* (*pt/pp* **planned**) progettare; (*intend*) prevedere
plane¹ /pleɪn/ *n* (*tree*) platano *m*
plane² *n* aeroplano *m*
plane³ *n* (*tool*) pialla *f* ● *vt* piallare
planet /ˈplænɪt/ *n* pianeta *m*
plank /plæŋk/ *n* asse *f*
planning /ˈplænɪŋ/ *n* pianificazione *f*. **~ permission** *n* licenza *f* edilizia
plant /plɑːnt/ *n* pianta *f*; (*machinery*) impianto *m*; (*factory*) stabilimento *m* ● *vt* piantare. **~ation** *n* piantagione *f*
plaque /plɑːk/ *n* placca *f*
plasma /ˈplæzmə/ *n* plasma *m*
plaster /ˈplɑːstə(r)/ *n* intonaco *m*; (*Med*) gesso *m*; (*sticking ~*) cerotto *m*;

~ **of Paris** gesso *m* ● *vt* intonacare (wall); (*cover*) ricoprire. **~ed** *adj* ☒ sbronzo. **~er** *n* intonacatore *m*

plastic /'plæstɪk/ *n* plastica *f* ● *adj* plastico

plastic surgery *n* chirurgia *f* plastica

plate /pleɪt/ *n* piatto *m*; (*flat sheet*) placca *f*; (*gold and silverware*) argenteria *f*; (*in book*) tavola *f* [fuori testo] ● *vt* (*cover with metal*) placcare

platform /'plætfɔ:m/ *n* (*stage*) palco *m*; (*Rail*) marciapiede *m*; (*Pol*) piattaforma *f*; **~ 5** binario 5

platinum /'plætɪnəm/ *n* platino *m* ● *attrib* di platino

platitude /'plætɪtju:d/ *n* luogo *m* comune

platonic /plə'tɒnɪk/ *adj* platonico

plausible /'plɔ:zəbl/ *adj* plausibile

play /pleɪ/ *n* gioco *m*; (*Theat*), (*TV*) rappresentazione *f*; (*Radio*) sceneggiato *m* radiofonico; **~ on words** gioco *m* di parole ● *vt* giocare a; (*act*) recitare; suonare (instrument); giocare (card) ● *vi* giocare; (*Mus*) suonare; **~ safe** non prendere rischi. □ **~ down** *vt* minimizzare. □ **~ up** *vi* 🄸 fare i capricci

play: ~er *n* giocatore, -trice *mf*. **~ful** *adj* scherzoso. **~ground** *n* (*Sch*) cortile *m* (*per la ricreazione*). **~group** *n* asilo *m*

p

playing: ~-card *n* carta *f* da gioco. **~-field** *n* campo *m* da gioco

play: ~-pen *n* box *m inv*. **~wright** /-raɪt/ *n* drammaturgo, -a *mf*

plc *n abbr* (public limited company) s.r.l.

plea /pli:/ *n* richiesta *f*; **make a ~ for** fare un appello a

plead /pli:d/ *vi* fare appello (**for** a); **~ guilty** dichiararsi colpevole; **~ with sb** implorare qcno

pleasant /'plez(ə)nt/ *adj* piacevole. **~ly** *adv* piacevolmente; (say, smile) cordialmente

pleas|e /pli:z/ *adv* per favore; **~e do** prego ● *vt* far contento; **~e oneself** fare il proprio comodo; **~e yourself!** come vuoi!; *pej* fai come ti pare!. **~ed** *adj* lieto; **~ed with/about** contento di. **~ing** *adj* gradevole

pleasure /'pleʒə(r)/ *n* piacere *m*; **with ~** con piacere, volentieri

pleat /pli:t/ *n* piega *f* ● *vt* pieghettare. **~ed 'skirt** *n* gonna *f* a pieghe

pledge /pledʒ/ *n* pegno *m*; (*promise*) promessa *f* ● *vt* impegnarsi a; (*pawn*) impegnare

plentiful /'plentɪfl/ *adj* abbondante

plenty /'plentɪ/ *n* abbondanza *f*; **~ of money** molti soldi; **~ of people** molta gente; **I've got ~** ne ho in abbondanza

pliable /'plaɪəbl/ *adj* flessibile

pliers /'plaɪəz/ *npl* pinze *fpl*

plight /plaɪt/ *n* condizione *f*

plimsolls /'plɪmsəlz/ *npl* scarpe *fpl* da ginnastica

plod /plɒd/ *vi* (*pt/pp* **plodded**) trascinarsi; (*work hard*) sgobbare

plot /plɒt/ *n* complotto *m*; (*of novel*) trama *f*; **~ of land** appezzamento *m* [di terreno] ● *vt/i* complottare

plough /plaʊ/ *n* aratro *m*; **~man's lunch** *piatto m di formaggi e sottaceti, servito con pane.* ● *vt/i* arare. □ **~ back** *vt* (*Comm*) reinvestire

ploy /plɔɪ/ *n* 🄸 manovra *f*

pluck /plʌk/ *n* fegato *m* ● *vt* strappare; depilare (eyebrows); spennare (bird); cogliere (flower). □ **~ up** *vt* **~ up courage** farsi coraggio

plucky /'plʌkɪ/ *adj* (**-ier, -iest**) coraggioso

plug /plʌg/ *n* tappo *m*; (*Electr*) spina *f*; (*Auto*) candela *f*; (🄸: *advertisement*) pubblicità *f inv* ● *vt* (*pt/pp* **plugged**) tappare; (🄸: *advertise*) pubblicizzare con insistenza. □ **~ in** *vt* (*Electr*) inserire la spina di

plum /plʌm/ *n* prugna *f*; (*tree*) prugno *m*

plumage /'plu:mɪdʒ/ *n* piumaggio *m*

plumb|er /'plʌmə(r)/ *n* idraulico *m*. **~ing** *n* impianto *m* idraulico

plume /plu:m/ *n* piuma *f*

plump /plʌmp/ *adj* paffuto ● **plump for** *vt* scegliere

plunge /plʌndʒ/ *n* tuffo *m*; **take the ~** 🄸 buttarsi ● *vt* tuffare; *fig* sprofondare ● *vi* tuffarsi

plural /'plʊərəl/ *adj* plurale ● *n* plurale *m*

plus /plʌs/ *prep* più ● *adj* in più; **500 ~** più di 500 ● *n* più *m*; (*advantage*) extra *m inv*

plush /'plʌʃ[ɪ]/ *adj* lussuoso

plutonium /pluˈtəʊnɪəm/ *n* plutonio *m*

ply /plaɪ/ *vt* (*pt/pp* **plied**) **~ sb with drink** continuare a offrire da bere a qcno. **~wood** *n* compensato *m*

p.m. *abbr* (post meridiem) del pomeriggio

PM *n abbr* Prime Minister

pneumonia /nju:ˈməʊnɪə/ *n* polmonite *f*

P.O. *abbr* Post Office

poach /pəʊtʃ/ *vt* (*Culin*) bollire; cacciare di frodo (deer); pescare di frodo (salmon); **~ed egg** uovo *m* in camicia. **~er** *n* bracconiere *m*

pocket /ˈpɒkɪt/ *n* tasca *f*; **be out of ~** rimetterci ● *vt* intascare. **~-book** *n* taccuino *m*; (*wallet*) portafoglio *m*. **~-money** *n* denaro *m* per le piccole spese

pod /pɒd/ *n* baccello *m*

poem /ˈpəʊɪm/ *n* poesia *f*

poet /ˈpəʊɪt/ *n* poeta *m*. **~ic** *adj* poetico

poetry /ˈpəʊɪtrɪ/ *n* poesia *f*

poignant /ˈpɔɪnjənt/ *adj* emozionante

point /pɔɪnt/ *n* punto *m*; (*sharp end*) punta *f*; (*meaning, purpose*) senso *m*; (*Electr*) presa *f* [di corrente]; **~s** *pl* (*Rail*) scambio *m*; **~ of view** punto *m* di vista; **good/bad ~s** aspetti *mpl* positivi/negativi; **what is the ~?** a che scopo?; **the ~ is** il fatto è; **I don't see the ~** non vedo il senso; **up to a ~** fino a un certo punto; **be on the ~ of doing sth** essere sul punto di fare qcsa ● *vt* puntare (**at** verso) ● *vi* (*with finger*) puntare il dito; **~ at/to** (person:) mostrare col dito; (indicator:) indicare. □ **~ out** *vt* far notare (fact); **~ sth out to sb** far notare qcsa a qcno

point-ˈblank *adj* a bruciapelo

point|ed /ˈpɔɪntɪd/ *adj* appuntito; (question) diretto. **~ers** *npl* (*advice*) consigli *mpl*. **~less** *adj* inutile

poise /pɔɪz/ *n* padronanza *f*. **~d** *adj* in equilibrio; **~d to** sul punto di

poison /ˈpɔɪzn/ *n* veleno *m* ● *vt* avvelenare. **~ous** *adj* velenoso

poke /pəʊk/ *n* [piccola] spinta *f* ● *vt* spingere; (fire) attizzare; (*put*) ficcare; **~ fun at** prendere in giro. □ **~ about** *vi* frugare

poker¹ /ˈpəʊkə(r)/ *n* attizzatoio *m*

poker² *n* (*Cards*) poker *m*

poky /ˈpəʊkɪ/ *adj* (**-ier, -iest**) angusto

Poland /ˈpəʊlənd/ *n* Polonia *f*

polar /ˈpəʊlə(r)/ *adj* polare. **~ ˈbear** *n* orso *m* bianco. **~ize** *vt* polarizzare

pole¹ *n* palo *m*

pole² *n* (*Geog, Electr*) polo *m*

Pole /pəʊl/ *n* polacco, -a *mf*

police /pəˈli:s/ *npl* polizia *f* ● *vt* pattugliare (area)

police: ~man *n* poliziotto *m*. **~ station** *n* commissariato *m*. **~woman** *n* donna *f* poliziotto

policy¹ /ˈpɒlɪsɪ/ *n* politica *f*

policy² *n* (*insurance*) polizza *f*

polio /ˈpəʊlɪəʊ/ *n* polio *f*

polish /ˈpɒlɪʃ/ *n* (*shine*) lucentezza *f*; (*substance*) lucido *m*; (*for nails*) smalto *m*; *fig* raffinatezza *f* ● *vt* lucidare; *fig* smussare. □ **~ off** *vt* [!] finire in fretta; spazzolare (food)

Polish /ˈpəʊlɪʃ/ *adj* polacco ● *n* (*language*) polacco *m*

polished /ˈpɒlɪʃt/ *adj* (manner) raffinato; (performance) senza sbavature

polite /pəˈlaɪt/ *adj* cortese. **~ly** *adv* cortesemente. **~ness** *n* cortesia *f*

politic|al /pəˈlɪtɪkl/ *adj* politico. **~ally** *adv* dal punto di vista politico. **~ian** *n* politico *m*

politics /ˈpɒlɪtɪks/ *n* politica *f*

poll /pəʊl/ *n* votazione *f*; (*election*) elezioni *fpl*; **opinion ~** sondaggio *m* d'opinione; **go to the ~s** andare alle urne ● *vt* ottenere (votes)

pollen /ˈpɒlən/ *n* polline *m*

pollut|e /pəˈlu:t/ *vt* inquinare. **~ion** *n* inquinamento *m*

polo /ˈpəʊləʊ/ *n* polo *m*. **~-neck** *n* collo *m* alto. **~ shirt** *n* dolcevita *f*

polythene /ˈpɒlɪθi:n/ *n* politene *m*. **~ bag** *n* sacchetto *m* di plastica

polyunˈsaturated *adj* polinsaturo

pomp /pɒmp/ *n* pompa *f*

pompous /ˈpɒmpəs/ *adj* pomposo

pond /pɒnd/ *n* stagno *m*

ponder /ˈpɒndə(r)/ *vt/i* ponderare

pony /ˈpəʊnɪ/ *n* pony *m*. **~-tail** *n* coda *f* di cavallo. **~-trekking** *n* escursioni *fpl* col pony

poodle /ˈpu:dl/ *n* barboncino *m*

pool[1] /puːl/ *n* (*of water, blood*) pozza *f*; [**swimming**] ~ piscina *f*
pool[2] *n* (*common fund*) cassa *f* comune; (*in cards*) piatto *m*; (*game*) biliardo *m* a buca. **~s** *npl* ≈ totocalcio *msg* ● *vt* mettere insieme
poor /pʊə(r)/ *adj* povero; (*not good*) scadente; **in ~ health** in cattiva salute ● *npl* **the ~** i poveri. **~ly** *adj* **be ~ly** non stare bene ● *adv* male
pop[1] /pɒp/ *n* botto *m*; (*drink*) bibita *f* gasata ● *v* (*pt*/*pp* **popped**) ● *vt* (*[!]: put*) mettere; (*burst*) far scoppiare ● *vi* (*burst*) scoppiare. □ **~ in**/**out** *vi* [!] fare un salto/un salto fuori
pop[2] *n* [!] musica *f* pop ● *attrib* pop
'**popcorn** *n* popcorn *m inv*
pope /pəʊp/ *n* papa *m*
poplar /'pɒplə(r)/ *n* pioppo *m*
poppy /'pɒpɪ/ *n* papavero *m*
popular /'pɒpjʊlə(r)/ *adj* popolare; (belief) diffuso. **~ity** *n* popolarità *f inv*
populat|e /'pɒpjʊleɪt/ *vt* popolare. **~ion** *n* popolazione *f*
'**pop-up** *n* popup *m inv*
porcelain /'pɔːsəlɪn/ *n* porcellana *f*
porch /pɔːtʃ/ *n* portico *m*; *Am* veranda *f*
porcupine /'pɔːkjʊpaɪn/ *n* porcospino *m*
pore[1] /pɔː(r)/ *n* poro *m*
pore[2] *vi* **~ over** immergersi in
pork /pɔːk/ *n* carne *f* di maiale
porn /pɔːn/ *n* [!] porno *m*. **~o** *adj* [!] porno *inv*
pornograph|ic /pɔːnə'græfɪk/ *adj* pornografico. **~y** *n* pornografia *f*
porpoise /'pɔːpəs/ *n* focena *f*
porridge /'pɒrɪdʒ/ *n* farinata *f* di fiocchi d'avena
port[1] /pɔːt/ *n* porto *m*
port[2] *n* (*Naut: side*) babordo *m*
port[3] *n* (*wine*) porto *m*
portable /'pɔːtəbl/ *adj* portatile
porter /'pɔːtə(r)/ *n* portiere *m*; (*for luggage*) facchino *m*
'**porthole** *n* oblò *m inv*
portion /'pɔːʃn/ *n* parte *f*; (*of food*) porzione *f*
portrait /'pɔːtrɪt/ *n* ritratto *m*
portray /pɔː'treɪ/ *vt* ritrarre; (*represent*) descrivere; (actor:) impersonare. **~al** *n* ritratto *m*
Portug|al /'pɔːtjʊgl/ *n* Portogallo *m*. **~uese** *adj* portoghese ● *n* portoghese *mf*
pose /pəʊz/ *n* posa *f* ● *vt* porre (problem, question) ● *vi* (*for painter*) posare; **~ as** atteggiarsi a
posh /pɒʃ/ *adj* [!] lussuoso; (people) danaroso
position /pə'zɪʃn/ *n* posizione *f*; (*job*) posto *m*; (*status*) ceto *m* [sociale] ● *vt* posizionare
positive /'pɒzɪtɪv/ *adj* positivo; (*certain*) sicuro; (*progress*) concreto ● *n* positivo *m*. **~ly** *adv* positivamente; (*decidedly*) decisamente
possess /pə'zes/ *vt* possedere. **~ion** *n* possesso *m*; **~ions** *pl* beni *mpl*
possess|ive /pə'zesɪv/ *adj* possessivo. **~iveness** *n* carattere *m* possessivo. **~or** *n* possessore, -ditrice *mf*
possibility /pɒsə'bɪlətɪ/ *n* possibilità *f inv*
possib|le /'pɒsɪbl/ *adj* possibile. **~ly** *adv* possibilmente; **I couldn't ~ly accept** non mi è possibile accettare; **he can't ~ly be right** non è possibile che abbia ragione; **could you ~ly...?** potrebbe per favore...?
post[1] /pəʊst/ *n* (*pole*) palo *m* ● *vt* affiggere (notice)
post[2] *n* (*place of duty*) posto *m* ● *vt* appostare; (*transfer*) assegnare
post[3] *n* (*mail*) posta *f*; **by ~** per posta ● *vt* spedire; (*put in letter-box*) imbucare; (*as opposed to fax*) mandare per posta; **keep sb ~ed** tenere qcno al corrente
post- *pref* dopo
postage /'pəʊstɪdʒ/ *n* affrancatura *f*. **~ stamp** *n* francobollo *m*
postal /'pəʊstl/ *adj* postale. **~ order** *n* vaglia *m* postale
post: ~-box *n* cassetta *f* delle lettere. **~card** *n* cartolina *f*. **~code** *n* codice *m* postale
poster /'pəʊstə(r)/ *n* poster *m inv*; (*advertising, election*) cartellone *m*
posterity /pɒ'sterətɪ/ *n* posterità *f*
posthumous /'pɒstjʊməs/ *adj* postumo. **~ly** *adv* dopo la morte
post: ~man *n* postino *m*. **~mark** *n* timbro *m* postale
post-mortem /-'mɔːtəm/ *n* autopsia *f*
'**post office** *n* ufficio *m* postale

postpone /pəʊst'pəʊn/ *vt* rimandare. **~ment** *n* rinvio *m*

posture /'pɒstʃə(r)/ *n* posizione *f*

pot /pɒt/ *n* vaso *m*; (*for tea*) teiera *f*; (*for coffee*) caffettiera *f*; (*for cooking*) pentola *f*; **~s of money** [!] un sacco di soldi; **go to ~** [!] andare in malora

potato /pə'teɪtəʊ/ *n* (*pl* **-es**) patata *f*

poten|t /'pəʊtənt/ *adj* potente. **~tate** *n* potentato *m*

potential /pə'tenʃl/ *adj* potenziale ● *n* potenziale *m*. **~ly** *adv* potenzialmente

pot: ~-hole *n* cavità *f inv*; (*in road*) buca *f*. **~-shot** *n* **take a ~-shot at** sparare a casaccio a

potter[1] /'pɒtə(r)/ *vi* **~ about** gingillarsi

potter[2] *n* vasaio, -a *mf*. **~y** *n* lavorazione *f* della ceramica; (*articles*) ceramiche *fpl*; (*place*) laboratorio *m* di ceramiche

potty /'pɒtɪ/ *adj* (**-ier, -iest**) [!] matto ● *n* vasino *m*

pouch /paʊtʃ/ *n* marsupio *m*

poultry /'pəʊltrɪ/ *n* pollame *m*

pounce /paʊns/ *vi* balzare; **~ on** saltare su

pound[1] /paʊnd/ *n* libbra *f* (= *0,454 kg*); (*money*) sterlina *f*

pound[2] *vt* battere ● *vi* (heart:) battere forte; (*run heavily*) correre pesantemente

pour /pɔ:(r)/ *vt* versare ● *vi* riversarsi; (*with rain*) piovere a dirotto. □ **~ out** *vi* riversarsi fuori ● *vt* versare (drink); sfogare (troubles)

pout /paʊt/ *vi* fare il broncio ● *n* broncio *m*

poverty /'pɒvətɪ/ *n* povertà *f*

powder /'paʊdə(r)/ *n* polvere *f*; (*cosmetic*) cipria *f* ● *vt* polverizzare; (*face*) incipriare. **~y** *adj* polveroso

power /'paʊə(r)/ *n* potere *m*; (*Electr*) corrente *f* [elettrica]; (*Math*) potenza *f*. **~ cut** *n* interruzione *f* di corrente. **~ed** *adj* **~ed by electricity** dotato di corrente [elettrica]. **~ful** *adj* potente. **~less** *adj* impotente. **~-station** *n* centrale *f* elettrica

PR *n abbr* public relations

practicable /'præktɪkəbl/ *adj* praticabile

practical /'præktɪkl/ *adj* pratico. **~ 'joke** *n* burla *f*. **~ly** *adv* praticamente

practice /'præktɪs/ *n* pratica *f*; (*custom*) usanza *f*; (*habit*) abitudine *f*; (*exercise*) esercizio *m*; (*Sport*) allenamento *m*; **in ~** (*in reality*) in pratica; **out of ~** fuori esercizio; **put into ~** mettere in pratica

practise /'præktɪs/ *vt* fare pratica in; (*carry out*) mettere in pratica; esercitare (profession) ● *vi* esercitarsi; (doctor:) praticare. **~d** *adj* esperto

praise /preɪz/ *n* lode *f* ● *vt* lodare. **~worthy** *adj* lodevole

pram /præm/ *n* carrozzella *f*

prank /præŋk/ *n* tiro *m*

prawn /prɔ:n/ *n* gambero *m*. **~ 'cocktail** *n* cocktail *m inv* di gamberetti

pray /preɪ/ *vi* pregare. **~er** *n* preghiera *f*

preach /pri:tʃ/ *vt/i* predicare. **~er** *n* predicatore, -trice *mf*

pre-ar'range /pri:-/ *vt* predisporre

precarious /prɪ'keərɪəs/ *adj* precario. **~ly** *adv* in modo precario

precaution /prɪ'kɔ:ʃn/ *n* precauzione *f*; **as a ~** per precauzione. **~ary** *adj* preventivo

precede /prɪ'si:d/ *vt* precedere

preceden|ce /'presɪdəns/ *n* precedenza *f*. **~t** *n* precedente *m*

preceding /prɪ'si:dɪŋ/ *adj* precedente

precinct /'pri:sɪŋkt/ *n* (*traffic-free*) zona *f* pedonale; (*Am: district*) circoscrizione *f*

precious /'preʃəs/ *adj* prezioso; (style) ricercato ● *adv* [!] **~ little** ben poco

precipice /'presɪpɪs/ *n* precipizio *m*

precipitate /prɪ'sɪpɪteɪt/ *vt* precipitare

precis|e /prɪ'saɪs/ *adj* preciso. **~ely** *adv* precisamente. **~ion** *n* precisione *f*

precursor /pri:'kɜ:sə(r)/ *n* precursore *m*

predator /'predətə(r)/ *n* predatore, -trice *mf*. **~y** *adj* rapace

predecessor /'pri:dɪsesə(r)/ *n* predecessore *m*

predicament /prɪ'dɪkəmənt/ *n* situazione *f* difficile

predict /prɪ'dɪkt/ *vt* predire. **~able** *adj* prevedibile. **~ion** *n* previsione *f*

preen /priːn/ *vt* lisciarsi; ~ **oneself** *fig* farsi bello

pre|fab /ˈpriːfæb/ *n* 🅘 casa *f* prefabbricata. ~ˈ**fabricated** *adj* prefabbricato

preface /ˈprefɪs/ *n* prefazione *f*

prefect /ˈpriːfekt/ *n* (*Sch*) *studente, -tessa mf della scuola superiore con responsabilità disciplinari, ecc*

prefer /prɪˈfɜː(r)/ *vt* (*pt/pp* **preferred**) preferire

prefera|ble /ˈprefərəbl/ *adj* preferibile (**to** a). ~**bly** *adv* preferibilmente

preferen|ce /ˈprefərəns/ *n* preferenza *f*. ~**tial** *adj* preferenziale

pregnan|cy /ˈpregnənsɪ/ *n* gravidanza *f*. ~**t** *adj* incinta

prehiˈstoric /priː-/ *adj* preistorico

prejudice /ˈpredʒʊdɪs/ *n* pregiudizio *m* ● *vt* influenzare (**against** contro); (*harm*) danneggiare. ~**d** *adj* prevenuto

preliminary /prɪˈlɪmɪnərɪ/ *adj* preliminare

prelude /ˈpreljuːd/ *n* preludio *m*

premature /ˈpremətjʊə(r)/ *adj* prematuro

preˈmeditated /priː-/ *adj* premeditato

premier /ˈpremɪə(r)/ *adj* primario ● *n* (*Pol*) primo ministro *m*, premier *m inv*

première /ˈpremɪeə(r)/ *n* prima *f*

premises /ˈpremɪsɪz/ *npl* locali *mpl*; **on the** ~ sul posto

premium /ˈpriːmɪəm/ *n* premio *m*; **be at a** ~ essere una cosa rara

premonition /preməˈnɪʃn/ *n* presentimento *m*

preoccupied /priːˈɒkjʊpaɪd/ *adj* preoccupato

preparation /prepəˈreɪʃn/ *n* preparazione *f*. ~**s** preparativi *mpl*

preparatory /prɪˈpærətrɪ/ *adj* preparatorio ● *adv* ~ **to** per

prepare /prɪˈpeə(r)/ *vt* preparare ● *vi* prepararsi (**for** per); ~**d to** disposto a

preposition /prepəˈzɪʃn/ *n* preposizione *f*

preposterous /prɪˈpɒstərəs/ *adj* assurdo

prerequisite /priːˈrekwɪzɪt/ *n* condizione *f* sine qua non

prescribe /prɪˈskraɪb/ *vt* prescrivere

prescription /prɪˈskrɪpʃn/ *n* (*Med*) ricetta *f*

presence /ˈprezns/ *n* presenza *f*; ~ **of mind** presenza *f* di spirito

present¹ /ˈpreznt/ *adj* presente ● *n* presente *m*; **at** ~ attualmente

present² *n* (*gift*) regalo *m*; **give sb sth as a** ~ regalare qcsa a qcno

present³ /prɪˈzent/ *vt* presentare; ~ **sb with an award** consegnare un premio a qcno. ~**able** *adj* **be** ~**able** essere presentabile

presentation /preznˈteɪʃn/ *n* presentazione *f*

presently /ˈprezntlɪ/ *adv* fra poco; (*Am: now*) attualmente

preservation /prezəˈveɪʃn/ *n* conservazione *f*

preservative /prɪˈzɜːvətɪv/ *n* conservante *m*

preserve /prɪˈzɜːv/ *vt* preservare; (*maintain*, (*Culin*) conservare ● *n* (*in hunting & fig*) riserva *f*; (*jam*) marmellata *f*

preside /prɪˈzaɪd/ *vi* presiedere (**over** a)

presidency /ˈprezɪdənsɪ/ *n* presidenza *f*

president /ˈprezɪdənt/ *n* presidente *m*. ~**ial** *adj* presidenziale

press /pres/ *n* (*machine*) pressa *f*; (*newspapers*) stampa *f* ● *vt* premere; pressare (flower); (*iron*) stirare; (*squeeze*) stringere ● *vi* (*urge*) incalzare. □ ~ **for** *vi* fare pressione per; **be** ~**ed for** essere a corto di. □ ~ **on** *vi* andare avanti

press: ~ **conference** *n* conferenza *f* stampa. ~ **cutting** *n* ritaglio *m* di giornale. ~**ing** *adj* urgente. ~**-up** *n* flessione *f*

pressure /ˈpreʃə(r)/ *n* pressione *f* ● *vt* = **pressurize.** ~**-cooker** *n* pentola *f* a pressione. ~ **group** *n* gruppo *m* di pressione

pressurize /ˈpreʃəraɪz/ *vt* far pressione su. ~**d** *adj* pressurizzato

prestig|e /preˈstiːʒ/ *n* prestigio *m*. ~**ious** *adj* prestigioso

presumably /prɪˈzjuːməblɪ/ *adv* presumibilmente

presume /prɪˈzjuːm/ *vt* presumere; ~ **to do sth** permettersi di fare qcsa

presupˈpose /priː-/ *vt* presupporre

pretence /prɪˈtens/ *n* finzione *f*; (*pre-*

text) pretesto *m*; **it's all ~** è tutta una scena

pretend /prɪ'tend/ *vt* fingere; (*claim*) pretendere ● *vi* fare finta

pretentious /prɪ'tenʃəs/ *adj* pretenzioso

pretext /'pri:tekst/ *n* pretesto *m*

pretty /'prɪtɪ/ *adj* (**-ier, -iest**) carino ● *adv* ([!]: *fairly*) abbastanza

prevail /prɪ'veɪl/ *vi* prevalere; **~ on sb to do sth** convincere qcno a fare qcsa. **~ing** *adj* prevalente

prevalen|ce /'prevələns/ *n* diffusione *f*. **~t** *adj* diffuso

prevent /prɪ'vent/ *vt* impedire; **~ sb** [**from**] **doing sth** impedire a qcno di fare qcsa. **~ion** *n* prevenzione *f*. **~ive** *adj* preventivo

preview /'pri:vju:/ *n* anteprima *f*

previous /'pri:vɪəs/ *adj* precedente. **~ly** *adv* precedentemente

prey /preɪ/ *n* preda *f*; **bird of ~** uccello *m* rapace ● *vi* **~ on** far preda di; **~ on sb's mind** attanagliare qcno

price /praɪs/ *n* prezzo *m* ● *vt* (*Comm*) fissare il prezzo di. **~less** *adj* inestimabile; ([!]: *amusing*) spassosissimo. **~y** *adj* [!] caro

prick /prɪk/ *n* puntura *f* ● *vt* pungere. □ **~ up** *vt* **~ up one's ears** rizzare le orecchie

prickl|e /'prɪkl/ *n* spina *f*; (*sensation*) formicolio *m*. **~y** *adj* pungente; (person) irritabile

pride /praɪd/ *n* orgoglio *m* ● *vt* **~ oneself on** vantarsi di

priest /pri:st/ *n* prete *m*

prim /prɪm/ *adj* (**primmer, primmest**) perbenino

primarily /'praɪmərɪlɪ/ *adv* in primo luogo

primary /'praɪmərɪ/ *adj* primario; (*chief*) principale. **~ school** *n* scuola *f* elementare

prime¹ /praɪm/ *adj* principale, primo; (*first-rate*) eccellente ● *n* **be in one's ~** essere nel fiore degli anni

prime² *vt* preparare (surface, person)

Prime Minister *n* Primo *m* Ministro

primeval /praɪ'mi:vl/ *adj* primitivo

primitive /'prɪmɪtɪv/ *adj* primitivo

primrose /'prɪmrəʊz/ *n* primula *f*

prince /prɪns/ *n* principe *m*

princess /prɪn'ses/ *n* principessa *f*

principal /'prɪnsəpl/ *adj* principale ● *n* (*Sch*) preside *m*

principally /'prɪnsəplɪ/ *adv* principalmente

principle /'prɪnsəpl/ *n* principio *m*; **in ~** in teoria; **on ~** per principio

print /prɪnt/ *n* (*mark, trace*) impronta *f*; (*Phot*) copia *f*; (*picture*) stampa *f*; **in ~** (*printed out*) stampato; (book) in commercio; **out of ~** esaurito ● *vt* stampare; (*write in capitals*) scrivere in stampatello. **~ed matter** *n* stampe *fpl*

print|er /'prɪntə(r)/ *n* stampante *f*; (*Typ*) tipografo, -a *mf*. **~er port** *n* (*Comput*) porta *f* per la stampante. **~ing** *n* tipografia *f*

'printout *n* (*Comput*) stampa *f*

prior /'praɪə(r)/ *adj* precedente. **~ to** *prep* prima di

priority /praɪ'ɒrətɪ/ *n* precedenza *f*; (*matter*) priorità *f inv*

prise /praɪz/ *vt* **~ open/up** forzare

prison /'prɪz(ə)n/ *n* prigione *f*. **~er** *n* prigioniero, -a *mf*

privacy /'prɪvəsɪ/ *n* privacy *f inv*

private /'praɪvət/ *adj* privato; (car, secretary, letter) personale ● *n* (*Mil*) soldato *m* semplice; **in ~** in privato. **~ly** *adv* (funded, educated etc) privatamente; (*in secret*) in segreto; (*confidentially*) in privato; (*inwardly*) interiormente

privation /praɪ'veɪʃn/ *n* privazione *f*; **~s** *npl* stenti *mpl*

privilege /'prɪvəlɪdʒ/ *n* privilegio *m*. **~d** *adj* privilegiato

prize /praɪz/ *n* premio *m* ● *adj* (*idiot etc*) perfetto ● *vt* apprezzare. **~-giving** *n* premiazione *f*. **~-winner** *n* vincitore, -trice *mf*. **~-winning** *adj* vincente

pro /prəʊ/ *n* ([!]: *professional*) professionista *mf*; **the ~s and cons** il pro e il contro

probability /prɒbə'bɪlətɪ/ *n* probabilità *f inv*

probabl|e /'prɒbəbl/ *adj* probabile. **~y** *adv* probabilmente

probation /prə'beɪʃn/ *n* prova *f*; (*Jur*) libertà *f* vigilata. **~ary** *adj* in prova; **~ary period** periodo *m* di prova

p

probe /prəʊb/ *n* sonda *f*; (*fig: investigation*) indagine *f* ● *vt* sondare; (*investigate*) esaminare a fondo

problem /'prɒbləm/ *n* problema *m* ● *adj* difficile. **~atic** *adj* problematico

procedure /prə'si:dʒə(r)/ *n* procedimento *m*

proceed /prə'si:d/ *vi* procedere ● *vt* **~ to do sth** proseguire facendo qcsa

proceedings /prə'si:dɪŋz/ *npl* (*report*) atti *mpl*; (*Jur*) azione *fsg* legale

proceeds /'prəʊsi:dz/ *npl* ricavato *msg*

process /'prəʊses/ *n* processo *m*; (*procedure*) procedimento *m*; **in the ~** nel far ciò ● *vt* trattare; (*Admin*) occuparsi di; (*Phot*) sviluppare

procession /prə'seʃn/ *n* processione *f*

processor /'prəʊsesə(r)/ *n* (*Comput*) processore *m*; (*for food*) robot *m inv* da cucina

proclaim /prə'kleɪm/ *vt* proclamare

procure /prə'kjʊə(r)/ *vt* ottenere

prod /prɒd/ *n* colpetto *m* ● *vt* (*pt/pp* **prodded**) punzecchiare; *fig* incitare

produce¹ /'prɒdju:s/ *n* prodotti *mpl*; **~ of Italy** prodotto in Italia

produce² /prə'dju:s/ *vt* produrre; (*bring out*) tirar fuori; (*cause*) causare; ([!]: *give birth to*) fare. **~r** *n* produttore *m*

product /'prɒdʌkt/ *n* prodotto *m*. **~ion** *n* produzione *f*; (*Theat*) spettacolo *m*

productiv|e /prə'dʌktɪv/ *adj* produttivo. **~ity** *n* produttività *f*

profession /prə'feʃn/ *n* professione *f*. **~al** *adj* professionale; (*not amateur*) professionista; (*piece of work*) da professionista; (*man*) di professione ● *n* professionista *mf*. **~ally** *adv* professionalmente

professor /prə'fesə(r)/ *n* professore *m* [universitario]

proficien|cy /prə'fɪʃnsɪ/ *n* competenza *f*. **~t** *adj* **be ~t in** essere competente in

profile /'prəʊfaɪl/ *n* profilo *m*

profit /'prɒfɪt/ *n* profitto *m* ● *vi* **~ from** trarre profitto da. **~able** *adj* proficuo. **~ably** *adv* in modo proficuo

profound /prə'faʊnd/ *adj* profondo. **~ly** *adv* profondamente

profus|e /prə'fju:s/ *adj* **~e apologies/flowers** una profusione di scuse/fiori. **~ion** *n* profusione *f*; **in ~ion** in abbondanza

prognosis /prɒg'nəʊsɪs/ *n* (*pl* **-oses**) prognosi *f inv*

program /'prəʊgræm/ *n* programma *m* ● *vt* (*pt/pp* **programmed**) programmare

programme /'prəʊgræm/ *n Br* programma *m*. **~r** *n* (*Comput*) programmatore, -trice *mf*

progress¹ /'prəʊgres/ *n* progresso *m*; **in ~** in corso; **make ~** *fig* fare progressi

progress² /prə'gres/ *vi* progredire; *fig* fare progressi

progressive /prə'gresɪv/ *adj* progressivo; (*reforming*) progressista. **~ly** *adv* progressivamente

prohibit /prə'hɪbɪt/ *vt* proibire. **~ive** *adj* proibitivo

project¹ /'prɒdʒekt/ *n* progetto *m*; (*Sch*) ricerca *f*

project² /prə'dʒekt/ *vt* proiettare (film, image) ● *vi* (*jut out*) sporgere

projector /prə'dʒektə(r)/ *n* proiettore *m*

prolific /prə'lɪfɪk/ *adj* prolifico

prologue /'prəʊlɒg/ *n* prologo *m*

prolong /prə'lɒŋ/ *vt* prolungare

promenade /prɒmə'nɑ:d/ *n* lungomare *m inv*

prominent /'prɒmɪnənt/ *adj* prominente; (*conspicuous*) di rilievo

promiscu|ity /prɒmɪ'skju:ətɪ/ *n* promiscuità *f*. **~ous** *adj* promiscuo

promis|e /'prɒmɪs/ *n* promessa *f* ● *vt* promettere; **~e sb that** promettere a qcno che; **I ~ed to** l'ho promesso. **~ing** *adj* promettente

promot|e /prə'məʊt/ *vt* promuovere; **be ~ed** (*Sport*) essere promosso. **~ion** *n* promozione *f*

prompt /prɒmpt/ *adj* immediato; (*punctual*) puntuale ● *adv* in punto ● *vt* incitare (**to** a); (*Theat*) suggerire a ● *vi* suggerire. **~er** *n* suggeritore, -trice *mf*. **~ly** *adv* puntualmente

Proms /prɒmz/ *npl* rassegna *f* di concerti estivi di musica classica presso l'Albert Hall a Londra

Proms | *Proms* sono una serie di concerti di musica classica che ogni estate, per otto settimane, si tengono giornalmente all'Albert Hall di Londra. Istituiti nel 1895 per iniziativa di Sir Henry Wood, il loro nome è l'abbreviazione di *promenade concerts*, concerti durante i quali a parte del pubblico in sala sono riservati posti in piedi.

prone /prəʊn/ *adj* **be ~ to do sth** essere incline a fare qcsa

pronoun /ˈprəʊnaʊn/ *n* pronome *m*

pronounce /prəˈnaʊns/ *vt* pronunciare; (*declare*) dichiarare. **~d** *adj* (*noticeable*) pronunciato

pronunciation /prənʌnsɪˈeɪʃn/ *n* pronuncia *f*

proof /pruːf/ *n* prova *f*; (*Typ*) bozza *f*, prova *f* ● *adj* **~ against** a prova di

propaganda /prɒpəˈgændə/ *n* propaganda *f*

propel /prəˈpel/ *vt* (*pt/pp* **propelled**) spingere. **~ler** *n* elica *f*

proper /ˈprɒpə(r)/ *adj* corretto; (*suitable*) adatto; ([!]: *real*) vero [e proprio]. **~ly** *adv* correttamente. **~ ˈname, ~ ˈnoun** *n* nome *m* proprio

property /ˈprɒpətɪ/ *n* proprietà *f inv*. **~ developer** *n* agente *m* immobiliare. **~ market** *n* mercato *m* immobiliare

prophecy /ˈprɒfəsɪ/ *n* profezia *f*

prophesy /ˈprɒfɪsaɪ/ *vt* (*pt/pp* **-ied**) profetizzare

prophet /ˈprɒfɪt/ *n* profeta *m*. **~ic** *adj* profetico

proportion /prəˈpɔːʃn/ *n* proporzione *f*; (*share*) parte *f*; **~s** *pl* (*dimensions*) proporzioni *fpl*. **~al** *adj* proporzionale. **~ally** *adv* in proporzione

proposal /prəˈpəʊzl/ *n* proposta *f*; (*of marriage*) proposta *f* di matrimonio

propose /prəˈpəʊz/ *vt* proporre; (*intend*) proporsi ● *vi* fare una proposta di matrimonio

proposition /prɒpəˈzɪʃn/ *n* proposta *f*; ([!]: *task*) impresa *f*

proprietor /prəˈpraɪətə(r)/ *n* proprietario, -a *mf*

prose /prəʊz/ *n* prosa *f*

prosecut|e /ˈprɒsɪkjuːt/ *vt* intentare azione contro. **~ion** *n* azione *f* giudiziaria; **the ~ion** l'accusa *f*. **~or** *n* [**Public**] **P~or** il Pubblico Ministero *m*

prospect¹ /ˈprɒspekt/ *n* (*expectation*) prospettiva *f*

prospect² /prəˈspekt/ *vi* **~ for** cercare

prospect|ive /prəˈspektɪv/ *adj* (*future*) futuro; (*possible*) potenziale. **~or** *n* cercatore *m*

prospectus /prəˈspektəs/ *n* prospetto *m*

prosper /ˈprɒspə(r)/ *vi* prosperare; (*person:*) stare bene finanziariamente. **~ity** *n* prosperità *f*

prosperous /ˈprɒspərəs/ *adj* prospero

prostitut|e /ˈprɒstɪtjuːt/ *n* prostituta *f*. **~ion** *n* prostituzione *f*

prostrate /ˈprɒstreɪt/ *adj* prostrato; **~ with grief** *fig* prostrato dal dolore

protagonist /prəʊˈtægənɪst/ *n* protagonista *mf*

protect /prəˈtekt/ *vt* proteggere (**from** da). **~ion** *n* protezione *f*. **~ive** *adj* protettivo. **~or** *n* protettore, -trice *mf*

protein /ˈprəʊtiːn/ *n* proteina *f*

protest¹ /ˈprəʊtest/ *n* protesta *f*

protest² /prəˈtest/ *vt/i* protestare

Protestant /ˈprɒtɪstənt/ *adj* protestante ● *n* protestante *mf*

protester /prəˈtestə(r)/ *n* contestatore, -trice *mf*

protocol /ˈprəʊtəkɒl/ *n* protocollo *m*

protrude /prəˈtruːd/ *vi* sporgere

proud /praʊd/ *adj* fiero (**of** di). **~ly** *adv* fieramente

prove /pruːv/ *vt* provare ● *vi* **~ to be a lie** rivelarsi una bugia. **~n** *adj* dimostrato

proverb /ˈprɒvɜːb/ *n* proverbio *m*. **~ial** *adj* proverbiale

provide /prəˈvaɪd/ *vt* fornire; **~ sb with sth** fornire qcsa a qcno ● *vi* **~ for** (*law:*) prevedere

provided /prəˈvaɪdɪd/ *conj* **~ [that]** purché

providen|ce /ˈprɒvɪdəns/ *n* provvidenza *f*. **~tial** *adj* provvidenziale

providing /prəˈvaɪdɪŋ/ *conj* = **provided**

provinc|e /ˈprɒvɪns/ *n* provincia *f*; *fig* campo *m*. **~ial** *adj* provinciale

provision /prəˈvɪʒn/ *n* (*of food, water*) approvvigionamento *m* (**of** di); (*of law*)

p

disposizione *f*; **~s** *pl* provviste *fpl*. **~al** *adj* provvisorio

provocat|ion /prɒvə'keɪʃn/ *n* provocazione *f*. **~ive** *adj* provocatorio; (*sexually*) provocante. **~ively** *adv* in modo provocatorio

provoke /prə'vəʊk/ *vt* provocare

prow /praʊ/ *n* prua *f*

prowess /'praʊɪs/ *n* abilità *f inv*

prowl /praʊl/ *vi* aggirarsi ● *n* **on the ~** in cerca di preda. **~er** *n* tipo *m* sospetto

proximity /prɒk'sɪmətɪ/ *n* prossimità *f*

proxy /'prɒksɪ/ *n* procura *f*; (*person*) persona *f* che agisce per procura

prude /pru:d/ *n* **be a ~** essere eccessivamente pudico

pruden|ce /'pru:dəns/ *n* prudenza *f*. **~t** *adj* prudente; (*wise*) oculatezza *f*

prudish /'pru:dɪʃ/ *adj* eccessivamente pudico

prune[1] /pru:n/ *n* prugna *f* secca

prune[2] *vt* potare

pry /praɪ/ *vi* (*pt/pp* **pried**) ficcare il naso

psalm /sɑ:m/ *n* salmo *m*

psychiatric /saɪkɪ'ætrɪk/ *adj* psichiatrico

psychiatr|ist /saɪ'kaɪətrɪst/ *n* psichiatra *mf*. **~y** *n* psichiatria *f*

P

psychic /'saɪkɪk/ *adj* psichico; **I'm not ~** non sono un indovino

psychological /saɪkə'lɒdʒɪkl/ *adj* psicologico

psycholog|ist /saɪ'kɒlədʒɪst/ *n* psicologo, -a *mf*. **~y** *n* psicologia *f*

pub /pʌb/ *n* [!] pub *m inv*

> **Pub** In Gran Bretagna, molti *pubs* (abbreviazione di *public house*) fanno parte di catene e sono proprietà di grandi birrerie, altri invece sono indipendenti (*free houses*). Oltre che per bere, si va al *pub* per socializzare e giocare a freccette, biliardo, ecc.; alcuni organizzano serate di quiz a gruppi. L'orario di apertura è diverso a seconda della licenza dell'esercizio, ma quello piò comune va dalle 11 alle 23.

puberty /'pju:bətɪ/ *n* pubertà *f*

public /'pʌblɪk/ *adj* pubblico ● *n* **the ~** il pubblico; **in ~** in pubblico. **~ly** *adv* pubblicamente

publican /'pʌblɪkən/ *n* gestore, -trice *mf*/proprietario, -a *mf* di un pub

publication /pʌblɪ'keɪʃn/ *n* pubblicazione *f*

public: ~ 'holiday *n* festa *f* nazionale. **~ 'house** *n* pub *m*

publicity /pʌb'lɪsətɪ/ *n* pubblicità *f*

publicize /'pʌblɪsaɪz/ *vt* pubblicizzare

public: ~ relations pubbliche relazioni *fpl*. **~ 'school** *n* scuola *f* privata; *Am* scuola *f* pubblica

> **public schools** In Inghilterra sono, al contrario di quanto il nome farebbe pensare, scuole secondarie private a pagamento, in cui spesso gli allievi risiedono in collegio.

publish /'pʌblɪʃ/ *vt* pubblicare. **~er** *n* editore *m*; (*firm*) editore *m*, casa *f* editrice. **~ing** *n* editoria *f*

pudding /'pʊdɪŋ/ *n* dolce *m* cotto al vapore; (*course*) dolce *m*

puddle /'pʌdl/ *n* pozzanghera *f*

puff /pʌf/ *n* (*of wind*) soffio *m*; (*of smoke*) tirata *f*; (*for powder*) piumino *m* ● *vt* sbuffare. **puff at** *vt* tirare boccate da (pipe). □ **~ out** *vt* lasciare senza fiato (person); spegnere (candle). **~ed** *adj* (*out of breath*) senza fiato. **~ pastry** *n* pasta *f* sfoglia

puffy /'pʌfɪ/ *adj* gonfio

pull /pʊl/ *n* trazione *f*; (*fig: attraction*) attrazione *f*; ([!]: *influence*) influenza *f* ● *vt* tirare; estrarre (tooth); stirarsi (muscle); **~ faces** far boccace; **~ oneself together** cercare di controllarsi; **~ one's weight** mettercela tutta; **~ sb's leg** [!] prendere in giro qcno. □ **~ down** *vt* (*demolish*) demolire. □ **~ in** *vi* (*Auto*) accostare. □ **~ off** *vt* togliere; [!] azzeccare. □ **~ out** *vt* tirar fuori ● *vi* (*Auto*) spostarsi; (*of competition*) ritirarsi. □ **~ through** *vi* (*recover*) farcela. □ **~ up** *vt* sradicare (plant); (*reprimand*) rimproverare ● *vi* (*Auto*) fermarsi

pullover /'pʊləʊvə(r)/ *n* pullover *m*

pulp /pʌlp/ *n* poltiglia *f*; (*of fruit*) polpa *f*; (*for paper*) pasta *f*

pulpit /ˈpʊlpɪt/ *n* pulpito *m*
pulse /pʌls/ *n* polso *m*
pummel /ˈpʌml/ *vt* (*pt/pp* **pummelled**) prendere a pugni
pump /pʌmp/ *n* pompa *f* ● *vt* pompare; [!] cercare di estrorcere da. □ **~ up** *vt* (*inflate*) gonfiare
pumpkin /ˈpʌmpkɪn/ *n* zucca *f*
pun /pʌn/ *n* gioco *m* di parole
punch¹ /pʌntʃ/ *n* pugno *m*; (*device*) pinza *f* per forare ● *vt* dare un pugno a; forare (ticket); perforare (hole)
punch² *n* (*drink*) ponce *m inv*
punctual /ˈpʌŋktjʊəl/ *adj* puntuale. **~ity** *n* puntualità *f*. **~ly** *adv* puntualmente
punctuat|e /ˈpʌŋktjʊeɪt/ *vt* punteggiare. **~ion** *n* punteggiatura *f*. **~ion mark** *n* segno *m* di interpunzione
puncture /ˈpʌŋktʃə(r)/ *n* foro *m*; (*tyre*) foratura *f* ● *vt* forare
punish /ˈpʌnɪʃ/ *vt* punire. **~able** *adj* punibile. **~ment** *n* punizione *f*
punk /pʌŋk/ *n* punk *m inv*
punt /pʌnt/ *n* (*boat*) barchino *m*
punter /ˈpʌntə(r)/ *n* (*gambler*) scommettitore, -trice *mf*; (*client*) consumatore, -trice *mf*
puny /ˈpju:nɪ/ *adj* (**-ier, -iest**) striminzito
pup /pʌp/ *n* = **puppy**
pupil /ˈpju:pl/ *n* alluno, -a *mf*; (*of eye*) pupilla *f*
puppet /ˈpʌpɪt/ *n* marionetta *f*; (*glove ~, fig*) burattino *m*
puppy /ˈpʌpɪ/ *n* cucciolo *m*
purchase /ˈpɜ:tʃəs/ *n* acquisto *m*; (*leverage*) presa *f* ● *vt* acquistare. **~r** *n* acquirente *mf*
pure /pjʊə(r)/ *adj* puro. **~ly** *adv* puramente
purgatory /ˈpɜ:gətrɪ/ *n* purgatorio *m*
purge /pɜ:dʒ/ (*Pol*) *n* epurazione *f* ● *vt* epurare
puri|fication /pjʊərɪfɪˈkeɪʃn/ *n* purificazione *f*. **~fy** *vt* (*pt/pp* **-ied**) purificare
puritan /ˈpjʊərɪtən/ *n* puritano, -a *mf*. **~ical** *adj* puritano
purity /ˈpjʊərɪtɪ/ *n* purità *f*
purple /ˈpɜ:pl/ *adj* viola
purpose /ˈpɜ:pəs/ *n* scopo *m*; (*determination*) fermezza *f*; **on ~** apposta. **~-built** *adj* costruito ad hoc. **~ful** *adj* deciso. **~fully** *adv* con decisione. **~ly** *adv* apposta
purr /pɜ:(r)/ *vi* (cat:) fare le fusa
purse /pɜ:s/ *n* borsellino *m*; (*Am: handbag*) borsa *f* ● *vt* increspare (lips)
pursue /pəˈsju:/ *vt* inseguire; *fig* proseguire. **~r** *n* inseguitore, -trice *mf*
pursuit /pəˈsju:t/ *n* inseguimento *m*; (*fig: of happiness*) ricerca *f*; (*pastime*) attività *f inv*; **in ~** all'inseguimento
pus /pʌs/ *n* pus *m*
push /pʊʃ/ *n* spinta *f*; (*fig: effort*) sforzo *m*; (*drive*) iniziativa *f*; **at a ~** in caso di bisogno; **get the ~** [!] essere licenziato ● *vt* spingere; premere (button); (*pressurize*) far pressione su; **be ~ed for time** [!] non avere tempo ● *vi* spingere. □ **~ aside** *vt* scostare. □ **~ back** *vt* respingere. □ **~ off** *vt* togliere ● *vi* ([!]*: leave*) levarsi dai piedi. □ **~ on** *vi* (*continue*) continuare. □ **~ up** *vt* alzare (price)
push: ~-chair *n* passeggino *m*. **~-up** *n* flessione *f*
pushy /ˈpʊʃɪ/ *adj* [!] troppo intraprendente
put /pʊt/ *vt* (*pt/pp* **put**, *pres p* **putting**) mettere; **~ the cost of sth at** valutare il costo di qcsa ● *vi* **~ to sea** salpare. □ **~ aside** *vt* mettere da parte. □ **~ away** *vt* mettere via. □ **~ back** *vt* rimettere; mettere indietro (clock). □ **~ by** mettere da parte. □ **~ down** *vt* mettere giù; (*suppress*) reprimere; (*kill*) sopprimere; (*write*) annotare; **~ one's foot down** [!] essere fermo; (*Auto*) dare un'accelerata; **~ down to** (*attribute*) attribuire. □ **~ forward** *vt* avanzare; mettere avanti (clock). □ **~ in** *vt* (*insert*) introdurre; (*submit*) presentare ● *vi* **~ in for** far domanda di. □ **~ off** *vt* spegnere (light); (*postpone*) rimandare; **~ sb off** tenere a bada qcno; (*deter*) smontare qcno; (*disconcert*) distrarre qcno; **~ sb off sth** (*disgust*) disgustare qcno di qcsa. □ **~ on** *vt* mettersi (clothes); mettere (brake); (*Culin*) mettere su; accendere (light); mettere in scena (play); prendere (accent); **~ on weight** mettere su qualche chilo. □ **~ out** *vt* spegnere (fire, light); tendere (hand); (*inconvenience*) creare degli inconvenienti a. □ **~ through** *vt* far passare; (*Teleph*) **I'll ~**

p

you through to him glielo passo. □ **~ up** *vt* alzare; erigere (building); montare (tent); aprire (umbrella); affiggere (notice); aumentare (price); ospitare (guest); **~ sb up to sth** mettere qcsa in testa a qcno ● *vi* (*at hotel*) stare; **~ up with** sopportare ● *adj* **stay ~!** rimani lì!

puzzl|e /'pʌzl/ *n* enigma *m*; (*jigsaw*) puzzle *m inv* ● *vt* lasciare perplesso ● *vi* **~e over** scervellarsi su. **~ing** *adj* inspiegabile

pygmy /'pɪgmɪ/ *n* pigmeo, -a *mf*

pyjamas /pə'dʒɑːməz/ *npl* pigiama *msg*

pylon /'paɪlən/ *n* pilone *m*

pyramid /'pɪrəmɪd/ *n* piramide *f*

python /'paɪθn/ *n* pitone *m*

Qq

quack¹ /kwæk/ *n* qua qua *m inv* ● *vi* fare qua qua

quack² *n* (*doctor*) ciarlatano *m*

quadrangle /'kwɒdræŋgl/ *n* quadrangolo *m*; (*court*) cortile *m* quadrangolare

quadruped /'kwɒdrʊped/ *n* quadrupede *m*

quadruple /'kwɒdrʊpl/ *adj* quadruplo ● *vt* quadruplicare ● *vi* quadruplicarsi. **~ts** *npl* quattro gemelli *mpl*

quagmire /'kwɒgmaɪə(r)/ *n* pantano *m*

quaint /kweɪnt/ *adj* pittoresco; (*odd*) bizzarro

quake /kweɪk/ *n* [!] terremoto *m* ● *vi* tremare

qualif|ication /kwɒlɪfɪ'keɪʃn/ *n* qualifica *f*. **~ied** *adj* qualificato; (*limited*) con riserva

qualify /'kwɒlɪfaɪ/ *v* (*pt/pp* **-ied**) ● *vt* (course:) dare la qualifica a (**as** di); (*entitle*) dare diritto a; (*limit*) precisare ● *vi* ottenere la qualifica; (*Sport*) qualificarsi

quality /'kwɒlətɪ/ *n* qualità *f inv*

qualm /kwɑːm/ *n* scrupolo *m*

quandary /'kwɒndərɪ/ *n* dilemma *m*

quantity /'kwɒntətɪ/ *n* quantità *f inv*; **in ~** in grande quantità

quarantine /'kwɒrəntiːn/ *n* quarantena *f*

quarrel /'kwɒrəl/ *n* lite *f* ● *vi* (*pt/pp* **quarrelled**) litigare. **~-some** *adj* litigioso

quarry¹ /'kwɒrɪ/ *n* (*prey*) preda *f*

quarry² *n* cava *f*

quart /kwɔːt/ *n* 1.14 *litro*

quarter /'kwɔːtə(r)/ *n* quarto *m*; (*of year*) trimestre *m*; *Am* 25 centesimi *mpl*; **~s** *pl* (*Mil*) quartiere *msg*; **at [a] ~ to six** alle sei meno un quarto ● *vt* dividere in quattro. **~-'final** *n* quarto *m* di finale

quarterly /'kwɔːtəlɪ/ *adj* trimestrale ● *adv* trimestralmente

quartz /kwɔːts/ *n* quarzo *m*. **~ watch** *n* orologio *m* al quarzo

quay /kiː/ *n* banchina *f*

queasy /'kwiːzɪ/ *adj* **I feel ~** ho la nausea

queen /kwiːn/ *n* regina *f*. **~ mother** *n* regina *f* madre

queer /kwɪə(r)/ *adj* strano; (*dubious*) sospetto; ([!]*: homosexual*) finocchio ● *n* [!] finocchio *m*

quench /kwentʃ/ *vt* **~ one's thirst** dissetarsi

query /'kwɪərɪ/ *n* domanda *f*; (*question mark*) punto *m* interrogativo ● *vt* (*pt/pp* **-ied**) interrogare; (*doubt*) mettere in dubbio

quest /kwest/ *n* ricerca *f* (**for** di)

question /'kwestʃn/ *n* domanda *f*; (*for discussion*) questione *f*; **out of the ~** fuori discussione; **without ~** senza dubbio; **in ~** in questione ● *vt* interrogare; (*doubt*) mettere in dubbio. **~able** *adj* discutibile. **~ mark** *n* punto *m* interrogativo

questionnaire /kwestʃə'neə(r)/ *n* questionario *m*

queue /kjuː/ *n* coda *f*, fila *f* ● *vi* **~ [up]** mettersi in coda (**for** per)

quick /kwɪk/ *adj* veloce; **be ~** sbrigati!; **have a ~ meal** fare uno spuntino ● *adv* in fretta ● *n* **be cut to the ~** *fig* essere punto sul vivo. **~ly** *adv* in fretta. **~-tempered** *adj* collerico

quid /kwɪd/ *n inv* [!] sterlina *f*

quiet /'kwaɪət/ *adj* (*calm*) tranquillo; (*silent*) silenzioso; (*voice, music*) basso;

keep ~ about [!] non raccontare a nessuno ● *n* quiete *f*; **on the** ~ di nascosto. **~ly** *adv* (*peacefully*) tranquillamente; (say) a bassa voce

quiet|en /ˈkwaɪətn/ *vt* calmare. □ ~ **down** *vi* calmarsi. **~ness** *n* quiete *f*

quilt /kwɪlt/ *n* piumino *m*. **~ed** *adj* trapuntato

quintet /kwɪnˈtet/ *n* quintetto *m*

quirk /kwɜːk/ *n* stranezza *f*

quit /kwɪt/ *v* (*pt/pp* **quitted, quit**) ● *vt* lasciare; (*give up*) smettere (**doing** di fare) ● *vi* ([!]: *resign*) andarsene; (*Comput*) uscire; **give sb notice to** ~ (landlord:) dare a qcno il preavviso di sfratto

quite /kwaɪt/ *adv* (*fairly*) abbastanza; (*completely*) completamente; (*really*) veramente; ~ [**so**]**!** proprio così!; ~ **a few** parecchi

quits /kwɪts/ *adj* pari

quiver /ˈkwɪvə(r)/ *vi* tremare

quiz /kwɪz/ *n* (*game*) quiz *m inv* ● *vt* (*pt/pp* **quizzed**) interrogare

quota /ˈkwəʊtə/ *n* quota *f*

quotation /kwəʊˈteɪʃn/ *n* citazione *f*; (*price*) preventivo *m*; (*of shares*) quota *f*. ~ **marks** *npl* virgolette *fpl*

quote /kwəʊt/ *n* [!] = **quotation**; **in ~s** tra virgolette ● *vt* citare; quotare (price)

Rr

rabbi /ˈræbaɪ/ *n* rabbino *m*; (*title*) rabbi

rabbit /ˈræbɪt/ *n* coniglio *m*

rabies /ˈreɪbiːz/ *n* rabbia *f*

race¹ /reɪs/ *n* (*people*) razza *f*

race² *n* corsa *f* ● *vi* correre ● *vt* gareggiare con; fare correre (horse)

race: ~course *n* ippodromo *m*. **~horse** *n* cavallo *m* da corsa. **~-track** *n* pista *m*

racial /ˈreɪʃl/ *adj* razziale. **~ism** *n* razzismo *m*

racing /ˈreɪsɪŋ/ *n* corse *fpl*; (*horse-*) corse *fpl* dei cavalli. ~ **car** *n* macchina *f* da corsa. ~ **driver** *n* corridore *m* automobilistico

racis|m /ˈreɪsɪzm/ *n* razzismo *m*. **~t** *adj* razzista ● *n* razzista *mf*

rack¹ /ræk/ *n* (*for bikes*) rastrelliera *f*; (*for luggage*) portabagagli *m inv*; (*for plates*) scolapiatti *m inv* ● *vt* ~ **one's brains** scervellarsi

rack² *n* **go to ~ and ruin** andare in rovina

racket¹ /ˈrækɪt/ *n* (*Sport*) racchetta *f*

racket² *n* (*din*) chiasso *m*; (*swindle*) truffa *f*; (*crime*) racket *m inv*, giro *m*

radar /ˈreɪdɑː(r)/ *n* radar *m inv*

radian|ce /ˈreɪdɪəns/ *n* radiosità *f inv*. **~t** *adj* raggiante

radiat|e /ˈreɪdɪeɪt/ *vt* irradiare ● *vi* (heat:) irradiarsi. **~ion** *n* radiazione *f*

radiator /ˈreɪdɪeɪtə(r)/ *n* radiatore *m*

radical /ˈrædɪkl/ *adj* radicale ● *n* radicale *mf*. **~ly** *adv* radicalmente

radio /ˈreɪdɪəʊ/ *n* radio *f inv*

radio|ˈactive *adj* radioattivo. **~acˈtivity** *n* radioattività *f*

radish /ˈrædɪʃ/ *n* ravanello *m*

radius /ˈreɪdɪəs/ *n* (*pl* **-dii** /-dɪaɪ/) raggio *m*

raffle /ˈræfl/ *n* lotteria *f*

raft /rɑːft/ *n* zattera *f*

rafter /ˈrɑːftə(r)/ *n* trave *f*

rag /ræg/ *n* straccio *m*; (*pej: newspaper*) giornalaccio *m*; **in ~s** stracciato

rage /reɪdʒ/ *n* rabbia *f*; **all the** ~ [!] all'ultima moda ● *vi* infuriarsi; (storm:) infuriare; (epidemic:) imperversare

ragged /ˈrægɪd/ *adj* logoro; (edge) frastagliato

raid /reɪd/ *n* (*by thieves*) rapina *f*; (*Mil*) incursione *f*, raid *m inv*; (*police*) irruzione *f* ● *vt* (*Mil*) fare un'incursione in; (police, burglars:) fare irruzione in. **~er** *n* (*of bank*) rapinatore, -trice *mf*

rail /reɪl/ *n* ringhiera *f*; (*hand~*) ringhiera *f*; (*Naut*) parapetto *m*; **by** ~ per ferrovia

ˈrailroad *n Am* = **railway**

ˈrailway *n* ferrovia *f*. **~man** *n* ferroviere *m*. ~ **station** *n* stazione *f* ferroviaria

rain /reɪn/ *n* pioggia *f* ● *vi* piovere

rain: ~bow *n* arcobaleno *m*. **~coat** *n* impermeabile *m*. **~fall** *n* precipitazione *f* [atmosferica]

q r

rainy /ˈreɪnɪ/ *adj* (**-ier, -iest**) piovoso

raise /reɪz/ *n Am* aumento *m* ● *vt* alzare; levarsi (hat); allevare (children, animals); sollevare (question); ottenere (money)

raisin /ˈreɪzn/ *n* uva *f* passa

rake /reɪk/ *n* rastrello *m* ● *vt* rastrellare. □ ~ **up** *vt* raccogliere col rastrello; [!] rivangare

rally /ˈrælɪ/ *n* raduno *m*; (*Auto*) rally *m inv*; (*Tennis*) scambio *m* ● *vt* (*pt/pp* **-ied**) radunare ● *vi* radunarsi; (*recover strength*) riprendersi

ram /ræm/ *n* montone *m*; (*Astr*) Ariete *m* ● *vt* (*pt/pp* **rammed**) cozzare contro

RAM /ræm/ *n* [memoria *f*] RAM *f*

rambl|e /ˈræmbl/ *n* escursione *f* ● *vi* gironzolare; (*in speech*) divagare. **~er** *n* escursionista *mf*; (*rose*) rosa *f* rampicante. **~ing** *adj* (*in speech*) sconnesso; (club) escursionistico

ramp /ræmp/ *n* rampa *f*; (*Aeron*) scaletta *f* mobile (*di aerei*)

rampage /ˈræmpeɪdʒ/ *n* **be/go on the ~** scatenarsi ● *vi* **~ through the streets** scatenarsi per le strade

ramshackle /ˈræmʃækl/ *adj* sgangherato

ran /ræn/ ▷**RUN**

ranch /rɑːntʃ/ *n* ranch *m*

random /ˈrændəm/ *adj* casuale; **~ sample** campione *m* a caso ● *n* **at ~** a casaccio

rang /ræŋ/ ▷**RING**[2]

r **range** /reɪndʒ/ *n* serie *f*; (*Comm, Mus*) gamma *f*; (*of mountains*) catena *f*; (*distance*) raggio *m*; (*for shooting*) portata *f*; (*stove*) cucina *f* economica; **at a ~ of** a una distanza di ● *vi* estendersi; **~ from... to...** andare da... a.... **~r** *n* guardia *f* forestale

rank /ræŋk/ *n* (*row*) riga *f*; (*Mil*) grado *m*; (*social position*) rango *m*; **the ~ and file** la base *f*; **the ~s** (*Mil*) i soldati *mpl* semplici ● *vt* (*place*) annoverare (**among** tra) ● *vi* (*be placed*) collocarsi

ransack /ˈrænsæk/ *vt* rovistare; (*pillage*) saccheggiare

ransom /ˈrænsəm/ *n* riscatto *m*; **hold sb to ~** tenere qcno in ostaggio (*per il riscatto*)

rant /rænt/ *vi* **~ [and rave]** inveire; **what's he ~ing on about?** cosa sta blaterando?

rap /ræp/ *n* colpo *m* [secco]; (*Mus*) rap *m* ● *v* (*pt/pp* **rapped**) ● *vt* dare colpetti a ● *vi* **~ at** bussare a

rape /reɪp/ *n* (*sexual*) stupro *m* ● *vt* violentare, stuprare

rapid /ˈræpɪd/ *adj* rapido. **~ity** *n* rapidità *f*. **~ly** *adv* rapidamente

rapids /ˈræpɪdz/ *npl* rapida *fsg*

rapist /ˈreɪpɪst/ *n* violentatore *m*

raptur|e /ˈræptʃə(r)/ *n* estasi *f*. **~ous** *adj* entusiastico

rare[1] /reə(r)/ *adj* raro. **~ly** *adv* raramente

rare[2] *adj* (*Culin*) al sangue

rarefied /ˈreərɪfaɪd/ *adj* rarefatto

rarity /ˈreərətɪ/ *n* rarità *f inv*

rascal /ˈrɑːskl/ *n* mascalzone *m*

rash[1] /ræʃ/ *n* (*Med*) eruzione *f*

rash[2] *adj* avventato. **~ly** *adv* avventatamente

rasher /ˈræʃə(r)/ *n* fetta *f* di pancetta

rasp /rɑːsp/ *n* (*noise*) stridio *m*. **~ing** *adj* stridente

raspberry /ˈrɑːzbərɪ/ *n* lampone *m*

rat /ræt/ *n* topo *m*; ([!]: *person*) carogna *f*; **smell a ~** [!] sentire puzzo di bruciato

rate /reɪt/ *n* (*speed*) velocità *f*; (*of payment*) tariffa *f*; (*of exchange*) tasso *m*; **~s** *pl* (*taxes*) imposte *fpl* comunali sui beni immobili; **at any ~** in ogni caso; **at this ~** di questo passo ● *vt* stimare; **~ among** annoverare tra ● *vi* **~ as** essere considerato

rather /ˈrɑːðə(r)/ *adv* piuttosto; **~!** eccome!; **~ too...** un po' troppo...

rating /ˈreɪtɪŋ/ *n* **~s** *pl* (*Radio, TV*) indice *m* d'ascolto, audience *f inv*

ratio /ˈreɪʃɪəʊ/ *n* rapporto *m*

ration /ˈræʃn/ *n* razione *f* ● *vt* razionare

rational /ˈræʃənl/ *adj* razionale. **~ize** *vt/i* razionalizzare

rattle /ˈrætl/ *n* tintinnio *m*; (*toy*) sonaglio *m* ● *vi* tintinnare ● *vt* (*shake*) scuotere; [!] innervosire. □ **~ off** *vt* [!] sciorinare

raucous /ˈrɔːkəs/ *adj* rauco

rave /reɪv/ *vi* vaneggiare; **~ about** andare in estasi per

raven /'reɪvn/ *n* corvo *m* imperiale
ravenous /'rævənəs/ *adj* (person) affamato
ravine /rə'vi:n/ *n* gola *f*
raving /'reɪvɪŋ/ *adj* **~ mad** [!] matto da legare
ravishing /'rævɪʃɪŋ/ *adj* incantevole
raw /rɔ:/ *adj* crudo; (*not processed*) grezzo; (weather) gelido; (*inexperienced*) inesperto; **get a ~ deal** [!] farsi fregare. **~ ma'terials** *npl* materie *fpl* prime
ray /reɪ/ *n* raggio *m*; **~ of hope** barlume *m* di speranza
raze /reɪz/ *vt* **~ to the ground** radere al suolo
razor /'reɪzə(r)/ *n* rasoio *m*. **~ blade** *n* lametta *f* da barba
re /ri:/ *prep* con riferimento a
reach /ri:tʃ/ *n* portata *f*; **within ~** a portata di mano; **out of ~ of** fuori dalla portata di; **within easy ~** facilmente raggiungibile ● *vt* arrivare a (place, decision); (*contact*) contattare; (*pass*) passare; **I can't ~ it** non ci arrivo ● *vi* arrivare (**to** a); **~ for** allungare la mano per prendere
re'act /rɪ-/ *vi* reagire
re'action /rɪ-/ *n* reazione *f*. **~ary** *adj* reazionario, -a *mf*
reactor /rɪ'æktə(r)/ *n* reattore *m*
read /ri:d/ *vt* (*pt/pp* **read** /red/) leggere; (*Univ*) studiare ● *vi* leggere; (instrument:) indicare. □ **~ out** *vt* leggere ad alta voce
readable /'ri:dəbl/ *adj* piacevole a leggersi; (*legible*) leggibile
reader /'ri:də(r)/ *n* lettore, -trice *mf*; (*book*) antologia *f*
readi|ly /'redɪlɪ/ *adv* volentieri; (*easily*) facilmente. **~ness** *n* disponibilità *f inv*; **in ~ness** pronto
reading /'ri:dɪŋ/ *n* lettura *f*
rea'djust /ri:-/ *vt* regolare di nuovo ● *vi* riabituarsi (**to** a)
ready /'redɪ/ *adj* (**-ier, -iest**) pronto; (*quick*) veloce; **get ~** prepararsi
ready-'made *adj* confezionato
real /ri:l/ *adj* vero; (increase) reale ● *adv Am* [!] veramente. **~ estate** *n* beni *mpl* immobili
realis|m /'rɪəlɪzm/ *n* realismo *m*. **~t** *n* realista *mf*. **~tic** *adj* realistico
reality /rɪ'ælətɪ/ *n* realtà *f inv*; **~ TV** *n* reality TV *f*
realization /rɪəlaɪ'zeɪʃn/ *n* realizzazione *f*
realize /'rɪəlaɪz/ *vt* realizzare
really /'rɪəlɪ/ *adv* davvero
realm /relm/ *n* regno *m*
realtor /'rɪəltə(r)/ *n Am* agente *mf* immobiliare
reap /ri:p/ *vt* mietere
reap'pear /ri:-/ *vi* riapparire
rear[1] /rɪə(r)/ *adj* posteriore; (*Auto*) di dietro; **~ end** [!] didietro *m* ● *n* **the ~** (*of building*) il retro *m*; (*of bus, plane*) la parte *f* posteriore; **from the ~** da dietro
rear[2] *vt* allevare ● *vi* **~ [up]** (horse:) impennarsi
rear'range /ri:-/ *vt* cambiare la disposizione di
reason /'ri:zn/ *n* ragione *f*; **within ~** nei limiti del ragionevole ● *vi* ragionare; **~ with** cercare di far ragionare. **~able** *adj* ragionevole. **~ably** *adv* (*in reasonable way, fairly*) ragionevolmente
reas'sur|ance /ri:-/ *n* rassicurazione *f*. **~e** *vt* rassicurare; **~e sb of sth** rassicurare qcno su qcsa. **~ing** *adj* rassicurante
rebate /'ri:beɪt/ *n* rimborso *m*; (*discount*) deduzione *f*
rebel[1] /'rebl/ *n* ribelle *mf*
rebel[2] /rɪ'bel/ *vi* (*pt/pp* **rebelled**) ribellarsi. **~lion** *n* ribellione *f*. **~lious** *adj* ribelle
re'bound[1] /rɪ-/ *vi* rimbalzare; *fig* ricadere
'rebound[2] /ri:-/ *n* rimbalzo *m*
rebuff /rɪ'bʌf/ *n* rifiuto *m*
re'build /ri:-/ *vt* (*pt/pp* **-built**) ricostruire
rebuke /rɪ'bju:k/ *vt* rimproverare
re'call /rɪ-/ *n* richiamo *m*; **beyond ~** irrevocabile ● *vt* richiamare; riconvocare (diplomat, parliament); (*remember*) rievocare
recap /'ri:kæp/ *vt/i* [!] = **recapitulate** ● *n* ricapitolazione *f*
recapitulate /ri:kə'pɪtjʊleɪt/ *vt/i* ricapitolare
re'capture /ri:-/ *vt* riconquistare; ricatturare (person, animal)
reced|e /rɪ'si:d/ *vi* allontanarsi. **~ing**

adj (forehead, chin) sfuggente; **have ~ing hair** essere stempiato
receipt /rɪ'si:t/ *n* ricevuta *f*; (*receiving*) ricezione *f*; **~s** *pl* (*Comm*) entrate *fpl*
receive /rɪ'si:v/ *vt* ricevere. **~r** *n* (*Teleph*) ricevitore *m*; (*Radio, TV*) apparecchio *m* ricevente; (*of stolen goods*) ricettatore, -trice *mf*
recent /'ri:snt/ *adj* recente. **~ly** *adv* recentemente
reception /rɪ'sepʃn/ *n* ricevimento *m*; (*welcome*) accoglienza *f*; (*Radio*) ricezione *f*; **~ [desk]** (*in hotel*) reception *f inv*. **~ist** *n* persona *f* alla reception
receptive /rɪ'septɪv/ *adj* ricettivo
recess /rɪ'ses/ *n* rientranza *f*; (*holiday*) vacanza *f*; *Am* (*Sch*) intervallo *m*
recession /rɪ'seʃn/ *n* recessione *f*
re'charge /ri:-/ *vt* ricaricare
recipe /'resəpɪ/ *n* ricetta *f*
recipient /rɪ'sɪpɪənt/ *n* (*of letter*) destinatario, -a *mf*; (*of money*) beneficiario, -a *mf*
recital /rɪ'saɪtl/ *n* recital *m inv*
recite /rɪ'saɪt/ *vt* recitare; (*list*) elencare
reckless /'reklɪs/ *adj* (action, decision) sconsiderato; **be a ~ driver** guidare in modo spericolato. **~ly** *adv* in modo sconsiderato. **~ness** *n* sconsideratezza *f*
reckon /'rekən/ *vt* calcolare; (*consider*) pensare. □ **~ on/with** *vt* fare i conti con
re'claim /rɪ-/ *vt* reclamare; bonificare (land)
reclin|e /rɪ'klaɪn/ *vi* sdraiarsi. **~ing** *adj* (seat) reclinabile
recluse /rɪ'klu:s/ *n* recluso, -a *mf*
recognition /rekəg'nɪʃn/ *n* riconoscimento *m*; **beyond ~** irriconoscibile
recognize /'rekəgnaɪz/ *vt* riconoscere
re'coil /rɪ-/ *vi* (*in fear*) indietreggiare
recollect /rekə'lekt/ *vt* ricordare. **~ion** *n* ricordo *m*
recommend /rekə'mend/ *vt* raccomandare. **~ation** *n* raccomandazione *f*
recon|cile /'rekənsaɪl/ *vt* riconciliare; conciliare (facts); **~cile oneself to** rassegnarsi a. **~ciliation** *n* riconciliazione *f*
reconnaissance /rɪ'kɒnɪsns/ *n* (*Mil*) ricognizione *f*
reconnoitre /rekə'nɔɪtə(r)/ *vi* (*pres p* **-tring**) fare una recognizione
recon'sider /ri:-/ *vt* riconsiderare
recon'struct /ri:-/ *vt* ricostruire. **~ion** *n* ricostruzione *f*
record[1] /rɪ'kɔ:d/ *vt* registrare; (*make a note of*) annotare
record[2] /'rekɔ:d/ *n* (*file*) documentazione *f*; (*Mus*) disco *m*; (*Sport*) record *m inv*; **~s** *pl* (*files*) schedario *msg*; **keep a ~ of** tener nota di; **off the ~** in via ufficiosa; **have a [criminal] ~** avere la fedina penale sporca
recorder /rɪ'kɔ:də(r)/ *n* (*Mus*) flauto *m* dolce
recording /rɪ'kɔ:dɪŋ/ *n* registrazione *f*
'record-player *n* giradischi *m inv*
recount /rɪ'kaʊnt/ *vt* raccontare
re-'count[1] /ri:-/ *vt* ricontare
're-count[2] /'ri:-/ *n* (*Pol*) nuovo conteggio *m*
recover /rɪ'kʌvə(r)/ *vt/i* recuperare. **~y** *n* recupero *m*; (*of health*) guarigione *m*
re-'cover /ri:-/ *vt* rifoderare
recreation /rekrɪ'eɪʃn/ *n* ricreazione *f*. **~al** *adj* ricreativo
recruit /rɪ'kru:t/ *n* (*Mil*) recluta *f*; **new ~** (*member*) nuovo, -a adepto, -a *mf*; (*worker*) neoassunto, -a *mf* ● *vt* assumere (staff). **~ment** *n* assunzione *f*
rectang|le /'rektæŋgl/ *n* rettangolo *m*. **~ular** *adj* rettangolare
rectify /'rektɪfaɪ/ *vt* (*pt/pp* **-ied**) rettificare
recuperate /rɪ'ku:pəreɪt/ *vi* ristabilirsi
recur /rɪ'kɜ:(r)/ *vi* (*pt/pp* **recurred**) ricorrere; (illness:) ripresentarsi
recurren|ce /rɪ'kʌrəns/ *n* ricorrenza *f*; (*of illness*) ricomparsa *f*. **~t** *adj* ricorrente
recycle /ri:'saɪkl/ *vt* riciclare
red /red/ *adj* (**redder, reddest**) rosso ● *n* rosso *m*; **in the ~** (*account*) scoperto. **R~ Cross** *n* Croce *f* rossa
redd|en /'redn/ *vt* arrossare ● *vi* arrossire. **~ish** *adj* rossastro
re'decorate /ri:-/ *vt* (*paint*) ridipingere; (*wallpaper*) ritappezzare
redeem /rɪ'di:m/ *vt* **~ing quality** unico aspetto *m* positivo
redemption /rɪ'dempʃn/ *n* riscatto *m*
red: ~-haired *adj* con i capelli rossi. **~-'handed** *adj* **catch sb ~-handed**

cogliere qcno con le mani nel sacco. **~ 'herring** *n* diversione *f*. **~-hot** *adj* rovente

red: ~ 'light *n* (*Auto*) semaforo *m* rosso

re'double /riː-/ *vt* raddoppiare

red 'tape *n* [!] burocrazia *f*

reduc|e /rɪ'djuːs/ *vt* ridurre; (*Culin*) far consumare. **~tion** *n* riduzione *f*

redundan|cy /rɪ'dʌndənsɪ/ *n* licenziamento *m*; (*payment*) cassa *f* integrazione. **~t** *adj* superfluo; **make ~t** licenziare; **be made ~t** essere licenziato

reed /riːd/ *n* (*Bot*) canna *f*

reef /riːf/ *n* scogliera *f*

reek /riːk/ *vi* puzzare (**of** di)

reel /riːl/ *n* bobina *f* ● *vi* (*stagger*) vacillare. □ **~ off** *vt fig* snocciolare

refectory /rɪ'fektərɪ/ *n* refettorio *m*; (*Univ*) mensa *f* universitaria

refer /rɪ'fɜː(r)/ *v* (*pt/pp* **referred**) ● *vt* rinviare (matter) (**to** a); indirizzare (person) ● *vi* **~ to** fare allusione a; (*consult*) rivolgersi a (book)

referee /refə'riː/ *n* arbitro *m*; (*for job*) garante *mf* ● *vt/i* (*pt/pp* **refereed**) arbitrare

reference /'refərəns/ *n* riferimento *m*; (*in book*) nota *f* bibliografica; (*for job*) referenza *f*; (*Comm*) **'your ~'** 'riferimento'; **with ~ to** con riferimento a; **make [a] ~ to** fare riferimento a. **~ book** *n* libro *m* di consultazione. **~ number** *n* numero *m* di riferimento

referendum /refə'rendəm/ *n* referendum *m inv*

re'fill¹ /riː-/ *vt* riempire di nuovo; ricaricare (pen, lighter)

'refill² /'riː-/ *n* (*for pen*) ricambio *m*

refine /rɪ'faɪn/ *vt* raffinare. **~d** *adj* raffinato. **~ment** *n* raffinatezza *f*; (*Techn*) raffinazione *f*. **~ry** *n* raffineria *f*

reflect /rɪ'flekt/ *vt* riflettere; **be ~ed in** essere riflesso in ● *vi* (*think*) riflettere (**on** su); **~ badly on sb** *fig* mettere in cattiva luce qcno. **~ion** *n* riflessione *f*; (*image*) riflesso *m*; **on ~ion** dopo riflessione. **~ive** *adj* riflessivo. **~or** *n* riflettore *m*

reflex /'riːfleks/ *n* riflesso *m* ● *attrib* di riflesso

reflexive /rɪ'fleksɪv/ *adj* riflessivo

reform /rɪ'fɔːm/ *n* riforma *f* ● *vt* riformare ● *vi* correggersi. **R~ation** *n* (*Relig*) riforma *f*. **~er** *n* riformatore, -trice *mf*

refrain¹ /rɪ'freɪn/ *n* ritornello *m*

refrain² *vi* astenersi (**from** da)

refresh /rɪ'freʃ/ *vt* rinfrescare. **~ing** *adj* rinfrescante. **~ments** *npl* rinfreschi *mpl*

refrigerat|e /rɪ'frɪdʒəreɪt/ *vt* conservare in frigo. **~or** *n* frigorifero *m*

re'fuel /riː-/ *v* (*pt/pp* **-fuelled**) ● *vt* rifornire (*di carburante*) ● *vi* fare rifornimento

refuge /'refjuːdʒ/ *n* rifugio *m*; **take ~** rifugiarsi

refugee /refjʊ'dʒiː/ *n* rifugiato, -a *mf*

'refund¹ /'riː-/ *n* rimborso *m*

re'fund² /rɪ-/ *vt* rimborsare

refusal /rɪ'fjuːzl/ *n* rifiuto *m*

refuse¹ /rɪ'fjuːz/ *vt/i* rifiutare; **~ to do sth** rifiutare di fare qcsa

refuse² /'refjuːs/ *n* rifiuti *mpl*. **~ collection** *n* raccolta *f* dei rifiuti

refute /rɪ'fjuːt/ *vt* confutare

re'gain /rɪ-/ *vt* riconquistare

regal /'riːgl/ *adj* regale

regard /rɪ'gɑːd/ *n* (*heed*) riguardo *m*; (*respect*) considerazione *f*; **~s** *pl* saluti *mpl*; **send/give my ~s to your brother** salutami tuo fratello ● *vt* (*consider*) considerare (**as** come); **as ~s** riguardo a. **~ing** *prep* riguardo a. **~less** *adv* lo stesso; **~less of** senza badare a

regatta /rɪ'gætə/ *n* regata *f*

regime /reɪ'ʒiːm/ *n* regime *m*

regiment /'redʒɪmənt/ *n* reggimento *m*. **~al** *adj* reggimentale. **~ation** *n* irreggimentazione *f*

region /'riːdʒən/ *n* regione *f*; **in the ~ of** *fig* approssimativamente. **~al** *adj* regionale

register /'redʒɪstə(r)/ *n* registro *m* ● *vt* registrare; mandare per raccomandata (letter); assicurare (luggage); immatricolare (vehicle); mostrare (feeling) ● *vi* (instrument:) funzionare; (student:) iscriversi (**for** a); **~ with** iscriversi nella lista di (doctor)

registrar /redʒɪ'strɑː(r)/ *n* ufficiale *m* di stato civile

registration /redʒɪ'streɪʃn/ *n* (*of vehicle*) immatricolazione *f*; (*of letter*) raccomandazione *f*; (*of luggage*) assicurazione *f*; (*for course*) iscrizione *f*. **~**

number *n* (*Auto*) targa *f*
registry office /ˈredʒɪstrɪ-/ *n* anagrafe *f*
regret /rɪˈgret/ *n* rammarico *m* • *vt* (*pt/pp* **regretted**) rimpiangere; **I ~ that** mi rincresce che. **~fully** *adv* con rammarico
regrettab|le /rɪˈgretəbl/ *adj* spiacevole. **~ly** *adv* spiacevolmente; (*before adjective*) deplorevolmente
regular /ˈregjʊlə(r)/ *adj* regolare; (*usual*) abituale • *n* cliente *mf* abituale. **~ity** *n* regolarità *f*. **~ly** *adv* regolarmente
regulat|e /ˈregʊleɪt/ *vt* regolare. **~ion** *n* (*rule*) regolamento *m*
rehears|al /rɪˈhɜːsl/ *n* (*Theat*) prova *f*. **~e** *vt/i* provare
reign /reɪn/ *n* regno *m* • *vi* regnare
reinforce /riːɪnˈfɔːs/ *vt* rinforzare. **~d 'concrete** *n* cemento *m* armato. **~ment** *n* rinforzo *m*
reiterate /riːˈɪtəreɪt/ *vt* reiterare
reject /rɪˈdʒekt/ *vt* rifiutare. **~ion** *n* rifiuto *m*; (*Med*) rigetto *m*
rejoic|e /rɪˈdʒɔɪs/ *vi liter* rallegrarsi. **~ing** *n* gioia *f*
rejuvenate /rɪˈdʒuːvəneɪt/ *vt* ringiovanire
relapse /rɪˈlæps/ *n* ricaduta *f* • *vi* ricadere
relate /rɪˈleɪt/ *vt* (*tell*) riportare; (*connect*) collegare • *vi* **~ to** riferirsi a; identificarsi con (person). **~d** *adj* imparentato (**to** a); (ideas etc) affine
relation /rɪˈleɪʃn/ *n* rapporto *m*; (*person*) parente *mf*. **~ship** *n* rapporto *m* (*blood tie*) parentela *f*; (*affair*) relazione *f*
relative /ˈrelətɪv/ *n* parente *mf* • *adj* relativo. **~ly** *adv* relativamente
relax /rɪˈlæks/ *vt* rilassare; allentare (pace, grip) • *vi* rilassarsi. **~ation** *n* rilassamento *m*, relax *m inv*; (*recreation*) svago *m*. **~ing** *adj* rilassante
relay¹ /riːˈleɪ/ *vt* ritrasmettere; (*Radio, TV*) trasmettere
relay² /ˈriːleɪ/ *n* (*Electr*) relais *m inv*; **work in ~s** fare i turni. **~ [race]** *n* [corsa *f* a] staffetta *f*
release /rɪˈliːs/ *n* rilascio *m*; (*of film*) distribuzione *f* • *vt* liberare; lasciare (hand); togliere (brake); distribuire (film); rilasciare (information etc)

relegate /ˈrelɪgeɪt/ *vt* relegare; **be ~d** (*Sport*) essere retrocesso
relent /rɪˈlent/ *vi* cedere. **~less** *adj* inflessibile; (*unceasing*) incessante. **~lessly** *adv* incessantemente
relevan|ce /ˈreləvəns/ *n* pertinenza *f*. **~t** *adj* pertinente (**to** a)
reliab|ility /rɪlaɪəˈbɪlətɪ/ *n* affidabilità *f*. **~le** *adj* affidabile a. **~ly** *adv* in modo affidabile; **be ~ly informed** sapere da fonte certa
relian|ce /rɪˈlaɪəns/ *n* fiducia *f* (**on** in). **~t** *adj* fiducioso (**on** in)
relic /ˈrelɪk/ *n* (*Relig*) reliquia *f*; **~s** *npl* resti *mpl*
relief /rɪˈliːf/ *n* sollievo *m*; (*assistance*) soccorso *m*; (*distraction*) diversivo *m*; (*replacement*) cambio *m*; (*in art*) rilievo *m*; **in ~** in rilievo. **~ map** *n* carta *f* in rilievo. **~ train** *n* treno *m* supplementare
relieve /rɪˈliːv/ *vt* alleviare; (*take over from*) dare il cambio a; **~ of** liberare da (burden)
religion /rɪˈlɪdʒən/ *n* religione *f*
religious /rɪˈlɪdʒəs/ *adj* religioso. **~ly** *adv* (*conscientiously*) scrupolosamente
relinquish /rɪˈlɪŋkwɪʃ/ *vt* abbandonare; **~ sth to sb** rinunciare a qcsa in favore di qcno
relish /ˈrelɪʃ/ *n* gusto *m*; (*Culin*) salsa *f* • *vt fig* apprezzare
reluctan|ce /rɪˈlʌktəns/ *n* riluttanza *f*. **~t** *adj* riluttante. **~tly** *adv* a malincuore
rely /rɪˈlaɪ/ *vi* (*pt/pp* **-ied**) **~ on** dipendere da; (*trust*) contare su
remain /rɪˈmeɪn/ *vi* restare. **~der** *n* resto *m*. **~ing** *adj* restante. **~s** *npl* resti *mpl*; (*dead body*) spoglie *fpl*
remand /rɪˈmɑːnd/ *n* **on ~** in custodia cautelare • *vt* **~ in custody** rinviare con detenzione provvisoria
remark /rɪˈmɑːk/ *n* osservazione *f* • *vt* osservare. **~able** *adj* notevole. **~ably** *adv* notevolmente
remarry /riː-/ *vi* risposarsi
remedy /ˈremədɪ/ *n* rimedio *m* (**for** contro)• *vt* (*pt/pp* **-ied**) rimediare a
remember /rɪˈmembə(r)/ *vt* ricordare, ricordarsi; **~ to do sth** ricordarsi di fare qcsa; **~ me to him** salutamelo • *vi* ricordarsi

remind /rɪ'maɪnd/ *vt* ~ **sb of sth** ricordare qcsa a qcno. ~**er** *n* ricordo *m*; (*memo*) promemoria *m*; (*letter*) lettera *f* di sollecito

reminisce /remɪ'nɪs/ *vi* rievocare il passato. ~**nces** *npl* reminiscenze *fpl*. ~**nt** *adj* **be** ~ **of** richiamare alla memoria

remnant /'remnənt/ *n* resto *m*; (*of material*) scampolo *m*; (*trace*) traccia *f*

remorse /rɪ'mɔːs/ *n* rimorso *m*. ~**ful** *adj* pieno di rimorso. ~**less** *adj* spietato. ~**lessly** *adv* senza pietà

remote /rɪ'məʊt/ *adj* remoto; (*slight*) minimo. ~ **access** *n* (*Comput*) accesso *m* remoto. ~ **con'trol** *n* telecomando *m*. ~**-con'trolled** *adj* telecomandato. ~**ly** *adv* lontanamente; **be not** ~**ly...** non essere lontanamente...

re'movable /rɪ-/ *adj* rimovibile

removal /rɪ'muːvl/ *n* rimozione *f*; (*from house*) trasloco *m*. ~ **van** *n* camion *m inv* da trasloco

remove /rɪ'muːv/ *vt* togliere; togliersi (clothes); eliminare (stain, doubts)

render /'rendə(r)/ *vt* rendere (service)

renegade /'renɪgeɪd/ *n* rinnegato, -a *mf*

renew /rɪ'njuː/ *vt* rinnovare (contract). ~**al** *n* rinnovo *m*

renounce /rɪ'naʊns/ *vt* rinunciare a

renovat|e /'renəveɪt/ *vt* rinnovare. ~**ion** *n* rinnovo *m*

renown /rɪ'naʊn/ *n* fama *f*. ~**ed** *adj* rinomato

rent /rent/ *n* affitto *m* • *vt* affittare; ~ [**out**] dare in affitto. ~**al** *n* affitto *m*

renunciation /rɪnʌnsɪ'eɪʃn/ *n* rinuncia *f*

re'open /riː-/ *vt/i* riaprire

re'organize /riː-/ *vt* riorganizzare

rep /rep/ *n* (*Comm*) [!] rappresentante *mf*; (*Theat*) ≈ teatro *m* stabile

repair /rɪ'peə(r)/ *n* riparazione *f*; **in good/bad** ~ in cattive/buone condizioni • *vt* riparare

repatriat|e /riː'pætrɪeɪt/ *vt* rimpatriare. ~**ion** *n* rimpatrio *m*

re'pay /riː-/ *vt* (*pt/pp* **-paid**) ripagare. ~**ment** *n* rimborso *m*

repeal /rɪ'piːl/ *n* abrogazione *f* • *vt* abrogare

repeat /rɪ'piːt/ *n* (*TV*) replica *f* • *vt/i* ripetere; ~ **oneself** ripetersi. ~**ed** *adj* ripetuto. ~**edly** *adv* ripetutamente

repel /rɪ'pel/ *vt* (*pt/pp* **repelled**) respingere; *fig* ripugnare. ~**lent** *adj* ripulsivo

repent /rɪ'pent/ *vi* pentirsi. ~**ance** *n* pentimento *m*. ~**ant** *adj* pentito

repertoire /'repətwɑː(r)/ *n* repertorio *m*

repetit|ion /repɪ'tɪʃn/ *n* ripetizione *f*. ~**ive** *adj* ripetitivo

re'place /rɪ-/ *vt* (*put back*) rimettere a posto; (*take the place of*) sostituire; ~ **sth with sth** sostituire qcsa con qcsa. ~**ment** *n* sostituzione *m*; (*person*) sostituto, -a *mf*. ~**ment part** *n* pezzo *m* di ricambio

'replay /'riː-/ *n* (*Sport*) partita *f* ripetuta; [**action**] ~ replay *m inv*

replenish /rɪ'plenɪʃ/ *vt* rifornire (stocks); (*refill*) riempire di nuovo

replica /'replɪkə/ *n* copia *f*

reply /rɪ'plaɪ/ *n* risposta *f* (**to** a) • *vt/i* (*pt/pp* **replied**) rispondere

report /rɪ'pɔːt/ *n* rapporto *m*; (*TV, Radio*) servizio *m*; (*Journ*) cronaca *f*; (*Sch*) pagella *f*; (*rumour*) diceria *f* • *vt* riportare; ~ **sb to the police** denunciare qcno alla polizia • *vi* riportare; (*present oneself*) presentarsi (**to** a). ~**edly** *adv* secondo quanto si dice. ~**er** *n* cronista *mf*, reporter *mf inv*

reprehensible /reprɪ'hensəbl/ *adj* riprovevole

represent /reprɪ'zent/ *vt* rappresentare

representative /reprɪ'zentətɪv/ *adj* rappresentativo • *n* rappresentante *mf*

repress /rɪ'pres/ *vt* reprimere. ~**ion** *n* repressione *f*. ~**ive** *adj* repressivo

reprieve /rɪ'priːv/ *n* commutazione *f* della pena capitale; (*postponement*) sospensione *f* della pena capitale; *fig* tregua *f* • *vt* sospendere la sentenza a; *fig* risparmiare

reprimand /'reprɪmɑːnd/ *n* rimprovero *m* • *vt* rimproverare

reprisal /rɪ'praɪzl/ *n* rappresaglia *f*; **in** ~ **for** per rappresaglia contro

reproach /rɪ'prəʊtʃ/ *n* ammonimento *m* • *vt* ammonire. ~**ful** *adj* riprovevole. ~**fully** *adv* con aria di rimprovero

repro'duc|e /riː-/ *vt* riprodurre • *vi* riprodursi. ~**tion** *n* riproduzione *f*.

~tive *adj* riproduttivo
reprove /rɪ'pru:v/ *vt* rimproverare
reptile /'reptaɪl/ *n* rettile *m*
republic /rɪ'pʌblɪk/ *n* repubblica *f*. **~an** *adj* repubblicano ● *n* repubblicano, -a *mf*
repugnan|ce /rɪ'pʌgnəns/ *n* ripugnanza *f*. **~t** *adj* ripugnante
repuls|ion /rɪ'pʌlʃn/ *n* repulsione *f*. **~ive** *adj* ripugnante
reputable /'repjʊtəbl/ *adj* affidabile
reputation /repjʊ'teɪʃn/ *n* reputazione *f*
request /rɪ'kwest/ *n* richiesta *f* ● *vt* richiedere. **~ stop** *n* fermata *f* a richiesta
require /rɪ'kwaɪə(r)/ *vt* (*need*) necessitare di; (*demand*) esigere. **~d** *adj* richiesto; **I am ~d to do** si esige che io faccia. **~ment** *n* esigenza *f*; (*condition*) requisito *m*
rescue /'reskju:/ *n* salvataggio *m* ● *vt* salvare. **~r** *n* salvatore, -trice *mf*
research /rɪ'sɜ:tʃ/ *n* ricerca *f* ● *vt* fare ricerche su; (*Journ*) fare un'inchiesta su ● *vi* **~ into** fare ricerche su. **~er** *n* ricercatore, -trice *mf*
resem|blance /rɪ'zembləns/ *n* rassomiglianza *f*. **~ble** *vt* rassomigliare a
resent /rɪ'zent/ *vt* risentirsi per. **~ful** *adj* pieno di risentimento. **~fully** *adv* con risentimento. **~ment** *n* risentimento *m*
reservation /rezə'veɪʃn/ *n* (*booking*) prenotazione *f*; (*doubt, enclosure*) riserva *f*
reserve /rɪ'zɜ:v/ *n* riserva *f*; (*shyness*) riserbo *m* ● *vt* riservare; riservarsi (right). **~d** *adj* riservato
reservoir /'rezəvwɑ:(r)/ *n* bacino *m* idrico
re'shuffle /ri:-/ *n* (*Pol*) rimpasto *m* ● *vt* (*Pol*) rimpastare
residence /'rezɪdəns/ *n* residenza *f*; (*stay*) soggiorno *m*. **~ permit** *n* permesso *m* di soggiorno
resident /'rezɪdənt/ *adj* residente ● *n* residente *mf*. **~ial** *adj* residenziale
residue /'rezɪdju:/ *n* residuo *m*
resign /rɪ'zaɪn/ *vt* dimettersi da; **~ oneself to** rassegnarsi a ● *vi* dare le dimissioni. **~ation** *n* rassegnazione *f*; (*from job*) dimissioni *fpl*. **~ed** *adj* rassegnato
resilient /rɪ'zɪlɪənt/ *adj* elastico; *fig* con buone capacità di ripresa
resin /'rezɪn/ *n* resina *f*
resist /rɪ'zɪst/ *vt* resistere a ● *vi* resistere. **~ance** *n* resistenza *f*. **~ant** *adj* resistente
resolut|e /'rezəlu:t/ *adj* risoluto. **~ely** *adv* con risolutezza. **~ion** *n* risolutezza *f*
resolve /rɪ'zɒlv/ *vt* **~ to do** decidere di fare
resort /rɪ'zɔ:t/ *n* (*place*) luogo *m* di villeggiatura; **as a last ~** come ultima risorsa ● *vi* **~ to** ricorrere a
resource /rɪ'sɔ:s/ *n* **~s** *pl* risorse *fpl*. **~ful** *adj* pieno di risorse; (solution) ingegnoso. **~fulness** *n* ingegnosità *f inv*
respect /rɪ'spekt/ *n* rispetto *m*; (*aspect*) aspetto *m*; **with ~ to** per quanto riguarda ● *vt* rispettare
respect|able /rɪ'spektəbl/ *adj* rispettabile. **~ably** *adv* rispettabilmente. **~ful** *adj* rispettoso
respective /rɪ'spektɪv/ *adj* rispettivo. **~ly** *adv* rispettivamente
respiration /respɪ'reɪʃn/ *n* respirazione *f*
respite /'respaɪt/ *n* respiro *m*
respond /rɪ'spɒnd/ *vi* rispondere; (*react*) reagire (**to** a); (patient:) rispondere (**to** a)
response /rɪ'spɒns/ *n* risposta *f*; (*reaction*) reazione *f*
responsibility /rɪspɒnsɪ'bɪlətɪ/ *n* responsabilità *f inv*
responsib|le /rɪ'spɒnsəbl/ *adj* responsabile; (job) impegnativo
responsive /rɪ'spɒnsɪv/ *adj* **be ~** (audience etc:) reagire; (brakes:) essere sensibile
rest¹ /rest/ *n* riposo *m*; (*Mus*) pausa *f*; **have a ~** riposarsi ● *vt* riposare; (*lean*) appoggiare (**on** su); (*place*) appoggiare ● *vi* riposarsi; (elbows:) appoggiarsi; (hopes:) riposare
rest² *n* **the ~** il resto *m*; (*people*) gli altri *mpl* ● *vi* **it ~s with you** sta a te
restaurant /'restərɒnt/ *n* ristorante *m*. **~ car** *n* vagone *m* ristorante
restful /'restfl/ *adj* riposante
restive /'restɪv/ *adj* irrequieto

r

restless /ˈrestlɪs/ *adj* nervoso

restoration /restəˈreɪʃn/ *n* (*of building*) restauro *m*

restore /rɪˈstɔː(r)/ *vt* ristabilire; restaurare (building); (*give back*) restituire

restrain /rɪˈstreɪn/ *vt* trattenere; **~ oneself** controllarsi. **~ed** *adj* controllato. **~t** *n* restrizione *f*; (*moderation*) ritegno *m*

restrict /rɪˈstrɪkt/ *vt* limitare; **~ to** limitarsi a. **~ion** *n* limite *m*; (*restraint*) restrizione *f*. **~ive** *adj* limitativo

ˈrest room *n Am* toilette *f inv*

result /rɪˈzʌlt/ *n* risultato *m*; **as a ~** a causa (**of** di) ● *vi* **~ from** risultare da; **~ in** portare a

resume /rɪˈzjuːm/ *vt/i* riprendere

résumé /ˈrezjʊmeɪ/ *n* riassunto *m*; *Am* curriculum vitae *m inv*

resurrect /rezəˈrekt/ *vt fig* risuscitare. **~ion** *n* **the R~ion** (*Relig*) la Risurrezione

resuscitat|e /rɪˈsʌsɪteɪt/ *vt* rianimare. **~ion** *n* rianimazione *f*

retail /ˈriːteɪl/ *n* vendita *f* al minuto *o* al dettaglio ● *adj & adv* al minuto ● *vt* vendere al minuto ● *vi* **~ at** essere venduto al pubblico al prezzo di. **~er** *n* dettagliante *mf*

retain /rɪˈteɪn/ *vt* conservare; (*hold back*) trattenere

retaliat|e /rɪˈtælɪeɪt/ *vi* vendicarsi. **~ion** *n* rappresaglia *f*; **in ~ion for** per rappresaglia contro

retarded /rɪˈtɑːdɪd/ *adj* ritardato

rethink /riːˈθɪŋk/ *vt* (*pt/pp* **rethought**) ripensare

reticen|ce /ˈretɪsəns/ *n* reticenza *f*. **~t** *adj* reticente

retina /ˈretɪnə/ *n* retina *f*

retinue /ˈretɪnjuː/ *n* seguito *m*

retire /rɪˈtaɪə(r)/ *vi* andare in pensione; (*withdraw*) ritirarsi ● *vt* mandare in pensione (employee). **~d** *adj* in pensione. **~ment** *n* pensione *f*; **since my ~ment** da quando sono andato in pensione

retiring /rɪˈtaɪərɪŋ/ *adj* riservato

retort /rɪˈtɔːt/ *n* replica *f* ● *vt* ribattere

reˈtrace /rɪ-/ *vt* ripercorrere; **~ one's steps** ritornare sui propri passi

retract /rɪˈtrækt/ *vt* ritirare; ritrattare (statement, evidence) ● *vi* ritrarsi

reˈtrain /riː-/ *vt* riqualificare ● *vi* riqualificarsi

retreat /rɪˈtriːt/ *n* ritirata *f*; (*place*) ritiro *m* ● *vi* ritirarsi; (*Mil*) battere in ritirata

reˈtrial /riː-/ *n* nuovo processo *m*

retrieval /rɪˈtriːvəl/ *n* recupero *m*

retrieve /rɪˈtriːv/ *vt* recuperare

retrograde /ˈretrəgreɪd/ *adj* retrogrado

retrospect /ˈretrəspekt/ *n* **in ~** guardando indietro. **~ive** *adj* retrospettivo; (legislation) retroattivo ● *n* retrospettiva *f*

return /rɪˈtɜːn/ *n* ritorno *m*; (*giving back*) restituzione *f*; (*Comm*) profitto *m*; (*ticket*) biglietto *m* di andata e ritorno; **by ~ [of post]** a stretto giro di posta; **in ~** in cambio (**for** di); **many happy ~s!** cento di questi giorni! ● *vi* ritornare ● *vt* (*give back*) restituire; ricambiare (affection, invitation); (*put back*) rimettere; (*send back*) mandare indietro; (*elect*) eleggere

return: ~ match *n* rivincita *f*. **~ ticket** *n* biglietto *m* di andata e ritorno

reunion /riːˈjuːnjən/ *n* riunione *f*

reunite /riːjʊˈnaɪt/ *vt* riunire

rev /rev/ *n* (*Auto*), [!] giro *m* (*di motore*) ● *v* (*pt/pp* **revved**) ● *vt* **~ [up]** far andare su di giri ● *vi* andare su di giri

reveal /rɪˈviːl/ *vt* rivelare; (dress:) scoprire. **~ing** *adj* rivelatore; (dress) osé

revel /ˈrevl/ *vi* (*pt/pp* **revelled**) **~ in sth** godere di qcsa

revelation /revəˈleɪʃn/ *n* rivelazione *f*

revelry /ˈrevlrɪ/ *n* baldoria *f*

revenge /rɪˈvendʒ/ *n* vendetta *f*; (*Sport*) rivincita *f*; **take ~** vendicarsi ● *vt* vendicare

revenue /ˈrevənjuː/ *n* reddito *m*

revere /rɪˈvɪə(r)/ *vt* riverire. **~nce** *n* riverenza *f*

Reverend /ˈrevərənd/ *adj* reverendo

reverent /ˈrevərənt/ *adj* riverente

reverse /rɪˈvɜːs/ *adj* opposto; **in ~ order** in ordine inverso ● *n* contrario *m*; (*back*) rovescio *m*; (*Auto*) marcia *m* indietro ● *vt* invertire; **~ the car into the garage** entrare in garage a marcia indietro; **~ the charges** (*Teleph*) fare una telefonata a carico ● *vi* (*Auto*) fare marcia indietro

revert /rɪ'vɜːt/ *vi* ~ **to** tornare a

review /rɪ'vjuː/ *n* (*survey*) rassegna *f*; (*re-examination*) riconsiderazione *f*; (*Mil*) rivista *f*; (*of book, play*) recensione *f* • *vt* riesaminare (situation); (*Mil*) passare in rivista; recensire (book, play). **~er** *n* critico, -a *mf*

revis|e /rɪ'vaɪz/ *vt* rivedere; (*for exam*) ripassare. **~ion** *n* revisione *f*; (*for exam*) ripasso *m*

revive /rɪ'vaɪv/ *vt* resuscitare; rianimare (person) • *vi* riprendersi; (person:) rianimarsi

revolt /rɪ'vəʊlt/ *n* rivolta *f* • *vi* ribellarsi • *vt* rivoltare. **~ing** *adj* rivoltante

revolution /revə'luːʃn/ *n* rivoluzione *f*; (*Auto*) **~s per minute** giri *mpl* al minuto. **~ary** *adj & n* rivoluzionario, -a *mf*. **~ize** *vt* rivoluzionare

revolve /rɪ'vɒlv/ *vi* ruotare; **~ around** girare intorno

revolv|er /rɪ'vɒlvə(r)/ *n* rivoltella *f*, revolver *m inv*. **~ing** *adj* ruotante

revue /rɪ'vjuː/ *n* rivista *f*

revulsion /rɪ'vʌlʃn/ *n* ripulsione *f*

reward /rɪ'wɔːd/ *n* ricompensa *f* • *vt* ricompensare. **~ing** *adj* gratificante

re'write /riː-/ *vt* (*pt* **rewrote**, *pp* **rewritten**) riscrivere

rhetoric /'retərɪk/ *n* retorica *f*. **~al** *adj* retorico

rhinoceros /raɪ'nɒsərəs/ *n* rinoceronte *m*

rhubarb /'ruːbɑːb/ *n* rabarbaro *m*

rhyme /raɪm/ *n* rima *f*; (*poem*) filastrocca *f* • *vi* rimare

rhythm /'rɪðm/ *n* ritmo *m*. **~ic[al]** *adj* ritmico. **~ically** *adv* con ritmo

rib /rɪb/ *n* costola *f*

ribbon /'rɪbən/ *n* nastro *m*; **in ~s** a brandelli

rice /raɪs/ *n* riso *m*

rich /rɪtʃ/ *adj* ricco; (food) pesante • *n* **the ~** *pl* i ricchi *mpl*; **~es** *pl* ricchezze *fpl*. **~ly** *adv* riccamente; (deserve) largamente

ricochet /'rɪkəʃeɪ/ *vi* rimbalzare • *n* rimbalzo *m*

rid /rɪd/ *vt* (*pt/pp* **rid**, *pres p* **ridding**) sbarazzare (**of** di); **get ~ of** sbarazzarsi di

riddance /'rɪdns/ *n* **good ~!** che liberazione!

ridden /'rɪdn/ ▹**RIDE**

riddle /'rɪdl/ *n* enigma *m*

ride /raɪd/ *n* (*on horse*) cavalcata *f*; (*in vehicle*) giro *m*; (*journey*) viaggio *m*; **take sb for a ~** [!] prendere qcno in giro • *v* (*pt* **rode**, *pp* **ridden**) • *vt* montare (horse); andare su (bicycle) • *vi* andare a cavallo; (jockey, showjumper:) cavalcare; (cyclist:) andare in bicicletta; (*in vehicle*) viaggiare. **~r** *n* cavallerizzo, -a *mf*; (*in race*) fantino *m*; (*on bicycle*) ciclista *mf*; (*in document*) postilla *f*

ridge /rɪdʒ/ *n* spigolo *m*; (*on roof*) punta *f*; (*of mountain*) cresta *f*

ridicule /'rɪdɪkjuːl/ *n* ridicolo *m* • *vt* mettere in ridicolo

ridiculous /rɪ'dɪkjʊləs/ *adj* ridicolo

rife /raɪf/ *adj* **be ~** essere diffuso; **~ with** pieno di

rifle /'raɪfl/ *n* fucile *m*; **~-range** tiro *m* al bersaglio • *vt* **~ [through]** mettere a soqquadro

rift /rɪft/ *n* fessura *f*; *fig* frattura *f*

rig[1] /rɪg/ *n* equipaggiamento *m*; (*at sea*) piattaforma *f* per trivellazioni subacquee • **rig out** *vt* (*pt/pp* **rigged**) equipaggiare. ▫ **~ up** *vt* allestire

rig[2] *vt* (*pt/pp* **rigged**) manovrare (election)

right /raɪt/ *adj* giusto; (*not left*) destro; **be ~** (person:) aver ragione; (clock:) essere giusto; **put ~** mettere all'ora (clock); correggere (person); rimediare a (situation); **that's ~!** proprio così! • *adv* (*correctly*) bene; (*not left*) a destra; (*directly*) proprio; (*completely*) completamente; **~ away** immediatamente • *n* giusto *m*; (*not left*) destra *f*; (*what is due*) diritto *m*; **on/to the ~** a destra; **be in the ~** essere nel giusto; **know ~ from wrong** distinguere il bene dal male; **by ~s** secondo giustizia; **the R~** (*Pol*) la destra *f* • *vt* raddrizzare; **~ a wrong** *fig* riparare a un torto. **~ angle** *n* angolo *m* retto

rightful /'raɪtfl/ *adj* legittimo

right: ~-'handed *adj* che usa la mano destra. **~-hand 'man** *n fig* braccio *m* destro

rightly /'raɪtlɪ/ *adv* giustamente

right: ~ of way *n* diritto *m* di transito; (*path*) passaggio *m*; (*Auto*) precedenza *f*. **~-'wing** *adj* (*Pol*) di destra • *n* (*Sport*) ala *f* destra

rigid /ˈrɪdʒɪd/ *adj* rigido. **~ity** *n* rigidità *f inv*

rigorous /ˈrɪɡərəs/ *adj* rigoroso

rim /rɪm/ *n* bordo *m*; (*of wheel*) cerchione *m*

rind /raɪnd/ *n* (*on fruit*) scorza *f*; (*on cheese*) crosta *f*; (*on bacon*) cotenna *f*

ring[1] /rɪŋ/ *n* (*circle*) cerchio *m*; (*on finger*) anello *m*; (*boxing*) ring *m inv*; (*for circus*) pista *f*; **stand in a ~** essere in cerchio

ring[2] *n* suono *m*; **give sb a ~** (*Teleph*) dare un colpo di telefono a qcno ● *v* (*pt* **rang**, *pp* **rung**) ● *vt* suonare; **~ [up]** (*Teleph*) telefonare a ● *vi* suonare; (*Teleph*) **~ [up]** telefonare. □ **~ back** *vt/i* (*Teleph*) richiamare. □ **~ off** *vi* (*Teleph*) riattaccare

ring: ~leader *n* capobanda *m*. **~ road** *n* circonvallazione *f*

rink /rɪŋk/ *n* pista *f* di pattinaggio

rinse /rɪns/ *n* risciacquo *m*; (*hair colour*) cachet *m inv* ● *vt* sciacquare

riot /ˈraɪət/ *n* rissa *f*; (*of colour*) accozzaglia *f*; **~s** *pl* disordini *mpl*; **run ~** impazzare ● *vi* creare disordini. **~er** *n* dimostrante *mf*. **~ous** *adj* sfrenato

rip /rɪp/ *n* strappo *m* ● *vt* (*pt/pp* **ripped**) strappare; **~ open** aprire con uno strappo. □ **~ off** *vt* [!] fregare

ripe /raɪp/ *adj* maturo; (cheese) stagionato

ripen /ˈraɪpn/ *vi* maturare; (cheese:) stagionarsi ● *vt* far maturare; stagionare (cheese)

ˈrip-off *n* [!] frode *f*

ripple /ˈrɪpl/ *n* increspatura *f*; (*sound*) mormorio *m* ●

rise /raɪz/ *n* (*of sun*) levata *f*; (*fig: to fame, power*) ascesa *f*; (*increase*) aumento *m*; **give ~ to** dare adito a ● *vi* (*pt* **rose**, *pp* **risen**) alzarsi; (sun:) sorgere; (dough:) lievitare; (prices, water level:) aumentare; (*to power, position*) arrivare (**to** a). **~r** *n* **early ~r** persona *f* mattiniera

rising /ˈraɪzɪŋ/ *adj* (sun) levante; **~ generation** nuova generazione *f* ● *n* (*revolt*) sollevazione *f*

risk /rɪsk/ *n* rischio *m*; **at one's own ~** a proprio rischio e pericolo ● *vt* rischiare

risky /ˈrɪskɪ/ *adj* (**-ier, -iest**) rischioso

rite /raɪt/ *n* rito *m*; **last ~s** estrema unzione *f*

ritual /ˈrɪtjʊəl/ *adj* rituale ● *n* rituale *m*

rival /ˈraɪvl/ *adj* rivale ● *n* rivale *mf*; **~s** *pl* (*Comm*) concorrenti *mpl* ● *vt* (*pt/pp* **rivalled**) rivaleggiare con. **~ry** *n* rivalità *f inv*; (*Comm*) concorrenza *f*

river /ˈrɪvə(r)/ *n* fiume *m*. **~-bed** *n* letto *m* del fiume

rivet /ˈrɪvɪt/ *n* rivetto *m* ● *vt* rivettare; **~ed by** *fig* inchiodato da

road /rəʊd/ *n* strada *f*, via *f*; **be on the ~** viaggiare

road: ~-map *n* carta *f* stradale. **~side** *n* bordo *m* della strada. **~-works** *npl* lavori *mpl* stradali. **~worthy** *adj* sicuro

roam /rəʊm/ *vi* girovagare

roar /rɔː(r)/ *n* ruggito *m*; **~s of laughter** scroscio *msg* di risa ● *vi* ruggire; (lorry, thunder:) rombare; **~ with laughter** ridere fragorosamente. **~ing** *adj* **do a ~ing trade** [!] fare affari d'oro

roast /rəʊst/ *adj* arrosto; **~ pork** arrosto *m* di maiale ● *n* arrosto *m* ● *vt* arrostire (meat) ● *vi* arrostirsi

rob /rɒb/ *vt* (*pt/pp* **robbed**) derubare (**of** di); svaligiare (bank). **~ber** *n* rapinatore *m*. **~bery** *n* rapina *f*

robe /rəʊb/ *n* tunica *f*; (*Am: bathrobe*) accappatoio *m*

robin /ˈrɒbɪn/ *n* pettirosso *m*

robot /ˈrəʊbɒt/ *n* robot *m inv*

robust /rəʊˈbʌst/ *adj* robusto

rock[1] /rɒk/ *n* roccia *f*; (*in sea*) scoglio *m*; (*sweet*) zucchero *m* candito. **on the ~s** (ship) incagliato; (marriage) finito; (drink) con ghiaccio

rock[2] *vt* cullare (baby); (*shake*) far traballare; (*shock*) scuotere ● *vi* dondolarsi

rock[3] *n* (*Mus*) rock *m inv*

rock-ˈbottom *adj* bassissimo ● *n* livello *m* più basso

rocket /ˈrɒkɪt/ *n* razzo *m* ● *vi* salire alle stelle

rocky /ˈrɒkɪ/ *adj* (**-ier, -iest**) roccioso; *fig* traballante

rod /rɒd/ *n* bacchetta *f*; (*for fishing*) canna *f*

rode /rəʊd/ ▷RIDE

rodent /ˈrəʊdnt/ *n* roditore *m*

rogue /rəʊɡ/ *n* farabutto *m*

role /rəʊl/ *n* ruolo *m*

roll /rəʊl/ *n* rotolo *m*; (*bread*) panino *m*; (*list*) lista *f*; (*of ship, drum*) rullio *m* ● *vi* rotolare; **be ~ing in money** [!] nuotare nell'oro ● *vt* spianare (lawn, pastry). □ **~ over** *vi* rigirarsi. □ **~ up** *vt* arrotolare; rimboccarsi (sleeves) ● *vi* [!] arrivare

'roll-call *n* appello *m*

roller /'rəʊlə(r)/ *n* rullo *m*; (*for hair*) bigodino *m*. **~ blades** *npl* pattini *npl* in linea. **~ blind** *n* tapparella *f*. **~-coaster** *n* montagne *fpl* russe. **~-skate** *n* pattino *m* a rotelle

'rolling-pin *n* mattarello *m*

Roman /'rəʊmən/ *adj* romano ● *n* romano, -a *mf*. **~ Catholic** *adj* cattolico ● *n* cattolico, -a *mf*

romance /rəʊ'mæns/ *n* (*love affair*) storia *f* d'amore; (*book*) romanzo *m* rosa

Romania /rəʊ'meɪnɪə/ *n* Romania *f*. **~n** *adj* rumeno ● *n* rumeno, -a *mf*

romantic /rəʊ'mæntɪk/ *adj* romantico. **~ally** *adv* romanticamente. **~ism** *n* romanticismo *m*

Rome /rəʊm/ *n* Roma *f*

romp /rɒmp/ *n* gioco *m* rumoroso ● *vi* giocare rumorosamente. **~ers** *npl* pagliaccetto *msg*

roof /ru:f/ *n* tetto *m*; (*of mouth*) palato *m* ● *vt* mettere un tetto su. **~-rack** *n* portabagagli *m inv*. **~-top** *n* tetto *m*

rook /rʊk/ *n* corvo *m*; (*in chess*) torre *f*

room /ru:m/ *n* stanza *f*; (*bedroom*) camera *f*; (*for functions*) sala *f*; (*space*) spazio *m*. **~y** *adj* spazioso; (clothes) ampio

r

roost /ru:st/ *vi* appollaiarsi

root[1] /ru:t/ *n* radice *f*; **take ~** metter radici ● **root out** *vt fig* scovare

root[2] *vi* **~ about** grufolare; **~ for sb** *Am* [!] fare il tifo per qcno

rope /rəʊp/ *n* corda *f*; **know the ~s** [!] conoscere i trucchi del mestiere ● **rope in** *vt* [!] coinvolgere

rose[1] /rəʊz/ *n* rosa *f*; (*of watering-can*) bocchetta *f*

rose[2] ▷RISE

rosé /'rəʊzeɪ/ *n* [vino *m*] rosé *m inv*

rot /rɒt/ *n* marciume *m*; ([!]: *nonsense*) sciocchezze *fpl* ● *vi* (*pt/pp* **rotted**) marcire

rota /'rəʊtə/ *n* tabella *f* dei turni

rotary /'rəʊtərɪ/ *adj* rotante

rotat|e /rəʊ'teɪt/ *vt* far ruotare; avvicendare (crops) ● *vi* ruotare. **~ion** *n* rotazione *f*; **in ~ion** a turno

rote /rəʊt/ *n* **by ~** meccanicamente

rotten /'rɒtn/ *adj* marcio; [!] schifoso; (person) penoso

rough /rʌf/ *adj* (*not smooth*) ruvido; (*ground*) accidentato; (*behaviour*) rozzo; (sport) violento; (area) malfamato; (crossing, time) brutto; (estimate) approssimativo ● *adv* (play) grossolanamente; **sleep ~** dormire sotto i ponti ● *vt* **~ it** vivere senza confort. □ **~ out** *vt* abbozzare

roughage /'rʌfɪdʒ/ *n* fibre *fpl*

rough|ly /'rʌflɪ/ *adv* rozzamente; (*more or less*) pressappoco. **~ness** *n* ruvidità *f*; (*of behaviour*) rozzezza *f*

roulette /ru:'let/ *n* roulette *f inv*

round /raʊnd/ *adj* rotondo ● *n* tondo *m*; (*slice*) fetta *f*; (*of visits, drinks*) giro *m*; (*of competition*) partita *f*; (*boxing*) ripresa *f*, round *m inv*; **do one's ~s** (doctor:) fare il giro delle visite ● *prep* intorno a; **open ~ the clock** aperto ventiquattr'ore ● *adv* **all ~** tutt'intorno; **ask sb ~** invitare qcno; **go/come ~ to** (a friend etc) andare da; **turn/look ~** girarsi; **~ about** (*approximately*) intorno a ● *vt* arrotondare; girare (corner). □ **~ down** *vt* arrotondare (*per difetto*). □ **~ off** *vt* (*end*) terminare. □ **~ on** *vt* aggredire. □ **~ up** *vt* radunare; arrotondare (prices)

roundabout /'raʊndəbaʊt/ *adj* indiretto ● *n* giostra *f*; (*for traffic*) rotonda *f*

round: ~ 'trip *n* viaggio *m* di andata e ritorno

rous|e /raʊz/ *vt* svegliare; risvegliare (suspicion, interest). **~ing** *adj* di incoraggiamento

route /ru:t/ *n* itinerario *m*; (*Aeron, Naut*) rotta *f*; (*of bus*) percorso *m*

routine /ru:'ti:n/ *adj* di routine ● *n* routine *f inv*; (*Theat*) numero *m*

row[1] /rəʊ/ *n* (*line*) fila *f*; **three years in a ~** tre anni di fila

row[2] *vi* (*in boat*) remare

row[3] /raʊ/ *n* [!] (*quarrel*) litigata *f*; (*noise*) baccano *m* ● *vi* [!] litigare

rowdy /'raʊdɪ/ *adj* (**-ier, -iest**) chiassoso

rowing boat /'rəʊɪŋ-/ *n* barca *f* a remi

royal /rɔɪəl/ *adj* reale

royalt|y /'rɔɪəltɪ/ *n* appartenenza *f* alla famiglia reale; (*persons*) i membri *mpl* della famiglia reale. **~ies** *npl* (*payments*) diritti *mpl* d'autore

rub /rʌb/ *n* **give sth a ~** dare una sfregata a qcsa ● *vt* (*pt/pp* **rubbed**) sfregare. □ **~ in** *vt* **don't ~ it in** [!] non rigirare il coltello nella piaga. □ **~ off** *vt* mandar via sfregando (stain); (*from blackboard*) cancellare ● *vi* andar via; **~ off on** essere trasmesso a. □ **~ out** *vt* cancellare

rubber /'rʌbə(r)/ *n* gomma *f*; (*eraser*) gomma *f* [da cancellare]. **~ band** *n* elastico *m*. **~y** *adj* gommoso

rubbish /'rʌbɪʃ/ *n* immondizie *fpl*; ([!]: *nonsense*) idiozie *fpl*; ([!]: *junk*) robaccia *f* ● *vt* [!] fare a pezzi. **~ bin** *n* pattumiera *f*. **~ dump** *n* discarica *f*; (*official*) discarica *f* comunale

rubble /'rʌbl/ *n* macerie *fpl*

ruby /'ru:bɪ/ *n* rubino *m* ● *attrib* di rubini; (lips) scarlatta

rucksack /'rʌksæk/ *n* zaino *m*

rudder /'rʌdə(r)/ *n* timone *m*

rude /ru:d/ *adj* scortese; (*improper*) spinto. **~ly** *adv* scortesemente. **~ness** *n* scortesia *f*

ruffian /'rʌfɪən/ *n* farabutto *m*

ruffle /'rʌfl/ *n* gala *f* ● *vt* scompigliare (hair)

rug /rʌg/ *n* tappeto *m*; (*blanket*) coperta *f*

rugby /'rʌgbɪ/ *n* **~ [football]** rugby *m*

rugged /'rʌgɪd/ *adj* (coastline) roccioso

ruin /'ru:ɪn/ *n* rovina *f*; **in ~s** in rovina ● *vt* rovinare. **~ous** *adj* estremamente costoso

rule /ru:l/ *n* regola *f*; (*control*) ordinamento *m*; (*for measuring*) metro *m*; **~s** regolamento *msg*; **as a ~** generalmente ● *vt* governare; dominare (colony, behaviour); **~ that** stabilire che ● *vi* governare. □ **~ out** *vt* escludere

ruler /'ru:lə(r)/ *n* capo *m* di Stato; (*sovereign*) sovrano, -a *mf*; (*measure*) righello *m*, regolo *m*

ruling /'ru:lɪŋ/ *adj* (class) dirigente; (party) di governo ● *n* decisione *f*

rum /rʌm/ *n* rum *m inv*

rumble /'rʌmbl/ *n* rombo *m*; (*of stomach*) brontolio *m* ● *vi* rombare; (stomach:) brontolare

rummage /'rʌmɪdʒ/ *vi* rovistare (**in**/**through** in)

rumour /'ru:mə(r)/ *n* diceria *f* ● *vt* **it is ~ed that** si dice che

run /rʌn/ *n* (*on foot*) corsa *f*; (*distance to be covered*) tragitto *m*; (*outing*) giro *m*; (*Theat*) rappresentazioni *fpl*; (*in skiing*) pista *f*; (*Am: ladder*) smagliatura *f* (*in calze*); **at a ~** di corsa; **~ of bad luck** periodo *m* sfortunato; **on the ~** in fuga; **have the ~ of** avere a disposizione; **in the long ~** a lungo termine ● *v* (*pt* **ran**, *pp* **run**, *pres p* **running**) ● *vi* correre; (river:) scorrere; (nose, make-up:) colare; (bus:) fare servizio; (play:) essere in cartellone; (colours:) sbiadire; (*in election*) presentarsi [come candidato] ● *vt* (*manage*) dirigere; tenere (house); (*drive*) dare un passaggio a; correre (risk); (*Comput*) lanciare; (*Journ*) pubblicare (article); (*pass*) far scorrere (eyes, hand); **~ a bath** far scorrere l'acqua per il bagno. □ **~ across** *vt* (*meet, find*) imbattersi in. □ **~ away** *vi* scappare [via]. □ **~ down** *vi* scaricarsi; (clock:) scaricarsi; (stocks:) esaurirsi ● *vt* (*Auto*) investire; (*reduce*) esaurire; ([!]: *criticize*) denigrare. □ **~ in** *vi* entrare di corsa. □ **~ into** *vi* (*meet*) imbattersi in; (*knock against*) urtare. □ **~ off** *vi* andare via di corsa ● *vt* stampare (copies). □ **~ out** *vi* uscire di corsa; (supplies, money:) esaurirsi; **~ out of** rimanere senza. □ **~ over** *vi* correre; (*overflow*) traboccare ● *vt* (*Auto*) investire. □ **~ through** *vi* scorrere. □ **~ up** *vi* salire di corsa; (*towards*) arrivare di corsa ● *vt* accumulare (debts, bill); (*sew*) cucire

'runaway *n* fuggitivo, -a *mf*

run-'down *adj* (area) in abbandono; (person) esaurito ● *n* analisi *f*

rung[1] /rʌŋ/ *n* (*of ladder*) piolo *m*

rung[2] ▷RING[2]

runner /'rʌnə(r)/ *n* podista *mf*; (*in race*) corridore, -trice *mf*; (*on sledge*) pattino *m*. **~ bean** *n* fagiolino *m*. **~-up** *n* secondo, -a *mf* classificato, -a

running /'rʌnɪŋ/ *adj* in corsa; (water) corrente; **four times ~** quattro volte di seguito ● *n* corsa *f*; (*management*) di-

r

rezione *f*; **be in the ~** essere in lizza. **~ 'commentary** *n* cronaca *f*

runny /'rʌnɪ/ *adj* semiliquido; **~ nose** naso che cola

runway *n* pista *f*

rupture /'rʌptʃə(r)/ *n* rottura *f*; (*Med*) ernia *f* ● *vt* rompere; **~ oneself** farsi venire l'ernia ● *vi* rompersi

rural /'rʊərəl/ *adj* rurale

ruse /ru:z/ *n* astuzia *f*

rush¹ /rʌʃ/ *n* (*Bot*) giunco *m*

rush² *n* fretta *f*; **in a ~** di fretta ● *vi* precipitarsi ● *vt* far premura a; **~ sb to hospital** trasportare qcno di corsa all'ospedale. **~-hour** *n* ora *f* di punta

Russia /'rʌʃə/ *n* Russia *f*. **~n** *adj & n* russo, -a *mf*; (*language*) russo *m*

rust /rʌst/ *n* ruggine *f* ● *vi* arrugginirsi

rustle /'rʌsl/ *vi* frusciare ● *vt* far frusciare; *Am* rubare (cattle). □ **~ up** *vt* [!] rimediare

'rustproof *adj* a prova di ruggine

rusty /'rʌstɪ/ *adj* (**-ier, -iest**) arrugginito

rut /rʌt/ *n* solco *m*; **in a ~** [!] nella routine

ruthless /'ru:θlɪs/ *adj* spietato. **~ness** *n* spietatezza *f*

rye /raɪ/ *n* segale *f*

Ss

sabot|age /'sæbətɑ:ʒ/ *n* sabotaggio *m* ● *vt* sabotare. **~eur** *n* sabotatore, -trice *mf*

saccharin /'sæʃeɪ/ *n* saccarina *f*

sachet /'sæʃeɪ/ *n* bustina *f*; (*scented*) sacchetto *m* profumato

sack¹ /sæk/ *vt* (*plunder*) saccheggiare

sack² *n* sacco *m*; **get the ~** [!] essere licenziato ● *vt* [!] licenziare. **~ing** *n* tela *f* per sacchi; ([!]: *dismissal*) licenziamento *m*

sacrament /'sækrəmənt/ *n* sacramento *m*

sacred /'seɪkrɪd/ *adj* sacro

sacrifice /'sækrɪfaɪs/ *n* sacrificio *m* ● *vt* sacrificare

sacrilege /'sækrɪlɪdʒ/ *n* sacrilegio *m*

sad /sæd/ *adj* (**sadder, saddest**) triste. **~den** *vt* rattristare

saddle /'sædl/ *n* sella *f* ● *vt* sellare; **I've been ~d with...** *fig* mi hanno affibbiato...

sad|ly /'sædlɪ/ *adv* tristemente; (*unfortunately*) sfortunatamente. **~ness** *n* tristezza *f*

safe /seɪf/ *adj* sicuro; (*out of danger*) salvo; (object) al sicuro; **~ and sound** sano e salvo ● *n* cassaforte *f*. **~guard** *n* protezione *f* ● *vt* proteggere. **~ly** *adv* in modo sicuro; (arrive) senza incidenti; (assume) con certezza

safety /'seɪftɪ/ *n* sicurezza *f*. **~-belt** *n* cintura *f* di sicurezza. **~-deposit box** *n* cassetta *f* di sicurezza. **~-pin** *n* spilla *f* di sicurezza *o* da balia. **~-valve** *n* valvola *f* di sicurezza

sag /sæg/ *vi* (*pt/pp* **sagged**) abbassarsi

saga /'sɑ:gə/ *n* saga *f*

sage /seɪdʒ/ *n* (*herb*) salvia *f*

Sagittarius /sædʒɪ'teərɪəs/ *n* Sagittario *m*

said /sed/ ▷**SAY**

sail /seɪl/ *n* vela *f*; (*trip*) giro *m* in barca a vela ● *vi* navigare; (*Sport*) praticare la vela; (*leave*) salpare ● *vt* pilotare

sailing /'seɪlɪŋ/ *n* vela *f*. **~-boat** *n* barca *f* a vela. **~-ship** *n* veliero *m*

sailor /'seɪlə(r)/ *n* marinaio *m*

saint /seɪnt/ *n* santo, -a *mf*. **~ly** *adj* da santo

sake /seɪk/ *n* **for the ~ of** (person) per il bene di; (peace) per amor di; **for the ~ of it** per il gusto di farlo

salad /'sæləd/ *n* insalata *f*. **~ bowl** *n* insalatiera *f*. **~ cream** *n salsa f per condire l'insalata*. **~-dressing** *n* condimento *m* per insalata

salary /'sælərɪ/ *n* stipendio *m*

sale /seɪl/ *n* vendita *f* (*at reduced prices*) svendita *f*; **for/on ~** in vendita

sales|man /'seɪlzmən/ *n* venditore *m*; (*traveller*) rappresentante *m*. **~woman** *n* venditrice *f*

saliva /sə'laɪvə/ *n* saliva *f*

salmon /'sæmən/ *n* salmone *m*

saloon /sə'lu:n/ *n* (*Auto*) berlina *f*; (*Am: bar*) bar *m*

salt /sɔ:lt/ *n* sale *m* ● *adj* salato; (fish, meat) sotto sale ● *vt* salare; (*cure*) mettere sotto sale. **~-cellar** *n* saliera *f*. **~ 'water** *n* acqua *f* di mare. **~y** *adj* salato

salute /sə'lu:t/ (*Mil*) *n* saluto *m* • *vt* salutare • *vi* fare il saluto

salvage /'sælvɪdʒ/ *n* (*Naut*) recupero *m* • *vt* recuperare

salvation /sæl'veɪʃn/ *n* salvezza *f*. **S~ 'Army** *n* Esercito *m* della Salvezza

same /seɪm/ *adj* stesso (**as** di) • *pron* **the ~** lo stesso; **be all the ~** essere tutti uguali • *adv* **the ~** nello stesso modo; **all the ~** (*however*) lo stesso; **the ~ to you** altrettanto

sample /'sɑ:mpl/ *n* campione *m* • *vt* testare

sanction /'sæŋkʃn/ *n* (*approval*) autorizzazione *f*; (*penalty*) sanzione *f* • *vt* autorizzare

sanctuary /'sæŋktjʊərɪ/ *n* (*Relig*) santuario *m*; (*refuge*) asilo *m*; (*for wildlife*) riserva *f*

sand /sænd/ *n* sabbia *f* • *vt* **~ [down]** carteggiare

sandal /'sændl/ *n* sandalo *m*

sandpaper *n* carta *f* vetrata • *vt* cartavetrare

sandwich /'sænwɪdʒ/ *n* tramezzino *m* • *vt* **~ed between** schiacciato tra

sandy /'sændɪ/ *adj* (**-ier, -iest**) (beach, soil) sabbioso; (hair) biondiccio

sane /seɪn/ *adj* (*not mad*) sano di mente; (*sensible*) sensato

sang /sæŋ/ ▷**SING**

sanitary /'sænɪtərɪ/ *adj* igienico; (system) sanitario. **~ napkin** *n Am*, **~ towel** *n* assorbente *m* igienico

sanitation /sænɪ'teɪʃn/ *n* impianti *mpl* igienici

sanity /'sænətɪ/ *n* sanità *f inv* di mente; (*common sense*) buon senso *m*

sank /sæŋk/ ▷**SINK**

sapphire /'sæfaɪə(r)/ *n* zaffiro *m* • *adj* blu zaffiro

sarcas|m /'sɑ:kæzm/ *n* sarcasmo *m*. **~tic** *adj* sarcastico

sardine /sɑ:'di:n/ *n* sardina *f*

sash /sæʃ/ *n* fascia *f*; (*for dress*) fusciacca *f*

sat /sæt/ ▷**SIT**

satchel /'sætʃl/ *n* cartella *f*

satellite /'sætəlaɪt/ *n* satellite *m*. **~ dish** *n* antenna *f* parabolica. **~ television** *n* televisione *f* via satellite

satin /'sætɪn/ *n* raso *m* • *attrib* di raso

satire /'sætaɪə(r)/ *n* satira *f*

satirical /sə'tɪrɪkl/ *adj* satirico

satisfaction /sætɪs'fækʃn/ *n* soddisfazione *f*; **be to sb's ~** soddisfare qcno

satisfactor|y /sætɪs'fæktərɪ/ *adj* soddisfacente. **~ily** *adv* in modo soddisfacente

satisf|y /'sætɪsfaɪ/ *vt* (*pt/pp* **-fied**) soddisfare; (*convince*) convincere; **be ~ied** essere soddisfatto. **~ying** *adj* soddisfacente

satphone /'sætfəʊn/ *n* telefono *m* satellitare

saturat|e /'sætʃəreɪt/ *vt* inzuppare (**with** di); (*Chem*), *fig* saturare (**with** di). **~ed** *adj* saturo

Saturday /'sætədeɪ/ *n* sabato *m*

sauce /sɔ:s/ *n* salsa *f*; (*cheek*) impertinenza *f*. **~pan** *n* pentola *f*

saucer /'sɔ:sə(r)/ *n* piattino *m*

saucy /'sɔ:sɪ/ *adj* (**-ier, -iest**) impertinente

Saudi Arabia /saʊdɪə'reɪbɪə/ *n* Arabia *f* Saudita

sauna /'sɔ:nə/ *n* sauna *f*

saunter /'sɔ:ntə(r)/ *vi* andare a spasso

sausage /'sɒsɪdʒ/ *n* salsiccia *f*; (*dried*) salame *m*

savage /'sævɪdʒ/ *adj* feroce; (tribe, custom) selvaggio • *n* selvaggio, -a *mf* • *vt* fare a pezzi. **~ry** *n* ferocia *f*

save /seɪv/ *n* (*Sport*) parata *f* • *vt* salvare (**from** da); (*keep, collect*) tenere; risparmiare (time, money); (*avoid*) evitare; (*Sport*) parare (goal); (*Comput*) salvare, memorizzare • *vi* **~ [up]** risparmiare • *prep* salvo

saver /'seɪvə(r)/ *n* risparmiatore, -trice *mf*

savings /'seɪvɪŋz/ *npl* (*money*) risparmi *mpl*. **~ account** *n* libretto *m* di risparmio. **~ bank** *n* cassa *f* di risparmio

saviour /'seɪvjə(r)/ *n* salvatore *m*

savour /'seɪvə(r)/ *n* sapore *m* • *vt* assaporare. **~y** *adj* salato; *fig* rispettabile

saw[1] /sɔ:/ *see* **see**1

saw[2] *n* sega *f* • *vt/i* (*pt* **sawed**, *pp* **sawn** *or* **sawed**) segare. **~dust** *n* segatura *f*

saxophone /'sæksəfəʊn/ *n* sassofono *m*

say /seɪ/ *n* **have one's ~** dire la propria; **have a ~** avere voce in capitolo ● *vt/i* (*pt/pp* **said**) dire; **that is to ~** cioè; **that goes without ~ing** questo è ovvio; **when all is said and done** alla fine dei conti. **~ing** *n* proverbio *m*

scab /skæb/ *n* crosta *f*; *pej* crumiro *m*

scald /skɔːld/ *vt* scottare; (*milk*) scaldare ● *n* scottatura *f*

scale[1] /skeɪl/ *n* (*of fish*) scaglia *f*

scale[2] *n* scala *f*; **on a grand ~** su vasta scala ● *vt* (*climb*) scalare. □ **~ down** *vt* diminuire

scales /skeɪlz/ *npl* (*for weighing*) bilancia *fsg*

scalp /skælp/ *n* cuoio *m* capelluto

scamper /'skæmpə(r)/ *vi* **~ away** sgattaiolare via

scan /skæn/ *n* (*Med*) scanning *m inv*, scansioscintigrafia *f* ● *vt* (*pt/pp* **scanned**) scrutare; (*quickly*) dare una scorsa a; (*Med*) fare uno scanning di

scandal /'skændl/ *n* scandalo *m*; (*gossip*) pettegolezzi *mpl*. **~ize** *vt* scandalizzare. **~ous** *adj* scandaloso

Scandinavia /skændɪ'neɪvɪə/ *n* Scandinavia *f*. **~n** *adj & n* scandinavo, -a *mf*

scanner /'skænə(r)/ *n* (*Comput*) scanner *m inv*

scant /skænt/ *adj* scarso

scant|y /'skæntɪ/ *adj* (**-ier, -iest**) scarso; (clothing) succinto. **~ily** *adv* scarsamente; (clothed) succintamente

scapegoat /'skeɪp-/ *n* capro *m* espiatorio

scar /skɑː(r)/ *n* cicatrice *f* ● *vt* (*pt/pp* **scarred**) lasciare una cicatrice a

scarc|e /skeəs/ *adj* scarso; *fig* raro; **make oneself ~e** [!] svignarsela. **~ely** *adv* appena; **~ely anything** quasi niente. **~ity** *n* scarsezza *f*

scare /skeə(r)/ *n* spavento *m*; (*panic*) panico *m* ● *vt* spaventare; **be ~d** aver paura (**of** di)

'scarecrow *n* spaventapasseri *m inv*

scarf /skɑːf/ *n* (*pl* **scarves**) sciarpa *f*; (*square*) foulard *m inv*

scarlet /'skɑːlət/ *adj* scarlatto. **~ 'fever** *n* scarlattina *f*

scary /'skeərɪ/ *adj* **be ~** far paura

scathing /'skeɪðɪŋ/ *adj* mordace

scatter /'skætə(r)/ *vt* spargere; (*disperse*) disperdere ● *vi* disperdersi. **~-brained** *adj* [!] scervellato. **~ed** *adj* sparso

scavenge /'skævɪndʒ/ *vi* frugare nella spazzatura. **~r** *n persona f che fruga nella spazzatura*

scenario /sɪ'nɑːrɪəʊ/ *n* scenario *m*

scene /siːn/ *n* scena *f*; (*quarrel*) scenata *f*; **behind the ~s** dietro le quinte

scenery /'siːnərɪ/ *n* scenario *m*

scenic /'siːnɪk/ *adj* panoramico

scent /sent/ *n* odore *m*; (*trail*) scia *f*; (*perfume*) profumo *m*. **~ed** *adj* profumato (**with** di)

sceptic|al /'skeptɪkl/ *adj* scettico. **~ism** *n* scetticismo *m*

schedule /'ʃedjuːl/ *n* piano *m*, programma *m*; (*of work*) programma *m*; (*timetable*) orario *m*; **behind ~** indietro; **on ~** nei tempi previsti; **according to ~** secondo i tempi previsti ● *vt* prevedere. **~d flight** *n* volo *m* di linea

scheme /skiːm/ *n* (*plan*) piano *m*; (*plot*) macchinazione *f* ● *vi pej* macchinare

scholar /'skɒlə(r)/ *n* studioso, -a *mf*. **~ly** *adj* erudito. **~ship** *n* erudizione *f*; (*grant*) borsa *f* di studio

school /skuːl/ *n* scuola *f*; (*in university*) facoltà *f*; (*of fish*) branco *m*

school: ~boy *n* scolaro *m*. **~girl** *n* scolara *f*. **~ing** *n* istruzione *f*. **~-teacher** *n* insegnante *mf*

sciatica /saɪ'ætɪkə/ *n* sciatica *f*

scien|ce /'saɪəns/ *n* scienza *f*; **~ce fiction** fantascienza *f*. **~tific** *adj* scientifico. **~tist** *n* scienziato, -a *mf*

scissors /'sɪzəz/ *npl* forbici *fpl*

scoff[1] /skɒf/ *vi* **~ at** schernire

scoff[2] *vt* [!] divorare

scold /skəʊld/ *vt* sgridare. **~ing** *n* sgridata *f*

scoop /skuːp/ *n* paletta *f*; (*Journ*) scoop *m inv* ● **scoop out** *vt* svuotare. □ **~ up** *vt* tirar su

scope /skəʊp/ *n* portata *f*; (*opportunity*) opportunità *f inv*

scorch /skɔːtʃ/ *vt* bruciare. **~er** *n* [!] giornata *f* torrida. **~ing** *adj* caldissimo

score /skɔː(r)/ *n* punteggio *m*; (*individual*) punteggio *m*; (*Mus*) partitura *f*; (*for film, play*) musica *f*; **a ~ [of]** (*twenty*) una ventina [di]; **keep [the] ~** tenere il punteggio; **on that ~** a questo proposito ● *vt* segnare (goal); (*cut*) incidere ● *vi* far punti; (*in football etc*) segnare; (*keep score*) tenere il punteggio. **~r** *n* segnapunti *m inv*; (*of goals*) giocatore, -trice *mf* che segna

scorn /skɔ:n/ *n* disprezzo *m* ● *vt* disprezzare. **~ful** *adj* sprezzante

Scorpio /'skɔ:pɪəʊ/ *n* Scorpione *m*

scorpion /'skɔ:pɪən/ *n* scorpione *m*

Scot /skɒt/ *n* scozzese *mf*

scotch *vt* far cessare

Scotch /skɒtʃ/ *adj* scozzese ● *n* (*whisky*) whisky *m* [scozzese]

Scot|land /'skɒtlənd/ *n* Scozia *f*. **~s**, **~tish** *adj* scozzese

> **Scottish Parliament** Istituito nel 1999 con sede a Edimburgo, il Parlamento scozzese ha funzione legislativa e esecutiva riguardo agli affari interni della Scozia. Dei 129 parlamentari o *MSPs* (*Members of the Scottish Parliament*), 73 sono eletti direttamente dai cittadini scozzesi secondo un sistema di maggioranza relativa; i restanti 56 (*Additional Members*) vengono eletti col sistema proporzionale.

scoundrel /'skaʊndrəl/ *n* mascalzone *m*

scour[1] /'skaʊə(r)/ *vt* (*search*) perlustrare

scour[2] *vt* (*clean*) strofinare

scourge /skɜ:dʒ/ *n* flagello *m*

scout /skaʊt/ *n* (*Mil*) esploratore *m* ● *vi* **~ for** andare in cerca di

Scout *n* [**Boy**] **~** [boy]scout *m inv*

scowl /skaʊl/ *n* sguardo *m* torvo ● *vi* guardare [di] storto

scram /skræm/ *vi* [!] levarsi dai piedi

scramble /'skræmbl/ *n* (*climb*) arrampicata *f* ● *vi* (*clamber*) arrampicarsi; **~ for** azzuffarsi per ● *vt* (*Teleph*) creare delle interferenze in; (*eggs*) strapazzare

scrap[1] /skræp/ *n* ([!]: *fight*) litigio *m*

scrap[2] *n* pezzetto *m*; (*metal*) ferraglia *f*; **~s** *pl* (*of food*) avanzi *mpl* ● *vt* (*pt/pp* **scrapped**) buttare via

'scrap-book *n* album *m inv*

scrape /skreɪp/ *vt* raschiare; (*damage*) graffiare. □ **~ through** *vi* passare per un pelo. □ **~ together** *vt* racimolare

scraper /'skreɪpə(r)/ *n* raschietto *m*

'scrap-yard *n* deposito *m* di ferraglia; (*for cars*) cimitero *m* delle macchine

scratch /skrætʃ/ *n* graffio *m*; (*to relieve itch*) grattata *f*; **start from ~** partire da zero; **up to ~** (work) all'altezza ● *vt* graffiare; (*to relieve itch*) grattare ● *vi* grattarsi. **~ card** *n* gratta e vinci *m inv*

scrawl /skrɔ:l/ *n* scarabocchio *m* ● *vt/i* scarabocchiare

scream /skri:m/ *n* strillo *m* ● *vt/i* strillare

screech /skri:tʃ/ *n* stridore *m* ● *vi* stridere ● *vt* strillare

screen /skri:n/ *n* paravento *m*; (*Cinema, TV*) schermo *m* ● *vt* proteggere; (*conceal*) riparare; proiettare (film); (*candidates*) passare al setaccio; (*Med*) sottoporre a visita medica. **~ing** *n* (*Med*) visita *f* medica; (*of film*) proiezione *f*. **~play** *n* sceneggiatura *f*

screw /skru:/ *n* vite *f* ● *vt* avvitare. □ **~ up** *vt* (*crumple*) accartocciare; strizzare (eyes); storcere (face); ([✖]: *bungle*) mandare all'aria. **~driver** cacciavite *m*

scribble /'skrɪbl/ *n* scarabocchio *m* ● *vt/i* scarabocchiare

script /skrɪpt/ *n* scrittura *f* (*a mano*); (*of film*) sceneggiatura *f*

scroll /skrəʊl/ *n* rotolo *m* (*di pergamena*); (*decoration*) voluta *f*. □ **~ down** *vi* scorrere in giù

scrounge /skraʊndʒ/ *vt/i* scroccare. **~r** *n* scroccone, -a *mf*

scrub[1] /skrʌb/ *n* (*land*) boscaglia *f*

scrub[2] *vt/i* (*pt/pp* **scrubbed**) strofinare; ([!]: *cancel*) cancellare (plan)

scruff /skrʌf/ *n* **by the ~ of the neck** per la collottola

scruffy /'skrʌfɪ/ *adj* (**-ier, -iest**) trasandato

scruple /'skru:pl/ *n* scrupolo *m*

scrupulous /'skru:pjʊləs/ *adj* scrupoloso

scrutin|ize /'skru:tɪnaɪz/ *vt* scrutinare. **~y** *n* (*look*) esame *m* minuzioso

scuffle /'skʌfl/ *n* tafferuglio *m*

sculpt /skʌlpt/ *vt/i* scolpire. **~or** *n* scultore *m*. **~ure** *n* scultura *f*

scum /skʌm/ *n* schiuma *f*; (*people*) feccia *f*

scurry /'skʌrɪ/ *vi* (*pt/pp* **-ied**) affrettare il passo

scuttle /'skʌtl/ *vi* (*hurry*) **~ away** correre via

S

sea /siː/ *n* mare *m*; **at ~** in mare; *fig* confuso; **by ~** via mare. **~board** *n* costiera *f*. **~food** *n* frutti *mpl* di mare. **~gull** *n* gabbiano *m*

seal[1] /siːl/ *n* (*Zool*) foca *f*

seal[2] *n* sigillo *m*; (*Techn*) chiusura *f* ermetica ● *vt* sigillare; (*Techn*) chiudere ermeticamente. □ **~ off** *vt* bloccare (area)

'sea-level *n* livello *m* del mare

seam /siːm/ *n* cucitura *f*; (*of coal*) strato *m*

'seaman *n* marinaio *m*

seamy /'siːmɪ/ *adj* sordido; (area) malfamato

seance /'seɪɑːns/ *n* seduta *f* spiritica

search /sɜːtʃ/ *n* ricerca *f*; (*official*) perquisizione *f*; **in ~ of** alla ricerca di ● *vt* frugare (**for** alla ricerca di); perlustrare (area); (*officially*) perquisire ● *vi* **~ for** cercare. **~ing** *adj* penetrante

search: ~light *n* riflettore *m*. **~-party** *n* squadra *f* di ricerca

sea: ~sick *adj* **be/get ~** avere il mal di mare. **~side** *n* **at/to the ~side** al mare

season /'siːzn/ *n* stagione *f* ● *vt* (*flavour*) condire. **~able** *adj*, **~al** *adj* stagionale. **~ing** *n* condimento *m*

'season ticket *n* abbonamento *m*

seat /siːt/ *n* (*chair*) sedia *f*; (*in car*) sedile *m*; (*place to sit*) posto *m* [a sedere]; (*bottom*) didietro *m*; (*of government*) sede *f*; **take a ~** sedersi ● *vt* mettere a sedere; (*have seats for*) aver posti [a sedere] per; **remain ~ed** mantenere il proprio posto. **~-belt** *n* cintura *f* di sicurezza

S

sea: ~weed *n* alga *f* marina. **~worthy** *adj* in stato di navigare

seclu|ded /sɪ'kluːdɪd/ *adj* appartato. **~sion** *n* isolamento *m*

second[1] /sɪ'kɒnd/ *vt* (*transfer*) distaccare

second[2] /'sekənd/ *adj* secondo; **on ~ thoughts** ripensandoci meglio ● *n* secondo *m*; **~s** *pl* (*goods*) merce *fsg* di seconda scelta; **have ~s** (*at meal*) fare il bis; **John the S~** Giovanni Secondo ● *adv* (*in race*) al secondo posto ● *vt* assistere; appoggiare (proposal)

secondary /'sekəndrɪ/ *adj* secondario. **~ school** *n* ≈ scuola *f* media (*inferiore e superiore*)

second: ~ 'class *adv* (travel, send) in seconda classe. **~-class** *adj* di seconda classe

'second hand *n* (*on clock*) lancetta *f* dei secondi

second-'hand *adj & adv* di seconda mano

secondly /'sekəndlɪ/ *adv* in secondo luogo

second-'rate *adj* di second'ordine

secrecy /'siːkrəsɪ/ *n* segretezza *f*; **in ~** in segreto

secret /'siːkrɪt/ *adj* segreto ● *n* segreto *m*

secretarial /sekrə'teərɪəl/ *adj* (work, staff) di segreteria

secretary /'sekrətərɪ/ *n* segretario, -a *mf*

secretive /'siːkrətɪv/ *adj* riservato. **~ness** *n* riserbo *m*

sect /sekt/ *n* setta *f*. **~arian** *adj* settario

section /'sekʃn/ *n* sezione *f*

sector /'sektə(r)/ *n* settore *m*

secular /'sekjʊlə(r)/ *adj* secolare; (education) laico

secure /sɪ'kjʊə(r)/ *adj* sicuro ● *vt* proteggere; chiudere bene (door); rendere stabile (ladder); (*obtain*) assicurarsi. **~ly** *adv* saldamente

securit|y /sɪ'kjʊərətɪ/ *n* sicurezza *f*; (*for loan*) garanzia *f*. **~ies** *npl* titoli *mpl*

sedate[1] /sɪ'deɪt/ *adj* posato

sedate[2] *vt* somministrare sedativi a

sedation /sɪ'deɪʃn/ *n* somministrazione *f* di sedativi; **be under ~** essere sotto l'effetto di sedativi

sedative /'sedətɪv/ *adj* sedativo ● *n* sedativo *m*

sediment /'sedɪmənt/ *n* sedimento *m*

seduce /sɪ'djuːs/ *vt* sedurre

seduct|ion /sɪ'dʌkʃn/ *n* seduzione *f*. **~ive** *adj* seducente

see /siː/ *v* (*pt* **saw**, *pp* **seen**) ● *vt* vedere; (*understand*) capire; (*escort*) accompagnare; **go and ~** andare a vedere; (*visit*) andare a trovare; **~ you!** ci vediamo!; **~ you later!** a più tardi!; **~ing that** visto che ● *vi* vedere; (*understand*) capire; **~ that** (*make sure*) assicurarsi che; **~ about** occuparsi di. □ **~ off** *vt* veder partire; (*chase away*) mandar via. □ **~ through** *vi* vedere attraverso; *fig* non farsi ingannare da ● *vt* portare a buon fine. □ ~ **to** *vi* occuparsi di

seed /si:d/ *n* seme *m*; (*Tennis*) testa *f* di serie; **go to ~** fare seme; *fig* lasciarsi andare. **~ed player** *n* (*Tennis*) testa *f* di serie. **~ling** *n* pianticella *f*

seedy /ˈsi:dɪ/ *adj* (**-ier, -iest**) squallido

seek /si:k/ *vt* (*pt*/*pp* **sought**) cercare

seem /si:m/ *vi* sembrare. **~ingly** *adv* apparentemente

seen /si:n/ ▷**SEE**[1]

seep /si:p/ *vi* filtrare

see-saw /ˈsi:sɔ:/ *n* altalena *f*

seethe /si:ð/ *vi* ~ **with anger** ribollire di rabbia

ˈsee-through *adj* trasparente

segment /ˈsegmənt/ *n* segmento *m*; (*of orange*) spicchio *m*

segregat|e /ˈsegrɪgeɪt/ *vt* segregare. **~ion** *n* segregazione *f*

seize /si:z/ *vt* afferrare; (*Jur*) confiscare. □ ~ **up** *vi* (*Techn*) bloccarsi

seizure /ˈsi:ʒə(r)/ *n* (*Jur*) confisca *f*; (*Med*) colpo *m* [apoplettico]

seldom /ˈseldəm/ *adv* raramente

select /sɪˈlekt/ *adj* scelto; (*exclusive*) esclusivo ● *vt* scegliere; selezionare (team). **~ion** *n* selezione *f*. **~ive** *adj* selettivo. **~or** *n* (*Sport*) selezionatore, -trice *mf*

self /self/ *n* io *m*

self: **~-adˈdressed** *adj* con il proprio indirizzo. **~-ˈcatering** *adj* in appartamento attrezzato di cucina. **~-ˈcentred** *adj* egocentrico. **~-ˈconfidence** *n* fiducia *f* in se stesso. **~-ˈconfident** *adj* sicuro di sé. **~-ˈconscious** *adj* impacciato. **~-conˈtained** *adj* (flat) con ingresso indipendente. **~-conˈtrol** *n* autocontrollo *m*. **~-deˈfence** *n* autodifesa *f*; (*Jur*) legittima difesa *f*. **~-emˈployed** *adj* che lavora in proprio. **~-ˈevident** *adj* ovvio. **~-inˈdulgent** *adj* indulgente con se stesso. **~-ˈinterest** *n* interesse *m* personale

self|ish /ˈselfɪʃ/ *adj* egoista. **~ishness** *n* egoismo *m*. **~less** *adj* disinteressato

self: **~-pity** *n* autocommiserazione *f*. **~-ˈportrait** *n* autoritratto *m*. **~-reˈspect** *n* amor *m* proprio. **~-ˈrighteous** *adj* presuntuoso. **~-ˈsacrifice** *n* abnegazione *f*. **~-ˈsatisfied** *adj* compiaciuto di sé. **~-ˈservice** *n* self-service *m inv* ● *attrib* self-service. **~-sufˈficient** *adj* autosufficiente

sell /sel/ *v* (*pt*/*pp* **sold**) ● *vt* vendere; **be sold out** essere esaurito ● *vi* vendersi. □ ~ **off** *vt* liquidare

seller /ˈselə(r)/ *n* venditore, -trice *mf*

Sellotape® /ˈseləʊ-/ *n* nastro *m* adesivo, scotch® *m*

ˈsell-out *n* ([!]: *betrayal*) tradimento *m*; **be a ~** (concert:) fare il tutto esaurito

semblance /ˈsembləns/ *n* parvenza *f*

semester /sɪˈmestə(r)/ *n Am* semestre *m*

semi /ˈsemɪ/: **~breve** /ˈsemɪbri:v/ *n* semibreve *f*. **~circle** *n* semicerchio *m*. **~ˈcircular** *adj* semicircolare. **~ˈcolon** *n* punto e virgola *m*. **~-deˈtached** *adj* gemella ● *n* casa *f* gemella. **~-ˈfinal** *n* semifinale *f*

seminar /ˈsemɪnɑ:(r)/ *n* seminario *m*. **~y** *n* seminario *m*

senat|e /ˈsenət/ *n* senato *m*. **~or** *n* senatore *m*

send /send/ *vt/i* (*pt*/*pp* **sent**) mandare; **~ for** mandare a chiamare (person); far venire (thing). **~er** *n* mittente *mf*. **~-off** *n* commiato *m*

senil|e /ˈsi:naɪl/ *adj* arteriosclerotico; (*Med*) senile. **~ity** *n* senilismo *m*

senior /ˈsi:nɪə(r)/ *adj* più vecchio; (*in rank*) superiore ● *n* (*in rank*) superiore *mf*; (*in sport*) senior *mf*; **she's two years my ~** è più vecchia di me di due anni. **~ ˈcitizen** *n* anziano, -a *mf*

seniority /si:nɪˈɒrətɪ/ *n* anzianità *f inv* di servizio

sensation /senˈseɪʃn/ *n* sensazione *f*. **~al** *adj* sensazionale. **~ally** *adv* in modo sensazionale

sense /sens/ *n* senso *m*; (*common ~*) buon senso *m*; **in a ~** in un certo senso; **make ~** aver senso ● *vt* sentire. **~less** *adj* insensato; (*unconscious*) privo di sensi

sensibl|e /ˈsensəbl/ *adj* sensato; (*suitable*) appropriato. **~y** *adv* in modo appropriato

sensitiv|e /ˈsensətɪv/ *adj* sensibile; (*touchy*) suscettibile. **~ely** *adv* con sensibilità. **~ity** *n* sensibilità *f inv*

sensual /ˈsensjʊəl/ *adj* sensuale. **~ity** *n* sensualità *f inv*

S

sensuous /ˈsensjʊəs/ *adj* voluttuoso
sent /sent/ ▷**SEND**
sentence /ˈsentəns/ *n* frase *f*; (*Jur*) sentenza *f*; (*punishment*) condanna *f* ● *vt* ~ **to** condannare a
sentiment /ˈsentɪmənt/ *n* sentimento *m*; (*opinion*) opinione *f*; (*sentimentality*) sentimentalismo *m*. **~al** *adj* sentimentale; *pej* sentimentalista. **~ality** *n* sentimentalità *f inv*
sentry /ˈsentrɪ/ *n* sentinella *f*
separable /ˈsepərəbl/ *adj* separabile
separate[1] /ˈsepərət/ *adj* separato. **~ly** *adv* separatamente
separat|e[2] /ˈsepəreɪt/ *vt* separare ● *vi* separarsi. **~ion** *n* separazione *f*
September /sepˈtembə(r)/ *n* settembre *m*
septic /ˈseptɪk/ *adj* settico; **go ~** infettarsi. **~ tank** *n* fossa *f* biologica
sequel /ˈsiːkwəl/ *n* seguito *m*
sequence /ˈsiːkwəns/ *n* sequenza *f*
Serbia /ˈsɜːbɪə/ *n* Serbia *f*
serenade /serəˈneɪd/ *n* serenata *f* ● *vt* fare una serenata a
seren|e /sɪˈriːn/ *adj* sereno. **~ity** *n* serenità *f inv*
sergeant /ˈsɑːdʒənt/ *n* sergente *m*
serial /ˈsɪərɪəl/ *n* racconto *m* a puntate; (*TV*) sceneggiato *m* a puntate; (*Radio*) commedia *f* radiofonica. **~ize** *vt* pubblicare a puntate; (*Radio, TV*) trasmettere a puntate. **~ killer** *n* serial killer *mf inv*. **~ number** *n* numero *m* di serie. **~ port** *n* (*Comput*) porta *f* seriale
series /ˈsɪəriːz/ *n* serie *f inv*
serious /ˈsɪərɪəs/ *adj* serio; (illness, error) grave. **~ly** *adv* seriamente; (ill) gravemente; **take ~ly** prendere sul serio. **~ness** *n* serietà *f inv*; (*of situation*) gravità *f inv*
sermon /ˈsɜːmən/ *n* predica *f*
serum /ˈsɪərəm/ *n* siero *m*
servant /ˈsɜːvənt/ *n* domestico, -a *mf*
serve /sɜːv/ *n* (*Tennis*) servizio *m* ● *vt* servire; scontare (sentence); **~ its purpose** servire al proprio scopo; **it ~s you right!** ben ti sta!; **~s two** per due persone ● *vi* prestare servizio; (*Tennis*) servire; **~ as** servire da. **~r** *n* (*Comput*) server *m inv*
service /ˈsɜːvɪs/ *n* servizio *m*; (*Relig*) funzione *f*; (*maintenance*) revisione *f*; **~s** *pl* forze *fpl* armate; (*on motorway*) area *f* di servizio; **in the ~s** sotto le armi; **of ~ to** utile a; **out of ~** (machine:) guasto ● *vt* (*Techn*) revisionare. **~able** *adj* utilizzabile; (*hard-wearing*) resistente; (*practical*) pratico
service: ~ charge *n* servizio *m*. **~ station** *n* stazione *f* di servizio
serviette /sɜːvɪˈet/ *n* tovagliolo *m*
servile /ˈsɜːvaɪl/ *adj* servile
session /ˈseʃn/ *n* seduta *f*; (*Jur*) sessione *f*; (*Univ*) anno *m* accademico
set /set/ *n* serie *f*, set *m inv*; (*of crockery, cutlery*) servizio *m*; (*Radio, TV*) apparecchio *m*; (*Math*) insieme *m*; (*Theat*) scenario *m*; (*Cinema, Tennis*) set *m inv*; (*of people*) circolo *m*; (*of hair*) messa *f* in piega ● *adj* (*ready*) pronto; (*rigid*) fisso; (book) in programma; **be ~ on doing sth** essere risoluto a fare qcsa; **be ~ in one's ways** essere abitudinario ● *v* (*pt/pp* **set**, *pres p* **setting**) ● *vt* mettere, porre; mettere (alarm clock); assegnare (task, homework); fissare (date, limit); chiedere (questions); montare (gem); assestare (bone); apparecchiare (table); **~ fire to** dare fuoco a; **~ free** liberare ● *vi* (sun:) tramontare; (jelly, concrete:) solidificare; **~ about doing sth** mettersi a fare qcsa. □ **~ back** *vt* mettere indietro; (*hold up*) ritardare; ([!]: *cost*) costare a. □ **~ off** *vi* partire ● *vt* avviare; mettere (alarm); fare esplodere (bomb). □ **~ out** *vi* partire; **~ out to do sth** proporsi di fare qcsa ● *vt* disporre; (*state*) esporre. □ **~ to** *vi* mettersi all'opera. □ **~ up** *vt* fondare (company); istituire (committee)
'set-back *n* passo *m* indietro
settee /seˈtiː/ *n* divano *m*
setting /ˈsetɪŋ/ *n* scenario *m*; (*position*) posizione *f*; (*of sun*) tramonto *m*; (*of jewel*) montatura *f*
settle /ˈsetl/ *vt* (*decide*) definire; risolvere (argument); fissare (date); calmare (nerves); saldare (bill) ● *vi* (*to live*) stabilirsi; (snow, dust, bird:) posarsi; (*subside*) assestarsi; (sediment:) depositarsi. □ **~ down** *vi* sistemarsi; (*stop making noise*) calmarsi. □ **~ for** *vt* accontentarsi di. □ **~ up** *vi* regolare i conti
settlement /ˈsetlmənt/ *n* (*agreement*) accordo *m*; (*of bill*) saldo *m*; (*colony*) insediamento *m*

settler /ˈsetlə(r)/ *n* colonizzatore, -trice *mf*

ˈset-to *n* [!] zuffa *f*; (*verbal*) battibecco *m*

ˈset-up *n* situazione *f*

seven /ˈsevn/ *adj* sette. **~ˈteen** *adj* diciassette. **~ˈteenth** *adj* diciasettesimo

seventh /ˈsevnθ/ *adj* settimo

seventieth /ˈsevntɪɪθ/ *adj* settantesimo

seventy /ˈsevntɪ/ *adj* settanta

sever /ˈsevə(r)/ *vt* troncare (relations)

several /ˈsevrəl/ *adj & pron* parecchi

sever|e /sɪˈvɪə(r)/ *adj* severo; (pain) violento; (illness) grave; (winter) rigido. **~ely** *adv* severamente; (ill) gravemente. **~ity** *n* severità *f inv*; (*of pain*) violenza *f*; (*of illness*) gravità *f*; (*of winter*) rigore *m*

sew /səʊ/ *vt/i* (*pt* **sewed**, *pp* **sewn** *or* **sewed**) cucire. ▫ **~ up** *vt* ricucire

sewage /ˈsu:ɪdʒ/ *n* acque *fpl* di scolo

sewer /ˈsu:ə(r)/ *n* fogna *f*

sewing /ˈsəʊɪŋ/ *n* cucito *m*; (*work*) lavoro *m* di cucito. **~ machine** *n* macchina *f* da cucire

sewn /səʊn/ ▹**SEW**

sex /seks/ *n* sesso *m*; **have ~** avere rapporti sessuali. **~ist** *adj* sessista. **~ offender** *n* colpevole *mf* di delitti a sfondo sessuale

sexual /ˈseksjʊəl/ *adj* sessuale. **~ ˈintercourse** *n* rapporti *mpl* sessuali. **~ity** *n* sessualità *f inv*. **~ly** *adv* sessualmente

sexy /ˈseksɪ/ *adj* (**-ier, -iest**) sexy

shabb|y /ˈʃæbɪ/ *adj* (**-ier, -iest**) scialbo; (treatment) meschino. **~iness** *n* trasandatezza *f*; (*of treatment*) meschinità *f inv*

shack /ʃæk/ *n* catapecchia *f* ● **shack up with** *vt* [!] vivere con

shade /ʃeɪd/ *n* ombra *f*; (*of colour*) sfumatura *f*; (*for lamp*) paralume *m*; (*Am: for window*) tapparella *f*; **a ~ better** un tantino meglio ● *vt* riparare dalla luce; (*draw lines on*) ombreggiare. **~s** *npl* [!] occhiali *mpl* da sole

shadow /ˈʃædəʊ/ *n* ombra *f*; **S~ Cabinet** governo *m* ombra ● *vt* (*follow*) pedinare. **~y** *adj* ombroso

shady /ˈʃeɪdɪ/ *adj* (**-ier, -iest**) ombroso; ([!]*: disreputable*) losco

shaft /ʃɑ:ft/ *n* (*Techn*) albero *m*; (*of light*) raggio *m*; (*of lift, mine*) pozzo *m*; **~s** *pl* (*of cart*) stanghe *fpl*

shaggy /ˈʃægɪ/ *adj* (**-ier, -iest**) irsuto; (animal) dal pelo arruffato

shake /ʃeɪk/ *n* scrollata *f* ● *v* (*pt* **shook**, *pp* **shaken**) ● *vt* scuotere; agitare (bottle); far tremare (building); **~ hands with** stringere la mano a ● *vi* tremare. ▫ **~ off** *vt* scrollarsi di dosso. **~-up** *n* (*Pol*) rimpasto *m*; (*Comm*) ristrutturazione *f*

shaky /ˈʃeɪkɪ/ *adj* (**-ier, -iest**) tremante; (table etc) traballante; (*unreliable*) vacillante

shall /ʃæl/ *v aux* **I ~ go** andrò; **we ~ see** vedremo; **what ~ I do?** cosa faccio?; **I'll come too, ~ I?** vengo anch'io, no?; **thou shalt not kill** *liter* non uccidere

shallow /ˈʃæləʊ/ *adj* basso, poco profondo; (dish) poco profondo; *fig* superficiale

sham /ʃæm/ *adj* falso ● *n* finzione *f*; (*person*) spaccone, -a *mf* ● *vt* (*pt/pp* **shammed**) simulare

shambles /ˈʃæmblz/ *n* baraonda *fsg*

shame /ʃeɪm/ *n* vergogna *f*; **it's a ~ that** è un peccato che; **what a ~!** che peccato! **~-faced** *adj* vergognoso

shame|ful /ˈʃeɪmfl/ *adj* vergognoso. **~less** *adj* spudorato

shampoo /ʃæmˈpu:/ *n* shampoo *m inv* ● *vt* fare uno shampoo a

shape /ʃeɪp/ *n* forma *f*; (*figure*) ombra *f*; **take ~** prendere forma; **get back in ~** ritornare in forma ● *vt* dare forma a (**into** di) ● *vi* **~ [up]** mettere la testa a posto; **~ up nicely** mettersi bene. **~less** *adj* informe

share /ʃeə(r)/ *n* porzione *f*; (*Comm*) azione *f* ● *vt* dividere; condividere (views) ● *vi* dividere. **~holder** *n* azionista *mf*

shark /ʃɑ:k/ *n* squalo *m*, pescecane *m*; *fig* truffatore, -trice *mf*

sharp /ʃɑ:p/ *adj* (knife etc) tagliente; (pencil) appuntito; (drop) a picco; (reprimand) severo; (outline) marcato; (*alert*) acuto; (*unscrupulous*) senza scrupoli; **~ pain** fitta *f* ● *adv* in punto; (*Mus*) fuori tono; **look ~!** sbrigati! ● *n* (*Mus*) diesis *m inv*. **~en** *vt* affilare (knife); appuntire (pencil)

shatter /ˈʃætə(r)/ *vt* frantumare; *fig* mandare in frantumi; **~ed** ([!]: *exhausted*) a pezzi ● *vi* frantumarsi

shav|e /ʃeɪv/ *n* rasatura *f*; **have a ~e** farsi la barba ● *vt* radere ● *vi* radersi. **~er** *n* rasoio *m* elettrico. **~ing-brush** *n* pennello *m* da barba; **~ing foam** *n* schiuma *f* da barba; **~ing soap** *n* sapone *m* da barba

shawl /ʃɔ:l/ *n* scialle *m*

she /ʃi:/ *pron* lei

sheaf /ʃi:f/ *n* (*pl* **sheaves**) fascio *m*

shear /ʃɪə(r)/ *vt* (*pt* **sheared**, *pp* **shorn** *or* **sheared**) tosare

shears /ʃɪəz/ *npl* (*for hedge*) cesoie *fpl*

shed[1] /ʃed/ *n* baracca *f*; (*for cattle*) stalla *f*

shed[2] *vt* (*pt*/*pp* **shed**, *pres p* **shedding**) perdere; versare (blood, tears); **~ light on** far luce su

sheep /ʃi:p/ *n inv* pecora *f*. **~-dog** *n* cane *m* da pastore

sheepish /ˈʃi:pɪʃ/ *adj* imbarazzato. **~ly** *adv* con aria imbarazzata

sheer /ʃɪə(r)/ *adj* puro; (*steep*) a picco; (*transparent*) trasparente ● *adv* a picco

sheet /ʃi:t/ *n* lenzuolo *m*; (*of paper*) foglio *m*; (*of glass, metal*) lastra *f*

shelf /ʃelf/ *n* (*pl* **shelves**) ripiano *m*; (*set of shelves*) scaffale *m*

shell /ʃel/ *n* conchiglia *f*; (*of egg, snail, tortoise*) guscio *m*; (*of crab*) corazza *f*; (*of unfinished building*) ossatura *f*; (*Mil*) granata *f* ● *vt* sgusciare (peas); (*Mil*) bombardare. □ **~ out** *vi* [!] sborsare

ˈshellfish *n inv* mollusco *m*; (*Culin*) frutti *mpl* di mare

shelter /ˈʃeltə(r)/ *n* rifugio *m*; (*air raid* ~) rifugio *m* antiaereo ● *vt* riparare (**from** da); *fig* mettere al riparo; (*give lodging to*) dare asilo a ● *vi* rifugiarsi. **~ed** *adj* (spot) riparato; (life) ritirato

shelve /ʃelv/ *vt* accantonare (project)

shelving /ˈʃelvɪŋ/ *n* (*shelves*) ripiani *mpl*

shepherd /ˈʃepəd/ *n* pastore *m* ● *vt* guidare. **~'s pie** *n pasticcio m di carne tritata e patate*

sherry /ˈʃerɪ/ *n* sherry *m*

shield /ʃi:ld/ *n* scudo *m*; (*for eyes*) maschera *f*; (*Techn*) schermo *m* ● *vt* proteggere (**from** da)

shift /ʃɪft/ *n* cambiamento *m*; (*in position*) spostamento *m*; (*at work*) turno *m* ● *vt* spostare; (*take away*) togliere; riversare (blame) ● *vi* spostarsi; (wind:) cambiare; ([!]: *move quickly*) darsi una mossa

shifty /ˈʃɪftɪ/ *adj* (**-ier, -iest**) *pej* losco; (eyes) sfuggente

shimmer /ˈʃɪmə(r)/ *n* luccichio *m* ● *vi* luccicare

shin /ʃɪn/ *n* stinco *m*

shine /ʃaɪn/ *n* lucentezza *f*; **give sth a ~** dare una lucidata a qcsa ● *v* (*pt*/*pp* **shone**) ● *vi* splendere; (*reflect light*) brillare; (hair, shoes:) essere lucido ● *vt* **~ a light on** puntare una luce su

shingle /ˈʃɪŋgl/ *n* (*pebbles*) ghiaia *f*

shiny /ˈʃaɪnɪ/ *adj* (**-ier, -iest**) lucido

ship /ʃɪp/ *n* nave *f* ● *vt* (*pt*/*pp* **shipped**) spedire; (*by sea*) spedire via mare

ship: ~ment *n* spedizione *f*; (*consignment*) carico *m*. **~ping** *n* trasporto *m*; (*traffic*) imbarcazioni *fpl*. **~shape** *adj & adv* in perfetto ordine. **~wreck** *n* naufragio *m*. **~wrecked** *adj* naufragato. **~yard** *n* cantiere *m* navale

shirk /ʃɜ:k/ *vt* scansare. **~er** *n* scansafatiche *mf inv*

shirt /ʃɜ:t/ *n* camicia *f*; **in ~-sleeves** in maniche di camicia

shit /ʃɪt/ [!] *n & int* merda *f* ● *vi* (*pt*/*pp* **shit**) cagare

shiver /ˈʃɪvə(r)/ *n* brivido *m* ● *vi* rabbrividire

shoal /ʃəʊl/ *n* (*of fish*) banco *m*

shock /ʃɒk/ *n* (*impact*) urto *m*; (*Electr*) scossa *f* [elettrica]; *fig* colpo *m*, shock *m inv*; (*Med*) shock *m inv*; **get a ~** (*Electr*) prendere la scossa ● *vt* scioccare. **~ing** *adj* scioccante; ([!]: weather, handwriting etc) tremendo

shod /ʃɒd/ ▷**SHOE**

shoddy /ˈʃɒdɪ/ *adj* (**-ier, -iest**) scadente

shoe /ʃu:/ *n* scarpa *f*; (*of horse*) ferro *m* ● *vt* (*pt*/*pp* **shod**, *pres p* **shoeing**) ferrare (horse)

shoe: ~horn *n* calzante *m*. **~-lace** *n* laccio *m* da scarpa

shone /ʃɒn/ ▷**SHINE**

shoo /ʃu:/ *vt* **~ away** cacciar via ● *int* sciò

shook /ʃʊk/ ▷**SHAKE**

shoot /ʃu:t/ *n* (*Bot*) germoglio *m*; (*hunt*) battuta *f* di caccia ● *v* (*pt*/*pp* **shot**) ● *vt* sparare; girare (film) ● *vi* (*hunt*) andare a caccia. □ ~ **down** *vt* abbattere. □ ~ **out** *vi* (*rush*) precipitarsi fuori. □ ~ **up** *vi* (*grow*) crescere in fretta; (prices:) salire di colpo

shop /ʃɒp/ *n* negozio *m*; (*workshop*) officina *f*; **talk** ~ [!] parlare di lavoro ● *vi* (*pt/pp* **shopped**) far compere; **go ~ping** andare a fare compere. □ ~ **around** *vi* confrontare i prezzi

shop: ~ **assistant** *n* commesso, -a *mf*. **~keeper** *n* negoziante *mf*. **~-lifter** *n* taccheggiatore, -trice *mf*. **~-lifting** *n* taccheggio *m*; **~per** *n* compratore, -trice *mf*

shopping /'ʃɒpɪŋ/ *n* compere *fpl*; (*articles*) acquisti *mpl*; **do the ~** fare la spesa. ~ **bag** *n* borsa *f* per la spesa. ~ **centre** *n* centro *m* commerciale. ~ **trolley** *n* carrello *m*

shop: **~-steward** *n* rappresentante *mf* sindacale. **~-'window** *n* vetrina *f*

shore /ʃɔ:(r)/ *n* riva *f*

shorn /ʃɔ:n/ ▷SHEAR

short /ʃɔ:t/ *adj* corto; (*not lasting*) breve; (person) basso; (*curt*) brusco; **a ~ time ago** poco tempo fa; **be ~ of** essere a corto di; **be in ~ supply** essere scarso; *fig* essere raro; **Mick is ~ for Michael** Mick è il diminutivo di Michael ● *adv* bruscamente; **in ~** in breve; ~ **of doing** a meno di fare; **go ~** essere privato (**of** di); **stop ~ of doing sth** non arrivare fino a fare qcsa; **cut ~** interrompere (meeting, holiday); **to cut a long story ~** per farla breve

shortage /'ʃɔ:tɪdʒ/ *n* scarsità *f inv*

short: **~bread** *n* biscotto *m* di pasta frolla. ~ **'circuit** *n* corto *m* circuito. **~coming** *n* difetto *m*. ~ **'cut** *n* scorciatoia *f*

shorten /'ʃɔ:tn/ *vt* abbreviare; accorciare (garment)

shorthand *n* stenografia *f*

short|ly /'ʃɔ:tlɪ/ *adv* presto; **~ly before/after** poco prima/dopo. **~ness** *n* brevità *f inv*; (*of person*) bassa statura *f*

shorts /ʃɔ:ts/ *npl* calzoncini *mpl* corti

short-'sighted *adj* miope

shot /ʃɒt/ ▷SHOOT ● *n* colpo *m*; (*person*) tiratore *m*; (*Phot*) foto *f*; (*injection*) puntura *f*; ([!]: *attempt*) prova *f*; **like a ~** [!] come un razzo. **~gun** *n* fucile *m* da caccia

should /ʃʊd/ *v aux* **I ~ go** dovrei andare; **I ~ have seen him** avrei dovuto vederlo; **I ~ like** mi piacerebbe; **this ~ be enough** questo dovrebbe bastare; **if he ~ come** se dovesse venire

shoulder /'ʃəʊldə(r)/ *n* spalla *f* ● *vt* mettersi in spalla; *fig* accollarsi. **~-bag** *n* borsa *f* a tracolla. **~-blade** *n* scapola *f*. **~-strap** *n* spallina *f*; (*of bag*) tracolla *f*

shout /ʃaʊt/ *n* grido *m* ● *vt/i* gridare. □ ~ **at** *vi* alzar la voce con. □ ~ **down** *vt* azzittire gridando

shove /ʃʌv/ *n* spintone *m* ● *vt* spingere; ([!]: *put*) ficcare ● *vi* spingere. □ ~ **off** *vi* [!] togliersi di torno

shovel /'ʃʌvl/ *n* pala *f* ● *vt* (*pt/pp* **shovelled**) spalare

show /ʃəʊ/ *n* (*display*) manifestazione *f*; (*exhibition*) mostra *f*; (*ostentation*) ostentazione *f*; (*Theat*), (*TV*) spettacolo *m*; (*programme*) programma *m*; **on ~** esposto ● *v* (*pt* **showed**, *pp* **shown**) ● *vt* mostrare; (*put on display*) esporre; proiettare (film) ● *vi* (film:) essere proiettato; **your slip is ~ing** ti si vede la sottoveste. □ ~ **in** *vt* fare accomodare. □ ~ **off** *vi* [!] mettersi in mostra ● *vt* mettere in mostra. □ ~ **up** *vi* risaltare; ([!]: *arrive*) farsi vedere ● *vt* ([!]: *embarrass*) far fare una brutta figura a

'show-down *n* regolamento *m* dei conti

shower /'ʃaʊə(r)/ *n* doccia *f*; (*of rain*) acquazzone *m*; **have a ~** fare la doccia ● *vt* ~ **with** coprire di ● *vi* fare la doccia. **~proof** *adj* impermeabile. **~y** *adj* da acquazzoni

'show-jumping *n* concorso *m* ippico

shown /ʃəʊn/ ▷SHOW

'show-off *n* esibizionista *mf*

showy /'ʃəʊɪ/ *adj* appariscente

shrank /ʃræŋk/ ▷SHRINK

shred /ʃred/ *n* brandello *m*; *fig* briciolo *m* ● *vt* (*pt/pp* **shredded**) fare a brandelli; (*Culin*) tagliuzzare. **~der** *n* distruttore *m* di documenti

shrewd /ʃru:d/ *adj* accorto. **~ness** *n* accortezza *f*

shriek /ʃri:k/ *n* strillo *m* ● *vt/i* strillare

shrift /ʃrɪft/ *n* **give sb short ~** liquidare qcno rapidamente

shrill /ʃrɪl/ *adj* penetrante

shrimp /ʃrɪmp/ *n* gamberetto *m*

shrine /ʃraɪn/ *n* (*place*) santuario *m*

shrink /ʃrɪŋk/ *vi* (*pt* **shrank**, *pp* **shrunk**) restringersi; (*draw back*) ritrarsi (**from** da)

shrivel /ˈʃrɪvl/ *vi* (*pt/pp* **shrivelled**) raggrinzare

shroud /ʃraʊd/ *n* sudario *m*; *fig* manto *m*

Shrove /ʃrəʊv/ *n* ~ **'Tuesday** martedì *m* grasso

shrub /ʃrʌb/ *n* arbusto *m*

shrug /ʃrʌg/ *n* scrollata *f* di spalle ● *vt/i* (*pt/pp* **shrugged**) ~ [**one's shoulders**] scrollare le spalle

shrunk /ʃrʌŋk/ ▷SHRINK. ~**en** *adj* rimpicciolito

shudder /ˈʃʌdə(r)/ *n* fremito *m* ● *vi* fremere

shuffle /ˈʃʌfl/ *vi* strascicare i piedi ● *vt* mescolare (cards)

shun /ʃʌn/ *vt* (*pt/pp* **shunned**) rifuggire

shunt /ʃʌnt/ *vt* smistare

shush /ʃʊʃ/ *int* zitto!

shut /ʃʌt/ *v* (*pt/pp* **shut**, *pres p* **shutting**) ● *vt* chiudere ● *vi* chiudersi; (shop:) chiudere. □ ~ **down** *vt/i* chiudere. □ ~ **up** *vt* chiudere; [!] far tacere ● *vi* [!] stare zitto; ~ **up!** stai zitto!

shutter /ˈʃʌtə(r)/ *n* serranda *f*; (*Phot*) otturatore *m*

shuttle /ˈʃʌtl/ *n* navetta *f* ● *vi* far la spola

shuttle: ~**cock** *n* volano *m*. ~ **service** *n* servizio *m* pendolare

shy /ʃaɪ/ *adj* (*timid*) timido. ~**ness** *n* timidezza *f*

Sicil|y /ˈsɪsɪlɪ/ *n* Sicilia *f*. ~**ian** *adj & n* siciliano, -a *mf*

sick /sɪk/ *adj* ammalato; (humour) macabro; **be** ~ (*vomit*) vomitare; **be** ~ **of sth** [!] essere stufo di qcsa; **feel** ~ aver la nausea

sick|ly /ˈsɪklɪ/ *adj* (**-ier, -iest**) malaticcio. ~**ness** *n* malattia *f*; (*vomiting*) nausea *f*. ~**ness benefit** *n* indennità *f* di malattia

side /saɪd/ *n* lato *m*; (*of person, mountain*) fianco *m*; (*of road*) bordo *m*; **on the** ~ (*as sideline*) come attività secondaria; ~ **by** ~ fianco a fianco; **take** ~**s** immischiarsi; **take sb's** ~ prendere le parti di qcno; **be on the safe** ~ andare sul sicuro ● *attrib* laterale ● *vi* ~ **with** parteggiare per

side: ~**board** *n* credenza *f*. ~**-effect** *n* effetto *m* collaterale. ~**lights** *npl* luci *fpl* di posizione. ~**line** *n* attività *f inv* complementare. ~**-show** *n* attrazione *f*. ~**-step** *vt* schivare. ~**-track** *vt* sviare. ~**walk** *n Am* marciapiede *m*. ~**ways** *adv* obliquamente

siding /ˈsaɪdɪŋ/ *n* binario *m* di raccordo

sidle /ˈsaɪdl/ *vi* camminare furtivamente (**up to** verso)

siege /siːdʒ/ *n* assedio *m*

sieve /sɪv/ *n* setaccio *m* ● *vt* setacciare

sift /sɪft/ *vt* setacciare; ~ [**through**] *fig* passare al setaccio

sigh /saɪ/ *n* sospiro *m* ● *vi* sospirare

sight /saɪt/ *n* vista *f*; (*on gun*) mirino *m*; **the** ~**s** *pl* le cose da vedere; **at first** ~ a prima vista; **be within/out of** ~ essere/non essere in vista; **lose** ~ **of** perdere di vista; **know by** ~ conoscere di vista. **have bad** ~ vederci male ● *vt* avvistare

'sightseeing *n* **go** ~ andare a visitare posti

sign /saɪn/ *n* segno *m*; (*notice*) insegna *f* ● *vt/i* firmare. □ ~ **on** *vi* (*as unemployed*) presentarsi all'ufficio di collocamento; (*Mil*) arruolarsi

signal /ˈsɪgnl/ *n* segnale *m* ● *v* (*pt/pp* **signalled**) ● *vt* segnalare ● *vi* fare segnali; ~ **to sb** far segno a qcno (**to** di). ~**-box** *n* cabina *f* di segnalazione

signature /ˈsɪgnətʃə(r)/ *n* firma *f*. ~ **tune** *n* sigla *f* [musicale]

significan|ce /sɪgˈnɪfɪkəns/ *n* significato *m*. ~**t** *adj* significativo

signify /ˈsɪgnɪfaɪ/ *vt* (*pt/pp* **-ied**) indicare

signpost /ˈsaɪn-/ *n* segnalazione *f* stradale

silence /ˈsaɪləns/ *n* silenzio *m* ● *vt* far tacere. ~**r** *n* (*on gun*) silenziatore *m*; (*Auto*) marmitta *f*

silent /ˈsaɪlənt/ *adj* silenzioso; (film) muto; **remain** ~ rimanere in silenzio. ~**ly** *adv* silenziosamente

silhouette /sɪlʊˈet/ *n* sagoma *f*, silhouette *f inv* ● *vt* **be** ~**d** profilarsi

silicon /ˈsɪlɪkən/ *n* silicio *m*. **~ chip** piastrina *f* di silicio

silk /sɪlk/ *n* seta *f* ● *attrib* di seta. **~worm** *n* baco *m* da seta

silky /ˈsɪlkɪ/ *adj* (**-ier, -iest**) come la seta

silly /ˈsɪlɪ/ *adj* (**-ier, -iest**) sciocco

silt /sɪlt/ *n* melma *f*

silver /ˈsɪlvə(r)/ *adj* d'argento; (paper) argentato ● *n* argento *m*; (*silverware*) argenteria *f*

silver: ~-plated *adj* placcato d'argento. **~ware** *n* argenteria *f*

similar /ˈsɪmɪlə(r)/ *adj* simile. **~ity** *n* somiglianza *f*. **~ly** *adv* in modo simile

simile /ˈsɪmɪlɪ/ *n* similitudine *f*

simmer /ˈsɪmə(r)/ *vi* bollire lentamente ● *vt* far bollire lentamente. □ **~ down** *vi* calmarsi

simple /ˈsɪmpl/ *adj* semplice; (person) sempliciotto. **~-'minded** *adj* sempliciotto

simplicity /sɪmˈplɪsətɪ/ *n* semplicità *f inv*

simply /ˈsɪmplɪ/ *adv* semplicemente

simulat|e /ˈsɪmjʊleɪt/ *vt* simulare. **~ion** *n* simulazione *f*

simultaneous /sɪmlˈteɪnɪəs/ *adj* simultaneo

sin /sɪn/ *n* peccato *m* ● *vi* (*pt/pp* **sinned**) peccare

since /sɪns/
- *prep* da **I've been waiting ~ Monday** aspetto da lunedì
- *adv* da allora
- *conj* da quando; (*because*) siccome

sincere /sɪnˈsɪə(r)/ *adj* sincero. **~ly** *adv* sinceramente; **Yours ~ly** distinti saluti

sincerity /sɪnˈserətɪ/ *n* sincerità *f inv*

sinful /ˈsɪnfl/ *adj* peccaminoso

sing /sɪŋ/ *vt/i* (*pt* **sang**, *pp* **sung**) cantare

singe /sɪndʒ/ *vt* (*pres p* **singeing**) bruciacchiare

singer /ˈsɪŋə(r)/ *n* cantante *mf*

single /ˈsɪŋgl/ *adj* solo; (*not double*) semplice; (*unmarried*) celibe; (woman) nubile; (room) singolo; (bed) a una piazza ● *n* (*ticket*) biglietto *m* di sola andata; (*record*) singolo *m*; **~s** *pl* (*Tennis*) singolo *m* ● **single out** *vt* scegliere; (*distinguish*) distinguere

single-handed *adj & adv* da solo

singular /ˈsɪŋgjʊlə(r)/ *adj* (*Gram*) singolare ● *n* singolare *m*. **~ly** *adv* singolarmente

sinister /ˈsɪnɪstə(r)/ *adj* sinistro

sink /sɪŋk/ *n* lavandino *m* ● *v* (*pt* **sank**, *pp* **sunk**) ● *vi* affondare ● *vt* affondare (ship); scavare (shaft); investire (money). □ **~ in** *vi* penetrare; **it took a while to ~ in** ([!]: *be understood*) c'è voluto un po' a capirlo

sinner /ˈsɪnə(r)/ *n* peccatore, -trice *mf*

sip /sɪp/ *n* sorso *m* ● *vt* (*pt/pp* **sipped**) sorseggiare

siphon /ˈsaɪfn/ *n* (*bottle*) sifone *m* ● **siphon off** *vt* travasare (*con sifone*)

sir /sɜː(r)/ *n* signore *m*; **S~** (*title*) Sir *m*; **Dear S~s** Spettabile ditta

siren /ˈsaɪrən/ *n* sirena *f*

sister /ˈsɪstə(r)/ *n* sorella *f*; (*nurse*) [infermiera *f*] caposala *f*. **~-in-law** *n* (*pl* **~s-in-law**) cognata *f*. **~ly** *adj* da sorella

sit /sɪt/ *v* (*pt/pp* **sat**, *pres p* **sitting**) ● *vi* essere seduto; (*sit down*) sedersi; (committee:) riunirsi ● *vt* sostenere (exam). □ **~ back** *vi fig* starsene con le mani in mano. □ **~ down** *vi* mettersi a sedere. □ **~ up** *vi* mettersi seduto; (*not slouch*) star seduto diritto; (*stay up*) stare alzato

site /saɪt/ *n* posto *m*; (*Archaeol*) sito *m*; (*building ~*) cantiere *m* ● *vt* collocare

sit-in /ˈsɪtɪn/ *n* occupazione *f* (*di fabbrica, ecc.*)

sitting /ˈsɪtɪŋ/ *n* seduta *f*; (*for meals*) turno *m*. **~-room** *n* salotto *m*

situat|e /ˈsɪtjʊeɪt/ *vt* situare. **~ed** *adj* situato. **~ion** *n* situazione *f*; (*location*) posizione *f*; (*job*) posto *m*

six /sɪks/ *adj* sei. **~teen** *adj* sedici. **~teenth** *adj* sedicesimo

sixth /sɪksθ/ *adj* sesto

sixtieth /ˈsɪkstɪɪθ/ *adj* sessantesimo

sixty /ˈsɪkstɪ/ *adj* sessanta

size /saɪz/ *n* dimensioni *fpl*; (*of clothes*) taglia *f*, misura *f*; (*of shoes*) numero *m*; **what ~ is the room?** che dimensioni ha la stanza? ● **size up** *vt* [!] valutare

sizzle /ˈsɪzl/ *vi* sfrigolare

skate[1] /skeɪt/ *n inv* (*fish*) razza *f*

skate[2] *n* pattino *m* ● *vi* pattinare

S

skateboard /ˈskeɪtbɔːd/ *n* skateboard *m inv*

skater /ˈskeɪtə(r)/ *n* pattinatore, -trice *mf*

skating /ˈskeɪtɪŋ/ *n* pattinaggio *m*. **~-rink** *n* pista *f* di pattinaggio

skeleton /ˈskelɪtn/ *n* scheletro *m*. **~ ˈkey** *n* passe-partout *m inv*. **~ ˈstaff** *n* personale *m* ridotto

sketch /sketʃ/ *n* schizzo *m*; (*Theat*) sketch *m inv* ● *vt* fare uno schizzo di

sketch|y /ˈsketʃɪ/ *adj* (**-ier, -iest**) abbozzato. **~ily** *adv* in modo abbozzato

ski /skiː/ *n* sci *m inv* ● *vi* (*pt/pp* **skied**, *pres p* **skiing**) sciare; **go ~ing** andare a sciare

skid /skɪd/ *n* slittata *f* ● *vi* (*pt/pp* **skidded**) slittare

skier /ˈskiːə(r)/ *n* sciatore, -trice *mf*

skiing /ˈskiːɪŋ/ *n* sci *m*

skilful /ˈskɪlfl/ *adj* abile

ˈski-lift *n* impianto *m* di risalita

skill /skɪl/ *n* abilità *f inv*. **~ed** *adj* dotato; (worker) specializzato

skim /skɪm/ *vt* (*pt/pp* **skimmed**) schiumare; scremare (milk). □ **~ off** *vt* togliere. □ **~ through** *vt* scorrere

skimp /skɪmp/ *vi* **~ on** lesinare su

skimpy /ˈskɪmpɪ/ *adj* (**-ier, -iest**) succinto

skin /skɪn/ *n* pelle *f*; (*on fruit*) buccia *f* ● *vt* (*pt/pp* **skinned**) spellare

skin: ~-deep *adj* superficiale. **~-diving** *n* nuoto *m* subacqueo

skinny /ˈskɪnɪ/ *adj* (**-ier, -iest**) molto magro

skip¹ /skɪp/ *n* (*container*) benna *f*

skip² *n* salto *m* ● *v* (*pt/pp* **skipped**) ● *vi* saltellare; (*with rope*) saltare la corda ● *vt* omettere.

skipper /ˈskɪpə(r)/ *n* skipper *m inv*

skipping-rope /ˈskɪpɪŋrəʊp/*n* corda *f* per saltare

skirmish /ˈskɜːmɪʃ/ *n* scaramuccia *f*

skirt /skɜːt/ *n* gonna *f* ● *vt* costeggiare

skittle /ˈskɪtl/ *n* birillo *m*

skulk /skʌlk/ *vi* aggirarsi furtivamente

skull /skʌl/ *n* cranio *m*

sky /skaɪ/ *n* cielo *m*. **~light** *n* lucernario *m*. **~ marshal** *n* guardia *f* armata a bordo di un aereo. **~scraper** *n* grattacielo *m*

slab /slæb/ *n* lastra *f*; (*slice*) fetta *f*; (*of chocolate*) tavoletta *f*

slack /slæk/ *adj* lento; (person) fiacco ● *vi* fare lo scansafatiche. □ **~ off** *vi* rilassarsi

slacken /ˈslækn/ *vi* allentare; **~ [off]** (trade:) rallentare; (speed, rain:) diminuire ● *vt* allentare; diminuire (speed)

slain /sleɪn/ ▷**SLAY**

slam /slæm/ *v* (*pt/pp* **slammed**) ● *vt* sbattere; (🅸: *criticize*) stroncare ● *vi* sbattere

slander /ˈslɑːndə(r)/ *n* diffamazione *f* ● *vt* diffamare. **~ous** *adj* diffamatorio

slang /slæŋ/ *n* gergo *m*. **~y** *adj* gergale

slant /slɑːnt/ *n* pendenza *f*; (*point of view*) angolazione *f*; **on the ~** in pendenza ● *vt* pendere; *fig* distorcere (report) ● *vi* pendere

slap /slæp/ *n* schiaffo *m* ● *vt* (*pt/pp* **slapped**) schiaffeggiare; (*put*) schiaffare ● *adv* in pieno

slap: ~dash *adj* 🅸 frettoloso

slash /slæʃ/ *n* taglio *m* ● *vt* tagliare; ridurre drasticamente (prices)

slat /slæt/ *n* stecca *f*

slate /sleɪt/ *n* ardesia *f* ● *vt* 🅸 fare a pezzi

slaughter /ˈslɔːtə(r)/ *n* macello *m*; (*of people*) massacro *m* ● *vt* macellare; massacrare (people). **~house** *n* macello *m*

slave /sleɪv/ *n* schiavo, -a *mf* ● *vi* **~ [away]** lavorare come un negro. **~-driver** *n* schiavista *mf*

slav|ery /ˈsleɪvərɪ/ *n* schiavitù *f inv*. **~ish** *adj* servile

slay /sleɪ/ *vt* (*pt* **slew**, *pp* **slain**) ammazzare

sleazy /ˈsliːzɪ/ *adj* (**-ier, -iest**) sordido

sledge /sledʒ/ *n* slitta *f*. **~-hammer** *n* martello *m*

sleek /sliːk/ *adj* liscio, lucente; (*well-fed*) pasciuto

sleep /sliːp/ *n* sonno *m*; **go to ~** addormentarsi; **put to ~** far addormentare ● *v* (*pt/pp* **slept**) ● *vi* dormire ● *vt* **~s six** ha sei posti letto. **~er** *n* (*Rail*) treno *m* con vagoni letto; (*compartment*) vagone *m* letto; **be a light/heavy ~er** avere il sonno leggero/pesante

sleeping: ~-bag *n* sacco *m* a pelo. **~-car** *n* vagone *m* letto. **~-pill** *n* sonnifero *m*

sleepless *adj* insonne

sleepy /'sli:pɪ/ *adj* (**-ier, -iest**) assonnato; **be ~** aver sonno

sleet /sli:t/ *n* nevischio *m* ● *vi* **it is ~ing** nevischia

sleeve /sli:v/ *n* manica *f*; (*for record*) copertina *f*. **~less** *adj* senza maniche

sleigh /sleɪ/ *n* slitta *f*

slender /'slendə(r)/ *adj* snello; (fingers, stem) affusolato; *fig* scarso; (chance) magro

slept /slept/ ▷SLEEP

slew[1] /slu:/ *vi* girare

slew[2] ▷SLAY

slice /slaɪs/ *n* fetta *f* ● *vt* affettare; **~d bread** pane *m* a cassetta

slick /slɪk/ *adj* liscio; (*cunning*) astuto ● *n* (*of oil*) chiazza *f* di petrolio

slid|e /slaɪd/ *n* scivolata *f*; (*in playground*) scivolo *m*; (*for hair*) fermaglio *m* (*per capelli*); (*Phot*) diapositiva *f* ● *v* (*pt/pp* **slid**) ● *vi* scivolare ● *vt* far scivolare. **~-rule** *n* regolo *m* calcolatore. **~ing** *adj* scorrevole; (door, seat) scorrevole; **~ing scale** scala *f* mobile

slight /slaɪt/ *adj* leggero; (importance) poco; (*slender*) esile. **~est** *adj* minimo; **not in the ~est** niente affatto ● *vt* offendere ● *n* offesa *f*. **~ly** *adv* leggermente

slim /slɪm/ *adj* (**slimmer, slimmest**) snello; *fig* scarso; (chance) magro ● *vi* dimagrire

slim|e /slaɪm/ *n* melma *f*. **~y** *adj* melmoso; *fig* viscido

sling /slɪŋ/ *n* (*Med*) benda *f* al collo ● *vt* (*pt/pp* **slung**) [!] lanciare

slip /slɪp/ *n* scivolata *f*; (*mistake*) lieve errore *m*; (*petticoat*) sottoveste *f*; (*for pillow*) federa *f*; (*paper*) scontrino *m*; **give sb the ~** [!] sbarazzarsi di qcno; **~ of the tongue** lapsus *m inv* ● *v* (*pt/pp* **slipped**) ● *vi* scivolare; (*go quickly*) sgattaiolare; (*decline*) retrocedere ● *vt* **he ~ped it into his pocket** se l'è infilato in tasca; **~ sb's mind** sfuggire di mente a qcno. □ **~ away** *vi* sgusciar via; (time:) sfuggire. □ **~ into** *vi* infilarsi (clothes). □ **~ up** *vi* [!] sbagliare

slipper /'slɪpə(r)/ *n* pantofola *f*

slippery /'slɪpərɪ/ *adj* scivoloso

slip-road *n* bretella *f*

slipshod /'slɪpʃɒd/ *adj* trascurato

'slip-up *n* [!] sbaglio *m*

slit /slɪt/ *n* spacco *m*; (*tear*) strappo *m*; (*hole*) fessura *f* ● *vt* (*pt/pp* **slit**) tagliare

slither /'slɪðə(r)/ *vi* scivolare

slobber /'slɒbə(r)/ *vi* sbavare

slog /slɒg/ *n* [**hard**] **~** sgobbata *f* ● *vi* (*pt/pp* **slogged**) (*work*) sgobbare

slogan /'sləʊgən/ *n* slogan *m inv*

slop /slɒp/ *v* (*pt/pp* **slopped**) ● *vt* versare. □ **~ over** *vi* versarsi

slop|e /sləʊp/ *n* pendenza *f*; (*ski* **~**) pista *f* ● *vi* essere inclinato, inclinarsi. **~ing** *adj* in pendenza

sloppy /'slɒpɪ/ *adj* (**-ier, -iest**) (work) trascurato; (worker) negligente; (*in dress*) sciatto; (*sentimental*) sdolcinato

slosh /slɒʃ/ *vi* [!] (person, feet:) sguazzare; (water:) scrosciare ● *vt* ([!]: *hit*) colpire

slot /slɒt/ *n* fessura *f*; (*time-*~) spazio *m* ● *v* (*pt/pp* **slotted**) ● *vt* infilare. □ **~ in** *vi* incastrarsi

'slot-machine *n* distributore *m* automatico; (*for gambling*) slot-machine *f inv*

slouch /slaʊtʃ/ *vi* (*in chair*) stare scomposto

Slovakia /slə'vækɪə/ *n* Slovacchia *f*

Slovenia /slə'vi:nɪə/ *n* Slovenia *f*

slovenl|y /'slʌvnlɪ/ *adj* sciatto. **~iness** *n* sciatteria *f*

slow /sləʊ/ *adj* lento; **be ~** (clock:) essere indietro; **in ~ motion** al rallentatore ● *adv* lentamente ● **~ down/up** *vt/i* rallentare

slowly *adv* lentamente

sludge /slʌdʒ/ *n* fanghiglia *f*

slug /slʌg/ *n* lumacone *m*; (*bullet*) pallottoia *f*. **~gish** *adj* lento

slum /slʌm/ *n* (*house*) tugurio *m*; **~s** *pl* bassifondi *mpl*

slumber /'slʌmbə(r)/ *vi* dormire

slump /slʌmp/ *n* crollo *m*; (*economic*) depressione *f* ● *vi* crollare

slung /slʌŋ/ ▷SLING

slur /slɜ:(r)/ *n* (*discredit*) calunnia *f* ● *vt* (*pt/pp* **slurred**) biascicare

slush /slʌʃ/ *n* pantano *m* nevoso; *fig* sdolcinatezza *f*. **~ fund** *n* fondi *mpl* neri. **~y** *adj* fangoso; (*sentimental*) sdolcinato

sly /slaɪ/ *adj* (**-er, -est**) scaltro ● *n* **on the ~** di nascosto

S

smack¹ /smæk/ *n* (*on face*) schiaffo *m*; (*on bottom*) sculaccione *m* ● *vt* (*on face*) schiaffeggiare; (*on bottom*) sculacciare; ~ **one's lips** far schioccare le labbra ● *adv* [!] in pieno

smack² *vi* ~ **of** *fig* sapere di

small /smɔːl/ *adj* piccolo; **be out/work** *etc* **until the ~ hours** fare le ore piccole ● *adv* **chop up ~** fare a pezzettini ● *n* **the ~ of the back** le reni *fpl*

small: ~ **ads** *npl* annunci *mpl* [commerciali]. ~ **'change** *n* spiccioli *mpl*. ~**pox** *n* vaiolo *m*. ~ **talk** *n* chiacchiere *fpl*

smart /smɑːt/ *adj* elegante; (*clever*) intelligente; (*brisk*) svelto; **be ~** ([!]: *cheeky*) fare il furbo ● *vi* (*hurt*) bruciare

smash /smæʃ/ *n* fragore *m*; (*collision*) scontro *m*; (*Tennis*) schiacciata *f* ● *vt* spaccare; (*Tennis*) schiacciare ● *vi* spaccarsi; (*crash*) schiantarsi (**into** contro). ~ [**hit**] *n* successo *m*. ~**ing** *adj* [!] fantastico

smattering /'smætərɪŋ/ *n* infarinatura *f*

smear /smɪə(r)/ *n* macchia *f*; (*Med*) striscio *m* ● *vt* imbrattare; (*coat*) spalmare (**with** di); *fig* calunniare

smell /smel/ *n* odore *m*; (*sense*) odorato *m* ● *v* (*pt/pp* **smelt** *or* **smelled**) ● *vt* odorare; (*sniff*) annusare ● *vi* odorare (**of** di)

smelly /'smelɪ/ *adj* (**-ier, -iest**) puzzolente

smelt¹ /smelt/ ▷SMELL

smelt² *vt* fondere

smile /smaɪl/ *n* sorriso *m* ● *vi* sorridere; ~ **at** sorridere a (sb); sorridere di (sth)

smirk /smɜːk/ *n* sorriso *m* compiaciuto

smithereens /smɪðə'riːnz/ *npl* **to/in ~** in mille pezzi

smock /smɒk/ *n* grembiule *m*

smog /smɒg/ *n* smog *m inv*

smoke /sməʊk/ *n* fumo *m* ● *vt/i* fumare. ~**less** *adj* senza fumo; (fuel) che non fa fumo

smoker /'sməʊkə(r)/ *n* fumatore, -trice *mf*; (*Rail*) vagone *m* fumatori

smoky /'sməʊkɪ/ *adj* (**-ier, -iest**) fumoso; (taste) di fumo

smooth /smuːð/ *adj* liscio; (movement) scorrevole; (sea) calmo; (manners) mellifluo ● *vt* lisciare. □ ~ **out** *vt* lisciare. ~**ly** *adv* in modo scorrevole

smother /'smʌðə(r)/ *vt* soffocare

smoulder /'sməʊldə(r)/ *vi* fumare; (*with rage*) consumarsi

smudge /smʌdʒ/ *n* macchia *f* ● *vt/i* imbrattare

smug /smʌg/ *adj* (**smugger, smuggest**) compiaciuto. ~**ly** *adv* con aria compiaciuta

smuggl|e /'smʌgl/ *vt* contrabbandare. ~**er** *n* contrabbandiere, a *mf*. ~**ing** *n* contrabbando *m*

snack /snæk/ *n* spuntino *m*. ~**-bar** *n* snack bar *m inv*

snag /snæg/ *n* (*problem*) intoppo *m*

snail /sneɪl/ *n* lumaca *f*; **at a ~'s pace** a passo di lumaca

snake /sneɪk/ *n* serpente *m*

snap /snæp/ *n* colpo *m* secco; (*photo*) istantanea *f* ● *attrib* (decision) istantaneo ● *v* (*pt/pp* **snapped**) ● *vi* (*break*) spezzarsi; ~ **at** (dog:) cercare di azzannare; (person:) parlare seccamente a ● *vt* (*break*) spezzare; (*say*) dire seccamente; (*Phot*) fare un'istantanea di. □ ~ **up** *vt* afferrare

snappy /'snæpɪ/ *adj* (**-ier, -iest**) scorbutico; (*smart*) elegante; **make it ~!** sbrigati!

'snapshot *n* istantanea *f*

snare /sneə(r)/ *n* trappola *f*

snarl /snɑːl/ *n* ringhio *m* ● *vi* ringhiare

snatch /snætʃ/ *n* strappo *m*; (*fragment*) brano *m*; (*theft*) scippo *m*; **make a ~ at** cercare di afferrare qcsa ● *vt* strappare [di mano] (**from** a); (*steal*) scippare; rapire (child)

sneak /sniːk/ *n* [!] spia *mf* ● *vi* ([!]: *tell tales*) fare la spia ● *vt* (*take*) rubare; ~ **a look at** dare una sbirciata a. □ ~ **in/out** *vi* sgattaiolare dentro/fuori

sneakers /'sniːkəz/ *npl Am* scarpe *fpl* da ginnastica

sneaky /'sniːkɪ/ *adj* sornione

sneer /snɪə(r)/ *n* ghigno *m* ● *vi* sogghignare; (*mock*) ridere di

sneeze /sniːz/ *n* starnuto *m* ● *vi* starnutire

snide /snaɪd/ *adj* [!] insinuante

sniff /snɪf/ *n* (*of dog*) annusata *f* ● *vi* tirare su col naso ● *vt* odorare (flower);

S

sniffare (glue, cocaine); (dog:) annusare

snigger /'snɪgə(r)/ *n* risatina *f* soffocata ● *vi* ridacchiare

snip /snɪp/ *n* taglio *m*; (🄸: *bargain*) affare *m* ● *vt/i* (*pt/pp* **snipped**) ~ [**at**] tagliare

snippet /'snɪpɪt/ *n* **a ~ of information/news** una breve notizia/informazione

snivel /'snɪvl/ *vi* (*pt/pp* **snivelled**) piagnucolare. **~ling** *adj* piagnucoloso

snob /snɒb/ *n* snob *mf*. **~bery** *n* snobismo *m*. **~bish** *adj* da snob

snooker /'snu:kə(r)/ *n* snooker *m*

snoop /snu:p/ *n* spia *f* ● *vi* 🄸 curiosare

snooze /snu:z/ *n* sonnellino *m* ● *vi* fare un sonnellino

snore /snɔ:(r)/ *vi* russare

snorkel /'snɔ:kl/ *n* respiratore *m*

snort /snɔ:t/ *n* sbuffo *n* ● *vi* sbuffare

snout /snaʊt/ *n* grugno *m*

snow /snəʊ/ *n* neve *f* ● *vi* nevicare; **~ed under with** *fig* sommerso di

snow: ~ball *n* palla *f* di neve ● *vi* fare a palle di neve. **~board** *n* snowboard *m*. **~-drift** *n* cumulo *m* di neve. **~fall** *n* nevicata *f*. **~flake** *n* fiocco *m* di neve. **~man** *n* pupazzo *m* di neve. **~-plough** *n* spazzaneve *m*. **~storm** *n* tormenta *f*. **~y** *adj* nevoso

snub /snʌb/ *n* sgarbo *m* ● *vt* (*pt/pp* **snubbed**) snobbare

'snub-nosed *adj* dal naso all'insù

snug /snʌg/ *adj* (**snugger, snuggest**) comodo; (*tight*) aderente

so /səʊ/

● *adv* così; **so far** finora; **so am I** anch'io; **so I see** così pare; **that is so** è così; **so much** così tanto; **so much the better** tanto meglio; **so it is** proprio così; **if so** se è così; **so as to** in modo da; **so long!** 🄸 a presto!

● *pron* **I hope/think/am afraid so** spero/penso/temo di sì; **I told you so** te l'ho detto; **because I say so** perché lo dico io; **I did so!** è vero!; **so saying/doing,...** così dicendo/facendo,...; **or so** circa; **very much so** sì, molto; **and so forth** *or* **on** e così via

● *conj* (*therefore*) perciò; (*in order that*) così; **so that** affinché; **so there** ecco!; **so what!** e allora?; **so where have you been?** allora, dove sei stato?

soak /səʊk/ *vt* mettere a bagno ● *vi* stare a bagno; **~ into** (liquid:) penetrare. □ **~ up** *vt* assorbire

soaking /'səʊkɪŋ/ *n* ammollo *m* ● *adj & adv* **~** [**wet**] 🄸 inzuppato

so-and-so /'səʊənsəʊ/ *n* Tal dei Tali *mf*; (*euphemism*) specie *f* di imbecille

soap /səʊp/ *n* sapone *m*. **~ opera** *n* telenovela *f*, soap opera *f inv*. **~ powder** *n* detersivo *m* in polvere

soapy /'səʊpɪ/ *adj* (**-ier, -iest**) insaponato

soar /sɔ:(r)/ *vi* elevarsi; (prices:) salire alle stelle

sob /sɒb/ *n* singhiozzo *m* ● *vi* (*pt/pp* **sobbed**) singhiozzare

sober /'səʊbə(r)/ *adj* sobrio; (*serious*) serio ● **sober up** *vi* ritornare sobrio

'so-called *adj* cosiddetto

soccer /'sɒkə(r)/ *n* calcio *m*

sociable /'səʊʃəbl/ *adj* socievole

social /'səʊʃl/ *adj* sociale; (*sociable*) socievole

socialis|m /'səʊʃəlɪzm/ *n* socialismo *m*. **~t** *adj* socialista ● *n* socialista *mf*

socialize /'səʊʃəlaɪz/ *vi* socializzare

social: ~ se'curity *n* previdenza *f* sociale. **~ worker** *n* assistente *mf* sociale

society /sə'saɪətɪ/ *n* società *f inv*

sociolog|ist /səʊsɪ'ɒlədʒɪst/ *n* sociologo, -a *mf*. **~y** *n* sociologia *f*

S

sock¹ /sɒk/ *n* calzino *m*; (*kneelength*) calza *f*

sock² *n* 🄸 pugno *m* ● *vt* 🄸 dare un pugno a

socket /'sɒkɪt/ *n* (*wall plug*) presa *f* [di corrente]; (*for bulb*) portalampada *m inv*

soda /'səʊdə/ *n* soda *f*; *Am* gazzosa *f*. **~ water** *n* seltz *m inv*

sodium /'səʊdɪəm/ *n* sodio *m*

sofa /'səʊfə/ *n* divano *m*. **~ bed** *n* divano *m* letto

soft /sɒft/ *adj* morbido, soffice; (voice) sommesso; (light, colour) tenue; (*not strict*) indulgente; (🄸: *silly*) stupido;

have a ~ spot for sb avere un debole per qcno. **~ drink** *n* bibita *f* analcolica

soften /ˈsɒfn/ *vt* ammorbidire; *fig* attenuare ● *vi* ammorbidirsi

softly /ˈsɒftlɪ/ *adv* (say) sottovoce; (treat) con indulgenza; (play music) in sottofondo

software *n* software *m*

soggy /ˈsɒgɪ/ *adj* (**-ier, -iest**) zuppo

soil[1] /sɔɪl/ *n* suolo *m*

soil[2] *vt* sporcare

solar /ˈsəʊlə(r)/ *adj* solare

sold /səʊld/ ▷SELL

solder /ˈsəʊldə(r)/ *n* lega *f* da saldatura ● *vt* saldare

soldier /ˈsəʊldʒə(r)/ *n* soldato *m* ● **soldier on** *vi* perseverare

sole[1] /səʊl/ *n* (*of foot*) pianta *f*; (*of shoe*) suola *f*

sole[2] *n* (*fish*) sogliola *f*

sole[3] *adj* unico, solo. **~ly** *adv* unicamente

solemn /ˈsɒləm/ *adj* solenne. **~ity** *n* solennità *f inv*

solicitor /səˈlɪsɪtə(r)/ *n* avvocato *m*

solid /ˈsɒlɪd/ *adj* solido; (oak, gold) massiccio ● *n* (*figure*) solido *m*; **~s** *pl* (*food*) cibi *mpl* solidi

solidarity /sɒlɪˈdærətɪ/ *n* solidarietà *f inv*

solidify /səˈlɪdɪfaɪ/ *vi* (*pt/pp* **-ied**) solidificarsi

solitary /ˈsɒlɪtərɪ/ *adj* solitario; (*sole*) solo. **~ conˈfinement** *n* cella *f* di isolamento

solitude /ˈsɒlɪtjuːd/ *n* solitudine *f*

S

solo /ˈsəʊləʊ/ *n* (*Mus*) assolo *m* ● *adj* (flight) in solitario ● *adv* in solitario. **~ist** *n* solista *mf*

solstice /ˈsɒlstɪs/ *n* solstizio *m*

soluble /ˈsɒljʊbl/ *adj* solubile

solution /səˈluːʃn/ *n* soluzione *f*

solve /sɒlv/ *vt* risolvere

solvent /ˈsɒlvənt/ *adj* solvente ● *n* solvente *m*

sombre /ˈsɒmbə(r)/ *adj* tetro; (clothes) scuro

some /sʌm/ *adj* (*a certain amount of*) del; (*a certain number of*) qualche, alcuni; **~ day** un giorno o l'altro; **I need ~ money/books** ho bisogno di soldi/libri; **do ~ shopping** fare qualche acquisto ● *pron* (*a certain amount*) un po'; (*a certain number*) alcuni; **I want ~** ne voglio

some: ~body /-bədɪ/ *pron & n* qualcuno *m*. **~how** *adv* in qualche modo; **~how or other** in un modo o nell'altro. **~one** *pron & n* = **somebody**

somersault /ˈsʌməsɔːlt/ *n* capriola *f*; **turn a ~** fare una capriola

ˈsomething *pron* qualche cosa, qualcosa; **~ different** qualcosa di diverso; **~ like** un po' come; (*approximately*) qualcosa come; **see ~ of sb** vedere qcno un po'

some: ~time *adv* un giorno o l'altro; **~times** *adv* qualche volta. **~what** *adv* piuttosto. **~where** *adv* da qualche parte ● *pron* **~where to eat** un posto in cui mangiare

son /sʌn/ *n* figlio *m*

sonata /səˈnɑːtə/ *n* sonata *f*

song /sɒŋ/ *n* canzone *f*

sonic /ˈsɒnɪk/ *adj* sonico. **~ ˈboom** *n* bang *m inv* sonico

ˈson-in-law *n* (*pl* **~s-in-law**) genero *m*

sonnet /ˈsɒnɪt/ *n* sonetto *m*

soon /suːn/ *adv* presto; (*in a short time*) tra poco; **as ~ as** [non] appena; **as ~ as possible** il più presto possibile; **~er or later** prima o poi; **the ~er the better** prima è, meglio è; **no ~er had I arrived than...** ero appena arrivato quando...; **I would ~er go** preferirei andare; **~ after** subito dopo

soot /sʊt/ *n* fuliggine *f*

sooth|e /suːð/ *vt* calmare

sooty /ˈsʊtɪ/ *adj* fuligginoso

sophisticated /səˈfɪstɪkeɪtɪd/ *adj* sofisticato

sopping /ˈsɒpɪŋ/ *adj & adv* **be ~ [wet]** essere bagnato fradicio

soppy /ˈsɒpɪ/ *adj* (**-ier, -iest**) [!] svenevole

soprano /səˈprɑːnəʊ/ *n* soprano *m*

sordid /ˈsɔːdɪd/ *adj* sordido

sore /sɔː(r)/ *adj* dolorante; (*Am: vexed*) arrabbiato; **it's ~** fa male; **have a ~ throat** avere mal di gola ● *n* piaga *f*. **~ly** *adv* (tempted) seriamente

sorrow /ˈsɒrəʊ/ *n* tristezza *f*. **~ful** *adj* triste

sorry /ˈsɒrɪ/ *adj* (**-ier, -iest**) (*sad*) spiacente; (*wretched*) pietoso; **you'll be ~!** te ne pentirai!; **I am ~** mi dispiace; **be** *or* **feel ~ for** provare compassione per; **~!** scusa!; (*more polite*) scusi!

sort /sɔ:t/ *n* specie *f*; ([!]: *person*) tipo *m*; **it's a ~ of fish** è un tipo di pesce; **be out of ~s** ([!]: *unwell*) stare poco bene ● *vt* classificare. □ **~ out** *vt* selezionare (papers); *fig* risolvere (problem); occuparsi di (person)

'so-so *adj & adv* così così

sought /sɔ:t/ ▷**SEEK**

soul /səʊl/ *n* anima *f*

sound[1] /saʊnd/ *adj* sano; (*sensible*) saggio; (*secure*) solido; (thrashing) clamoroso ● *adv* **~ asleep** profondamente addormentato

sound[2] *n* suono *m*; (*noise*) rumore *m*; **I don't like the ~ of it** [!] non mi suona bene ● *vi* suonare; (*seem*) aver l'aria ● *vt* (*pronounce*) pronunciare; (*Med*) auscoltare (chest). **~ barrier** *n* muro *m* del suono. **~ card** *n* (*Comput*) scheda *f* sonora. **~less** *adj* silenzioso. □ **~ out** *vt fig* sondare

soundly /'saʊndlɪ/ *adv* (sleep) profondamente; (defeat) clamorosamente

'sound: ~proof *adj* impenetrabile al suono. **~-track** *n* colonna *f* sonora

soup /su:p/ *n* minestra *f*. **~ed-up** *adj* [!] (engine) truccato

sour /'saʊə(r)/ *adj* agro; (*not fresh & fig*) acido

source /sɔ:s/ *n* fonte *f*

south /saʊθ/ *n* sud *m*; **to the ~ of** a sud di ● *adj* del sud, meridionale ● *adv* verso il sud

south: S~ 'Africa *n* Sudafrica *m*. **S~ A'merica** *n* America *f* del Sud. **S~ American** *adj & n* sud-americano, -a *mf*. **~-'east** *n* sud-est *m*

southerly /'sʌðəlɪ/ *adj* del sud

southern /'sʌðən/ *adj* del sud, meridionale; **~ Italy** il Mezzogiorno *m*. **~er** *n* meridionale *mf*

'southward[s] /-wəd[z]/ *adv* verso sud

souvenir /su:və'nɪə(r)/ *n* ricordo *m*, souvenir *m inv*

sovereign /'sɒvrɪn/ *adj* sovrano ● *n* sovrano, -a *mf*. **~ty** *n* sovranità *f inv*

Soviet /'səʊvɪət/ *adj* sovietico; **~ Union** Unione *f* Sovietica

sow[1] /saʊ/ *n* scrofa *f*

sow[2] /səʊ/ *vt* (*pt* **sowed**, *pp* **sown** *or* **sowed**) seminare

soya /'sɔɪə/ *n* **~ bean** soia *f*

spa /spɑ:/ *n* stazione *f* termale

space /speɪs/ *n* spazio *m* ● *adj* (research etc) spaziale ● *vt* **~ [out]** distanziare

space: ~ship *n* astronave *f*. **~ shuttle** *n* navetta *f* spaziale

spade /speɪd/ *n* vanga *f*; (*for child*) paletta *f*; **~s** *pl* (*in cards*) picche *fpl*. **~work** *n* lavoro *m* preparatorio

Spain /speɪn/ *n* Spagna *f*

spam /spæm/ spam *m*

span[1] /spæn/ *n* spanna *f*; (*of arch*) luce *f*; (*of time*) arco *m*; (*of wings*) apertura *f* ● *vt* (*pt/pp* **spanned**) estendersi su

span[2] ▷**SPICK**

Span|iard /'spænjəd/ *n* spagnolo, -a *mf*. **~ish** *adj* spagnolo ● *n* (*language*) spagnolo *m*; **the ~ish** *pl* gli spagnoli

spank /spæŋk/ *vt* sculacciare. **~ing** *n* sculacciata *f*

spanner /'spænə(r)/ *n* chiave *f* inglese

spare /speə(r)/ *adj* (*surplus*) in più; (*additional*) di riserva ● *n* (*part*) ricambio *m* ● *vt* risparmiare; (*do without*) fare a meno di; **can you ~ five minutes?** avresti cinque minuti?; **to ~** (*surplus*) in eccedenza. **~ part** *n* pezzo *m* di ricambio. **~ time** *n* tempo *m* libero. **~ 'wheel** *n* ruota *f* di scorta

spark /spɑ:k/ *n* scintilla *f*. **~ing-plug** *n* (*Auto*) candela *f*

sparkl|e /'spɑ:kl/ *n* scintillio *m* ● *vi* scintillare. **~ing** *adj* frizzante; (wine) spumante

sparrow /'spærəʊ/ *n* passero *m*

sparse /spɑ:s/ *adj* rado. **~ly** *adv* scarsamente; **~ly populated** a bassa densità di popolazione

spasm /'spæzm/ *n* spasmo *m*. **~odic** *adj* spasmodico

spat /spæt/ ▷**SPIT**[1]

spate /speɪt/ *n* (*series*) successione *f*; **be in full ~** essere in piena

spatial /'speɪʃl/ *adj* spaziale

spatter /'spætə(r)/ *vt* schizzare

spawn /spɔ:n/ *n* uova *fpl* (*di pesci, rane, ecc.*) ● *vi* deporre le uova ● *vt fig* generare

speak /spi:k/ *v* (*pt* **spoke**, *pp* **spoken**) ● *vi* parlare (**to** a); **~ing!** (*Teleph*) sono io! ● *vt* dire; ~ **one's mind** dire quello che si pensa. □ ~ **for** *vi* parlare a nome di. □ ~ **up** *vi* parlare più forte; ~ **up for oneself** parlare per se stesso

speaker /'spi:kə(r)/ *n* parlante *mf*; (*in public*) oratore, -trice *mf*; (*of stereo*) cassa *f*

spear /spɪə(r)/ *n* lancia *f*

special /'speʃl/ *adj* speciale. **~ist** *n* specialista *mf*. **~ity** *n* specialità *f inv*

special|ize /'speʃəlaɪz/ *vi* specializzarsi. **~ly** *adv* specialmente; (*particularly*) particolarmente

species /'spi:ʃi:z/ *n* specie *f inv*

specific /spə'sɪfɪk/ *adj* specifico. **~ally** *adv* in modo specifico

specify /'spesɪfaɪ/ *vt* (*pt/pp* **-ied**) specificare

specimen /'spesɪmən/ *n* campione *m*

speck /spek/ *n* macchiolina *f*; (*particle*) granello *m*

specs /speks/ *npl* [!] occhiali *mpl*

spectacle /'spektəkl/ *n* (*show*) spettacolo *m*. **~s** *npl* occhiali *mpl*

spectacular /spek'tækjʊlə(r)/ *adj* spettacolare

spectator /spek'teɪtə(r)/ *n* spettatore, -trice *mf*

spectre /'spektə(r)/ *n* spettro *m*

spectrum /'spektrəm/ *n* (*pl* **-tra**) spettro *m*; *fig* gamma *f*

speculat|e /'spekjʊleɪt/ *vi* speculare. **~ion** *n* speculazione *f*. **~ive** *adj* speculativo. **~or** *n* speculatore, -trice *mf*

sped /sped/ ▷**SPEED**

speech /spi:tʃ/ *n* linguaggio *m*; (*address*) discorso *m*. **~less** *adj* senza parole

speed /spi:d/ *n* velocità *f inv*; (*gear*) marcia *f*; **at** ~ a tutta velocità ● *vi* (*pt/pp* **sped**) andare veloce; (*pt/pp* **speeded**) (*go too fast*) andare a velocità eccessiva. □ ~ **up** (*pt/pp* **speeded up**) *vt/i* accelerare

speed: **~boat** *n* motoscafo *m*. ~ **camera** *n* Autovelox® *m inv*. ~ **dating** *n* speed dating *m*. ~ **limit** *n* limite *m* di velocità

speedometer /spi:'dɒmɪtə(r)/ *n* tachimetro *m*

speed|y /'spi:dɪ/ *adj* (**-ier, -iest**) rapido. **~ily** *adv* rapidamente

spell[1] /spel/ *n* (*turn*) turno *m*; (*of weather*) periodo *m*

spell[2] *v* (*pt/pp* **spelled, spelt**) ● *vt* **how do you ~...?** come si scrive...?; **could you ~ that for me?** me lo può compitare?; ~ **disaster** essere disastroso ● *vi* **he can't ~** fa molti errori d'ortografia

spell[3] *n* (*magic*) incantesimo *m*. **~bound** *adj* affascinato

spelling /'spelɪŋ/ *n* ortografia *f*

spelt /spelt/ ▷**SPELL**[2]

spend /spend/ *vt/i* (*pt/pp* **spent**) spendere; passare (time)

sperm /spɜ:m/ *n* spermatozoo *m*; (*semen*) sperma *m*

spew /spju:/ *vt/i* vomitare

spher|e /sfɪə(r)/ *n* sfera *f*. **~ical** *adj* sferico

spice /spaɪs/ *n* spezia *f*; *fig* pepe *m*

spick /spɪk/ *adj* ~ **and span** lindo

spicy /'spaɪsɪ/ *adj* piccante

spider /'spaɪdə(r)/ *n* ragno *m*

spik|e /spaɪk/ *n* punta *f*; (*Bot, Zool*) spina *f*; (*on shoe*) chiodo *m*. **~y** *adj* (plant) pungente

spill /spɪl/ *v* (*pt/pp* **spilt** *or* **spilled**) ● *vt* versare (blood) ● *vi* rovesciarsi

spin /spɪn/ *v* (*pt/pp* **spun**, *pres p* **spinning**) ● *vt* far girare; filare (wool); centrifugare (washing) ● *vi* girare; (washing machine:) centrifugare ● *n* rotazione *f*; (*short drive*) giretto *m*. □ ~ **out** *vt* far durare

spinach /'spɪnɪdʒ/ *n* spinaci *mpl*

spin-'drier *n* centrifuga *f*

spine /spaɪn/ *n* spina *f* dorsale; (*of book*) dorso *m*; (*Bot, Zool*) spina *f*. **~less** *adj fig* smidollato

'spin-off *n* ricaduta *f*

spiral /'spaɪrəl/ *adj* a spirale ● *n* spirale *f* ● *vi* (*pt/pp* **spiralled**) formare una spirale. ~ **'staircase** *n* scala *f* a chiocciola

spire /'spaɪə(r)/ *n* guglia *f*

spirit /'spɪrɪt/ *n* spirito *m*; (*courage*) ardore *m*; **~s** *pl* (*alcohol*) liquori *mpl*; **in good ~s** di buon umore; **in low ~s** abbattuto

spirited /'spɪrɪtɪd/ *adj* vivace; (*courageous*) pieno d'ardore

spiritual /'spɪrɪtjʊəl/ *adj* spirituale ● *n* spiritual *m*. **~ism** *n* spiritismo *m*. **~ist** *n* spiritista *mf*

S

spit¹ /spɪt/ *n* (*for roasting*) spiedo *m*

spit² *n* sputo *m* ● *vt/i* (*pt/pp* **spat**, *pres p* **spitting**) sputare; (cat:) soffiare; (fat:) sfrigolare; **it's ~ting [with rain]** pioviggina; **the ~ting image of** il ritratto spiccicato di

spite /spaɪt/ *n* dispetto *m*; **in ~ of** malgrado ● *vt* far dispetto a. **~ful** *adj* indispettito

spittle /'spɪtl/ *n* saliva *f*

splash /splæʃ/ *n* schizzo *m*; (*of colour*) macchia *f*; ([!]: *drop*) goccio *m* ● *vt* schizzare; **~ sb with sth** schizzare qcno di qcsa ● *vi* schizzare. □ **~ about** *vi* schizzarsi. □ **~ down** *vi* (spacecraft:) ammarare

splendid /'splendɪd/ *adj* splendido

splendour /'splendə(r)/ *n* splendore *m*

splint /splɪnt/ *n* (*Med*) stecca *f*

splinter /'splɪntə(r)/ *n* scheggia *f* ● *vi* scheggiarsi

split /splɪt/ *n* fessura *f*; (*quarrel*) rottura *f*; (*division*) scissione *f*; (*tear*) strappo *m* ● *v* (*pt/pp* **split**, *pres p* **splitting**) ● *vt* spaccare; (*share, divide*) dividere; (*tear*) strappare ● *vi* spaccarsi; (*tear*) strapparsi; (*divide*) dividersi; **~ on sb** [!] denunciare qcno ● *adj* **a ~ second** una frazione *f* di secondo. □ **~ up** *vt* dividersi ● *vi* (couple:) separarsi

splutter /'splʌtə(r)/ *vi* farfugliare

spoil /spɔɪl/ *n* **~s** *pl* bottino *msg* ● *v* (*pt/pp* **spoilt** *or* **spoiled**) ● *vt* rovinare; viziare (person) ● *vi* andare a male. **~sport** *n* guastafeste *mf inv*

spoke¹ /spəʊk/ *n* raggio *m*

spoke², **spoken** /'spəʊkn/ ▷**SPEAK**

'spokesman *n* portavoce *m inv*

sponge /spʌndʒ/ *n* spugna *f* ● *vt* pulire (*con la spugna*) ● *vi* **~ on** scroccare da. **~-cake** *n* pan *m* di Spagna

sponsor /'spɒnsə(r)/ *n* garante *m*; (*Radio, TV*) sponsor *m inv*; (*god-parent*) padrino *m*, madrina *f*; (*for membership*) socio, -a *mf* garante ● *vt* sponsorizzare. **~ship** *n* sponsorizzazione *f*

spontaneous /spɒn'teɪnɪəs/ *adj* spontaneo

spoof /spu:f/ *n* [!] parodia *f*

spooky /'spu:kɪ/ *adj* (**-ier, -iest**) [!] sinistro

spool /spu:l/ *n* bobina *f*

spoon /spu:n/ *n* cucchiaio *m* ● *vt* mettere col cucchiaio. **~-feed** *vt* (*pt/pp* **-fed**) *fig* imboccare. **~ful** *n* cucchiaiata *f*

sporadic /spə'rædɪk/ *adj* sporadico

sport /spɔ:t/ *n* sport *m inv* ● *vt* sfoggiare. **~ing** *adj* sportivo; **~ing chance** possibilità *f inv*

sports: ~car *n* automobile *f* sportiva. **~man** *n* sportivo *m*. **~woman** *n* sportiva *f*

spot /spɒt/ *n* macchia *f*; (*pimple*) brufolo *m*; (*place*) posto *m*; (*in pattern*) pois *m inv*; (*of rain*) goccia *f*; (*of water*) goccio *m*; **~s** *pl* (*rash*) sfogo *msg*; **a ~ of** [!] un po' di; **a ~ of bother** qualche problema; **on the ~** sul luogo; (*immediately*) immediatamente; **in a [tight] ~** [!] in difficoltà ● *vt* (*pt/pp* **spotted**) macchiare; ([!]: *notice*) individuare

spot: ~ 'check *n* (*without warning*) controllo *m* a sorpresa; **do a ~ check on sth** dare una controllata a qcsa. **~less** *adj* immacolato. **~light** *n* riflettore *m*

spotted /'spɒtɪd/ *adj* (material) a pois

spotty /'spɒtɪ/ *adj* (**-ier, -iest**) (*pimply*) brufoloso

spouse /spaʊz/ *n* consorte *mf*

spout /spaʊt/ *n* becco *m* ● *vi* zampillare (**from** da)

sprain /spreɪn/ *n* slogatura *f* ● *vt* slogare

sprang /spræŋ/ ▷**SPRING²**

spray /spreɪ/ *n* spruzzo *m*; (*preparation*) spray *m inv*; (*container*) spruzzatore *m inv* ● *vt* spruzzare. **~-gun** *n* pistola *f* a spruzzo

spread /spred/ *n* estensione *f*; (*of disease*) diffusione *f*; (*paste*) crema *f*; ([!]: *feast*) banchetto *m* ● *v* (*pt/pp* **spread**) ● *vt* spargere; spalmare (butter, jam); stendere (cloth, arms); diffondere (news, disease); dilazionare (payments); **~ sth with** spalmare qcsa di ● *vi* spargersi; (butter:) spalmarsi; (disease:) diffondersi. **~sheet** *n* (*Comput*) foglio *m* elettronico. □ **~ out** *vt* sparpagliare ● *vi* sparpagliarsi

spree /spri:/ *n* [!] **go on a ~** far baldoria; **go on a shopping ~** fare spese folli

sprightly /'spraɪtlɪ/ *adj* (**-ier, -iest**) vivace

S

spring¹ /sprɪŋ/ *n* primavera *f* ● *attrib* primaverile

spring² *n* (*jump*) balzo *m*; (*water*) sorgente *f*; (*device*) molla *f*; (*elasticity*) elasticità *f inv* ● *v* (*pt* **sprang**, *pp* **sprung**) ● *vi* balzare; (*arise*) provenire (**from** da) ● *vt* **he just sprang it on me** me l'ha detto a cose fatte compiuto. □ **~ up** balzare; *fig* spuntare

spring: ~board *n* trampolino *m*. **~time** *n* primavera *f*

sprinkl|e /'sprɪŋkl/ *vt* (*scatter*) spruzzare (liquid); spargere (flour, cocoa); **~ sth with** spruzzare qcsa di (liquid); cospargere qcsa di (flour, cocoa). **~er** *n* sprinkler *m inv*; (*for lawn*) irrigatore *m*. **~ing** *n* (*of liquid*) spruzzatina *f*; (*of pepper, salt*) pizzico *m*; (*of flour, sugar*) spolveratina *f*; (*of knowledge*) infarinatura *f*; (*of people*) pugno *m*

sprint /sprɪnt/ *n* sprint *m inv* ● *vi* fare uno sprint; (*Sport*) sprintare. **~er** *n* sprinter *mf inv*

sprout /spraʊt/ *n* germoglio *m*; [**Brussels**] **~s** *pl* cavolini *mpl* di Bruxelles ● *vi* germogliare

sprung /sprʌŋ/ ▷SPRING² ● *adj* molleggiato

spud /spʌd/ *n* 🄸 patata *f*

spun /spʌn/ ▷SPIN

spur /spɜː(r)/ *n* sperone *m*; (*stimulus*) stimolo *m*; (*road*) svincolo *m*; **on the ~ of the moment** su due piedi ● *vt* (*pt/pp* **spurred**) **~** [**on**] *fig* spronare [a]

spurn /spɜːn/ *vt* sdegnare

spurt /spɜːt/ *n* getto *m*; (*Sport*) scatto *m*; **put on a ~** fare uno scatto ● *vi* sprizzare; (*increase speed*) scattare

spy /spaɪ/ *n* spia *f* ● *v* (*pt/pp* **spied**) ● *vi* spiare ● *vt* (🄸: *see*) spiare. □ **~ on** *vi* spiare

squabble /'skwɒbl/ *n* bisticcio *m* ● *vi* bisticciare

squad /skwɒd/ *n* squadra *f*; (*Sport*) squadra

squadron /'skwɒdrən/ *n* (*Mil*) squadrone *m*; (*Aeron*), (*Naut*) squadriglia *f*

squalid /'skwɒlɪd/ *adj* squallido

squalor /'skwɒlə(r)/ *n* squallore *m*

squander /'skwɒndə(r)/ *vt* sprecare

square /skweə(r)/ *adj* quadrato; (meal) sostanzioso; (🄸: *old-fashioned*) vecchio stampo; **all ~** 🄸 pari ● *n* quadrato *m*; (*in city*) piazza *f*; (*on chessboard*) riquadro *m* ● *vt* (*settle*) far quadrare; (*Math*) elevare al quadrato ● *vi* (*agree*) armonizzare

squash /skwɒʃ/ *n* (*drink*) spremuta *f*; (*sport*) squash *m*; (*vegetable*) zucca *f* ● *vt* schiacciare; soffocare (rebellion)

squat /skwɒt/ *adj* tarchiato ● *n* 🄸 edificio *m* occupato abusivamente ● *vi* (*pt/pp* **squatted**) accovacciarsi; **~ in** occupare abusivamente. **~ter** *n* occupante *mf* abusivo, -a

squawk /skwɔːk/ *n* gracchio *m* ● *vi* gracchiare

squeak /skwiːk/ *n* squittio *m*; (*of hinge, brakes*) scricchiolio *m* ● *vi* squittire; (hinge, brakes:) scricchiolare

squeal /skwiːl/ *n* strillo *m*; (*of brakes*) cigolio *m* ● *vi* strillare; ☒ spifferare

squeamish /'skwiːmɪʃ/ *adj* dallo stomaco delicato

squeeze /skwiːz/ *n* stretta *f*; (*crush*) pigia pigia *m inv* ● *vt* premere; (*to get juice*) spremere; stringere (hand); (*force*) spingere a forza; (🄸: *extort*) estorcere (**out of** da). □ **~ in/out** *vi* sgusciare dentro/fuori. □ **~ up** *vi* stringersi

squid /skwɪd/ *n* calamaro *m*

squiggle /'skwɪgl/ *n* scarabocchio *m*

squint /skwɪnt/ *n* strabismo *m* ● *vi* essere strabico

squirm /skwɜːm/ *vi* contorcersi; (*feel embarrassed*) sentirsi imbarazzato

squirrel /'skwɪrəl/ *n* scoiattolo *m*

squirt /skwɜːt/ *n* spruzzo *m*; (🄸: *person*) presuntuoso *m* ● *vt/i* spruzzare

St *abbr* (Saint) S; *abbr* Street

stab /stæb/ *n* pugnalata *f*, coltellata *f*; (*sensation*) fitta *f*; (🄸: *attempt*) tentativo *m* ● *vt* (*pt/pp* **stabbed**) pugnalare, accoltellare

stability /stə'bɪlətɪ/ *n* stabilità *f inv*

stabilize /'steɪbɪlaɪz/ *vt* stabilizzare ● *vi* stabilizzarsi

stable¹ /'steɪbl/ *adj* stabile

stable² *n* stalla *f*; (*establishment*) scuderia *f*

stack /stæk/ *n* catasta *f*; (*of chimney*) comignolo *m*; (*chimney*) ciminiera *f*; (🄸: *large quantity*) montagna *f* ● *vt* accatastare

stadium /'steɪdɪəm/ *n* stadio *m*

staff /stɑːf/ *n* (*stick*) bastone *m*; (*employees*) personale *m*; (*teachers*) corpo *m* insegnante; (*Mil*) Stato *m* Maggiore ● *vt* fornire di personale. **~-room** *n* (*Sch*) sala *f* insegnanti

stag /stæg/ *n* cervo *m*

stage /steɪdʒ/ *n* palcoscenico *m*; (*profession*) teatro *m*; (*in journey*) tappa *f*; (*in process*) stadio *m*; **go on the ~** darsi al teatro; **by** *or* **in ~s** a tappe ● *vt* mettere in scena; (*arrange*) organizzare

stagger /ˈstægə(r)/ *vi* barcollare ● *vt* sbalordire; scaglionare (holidays etc); **I was ~ed** sono rimasto sbalordito ● *n* vacillamento *m*. **~ing** *adj* sbalorditivo

stagnant /ˈstægnənt/ *adj* stagnante

stagnat|e /stægˈneɪt/ *vi fig* [ri]stagnare. **~ion** *n fig* inattività *f*

ˈstag party *n* addio *m* al celibato

staid /steɪd/ *adj* posato

stain /steɪn/ *n* macchia *f*; (*for wood*) mordente *m* ● *vt* macchiare; (wood) dare il mordente a; **~ed glass** vetro *m* colorato; **~ed-glass window** vetrata *f* colorata. **~less** *adj* senza macchia; (steel) inossidabile. **~ remover** *n* smacchiatore *m*

stair /steə(r)/ *n* gradino *m*; **~s** *pl* scale *fpl*. **~case** *n* scale *fpl*

stake /steɪk/ *n* palo *m*; (*wager*) posta *f*; (*Comm*) partecipazione *f*; **at ~** in gioco ● *vt* puntellare; (*wager*) scommettere

stale /steɪl/ *adj* stantio; (air) viziato; (*uninteresting*) trito [e ritrito]. **~mate** *n* (*in chess*) stallo *m*; (*deadlock*) situazione *f* di stallo

stalk[1] /stɔːk/ *n* gambo *m*

stalk[2] *vt* inseguire ● *vi* camminare impettito

stall /stɔːl/ *n* box *m inv*; (*in market*) bancarella *f*; **~s** *pl* (*Theat*) platea *f* ● *vi* (engine:) spegnersi; *fig* temporeggiare ● *vt* far spegnere (engine); tenere a bada (person)

stallion /ˈstæljən/ *n* stallone *m*

stalwart /ˈstɔːlwət/ *adj* fedele

stamina /ˈstæmɪnə/ *n* [capacità *f inv* di] resistenza *f*

stammer /ˈstæmə(r)/ *n* balbettio *m* ● *vt/i* balbettare

stamp /stæmp/ *n* (*postage ~*) francobollo *m*; (*instrument*) timbro *m*; *fig* impronta *f* ● *vt* affrancare (letter); timbrare (bill); battere (feet). □ **~ out** *vt* spegnere; *fig* soffocare

stampede /stæmˈpiːd/ *n* fuga *f* precipitosa; [!] fuggi-fuggi *m* ● *vi* fuggire precipitosamente

stance /stɑːns/ *n* posizione *f*

stand /stænd/ *n* (*for bikes*) rastrelliera *f*; (*at exhibition*) stand *m inv*; (*in market*) bancarella *f*; (*in stadium*) gradinata *f inv*; *fig* posizione *f* ● *v* (*pt/pp* **stood**) ● *vi* stare in piedi; (*rise*) alzarsi [in piedi]; (*be*) trovarsi; (*be candidate*) essere candidato (**for** a); (*stay valid*) rimanere valido; **~ still** non muoversi; **I don't know where I ~** non so qual'è la mia posizione; **~ firm** *fig* tener duro; **~ together** essere solidali; **~ to lose/gain** rischiare di perdere/vincere; **~ to reason** essere logico ● *vt* (*withstand*) resistere a; (*endure*) sopportare; (*place*) mettere; **~ a chance** avere una possibilità; **~ one's ground** tener duro; **~ the test of time** superare la prova del tempo; **~ sb a beer** offrire una birra a qcno. □ **~ by** *vi* stare a guardare; (*be ready*) essere pronto ● *vt* (*support*) appoggiare. □ **~ down** *vi* (*retire*) ritirarsi. □ **~ for** *vt* (*mean*) significare; (*tolerate*) tollerare. □ **~ in for** *vt* sostituire. □ **~ out** *vi* spiccare. □ **~ up** *vi* alzarsi [in piedi]. □ **~ up for** *vt* prendere le difese di; **~ up for oneself** farsi valere. □ **~ up to** *vt* affrontare

standard /ˈstændəd/ *adj* standard; **be ~ practice** essere pratica corrente ● *n* standard *m inv*; (*Techn*) norma *f*; (*level*) livello *m*; (*quality*) qualità *f inv*; (*flag*) stendardo *m*; **~s** *pl* (*morals*) valori *mpl*; **~ of living** tenore *m* di vita. **~ize** *vt* standardizzare

ˈstandard lamp *n* lampada *f* a stelo

ˈstand-by *n* riserva *f*; **on ~** (*at airport*) in lista d'attesa

ˈstand-in *n* controfigura *f*

standing /ˈstændɪŋ/ *adj* (*erect*) in piedi; (*permanent*) permanente ● *n* posizione *f*; (*duration*) durata *f*. **~ ˈorder** *n* addebitamento *m* diretto. **~-room** *n* posti *mpl* in piedi

stand: ~point *n* punto *m* di vista. **~still** *n* **come to a ~still** fermarsi; **at a ~still** in un periodo di stasi

stank /stæŋk/ ▸**STINK**

S

staple¹ /ˈsteɪpl/ *n* (*product*) prodotto *m* principale

staple² *n* graffa *f* ● *vt* pinzare. **~r** *n* pinzatrice *f*, cucitrice *f*

star /stɑː(r)/ *n* stella *f*; (*asterisk*) asterisco *m*; (*Cinema, Sport, Theat*) divo, -a *mf*, stella *f* ● *vi* (*pt/pp* **starred**) essere l'interprete principale

starboard /ˈstɑːbəd/ *n* tribordo *m*

starch /stɑːtʃ/ *n* amido *m* ● *vt* inamidare. **~y** *adj* ricco di amido; *fig* compito

stare /steə(r)/ *n* sguardo *m* fisso ● *vi* **it's rude to ~** è da maleducati fissare la gente; **~ at** fissare; **~ into space** guardare nel vuoto

ˈstarfish *n* stella *f* di mare

stark /stɑːk/ *adj* austero; (contrast) forte ● *adv* completamente; **~ naked** completamente nudo

starling /ˈstɑːlɪŋ/ *n* storno *m*

starry /ˈstɑːrɪ/ *adj* stellato

start /stɑːt/ *n* inizio *m*; (*departure*) partenza *f*; (*jump*) sobbalzo *m*; **from the ~** [fin] dall'inizio; **for a ~** tanto per cominciare; **give sb a ~** (*Sport*) dare un vantaggio a qcno ● *vi* [in]cominciare; (*set out*) avviarsi; (engine, car:) partire; (*jump*) trasalire; **to ~ with,...** tanto per cominciare,... ● *vt* [in]cominciare; (*cause*) dare inizio a; (*found*) mettere su; mettere in moto (car); mettere in giro (rumour). **~er** *n* (*Culin*) primo *m* [piatto *m*]; (*in race: giving signal*) starter *m inv*; (*participant*) concorrente *mf*; (*Auto*) motorino *m* d'avviamento. **~ing-point** *n* punto *m* di partenza

startle /ˈstɑːtl/ *vt* far trasalire; (news:) sconvolgere

starvation /stɑːˈveɪʃn/ *n* fame *f*

starve /stɑːv/ *vi* morire di fame ● *vt* far morire di fame

state /steɪt/ *n* stato *m*; (*grand style*) pompa *f*; **~ of play** punteggio *m*; **be in a ~** (person:) essere agitato; **lie in ~** essere esposto ● *attrib* di Stato; (*Sch*) pubblico; (*with ceremony*) di gala ● *vt* dichiarare; (*specify*) precisare. **~less** *adj* apolide

stately /ˈsteɪtlɪ/ *adj* (**-ier, -iest**) maestoso. **~ ˈhome** *n* dimora *f* signorile

statement /ˈsteɪtmənt/ *n* dichiarazione *f*; (*Jur*) deposizione *f*; (*in banking*) estratto *m* conto; (*account*) rapporto *m*

> **i** **state schools** In Gran Bretagna sono le scuole elementari, medie e superiori pubbliche, contrapposte alle *public schools* (scuole private).

ˈstatesman *n* statista *mf*

static /ˈstætɪk/ *adj* statico

station /ˈsteɪʃn/ *n* stazione *f*; (*police*) commissariato *m* ● *vt* appostare (guard); **be ~ed in Germany** essere di stanza in Germania. **~ary** *adj* immobile

ˈstation-wagon *n Am* familiare *f*

statistic|al /stəˈtɪstɪkl/ *adj* statistico. **~s** *n & pl* statistica *f*

statue /ˈstætjuː/ *n* statua *f*

stature /ˈstætʃə(r)/ *n* statura *f*

status /ˈsteɪtəs/ *n* condizione *f*; (*high rank*) alto rango *m*. **~ symbol** *n* status symbol *m inv*

statut|e /ˈstætjuːt/ *n* statuto *m*. **~ory** *adj* statutario

staunch /stɔːntʃ/ *adj* fedele. **~ly** *adv* fedelmente

stave /steɪv/ *vt* **~ off** tenere lontano

stay /steɪ/ *n* soggiorno *m* ● *vi* restare, rimanere; (*reside*) alloggiare; **~ the night** passare la notte; **~ put** non muoversi ● *vt* **~ the course** resistere fino alla fine. □ **~ away** *vi* stare lontano. □ **~ behind** *vi* non andare con gli altri. □ **~ in** *vi* (*at home*) stare in casa; (*Sch*) *restare a scuola dopo le lezioni*. □ **~ up** *vi* stare su; (person:) stare alzato

stead /sted/ *n* **in his ~** in sua vece; **stand sb in good ~** tornare utile a qcno. **~fast** *adj* fedele; (refusal) fermo

steadily /ˈstedɪlɪ/ *adv* (*continually*) continuamente

steady /ˈstedɪ/ *adj* (**-ier, -iest**) saldo, fermo; (breathing) regolare; (job, boyfriend) fisso; (*dependable*) serio

steak /steɪk/ *n* (*for stew*) spezzatino *m*; (*for grilling, frying*) bistecca *f*

steal /stiːl/ *v* (*pt* **stole**, *pp* **stolen**) ● *vt* rubare (**from** da). □ **~ in**/**out** *vi* entrare/uscire furtivamente

stealth /stelθ/ *n* **by ~** di nascosto. **~y** *adj* furtivo

steam /stiːm/ *n* vapore *m*; **under one's own ~** [!] da solo ● *vt* (*Culin*)

S

cucinare a vapore • *vi* fumare. □ ~ **up** *vi* appannarsi

'steam-engine *n* locomotiva *f*

steamer /'sti:mə(r)/ *n* piroscafo *m*; (*saucepan*) pentola *f* a vapore

'steamroller *n* rullo *m* compressore

steamy /'sti:mɪ/ *adj* appannato

steel /sti:l/ *n* acciaio *m* • *vt* ~ **oneself** temprarsi

steep¹ /sti:p/ *vt* (*soak*) lasciare a bagno

steep² *adj* ripido; ([!]: price) esorbitante. ~**ly** *adv* ripidamente

steeple /'sti:pl/ *n* campanile *m*. ~**chase** *n* corsa *f* ippica a ostacoli

steer /stɪə(r)/ *vt/i* guidare; ~ **clear of** stare alla larga da. ~**ing** *n* (*Auto*) sterzo *m*. ~**ing-wheel** *n* volante *m*

stem¹ /stem/ *n* stelo *m*; (*of glass*) gambo *m*; (*of word*) radice *f* • *vi* (*pt/pp* **stemmed**) ~ **from** derivare da

stem² *vt* (*pt/pp* **stemmed**) contenere

stench /stentʃ/ *n* fetore *m*

step /step/ *n* passo *m*; (*stair*) gradino *m*; ~**s** *pl* (*ladder*) scala *f* portatile; **in** ~ al passo; **be out of** ~ non stare al passo; ~ **by** ~ un passo alla volta • *vi* (*pt/pp* **stepped**) ~ **into** entrare in; ~ **out of** uscire da; ~ **out of line** sgarrare. □ ~ **down** *vi fig* dimettersi. □ ~ **forward** *vi* farsi avanti. □ ~ **in** *vi fig* intervenire. □ ~ **up** *vt* (*increase*) aumentare

step: ~**brother** *n* fratellastro *m*. ~**daughter** *n* figliastra *f*. ~**father** *n* patrigno *m*. ~**-ladder** *n* scala *f* portatile. ~**mother** *n* matrigna *f*

'stepping-stone *n* pietra *f* per guadare; *fig* trampolino *m*

step: ~**sister** *n* sorellastra *f*. ~**son** *n* figliastro *m*

stereo /'sterɪəʊ/ *n* stereo *m*; **in** ~ in stereofonia. ~**phonic** *adj* stereofonico

stereotype /'sterɪətaɪp/ *n* stereotipo *m*. ~**d** *adj* stereotipato

steril|e /'steraɪl/ *adj* sterile. ~**ity** *n* sterilità *f inv*

sterling /'stɜ:lɪŋ/ *adj fig* apprezzabile; ~ **silver** argento *m* pregiato • *n* sterlina *f*

stern¹ /stɜ:n/ *adj* severo

stern² *n* (*of boat*) poppa *f*

stethoscope /'steθəskəʊp/ *n* stetoscopio *m*

stew /stju:/ *n* stufato *m*; **in a** ~ [!] agitato • *vt/i* cuocere in umido; ~**ed fruit** frutta *f* cotta

steward /'stju:əd/ *n* (*at meeting*) organizzatore, -trice *mf*; (*on ship, aircraft*) steward *m inv*. ~**ess** *n* hostess *f inv*

stick¹ /stɪk/ *n* bastone *m*; (*of celery, rhubarb*) gambo *m*; (*Sport*) mazza *f*

stick² *v* (*pt/pp* **stuck**) • *vt* (*stab*) [con-]ficcare; (*glue*) attaccare; ([!]: *put*) mettere; ([!]: *endure*) sopportare • *vi* (*adhere*) attaccarsi (**to** a); (*jam*) bloccarsi; ~ **to** attenersi a (facts); mantenere (story); perseverare in (task); ~ **at it** [!] tener duro; ~ **at nothing** [!] non fermarsi di fronte a niente; **be stuck** (vehicle, person:) essere bloccato; (drawer:) essere incastrato; **be stuck with sth** [!] farsi incastrare con qcsa. □ ~ **out** *vi* (*project*) sporgere; ([!]: *catch the eye*) risaltare • *vt* [!] fare (tongue). □ ~ **up for** *vt* [!] difendere

sticker /'stɪkə(r)/ *n* autoadesivo *m*

'sticking plaster *n* cerotto *m*

stickler /'stɪklə(r)/ *n* **be a** ~ **for** tenere molto a

sticky /'stɪkɪ/ *adj* (**-ier, -iest**) appiccicoso; (*adhesive*) adesivo; (*fig: difficult*) difficile

stiff /stɪf/ *adj* rigido; (brush, task) duro; (person) controllato; (drink) forte; (penalty) severo; (price) alto; **bored** ~ [!] annoiato a morte; ~ **neck** torcicollo *m*. ~**en** *vt* irrigidire • *vi* irrigidirsi. ~**ness** *n* rigidità *f inv*

stifl|e /'staɪfl/ *vt* soffocare. ~**ing** *adj* soffocante

still¹ /stɪl/ *n* distilleria *f*

still² *adj* fermo; (drink) non gasato; **keep/stand** ~ stare fermo • *n* quiete *f*; (*photo*) posa *f* • *adv* ancora; (*nevertheless*) nondimeno, comunque; **I'm** ~ **not sure** non sono ancora sicuro

'stillborn *adj* nato morto

still 'life *n* natura *f* morta

stilted /'stɪltɪd/ *adj* artificioso

stilts /stɪlts/ *npl* trampoli *mpl*

stimulant /'stɪmjʊlənt/ *n* eccitante *m*

stimulat|e /'stɪmjʊleɪt/ *vt* stimolare. ~**ion** *n* stimolo *m*

stimulus /'stɪmjʊləs/ *n* (*pl* **-li** /-laɪ/) stimolo *m*

sting /stɪŋ/ *n* puntura *f*; (*from nettle,*

jellyfish) sostanza *f* irritante; (*organ*) pungiglione *m* ● *v* (*pt/pp* **stung**) ● *vt* pungere; (jellyfish:) pizzicare ● *vi* (insect:) pungere. **~ing nettle** *n* ortica *f*

stingy /'stɪndʒɪ/ *adj* (**-ier, -iest**) tirchio

stink /stɪŋk/ *n* puzza *f* ● *vi* (*pt* **stank**, *pp* **stunk**) puzzare

stipulat|e /'stɪpjʊleɪt/ *vt* porre come condizione. **~ion** *n* condizione *f*

stir /stɜː(r)/ *n* mescolata *f*; (*commotion*) trambusto *m* ● *v* (*pt/pp* **stirred**) ● *vt* muovere; (*mix*) mescolare ● *vi* muoversi

stirrup /'stɪrəp/ *n* staffa *f*

stitch /stɪtʃ/ *n* punto *m*; (*in knitting*) maglia *f*; (*pain*) fitta *f*; **have sb in ~es** [!] far ridere qcno a crepapelle ● *vt* cucire

stock /stɒk/ *n* (*for use or selling*) scorta *f*, stock *m inv*; (*livestock*) bestiame *m*; (*lineage*) stirpe *f*; (*Fin*) titoli *mpl*; (*Culin*) brodo *m*; **in ~** disponibile; **out of ~** esaurito; **take ~** *fig* fare il punto ● *adj* solito ● *vt* (shop:) vendere; approvvigionare (shelves). □ **~ up** *vi* far scorta (**with** di)

stock: ~broker *n* agente *m* di cambio. **S~ Exchange** *n* Borsa *f* Valori

stocking /'stɒkɪŋ/ *n* calza *f*

stock: ~pile *vt* fare scorta di ● *n* riserva *f*. **~-'still** *adj* immobile. **~-taking** *n* (*Comm*) inventario *m*

stocky /'stɒkɪ/ *adj* (**-ier, -iest**) tarchiato

stodgy /'stɒdʒɪ/ *adj* indigesto

stoke /stəʊk/ *vt* alimentare

stole[1] /stəʊl/ *n* stola *f*

stole[2], **stolen** /'stəʊln/ ▷**STEAL**

stomach /'stʌmək/ *n* pancia *f*; (*Anat*) stomaco *m* ● *vt* [!] reggere. **~-ache** *n* mal *m* di pancia

stone /stəʊn/ *n* pietra *f*; (*in fruit*) nocciolo *m*; (*Med*) calcolo *m*; (*weight*) *6,348 kg* ● *adj* di pietra; (wall, Age) della pietra ● *vt* snocciolare (fruit). **~-cold** *adj* gelido. **~-'deaf** *adj* [!] sordo come una campana

stony /'stəʊnɪ/ *adj* pietroso; (glare) glaciale

stood /stʊd/ ▷**STAND**

stool /stuːl/ *n* sgabello *m*

stoop /stuːp/ *n* curvatura *f* ● *vi* stare curvo; (*bend down*) chinarsi; *fig* abbassarsi

stop /stɒp/ *n* (*break*) sosta *f*; (*for bus, train*) fermata *f*; (*Gram*) punto *m*; **come to a ~** fermarsi; **put a ~ to sth** mettere fine a qcsa ● *v* (*pt/pp* **stopped**) ● *vt* fermare; arrestare (machine); (*prevent*) impedire; **~ sb doing sth** impedire a qcno di fare qcsa; **~ doing sth** smettere di fare qcsa; **~ that!** smettila! ● *vi* fermarsi; (rain:) smettere ● *int* fermo!. □ **~ off** *vi* fare una sosta. □ **~ up** *vt* otturare (sink); tappare (hole). □ **~ with** *vi* ([!]: *stay with*) fermarsi da

stop: ~gap *n* palliativo *m*; (*person*) tappabuchi *m inv*. **~-over** *n* sosta *f*; (*Aeron*) scalo *m*

stoppage /'stɒpɪdʒ/ *n* ostruzione *f*; (*strike*) interruzione *f*; (*deduction*) trattenute *fpl*

stopper /'stɒpə(r)/ *n* tappo *m*

stop-watch *n* cronometro *m*

storage /'stɔːrɪdʒ/ *n* deposito *m*; (*in warehouse*) immagazzinaggio *m*; (*Comput*) memoria *f*

store /stɔː(r)/ *n* (*stock*) riserva *f*; (*shop*) grande magazzino *m*; (*depot*) deposito *m*; **in ~** in deposito; **what the future has in ~ for me** cosa mi riserva il futuro; **set great ~ by** tenere in gran conto ● *vt* tenere; (*in warehouse*, (*Comput*)) immagazzinare. **~-room** *n* magazzino *m*

storey /'stɔːrɪ/ *n* piano *m*

stork /stɔːk/ *n* cicogna *f*

storm /stɔːm/ *n* temporale *m*; (*with thunder*) tempesta *f* ● *vt* prendere d'assalto. **~y** *adj* tempestoso

story /'stɔːrɪ/ *n* storia *f*; (*in newspaper*) articolo *m*

stout /staʊt/ *adj* (shoes) resistente; (*fat*) robusto; (defence) strenuo

stove /stəʊv/ *n* stufa *f*; (*for cooking*) cucina *f* [economica]

stow /stəʊ/ *vt* metter via. **~away** *n* passeggero, -a *mf* clandestino, -a

straggl|e /'strægl/ *vi* crescere disordinatamente; (*dawdle*) rimanere indietro. **~er** *n* persona *f* che rimane indietro. **~y** *adj* in disordine

straight /streɪt/ *adj* diritto, dritto; (answer, question, person) diretto; (*tidy*) in ordine; (drink, hair) liscio ● *adv* diritto, dritto; (*directly*) direttamente; **~ away** immediatamente; **~ on** *or* **ahead** diritto; **~ out** *fig* apertamente; **go ~** [!] rigare diritto; **put sth ~** mettere qcsa in ordine; **sit/stand up ~** stare diritto

straighten /'streɪtn/ *vt* raddrizzare ● *vi* raddrizzarsi; **~** [**up**] (person:) mettersi diritto. □ **~ out** *vt fig* chiarire (situation)

straight'forward *adj* franco; (*simple*) semplice

strain¹ /streɪn/ *n* (*streak*) vena *f*; (*Bot*) varietà *f inv*; (*of virus*) forma *f*

strain² *n* tensione *f*; (*injury*) stiramento *m*; **~s** *pl* (*of music*) note *fpl* ● *vt* tirare; sforzare (eyes, voice); stirarsi (muscle); (*Culin*) scolare ● *vi* sforzarsi. **~ed** *adj* (relations) teso. **~er** *n* colino *m*

strait /streɪt/ *n* stretto *m*; **in dire ~s** in serie difficoltà. **~-jacket** *n* camicia *f* di forza. **~-'laced** *adj* puritano

strand¹ /strænd/ *n* (*of thread*) gugliata *f*; (*of beads*) filo *m*; (*of hair*) capello *m*

strand² *vt* **be ~ed** rimanere bloccato

strange /streɪndʒ/ *adj* strano; (*not known*) sconosciuto; (*unaccustomed*) estraneo. **~ly** *adv* stranamente; **~ly enough** curiosamente. **~r** *n* estraneo, -a *mf*

strangle /'stræŋgl/ *vt* strangolare; *fig* reprimere

strap /stræp/ *n* cinghia *f* (*to grasp in vehicle*) maniglia *f*; (*of watch*) cinturino *m*; (*shoulder ~*) bretella *f*, spallina *f* ● *vt* (*pt/pp* **strapped**) legare; **~ in** *or* **down** assicurare

strategic /strə'ti:dʒɪk/ *adj* strategico

strategy /'strætədʒɪ/ *n* strategia *f*

straw /strɔ:/ *n* paglia *f*; (*single piece*) fuscello *m*; (*for drinking*) cannuccia *f*; **the last ~** l'ultima goccia

strawberry /'strɔ:bərɪ/ *n* fragola *f*

stray /streɪ/ *adj* (*animal*) randagio ● *n* randagio *m* ● *vi* andarsene per conto proprio; (*deviate*) deviare (**from** da)

streak /stri:k/ *n* striatura *f*; (*fig: trait*) vena *f* ● *vi* sfrecciare. **~y** *adj* striato; (bacon) grasso

stream /stri:m/ *n* ruscello *m*; (*current*) corrente *f*; (*of blood, people*) flusso *m*; (*Sch*) classe *f* ● *vi* scorrere. □ **~ in/out** *vi* entrare/uscire a fiotti

streamer /'stri:mə(r)/ *n* (*paper*) stella *f* filante; (*flag*) pennone *m*

'streamline *vt* rendere aerodinamico; (*simplify*) snellire. **~d** *adj* aerodinamico

street /stri:t/ *n* strada *f*. **~car** *n Am* tram *m inv*. **~lamp** *n* lampione *m*

strength /streŋθ/ *n* forza *f*; (*of wall, bridge etc*) solidità *f inv*; **~s** punti *mpl* forti; **on the ~ of** grazie a. **~en** *vt* rinforzare

strenuous /'strenjʊəs/ *adj* faticoso; (attempt, denial) energico

stress /stres/ *n* (*emphasis*) insistenza *f*; (*Gram*) accento *m* tonico; (*mental*) stress *m inv*; (*Mech*) spinta *f* ● *vt* (*emphasize*) insistere su; (*Gram*) mettere l'accento [tonico] su. **~ed** *adj* (*mentally*) stressato. **~ful** *adj* stressante

stretch /stretʃ/ *n* stiramento *m*; (*period*) periodo *m* di tempo; (*of road*) estensione *f*; (*elasticity*) elasticità *f inv*; **at a ~** di fila; **have a ~** stirarsi ● *vt* tirare; allargare (shoes, arms etc); (person:) allungare ● *vi* (*become wider*) allargarsi; (*extend*) estendersi; (person:) stirarsi. **~er** *n* barella *f*

strict /strɪkt/ *adj* severo; (*precise*) preciso. **~ly** *adv* severamente; **~ly speaking** in senso stretto

stride /straɪd/ *n* [lungo] passo *m*; **take sth in one's ~** accettare qcsa con facilità ● *vi* (*pt* **strode**, *pp* **stridden**) andare a gran passi

strident /'straɪdənt/ *adj* stridente; (colour) vistoso

strife /straɪf/ *n* conflitto *m*

strike /straɪk/ *n* sciopero *m*; (*Mil*) attacco *m*; **on ~** in sciopero ● *v* (*pt/pp* **struck**) ● *vt* colpire; accendere (match); trovare (oil, gold); (*delete*) depennare; (*occur to*) venire in mente a; (*Mil*) attaccare ● *vi* (lightning:) cadere; (clock:) suonare; (*Mil*) attaccare; (workers:) scioperare; **~ lucky** azzeccarla. □ **~ off, strike out** *vt* eliminare. □ **~ up** *vt* fare (friendship); attaccare (conversation). **~-breaker** *n persona f che non aderisce a uno sciopero*

striker /'straɪkə(r)/ *n* scioperante *mf*

striking /'straɪkɪŋ/ *adj* impressionante; (*attractive*) affascinante

string /strɪŋ/ *n* spago *m*; (*of musical instrument, racket*) corda *f*; (*of pearls*) filo *m*; (*of lies*) serie *f*; **the ~s** (*Mus*) gli archi; **pull ~s** [!] usare le proprie conoscenze ● *vt* (*pt/pp* **strung**) (*thread*) infilare (beads). **~ed** *adj* (instrument) a corda

stringent /'strɪndʒnt/ *adj* rigido

S

strip /strɪp/ *n* striscia *f* ● *v* (*pt/pp* **stripped**) ● *vt* spogliare; togliere le lenzuola da (bed); scrostare (wood, furniture); smontare (machine); (*deprive*) privare (**of** di) ● *vi* (*undress*) spogliarsi. ~ **cartoon** *n* striscia *f*. ~ **club** *n* locale *m* di strip-tease

stripe /straɪp/ *n* striscia *f*; (*Mil*) gallone *m*. ~**d** *adj* a strisce

strip-'tease *n* spogliarello *m*, strip-tease *m inv*

strive /straɪv/ *vi* (*pt* **strove**, *pp* **striven**) sforzarsi (**to** di); ~ **for** sforzarsi di ottenere

strode /strəʊd/ ▷**STRIDE**

stroke¹ /strəʊk/ *n* colpo *m*; (*of pen*) tratto *m*; (*in swimming*) bracciata *f*; (*Med*) ictus *m inv*; ~ **of luck** colpo *m* di fortuna; **put sb off his** ~ far perdere il filo a qcno

stroke² *vt* accarezzare

stroll /strəʊl/ *n* passeggiata *f* ● *vi* passeggiare. ~**er** *n* (*Am: push-chair*) passeggino *m*

strong /strɒŋ/ *adj* (**-er** /-gə(r)/, **-est** /-gɪst/) forte; (argument) valido

strong: ~**hold** *n* roccaforte *f*. ~**ly** *adv* fortemente. ~**-room** *n* camera *f* blindata

stroppy /'strɒpɪ/ *adj* scorbutico

strove /strəʊv/ ▷**STRIVE**

struck /strʌk/ ▷**STRIKE**

structural /'strʌktʃərəl/ *adj* strutturale. ~**ly** *adv* strutturalmente

structure /'strʌktʃə(r)/ *n* struttura *f*

struggle /'strʌgl/ *n* lotta *f*; **without a** ~ senza lottare ● *vi* lottare; ~ **for breath** respirare con fatica; ~ **to do sth** fare fatica a fare qcsa; ~ **to one's feet** alzarsi con fatica

strum /strʌm/ *vt/i* (*pt/pp* **strummed**) strimpellare

strung /strʌŋ/ ▷**STRING**

strut¹ /strʌt/ *n* (*component*) puntello *m*

strut² *vi* (*pt/pp* **strutted**) camminare impettito

stub /stʌb/ *n* mozzicone *m*; (*counterfoil*) matrice *f* ● *vt* (*pt/pp* **stubbed**) ~ **one's toe** sbattere il dito del piede (**on** contro). □ ~ **out** *vt* spegnere (cigarette)

stubb|le /'stʌbl/ *n* barba *f* ispida. ~**ly** *adj* ispido

stubborn /'stʌbən/ *adj* testardo; (refusal) ostinato

stuck /stʌk/ ▷**STICK²**. ~**-'up** *adj* [!] snob

stud¹ /stʌd/ *n* (*on boot*) tacchetto *m*; (*on jacket*) borchia *f*; (*for ear*) orecchino *m* [a bottone]

stud² *n* (*of horses*) scuderia *f*

student /'stju:dənt/ *n* studente *m*, studentessa *f*; (*school child*) scolaro, -a *mf*. ~ **nurse** *n* studente, studentessa infermiere, -a

studio /'stju:dɪəʊ/ *n* studio *m*

studious /'stju:dɪəs/ *adj* studioso; (attention) studiato

study /'stʌdɪ/ *n* studio *m* ● *vt/i* (*pt/pp* **studied**) studiare

stuff /stʌf/ *n* materiale *m*; ([!]: *things*) roba *f* ● *vt* riempire; (*with padding*) imbottire; (*Culin*) farcire; ~ **sth into a drawer/one's pocket** ficcare qcsa alla rinfusa in un cassetto/in tasca. ~**ing** *n* (*padding*) imbottitura *f*; (*Culin*) ripieno *m*

stuffy /'stʌfɪ/ *adj* (**-ier, -iest**) che sa di chiuso; (*old-fashioned*) antiquato

stumbl|e /'stʌmbl/ *vi* inciampare; ~**e across** *or* **on** imbattersi in. ~**ing-block** *n* ostacolo *m*

stump /stʌmp/ *n* ceppo *m*; (*of limb*) moncone *m*. ~**ed** *adj* [!] perplesso ● **stump up** *vt/i* [!] sganciare

stun /stʌn/ *vt* (*pt/pp* **stunned**) stordire; (*astonish*) sbalordire

stung /stʌŋ/ ▷**STING**

stunk /stʌŋk/ ▷**STINK**

stunning /'stʌnɪŋ/ *adj* [!] favoloso; (blow, victory) sbalorditivo

stunt¹ /stʌnt/ *n* [!] trovata *f* pubblicitaria

stunt² *vt* arrestare lo sviluppo di. ~**ed** *adj* stentato

stupendous /stju:'pendəs/ *adj* stupendo. ~**ly** *adv* stupendamente

stupid /'stju:pɪd/ *adj* stupido. ~**ity** *n* stupidità *f*. ~**ly** *adv* stupidamente

stupor /'stju:pə(r)/ *n* torpore *m*

sturdy /'stɜ:dɪ/ *adj* (**-ier, -iest**) robusto; (furniture) solido

stutter /'stʌtə(r)/ *n* balbuzie *f* ● *vt/i* balbettare

sty, **stye** /staɪ/ *n* (*pl* **styes**) (*Med*) orzaiolo *m*

style /staɪl/ *n* stile *m*; (*fashion*) moda *f*;

(*sort*) tipo m; (*hair*~) pettinatura *f*; **in ~** in grande stile

stylish /'staɪlɪʃ/ *adj* elegante. **~ly** *adv* con eleganza

stylist /'staɪlɪst/ *n* stilista *mf*; (*hair*-~) parrucchiere, -a *mf*. **~ic** *adj* stilistico

stylus /'staɪləs/ *n* (*on record player*) puntina *f*

suave /swɑ:v/ *adj* dai modi garbati

sub'conscious /sʌb-/ *adj* subcosciente ● *n* subcosciente *m*. **~ly** *adv* in modo inconscio

'subdivi|de *vt* suddividere. **~sion** *n* suddivisione *f*

subject[1] /'sʌbdʒɪkt/ *adj* **~ to** soggetto a; (*depending on*) subordinato a; **~ to availability** nei limiti della disponibilità ● *n* soggetto *m*; (*of ruler*) suddito, -a *mf*; (*Sch*) materia *f*

subject[2] /səb'dʒekt/ *vt* (*to attack, abuse*) sottoporre; assoggettare (country)

subjective /səb'dʒektɪv/ *adj* soggettivo. **~ly** *adv* soggettivamente

subjunctive /səb'dʒʌŋktɪv/ *adj & n* congiuntivo *m*

sublime /sə'blaɪm/ *adj* sublime. **~ly** *adv* sublimamente

subma'rine *n* sommergibile *m*

submerge /səb'mɜ:dʒ/ *vt* immergere; **be ~d** essere sommerso ● *vi* immergersi

submiss|ion /səb'mɪʃn/ *n* sottomissione *f*. **~ive** *adj* sottomesso

submit /səb'mɪt/ *v* (*pt/pp* **-mitted**, *pres p* **-mitting**) ● *vt* sottoporre ● *vi* sottomettersi

subordinate /sə'bɔ:dɪneɪt/ *vt* subordinare (**to** a)

subscribe /səb'skraɪb/ *vi* contribuire; **~ to** abbonarsi a (newspaper); sottoscrivere (fund); *fig* aderire a. **~r** *n* abbonato, -a *mf*

subscription /səb'skrɪpʃn/ *n* (*to club*) sottoscrizione *f*; (*to newspaper*) abbonamento *m*

subsequent /'sʌbsɪkwənt/ *adj* susseguente. **~ly** *adv* in seguito

subside /səb'saɪd/ *vi* sprofondare; (ground:) avvallarsi; (storm:) placarsi

subsidiary /səb'sɪdɪərɪ/ *adj* secondario ● *n* **~** [**company**] filiale *f*

subsid|ize /'sʌbsɪdaɪz/ *vt* sovvenzionare. **~y** *n* sovvenzione *f*

substance /'sʌbstəns/ *n* sostanza *f*

sub'standard *adj* di qualità inferiore

substantial /səb'stænʃl/ *adj* solido; (meal) sostanzioso; (*considerable*) notevole. **~ly** *adv* notevolmente; (*essentially*) sostanzialmente

substitut|e /'sʌbstɪtju:t/ *n* sostituto *m* ● *vt* **~e A for B** sostituire B con A ● *vi* **~e for sb** sostituire qcno. **~ion** *n* sostituzione *f*

subterranean /sʌbtə'reɪnɪən/ *adj* sotterraneo

'subtitle *n* sottotitolo *m*

sub|tle /'sʌtl/ *adj* sottile; (taste, perfume) delicato. **~tlety** *n* sottigliezza *f*. **~tly** *adv* sottilmente

subtract /səb'trækt/ *vt* sottrare. **~ion** *n* sottrazione *f*

suburb /'ʃʌbɜ:b/ *n* sobborgo *m*; **in the ~s** in periferia. **~an** *adj* suburbano. **~ia** *n* i sobborghi *mpl*

subversive /səb'vɜ:sɪv/ *adj* sovversivo

'subway *n* sottopassagio *m*; (*Am: railway*) metropolitana *f*

succeed /sək'si:d/ *vi* riuscire; (*follow*) succedere a; **~ in doing** riuscire a fare ● *vt* succedere a (king). **~ing** *adj* successivo

success /sək'ses/ *n* successo *m*; **be a ~** (*in life*) aver successo. **~ful** *adj* riuscito; (businessman, artist etc) di successo. **~fully** *adv* con successo

succession /sək'seʃn/ *n* successione *f*; **in ~** di seguito

successive /sək'sesɪv/ *adj* successivo. **~ly** *adv* successivamente

successor /sək'sesə(r)/ *n* successore *m*

succulent /'ʃʌkjʊlənt/ *adj* succulento

succumb /sə'kʌm/ *vi* soccombere (**to** a)

such /sʌtʃ/ *adj* tale; **~ a book** un libro di questo genere; **~ a thing** una cosa di questo genere; **~ a long time ago** talmente tanto tempo fa; **there is no ~ thing** non esiste una cosa così; **there is no ~ person** non esiste una persona così ● *pron* **as ~** come tale; **~ as** chi; **and ~** e simili; **~ as it is** così com'è. **~like** *pron* [!] di tal genere

suck /ʃʌk/ *vt* succhiare. □ **~ up** *vt* assorbire. □ **~ up to** *vt* [!] fare il lecchino con

S

sucker /ˈʃʌkə(r)/ *n* (*Bot*) pollone *m*; ([!]: *person*) credulone, -a *mf*

suction /ˈsʌkʃn/ *n* aspirazione *f*

sudden /ˈsʌdn/ *adj* improvviso ● *n* **all of a ~** all'improvviso. **~ly** *adv* improvvisamente

sue /suː/ *vt* (*pres p* **suing**) fare causa a (**for** per) ● *vi* fare causa

suede /sweɪd/ *n* pelle *f* scamosciata

suet /ˈsuːɪt/ *n* grasso *m* di rognone

suffer /ˈsʌfə(r)/ *vi* soffrire (**from** per) ● *vt* soffrire; subire (loss etc); (*tolerate*) subire. **~ing** *n* sofferenza *f*

suffice /səˈfaɪs/ *vi* bastare

sufficient /səˈfɪʃənt/ *adj* sufficiente. **~ly** *adv* sufficientemente

suffix /ˈsʌfɪks/ *n* suffisso *m*

suffocat|e /ˈsʌfəkeɪt/ *vt/i* soffocare. **~ion** *n* soffocamento *m*

sugar /ˈʃʊgə(r)/ *n* zucchero *m* ● *vt* zuccherare. **~ basin**, **~-bowl** *n* zuccheriera *f*. **~y** *adj* zuccheroso; *fig* sdolcinato

suggest /səˈdʒest/ *vt* suggerire; (*indicate, insinuate*) fare pensare a. **~ion** *n* suggerimento *m*; (*trace*) traccia *f*. **~ive** *adj* allusivo. **~ively** *adv* in modo allusivo

suicidal /suːɪˈsaɪdl/ *adj* suicida

suicide /ˈsuːɪsaɪd/ *n* suicidio *m*; (*person*) suicida *mf*; **commit ~** suicidarsi

suit /suːt/ *n* vestito *m*; (*woman's*) tailleur *m inv*; (*in cards*) seme *m*; (*Jur*) causa *f*; **follow ~** *fig* fare lo stesso ● *vt* andar bene a; (*adapt*) adattare (**to** a); (*be convenient for*) andare bene per; **be ~ed to** *or* **for** essere adatto a; **~ yourself!** fa' come vuoi!

S

suitabl|e /ˈsuːtəbl/ *adj* adatto. **~y** *adv* convenientemente

ˈsuitcase *n* valigia *f*

suite /swiːt/ *n* suite *f inv*; (*of furniture*) divano *m* e poltrone *fpl* assortiti

sulk /sʌlk/ *vi* fare il broncio. **~y** *adj* imbronciato

sullen /ˈsʌlən/ *adj* svogliato

sulphur /ˈsʌlfə(r)/ *n* zolfo *m*. **~ic acid** *n* acido *m* solforico

sultana /sʌlˈtɑːnə/ *n* uva *f* sultanina

sultry /ˈsʌltrɪ/ *adj* (**-ier, -iest**) (weather) afoso; *fig* sensuale

sum /sʌm/ *n* somma *f*; (*Sch*) addizione *f* ● **~ up** (*pt/pp* **summed**) *vi* riassumere ● *vt* valutare

summar|ize /ˈsʌməraɪz/ *vt* riassumere. **~y** *n* sommario *m* ● *adj* sommario; (dismissal) sbrigativo

summer /ˈsʌmə(r)/ *n* estate *f*. **~-house** *n* padiglione *m*. **~time** *n* (*season*) estate *f*

> **i**
> **Summer camp** Negli Stati Uniti indica il campeggio estivo cui moltissimi ragazzi si recano per socializzare e praticare attività ricreative e sportive all'aria aperta; tra queste il nuoto, il canottaggio, l'arrampicata e i corsi di sopravvivenza.

summery /ˈsʌmərɪ/ *adj* estivo

summit /ˈsʌmɪt/ *n* cima *f*. **~ conference** *n* vertice *m*

summon /ˈsʌmən/ *vt* convocare; (*Jur*) citare. □ **~ up** *vt* raccogliere (strength); rievocare (memory)

summons /ˈsʌmənz/ *n* (*Jur*) citazione *f* ● *vt* citare in giudizio

sumptuous /ˈsʌmptjʊəs/ *adj* sontuoso. **~ly** *adv* sontuosamente

sun /sʌn/ *n* sole *m* ● *vt* (*pt/pp* **sunned**) **~ oneself** prendere il sole

sun: ~bathe *vi* prendere il sole. **~burn** *n* scottatura *f* (*solare*). **~burnt** *adj* scottato (*dal sole*)

Sunday /ˈsʌndeɪ/ *n* domenica *f*

ˈsunflower *n* girasole *m*

sung /sʌŋ/ ▷**SING**

ˈsun-glasses *npl* occhiali *mpl* da sole

sunk /sʌŋk/ ▷**SINK**

sunken /ˈsʌŋkn/ *adj* incavato

ˈsunlight *n* [luce *f* del] sole *m*

sunny /ˈsʌnɪ/ *adj* (**-ier, -iest**) assolato

sun: ~rise *n* alba *f*. **~-roof** *n* (*Auto*) tettuccio *m* apribile. **~set** *n* tramonto *m*. **~shine** *n* [luce *f* del] sole *m*. **~stroke** *n* insolazione *f*. **~-tan** *n* abbronzatura *f*. **~-tan oil** *n* olio *m* solare

super /ˈsuːpə(r)/ *adj* [!] fantastico

superb /sʊˈpɜːb/ *adj* splendido

supercilious /suːpəˈsɪlɪəs/ *adj* altezzoso

superficial /suːpəˈfɪʃl/ *adj* superficiale. **~ly** *adv* superficialmente

superfluous /sʊ'pɜːflʊəs/ *adj* superfluo

super'human *adj* sovrumano

superintendent /suːpərɪn'tendənt/ *n* (*of police*) commissario *m* di polizia

superior /suː'pɪərɪə(r)/ *adj* superiore ● *n* superiore, -a *mf*. **~ity** *n* superiorità *f*

superlative /suː'pɜːlətɪv/ *adj* eccellente ● *n* superlativo *m*

'supermarket *n* supermercato *m*

super'natural *adj* soprannaturale

'superpower *n* superpotenza *f*

supersede /suːpə'siːd/ *vt* rimpiazzare

super'sonic *adj* supersonico

superstiti|on /suːpə'stɪʃn/ *n* superstizione *f*. **~ous** *adj* superstizioso

supervis|e /'suːpəvaɪz/ *vt* supervisionare. **~ion** *n* supervisione *f*. **~or** *n* supervisore *m*

supper /'sʌpə(r)/ *n* cena *f*

supple /'sʌpl/ *adj* slogato

supplement /'sʌplɪmənt/ *n* supplemento *m* ● *vt* integrare. **~ary** *adj* supplementare

supplier /sə'plaɪə(r)/ *n* fornitore, -trice *mf*

supply /sə'plaɪ/ *n* fornitura *f*; (*in economics*) offerta *f*; **supplies** *pl* (*Mil*) approvvigionamenti *mpl* ● *vt* (*pt/pp* **-ied**) fornire; **~ sb with sth** fornire qcsa a qcno

support /sə'pɔːt/ *n* sostegno *m*; (*base*) supporto *m*; (*keep*) sostentamento *m* ● *vt* sostenere; mantenere (family); (*give money to*) mantenere finanziariamente; (*Sport*) fare il tifo per. **~er** *n* sostenitore, -trice *mf*; (*Sport*) tifoso, -a *mf*. **~ive** *adj* incoraggiante

suppose /sə'pəʊz/ *vt* (*presume*) supporre; (*imagine*) pensare; **be ~d to do** dover fare; **not be ~d to** [!] non avere il permesso di; **I ~ so** suppongo di sì. **~dly** *adv* presumibilmente

suppress /sə'pres/ *vt* sopprimere. **~ion** *n* soppressione *f*

supremacy /suː'preməsɪ/ *n* supremazia *f*

supreme /suː'priːm/ *adj* supremo

sure /ʃʊə(r)/ *adj* sicuro, certo; **make ~** accertarsi; **be ~ to do it** mi raccomando di farlo ● *adv Am* [!] certamente; **~ enough** infatti. **~ly** *adv* certamente; (*Am: gladly*) volentieri

surety /'ʃʊərətɪ/ *n* garanzia *f*; **stand ~ for** garantire

surf /sɜːf/ *n* schiuma *f* ● *vt* (*Comput*) **~ the Net** surfare in Internet

surface /'sɜːfɪs/ *n* superficie *f*; **on the ~** *fig* in apparenza ● *vi* (*emerge*) emergere. **~ mail** *n* **by ~ mail** per posta ordinaria

'surfboard *n* tavola *f* da surf

surfing /'sɜːfɪŋ/ *n* surf *m inv*

surge /sɜːdʒ/ *n* (*of sea*) ondata *f*; (*of interest*) aumento *m*; (*in demand*) impennata *f*; (*of anger, pity*) impeto *m* ● *vi* riversarsi; **~ forward** buttarsi in avanti

surgeon /'sɜːdʒən/ *n* chirurgo *m*

surgery /'sɜːdʒərɪ/ *n* chirurgia *f*; (*place, consulting room*) ambulatorio *m*; (*hours*) ore *fpl* di visita; **have ~** subire un'intervento [chirurgico]

surgical /'sɜːdʒɪkl/ *adj* chirurgico

surly /'sɜːlɪ/ *adj* (**-ier, -iest**) scontroso

surmise /sə'maɪz/ *vt* supporre

surmount /sə'maʊnt/ *vt* sormontare

surname /'sɜːneɪm/ *n* cognome *m*

surpass /sə'pɑːs/ *vt* superare

surplus /'sɜːpləs/ *adj* d'avanzo ● *n* sovrappiù *m*

surpris|e /sə'praɪz/ *n* sorpresa *f* ● *vt* sorprendere; **be ~ed** essere sorpreso (**at** da). **~ing** *adj* sorprendente. **~ingly** *adv* sorprendentemente

surrender /sə'rendə(r)/ *n* resa *f* ● *vi* arrendersi ● *vt* cedere

surreptitious /sʌrəp'tɪʃəs/ *adj & adv* di nascosto

surround /sə'raʊnd/ *vt* circondare. **~ing** *adj* circostante. **~ings** *npl* dintorni *mpl*

surveillance /sə'veɪləns/ *n* sorveglianza *f*

survey¹ /'sɜːveɪ/ *n* sguardo *m*; (*poll*) sondaggio *m*; (*investigation*) indagine *f*; (*of land*) rilevamento *m*; (*of house*) perizia *f*

survey² /sə'veɪ/ *vt* esaminare; fare un rilevamento di (land); fare una perizia di (building). **~or** *n* perito *m*; (*of land*) topografo, -a *mf*

survival /sə'vaɪvl/ *n* sopravvivenza *f*; (*relic*) resto *m*

surviv|e /sə'vaɪv/ *vt* sopravvivere a ● *vi* sopravvivere. **~or** *n* superstite *mf*; **be**

a **~or** [!] riuscire sempre a cavarsela

susceptible /sə'septəbl/ *adj* influenzabile; **~ to** sensibile a

suspect¹ /sə'spekt/ *vt* sospettare; (*assume*) supporre

suspect² /'sʌspekt/ *adj & n* sospetto, -a *mf*

suspend /sə'spend/ *vt* appendere; (*stop, from duty*) sospendere. **~er belt** *n* reggicalze *m inv*. **~ders** *npl* giarretiere *fpl*; (*Am: braces*) bretelle *mpl*

suspense /sə'spens/ *n* tensione *f*; (*in book etc*) suspense *f*

suspension /sə'spenʃn/ *n* (*Auto*) sospensione *f*. **~ bridge** *n* ponte *m* sospeso

suspici|on /sə'spɪʃn/ *n* sospetto *m*; (*trace*) pizzico *m*; **under ~on** sospettato. **~ous** *adj* sospettoso; (*arousing suspicion*) sospetto. **~ously** *adv* sospettosamente; (*arousing suspicion*) in modo sospetto

sustain /sə'steɪn/ *vt* sostenere; mantenere (life); subire (injury)

swab /swɒb/ *n* (*Med*) tampone *m*

swagger /'swægə(r)/ *vi* pavoneggiarsi

swallow¹ /'swɒləʊ/ *vt/i* inghiottire. □**~ up** *vt* divorare; (earth, crowd:) inghiottire

swallow² *n* (*bird*) rondine *f*

swam /swæm/ ▷**SWIM**

swamp /swɒmp/ *n* palude *f* ● *vt fig* sommergere. **~y** *adj* paludoso

swan /swɒn/ *n* cigno *m*

swap /swɒp/ *n* [!] scambio *m* ● *vt* (*pt/pp* **swapped**) [!] scambiare (**for** con) ● *vi* fare cambio

swarm /swɔːm/ *n* sciame *m* ● *vi* sciamare; **be ~ing with** brulicare di

swarthy /'swɔːðɪ/ *adj* (**-ier, -iest**) di carnagione scura

swat /swɒt/ *vt* (*pt/pp* **swatted**) schiacciare

sway /sweɪ/ *n fig* influenza *f* ● *vi* oscillare; (person:) ondeggiare ● *vt* (*influence*) influenzare

swear /sweə(r)/ *v* (*pt* **swore**, *pp* **sworn**) ● *vt* giurare ● *vi* giurare; (*curse*) dire parolacce; **~ at sb** imprecare contro qcno; **~ by** [!] credere ciecamente in. **~-word** *n* parolaccia *f*

sweat /swet/ *n* sudore *m* ● *vi* sudare

sweater /'swetə(r)/ *n* golf *m inv*

swede /swiːd/ *n* rapa *f* svedese

Swed|e *n* svedese *mf*. **~en** *n* Svezia *f*. **~ish** *adj* svedese

sweep /swiːp/ *n* scopata *f*, spazzata *f*; (*curve*) curva *f*; (*movement*) movimento *m* ampio; **make a clean ~** *fig* fare piazza pulita ● *v* (*pt/pp* **swept**) ● *vt* scopare, spazzare; (wind:) spazzare ● *vi* (*go swiftly*) andare rapidamente; (wind:) soffiare. □**~ away** *vt fig* spazzare via. □**~ up** *vt* spazzare

sweeping /'swiːpɪŋ/ *adj* (gesture) ampio; (statement) generico; (changes) radicale

sweet /swiːt/ *adj* dolce; **have a ~ tooth** essere goloso ● *n* caramella *f*; (*dessert*) dolce *m*. **~ corn** *n* mais *m*

sweeten /'swiːtn/ *vt* addolcire. **~er** *n* dolcificante *m*

sweetheart *n* innamorato, -a *mf*; **hi, ~** ciao, tesoro

swell /swel/ ● *v* (*pt* **swelled**, *pp* **swollen** *or* **swelled**) ● *vi* gonfiarsi; (*increase*) aumentare ● *vt* gonfiare; (*increase*) far salire. **~ing** *n* gonfiore *m*

swept /swept/ ▷**SWEEP**

swerve /swɜːv/ *vi* deviare bruscamente

swift /swɪft/ *adj* rapido. **~ly** *adv* rapidamente

swig /swɪg/ *n* [!] sorso *m* ● *vt* (*pt/pp* **swigged**) [!] scolarsi

swim /swɪm/ *n* **have a ~** fare una nuotata ● *v* (*pt* **swam**, *pp* **swum**) ● *vi* nuotare; (room:) girare; **my head is ~ming** mi gira la testa ● *vt* percorrere a nuoto. **~mer** *n* nuotatore, -trice *mf*

swimming /'swɪmɪŋ/ *n* nuoto *m*. **~-baths** *npl* piscina *fsg*. **~ costume** *n* costume *m* da bagno. **~-pool** *n* piscina *f*. **~ trunks** *npl* calzoncini *mpl* da bagno

'swim-suit *n* costume *m* da bagno

swindle /'swɪndl/ *n* truffa *f* ● *vt* truffare. **~r** *n* truffatore, -trice *mf*

swine /swaɪn/ *n* [!] porco *m*

swing /swɪŋ/ *n* oscillazione *f*; (*shift*) cambiamento *m*; (*seat*) altalena *f*; (*Mus*) swing *m*; **in full ~**in piena attività ● *v* (*pt/pp* **swung**) ● *vi* oscillare; (*on swing, sway*) dondolare; (*dangle*) penzolare; (*turn*) girare ● *vt* oscillare; far deviare (vote). **~-'door** *n* porta *f* a vento

swipe /swaɪp/ *n* [!] botta *f* ● *vt* [!] colpire; (*steal*) rubare; far passare nella macchinetta (credit card); **~ card** *n* pass *m inv* magnetico

Swiss /swɪs/ *adj & n* svizzero, -a *mf*; **the ~** *pl* gli svizzeri. **~ 'roll** *n rotolo m di pan di Spagna ripieno di marmellata*

switch /swɪtʃ/ *n* interruttore *m*; (*change*) mutamento *m* ● *vt* cambiare; (*exchange*) scambiare ● *vi* cambiare; **~ to** passare a. □ **~ off** *vt* spegnere. □ **~ on** *vt* accendere

switchboard *n* centralino *m*

Switzerland /'swɪtsələnd/ *n* Svizzera *f*

swivel /'swɪvl/ *v* (*pt/pp* **swivelled**) ● *vt* girare ● *vi* girarsi

swollen /'swəʊlən/ ▷**SWELL** ● *adj* gonfio. **~-'headed** *adj* presuntuoso

swoop /swu:p/ *n* (*by police*) incursione *f* ● *vi* **~ [down]** (bird:) piombare; *fig* fare un'incursione

sword /sɔ:d/ *n* spada *f*

swore /swɔ:(r)/ ▷**SWEAR**

sworn /swɔ:n/ ▷**SWEAR**

swot /swɒt/ *n* 🄸 sgobbone, -a *mf* ● *vt* (*pt/pp* **swotted**) 🄸 sgobbare

swum /swʌm/ ▷**SWIM**

swung /swʌŋ/ ▷**SWING**

syllable /'sɪləbl/ *n* sillaba *f*

syllabus /'sɪləbəs/ *n* programma *m* [dei corsi]

symbol /'sɪmbl/ *n* simbolo *m* (**of** di). **~ic** *adj* simbolico. **~ism** *n* simbolismo *m*. **~ize** *vt* simboleggiare

symmetr|ical /sɪ'metrɪkl/ *adj* simmetrico. **~y** *n* simmetria *f*

sympathetic /sɪmpə'θetɪk/ *adj* (*understanding*) comprensivo; (*showing pity*) compassionevole. **~ally** *adv* con comprensione/compassione

sympathize /'sɪmpəθaɪz/ *vi* capire; (*in grief*) solidarizzare; **~ with sb** capire qcno/solidarizzare con qcno. **~r** *n* (*Pol*) simpatizzante *mf*

sympathy /'sɪmpəθɪ/ *n* comprensione *f*; (*pity*) compassione *f*; (*condolences*) condoglianze *fpl*; **in ~ with** (strike) per solidarietà con

symphony /'sɪmfənɪ/ *n* sinfonia *f*

symptom /'sɪmptəm/ *n* sintomo *m*. **~atic** *adj* sintomatico (**of** di)

synagogue /'sɪnəgɒg/ *n* sinagoga *f*

synchronize /'sɪŋkrənaɪz/ *vt* sincronizzare

syndicate /'sɪndɪkət/ *n* gruppo *m*

synonym /'sɪnənɪm/ *n* sinonimo *m*. **~ous** *adj* sinonimo

syntax /'sɪntæks/ *n* sintassi *f inv*

synthesize /'sɪnθəsaɪz/ *vt* sintetizzare. **~r** *n* (*Mus*) sintetizzatore *m*

synthetic /sɪn'thetɪk/ *adj* sintetico ● *n* fibra *f* sintetica

syringe /sɪ'rɪndʒ/ *n* siringa *f*

syrup /'sɪrəp/ *n* sciroppo *m*; *treacle* tipo *m* di melassa

system /'sɪstəm/ *n* sistema *m*. **~atic** *adj* sistematico

Tt

tab /tæb/ *n* linguetta *f*; (*with name*) etichetta *f*; **keep ~s on** 🄸 sorvegliare; **pick up the ~** 🄸 pagare il conto

table /'teɪbl/ *n* tavolo *m*; (*list*) tavola *f*; **at [the] ~** a tavola; **~ of contents** tavola *f* delle materie ● *vt* proporre. **~-cloth** *n* tovaglia *f*. **~spoon** *n* cucchiaio *m* da tavola. **~spoon[ful]** *n* cucchiaiata *f*

tablet /'tæblɪt/ *n* pastiglia *f*; (*slab*) lastra *f*; **~ of soap** saponetta *f*

'table tennis *n* tennis *m* da tavolo; (*everyday level*) ping pong *m*

tabloid /'tæblɔɪd/ *n* [giornale *m* formato] tabloid *m inv*; *pej* giornale *m* scandalistico

taboo /tə'bu:/ *adj* tabù *inv* ● *n* tabù *m inv*

tacit /'tæsɪt/ *adj* tacito

taciturn /'tæsɪtɜ:n/ *adj* taciturno

tack /tæk/ *n* (*nail*) chiodino *m*; (*stitch*) imbastitura *f*; (*Naut*) virata *f*; *fig* linea *f* di condotta ● *vt* inchiodare; (*sew*) imbastire ● *vi* (*Naut*) virare

tackle /'tækl/ *n* (*equipment*) attrezzatura *f*; (*football etc*) contrasto *m*, tackle *m inv* ● *vt* affrontare

tacky /'tækɪ/ *adj* (paint) non ancora asciutto; (glue) appiccicoso; *fig* pacchiano

tact /tækt/ *n* tatto *m*. **~ful** *adj* pieno di

tatto; (remark) delicato. **~fully** *adv* con tatto

tactic|al /'tæktɪkl/ *adj* tattico. **~s** *npl* tattica *fsg*

tactless /'tæktlɪs/ *adj* privo di tatto. **~ly** *adv* senza tatto. **~ness** *n* mancanza *f* di tatto; (*of remark*) indelicatezza *f*

tadpole /'tædpəʊl/ *n* girino *m*

tag[1] /tæg/ *n* (*label*) etichetta *f* ● *vt* (*pt/pp* **tagged**) attaccare l'etichetta a. □ **~ along** *vi* seguire passo passo

tag[2] *n* (*game*) acchiapparello *m*

tail /teɪl/ *n* coda *f*; **~s** *pl* (*tailcoat*) frac *m inv* ● *vt* ([!]: *follow*) pedinare. □ **~ off** *vi* diminuire

tail light *n* fanalino *m* di coda

tailor /'teɪlə(r)/ *n* sarto *m*. **~-made** *adj* fatto su misura

taint /teɪnt/ *vt* contaminare

take /teɪk/ *n* (*Cinema*) ripresa *f* ● *v* (*pt* **took**, *pp* **taken**) ● *vt* prendere; (*to a place*) portare (person, object); (*contain*) contenere (passengers etc); (*endure*) sopportare; (*require*) occorrere; (*teach*) insegnare; (*study*) studiare (subject); fare (exam, holiday, photograph, walk, bath); sentire (pulse); misurare (sb's temperature); **~ sb prisoner** fare prigioniero qcno; **be ~n ill** ammalarsi; **~ sth calmly** prendere con calma qcsa ● *vi* (plant:) attecchire. □ **~ after** *vt* assomigliare a. □ **~ away** *vt* (*with one*) portare via; (*remove*) togliere; (*subtract*) sottrarre; **'to ~ away'** 'da asporto'. □ **~ back** *vt* riprendere; ritirare (statement); (*return*) riportare [indietro]. □ **~ down** *vt* portare giù; (*remove*) tirare giù; (*write down*) prendere nota di. □ **~ in** *vt* (*bring indoors*) portare dentro; (*to one's home*) ospitare; (*understand*) capire; (*deceive*) ingannare; riprendere (garment); (*include*) includere. □ **~ off** *vt* togliersi (clothes); (*deduct*) togliere; (*mimic*) imitare; **~ time off** prendere delle vacanze; **~ oneself off** andarsene ● *vi* (*Aeron*) decollare. □ **~ on** *vt* farsi carico di; assumere (employee); (*as opponent*) prendersela con. □ **~ out** *vt* portare fuori; togliere (word, stain); (*withdraw*) ritirare (money, books); **~ out a subscription to sth** abbonarsi a qcsa; **~ it out on sb** [!] prendersela con qcno. □ **~ over** *vt* assumere il controllo di (firm) ● *vi* **~ over from sb** sostituire qcno; (*permanently*) succedere a qcno. □ **~ to** *vt* (*as a habit*) darsi a; **I took to her** (*liked*) mi è piaciuta. □ **~ up** *vt* portare su; accettare (offer); intraprendere (profession); dedicarsi a (hobby); prendere (time); occupare (space); tirare su (floorboards); accorciare (dress); **~ sth up with sb** discutere qcsa con qcno ● *vi* **~ up with sb** legarsi a qcno

take: ~-off *n* (*Aeron*) decollo *m*. **~-over** *n* rilevamento *m*

takings /'teɪkɪŋz/ *npl* incassi *mpl*

tale /teɪl/ *n* storia *f*; *pej* fandonia *f*

talent /'tælənt/ *n* talento *m*. **~ed** *adj* [ricco] di talento

talk /tɔːk/ *n* conversazione *f*; (*lecture*) conferenza *f*; (*gossip*) chiacchere *fpl*; **make small ~** parlare del più e del meno ● *vi* parlare ● *vt* parlare di (politics etc); **~ sb into sth** convincere qcno di qcsa. □ **~ over** *vt* discutere

talkative /'tɔːkətɪv/ *adj* loquace

tall /tɔːl/ *adj* alto. **~boy** *n* cassettone *m*. **~ order** *n* impresa *f* difficile. **~ 'story** *n* frottola *f*

tally /'tælɪ/ *n* conteggio *m*; **keep a ~ of** tenere il conto di ● *vi* coincidere

tambourine /tæmbə'riːn/ *n* tamburello *m*

tame /teɪm/ *adj* (animal) domestico; (*dull*) insulso ● *vt* domare. **~ly** *adv* docilmente. **~r** *n* domatore, -trice *mf*

tamper /'tæmpə(r)/ *vi* **~ with** manomettere

tampon /'tæmpɒn/ *n* tampone *m*

tan /tæn/ *adj* marrone rossiccio ● *n* marrone *m* rossiccio; (*from sun*) abbronzatura *f* ● *v* (*pt/pp* **tanned**) ● *vt* conciare (hide) ● *vi* abbronzarsi

tang /tæŋ/ *n* sapore *m* forte; (*smell*) odore *m* penetrante

tangent /'tændʒənt/ *n* tangente *f*

tangible /'tændʒɪbl/ *adj* tangibile

tangle /'tæŋgl/ *n* groviglio *m*; (*in hair*) nodo *m* ● *vt* **~[up]** aggrovigliare ● *vi* aggrovigliarsi

tango /'tæŋgəʊ/ *n* tango *m inv*

tank /tæŋk/ *n* contenitore *m*; (*for petrol*) serbatoio *m*; (*fish* **~**) acquario *m*; (*Mil*) carro *m* armato

tanker /'tæŋkə(r)/ *n* nave *f* cisterna; (*lorry*) autobotte *f*

tantrum /'tæntrəm/ *n* scoppio *m* d'ira

tap /tæp/ *n* rubinetto *m*; (*knock*) colpo *m*; **on ~** a disposizione ● (*pt/pp* **tapped**) ● *vt* dare un colpetto a; sfruttare (resources); mettere sotto controllo (telephone) ● *vi* picchiettare. **~-dance** *n* tip tap *m* ● *vi* ballare il tip tap

tape /teɪp/ *n* nastro *m*; (*recording*) cassetta *f* ● *vt* legare con nastro; (*record*) registrare

tape-measure *n* metro *m* [a nastro]

taper /ˈteɪpə(r)/ *n* candela *f* sottile ● **taper off** *vi* assottigliarsi

tape recorder *n* registratore *m*

tapestry /ˈtæpɪstrɪ/ *n* arazzo *m*

tar /tɑː(r)/ *n* catrame *m* ● *vt* (*pt/pp* **tarred**) incatramare

target /ˈtɑːgɪt/ *n* bersaglio *m*; *fig* obiettivo *m*

tarnish /ˈtɑːnɪʃ/ *vi* ossidarsi ● *vt* ossidare; *fig* macchiare

tart[1] /tɑːt/ *adj* aspro; *fig* acido

tart[2] *n* crostata *f*; (*individual*) crostatina *f*; (⊠: *prostitute*) donnaccia *f* ● **tart up** *vt* ! **~ oneself up** agghindarsi

tartan /ˈtɑːtn/ *n* tessuto *m* scozzese, tartan *m inv* ● *attrib* di tessuto scozzese

task /tɑːsk/ *n* compito *m*; **take sb to ~** riprendere qcno. **~ force** *n* (*Pol*) commissione *f*; (*Mil*) task-force *f inv*

tassel /ˈtæsl/ *n* nappa *f*

taste /teɪst/ *n* gusto *m*; (*sample*) assaggio *m*; **get a ~ of sth** *fig* assaporare il gusto di qcsa ● *vt* sentire il sapore di; (*sample*) assaggiare ● *vi* sapere (**of** di); **it ~s lovely** è ottimo. **~ful** *adj* di [buon] gusto. **~fully** *adv* con gusto. **~less** *adj* senza gusto. **~lessly** *adv* con cattivo gusto

tasty /ˈteɪstɪ/ *adj* (**-ier, -iest**) saporito

tat /tæt/ ▷TIT[2]

tatter|ed /ˈtætəd/ *adj* cencioso; (pages) stracciato. **~s** *npl* **in ~s** a brandelli

tattoo[1] /tæˈtuː/ *n* tatuaggio *m* ● *vt* tatuare

tattoo[2] *n* (*Mil*) parata *f* militare

tatty /ˈtætɪ/ *adj* (**-ier, -iest**) (clothes, person) trasandato; (book) malandato

taught /tɔːt/ ▷TEACH

taunt /tɔːnt/ *n* scherno *m* ● *vt* schernire

Taurus /ˈtɔːrəs/ *n* Toro *m*

taut /tɔːt/ *adj* teso

tax /tæks/ *n* tassa *f*; (*on income*) imposte *fpl*; **before ~** (price) tasse escluse; (salary) lordo ● *vt* tassare; *fig* mettere alla prova; **~ with** accusare di. **~able** *adj* tassabile. **~ation** *n* tasse *fpl*. **~ evasion** *n* evasione *f* fiscale. **~-free** *adj* esentasse. **~ haven** *n* paradiso *m* fiscale

taxi /ˈtæksɪ/ *n* taxi *m inv* ● *vi* (*pt/pp* **taxied**, *pres p* **taxiing**) (aircraft:) rullare. **~ driver** *n* tassista *mf*. **~ rank** *n* posteggio *m* per taxi

ˈtaxpayer *n* contribuente *mf*

tea /tiː/ *n* tè *m inv*. **~-bag** *n* bustina *f* di tè. **~-break** *n* intervallo *m* per il tè

teach /tiːtʃ/ *vt/i* (*pt/pp* **taught**) insegnare; **~ sb sth** insegnare qcsa a qcno. **~er** *n* insegnante *mf*; (*primary*) maestro, -a *mf*. **~ing** *n* insegnamento *m*

teacup *n* tazza *f* da tè

team /tiːm/ *n* squadra *f*; *fig* équipe *f inv* ● **team up** *vi* unirsi

ˈteam-work *n* lavoro *m* di squadra; *fig* lavoro *m* d'équipe

ˈteapot *n* teiera *f*

tear[1] /teə(r)/ *n* strappo *m* ● *v* (*pt* **tore**, *pp* **torn**) ● *vt* strappare ● *vi* strappare; (material:) strapparsi; (*run*) precipitarsi. □ **~ apart** *vt* (*fig: criticize*) fare a pezzi; (*separate*) dividere. □ **~ away** *vt* **~ oneself away** andare via; **~ oneself away from** staccarsi da (television). □ **~ open** *vt* aprire strappando. □ **~ up** *vt* strappare; rompere (agreement)

tear[2] /tɪə(r)/ *n* lacrima *f*. **~ful** *adj* (person) in lacrime; (farewell) lacrimevole. **~fully** *adv* in lacrime. **~gas** *n* gas *m* lacrimogeno

tease /tiːz/ *vt* prendere in giro (person); tormentare (animal)

tea: ~-set *n* servizio *m* da tè. **~spoon** *n* cucchiaino *m* [da tè]

teat /tiːt/ *n* capezzolo *m*; (*on bottle*) tettarella *f*

ˈtea-towel *n* strofinaccio *m* [per i piatti]

technical /ˈteknɪkl/ *adj* tecnico. **~ity** *n* tecnicismo *m*; (*Jur*) cavillo *m* giuridico. **~ly** *adv* tecnicamente; (*strictly*) strettamente

technician /tekˈnɪʃn/ *n* tecnico, -a *mf*

technique /tekˈniːk/ *n* tecnica *f*

technological /teknə'lɒdʒɪkl/ *adj* tecnologico
technology /tek'nɒlədʒɪ/ *n* tecnologia *f*
tedious /'ti:dɪəs/ *adj* noioso
tedium /'ti:dɪəm/ *n* tedio *m*
teem /ti:m/ *vi* (*rain*) piovere a dirotto; **be ~ing with** (*full of*) pullulare di
teenage /'ti:neɪdʒ/ *adj* per ragazzi; **~ boy/girl** adolescente *mf*. **~r** *n* adolescente *mf*
teens /ti:nz/ *npl* **the ~** l'adolescenza *fsg*; **be in one's ~** essere adolescente
teeny /'ti:nɪ/ *adj* (**-ier, -iest**) piccolissimo
teeter /'ti:tə(r)/ *vi* barcollare
teeth /ti:θ/ ▷TOOTH
teeth|e /ti:ð/ *vi* mettere i [primi] denti. **~ing troubles** *npl fig* difficoltà *fpl* iniziali
telecommunications /telɪkəmju:nɪ'keɪʃnz/ *npl* telecomunicazioni *fpl*
telegram /'telɪgræm/ *n* telegramma *m*
telepathy /tɪ'lepəθɪ/ *n* telepatia *f*
telephone /'telɪfəʊn/ *n* telefono *m*; **be on the ~** avere il telefono; (*be telephoning*) essere al telefono ● *vt* telefonare a ● *vi* telefonare
telephone: ~ booth *n*, **~ box** *n* cabina *f* telefonica. **~ directory** *n* elenco *m* telefonico
telephonist /tɪ'lefənɪst/ *n* telefonista *mf*
telescop|e /'telɪskəʊp/ *n* telescopio *m*. **~ic** *adj* telescopico
televise /'telɪvaɪz/ *vt* trasmettere per televisione
television /'telɪvɪʒn/ *n* televisione *f*; **watch ~** guardare la televisione. **~ set** *n* televisore *m*
teleworking /'telɪwɜ:kɪŋ/ *n* telelavoro *m*
telex /'teleks/ *n* telex *m inv*
tell /tel/ *vt* (*pt/pp* **told**) dire; raccontare (story); (*distinguish*) distinguere (**from** da); **~ sb sth** dire qcsa a qcno; **~ the time** dire l'ora; **I couldn't ~ why...** non sapevo perché... ● *vi* (*produce an effect*) avere effetto; **time will ~** il tempo ce lo dirà; **his age is beginning to ~** l'età comincia a farsi sentire [per lui]; **you mustn't ~** non devi dire niente. □ **~ off** *vt* sgridare
teller /'telə(r)/ *n* (*in bank*) cassiere, -a *mf*
telling /'telɪŋ/ *adj* significativo; (argument) efficace
telly /'telɪ/ *n* ⓘ tv *f inv*
temp /temp/ *n* ⓘ impiegato, -a *mf* temporaneo, -a
temper /'tempə(r)/ *n* (*disposition*) carattere *m*; (*mood*) umore *m*; (*anger*) collera *f*; **lose one's ~** arrabbiarsi; **be in a ~** essere arrabbiato; **keep one's ~** mantenere la calma
temperament /'temprəmənt/ *n* temperamento *m*. **~al** *adj* (*moody*) capriccioso
temperate /'tempərət/ *adj* (climate) temperato
temperature /'temprətʃə(r)/ *n* temperatura *f*; **have a ~** avere la febbre
temple¹ /'templ/ *n* tempio *m*
temple² *n* (*Anat*) tempia *f*
tempo /'tempəʊ/ *n* ritmo *m*; (*Mus*) tempo *m*
temporar|y /'tempərərɪ/ *adj* temporaneo; (measure, building) provvisorio. **~ily** *adv* temporaneamente; (introduced, erected) provvisoriamente
tempt /tempt/ *vt* tentare; sfidare (fate); **~ sb to** indurre qcno a; **be ~ed** essere tentato (**to** di); **I am ~ed by the offer** l'offerta mi tenta. **~ation** *n* tentazione *f*. **~ing** *adj* allettante; (food, drink) invitante
ten /ten/ *adj* dieci
tenaci|ous /tɪ'neɪʃəs/ *adj* tenace. **~ty** *n* tenacia *f*
tenant /'tenənt/ *n* inquilino, -a *mf*; (*Comm*) locatario, -a *mf*
tend *vi* **~ to do sth** tendere a far qcsa
tendency /'tendənsɪ/ *n* tendenza *f*
tender¹ /'tendə(r)/ *n* (*Comm*) offerta *f*; **be legal ~** avere corso legale ● *vt* offrire; presentare (resignation)
tender² *adj* tenero; (*painful*) dolorante. **~ly** *adv* teneramente. **~ness** *n* tenerezza *f*; (*painfulness*) dolore *m*
tendon /'tendən/ *n* tendine *m*
tennis /'tenɪs/ *n* tennis *m*. **~-court** *n* campo *m* da tennis. **~ player** *n* tennista *mf*
tenor /'tenə(r)/ *n* tenore *m*
tense¹ /tens/ *n* (*Gram*) tempo *m*

tense² *adj* teso ● *vt* tendere (muscle). ▫ **~ up** *vi* tendersi

tension /'tenʃn/ *n* tensione *f*

tent /tent/ *n* tenda *f*

tentacle /'tentəkl/ *n* tentacolo *m*

tentative /'tentətɪv/ *adj* provvisorio; (smile, gesture) esitante. **~ly** *adv* timidamente; (accept) provvisoriamente

tenterhooks /'tentəhʊks/ *npl* **be on ~** essere sulle spine

tenth /tenθ/ *adj* decimo ● *n* decimo, -a *mf*

tenuous /'tenjʊəs/ *adj fig* debole

tepid /'tepɪd/ *adj* tiepido

term /tɜːm/ *n* periodo *m*; (*Sch*) (*Univ*) trimestre *m*; (*expression*) termine *m*; **~s** *pl* (*conditions*) condizioni *fpl*; **~ of office** carica *f*; **in the short/long ~** a breve/lungo termine; **be on good/bad ~s** essere in buoni/cattivi rapporti; **come to ~s with** accettare (past, fact); **easy ~s** facilità *f* di pagamento

terminal /'tɜːmɪn(ə)l/ *adj* finale; (*Med*) terminale ● *n* (*Aeron*) terminal *m inv*; (*Rail*) stazione *f* di testa; (*of bus*) capolinea *m*; (*on battery*) morsetto *m*; (*Comput*) terminale *m*. **~ly** *adv* **be ~ly ill** essere in fase terminale

terminat|e /'tɜːmɪneɪt/ *vt* terminare; rescindere (contract); interrompere (pregnancy) ● *vi* terminare; **~e in** finire in. **~ion** *n* termine *m*; (*Med*) interruzione *f* di gravidanza

terminology /tɜːmɪ'nɒlədʒɪ/ *n* terminologia *f*

terrace /'terəs/ *n* terrazza *f*; (*houses*) fila *f* di case a schiera; **the ~s** (*Sport*) le gradinate. **~d house** *n* casa *f* a schiera

terrain /te'reɪn/ *n* terreno *m*

terrible /'terəbl/ *adj* terribile

terrific /tə'rɪfɪk/ *adj* 🅸 (*excellent*) fantastico; (*huge*) enorme. **~ally** *adv* 🅸 terribilmente

terri|fy /'terɪfaɪ/ *vt* (*pt/pp* **-ied**) atterrire; **be ~fied** essere terrorizzato. **~fying** *adj* terrificante

territorial /terɪ'tɔːrɪəl/ *adj* territoriale

territory /'terɪtərɪ/ *n* territorio *m*

terror /'terə(r)/ *n* terrore *m*. **~ism** *n* terrorismo *m*. **~ist** *n* terrorista *mf*. **~ize** *vt* terrorizzare

terse /tɜːs/ *adj* conciso

test /test/ *n* esame *m*; (*in laboratory*) esperimento *m*; (*of friendship, machine*) prova *m*; (*of intelligence, aptitude*) test *m inv*; **put to the ~** mettere alla prova ● *vt* esaminare; provare (machine)

testament /'testəmənt/ *n* testamento *m*; **Old/New T~** Antico/Nuovo Testamento *m*

testicle /'testɪkl/ *n* testicolo *m*

testify /'testɪfaɪ/ *vt/i* (*pt/pp* **-ied**) testimoniare

testimonial /testɪ'məʊnɪəl/ *n* lettera *f* di referenze

testimony /'testɪmənɪ/ *n* testimonianza *f*

'test: ~ match *n* partita *f* internazionale. **~-tube** *n* provetta *f*

tether /'teðə(r)/ *n* **be at the end of one's ~** non poterne più

text /tekst/ *n* testo *m*. **~book** *n* manuale *m*

textile /'tekstaɪl/ *adj* tessile ● *n* stoffa *f*

text message *n* sms *m inv*, breve messaggio *m* di testo

texture /'tekstʃə(r)/ *n* (*of skin*) grana *f*; (*of food*) consistenza *f*; **of a smooth ~** (*to the touch*) soffice al tatto

Thames /temz/ *n* Tamigi *m*

than /ðən/, *accentato* /ðæn/ *conj* che; (*with numbers, names*) di; **older ~ me** più vecchio di me

thank /θæŋk/ *vt* ringraziare; **~ you [very much]** grazie [mille]. **~ful** *adj* grato. **~fully** *adv* con gratitudine; (*happily*) fortunatamente. **~less** *adj* ingrato

thanks /θæŋks/ *npl* ringraziamenti *mpl*; **~!** 🅸 grazie!; **~ to** grazie a

that /ðæt/

● *adj & pron* (*pl* **those**) quel, quei *pl*; (*before s + consonant, gn, ps and z*) quello, quegli *pl*; (*before vowel*) quell' *mf*, quegli *mpl*, quelle *fpl*; **~ woman** quella donna; **I don't like those** quelli non mi piacciono; **~ is** cioè; **is ~ you?** sei tu?; **who is ~?** chi è?; **what did you do after ~?** cosa hai fatto dopo?; **like ~** in questo modo, così; **a man like ~** un uomo così; **~ is why** ecco perché; **~'s it!** (*you've understood*) ecco!; (*I've finished*) ecco fatto!; (*I've had enough*) basta così!; (*there's* *nothing more*) tutto qui!; **~'s ~!** (*with job*) ecco fatto!; (*with relationship*) è tutto finito!; **and ~'s ~!** punto e basta! **all ~ I know** tutto quello che so

● *adv* così; **it wasn't ~ good** non era poi così buono

● *rel pron* che; **the man ~ I spoke to** l'uomo con cui ho parlato; **the day ~ I saw him** il giorno in cui l'ho visto; **all ~ I know** tutto quello che so

● *conj* che; **I think ~...** penso che...

thaw /θɔː/ *n* disgelo *m* ● *vt* fare scongelare (food) ● *vi* (food:) scongelarsi; **it's ~ing** sta sgelando

the /ðə/, *di fronte a una vocale* /ðiː/

● *def art* il, la *f*; i *mpl*, le *fpl*; (*before s + consonant, gn, ps and z*) lo, gli *mpl*; (*before vowel*) l' *mf*, gli *mpl*, le *fpl*; **at ~ cinema/station** al cinema/alla stazione; **from ~ cinema/station** dal cinema/dalla stazione

● *adv* **~ more ~ better** più ce n'è meglio è; (*with reference to pl*) più ce ne sono, meglio è; **all ~ better** tanto meglio

theatre /ˈθɪətə(r)/ *n* teatro *m*; (*Med*) sala *f* operatoria

theatrical /θɪˈætrɪkl/ *adj* teatrale; (*showy*) melodrammatico

theft /θeft/ *n* furto *m*

their /ðeə(r)/ *adj* il loro *m*, la loro *f*, i loro *mpl*, le loro *fpl*; **~ mother/father** la loro madre/il loro padre

theirs /ðeəz/ *poss pron* il loro *m*, la loro *f*, i loro *mpl*, le loro *fpl*; **a friend of ~** un loro amico; **friends of ~** dei loro amici; **those are ~** quelli sono loro; (*as opposed to ours*) quelli sono i loro

t

them /ðem/ *pron* (*direct object*) li *m*, le *f*; (*indirect object*) gli, loro *fml*; (*after prep: with people*) loro; (*after preposition: with things*) essi; **we haven't seen ~** non li/le abbiamo visti/viste; **give ~ the money** dai loro *or* dagli i soldi; **give it to ~** daglielo; **I've spoken to ~** ho parlato con loro; **it's ~** sono loro

theme /θiːm/ *n* tema *m*. **~ park** *n* parco *m* a tema. **~ song** *n* motivo *m* conduttore

them'selves *pron* (*reflexive*) si; (*emphatic*) se stessi; **they poured ~ a drink** si sono versati da bere; **they said so ~** lo hanno detto loro stessi; **they kept it to ~** se lo sono tenuti per sé; **by ~** da soli

then /ðen/ *adv* allora; (*next*) poi; **by ~** (*in the past*) ormai; (*in the future*) per allora; **since ~** sin da allora; **before ~** prima di allora; **from ~ on** da allora in poi; **now and ~** ogni tanto; **there and ~** all'istante ● *adj* di allora

theoretical /θɪəˈretɪkl/ *adj* teorico

theory /ˈθɪərɪ/ *n* teoria *f*; **in ~** in teoria

therapeutic /θerəˈpjuːtɪk/ *adj* terapeutico

therap|ist /ˈθerəpɪst/ *n* terapista *mf*. **~y** *n* terapia *f*

there /ðeə(r)/ *adv* là, lì; **down/up ~** laggiù/lassù; **~ is/are** c'è/ci sono; **~ he/she is** eccolo/eccola ● *int* **~, ~!** dai, su!

there: ~abouts *adv* **[or] ~abouts** (*roughly*) all'incirca. **~fore** /-fɔː(r)/ *adv* perciò

thermometer /θəˈmɒmɪtə(r)/ *n* termometro *m*

thermostat /ˈθɜːməstæt/ *n* termostato *m*

thesaurus /θɪˈsɔːrəs/ *n* dizionario *m* dei sinonimi

these /ðiːz/ ▷ THIS

thesis /ˈθiːsɪs/ *n* (*pl* **-ses** /-siːz/) tesi *f inv*

they /ðeɪ/ *pron* loro; **~ are tired** sono stanchi; **we're going, but ~ are not** noi andiamo, ma loro no; **~ say** (*generalizing*) si dice; **~ are building a new road** stanno costruendo una nuova strada

thick /θɪk/ *adj* spesso; (forest) fitto; (liquid) denso; (hair) folto; ([!]: *stupid*) ottuso; ([!]: *close*) molto unito; **be 5 mm ~** essere 5 mm di spessore ● *adv* densamente ● *n* **in the ~ of** nel mezzo di. **~en** *vt* ispessire (sauce) ● *vi* ispessirsi; (fog:) infittirsi. **~ly** *adv* densamente; (cut) a fette spesse. **~ness** *n* spessore *m*

thief /θiːf/ *n* (*pl* **thieves**) ladro, -a *mf*

thigh /θaɪ/ *n* coscia *f*

thimble /ˈθɪmbl/ *n* ditale *m*

thin /θɪn/ *adj* (**thinner, thinnest**) sottile; (shoes, sweater) leggero; (liquid) liquido; (person) magro; (fig: excuse, plot) inconsistente ● *adv* = **thinly** ● *v* (*pt/pp* **thinned**) ● *vt* diluire (liquid) ● *vi* diradarsi. □ ~ **out** *vi* diradarsi. ~**ly** *adv* (populated) scarsamente; (disguised) leggermente; (cut) a fette sottili

thing /θɪŋ/ *n* cosa *f*; ~**s** *pl* (*belongings*) roba *fsg*; **for one** ~ in primo luogo; **the right** ~ la cosa giusta; **just the** ~**!** proprio quel che ci vuole!; **how are** ~**s?** come vanno le cose?; **the latest** ~ [!] l'ultima cosa; **the best** ~ **would be** la cosa migliore sarebbe; **poor** ~**!** poveretto!

think /θɪŋk/ *vt/i* (*pt/pp* **thought**) pensare; (*believe*) credere; **I** ~ **so** credo di sì; **what do you** ~**?** (*what is your opinion?*) cosa ne pensi?; ~ **of/about** pensare a; **what do you** ~ **of it?** cosa ne pensi di questo?. □ ~ **over** *vt* riflettere su. □ ~ **up** *vt* escogitare

third /θɜːd/ *adj & n* terzo, -a *mf*. ~**ly** *adv* terzo. ~**-rate** *adj* scadente

thirst /θɜːst/ *n* sete *f*. ~**ily** *adv* con sete. ~**y** *adj* assetato; **be** ~**y** aver sete

thirteen /θɜːˈtiːn/ *adj* tredici. ~**th** *adj* tredicesimo

thirtieth /ˈθɜːtɪɪθ/ *adj* trentesimo

thirty /ˈθɜːtɪ/ *adj* trenta

this /ðɪs/ *adj* (*pl* **these**) questo; ~ **man/woman** quest'uomo/questa donna; **these men/women** questi uomini/queste donne; ~ **one** questo; ~ **morning/evening** stamattina/stasera ● *pron* (*pl* **these**) questo; **we talked about** ~ **and that** abbiamo parlato del più e del meno; **like** ~ così; ~ **is Peter** questo è Peter; (*Teleph*) sono Peter; **who is** ~ chi è?; (*Teleph*) chi parla? ● *adv* così; ~ **big** così grande

thistle /ˈθɪsl/ *n* cardo *m*

thorn /θɔːn/ *n* spina *f*. ~**y** *adj* spinoso

thorough /ˈθʌrə/ *adj* completo; (knowledge) profondo; (clean, search, training) a fondo; (person) scrupoloso

thorough: ~**bred** *n* purosangue *m inv*. ~**fare** *n* via *f* principale; **'no** ~**fare'** 'strada non transitabile'

thorough|ly /ˈθʌrəlɪ/ *adv* (clean, search, know sth) a fondo; (*extremely*) estremamente. ~**ness** *n* completezza *f*

those /ðəʊz/ ▷**THAT**

though /ðəʊ/ *conj* sebbene; **as** ~ come se ● *adv* [!] tuttavia

thought /θɔːt/ ▷**THINK** ● *n* pensiero *m*; (*idea*) idea *f*. ~**ful** *adj* pensieroso; (*considerate*) premuroso. ~**fully** *adv* pensierosamente; (*considerately*) premurosamente. ~**less** *adj* (*inconsiderate*) sconsiderato. ~**lessly** *adv* con noncuranza

thousand /ˈθaʊznd/ *adj* **one/a** ~ mille *m inv* ● *n* mille *m inv*; ~**s of** migliaia *fpl* di. ~**th** *adj* millesimo ● *n* millesimo, -a *mf*

thrash /θræʃ/ *vt* picchiare; (*defeat*) sconfiggere. □ ~ **out** *vt* mettere a punto

thread /θred/ *n* filo *m*; (*of screw*) filetto *m* ● *vt* infilare (beads); ~ **one's way through** farsi strada fra. ~**bare** *adj* logoro

threat /θret/ *n* minaccia *f*

threaten /ˈθretn/ *vt* minacciare (**to do** di fare) ● *vi fig* incalzare. ~**ing** *adj* minaccioso; (sky, atmosphere) sinistro

three /θriː/ *adj* tre. ~**fold** *adj & adv* triplo. ~**some** *n* trio *m*

threshold /ˈθreʃəʊld/ *n* soglia *f*

threw /θruː/ ▷**THROW**

thrift /θrɪft/ *n* economia *f*. ~**y** *adj* parsimonioso

thrill /θrɪl/ *n* emozione *f*; (*of fear*) brivido *m* ● *vt* entusiasmare; **be** ~**ed with** essere entusiasta di. ~**er** *n* (*book*) [romanzo *m*] giallo *m*; (*film*) [film *m*] giallo *m*. ~**ing** *adj* eccitante

thrive /θraɪv/ *vi* (*pt* **thrived** *or* **throve**, *pp* **thrived** *or* **thriven** /ˈθrɪvn/) (business:) prosperare; (child, plant:) crescere bene; **I** ~ **on pressure** mi piace essere sotto tensione

throat /θrəʊt/ *n* gola *f*; **sore** ~ mal *m* di gola

throb /θrɒb/ *n* pulsazione *f*; (*of heart*) battito *m* ● *vi* (*pt/pp* **throbbed**) (*vibrate*) pulsare; (heart:) battere

throes /θrəʊz/ *npl* **in the** ~ **of** *fig* alle prese con

throne /θrəʊn/ *n* trono *m*

throng /θrɒŋ/ *n* calca *f*

throttle /ˈθrɒtl/ *n* (*on motorbike*) manopola *f* di accelerazione ● *vt* strozzare

through /θruː/ *prep* attraverso; (*during*) durante; (*by means of*) tramite; (*thanks* *to*) grazie a; **Saturday ~ Tuesday** *Am* da sabato a martedì incluso ● *adv* attraverso; **~ and ~** fino in fondo; **wet ~** completamente bagnato; **read sth ~** dare una lettura a qcsa; **let ~** lasciar passare (sb) ● *adj* (train) diretto; **be ~** (*finished*) aver finito; (*Teleph*) avere la comunicazione

throughout /θruːˈaʊt/ *prep* per tutto ● *adv* completamente; (*time*) per tutto il tempo

throw /θrəʊ/ *n* tiro *m* ● *vt* (*pt* **threw**, *pp* **thrown**) lanciare; (*throw away*) gettare; azionare (switch); disarcionare (rider); ([!]: *disconcert*) disorientare; [!] dare (party). □ **~ away** *vt* gettare via. □ **~ out** *vt* gettare via; rigettare (plan); buttare fuori (person). □ **~ up** *vt* alzare ● *vi* (*vomit*) vomitare

thrush /θrʌʃ/ *n* tordo *m*

thrust /θrʌst/ *n* spinta *f* ● *vt* (*pt/pp* **thrust**) (*push*) spingere; (*insert*) conficcare; **~ [up]on** imporre a

thud /θʌd/ *n* tonfo *m*

thug /θʌg/ *n* deliquente *m*

thumb /θʌm/ *n* pollice *m*; **as a rule of ~** come regola generale; **under sb's ~** succube di qcno ● *vt* **~ a lift** fare l'autostop. **~-index** *n* indice *m* a rubrica. **~tack** *n Am* puntina *f* da disegno

thump /θʌmp/ *n* colpo *m*; (*noise*) tonfo *m* ● *vt* battere su (table, door); battere (fist); colpire (person) ● *vi* battere (**on** su); (heart:) battere forte. □ **~ about** *vi* camminare pesantemente

thunder /ˈθʌndə(r)/ *n* tuono *m*; (*loud noise*) rimbombo *m* ● *vi* tuonare; (*make loud noise*) rimbombare. **~clap** *n* rombo *m* di tuono. **~storm** *n* temporale *m*. **~y** *adj* temporalesco

Thursday /ˈθɜːzdeɪ/ *n* giovedì *m inv*

thus /ðʌs/ *adv* così

thwart /θwɔːt/ *vt* ostacolare

Tiber /ˈtaɪbə(r)/ *n* Tevere *m*

tick /tɪk/ *n* (*sound*) ticchettio *m*; (*mark*) segno *m*; ([!]: *instant*) attimo *m* ● *vi* ticchettare. □ **~ off** *vt* spuntare; [!] sgridare. □ **~ over** *vi* (engine:) andare al minimo

ticket /ˈtɪkɪt/ *n* biglietto *m*; (*for item deposited, library*) tagliando *m*; (*label*) cartellino *m*; (*fine*) multa *f*. **~-collector** *n* controllore *m*. **~-office** *n* biglietteria *f*

tick|le /ˈtɪkl/ *n* solletico *m* ● *vt* fare il solletico a; (*amuse*) divertire ● *vi* fare prurito. **~lish** *adj* che soffre il solletico

tide /taɪd/ *n* marea *f*; (*of events*) corso *m*; **the ~ is in/out** c'è alta/bassa marea ● **tide over** *vt* **~ sb over** aiutare qcno a andare avanti

tidily /ˈtaɪdɪlɪ/ *adv* in modo ordinato

tidiness /ˈtaɪdɪnɪs/ *n* ordine *m*

tidy /ˈtaɪdɪ/ *adj* (**-ier, -iest**) ordinato; ([!]: amount) bello ● *vt* (*pt/pp* **-ied**) **~ [up]** ordinare; **~ oneself up** mettersi in ordine

tie /taɪ/ *n* cravatta *f*; (*cord*) legaccio *m*; (*fig: bond*) legame *m*; (*restriction*) impedimento *m*; (*Sport*) pareggio *m* ● *v* (*pres p* **tying**) ● *vt* legare; fare (knot); **be ~d** (*in competition*) essere in parità ● *vi* pareggiare. □ **~ in with** *vi* corrispondere a. □ **~ up** *vt* legare; vincolare (capital); **be ~d up** (*busy*) essere occupato

tier /tɪə(r)/ *n* fila *f*; (*of cake*) piano *m*; (*in stadium*) gradinata *f*

tiger /ˈtaɪgə(r)/ *n* tigre *f*

tight /taɪt/ *adj* stretto; (*taut*) teso; ([!]: *drunk*) sbronzo; ([!]: *mean*) spilorcio; **~ corner** [!] brutta situazione *f* ● *adv* strettamente; (hold) forte; (closed) bene

tighten /ˈtaɪtn/ *vt* stringere; avvitare (screw); intensificare (control) ● *vi* stringersi

tight: ~-ˈfisted *adj* tirchio. **~ly** *adv* strettamente; (hold) forte; (closed) bene. **~rope** *n* fune *f* (*da funamboli*)

tights /taɪts/ *npl* collant *m inv*

tile /taɪl/ *n* mattonella *f*; (*on roof*) tegola *f* ● *vt* rivestire di mattonelle (wall)

till[1] /tɪl/ *prep & conj* = **until**

till[2] *n* cassa *f*

tilt /tɪlt/ *n* inclinazione *f*; **at full ~** a tutta velocità ● *vt* inclinare ● *vi* inclinarsi

timber /ˈtɪmbə(r)/ *n* legname *m*

time /taɪm/ *n* tempo *m*; (*occasion*) volta *f*; (*by clock*) ora *f*; **two ~s four** due volte quattro; **at any ~** in qualsiasi momento; **this ~** questa volta; **at ~s, from ~ to ~** ogni tanto; **~ and again** cento volte; **two at a ~** due alla volta; **on ~** in orario; **in ~** in tempo; (*eventually*) col tempo; **in no ~ at all** velocemente; **in a year's ~** fra un anno; **behind ~** in ritardo; **behind**

t

the **~s** antiquato; **for the ~ being** per il momento; **what is the ~?** che ora è?; **by the ~ we arrive** quando arriviamo; **did you have a nice ~?** ti sei divertito?; **have a good ~!** divertiti! ● *vt* scegliere il momento per; cronometrare (race); **be well ~d** essere ben calcolato

time: ~ bomb *n* bomba *f* a orologeria. **~ly** *adj* opportuno. **~-table** *n* orario *m*

timid /'tɪmɪd/ *adj* (*shy*) timido; (*fearful*) timoroso

tin /tɪn/ *n* stagno *m*; (*container*) barattolo *m* ● *vt* (*pt/pp* **tinned**) inscatolare. **~ foil** *n* [carta *f*] stagnola *f*

tinge /tɪndʒ/ *n* sfumatura *f* ● *vt* **~d with** *fig* misto a

tingle /'tɪŋgl/ *vi* pizzicare

tinker /'tɪŋkə(r)/ *vi* armeggiare

tinkle /'tɪŋkl/ *n* tintinnio *m*; (!: *phone call*) colpo *m* di telefono ● *vi* tintinnare

tinned /tɪnd/ *adj* in scatola

'tin opener *n* apriscatole *m inv*

tint /tɪnt/ *n* tinta *f* ● *vt* tingersi (hair)

tiny /'taɪnɪ/ *adj* (**-ier, -iest**) minuscolo

tip¹ /tɪp/ *n* punta *f*

tip² *n* (*money*) mancia *f*; (*advice*) consiglio *m*; (*for rubbish*) discarica *f* ● *v* (*pt/pp* **tipped**) ● *vt* (*tilt*) inclinare; (*overturn*) capovolgere; (*pour*) versare; (*reward*) dare una mancia a ● *vi* inclinarsi; (*overturn*) capovolgersi. □ **~ off** *vt* **~ sb off** (*inform*) fare una soffiata a qcno. □ **~ out** *vt* rovesciare. □ **~ over** *vt* capovolgere ● *vi* capovolgersi

tipped /tɪpt/ *adj* (cigarette) col filtro

tipsy /'tɪpsɪ/ *adj* ! brillo

tiptoe /'tɪptəʊ/ *n* **on ~** in punta di piedi

tiptop /tɪp'tɒp/ *adj* ! in condizioni perfette

tire /'taɪə(r)/ *vt* stancare ● *vi* stancarsi. **~d** *adj* stanco; **~d of** stanco di; **~d out** stanco morto. **~less** *adj* instancabile. **~some** *adj* fastidioso

tiring /'taɪərɪŋ/ *adj* stancante

tissue /'tɪʃu:/ *n* tessuto *m*; (*handkerchief*) fazzolettino *m* di carta. **~-paper** *n* carta *f* velina

tit¹ /tɪt/ *n* (*bird*) cincia *f*

tit² *n* **~ for tat** pan per focaccia

title /'taɪtl/ *n* titolo *m*. **~-deed** *n* atto *m* di proprietà. **~-role** *n* ruolo *m* principale

to /tu:/, *atono* /tə/

● *prep* a; (*to countries*) in; (*towards*) verso; (*up to, until*) fino a; **I'm going to John's/the butcher's** vado da John/dal macellaio; **come/go to sb** venire/andare da qcno; **to Italy/Switzerland** in Italia/Svizzera; **I've never been to Rome** non sono mai stato a Roma; **go to the market** andare al mercato; **to the toilet/my room** in bagno/camera mia; **to an exhibition** a una mostra; **to university** all'università; **twenty/quarter to eight** le otto meno venti/un quarto; **5 to 6 kilos** da 5 a 6 chili; **to the end** alla fine; **to this day** fino a oggi; **to the best of my recollection** per quanto mi possa ricordare; **give/say sth to sb** dare/dire qcsa a qcno; **give it to me** dammelo; **there's nothing to it** è una cosa da niente

● *verbal constructions* **to go** andare; **learn to swim** imparare a nuotare; **I want to/have to go** voglio/devo andare; **it's easy to forget** è facile da dimenticare; **too ill/tired to go** troppo malato/stanco per andare; **you have to** devi; **I don't want to** non voglio; **live to be 90** vivere fino a 90 anni; **he was the last to arrive** è stato l'ultimo ad arrivare; **to be honest,...** per essere sincero,...

● *adv* **pull to** chiudere; **to and fro** avanti e indietro

toad /təʊd/ *n* rospo *m*. **~stool** *n* fungo *m* velenoso

toast /təʊst/ *n* pane *m* tostato; (*drink*) brindisi *m* ● *vt* tostare (bread); (*drink a ~ to*) brindare a. **~er** *n* tostapane *m inv*

tobacco /tə'bækəʊ/ *n* tabacco *m*. **~nist's [shop]** *n* tabaccheria *f*

toboggan /tə'bɒgən/ *n* toboga *m* ● *vi* andare in toboga

today /tə'deɪ/ *adj & adv* oggi *m*; **a week ~** una settimana a oggi; **~'s paper** il giornale di oggi

t

toddler /'tɒdlə(r)/ *n* bambino, -a *mf* ai primi passi
toe /təʊ/ *n* dito *m* del piede; (*of footwear*) punta *f*; **big ~** alluce *m* ● *vt* **~ the line** rigar diritto. **~nail** *n* unghia *f* del piede
toffee /'tɒfɪ/ *n* caramella *f* al mou
together /tə'geðə(r)/ *adv* insieme; (*at the same time*) allo stesso tempo; **~ with** insieme a
toilet /'tɔɪlɪt/ *n* (*lavatory*) gabinetto *m*. **~ paper** *n* carta *f* igienica
toiletries /'tɔɪlɪtrɪz/ *npl* articoli *mpl* da toilette
toilet roll *n* rotolo *m* di carta igienica
token /'təʊkən/ *n* segno *m*; (*counter*) gettone *m*; (*voucher*) buono *m* ● *attrib* simbolico
told /təʊld/ ▷**TELL** ● *adj* **all ~** in tutto
tolerabl|e /'tɒl(ə)rəbl/ *adj* tollerabile; (*not bad*) discreto. **~y** *adv* discretamente
toleran|ce /'tɒl(ə)r(ə)ns/ *n* tolleranza *f*. **~t** *adj* tollerante. **~tly** *adv* con tolleranza
tolerate /'tɒləreɪt/ *vt* tollerare
toll[1] /təʊl/ *n* pedaggio *m*; **death ~** numero *m* di morti
toll[2] *vi* suonare a morto
tomato /tə'mɑːtəʊ/ *n* (*pl* **-es**) pomodoro *m*. **~ ketchup** *n* ketchup *m*. **~ purée** *n* concentrato *m* di pomodoro
tomb /tuːm/ *n* tomba *f*
'tombstone *n* pietra *f* tombale
tomorrow /tə'mɒrəʊ/ *adj & adv* domani *m*; **~ morning** domani mattina; **the day after ~** dopodomani; **see you ~!** a domani!
ton /tʌn/ *n* tonnellata *f* (= *1,016 kg.*); **~s of** [!] un sacco di
tone /təʊn/ *n* tono *m*; (*colour*) tonalità *f inv* ● **tone down** *vt* attenuare. □ **~ up** *vt* tonificare (muscles)
tongs /tɒŋz/ *npl* pinze *fpl*
tongue /tʌŋ/ *n* lingua *f*; **~ in cheek** (say) ironicamente. **~-twister** *n* scioglilingua *m inv*
tonic /'tɒnɪk/ *n* tonico *m*; (*for hair*) lozione *f* per i capelli; *fig* toccasana *m inv*; **~** [**water**] acqua *f* tonica
tonight /tə'naɪt/ *adv* stanotte; (*evening*) stasera ● *n* questa notte *f*; (*evening*) questa sera *f*
tonne /tʌn/ *n* tonnellata *f* metrica
tonsil /'tɒnsl/ *n* (*Anat*) tonsilla *f*. **~litis** *n* tonsillite *f*
too /tuː/ *adv* troppo; (*also*) anche; **~ many** troppi; **~ much** troppo; **~ little** troppo poco
took /tʊk/ ▷**TAKE**
tool /tuːl/ *n* attrezzo *m*
tooth /tuːθ/ *n* (*pl* **teeth**) dente *m*
tooth: ~ache *n* mal *m* di denti. **~brush** *n* spazzolino *m* da denti. **~paste** *n* dentifricio *m*. **~pick** *n* stuzzicadenti *m inv*
top[1] /tɒp/ *n* (*toy*) trottola *f*
top[2] *n* cima *f*; (*Sch*) primo, -a *mf*; (*upper part or half*) parte *f* superiore; (*of page, list, road*) inizio *m*; (*upper surface*) superficie *f*; (*lid*) coperchio *m*; (*of bottle*) tappo *m*; (*garment*) maglia *f*; (*blouse*) camicia *f*; (*Auto*) marcia *f* più alta; **at the ~** *fig* al vertice; **at the ~ of one's voice** a squarciagola; **on ~/on ~ of** sopra; **on ~ of that** (*besides*) per di più; **from ~ to bottom** da cima a fondo ● *adj* in alto; (official, floor) superiore; (pupil, musician etc) migliore; (speed) massimo ● *vt* (*pt/pp* **topped**) essere in testa a (list); (*exceed*) sorpassare; **~ped with ice-cream** ricoperto di gelato. □ **~ up** *vt* riempire
top: ~ 'floor *n* ultimo piano *m*. **~ hat** *n* cilindro *m*. **~-heavy** *adj* con la parte superiore sovraccarica
topic /'tɒpɪk/ *n* soggetto *m*; (*of conversation*) argomento *m*. **~al** *adj* d'attualità
topless *adj & adv* topless
topple /'tɒpl/ *vt* rovesciare ● *vi* rovesciarsi. □ **~ off** *vi* cadere
top-'secret *adj* segretissimo, top secret *inv*
torch /tɔːtʃ/ *n* torcia *f* [elettrica]; (*flaming*) fiaccola *f*
tore /tɔː(r)/ ▷**TEAR[1]**
torment[1] /'tɔːment/ *n* tormento *m*
torment[2] /tɔː'ment/ *vt* tormentare
torn /tɔːn/ ▷**TEAR[1]** ● *adj* bucato
tornado /tɔː'neɪdəʊ/ *n* (*pl* **-es**) tornado *m inv*
torpedo /tɔː'piːdəʊ/ *n* (*pl* **-es**) siluro *m* ● *vt* silurare
torrent /'tɒrənt/ *n* torrente *m*. **~ial** *adj* (rain) torrenziale
tortoise /'tɔːtəs/ *n* tartaruga *f*

t

torture /ˈtɔːtʃə(r)/ *n* tortura *f* ● *vt* torturare

Tory /ˈtɔːrɪ/ *adj & n* [!] conservatore, -trice *mf*

toss /tɒs/ *vt* gettare; (*into the air*) lanciare in aria; (*shake*) scrollare; (horse:) disarcionare; mescolare (salad); rivoltare facendo saltare in aria (pancake); **~ a coin** fare testa o croce ● *vi* **~ and turn** (*in bed*) rigirarsi; **let's ~ for it** facciamo testa o croce

tot[1] /tɒt/ *n* bimbetto, -a *mf*; ([!]: *of liquor*) goccio *m*

tot[2] *vt* (*pt/pp* **totted**) **~ up** [!] fare la somma di

total /ˈtəʊtl/ *adj* totale ● *n* totale *m* ● *vt* (*pt/pp* **totalled**) ammontare a; (*add up*) sommare

totalitarian /təʊtælɪˈteərɪən/ *adj* totalitario

totally /ˈtəʊtəlɪ/ *adv* totalmente

totter /ˈtɒtə(r)/ *vi* barcollare; (government:) vacillare

touch /tʌtʃ/ *n* tocco *m*; (*sense*) tatto *m*; (*contact*) contatto *m*; (*trace*) traccia *f*; (*of irony, humour*) tocco *m*; **get/be in ~** mettersi/essere in contatto ● *vt* toccare; (*lightly*) sfiorare; (*equal*) eguagliare; (*fig: move*) commuovere ● *vi* toccarsi. □ **~ down** *vi* (*Aeron*) atterrare. □ **~ on** *vt fig* accennare a. **touch up** *vt* ritoccare (painting). **~ing** *adj* commovente. **~screen** *n* touch screen *m inv*. **~-tone** *adj* a tastiera. **~y** *adj* permaloso; (subject) delicato

tough /tʌf/ *adj* duro; (*severe, harsh*) severo; (*durable*) resistente; (*resilient*) forte

toughen /ˈtʌfn/ *vt* rinforzare. □ **~ up** *vt* rendere più forte (person)

tour /tʊə(r)/ *n* giro *m*; (*of building, town*) visita *f*; (*Theat*), (*Sport*) tournée *f inv*; (*of duty*) servizio *m* ● *vt* visitare ● *vi* fare un giro turistico; (*Theat*) essere in tournée

touris|m /ˈtʊərɪzm/ *n* turismo *m*. **~t** *n* turista *mf* ● *attrib* turistico. **~t office** *n* ufficio *m* turistico

tournament /ˈtʊənəmənt/ *n* torneo *m*

tousle /ˈtaʊzl/ *vt* spettinare

tout /taʊt/ *n* (*ticket* **~**) bagarino *m*; (*horse-racing*) informatore *m* ● *vi* **~ for** sollecitare

tow /təʊ/ *n* rimorchio *m*; **'on ~'** 'a rimorchio'; **in ~** [!] al seguito ● *vt* rimorchiare. □ **~ away** *vt* portare via col carro attrezzi

toward[s] /təˈwɔːd(z)/ *prep* verso (*with respect to*) nei riguardi di

towel /ˈtaʊəl/ *n* asciugamano *m*. **~ling** *n* spugna *f*

tower /ˈtaʊə(r)/ *n* torre *f* ● *vi* **~ above** dominare. **~ block** *n* palazzone *m*. **~ing** *adj* torreggiante; (rage) violento

town /taʊn/ *n* città *f inv*. **~ 'hall** *n* municipio *m*

toxic /ˈtɒksɪk/ *adj* tossico

toy /tɔɪ/ *n* giocattolo *m*. **~shop** *n* negozio *m* di giocattoli. □ **~ with** *vt* giocherellare con

trace /treɪs/ *n* traccia *f* ● *vt* seguire le tracce di; (*find*) rintracciare; (*draw*) tracciare; (*with tracing-paper*) ricalcare

track /træk/ *n* traccia *f*; (*path*, (*Sport*)) pista *f*; (*Rail*) binario *m*; **keep ~ of** tenere d'occhio ● *vt* seguire le tracce di. □ **~ down** *vt* scovare

tracksuit *n* tuta *f* da ginnastica

tractor /ˈtræktə(r)/ *n* trattore *m*

trade /treɪd/ *n* commercio *m*; (*line of business*) settore *m*; (*craft*) mestiere *m*; **by ~** di mestiere ● *vt* commerciare; **~ sth for sth** scambiare qcsa per qcsa ● *vi* commerciare. □ **~ in** *vt* (*give in part exchange*) dare in pagamento parziale

ˈtrade mark *n* marchio *m* di fabbrica

trader /ˈtreɪdə(r)/ *n* commerciante *mf*

trades ˈunion *n* sindacato *m*

tradition /trəˈdɪʃn/ *n* tradizione *f*. **~al** *adj* tradizionale. **~ally** *adv* tradizionalmente

traffic /ˈtræfɪk/ *n* traffico *m* ● *vi* (*pt/pp* **trafficked**) trafficare

traffic: ~ circle *n Am* isola *f* rotatoria. **~ jam** *n* ingorgo *m*. **~ lights** *npl* semaforo *msg*. **~ warden** *n* vigile *m* [urbano]; (*woman*) vigilessa *f*

tragedy /ˈtrædʒədɪ/ *n* tragedia *f*

tragic /ˈtrædʒɪk/ *adj* tragico. **~ally** *adv* tragicamente

trail /treɪl/ *n* traccia *f*; (*path*) sentiero *m* ● *vi* strisciare; (plant:) arrampicarsi; **~ [behind]** rimanere indietro; (*in competition*) essere in svantaggio ● *vt* trascinare

trailer /ˈtreɪlə(r)/ *n* (*Auto*) rimorchio *m*; (*Am: caravan*) roulotte *f inv*; (*film*) presentazione *f* (*di un film*)

train /treɪn/ *n* treno *m*; **~ of thought**

filo *m* dei pensieri • *vt* formare professionalmente; (*Sport*) allenare; (*aim*) puntare; educare (child); addestrare (animal, soldier) • *vi* fare il tirocinio; (*Sport*) allenarsi. **~ed** *adj* (animal) addestrato (**to do** a fare)

trainee /treɪ'ni:/ *n* apprendista *mf*

train|er /'treɪnə(r)/ *n* (*Sport*) allenatore, -trice *mf*; (*in circus*) domatore, -trice *mf*; (*of dog, race-horse*) addestratore, -trice *mf*; **~ers** *pl* scarpe *fpl* da ginnastica. **~ing** *n* tirocinio *m*; (*Sport*) allenamento *m*; (*of animal, soldier*) addestramento *m*

trait /treɪt/ *n* caratteristica *f*

traitor /'treɪtə(r)/ *n* traditore, -trice *mf*

tram /træm/ *n* tram *m inv*. **~-lines** *npl* rotaie *fpl* del tram

tramp /træmp/ *n* (*hike*) camminata *f*; (*vagrant*) barbone, -a *mf*; (*of feet*) calpestio *m* • *vi* camminare con passo pesante; (*hike*) percorrere a piedi

trample /'træmpl/ *vt/i* ~ [**on**] calpestare

trampoline /'træmpəli:n/ *n* trampolino *m*

trance /trɑ:ns/ *n* trance *f inv*

tranquil /'træŋkwɪl/ *adj* tranquillo. **~lity** *n* tranquillità *f*

tranquillizer /'træŋkwɪlaɪzə(r)/ *n* tranquillante *m*

transatlantic /trænzət'læntɪk/ *adj* transatlantico

transcend /træn'send/ *vt* trascendere

transfer¹ /'trænsfɜ:(r)/ *n* trasferimento *m*; (*Sport*) cessione *f*; (*design*) decalcomania *f*

transfer² /træns'fɜ:(r)/ *v* (*pt/pp* **transferred**) • *vt* trasferire; (*Sport*) cedere • *vi* trasferirsi; (*when travelling*) cambiare. **~able** *adj* trasferibile

transform /træns'fɔ:m/ *vt* trasformare. **~ation** *n* trasformazione *f*. **~er** *n* trasformatore *m*

transfusion /træns'fju:ʒn/ *n* trasfusione *f*

transient /'trænzɪənt/ *adj* passeggero

transistor /træn'zɪstə(r)/ *n* transistor *m inv*; (*radio*) radiolina *f* a transistor

transit /'trænzɪt/ *n* transito *m*; **in ~** (goods) in transito

transition /træn'zɪʃn/ *n* transizione *f*. **~al** *adj* di transizione

transitive /'trænzɪtɪv/ *adj* transitivo

translat|e /trænz'leɪt/ *vt* tradurre. **~ion** *n* traduzione *f*. **~or** *n* traduttore, -trice *mf*

transmission /trænz'mɪʃn/ *n* trasmissione *f*

transmit /trænz'mɪt/ *vt* (*pt/pp* **transmitted**) trasmettere. **~ter** *n* trasmettitore *m*

transparen|cy /træn'spærənsɪ/ *n* (*Phot*) diapositiva *f*. **~t** *adj* trasparente

transplant¹ /'trænsplɑ:nt/ *n* trapianto *m*

transplant² /træns'plɑ:nt/ *vt* trapiantare

transport¹ /'trænspɔ:t/ *n* trasporto *m*

transport² /træn'spɔ:t/ *vt* trasportare. **~ation** *n* trasporto *m*

trap /træp/ *n* trappola *f*; (**!**: *mouth*) boccaccia *f* • *vt* (*pt/pp* **trapped**) intrappolare; schiacciare (finger in door). **~'door** *n* botola *f*

trapeze /trə'pi:z/ *n* trapezio *m*

trash /træʃ/ *n* robaccia *f*; (*rubbish*) spazzatura *f*; (*nonsense*) schiocchezze *fpl*. **~can** *n Am* secchio *m* della spazzatura. **~y** *adj* scadente

travel /'trævl/ *n* viaggi *mpl* • *v* (*pt/pp* **travelled**) • *vi* viaggiare; (*to work*) andare • *vt* percorrere (distance). **~ agency** *n* agenzia *f* di viaggi. **~ agent** *n* agente *mf* di viaggio

traveller /'trævələ(r)/ *n* viaggiatore, -trice *mf*; (*Comm*) commesso *m* viaggiatore; **~s** *pl* (*gypsies*) zingari *mpl*. **~'s cheque** *n* traveller's cheque *m inv*

trawler /'trɔ:lə(r)/ *n* peschereccio *m*

tray /treɪ/ *n* vassoio *m*; (*for baking*) teglia *f*; (*for documents*) vaschetta *f* sparticarta; (*of printer, photocopier*) vassoio *m*

treacher|ous /'tretʃərəs/ *adj* traditore; (weather, currents) pericoloso. **~y** *n* tradimento *m*

treacle /'tri:kl/ *n* melassa *f*

tread /tred/ *n* andatura *f*; (*step*) gradino *m*; (*of tyre*) battistrada *m inv* • *v* (*pt* **trod**, *pp* **trodden**) • *vi* (*walk*) camminare. □ **~ on** *vt* calpestare (grass); pestare (foot)

treason /'tri:zn/ *n* tradimento *m*

treasure /'treʒə(r)/ *n* tesoro *m* • *vt* tenere in gran conto. **~r** *n* tesoriere, -a *mf*

t

treasury /'treʒərɪ/ *n* **the T~** il Ministero del Tesoro

treat /tri:t/ *n* piacere *m*; (*present*) regalo *m*; **give sb a ~** fare una sorpresa a qcno ● *vt* trattare; (*Med*) curare; **~ sb to sth** offrire qcsa a qcno

treatise /'tri:tɪz/ *n* trattato *m*

treatment /'tri:tmənt/ *n* trattamento *m*; (*Med*) cura *f*

treaty /'tri:tɪ/ *n* trattato *m*

treble /'trebl/ *adj* triplo ● *n* (*Mus: voice*) voce *f* bianca ● *vt* triplicare ● *vi* triplicarsi. **~ clef** *n* chiave *f* di violino

tree /tri:/ *n* albero *m*

trek /trek/ *n* scarpinata *f*; (*as holiday*) trekking *m inv* ● *vi* (*pt/pp* **trekked**) farsi una scarpinata; (*on holiday*) fare trekking

tremble /'trembl/ *vi* tremare

tremendous /trɪ'mendəs/ *adj* (*huge*) enorme; ([!]: *excellent*) formidabile. **~ly** *adv* (*very*) straordinariamente; (*adj lot*) enormemente

tremor /'tremə(r)/ *n* tremito *m*; [earth] ~ scossa *f* [sismica]

trench /trentʃ/ *n* fosso *m*; (*Mil*) trincea *f*. **~ coat** *n* trench *m inv*

trend /trend/ *n* tendenza *f*; (*fashion*) moda *f*. **~y** *adj* (**-ier, -iest**) [!] di *or* alla moda

trepidation /trepɪ'deɪʃn/ *n* trepidazione *f*

trespass /'trespəs/ *vi* **~ on** introdursi abusivamente in; *fig* abusare di. **~er** *n* intruso, -a *mf*

trial /'traɪəl/ *n* (*Jur*) processo *m*; (*test, ordeal*) prova *f*; **on ~** in prova; (*Jur*) in giudizio; **by ~ and error** per tentativi

triang|le /'traɪæŋgl/ *n* triangolo *m*. **~ular** *adj* triangolare

tribe /traɪb/ *n* tribù *f inv*

tribulation /trɪbjʊ'leɪʃn/ *n* tribolazione *f*

tribunal /traɪ'bju:nl/ *n* tribunale *m*

tributary /'trɪbjʊtərɪ/ *n* affluente *m*

tribute /'trɪbju:t/ *n* tributo *m*; **pay ~** rendere omaggio

trick /trɪk/ *n* trucco *m*; (*joke*) scherzo *m*; (*in cards*) presa *f*; **do the ~** [!] funzionare; **play a ~ on** fare uno scherzo a ● *vt* imbrogliare

trickle /'trɪkl/ *vi* colare

trick|ster /'trɪkstə(r)/ *n* imbroglione, -a *mf*. **~y** *adj* (**-ier, -iest**) *adj* (operation) complesso; (situation) delicato

tricycle /'traɪsɪkl/ *n* triciclo *m*

tried /traɪd/ ⊳**TRY**

trifl|e /'traɪfl/ *n* inezia *f*; (*Culin*) zuppa *f* inglese. **~ing** *adj* insignificante

trigger /'trɪgə(r)/ *n* grilletto *m* ● *vt* **~** [**off**] scatenare

trim /trɪm/ *adj* (**trimmer, trimmest**) curato; (figure) snello ● *n* (*of hair, hedge*) spuntata *f*; (*decoration*) rifinitura *f*; **in good ~** in buono stato; (person) in forma ● *vt* (*pt/pp* **trimmed**) spuntare (hair etc); (*decorate*) ornare; (*Naut*) orientare. **~ming** *n* bordo *m*; **~mings** *pl* (*decorations*) guarnizioni *fpl*; **with all the ~mings** (*Culin*) guarnito

trinket /'trɪŋkɪt/ *n* ninnolo *m*

trio /'tri:əʊ/ *n* trio *m*

trip /trɪp/ *n* (*excursion*) gita *f*; (*journey*) viaggio *m*; (*stumble*) passo *m* falso ● *v* (*pt/pp* **tripped**) ● *vt* far inciampare ● *vi* inciampare (**on**/**over** in). □ **~ up** *vt* far inciampare

tripe /traɪp/ *n* trippa *f*; ([✖]: *nonsense*) fesserie *fpl*

triple /'trɪpl/ *adj* triplo ● *vt* triplicare ● *vi* triplicarsi

triplets /'trɪplɪts/ *npl* tre gemelli *mpl*

triplicate /'trɪplɪkət/ *n* **in ~** in triplice copia

tripod /'traɪpɒd/ *n* treppiede *m inv*

trite /traɪt/ *adj* banale

triumph /'traɪʌmf/ *n* trionfo *m* ● *vi* trionfare (**over** su). **~ant** *adj* trionfante. **~antly** *adv* (exclaim) con tono trionfante

trivial /'trɪvɪəl/ *adj* insignificante. **~ity** *n* banalità *f inv*

trolley /'trɒlɪ/ *n* carrello *m*; (*Am: tram*) tram *m inv*. **~ bus** *n* filobus *m inv*

trombone /trɒm'bəʊn/ *n* trombone *m*

troop /tru:p/ *n* gruppo *m*; **~s** *pl* truppe *fpl* ● *vi* **~ in**/**out** entrare/uscire in gruppo

trophy /'trəʊfɪ/ *n* trofeo *m*

tropic /'trɒpɪk/ *n* tropico *m*; **~s** *pl* tropici *mpl*. **~al** *adj* tropicale

trot /trɒt/ *n* trotto *m* ● *vi* (*pt/pp* **trotted**) trottare

trouble /'trʌbl/ *n* guaio *m*; (*difficulties*) problemi *mpl*; (*inconvenience*, (*Med*) disturbo *m*; (*conflict*) conflitto *m*; **be in ~**

t

essere nei guai; (swimmer, climber:) essere in difficoltà; **get into ~** finire nei guai; **get sb into ~** mettere qcno nei guai; **take the ~ to do sth** darsi la pena di far qcsa ● *vt* (*worry*) preoccupare; (*inconvenience*) disturbare; (conscience, old wound:) tormentare ● *vi* **don't ~!** non ti disturbare!. **~-maker** *n* **be a ~-maker** seminare zizzania. **~some** *adj* fastidioso

trough /trɒf/ *n* trogolo *m*; (*atmospheric*) depressione *f*

troupe /tru:p/ *n* troupe *f inv*

trousers /ˈtraʊzəz/ *npl* pantaloni *mpl*

trout /traʊt/ *n inv* trota *f*

trowel /ˈtraʊəl/ *n* (*for gardening*) paletta *f*; (*for builder*) cazzuola *f*

truant /ˈtru:ənt/ *n* **play ~** marinare la scuola

truce /tru:s/ *n* tregua *f*

truck /trʌk/ *n* (*lorry*) camion *m inv*

trudge /trʌdʒ/ *n* camminata *f* faticosa ● *vi* arrancare

true /tru:/ *adj* vero; **come ~** avverarsi

truffle /ˈtrʌfl/ *n* tartufo *m*

truly /ˈtru:lɪ/ *adv* veramente; **Yours ~** distinti saluti

trump /trʌmp/ *n* (*in cards*) atout *m inv*

trumpet /ˈtrʌmpɪt/ *n* tromba *f*. **~er** *n* trombettista *mf*

truncheon /ˈtrʌntʃn/ *n* manganello *m*

trunk /trʌŋk/ *n* (*of tree, body*) tronco *m*; (*of elephant*) proboscide *f*; (*for travelling, storage*) baule *m*; (*Am: of car*) bagagliaio *m*; **~s** *pl* calzoncini *mpl* da bagno

truss /trʌs/ *n* (*Med*) cinto *m* erniario

trust /trʌst/ *n* fiducia *f*; (*group of companies*) trust *m inv*; (*organization*) associazione *f*; **on ~** sulla parola ● *vt* fidarsi di; (*hope*) augurarsi ● *vi* **~ in** credere in; **~ to** affidarsi a. **~ed** *adj* fidato

trustee /trʌsˈti:/ *n* amministratore, -trice *mf* fiduciario, -a

ˈtrust|ful /ˈtrʌstfl/ *adj* fiducioso. **~ing** *adj* fiducioso. **~worthy** *adj* fidato

truth /tru:θ/ *n* (*pl* **-s** /tru:ðz/) verità *f inv*. **~ful** *adj* veritiero. **~fully** *adv* sinceramente

try /traɪ/ *n* tentativo *m*, prova *f*; (*in rugby*) meta *f* ● *v* (*pt/pp* **tried**) ● *vt* provare; (*be a strain on*) mettere a dura prova; (*Jur*) processare (person); discutere (case); **~ to do sth** provare a fare qcsa ● *vi* provare. □ **~ on** *vt* provarsi (garment). □ **~ out** *vt* provare

trying /ˈtraɪɪŋ/ *adj* duro; (person) irritante

T-shirt /ˈti:-/ *n* maglietta *f*

tub /tʌb/ *n* tinozza *f*; (*carton*) vaschetta *f*; (*bath*) vasca *f* da bagno

tuba /ˈtju:bə/ *n* (*Mus*) tuba *f*

tubby /ˈtʌbɪ/ *adj* (**-ier, -iest**) tozzo

tube /tju:b/ *n* tubo *m*; (*of toothpaste*) tubetto *m*; (*Rail*) metro *f*

tuberculosis /tju:bɜ:kjʊˈləʊsɪs/ *n* tubercolosi *f*

tubular /ˈtju:bjʊlə(r)/ *adj* tubolare

tuck /tʌk/ *n* piega *f* ● *vt* (*put*) infilare. □ **~ in** *vt* rimboccare; **~ sb in** rimboccare le coperte a qcno ● *vi* (🅘: *eat*) mangiare con appetito. □ **~ up** *vt* rimboccarsi (sleeves); (*in bed*) rimboccare le coperte a

Tuesday /ˈtju:zdeɪ/ *n* martedì *m inv*

tuft /tʌft/ *n* ciuffo *m*

tug /tʌg/ *n* strattone *m*; (*Naut*) rimorchiatore *m* ● *v* (*pt/pp* **tugged**) ● *vt* tirare ● *vi* dare uno strattone. **~ of war** *n* tiro *m* alla fune

tuition /tju:ˈɪʃn/ *n* lezioni *fpl*

tulip /ˈtju:lɪp/ *n* tulipano *m*

tumble /ˈtʌmbl/ *n* ruzzolone *m* ● *vi* ruzzolare. **~down** *adj* cadente. **~-drier** *n* asciugabiancheria *f*

tumbler /ˈtʌmblə(r)/ *n* bicchiere *m* (*senza stelo*)

tummy /ˈtʌmɪ/ *n* 🅘 pancia *f*

tumour /ˈtju:mə(r)/ *n* tumore *m*

tumult /ˈtju:mʌlt/ *n* tumulto *m*. **~uous** *adj* tumultuoso

tuna /ˈtju:nə/ *n* tonno *m*

tune /tju:n/ *n* motivo *m*; **out of/in ~** (instrument) scordato/accordato; (person) stonato/intonato; **to the ~ of** 🅘 per la modesta somma di ● *vt* accordare (instrument); sintonizzare (radio, TV); mettere a punto (engine). □ **~ in** *vt* sintonizzare ● *vi* sintonizzarsi (**to** su). □ **~ up** *vi* (orchestra:) accordare gli strumenti

tuneful /ˈtju:nfl/ *adj* melodioso

tuner /ˈtju:nə(r)/ *n* accordatore, -trice *mf*; (*Radio, TV*) sintonizzatore *m*

tunic /ˈtju:nɪk/ *n* tunica *f*; (*Mil*) giacca *f*; (*Sch*) ≈ grembiule *m*

tunnel /ˈtʌnl/ *n* tunnel *m inv* ● *vi* (*pt/pp*

tunnelled) scavare un tunnel

turban /ˈtɜːbən/ *n* turbante *m*

turbine /ˈtɜːbaɪn/ *n* turbina *f*

turbulen|ce /ˈtɜːbjʊləns/ *n* turbolenza *f*. **~t** *adj* turbolento

turf /tɜːf/ *n* erba *f*; (*segment*) zolla *f* erbosa ● **turf out** *vt* [!] buttar fuori

Turin /tjuːˈrɪn/ *n* Torino *f*

Turk /tɜːk/ *n* turco, -a *mf*

turkey /ˈtɜːkɪ/ *n* tacchino *m*

Turk|ey *n* Turchia *f*. **~ish** *adj* turco

turmoil /ˈtɜːmɔɪl/ *n* tumulto *m*

turn /tɜːn/ *n* (*rotation, short walk*) giro *m*; (*in road*) svolta *f*, curva *f*; (*development*) svolta *f*; (*Theat*) numero *m*; ([!]*: attack*) crisi *f inv*; **a ~ for the better**/**worse** un miglioramento/peggioramento; **do sb a good ~** rendere un servizio a qcno; **take ~s** fare a turno; **in ~** a turno; **out of ~** (speak) a sproposito; **it's your ~** tocca a te ● *vt* girare; voltare (back, eyes); dirigere (gun, attention) ● *vi* girare; (person:) girarsi; (leaves:) ingiallire; (*become*) diventare; **~ right**/**left** girare a destra/sinistra; **~ sour** inacidirsi; **~ to sb** girarsi verso qcno; *fig* rivolgersi a qcno. □ **~ against** *vi* diventare ostile a ● *vt* mettere contro. □ **~ away** *vt* mandare via (people); girare dall'altra parte (head) ● *vi* girarsi dall'altra parte. □ **~ down** *vt* piegare (collar); abbassare (heat, gas, sound); respingere (person, proposal). □ **~ in** *vt* ripiegare in dentro (edges); consegnare (lost object) ● *vi* ([!]*: go to bed*) andare a letto; **~ into the drive** entrare nel viale. □ **~ off** *vt* spegnere; chiudere (tap, water) ● *vi* (car:) girare. □ **~ on** *vt* accendere; aprire (tap, water); ([!]*: attract*) eccitare ● *vi* (*attack*) attaccare. □ **~ out** *vt* (*expel*) mandar via; spegnere (light, gas); (*produce*) produrre; (*empty*) svuotare (room, cupboard) ● *vi* (*transpire*) risultare; **~ out well**/**badly** (cake, dress:) riuscire bene/male; (situation:) andare bene/male. □ **~ over** *vt* girare ● *vi* girarsi; **please ~ over** vedi retro. □ **~ round** *vi* girarsi; (car:) girare. □ **~ up** *vt* tirare su (collar); alzare (heat, gas, sound, radio) ● *vi* farsi vedere

turning /ˈtɜːnɪŋ/ *n* svolta *f*. **~-point** *n* svolta *f* decisiva

turnip /ˈtɜːnɪp/ *n* rapa *f*

turn: ~over *n* (*Comm*) giro *m* d'affari; (*of staff*) ricambio *m*. **~pike** *n Am* autostrada *f*. **~stile** *n* cancelletto *m* girevole. **~table** *n* piattaforma *f* girevole; (*on record-player*) piatto *m* (*di giradischi*). **~-up** *n* (*of trousers*) risvolto *m*

turquoise /ˈtɜːkwɔɪz/ *adj* (*colour*) turchese ● *n* turchese *m*

turret /ˈtʌrɪt/ *n* torretta *f*

turtle /ˈtɜːtl/ *n* tartaruga *f* acquatica

tusk /tʌsk/ *n* zanna *f*

tussle /ˈtʌsl/ *n* zuffa *f* ● *vi* azzuffarsi

tutor /ˈtjuːtə(r)/ *n* insegnante *mf* privato, -a; (*Univ*) *insegnante mf universitario, -a che segue individualmente un ristretto numero di studenti*. **~ial** *n* discussione *f* col tutor

tuxedo /tʌkˈsiːdəʊ/ *n Am* smoking *m inv*

TV *n abbr* (television) tv *f inv*, tivù *f inv*

twang /twæŋ/ *n* (*in voice*) suono *m* nasale ● *vt* far vibrare

tweezers /ˈtwiːzəz/ *npl* pinzette *fpl*

twelfth /twelfθ/ *adj* dodicesimo

twelve /twelv/ *adj* dodici

twentieth /ˈtwentɪɪθ/ *adj* ventesimo

twenty /ˈtwentɪ/ *adj* venti

twice /twaɪs/ *adv* due volte

twiddle /ˈtwɪdl/ *vt* giocherellare con; **~ one's thumbs** *fig* girarsi i pollici

twig[1] /twɪg/ *n* ramoscello *m*

twig[2] *vt/i* (*pt/pp* **twigged**) [!] intuire

twilight /ˈtwaɪ-/ *n* crepuscolo *m*

twin /twɪn/ *n* gemello, -a *mf* ● *attrib* gemello. **~ beds** *npl* letti *mpl* gemelli

twine /twaɪn/ *n* spago *m* ● *vi* intrecciarsi; (plant:) attorcigliarsi ● *vt* intrecciare

twinge /twɪndʒ/ *n* fitta *f*; **~ of conscience** rimorso *m* di coscienza

twinkle /ˈtwɪŋkl/ *n* scintillio *m* ● *vi* scintillare

twirl /twɜːl/ *vt* far roteare ● *vi* volteggiare ● *n* piroetta *f*

twist /twɪst/ *n* torsione *f*; (*curve*) curva *f*; (*in rope*) attorcigliata *f*; (*in book, plot*) colpo *m* di scena ● *vt* attorcigliare (rope); torcere (metal); girare (knob, cap); (*distort*) distorcere; **~ one's ankle** storcersi la caviglia ● *vi* attorcigliarsi; (road:) essere pieno di curve

twit /twɪt/ *n* [!] cretino, -a *mf*

t

twitch /twɪtʃ/ *n* tic *m inv*; (*jerk*) strattone *m* ● *vi* contrarsi
twitter /'twɪtə(r)/ *n* cinguettio *m* ● *vi* cinguettare; (person:) cianciare
two /tu:/ *adj* due
two: ~-faced *adj* falso. **~-piece** *adj* (*swimsuit*) due pezzi *m inv*; (*suit*) completo *m*. **~-way** *adj* (traffic) a doppio senso di marcia
tycoon /taɪ'ku:n/ *n* magnate *m*
tying /'taɪɪŋ/ ▷TIE
type /taɪp/ *n* tipo *m*; (*printing*) carattere *m* [tipografico] ● *vt* scrivere a macchina ● *vi* scrivere a macchina. **~writer** *n* macchina *f* da scrivere. **~written** *adj* dattiloscritto
typical /'tɪpɪkl/ *adj* tipico. **~ly** *adv* tipicamente; (*as usual*) come al solito
typify /'tɪpɪfaɪ/ *vt* (*pt/pp* **-ied**) essere tipico di
typing /'taɪpɪŋ/ *n* dattilografia *f*
typist /'taɪpɪst/ *n* dattilografo, -a *mf*
tyrannical /tɪ'rænɪkl/ *adj* tirannico
tyranny /'tɪrənɪ/ *n* tirannia *f*
tyrant /'taɪrənt/ *n* tiranno, -a *mf*
tyre /'taɪə(r)/ *n* gomma *f*, pneumatico *m*

Uu

udder /'ʌdə(r)/ *n* mammella *f* (*di vacca, capra etc*)
UK *n abbr* United Kingdom
ulcer /'ʌlsə(r)/ *n* ulcera *f*
ultimate /'ʌltɪmət/ *adj* definitivo; (*final*) finale; (*fundamental*) fondamentale. **~ly** *adv* alla fine
ultimatum /ʌltɪ'meɪtəm/ *n* ultimatum *m inv*
ultra'violet *adj* ultravioletto
umbrella /ʌm'brelə/ *n* ombrello *m*
umpire /'ʌmpaɪə(r)/ *n* arbitro *m* ● *vt/i* arbitrare
umpteen /ʌmp'ti:n/ *adj* [!] innumerevole. **~th** *adj* [!] ennesimo; **for the ~th time** per l'ennesima volta
UN *n abbr* (United Nations) ONU *f*
un'able /ʌn-/ *adj* **be ~ to do sth** non potere fare qcsa; (*not know how*) non sapere fare qcsa
unac'companied *adj* non accompagnato; (luggage) incustodito
unac'customed *adj* insolito; **be ~ to** non essere abituato a
un'aided *adj* senza aiuto
unanimous /ju:'nænɪməs/ *adj* unanime. **~ly** *adv* all'unanimità
un'armed *adj* disarmato; **~ combat** *n* lotta *f* senza armi
unat'tended *adj* incustodito
una'voidable *adj* inevitabile
una'ware *adj* **be ~ of sth** non rendersi conto di qcsa. **~s** *adv* **catch sb ~s** prendere qcno alla sprovvista
un'bearabl|e *adj* insopportabile. **~y** *adv* insopportabilmente
unbeat|able /ʌn'bi:təbl/ *adj* imbattibile. **~en** *adj* imbattuto
unbe'lievable *adj* incredibile
un'biased *adj* obiettivo
un'block *vt* sbloccare
un'bolt *vt* togliere il chiavistello di
un'breakable *adj* infrangibile
un'button *vt* sbottonare
uncalled-for /ʌn'kɔ:ldfɔ:(r)/ *adj* fuori luogo
un'canny *adj* sorprendente; (silence, feeling) inquietante
un'certain *adj* incerto; (weather) instabile; **in no ~ terms** senza mezzi termini. **~ty** *n* incertezza *f*
un'charitable *adj* duro
uncle /'ʌŋkl/ *n* zio *m*

> *i* **Uncle Sam** Personaggio immaginario che rappresenta gli Stati Uniti, il suo governo e i suoi cittadini. Nell'iconografia è tradizionalmente rappresentato con la barba bianca, vestito dei colori nazionali bianco, rosso e azzurro, con un gran cappello a cilindro con le stelle della bandiera americana. Spesso utilizzato quando si fa appello al patriottismo americano.

un'comfortabl|e *adj* scomodo; imbarazzante (silence, situation); **feel ~e** *fig* sentirsi a disagio. **~y** *adv* (sit) scomodamente; (*causing alarm etc*) spaventosamente

t u

un'common *adj* insolito
un'compromising *adj* intransigente
uncon'ditional *adj* incondizionato. **~ly** *adv* incondizionatamente
un'conscious *adj* privo di sensi; (*unaware*) inconsapevole; **be ~ of sth** non rendersi conto di qcsa. **~ly** *adv* inconsapevolmente
uncon'ventional *adj* poco convenzionale
un'cork *vt* sturare
uncouth /ʌn'ku:θ/ *adj* zotico
un'cover *vt* scoprire; portare alla luce (buried object)
unde'cided *adj* indeciso; (*not settled*) incerto
undeniabl|e /ʌndɪ'naɪəbl/ *adj* innegabile. **~y** *adv* innegabilmente
under /'ʌndə(r)/ *prep* sotto; (*less than*) al di sotto di; **~ there** lì sotto; **~ repair/construction** in riparazione/costruzione; **~ way** *fig* in corso ● *adv* (**~** *water*) sott'acqua; (*unconscious*) sotto anestesia
'undercarriage *n* (*Aeron*) carrello *m*
'underclothes *npl* biancheria *fsg* intima
under'cover *adj* clandestino
'undercurrent *n* corrente *f* sottomarina; *fig* sottofondo *m*
'underdog *n* perdente *m*
under'done *adj* (meat) al sangue
under'estimate *vt* sottovalutare
under'fed *adj* denutrito
under'foot *adv* sotto i piedi; **trample ~** calpestare
under'go *vt* (*pt* **-went**, *pp* **-gone**) subire (operation, treatment); **~ repair** essere in riparazione
under'graduate *n* studente, -tessa *mf* universitario, -a
under'ground[1] *adv* sottoterra
'underground[2] *adj* sotterraneo; (*secret*) clandestino ● *n* (*railway*) metropolitana *f*. **~ car park** *n* parcheggio *m* sotterraneo
'undergrowth *n* sottobosco *m*
'underhand *adj* subdolo
under'lie *vt* (*pt* **-lay**, *pp* **-lain**, *pres p* **-lying**) *fig* essere alla base di
under'line *vt* sottolineare
under'lying *adj fig* fondamentale
under'mine *vt fig* minare
underneath /ʌndə'ni:θ/ *prep* sotto; **~ it** sotto ● *adv* sotto
under'paid *adj* mal pagato
'underpants *npl* mutande *fpl*
'underpass *n* sottopassaggio *m*
under'privileged *adj* non abbiente
under'rate *vt* sottovalutare
'undershirt *n Am* maglia *f* della pelle
under'stand *vt* (*pt/pp* **-stood**) capire; **I ~ that...** (*have heard*) mi risulta che... ● *vi* capire. **~able** *adj* comprensibile. **~ably** *adv* comprensibilmente
under'standing *adj* comprensivo ● *n* comprensione *f*; (*agreement*) accordo *m*; **on the ~ that** a condizione che
'understatement *n* understatement *m inv*
under'take *vt* (*pt* **-took**, *pp* **-taken**) intraprendere; **~ to do sth** impegnarsi a fare qcsa
'undertaker *n* impresario *m* di pompe funebri; [**firm of**] **~s** *n* impresa *f* di pompe funebri
under'taking *n* impresa *f*; (*promise*) promessa *f*
'undertone *n fig* sottofondo *m*; **in an ~** sottovoce
under'value *vt* sottovalutare
'underwater[1] *adj* subacqueo
under'water[2] *adv* sott'acqua
'underwear *n* biancheria *f* intima
under'weight *adj* sotto peso
'underworld *n* (*criminals*) malavita *f*
unde'sirable *adj* indesiderato; (person) poco raccomandabile
un'dignified *adj* non dignitoso
un'do *vt* (*pt* **-did**, *pp* **-done**) disfare; slacciare (dress, shoes); sbottonare (shirt); *fig*, (*Comput*) annullare
un'doubted *adj* indubbio. **~ly** *adv* senza dubbio
un'dress *vt* spogliare; **get ~ed** spogliarsi ● *vi* spogliarsi
un'due *adj* eccessivo
un'duly *adv* eccessivamente
un'earth *vt* dissotterrare; *fig* scovare; scoprire (secret). **~ly** *adj* soprannaturale; **at an ~ly hour** [!] a un'ora impossibile
uneco'nomic *adj* poco remunerativo

unem'ployed *adj* disoccupato ● *npl* **the ~** i disoccupati
unem'ployment *n* disoccupazione *f*. **~ benefit** *n* sussidio *m* di disoccupazione
un'ending *adj* senza fine
un'equal *adj* disuguale; (struggle) impari; **be ~ to a task** non essere all'altezza di un compito
unequivocal /ʌnɪ'kwɪvəkl/ *adj* inequivocabile; (person) esplicito
un'ethical *adj* immorale
un'even *adj* irregolare; (distribution) ineguale; (number) dispari
unex'pected *adj* inaspettato. **~ly** *adv* inaspettatamente
un'fair *adj* ingiusto. **~ly** *adv* ingiustamente. **~ness** *n* ingiustizia *f*
un'faithful *adj* infedele
unfa'miliar *adj* sconosciuto; **be ~ with** non conoscere
un'fasten *vt* slacciare; (*detach*) staccare
un'favourable *adj* sfavorevole; (impression) negativo
un'feeling *adj* insensibile
un'fit *adj* inadatto; (*morally*) indegno; (*Sport*) fuori forma; **~ for work** non in grado di lavorare
un'fold *vt* spiegare; (*spread out*) aprire; *fig* rivelare ● *vi* (view:) spiegarsi
unfore'seen *adj* imprevisto
unforgettable /ʌnfə'getəbl/ *adj* indimenticabile
unforgivable /ʌnfə'gɪvəbl/ *adj* imperdonabile
un'fortunate *adj* sfortunato; (*regrettable*) spiacevole; (remark, choice) infelice. **~ly** *adv* purtroppo
un'founded *adj* infondato
unfurl /ʌn'fɜ:l/ *vt* spiegare
ungainly /ʌn'geɪnlɪ/ *adj* sgraziato
un'grateful *adj* ingrato. **~ly** *adv* senza riconoscenza
un'happy *adj* infelice; (*not content*) insoddisfatto (**with** di)
un'harmed *adj* incolume
un'healthy *adj* poco sano; (*insanitary*) malsano
un'hurt *adj* illeso
unification /ju:nɪfɪ'keɪʃn/ *n* unificazione *f*
uniform /'ju:nɪfɔ:m/ *adj* uniforme ● *n* uniforme *f*. **~ly** *adv* uniformemente
unify /'ju:nɪfaɪ/ *vt* (*pt/pp* **-ied**) unificare
uni'lateral /ju:nɪ-/ *adj* unilaterale
uni'maginable *adj* inimmaginabile
unim'portant *adj* irrilevante
unin'habited *adj* disabitato
unin'tentional *adj* involontario. **~ly** *adv* involontariamente
union /'ju:nɪən/ *n* unione *f*; (*trade* **~**) sindacato *m*. **U~ Jack** *n* bandiera *f* del Regno Unito
unique /ju:'ni:k/ *adj* unico. **~ly** *adv* unicamente
unison /'ju:nɪsn/ *n* **in ~** all'unisono
unit /'ju:nɪt/ *n* unità *f inv*; (*department*) reparto *m*; (*of furniture*) elemento *m*
unite /ju:'naɪt/ *vt* unire ● *vi* unirsi
unity /'ju:nətɪ/ *n* unità *f*; (*agreement*) accordo *m*
universal /ju:nɪ'vɜ:sl/ *adj* universale. **~ly** *adv* universalmente
universe /'ju:nɪvɜ:s/ *n* universo *m*
university /ju:nɪ'vɜ:sətɪ/ n università *f* ● *attrib* universitario
un'just *adj* ingiusto
un'kind *adj* scortese. **~ly** *adv* in modo scortese. **~ness** *n* mancanza *f* di gentilezza
un'known *adj* sconosciuto
un'lawful *adj* illecito, illegale
unleaded /ʌn'ledɪd/ *adj* senza piombo
un'leash *vt fig* scatenare
unless /ən'les/ *conj* a meno che; **~ I am mistaken** se non mi sbaglio
un'like *adj* (*not the same*) diversi ● *prep* diverso da; **that's ~ him** non è da lui; **~ me, he...** diversamente da me, lui...
un'likely *adj* improbabile
un'limited *adj* illimitato
un'load *vt* scaricare
un'lock *vt* aprire (*con chiave*)
un'lucky *adj* sfortunato; **it's ~ to...** porta sfortuna...
un'married *adj* non sposato. **~ 'mother** *n* ragazza *f* madre
un'mask *vt fig* smascherare
unmistakabl|e /ʌnmɪ'steɪkəbl/ *adj* inconfondibile. **~y** *adv* chiaramente
un'natural *adj* innaturale; *pej* anormale. **~ly** *adv* in modo innaturale; *pej* in modo anormale

u

un'necessar|y *adj* inutile. **~ily** *adv* inutilmente
un'noticed *adj* inosservato
unob'tainable *adj* (product) introvabile; (phone number) non ottenibile
unob'trusive *adj* discreto. **~ly** *adv* in modo discreto
unof'ficial *adj* non ufficiale. **~ly** *adv* ufficiosamente
un'pack *vi* disfare le valigie ● *vt* svuotare (parcel); spacchettare (books); **~ one's case** disfare la valigia
un'paid *adj* da pagare; (*work*) non retribuito
un'pleasant *adj* sgradevole; (person) maleducato. **~ly** *adv* sgradevolmente; (behave) maleducatamente. **~ness** *n* (*bad feeling*) tensioni *fpl*
un'plug *vt* (*pt/pp* **-plugged**) staccare
un'popular *adj* impopolare
un'precedented *adj* senza precedenti
unpre'dictable *adj* imprevedibile
unpre'pared *adj* impreparato
unpro'fessional *adj* non professionale; **it's ~** è una mancanza di professionalità
un'profitable *adj* non redditizio
un'qualified *adj* non qualificato; (*fig: absolute*) assoluto
un'questionable *adj* incontestabile
unravel /ʌn'rævl/ *vt* (*pt/pp* **-ravelled**) districare; (*in knitting*) disfare
un'real *adj* irreale; [!] inverosimile
un'reasonable *adj* irragionevole
unre'lated *adj* (fact) senza rapporto (**to** con); (person) non imparentato (**to** con)
unre'liable *adj* inattendibile; (person) inaffidabile, che non dà affidamento
un'rest *n* fermenti *mpl*
un'rivalled *adj* ineguagliato
un'roll *vt* srotolare ● *vi* srotolarsi
unruly /ʌn'ru:lɪ/ *adj* indisciplinato
un'safe *adj* pericoloso
unsatis'factory *adj* poco soddisfacente
un'savoury *adj* equivoco
unscathed /ʌn'skeɪðd/ *adj* illeso
un'screw *vt* svitare
un'scrupulous *adj* senza scrupoli
un'seemly *adj* indecoroso
un'selfish *adj* disinteressato
un'settled *adj* in agitazione; (weather) variabile; (bill) non saldato
unshakeable /ʌn'ʃeɪkəbl/ *adj* categorico
unshaven /ʌn'ʃeɪvn/ *adj* non rasato
unsightly /ʌn'saɪtlɪ/ *adj* brutto
un'skilled *adj* non specializzato. **~ worker** *n* manovale *m*
un'sociable *adj* scontroso
unso'phisticated *adj* semplice
un'sound *adj* (building, reasoning) poco solido; (advice) poco sensato; **of ~ mind** malato di mente
un'stable *adj* instabile; (*mentally*) squilibrato
un'steady *adj* malsicuro
un'stuck *adj* **come ~** staccarsi; ([!]: *project*) andare a monte
unsuc'cessful *adj* fallimentare; **be ~** (*in attempt*) non aver successo. **~ly** *adv* senza successo
un'suitable *adj* (*inappropriate*) inadatto; (*inconvenient*) inopportuno
unthinkable /ʌn'θɪŋkəbl/ *adj* impensabile
un'tidiness *n* disordine *m*
un'tidy *adj* disordinato
un'tie *vt* slegare
until /ən'tɪl/ *prep* fino a; **not ~** non prima di; **~ the evening** fino alla sera; **~ his arrival** fino al suo arrivo ● *conj* finché, fino a quando; **not ~ you've seen it** non prima che tu l'abbia visto
un'told *adj* (wealth) incalcolabile; (suffering) indescrivibile; (story) inedito
un'true *adj* falso; **that's ~** non è vero
unused¹ /ʌn'ju:zd/ *adj* non [ancora] usato
unused² /ʌn'ju:st/ *adj* **be ~ to** non essere abituato a
un'usual *adj* insolito. **~ly** *adv* insolitamente
un'veil *vt* scoprire
un'wanted *adj* indesiderato
un'welcome *adj* sgradito
un'well *adj* indisposto
unwieldy /ʌn'wi:ldɪ/ *adj* ingombrante
un'willing *adj* riluttante. **~ly** *adv* malvolentieri
un'wind *v* (*pt/pp* **unwound**) ● *vt* svol-

gere, srotolare • *vi* svolgersi, srotolarsi; (!: *relax*) rilassarsi

un'wise *adj* imprudente

un'worthy *adj* non degno

un'wrap *vt* (*pt/pp* **-wrapped**) scartare (present, parcel)

un'written *adj* tacito

up /ʌp/ *adv* su; (*not in bed*) alzato; (road) smantellato; (theatre curtain, blinds) alzato; (shelves, tent) montato; (notice) affisso; (building) costruito; **prices are up** i prezzi sono aumentati; **be up for sale** essere in vendita; **up here/there** quassù/lassù; **time's up** tempo scaduto; **what's up?** ! cosa è successo?; **up to** (*as far as*) fino a; **be up to** essere all'altezza di (task); **what's he up to?** ! cosa sta facendo?; (*plotting*) cosa sta combinando?; **I'm up to page 100** sono arrivato a pagina 100; **feel up to it** sentirsela; **be one up on sb** ! essere in vantaggio su qcno; **go up** salire; **lift up** alzare; **up against** *fig* alle prese con • *prep* su; **the cat ran/is up the tree** il gatto è salito di corsa/è sull'albero; **further up this road** più avanti su questa strada; **row up the river** risalire il fiume; **go up the stairs** salire su per le scale; **be up the pub** ! essere al pub; **be up on** *or* **in sth** essere bene informato su qcsa • *n* **ups and downs** *npl* alti *mpl* e bassi

'upbringing *n* educazione *f*

up'date¹ *vt* aggiornare

'update² *n* aggiornamento *m*

up'grade *vt* promuovere (person); modernizzare (equipment)

upheaval /ʌp'hi:vl/ *n* scompiglio *m*

up'hill *adj* in salita; *fig* arduo • *adv* in salita

u

up'hold *vt* (*pt/pp* **upheld**) sostenere (principle); confermare (verdict)

upholster /ʌp'həʊlstə(r)/ *vt* tappezzare. **~er** *n* tappezziere, -a *mf*. **~y** *n* tappezzeria *f*

'upkeep *n* mantenimento *m*

up-'market *adj* di qualità

upon /ə'pɒn/ *prep* su; **~ arriving home** una volta arrivato a casa

upper /'ʌpə(r)/ *adj* superiore • *n* (*of shoe*) tomaia *f*

upper class *n* alta borghesia *f*

'upright *adj* dritto; (piano) verticale; (*honest*) retto • *n* montante *m*

'uprising *n* rivolta *f*

'uproar *n* tumulto *m*; **be in an ~** essere in trambusto

up'set¹ *vt* (*pt/pp* **upset**, *pres p* **upsetting**) rovesciare; sconvolgere (plan); (*distress*) turbare; **get ~ about sth** prendersela per qcsa; **be very ~** essere sconvolto; **have an ~ stomach** avere l'intestino disturbato

'upset² *n* scombussolamento *m*

'upshot *n* risultato *m*

upside 'down *adv* sottosopra; **turn ~ ~** capovolgere

up'stairs¹ *adv* [al piano] di sopra

'upstairs² *adj* del piano superiore

'upstart *n* arrivato, -a *mf*

up'stream *adv* controcorrente

'uptake *n* **be slow on the ~** essere lento nel capire; **be quick on the ~** capire le cose al volo

up-to-'date *adj* moderno; (news) ultimo; (records) aggiornato

'upturn *n* ripresa *f*

upward /'ʌpwəd/ *adj* verso l'alto, in su; **~ slope** salita *f* • *adv* **~[s]** verso l'alto; **~s of** oltre

uranium /jʊ'reɪnɪəm/ *n* uranio *m*

urban /'ɜ:bən/ *adj* urbano

urge /ɜ:dʒ/ *n* forte desiderio *m* • *vt* esortare (**to** a). □ **~ on** *vt* spronare

urgen|cy /'ɜ:dʒənsɪ/ *n* urgenza *f*. **~t** *adj* urgente

urinate /'jʊərɪneɪt/ *vi* urinare

urine /'jʊərɪn/ *n* urina *f*

us /ʌs/ *pron* ci; (*after prep*) noi; **they know us** ci conoscono; **give us the money** dateci i soldi; **give it to us** datecelo; **they showed it to us** ce l'hanno fatto vedere; **they meant us, not you** intendevano noi, non voi; **it's us** siamo noi; **she hates us** ci odia

US[A] *n[pl]* *abbr* (**United States [of America]**) U.S.A. *mpl*

usage /'ju:sɪdʒ/ *n* uso *m*

use¹ /ju:s/ *n* uso *m*; **be of ~** essere utile; **be of no ~** essere inutile; **make ~ of** usare; (*exploit*) sfruttare; **it is no ~** è inutile; **what's the ~?** a che scopo?

use² /ju:z/ *vt* usare. □ **~ up** *vt* consumare

used¹ /ju:zd/ *adj* usato

used² /ju:st/ *pt* **be ~ to sth** essere abituato a qcsa; **get ~ to** abituarsi a; **he ~ to live here** viveva qui

useful /'ju:sfl/ *adj* utile. **~ness** *n* utilità *f*

useless /'ju:slɪs/ *adj* inutile; (!: person) incapace

user /'ju:zə(r)/ *n* utente *mf*. **~-'friendly** *adj* facile da usare

usher /'ʌʃə(r)/ *n* (*Theat*) maschera *f*; (*Jur*) usciere *m*; (*at wedding*) *persona f che accompagna gli invitati a un matrimonio ai loro posti in chiesa* • **usher in** *vt* fare entrare

usherette /ʌʃə'ret/ *n* maschera *f*

usual /'ju:ʒʊəl/ *adj* usuale; **as ~** come al solito. **~ly** *adv* di solito

utensil /ju:'tensl/ *n* utensile *m*

utilize /'ju:tɪlaɪz/ *vt* utilizzare

utmost /'ʌtməʊst/ *adj* estremo • *n* **one's ~** tutto il possibile

utter¹ /'ʌtə(r)/ *adj* totale. **~ly** *adv* completamente

utter² *vt* emettere (sigh, sound); proferire (word). **~ance** *n* dichiarazione *f*

U-turn /'ju:-/ *n* (*Auto*) inversione *f* a U; *fig* marcia *f* in dietro

Vv

vacan|cy /'veɪk(ə)nsɪ/ *n* (*job*) posto *m* vacante; (*room*) stanza *f* disponibile. **~t** *adj* libero; (position) vacante; (look) assente

vacate /və'keɪt/ *vt* lasciare libero

vacation /və'keɪʃn/ *n* vacanza *f*

vaccinat|e /'væksɪneɪt/ *vt* vaccinare. **~ion** *n* vaccinazione *f*

vaccine /'væksi:n/ *n* vaccino *m*

vacuum /'vækjʊəm/ *n* vuoto *m* • *vt* passare l'aspirapolvere in/su. **~ cleaner** *n* aspirapolvere *m inv*. **~ flask** *n* thermos® *m inv*. **~-packed** *adj* confezionato sottovuoto

vagina /və'dʒaɪnə/ *n* (*Anat*) vagina *f*

vague /veɪg/ *adj* vago; (outline) impreciso; (*absent-minded*) distratto; **I'm still ~ about it** non ho ancora le idee chiare in proposito. **~ly** *adv* vagamente

vain /veɪn/ *adj* vanitoso; (hope, attempt) vano; **in ~** invano. **~ly** *adv* vanamente

valentine /'væləntaɪn/ *n* (*card*) biglietto *m* di San Valentino

valiant /'vælɪənt/ *adj* valoroso

valid /'vælɪd/ *adj* valido. **~ate** *vt* (*confirm*) convalidare. **~ity** *n* validità *f*

valley /'vælɪ/ *n* valle *f*

valour /'vælə(r)/ *n* valore *m*

valuable /'væljʊəbl/ *adj* di valore; *fig* prezioso. **~s** *npl* oggetti *mpl* di valore

valuation /væljʊ'eɪʃn/ *n* valutazione *f*

value /'vælju:/ *n* valore *m*; (*usefulness*) utilità *f* • *vt* valutare; (*cherish*) apprezzare. **~ 'added tax** *n* imposta *f* sul valore aggiunto

valve /vælv/ *n* valvola *f*

vampire /'væmpaɪə(r)/ *n* vampiro *m*

van /væn/ *n* furgone *m*

vandal /'vændl/ *n* vandalo, -a *mf*. **~ism** *n* vandalismo *m*. **~ize** *vt* vandalizzare

vanilla /və'nɪlə/ *n* vaniglia *f*

vanish /'vænɪʃ/ *vi* svanire

vanity /'vænətɪ/ *n* vanità *f*. **~ bag** *or* **case** *n* beauty-case *m inv*

vapour /'veɪpə(r)/ *n* vapore *m*

variable /'veərɪəbl/ *adj* variabile; (*adjustable*) regolabile

variance /'veərɪəns/ *n* **be at ~** essere in disaccordo

variant /'veərɪənt/ *n* variante *f*

variation /veərɪ'eɪʃn/ *n* variazione *f*

varied /'veərɪd/ *adj* vario; (diet) diversificato; (life) movimentato

variety /və'raɪətɪ/ *n* varietà *f inv*

various /'veərɪəs/ *adj* vario

varnish /'vɑ:nɪʃ/ *n* vernice *f*; (*for nails*) smalto *m* • *vt* verniciare; **~ one's nails** mettersi lo smalto

vary /'veərɪ/ *vt/i* (*pt/pp* **-ied**) variare. **~ing** *adj* variabile; (*different*) diverso

vase /vɑ:z/ *n* vaso *m*

vast /vɑ:st/ *adj* vasto; (difference, amusement) enorme. **~ly** *adv* (superior) di gran lunga; (different, amused) enormemente

vat /væt/ *n* tino *m*

u

VAT /viːeɪ'tiː/, /væt/ *n abbr* (value added tax) I.V.A. *f*

vault[1] /vɔːlt/ *n* (*roof*) volta *f*; (*in bank*) caveau *m inv*; (*tomb*) cripta *f*

vault[2] *n* salto *m* ● *vt/i* ~ [**over**] saltare

VDU *n abbr* (visual display unit) VDU *m*

veal /viːl/ *n* carne *f* di vitello ● *attrib* di vitello

veer /vɪə(r)/ *vi* cambiare direzione; (*Auto, Naut*) virare

vegetable /'vedʒtəbl/ *n* (*food*) verdura *f*; (*when growing*) ortaggio *m* ● *attrib* (oil, fat) vegetale

vegetarian /vedʒɪ'teərɪən/ *adj & n* vegetariano, -a *mf*

vehicle /'viːɪkl/ *n* veicolo *m*; (*fig: medium*) mezzo *m*

veil /veɪl/ *n* velo *m* ● *vt* velare

vein /veɪn/ *n* vena *f*; (*mood*) umore *m*; (*manner*) tenore *m*. **~ed** *adj* venato

velocity /vɪ'lɒsətɪ/ *n* velocità *f*

velvet /'velvɪt/ *n* velluto *m*. **~y** *adj* vellutato

vendetta /ven'detə/ *n* vendetta *f*

vending-machine /'vendɪŋ-/ *n* distributore *m* automatico

veneer /və'nɪə(r)/ *n* impiallacciatura *f*; *fig* vernice *f*. **~ed** *adj* impiallacciato

venereal /vɪ'nɪərɪəl/ *adj* **~ disease** malattia *f* venerea

Venetian /və'niːʃn/ *adj & n* veneziano, -a *mf*. **v~ blind** *n* persiana *f* alla veneziana

vengeance /'vendʒəns/ *n* vendetta *f*; **with a ~** [!] a più non posso

venison /'venɪsn/ *n* (*Culin*) carne *f* di cervo

venom /'venəm/ *n* veleno *m*. **~ous** *adj* velenoso

vent[1] /vent/ *n* presa *f* d'aria; **give ~ to** *fig* dar libero sfogo a ● *vt fig* sfogare (anger)

vent[2] *n* (*in jacket*) spacco *m*

V

ventilat|e /'ventɪleɪt/ *vt* ventilare. **~ion** *n* ventilazione *f*; (*installation*) sistema *m* di ventilazione. **~or** *n* ventilatore *m*

ventriloquist /ven'trɪləkwɪst/ *n* ventriloquo, -a *mf*

venture /'ventʃə(r)/ *n* impresa *f* ● *vt* azzardare ● *vi* avventurarsi

venue /'venjuː/ *n* luogo *m* (*di convegno, concerto, ecc.*)

veranda /və'rændə/ *n* veranda *f*

verb /vɜːb/ *n* verbo *m*. **~al** *adj* verbale

verdict /'vɜːdɪkt/ *n* verdetto *m*; (*opinion*) parere *m*

verge /vɜːdʒ/ *n* orlo *m*; **be on the ~ of doing sth** essere sul punto di fare qcsa ● **verge on** *vt fig* rasentare

verify /'verɪfaɪ/ *vt* (*pt/pp* **-ied**) verificare; (*confirm*) confermare

vermin /'vɜːmɪn/ *n* animali *mpl* nocivi

versatil|e /'vɜːsətaɪl/ *adj* versatile. **~ity** *n* versatilità *f*

verse /vɜːs/ *n* verso *m*; (*of Bible*) versetto *m*; (*poetry*) versi *mpl*

versed /vɜːst/ *adj* **~ in** versato in

versus /'vɜːsəs/ *prep* contro

vertebra /'vɜːtɪbrə/ *n* (*pl* **-brae** /-briː/) (*Anat*) vertebra *f*

vertical /'vɜːtɪkl/ *adj & n* verticale *m*

vertigo /'vɜːtɪgəʊ/ *n* (*Med*) vertigine *f*

verve /vɜːv/ *n* verve *f*

very /'verɪ/ *adv* molto; **~ much** molto; **~ little** pochissimo; **~ many** moltissimi; **~ few** pochissimi; **~ probably** molto probabilmente; **~ well** benissimo; **at the ~ most** tutt'al più; **at the ~ latest** al più tardi ● *adj* **the ~ first** il primissimo; **the ~ thing** proprio ciò che ci vuole; **at the ~ end/beginning** proprio alla fine/all'inizio; **that ~ day** proprio quel giorno; **the ~ thought** la sola idea; **only a ~ little** solo un pochino

vessel /'vesl/ *n* nave *f*

vest /vest/ *n* maglia *f* della pelle; (*Am: waistcoat*) gilè *m inv*. **~ed interest** *n* interesse *m* personale

vestige /'vestɪdʒ/ *n* (*of past*) vestigio *m*

vet /vet/ *n* veterinario, -a *mf* ● *vt* (*pt/pp* **vetted**) controllare minuziosamente

veteran /'vetərən/ *n* veterano, -a *mf*

veterinary /'vetərɪnərɪ/ *adj* veterinario. **~ surgeon** *n* medico *m* veterinario

veto /'viːtəʊ/ *n* (*pl* **-es**) veto *m* ● *vt* proibire

vex /veks/ *vt* irritare. **~ation** *n* irritazione *f*. **~ed** *adj* irritato; **~ed question** questione *f* controversa

via /'vaɪə/ *prep* via; (*by means of*) attraverso

viable /'vaɪəbl/ *adj* (life form, relationship, company) in grado di sopravvivere; (proposition) attuabile

viaduct /'vaɪədʌkt/ *n* viadotto *m*

vibrat|e /vaɪ'breɪt/ *vi* vibrare. **~ion** *n* vibrazione *f*

vicar /'vɪkə(r)/ *n* parroco *m* (*protestante*). **~age** *n* casa *f* parrocchiale

vice[1] /vaɪs/ *n* vizio *m*

vice[2] *n* (*Techn*) morsa *f*

vice versa /vaɪsɪ'vɜ:sə/ *adv* viceversa

vicinity /vɪ'sɪnətɪ/ *n* vicinanza *f*; **in the ~ of** nelle vicinanze di

vicious /'vɪʃəs/ *adj* cattivo; (attack) brutale; (animal) pericoloso. **~ 'circle** *n* circolo *m* vizioso. **~ly** *adv* (attack) brutalmente

victim /'vɪktɪm/ *n* vittima *f*. **~ize** *vt* fare delle rappresaglie contro

victor /'vɪktə(r)/ *n* vincitore *m*

victor|ious /vɪk'tɔ:rɪəs/ *adj* vittorioso. **~y** *n* vittoria *f*

video /'vɪdɪəʊ/ *n* video *m*; (*cassette*) videocassetta *f*; (*recorder*) videoregistratore *m* ● *attrib* video ● *vt* registrare

video: ~ recorder *n* videoregistratore *m*. **~-tape** *n* videocassetta *f*

vie /vaɪ/ *vi* (*pres p* **vying**) rivaleggiare

view /vju:/ *n* vista *f*; (*photographed, painted*) veduta *f*; (*opinion*) visione *f*; **look at the ~** guardare il panorama; **in my ~** secondo me; **in ~ of** in considerazione di; **on ~** esposto; **with a ~ to** con l'intenzione di ● *vt* visitare (house); (*consider*) considerare ● *vi* (*TV*) guardare. **~er** *n* (*TV*) telespettatore, -trice *mf*; (*Phot*) visore *m*

view: ~finder *n* (*Phot*) mirino *m*. **~point** *n* punto *m* di vista

vigilan|ce /'vɪdʒɪləns/ *n* vigilanza *f*. **~t** *adj* vigile

vigorous /'vɪgərəs/ *adj* vigoroso

vigour /'vɪgə(r)/ *n* vigore *m*

vile /vaɪl/ *adj* disgustoso; (weather) orribile; (temper, mood) pessimo

village /'vɪlɪdʒ/ *n* paese *m*. **~r** *n* paesano, -a *mf*

villain /'vɪlən/ *n* furfante *m*; (*in story*) cattivo *m*

vindicate /'vɪndɪkeɪt/ *vt* (*from guilt*) discolpare; **you are ~d** ti sei dimostrato nel giusto

vindictive /vɪn'dɪktɪv/ *adj* vendicativo

vine /vaɪn/ *n* vite *f*

vinegar /'vɪnɪgə(r)/ *n* aceto *m*

vineyard /'vɪnjɑ:d/ *n* vigneto *m*

vintage /'vɪntɪdʒ/ *adj* (wine) d'annata ● *n* (*year*) annata *f*

viola /vɪ'əʊlə/ *n* (*Mus*) viola *f*

violat|e /'vaɪəleɪt/ *vt* violare. **~ion** *n* violazione *f*

violen|ce /'vaɪələns/ *n* violenza *f*. **~t** *adj* violento

violet /'vaɪələt/ *adj* violetto ● *n* (*flower*) violetta *f*; (*colour*) violetto *m*

violin /vaɪə'lɪn/ *n* violino *m*. **~ist** *n* violinista *mf*

VIP *n abbr* (very important person) vip *mf*

virgin /'vɜ:dʒɪn/ *adj* vergine ● *n* vergine *f*. **~ity** *n* verginità *f*

Virgo /'vɜ:gəʊ/ *n* Vergine *f*

viril|e /'vɪraɪl/ *adj* virile. **~ity** *n* virilità *f*

virtual /'vɜ:tjʊəl/ *adj* effettivo. **~ reality** *n* realtà *f* virtuale. **~ly** *adv* praticamente

virtue /'vɜ:tju:/ *n* virtù *f inv*; (*advantage*) vantaggio *m*; **by** *or* **in ~ of** a causa di

virtuous /'vɜ:tjʊəs/ *adj* virtuoso

virulent /'vɪrʊlənt/ *adj* virulento

virus /'vaɪərəs/ *n* virus *m inv*

visa /'vi:zə/ *n* visto *m*

visibility /vɪzə'bɪlətɪ/ *n* visibilità *f*

visibl|e /'vɪzəbl/ *adj* visibile. **~y** *adv* visibilmente

vision /'vɪʒn/ *n* visione *f*; (*sight*) vista *f*

visit /'vɪzɪt/ *n* visita *f* ● *vt* andare a trovare (person); andare da (doctor etc); visitare (town, building). **~ing hours** *npl* orario *m* delle visite. **~or** *n* ospite *mf*; (*of town, museum*) visitatore, -trice *mf*; (*in hotel*) cliente *mf*

visor /'vaɪzə(r)/ *n* visiera *f*; (*Auto*) parasole *m*

visual /'vɪzjʊəl/ *adj* visivo. **~ aids** *npl* supporto *m* visivo. **~ dis'play unit** *n* visualizzatore *m*. **~ly** *adv* visualmente; **~ly handicapped** non vedente

visualize /'vɪzjʊəlaɪz/ *vt* visualizzare

vital /'vaɪtl/ *adj* vitale. **~ity** *n* vitalità *f*. **~ly** *adv* estremamente

vitamin /'vɪtəmɪn/ *n* vitamina *f*

vivaci|ous /vɪ'veɪʃəs/ *adj* vivace. **~ty** *n* vivacità *f*

vivid /'vɪvɪd/ *adj* vivido. **~ly** *adv* in modo vivido

vocabulary /və'kæbjʊlərɪ/ *n* vocabolario *m*; (*list*) glossario *m*

vocal /ˈvəʊkl/ *adj* vocale; (*vociferous*) eloquente. **~ cords** *npl* corde *fpl* vocali

vocalist /ˈvəʊkəlɪst/ *n* vocalista *mf*

vocation /vəˈkeɪʃn/ *n* vocazione *f*. **~al** *adj* di orientamento professionale

vociferous /vəˈsɪfərəs/ *adj* vociante

vogue /vəʊg/ *n* moda *f*; **in ~** in voga

voice /vɔɪs/ *n* voce *f* ● *vt* esprimere. **~mail** *n* posta *f* elettronica vocale

void /vɔɪd/ *adj* (*not valid*) nullo; **~ of** privo di ● *n* vuoto *m*

volatile /ˈvɒlətaɪl/ *adj* volatile; (*person*) volubile

volcanic /vɒlˈkænɪk/ *adj* vulcanico

volcano /vɒlˈkeɪnəʊ/ *n* vulcano *m*

volley /ˈvɒlɪ/ *n* (*of gunfire*) raffica *f*; (*Tennis*) volée *f inv*

volt /vəʊlt/ *n* volt *m inv*. **~age** *n* (*Electr*) voltaggio *m*

volume /ˈvɒljuːm/ *n* volume *m*; (*of work, traffic*) quantità *f inv*. **~ control** *n* volume *m*

voluntar|y /ˈvɒləntərɪ/ *adj* volontario. **~y work** *n* volontariato *m*. **~ily** *adv* volontariamente

volunteer /vɒlənˈtɪə(r)/ *n* volontario, -a *mf* ● *vt* offrire volontariamente (information) ● *vi* offrirsi volontario; (*Mil*) arruolarsi come volontario

vomit /ˈvɒmɪt/ *n* vomito *m* ● *vt/i* vomitare

voracious /vəˈreɪʃəs/ *adj* vorace

vot|e /vəʊt/ *n* voto *m*; (*ballot*) votazione *f*; (*right*) diritto *m* di voto; **take a ~e on** votare su ● *vi* votare ● *vt* **~e sb president** eleggere qcno presidente. **~er** *n* elettore, -trice *mf*. **~ing** *n* votazione *f*

vouch /vaʊtʃ/ *vi* **~ for** garantire per. **~er** *n* buono *m*

vow /vaʊ/ *n* voto *m* ● *vt* giurare

vowel /ˈvaʊəl/ *n* vocale *f*

voyage /ˈvɔɪɪdʒ/ *n* viaggio *m* [marittimo]; (*in space*) viaggio *m* [nello spazio]

vulgar /ˈvʌlgə(r)/ *adj* volgare. **~ity** *n* volgarità *f inv*

vulnerable /ˈvʌlnərəbl/ *adj* vulnerabile

vulture /ˈvʌltʃə(r)/ *n* avvoltoio *m*

vying /ˈvaɪɪŋ/ ▷**VIE**

Ww

wad /wɒd/ *n* batuffolo *m*; (*bundle*) rotolo *m*. **~ding** *n* ovatta *f*

waddle /ˈwɒdl/ *vi* camminare ondeggiando

wade /weɪd/ *vi* guadare; **~ through** [!] procedere faticosamente in (book)

wafer /ˈweɪfə(r)/ *n* cialda *f*, wafer *m inv*; (*Relig*) ostia *f*

waffle[1] /ˈwɒfl/ *vi* [!] blaterare

waffle[2] *n* (*Culin*) cialda *f*

waft /wɒft/ *vt* trasportare ● *vi* diffondersi

wag /wæg/ *v* (*pt/pp* **wagged**) ● *vt* agitare ● *vi* agitarsi

wage[1] /weɪdʒ/ *vt* dichiarare (war); lanciare (campaign)

wage[2] *n*, & **~s** *pl* salario *msg*. **~ packet** *n* busta *f* paga

waggle /ˈwægl/ *vt* dimenare ● *vi* dimenarsi

wagon /ˈwægən/ *n* carro *m*; (*Rail*) vagone *m* merci

wail /weɪl/ *n* piagnucolio *m*; (*of wind*) lamento *m*; (*of baby*) vagito *m* ● *vi* piagnucolare; (wind:) lamentarsi; (baby:) vagire

waist /weɪst/ *n* vita *f*. **~coat** *n* gilè *m inv*; (*of man's suit*) panciotto *m*. **~line** *n* vita *f*

wait /weɪt/ *n* attesa *f*; **lie in ~ for** appostarsi per sorprendere ● *vi* aspettare; **~ for** aspettare ● *vt* **~ one's turn** aspettare il proprio turno. □ **~ on** *vt* servire

waiter /ˈweɪtə(r)/ *n* cameriere *m*

waiting: ~-list *n* lista *f* d'attesa. **~-room** *n* sala *f* d'aspetto

waitress /ˈweɪtrɪs/ *n* cameriera *f*

waive /weɪv/ *vt* rinunciare a (claim); non tener conto di (rule)

wake[1] /weɪk/ *n* veglia *f* funebre ● *v* (*pt* **woke**, *pp* **woken**) **~ [up]** ● *vt* svegliare ● *vi* svegliarsi

wake[2] *n* (*Naut*) scia *f*; **in the ~ of** *fig* nella scia di

Wales /weɪlz/ *n* Galles *m*

walk /wɔːk/ *n* passeggiata *f*; (*gait*) andatura *f*; (*path*) sentiero *m*; **go for a ~** andare a fare una passeggiata ● *vi* camminare; (*as opposed to drive etc*) andare a piedi; (*ramble*) passeggiare ● *vt* portare a spasso (dog); percorrere (streets). □ **~ out** *vi* (husband, employee:) andarsene; (workers:) scioperare. □ **~ out on** *vt* lasciare

walker /ˈwɔːkə(r)/ *n* camminatore, -trice *mf*; (*rambler*) escursionista *mf*

walk-out *n* sciopero *m*

wall /wɔːl/ *n* muro *m*; **go to the ~** [!] andare a rotoli; **drive sb up the ~** [!] far diventare matto qcno ● **wall up** *vt* murare

wallet /ˈwɒlɪt/ *n* portafoglio *m*

wallop /ˈwɒləp/ *n* [!] colpo *m* ● *vt* (*pt/pp* **walloped**) [!] colpire

wallow /ˈwɒləʊ/ *vi* sguazzare; (*in self-pity, grief*) crogiolarsi

ˈwallpaper *n* tappezzeria *f* ● *vt* tappezzare

> *i* **Wall Street** Via di Manhattan, a New York, dove hanno sede la Borsa e altri istituti finanziari. Quando si parla di *Wall Street* ci si riferisce appunto a tali istituti.

walnut /ˈwɔːlnʌt/ *n* noce *f*

waltz /wɔːlts/ *n* valzer *m inv* ● *vi* ballare il valzer

wand /wɒnd/ *n* (*magic ~*) bacchetta *f* [magica]

wander /ˈwɒndə(r)/ *vi* girovagare; (*fig: digress*) divagare. □ **~ about** *vi* andare a spasso

wane /weɪn/ *n* **be on the ~** essere in fase calante ● *vi* calare

wangle /ˈwæŋgl/ *vt* [!] rimediare (invitation, holiday)

want /wɒnt/ *n* (*hardship*) bisogno *m*; (*lack*) mancanza *f* ● *vt* volere; (*need*) aver bisogno di; **~ [to have] sth** volere qcsa; **~ to do sth** voler fare qcsa; **we ~ to stay** vogliamo rimanere; **I ~ you to go** voglio che tu vada; **it ~s painting** ha bisogno d'essere dipinto; **you ~ to learn to swim** bisogna che impari a nuotare ● *vi* **~ for** mancare di. **~ed** *adj* ricercato. **~ing** *adj* **be ~ing** mancare; **be ~ing in** mancare di

WAP /wæp/ *n abbr* (wireless application protocol) WAP *m inv*

war /wɔː(r)/ *n* guerra *f*; *fig* lotta *f* (**on** contro); **at ~** in guerra

ward /wɔːd/ *n* (*in hospital*) reparto *m*; (*child*) minore *m* sotto tutela ● **ward off** *vt* evitare; parare (blow)

warden /ˈwɔːdn/ *n* guardiano, -a *mf*

warder /ˈwɔːdə(r)/ *n* guardia *f* carceraria

wardrobe /ˈwɔːdrəʊb/ *n* guardaroba *m*

warehouse /ˈweəhaʊs/ *n* magazzino *m*

war: ~fare *n* guerra *f*. **~head** *n* testata *f*

warm /wɔːm/ *adj* caldo; (welcome) caloroso; **be ~** (person:) aver caldo; **it is ~** (weather) fa caldo ● *vt* scaldare. □ **~ up** *vt* scaldare ● *vi* scaldarsi; *fig* animarsi. **~-hearted** *adj* espansivo. **~ly** *adv* (greet) calorosamente; (dress) in modo pesante. **~th** *n* calore *m*

warn /wɔːn/ *vt* avvertire. **~ing** *n* avvertimento *m*; (*advance notice*) preavviso *m*

warp /wɔːp/ *vt* deformare; *fig* distorcere ● *vi* deformarsi

warped /wɔːpt/ *adj fig* contorto; (sexuality) deviato; (view) distorto

warrant /ˈwɒrənt/ *n* (*for arrest, search*) mandato *m* ● *vt* (*justify*) giustificare; (*guarantee*) garantire. **~y** *n* garanzia *f*

warrior /ˈwɒrɪə(r)/ *n* guerriero, -a *mf*

ˈwarship *n* nave *f* da guerra

wart /wɔːt/ *n* porro *m*

ˈwartime *n* tempo *m* di guerra

war|y /ˈweərɪ/ *adj* (**-ier, -iest**) (*careful*) cauto; (*suspicious*) diffidente

was /wɒz/ ▷**BE**

wash /wɒʃ/ *n* lavata *f*; (*clothes*) bucato *m*; (*in washing machine*) lavaggio *m*; **have a ~** darsi una lavata ● *vt* lavare; (sea:) bagnare; **~ one's hands** lavarsi le mani ● *vi* lavarsi. □ **~ out** *vt* sciacquare (soap); sciacquarsi (mouth). □ **~ up** *vt* lavare ● *vi* lavare i piatti; *Am* lavarsi

washable /ˈwɒʃəbl/ *adj* lavabile

wash-basin *n* lavandino *m*

washer /ˈwɒʃə(r)/ *n* (*Techn*) guarnizione *f*; (*machine*) lavatrice *f*

washing /ˈwɒʃɪŋ/ *n* bucato *m*. **~-machine** *n* lavatrice *f*. **~-powder** *n* detersivo *m*. **~-ˈup** *n* **do the ~-up** lavare i piatti. **~-'up liquid** *n* detersivo *m* per i piatti

wash: ~-out *n* disastro *m*. **~-room** *n* bagno *m*

wasp /wɒsp/ *n* vespa *f*

waste /weɪst/ *n* spreco *m*; (*rubbish*) rifiuto *m*; **~ of time** perdita *f* di tempo ● *adj* (product) di scarto; (land) desolato; **lay ~** devastare ● *vt* sprecare. □ **~ away** *vi* deperire

waste: ~-di'sposal unit *n* eliminatore *m* di rifiuti. **~ful** *adj* dispendioso. **~-'paper basket** *n* cestino *m* per la carta [straccia]

watch /wɒtʃ/ *n* guardia *f*; (*period of duty*) turno *m* di guardia; (*timepiece*) orologio *m*; **be on the ~** stare all'erta ● *vt* guardare (film, match, television); (*be careful of, look after*) stare attento a ● *vi* guardare. □ **~ out** *vi* (*be careful*) stare attento (**for** a). □ **~ out for** *vt* (*look for*) fare attenzione all'arrivo di (person)

watch: ~-dog *n* cane *m* da guardia. **~man** *n* guardiano *m*

water /'wɔːtə(r)/ *n* acqua *f* ● *vt* annaffiare (garden, plant); (*dilute*) annacquare ● *vi* (eyes:) lacrimare; **my mouth was ~ing** avevo l'acquolina in bocca. □ **~ down** *vt* diluire; *fig* attenuare

water: ~-colour *n* acquerello *m*. **~cress** *n* crescione *m*. **~fall** *n* cascata *f*

'watering-can *n* annaffiatoio *m*

water: ~-lily *n* ninfea *f*. **~ logged** *adj* inzuppato. **~proof** *adj* impermeabile. **~-skiing** *n* sci *m* nautico. **~tight** stagno; *fig* irrefutabile. **~way** *n* canale *m* navigabile

watery /'wɔːtərɪ/ *adj* acquoso; (eyes) lacrimoso

watt /wɒt/ *n* watt *m inv*

wave /weɪv/ *n* onda *f*; (*gesture*) cenno *m*; *fig* ondata *f* ● *vt* agitare; **~ one's hand** agitare la mano ● *vi* far segno; (flag:) sventolare. **~length** *n* lunghezza *f* d'onda

W

waver /'weɪvə(r)/ *vi* vacillare; (*hesitate*) esitare

wavy /'weɪvɪ/ *adj* ondulato

wax[1] /wæks/ *vi* (moon:) crescere; (*fig: become*) diventare

wax[2] *n* cera *f*; (*in ear*) cerume *m* ● *vt* dare la cera a. **~works** *n* museo *m* delle cere

way /weɪ/ *n* percorso *m*; (*direction*) direzione *f*; (*manner, method*) modo *m*; **~s** *pl* (*customs*) abitudini *fpl*; **be in the ~** essere in mezzo; **on the ~ to Rome** andando a Roma; **I'll do it on the ~** lo faccio mentre vado; **it's on my ~** è sul mio percorso; **a long ~ off** lontano; **this ~** da questa parte; (*like this*) così; **by the ~** a proposito; **by ~ of** come; (*via*) via; **either ~** (*whatever we do*) in un modo o nell'altro; **in some ~s** sotto certi aspetti; **in a ~** in un certo senso; **in a bad ~** (person) molto grave; **out of the ~** fuori mano; **under ~** in corso; **lead the ~** far strada; *fig* aprire la strada; **make ~** far posto (**for** a); **give ~** (*Auto*) dare la precedenza; **go out of one's ~** *fig* scomodarsi (**to** per); **get one's [own] ~** averla vinta ● *adv* **~ behind** molto indietro. **~ 'in** *n* entrata *f*

way'lay *vt* (*pt/pp* **-laid**) aspettare al varco (person)

way 'out *n* uscita *f*; *fig* via *f* d'uscita

way-'out *adj* [!] eccentrico

we /wiː/ *pron* noi; **we're the last** siamo gli ultimi; **they're going, but we're not** loro vanno, ma noi no

weak /wiːk/ *adj* debole; (liquid) leggero. **~en** *vt* indebolire ● *vi* indebolirsi. **~ling** *n* smidollato, -a *mf*. **~ness** *n* debolezza *f*; (*liking*) debole *m*

wealth /welθ/ *n* ricchezza *f*; *fig* gran quantità *f*. **~y** *adj* (**-ier, -iest**) ricco

weapon /'wepən/ *n* arma *f*; **~s of mass destruction** *npl* armi *mpl* di distruzione di massa

wear /weə(r)/ *n* (*clothing*) abbigliamento *m*; **for everyday ~** da portare tutti i giorni; **~ [and tear]** usura *f* ● *v* (*pt* **wore**, *pp* **worn**) ● *vt* portare; (*damage*) consumare; **~ a hole in sth** logorare qcsa fino a fare un buco; **what shall I ~?** cosa mi metto? ● *vi* consumarsi; (*last*) durare. □ **~ off** *vi* scomparire; (effect:) finire. □ **~ out** *vt* consumare [fino in fondo]; (*exhaust*) estenuare ● *vi* estenuarsi

wear|y /'wɪərɪ/ *adj* (**-ier, -iest**) sfinito ● *v* (*pt/pp* **wearied**) ● *vt* sfinire ● *vi* **~y of** stancarsi di. **~ily** *adv* stancamente

weather /'weðə(r)/ *n* tempo *m*; **in this ~** con questo tempo; **under the ~** [!] giù di corda ● *vt* sopravvivere a (storm)

weather: ~-beaten *adj* (face) segnato dalle intemperie. **~ forecast** *n* previsioni *fpl* del tempo

weave¹ /wi:v/ *vi* (*pt/pp* **weaved**) (*move*) zigzagare

weave² *n* tessuto *m* ● *vt* (*pt* **wove**, *pp* **woven**) tessere; intrecciare (flowers etc); intrecciare le fila di (story etc). **~r** *n* tessitore, -trice *mf*

web /web/ *n* rete *f*; (*spider's*) ragnatela *f*. **W~** (*Comput*) Web *m inv*, Rete *f*. **~bed feet** *npl* piedi *mpl* palmati. **~cam** *n* webcam *f inv*. **~ master** *n* webmaster *m inv*. **~ page** *n* pagina *f* web. **~ site** *n* sito *m* web

wed /wed/ *vt* (*pt/pp* **wedded**) sposare ● *vi* sposarsi. **~ding** *n* matrimonio *m*

wedding: ~ cake *n* torta *f* nuziale. **~-ring** *n* fede *f*

wedge /wedʒ/ *n* zeppa *f*; (*for splitting wood*) cuneo *m*; (*of cheese*) fetta *f* ● *vt* (*fix*) fissare

Wednesday /ˈwenzdeɪ/ *n* mercoledì *m inv*

wee¹ /wi:/ *adj* [!] piccolo

wee² *vi* [!] fare la pipì

weed /wi:d/ *n* erbaccia *f*; ([!]: *person*) mollusco *m* ● *vt* estirpare le erbacce da. ▫ **~ out** *vt fig* eliminare

ˈweed-killer *n* erbicida *m*

weedy /ˈwi:dɪ/ *adj* [!] mingherlino

week /wi:k/ *n* settimana *f*. **~day** *n* giorno *m* feriale. **~end** *n* fine settimana *m*

weekly /ˈwi:klɪ/ *adj* settimanale ● *n* settimanale *m* ● *adv* settimanalmente

weep /wi:p/ *vi* (*pt/pp* **wept**) piangere

weigh /weɪ/ *vt/i* pesare; **~ anchor** levare l'ancora. ▫ **~ down** *vt fig* piegare. ▫ **~ up** *vt fig* soppesare; valutare (person)

weight /weɪt/ *n* peso *m*; **put on/lose ~** ingrassare/dimagrire. **~ing** *n* (*allowance*) indennità *f inv*

weight-lifting *n* sollevamento *m* pesi

weir /wɪə(r)/ *n* chiusa *f*

weird /wɪəd/ *adj* misterioso; (*bizarre*) bizzarro

welcome /ˈwelkəm/ *adj* benvenuto; **you're ~!** prego!; **you're ~ to have it/to come** prendilo/vieni pure ● *n* accoglienza *f* ● *vt* accogliere; (*appreciate*) gradire

weld /weld/ *vt* saldare. **~er** *n* saldatore *m*

welfare /ˈwelfeə(r)/ *n* benessere *m*; (*aid*) assistenza *f*. **W~ State** *n* Stato *m* assistenziale

well¹ /wel/ *n* pozzo *m*; (*of staircase*) tromba *f*

well² *adv* (**better, best**) bene; **as ~** anche; **as ~ as** (*in addition*) oltre a; **~ done!** bravo!; **very ~** benissimo ● *adj* **he is not ~** non sta bene; **get ~ soon!** guarisci presto! ● *int* beh!; **~ I never!** ma va!

well-behaved *adj* educato

well: ~-known *adj* famoso. **~-off** *adj* benestante. **~-to-do** *adj* ricco

Welsh /welʃ/ *adj & n* gallese; **the ~** *pl* i gallesi. **~man** *n* gallese *m*. **~ rabbit** *n* toast *m inv* al formaggio

> *i* **Welsh Assembly** Istituita nel 1999 con sede a Cardiff, la *Welsh Assembly* ha poteri legislativi secondari limitati (non ha poteri riguardo al sistema fiscale al contrario dello *Scottish Parliament*). L'Assemblea è composta di 60 rappresentanti, 40 dei quali (*Assembly Members* o *AMs*) eletti a suffragio diretto, i restanti 20 eletti sulla base di liste regionali e col sistema proporzionale.

went /went/ ▹**GO**

wept /wept/ ▹**WEEP**

were /wɜ:(r)/ ▹**BE**

west /west/ *n* ovest *m*; **to the ~ of** a ovest di; **the W~** l'Occidente *m* ● *adj* occidentale ● *adv* verso occidente; **go ~** [!] andare in malora. **~erly** *adj* verso ovest; occidentale (wind). **~ern** *adj* occidentale ● *n* western *m inv*

West: ~ ˈIndian *adj & n* antillese *mf*. **~ ˈIndies** /ˈɪndɪz/ *npl* Antille *fpl*

ˈwestward[s] /-wəd[z]/ *adv* verso ovest

wet /wet/ *adj* (**wetter, wettest**) bagnato; fresco (paint); (*rainy*) piovoso; ([!]: person) smidollato; **get ~** bagnarsi ● *vt* (*pt/pp* **wet, wetted**) bagnare. **~ ˈblanket** *n* guastafeste *mf inv*

whack /wæk/ *n* [!] colpo *m* ● *vt* [!]

W

dare un colpo a. **~ed** *adj* [!] stanco morto. **~ing** *adj* ([!]: *huge*) enorme

whale /weɪl/ *n* balena *f*; **have a ~ of a time** [!] divertirsi un sacco

wham /wæm/ *int* bum

wharf /wɔːf/ *n* banchina *f*

what /wɒt/ *pron* che, [che] cosa; **~ for?** perché?; **~ is that for?** a che cosa serve?; **~ is it?** (*what do you want*) cosa c'è?; **~ is it like?** com'è?; **~ is your name?** come ti chiami?; **~ is the weather like?** com'è il tempo?; **~ is the film about?** di cosa parla il film?; **~ is he talking about?** di cosa sta parlando?; **he asked me ~ she had said** mi ha chiesto cosa ha detto; **~ about going to the cinema?** e se andassimo al cinema?; **~ about the children?** (*what will they do*) e i bambini?; **~ if it rains?** e se piove? ● *adj* quale, che; **take ~ books you want** prendi tutti i libri che vuoi; **~ kind of a** che tipo di; **at ~ time?** a che ora? ● *adv* che; **~ a lovely day!** che bella giornata! ● *int* **~!** [che] cosa!; **~?** [che] cosa?

what'ever *adj* qualunque ● *pron* qualsiasi cosa; **~ is it?** cos'è?; **~ he does** qualsiasi cosa faccia; **~ happens** qualunque cosa succeda; **nothing ~** proprio niente

whatso'ever *adj & pron* = **whatever**

wheat /wiːt/ *n* grano *m*, frumento *m*

wheel /wiːl/ *n* ruota *f*; (*steering* ~) volante *m*; **at the ~** al volante ● *vt* (*push*) spingere ● *vi* (*circle*) ruotare; **~ [round]** ruotare

wheel: ~barrow *n* carriola *f*. **~chair** *n* sedia *f* a rotelle. **~-clamp** *n* ceppo *m* bloccaruote

wheeze /wiːz/ *vi* ansimare

when /wen/ *adv & conj* quando; **the day ~** il giorno in cui; **~ swimming/reading** nuotando/leggendo

when'ever *adv & conj* in qualsiasi momento; (*every time that*) ogni volta che; **~ did it happen?** quando è successo?

where /weə(r)/ *adv & conj* dove; **the street ~ I live** la via in cui abito; **~ do you come from?** da dove vieni?

whereabouts[1] /weərə'baʊts/ *adv* dove

'whereabouts[2] *n* **nobody knows his ~** nessuno sa dove si trova

where'as *conj* dal momento che; (*in contrast*) mentre

wher'ever *adv & conj* dovunque; **~ is he?** dov'è mai?; **~ possible** dovunque sia possibile

whet /wet/ *vt* (*pt/pp* **whetted**) aguzzare (appetite)

whether /'weðə(r)/ *conj* se; **~ you like it or not** che ti piaccia o no

which /wɪtʃ/ *adj & pron* quale; **~ one?** quale?; **~ one of you?** chi di voi?; **~ way?** (*direction*) in che direzione? ● *rel pron* (*object*) che; **~ he does frequently** cosa che fa spesso; **after ~** dopo di che; **on/in ~** su/in cui

which'ever *adj & pron* qualunque; **~ it is** qualunque sia; **~ one of you** chiunque tra voi

while /waɪl/ *n* **a long ~** un bel po'; **a little ~** un po' ● *conj* mentre; (*as long as*) finché; (*although*) sebbene ● **while away** *vt* passare (time)

whilst /waɪlst/ *conj see* **while**

whim /wɪm/ *n* capriccio *m*

whimper /'wɪmpə(r)/ *vi* piagnucolare; (dog:) mugolare

whine /waɪn/ *n* lamento *m*; (*of dog*) guaito *m* ● *vi* lamentarsi; (dog:) guaire

whip /wɪp/ *n* frusta *f*; (*Pol: person*) *parlamentare mf incaricato, -a di assicurarsi della presenza dei membri del suo partito alle votazioni* ● *vt* (*pt/pp* **whipped**) frustare; (*Culin*) sbattere; (*snatch*) afferrare; ([!]: *steal*) fregare. □ **~ up** *vt* (*incite*) stimolare; [!] improvvisare (meal). **~ped 'cream** *n* panna *f* montata

whirl /wɜːl/ *n* (*movement*) rotazione *f*; **my mind's in a ~** ho le idee confuse ● *vi* girare rapidamente ● *vt* far girare rapidamente. **~pool** *n* vortice *m*. **~wind** *n* turbine *m*

whirr /wɜː(r)/ *vi* ronzare

whisk /wɪsk/ *n* (*Culin*) frullino *m* ● *vt* (*Culin*) frullare. □ **~ away** *vt* portare via

whisker /'wɪskə(r)/ *n* **~s** (*of cat*) baffi *mpl*; (*on man's cheek*) basette *fpl*; **by a ~** per un pelo

whisky /'wɪskɪ/ *n* whisky *m inv*

whisper /'wɪspə(r)/ *n* sussurro *m*; (*rumour*) diceria *f* ● *vt/i* sussurrare

whistle /'wɪsl/ *n* fischio *m*; (*instrument*) fischietto *m* ● *vt* fischiettare ● *vi* fischiettare; (referee) fischiare

white /waɪt/ *adj* bianco; **go ~** (*pale*) sbiancare ● *n* bianco *m*; (*of egg*) albume *m*; (*person*) bianco, -a *mf*

white: ~ 'coffee *n* caffè *m inv* macchiato. **~-'collar worker** *n* colletto *m* bianco

white 'lie *n* bugia *f* pietosa

whiten /'waɪtn/ *vt* imbiancare ● *vi* sbiancare

'whitewash *n* intonaco *m*; *fig* copertura *f* ● *vt* dare una mano d'intonaco a; *fig* coprire

Whitsun /'wɪtsn/ *n* Pentecoste *f*

who /hu:/ *inter pron* chi ● *rel pron* che; **the children, ~ were all tired,...** i bambini, che erano tutti stanchi,...

who'ever *pron* chiunque; **~ he is** chiunque sia; **~ can that be?** chi può mai essere?

whole /həʊl/ *adj* tutto; (*not broken*) intatto; **the ~ truth** tutta la verità; **the ~ world** il mondo intero; **the ~ lot** (*everything*) tutto; (*pl*) tutti; **the ~ lot of you** tutti voi ● *n* tutto *m*; **as a ~** nell'insieme; **on the ~** tutto considerato; **the ~ of Italy** tutta l'Italia

whole: ~-'hearted *adj* di tutto cuore. **~meal** *adj* integrale

'wholesale *adj & adv* all'ingrosso; *fig* in massa. **~r** *n* grossista *mf*

wholesome /'həʊlsəm/ *adj* sano

wholly /'həʊlɪ/ *adv* completamente

whom /hu:m/ *rel pron* che; **the man ~ I saw** l'uomo che ho visto; **to/with ~** a/con cui ● *inter pron* chi; **to ~ did you speak?** con chi hai parlato?

whooping cough /'hu:pɪŋ/ *n* pertosse *f*

whore /hɔ:(r)/ *n* [!] puttana *f*

whose /hu:z/ *rel pron* il cui; **people ~ name begins with D** le persone i cui nomi cominciano con la D ● *inter pron* di chi; **~ is that?** di chi è quello? ● *adj* **~ car did you use?** di chi è la macchina che hai usato?

why /waɪ/ *adv* (*inter*) perché; **the reason ~** la ragione per cui; **that's ~** per questo ● *int* diamine

wick /wɪk/ *n* stoppino *m*

wicked /'wɪkɪd/ *adj* cattivo; (*mischievous*) malizioso

wicker /'wɪkə(r)/ *n* vimini *mpl* ● *attrib* di vimini

wide /waɪd/ *adj* largo; (experience, knowledge) vasto; (difference) profondo; (*far from target*) lontano; **10 cm ~** largo 10 cm; **how ~ is it?** quanto è largo? ● *adv* (*off target*) lontano dal bersaglio; **~ awake** del tutto sveglio; **~ open** spalancato; **far and ~** in lungo e in largo. **~ly** *adv* largamente; (known, accepted) generalmente; (different) profondamente

widen /'waɪdn/ *vt* allargare ● *vi* allargarsi

'widespread *adj* diffuso

widow /'wɪdəʊ/ *n* vedova *f*. **~ed** *adj* vedovo. **~er** *n* vedovo *m*

width /wɪdθ/ *n* larghezza *f*; (*of material*) altezza *f*

wield /wi:ld/ *vt* maneggiare; esercitare (power)

wife /waɪf/ *n* (*pl* **wives**) moglie *f*

wig /wɪg/ *n* parrucca *f*

wiggle /'wɪgl/ *vi* dimenarsi ● *vt* dimenare

wild /waɪld/ *adj* selvaggio; (animal, flower) selvatico; (*furious*) furibondo; (applause) fragoroso; (idea) folle; (*with joy*) pazzo; (guess) azzardato; **be ~ about** (*keen on*) andare pazzo per ● *adv* **run ~** crescere senza controllo ● *n* **in the ~** allo stato naturale; **the ~s** *pl* le zone *fpl* sperdute

wilderness /'wɪldənɪs/ *n* deserto *m*; (*fig: garden*) giungla *f*

'wildfire *n* **spread like ~** allargarsi a macchia d'olio

wild: ~-'goose chase *n* ricerca *f* inutile. **~life** *n* animali *mpl* selvatici

will[1] /wɪl/ *v aux* **he ~ arrive tomorrow** arriverà domani; **I won't tell him** non glielo dirò; **you ~ be back soon, won't you?** tornerai presto, no?; **he ~ be there, won't he?** sarà là, no?; **she ~ be there by now** sarà là ormai; **~ you go?** (*do you intend to go*) pensi di andare?; **~ you go to the baker's and buy...?** puoi andare dal panettiere a comprare...?; **~ you be quiet!** vuoi stare calmo!; **~ you have some wine?** vuoi del vino?; **the engine won't start** la macchina non parte

will² *n* volontà *f inv*; (*document*) testamento *m*
willing /ˈwɪlɪŋ/ *adj* disposto; (*eager*) volonteroso. **~ly** *adv* volentieri. **~ness** *n* buona volontà *f*
willow /ˈwɪləʊ/ *n* salice *m*
ˈwill-power *n* forza *f* di volontà
wilt /wɪlt/ *vi* appassire
win /wɪn/ *n* vittoria *f*; **have a ~** riportare una vittoria ● *v* (*pt/pp* **won**; *pres p* **winning**) ● *vt* vincere; conquistare (fame) ● *vi* vincere. □ **~ over** *vt* convincere
wince /wɪns/ *vi* contrarre il viso
winch /wɪntʃ/ *n* argano *m*
wind¹ /wɪnd/ *n* vento *m*; (*breath*) fiato *m*; (🄸: *flatulence*) aria *f*; **get/have the ~ up** 🄸 aver fifa; **get ~ of** aver sentore di; **in the ~** nell'aria ● *vt* **~ sb** lasciare qcno senza fiato
wind² /waɪnd/ *v* (*pt/pp* **wound**) ● *vt* (*wrap*) avvolgere; (*move by turning*) far girare; (clock) caricare ● *vi* (road:) serpeggiare. □ **~ up** *vt* caricare (clock); concludere (proceedings); 🄸 prendere in giro (sb)
windfall /ˈwɪndfɔːl/ *n fig* fortuna *f* inaspettata
ˈwind farm *n* centrale *f* eolica
winding /ˈwaɪndɪŋ/ *adj* tortuoso
wind: ~ instrument *n* strumento *m* a fiato. **~mill** *n* mulino *m* a vento
window /ˈwɪndəʊ/ *n* finestra *f*; (*of car*) finestrino *m*; (*of shop*) vetrina *f*
window: ~-box *n* cassetta *f* per i fiori. **~-sill** *n* davanzale *m*
ˈwindscreen *n*, *Am* **ˈwindshield** *n* parabrezza *m inv*. **~ washer** *n* getto *m* d'acqua. **~-wiper** *n* tergicristallo *m*
wine /waɪn/ *n* vino *m*
wine: ~glass *n* bicchiere *m* da vino. **~-list** *n* carta *f* dei vini
ˈwine-tasting *n* degustazione *f* di vini
wing /wɪŋ/ *n* ala *f*; (*Auto*) parafango *m*; **~s** *pl* (*Theat*) quinte *fpl*. **~er** *n* (*Sport*) ala *f*
wink /wɪŋk/ *n* strizzata *f* d'occhio; **not sleep a ~** non chiudere occhio ● *vi* strizzare l'occhio; (light:) lampeggiare
winner /ˈwɪnə(r)/ *n* vincitore, -trice *mf*
wint|er /ˈwɪntə(r)/ *n* inverno *m*. **~ry** *adj* invernale
wipe /waɪp/ *n* passata *f*; (*to dry*) asciugata *f* ● *vt* strofinare; (*dry*) asciugare. □ **~ off** *vt* asciugare; (*erase*) cancellare. □ **~ out** *vt* annientare; eliminare (village); estinguere (debt). □ **~ up** *vt* asciugare (dishes)
wire /ˈwaɪə(r)/ *n* fil *m* di ferro; (*electrical*) filo *m* elettrico
wiring /ˈwaɪərɪŋ/ *n* impianto *m* elettrico
wisdom /ˈwɪzdəm/ *n* saggezza *f*; (*of action*) sensatezza *f*. **~ tooth** *n* dente *m* del giudizio
wise /waɪz/ *adj* saggio; (*prudent*) sensato. **~ly** *adv* saggiamente; (act) sensatamente
wish /wɪʃ/ *n* desiderio *m*; **make a ~** esprimere un desiderio; **with best ~es** con i migliori auguri ● *vt* desiderare; **~ sb well** fare tanti auguri a qcno; **I ~ you every success** ti auguro buona fortuna; **I ~ you could stay** vorrei che tu potessi rimanere ● *vi* **~ for sth** desiderare qcsa. **~ful** *adj* **~ful thinking** illusione *f*
wistful /ˈwɪstfl/ *adj* malinconico
wit /wɪt/ *n* spirito *m*; (*person*) persona *f* di spirito; **be at one's ~s' end** non saper che pesci pigliare
witch /wɪtʃ/ *n* strega *f*. **~craft** *n* magia *f*. **~-hunt** *n* caccia *f* alle streghe
with /wɪð/ *prep* con; (*fear, cold, jealousy etc*) di; **I'm not ~ you** 🄸 non ti seguo; **can I leave it ~ you?** (*task*) puoi occupartene tu?; **~ no regrets/money** senza rimpianti/soldi; **be ~ it** 🄸 essere al passo coi tempi; (*alert*) essere concentrato
withˈdraw *v* (*pt* **-drew**, *pp* **-drawn**) ● *vt* ritirare; prelevare (money) ● *vi* ritirarsi. **~al** *n* ritiro *m*; (*of money*) prelevamento *m*; (*from drugs*) crisi *f inv* di astinenza; (*Psych*) chiusura *f* in se stessi. **~al symptoms** *npl* sintomi *mpl* da crisi di astinenza
withˈdrawn ▷**WITHDRAW** ● *adj* (person) chiuso in se stesso
wither /ˈwɪðə(r)/ *vi* (flower:) appassire
withˈhold *vt* (*pt/pp* **-held**) rifiutare (consent) (**from** a); nascondere (information) (**from** a); trattenere (smile)
withˈin *prep* in; (*before the end of*) entro; **~ the law** legale ● *adv* all'interno

W

with'out *prep* senza; **~ stopping** senza fermarsi

with'stand *vt* (*pt/pp* **-stood**) resistere a

witness /'wɪtnɪs/ *n* testimone *mf* ● *vt* autenticare (signature); essere testimone di (accident). **~-box** *n*, *Am* **~-stand** *n* banco *m* dei testimoni

witticism /'wɪtɪsɪzm/ *n* spiritosaggine *f*

witty /'wɪtɪ/ *adj* (**-ier, -iest**) spiritoso

wives /waɪvz/ ▷**WIFE**

wizard /'wɪzəd/ *n* mago *m*. **~ry** *n* stregoneria *f*

wobb|le /'wɒbl/ *vi* traballare. **~ly** *adj* traballante

woe /wəʊ/ *n* afflizione *f*

woke, **woken** /wəʊk/, /'wəʊkn/ ▷**WAKE**[1]

wolf /wʊlf/ *n* (*pl* **wolves** /wʊlvz/) lupo *m*; ([!]: *womanizer*) donnaiolo *m* ● *vt* **~** [**down**] divorare. **~ whistle** *n* fischio *m* ● *vi* **~-whistle at sb** fischiare dietro a qcno

woman /'wʊmən/ *n* (*pl* **women**) donna *f*. **~izer** *n* donnaiolo *m*. **~ly** *adj* femmineo

womb /wu:m/ *n* utero *m*

women /'wɪmɪn/ ▷**WOMAN**. **W~'s Libber** *n* femminista *f*. **W~'s Liberation** *n* movimento *m* femminista

won /wʌn/ ▷**WIN**

wonder /'wʌndə(r)/ *n* meraviglia *f*; (*surprise*) stupore *m*; **no ~!** non c'è da stupirsi!; **it's a ~ that...** è incredibile che... ● *vi* restare in ammirazione; (*be surprised*) essere sorpreso; **I ~** è quello che mi chiedo; **I ~ whether she is ill** mi chiedo se è malata?. **~ful** *adj* meraviglioso. **~fully** *adv* meravigliosamente

wood /wʊd/ *n* legno *m*; (*for burning*) legna *f*; (*forest*) bosco *m*; **out of the ~** *fig* fuori pericolo; **touch ~!** tocca ferro!

wood: ~ed /-ɪd/ *adj* boscoso. **~en** *adj* di legno; *fig* legnoso. **~ wind** *n* strumenti *mpl* a fiato. **~work** *n* (*wooden parts*) parti *fpl* in legno; (*craft*) falegnameria *f*. **~worm** *n* tarlo *m*. **~y** *adj* legnoso; (hill) boscoso

wool /wʊl/ *n* lana *f* ● *attrib* di lana. **~len** *adj* di lana. **~lens** *npl* capi *mpl* di lana

woolly /'wʊlɪ/ *adj* (**-ier, -iest**) (sweater) di lana; *fig* confuso

word /wɜ:d/ *n* parola *f*; (*news*) notizia *f*; **by ~ of mouth** a viva voce; **have a ~ with** dire due parole a; **have ~s** bisticciare; **in other ~s** in altre parole. **~ing** *n* parole *fpl*. **~ processor** *n* programma *m* di videoscrittura, word processor *m inv*

wore /wɔ:(r)/ ▷**WEAR**

work /wɜ:k/ *n* lavoro *m*; (*of art*) opera *f*; **~s** *pl* (*factory*) fabbrica *fsg*; (*mechanism*) meccanismo *msg*; **at ~** al lavoro; **out of ~** disoccupato ● *vi* lavorare; (machine, ruse:) funzionare; (*study*) studiare ● *vt* far funzionare (machine); far lavorare (employee); far studiare (student). □ **~ off** *vt* sfogare (anger); lavorare per estinguere (debt); fare sport per smaltire (weight). □ **~ out** *vt* elaborare (plan); risolvere (problem); calcolare (bill); **I ~ed out how he did it** ho capito come l'ha fatto ● *vi* evolvere. □ **~ up** *vt* **I've ~ed up an appetite** mi è venuto appetito; **don't get ~ed up** (*anxious*) non farti prendere dal panico; (*angry*) non arrabbiarti

workable /'wɜ:kəbl/ *adj* (*feasible*) fattibile

worker /'wɜ:kə(r)/ *n* lavoratore, -trice *mf*; (*manual*) operaio, -a *mf*

working /'wɜ:kɪŋ/ *adj* (clothes etc) da lavoro; (day) feriale; **in ~ order** funzionante. **~ class** *n* classe *f* operaia. **~-class** *adj* operaio

work: ~man *n* operaio *m*. **~manship** *n* lavorazione *f*. **~shop** *n* officina *f*; (*discussion*) dibattito *m*

world /wɜ:ld/ *n* mondo *m*; **a ~ of difference** una differenza abissale; **out of this ~** favoloso; **think the ~ of sb** andare matto per qcno. **~ly** *adj* materiale; (person) materialista. **~-'wide** *adj* mondiale ● *adv* mondialmente

worm /wɜ:m/ *n* verme *m* ● *vt* **~ one's way into sb's confidence** conquistarsi la fiducia di qcno in modo subdolo. **~-eaten** *adj* tarlato

worn /wɔ:n/ ▷**WEAR** ● *adj* sciupato. **~-out** *adj* consumato; (person) sfinito

worried /'wʌrɪd/ *adj* preoccupato

worr|y /'wʌrɪ/ *n* preoccupazione *f* ● *v* (*pt/pp* **worried**) ● *vt* preoccupare; (*bother*) disturbare ● *vi* preoccuparsi.

~**ing** *adj* preoccupante

worse /wɜːs/ *adj* peggiore ● *adv* peggio ● *n* peggio *m*

worsen /ˈwɜːsn/ *vt/i* peggiorare

worship /ˈwɜːʃɪp/ *n* culto *m*; (*service*) funzione *f*; **Your/His W~** (*to judge*) signor giudice/il giudice ● *v* (*pt/pp* **-shipped**) ● *vt* venerare ● *vi* andare a messa

worst /wɜːst/ *adj* peggiore ● *adv* peggio [di tutti] ● *n* **the ~** il peggio; **get the ~ of it** avere la peggio; **if the ~ comes to the ~** nella peggiore delle ipotesi

worth /wɜːθ/ *n* valore *m*; **£10 ~ of petrol** 10 sterline di benzina ● *adj* **be ~** valere; **be ~ it** *fig* valerne la pena; **it's ~ trying** vale la pena di provare; **it's ~ my while** mi conviene. ~**less** *adj* senza valore. ~**while** *adj* che vale la pena; (cause) lodevole

worthy /ˈwɜːðɪ/ *adj* degno; (cause, motive) lodevole

would /wʊd/ *v aux* **I ~ do it** lo farei; **~ you go?** andresti?; **~ you mind if I opened the window?** ti dispiace se apro la finestra?; **he ~ come if he could** verrebbe se potesse; **he said he ~n't** ha detto di no; **~ you like a drink?** vuoi qualcosa da bere?; **what ~ you like to drink?** cosa prendi da bere?; **you ~n't, ~ you?** non lo faresti, vero?

wound¹ /wuːnd/ *n* ferita *f* ● *vt* ferire

wound² /waʊnd/ ▷**WIND²**

wrangle /ˈræŋgl/ *n* litigio *m* ● *vi* litigare

wrap /ræp/ *n* (*shawl*) scialle *m* ● *vt* (*pt/pp* **wrapped**) **~ [up]** avvolgere; (present) incartare; **be ~ped up in** *fig* essere completamente preso da ● *vi* **~ up warmly** coprirsi bene. ~**per** *n* (*for sweet*) carta *f* [di caramella]. ~**ping** *n* materiale *m* da imballaggio. ~**ping paper** *n* carta *f* da pacchi; (*for gift*) carta *f* da regalo

wrath /rɒθ/ *n* ira *f*

wreak /riːk/ *vt* **~ havoc with sth** scombussolare qcsa

wreath /riːθ/ *n* (*pl* **~s** /-ðz/) corona *f*

wreck /rek/ *n* (*of ship*) relitto *m*; (*of car*) carcassa *f*; (*person*) rottame *m* ● *vt* far naufragare; demolire (car). ~**age** *n* rottami *mpl*; *fig* brandelli *mpl*

wrench /rentʃ/ *n* (*injury*) slogatura *f*; (*tool*) chiave *f* inglese; (*pull*) strattone *m* ● *vt* (*pull*) strappare; slogarsi (wrist, ankle etc)

wrestl|e /ˈresl/ *vi* lottare corpo a corpo; *fig* lottare. ~**er** *n* lottatore, -trice *mf*. ~**ing** *n* lotta *f* libera; (*all-in*) catch *m*

wretch /retʃ/ *n* disgraziato, -a *mf*. ~**ed** *adj* odioso; (weather) orribile; **feel ~ed** (*unhappy*) essere triste; (*ill*) sentirsi malissimo

wriggle /ˈrɪgl/ *n* contorsione *f* ● *vi* contorcersi; (*move forward*) strisciare; **~ out of sth** [!] sottrarsi a qcsa

wring /rɪŋ/ *vt* (*pt/pp* **wrung**) torcere (sb's neck); strizzare (clothes); **~ one's hands** torcersi le mani; ~**ing wet** inzuppato

wrinkle /ˈrɪŋkl/ *n* grinza *f*; (*on skin*) ruga *f* ● *vt/i* raggrinzire. ~**d** *adj* (skin, face) rugoso; (clothes) raggrinzito

wrist /rɪst/ *n* polso *m*. ~**-watch** *n* orologio *m* da polso

writ /rɪt/ *n* (*Jur*) mandato *m*

write /raɪt/ *vt/i* (*pt* **wrote**, *pp* **written**, *pres p* **writing**) scrivere. □ **~ down** *vt* annotare. □ **~ off** *vt* cancellare (debt); distruggere (car)

ˈwrite-off *n* (*car*) rottame *m*

writer /ˈraɪtə(r)/ *n* autore, -trice *mf*; **she's a ~** è una scrittrice

writhe /raɪð/ *vi* contorcersi

writing /ˈraɪtɪŋ/ *n* (*occupation*) scrivere *m*; (*words*) scritte *fpl*; (*handwriting*) scrittura *f*; **in ~** per iscritto. ~**-paper** *n* carta *f* da lettera

written /ˈrɪtn/ ▷**WRITE**

wrong /rɒŋ/ *adj* sbagliato; **be ~** (person:) sbagliare; **what's ~?** cosa c'è che non va? ● *adv* (spelt) in modo sbagliato; **go ~** (person:) sbagliare; (machine:) funzionare male; (plan:) andar male ● *n* ingiustizia *f*; **in the ~** dalla parte del torto; **know right from ~** distinguere il bene dal male ● *vt* fare torto a. ~**ful** *adj* ingiusto. ~**ly** *adv* in modo sbagliato; (accuse, imagine) a torto; (informed) male

wrote /rəʊt/ ▷**WRITE**

wroughtˈiron /rɔːt-/ *n* ferro *m* battuto ● *attrib* di ferro battuto

W

wrung /rʌŋ/ ▷**WRING**

wry /raɪ/ *adj* (**-er, -est**) (humour, smile) beffardo

Xmas /ˈkrɪsməs/ *n* [!] Natale *m*

ˈ**X-ray** *n* (*picture*) radiografia *f*; **have an ~** farsi fare una radiografia ● *vt* passare ai raggi X

yacht /jɒt/ *n* yacht *m inv*; (*for racing*) barca *f* a vela. **~ing** *n* vela *f*

yank /jæŋk/ *vt* [!] tirare

Yank *n* [!] americano, -a *mf*

yap /jæp/ *vi* (*pt/pp* **yapped**) (dog:) guaire

yard¹ /jɑːd/ *n* cortile *m*; (*for storage*) deposito *m*

yard² *n* iarda *f* (= *91,44 cm*). **~stick** *n fig* pietra *f* di paragone

yarn /jɑːn/ *n* filo *m*; ([!]*: tale*) storia *f*

yawn /jɔːn/ *n* sbadiglio *m* ● *vi* sbadigliare. **~ing** *adj* **~ing gap** sbadiglio *m*

yeah /jeə/ *adv* sì

year /jɪə(r)/ *n* anno *m*; (*of wine*) annata *f*; **for ~s** [!] da secoli. **~-book** *n* annuario *m*. **~ly** *adj* annuale ● *adv* annualmente

yearn /jɜːn/ *vi* struggersi. **~ing** *n* desiderio *m* struggente

yeast /jiːst/ *n* lievito *m*

yell /jel/ *n* urlo *m* ● *vi* urlare

yellow /ˈjeləʊ/ *adj & n* giallo *m*

yelp /jelp/ *n* (*of dog*) guaito *m* ● *vi* (dog:) guaire

yes /jes/ *adv* sì ● *n* sì *m inv*

yesterday /ˈjestədeɪ/ *adj & adv* ieri *m inv*; **~'s paper** il giornale di ieri; **the day before ~** l'altroieri

yet /jet/ *adv* ancora; **as ~** fino ad ora; **not ~** non ancora; **the best ~** il migliore finora ● *conj* eppure

yield /jiːld/ *n* produzione *f*; (profit) reddito *m* ● *vt* produrre; fruttare (profit) ● *vi* cedere; *Am* (*Auto*) dare la precedenza

yoga /ˈjəʊgə/ *n* yoga *m*

yoghurt /ˈjɒgət/ *n* yogurt *m inv*

yoke /jəʊk/ *n* giogo *m*; (*of garment*) carré *m inv*

yokel /ˈjəʊkl/ *n* zotico, -a *mf*

yolk /jəʊk/ *n* tuorlo *m*

you /juː/ *pron* (*subject*) tu, voi *pl*; (*formal*) lei, voi *pl*; (*direct/indirect object*) ti, vi *pl*; (*formal: direct object*) la; (*formal: indirect object*) le; (*after prep*) te, voi *pl*; (*formal: after prep*) lei;

> **!** **tu** is used when speaking to friends, children and animals. **lei** is used to speak to someone you do not know. **voi** is used to speak to more than one person. Note that *you* is often not translated when it is the subject of the sentence

~ are very kind (*sg*) sei molto gentile; (*formal*) è molto gentile; (*pl & formal pl*) siete molto gentili; **~ can stay, but he has to go** (*sg*) tu puoi rimanere, ma lui deve andarsene; (*pl*) voi potete rimanere, ma lui deve andarsene; **all of ~** tutti voi; **I'll give ~ the money** (*sg*) ti darò i soldi; (*pl*) vi darò i soldi; **I'll give it to ~** (*sg*) te/(*pl*) ve lo darò; **it was ~!** (*sg*) eri tu!; (*pl*) eravate voi!; **~ have to be careful** (*one*) si deve fare attenzione

young /jʌŋ/ *adj* giovane ● *npl* (*animals*) piccoli *mpl*; **the ~** (*people*) i giovani *mpl*. **~ lady** *n* signorina *f*. **~ man** *n* giovanotto. **~ster** *n* ragazzo, -a *mf*; (*child*) bambino, -a *mf*

your /jɔː(r)/ *adj* il tuo *m*, la tua *f*, i tuoi *mpl*, le tue *fpl*; (*formal*) il suo *m*, la sua *f*, i suoi *mpl*, le sue *fpl*; (*pl & formal pl*) il vostro *m*, la vostra *f*, i vostri *mpl*, le vostre *fpl*; **~ mother/father** tua madre/tuo padre; (*formal*) sua madre/suo padre; (*pl & formal pl*) vostra madre/ vostro padre

yours /jɔːz/ *poss pron* il tuo *m*, la tua *f*, i tuoi *mpl*, le tue *fpl*; (*formal*) il suo *m*, la sua *f*, i suoi *mpl*, le sue *fpl*; (*pl & formal pl*) il vostro *m*, la vostra *f*, i vostri *mpl*, le vostre *fpl*; **a friend of ~** un tuo/ suo/vostro amico; **friends of ~** dei tuoi/vostri/suoi amici; **that is ~** quello è tuo/vostro/suo; (*as opposed to mine*) quello è il tuo/il vostro/il suo

your'self *pron* (*reflexive*) ti; (*formal*) si; (*emphatic*) te stesso; (*formal*) sé, se stesso; **do pour ~ a drink** versati da bere; (*formal*) si versi da bere; **you said so ~** lo hai detto tu stesso; (*formal*) lo ha detto lei stesso; **you can be proud of ~** puoi essere fiero di te/di sé; **by ~** da solo

your'selves *pron* (*reflexive*) vi; (*emphatic*) voi stessi; **do pour ~ a drink** versatevi da bere; **you said so ~** lo avete detto voi stessi; **you can be proud of ~** potete essere fieri di voi; **by ~** da soli

youth /juːθ/ *n* (*pl* **youths** /-ðːz/) gioventù *f inv*; (*boy*) giovanetto *m*; **the ~** (*young people*) i giovani *mpl*. **~ful** *adj* giovanile. **~ hostel** *n* ostello *m* [della gioventù]

Yugoslav /ˈjuːgəslɑːv/ *adj & n* jugoslavo, -a *mf*

Yugoslavia /-ˈslɑːvɪə/ *n* Jugoslavia *f*

Zz

zeal /ziːl/ *n* zelo *m*

zealous /ˈzeləs/ *adj* zelante. **~ly** *adv* con zelo

zebra /ˈzebrə/ *n* zebra *f*. **~-ˈcrossing** *n* passaggio *m* pedonale, zebre *fpl*

zero /ˈzɪərəʊ/ *n* zero *m*

zest /zest/ *n* gusto *m*

zigzag /ˈzɪgzæg/ *n* zigzag *m inv* • *vi* (*pt/ pp* **-zagged**) zigzagare

zilch /zɪltʃ/ *n* [!] zero *m* assoluto

zinc /zɪŋk/ *n* zinco *m*

zip /zɪp/ *n* **~** [**fastener**] cerniera *f* [lampo] • *vt* (*pt/pp* **zipped**) **~** [**up**] chiudere con la cerniera [lampo]

'Zip code *n Am* codice *m* postale

zipper /ˈzɪpə(r)/ *n Am* cerniera *f* [lampo]

zodiac /ˈzəʊdɪæk/ *n* zodiaco *m*

zombie /ˈzɒmbɪ/ *n* [!] zombi *mf inv*

zone /zəʊn/ *n* zona *f*

zoo /zuː/ *n* zoo *m inv*

zoolog|ist /zəʊˈɒlədʒɪst/ *n* zoologo, -a *mf*. **~y** zoologia *f*

zoom /zuːm/ *vi* sfrecciare. **~ lens** *n* zoom *m inv*

Verbi inglesi irregolari

Infinito	*Passato*	*Participio passato*
be	was	been
bear	bore	borne
beat	beat	beaten
become	became	become
begin	began	begun
bend	bent	bent
bet	bet, betted	bet, betted
bid	bade, bid	bidden, bid
bind	bound	bound
bite	bit	bitten
bleed	bled	bled
blow	blew	blown
break	broke	broken
breed	bred	bred
bring	brought	brought
build	built	built
burn	burnt, burned	burnt, burned
burst	burst	burst
buy	bought	bought
catch	caught	caught
choose	chose	chosen
cling	clung	clung
come	came	come
cost	cost, costed (*vt*)	cost, costed
cut	cut	cut
deal	dealt	dealt
dig	dug	dug
do	did	done
draw	drew	drawn
dream	dreamt, dreamed	dreamt, dreamed
drink	drank	drunk
drive	drove	driven
eat	ate	eaten
fall	fell	fallen
feed	fed	fed
feel	felt	felt
fight	fought	fought
find	found	found
flee	fled	fled
fly	flew	flown
freeze	froze	frozen
get	got	got, gotten *US*
give	gave	given
go	went	gone
grow	grew	grown
hang	hung, hanged	hung, hanged
have	had	had
hear	heard	heard
hide	hid	hidden
hit	hit	hit
hold	held	held
hurt	hurt	hurt
keep	kept	kept
kneel	knelt	knelt
know	knew	known
lay	laid	laid
lead	led	led
lean	leaned, leant	leaned, leant
learn	learnt, learned	learnt, learned
leave	left	left
lend	lent	lent
let	let	let
lie	lay	lain
lose	lost	lost
make	made	made
mean	meant	meant
meet	met	met
pay	paid	paid
put	put	put
read	read	read
ride	rode	ridden
ring	rang	rung
rise	rose	risen
run	ran	run
say	said	said
see	saw	seen
seek	sought	sought
sell	sold	sold
send	sent	sent

Infinito	*Passato*	*Participio passato*
set	set	set
sew	sewed	sewn, sewed
shake	shook	shaken
shine	shone	shone
shoe	shod	shod
shoot	shot	shot
show	showed	shown
shut	shut	shut
sing	sang	sung
sink	sank	sunk
sit	sat	sat
sleep	slept	slept
sling	slung	slung
smell	smelt, smelled	smelt, smelled
speak	spoke	spoken
spell	spelled, spelt	spelled, spelt
spend	spent	spent
spit	spat	spat
spoil	spoilt, spoiled	spoilt, spoiled
spread	spread	spread
spring	sprang	sprung
stand	stood	stood
steal	stole	stolen
stick	stuck	stuck
sting	stung	stung
stride	strode	stridden
strike	struck	struck
swear	swore	sworn
sweep	swept	swept
swell	swelled	swollen, swelled
swim	swam	swum
swing	swung	swung
take	took	taken
teach	taught	taught
tear	tore	torn
tell	told	told
think	thought	thought
throw	threw	thrown
thrust	thrust	thrust
tread	trod	trodden
under-stand	under-stood	understood
wake	woke	woken
wear	wore	worn
win	won	won
write	wrote	written

Italian verb tables

1. in **-are** (*eg* **compr|are**)

Present **~o**, **~i**, **~a**, **~iamo**, **~ate**, **~ano**
Imperfect **~avo**, **~avi**, **~ava**, **~avamo**, **~avate**, **~avano**
Past historic **~ai**, **~asti**, **~ò**, **~ammo**, **~aste**, **~arono**
Future **~erò**, **~erai**, **~erà**, **~eremo**, **~erete**, **~eranno**
Present subjunctive **~i**, **~i**, **~i**, **~iamo**, **~iate**, **~ino**
Past subjunctive **~assi**, **~assi**, **~asse**, **~assimo**, **~aste**, **~assero**
Present participle **~ando**
Past participle **~ato**
Imperative **~a** (*fml* **~i**), **~iamo**, **~ate**
Conditional **~erei**, **~eresti**, **~erebbe**, **~eremmo**, **~ereste**, **~erebbero**

2. in **-ere** (*eg* **vend|ere**)

Pres **~o**, **~i**, **~e**, **~iamo**, **~ete**, **~ono**
Impf **~evo**, **~evi**, **~eva**, **~evamo**, **~evate**, **~evano**
Past hist **~ei** *or* **~etti**, **~esti**, **~è** *or* **~ette**, **~emmo**, **~este**, **~erono** *or* **~ettero**
Fut **~erò**, **~erai**, **~erà**, **~eremo**, **~erete**, **~eranno**
Pres sub **~a**, **~a**, **~a**, **~iamo**, **~iate**, **~ano**
Past sub **~essi**, **~essi**, **~esse**, **~essimo**, **~este**, **~essero**
Pres part **~endo**
Past part **~uto**
Imp **~i** (*fml* **~a**), **~iamo**, **~ete**
Cond **~erei**, **~eresti**, **~erebbe**, **~eremmo**, **~ereste**, **~erebbero**

3. in **-ire** (*eg* **dorm|ire**)

Pres **~o**, **~i**, **~e**, **~iamo**, **~ite**, **~ono**
Impf **~ivo**, **~ivi**, **~iva**, **~ivamo**, **~ivate**, **~ivano**
Past hist **~ii**, **~isti**, **~i**, **~immo**, **~iste**, **~irono**
Fut **~irò**, **~irai**, **~irà**, **~iremo**, **~irete**, **~iranno**
Pres sub **~a**, **~a**, **~a**, **~iamo**, **~iate**, **~ano**
Past sub **~issi**, **~issi**, **~isse**, **~issimo**, **~iste**, **~issero**
Pres part **~endo**
Past part **~ito**
Imp **~i** (*fml* **~a**), **~iamo**, **~ite**
Cond **~irei**, **~iresti**, **~irebbe**, **~iremmo**, **~ireste**, **~irebbero**

Notes

• Many verbs in the third conjugation take *isc* between the stem and the ending in the first, second, and third person singular and in the third person plural of the present, the present subjunctive, and the imperative:
fin|ire *Pres* **~isco**, **~isci**, **~isce**, **~iscono.** *Pres sub* **~isca**, **~iscano** *Imp* **~isci.**

• The three forms of the imperative are the same as the corresponding forms of the present for the second and third conjugation. In the first conjugation the forms are also the same except for the second person singular: present *compri*, imperative *compra*. The negative form of the second person singular is formed by putting *non* before the infinitive for all conjugations: *non comprare*. In polite forms the third person of the present subjunctive is used instead for all conjugations: *compri*.

Irregular verbs:

Certain forms of all irregular verbs are regular (except for *essere*). These are: the second person plural of the present, the past subjunctive, and the present participle. All forms not listed below are regular and can be derived from the parts given. Only those irregular verbs considered to be the most useful are shown in the tables.

accadere *as* **cadere**

accendere
Past hist accesi, accendesti
Past part acceso

affliggere
Past hist afflissi, affliggesti
Past part afflitto

ammettere *as* **mettere**

andare
Pres vado, vai, va, andiamo, andate, vanno
Fut andrò *etc*
Pres sub vada, vadano
Imp va', vada, vadano

apparire
Pres appaio *or* apparisco, appari *or* apparisci, appare *or* apparisce, appaiono *or* appariscono
Past hist apparvi *or* apparsi, apparisti, apparve *or* apparì *or* apparse, apparvero *or* apparirono *or* apparsero
Pres sub appaia *or* apparisca

aprire
Pres apro
Past hist aprii, apristi
Pres sub apra
Past part aperto

avere
Pres ho, hai, ha, abbiamo, hanno
Past hist ebbi, avesti, ebbe, avemmo, aveste, ebbero
Fut avrò *etc*
Pres sub abbia *etc*
Imp abbi, abbia, abbiate, abbiano

bere
Pres bevo *etc*
Impf bevevo *etc*
Past hist bevvi *or* bevetti, bevesti
Fut berrò *etc*
Pres sub beva *etc*
Past sub bevessi *etc*
Pres part bevendo
Cond berrei *etc*

cadere
Past hist caddi, cadesti
Fut cadrò *etc*

chiedere
Past hist chiesi, chiedesti
Pres sub chieda *etc*
Past part chiesto *etc*

chiudere
Past hist chiusi, chiudesti
Past part chiuso

cogliere
Pres colgo, colgono
Past hist colsi, cogliesti
Pres sub colga
Past part colto

correre
Past hist corsi, corresti
Past part corso

crescere
Past hist crebbi
Past part cresciuto

cuocere
Pres cuocio, cuociamo, cuociono
Past hist cossi, cocesti
Past part cotto

dare
Pres do, dai, dà, diamo, danno
Past hist diedi *or* detti, desti
Fut darò *etc*
Pres sub dia *etc*
Past sub dessi *etc*
Imp da' (*fml* dia)

dire
Pres dico, dici, dice, diciamo, dicono
Impf dicevo *etc*
Past hist dissi, dicesti
Fut dirò *etc*

Pres sub dica, diciamo, diciate, dicano
Past sub dicessi *etc*
Pres part dicendo
Past part detto
Imp di' (*fml* dica)

dovere
Pres devo *or* debbo, devi, deve, dobbiamo, devono *or* debbono
Fut dovrò *etc*
Pres sub deva *or* debba, dobbiamo, dobbiate, devano *or* debbano
Cond dovrei *etc*

essere
Pres sono, sei, è, siamo, siete, sono
Impf ero, eri, era, eravamo, eravate, erano
Past hist fui, fosti, fu, fummo, foste, furono
Fut sarò *etc*
Pres sub sia *etc*
Past sub fossi, fossi, fosse, fossimo, foste, fossero
Past part stato
Imp sii (*fml* sia), siate
Cond sarei *etc*

fare
Pres faccio, fai, fa, facciamo, fanno
Impf facevo *etc*
Past hist feci, facesti
Fut farò *etc*
Pres sub faccia *etc*
Past sub facessi *etc*
Pres part facendo
Past part fatto
Imp fa' (*fml* faccia)
Cond farei *etc*

fingere
Past hist finsi, fingesti, finsero
Past part finto

giungere
Past hist giunsi, giungesti, giunsero
Past part giunto

leggere
Past hist lessi, leggesti
Past part letto

mettere
Past hist misi, mettesti
Past part messo

morire
Pres muoio, muori, muore, muoiono
Fut morirò *or* morrò *etc*
Pres sub muoia
Past part morto

muovere
Past hist mossi, movesti
Past part mosso

nascere
Past hist nacqui, nascesti
Past part nato

offrire
Past hist offersi *or* offrii, offristi
Pres sub offra
Past part offerto

parere
Pres paio, pari, pare, pariamo, paiono
Past hist parvi *or* parsi, paresti
Fut parrò *etc*
Pres sub paia, paiamo *or* pariamo, pariate, paiano
Past part parso

piacere
Pres piaccio, piaci, piace, piacciamo, piacciono
Past hist piacqui, piacesti, piacque, piacemmo, piaceste, piacquero
Pres sub piaccia *etc*
Past part piaciuto

porre
Pres pongo, poni, pone, poniamo, ponete, pongono
Impf ponevo *etc*
Past hist posi, ponesti
Fut porrò *etc*
Pres sub ponga, poniamo, poniate, pongano
Past sub ponessi *etc*

potere
Pres posso, puoi, può, possiamo, possono
Fut potrò *etc*
Pres sub possa, possiamo, possiate, possano
Cond potrei *etc*

prendere
Past hist presi, prendesti
Past part preso

ridere
Past hist risi, ridesti
Past part riso

rimanere
Pres rimango, rimani, rimane, rimaniamo, rimangono
Past hist rimasi, rimanesti
Fut rimarrò *etc*
Pres sub rimanga
Past part rimasto
Cond rimarrei

salire
Pres salgo, sali, sale, saliamo, salgono
Pres sub salga, saliate, salgano

sapere
Pres so, sai, sa, sappiamo, sanno
Past hist seppi, sapesti
Fut saprò *etc*
Pres sub sappia *etc*
Imp sappi (*fml* sappia), sappiate
Cond saprei *etc*

scegliere
Pres scelgo, scegli, sceglie, scegliamo, scelgono
Past hist scelsi, scegliesti *etc*
Past part scelto

scrivere
Past hist scrissi, scrivesti *etc*
Past part scritto

sedere
Pres siedo *or* seggo, siedi, siede, siedono
Pres sub sieda *or* segga

spegnere
Pres spengo, spengono
Past hist spensi, spegnesti
Past part spento

stare
Pres sto, stai, sta, stiamo, stanno
Past hist stetti, stesti
Fut starò *etc*
Pres sub stia *etc*
Past sub stessi *etc*
Past part stato
Imp sta' (*fml* stia)

tacere
Pres taccio, tacciono
Past hist tacqui, tacque, tacquero
Pres sub taccia

tendere
Past hist tesi
Past part teso

tenere
Pres tengo, tieni, tiene, tengono
Past hist tenni, tenesti
Fut terrò *etc*
Pres sub tenga

togliere
Pres tolgo, tolgono
Past hist tolsi, tolse, tolsero
Pres sub tolga, tolgano
Past part tolto
Imp fml tolga

trarre
Pres traggo, trai, trae, traiamo, traete, traggono
Past hist trassi, traesti
Fut trarrò *etc*
Pres sub tragga
Past sub traessi *etc*
Past part tratto

uscire
Pres esco, esci, esce, escono
Pres sub esca
Imp esci (*fml* esca)

valere
Pres valgo, valgono
Past hist valsi, valesti
Fut varrò *etc*
Pres sub valga, valgano
Past part valso
Cond varrei *etc*

vedere
Past hist vidi, vedesti
Fut vedrò *etc*
Past part visto *or* veduto
Cond vedrei *etc*

venire

Pres vengo, vieni, viene, vengono
Past hist venni, venisti
Fut verrò *etc*

vivere

Past hist vissi, vivesti
Fut vivrò *etc*
Past part vissuto
Cond vivrei *etc*

volere

Pres voglio, vuoi, vuole, vogliamo, vogliono
Past hist volli, volesti
Fut verrò *etc*
Pres sub voglia *etc*
Imp vogliate
Cond vorrei *etc*

Numbers/Numeri

Cardinal numbers/ Numeri cardinali

0	zero **zero**
1	one **uno**
2	two **due**
3	three **tre**
4	four **quattro**
5	five **cinque**
6	six **sei**
7	seven **sette**
8	eight **otto**
9	nine **nove**
10	ten **dieci**
11	eleven **undici**
12	twelve **dodici**
13	thirteen **tredici**
14	fourteen **quattordici**
15	fifteen **quindici**
16	sixteen **sedici**
17	seventeen **diciassette**
18	eighteen **diciotto**
19	nineteen **diciannove**
20	twenty **venti**
21	twenty-one **ventuno**
22	twenty-two **ventidue**
30	thirty **trenta**
40	forty **quaranta**
50	fifty **cinquanta**
60	sixty **sessanta**
70	seventy **settanta**
80	eighty **ottanta**
90	ninety **novanta**
100	a hundred **cento**
101	a hundred and one **centouno**
110	a hundred and ten **centodieci**
200	two hundred **duecento**
1,000	a thousand **mille**
10,000	ten thousand **diecimila**
100,000	a hundred thousand **centomila**
1,000,000	a million **un milione**

Ordinal numbers/ Numeri ordinali

1st	first **primo**
2nd	second **secondo**
3rd	third **terzo**
4th	fourth **quarto**
5th	fifth **quinto**
6th	sixth **sesto**
7th	seventh **settimo**
8th	eighth **ottavo**
9th	ninth **nono**
10th	tenth **decimo**
11th	eleventh **undicesimo**
20th	twentieth **ventesimo**
21st	twenty-first **ventunesimo**
30th	thirtieth **trentesimo**
40th	fortieth **quarantesimo**
50th	fiftieth **cinquantesimo**
100th	hundredth **centesimo**
1,000th	thousandth **millesimo**